CRIMINAL JUSTICE

CRIMINAL JUSTICE

Fourth Edition

ANDREW SANDERS
RICHARD YOUNG
AND
MANDY BURTON

OXFORD
UNIVERSITY PRESS

OXFORD
UNIVERSITY PRESS

Great Clarendon Street, Oxford OX2 6DP

Oxford University Press is a department of the University of Oxford.
It furthers the University's objective of excellence in research, scholarship,
and education by publishing worldwide in

Oxford New York

Auckland Cape Town Dar es Salaam Hong Kong Karachi
Kuala Lumpur Madrid Melbourne Mexico City Nairobi
New Delhi Shanghai Taipei Toronto

With offices in

Argentina Austria Brazil Chile Czech Republic France Greece
Guatemala Hungary Italy Japan Poland Portugal Singapore
South Korea Switzerland Thailand Turkey Ukraine Vietnam

Oxford is a registered trade mark of Oxford University Press
in the UK and in certain other countries

Published in the United States
by Oxford University Press Inc., New York

© Oxford University Press 2010

British Library Cataloguing in Publication Data

Data available

Library of Congress Cataloging in Publication Data
Sanders, Andrew, 1952–
Criminal justice / Andrew Sanders, Richard Young and
Mandy Burton.—4th ed.
p. cm.
Includes bibliographical references and index.
ISBN 978-0-19-954131-7 (pbk.)
1. Criminal justice, Administration of—Great Britain. 2. Criminal
procedure—Great Britain. I. Young, Richard (Richard P.). II. Burton,
Mandy. III. Title.
KD7876.S36 2010
345.42'05—dc22   2010014845

Typeset by Newgen Imaging Systems (P) Ltd., Chennai, India
Printed in Great Britain
on acid-free paper by
Ashford Colour Press Ltd, Gosport, Hampshire

ISBN 978-0-19-954131-7

1 3 5 7 9 10 8 6 4 2

This book is dedicated to the memory of

Michael Young
(1948–1993)

Sylvia Sanders
(1921–1983)

John Wagstaffe
(1918–2002)

Contents

Preface

Less than four years have elapsed since the third edition of this text was published in 2007. In the preface to that edition we observed that there had been a huge number of developments in criminal justice since the previous edition in 2000. Despite this, we said, the fundamentals of the subject remained the same.

This is all as true now as it was in 2007. There has been constant legislative change, and policy development. There has been less academic research than in previous years, but inspectorates and other government agencies have been busier than ever. We will see that their reports and evaluations are often as revealing as academic research is of criminal justice failings and problems. And the fundamentals? These are, primarily, that criminal justice continues on the course we have charted ever since the first edition in 1994. That is, the appearance of fairness in the black letter of the law is frequently not matched by the reality (ie by the way the system really works); the rights of the accused, and the civil liberties of us all, are being steadily eroded; and minorities and the less privileged suffer from the heavy hand of the state disproportionately. The government tries to justify all this in the name of protecting victims, bringing more offenders to justice, fighting terrorism and using resources efficiently.

Readers should decide for themselves whether the gains outweigh the losses, and whether the government really believes its own justifications. We are clear in our views, and continue to make them clear throughout the book: we don't think the gains outweigh the losses and we believe the government is often dishonest. The dismissal in 2009 of the Independent Chair of the Advisory Council on the Misuse of Drugs – the unfortunately named Professor Nutt – is a striking example. The Home Secretary said that he could not have a government advisor publicly criticising government policy (in this case, on the upgrading of cannabis) even when the criticism was based on evidence it was the Council's duty to gather and disseminate. In the Preface to the third edition we said that we might be able to report in later editions that someone had listened to reason and evidence, and that criminal justice had changed direction. Sadly, we were too optimistic: no-one is listening. Not in government at any rate. Or maybe they are – but fear that if they take notice they, too, will be sacked.

Nonetheless, no academic subject is an exact science. We do not expect everyone to agree with us, and do not want people to feel obliged to agree simply because we are 'experts'. We only ask that you allow your assumptions to be challenged and your intellect to be engaged. If your sense of injustice and your desire to make the world a better place for those without the power to challenge those in authority is heightened, so much the better. Then make up your own minds. We do not pretend to be objective: we say what we think is wrong with the system, and how we think it should be improved. We encourage you to do the same. Studying academic subjects should not only involve learning what the rules are. Academics and students alike should evaluate those rules and ask whether they are fair.

This edition follows the pattern of previous editions. For the first time there are no structural changes. As before, we have written a socio-legal textbook for students. That means that we go behind the legislation and cases to examine the policy behind the law, and whether those policies are successful. To do that we necessarily look at research on how the system works and who is affected by it – often in unintended and brutal ways. There is enough 'law' here for law students, and enough criminology for social science students. We hope that readers will get a feel for what it is like to be at the receiving end of criminal justice – not just accused people, but victims, police officers and lawyers too. The inclusion in this edition of lots of references to websites hosting video evidence of how the police use their powers (and their power) should help bring the reality of the system home.

As in previous editions, we do not pretend to cover all of the sprawling mess that now constitutes our criminal justice system. In particular, we say very little about sentencing and punishment. The book would be too big if we tried, and there are plenty of other good books on penology. However, the approach we adopt can be applied to any criminal justice topic, and we encourage readers to look into issues we do not discuss and evaluate them for yourselves. Major developments up to the end of 2009 are covered, and web links were tested soon after. Nonetheless, the furious pace of change in criminal justice means that much of the detail in the book will become out of date in a distressingly short space of time. However, we refer readers to our new Online Resource Centre, where we will endeavour to cover important changes as they occur.

Too many people helped us in so many different ways that we cannot name them all, so we will not identify any. If we did they'd be all too likely to find themselves on a database somewhere. But we cannot let the love and support of our partners, Jo, Hannah and Chee (even if our various children are now too numerous to name), go unnoticed. Three partners? What's going on? Well, the best change since the last edition has been the addition of Dr Mandy Burton to the writing team, and Andrew and Richard take this opportunity to thank her for joining with us. We must also thank Melanie Jackson of OUP for keeping faith with us and putting up with the inevitable delays. Only three months late this time; a record.

And now, finally, aren't we missing something? Perhaps the most significant event of the last four years is the financial crisis and subsequent virtual melt-down of most Western economies. Individuals who behaved as irresponsibly as the financial institutions did would probably be prosecuted. Individuals as lax as the government and its regulatory agencies were in watching over those financial institutions would probably, again, be prosecuted. But there is no mention of the crisis in this book. Because there isn't one law for us all. Many of the banks have been bailed out by government. They have made profits and the bankers responsible for the crisis have been rewarded with bonuses yet again.

We've all been robbed and we will be paying, literally, for the failings of the banks, bankers, regulators and government for years to come. Criminal justice will take its share of the consequent financial cuts (as indeed will higher education) and by the end of this book you'll have a good idea of who will suffer most as a result. But no-one, at the time of writing, has been prosecuted, and much of the wrongdoing was not criminal. It's an object-lesson in how what is not criminal is often worse than that which is. We hope that reading this book will give you some insight into why this is and why some people are protected while others are not.

It's not all doom and gloom, however, and the observant reader will still find the occasional joke tucked away in the pages that follow. While Criminal Justice may have gone for a Burton, our sense of hope, and dark humour, lingers on.

Mandy Burton, Leicester
Andrew Sanders, Birmingham
Richard Young, Tickenham Village Hall

Table of Cases

Table of Statutes

(The articles of the European Convention on Human Rights are tabled under Sch 1 of the Human Rights Act 1998)

Statutory Instruments

1

The aims and values of 'criminal justice'

Let no-one be in any doubt, the rules of the game are changing.
(Former Prime Minister Tony Blair, 5 August 2005).

Key issues:

- The structure of the criminal justice system
- Blurring civil and criminal boundaries: ASBOs and similar
- Proving guilt and innocence: burden and standard of proof
- Adversarial and inquisitorial approaches
- Recent trends in crime and criminal justice
- Packer's 'due process' and 'crime control' models
- The human rights approach to criminal justice
- The managerial approach to criminal justice
- Where do victims fit into these approaches?
- Our approach: the 'freedom' model

1.1 The nature and structure of 'criminal justice'

A book with a title as vague as 'criminal justice' should begin by saying what it is about. In thinking about criminal justice we all have our own images and assumptions. In this chapter we spell out our own assumptions. We also explain the theoretical framework within which we think criminal justice in England and Wales can most usefully be understood, criticised and reformed. We see the criminal justice system as a complex social institution[1] which regulates potential, alleged and actual criminal

---

1 See further Garland D, *Punishment and Modern Society* (Oxford: Clarendon Press, 1990) p 282.

activity within limits designed to protect people from wrongful treatment and wrongful conviction. In the first three editions of this book we focused mainly on police, prosecution and court powers and procedures in respect of *alleged* crime, resulting in either 'diversion' out of the system (eg, through the imposition of a police or prosecution caution) or court proceedings. But recent years have witnessed a reconfiguration of criminal law and criminal justice in favour of crime pre-emption through risk management techniques.[2] Underpinning this shift in orientation is the ideological view that public safety and the interests of victims should be given greater weight than civil liberties and the rights of suspects. It follows that while the determination of guilt and innocence is still hugely important, this must now be considered alongside the control of *potential* criminal activity through risk management devices such as dispersal and anti-social behaviour orders (see 1.2.2). In this section we introduce some of the key issues and tensions inherent in this reconfiguration of 'criminal justice' and also discuss the key terms 'criminal' and 'justice'. First we outline the structure and core terminology of the traditional English[3] criminal process for readers unfamiliar with this jurisdiction, and explain how this relates to the organisation of this book.

1.1.1 The structure of the English criminal process

1.1.1.1 Criminal process

Anyone who thinks a crime may have been committed may (but need not)[4] report this to a law enforcement body. As we will see in ch 7, there are many enforcement bodies. First, there are 43 'local' police forces, roughly corresponding with local authority areas. Second, there are also some national police bodies such as the Serious Organised Crime Agency and the British Transport Police. Third, many types of crime that would be called 'administrative offences' in some other countries – eg health and safety violations, pollution, tax evasion – are dealt with by specialist agencies such as the Health and Safety Executive. In addition, a lot of 'policing' is done by private agencies, such as security firms, which, like ordinary witnesses and victims, generally call in the police if they detect suspected crimes and want further action taken. The police may seek to find evidence of guilt through the use of powers such as stop-search (see ch 2), arrest (ch 3), detention and interrogation (chs 4–5) and a variety of other non-interrogative means including electronic surveillance (ch 6). Enforcement bodies are not obliged

---

[2] The extent to which this is merely a pendulum-like swing back to a risk management approach is debatable. See, for example, Bonner D, *Executive Measures, Terrorism and National Security: Have the Rules of the Game Changed?* (Aldershot: Ashgate, 2007).

[3] By 'English' we actually refer to England and Wales. Scotland is somewhat different, but increasingly less so as the two systems are converging.

[4] While this is a general principle, there are exceptions. For example, s 117 of the Anti-terrorism, Crime and Security Act 2001 (inserting s 38B into the Terrorism Act 2000) created the offence of failing to disclose to the police information thought to be of material assistance either in preventing an act of terrorism or in the apprehension, prosecution or conviction of a person for an offence involving the instigation, preparation or commission of an act of terrorism.

to prosecute even if they have overwhelming evidence of guilt. If the police do wish to prosecute, they pass the case on to the Crown Prosecution Service (CPS). The CPS decides whether to take matters further, and – if so – will prosecute, sometimes hiring specialist lawyers (barristers) for very serious cases. Specialised enforcement agencies (such as the Health and Safety Executive) generally prosecute their own cases. Also, private policing bodies and individual victims may prosecute in their own right, though this is now unusual (see further ch 7).

All prosecuted cases start in the lowest (magistrates') courts – or, where the defendant is 18 or under, the youth courts (ch 9). In this lowest tier of the criminal courts, most cases are decided by a bench of three lay magistrates supported by a legal adviser, though increasingly professional judges (once referred to as stipendiary magistrates, but now known as District Judges) decide cases alone. Very serious cases are quickly transferred out of the magistrates' and youth courts to the Crown Court (ch 10). Here proceedings are more formal, and there is a professional judge (and, in contested cases, a jury).

The division of business between the magistrates' courts and the Crown Court is determined by the initial legal classification of an offence as either 'summary' (triable in the magistrates' courts only), 'either-way' (triable in either the magistrates' courts or the Crown Court) or 'triable on indictment only' (triable only in the Crown Court). The latter two types of offence are sometimes lumped together under the label 'indictable offences'. Regardless of this classification, most prosecuted cases are uncontested, because the defendant pleads guilty (ch 8).

People who are convicted of crimes may appeal to a higher court (ch 11): from the magistrates,/youth courts to the Crown Court (where a completely new hearing of the matter takes place) and/or the Court of Appeal; and from the Crown Court to the Court of Appeal. Exceptionally, a further appeal is sometimes allowed to the House of Lords (redesignated as the Supreme Court from 1 October 2009). Appeals to courts other than the Crown Court are generally restricted to points of law, although fresh evidence is sometimes admitted. Once normal appeal rights are exhausted the final avenue open to the convicted defendant is to persuade an administrative body, the Criminal Cases Review Commission (CCRC), that there is some fresh evidence or argument that, if put before an appeal court, would give rise to a real possibility of the conviction being overturned. If, following investigation, the CCRC accepts that there is such a possibility the case will be referred to an appellate court for determination.

Convictions can be 'quashed' by the Court of Appeal if a defendant is found to have been denied a fair trial, as in cases where the police fail to disclose evidence that undermined the prosecution case. Such malpractice, if adjudged severe enough, is said to render the conviction 'unsafe', and to amount to a 'miscarriage of justice', although such breaches of due process do not necessarily mean that the defendants concerned are factually innocent of the crime in question.[5] This means that there are two main

---

[5] See the discussion by Naughton M, *Rethinking Miscarriages of Justice: Beyond the Tip of the Iceberg* (Basingstoke: Palgrave Macmillan, 2007).

types of 'wrongful conviction' (which often overlap). One is where the defendant (whether actually guilty or not) is convicted unfairly; in most of these cases, the lack of fair trial makes it impossible to judge whether the defendant is guilty or not. The other is where an innocent defendant is convicted (whether fairly or not). The conviction through unfair means of those perceived or known to be actually innocent is the type of miscarriage of justice that gives rise to most public concern.

Public concern can also be aroused by the acquittal of those perceived to be guilty, and some have argued that such acquittals amount to a different kind of miscarriage of justice.[6] The CPS is sometimes allowed to appeal against acquittals, especially when there is an alleged error of law, such as a refusal to let a jury hear prosecution evidence because the trial judge considers that the police lacked the legal power to secure that evidence. In rare cases, where new and compelling evidence of guilt emerges, entirely fresh proceedings can be brought against someone previously acquitted.[7]

The decisions of the higher appeal courts apply to all future cases with similar circumstances. In this way, the 'common law' is in a continual process of evolution.[8] Another way in which common law is created in the criminal justice area is through challenges to the decisions of state agencies ('judicial review'). For example, a victim of a crime can ask a court (usually the High Court, making this a civil, not a criminal, case) to rule on the lawfulness of a decision by the CPS not to prosecute. Again, such decisions set 'precedents' that not only guide the decisions of courts, but also of enforcement agencies, thereafter. Judicial review is one of a number of mechanisms that regulate the operation and policies of the criminal justice system. Others include government inspectorates and the Independent Police Complaints Commission (see ch 12).

An element of criminal justice which is often forgotten is criminal defence. Anyone arrested and taken to a police station is entitled to receive free legal advice from an accredited adviser (who is not necessarily a fully qualified lawyer) either over the telephone or in person. The state also provides funding for free legal representation in the magistrates' courts and the Crown Court subject to a means test and a merits test. The former test means that middle class defendants (a relatively small proportion of the whole, leaving motoring offences aside) generally pay for their own defence or represent themselves. The latter test means that rich and poor alike must pay for their own legal representation for the more mundane charges (such as speeding offences or television licence evasion) that form the majority of cases in the magistrates' courts. Thus a large proportion of defendants facing summary charges either represent themselves or rely on a duty solicitor present each day at court. In the Crown Court, by

---

[6] Then Prime Minister Tony Blair argued that: 'It is perhaps the biggest miscarriage of justice in today's system when the guilty walk away unpunished' (cited and critiqued in Naughton, 2007: 21).

[7] Criminal Justice Act 2003, part 10.

[8] Britain has no criminal code. Legislation has been built up piecemeal, so courts have to fill in the gaps more than in 'civil law' systems, thus creating case law (often known as 'the common law'). Moreover Britain has no constitution to guide how gaps should be filled. This also means that case law is subordinate to legislation. Even if legislation contravenes the European Convention on Human Rights, which was enshrined in the law in 1998 (see 1.6) it is simply declared 'incompatible' rather than being rendered invalid.

contrast, the overwhelming majority of defendants are relatively poor and face serious charges, and so are usually represented by solicitors and barristers at the state's expense. Issues relating to criminal defence are dealt with throughout this book.

1.1.1.2 Civil and criminal boundary

It is difficult to define the difference between 'civil' and 'criminal' matters. In general the former are dealt with in civil courts (district courts, county courts and the High Court), and are for individuals to pursue rather than the state. Many 'wrongs', such as torts (eg negligence) and breach of contract, are civil matters. It is not possible to prosecute or seek the state punishment of the wrongdoer, but the wronged person (the plaintiff) can sue with a view to obtaining a civil remedy, such as compensatory damages.

However the boundaries between the civil and criminal spheres are becoming increasingly blurred. First, some matters involving civil and criminal elements are most effectively dealt with at one time. Domestic violence, in particular, may involve a crime (assault) which merits punishment but also an ongoing threat to safety necessitating a civil injunction requiring the aggressor to keep away from the family home.[9] The shift towards crime pre-emption encourages and reinforces this blending of civil and criminal justice. Second, while criminal courts normally punish for crimes, leaving civil courts to compensate for loss,[10] at the sentencing stage criminal courts frequently order defendants to compensate victims. However, victims are reliant upon the prosecution to seek this on their behalf and are not able to participate in criminal proceedings in the way that they can in a civil claim. Third, the actions (and inactions) of the criminal justice agencies such as the police and CPS can be subjected to scrutiny in the civil justice system through judicial review (as noted above), or an action for professional negligence or breach of the Human Rights Act 1998.

Finally, there are important new hybrid laws. Under the Proceeds of Crime Act 2002 (consolidated by the Serious Crime Act 2007) civil courts may allow enforcement agencies to seize or retain property that is more likely than not to have been obtained criminally without having to prove anyone guilty of a crime.[11] Then there are 'civil behavioural orders' that embody civil evidential standards, but are dealt with in criminal courts. Over the last 12 years, around a dozen have been created (see table 1.1).[12] For example, under the Crime and Disorder Act 1998, as extended by subsequent legislation, the police, local authorities, housing action trusts or registered social landlords can apply for an anti-social behaviour order (ASBO). Applications can be made to the magistrates' court or as part of proceedings (such as for housing possession) in the

---

[9] There is pressure to design processes, and even special courts, to deal with overlapping civil and criminal proceedings in domestic violence cases. See further ch 9.

[10] Although, to muddy the waters further, civil courts sometimes award punitive damages.

[11] Millington T and Williams S, *The Proceeds of Crime* (Oxford: OUP, 2007).

[12] This does not include other hybrid laws, such as civil protection orders for victims of domestic violence, that have criminal sanctions, and therefore criminal justice enforcement processes, for breach.

county court.[13] In either case the procedure involved is civil, not criminal.[14] Although this means that hearsay evidence is admissible,[15] the criminal – not civil – standard of proof is required (see 1.2.2 below). ASBOs are intended to prevent further 'anti-social' acts by the defendant, and can include prohibitions such as curfews, or commands to avoid certain places or individuals.[16] Doing anything in breach of the order (whether otherwise criminal or not), without reasonable excuse, is a criminal offence carrying a penalty of up to five years' imprisonment. The ASBO thus acts like a personalised criminal law, and one that has real bite.[17] Over half of the 51 individuals who breached their ASBO and were taken to court in 2000 received a custodial sentence, including 13 juveniles.[18] By the end of December 2007 the total number of ASBOs imposed by courts had reached 14,975 of which 6,028 were known to have been imposed on those aged 10–17.[19] The blurring of civil and criminal law has thus facilitated a substantial expansion of formal state control of individuals. Further expansion has taken place through a reworking of the criminal law itself, as indicated below.

1.1.2 Criminal law and criminal behaviour

What is defined as criminal varies from society to society and across time. Take England and Wales in the first decade of the twenty-first century. Its criminal law is generally thought of as proscribing people and corporate bodies from culpably (ie, intentionally or recklessly) acting in particularly harmful or socially undesirable ways. However, much of such behaviour is not criminalised (invasions of privacy, police abuse of suspects' rights, and the wasteful misuse of the earth's resources are possible examples) and many feel that much of what is criminalised should not be (examples might be smoking cannabis and swearing by football fans). Moreover, the law criminalises many forms of behaviour where the actor has acted negligently or even, in the case of some strict liability offences, where every care was taken to avoid harm.

---

[13] Criminal courts may also make an order of their own volition following normal criminal proceedings for an alleged offence which resulted in conviction, but only in addition to the sentence given for that offence: Crime and Disorder Act 1998, s 1C, as inserted by s 64 of the Police Reform Act 2002.

[14] *R (on the application of McCann) v Manchester Crown Court* [2002] 4 All ER 593.

[15] The rule against hearsay evidence in criminal proceedings is designed to prevent a party using evidence of an out-of-court statement for the purpose of proving the truth of any fact asserted in that statement. It ensures that direct evidence is given by those with personal knowledge of the relevant matters, thus allowing cross-examination to take place, demeanour to be assessed, and so forth. See Roberts P and Zuckerman A, *Criminal Evidence* (Oxford: OUP, 2004) ch 12.

[16] Appellate courts are edging their way to requiring ABSOs to be clear, precise, targeted at the relevant anti-social behaviour, and proportionate to the risk to be guarded against. See *Dean Boness & ors* [2005] EWCA Crim 2395. Despite this, less than 1% of all applications for ASBOs are rejected.

[17] For a normative critique see Simester A and Von Hirsch A, 'Regulating Offensive Conduct Through Two-Step Prohibitions' in Simester A and Von Hirsch A (eds), *Incivilities: Regulating Offensive Behaviour* (Oxford: Hart, 2006).

[18] Campbell S, *A Review of Anti-social Behaviour Orders* (Home Office Research Study 236) (London: Home Office, 2002) p 76.

[19] <http://www.crimereduction.homeoffice.gov.uk/asbos/asbos2.htm> (accessed 5 January 2010).

Table 1.1 Examples of civil orders introduced to tackle criminal and sub-criminal behaviour[20]

Title of Order	Behaviour to be Prevented	Act	Duration of Order	Punishment for Breach
Anti-Social Behaviour Order	Anti-social behaviour	Crime and Disorder Act 1998	Min – 2 years Max – indefinitely	Max – 5 years' imprisonment
Drinking Ban Orders	Drinking related anti-social behaviour	Violent Crime Reduction Act 2006	Min – 2 months Max – 2 years	Max – Level Four Fine
Forced Marriage Protection Orders	Forced marriages	Forced Marriage Civil Protection Act 2007	Max – indefinitely	Contempt of Court – 2 years max
Non-Molestation Orders	Domestic violence	Domestic Violence, Crime and Victims Act 2004	Max – indefinitely	Max – 5 years' imprisonment
Parenting Orders	Juvenile anti-social behaviour or criminality	Crime and Disorder Act 1998	Max – 12 months	Max – Level Three Fine
Protection from Harassment Order	Stalking and general harassing behaviour	Protection from Harassment Act 1997	Max – indefinitely	Max – 5 years' imprisonment
Risk of Sexual Harm Orders	Sexual offending	Sexual Offences Act 2003	Min – 2 years Max – indefinitely	Max – 5 years' imprisonment
Serious Crime Prevention Orders	Serious crime	Serious Crime Act 2007	Max – 5 years	Max – 5 years' imprisonment
Sexual Offences Prevention Order	Sexual offending	Sexual Offences Act 2003	Min – 5 years Max – indefinitely	Max – 5 years' imprisonment
Terrorist Control Orders	Terrorism	Prevention of Terrorism Act 2005	12 months	Max – 5 years' imprisonment
Violent Offender Orders	Violent offending	Criminal Justice and Immigration Act 2008	Min – 2 years Max – 5 years	Max – 5 years' imprisonment

[20] Brown K, 'Charting the Expansion in the Number of Civil Orders to Tackle Criminal and Sub-Criminal Behaviour' (unpublished). Many thanks to Kevin for permission to reproduce this table from his paper.

Decisions concerning which acts are to be criminalised are sometimes based on coherently expressed principles supported by an informed consensus; more often they are the products of historical accident, political and administrative expedience, and shifting, incoherent ideological notions of the appropriate reach of the criminal law.[21] Thus the recent lurch towards crime pre-emption is reflected in the 'general tendency to expand the boundaries of criminal liability...with growing emphasis on inchoate liability and offences of preparation far removed from the perpetration of harm'.[22] In the first nine years of the Labour Government (1997 to 2006) over 3,000 new criminal offences were created. While many are either trivial or brought old laws up to date, many others criminalised previously lawful behaviour.[23]

Similar observations might be made about the way in which harmful (and potentially harmful) behaviours are in practice identified as criminal and responded to as such. For example, it may be that rowdy behaviour by unemployed scruffy youths will be interpreted in quite a different way from that engaged in by university students following their final examinations. One person's public disorder is another's youthful high spirits. These kinds of interpretative decisions are also influenced by shifts in ideology. Thus, for example, feminist writers and activists have raised public awareness of domestic violence to the point where many more victims and police officers now interpret what takes place within the 'private' sphere of the home as criminal.[24] And the Government's focus on 'anti-social behaviour' has probably increased awareness, intolerance and formal reporting to the police, of people and acts previously seen as merely irritating or unconventional.[25]

Since criminal laws and perceptions of criminality are social constructs it is not surprising that much criminal justice activity reflects the interests of powerful groups and actors. There are many more criminal laws and regulatory resources aimed at harmful behaviour by individuals (particularly children and young people) than at harmful corporate activity, for example. And, as we shall see in ch 7, benefits fraud is prosecuted far more frequently than is tax fraud. Much criminal justice activity supports widely held social values while at the same time compounding wider social divisions and making no concessions for the social causes of crime.[26] For example,

---

[21]   See further Hillyard P, Pantazis C, Tombs S and Gordon D (eds), *Beyond Criminology: Taking Harm Seriously* (London: Pluto Press, 2004).

[22]   Virgo G, 'Terrorism: Possession of Articles' (2008) 67(2) CLJ 236.

[23]   Young R, 'Street Policing after PACE' in Cape E and Young R (eds), *Regulating Policing* (Oxford: Hart, 2008).

[24]   See further, Wells C, 'The Impact of Feminist Thinking on Criminal Law and Justice: Contradiction, Complexity, Conviction and Connection' [2004] Crim LR 503.

[25]   Tonry M, *Punishment and Politics: Evidence and Emulation in the Making of English Crime Control Policy* (Cullompton: Willan, 2004) 57.

[26]   Thus, measures to tackle 'anti-social' behaviour are often targeted on the most disadvantaged communities and are about punitive responses rather than increased support (Brown A, 'Anti-Social Behaviour, Crime Control and Social Control' (2004) 43 Howard J Crim Justice 203; Koffmann L, 'Holding Parents to Account: Tough on Children, Tough on the Causes of Children' (2008) 35(1) JLS 113. See, more generally, Cook D, *Criminal and Social Justice* (London: Sage, 2006).

theft laws protect poor people as well as wealthy people, but the prosecution and punishment of shoplifting has a greater impact on the poor than the wealthy, and upholds the value of private property whilst ignoring (or even reinforcing) poverty.

In summary, the enforcement of the criminal law upholds social order for the benefit of all, reinforces a hierarchical social order which benefits some while disadvantaging others, and, in an unequal society, is bound to be morally problematic. Consensus and conflict are thus likely to be interwoven in all attempts at 'maintaining order' and controlling crime.

1.2 **Guilt and innocence**

In a democracy, state punishment can be legitimately inflicted only on those found guilty of crime. The criminal justice system insists on proof of guilt, rather than simply taking the word of the victim or the police. But proving guilt is not straightforward. If accused persons are truly criminal they will often be concerned to hide the truth. So should we always disbelieve them? Of course not – the police or prosecution witnesses may be mistaken, or they may be correct about some of the facts (for example, whether the accused punched someone) but simply not know other important details (for example, whether the punch was in self-defence). Occasionally prosecution witnesses themselves hide the truth, or even lie. Thus David Carrington-Jones spent nearly seven years in prison for a rape he always denied, even though he knew this would make early release on parole unlikely. His conviction was quashed in 2008 when the Court of Appeal heard evidence that the complainant had a track-record of making unsubstantiated allegations of rape (against her step-father, brother, fiancé and a customer at work), two of which she later admitted were false.[27]

It follows that when accused persons dispute guilt it is as likely that they are innocent as guilty, unless there is evidence pointing one way or the other. And it is rare for that evidence to prove *conclusively* that someone is guilty, in the way we (often naively) expect scientific and medical tests to provide conclusive truth. The only way to completely prevent the conviction of the factually innocent would be to insist on incontrovertible proof, which would lead to very few (if any) convictions. This was recognised by the Court of Appeal in *Ward* (1993) 96 Cr App Rep 1 when it said that criminal justice:

should be developed so as to reduce the risk of conviction of the innocent to an absolute minimum. At the same time we are very much alive to the fact that, although the avoidance of the conviction of the innocent must unquestionably be the primary consideration, the

---

[27] *The Mail on Sunday*, 16 October 2008. The media frequently fuel a view that false allegations of rape are common. In fact there is no reliable evidence on the prevalence of false allegations, but they do undoubtedly occur. See Rumney P, 'False Allegations of Rape' (2006) 65(1) CLJ 128.

public interest would not be served by a multiplicity of rules which merely impede effective law enforcement' (at 52).

This judgment, however, fudges two key issues. No-one in their right mind would advocate a multiplicity of rules which 'merely' impeded effective law enforcement. Rules protecting suspects from wrongful conviction, harsh treatment or invasions of privacy often do impede 'effective' law enforcement, but, in a democracy, this price is seen as worth paying in order to protect the liberty and dignity of the individual suspect. Second, does the Court of Appeal really mean that the risk of wrongful conviction of the innocent should be reduced to an 'absolute minimum'? That vast numbers of guilty persons shall, if necessary to achieve this, go free?

Let us leave aside such rhetorical flourishes and ask to what extent is the acquittal of the innocent defendant a priority of English criminal justice in fact? The main theoretical safeguard offered to suspects in the English system of criminal justice (and also under the European Convention on Human Rights) is the presumption of innocence. This presumption finds expression in the principle that guilt must be proved beyond reasonable doubt. There are two aspects to this principle; firstly it places the burden of proof on the prosecution; and, secondly, it stipulates a high standard of proof.

1.2.1 **The burden of proof**

Viscount Sankey LC described the burden of proof in *Woolmington v DPP*[28] as the 'golden thread' which ran throughout criminal law. 'No matter what the charge or where the trial, the principle that the prosecution must prove the guilt of the prisoner is part of the common law of England and no attempt to whittle it down can be entertained.' In recognition of parliamentary supremacy over the courts, Lord Sankey noted, however, that this common law principle was subject to statutory exceptions. These are numerous; in the mid 1990s, Ashworth and Blake calculated that 219 out of the 540 indictable offences in common use involved a shifting from the prosecution to the defence of the burden of proof in relation to some elements of the offence. For example there are many prosecutions under s 5 of the Public Order Act 1986 for using threatening, abusive or insulting words or behaviour within the hearing or sight of a person likely to be caused harassment, alarm or distress thereby. All the prosecution need prove is that defendants did as alleged (not that any alarm, etc was caused). Accused persons then escape liability only if they can prove on the balance of probabilities that their conduct was reasonable.

Shifts in the burden of proof, sometimes referred to as a reverse onus, never require the defendant to prove something 'beyond reasonable doubt' but only, at most, 'on the balance of probabilities'. Nonetheless, this means that a court can convict in cases where the defendant's story is as likely to be true as false. This might appear to be contrary to the European Convention on Human Rights (ECHR), Art 6(2) of which states

---

[28] *Woolmington v DPP* [1935] AC 462 at 481–2.

that: 'Everyone charged with a criminal offence shall be presumed innocent until proved guilty according to law.' But, following a European Court of Human Rights (ECtHR) ruling that reverse onuses did not necessarily violate the Convention,[29] the House of Lords in *Lambert*[30] stated that Art 6(2) permits a statute to place a burden of proof on a defendant, if that burden is proportionate to the aim being pursued, which must itself be legitimate. In determining these issues, a court must take account of such factors as the gravity of the conduct dealt with by the offence in question, the justification for placing a burden on the defendant, and the degree of difficulty in discharging that burden. It follows that the courts will have to proceed on a case-by-case basis, deciding for each offence whether a shift in burden is proportionate or not.

Parliament has responded to the human rights era supposedly ushered in by the Human Rights Act 1998 (which made ECHR rights enforceable within the domestic court system) by stipulating that some of the more serious statutory offences which appear on their face to require the defendant to prove some matter should be read as only imposing a burden to adduce sufficient evidence to make the issue a live one. For example, when the main terrorism offences were consolidated in the Terrorism Act 2000 the opportunity was taken (in s 57(2)) to recast the offence created by s 82 of the Criminal Justice and Public Order Act 1994 (possessing an article for suspected terrorist purposes) in precisely this way. Now, if a defendant adduces evidence sufficient to raise the issue that she or he had an item in their possession for a non-terrorist purpose then an acquittal must follow unless the prosecution proves beyond reasonable doubt that no such purpose existed. On the other hand a number of terrorist offences were re-enacted with a shift in burden still in place. It is possible some of these reverse onus provisions will be successfully challenged, but many are undoubtedly here to stay.[31]

1.2.2 The standard of proof

If a court was allowed to find a person guilty on the balance of probabilities (the standard of proof generally applied in civil cases) then many more factually guilty persons could be successfully prosecuted, but so too could many more who were factually innocent. If, on the other hand, it was required that guilt be proven beyond any doubt at all, whether reasonable or not, then few successful prosecutions could be brought. This would protect people who were actually innocent, but would allow the vast majority of guilty suspects to escape conviction. The standard of proof required (guilt beyond reasonable doubt) amounts to a compromise between two potentially conflicting aims: to convict the guilty and acquit the innocent. The particular standard chosen expresses a preference for erroneous acquittals over erroneous convictions.

---

[29] *Salabiaku v France* (1988) EHRR 379.

[30] *Lambert* [2001] 2 Cr App R 511. See also *Attorney General's Reference No 4 of 2002; Sheldrake v DPP* [2004] UKHL 43.

[31] See further, Dennis I, 'Reverse Onuses and the Presumption of Innocence: In Search of Principle' [2005] Crim LR 901.

In recent years the Government, as part of the lurch towards pre-emption, has sought to reduce the practical impact of the standard of proof. For example, the Government had hoped that the civil standard of proof would be applied in initial ASBO proceedings so that an order would be made if on the balance of probabilities it was found that a person had acted 'anti-socially'. Though the courts held that the implications of making an ASBO were sufficiently serious to justify the use of the criminal standard of proof,[32] civil standards are still applied to the making of other civil orders that have criminal sanctions for breach.[33]

In any event the insistence that a crime or anti-social behaviour be proven 'beyond reasonable doubt' by the prosecution does little to protect defendants if that crime or behaviour is so vague or commonplace that almost anything could come within the definition. Thus s 57 of the Terrorism Act 2000 makes it an offence if the accused 'possesses an article in circumstances which give rise to a reasonable suspicion that his possession is for a purpose connected with the commission, preparation or instigation of an act of terrorism'. There is no requirement to prove that possession *was* for such a purpose but only that there is a reasonable suspicion that this is so. As we shall see in ch 2, reasonable suspicion is an elastic concept that requires little by way of hard, objective evidence consistent with guilt. Note also that the terms 'article' and 'connected with' could hardly be broader.[34] Some might argue that breadth and elasticity is needed to enable the early disruption of activity which, if not pre-empted, might wreak large-scale death and destruction. But such pre-emptive thinking can also be seen in the definition of low-level crime. To take the ASBO example again, neither the behaviour which prompts the making of the order, nor the behaviour in breach of that order need be criminal in and of itself (although sometimes it is).[35] Some ASBOs prohibit children from walking to their siblings' school, thus putting parents needing to collect the latter into an impossible quandary. Others have prohibited people with suicidal tendencies from entering high buildings or jumping into rivers.[36] Moreover, there is good reason to doubt that the high standard of proof beyond reasonable doubt

---

[32] *R (on the application of McCann) v Manchester Crown Court* [2002] 4 All ER 593.

[33] For example restraining orders under the Protection from Harassment Act 1997. See *Hipgrave v Jones* [2005] 2 FLR 174. However, in *Birmingham City Council v Shafi, Ellis* [2008] EWCA 1186 a council sought an injunction where an ASBO would have been appropriate. It did this to try to avoid the criminal standard of proof, but the Court of Appeal said that in such circumstances the criminal standard should apply.

[34] The courts have ruled that paper and electronic documents and records fall within the definition of an 'article': *Rowe* [2007] QB 975, but that, in the interests of legal certainty, there must be some direct connection between possession of the article and its use for terrorism: *Zafar* [2008] 2 WLR 1013. See also the preceding sub-section for an explanation of how the defendant can place a much heavier burden on the prosecution of proving that no non-terrorist purpose existed.

[35] In which case it can be argued an ASBO is inappropriate because it may be used to circumvent the maximum penalty for overlapping criminal offences: *Stevens* [2006] EWCA 255.

[36] Inappropriate and draconian uses of the orders against, for example, children, beggars, prostitutes and those with mental health problems, are becoming increasingly frequent. See further Macdonald S, 'A Suicidal Woman, Roaming Pigs and a Noisy Trampolinist: Refining the ASBOs Definition of Anti Social Behaviour' (2006) 69 MLR 183; Macdonald S and Telford M, 'The Use of ASBOS against Young People in England and Wales: Lessons from Scotland' (2007) 27(4) Legal Studies 604.

is actually applied in the courts, for less than 1% of applications for ASBOs (from 1999 to 2005) were turned down.[37]

These problems also apply to 'behaviour liable to cause a breach of the peace' (see ch 3) and some unambiguously criminal offences such as behaviour 'likely to cause alarm or distress'.[38] Police officers can 'prove' beyond reasonable doubt that something was 'likely' or 'liable' by stating that they believed it was likely or liable – no other witnesses are needed. A related police power, created by the Anti-social Behaviour Act 2003, is the 'dispersal order'. If the police designate an area a 'dispersal zone' (and over 1,000 were so designated in England and Wales between 2004 and 2006) they can tell any 'groups' of two or more people to disperse if they believe a member of the public is likely to be harassed, alarmed or distressed by their continuing presence. It is a criminal offence to not do as the police say.[39]

The lesson to be drawn from this section is that, rather than be taken in by oratorical claims concerning supposedly fundamental principles, one must consider in detail the actual rules and their operation. We must, in other words, be alive to the possibility that the rhetorical goals of criminal justice are not necessarily the same as the goals that are actually pursued. In particular, we have seen that the recent shift towards preventive orders means that proof of guilt is not always a precondition of intrusive control by the agents of criminal justice.

1.3 Adversarial and inquisitorial theories of criminal justice

Evidence relating to guilt and innocence has to be gathered, put in some coherent order and then presented. This is done in accordance with rules, principles and policies of criminal procedure and evidence. There are two broad approaches to criminal justice fact-finding – the adversarial and the inquisitorial.[40] The adversarial principle that it is for the prosecution to bring a case to court and prove guilt is a characteristic of the English system and of other common law systems such as Australia, Canada and the USA. Civil law systems, such as France or Germany, are generally said to be based on inquisitorial principles.

---

[37] Data obtained from Home Office website in April 2007 (thanks again to Kevin Brown for this reference).

[38] Public Order Act 1986, s 5 (the defendant must have intended or been aware that his or her behaviour was threatening, abusive, insulting or disorderly). Further examples of the breadth of the criminal law are given in 10.4.

[39] See further Crawford A and Lister S, *The Use and Impact of Dispersal Orders* (London: Policy Press, 2007); Crawford A, 'Dispersal Powers and the Symbolic Role of Anti-Social Behaviour Legislation' (2008a) 71(5) MLR 753.

[40] 'Popular' or 'informal' justice, as found, for example, in African tribal systems, arguably represents a third broad approach. See further Vogler R, *A World View of Criminal Justice* (Aldershot: Ashgate, 2005).

In an inquisitorial system the dominant role in conducting a criminal inquiry is supposed to be played by the court.[41] A dossier is prepared to enable the judge taking the case to master its details. The judge then makes decisions about which witnesses to call and examines them in person, with the prosecution and defence lawyers consigned to a subsidiary role. In some inquisitorial systems the dossier is prepared (in serious cases) by an examining magistrate (juge d'instruction), with wide investigative powers, but more frequently this is done by the prosecutor and police.

In the 'pure' adversarial system, by contrast, the burden of preparing the case for court falls on the parties themselves. The judge (sometimes with a jury) acts as an umpire, listening to the evidence produced by the parties, ensuring that the proceedings are conducted with procedural propriety, and announcing a decision at the conclusion of the case. If the parties choose not to call a certain witness, then however relevant that person's evidence might have been, there is nothing the court can do about it. The adversarial contest in court thus resembles a game in which truth might appear to be the loser.[42] Indeed, it is sometimes said that adversarial systems focus on proof, and inquisitorial systems on truth.[43] But this is too simplistic. Both systems are concerned with establishing the facts to the required degree of certainty,[44] but they differ on the best way of achieving that end.

Adversarial theory holds that 'truth is best discovered by powerful statements on both sides of the question'[45] which are then evaluated by a passive and impartial adjudicator. This recognises that the events leading up to a criminal offence, and the intentions or knowledge of the parties involved, are always open to interpretation and dispute. The danger in an inquisitorial system is that whoever conducts the investigation (whether the police, a prosecutor or an examining magistrate) will come to favour one particular view of the matter, and that this will influence the construction of the dossier. Material helpful to the accused may be excluded. There is also the danger that a trial judge, having formed an initial view of the case based on a reading of the dossier, will give too much weight to evidence adduced at the trial which is consistent with the pre-existing theory, and too little to that which conflicts with it:

In one study, two groups of professional judges were compared. They heard identical cases, but one group read the file beforehand and the other did not. All of those who read the

---

[41] Our discussion here is of an 'ideal type' for in practice there are considerable differences between systems which are labelled 'inquisitorial': Damaska M, 'Evidentiary Barriers to Conviction and Two Models of Criminal Procedure: A Comparative Study' (1973) 121 U Penn LR 506.

[42] See Frankel M, 'The Search for the Truth: An Umpireal View' (1975) 123 U Penn LR 1031.

[43] See the critique of the adversarial system by a (then) Chief Constable, Pollard C, 'Public Safety, Accountability and the Courts' [1996] Crim LR 152, and the reply by Ashworth A, 'Crime, Community and Creeping Consequentialism' [1996] Crim LR 220.

[44] It is in this sense that 'truth' must be understood in the discussion that follows. In reality, a criminal trial focuses on whether the evidence of guilt presented meets the 'beyond reasonable doubt' test. If it does not then that is the end of the matter, and the question of whether somebody else might have committed the offence will not be examined further.   [45] Ex p Lloyd (1822) Mont 70, 72 n.

file beforehand convicted the defendant. Only twenty-seven per cent of the others did so. The prosecutor's opinion and the documents supporting it strongly influenced prior expectations.[46]

In dossier-based systems the spoken word is so distrusted that once something is memorialised in the dossier it is hard to dislodge that later in, for example, a trial.[47] Far better, according to the adversarial theory, that the judge remain impartial throughout and allow the parties to put forward their interpretations of the facts and law in the way most favourable to them. By opening up a range of possible views, it is more likely that the 'real truth' will emerge:

The arguments of counsel hold the case, as it were, in suspension between two opposing interpretations of it. While the proper classification of the case is thus kept unresolved, there is time to explore all of its peculiarities and nuances.[48]

So, while inquisitorial systems are rightly portrayed as involving a pre-eminent commitment to search for the truth, the way in which that search is conducted can shape the 'truth' that is proclaimed in court. Adversarial systems, by contrast, with their emphasis on the parties proving their case, can lose sight of the truth for different reasons: one or both of the parties might deliberately suppress relevant evidence for tactical reasons, or engage in aggressive cross-examination designed to so humiliate or confuse a witness that their evidence will be perceived as unreliable.[49] Or one party (almost invariably the defendant) might lack adequate access to the resources or expertise needed to counterbalance the arguments of their opponent.[50] In practice, there is no reliable evidence on which system is better at getting at the truth, nor is such evidence likely to be obtainable.[51]

Adversarial and inquisitorial models express different conceptions of how power should be allocated in society.[52] These differences result in the adversarial model attaching less weight to the goal of reliable fact-finding than the inquisitorial model, not because that goal is seen as unimportant, but rather because of an acknowledgement that the pursuit of other important aims necessarily implies a reduced relative

---

[46] McEwan J, 'The Adversarial and Inquisitorial Models of Criminal Trial' in Duff A, Farmer L, Marshall S and Tadros V (eds), *The Trial on Trial* (Oxford: Hart, 2004) p 64. See further Fuller L, 'The Forms and Limits of Adjudication' (1978) 92 Harv LR 353 at p 383.

[47] Hodgson J, 'Hierarchy, Bureaucracy and Ideology in French Criminal Justice' (2002) 29 JLS 227.

[48] Fuller (1978: 383). For an accessible exploration of this point see Jackson J and Doran S, *Judge without Jury* (Oxford: OUP, 1995) ch 3.

[49] This has been a particular problem in rape trials, where the adversarial model has come under particular attack. Temkin J, 'Prosecuting and Defending Rape' (2000) 27 JLS 219 at p 241 refers to defence barristers' cross examinations intended to 'depict women as "sluts" so that juries would conclude that they were undeserving of the law's protection...because they simply assumed it was their duty to do their utmost for their client'.   [50] See generally McEwan (2004).

[51] Redmayne M, *Expert Evidence and Criminal Justice* (Oxford: OUP, 2001) p 213, n 92.

[52] See Damaska M, *The Faces of Justice and State Authority* (New Haven: Yale, 1986) and the accessible discussion by Jackson J, 'Evidence: Legal Perspective' in Bull R and Carson D (eds), *Handbook of Psychology in Legal Contexts* (Chichester: Wiley, 1995).

weighting for 'truth-discovery'.[53] The adversarial model assumes that the state is committed to proving cases against individual citizens in order to fulfil its duty of enforcing the criminal law. In order to guard against the state abusing its powerful position, safeguards must be provided. One such safeguard is an expression of the constitutional doctrine of the separation of powers: the state provides a forum in which one branch of government (the judicial, ie the criminal courts) considers the case built and presented by another (the executive, ie the police and the prosecution). The passivity of magistrates and judges required by adversarial theory can also be seen as an expression of this mistrust of official power, as can the use of lay people (juries and most magistrates) to deliver verdicts on guilt or innocence. These devices all seek, amongst other things, to guarantee the impartiality of adjudication.

The adversarial model is also sensitive to the need to ensure that prosecution evidence is collected by fair and lawful means. Thus, for example, defence lawyers are meant to play an active part at the investigative stage of a criminal case (advising the suspect, applying for bail, and so forth) and there are limits on the length of time suspects can be held by the police for questioning. The importance attached in an adversarial system to the integrity of the procedures followed in collecting evidence and proving guilt can also be seen in the development of rules of evidence aimed at promoting both the fairness and reliability of verdicts pronounced by a court.[54]

In the inquisitorial system, by contrast, the underlying assumption is that the state can be (largely) trusted to conduct a neutral investigation into the truth. Therefore safeguards such as passive adjudicators, a strict separation of investigative and adjudicative powers, rules of evidence and defence lawyers are seen as less important. Many suspects are subjected to lengthy periods of pre-charge incarceration without access to legal advice. Leigh and Zedner have noted that 'while nothing in French law requires the overuse of detention, a tendency to do so seems deeply ingrained in the legal culture and doubtless derives from a desire not to release a suspect until the truth has been ascertained'.[55] All too often the supposed safeguard against oppressive police practices offered by judicial or prosecution control of the investigation process is a chimera. According to the author of the most in-depth empirical study of the French system, judicial supervision does not involve a careful and impartial pursuit of alternative theories and lines of enquiry. Rather:

The guilt of the suspect is presumed and denials are rejected. Evidence of violence committed on the suspect by the police was ignored and left for the defence to raise at court; the word of the victim or of the police was consistently preferred over that of the suspect; serious cases meant an almost automatic request for a remand in custody, even where the evidence was

---

[53] Damaska M, 'Evidentiary Barriers to Conviction and Two Models of Criminal Procedure: A Comparative Study' (1973) 121 U Penn LR 506 at 579–80, n 197.

[54] See generally Roberts and Zuckerman (2004).

[55] Leigh L and Zedner L, *A Report on the Administration of Criminal Justice in the Pre-Trial Phase in England and Germany* (Royal Commission on Criminal Justice, Research Study No 1) (London: HMSO, 1992) p 53.

thin. At trial, the most serious charge which the evidence might support was preferred: the public interest demanded that nothing should risk going unpunished.[56]

The problem of abuse in the inquisitorial system, and doubts about the effectiveness of the juge d'instruction, led to the abolition of this role in Germany in 1975. Corruption amongst investigative judges led to abolition in Italy in 1988, and substantial reforms to the French system were made in 1993 and 2000.[57] Whether adequate safeguards for suspects in France were put in place as a result of these changes seems doubtful. Reforms to institutional arrangements are unlikely to achieve much so long as the prevailing legal culture assumes the guilt of suspects and prioritises the 'community interest' in the efficient conviction of the guilty.[58]

In order to avoid giving the impression that everything in the English adversarial garden is rosy, in the next section we supplement our account of the theoretical underpinnings of English criminal justice with a short account of its own weed-ridden history.

1.4 **Recent trends in criminal justice and crime**

In 1981, the Royal Commission on Criminal Procedure (the Philips Commission), originally set up because of the wrongful conviction of three youths for the murder of Maxwell Confait,[59] published its blueprint for a 'fair, open, workable and efficient' system.[60] It recommended that there should be a 'fundamental balance' in criminal justice between the rights of suspects and the powers of the police.[61] Although not all of its proposals were accepted, its report led to the Police and Criminal Evidence Act 1984 (PACE) and the Prosecution of Offences Act 1985. PACE, together with its associated Codes of Practice, provided, for the first time, a detailed legislative framework for the operation of police powers and suspects' rights. The 1985 Act created the Crown Prosecution Service to take over the prosecution function from the police. Lawyers, rather than the police, now have the final say on whether cases should be prosecuted. The aim was, in part, to try to ensure that the defects in criminal procedure exposed by the 'Confait Affair' – such as undue pressure on suspects to confess, the unavailability of legal advice for suspects in

---

[56] Hodgson J, 'The Police, the Prosecutor and the Juge D'Instruction' (2001) 41 B J Crim 342 at 357. For full length treatment see Hodgson J, *French Criminal Justice* (Oxford: Hart, 2005).

[57] See generally Jorg et al, 'Are Inquisitorial and Adversarial Systems Converging?' in Harding et al (eds), *Criminal Justice in Europe* (Oxford: Clarendon, 1995).

[58] On the legal culture in France see Hodgson J, 'Codified Criminal Procedure and Human Rights: Some Observations on the French Experience' [2003] Crim LR 165.

[59] See the official inquiry into what became known as the 'Confait Affair': *Report of an Inquiry into the Circumstances leading to the Trial of Three Persons on Charges arising out of the Death of Maxwell Confait and the Fire at 27 Doggett Road, London SE6* (HCP 90) (London: HMSO, 1977).

[60] Royal Commission on Criminal Procedure (RCCP), Report (Cmnd 8092) (London: HMSO, 1981) para 10.1.   [61] RCCP (1981) paras 1.11 to 1.35.

police stations, and the absence of an independent check on police decisions – would be eliminated, thereby reducing the risk of further miscarriages of justice.

However, in the years following these Acts of Parliament, a string of similar cases came to light including the 'Guildford Four', the 'Maguires', the 'Birmingham Six', Stefan Kiszko, Judith Ward, the 'Cardiff Three', the 'Tottenham Three', the Taylor sisters, and the 'Bridgewater Four'. Long terms of imprisonment were served by nearly all of the defendants in these cases. Paddy Nicholls, whose conviction was quashed on 12 June 1998, served 23 years for the 'murder' of someone later shown to have almost certainly died of natural causes.[62] The causes of the miscarriages of justice varied from case to case, but common features were the suppression by the police and prosecution agencies of evidence helpful to the defence, incriminating evidence (including false confessions) secured from suspects by the police use of psychological pressure and tricks, deficiencies in the production and interpretation of expert evidence, and the distortion, manipulation and occasional fabrication of prosecution evidence (again, including confession evidence).[63] By implication, a further cause was the inadequate resources available to the defence to guard against or uncover these defects prior to conviction. For all these reasons, the adversarial truth-discovery mechanism of hearing powerful arguments on both sides of the question had been undermined. Juries had understandably convicted on the basis of what had seemed in court to be overwhelming prosecution cases.

Some of the people involved in these cases were tried before the changes in the law ushered in by the Philips Commission, but others (such as the 'Cardiff Three', where three young men were wrongly convicted of offences connected with murder of a prostitute)[64] were convicted under the new regime. Also, by July 1993, the convictions of 14 people had been quashed because of irregularities by one particular group of police officers (the West Midlands Serious Crime Squad), most of these being post-PACE cases.[65] The pressure created by these spectacular miscarriages led to the establishment of the Royal Commission on Criminal Justice (the Runciman Commission), which reported in 1993.[66] Yet the Runciman Commission advocated few major changes to the criminal process, arguing that there was no reason to believe that the 'great majority' of verdicts were 'not correct'.[67] Moreover, its recommendations taken

---

[62]   *The Guardian*, 13 June 1998.

[63]   For useful accounts of some of the main cases see Rozenberg J, 'Miscarriages of Justice' in Stockdale E and Casale S (eds), *Criminal Justice under Stress* (London: Blackstone, 1992), and ch 2 of Walker C and Starmer K (eds), *Miscarriages of Justice* (London: Blackstone Press, 1999).

[64]   The real murderer was convicted in 2003, 11 years after their convictions were quashed. Three witnesses, who were bullied into giving false evidence against them, were jailed in 2008. Thirteen serving and former police officers are, at the time of writing, facing charges of conspiracy to pervert the course of justice: *The Guardian*, 22 December 2008, 4 and 9 March 2009.

[65]   Many of these cases are discussed in Kaye T, *'Unsafe and Unsatisfactory?' Report of the Independent Inquiry into the Working Practices of the West Midlands Police Serious Crime Squad* (London: Civil Liberties Trust, 1991).

[66]   Royal Commission on Criminal Justice (RCCJ), Report (Cm 2263) (London: HMSO, 1993).

[67]   RCCJ (1993) para 23.

overall favoured the interests of the police and prosecution agencies more than those of suspects.[68]

An obvious question raised by this sequence of events is whether the Runciman Commission was right to think that the framework established by PACE and the Prosecution of Offences Act 1985 was basically sound. One view is that something more than mere tinkering was needed if suspects were to be adequately protected, as indicated by continuing patterns of police malpractice and wrongful convictions.[69] An opposite view is that the mid 1980s legislation had already swung the pendulum so far in favour of safeguards for suspects that the ability of the police to bring criminals to justice had been unduly hampered, the occasional dramatic miscarriage or corruption case notwithstanding.

The latter view prevailed under the Conservative Government in the years immediately following the publication of the Runciman Commission's report. Taken together, the Criminal Justice and Public Order Act 1994, the Criminal Procedure and Investigations Act 1996, and the Police Act 1997 provided the police and prosecution with important new powers and significantly reduced the rights and safeguards of suspects. The Labour Government in power since 1997 has dismantled suspects' rights and increased police powers at an even greater rate. The torrent of legislation on the subject includes the Crime and Disorder Act 1998, the Youth Justice and Criminal Evidence Act 1999, the Regulation of Investigatory Powers Act 2000, the Police Reform Act 2002, the Anti-social Behaviour Act 2003, the Criminal Justice Act 2003, the Domestic Violence, Crime and Victims Act 2004, the Clean Neighbourhoods and Environment Act 2005, the Serious Organised Crime and Police Act 2005, the Violent Crime Reduction Act 2006, the Serious Crime Act 2007, the Criminal Justice and Immigration Act 2008 and numerous anti-terrorism Acts. When former Prime Minister Blair said that 'the rules of the game are changing' (as quoted at the start of this chapter) he was not exaggerating.[70] They are likely to continue to change over the next few years. Announcing a review of PACE, the Home Office Minister of State said its aim was 'serving the needs of victims and witnesses and helping raise the efficiency and effectiveness of the police service'. Protecting suspects came low in a list of criteria for changing the law.[71] Thus the final consultation document contained a long list of proposed extra police powers (such as easier authorisation of lengthy detention of suspects, and more opportunities for police questioning of suspects) but no new or

[68] For critiques see Young R and Sanders A, 'The Royal Commission on Criminal Justice: A Confidence Trick?' (1994) 15 OJLS 435; McConville M and Bridges L (eds), *Criminal Justice in Crisis* (Aldershot: Edward Elgar, 1994) and Field S and Thomas P (eds), *Justice and Efficiency? The Royal Commission on Criminal Justice* (London: Blackwell, 1994) (also published as (1994) 21 JLS No 1).

[69] For evidence of police and prosecution malpractice of a kind likely to contribute to miscarriages of justice see chs 2–7. For quashed convictions and successful civil actions against the police since the RCCJ reported, see chs 6 (at 6) and 11–12. For accounts of the most notorious miscarriages of justice uncovered in recent times, go to <http://www.innocent.org.uk/cases/index.html> (accessed 5 January 2010).

[70] Although we should here note that the recent lurch towards 'preventive' anti-terrorist legislation has many historical precedents: Bonner (2007).

[71] See Cape E, 'Modernising Police Powers – Again?' [2007] Crim LR 934 for discussion and detailed references to the Minister's initial consultation document.

strengthened rights for suspects.[72] As this was issued in August 2008, we do not know yet how many of these proposals will be implemented.

We also need to consider briefly the crime problem. For if it is getting worse, the Government's view that the 'rules of the game' remain overly generous to the accused may have some merit. But if crime rates are steady or in decline, and detection rates steady or rising, the Government's position will be much weaker.

Trends in crime are measured in two ways. In addition to collating the crimes recorded by the police, the government also interviews large samples of adult house-holders to estimate roughly how many crimes are not recorded (largely because many victims do not report crimes to the police). In 2007/08 there were around 10 million crimes in total (of which victims were aware). Just under 5 million of these crimes were recorded by the police. Perhaps to the surprise of many readers, on both meas-ures this reflects a drop on the previous year. Indeed, crime levels have fallen in most years since 1995, and are now around their 1981 level. This is all true of serious as well as less serious crime. Of the five million 'official' crimes, 1% are sexual offences, 2% robberies, and nearly 20% other violent crime (in half of which there was no injury). Burglary constitutes another 12%. Most of the rest – that is, around two thirds of the total – consists of non-violent theft and criminal damage. The use of weapons (around one quarter of all violent crime) has remained stable over the last 10 years. The police detected a higher proportion of 'official' crime (28%) in 2007/8 than in the previous year (26%), though the absolute number of detections fell slightly.[73] As the economic recession gets worse we might expect an increase in acquisitive crime. Figures for the last three months of 2008 are ambiguous. Most 'official' crime continued to fall, apart from burglary, which rose by 4%. The 'unofficial' crime total remained stable, but per-sonal thefts rose sharply (unlike burglary, which remained stable).[74] To sum up, crime is falling or stable, and those who commit crime have a higher chance of being caught than previously. The crime problem, then, while always a matter of concern, provides no more reason now than it did several years ago to strengthen police powers and reduce the rights of suspects. Much the same can be said of terrorism. England and Wales has for centuries experienced occasional acts of terrorism as well as more con-certed terrorist campaigns and it is arguable that the threat now posed by Al-Qaeda and other fundamentalist groups is not qualitatively different from that, say, posed in the 1970s and 1980s by the provisional Irish Republican Army (IRA).[75] To the extent

---

[72] Home Office, *PACE Review: Government proposals in response to the Review of the Police and Criminal Evidence Act 1984* (London: Home Office Policing Powers and Protection Unit, 2008).

[73] Kershaw et al, *Crime in England and Wales, 2007/8* (Statistical Bulletin 07/08) (London: Home Office, 2008). For a short but excellent discussion see Reiner R, 'Success or Statistics? New Labour and Crime Control' (2007) 67 Criminal Justice Matters 4.

[74] Home Office (2009c) *Crime in England and Wales: Quarterly Update to December 2008* (London: Home Office Statistical Bulletin 06/09).

[75] See Feldman D, 'Human Rights, Terrorism and Risk: The Roles of Politicians and Judges' [2006] PL 364 at 367–70; Bonner (2007: 8–10). For a contrary view see Greer, S 'Human Rights and the Struggle against Terrorism in the United Kingdom' (2008) 2 EHRLR 163.

that the threat is novel (for example, the use of suicide bombers), most of the laws passed to counter it seem unlikely to be effective. The avalanche of anti-terrorist laws passed in recent years cannot be justified by the facts, however brute some of those facts may appear to be.[76]

More fundamentally, decisions about how much power to give the police and prosecution agencies can never be factually determined but rather express value choices about the appropriate goals of criminal justice, the order in which they should be prioritised, and the appropriate means to achieve them. Is there any way of clarifying the implications of such choices, thus providing us with the normative material we need in order to come to a more rational decision about the appropriate means and ends of criminal justice?

These were the kinds of problem which, over 30 years ago, an American writer, Herbert Packer, tackled when he developed his two models of the criminal process: due process and crime control.[77] These models have been used by many commentators on criminal justice as tools of analysis.[78] They have also been subjected to much criticism. In the next section we explain the models, and comment on their strengths and weaknesses.

1.5 **Crime control and due process**

Packer developed his models in order to illuminate what he saw as the two conflicting value systems that competed for priority in the operation of the criminal process. Neither purported to describe any specific system, and neither was to be taken as the ideal. Rather, they represented extremes on a spectrum of possible ways of doing criminal justice. Use of the models enables one to plot the position of current criminal justice practices at each stage of the criminal process, as well as to highlight the direction of actual and foreseeable trends.

1.5.1 **Crime control**

In this model the repression of criminal conduct is viewed as by far the most important function to be performed by the criminal process. In the absence of such repression, a

---

[76] For a measured analysis see Greer (2008).

[77] Packer H, *The Limits of the Criminal Sanction* (Stanford: Stanford UP, 1968) ch 8.

[78] See, for example, McConville M and Baldwin J, *Courts, Prosecution, and Conviction* (Oxford: Clarendon, 1981) pp 3–7; Padfield N, *Text and Materials on the Criminal Justice Process* 3rd edn (London: LexisNexis, 2003) pp 27–30 and the first edition of this book. For refinements and other approaches see, for example, Bottoms A and McClean J, *Defendants in the Criminal Process* (London: Routledge, 1976) pp 226–32; King M, *The Framework of Criminal Justice* (London: Croom Helm, 1981) ch 2, Norrie A, ' "Simulacra of Morality?" Beyond the Ideal/Actual Antinomies of Criminal Justice' in Duff A (ed), *Criminal Law: Principle and Critique* (New York: CUP, 1998), Roach K, 'Four Models of the Criminal Process' (1999a) 89 J Crim Law and Criminology 671 and the rest of this book.

general disregard for the criminal law would develop and citizens would live in constant fear. In order to uphold social freedom, the model must achieve a high rate of detection and conviction. But because crime levels are high and resources are limited the model depends for success on speed and on minimising the opportunities for challenge. Formal fact-finding through examination and cross-examination in court is slow and wasteful. Speed can best be achieved by allowing the police to establish the facts through interrogation. To further guarantee speed, procedures must be uniform and routine, so that the model as a whole resembles a conveyor belt in its operation.

The quality control in this system is entrusted in large measure to the police. By the application of their expertise the probably innocent are quickly screened out of the process while the probably guilty are passed quickly through the remaining stages of the process. Indeed, the model goes further in claiming that the pre-trial administrative processes are more likely to produce reliable evidence of guilt than formal court procedures. The ideal mechanisms for truncating these procedures are guilty pleas. They eliminate lengthy and expensive trials. The police will thus seek to extract confessions from those whom they presume to be guilty as this makes it very difficult for the suspect to do other than admit guilt at court. For as Packer[79] concludes of the crime control model, 'when reduced to its barest essentials and operating at its most successful pitch, it offers two possibilities: an administrative fact-finding process leading (1) to exoneration of the suspect or (2) to the entry of a plea of guilty'.

The crime control model accepts that some (but not many) mistakes will be made in identifying the probably guilty and the probably innocent, and considers this a price worth paying for the efficient repression of crime. On the other hand, if too many guilty people escaped liability, or the system was perceived to be generally unreliable (as would be the case if it was shown that innocent people were being prosecuted on a large scale) then the deterrent efficacy of the criminal law would be weakened. Limited safeguards against miscarriages of justice, including an appellate system, are therefore accepted as necessary, but primarily in order to promote confidence in the system. Confidence is promoted in part by displaying confidence in itself, so cases are regarded as closed following verdicts in all but the most compelling circumstances.

While the crime control model can tolerate rules forbidding illegal arrests or coercive interrogations (since such rules might promote reliability) those rules should not be enforced through the exclusion, in court, of illegally obtained evidence, or the quashing of convictions simply because the rules have been breached. To let the guilty go free on such technicalities undermines crime control to an unacceptable extent.

1.5.2 Due process

The due process model lacks confidence in informal pre-trial fact-finding processes. Many factors may contribute to a mistaken belief in guilt resulting in the production

---

[79] Packer (1968: 162–3).

of unreliable evidence against the suspect. For example, witnesses to disturbing events tend to make errors in recollecting details, or may be animated by a bias that the police either encourage or will not seek to discover. Similarly, confessions by suspects in police custody are as likely to signify psychological coercion by officers convinced they have apprehended the right suspect as they are to demonstrate guilt. Due process therefore insists on formal, adjudicative, adversary fact-finding processes in which the case against the accused is tested before a public and impartial court.

Because of this concern with error, the due process model also rejects the crime control desire for finality. There must always be a possibility of a case being reopened to take account of some new fact that has come to light since the last public hearing. Unlike crime control, the due process model insists on the prevention and elimination of miscarriages of justice as an end in itself: 'The aim of the process is at least as much to protect the factually innocent as it is to convict the factually guilty.'[80]

Other values upheld by the due process model include the primacy of the individual citizen, and thus the complementary need for limits on official power. Controls are needed to prevent state officials exercising coercive powers in an oppressive manner even if this impairs the efficiency of the system. In certain situations, concern with abuse of power in the due process model takes precedence over reliability. Suppose, for example, that the police had illegally obtained evidence that established that a suspect had almost certainly committed a murder. The due process model would insist that the evidence be excluded at trial; if there was no other evidence of guilt, the suspect would walk free because of the procedural irregularity. It is only by demonstrating to officials that there is nothing to be gained by abusing power and breaking rules that adherence to them can be guaranteed. The due process model is also concerned with the upholding of moral standards as a matter of principle. In the belief that an important way to encourage and affirm law-abiding behaviour is by example, unlawfully obtained evidence has to be excluded.[81] To do otherwise would be to undermine the moral condemnation which is meant to be conveyed by a finding of guilt.[82]

The due process model also upholds the ideal of equality – that everyone should be placed in the same position as regards the resources at their disposal to conduct an effective defence of a criminal charge. Thus, whenever the system affords a theoretical right for a lawyer to advise or represent a client, the due process model insists that those who cannot afford a lawyer should be provided with one for free. Lawyers play a central part in this model since they should bring into play the remedies and sanctions which due process offers as checks against the operation of the system.

Finally, the due process model is sceptical about the morality of the criminal sanction. It notes that in practice this sanction is used primarily against the psychologically and economically impaired. To seek to condemn and deter these people for their

---

[80] Packer (1968: 165).   [81] Packer (1968: 231–2).

[82] In his 'reconstruction' of Packer's models, Aranella (1996: 21), points out that: 'A public trial, if fairly conducted, sends its own message about dignity, fairness, and justice that contributes to the moral force of the criminal sanction.'

supposedly free-will decision to breach the criminal law smacks of cruel hypocrisy, particularly when there is a failure to provide for the individualised and humane rehabilitation of offenders. 'In short', as Packer (1968: 171) puts it, 'doubts about the ends for which power is being exercised create pressure to limit the discretion with which that power is exercised'.

At the risk of oversimplification, one can summarise the main conflict in values between the two models in the following way. Crime control values prioritise the conviction of the guilty, even at the risk of the conviction of some (fewer) innocents, and with the cost of infringing the liberties of suspects to achieve its goals; while due process values prioritise the acquittal of the innocent, even if risking the frequent acquittal of the guilty, and giving high priority to the protection of civil liberties as an end in itself. Further, whereas due process seeks to maximise adversarialism by introducing obstacles and hurdles for the prosecution to surmount at every stage, crime control seeks ways of ensuring that the adversarial contest never gets beyond the encounter between the police and the suspect in the police station. Due process and adversarial ideology thus can work harmoniously together, whereas crime control values tend to subvert adversarial procedures. Indeed, with its emphasis on trusting the police and prosecution to get at the truth in a reliable manner, the crime control model expresses some of the ideological elements which underpin the inquisitorial model. Both models employ powerful arguments and Packer (1968: 154) himself suggested that anyone who supported one model to the complete exclusion of the other 'would be rightly viewed as a fanatic'.

1.5.3 What are the goals of crime control and due process?

Some criticisms of Packer's analytical framework (and how it has been used) derive from a misunderstanding about the goals and values each model encompasses.[83] Ashworth and Redmayne, for example, suggest that the 'models might be reconstructed so as to suggest that crime control is the underlying purpose of the system, but that pursuit of this purpose should be qualified out of respect to due process; or so as to suggest that crime control and due process should be recognized as the two main objectives of the system'.[84] Similarly Smith argues that 'the Crime Control Model is concerned with the fundamental goal of the criminal justice system, whereas the Due Process Model is concerned with setting limits to the pursuit of that goal. Due Process is not a goal in itself.'[85] These criticisms place too much weight on the labels Packer applied to his models. In particular, it is mistaken to regard the due process model as merely a negative model in which the only aim is to protect suspects. The two models share

---

[83] For fuller discussion of abuse of Packer's models see Roberts P, 'Comparative Criminal Justice Goes Global' (2008) 28 OJLS 369 at 378–9, and the third edition of this work at pp 22–5.

[84] Ashworth A and Redmayne M, *The Criminal Process* 3rd edn (Oxford: OUP, 2005) p 39.

[85] Smith D, 'Case Construction and the Goals of Criminal Process' (1997a) 37 BJ Crim 319 at 335. See, to similar effect, Aranella (1996: 19), and Damaska (1973: 575).

much common ground including the assumptions that the 'criminal process ordinarily ought to be invoked by those charged with the responsibility for doing so when it appears that a crime has been committed' and that 'a degree of scrutiny and control must be exercised with respect to the activities of law enforcement officers,...the security and privacy of the individual may not be invaded at will'.[86] It thus follows that both models incorporate the belief that law enforcement is socially desirable[87] (because of its crime preventive effects) and both incorporate the belief that there must be some limits to the power of the government to pursue this underlying aim. The difference between the models, put simply, is that they represent different points of view about what those limits should be.

Choongh criticises Packer from an empirical standpoint, arguing that neither of his models adequately explains the experiences of a significant minority of those who are arrested and detained at the police station. For these detainees there is never any intention by the police to invoke the criminal process:

Arrest and detention is not, for this group of individuals, the stepping stone onto Packer's conveyor belt or the first stage of an obstacle course. It represents instead a self-contained policing system which makes use of a legal canopy to subordinate sections of society viewed as anti-police and innately criminal.[88]

He argues that the police are here operating a 'social disciplinary' model, which encompasses the belief that:

an acceptable and efficient way to police society is to identify classes of people who in various ways reject prevailing norms because it is amongst these classes that the threat of crime is at its most intense...the police are then justified in subjecting them to surveillance and subjugation, regardless of whether the individuals selected for this treatment are violating the criminal law at any given moment.[89]

However, Packer was constructing models of the criminal process, not of policing; it is not surprising that 'social disciplining' was not central in his analysis. Policing encompasses many activities: maintaining surveillance over public space, quelling disorder, responding to emergencies, rescuing pets, finding missing persons, directing traffic and so on. Only some of these are associated with controlling crime and even fewer are necessarily related to the formal criminal process. What Choongh's work usefully does is highlight the way in which the police sometimes use resources provided by the criminal process (such as interrogation powers) to pursue some part of the broader police mission. Nonetheless, Packer was too astute an observer to have overlooked that

---

[86] Packer (1968: 155–6).

[87] Note the comment by Packer (1968: 163) that the due process model 'does not rest on the idea that it is not socially desirable to repress crime, although critics of its application have been known to claim so'. See also Duff P, 'Crime Control, Due Process and "The Case for the Prosecution" ' (1998) 38 BJ Crim 611.

[88] Choongh S, 'Policing the Dross: A Social Disciplinary Model of Policing' (1998) 38 BJ Crim 623 at p 625.

[89] Choongh (1998: 627). See also Choongh S, *Policing as Social Discipline* (Oxford: Clarendon, 1997).

police powers could be used to subject whole classes of people to surveillance and sub-ordination.[90] Thus he noted that the crime control model rejected the due process idea that arrest should only be allowed when there was reason to believe that a specific indi-vidual had committed a specific crime.[91] Rather, 'people who are known to the police as previous offenders should be subject to arrest at any time for the limited purpose of determining whether they have been engaging in anti-social activities...'[92] Secondly:

anyone who behaves in a manner suggesting that he may be up to no good should be sub-ject to arrest for investigation: it may turn out that he has committed an offence, but more importantly, the very fact of stopping him for questioning, either on the street or at the sta-tion house, may prevent the commission of a crime. As a third instance, those who make a living out of criminal activity should be made to realise that their presence in the commu-nity is unwanted if they persist in their criminal occupations; periodic checks of their activ-ity, whether or not this involves an arrest, will help to bring that attitude home to them.[93]

Packer clearly linked these forms of 'social disciplining' to the ultimate goal of con-trolling crime. So does Choongh, albeit unwittingly.[94] The type of 'social disciplining' documented in Choongh's work highlights an important strand of crime control ide-ology but does not justify the construction of a new model of the criminal process.

  We have now clarified what adherents to crime control and due process models see as the purpose of criminal justice. Whether one believes the system is (or should be) governed predominantly by due process or crime control values, the purpose of the system would (or should) remain the same: to control crime, but with some protec-tions for suspects. Where one locates an actual criminal process on the spectrum of possibilities represented by the two models depends largely on the nature and extent of those protections.

1.5.4 English criminal justice: due process or crime control?

The English criminal justice system, like the American, is usually characterised as one which emphasises adversarial procedures and due process safeguards. In terms of the formal structure we can observe these safeguards intensifying as a person's liberty is progressively constrained.[95] The least constraining exercise of police power is simple questioning of someone who is merely a citizen, not a suspect. Since the questions are not aimed at incriminating the individual no due process protections are needed, but

---

[90] Packer (1968: 178), also noted that the criminal law itself might be so vaguely defined (eg, vagrancy and disorderly conduct laws) as to make 'social disciplining' lawful.   [91] Packer (1968: 176).

[92] Packer (1968: 177). Compare with Choongh (1998: 628): 'Having arrested individuals once, this in itself becomes reason for keeping them under surveillance...an individual becomes permanently suspect rather than a suspect for a particular offence.'   [93] Packer (1968: 177).

[94] See Choongh (1998: 629, 632) for example.

[95] All the points made in this sub-section are discussed in later chapters, at which point supporting refer-ences are provided.

no compulsion can be exercised either. The police are here in an information-gathering or inquisitorial mode.

As soon as the police have any reason to suspect the individual an 'adversarial' relationship is formed; the citizen becomes a suspect. The police now have the task of collecting evidence of what they believe the suspect has done so that this can be proven to the satisfaction of the courts. To assist them in this task the law provides them with various powers and, in order to guard against the misuse of these powers, due process protections begin. In general, only if there is 'reasonable suspicion' can coercive powers be exercised to search or to arrest a suspect. On arrest the suspect is usually taken to a police station and detained. This requires further due process justification because civil liberties are further eroded by detention and its associated procedures such as interrogation and strip-searches. Only if detention is adjudged to be 'necessary' (ie, in a broad sense of furthering the investigation) can it be authorised. If detention is authorised, further forms of due process protection come into play, such as the right to legal advice. In order to charge and prosecute a detainee, more evidence is required and further protections are provided – vetting of the case by the CPS and a grant of legal aid to prepare a defence. In order to convict there must be yet more evidence (proof beyond a reasonable doubt). The increasingly stringent nature of these protections is in accordance with Packer's portrayal of due process as an obstacle course with each successive stage presenting impediments to carrying the citizen any further along the process. This should mean that few factually innocent persons are found legally guilty, or are carried too far down the course, but it will also mean that many factually guilty persons will be ejected from the system for lack of the required standard of evidence.

If we look at the way the system actually operates, however, it displays certain features characteristic of a crime control model. Decisions to arrest and stop-search are often made on police instinct rather than reasonable suspicion, detention for the purpose of obtaining a confession is habitually and uniformly authorised, and there are huge incentives to confess and plead guilty. Perhaps most telling is the fact that the great majority (over 90%) of defendants whose cases proceed to trial plead guilty and forego their right to an adversarial battle. The prosecution evidence is not tested, and 'proof' beyond reasonable doubt is constituted by the plea itself. The probability in such a system is that many more factually innocent persons will be found legally guilty, and that many more factually guilty persons will be convicted, than if the system actually operated in the formal manner described earlier. In Packer's imagery, the system operates as a conveyor belt, moving suspects through a series of routinised procedures which lead, in the vast majority of those cases that reach court, to conviction.

Packer's conclusion[96] in the American context was that the actual operation of the criminal process conformed closely to crime control, but that the law governing that process (as developed, in particular, by the Supreme Court) expressed due process ideology. He identified a gap, in other words, between the law in books and the law

---

[96] Packer (1968: 239–40).

in action. But as Packer himself pointed out, it was perfectly possible for the Supreme Court to change tack and develop case law which expressed crime control values. If the rules themselves were in harmony with the crime control model, then there would be no need for the police to break them in order to achieve their central goal (if such it is) of repressing crime efficiently. The only gap that would then exist would be between the law in books and due process ideology.

The question of where on the spectrum between crime control and due process English criminal justice is today to be located must, therefore, take account of both the formal law as laid down in statutes and case law, and the actual operation of the system by officials operating within that legal framework. The first edition of this book, published in 1994, attempted to do this and concluded that the criminal process was far more oriented towards the crime control model than surface appearances might suggest, that there was a historical drift towards the crime control model, but that due process inspired safeguards remained, and would continue to remain, important. Subsequent events have confirmed that assessment, although the drift towards crime control has accelerated. For example, we shall see in the next chapter that many stop-search powers can be used lawfully even without reasonable suspicion.

Packer's models are the most enduring theoretical framework of criminal justice.[97] However, Packer's models do not identify all the major interests in the criminal process, nor all the major conflicts between them. Although still valuable, these models constitute an inadequate framework for the analysis of criminal justice. The most influential alternative is the human rights approach.

1.6 **The fundamental (human) rights approach**

The human rights approach starts from the position that citizens are rational, rights-bearing subjects. State power must therefore be subject to limits that respect the dignity of the individual. It follows that 'balancing' of conflicting criminal justice aims and interests should not be driven by consequentialist calculations of which set of arrangements would produce the most overall benefit to society. Rather, individual rights must be assigned some special weight in the balancing process. The goal of bringing cases to effective trial in the service of crime control is authoritatively constrained by human rights principles instead of (as in Packer's models) merely compromised to a varying extent by conflicting due process principles.[98] This philosophical position has been translated into positive law as a result of the United Nations Declaration of Human Rights (1948) and various regional human rights instruments. For the UK, human rights law derives from the European Convention on Human Rights (ECHR).

---

[97] Roach K, *Due Process and Victims' Rights: The New Law and Politics of Criminal Justice* (Toronto: University of Toronto Press, 1999b).   [98] Ashworth and Redmayne (2005: 28–37).

The UK has been bound at the international level by the ECHR since 1953.[99] For over 40 years thereafter, breaches of the rights set out in the Convention could only be challenged directly before the European Court of Human Rights (ECtHR) in Strasbourg. If the Court ruled that a breach had occurred the UK was obliged to amend the offending law or practice. The recognition that this procedure was cumbersome, slow and embarrassing to domestic political and judicial elites eventually led to the passing of the Human Rights Act 1998.[100] This requires British courts to take account of the Convention and the decisions of the European Court. If a common law precedent is found to be inconsistent with the Convention, the latter must be followed. The position with statutes is different, reflecting a concern to maintain the supremacy of Parliament over the courts. Thus, statutory provisions should be interpreted so far as is possible in accordance with the ECHR, and the House of Lords has repeatedly emphasised the radical and expansive nature of this interpretive obligation.[101] But if a court finds that a UK statute cannot be interpreted in accordance with the Convention, the court may make a 'declaration of incompatibility'. This does not invalidate the offending legislation. A new 'fast-track' procedure allows (but does not require) Parliament to amend the incompatible legislation.[102]

The rights enshrined in the ECHR and elaborated through decisions of the ECtHR thus provide us with criteria with which to evaluate our criminal justice system. There are a number of problems with using them in this way though.

1.6.1 Vagueness and inconsistency

Many ECHR rights are vague in the sense that their scope is uncertain. Take, for example, the Art 3 prohibition of inhuman or degrading treatment. Is it degrading to be arrested in public, or to have saliva scraped from inside one's mouth, for example? This vagueness is, of course, a quality of all legal rules, since they are inevitably 'open-textured' to a greater or lesser degree.[103] Rules always require interpretation and consideration of how they are to be applied in any given situation. But, like most international treaties, ECHR rights are particularly vague (and modest in scope), reflecting the need to achieve consensus amongst states with radically different legal traditions. One consequence of this is that no-one can simply ask the ECtHR (or a domestic court) to review the compatibility of national laws with the Convention in the abstract. Rather, specific individuals have to make a case that their human rights were infringed on a specific

---

[99] In addition, criminal justice in this country is now subject in a growing number of areas to European Community law and, therefore, to judicial supervision from the European Court of Justice. See, eg, Dine J, 'European Community Criminal Law?' [1993] Crim LR 246; and Baker E, 'Taking European Criminal Law Seriously' [1998] Crim LR 361.

[100] Young J, 'The Politics of the Human Rights Act' (1999) 26(1) JLS 27.

[101] Eg, *A (No 2)* [2001] UKHL 25, [2002] 1 AC 45; *Ghaidan v Godin-Mendoza* [2004] UKHL 30.

[102] A useful introduction to the Act and its reception is provided by Wadham et al, *Blackstone's Guide to the Human Rights Act 1998*, 4th edn (Oxford: OUP, 2007).

[103] Hart H, *The Concept of Law* (Oxford: Clarendon, 1961).

occasion.[104] This means that judgments are sensitive to the facts of a particular case and may not provide definitive or indicative answers to the question of whether a law or legal practice in itself might be in breach of the Convention (in other factual circumstances or all circumstances). Even under ideal conditions it would take much litigation before the parameters of human rights requirements become reasonably clear. But the ECtHR is overloaded and lacks the capacity to adjudicate most applications it receives in the way it would need to in order to shape the law coherently and consistently with its earlier decisions.[105] Moreover, the Human Rights Act merely requires domestic courts to take account of (rather than regard themselves as bound by) decisions of the ECtHR. Even were this not so, the particularly open-textured nature of the Convention rights and the fact they often conflict with each other and with other important interests leaves an enormous amount of discretion to judicial elites in determining 'our human rights' and judges will naturally differ in their determinations of such issues. Uncertainty of scope, inconsistency and incoherence are thus key features of Convention rights, notwithstanding the large degree of consensus around some issues (eg, use of physical violence to extract a confession is impermissible).

1.6.2 Human rights can be 'qualified'

While the term 'human rights' might be thought of as connoting something inviolable, this is not true of most Convention rights. The exceptions are the rights to life (Art 2) and not to be subjected to torture or inhuman or degrading treatment or punishment (Art 3). These are 'absolute' in the sense that they cannot be legitimately traded off against other rights or interests, or derogated from during times of national emergency. At the other extreme are 'qualified' rights, such as freedom of association (Art 11) and privacy (Art 8). For example, no invasion of Art 8 is allowed unless it is:

in accordance with the law and is necessary in a democratic society in the interests of national security, public safety or the economic well-being of the country, for the prevention of disorder or crime, for the protection of health or morals, or for the protection of the rights and freedoms of others.

It is difficult to think of a law infringing a qualified right that could not be defensibly linked to the furtherance of the many 'interests' and goals of 'protection' listed here,[106]

---

[104] See the discussion by Munday R, 'Inferences from Silence and European Human Rights Law' [1996] Crim LR 370.

[105] Greer S, 'Protocol 14 and the Future of the European Court of Human Rights' [2005] PL 83. For a fuller analysis of the crisis currently besetting the Convention system see Greer S, *The European Convention on Human Rights: Achievements, Problems and Prospects* (Cambridge: Cambridge University Press, 2006). Also see Amos M, 'The Impact of the Human Rights Act on the United Kingdom's performance before the European Court of Human Rights' [2007] PL 655 at 657 and 671.

[106] 'There is hardly a case in which either the domestic courts or Strasbourg has found the state to be acting for an illegitimate aim, so broad are the specified categories': Phillipson G, 'Bills of Rights as a Threat to Human Rights: The Alleged "Crisis of Legalism"' [2007] PL 217 at 220.

so the real question tends to be whether such an infringement is 'necessary in a democratic society'. This is known as the 'proportionality test' and requires that infringements of rights must be limited and proportionate to the aim sought to be secured. Thus, a major infringement of a Convention right to secure some marginal increase in crime control should always fail this test. Whether the proportionality test is difficult for the state to satisfy in practice is debatable, however, as we shall see throughout this book. For example, in ch 6 we show that the human rights era has made little difference to the ability of the police to invade people's privacy through the use of electronic surveillance ('bugging') devices.

1.6.3 Human rights can be 'derogated' from

Most Convention rights come somewhere between 'qualified' and 'absolute' rights. These 'strong' rights include the right to liberty and security of the person (Art 5) and the right to a fair trial (Art 6). Article 15 of the ECHR provides that, at a time of 'public emergency threatening the life of the nation' the state can take measures derogating from (ie, in breach of) these 'strong' rights. Such measures must be 'strictly required by the exigencies of the situation'. These tests are far more easily satisfied than one might imagine given the drastic imagery they embody. Thus the UK entered a derogation in respect of the 'emergency' legislation prompted by the situation in Northern Ireland and its related breaches of the Art 5 criteria governing the legality of arrest and extended detention. The derogation was adjudged valid by the European Court on successive occasions.[107] This derogation was finally withdrawn on 19 February 2001.

Does this signify a change in political and legal culture since the Labour Government 'brought rights home' through the passing of the Human Rights Act 1998? Not if s 23 of the Anti-terrorism, Crime and Security Act 2001 is anything to go by. This provided for the indefinite detention without trial of foreign nationals reasonably believed by the Home Secretary to be a terrorist or to pose a risk to national security. This clearly breached Art 5 of the ECHR, as well as amounting to racial discrimination, and the government duly registered a new derogation from the Convention, notwithstanding much criticism that this form of 'internment' was not 'strictly required by the exigencies of the situation'.[108] But in 2004 the House of Lords in *A and Others* declared this to be incompatible with the European Convention because indefinite detention of foreign nationals suspected of terrorism was adjudged to be disproportionate (ie, not strictly required by the exigencies of the situation) and discriminatory.[109]

---

[107] *Ireland v UK* (1978) 2 EHRR 25; *Brannigan and McBride v UK* (1993) 17 EHRR 539; *Marshall v United Kingdom* (App No 41571/98, Judgment of Court 10 July 2001). See generally Marks S, 'Civil Liberties at the Margin: The UK Derogation and the European Court of Human Rights' (1995) 15 OJLS 68.

[108] For a full account of this episode, and analysis of the internment power, see Walker (2002a: 8–11, 217–36).

[109] *A and ors v Secretary of State for the Home Department* [2004] UK HL 56. While freedom from discrimination in general is not prohibited by the ECHR, Art 5 (and other) rights 'shall be secured without

The scope for derogation makes the human rights framework unstable. Moreover, attempting to assess whether our criminal justice system lives up to human rights standards often involves waiting for a view from the courts as to whether we are facing a national emergency. As different levels of court may differ on this question, and the conditions of the 'emergency' are bound to shift over time, this creates yet more uncertainty and inconsistency, rendering attempts to evaluate criminal justice in accordance with human rights standards a rather speculative exercise.

1.6.4 Human rights offer little more than a minimalist safety net

A and Others was an uncharacteristically bold decision. Domestic courts usually interpret the ECHR in minimalist ways that do not interfere with domestic criminal justice laws and practices. Since they do not show a similar reluctance to interfere in some other areas of social policy,[110] it is difficult to attribute this minimalism to a concern with upholding parliamentary supremacy or as demonstrating deference to the supposedly specialised knowledge and skills of the Executive (although no doubt these factors play a part too). Rather, the judges' assessments of when the community interest in law enforcement outweighs human rights usually express crime control values.[111] Thus when, following the decision in *A & Others*, Parliament replaced indefinite detention in prison with a system of 'control orders' which greatly restrict the movement, activities and associations of those subject to them, the House of Lords only narrowly held that an order imposing an 18-hour daily curfew resulted in a breach of Art 5,[112] while an order imposing a 14-hour daily curfew was unanimously found *not* to involve a deprivation of liberty.[113] As Ewing and Tham observe: '...the standard at which the level of rights' violations is set is now so low that even serious restraints on liberty can cross the hurdle of legality with relative ease'.[114] The Government's own Department for Constitutional Affairs noted in 2006 that 'the Human Rights Act has not seriously impeded the achievement of the Government's objectives on crime, terrorism or immigration' and added that arguments 'that the Human Rights Act has significantly altered the constitutional

---

discrimination' (Art 14). The Prevention of Terrorism Act 2005 repealed s 23, but introduced a new system of control orders (see further ch 4).

[110] The classic analysis is that by Griffith J, *The Politics of the Judiciary*, 5th edn (London: HarperCollins, 1997). For brief discussion of how the judges are more willing to protect rights of a cultural nature than those which challenge political or economic arrangements, see Lustgarten L, 'Human Rights: Where Do We Go From Here?' (2006) 69(5) MLR 843 at 848.

[111] For an early analysis see Ashworth A, 'Criminal Proceedings After the Human Rights Act: The First Year' [2001] Crim LR 855. See also the critique of *Brown v Stott* [2001] 2 WLR 817 by Ashworth and Redmayne (2005: 41) which, they say, set 'the tone for many of the subsequent decisions under the Human Rights Act'.

[112] *JJ* [2007] UK HL 45; [2007] 3 WLR 642.   [113] *MB and AF* [2007] UK HL 46; [2007] 3 WLR 681.

[114] Ewing K and Tham J-C, 'The Continuing Futility of the Human Rights Act' [2008] PL 668 at 682.

balance between Parliament, the Executive and the Judiciary have been considerably exaggerated'.[115]

Admittedly, the courts, Parliament, and all other public authorities must now incorporate the human rights framework into their decision-making.[116] But even this brief discussion of governmental and judicial decision-making shows that the ECHR leaves a huge amount of room for manoeuvre. This should not be taken as implying that human rights are unimportant. They provide a legal safety net, preventing the state from creating the kind of harsh and repressive criminal justice typical of totalitarian states.[117] The influence of the Convention should be seen as much in what the state has not done in the criminal justice arena as in what it has done. But while the ECHR 'safety net' must be welcomed, we must also recognise that it has little influence beyond that.

1.6.5 Human rights coverage is patchy

A further problem with using human rights as evaluative criteria is that they provide no guidance on numerous important and controversial questions such as should interrogation be judicially controlled, should juries or other lay elements always have a role in trials, and should decisions to prosecute be made by law enforcers or lawyers? Even supporters of the ECHR recognise that in many respects the protection it offers to human rights is deficient.[118] For example, it makes virtually no special provision for the rights of vulnerable groups of suspects, such as juveniles or the mentally disordered, nor is there any explicit reference to the interests of victims or witnesses. The ECtHR has made the deficiency good to some extent by stating that the Art 6 right to a fair trial applies to victims and witnesses as well as the accused.[119] The ability of the human rights approach to take this kind of issue into account is a major advance on the Packer models, where the Accused v State spectrum has little place for victim considerations. There is no reason why a human rights framework should be limited to the ECHR. But how far should it go? The UK has European Union obligations to victims that go further (see ch 13) but are/should they be accorded the status of 'human rights'? If so, should they be absolute,

---

[115] Department for Constitutional Affairs, *Review of the Implementation of the Human Rights Act* (2006a), <http://www.justice.gov.uk/docs/full_review.pdf> p 4, (accessed 5 January 2010), also cited by Ewing and Tham (2008: 691).

[116] Various mechanisms have been put in place to achieve this. For example, there is now a Parliamentary Joint Committee on Human Rights which assesses the implications for human rights of proposed legislation, s 19 of the Human Rights Act 1998 requires Ministers in charge of a Bill to state their view as to whether the measure is compatible with Convention rights, and some of the most controversial anti-terrorist legislation is kept under a variety of forms of extra-governmental review (on the latter, see Walker (2002a: 267–71)).

[117] This has been particularly important at times when a weak government has been tempted to turn to populist 'tough on crime' measures in an attempt to revive its flagging political fortunes. See Garland D, 'The Limits of the Sovereign State: Strategies of Crime Control in Contemporary Society' (1996) 36 BJ Crim 445 at 462.   [118] See, for example, Ashworth and Redmayne (2005: 45).

[119] See, in particular, *Doorson v Netherlands* (1996) 22 EHRR 330 where the defendant's right to examine prosecution witnesses was restricted in the interests of protecting witnesses who had a well-grounded fear of reprisals should their identities be revealed. Discussed in ch 13.

strong or qualified? Equally important are interests of a more collective kind. Arguably protecting the environment is at least as urgent as most of the rights in the ECHR, but can we realistically envisage a 'right' to a safe environment? How would this fit into the human rights framework? Lee argues that it is impossible to do so – and, were it possible, he further argues, it would not be desirable as it would be too limited.[120] If he is right, the human rights framework's claim to be comprehensive fails before what will surely be the greatest challenge facing humanity in the twenty-first century.

1.6.6 The maximalist (legalistic) alternative and the margin of appreciation

All of this will be disappointing to those academics, practitioners and pressure groups who would like to see human rights play a much greater part in criminal justice. These 'maximalists' attempt to solve the 'no more than a safety net' problem, as well as the problem of patchy coverage, by seeking (through doctrinal argument and test cases that draw on those arguments) to elaborate and extend the scope of the rights enshrined in the ECHR and thus (through the Human Rights Act (HRA) 1998) in English law. In an unusually powerful cross-fertilisation of ideas between academic and practising lawyers, many specific legislative and common law rules in almost every area of criminal justice have been tested against the ECHR, and some detailed laws have been 'read off' from it. Cases have been decided by the ECtHR and by English courts under the HRA on, to take just a few examples, the reverse onus, drawing inferences of guilt from silence, and legislative presumptions against bail for very serious crimes.[121] Yet, as we shall see, few of these legal challenges are success-ful. This is because in deciding between 'maximalist' and 'minimalist' positions, the ECtHR, through its 'margin of appreciation' doctrine, subjects a state's assessment of the need to invade rights to a relatively undemanding standard of judicial review. We have seen that, even when a state derogates from the ECHR the ECtHR rarely inter-feres with this, again judging that the state is best placed to judge when invasions of rights are 'needed' in order to deal with an 'emergency'. As Ormerod observes:

On one level, it is impossible to regard Strasbourg rulings otherwise than as pronouncements of the very minimum protection to be afforded... The margin of appreciation afforded to all States in all aspects of the Convention is well established...[122]

When policy-makers draft legislation and guidance they intend it to be 'human rights compliant' in this minimalist sense. Gearty says of those elements of the Terrorism Act 2000 that did not require derogation:

It is noteworthy that none of these concessions to human rights law involved the bald elimi-nation (as opposed to mere procedural elaboration) of powers desired by the executive; right

---

[120] Lee R, 'Resources, Rights and Environmental Regulation' (2005) 32 JLS 111.

[121] On the reverse onus see 1.2.1. The other examples are dealt with in chs 5 and 9 respectively.

[122] Ormerod D, 'ECHR and the Exclusion of Evidence: Trial Remedies for Article 8 Breaches' [2003] Crim LR 61 at 65.

from the start the human rights standard set by the Act [the HRA]...has been a relatively low one, with the consequence that only a rather undemanding jump by the executive brings its repressive practices within the zone of human rights compliance.[123]

As we have seen, UK courts usually (though not always) are similarly minimalist.[124] By contrast, 'maximalists' want as much criminal justice law and policy as possible to be 'read off' from the ECHR. They rightly see the 'human rights compliance' approach of the policy makers as giving them almost as much room to manoeuvre as they had before the HRA, allowing the drift towards the crime control end of the spectrum documented in 1.4 and 1.5.4. We characterise 'maximalists' as 'legalistic' because, whenever the ECHR is open to interpretation, they attempt to argue that the law *is* what they (and, often, we) *want* it to be. We have seen that neither courts nor governments are taken in by this.[125] Thus maximalism is unlikely to reverse the crime control trend.[126]

1.6.7 Conflicts between rights and with the priorities of the state

In its purest form a human rights framework would simply establish inviolable rights to every category of person and in every type of situation where significant freedom is threatened. This would ignore two major problems. First, the more rights there are, the more scope there is for some rights to conflict with others. Second, a real criminal justice system has to be reasonably effective in bringing cases to trial and convicting when there is strong legally obtained evidence.

Both problems are tackled in part via the hierarchy of 'absolute', 'strong' and 'qualified' rights discussed earlier. If a case involved a conflict between the right to a fair trial (strong) and to privacy (qualified) the former would trump the latter. And effectiveness can be balanced against 'qualified' rights and used to justify derogation from 'strong' rights. But what about when rights in the same position in the hierarchy clash? The classic example is when the rights of complainants to a fair trial clash with those of defendants. This first arose in the domestic courts in *A*, which concerned the prohibition of the use of sexual history evidence in rape cases: a vital element in the right

---

[123] Gearty C '11 September 2001, Counter-terrorism, and the Human Rights Act' (2005) 32 JLS 18 at 21–2.

[124] 'It is of course open to member states to provide for rights more generous than those guaranteed by the Convention but such provision should not be the product of interpretation of the Convention by national courts...The duty of national courts is to keep pace with the Strasbourg jurisprudence as it evolves over time...' per Lord Bingham in *R (on the application of Ullah) v Special Adjudicator* [2004] UKHL 26; [2004] 2 AC 323 at [20]. For critique see Lewis J, 'The European Ceiling on Human Rights' [2007] PL 720.

[125] See, again, Lord Bingham in *R (on the application of Ullah) v Special Adjudicator* [2004] UKHL 26; [2004] 2 AC 323 [20].

[126] This is one reason why some people argue that human rights policies, and the laws that stem from them, should be argued for at the political level rather than in the courts. See, for example, Gearty C, *Can Human Rights Survive?* (Cambridge: Cambridge University Press, 2006); Campbell T, *Rights: A Critical Introduction* (London: Routledge, 2006); Munro V, 'Of Rights and Rhetoric: Discourses of Degradation and Exploitation in the Context of Sex Trafficking' (2008) 35 JLS 240.

of complainants to a fair trial, but arguably undermining of the defendant's right to a fair trial.[127] The more rights are assigned to victims and witnesses (and maximalists, remember, seek to assign more and more rights to deserving parties) the more clashes like this there will be.

The way human rights advocates deal with the demands of effectiveness is illustrated in Ashworth's discussion of why the principle that the innocent should be protected against wrongful conviction should not be regarded as absolute.[128] First, he acknowledges that attempts to introduce ever-more elaborate safeguards against wrongful conviction could only be achieved by diverting resources from other important social needs, such as education, health, and social security (which could themselves be described in the language of human rights). To put it bluntly, how many hospitals (and how many life-saving operations) are we prepared to sacrifice for the sake of achieving some marginal (and unquantifiable) increase in the protection of innocent people against wrongful conviction? Second, the more elaborate safeguards against wrongful conviction became, the more difficult it might be to convict the actually guilty. Ashworth's conclusion is that the criminal process should be organised in such a way as to render the risk of wrongful conviction 'acceptably low', and that this objective necessitates research both into the sources of error and the consequences of erecting safeguards against them.[129] This leaves open the questions of what is to count as 'acceptably low', how much we are prepared to spend on achieving this, how much we are prepared to infringe the rights of victims in erecting such safeguards, and how we are to know when the actually guilty have been acquitted (and the innocent protected).

Overall, the hierarchy in the ECHR provides inadequate answers to the problems of conflicts of rights and with state priorities. The more maximalist the approach, the greater will be these problems. But the more minimalist the approach, the more gaps that will need to be filled without clear guiding principles. Beyond a fairly basic 'safety net' there will remain considerable room for debate over the specific content of most laws and policies, allowing a vast amount of permissible space between the crime control and due process ends of Packer's spectrum, not to mention much leeway concerning the rights of victims. We are therefore still left with the question of how to evaluate the criminal justice system.

---

[127] [2001] 2 Cr App R 351. The decision predictably provoked controversy amongst academics. Nicol D, 'Law and Politics after the Human Rights Act' [2006] PL 722 at 739, for example, saw the House of Lords as 'blinded by its zeal for the rights of male defendants' showing scant regard for the rights of women, 'the underprivileged majority of the population'. Hickman T, 'The Courts and Politics after the Human Rights Act: A Comment' [2008] PL 84 at 93, responded by arguing that the House 'came down fearlessly in favour of the vulnerable minority with the most immediate call on the courts for protection; namely accused persons...' Among the many later cases on the point are W [2005] Crim LR 965; and, on witness anonymity, Davis [2007] Crim LR 70. See also G [2008] UKHL 37 for an example of a clash of Art 8 rights held by a complainant and an accused in relation to the offence of rape of a child under 13.

[128] Ashworth A, The Criminal Process, 2nd edn (Oxford: OUP, 1998) pp 50–2.

[129] Ashworth (1998a: 51).

1.6.8 Individualistic rights and legalistic remedies

A final problem is that the ECHR offers highly individualistic remedies to abuses of power. Its core method of enforcement relies on somebody pursuing a complaint about the treatment they have suffered.[130] This may not be appropriate where abuses of power are taking place against a disorganised and marginalised community as a whole, particularly where members of that community have no faith in law, lawyers or legal institutions. For in such a situation, no-one may be prepared to complain about what is happening, at least not until some considerable time has elapsed. Even then, an infringement might take years to establish; in the meantime, members of a whole community may continue to have their rights abused. There is also the point that it is unrealistic to expect the courts, in their limited and time-pressured role of deciding individual cases, to develop research-based, principled and satisfactory guidelines for – for example – law enforcement bodies on what might constitute an abusive policing method.[131] Another way of guarding against abuse is excluding from trial evidence obtained in breach of the ECHR. But much of the ECtHR's case law on remedies is 'confusing and unconvincing'[132] and UK courts do not exclude evidence that is obtained in breach of 'qualified' rights. Rights without adequate remedies are largely meaningless.[133]

What is needed in addition to legalistic remedies such as are offered under the ECHR are proactive methods of guarding against systemic abuses. One such method is the committee established under the 1989 European Convention for the Prevention of Torture and Inhuman or Degrading Treatment or Punishment. The committee may visit the prisons and police stations of any member country and report on conditions which may be in breach of Art 3 of the European Convention on Human Rights. Thus, prisoners in England and Wales, a marginalised group if ever there was one, were found to be on the receiving end of practices that breached this Article.[134] But this does not cover all the rights supposedly protected by the European Convention. In some fields of social life regulatory agencies have been created to encourage, monitor and, more exceptionally, enforce (or assist individuals in enforcing) compliance with legal norms – for example, the Equal

---

[130] Under s 7 of the Human Rights Act 1998 those who can invoke Convention rights in legal proceedings are restricted to 'victims' of unlawful acts. This means that campaigning groups, such as Liberty do not have standing in their own right to bring proceedings. Instead, they seek to identify suitable emergent 'test cases' where they can either act on behalf of the 'victim' or intervene in the case as an interested 'third party': Maiman R, '"We've had to raise our game": Liberty's Litigation Strategy under the Human Rights Act 1998' in Halliday S and Schmidt P (eds), *Human Rights Brought Home* (Oxford: Hart, 2004).

[131] See Ashworth A, 'Re-drawing the Boundaries of Entrapment' [2002] Crim LR 161, especially at pp 178–9. In the non-crime field see *HL v UK* 45008/99 (5 October 2004) discussed by Clements L, 'Winners and Losers' (2005) 32(1) JLS 34 at p 35.

[132] A judgement made by Ashworth in the context of ECtHR cases on the implications of breaches of Convention rights on the fairness of any subsequent trial. See his commentary on *PG and JH v United Kingdom* [2002] Crim LR 308 at 310.   [133] For detailed analysis of these points, see ch 12.

[134] See further Evans M and Morgan R, 'The European Convention for the Prevention of Torture: Operational Practice' (1992) 41 ICLQ 590.

Opportunities Commission, the Commission for Racial Equality and the Disability Rights Commission, now brought together under the Equality Act 2006 as the Equality and Human Rights Commission (EHRC). In the field of criminal justice such generic institutions are supplemented by more focused regulatory bodies such as the Independent Police Complaints Commission (see further ch 12) and government inspectorates.

Non-judicial regulatory bodies have grown substantially in power and importance over the last 20 years or so, and we welcome this. As Lustgarten observes, 'human rights scholars have focused far too much on courts and the judiciary.... [T]he primary mechanism for securing what legal rights try to achieve is the harnessing of the power of state administrative institutions, not recourse to the courts to stop abuses or to goad resisting governments into taking faltering steps.'[135] Thus, in evaluating the operation of criminal justice, and in thinking about how to protect the interests embodied in human rights[136] we need to look at how regulatory bodies might most effectively encourage the police and prosecution agencies to respect rights (and what might make the latter choose to do so anyway). But we need to be realistic about this. Governments can undermine the power of regulatory bodies by starving them of resources,[137] or can control their activities by determining both their agendas and those of the agencies they are supposed to regulate. Despite these constraints, government inspectorates in the criminal justice field have uncovered problems that have led to progressive change, and some of our critique of criminal justice in subsequent chapters draws on their reports.[138] But, as we show in the next section, the agenda that has been set by government is not one that prioritises human rights.

1.7 **Managerialism and the rise of actuarial justice**

The main elements of criminal justice – the police, CPS, and the courts, and (though not covered in this book) the probation, prisons and Youth Justice services – are part of the public sector, financed predominantly by public revenue. The vast bulk of defence work is similarly paid for out of the public purse in the form of legal aid. Like the rest of the public sector, criminal justice has been much influenced by the

---

[135] Lustgarten (2006: 854).

[136] For valuable essays on this theme see Galligan D and Sandler D, 'Implementing Human Rights' in Halliday and Schmidt (2004); Douzinas C 'Left or Rights?' (2007) 34 JLS 617.

[137] Parliament created a Human Rights Commission for Northern Ireland under the Northern Ireland Act 1998. It has not been particularly successful, in part because the legal and financial resources provided to it by the Government have proved inadequate: Livingstone S and Murray R, 'The Effectiveness of National Human Rights Institutions' in Halliday and Schmidt (2004).

[138] Look in the bibliography for reports by, for example, HM CPS Inspectorate. In the field of penal policy the HM Prisons Inspectorate has played a vital role in keeping the values of humanity and decency alive.

'new public management' promoted by successive governments from the early 1980s onwards.[139] The main motivating forces for this programme was an ideological preference for the disciplines of the market to achieve value-for-money, and control public expenditure.[140] Efficiency, effectiveness and economy became the trinity which public sector officials were required to worship. Among the main mechanisms borrowed from the private sector in this programme were the fostering of 'consumer' power, the introduction of competition in the provision of services to those 'consumers', the setting of clear objectives which would allow each service provider to be audited on their performance and (in theory) greater autonomy for local 'managers' and service-providers to enable them to be more responsive to consumer demand.

New public management has impacted on all criminal justice agencies. Here, we will take the police as an example. From the mid 1980s onwards chief police officers and local police authorities have been obliged to formulate objectives and priorities for their force which reflect the wishes and needs of the public and take into account the views and experience of front-line officers. Her Majesty's Inspectors of Constabulary (HMIC) are required to report on how effectively chief police officers identify and respond to policing problems using these methods. Increased funding is conditional on the police being able to demonstrate (for example, through 'output and performance measures') that objectives are being met. Investigations by the Audit Commission that promote economy, efficiency and effectiveness have intensified this scrutiny.

On coming to power in 1997 the Labour government reshaped the agenda of managerialism by promoting a wide range of programmes and devices designed above all to prevent crime and manage risk. We have already seen how the Crime and Disorder Act 1998 and subsequent legislation created a long list of civil behavioural orders (table 1.1). More generally the 1998 Act required local authorities and the police to work together in formulating and implementing local strategies to reduce crime and disorder (ss 5 and 6). Other bodies, such as probation services, health authorities and police authorities, were also required to cooperate in this endeavour. Performance targets were established to measure the extent to which local strategic objectives were achieved.

Many theorists have seen in such developments further evidence of the rise of what they refer to (variously) as 'the new penology', 'actuarial justice', 'neo-liberalism', 'the new regulatory state' or the 'risk society'.[141] As confidence in the ability of the police and courts to reduce crime levels by detecting and sentencing offenders has declined,

---

[139] McLaughlin E and Murji K, 'The End of Public Policing? Police Reform and "The New Managerialism"' in Noaks et al (eds), *Contemporary Issues in Criminology* (Cardiff: University of Wales Press, 1995).

[140] See the discussion by Savage S and Charman S, 'Managing Change' in Leishman et al (eds), *Core Issues in Policing* (Harlow: Longman, 1996).

[141] There is an enormous literature associated with these terms. Accessible entry points include Braithwaite J, 'The New Regulatory State and the Transformation of Criminology' (2000) 40 (2) BJ Crim 222; Garland D, '"Governmentality" and the Problem of Crime' in Smandych R (ed), *Governable Places: Readings on Governmentality and Crime Control* (Aldershot: Ashgate, 1999), Ericson R and Haggerty K, 'Governing the Young', in the same collection; and Feeley M and Simon J, 'Actuarial Justice: The Emerging New Criminal Law' in Nelken D (ed), *The Futures of Criminology* (London: Sage, 1994).

there has been a growing emphasis on deterring and preventing crime through the monitoring, manipulation and control of situations and populations deemed, in the aggregate, criminogenic. Private security guards, CCTV, improved car and home security devices, better street lighting, the closer regulation of 'deviant' or threatening groups (unlicensed traders, the homeless, disorderly youth, 'neighbours from hell', 'bogus' asylum seekers and so forth) all provide evidence of this pre-emptive trend. As Garland puts it: 'Whereas older strategies sought to govern crime directly, through the specialist apparatus of criminal justice, this new approach entails a more indirect form of government-at-a-distance, involving "interagency" cooperation and the responsibilization of private individuals and organizations.'[142] As ours is a textbook about the 'specialist apparatus of criminal justice' rather than about crime control in general, we will confine discussion of these new strategies to their impact on that apparatus – for instance, encouraging a crime-preventive mentality in public policing, and affecting the way in which the police use their powers ostensibly aimed at detecting individual offenders (see further ch 2).[143] At the same time, managerial techniques have been adopted, particularly through the Police Reform Act 2002, to make the activities of criminal justice agencies more transparent and governable.

This Act gives the Home Secretary the power to require a police force to take remedial action where they are judged to be inefficient or ineffective in reaching targets set by government. It also empowers the government to establish an Annual Policing Plan setting out strategic priorities for policing and requiring local police authorities to produce a three-year strategy plan consistent with the national priorities. The first plan required the police to adopt 17 key performance indicators relating to a wide variety of crimes. Many other detailed performance indicators, strategic priorities and targets were also imposed on the police. The local strategic plans not only had to incorporate all of this detail, but could be established only following consultation with other local bodies such as the crime and disorder reduction partnerships, youth offender teams, drug action teams and the new criminal justice boards, all of whom have their own multiple sets of priorities, performance indicators and targets (again, mostly set by central government).

The initial policing plans set by government were criticised as being overly prescriptive and leaving little room for any local democratic influence over policing policy.[144] The third national policing plan (covering 2005–2008) accordingly set out fewer targets. The 'five key priorities' were:

(a) to reduce overall crime, including violent and drug-related crime, in line with the government's Public Service Agreements (this required the police to reduce crime by 15% between 2002–03 and 2007–08);

---

[142] Garland (1991: 21).

[143] Indeed what Choongh sees as the 'social disciplining' by the police of problem populations (see above) might be better understood in terms of actuarial risk management.

[144] Jones T, 'The Accountability of Policing' in Newburn T (ed), *The Handbook of Policing*, 2nd edn (Cullompton: Willan, 2008).

(b) to provide a citizen-focused police service ('putting the law-abiding citizen first') which responds to the needs of communities and individuals, especially victims and witnesses, and inspires public confidence in the police, particularly among minority ethnic communities;

(c) to take action with partners to increase sanction detection rates (ie bring more offenders 'to justice') and target prolific and other priority offenders;

(d) to reduce people's concern about crime, and anti-social behaviour and disorder;

(e) to combat serious and organised crime.[145]

There are some obvious silences and gaps here, such as 'respecting the human rights of suspects' and 'reducing people's concern about police practices that increase the likelihood of miscarriages of justice'. This is perhaps not surprising given that the required targeting of 'prolific and other priority offenders' and the push for more convictions smacks both of actuarial justice (subjecting risky populations to closer regulation) and an impatience with civil liberties and due process safeguards. The national policing plan is now encompassed within the government's national community safety plan 2008–2011.[146] The key 'Public Service Agreement' for this period is 'make communities safer'. Under this banal banner march four 'priority actions':

1. reduce the most serious violence, including tackling serious sexual offences and domestic violence;

2. continue to make progress on serious acquisitive crime through a focus on the issues of greatest priority in each locality and the most harmful offenders – particularly drug-misusing offenders;

3. tackle the crime, disorder and anti-social behaviour issues of greatest importance in each locality, increasing public confidence in the local agencies involved in dealing with these issues;

4. reduce reoffending through the improved management of offenders.

Overall, it seems clear that the dominant managerial impetus has been the pursuit of ever more effective, efficient and economic crime control legitimated by reference to the interests and views of the 'law-abiding citizen'. But this is at the expense of the protection of due process values and human rights, and 'target-driven' policing ends up focusing on the targets rather than the actual crime problems for which they are poor surrogates.[147] An internal police inquiry into the mishandling of rape complaints

---

[145] Home Office, *National Policing Plan 2005–2008: Safer, Stronger Communities* (London: Home Office, 2004c). For recent discussions see Jones (2008), and Golding B and Savage S, 'Leadership and Performance Management' in Newburn (2008).

[146] Available from <http://www.crimereduction.homeoffice.gov.uk/activecommunities/activecommunities088.pdf> (accessed 5 January 2010).

[147] Flanagan R, *The Review of Policing: Final Report* (London: HMIC, 2008).

provides a good example: '[police] management treated car crime as a higher priority than sex offences, because it was under pressure to meet targets for solving cases'.[148] Those who support this emphasis within managerialism would no doubt argue that targets can be tweaked to better guide performance, and that crime control and the protection of human rights are complementary. That is, deterring and punishing crime protects and upholds the human rights of victims, and the interests of the latter should carry greater weight than those of suspects and offenders. The rise of victims as 'consumers' means that the criminal justice agencies are required to measure their 'success' with reference to victim satisfaction. An example of this is domestic violence courts, where all agencies are rated according to levels of victim satisfaction as well as more traditional criminal justice targets such as increasing guilty pleas.[149] This approach begs the question: what weight should be given to victims within the criminal justice system? It also returns us to the issue of an appropriate framework for clarifying how the conflicts between competing interests are resolved.

1.8 **Victims**

We have noted that the due process and crime control models have little to say about the place of the victim within criminal justice. At the time Packer was writing in the late 1960s, few criminologists gave much thought to victims. But surveys in the 1980s demonstrated their importance in reporting crime to the police, providing information on likely suspects, and acting as witnesses in prosecutions.[150] They also revealed that victims became increasingly dissatisfied with the criminal process over time.[151] Failures to keep them informed about the progress of 'their' case were felt particularly keenly. This is important from an instrumental standpoint as research also suggests that where victims perceive that the values and goals of the criminal process are insensitive to their interests, they are correspondingly less likely to come forward and participate in criminal justice.[152] This realisation led to calls for reform in police practices, pre-trial procedures and in sentencing.

Criminal justice changed slowly. The Victim's Charter, first published in 1990, was symbolically significant in setting out the services a victim could expect from various criminal justice agencies. As we shall see in ch 13, the Charter and more recent developments, such as the Victim's Code issued under the Domestic Violence, Crime and Victims Act 2004, stop short of bestowing enforceable rights on victims. But these

---

[148] *The Guardian*, 17 March 2009. Also see *The Guardian*, 16 March 2009.   [149] See ch 9.

[150] See, for example, Hough M and Mayhew P, Taking Account of Crime (Home Office Research Study No 111) (London: HMSO, 1985).

[151] Shapland et al, *Victims in the Criminal Justice System* (Aldershot: Gower, 1985).

[152] See van Dijk J, 'Implications of the International Crime Victims Survey for a Victim Perspective' in Crawford A and Goodey J (eds), *Integrating a Victim Perspective within Criminal Justice* (Aldershot: Ashgate, 2000).

'service rights' do make a concrete contribution to the well-being of victims without undermining the rights of suspects and defendants. We shall see that victims have also become more involved in decisions about 'their' cases. These 'procedural rights' are far more controversial. Like 'service rights' they are not generally enforceable. This is partly because the adversarial system envisages a contest between the state, representing the public interest, and the individual suspect. This structure does not easily accommodate a third party input such as that of the victim.

Are victims better served by a due process or crime control model of adversarial justice? At first sight the crime control model appears to embody a greater concern for the victim, except where it is distorted by managerialist targets, as illustrated by the downgrading of rape complaints discussed in 1.7. It offers the prospect of a higher rate of conviction and, by disposing of cases expeditiously through encouraging defendants to plead guilty, reduces the need for victims to come to court and give evidence. This is particularly important in cases involving violence, such as child abuse, sexual offences and other forms of assault, where giving evidence in public, particularly in cross-examination, may prove highly distressing.[153] A clear example is rape, where the previous sexual history of the victim was in the past often treated by the courts as relevant in some general sense to the issue of consent.[154] As McEwan put it, 'There is little incentive for rape victims to come forward when the system which is supposed to protect the public from crime serves them up in court like laboratory specimens on a microscope slide.'[155]

But some victims want to have 'their day in court' and some defendants – some of whom are innocent – refuse to plead guilty. Pressure to make the trial experience less of an ordeal for victims has thus mounted. Sometimes inroads have been made into the due process rights of the defendant in order better to protect the vulnerable victim. For example, the law now allows the admission of documentary (which includes videotaped) evidence in some cases, including where the statement is made to a police officer and the maker does not give oral evidence through fear.[156] And some victims are now allowed to give their evidence behind screens. But, like a see-saw, as trial procedures become more just or bearable for victims the defendant's ability to contest the prosecution case may become increasingly undermined. These special measures 'inevitably carry the risk of creating the impression that the defendant is too terrifying to be

---

[153] Brereton D, 'How Different are Rape Trials?: A Comparison of the Cross-Examination of Complainants in Rape and Assault Trials' (1997) 37 BJ Crim 242.

[154] The Youth Justice and Criminal Evidence Act 1999 was intended to change this by restricting judicial discretion, but did so to such an extent that the House of Lords found it infringed the defendant's right to a fair trial: *A (No 2)* [2001] UKHL 25. In practice, judicial training may be having more beneficial effect: Kibble N, 'Judicial Perspectives on the Operation of s 41 and the Relevance and Admissibility of Prior Sexual History: Four Scenarios' [2005] Crim LR 190 at p 205.

[155] McEwan J, 'Documentary Hearsay Evidence – Refuge for the Vulnerable Witness?' [1989] Crim LR 629.

[156] See ss 23–26 of the Criminal Justice Act 1988. The Youth Justice and Criminal Evidence Act 1999 also aims to make the giving of evidence more bearable for some victims and witnesses. All these provisions are discussed in more detail in chs 10 and 13.

faced directly'.[157] Moreover, when evidence is admitted solely in documentary form the defence is given no opportunity to cross-examine the maker of the statement concerning its contents. This makes it less likely that defendants can win in court, and thus less likely that they will contest the matter in the first place. Such measures have been held to be compatible with the Art 6 right to a fair trial so long as the rights of the defence are curtailed as little as possible.[158] That rider notwithstanding, it is evident that crime control and concern for victims can be made to walk hand in hand. The rhetoric of victims' rights has proved a powerful criminal justice policy-making tool, so much so that it has been argued by some that victims' rights are harnessed for crime control. Roach for example argues that a punitive model of victims' rights has emerged replicating some of the assumptions of crime control, He states: 'Victims rights have become the new rights bearing face of crime control'.[159] The rights of victims are pitted against the due process claims of defendants as if a conflict between the two were inevitable.

The benefits that the due process model offers victims are more subtle than those tendered by crime control. Typical crime control techniques employed to secure guilty pleas are offers of reduced charges or reduced sentences, as we shall explore in ch 8. To take the example of rape again, charge bargaining may result in victims learning to their horror that the legal process has labelled the act in question as some lesser wrong such as indecent assault. Similarly, sentence discounts for pleas of guilty may result in convicted offenders receiving a more lenient penalty than victims consider just.[160] Due process, by contrast, opposes such strategies, which means that where a conviction occurs it is likely that the offence proved and the sentence imposed will more accurately reflect the victim's suffering and the victim may also have had the opportunity of giving an account to the court, and perhaps feeling that it has been accepted by virtue of the conviction. Some vulnerable victims are more concerned that their story be heard and that they be taken seriously than that they be protected from the rough and tumble of an adversarial trial. Many learning disabled victims, for instance, want to make their public accusation even if the poor memory or communication skills which are a result of their disability make a conviction unlikely.[161]

More fundamentally, with the due process model's insistence on proof of (rather than belief in) guilt, it offers superior protection to that achieved by crime control against miscarriages of justice. A wrongful conviction represents an injury to the

---

[157] McEwan (2004: 61). Prioritising protection for victims may not be in the best interests of the prosecution either in some circumstances. For example, where the police video-recorded interview with a victim is allowed to be their evidence-in-chief in court the prosecution is denied the chance to lead evidence in an order which fits the narrative they wish to construct. For discussion see Cooper D, 'Pigot Unfulfilled: Video-recorded Cross-Examination under section 28 of the Youth Justice and Criminal Evidence Act 1999' [2005] Crim LR 456.

[158] For example, the ECtHR has made clear that evidence not subject to cross-examination should not be the sole or main evidence on which a conviction is founded. See further *Kostovski v Netherlands* [1989] ECHR 20; *Doorson v Netherlands* op cit.   [159] Roach (1999b) 31–2.

[160] Fenwick H, 'Charge Bargaining and Sentence Discount: the Victim's Perspective' (1997) 5 Int R Victimology 23.

[161] Sanders et al, *Victims with Learning Disabilities* (Oxford: Oxford Centre for Criminology, 1997).

victim (and to wider society), as well as to the defendant, because it means that the offender has not been correctly identified and convicted. When Stefan Kiszko was cleared in 1992 of the murder of Lesley Molseed after spending 16 years in prison, her father summed up the family's feelings: 'For us, it is just like Lesley had been murdered last week.' As counsel for Mr Kiszko put it: 'We acknowledge their pain in having to listen to some of the details surrounding their daughter's death and the new pain of learning that her killer has not, after all, been caught.'[162] In addition, the lengthy campaigns usually needed to bring miscarriages of justice to light must make it nigh impossible for those victimised to put their experiences behind them. And once a conviction has been quashed, reopening and solving a long-closed case is far from easy. Lesley Molseed's actual killer was finally convicted in November 2007, 32 years after her murder.

But while systems in which crime control values predominate may convict more factually innocent persons than would due process-based systems, the former model would also convict far more factually guilty persons. Overall, more victims will be able to see 'their' offenders brought to justice, albeit of a flawed kind, in a crime control-oriented system. Thus, the dilemma that Packer highlighted through the use of his two models of criminal justice exists also in relation to arguments about the treatment of victims. The claims of victims must be weighed against the competing claims of efficiency, defendants and the need to preserve the moral integrity of the criminal process. However, in weighing the social costs of 'wrongful' convictions and acquittals against each other, it is important to remember that the interests of victims do not fall solely onto one side of the scales.

It must also be recognised that people who report alleged crimes to the police are not always victims. Shop owners have been known to burn down their own premises in order to cash in on their insurance policies. Business people have sometimes staged robberies and burglaries for the same reason, or in order to cover up earlier asset losses through their own fraud or thieving. False allegations of rape are undoubtedly rare, but they happen.[163] Our natural sympathy for victims of crime should not blind us to the fact that one of the objects of the 'adversarial model' is to discover whether prosecution witnesses, including 'victims', are telling the truth or not. A system in which 'victims' were treated with kid gloves or were allowed to decide the fate of suspects and defendants would be as indefensible as one which ritually humiliated them.

In earlier sections we saw that conventional theoretical frameworks (including those of human rights and managerialism) see the main purpose of criminal justice as being to control crime with due process restraints operating to a greater or lesser extent in a subsidiary fashion. Both purposes – crime control and restraints

---

162 *The Guardian*, 18 February 1992. Similarly, when the three surviving members of the 'Bridgewater Four' had their convictions quashed after serving 19 years in prison, one of them observed: 'Not only have the police been devious and deceitful by getting innocent men in prison; far worse, after having a child killed the police have deceived Mr and Mrs Bridgewater': *The Guardian*, 22 February 1997.

163 See discussion of David Carrington-Jones' case (see 1.2) and Rumney (1999).

on power – can, as we have seen, work against the interests of victims. The interests of victims are furthered in conventional frameworks only as a by-product of their main goals.[164] It has been argued by Doak, however, that the HRA heralds a new phase in the development of victims' rights; that victims can increasingly expect to see their rights safeguarded in domestic law. He makes the argument for 'a principled rights based framework' which evolves to keep pace with international consensus, but rightly acknowledges that his approach can be critiqued for being 'vague and unpredictable'.[165] While this legalistic approach to human rights works for victims some of the time it is easy to point to cases where victims have failed in their human rights claims, even in relation to 'absolute' rights such as the right to life under Art 2.[166] It is overly optimistic to think that a maximalist approach to victims' human rights will be taken, even if such an approach were thought desirable.[167] Human rights can be made to walk hand in hand with victims' rights, but can also work against victims. Female victims in particular may find that recognition of their rights is not a reliable by-product of human rights frameworks.[168] Only a 'victim centred' model of criminal justice would prioritise the interests of victims. As Cavadino and Dignan have noted, such a model has been proposed but never implemented, even experimentally.[169] We shall see in ch 13 that recent government policy documents claim that legislative changes have put victims 'at the centre of criminal justice'.[170] This is part of what the Prime Minister was referring to when he said 'the rules of the game are changing' (quoted at the start of this chapter), but as far as victims are concerned, this is more rhetoric than substance, despite the genuine enhancement of service rights some of those changes introduced.[171] Victim-centred models argue for replacing adversarial justice in which the state prosecutes citizens in the name

---

[164] Fenwick (1997).

[165] Doak J, *Victims' Rights, Human Rights and Criminal Justice* (Oxford: Hart Publishing, 2008) 248.

[166] For example in *Van Colle and Smith* [2008] UKHL the House of Lords rejected the argument that the victims' human rights had been breached by the failure of the police to protect them from serious and, in Van Colle's case, fatal violence. Smith's case was not under the HRA but he nevertheless relied on the ECHR to support his argument for a common law remedy. See further ch 13.

[167] In the context of domestic violence it has been argued that the courts should give greater recognition to victims' Art 3 and Art 8 rights. See Choudry S and Herring J, 'Righting Domestic Violence' (2006a) Int J of Law, Policy and Family 95; Choudry S and Herring J, 'Domestic Violence and the Human Rights Act 1998: A New Means of Legal Intervention?' [2006b] PL 752.

[168] Feminists have argued that human rights are men's rights (See McColgan A, *Women Under the Law: The False Promise of Human Rights* (London: Longman, 2000); McKinnon C, *Are Women Human?* (Harvard: Harvard University Press, 2006). Although the force of these arguments might be diminished by analysis of individual cases such as *MC v Bulgaria* 2003 ECtHR (App No 39272/98), and more recently *G* [2008] UKHL 37, the critique remains. See further Dembour M-B, *Who Believes in Human Rights?* (Cambridge: Cambridge University Press, 2006) ch 7.

[169] Dignan J and Cavadino M, 'Towards a Framework for Conceptualising and Evaluating Models of Criminal Justice from a Victim's Perspective' (1996) 4 Int R Victimology 153 at p 165.

[170] See, especially *Justice for All*, Cm 5563 (London: Home Office, 2002a).

[171] Jackson J, 'Justice for All: Putting Victims at the Heart of Criminal Justice' (2003) 30 JLS 309. The rhetoric of victims' rights has remained dominant in the politics of both the government and opposition parties. See for example *The Guardian*, 27 October 2008.

of the public interest with civil procedures which would be initiated by victims. Its obvious weakness 'is its failure to acknowledge that an offence may have broader social implications which go beyond the personal harm or loss experienced by the direct victim'.[172] For ourselves, we do not believe that the claims of victims, powerful though they are, should be allowed to override all other considerations discussed in this chapter. At present, victim concerns are increasingly thrown into the pot indiscriminately, leading to an even more tangled web of irreconcilable demands and priorities than existed hitherto. The interests of victims do need to be taken into account but in a systematic fashion. To do this, an alternative framework is needed.

1.9 **An alternative framework: the enhancement of freedom**

We have seen that everyone recognises that there are many different values and interests at stake in criminal justice. The most important are:

- convicting the guilty;
- protecting the innocent from wrongful conviction;
- protecting victims;
- protecting everyone (innocent and guilty) from arbitrary or oppressive treatment;
- maintaining order;
- securing public confidence in, and cooperation with, policing and prosecution; and
- pursuing these goals efficiently and effectively without disproportionate cost and consequent harm to other public services.

Criminal justice is controversial, not because this list of goals is controversial, but because people differ over which are most important and which are to be given low priority. Many people, especially politicians, like to pretend that they are all equally achievable, but we have seen that this is dangerously misleading. One of the great virtues of Packer's models is that they alert us to the irreconcilability of many of these purposes. However, we have seen that both models are incomplete (they do not cater for the interests of victims, in particular) and neither is normatively acceptable in itself (ie neither model represents an ideal to which we might aspire). We saw that the human rights perspective tries to overcome these two difficulties but that 'rights' perspectives are not the most fruitful or comprehensive ways to understand, critique or develop criminal justice.

---

[172] Dignan and Cavadino (1996: 165).

1.9.1 **Promoting freedom: the overriding purpose**

Let us tackle the problem from a different angle and ask what is the point of protecting victims, offenders and, indeed, anyone affected by crime and the justice system. In our view it is primarily to protect and enhance freedom.[173] Why make it a crime to thieve or assault? Because the losses and hurts they cause are (among other things) losses of freedom – freedom to enjoy one's possessions, to walk the streets without fear and so forth. We seek to convict thieves and violent offenders in the hope that the punishment or treatment consequent upon conviction will reduce their propensity to commit crime, and in the expectation that censuring their wrongdoing will reinforce everyone else's law-abiding instincts and behaviour. Either way the freedom of past and potential future victims should be enhanced through having their fear of crime reduced. In the same way, what is the point of protecting suspects and defendants, innocent or guilty? Again, protection is not a goal in itself, but a means to the end of promoting their freedom. And why do we insist that the police must obey the rule of law? Because their failure to do so undermines our sense that we live in a free society, where state officials cannot invade our lives in an arbitrary manner.

At first sight it may appear that we simply advocate a list of irreconcilable aims (protecting suspects, convicting the guilty, acquitting the innocent etc) in the same way that everyone else does. However, we see none of these objectives as goals in themselves. Instead we see them as means to achieving the overriding goal of freedom. This means that, in theory at least, the problem of allocating priority to conflicting goals is solved. All we have to do is to prioritise the goal that is likely to enhance freedom the most.[174] This last sentence will worry rights theorists.[175] So we should make clear our commitment to the protection of the basic human rights as set out in the ECHR (although we remain sceptical about maximalist attempts to elaborate and extend these rights). We have seen that this safety net approach safeguards our most fundamental protections for suspects and defendants. In other words, maximising freedom requires the protection given by basic human rights. But we shall see that this overriding goal requires a lot more too, as there are many things the state can do that are consistent with these human rights but inconsistent with maximising freedom. For example, a policy of using stop-search powers whenever the law would permit this would not infringe anyone's human rights, but neither would a more restrained use of the powers. We would opt for the latter policy because, for reasons fully explained in ch 2, it is better suited to preserving and enlarging the freedom of the public. It is in

---

[173] Note here the use of the word 'primarily'. We accept that other human values are important too (such as equality, welfare and so forth) but remain of the view that thinking of the criminal process as predominantly concerned with maximising freedom is realistic as well as normatively defensible. We thus reject the charge that the freedom model attempts 'to reduce all human values to a single metric' (Ashworth and Redmayne, 2005: 45).

[174] See Cavadino (1997) for a similar approach (albeit expressed in the language of rights): 'what will the overall result of an action be for the amount of positive freedom enjoyed by those involved?'

[175] Eg, Ashworth and Redmayne (2005: 44).

this sense that we are interested in the 'freedom of the community at large'.[176] In terms of philosophical pigeonholing, then, our approach can best be described as distribution-sensitive consequentialism. To put this another way, as part of our concern to maximise human freedom, we put a high value on justice and fairness. We thus reject outright any crude form of utilitarianism in which the freedom of the majority could 'trump' the basic freedoms, or human rights, of an unpopular minority.

What is most likely to enhance freedom will vary from circumstance to circumstance. Let us take a hypothetical example of a motorist forced to brake suddenly by someone driving carelessly. The irate victim reports the matter to the police. It is worth devoting some resources to catching and prosecuting the suspected offender, but not many. If the suspect claimed that her car was stolen on the day in question, and was then abandoned the next day near her home, would it be worth the expenditure involved in checking her alibis and looking for the (alleged) car thief? Would it be justifiable to hold her in custody and interrogate her? Those who share our implicit priorities would answer 'no' to both questions. Why? Because the freedom lost to the victims of this offence (both the irate complainant and future victims) by non-investigation is less than the freedom lost by the suspect if the police investigated the affair in the way that we would expect them to investigate a rape. And the expenditure involved would be out of all proportion to the benefits thereby gained. The police should be given better, more freedom enhancing, things to do with their limited time.

Because of shared implicit priorities and the simple nature of the example, the law and practice used to be at one with our analysis. Until a change in the law in 2005 (see ch 3) the police were not normally permitted to arrest and interrogate for minor offences. Now, under the new law, they can devote substantial resources to single road traffic incidents like this, though they are never likely to do so in practice. The real world is not so simple most of the time, of course; and our approach is not, most of the time, nearly so simple to put into practice as it is to state in theory.[177] In particular, given such problems as imperfect information, the pressures of time and personal prejudices, one could not expect a workable criminal justice system to depend on a fine weighing up by individual police officers and prosecutors of what would maximise human freedom in any given situation (ie, act-consequentialism). We therefore incline towards distribution sensitive rule-consequentialism[178] on the basis that adherence to rules designed to enhance freedom is likely in the long run to promote freedom more effectively than the act-consequentialist alternative.[179]

---

[176] A term that seems to worry rights theorists: Ashworth and Redmayne (2005: 44).

[177] As Berlin I, *Liberty*, (edited by Hardy H) (Oxford: OUP, 2002) p 41 puts it: 'the problem of how an overall increase of liberty in particular circumstances is to be secured...can be an agonising problem, not to be solved by any hard-and-fast rule'.

[178] A phrase taken from Hooker B, 'Rule-Consequentialists' in LaFollette H (ed), *The Blackwell Guide to Ethical Theory* (Oxford: Blackwell, 2000).

[179] These ideas are worked out in more detail in the context of prosecutor behaviour in Young R and Sanders A, 'The Ethics of Prosecution Lawyers' (2005) 7(2) Legal Ethics 190.

1.9.2 Should the freedom of victims predominate?

Our position implies that one should take into account the freedom of victims as well as the freedom of people accused of crime. To argue for these two measures of freedom to be balanced is one thing, but knowing how to do so is quite another.[180] Crime control adherents would argue that suspects and offenders should have fewer rights than victims and that their freedoms should have a low weighting. We disagree for several reasons:

All applications of state power reduce freedom, at least in the short run[181]

While it is true that criminal acts reduce freedom, the inescapable fact is that once a crime is committed the harm it causes is usually irreversible. The application of state power may do nothing to redress the balance. Indeed, less than one-tenth of all stop-searches lead to arrest, and less than one-half of all arrests lead to caution or prosecution (see chs 2 and 3). Unless the use of stop-search and arrest has a net deterrent effect in itself these are applications of power which reduce freedom in exchange for no gain whatsoever. If those stop-searched or arrested are innocent (and most will be) the loss of freedom will be all the more acutely felt. Our argument is that since society has a choice whether or not to allow the application of state power, it should only grant it if it is likely to enhance more freedom than it erodes. The use of power has therefore to be justified every time it is granted in principle (ie by law) and exercised in practice.[182]

Placing greater weight on victims' freedom would be counterproductive for the overall freedom of all (including victims)

Crime control adherents might argue that the payback for victims and the wider society from incursions on the freedom of suspects and offenders is small precisely because too much weighting is given to the rights of suspects and defendants. However, if it became easier to arrest, charge and convict, the proportion of people against whom action would be taken that were actually guilty would be lower even though their numbers would rise. Greater freedom for victims would be purchased at the expense of a disproportionately high freedom-cost to suspects.

There are also financial costs to increased law enforcement activity. Law enforcement is expensive. Police activity against suspects costs not only some of the freedom of those suspects, but community resources. Doing nothing would enable the money thereby saved to be used to enhance the lives (indeed, the positive freedom) of everyone through improved health, education, housing and so forth.

---

[180] For the argument that it is conceptually possible to measure freedom in an empirical sense see Carter I, *A Measure of Freedom* (Oxford: OUP, 1999). This book includes a defence of the view that freedom has a non-specific value (ie, that extends beyond specific freedoms protected through human rights) – see especially ch 2.   [181] See the discussion by Berlin (2002: 41).

[182] See also Cavadino (1997: 241).

The application of state power is often as damaging to the freedom of suspects and defendants as crime is to the freedom of victims

Even accepting the above, the crime control adherent would argue that it is worse to be a victim of crime than to be subjected to state coercion, and that the freedom of the suspect is more dispensable than that of the victim. Take another real-life example. One of our friends was walking alone late in the evening. Two men approached her and engaged her in unfriendly conversation against her will. Along with the fear of what they might do to her were her thoughts: what had she done to attract their attention? Was it the way she looked, something they knew about her, where she had been, her friends? She stood up for herself and they let her go. As she shook with fear and anger she wondered what might have happened had they not let her go, as she felt herself to be completely in their power.

We have just described what happened to our friend when she arrived at Birmingham airport, having just attended a Criminology conference in Belfast in 1997. Her encounter had been with (non-uniform) police, but it could equally have been with potential thugs. Now imagine her to be of Asian origin. Perhaps this would happen every time she travelled by air. She would begin to dread the journey and to fear looking anyone in the eye.[183] Or imagine someone living in the inner city, being subjected to this kind of treatment on the streets and in police stations, week after week.[184] But there are worse examples. When terrorists strike at the heart of our safety, as in London in July 2005, we sometimes say that it is worth paying any price to catch the criminals and stop it happening again. But perhaps that is because we cannot conceive of ourselves personally having to pay that price. In the four weeks after those bombings 44 people were arrested and not charged. One was Girma Belay, a 52-year-old Ethiopian refugee. His home was raided, guns were pointed at him, he was stripped naked and an officer 'punched and kicked me like he was a boxer training on his bag.' He was held in custody for six days where he was interrogated, photographed and treated like a criminal. An officer told him, when he was released, 'Sorry mate – wrong place, wrong time'. According to the journalist who interviewed him: 'Mr Belay is a shattered man. Tortured by flashbacks and gripped by fear, he…weeps when he describes what happened'.[185] The tragic fatal shooting of Jean Charles de Menezez, and the broader phenomenon of deaths in police custody (see ch 4), similarly reminds us of the falsity of the oft-heard phrase that the innocent have nothing to fear from increasing police power.

Loss of freedom is not always a matter of individual incidents for victims or suspects. Just as the suffering of a woman brutalised by her partner can only be comprehended if the pattern of victimisation over time is taken into account, so the loss of freedom of suspects subjected to repeated stops and so forth is completely different from that suffered by a one-off victim (or a one-off suspect).

---

[183] See Hillyard P, *Suspect Community* (London: Pluto Press, 1993).   [184] Choongh (1997).
[185] *The Guardian*, 4 August 2005.

Victims and accused people are not separate categories

So far in this book we have made an implicit assumption which is widely shared but is nonetheless erroneous: that victims and people accused of crime are separate groups of people. In reality, just as most people are victims of crime at least once in their adult life, so most people also offend at some time in their lives, many people do so many times, and many more are accused of this by the police. One-third of all men and 9% of women born in 1953 were convicted of at least one non-Road Traffic Act offence before the age of 46.[186] Just think how many committed offences and got away with them, as only a small minority of reported crimes end in conviction, and reported crimes are a tiny minority of the total number of crimes committed.[187] And who are the victims of crime? Disproportionately young working class men and members of ethnic minorities – the groups who are disproportionately represented among convicted offenders.[188] The very people who, as victims, crime control adherents would protect are those people whose freedom would be sacrificed the next day when they are, or are suspected of, offending.

Sometimes the overlap in the two categories is complete. We refer throughout the book to the murder of Stephen Lawrence, a young black teenager, in 1993. One aspect of this tragedy, and one of the reasons why the police never successfully prosecuted the murder, was that when the police arrived they arrested his friend, Duwayne Brooks, and ignored his frantic pleas to look for the murderers in the direction he was pointing. He was thereafter charged with numerous offences (but never convicted). The police eventually acknowledged his victim status, apologised for a catalogue of errors and paid £100,000 compensation. His solicitor commented: 'Mr Brooks felt that because he was a young black man he was treated as a suspect and not a victim and witness.'[189] The idea that his freedom would be more or less valuable depending on which of these categories we eventually agreed he belonged to is ludicrous.

It is essential that victims, suspects and offenders respect the criminal justice system

Much successful policing depends on information and cooperation from the community. Without community support the police would be even less effective than they are now. But support is not guaranteed, and there is evidence that it has been in decline until very recently. The proportion of the public who believe that the police do a 'very' or 'fairly' good job went down from 92% in 1982 to 82% in 1994, and those who thought they do a 'very good' job halved (from 43% to 24%).[190] As we saw above, increasing

---

[186] Prime et al, *Criminal Careers of those Born between 1953 and 1978*, Home Office Statistical Bulletin 4/01 (London: Home Office, 2001).   [187] See Kershaw et al (2008) and the discussion in ch 2.

[188] Morgan R and Newburn T, *The Future of Policing* (Oxford: Clarendon, 1997) pp 26–7. See also Hartless et al, 'More Sinned Against than Sinning: A Study of Young Teenagers' Experience of Crime' (1995) 35 BJ Crim 114.

[189] *The Guardian*, 10 March 2006. The aspects of the case involving Brooks are discussed further in ch 12, and the arrest aspects in ch 3.

[190] Bucke T, *Policing and the Public: Findings From the 1994 British Crime Survey* (Home Office Research Findings No 28) (London: Home Office, 1995).

confidence in the police has become a key managerial objective, and this has produced some improvement. Thus, in 2003/04, 47% of the population thought that the police in their local area were doing an 'excellent or good job', compared with 50% in 2005/06 and 53% in 2007/08.[191] Levels of satisfaction with the police are influenced by how the police do their job as well as by what they do and the results they get. Thus the least favourable views of the police are held by those who have come into contact with them directly, whether as victims or suspects.[192] Tyler's empirical study found that people have a deeply ingrained sense of 'fairness' and 'justice' which enables them to accept results they regard as wrong if they feel the process by which they were achieved was fair.[193] That is one reason why it is so important that the police respect the rule of law.

If society divided neatly into offenders and the rest, the way offenders are treated by the police might not harm the way 'the rest' viewed the police, and their co-operation might not be jeopardised. As we have seen, however, very large numbers of people are both occasional offenders (and even more are occasional suspects) and occasional victims. The overlap between suspect-communities and victim-communities means that if the police need to keep the victim-community on their side, they also need to do the same for the suspect-community. Tyler's research suggests that treating suspects fairly is the best way to persuade them to respect, and thus cooperate with, the law in future. In other words, adherence to due process and the human rights of suspects and defendants can be of instrumental value in preventing and detecting crime as well as of value in itself.[194]

1.9.3 **What is 'freedom'?**

We have so far used the term 'freedom' very loosely. As this is not a book of political philosophy we shall not attempt to define the term closely. This leaves us open to the charge that our 'fundamental concept' is 'under-determined'.[195] We are well aware that freedom, like human rights, is a contestable concept and can take negative or positive forms. We could spend much of this book defending our own preferred political philosophy and the set of reforms that would follow from it. But we prefer to concentrate instead on presenting a detailed analysis of how criminal justice actually works and providing some broadly drawn indications of how we think it should be reformed. We do this in the belief that a clear understanding of the reality of criminal justice is a necessary precondition of successful reform. And we are not convinced that it is either necessary or desirable in this book to tie our suggested reforms to a particular political philosophy. Instead, we believe that the vast majority of our suggestions for reform, or something on their lines, are palatable to most people who subscribe to

---

[191] Kershaw et al (2008: 118).   [192] Allen et al (2005: 10).
[193] Tyler T, *Why People Obey the Law* (New Haven: Yale University Press, 1990).
[194] See further Young (2008).   [195] Ashworth and Redmayne (2005: 44).

democratic values and the rule of law.[196] In that sense our model should be understood as a negative one, in that we are clearer about what we are against than what we are for. It should also be understood as a sensitising device which does not pretend to provide all the answers but rather alerts one to the kinds of questions and considerations to be taken into account.

However, the types of freedom which we believe the criminal justice system should enhance include those of the community at large. Thus the use of police powers against some communities more than others is a concern. As we shall see in later chapters, this is what happens with stop-search in relation to ethnic minorities, and the use of anti-terrorist powers in relation to people with Asian (previously Irish) connections. Equally important is the propensity of some communities to be victimised in certain ways more than others. For instance, many poor communities are badly affected by drug-related crime. But if the police attempt to control crime in such communities by instilling more fear in their inhabitants than do the criminals, the desirable ends will have been frustrated by the means. Poor communities suffer from 'non-traditional' forms of crime too. Working class people are harmed far more by dangerous working conditions than they are by street attacks and pub fights. And we are all far more at risk from illegal driving practices than we are from those who we conventionally think of as criminal. It follows that we must question the differential powers provided by the law to police 'normal' crime, corporate crime and road traffic, to take just a few examples; and to question the different ways in which law enforcement bodies use those powers and the different experiences of people suspected of these different crimes.

We are concerned about the actual ability of people to exercise freedom, rather than a theoretical aspiration. This is why it makes no sense only to analyse the law without seeing how it actually works. To tell arrested suspects, for instance, that they can look up their rights in a law book to ensure that they are being treated fairly is a classic example of a theoretical right of zero practical value.[197] Law students (and academics!) have trouble understanding what the rights of suspects are after lengthy study, so what chance would most suspects have? Even if they did understand them, would it really make any difference? Asked by Choongh if the police had told him what his rights were, one detained suspect said bitterly:

What rights? You wanna see your rights? Your rights is all on one piece of paper [suspect gets out the charge-sheet]. That's your rights, right here! . . . I'm gonna be here until the morning anyway, so there's no point is there.[198]

---

[196] A similar method is employed by Schwartz J, 'Relativism, Reflective Equilibrium, and Justice' (1997) 17 LS 128 who writes that: 'If we can rule out domination as unjust, the remaining arbitrariness among emancipatory conceptions seems harmless. At any rate, to rule out conceptions that license domination would be progress' (p 153).

[197] Under the PACE Code of Practice C, detained suspects have the right to consult the various codes of practice issued under that Act. See further ch 4.   [198] Choongh (1997: 178).

And so we approach the enhancement of freedom through criminal justice by arguing that it be achieved by methods which take account of the real circumstances in which they operate. Due process mechanisms and crime control powers need to be sensitive to the context within which they operate. Searches of suspected drug dealers which are carried out in such an oppressive, arbitrary and discriminatory way that they provoke widespread rioting and long-term alienation of whole neighbourhoods from the police do not enlarge freedom but undermine it. The lawful use of arrest powers in a non-discriminatory manner which cannot be shown to detect or prevent a significant amount of crime does not enlarge freedom but undermines it. Due process mechanisms which result in little protection for suspects but cause humiliation to victims or impede the police from detecting serious crime do not enlarge freedom but undermine it. Layers of bureaucracy that add nothing to due process protections and which divert criminal justice officials from achieving legitimate goals do not enlarge freedom but undermine it. And in deciding how much power to give the police, how much due process to provide to suspects, it makes sense to consider, within the particular social context concerned, how powers are likely to be used and experienced in practice, how much (preferably serious) crime we might thereby detect or prevent and how effective due process mechanisms are likely to be.

To summarise, the freedom approach starts with the understanding that criminal justice practices are inherently coercive or involve significant invasions of privacy. The police and other law enforcement agencies have powers that enable them to do things which would otherwise constitute torts or even crimes: for example detaining people, entering their homes, seizing their property. For all this to be justified, we need to be confident that:

(a) there is some objective basis for treating a person as a suspect;

(b) the treatment of the accused is not disproportionate to the nature of the offence or risk they are thought to pose;

(c) the powers used are reasonably effective at detecting or preventing crime and that they do not lead to unreasonably large numbers of people being convicted of crimes they did not commit;

(d) the benefits to be achieved by the use of coercive and invasive powers outweigh the disadvantages to individual suspects and other citizens;

(e) police, prosecution and court powers are not used unfairly, in a discriminatory manner or for other improper purposes; and

(f) preferably the law is enforced with consent – though 'consent' is a double-edged sword, for it allows officials to avoid resorting to their legal powers, thereby circumventing the controls and safeguards which should apply.

The weight to be attached to the above factors depends partly upon the political and social outlook of the observer. Some may want to keep controls on police powers to a minimum because their main anxiety is the level of crime. Others may be more anxious about the improper, disproportionate or overtly coercive use of 'ineffective' police powers. In the chapters that follow we attempt to objectively analyse the effectiveness and impact of each stage of the criminal process. This will help to understand how the overall freedom of all can be maximised.

1.9.4 Crime and social justice

If freedom is the main goal of criminal justice, and the use of resources has to be taken into account, it follows that criminal justice should not be analysed in isolation from other aspects of society which encroach on freedom. When considering the use of legal and financial resources to combat crime we should also consider other social needs in relation to, for instance, housing, employment, education, health and so forth. Given the considerable evidence that many indices of poverty (such as housing and employment problems) are related to conventional crime,[199] tackling these social problems might be more cost-effective than using the coercive powers of the state anyway.

One way of ensuring that we do not see crime in isolation from other social problems, and of highlighting the importance of social crime prevention as well as individual crime control is to look at two divergent trends in social policy: those of social inclusion and social exclusion. The exclusionary approach is characterised by Faulkner as one whereby:

Crime is to be prevented by efficiency of detection, certainty of conviction and severity of punishment... 'Criminals' are to be seen as an 'enemy' to be defeated and humiliated, in a 'war' in which the police are seen as the 'front line'.

He contrasts this with Locke's view that 'the end of law is not to abolish or restrain but to preserve and enlarge freedom'. On this inclusionary approach:

Authority will not be respected if it is simply imposed: it has to be accountable and it has to be legitimate in the sense that respect for it has to be earned and justified. Consideration for others and obedience to the law are learned by explanation, discussion, experience and example... Solutions to the problem of crime have to be sought by inclusion within the community itself – among parents, in schools, by providing opportunities and hope for young people – and not by exclusion from it.[200]

Greater fairness to all is possible without either undermining the ability of the system to bring the guilty to justice or to protect the innocent from wrongful conviction. This is because, as this book will show, the criminal process as it currently operates shows strong exclusionary tendencies – failing to seek solutions from within the community, and failing to show adequate respect to individual citizens, whether in the roles of suspects, witnesses or victims.

---

[199] Morgan and Newburn (1997).

[200] Faulkner D, *Darkness and Light: Justice, Crime and Management for Today* (London: Howard League, 1996) p 6.

1.10 **Conclusion**

In this chapter we have shown that criminal justice can have several different purposes, many of which conflict with each other (and with social goals in other spheres of life) some or all of the time. While these conflicts will never be eradicated, it is important to have a way of prioritising the different purposes of criminal justice – not just in an abstract way, but in relation to specific problems. Only then can we hope to get near achieving the best possible solutions, in terms of maximum benefits for minimum losses. Further, a rational system which applies consistent principles will be both fair and seen to be fair – which is a good thing in itself and has the added advantage of encouraging cooperation with the system and thus increasing the ability of criminal justice to control crime.

The previous section argued that a rational ordering of goals, which gives a clear steer to those carrying out the system's functions, is possible if we adopt freedom as the ultimate goal of criminal justice. This does not involve abandoning crime control, crime prevention, concern for human rights or cost-effectiveness. Instead it enables us to pursue all these goals to differing extents and in different ways according to the context in which one is operating. The weighting of competing goals, interests and rights will still be necessary under our framework, but adopting the language of freedom should help us to calculate the value of those weights in a persuasive way – in a common currency. We might, for example, more effectively convince the police to respect suspects' rights (and politicians to stop dismantling them) if we highlight how these rights do not constrain but rather facilitate the achievement of the ultimate criminal justice goal of promoting freedom. That represents a clear advance on the human rights paradigm, which, as we have seen, has singularly failed to arrest the historic drift towards crime control values.

It should be clear that we are arguing normatively – that is, we are arguing that enlarging freedom is what the system should be aiming at. Throughout the book we shall contrast the way the system actually operates with the way we believe it should operate according to this framework. However, this will not always be a huge difference. We shall see that, some of the time, the system implicitly operates according to a 'freedom' framework anyway. So, for instance, in domestic violence cases it can be argued that much police work is increasingly context-sensitive and primarily aims to protect women victims; law enforcement per se is a secondary goal. Domestic violence is a significant component of the work of the criminal justice system and so frequently appears in our discussions throughout this book.[201] Historically the criminal justice agencies have not taken victims of domestic violence seriously, but we will argue that there are ways that this can and is being done within the freedom framework advocated. For example, in relation to CPS decision-making in domestic violence cases, the

---

[201] Domestic violence represents 15% of all violent crime. See Kershaw et al (2008).

freedom framework can be used to argue against approaches that would force victims to participate in prosecution. At the same time it can be used to support prosecutions that do not need victims to give evidence.[202] The 'freedom' framework does implicitly influence the way the criminal justice system works. But because the freedom goal is never explicitly acknowledged, other goals sometimes creep in, creating incoherence and poor prioritisation. Our concern in the rest of the book will therefore be as much to describe the system analytically – to assess what it is trying to do and what it succeeds in doing – as it will be to advocate our normative position.

Another normative position, which we have shown is related to the 'freedom' objective, is that of an 'inclusive' society and, within it, an inclusive way of operating criminal justice. Again, we are as concerned to see the extent to which criminal justice is, or is not, inclusive as we are to argue for inclusiveness. Here we shall see that our normative goal and the harsh reality are even farther away from each other than is the case in relation to the freedom objective. The social exclusionary tendencies of the criminal process reflect exclusionary tendencies within wider society. These tendencies were exacerbated, if not actually encouraged, under the Conservative administrations in power from 1979 to 1997. The Labour administrations in power since then have employed inclusionary rhetoric but the policy emphasis has been on encouraging more into conventional paid work rather than reducing inequality.[203] This individualisation of social policy can also be seen in the criminal justice sphere, where the emphasis has been on remoralising or resocialising individual offenders so that they become responsible for 'reintegrating' themselves into 'law-abiding society'. Practical help and assistance to enable offenders to achieve this has been much less in evidence, as have the measures needed to tackle the conditions which generate conventional crime in the first place.[204] When offenders fail to take responsibility to stop their own offending, exclusionary measures such as tagging, curfews and prison remain the default option.[205]

It may be some time, then, before the inclusionary philosophy is applied in full to criminal justice. In the meantime, it is important to sketch out the potential of an inclusionary approach. Raising awareness of the issues at stake is a step along the road to rational reform.

Packer's conclusion to his analysis of American criminal law and criminal process has received little subsequent attention. But his final words[206] are as pertinent now as they were in the late 1960s: 'The criminal sanction is at once prime guarantor and prime threatener of human freedom. Used providently and humanely it is guarantor; used indiscriminately and coercively, it is threatener. The tensions that inhere in the criminal sanction can never be wholly resolved in favour of guaranty and against threat. But we can begin to try.' It is time we tried here too.

---

[202] See further ch 7.

[203] See Levitas R, *The Inclusive Society?: Social Exclusion and New Labour*, 2nd edn (Basingstoke: Palgrave Macmillan, 2005).   [204] See Clements (2005).

[205] See Gray P, 'The Politics of Risk and Young Offenders' Experiences of Social Exclusion and Restorative Justice' (2005) 45(6) BJ Crim 938.   [206] Packer (1968: 366).

Further reading

Ashworth A and Redmayne M, *The Criminal Process* (Oxford: OUP, 2005) chs 2 and 3

Bonner D, *Executive Measures, Terrorism and National Security: Have the Rules of the Game Changed?* (Aldershot: Ashgate, 2007)

Campbell T, *Rights: A Critical Introduction* (London: Routledge, 2006)

Cook, D, *Criminal and Social Justice* (London: Sage, 2006)

Gearty C, *Can Human Rights Survive?* (Cambridge: Cambridge University Press, 2006)

Hillyard P, Pantazis C, Tombs S and Gordon D (eds), *Beyond Criminology: Taking Harm Seriously* (London: Pluto Press, 2004)

McEwan J, 'The Adversarial and Inquisitorial Models of Criminal Trial' in Duff A, Farmer L, Marshall S and Tadros V (eds), *The Trial on Trial* (Oxford: Hart, 2004)

Tonry M, *Punishment and Politics: Evidence and Emulation in the Making of English Crime Control Policy* (Cullompton: Willan, 2004)

2

Stop and search

[The police are] just trying to let us know that they can do anything they want to us really, that they can stop us when they want and search us when they want, and bother us when they want.
(Drug user, quoted by Lister et al (2008: 41).

Key issues

- The relative infrequency with which police resort to formal legal powers
- The drift from reactive peacekeeping towards proactive targeting of crime and anti-social behaviour
- Factors influencing the use of police discretion
- Stop-search powers requiring reasonable suspicion (legal and working rules)
- Stop and search powers not requiring reasonable suspicion (the pre-emptive principle writ large)
- The importance of 'consent' and the rise of 'stop and account'
- Is stop and search racially discriminatory?
- Do the constraints and controls surrounding the use of stop-search actually work?
- Does stop-search diminish or enhance freedom?
- Stop-search and police-community relations
- Stop-search as social exclusion

2.1 **Introduction**

In a textbook on criminal justice, it is natural to concentrate on the law enforcement role of the police, so this chapter is concerned with the powers of the police to stop and search people. The main such power is provided by s 1 of the Police and Criminal

Evidence Act 1984 (PACE), which is the key statute regulating police powers. The object of stop-searches is to find stolen or prohibited items, such as drugs or offensive weapons, carried by pedestrians or occupants of vehicles. PACE stop-searches require that the police reasonably suspect that such items will be found. The police have additional statutory powers which do not require reasonable suspicion. Thus they may stop vehicles (ostensibly in order to carry out routine checks) and, in certain situations, may stop anyone on foot or in a vehicle to look for weapons, or items connected with terrorism, regardless of whether they have reasonable suspicion that such items will be found. In addition, the police have developed a non-statutory practice of stopping people and asking them to account for their behaviour or presence in a particular area (so-called 'stop and account'). These kinds of stops may or may not morph into a statutory stop-search, but they always involve an attempt to search the contents of someone's mind. Finally, there are 'stops' where the police do not necessarily suspect the stopped person of anything criminal but may, for example, seek their assistance as a witness. For the sake of clarity we will reserve the term 'stop-search' for stops that involve physical searches of people's bodies and vehicles, while references to other stops should be understood as likely to involve a search for useful information.

Each year, millions of people are stopped by the police. In the 2004/05 British Crime Survey (of a representative cross-section of adults living in households in England and Wales) 10% of adults were stopped once or more while in a vehicle and 3% were stopped at least once on foot.[1] The most common 'outcome' of these stops was to be 'just asked questions' (42% of vehicle stops; 70% of foot stops). Two per cent of all foot stops, and of all vehicle stops, resulted in an arrest.[2] Figures for youths are not routinely collected, but in 1998/99 a quarter of males aged between 14 and 15 had been stopped *on foot* in the preceding year as had 11% of females in the same age range.[3] Looking at it another way, counting just PACE stop-searches and 'stop and account', there were 3.3 million recorded stops in 2007/08.[4]

We can thus see that there are millions of stops and stop-searches each year with many of them generating evidence of crime sufficient to justify an arrest. This is not in itself surprising, given the tens of millions of crimes taking place each year.[5] Yet

---

[1] Allen et al, *Policing and the Criminal Justice System – Public Confidence and Perceptions: Findings from the 2004/05 British Crime Survey*, Home Office Online Report 07/06, table 2.03 (London: Home Office, 2006).   [2] Ibid, tables 2.08–2.09.

[3] Flood-Page et al, *Youth Crime: Findings from the 1998/99 Youth Lifestyles Survey* (Home Office Research Study 209) (London: Home Office, 2000) p 49.

[4] Source: Povey D and Smith K (eds), *Police Powers and Procedures, England and Wales 2007/08* (Home Office Statistical Bulletin 7/09) (London: Home Office, 2009), para 5.5.

[5] In addition to the ten million crimes uncovered by the British Crime Survey of adults living in households in 2007/08 (see 1.4), commercial and public sector victims experienced an estimated 35 million crimes in 1999–2000, 31 million of which involved theft from a shop: Brand S and Price R, *The Economic and Social Costs of Crime* (Home Office Research Study 217) (London: Home Office, 2000) table 2. There are also untold millions of drugs offences committed each year, as indicated by the fact that there were just under three million adult (aged 16–59) users of illicit drugs in 2007/08, just under a million of whom had used Class A drugs (such as cocaine, crack, LSD, ectasy and heroin): Hoare J and Flatley J, *Drug Misuse Declared: Findings from*

the key characteristic of policing is that formal legal powers are used relatively infrequently. Thus, the average police officer 'clears up' less than one crime per month[6] and an observational study of patrol officers (covering 170 hours) recorded a stop-search every 5.3 hours, and a recordable stop (ie, a 'stop and account') every 2.2 hours.[7] In understanding how the police use street policing powers, we need to begin by placing this activity in context by looking at what they do the rest of the time. This introductory discussion provides an essential building block not just for this chapter but also for those that follow on other policing powers.

2.1.1 **Crime and street policing in context**

In the mid 1960s, Banton made the point (subsequently confirmed by a plethora of research studies) that:

The policeman on patrol is primarily a 'peace officer' rather than a law officer. Relatively little of his time is spent enforcing the law in the sense of arresting offenders; far more is spent 'keeping the peace'...the most striking thing about patrol work is the high proportion of cases in which policemen do not enforce the law.[8]

As Morgan and Newburn note, '...the police handle everything from unexpected childbirths, skid row alcoholics, drug addicts, emergency psychiatric cases, family fights, landlord-tenant disputes, and traffic violations, to occasional incidents of crime'.[9] Some of the disputes and fights (and all traffic violations) will involve breaches of the criminal law. But whether and when this is so will often be a matter of judgement for the officers concerned. Since, in most of these cases, 'peacekeeping' will be their main objective, the question is how best to achieve this. If the peace can be kept

---

the 2007/08 British Crime Survey (London: Home Office, 2008) p 7. The number of motoring offences dealt with by official police action or a penalty charge notice in 2006 was 12.7 million, of which 1.7 million were prosecuted in court: Fiti et al, *Statistical Bulletin: Motoring Offences and Breath Test Statistics England and Wales 2006* (London: Ministry of Justice, 2008) p 3, table A.

[6] For the period 1995–2004/05 see: Nicholas et al, *Crime in England and Wales 2004/2005* (Home Office Statistical Bulletin 11/05) (London: Home Office, 2005) p 125. The equivalent reports have not included this data in more recent years, but it is easy to calculate that officers are still, on average, clearing up less than one crime per month. In 2007/8, 1,373,933 offences were 'cleared up' (Kershaw et al, *Crime in England and Wales 2007/08* (Home Office Statistical Bulletin 07/08) (London: Home Office, 2008) p 168), at a time when 141,589 officers (full-time equivalent) were in post (Bullock S, *Police Service Strength* (Home Office Statistical Bulletin 08/08) (London: Home Office, 2008) p 1. A cleared up crime is one where an offence has been officially recorded, a 'sanction' of some kind has been imposed on the offender (such as a formal warning, penalty notice, caution, charge or having an offence 'taken into consideration' at court), and any victim has been told that the crime has been cleared up. It also includes offences triable on indictment only where no sanction was imposed but the CPS considers that there would have been a realistic prospect of conviction if the case had been prosecuted in the Crown Court.

[7] Home Office, *An Evaluation of the Phased Implementation of the Recording of Police Stops* (London: Home Office, 2004d) p 13.

[8] Banton M, *The Policeman in the Community* (London: Tavistock, 1964) p 127.

[9] Morgan R and Newburn T, *The Future of Policing* (Oxford: OUP, 1997) p 79.

between the disputants by 'words of advice', as it often can, the law will only be enforced in serious cases. Research shows that patrol officers take a harsher stance when dealing with marginal populations, such as the homeless, youths 'hanging around' on the streets, and drug users.[10] Even here, however, the tendency is for the police to 'hassle' (through surveillance, questioning or 'moving people on') 'with remarkably few encounters resulting in the formal use of police powers'.[11] But if conflict continues, or there is a refusal to submit to police authority, the law can be invoked.

The fact that the police can choose whether or not to enforce the law underpins the way the criminal justice system works. Exactly the same is true of non-police agencies as well, which are discussed in detail in ch 7. This means, for instance, that the caseload of the courts is shaped not only by the way the law is enforced, but also by the way it is not enforced.

Another common observation about policing is that much of it takes place at the behest of the public. Thus police officers assigned to general patrol duties operate predominantly in reactive mode, responding to myriad and often mundane demands for service from the public. Opportunities for these officers to engage in proactive policing (using their initiative to deter, or uncover evidence of, criminal activity) occur relatively infrequently and, partly in consequence, are usually seized enthusiastically. Proactive policing is popular with the police since it fits with their self-image as skilful 'crime fighters' (see 2.1.4 below). Indeed, promotion and the securing and retention of high status jobs (such as detective work) still depend partly on 'activity', as measured by stops and quality arrests.[12] As a general shift inspector put it: 'I would never demand a quota for arrests, but I do expect them to take an interest in crime, to investigate crime, and to show arrests wherever possible.'[13] Proactive stops and stop-searches enable individual officers to demonstrate measurable crime-related activity in a way which peacekeeping usually does not. In addition, there have always been specialist groups of 'proactive' officers. For example, drug, vice and serious crime squads are expected to take the lead in tackling their spheres of criminal activity, and therefore stop-search on their own initiative.[14] Even for the minority of stop-searches which are reactive, the nature of the police response is not predetermined. The police have to sift and interpret what they are told by the public, and they do so on the basis of their own views, experiences and priorities.

[10] See, for example, Loader I, *Youth Policing and Democracy* (Basingstoke: Macmillan Press, 1996) pp 76–91; Lister et al, *Street Policing of Problem Drug Users* (York: Joseph Rowntree Foundation, 2008).

[11] Lister et al (2008) p 18.

[12] Fitzgerald M, *Stop and Search: Final Report* (London: Metropolitan Police, 1999) ch 3; Miller et al, *The Impact of Stops and Searches on Crime and the Community* (Police Research Series Paper 127) (London: Home Office, 2000) p 17; Long J, 'Keeping PACE: Some Front Line Policing Perspectives' in Cape E and Young R (eds), *Regulating Policing* (Oxford: Hart, 2008) pp 106–8.

[13] Fielding N, *Community Policing* (Oxford: Clarendon, 1995) p 52.

[14] See Maguire M and Norris C, *The Conduct and Supervision of Criminal Investigations* (Royal Commission on Criminal Justice Research Study No 5) (London: HMSO, 1992).

These priorities are partly set by the government, as explained in ch 1 (see 1.7). Thus, in the early 1990s the government decided that the 'peacekeeping' and community relations roles highlighted by Banton should no longer be prioritised on the ground that they used resources inefficiently. Police efficiency is now measured primarily in terms of crime-fighting, but instead of reactive policing, 'targeted' and 'intelligence-led' policing is encouraged.[15] This is highly proactive, in that specific offenders, offender-types, offences or geographical areas are targeted for pre-emptive police action on the basis of crime data, information from informants and so forth. Some of this work is done in partnership with local authorities and other local crime prevention agencies.[16]

The government has also required police forces to set up dedicated 'neighbourhood policing teams'.[17] These are intended to increase the visibility and familiarity of police at a local level ('reassurance policing'), deal more effectively with low-level anti-social behaviour and minor crime, and achieve a greater 'citizen focus' within policing.[18] Thus, for example, under the 'Partners and Communities Together' (PACT) initiative, representatives of the police and other agencies meet with members of the public to enable the latter to express and vote upon their local policing priorities. These do not bind the police although they are supposed to report back to the 'community' on action taken. All of this appears to be fuelling the more general trend towards pre-emption through proactive policing. As Lister et al note: 'As a result of these developments police managers are likely to remain under pressure to improve public perceptions of safety by increasing levels of visible street patrol as well as tackling signs of insecurity, for example visible signs of drug use, rough sleepers and beggars.'[19] It is worth stressing that the police are here engaged in a distinctive form of reactive policing. Rather than responding to reports of specific incidents or crimes, they are being asked to react to more generalised anxieties and concerns. The proactive use of stops and stop-search provides a key resource for the police in responding to this 'fear-led' pre-emptive agenda.

In this section we have sketched some contemporary forms of policing[20] and the drift away from reactive peacekeeping and towards proactively tackling crime and anti-social behaviour. We saw, in particular, that while 'the public' make demands on the police and shape some of what they do, the drift towards proactivity means that the

---

[15] See Ratcliffe J, *Intelligence-Led Policing* (Cullompton: Willan, 2008) pp 36–9.

[16] See eg Crawford A, *The Local Governance of Crime* (Oxford: Clarendon, 1997). Part 1 of the Crime and Disorder Act 1998 (CDA) put such partnerships on a statutory footing. A high profile example is the 'Street Crime Initiative', under which in 2002/03 a range of organisations and agencies sought to reduce street crime. This included the police targeting 320 'persistent young offenders' in areas of high street crime: Joint Inspectorates, *Streets Ahead: A Joint Inspection of the Street Crime Initiative* (London: Home Office Communication Directorate, 2003).

[17] See Home Office, *Building Communities, Beating Crime* (White Paper) Cm 6360 (London: Home Office, 2004a).

[18] For critical discussion, see Crawford A, ' "Reassurance Policing: Feeling is Believing" ' in Henry A and Smith D (eds), *Transformations of Policing* (Aldershot: Ashgate, 2007).   [19] Lister et al (2008: 4).

[20] For a fuller assessment see McLaughlin E, *The New Policing* (London: Sage, 2007).

police themselves, and the government, are more influential. We have stressed that the use of formal legal powers remains a relatively infrequent, highly discretionary affair. In the next section we look more systematically at the factors influencing the exercise of police discretion.

2.1.2   Factors influencing the exercise of discretion

Crimes abound almost everywhere, yet the police have finite resources. It follows that they necessarily exercise discretion when deciding who to stop and who to arrest. Given the volume of crime, one might expect that only the most serious offences and offenders would be selected. In reality the police devote a large amount of resources to mundane crime. In a study of assault, for example, Clarkson et al found no relationship between seriousness (except for the most extreme offences) and police investigation/court action.[21] If seriousness is not the prime determinant of police action, what is? The most important factors influencing the exercise of discretion, the effects of which will vary over time and from place to place, are:

Personal: where officers feel under pressure to stop-search and make arrests in order to justify themselves and enhance job prospects, they may target simple cases (such as cannabis possession). Such targeting may also occur where officers are bored, where they wish to get back to the police station, or because a new recruit is encouraged to 'start at the bottom' in order to gain confidence in practical policing. Some officers also allow strong personal dislike of particular social groups to influence their decision-making. For example, racial hatred has occasionally surfaced as a motivation for stop-searches.[22]

Working assumptions and working rules: working assumptions concern the way that patrol officers typically view the world around them and involve stereotypes about suspicious behaviour, people, and communities. Working rules are the norms that structure police behaviour, such as the rule that those who challenge police authority ('contempt of cop') should have police power brought to bear on them in order to reassert that very authority.

Procedural: offenders who have the protection of the privacy of their home or office, for instance, are less vulnerable than people on the street or in public places, where no warrants or other forms of prior authorisation for the use of policing powers are usually needed. This allows 'white collar' (ie business) crimes to be particularly well hidden.

---

[21] Clarkson et al, 'Assaults: The Relationship between Seriousness, Criminalisation and Punishment' [1994] Crim LR 4, table 2.

[22] See the transcript of an undercover BBC investigation ('The Secret Policeman') at: <http://www.ligali.org/pdf/bbc_transcript_secret_policeman.pdf> (accessed 5 January 2010) and the discussion in McLaughlin (2007) ch 6.

Changed forms of policing: store detectives, security guards, bouncers and other forms of private police now easily outnumber the public police.[23] Recent legislation provides for the accreditation of private police personnel who can then be provided with some of the powers that the public police possess in relation to relatively trivial crime (such as the power to impose a fixed penalty notice for a number of low-level offences,[24] or to confiscate alcohol and tobacco from children). These powers are also available to a new category of public quasi-police known as 'police community support officers' (PCSOs), who now play an important part in neighbourhood policing teams.[25] Technological innovations, such as CCTV, computerised databases, digital recording and swipe card access systems have further increased the amount and effectiveness of organised surveillance (a core feature of policing) taking place in society. Some people (eg lower class youths)[26] and places (eg shopping malls)[27] are increasingly 'over-policed' while others are neglected, and new demands are being placed on the public police to take action against particular individuals identified as suspicious or anti-social by CCTV controllers or security personnel.[28] Stop-searches based on cameras which have the capacity for automatic number plate recognition are also growing in importance, directing police resources 'to persons in vehicles committing offences, or involved in criminality'.[29]

Interpretational latitude: many substantive laws (eg carrying an offensive weapon) are ambiguous, as are many police powers (eg stop-search and arrest: see below and ch 3). Such ambiguities may deter a police officer from acting or may, conversely, allow officers to act much as they wish. The government's recent insistence that the police tackle low-level disorder and non-criminal activity deemed to be 'anti-social' means that the police (both public and private) now more often exercise discretion in situations of legal ambiguity.

Organisational: some police forces adopt particular policies in relation to certain offences (eg a 'zero tolerance' campaign against drunken driving, vice or domestic violence; or a tolerance policy concerning the possession of 'soft' drugs).

---

[23] Jones T and Newburn T, 'The Transformation of Policing? Understanding Current Trends in Policing Systems' (2002) 42(1) BJ Crim 129.

[24] These now include retail thefts under £200 and criminal damage under £500. See further Young R, 'Street Policing after PACE: The Drift to Summary Justice' in Cape and Young (2008).

[25] Created by the Police Reform Act 2002. See Ormerod D and Roberts A, 'The Police Reform Act 2002 – Increasing Centralisation, Maintaining Confidence and Contracting Out Crime Control' [2003] Crim LR 141, and Crawford (2007).

[26] Goldsmith C, 'Cameras, Cops and Contracts: What Anti-social Behaviour Management Feels like to Young People' in Squires P (ed), *ASBO Nation: The Criminalisation of Nuisance* (Bristol: The Policy Press, 2008).   [27] See, for example, McCahill M, *The Surveillance Web* (Cullompton: Willan, 2002) ch 4.

[28] See further Norris C, 'From Personal to Digital: CCTV, the Panopticon, and the Technological Mediation of Suspicion and Social Control' in Lyon D (ed), *Surveillance as Social Sorting: Privacy, Risk and Digital Discrimination* (London: Routledge, 2003). Note, though, that private security staff will tend to involve the public police only when this does not conflict with situational and commercial imperatives (eg, Hobbs et al, *Bouncers* (Oxford: OUP, 2003) pp 187–92).

[29] Home Office, *Stop & Search Manual* (London: Home Office, 2005a) p 17, para 1.9.

Societal pressures: both PACE and the Crime and Disorder Act 1998 require individual police forces to consult and work with local communities in relation to policing and crime reduction,[30] and we noted in the preceding section how every neighbourhood in the country now has its own dedicated policing team which is tasked with identifying and responding to local priorities. Wider societal pressures occur from time to time in relation to particular offences such as robbery or domestic violence.[31]

Political/managerial pressures: in recent times the police have been forced to respond to targets and priorities set by central government, inspectorates and the Audit Commission, causing them to focus more on some crimes and issues and less on others (see 1.7). As noted in the preceding section, the overall effect of such perform- ance targets has been to produce a shift away from peacekeeping towards 'cracking down' on disorder and crime.[32]

2.1.3 Does law influence the police? A typology of legal rules

Law was scarcely mentioned in our account of the factors influencing police discre- tion in the preceding section. This is not because legal rules play no part in police officers' thinking; it is because their relationship to police actions is sufficiently com- plex to merit separate treatment. When the police decide to act it is usually a policy or working rule which is most directly in play, not a legal rule. Take, for example, PACE. Many of its provisions brought the law into line with police practice or police aspirations. Thus, stop and search laws were extended by PACE from certain locali- ties to the country as a whole, *allowing* the police to search people they think are suspicious, but not *requiring* them to do so. In part, this enabled the police to opera- tionalise their working assumptions and rules more extensively than hitherto. Legal rules which allow the police to act more frequently in pursuit of their aspirations may be termed 'enabling rules'. In part, PACE made legal what the police were doing anyway. When the law is brought into line with pre-existing police practice the new rules are 'legitimising'.

We will see throughout chs 2–6 that many of the rules in PACE were not intended to control the police but rather were introduced to allow them more leeway. Bridges and Bunyan show that much of PACE was a product of 'the highly assertive evi- dence presented to the Royal Commission by various police spokesmen and pressure

---

[30] PACE, s 106, CDA, ss 5 and 6.

[31] See, for instance, Hall et al, *Policing the Crisis* (London: Macmillan, 1978) for an analysis of the 'mug- ging' scare of the 1970s. More recently media pressure led to the then Prime Minister treating a rise in street robbery as a national emergency, thus producing a major redeployment of policing resources: Joint Inspectorates (2003).

[32] See Fitzgerald et al, *Policing for London* (Cullompton, Willan, 2002) pp 110–28; Foster et al, *Assessing the Impact of the Stephen Lawrence Inquiry*, Home Office Research Study 294 (London, Home Office, 2005) 58.

	Rule expresses crime control values	Rule expresses due process values
Influences police	Enabling	Inhibitory
No influence on police	Legitimising	Presentational

Figure 2.1 Types of legal rule and effect on police behaviour

groups'.[33] It is no surprise to find that rules resulting from the initiative of the police generally embody more crime control values than due process values and run counter to the 'freedom' perspective presented in ch 1.

However, some PACE rules have a freedom-enhancing due process character. These rules are intended to inhibit the police from following their working rules (or are intended to give that impression), especially where the latter embody crime control values. If legal norms succeed in this ostensible aim they are 'inhibitory rules'. If they do not they are 'presentational rules' (see Fig 2.1).[34] Presentational rules can thus be defined as those which appear to be inhibitory but in fact are not. They create the appearance that the police are subjected to more effective legal constraint than is actually the case.

Few legal rules are as one-dimensional as this suggests, as most originate from mixed motives and/or messy compromises. For example, as soon as a rule legitimises a police practice (such as stop-search) it is likely to encourage greater use of that practice, and so has the effect of an enabling rule. And rules that begin their life as presentational may, over time, come to develop more inhibitory qualities as a result of more effective training, changes in incentive structures and so forth. Despite these complications, the typology helps us to understand the major themes of this book.

2.1.4 **Cop culture**

We have argued that many rules can be interpreted as the police want, and this is true of other factors influencing discretion such as community pressures. The desires of local or wider communities (which are rarely expressed with one voice and which often conflict) need to be sifted, interpreted and prioritised by the police. Similarly, offence 'seriousness' is not an objective category, and what is or is not 'anti-social behaviour' under the Crime and Disorder Act 1998, for instance, will depend in part on one's view of the world. The police world outlook – which influences the way the

---

[33] Bridges L and Bunyan T, 'Britain's New Urban Policing Strategy – The Police and Criminal Evidence Bill in Context' (1983) 10 JLS 85 at p 86. See also McConville et al, *The Case for the Prosecution* (London: Routledge, 1991) pp 173–8.

[34] This typology builds on the terms and concepts developed by Smith and Gray (1983).

police handle legal rules and non-legal influences – does not simply encapsulate that of society at large. It is moulded by 'cop culture'. This is:

rooted in constant problems which officers face in carrying out the role they are mandated to perform... Cop culture has developed as a patterned set of understandings that help officers cope with and adjust to the pressures and tensions confronting the police.[35]

Cop culture comprises a number of related elements.[36] The most important is 'authority'. A request by an officer to stop or to answer questions is always underpinned by the unspoken threat of the use of force (eg, stop-search or arrest), but this is only part of the *authority* of the officer. More important is the officer's symbolic role as the upholder of a (supposedly) impartial and universal law. This authority usually secures results without the need for coercion. Other related elements include a sense of 'danger', which is the officer's sense of the unpredictability of interactions with members of the public; the demand for deference from most members of the public, without which authority is undermined and order is threatened; the need, as we saw earlier, to produce 'results'; and a sense of mission to prevent 'them', the threatening 'Other', from ruining things for 'us'.

This is a dichotomous view of society which sees a relatively small section of society perpetually on the verge of revolt against the respectable majority. The sense of impending chaos and the importance of the 'thin blue line' holding it at bay permeates cop culture. This links to the police 'cult of masculinity'[37] evidenced by research conducted over several decades and 'an attitude of "on the streets we can't lose or we're finished."'[38]

Only the police know what it is really like 'out there'. If the naive, well-meaning, respectable majority knew what it was like, they would not make police officers work with one hand tied behind their backs. Thus Dixon quotes an officer saying: 'PACE was meant to protect decent people, but we don't deal with decent people.'[39] While the police see their interests and values as being those of the majority, cop culture is impatient with that majority for not realising how much it needs the police and how impractical the due process values of the 'English liberal intelligentsia'[40] are. The social isolation of officers from 'civilians' (both 'rough' and 'respectable'), and the social solidarity among officers, minimises the extent to which this view of the world is challenged. One result is, as we shall see, a very particular view of what constitutes 'suspicious' behaviour and impatience with any rules which get in the way of the 'fight

---

[35] Reiner R, *The Politics of the Police*, 3rd edn (Oxford: OUP, 2000) p 87.

[36] For a useful overview of the literature see Westmarland L, 'Police Cultures' in Newburn T (ed), *The Handbook of Policing*, 2nd edn (Cullompton: Willan, 2008). For a former police superintendent's critical account of cop culture see Young M, *An Inside Job* (Oxford: Clarendon Press, 1991).

[37] Smith and Gray (1983).   [38] Westmarland (2008: 268).

[39] Dixon D, *Law in Policing* (Oxford: Clarendon, 1997) p 104.

[40] Police officer quoted by Shiner M, 'National Implementation of the Recording of Police Stops' (London: Home Office, 2006) p 51.

against crime'. This means that legality is often sacrificed for efficiency.[41] Thus, cop culture acts as a powerful crime control engine at the heart of the machinery of criminal justice.

What we have said about 'cop culture' might lead one to believe that the police who subscribe to it see the world completely differently from the way others see it, and that cop culture is invariant. This would be a mistake. First, the differences between cop culture and that of the wider society can be overstated. For example, impatience with rules which appear to impede the fight against crime is widespread through society,[42] and Labour governments from 1997 onwards deliberately cultivated the dichotomous notion that a minority of criminals and anti-socials will undermine 'our way of life' unless pre-emptive and punitive measures are vigorously pursued by the police and others.[43] Second, there are differences within cop culture: between forces and within forces (for example between 'management cops' and 'street cops', and between different types of squad). There are differences between aspects of modern cop culture and that of the 1960s (especially in relation to race, gender and sexual orientation). The growing numbers of ethnic minority,[44] and female, police officers, and the establishment of groups such as the Black Police Officers Association, British Association of Women in Policing, and the Lesbian and Gay Police Association evidence and help sustain an ongoing (if painfully slow) process of 'cultural fragmentation' within the police.[45]

One reason why cop culture is generally thought to be completely distinct is that, when the police talk about what they do (and why they do it) they often exaggerate. Researchers, listening to what police officers say but not observing what they actually do, sometimes make the mistake of assuming that those officers are describing reality. In their talk, the police overemphasise the excitement and danger of their job, the awfulness of the 'toe-rags' they deal with and their ethnic distinctiveness, and their own macho qualities. Hoyle, for instance, in research carried out in the 1990s, found most officers expressing disparaging remarks about domestic disputes ('rubbish work'). But in reality she found that most officers handled these disputes sensitively.[46] Hoyle accordingly draws a distinction between 'canteen culture' (the way officers talk about their work and which incorporates in a strong form all the elements identified earlier)

---

[41] Goldsmith A, 'Taking Police Culture Seriously' (1990) 1 Policing and Society 91.

[42] See Chan J, 'Changing Police Culture' (1996) 36 BJ Crim 109.

[43] See, for example Nixon J and Parr S, 'Anti-social Behaviour: Voices from the Front Line' in Flint J (ed), *Housing, Urban Governance and Anti-Social Behaviour* (Bristol: Policy Press, 2006).

[44] The proportion of ethnic minority officers doubled from 2% in 1999 to 3.9% (5,511 officers) in April 2007, although the Home Secretary's 1999 target of 7% by 2009 'will almost certainly not be met': Equality and Human Rights Commission, *Police and Racism: What has been Achieved 10 Years after the Stephen Lawrence Inquiry Report* (2009) p 13. It should not, of course, be assumed that the dominant police culture will be broken down simply through ensuring greater socio-demographic diversity of recruits (see, for example, Cashmore, 2001).

[45] See Loader I and Mulcahy A, *Policing and the Condition of England* (Oxford: OUP, 2003) ch 6; Foster et al (2005: ch 4); McLauglin (2007: ch 6).

[46] Hoyle C, *Negotiating Domestic Violence* (Oxford: Clarendon Press, 1998).

and the actual working rules of the police. Similarly, Smith and Gray found that the police officers they observed behaved in far less racist ways than their views would lead one to expect.[47] By the same token we should not assume that the decreasing frequency of racist 'banter' in the canteen[48] (and the presence of anti-racist elements in modern police training) is reflected in an absence of racist behaviour on the streets. A gap between talk and action may exist here too, particularly where patrol officers are unaware that their actions are being observed by researchers. An undercover investigation into the police by a BBC reporter, broadcast as 'The Secret Policeman' on 21 October 2003, found that away from the training room (and from the canteen) a number of new recruits spoke 'privately' of their hatred of 'pakis' and five of them admitted (or boasted) that they intended to, or did, use their powers in racially discriminatory ways.[49]

In view of the gap between talk and action, Waddington (1999) argues that the concept of 'cop culture' is unhelpful. He argues that the way that policing works and discretion is exercised depends on the demands of the job and the nature of society; canteen culture, by contrast, serves the role of relieving tension and justifying sometimes distasteful and distressing actions, and bears no necessary relation to reality. In our view, Waddington goes too far. First, as we have noted already, the demands of the job and the nature of society (and society's demands) can be interpreted in different ways. Second, if the stories swapped in the canteen were to become totally divorced from reality they could no longer serve the function of justifying what the police do. As Britton says, '...when we tell a story we reveal to our listener(s) one or more central assumed truths about the world. These are important because they can then contribute to a more general taken-for-granted understanding of the world and become a basis for acting in it...'[50] Third, stories and jokes can be used in an instrumental way to find out how others are likely to behave as colleagues. For example, racist 'banter' is sometimes used to test whether new recruits (particularly those from an ethnic minority) can be trusted not to challenge racist policing.[51]

It follows that police culture will be a product in part of certain objective realities which change slowly (fundamental realities of policing, the way our society is structured, the vulnerable situation in which many victims of domestic violence find themselves and so forth), and in part a product of police attitudes and perceptions (attitudes to 'domestics' which fail to understand the predicament of the victims, to ethnic minorities, to discipline and so forth). Police culture can be seen as producing both 'canteen

---

[47] Smith and Gray (1983). Several other examples could be cited. See Waddington P, 'Police (Canteen) Sub-Culture: An Appreciation' (1999) 39 BJ Crim 286.

[48] Fitzgerald (1999: ch 5); Fitzgerald et al (2002: 127); Holdaway S and O'Neill M, 'Where has All the Racism Gone? Views of Racism within Constabularies after Macpherson' (2007) 30(3) Ethnic and Racial Studies 397 at 400–2.

[49] See McLaughlin (2007: ch 6).

[50] Britton N, 'Examining Police/Black Relations: What's in a Story' (2000b) 23(4) Ethnic and Racial Studies 696.

[51] Cashmore E, 'The Experiences of Ethnic Minority Police Officers in Britain: Under-recruitment and Racial Profiling in a Performance Culture' (2001) 24(4) Ethnic and Racial Studies 642 at 650.

culture' on the one hand and, on the other, specific 'working rules' which are usually less (but sometimes more) extreme than implied by what the police say when eating their mixed grills. As for police practices, they are a product of the interaction of those working rules with countervailing social pressures (for instance from ethnic minority communities who resent aspects of police practices) and legal constraints.[52]

One effect of police culture is to give priority to certain freedoms above others. Less value is put on the freedom involved in activities (especially those of 'them') which impinge on the freedoms of others (especially those of 'us') than is put on 'our' freedoms to be undisturbed. We shall therefore see in ch 3, that the police prioritise public order at the expense of tolerance and the rights of unpopular minorities. The aggressive policing of demonstrations, and treatment of demonstrators as suspects, that came to the fore with the death of Ian Tomlinson in April 2009 is a stark example.[53] This leads to a tendency to over-police (and under-protect) 'police property', ie, those who are perceived to be deviating from a 'respectable' norm. Yet the opposite is true of most non-police agencies (discussed in detail in ch 7). The latter are very reluctant to encroach on the freedom of those whom they police. Clearly the job of law enforcement per se in an adversary system does not produce the distinctive elements which comprise 'cop culture'.

One way of changing police practices might be to inculcate more democratic (or more inclusive) values in officers. This might be attempted through, for example, radical changes in recruitment and training practices, combined with the introduction of new performance indicators, a genuine commitment to working more closely with local communities, robust leadership and stronger disciplinary measures for those found to be flouting the officially espoused policies and practices.[54] Rather than getting closer to the community simply in order to glean more information from it, the police would need to engage in a continuing debate, one involving all sections and levels of society, about the proper means and ends of policing.[55] In the rest of this chapter we look at how the police as presently constituted operate powers to stop and search, and at some of the social consequences.

2.2 **The power to stop-search**

At the time of the Royal Commission on Criminal Procedure (Philips Commission) report in 1981, the law on stop-search was confused and incoherent, having developed in an ad hoc manner. For example, there were no national stop-search powers for

---

[52] See further Chan (1996: 115).   [53] See eg The *Guardian*, 1 May 2009.

[54] Evidence that such multi-layered strategies can be at least partially successful can be found in two case-studies from the United States and Australia respectively: Miller S, *Gender and Community Policing* (Boston MA: North Eastern University Pres, 1999); Chan J, *Changing Police Culture* (Cambridge: Cambridge University Press, 1997). See also the essays in (2008) 18(1) Policing and Society.

[55] Loader (1996: ch 7); Crawford (2007).

stolen goods or offensive weapons. On the other hand, local legislation for many big cities did allow stop-search for stolen goods.[56]

Most of these powers allowed the police to stop-search only if they 'reasonably suspected' a person of the offence in question. A major issue of concern in the 1970s and early 1980s was how far the police really were inhibited by the reasonable suspicion requirement. The early 1980s saw a number of riots in several inner-city areas where poverty and ethnic minority conflict with the police was commonplace.[57] A massive stop-search operation, 'Swamp 81', in particular, was identified as one of the 'triggers' of the Brixton riot of 1981.[58] Described by some as 'saturation policing', stop-search on this scale was manifestly not on a 'reasonable suspicion' basis.[59] Every empirical research project carried out in this period found that many stop-searches were problematic: they targeted young males (black or 'scruffy' males in particular), and were often arbitrary or based 'on grounds which police officers find it hard to specify'.[60] The Philips Commission knew that stop-search was difficult to control, and was aware of the damage which these powers could do to the relationship between police and black youths in particular. It recommended a single uniform power for the police to stop-search for stolen goods or 'articles which it is a criminal offence to possess', but it also believed that 'the exercise of the powers must be subject to strict safeguards'.[61] Along with many other of the Philips Commission's proposals, these recommendations were enacted in PACE (though we shall see that there are many other stop-search powers in addition to those in PACE). The bundle of laws and controls that resulted contained elements of all four of the types of rule we identified earlier: the extension of the powers nationwide *legitimised* pre-existing police working practices and, by cloaking officers with legal authority, *enabled* more intensive stop and search strategies in future. At the same time, *inhibitory* elements were incorporated (with limited success, thus rendering them largely *presentational*) in the form of 'safeguards'.

As we mentioned earlier, police powers are useable far more easily in public than in private. Thus PACE stop-search powers may be used only in public places, and non-dwelling places to which the public have ready access – including public transport, and (while open to the public) museums, sports grounds, cinemas, pubs, restaurants, night-clubs, banks and shops.[62] Section 1 of PACE is headed 'Power of constable to

---

[56] See Royal Commission on Criminal Procedure, *The Investigation and Prosecution of Criminal Offences in England and Wales: The Law and Procedure* (Cmnd 8092–1, app 1).

[57] For discussion, see Cashmore E and McLaughlin E (eds), *Out of Order?* (London: Routledge, 1991) p 113.   [58] See further 2.5.4 below.

[59] Scarman Sir L, *The Brixton Disorders: 10–12 April 1981* (Cmnd 8427) (London: HMSO, 1981).

[60] Willis C, *The Use, Effectiveness and Impact of Police Stop and Search Powers* (Home Office Research and Planning Unit Paper No 15) (London: Home Office, 1983) p 15; also see Smith and Gray (1983).

[61] Royal Commission on Criminal Procedure (RCCP), Report (Cmnd 8092) (London: HMSO, 1981) para 3.17.

[62] PACE, s 1(1). For a more detailed account of the spatial limitation of the power to stop and search see Clark D, *Bevan and Lidstone's The Investigation of Crime*, 3rd edn (London: LexisNexis, 2004) pp 91–5. Under s 4 of the Offensive Weapons Act 1996 (inserting s 139B into the Criminal Justice Act 1988), as widened by

stop and search persons, vehicles, etc'. This power can best be understood as comprising three main elements: a 'reasonable suspicion' criterion, the offences to which stop and search is applicable, and the power itself.

2.2.1 Reasonable suspicion and police suspicion

2.2.1.1 The slippery concept of reasonable suspicion

Under s 1(3) of PACE police officers may only stop-search if they have 'reasonable grounds for suspecting' that evidence of relevant offences will be found; and seizure may take place only of articles which, under s 1(7), the officer 'has reasonable grounds for suspecting' to be relevant. The requirement of 'reasonable suspicion' is aimed at inhibiting the police from stopping and searching indiscriminately – or, indeed, in inappropriately discriminatory ways – without unduly fettering their ability to detect crime.

The few cases on reasonable suspicion do little to define it, other than making it clear that it may be based on material, such as hearsay, that would not be admissible in court.[63] In *Francis*, for example, suspicion was created by the suspect driving in an area known for drugs, with a passenger. The last time the driver had been stopped her passenger (a different one) had been in possession of drugs. This was held not to constitute 'reasonable suspicion'.[64] In *Slade*, on the other hand, the suspect's proximity to an address known for its drugs connections, combined with the fact that he had noticed the officer and put his hand in his pocket while smiling 'smugly', was held to constitute reasonable suspicion.[65] It would be difficult to slip a Rizla paper between the material facts of these 'reasonable suspicion' cases which nonetheless reach different conclusions.

An attempt to clarify the concept of 'reasonable suspicion' is contained in PACE Code of Practice A.[66] This Code has been revised many times, sometimes with a view to enlarging the concept of reasonable suspicion, sometimes with a view to restricting

---

s 48 of the Violent Crime Reduction Act 2006, the police have the power to enter *schools* to search those premises and anyone on them for bladed or pointed articles and offensive weapons so long as they reasonably suspect that someone on those premises has such an item.

[63] *Shaaban Bin Hussien v Chong Fook Kam* [1970] AC 942; *Erskine v Hollin* [1971] RTR 199.

[64] LEXIS, CO/1434/91, June 1992. *Black* CO/877/95 (11th May 1995) QBD is to similar effect. See also *Tomlinson*, reported in LAG Bulletin, May 1992, p 21 and *French v DPP* [1996] EWHC Admin 283 (27 November 1996).

[65] LEXIS, CO/1678/96, October 1996. Also see *Lawrence* for a similar case: LEXIS CO/2775/94 May 1995.

[66] A number of Codes of Practice have been made by the Home Office under the authority of PACE. Codes of Practice are similar in effect to legislation, insofar as they must be taken into account by the courts, but they are brought into effect by statutory instrument. This makes them easy to amend in the light of experience. Code A applies not only to stop-search powers exercised under PACE, but also to those exercised under, for instance, the Terrorism Act 2000 and the Criminal Justice and Public Order Act 1994.

it. References in the text are to the version that came into force on 1 January 2009.[67] The core 'definition' of reasonable suspicion is contained in para 2.2:

Reasonable grounds for suspicion depend on the circumstances in each case. There must be an objective basis for that suspicion based on facts, information and/or intelligence which are relevant to the likelihood of finding an article of a certain kind...

This definition is little changed from when PACE was first enacted, and it leaves scope to identify certain groups as more suspicious than others. Paragraph 2.2 acknowledges this by going on to warn that:

Reasonable suspicion can never be supported on the basis of personal factors. It must rely on intelligence or information about, or some specific behaviour by, the person concerned. For example, other than in a witness description of a suspect, a person's race, age, appearance, or the fact that the person is known to have a previous conviction, cannot be used alone or in combination with any other factor, as the reason for searching that person. Reasonable suspicion cannot be based on generalisations or stereotypical images of certain groups or categories of people as more likely to be involved in criminal activity. A person's religion cannot be considered as reasonable grounds for suspicion and should never be considered as a reason to stop or stop and search an individual.

The final sentence is a twenty-first century addition which reflects growing concern that the police have begun to target Muslims in the wake of the terrorist atrocities on September 11 2001 in New York and in July 2005 in London.[68] It is remarkable that a legislative code of practice directs, in effect, that people should not be stopped just because they are black or Muslim, and is a rare example of the law attempting to take into account the social reality of policing on the streets. This message is amplified in, for example, para 1.1:

Powers to stop and search must be used fairly, responsibly, with respect for people being searched and without unlawful discrimination.

That such amplification has been deemed necessary suggests that, a quarter of a century on from the original enactment of PACE and the Codes of Practice, problems of controlling the use of police discretion have persisted. One indication that the law has proved largely ineffective in restraining the police is the enormous growth in recorded stop-searches since PACE was introduced, with the annual total rising from around 110,000 to one million in little over a decade (see table 2.1). However, all such statistics must be treated with caution, since they are the product of recording practices that may be inconsistent over time.

---

[67] The 2009 version of Code of Practice A can be downloaded from <http://police.homeoffice.gov.uk/> (accessed 5 January 2010).

[68] See, for example, Chakraborti N, 'Policing Muslim Communities' in Rowe M (ed) *Policing Beyond Macpherson* (Cullompton: Willan, 2007); Mythen G, Walklate S and Khan T, (2009) '"I'm a Muslim, but I'm Not a Terrorist": Victimization, Risky Identities and the Performance of Safety' 49(6) BJ Crim 736.

Table 2.1 Recorded stop-searches (where reasonable suspicion is required) and arrest rates[69]

Year	Stop-Searches	Arrests	% of stops leading to arrest
1986	109,800	18,900	17.2
1987	118,300	19,600	16.6
1988	149,600	23,700	15.8
1989	202,800	32,800	16.2
1990	256,900	39,200	15.3
1991	303,800	46,200	15.2
1992	351,700	48,700	13.8
1993	442,800	55,900	12.6
1994	576,000	70,300	12.2
1995	690,300	81,000	11.7
1996	814,500	87,700	10.8
1996/97	871,500	91,100	10.5
1997/98	1,050,700	108,700	10.3
1998/99	1,080,700	121,300	11.2
1999/00	857,200	108,500	12.7
2000/01	714,100	95,400	13.4
2001/02	741,000	98,700	13.3
2002/03	895,300	114,300	12.8
2003/04	749,400	95,100	12.7
2004/05	861,500	95,800	11.1
2005/06	888,700	102,700	11.6
2006/07	962,900	111,100	11.5
2007/08	1,045,923	119,567	11.4

Table 2.1 shows that the number of recorded stop-searches rose rapidly from the mid 1980s to the late 1990s before falling sharply at the turn of the century[70] and then picking

---

[69] Source: Povey D and Smith K (eds), *Police Powers and Procedures, England and Wales 2007/08*, 2nd edn (Home Office Statistical Bulletin 7/09) (London: Home Office, 2009) table 2a, and earlier bulletins in the same series. These figures largely relate to stop-search under PACE, s 1, but also s 43 of the Terrorism Act 2000, s 23 of the Misuse of Drugs Act 1971 and some other less important powers where 'reasonable suspicion' is required.

[70] The drop at the turn of the century appears to be a result of the high profile Macpherson Inquiry, which branded the Metropolitan Police as institutionally racist, drew attention to the damage that stop-search practices were doing to race relations and recommended tighter safeguards: Macpherson Sir W, *The Stephen Lawrence Inquiry – Report* (London: SO, 1999) recommendations 61–3. This prompted a temporary loss of confidence by the police (Fitzgerald (1999: ch 5); Fitzgerald et al (2002: 100–1); Miller et al (2000: 17)).

Table 2.2 Recorded stop-searches compared with BCS estimates of actual stop-searches

Year	Police-recorded stop-searches	British Crime Survey estimate of number of stop-searches	Percentage of searches recorded by police
1987	118,300	295,000	40.1%
1999/2000[71]	825,356	1,102,000	75.0%

up again, albeit with a dip in 2003/04. As the numbers of stop-searches continued to rise post-1995 (when crime levels were declining) changes in the levels of crime cannot be used to explain these trends. In any event, no strong relationship exists between the level of crime in a police force area and the level of recorded searches carried out in that area, as some forces with high crime rates make relatively little recorded use of stop-search (Miller et al, 2000: 13). In short, trends in the recorded use of stop-search do not appear to be driven by the amount of reasonably suspicious behaviour taking place but rather by police policies and practices. Indeed, much (but by no means all) of the apparent growth in stop-search shown in table 2.1 is the result of increased *recording* of stop-search activity by the police, as can be seen from table 2.2, which compares police figures with British Crime Survey estimates of the levels of stop-search (although only in relation to adults living in households) in the post-PACE era.

It seems, then, that stop-searches have risen substantially in the post-PACE era, but not so sharply as police records would suggest.

Table 2.1 also shows that the arrest rate (the percentage of stops resulting in an arrest) generally declined as the number of recorded stop-searches increased from 1986–1997/98. As the numbers of recorded stop-searches fell from 1999 onwards, the arrest rate began to increase, until the trends reversed again. There are a number of possible explanatory factors behind these trends, of which three will be noted here. First, the inverse relationship between levels of recorded stop-search and arrest rates may reflect the fact that the more often you perform a task, the less careful you tend to be.[72] Second, a growing proportion of stop-search activity is likely to be proactive in nature, where the level of suspicion is often relatively weak. The significance of this shift in the reactive/proactive mix is that high discretion searches (where the police are acting proactively) are only two-thirds as likely to result in an arrest as low discretion searches (where the police are responding to a specific incident or call from the

---

[71] Source: Clancy et al (2001: 67–8).

[72] Consistent with this, Miller et al (2000: 12) found that forces that use stop-search a lot, such as Cleveland, tend to have lower arrest rates than comparable police forces that use it less, such as Humberside. The figures for particular police forces for 2006/07 show a much more uncertain relationship between volume and arrest rates, however: Ministry of Justice, *Arrests for Recorded Crime (Notifiable Offences) and the Operation of Certain Police Powers under PACE England and Wales 2006/07* (London: MoJ, 2008c: 26) table P1.

public).[73] Third, and probably by far the most important, the police have, over time, recorded proportionately more of their stop-search activity that does not result in an arrest.[74] Thus Skogan noted that the 1988 British Crime Survey indicated a stop-search arrest rate of around 6% compared with close to 17% in the official figures.[75] It thus seems likely that the recorded arrest rates shown in table 2.1 overstate the actual arrest rate, and particularly so the further back in time one goes.

To sum up, the low actual arrest rate, and the fact that actual stop-search activity (for adults living in households) has increased fourfold since 1987, are good indications that PACE and the law on reasonable suspicion has had relatively little inhibitory effect on police stop-search activity.

2.2.1.2 Police suspicion, working assumptions and working rules

If the legal rules do little to constrain and structure police discretion, what does? Police officers often refer to 'instinct' and 'experience'. As Fielding observes, experience is valued, whereas 'books' or theory are not.[76] Research has repeatedly found that exhortations in probationer training to police 'by the book' are quickly overwhelmed by the more powerful influences through which traditional cop culture is reproduced, amongst which are the 'old sweats' who induct trainees into the 'realities of the street'.[77] Partly this involves learning how to deal with conflict and volatile situations. As one officer has put it: 'On the street, most times, you don't have time to go through a list of reasonable grounds before stopping [and searching]. It's not like a doctor making a diagnosis: you've got this problem and you have to solve it there and then and think about it afterwards.'[78] But most stop-searches are the result of individual officer discretion (high discretion searches) rather than the result of officers acting on intelligence already received or being called to a problematic incident (low discretion searches). Thus, in the majority of stop-searches officers are not 'problem-solving' but rather proactively seeking to detect, prevent or disrupt crime and disorder.[79] This results in officers targeting those who they think offer the best prospects for achieving these ends, almost regardless of the level of individualised suspicion. The young, particularly those from ethnic minorities or lower class backgrounds, suffer particularly from such high discretion searches, but so do 'druggy-looking people',[80] the homeless, asylum seekers, and other unpopular users of public space.

Just how quickly induction into the craft of street-policing can take place was exemplified by 'The Secret Policeman' programme. PC Andy Hall had served for 15 months

---

[73] As found in the Fitzgerald (1999: ch 3) study, from where the terms 'high' and 'low' discretion are taken.   [74] For an explanation of this trend see 2.4.1.

[75] Skogan W, *The Police and Public in England and Wales: A British Crime Survey Report* (Home Office Research Study 117) (London: HMSO, 1990) p 34, n 4.

[76] Fielding N, *Joining Forces* (London: Routledge, 1988).

[77] For a discussion of the relevant studies see Foster J, 'Police Cultures' in Newburn T (ed), *The Handbook of Policing*, 1st edn (Cullompton: Willan, 2003) pp 202–6.   [78] Cited in Fitzgerald (1999: ch 3).

[79] Fitzgerald (1999: ch 3).

[80] An expression used by one of the officers quoted by Fitzgerald (1999: ch 2).

in London but wanted to move to Manchester so had to undergo initial training again. During the course he spoke privately to a fellow probationer, PC Mark Daly, who was in fact an undercover BBC reporter. The secret recording of the conversation shows how the lessons of 'practical policing' may be taught even to probationers still in training school:

PC Hall:	I would never say this in class. If you did not discriminate and you did not bring out your prejudices, you'd be a shit copper, do you know that?
PC Daly:	Really?
PC Hall:	If you was on the street Mark, and you wouldn't stop anyone because of their colour, because of their race, because of how they dress, because of how they thingy, you'd be a shit copper. I mean we used to drive down the road and say 'he looks a dodgy c*** let's stop him.' That is practical policing. It is mate. And nine times out of ten you're right.[81] But in training environment you can't be seen to do it because it's discrimination. It's against the equal opportunities. But when you are on the street you will fucking pick it up.

This programme was made not long after the publication in 1999 of the Macpherson Report. The latter excoriated police services for their 'institutional racism', as manifested, amongst other things, by the disproportionate stop-searching of black and minority ethnic (BME) people (see 2.3 below).[82] This resulted in a huge (if often misguided) reform effort to improve police practice, and contributed to the virtual eradication of *openly* racist talk and action.[83] Police officers of PC Hall's ilk are thus unlikely nowadays to reveal to researchers such racially prejudiced thinking. Instead they are likely to explain their behaviour by reference to a vague concept, such as a 'hunch'. Some generalisations which inform practical decision-making are acknowledged more openly, however. Quinton et al found that: 'The individuals who were known to the police were often targeted in stops and searches. It was common practice, on the shift briefings in each of the pilot sites, for officers to be given the details of individuals and cars which would be "worth a stop".'[84] Fitzgerald found that officers were open about their targeting of those who were 'known' to the police by virtue of their criminal record and/or their associates. As one constable put it: 'The vast majority of the people we're dealing with are the same people all the time.' This assertion was supported by Fitzgerald's analysis of search records which found that about half of those searched, who were not arrested as a result, had previous convictions or cautions. She also found that of the 589 people searched on three or

---

[81] This is an expression of confidence in police fact-finding redolent of the crime control model. It would be more accurate to say that nine times out of ten the police are wrong (see table 2.1).

[82] Macpherson (1999: 29–30).   [83] Foster et al (2005) pp 35–40; Holdaway and O'Neill (2007).

[84] Quinton et al, *Police Stops, Decision-making and Practice* (Police Research Series Paper 130) (London: Home Office, 2000) pp 24–5. Scottish police similarly target the 'usual suspects' and their associates: McAra L and McVie S, 'The Usual Suspects? Street-Life, Young People and the Police' (2005) 5(1) Criminal Justice 5 at p 26.

more occasions within the first quarter of 1999 only two had no criminal record (Fitzgerald, 1999: ch 3).

Another important factor in police suspicion is incongruity – being where one does not belong: a scruffily dressed young male in a 'posh' area, for instance (Loader, 1996: 127–8), or for that matter someone dressed in a dinner jacket driving around a decaying inner-city area.[85] There is an even-handedness here which is more apparent than real. The rich may seem to be equally at risk of having police power exercised against them if they spend time in poor areas as are the poor in wealthy areas. But wealthy people are less likely to be in such areas, will not be offended if the police suggest that they do not 'belong', and generally possess fewer traits (race, previous convictions and so forth) which would, when added to incongruity, lead to suspiciousness. It is also far easier for the wealthy to avoid incongruity when out of their own area (by dressing scruffily) than it is for the poor.

Membership of an ethnic minority, especially if one is in an area with few ethnic minority people, is also important.[86] In 'The Secret Policeman' an experienced constable who was accompanying a new recruit on street patrol (as his tutor) was asked by the recruit (actually a BBC undercover reporter) what he thought of ethnic minorities. PC Turley replied:

...they'll try and pull a fast one on every time. Like round here if there's a car full of black people or a car full of Asians you pull it because we've got no really ethnic minorities round here. You can guarantee it will be full of shit coming across to rob or doing something.[87]

What comes out of this material, as well as much other research, pre and post PACE, and from Australia and the USA as well as the UK, is that much police discretion is based on stereotyping.[88] This process enables rough and ready but very speedy judgements about a person's character (their 'master status') to be made on the basis of visible signs (known as 'auxiliary traits').[89] These auxiliary traits include gender, age, scruffiness, attitude to the police, previous convictions and ethnic group.

---

[85] 'I focus on people not matching area – how they dress' (officer quoted by Quinton et al (2000: 23).

[86] See, for example, Loader and Mulcahy (2003) pp 157–8; Equality and Human Rights Commission (2008: 24), and Hallsworth S, 'Racial Targeting and Social Control: Looking behind the Police' (2006) 14 Critical Criminology 293 at 301–2.

[87] Occasionally even more extreme forms of racism interact with incongruity in decision-making. Black and Asian people are evidently seen by a (hopefully tiny) minority of officers as by definition incongruous in an Anglo-Saxon England constructed as 'naturally' white. Examples of this were recorded as part of 'The Secret Policeman' documentary: 'It's fucking proactive policing, yeah, innit? He's a Paki and I'm stopping him, because I'm fucking English. At the end of the day mate, we look after our own. You know that don't you?' (PC Andy Hall).

[88] For a psychological analysis of stereotyping, and the related phenomena of prejudice and ethnocentrism see Ainsworth P, *Psychology and Policing* (Cullompton: Willan, 2002) pp 27–32.

[89] The terminology is used by criminologists who adopt the 'social reaction' (or 'labelling') perspective. For an English example in this tradition see Gill O, 'Urban stereotypes and delinquent incidents' (1976) 16 BJ Crim 312.

A classic example of stereotyping is provided by the 50-year-old Bishop of Stepney, who finally expressed his anger after being stopped for the eighth time in as many years. When asked why he stopped the bishop's car, the officer simply said 'Open the boot': 'He asked me what I did, and I said, "I'm the Bishop of Stepney." He said "whoops", I revealed my dog collar and he looked as if he'd just seen a ghost.' The officer immediately told the bishop he could go, refusing to say why he had stopped him. The stereotyping in this case is clear. Middle-aged men normally have a respectable master status in the eyes of the police. However, the bishop's black auxiliary trait trumped his middle-aged auxiliary trait, giving him a 'suspicious' master status.[90] The black auxiliary trait was then trumped when his clerical collar was revealed, returning to him the 'respectable' master status he would have had, had he not been black.[91]

Research in the post-Macpherson era has confirmed the continuing firm police belief in the value of the working assumptions and rules we have outlined here.[92] As one officer declared:

I mean I'm sure sociologists, liberal types, would say that we're employing stereotypes to make those decisions, well yes, and it works. That's how we catch criminals.[93]

All that has changed in recent times is that young Asian males have become more pronounced targets for suspicion, particularly in the context of the 'war on terror'. To give just one example, in 2007 an officer with specialist responsibility for giving race and diversity lessons to recruits told a public meeting in Cumbria that any sightings of young Asian men in an area of the Lake District should be reported to the police, adding:

Whilst we are told not to stereotype, the reality is that groups of young Asian males need to be checked out.[94]

What would it take to get police officers to respect the law's requirement of reasonable suspicion? In 1995 a charitable body, NACRO, ran an experiment in one area of London in cooperation with the local police. The police were required to give a leaflet to everyone stop-searched in the area which explained their rights. No new rules were introduced, although the use of stop-search as a performance indicator in the area was stopped, and the commitment of the area's senior police to non-racist policing

---

[90] Research confirms that the trumping of a 'respectable age or class' by a 'disrespectable ethnicity' occurs quite frequently for some ethnic groups: Mooney J and Young J, 'Policing Ethnic Minorities: Stop and Search in North London' in Marlow and Loveday (2000). Similarly black women are seen by the police as more threatening than white women: Player E, 'Women and Crime in the City' in Downes D (ed), *Crime and the City* (Basingstoke: Macmillan, 1989) pp 122–5.

[91] Off duty black police officers sometimes suffer in much the same way. For an example see Havis S and Best D, *Stop and Search Complaints: A Police Complaints Authority Study* (London: Police Complaints Authority, 2004) p 31.   [92] For example, Lister et al (2008); Shiner (2006).

[93] Police officer quoted by Shiner (2006: 53).

[94] Quoted in Equality and Human Rights Commission (2008: 19).

was emphasised. In that year, the number of stop-searches was apparently halved, at a time when stop-searches across the capital in general continued to rise. It is likely that giving out a leaflet which set out the law concentrated the minds of officers on the rules and inhibited their use of the power.[95]

The experience of the NACRO experiment suggests that limited change can happen, but only with constant reinforcement, not only in relation to what the rules are, but also in relation to the effects of adhering to them (or not). This is a matter of both positive reinforcement (not rewarding, through performance indicators, stops simply on a volume basis) and negative reinforcement (the threat of disciplinary action for racism and rule-breaking, discussed in ch 12, and again illustrated by the police management attitude in Tottenham at the time of the experiment). Policing in general does not yet embody either form of reinforcement,[96] and so the conclusions of the authors of the NACRO study hold good in the main: 'the guidance on reasonable suspicion in the PACE Code of Practice is not clearly understood, or remembered, or put into practice... The 'culture' on divisions [ie on the street] will have a stronger impact on probationary officers than classroom teaching can hope to achieve' (NACRO 1997: 41).

The aftermath of the Macpherson Report confirms these conclusions. Macpherson's wounding critique of 'institutionally racist' stop-search practices, and the attempts to improve training and supervision in response, appear to have had the same (short-term) effect as the NACRO experiment of concentrating officers' minds on the rules. A large-scale Home Office funded study set up to assess the impact of the Macpherson Inquiry found that:

observed officers reported a climate in the aftermath of the Inquiry in which 'people were too afraid' to stop and search for fear of being accused of racism. This effect seemed to be particularly powerful in [the Met.], where officers said the use of searches dramatically declined... It also appears that the Inquiry brought into focus officers' uncertainty and confusion about the legitimate use of their powers. As one officer explained: 'It makes police officers scared. If I saw a black youth on a street corner I would probably not search him, unless he's done something physically tangible that I have seen, I won't do it.'[97]

This, of course, is exactly what reasonable suspicion requires – something tangible. As the researchers go on to observe:

It seems likely that because officers felt under increased scrutiny in the aftermath of the Inquiry, and that they might therefore be held to account for their actions, there were times when they

---

[95] NACRO, *Policing Local Communities: The Tottenham Experiment* (London: NACRO, 1997).

[96] In the wake of the Macpherson Report, the Government belatedly realised the damage caused by performance indicators that emphasise quantity rather than quality (Home Office, 2005a: 12, 25, 27, 38) but as their notion of quality encompasses a strong emphasis on the intelligence-gathering function of stop-search (eg 27–8) and an inadequate emphasis on the precondition of individualised reasonable suspicion of a specific offence (partly a product of the mixed-message sent out by their creation of, and support for, search powers that do not carry that precondition – see next sub-section), we remain sceptical that front-line police officers will change their ways. [97] Foster et al (2005: 29–30).

realised they could not always account for their conduct. Officers reported that the perceived increase in scrutiny meant that they could no longer go on 'fishing trips' where they knew they did not have proper grounds for searching. The climate before the Inquiry appeared to have made it either acceptable and/or possible for some officers to break rules in relation to stop and search. Since the Lawrence Inquiry Report this was perceived to be more difficult.[98]

The difficulty does not appear to be insurmountable, however, as indicated by the recent rises in the stop-search figures (see table 2.1), which have been particularly marked in the case of ethnic minorities.[99] And now that various influential opinion-leaders have claimed that the police as a whole are no longer 'institutionally racist',[100] it seems likely that the role of reasonable suspicion as an inhibitory factor is fading into the background once again. We should not make the mistake, however, of concluding that the reasonable suspicion requirement is purely presentational. That it has some inhibitory effect is indicated by the even lower arrest rates associated with stop-search powers that do not require this level of suspicion (see 2.2.2.2).[101]

2.2.2 The offences at which stop and search is targeted

A due process theorist would argue that stop-search powers could only be legitimate if they required the police to have reasonable suspicion of a specific offence. A crime control theorist would argue that the police should be able to act whenever their suspicions, however generalised, are aroused. PACE appears at first sight to take the due process approach, but matters are not quite so simple as this, as we shall now explore.

---

[98] Ibid, 30. British Crime Survey data from 1999 strongly suggests that the targeting by patrol officers of black people on foot did become less pronounced at this time, although this was not true for vehicle stops: Clancy et al (2001: 64–6).

[99] Thus, following general and fairly even falls across the board in 1999/2000, the two years to 2001/02 saw a further overall fall in the numbers of recorded stop-searches of white people, but very significant increases for black and Asian people. The years from 2004/05 to 2006/07 are marked by large percentage increases but most noticeably for Asian people in London, reflecting the increased concern about people of Muslim faith following the July 2005 attacks on the London transport system. The upshot is that racial disparities have widened markedly in recent years, despite repeated exhortations from government for the police to curb 'ethnic disproportionality'. Source: annual 'Statistics on Race and the Criminal Justice System' as published by the Home Office and, now, the Ministry of Justice (available from <http://www.justice.gov.uk/publications/raceandcjs.htm> – accessed 5 January 2010).

[100] Including Trevor Phillips, the Chair of the Equality and Human Rights Commission, in a speech made on 19 January 2009 (<http://news.bbc.co.uk/1/hi/uk_politics/7836766.stm> – accessed 5 January 2010), and Jack Straw, the Justice Secretary, in an interview broadcast on 22 February 2009 (<http://news.bbc.co.uk/1/hi/7904194.stm> – accessed 5 January 2010).

[101] It is likely that the growth in the use of such powers over the last decade (see table 2.2) means that some of the stop-search activity based on a weak level of suspicion which would previously have been cloaked in the authority of PACE now takes place under other legislation. This might help explain why the arrest rate for stop-searches requiring reasonable suspicion has not deteriorated as much as one might have expected in the period from 2003/04 onwards (see table 2.1). Another explanatory factor is likely to be that arrest became a more favoured outcome given the intense pressure from the Government for the police to 'bring more offenders to justice'.

2.2.2.1 Stop-searches requiring reasonable suspicion

Under s 1(3) of PACE, a police officer may stop and search only if 'he has reasonable grounds for suspecting that he will find stolen or prohibited articles or any article to which sub-section (8A) below applies or any firework...' 'Stolen articles' clearly include those stolen in contravention of s 1 of the Theft Act 1968, and probably include goods obtained by fraud or blackmail.[102] What is a 'prohibited article'? According to s 1(7) and (8), it is either (i) an offensive weapon or (ii) an article intended for use in burglary, theft, taking vehicles or fraud. Section 1(8A) was added by the Criminal Justice Act 1988. It allows searches for articles which, under s 139 of that Act, are unlawful if carried without a good excuse. Such articles include anything with blades or sharp points, including penknives if the blade is over three inches long. This enlarges the already extensive notion of the offensive weapon. Any item can be classed as an offensive weapon so long as it can be shown that the person possessed it with intention to cause injury. Similarly, a wide range of articles could be intended for use in committing crimes of dishonesty. The Criminal Justice Act 2003 (s 1) added items intended for use in causing criminal damage, and the Serious Organised Crime and Police Act 2005 (s 115) added prohibited fireworks,[103] to the ever-lengthening list of articles which can be the object of a stop-search. Broad as these powers are, they represent additions to (rather than replacements for) the miscellaneous powers mentioned earlier.[104] Thus, the police have long had a power to search where they reasonably suspect that a controlled drug will be found on a person or in a vehicle.[105]

2.2.2.2 Stop-searches *not* requiring reasonable suspicion

Extra powers to stop and search vehicles and pedestrians were introduced by the Criminal Justice and Public Order Act 1994 (CJPO), s 60.[106] These can be invoked by a senior officer where the police wish to stop-search for guns, knives or other weapons as provided under PACE, s 1, but there is no individualised reasonable suspicion. This originally allowed, for a period not normally exceeding 24 hours, the police to stop-search anyone where there is a reasonable belief *in relation to a particular locality* that 'incidents involving serious violence may take place'.[107] The Knives Act 1997 extended this power to cover situations where the senior officer (who now need only be

---

[102] Assuming that the extended definition of 'stolen goods' to be found in s 24(4) of the Theft Act 1968 applies here too.

[103] That is to say, prohibited under the Firework Regulations (SI 2004/1836) passed pursuant to the Fireworks Act 2003.

[104] In what follows we do not attempt an exhaustive list of all stop-search powers. A score of them are set out in Annex A to PACE Code of Practice A but even this list is declared to be only of the 'main' stop and search powers.   [105] Misuse of Drugs Act 1971, s 23.

[106] As with PACE, the pressure for increasing police power in this way came from the police themselves: Wasik M and Taylor R, *Blackstone's Guide to the Criminal Justice and Public Order Act 1994* (London: Blackstone Press, 1995) p 97.

[107] CJPO, s 60 (2). Also see Code A, para 1.8. See Clark (2004: 86–9) for details.

an Inspector) has a reasonable belief that persons are carrying 'dangerous instruments or offensive weapons', again with no requirement of reasonable suspicion against any particular individuals.[108] Section 87 of the Serious Crime Act 2007 extended this again, by enabling a s 60 authorisation to be made if the authorising officer reasonably believes that an incident involving serious violence has taken place in that officer's police area, that a weapon or dangerous instrument used in that incident is being carried in any locality within that area, and it is expedient to give an authorisation to find that article. The legislation is silent on the question of the selection of people to be searched under s 60. In practice, the police no doubt target much the same people as those stop-searched under PACE.

Wide-ranging powers are also provided by ss 44–47 of the Terrorism Act 2000 and the Anti-terrorism, Crime and Security Act 2001 (building on earlier anti-terrorism provisions). The police may stop any vehicle or person for the sole purpose of searching for articles of a kind which could be used in connection with terrorism 'whether or not the constable has any grounds for suspecting the presence of articles of that kind' (s 45(1)). While the 'sole purpose' restriction may sound impressive, we shall see below that arrests arising out of such stops need not be in connection with terrorism. Thus, if the police search for evidence of terrorism but find someone in possession of cannabis they can arrest for that offence instead. Authorisation has to be by an officer of at least the rank of Assistant Chief Constable who must judge it 'expedient for the prevention of acts of terrorism' (s 44(3)); and the period may last for 28 days (renewable). Authorisation must be confirmed by the Home Secretary, who has the power to set a shorter period. Like s 60 of the CJPO 1994, the power is confined to an area specified in a prior authorisation by a senior officer but, unlike the s 60 power, this area can extend to an entire police force area. An authorisation could therefore cover, for example, a whole city or the whole of Northern Ireland, or even straddle a number of areas (if authorising officers were to coordinate their activities), potentially covering the whole country.

Indeed, through the litigation that has become known as *Gillan* the courts learned that the Metropolitan Police together with the Home Secretary had, since the coming into force of s 44 on 19 February 2001, adopted the practice of issuing rolling (successive) authorisations for the whole of London. The Court of Appeal upheld this practice, commenting that: 'It did no more than enable the commander in a particular area to have the powers available when this was operationally required without going back

---

[108] Knives Act 1997, s 8, amending CJPO, s 60. This also allows the 24-hour period to be extended by a further 24 hours. Section 25 of the Crime and Disorder Act 1998 extended s 60 yet further by allowing police officers to require a person to remove items which the constable reasonably suspects are designed to prevent the person's identity being revealed. See also s 94 of the Anti-terrorism, Crime and Security Act 2001 which enables an officer of at least the rank of inspector to make an authorisation relating specifically to this power to require the removal of (and/or seize) identity-concealing items.

to the Secretary of State for confirmation of a particular use.'[109] Moreover, it appears that the Home Secretary has never refused confirmation of an authorisation or set an earlier expiry date than that established by the police.[110] In short, the capital's police have, with the connivance of the Home Secretary and the domestic courts, turned an apparently exceptional power into a routine one. It was only small comfort that when *Gillan* reached the House of Lords, Lord Bingham declared that the lack of any legal requirement of suspicion at the point of application of the power

cannot, realistically, be interpreted as a warrant to stop and search people who are obviously not terrorist suspects, which would be futile and time-wasting. It is to ensure that a constable is not deterred from stopping and searching a person whom he does suspect as a potential terrorist by the fear that he could not show reasonable grounds for his suspicion.[111]

This indicates that it may not be lawful for the police to stop-search everyone in a particular location under s 44, although quite which categories of person could ever be regarded as incapable of containing terrorist suspects remains unclear. In any event, the *Gillan* requirement laid down in the House of Lords (if such it is) that an officer must suspect someone of being a *potential* terrorist is self-evidently not a demanding one, and opens the door to the highly problematic practice of ethnic profiling.[112] There is little qualitative evidence available of how this power is used in practice by individual officers.[113] The account given to his police authority by a senior police commander in London gives some indication, however:

it's very, very flaky and I won't be at all convincing, I know that, but it would be around professional judgement, what they see around the circumstances: the behaviour of the individual and the circumstances all fall together, lead them to make a judgement. That is so flaky, you know, even I feel embarrassed saying that. But that is the truth as to what they do.[114]

The Metropolitan Police Authority responded: 'This arbitrary and discretionary practice can only leave the door wide open for officers to base their selection of whom to stop on prejudice, unconscious or otherwise.'[115]

---

[109]   *Gillan* [2004] EWCA Civ 1067 [51]. Confirmed by the House of Lords in *Gillan* [2006] UKHL 12.

[110]   *Gillan and Quinton v the United Kingdom* (App No 4158/05) Judgment 12 January 2010 [80].

[111]   *Gillan* [2006] UKHL 12 [35]. For critical commentary see [2006] Crim LR 752.

[112]   For critique, see Moeckli D, 'Stop and Search Under the Terrorism Act 2000: A Comment on *R (Gillan) v Commissioner of Police for the Metropolis*' (2007) 70(4) MLR 654. Code of Practice A itself acknowledges (para 2.5) that there 'may be circumstances...where it is appropriate for officers to take account of a person's ethnic origin in selecting persons to be stopped in response to a specific terrorist threat (for example, some international terrorist groups are associated with particular ethnic identities)'. Further guidance for the police can be found in the National Policing Improvement Agency, *Practice Advice on Stop and Search in Relation to Terrorism* (London: NPIA, 2008) which emphasises (somewhat bizarrely) that 'every person searched under section 44 should be told explicitly that they are not suspected of being a terrorist' (p 14) (available from <http://www.npia.police.uk/en/11700.htm> – accessed 5 January 2010).

[113]   But see Hallsworth (2006: 296–8) for some examples of patrol officers' thinking on who to target.

[114]   Quoted in Metropolitan Police Authority (2008: 51–2).

[115]   Ibid, p 52. Much the same could be said of the long-standing power of searching for the purpose of examination at ports of entry into England and Wales, which is now contained in the Terrorism Act 2000, Sch 7. This is yet another power where reasonable suspicion is not required.

Table 2.3 Arrests produced by stop-searches where no individualised reasonable suspicion is needed[116]

	s 60 of CJPO Act 1994 (violence and offensive weapons)			s 44 of Terrorism Act 2000 (terrorism-related articles)		
	Total searches	Arrests for offensive weapons	Unrelated arrests	Total searches	Arrests in connection with terrorism	Unrelated arrests
1997/98	7,970	103	332	n/a	n/a	n/a
1998/99	5,500	91	84	n/a	n/a	n/a
1999/00	6,840	36	195	n/a	n/a	n/a
2000/01	11,330	309	411	n/a	n/a	n/a
2001/02	18,900	203	485	10,200	20	169
2002/03	44,400	356	2,143	32,100	19	361
2003/04	40,400	299	1,248	33,800	19	472
2004/05	41,600	256	958	37,000	64	404
2005/06	36,300	192	1,522	50,047	105	458
2006/07	44,700	256	1,369	41,924	28	452
2007/08	53,250	311	1,750	124,687	73	1,198

While the availability of the powers reviewed in this sub-section depend, in the main, on a prior assessment by a senior officer that *serious* offences are in the offing, in practice they can be used in more mundane ways at the point of application. Thus whilst s 60 CJPO was 'sold' politically as a way of tackling serious violence, in reality it has become a useful police resource in responding to low-level disorder where no other power fits the bill. Thus one officer said he used s 60 for: 'Anyone causing trouble really – but people who aren't worth pulling [arresting] 'cause they haven't done enough' (Quinton et al, 2000: 50).[117] And it is telling that it was thought necessary to include in the official police guidance on the use of s 44 (NPIA, 2008: 17) that 'stop and search powers under the Terrorism Act 2000 must never be used as a public order tactic'.

Table 2.3 indicates the apparent[118] growth in the use of these stop-search powers and highlights the way they are useful to the police in uncovering evidence of offences quite unrelated to those at which the powers are ostensibly targeted.

---

[116] Source: Povey and Smith (2009), tables 2b and 2c.

[117] This is contrary to the Code of Practice (Note for Guidance 10) which states that the s 60 power should not be 'used to replace or circumvent the normal powers for dealing with routine crime problems'.

[118] We say 'apparent' because the relationship between recorded stop-searches and actual stop-searches under these provisions remains unclear. Undoubtedly there will be some under-recording, and the problem is likely to be extensive where the police engage in mass searches at busy times of the day (eg, at the entry to a railway station during rush hour). See further MPA (2008: 49).

Table 2.3 shows that the recorded use of the s 60 power grew by over 600% within a decade, with use of the s 44 power showing a similar trajectory, then trebling between 2007 and 2008. The importance of the lack of a reasonable suspicion criterion is demonstrated by very low – and deteriorating – arrest rates. In 2007/08, the arrest rate for s 60 stop-searches was 3.8% (compared with 7.2% in 1996), and for s 44 stop-searches was 1.0% (compared with 1.9% in 2001/02). In line with our discussion of stop-search powers requiring reasonable suspicion (see 2.2.1.1), we suggest that the deterioration in arrest rates is consistent with ever less discriminating use of the power reflecting the push towards pre-emption of crime and terrorism, and also consistent with greater recording of unproductive searches over time. The explosion of unproductive s 44 stop-searches became so great that even the police themselves acknowledge that they have 'the potential to have a negative impact, particularly on minority communities'.[119] The Metropolitan Police are therefore now planning to use s 44 powers only in specific locations and for specific reasons.[120] It is not known at the time of writing whether this signals a real change in policy, as similar statements by Yates' predecessor in 2006 – see 2.5.1 – were not acted on. But a shift of policy is now more likely following the UK government's defeat in the *Gillan* litigation before the European Court of Human Rights (Fourth Chamber) in January 2010. In brief, the Court decided that s 44 stop-searches constituted interferences with the right to respect for private life under Art 8. Further, it ruled that such an interference was not justifiable because the powers of authorisation and confirmation, as well as the powers of stop-search themselves, were 'neither sufficiently circumscribed nor subject to adequate legal safeguards against abuse'.[121] This is a powerful due process judgment and one that may well be challenged by the government before the Court's grand chamber. If the decision in *Gillan* is, or has to be, accepted, then changes in domestic law and policy are highly likely to follow; changes in practice perhaps less so.

2.2.2.3 Allied powers of stop and search

Section 163 of the Road Traffic Act 1988 provides police officers with a general power to stop vehicles, and related powers to require drivers to produce certain documentation, such as a driving licence (on which the driver's name, address and date of birth appears), certificate of insurance and MOT certificate. If drivers do not have these documents with them, then they can be required to produce them within seven days at a police station (or face prosecution for failing to do so). These 'stop and produce' powers can therefore be useful to the police both for gaining information about those using public space that attract their attention, and to cause inconvenience to those on whom they wish to impose their authority. There is no requirement that any specific offence is suspected, still less reasonably suspected. The only restriction that has been read in by the courts is that the stop would be unlawful if made

---

[119] John Yates, Head of Counter-Terrorism at the Metropolitan Police, writing in a consultation document, reported by *The Guardian*, 7 May 2009.   [120] Yates, ibid.

[121] *Gillan and Quinton v the United Kingdom* (App No 4158/05) Judgment 12 January 2010 [87].

capriciously, oppressively or exhibited some other form of malpractice. Thus it was held to be a lawful use of the power to stop cars at random with a view to checking whether there was evidence (eg smell of alcohol) that would justify a formal breath test.[122] If the police stop a car under this section, they do not have the right per se to search for stolen goods, drugs or prohibited articles. However, if in the course of the stop under s 163 police suspicion relating to, for instance, theft is aroused, then the police will be able to continue the stop and search for that second purpose. No official statistics are produced on the use of s 163 or its relationship to stop-search and arrests, and citizens stopped under this power do not have the right to a record of the encounter.

This is a very broad power and helps us understand the British Crime Survey finding (see 2.1) that over three times as many adults experience a non-consensual stop when driving a vehicle (where reasonable suspicion is not required) as experience one when on foot (where it usually is). The power can be used proactively as a means of generating the level of suspicion required to carry out a more extensive search, and the case of Smith[123] suggests that the courts are happy to give the police wide latitude in this respect. A police officer on motorised patrol decided to follow a hatchback with three occupants in it. The officer noticed that the rear occupant 'was fidgeting around and moving his left arm behind his back'. He decided to stop the car because (the court assumed) he suspected that this person might be in possession of drugs. On opening the driver's door the officer noticed Rizla cigarette papers on the dashboard and a smell of cannabis. He decided to search the rear occupant for drugs under s 23 of the Misuse of Drugs Act 1971. The rear occupant resisted and was charged with obstructing an officer in the execution of his duty. The question therefore arose of whether the officer had been acting in the execution of his duty when stopping the car. The defence argument was that the officer had stopped this car, which contained three black men, 'on spec' (ie, speculatively) and that this was a capricious exercise of the s 163 power. The court decided that the police officer's initial suspicion that the rear occupant was in possession of drugs (as evidenced by his 'fidgeting around and moving his left arm behind his back') was sufficient to defeat that argument. So, if you feel tempted to scratch your back when next in a car, check first that you are not being watched by the police. But do not become statue-like either, as that might be construed as just as suspicious; as might checking to see if you are being watched by the police before deciding on your posture.

Section 4 of PACE (as amended) enhances the s 163 power to stop vehicles in that it enables a senior officer to authorise a road check (the mass stopping of either all vehicles, or all vehicles that match a particular criterion) where reasonable grounds exist to believe that someone who is unlawfully at large, or who has committed (or who intends to commit) an indictable offence (or is a witness to such an offence) would

---

[122] *Chief Constable of Gwent v Dash* [1986] RTR 41.
[123] *R. (on the application of Smith) v DPP* (QBD (Admin Ct)) [2002] EWHC 113.

be in the locality where the checks are to take place. The number of road checks has reduced in recent years, no doubt because the police now feel that they have more effective ways of stopping vehicles, as by using s 44 of the Terrorism Act 2000. In 2007/08 there were 27 road checks, resulting in the stopping of 7,200 vehicles and just five arrests (an arrest rate of 0.07%).[124] Even in previous years, when there were more arrests (but still less than 1% of all stops), the arrests connected with the reason for the road check were smaller in number than unrelated arrests that follow the use of this power.

2.2.2.4 Does the law really require individualised suspicion of a specific offence?

The following two lists divide the main stop and search powers into those which do (list A), and those which do not (list B), require individualised reasonable suspicion at the time of the stop, indicating the type of criminal activity they are aimed at:

A – *powers requiring reasonable suspicion*
> s 1 PACE 1984 (prohibited fireworks, 'stolen' goods; articles for use in offences of dishonesty; offensive weapons; bladed objects without lawful excuse; items for use in criminal damage)
> s 23 Misuse of Drugs Act 1971 (drugs)
> s 41 and s 43 Terrorism Act 2000 (terrorist offences)[125]

B – *powers not requiring reasonable suspicion*
> s 163 Road Traffic Act 1988 (stop and produce driving documents)
> s 4 PACE (road checks in relation to indictable offences)
> s 60 CJPO 1994 (stop-search for offensive weapons/dangerous implements)
> ss 44–47 Terrorism Act 2000 (stop-search for articles connected with terrorism)
> Sch 7 Terrorism Act 2000 (terrorist activities: examinations at ports and airports)

List B powers are clearly enabling rules par excellence, lacking most of the due process elements one might expect to find when police powers are extended by statute. Although these powers are directed at specific activities (such as the threat of violence), it is typical for the majority of any resulting arrests to be made for reasons unconnected with the ostensible reasons for the stop and search, as table 2.3 shows in relation to both s 60 CJPO and s 44 Terrorism Act.

We need to reflect now on the extent to which stop and search powers really are directed at specific offences. Despite the great increases in police stop-search powers since PACE was enacted, it remains true that the police have no general powers to stop-search simply because someone is thought to be in some general sense 'suspicious'. Either the individual has to be suspected of something in particular (eg PACE, s 1) or something in particular has to be suspected in that vicinity (eg PACE, s 4; CJPO, s 60; Terrorism Act 2000 s 44), or someone has to belong to a category which is deemed

---

[124] Povey and Smith (2009) table 2d.
[125] See Walker C, *Blackstone's Guide to the Anti-Terrorism Legislation* (Oxford: OUP, 2002a) pp 118–49.

'suspicious' (eg Terrorism Act examinations). However, it will often not be possible to know why someone appears 'suspicious'. Only a conversation and/or search will reveal the knife, drugs, stolen credit card, soft-core pornography, medical records, love letters, anarchist literature, banker's bonus, or contraceptives about which the individual may be embarrassed. As the figures in table 2.3 show in relation to two powers, not only are such suspicions usually unfounded but they are indeed often unrelated to any subsequent arrest. Is the requirement that suspicion relate to a particular offence simply a presentational rule? In one of McConville et al's cases (1991: 28), a youth ran away when he saw the police, so he was chased and searched. A Krugerrand (gold coin) was found, so he was arrested. It turned out that he had this lawfully, but that hardly matters. The police often stop, search and arrest people who run away when they see police officers. This is, by any standards, suspicious behaviour. But of what can one reasonably suspect such people? In this particular case, was it really reasonable suspicion of theft? As one would expect from the national statistics displayed in table 2.3, the arrests which resulted from stops in this study were often unrelated to the reasons for the stops.

The way police-public encounters begin in relation to one issue and end in completely unrelated ways has been observed by others, before and after PACE.[126] Smith, however, suggests not just that unsuspected offences come to light following legitimate stops, but also that suspicion of an offence to which PACE, s 1 applies is sometimes used as a pretext when other offences are suspected:

observations at police stations suggest that police may often find illegal immigrants by carrying out stops and searches of black people in vehicles or on foot. There is no power to detain or search a person in the street on suspicion of immigration offences, but some other justification can be found for the original stop.[127]

However, in some areas and in some contexts, there are simply numerous mundane crimes (such as possession of cannabis) waiting to be discovered. The fact that there is no specific reason to stop particular individuals or cars in these contexts does not alter the fact that statistically the officer is more likely to notch up a successful 'collar' by stopping them than by stopping people randomly, or by stopping respectable-looking people in affluent suburbs. Most stops are in inner-city areas, largely because they are inner-city areas. These areas are not necessarily more criminogenic than others, but the crimes which predominate in them (drugs, car theft, burglary and street violence) are more amenable than most to discovery by stop and search. Not surprisingly, the attempt of legislators in the early 1980s through PACE, s 1 to require specific suspicion of specific offences as a condition of using stop and search powers is proving unsuccessful.

---

[126] See eg Southgate P, *Police-Public Encounters* (Home Office Research Study 90) (London: Home Office, 1986) p 8; Fitzgerald (1999: ch 5): '...many of the drugs arrests seemed to have come about largely by chance...the grounds for the original stop were not always apparent'.

[127] Smith D, 'Origins of Black Hostility to the Police' (1991) 2 Policing and Society 6.

2.2.3 Stop-search powers, consent and the rise of 'stop and account'

When we talk about 'the power' to stop-search, we are actually referring to a bundle of powers. For example, PACE, s 1(2)(b) states that a police officer 'may detain a person or vehicle for the purpose of…a search', and s 1(6) provides a power to seize certain property discovered in the course of this search. In addition, the police have an implicit power to question.[128] However, the power of an officer to question is slightly different from the other powers contained in s 1: suspects must submit to search and detention (and indeed 'reasonable force' may be used if the suspect objects),[129] but they need not answer questions. Any answers they do give may be sufficient to dispel the officer's reasonable suspicion, in which case the power to search is lost (Code A, para 10.2). Other stop-search powers discussed earlier, in the CJPO, Terrorism Act 2000 and elsewhere in PACE, also contain these powers to detain, question and seize as well as to stop and to search.

Early versions of the Code of Practice allowed police officers to search persons with their consent. Such consensual searches did not require the exercise of formal powers, and, as a corollary, none of the restrictions outlined earlier – such as suspicion of specific offences – applied. Nor did the other controls to be discussed in 2.4 below. Research conducted soon after PACE was enacted found most stops to be 'consensual' in the sense that 'a lot of people are not quite certain that they have the right to say no and then we sort of bamboozle them into allowing us to search'.[130] After various attempts to restrain the police from evading the PACE safeguards through the use of consensual searches were found to have failed, all versions of Code of Practice A from 2003 onwards have prohibited them completely:

An officer must not search a person, even with his or her consent, where no power to search is applicable. Even where a person is prepared to submit to a search voluntarily, the person must not be searched unless the necessary legal power exists, and the search must be in accordance with the relevant power and the provisions of this code (para 1.5).[131]

This provision, important as it is, has not resolved all of the problems inherent in the relationship between police power and public consent. First, it is sometimes simply ignored, as in one of the five forces examined in a recent study (Home Office 2005a: 39). Second, the Code of Practice also makes clear, in relation to searches requiring reasonable suspicion, that while there is no power to *stop or detain* a person against their will in order to find grounds for a search (para 2.11),[132] there is nothing to prevent an officer

---

[128] *Daniel v Morrison* (1979) 70 Cr App Rep 142.   [129] Code A, para 3.2.

[130] Police officer, quoted in Dixon et al, 'Consent and the Legal Regulation of Policing' (1990b) 17 JLS 345 at p 348.

[131] But note that (a) this para specifically exempts sports grounds and similar venues, where searches are often carried out routinely; (b) community support officers (quasi-police) can carry out certain searches *only* with the consent of suspects: Annex C to Code of Practice A.

[132] But see the discussion in 2.2 above on the Road Traffic Act power to stop vehicles regardless of any individualised suspicion (which falls outside the provisions of Code A).

without such grounds simply speaking to, or questioning, someone 'in the ordinary course' of their duties, and this is said to be so even if the person is unwilling to reply (Note 1). In theory this means an officer could try to break down a person's unwillingness to reply by following them down the street while putting an unanswered question repeatedly. In practice, the police often *ask people to stop* and to answer questions in order to gather information on incidents and to assess whether those present should be classified as suspects and searched or arrested accordingly. These kinds of stops became controversial as a result of the Macpherson Report's recommendation that all stops, including 'voluntary' ones, should be recorded.[133] While this recommendation was accepted, subject to its feasibility being assessed, the government restricted its ambit to encounters falling short of a search where someone is asked to account for themselves. Such encounters might arise as part of a statutory stop or stop-search (an involuntary stop) or in situations where the police had no statutory power to stop (a voluntary stop). A new set of regulatory provisions was duly inserted into Code A of PACE under the heading: 'Recording of encounters not governed by Statutory Powers'. The key provision reads:

When an officer requests a person in a public place to account for themselves, i.e. their actions, behaviour, presence in an area or possession of anything, a record of the encounter … must be completed at the time (para 4.12).

However, following yet another change to the Code of Practice (effective from 1 January 2009) only the officer's identifying details and the ethnic group of the detainee need be recorded (para 4.17). These types of stops have, unsurprisingly, become known as 'stop and account'. One might think that, as far as voluntary stop and accounts are concerned, a member of the public spoken to in this way could simply walk away, given that, by definition, the officer has no power to detain them. Unfortunately the law fails to address this crucial issue. Officers are told by the Code (para 4.18) that there 'is no power to require the person questioned to provide personal details' (such as ethnic background), but is silent on whether persons questioned have to account for themselves. The use of the word 'request' in para 4.12 (quoted above), suggests that they do not. But the Code of Practice neither requires officers to make this clear at the start of the encounter, nor stipulates whether or not a refusal to answer questions or an attempt to walk away could give grounds for the statutory power of stop-search (or even arrest) to be invoked.[134] Much of the surrounding post-Macpherson literature on stop and account assumes, without

---

[133] Prior to this, only stops that resulted in searches (ie 'stop-searches') had to be recorded. See further 2.4.1.

[134] If a police officer *detains* somebody without reasonable suspicion then any answers (or refusals to answer) the officer's subsequent questions cannot *retrospectively* provide the reasonable grounds for suspicion necessary to justify the initial detention (Code A, para 2.9). But this provision has no application to the case of a *consensual* stop and account. These supposedly consensual encounters thus provide the police with an opportunity to generate reasonable suspicion sufficient to justify a non-consensual stop and search. Code A (para 2.11) recognises this very point, but is silent on whether 'non-answers' can found reasonable suspicion.

argument or analysis, that the police can 'require', or even 'demand' an account.[135] Thus the Equality and Human Rights Commission (a body which really should know better) declared in 2009 that:

Figures were published for the first time this year revealing the police used their powers to stop members of the public in the street and demand they account for themselves on nearly two million occasions in 2006/7.[136]

Taken in combination with the law's silence on the ramifications of failing to give an account, such loose talk may be fuelling a perception that the police have acquired a new 'stop and account' power. What is happening here is, to some extent, merely a legitimation of long-standing police practice. As one Superintendent involved in piloting the Macpherson recommendation told Shiner (2006: 28):

All this is doing is introducing a form into the equation. Now what officers were doing before in this division, if I stop you and ask you to account for your actions, behaviour or possession, I've asked your name and address, I'm going to check you out on the radio...*I'm not going to let you walk away without knowing who you are.* So I'll take your details, I'll take your personal details, and I'll probably take a description of what you are wearing...[and write it down in my notebook]. Now what I always say to people is 'all this is just your medium for recording those details, that's all that's changed...you just write it down on a different piece of paper.' [emphasis added]

As Dixon et al (1990b) point out, when an officer asks someone on the street whether they would mind answering questions, this is usually perceived (correctly) not to be a genuine request, admitting either 'yes' or 'no' as an answer, but a polite way of insisting. But the drift towards thinking of 'stop and account' as a *power*, combined with the new formal record-keeping requirement (which helps turn these encounters into systematic intelligence-gathering opportunities),[137] may also be having an enabling effect. Consistent with that hypothesis, the number of stop and accounts rose from 1.4 million in 2005/06 (the first year in which records of these encounters were kept) to 2.35 million in 2007/08,[138] although this rise may be as much to do with better recording practices. What proportion of these stops were 'voluntary' as opposed to involuntary is not known. In practice this distinction is unlikely to be prominent in officers' thinking, and it will certainly remain wholly obscure to the people asked to provide accounts. Nor can we be sure that officers are keeping records consistently across the different types of stop and account. Thus we cannot know what proportion of stop and

---

[135] See, for example, Lister et al (2008: 44) who write of 'low-level uses of police powers such as stop and account', and Ministry of Justice, *Statistics on Race and the Criminal Justice System 2006/7* (London: MoJ, 2008d) which uses the term 'required' to account and repeatedly refers to 'stop and account' as a police 'power' (eg p 26).   [136] Equality and Human Rights Commission (2009: 22).

[137] As one officer told Shiner (2006: 24), 'stop and account in its basic form helps us to gain intelligence that we might not previously have got.' See further 2.5.1 on the intelligence-gathering role of stop-search practices.   [138] Ministry of Justice (2009b) table 4.9.

accounts are taking place on a 'voluntary' basis or accurately measure the enabling effects of these recent developments.[139]

There are other difficulties with consensual encounters. What, for instance, of suspects who do not simply refuse to answer questions, but who refuse rudely and aggressively (or start scratching their backs)? Is this 'behaviour of the person' creating reasonable suspicion?[140] And what of people who seek to avoid being spoken to by the police in the first place? Quinton et al (2000: 27) found that a quarter of the 90 police officers they interviewed regarded such elusive behaviour as a prompt for a stop. For example: 'You see someone and you just know he's not right. It's the way people react to you – won't look you in the eye; go in different directions; [they] give indication [they] don't want to speak or be seen.'[141] Moreover, breaking stop and search down into discrete actions takes no account of the social processes involved. In an encounter which begins with a consensual and innocuous conversation, suspicion may develop and the suspect may get impatient. The point in the 'flow of the encounter'[142] at which consent is no longer present and formal powers are, or should be, invoked cannot be identified with precision. Indeed, from the suspect's perspective, it may remain unclear that a non-consensual search has in fact taken place. This is because: 'The cooperation of the person to be searched must be sought in every case, even if the person initially objects to the search' (Code A, para 3.2). While it is understandable and desirable that the law should seek to restrain the use of forcible searches in this way, where suspects have cooperated in a search they are likely to understand that legal power has been exercised over them only if the police tell them (as they are supposed to do – see 2.4) that this is so.

Just to complicate matters still further, there are situations when members of the public *are* legally obliged to give limited information to police officers when questioned. For example, under s 50 of the Police Reform Act 2002 a constable in uniform who reasonably believes that someone has been, or is, acting anti-socially (within the meaning of s 1 of the Crime and Disorder Act 1998) can require that person to provide their name and address, and a failure to do so constitutes an offence.[143] The breadth of 'anti-social behaviour' (conduct likely to cause harassment, alarm or distress) means that it is now relatively easy for the police to insist that 'troublesome' people they 'consensually encounter' provide them with at least

---

[139] At the time of writing, no British Crime Survey figures on police stops for the same period were available, which means we cannot be sure whether 'stop and account' is having an enabling effect.

[140] See the arrest case of *Ricketts v Cox* (1981) 74 Cr App Rep 298, discussed in ch 3, below.

[141] See also Fitzgerald (1999: ch 4) who found that the grounds given for searches in police records included references to suspects being 'uncooperative', 'evasive to police questioning' and 'very anti-police'.

[142] See Shiner (2006: 19).

[143] A PCSO has the same power to demand a name and address, and can also so demand in the case of a wide range of other matters including fixed penalty offences, offences which appear to have caused injury alarm or distress to another person or loss of or damage to another person's property, certain licensing offences, and certain motoring matters. See Police Reform Act 2002, Sch 4, part 1 and SI 2007/3201.

some information. A simple refusal to answer any questions is often no longer a lawful option, and this provides the police with a legal wedge to prise open the door to more prolonged conversation. 'The potential for abuse by officers repeatedly harassing groups of youths is obvious'.[144] Research is now documenting the realisation of this potential, as with Goldsmith's account of one area of social housing in the south of England:

> Every young person who participated in the interviews reported being fairly regularly stopped and searched by the police. Routine stops were often made to take names and check that young people were not in possession of alcohol. Police suspicion was aroused by a variety of innocuous behaviours such as running down the street, as two 13-year-old girls found when they were stopped, running home from a youth work session. When asked about this incident at a forum meeting the local District Commander stated that 'running was a legitimate reason to stop a young person on this estate'.[145]

The liberal notion that we should be free to go about our business without any requirement to account for ourselves or provide personal details unless we engage in objectively suspicious or harmful behaviour is evidently under increasing threat. As noted above, it remains to be seen whether the UK's defeat in *Gillan* before the European Court of Rights (Fourth Section) in January 2010[146] will lead (a) to substantial amendments to domestic law, such as the introduction of a reasonable suspicion requirement for all stop-searches and stop-and-accounts and (b) substantial changes to actual police practice.

2.2.4 Citizens' powers to stop-search

A citizen's arrest is a familiar notion in England and Wales (see further 3.3.5) but a citizen's stop-search much less so. Most of us have, however, been stop-searched by someone other than a police officer at some point in our lives, most obviously when passing through security checks within an airport. Security personnel carry out routine stop-searches at the entrance to many courts, sporting events and various venues within the night-time economy. And shoppers (some honest, some not) who set off security alarms when leaving stores are likely to find themselves stop-searched by store detectives. All these stop-searches take place on the basis of *contract* or implied *consent*.

As part of the recent trend towards the pluralisation of policing, with many civilian bodies and individuals now seen as part and parcel of the crime control apparatus and 'responsibilised'[147] accordingly, *statutory* stop-search powers have been given to some categories of private citizen and members of the 'extended police

---

[144] Ormerod and Roberts (2003: 162).   [145] Goldsmith (2008: 234).
[146] *Gillan and Quinton v the United Kingdom* (App No 4158/05) Judgment 12 January 2010.
[147] Garland D, *The Culture of Control* (Oxford: OUP, 2001) ch 5.

family'. Most notably, PCSOs now have the following standard stop and search powers:[148]

- to carry out an authorised road check under s 4 of PACE;

- to stop and search pedestrians and vehicles under s 44 of the Terrorism Act 2000 when in the company, and under the supervision, of a constable;

- following a refusal to surrender alcohol or tobacco when lawfully required to do so, to search for alcohol or containers for alcohol (possessed by children,[149] or by anyone in designated areas[150]), or tobacco (in the case of children)[151] and to seize and dispose of the same.[152]

PCSOs do not (yet) have the standard s 1 PACE power to stop-search with reasonable suspicion, or the power to stop any vehicle (other than as part of a s 4 road check), or the s 60 CJPO power to search for weapons. While there may be good arguments for not providing PCSOs with all the search powers of police officers, the inconsistency in treatment does make it harder for people to know their rights when required to submit to a search by someone who, for most intents and purposes, looks and acts like a police officer.

Most notable (and controversial) of other civilian stop-search powers are those provided by ss 45–46 of the Violent Crime Reduction Act 2006. Under s 45, any member of staff of a school who reasonably suspects a pupil on those premises of having a blade or offensive weapon with them or in their possessions (eg in a school locker) may search them and their possessions (but only in their presence) if authorised to do so by the head teacher. *Anything* found during the search which is reasonably suspected to be evidence of an offence (eg cannabis) may be seized and must then be handed over to the police. Many school teachers were unhappy at having this crime control function foisted on to them and the Act accordingly provides that they (unlike school security personnel) may not be required by the head teacher to carry out such searches. Section 46 provides like powers for the further education sector.

2.3 Is stop and search racially discriminatory?

Now that we have introduced a wide range of stop and search powers we need to address a question that has provoked deep concern and much apparently conflicting evidence over the last decade: is the practice of stop and search characterised by racial

---

[148] PCSO powers were first provided for by the Police Reform Act 2002 (Sch 4), and then extended by Sch 8 of the Serious Organised Crime and Police Act 2005. Many of them were available only if the local Chief Constable so designated, but s 7 of the Police and Justice Act 2006 enabled the introduction of SI 2007/3202 which established a set of standard powers and duties applicable to all PCSOs.

[149] See Confiscation of Alcohol (Young Persons) Act 1997.

[150] See s 12 of the Criminal Justice and Police Act 2001, allowing for the designation of what might be termed alcohol exclusion zones.   [151] See s 7 of Children and Young Persons Act 1933.

[152] If they find drugs during such a search they may seize and dispose of these too.

Table 2.4 Proportion (%) of ethnic groups stopped and searched in England and Wales 2006/07[153]

	White	Black	Asian	Other	Unknown	Total[154]
General population[155]	91.3	2.8	4.7	1.2	0.0	100
Reasonable suspicion stop-searches[156]	72.3	15.9	8.1	1.5	2.1	100
s 60 CJPO stop-searches	57.1	29.6	10.1	1.4	1.7	100
s 44 Terrorism Act	69.8	9.7	14.8	4.4	1.3	100
Stop and account	85.7	6.3	4.9	1.1	1.9	100

discrimination? An obvious starting point for analysis is whether people of different ethnic backgrounds are stopped in proportion to their numbers in general population. In table 2.4 the relevant figures are presented for the stop and search powers where record-keeping on the part of the police is required.

While it is evident from table 2.4 that more white people are subjected to stop and search than BME people, as one would expect given that over 9 out of 10 people in England and Wales are white, we can also see that in the case of every stop and search power, black and Asian people are greatly *over-represented* in those searched. According to the government, a black person is just over seven times (and an Asian person 2.2 times) more likely to experience a reasonable suspicion stop-search than a white person, and similar ratios have been found for many years.[157] The most frequent type of 'search' is actually stop and account, for which figures were published for the first time in 2008. Here black people were nearly two and a half times more likely to be asked to account for themselves than white people.[158] As we might have expected from our earlier discussion, Asian people seem to be particularly singled out in the context of s 44 Terrorism Act stop-searches, and this was even more true in 2007/08 (when 18% of these searches were of Asians who constitute less than 5% of the population) whereas black people are vastly over-represented in the s 60 CJPO figures.[159]

These huge disparities could be a product of direct discrimination, indirect discrimination, or legitimate factors (or a combination of all three). Disproportion, even on this huge scale, does not necessarily mean discrimination, but obviously it raises

[153] Source: Ministry of Justice (2008d) ch 4.

[154] Individual figures in row may not sum to 100 due to rounding.

[155] 2001 census figures. It should be borne in mind that the census figures tell us what proportion of people are, for example, black, whereas police records of stop-searches tell us what proportion of stop-searches are of black people. As people are often targeted for repeated stop-searches, it is unsafe to infer from this table that, for example, 15.9% of black people were subjected to a reasonable suspicion stop-search in 2006/07.

[156] This row is mainly comprised of stop-searches under s 1 PACE and s 23 of the Misuse of Drugs Act.

[157] Ministry of Justice (2008d: 23–4) (available from <http://www.homeoffice.gov.uk/rds>, where earlier and subsequent reports in the same series may be consulted).   [158] Ministry of Justice (2008d: 26).

[159] Ministry of Justice, *Statistics on Race and the Criminal Justice System 2007/08* (2009b) ch 4.

a case to be answered. We do not attempt a definite answer here for it is a complex issue that goes far beyond stop-search. There is a huge amount of data and discussion that cannot be summarised in a few pages, and yet there are still gaps in the evidence. On this book's 'online resource centre' we do attempt to reach more firm conclusions. We also recommend that you read the report of the Equality and Human Rights Commission, the review of the evidence by Bowling and Phillips, and (in our opinion) a more contentious discussion by Stenson and Waddington.[160]

These are the main issues that need to be taken into account:

- It may be that black and Asian people simply behave more suspiciously than other people. However, we have seen that 'suspiciousness' is not an objective criterion, and much of the behaviour that looks suspicious to patrol officers (such as evasiveness) is itself a product of long-standing poor relations between ethnic minorities and the police.

- It may be that black and Asian people are more visible (or 'available') in areas and during time periods in which the police focus stop-search activity. This is likely to be true to some extent, as black and Asian people tend to be less affluent than white people, so they spend more time on the streets and in public places. But treating people who 'hang around' in public, for example, as suspicious, and going for these 'easy options' ('low hanging fruit' as the former Chair of the Youth Justice Board once put it) is again a matter of police choice based on unproven assumptions. Further, there is some evidence that in 'entrepreneurial spaces' (such as shopping malls), where risk-management techniques are used a lot, black males become targets for stop-search.[161]

- A clutch of northern forces, and forces in rural Wales, maintain low disproportionality rates while others, particularly in the south, maintain high rates. Also neighbouring forces often have very different rates. This suggests that the disproportionality figures are a product of police policy and practice rather than a simple reflection of suspicious behaviour.

- Racial discrimination can mean two different things. First, using powers unlawfully against black and Asian people more than against whites. Second, using powers lawfully against black and Asian people in circumstances where they are used less against whites. We simply have no robust evidence that disentangles these points. One suggestive study, but dating back to 1990, divided the reasons for the stops the researchers observed into 'tangible' and

---

[160] Equality and Human Rights Commission, *Police and Racism: What has been Achieved 10 Years after the Stephen Lawrence Inquiry Report?* (2009) esp pp 24–5; Bowling B and Phillips C, 'Disproportionate and Discriminatory: Reviewing the Evidence on Police Stop and Search' (2007) 70(6) MLR 936; Stenson K and Waddington P, 'Macpherson, Police Stops and Institutionalised Racism' in Rowe (2007). Also see the small-scale study: Sharp D and Atherton S, 'To Serve and Protect? The Experiences of Policing in the Community of Young People from Black and Other Ethnic Minority Groups' (2007) 47(5) BJ Crim 746.

[161] Hallsworth (2006: 301–2).

'intangible' reasons, and found that black people were more frequently stopped for 'intangible' reasons than were white people.[162]

• Disproportionality is at its worst in relation to stops under s 60 of CJPO (black people) and s 44 of the Terrorism Act (Asian people). These are the most important powers where no reasonable suspicion is required. Thus, almost by definition, BMEs are stopped more often, proportionately, where there is little or no objective evidence – and the very low arrest rates for stops under these powers illustrate this.

• Black and Asian people are, when stopped, far more frequently searched and arrested than are white people. Whether this means that their disproportionately bad treatment is compounded by search and arrest behaviour, or that the stops have more substance to them, is open to debate. But black and Asian people also report more dissatisfaction with police behaviour. This may be 'simply' due to being stopped more often, but may also be due to the way the police treat them, and their perception (whether justified or not) of being treated disproportionately badly. The question of the way in which police exercise these powers will be examined later.

2.4 Constraints and controls on the exercise of discretion

The Philips Commission was aware that the criterion of reasonable suspicion could become devalued in practice, and that random stops should be guarded against. Its solution was to introduce a battery of secondary controls:

We consider that the notification of the reason for the search to the person who has been stopped, the recording of searches by officers, and the monitoring of the records by supervising officers would be the most effective and practical ways of reducing the risk.[163]

2.4.1 Giving and recording reasons for stop-searches

A police officer must take reasonable steps to provide certain information to suspects *before* searching them, including the officer's name and police station, the object of the proposed search and the grounds for proposing to make it.[164] Except where it is

---

[162] Norris et al, 'Black and Blue: An Analysis of the Influence of Race on Being Stopped by the Police' (1992) 43 BJ Sociology 207.

[163] Royal Commission on Criminal Procedure, *Report* (Cmnd 8092) (London: HMSO, 1981) para 3.25.

[164] PACE, s 2. This, and s 3 discussed below, applies to searches under all legislation, not just PACE (see s 2(1)). They therefore apply to the powers discussed in 2.2 above. The requirement to give this information

impracticable, the officer must also make a written record of the search and provide the suspect with either a copy or an electronic receipt stating how the full record can be accessed.[165]

Section 3(6) of PACE provides that the record must state:

(1) the object of the search (ie stolen goods or prohibited articles);

(2) the grounds for making it (ie what has given rise to the suspicion);

(3) the time and date when it was made;

(4) the place where it was made;

(5) whether anything (and if so what) was found;

(6) whether any (and if so what) injury to a person or damage to property appears to the officer to have resulted from the search;

(7) the identity of the officer making the search.

One purpose of providing information before search, committing it to writing afterwards and providing suspects with access to those records is to enable suspects to hold police officers to account if they misuse their powers. This is intended to provide a remedy for those who are wrongly stopped, and the fear of complaints should produce more compliance in the first place. There are a number of reasons to question the realism of this.

First, research has consistently shown a significant level of non-compliance with the obligation to give reasons prior to search. For example, a survey of people aged between 12 and 30 living in households found that no reasons were given by the police in just under half of searches following vehicle stops and one-third of searches following a pedestrian stop (Flood-Page et al, 2000: 52). Some social groups are treated better than others in this respect. Thus the 2000 British Crime Survey (of adults living in households) found that 92% of those subjected to a vehicle-stop were given reasons, as were 80% of those stopped on foot (Clancy et al, 2001: 59–61). Both research studies took place at a time when 'consensual' searches, outside the scope of the PACE safeguards, were commonplace. Even so, one might have thought that it would be in the interests of the police to give reasons for a stop-search (whether 'consensual' or not) in order to maximise the prospect of obtaining the cooperation of the suspect. The non-provision of reasons makes sense in certain situations, however, including those where the suspects are deferential and cooperative anyway, or where the police are willing or even keen to stop-search without first obtaining cooperation (as where they wish to impose discipline or avoid the loss of authority involved in admitting that they are accountable to 'police property'). As one experienced constable put it: '. . . you can't lose face

---

was held to be mandatory in *R v Christopher Bristol* [2007] EWCA Crim 3214. See also *B v DPP* [2008] EWHC 1655 (Admin).

[165] Sections 2(3)(d) and 3; PACE Code of Practice A, paras 4.2, 4.2A and 4.10A.

in dealing with a member of the public, especially in a confrontational situation'.[166] Our analysis here is consistent with the higher rates of reason-giving found for stops of adults as compared with youths and young adults, and also consistent with some of the qualitative examples provided in this chapter (see 2.5.2 below) of the particularly aggressive stop-searches experienced by subordinated groups in society, such as the young, the homeless and ethnic minorities.

Secondly, there is significant under-recording of searches, although, as we demonstrated in table 2.2, the extent of under-recording has reduced over time. Why do the police fail to make records for some searches? Lustgarten (2003: 617) has suggested that imposing a requirement on the police that involves paperwork is intended in part to create a disincentive to 'unnecessary and oppressive use of powers'. But the disincentive may operate more in relation to record-keeping than in the use of powers. One officer, commenting on under-recording, explained simply: 'Some informal searches not included, checking "scallywags" – what's in their pockets.'[167] Indeed, it is perhaps exactly for oppressive or unnecessary searches that we should expect under-recording to occur since it may then simply be the suspect's word against the officer's word as to whether a search took place at all. It is in such searches too (carried out primarily against 'police property') that the police may feel they have little to fear from not recording (and not giving reasons to suspects) since they know that the oppressed rarely seek to hold officers accountable for their actions and even more rarely succeed (see 2.4.3). Where accountability becomes a live issue, as where the search leads to an arrest, or an articulate and rights-conscious suspect is encountered, a record is much more likely to be made. Many officers told Dixon et al (1990b) that they made a record only if they feared that there would be some sort of 'comeback'. If, for example, a middle class person who was aware of the law happened to be stopped 'you would probably revert to the standard opening speech procedure and complete a form' (Dixon et al, 1990b: 349). What emerges from the research is that recording and non-recording decisions are strongly influenced by whether or not officers believe that record-keeping will further *police* goals.[168] Such beliefs can be influenced by external factors of course. Thus the rise of managerialism and target-driven policing has led to some supervising officers encouraging recording on the basis that it provides good evidence of the *amount* of work the police do,[169] while the modern emphasis on intelligence-led policing and electronic databases has turned the stop and search record into an increasingly valued information-gathering tool, notwithstanding that the use of intelligence gathered in this way remains haphazard.[170] Thus the trend towards recording an ever greater proportion of stop-search activity is consistent with growing police confidence in the proactive use of the power and an increasing sense amongst officers both that there is nothing to fear from recording searches and that a useful contribution may be made to intelligence gathering (and demonstrating police activity) by doing so.

---

[166] Quoted by Fitzgerald (1999: ch4).   [167] Quoted by Bland et al (2000: 36).
[168] See further Bland et al (2000: 29–37) and 2.5.1 and 2.5.2 below.   [169] Home Office (2004d: 19).
[170] See, for example, Home Office (2004d: 8 & 19); Shiner (2006: 50–3).

Thirdly, the government has sought to 'reduce the bureaucracy' associated with stop-search by removing the long-standing requirement that the person searched be given a copy of the search record there and then. Thus, following a limited pilot, the 2009 version of Code of Practice A was amended so that the police now need only give a 'receipt' so long as this 'is produced by electronic means and states how the full record can be accessed' (para 4.2A). Where police officers are using the necessary electronic devices, those searched must now take the initiative by requesting a copy of the full record from their local police station, or by accessing it via the Internet. The Equality and Human Rights Commission (2008: 23) has expressed 'grave disquiet' at this retrograde shift:

It seems likely that many of those (predominantly young, male, black and working class) who receive a receipt will be daunted by the prospect of presenting themselves at a police station with their receipt and requesting the full record. They may feel that this will bring them to further police attention, and mark them out as potentially a 'troublemaker'. Also not everyone has access or the skills to use a website to get an electronic version of the report.

The fourth reason to question the usefulness of records as a safeguard for suspects is that historically they only applied to searches. The great majority of stops did not go this far, and therefore remained unrecorded. As we have seen (2.2.3), the Macpherson Report recommended that all stops should be recorded, 'consensual' or not, and regardless of whether they resulted in a search.[171] A pilot project to test the feasibility of this recommendation found that the police failed to complete a record in 79% of recordable instances (Bland et al, 2000: 31).[172] This figure looks even worse once one realises that the project did not require the police to record the 'frequent informal' stops where 'known criminals' or 'informants' were stopped by the police for the purpose of gathering 'criminal intelligence' because officers had objected that such recording might 'impact on their working practices' (Bland et al, 2000: 14–15). Thus members of the public in the pilot sites who reported being stopped and searched repeatedly, sometimes in the course of just one day, were almost never given records of these encounters.

As noted above, the 2003 version of the Code of Practice A introduced a nationwide requirement to record encounters that amounted to a 'stop and account' (implemented in 2005), thus continuing to exclude encounters where the police seek to gather more general criminal intelligence from 'informants'. The police complained that even this restricted definition of stops resulted in too much bureaucracy.[173] Home Office research indicated that three-quarters of stops were recorded in five minutes or less, with no adverse effect evident on either crime or the number of searches carried out.[174] On the other side of the argument, the Flanagan review of policing estimated that in

---

[171] Macpherson (1999) recommendation 61.

[172] Observational research conducted once phased implementation of the Macpherson recommendation began in five sites found a recording level of just under 45%: Home Office (2004d: 13).

[173] For an overview of police concerns see Wilding (2008: 131–8).   [174] Home Office (2004d: 2).

London alone 'Stop and Account consumes over 48,000 hours annually of officers' time', not counting the time supervisors spent checking each form, and recommended a drastic reduction in recording requirements.[175] The 2009 version of the Code accordingly removed the requirement to provide the person 'held to account' with a form recording the encounter. Instead police officers are now only obliged to record the ethnicity of the person stopped (with the intention being that this will be transmitted electronically back to the station), and to give that person a 'receipt'. Supervising officers will, at least in theory, still be able to check patterns of stop and account against individual officer details, but as they will no longer have access to information about why a person was stopped, or what the outcome of the stop was, the potential for meaningful supervision has been severely attenuated.[176] And the giving of a receipt rather than a form to those asked to account for themselves is subject to much the same critique as that expressed by the Equality and Human Rights Commission in the preceding paragraph.

The most obvious problem with requiring officers to provide reasons for stop-searches to suspects, and to record those reasons in writing, is that police officers will tend to give accounts designed more to fit the statutory criteria than the actual events. In particular, it is unrealistic to expect an officer to record on his stop-search form that his reason for exercising a power was that a 'Rastafarian out at night', was inherently suspicious[177] or that someone was stopped 'because he's a fucking Paki in a Jaguar',[178] yet we know that such prejudiced actions do occur. Only the bravest (or most foolish) officers would complete written records in such ways as to make clear the unlawfulness of a stop. So if there were a challenge to a particular stop, it would be the suspect's word against the officer's, just as if there were no written record. The record therefore may be more of a protection for the officer than it is for the suspect.

Lack of knowledge on the part of suspects further undermines the likelihood of police accountability. It is no use having a right not to be stopped and searched unlawfully if people do not know what that right entails. The difficulties discussed above in defining reasonable suspicion mean that it is virtually impossible to know what a right not to be stopped and searched unlawfully means. This problem has been greatly exacerbated by the post-PACE proliferation of stop-search powers, and the different pre-conditions for use that apply to each of these. Matters have only become worse with the advent of quasi-police, such as the Community Support Officer (CSO), who sometimes have stop-search powers and sometimes not.

Similarly, it is no use having a record made if people do not know of its existence. This is why the police are obliged under PACE to inform suspects that they are entitled

---

[175] Flanagan R, *The Review of Policing: Final Report*, (2008) pp 61–4 (available at <http://police.homeoffice. gov.uk/publications/police-reform/Review_of_policing_final_report/> – accessed 5 January 2010).

[176] See the critique by the Equality and Human Rights Commission (2008: 23).

[177] Officer quoted by Quinton et al (2000: 24).

[178] Reason given for a stop by PC Rob Pulling and PC Andy Hall in 'The Secret Policeman'. PC Pulling accepted that 'I'd obviously have to think of something else', ie, to give as the ostensible reason for the stop.

to a copy of the record. However, if the officer fails to inform the suspect, then the suspect will remain unaware of the entitlement to a copy of the record so will not know that the officer breached the legal duty to explain this. Bland et al (2000: 29) found that only 'a handful' of people had applied in the last year for a copy of their search record. The Code of Practice now obliges the searching officer to provide suspects with a copy of the record (or at least a receipt) there and then but the problem of non-compliance, and the suspect's lack of awareness that non-compliance has occurred, remains.

Dixon et al have argued that one major reform which is needed if PACE is to be at all effective in relation to powers on the street is for citizens to be fully educated about their rights and, by implication, not to have to rely on the police for this knowledge.[179] This would certainly help enhance police accountability, but the very complexity and ambiguity of the law (and the secrecy surrounding authorisations of s 44 stop-searches under the Terrorism Act 2000) means that the goal of full education is probably unattainable.[180] Take, for example, the Association of Police Authorities' leaflet on 'Stop & Search: Know Your Rights', designed to be carried in a purse or wallet. This makes no reference to reasonable suspicion and lapses into misleadingly broad statements such as 'You can be stopped and searched *anywhere* when an officer believes that you are carrying drugs, weapons or stolen property…' (emphasis in original).[181] From this one might infer that the police can forcibly enter your home and search you for drugs on the basis of mere belief, however unreasonable.[182] It appears to be impossible to create a statement of stop-search rights that is both accurate and handy-sized. But carrying around a chapter of this length and referring to it when stopped is hardly a practicable option (and is liable to get you arrested for challenging police authority, so do not put this idea to the test).[183]

2.4.2 Monitoring of search records

What of the Philips Commission's belief that scrutiny of search records by supervising officers would help guard against unlawful stop-searches? There are two major problems here. First, when a supervisory officer scrutinises such records, the scrutiny

[179] Dixon et al, 'Reality and Rules in the Construction and Regulation of Police Suspicion' (1989) 17 IJ Sociology of Law 185 at p 203.

[180] 'I am acutely aware of the confusion between stop and account and stop and search among both the public and police officers': Berry J, *Reducing Bureaucracy in Policing: Interim Report* (2009) p 9 (available from: <http://police.homeoffice.gov.uk/publications/police-reform/reducing-bureaucracy-report.html> – accessed 5 January 2010). Jan Berry was appointed the 'Independent Reducing Bureaucracy in Policing Advocate' by the Home Secretary on 1 October 2008. She was previously chair of the Police Federation (the main police trade union).

[181] Published by the APA in September 2008, and distributed by individual police authorities.

[182] See also the information on stop-search rights on the APA website, which seems to reduce the question of rights to whether one is given a form by the police or not (http://www.apa.police.uk/APA/ – last accessed 5 January 2010).

[183] Take the following example of a black man, regularly stopped and search throughout his life, who happens to be a church elder, a magistrate and a manager at the Equality and Human Rights Commission: 'In a recent incident he produced a leaflet that outlines the rules for stop and search. In response a police officer remarked: "Oh, we've got a clever one here."': Equality and Human Rights Commission (2008: 21).

is not of what the officer did or whether it was within the law but of the officer's account of what was done. A police officer fearing rigorous managerial supervision would be unlikely to portray a stop-search as anything other than lawful.[184]

But it seems that police officers do not fear this. For the second major problem with supervision is that it rarely occurs. Only a quarter of police supervisory officers questioned by Dixon et al mentioned checking paperwork as a form of supervision. Over three-quarters of the constables and sergeants interviewed said that their stops were not generally supervised (Dixon et al, 1989: 200–1). Over ten years later, in the late 1990s, separate studies by Bland et al (2000) and Fitzgerald (1999) found that nothing had changed. Fitzgerald, for example, states that the only supervision she discovered was where a probationer reported that his sergeant had put pressure on him to conduct unethical searches.[185] It is thus not surprising that all these studies report that some forms were completed tersely or even tautologically: grounds for search being stated as 'suspicious behaviour' (Dixon et al, 1989), 'drugs search', 'info received' and 'acting furtively' (Bland et al, 2000). NACRO (1997: 12) found that 'what did emerge very clearly was the uniformity and standard phrases given in the section on grounds for the search. Certain stock sentences were repeated frequently … it is clear that a standard method for completing these [forms] is instilled into officers.'[186] As the officers' supervising officers had initialled all these forms but not questioned them, the forms had no credibility as a form of accountability or for ensuring that stop-searches were carried out fairly. On the other hand, at least the requirement to record has the potential to focus officers' minds on the limits of their legal powers, and some officers do claim this has an influence on them (Bland et al, 2000: 71–2).

Recent versions of Code of Practice A have taken account of these research findings by stating that supervisors and senior officers with area- or force-wide responsibilities must monitor the use of stop-search powers, considering in particular whether there is any evidence that they are being exercised on the basis of stereotyped images or inappropriate generalisations.[187] In addition such scrutiny must be supported by the compilation of comprehensive statistical records of stops and searches at force, area and local level.[188] Paragraph 5.3 continues: 'Any apparently disproportionate use of the

---

[184] 'A few sergeants interviewed held very strong views on what could be expected from examining forms. They firmly pointed out that they could only check how well the form had been filled out. Because officers were effectively invisible on the streets, they were unhappy about signing off the form to say that the encounter was appropriate': (Home Office, 2004d: 19).

[185] Fitzgerald (1999: ch 5). Miller et al (2000: 16–17) provide a similar example. And see Bland et al (2000: 58–60, 44).

[186] Similarly, Fitzgerald (1999: ch 3) noted that the grounds given on records of stop-searches for drugs 'followed a strikingly similar formula even though they were written by different officers in different areas'.

[187] Paragraph 5.1. This is in line with the Race Relations (Amendment) Act 2000 which imposed a positive duty on the police 'to have due regard to the need – (a) to eliminate unlawful racial discrimination, and (b) to promote equality of opportunity and good relations between persons of different racial groups.' The Equality and Human Rights Commission has been given powers to oversee compliance with the 2000 Act.

[188] The increasing use of computers to record stop-search encounters will, in theory, enable discriminatory patterns to be detected more easily, thus rendering more visible than ever before the work of patrol

powers by particular officers or groups of officers or in relation to specific sections of the community should be identified and investigated.'[189] It is doubtful whether this is yet making any difference. When over eight thousand stop-searches were carried out on those protesting against a proposed coal-fired power station at Kingsnorth power station in August 2008, fewer than 25% of the forms were found by a police review to be legible.[190] These new obligations may nonetheless, in time, improve scrutiny and supervision of record-keeping, as well as the quality of the accounts offered on record. But the problem will remain that these accounts and records may bear little relation to the nature and pattern of the interactions that actually take place between the police and those they stop-search.

Police stop and search may be inherently difficult to supervise adequately due to its relatively low visibility. What is nonetheless open to criticism is the pretence that fully effective supervision is possible and that written records of stop-searches are an adequate check on their legality, and the failure to encourage supervisory officers to take their responsibilities seriously.[191] Adequate supervision may not be possible, but better supervision certainly is: senior officers can hardly be unaware of photographs of criminals on parade room walls with notes urging stops simply because of their criminal records.[192] One police commander of a town is reported to have responded to complaints of disproportionate stop-searches of ethnic minorities by checking the paperwork. His conclusion was that those searched 'in almost all cases were men known to be involved in street crime, whom sensible, intelligence-led policing suggests I should be keeping under surveillance and the very people I should be telling my men to stop and search'.[193] But responsibility for this problem goes higher still. Both the Home Office and the Association of Chief Police Officers strongly advocate 'intelligence-led' policing which targets 'the most persistent offenders' even though there is an awareness that this can result in an increase in disproportionality because of the ethnicity of those identified as suitable targets.[194] For instance, in May 2008

officers. As Ericson and Haggerty (1997: 434) point out, knowledge production provides 'for routine surveillance of both the population of citizens and the population of police'. Similarly, CCTV and cameras in patrol cars can be used to capture police deviance as well as citizen deviance.

[189] Paragraph 5.4 adds that: 'In order to promote public confidence... forces in consultation with police authorities must make arrangements for the records to be scrutinised by representatives of the community, and to explain the use of the powers at a local level' although concerns about preserving the anonymity of those searched means that scrutiny is likely to be confined in practice to statistics generated by the search records (Note 19).

[190] See <http://www.guardian.co.uk/environment/2009/jul/22/kingsnorth-police> (accessed 5 January 2010).

[191] Snapshot observations carried out by academics from the London School of Economics in four forces and one London borough revealed front-line supervision to be of highly variable quality, and working best where monitored and supported by senior line management: Home Office (2005a: 38–9).

[192] See the reference to this in 2.2.1 above.

[193] HC Stdg Comm D, 13 April 2000, col 27. Discussed by Lustgarten (2003: 612).

[194] Home Office (2005a: 40). At p 13 of this document, Basic Command Units are exhorted to 'risk-assess' police intelligence for racial bias in order to ensure there is no racial discrimination when identifying

the Home Secretary urged police forces across the country to follow the example of a four-day operation by Essex Police in which 14 persistent offenders were confronted at their homes, openly filmed, followed by surveillance and other police officers, and repeatedly stopped and searched (a total of 60 times).[195] In sum, the problems inherent in attempts to control low visibility and discretionary police work are compounded by laxity in the law and by a pervasive policing and political culture which emphasises 'results' rather than procedural propriety. Thus, day-to-day supervisory and oversight practices remain patchy and ineffective, with racial disparities in stop-search statistics and practices as pronounced as ever. The Equality and Human Rights Commission (2008: 24) quotes an unpublished HMIC report into police compliance with the race equality duty as follows:

HMIC found that generally, forces could not give a clear account of the reasons for disproportionality. It was apparent that, although a great deal of information is collected, inspected
forces lacked the in-house resources to analyse it in any detail, although some have since
introduced dedicated analysts... The inspection team found that forces were inconsistent in
implementation and adherence to stop and search policies.[196]

We think it fair to conclude, in the absence of any systematic research to the contrary, that the rules and policies on supervision remain largely presentational, doing
little to influence on-the-street decision-making.

2.4.3 Remedies

Where a stop is legally questionable, what is the probability and likely consequence of a successful challenge? If a stop is unsuccessful, suspects will usually want to put the matter behind them, and the absence of reasonable suspicion (assuming any is required) will rarely be an issue. If the stop is successful, in the sense of a crime being discovered, it will rarely be questioned because the initial illegality becomes overshad-
owed by the crime itself.[197] We have seen, however, that some groups are subjected

---

'targeted individuals and hot spot areas'. What remains unacknowledged in this Report is that 'targeting individuals and areas' is often incompatible with the PACE requirement that reasonable suspicion of some specific offence exists in relation to a particular individual at the particular time that the stop-search takes place.

[195] <http://www.guardian.co.uk/politics/2008/may/08/police.ukcrime> (last accessed 5 January 2010).

[196] Pressure from the police on HMIC to not publish this report seems to have been successful, although an anodyne two page summary can be tracked down at <http://webarchive.nationalarchives.gov. uk/20070708092741/> and <http://inspectorates.homeoffice.gov.uk/hmic/inspections/ptd/diversity/duty-calls-hmic-inspection.pdf> (accessed 5 January 2010).

[197] The position is different if the crime is not so much 'discovered' as generated by the unlawful search itself. Thus where a suspect's resistance to the unlawful search leads to them being prosecuted for obstructing an officer in the execution of his/her duty, the illegality of the search means that the officer is not execut-
ing a lawful duty, so an essential ingredient of the offence is missing: *R v Christopher Bristol* [2007] EWCA Crim 3214. Similarly, where a suspect is charged with assault or threatening behaviour following resistance to an unlawful arrest, no crime will be committed if the force used by the suspect is adjudged reasonable – see *B v DPP* [2008] EWHC 1655 (Admin).

to repeated stops and stop-searches and that they do not have the option of 'putting the matter behind them'. They are in a continuing conflictual relationship with the police and might see a legal challenge as the only way out. But many such groups are socially marginalised and perceive the law as remote and inaccessible. As one youth told Goldsmith (2008: 234):

we were all actually thinking about doing…like…getting a campaign to sue [the police] because we couldn't…literally it was so bad we'd be getting stopped every five minutes. But we just couldn't do it because we didn't know how and we can't pay.

Thus it is only rarely that stop-search practices are challenged, and such challenges tend to come from articulate and organised adults, such as the protester and the journalist in the *Gillan* case. In the unlikely event of a challenge being made to a stop and search, what actions or remedies are available?

It is striking that the ECHR, PACE, the Terrorism Act, the CJPO and so forth are all silent on this point, neither making it a crime nor a tort to stop and search someone unlawfully, to fail to provide information before search, or to make a record of it afterwards.[198] At common law, a failure by an officer to provide information prior to search renders the stop and search unlawful: *Pedro v Diss*.[199] Here the suspect used force to free himself from an unlawful detention and was, in consequence, charged with assaulting an officer in the execution of his duty. It was held that the unlawfulness of the detention meant that the officer was not acting in the execution of his duty, and so the assault was not criminal. These principles were affirmed by the Divisional Court in *Osman* where the officers had failed to give their names and station prior to a forcible search under s 60 of CJPO.[200]

A stop and search which was unlawful – whether because inadequate reasons were provided or because inadequate reasons existed (such as no reasonable suspicion in the case of a PACE search) – could constitute the tort of assault. However, there have been no reported cases of this, partly because such an action would be speculative, and partly, no doubt, because the loss or damages suffered as a result of an unlawful stop and search tends to be regarded by the domestic courts as insignificant.[201] If charges followed the discovery of stolen or prohibited articles, a motion to exclude from court evidence discovered as a result of the stop and search is possible although unlikely

---

[198] PACE, s 67(10) provides that a failure on the part of a police officer to comply with the provisions of Code of Practice A 'shall not of itself render him liable to any criminal or civil proceedings'.

[199] [1981] 2 All ER 59.

[200] *Osman (Mustapha) v Southwark Crown Court* (1999) 163 JP 725. But note that officers do not have to give their name and station prior to using their power under s 60(4)(a) of the CJPO 1994 requiring someone to remove or give up an item reasonably believed as an article intended to be used to disguise identity: *DPP v Avery* [2002] 1 Cr App R 31.

[201] See *Gillan* [2006] UKHL 12 [25] where Lord Bingham characterised a stop-search as akin to being 'kept from proceeding or kept waiting'. For critique see Ashworth A, 'Case Comment: Police Powers–Whether Authorisation Given under Terrorism Legislation Lawful' [2006] Crim LR 751, 755 (and see also 2.5.3, where a more realistic appraisal by the ECtHR is quoted).

to succeed.[202] If PACE stops are challenged in court (in either of these ways), and the officers' accounts differ from those of the suspect what would or could the court do? If defining the absence of reasonable suspicion is difficult, proving it is all the more so: these are low visibility decisions where there are seldom other civilian witnesses and where – because those stopped are so often people with previous convictions – suspects are easily 'discredited'.[203]

The main problem with all of the remedies discussed so far is that they are individualistic in nature. The most troubling aspect of stop-search, however, is the way in which the power is deployed disproportionately against certain social groups. In other words, remedies are needed that can take into account overall patterns of discretionary decision-making rather than focusing on the much narrower question of whether a particular constable had reasonable suspicion in a particular case. This is something the ECtHR sometimes takes into account, as it did in *Gillan* when deciding that s 44 Terrorism Act 2000 stop-search powers amounted to an unjustifiable breach of Art 8. It stated that '...there is a clear risk of arbitrariness in the grant of such a broad discretion to the police officer. While the present cases do not concern black applicants or those of Asian origin, the risks of the discriminatory use of the powers against such persons is a very real consideration...'[204] But it took more than six years from the date of the stop-searches in question to secure this judgment. Are there any more accessible domestic remedies? Following a recommendation of the Macpherson Report, the Race Relations (Amendment) Act 2000 makes it unlawful for any public authority to do any act which constitutes racial discrimination. This extension of the race discrimination legislation, combined with the impact of a recent European Council 'Race Directive' (2000/43), means that acts of direct discrimination (overt racist behaviour) as well as practices that amount to indirect discrimination (because they unjustifiably disadvantage people of a particular ethnic group) are all likely in future to be actionable in the domestic courts.[205] Another

---

[202] In *McCarthy* [1996] Crim LR 818 the Court of Appeal approved of a judge's decision not to exclude evidence obtained as a result of a stop-search where the police had lied about the true basis for the search. As ch 12 will show, *McCarthy* is consistent with the courts' normal interpretation of the exclusionary provisions of PACE.

[203] See the discussion of discrediting in the context of complaints against the police in ch 12, below.

[204] *Gillan and Quinton v the United Kingdom* (App No 4158/05) Judgment 12 January 2010 [85].

[205] The Equality and Human Rights Commission has the power to assist individual complainants and launch proactive investigations of its own. As to possible human rights arguments and remedies see further Feldman (2002: 302–7; 318–19), Moeckli (2007), and De Schutter O and Ringelheim J, 'Ethnic Profiling: A Rising Challenge for European Human Rights Law' (2008) 71(3) MLR 358. The ECHR does not mention stop-search, but Art 5(1) states that 'No one shall be deprived of his liberty save in the following cases and in accordance with a procedure prescribed by law.' The relevant following case is contained in Art 5(1)(b) which allows detention 'in order to secure the fulfilment of any obligation prescribed by law'. The European Commission has held that examinations under the terrorist legislation comply with this provision (see discussion of *McVeigh, O'Neill and Evans v UK* (1981) 25 DR 15 in 3.4), which means that it seemed arguable that all the other stop and search powers would also comply. Indeed, the English courts have taken the view that stop-search will rarely amount to a deprivation of liberty within the meaning of Art 5: *Gillan* [2006] UKHL 12. This case also indicates that the domestic courts are most unlikely to uphold the argument that

non-individualistic approach is to seek a judicial review in relation to a stop-search policy. In August 2008 Kent police used s 1 of PACE to stop-search everyone entering and leaving a peaceful climate camp demonstration against a proposed new power station. This included two children aged 11. The children, along with another man, sought judicial review arguing that such a blanket practice was unlawful. Shortly before the case was due to be heard the police finally disclosed a briefing document in which senior officers had asserted that all demonstrators should be searched because there were reasonable grounds to do so. On 29 January 2010 the police admitted 'total surrender' accepting an Order that the searches of the claimants had been 'unlawful', and constituted a violation of their human rights to privacy (breach of Art 8 of the ECHR), to freedom of expression (breach of Art 10) and freedom of association (breach of Art 11).[206]

One other possible remedy is the making of a complaint against the police officer concerned. PACE, s 67(8) originally made it a disciplinary offence to breach any of the provisions in the Codes of Practice, but this was repealed in the 1990s. Repeal sent a crime control signal to the police, although complaints can still lead to disciplinary action on some other footing such as 'incivility'. In practice, relatively few of the many people aggrieved by police actions ever make an official complaint (see ch 12). One factor behind the low complaint rate is the correct perception that the chances of having a complaint upheld are low. Of 100 cases involving formal complaints of stop-search practices, in just eight was the complaint substantiated. Thirty-one of the 100 cases were sent to the CPS for consideration of criminal culpability, but charges were brought in only one case (indecent assault) and the officer concerned was acquitted at Crown Court.[207] The low rates of substantiation and prosecution are partly because of the difficulty of establishing that an officer lacked reasonable suspicion or failed to give information prior to search or conducted the encounter in a disrespectful or abusive way,[208] and partly because of the failings or inadequacies of the police complaints machinery (see ch 12). The fear of a complaint or disciplinary action may nonetheless deter some officers from breaching the stop-search rules, particularly when the use of

---

stop-search threatens Art 11 (freedom of assembly) or Art 10 (freedom of expression) rights, or has a chilling effect upon their exercise, unless the powers were used wrongly (as *seems* to have happened in that case – and as certainly happened in the Kingsnorth case; see next footnote and accompanying text) in order to control or deter attendance at demonstrations. However, when *Gillan* reached the ECtHR the Fourth Section who determined the case dropped a heavy hint (without having needed to do so) that the degree of coercion involved in a stop-search was 'indicative of a deprivation of liberty within the meaning of Article 5...': *Gillan and Quinton v the United Kingdom* (App No 4158/05) Judgment 12 January 2010 [57]. As noted in the text, the ECtHR also found a breach of Art 8 in this case. It declined to comment on the arguments relating to Arts 10 and 11.

206 See <http://www.indymedia.org.uk/en/2010/01/445509.html> (last accessed 18 February 2010).

207 Havis and Best (2004: 36, 40).

208 This is particularly true where there are no independent witnesses (relatives or friends of the complainant do not count as sufficiently independent). If the person stop-searched is an off duty police officer, the chances of success are evidently greater: see Havis and Best (2004: 19, 31, 38).

the power becomes a matter of public controversy and officers sense that 'management' would not support their actions.[209]

In a few rare instances, the police have overstepped the boundaries of legality so blatantly and ineptly that the courts have felt obliged to take meaningful remedial action. In *Somers*, for example, the appellant had been driving a hire-car when he was stopped by police officers, supposedly acting under Road Traffic Act powers. They claimed they wished to check whether the car was stolen since a similar vehicle had been stolen in the same area shortly before. The appellant was placed in the police car and was not permitted, despite his request, to witness the police officers entering the hire-car. The officers made a check with the licensing authority which revealed that the car appeared to be genuine in the sense that it was owned by a hire-car company. Moreover, the appellant produced the hire agreement. The officers claimed, however, that they wanted to go further by checking the chassis number or the engine number and so entered the car to find the bonnet release switch. They claimed that while looking for this switch they found a bag of crack cocaine in a small compartment immediately below the radio and above the ventilation control. As Lord Justice Pill put it, 'It is not a place where, in the experience of anyone in court, a bonnet release would be found.'[210]

Other curious features of the case noted by the court included: (i) the persistence of the police investigation into the ownership of the car given that it was quite obvious that it was a hire-car legitimately in the possession of the appellant (the signs of the car-hire company were displayed prominently on the passenger door!); (ii) the failure of the police to find the bonnet release handle (and the fact that they gave up looking for it having 'found' the drugs); (iii) two other police cars were summoned to the scene, arriving within six minutes, despite the fact that the suspect was perfectly cooperative; (iv) no record was kept of the search; (v) the cooperation of the suspect had not been sought in carrying out the search; (vi) several officers had failed to note the incident in their pocket books; (vii) a copy of one of the relevant police documents appeared to have been doctored prior to it being sent to the defence.

The appellant's fingerprints were not found on the bag of drugs. Although he had previous convictions for 'serious offences', and had in 2002 been convicted of obstructing a police officer, he had no convictions for drug offences. By his own admission, he did not like or trust the police. The clear implication was that the police had planted the drugs in the car of a 'usual suspect' thought to merit severe social disciplining. He was convicted at first instance but the conviction was quashed as unsafe because the trial judge had not drawn the jury's attention sufficiently to the unsatisfactory nature of, and inconsistencies in, the police evidence. The prosecution had the cheek to ask for a retrial as this, they said, 'would give the opportunity for the Crown to iron out any curiosities within the

---

[209] As seems to have happened in the aftermath of the Macpherson Inquiry: Fitzgerald (1999: ch 5); Fitzgerald et al (2002: 101).   [210] *R v Somers* [2003] EWCA Crim 1356 [5].

case…'[211] This application was refused. Nonetheless, Mr Somers had served nine months in prison prior to his appeal being heard so it is difficult to argue that the quashing of the conviction amounted to a complete remedy. It is sometimes said that the innocent have nothing to fear from increases in police powers. Do you think Mr Somers would agree?

2.5 The impact of stop-search powers

The question for us in this section is whether the freedom gained for 'society' by catching criminals through stop-search exceeds or is less than the freedom lost by the people who are subjected to stop-search.

2.5.1 Success rates and crime control

How valuable are stop and search powers for the police? In 2.2.1.1 we saw that only around 11% of recorded 'reasonable suspicion' stop-searches now lead to arrest, and that the 'true' arrest rate is probably lower still.[212] Overall, arrests following stops constitute only 8% of all arrests (though 14%–19% of arrests by the Metropolitan Police over the last ten years)[213] and the contribution such arrests make to tackling crime directly is small.[214] Moreover, there '…are forces that have high levels of search arrests that achieve only low primary clear-up rates, as well as forces with lower levels of arrests from searches that achieve good clear-up rates' (Miller et al, 2000: 22). At first sight this is surprising, as every successful search-arrest counts as a cleared-up crime, whereas unsuccessful searches do not add to the stock of crimes to be cleared-up. But use of the power involves opportunity costs: while police officers are busy proactively stop-searching they cannot do anything about the other crimes that are clamouring for attention. Also, only about half of arrests following a search result in caution or conviction (Miller et al, 2000: 24–6). The cost-benefit analysis looks still worse if one looks at how frequently *stops* lead to a prosecution. For example, according to the 1992 British Crime Survey, only about 3% of pedestrian stops and 7% of car stops led to a prosecution,[215] and even here some of the latter will have been for minor road traffic offences, and some of the prosecutions will have failed. And the Independent Reviewer

---

[211] *R v Somers* [51].

[212] There are problems inherent in using arrest rates as a measure of the success of stop-search in tackling crime, for the police may use their discretion not to arrest even where they do detect crime (Wilding, 2008: 137). Fitzgerald (1999) provides examples, including where officers deal with cannabis possession by giving an informal warning and ensuring the disposal of the drug down a street-drain rather than arresting.

[213] Povey and Smith (2009) table 1c.

[214] One recorded search followed by an arrest takes place for every 106 British Crime Survey crimes susceptible to detection by a search, or for every 239 BCS crimes in total (Miller et al, 2000: 23–4).

[215] Skogan W, *Contacts between Police and Public – Findings from the 1992 British Crime Survey* (Home Office Research Study No 134) (London: Home Office, 1994) p 27, table 3.5.

of the terrorism legislation has noted that not a single s 44 stop-search has ever resulted in conviction for a terrorism offence.[216]

That the crime uncovered by 'reasonable suspicion' stop-search is often mundane is indicated by the fact that around two-fifths of all searches are for drugs, and just under a third of arrests arising from stop-searches are drug related, overwhelmingly for cannabis possession.[217] While Fitzgerald noted in 1999 that stop-search played a useful part in London (and no doubt elsewhere) in uncovering the more serious crime of carrying offensive weapons,[218] she has more recently warned that the cost in terms of groundless stops and consequent community resentment might now be too high. This was a response to Metropolitan Police claims that a fall in knife crime in 2008 was attributable to a huge increase in stop-searches and targeting of 'hot spots'.[219] In the absence of stop-search powers, such crimes would not necessarily remain undetected, for the police could arrest where they genuinely have reasonable suspicion. They would probably do so less often than they currently stop and search, given the greater legal formalities and consequences of arrest (see ch 3), but since a more selective policy should be based on more evidence, the fall in the number of detections should be relatively small.

Overall, then, the opportunity costs involved in extensive stop-searching, the infringement of civil liberties involved, and the low haul of productive arrests secured, all suggest that stop-search as currently practised is not a freedom-enhancing way of tackling crime. That, however, is not the end of the matter, for the widespread use of stop-search powers may be effective in deterring potential offenders. As one officer put it: 'If active criminals know that they can't go out without being searched that tends to put a damper on their activities.'[220] The effectiveness of such a policy is extremely doubtful. The problem was highlighted by Swamp 81.[221]

---

[216] Cited in *Gillan and Quinton v the United Kingdom* (App No 4158/05) Judgment 12 January 2010 [43].

[217] Povey and Smith (2009: table 2A); Fitzgerald (1999: ch 2).   [218] Fitzgerald (1999: ch 2).

[219] For discussion of the police claims and Fitzgerald's response, see *The Guardian*, 18 November 2008. The new Metropolitan Police Commissioner in January 2009 vowed to continue this policy (*The Guardian*, 29 January 2009). The wisdom of doing so has been called further into question by a subsequent analysis of the stop-search figures by Professor Fitzgerald published on 24 January 2010: <http://www.guardian.co.uk/uk/2010/jan/24/stop-and-search-operation-blunt> (accessed 19 February 2010).

[220] Quoted by Fitzgerald (1999: ch 2). See also (Chief Constable) Wilding (2008: 135) who writes: 'Is the power to stop account/stop and search a deterrent? I have no doubt that it is because I was in the Metropolitan Police when the Macpherson Report was published. Almost overnight stop and search practically ceased, we lost the streets and crime shot up.' The Macpherson Report was published in February 1999, and there was indeed an associated sharp drop in recorded stop-searches by the Metropolitan Police (but not other police forces) in that quarter: Wilkins G and Addicot C, *Operation of Certain Police Powers under PACE, Statistical Bulletin 9/00* (London: Home Office, 2000) p 2. It is an exaggeration, however, to say that stop-search practically ceased in the capital around this time – even when the Macpherson effect was at its most pronounced (in 2000/01), the Metropolitan Police carried out 169,900 recorded stop-searches requiring reasonable suspicion, 2,813 s 60 stop-searches, 2,678 s 44 stop-searches, and 28 road checks (in which 41,443 vehicles were stopped): Ayres et al, *Arrests for Notifiable Offences and the Operation of Certain Police Powers under PACE, Statistical Bulletin 19/01* (London: Home Office, 2001) pp 24–7, tables P1–P4. The notion that the reduction in stop-search activity resulted in street-crime 'shooting up' is also highly debatable. For more measured analysis see Hallsworth S, *Street Crime* (Cullompton: Willan, 2005) esp ch 9.

[221] Scarman (1981: para 3.27), discussed in 2.2, above.

This massive operation, in which the police made 943 stops, saturated the streets of Brixton for several days and triggered a riot. Even if one takes the riot out of the equation the effectiveness of such crackdowns in tackling street crime may be questioned. Scarman observed that:

the evidence is not clear that a street saturation operation does diminish street crime: it may well only drive it elsewhere. And, after the operation has ended, street crime returns.[222]

So extensive stop and search may impact upon crime at one time and in one place, but otherwise allows crime to flourish. This 'displacement' phenomenon can be overstated, but the resources needed to protect against it, and to sustain aggressive crackdowns in the long term, would be enormous, as indeed would be the damage done to police-community and intra-community relations by such a policy. That is all the more so now that the 'crime' being targeted includes low-level 'anti-social behaviour'. Thus intense surveillance and stop-searching in one deprived area of social housing led to bitter resentment amongst the targeted youths, who retreated to 'hidden' spaces, such as stairwells of flats and isolated park areas in order to avoid further contact with the police.[223] That outcome is hardly likely to be reassuring for local adults, and the potential for an escalation of tension within the community is obvious.[224] We should not be surprised then, to find that any crime-reductive effects of intensive stop-search are cancelled out by displacement and crime-fuelling effects. Miller et al's analysis of the available data concluded that: 'Generally speaking, changes in the level of stops and searches do not appear to affect the levels of crime.'[225] Some 'targeted policing' (discussed in 2.1) is of 'Swamp 81' variety, and s 60 CJPO and s 44 Terrorism Act powers now allow the police to do what they were not strictly allowed to do in Brixton in 1981. Little seems to have been learnt from that experience.

---

[222] Ibid, para 4.78. For recent evidence of displacement, see the study by Hallsworth (2005: 114): 'Gains made in one place by community safety effort were offset by increases in other areas as the street robbers moved on.' See also Lister et al (2008: 48–9) who found that drug users were not deterred by street policing from either drug using or the acquisitive crime which funded their habit.

[223] Goldsmith (2008: 235).

[224] See the account by Blincoe N, 'Me v the Kids' *The Guardian* ('Weekend' magazine), 7 February 2009.

[225] Miller et al (2000: 36). The authors of this study also looked at the possibility that stop-search disrupted criminal activity through nipping it in the bud, which would happen where those detected carrying drugs, offensive weapons or instruments useful for burglary would otherwise have gone on to supply drugs, commit acts of violence or burgle, as the case may be. They concluded that any such impact had only a marginal effect on crime levels, most probably achieving a reduction in crime susceptible to disruption in the order of 0.6% (p 30). Assessing whether a zero tolerance approach to minor crime and disorder (such as adopted in Cleveland) achieved its intended benefit of preventing the development of more serious crime problems was beyond the scope of this study, although the authors noted (p 37) that using stop-searches 'as part of order maintenance strategies has the distinct potential to impact negatively on community relations and hamper the long-term effectiveness of police work'. The contrary police claim that intensive stop-search strategies led to a fall in knife crime in 2008 (*The Guardian*, 18 November 2008) is not based on rigorous research of the calibre of Miller et al.

Another way in which stop and search may contribute to crime control is in augmenting 'criminal intelligence'. Police collators, for instance, build up computer databases of information about suspects and witnesses based on information derived from stop-searches.[226] Some police services use the amount of information submitted by uniformed officers as a criterion for promotion to CID, thus encouraging enthusiastic use of stop-search powers.[227] The Home Office and the Association of Chief Police Officers have given the following advice to front line officers:

Remember that when a stop-search does not lead to an arrest this in no way means that the stop and search was unlawful, inappropriate or of no value. Although the reason for conducting a stop and search is detection, any search can yield valuable intelligence, which must be captured. Do not underestimate the potential value of small pieces of information (Home Office 2005a: 28).

Written records in particular – ostensibly introduced as protections *for* suspects – provide the basis for systematic collation of information *about* suspects.[228] In some areas, more stops lead to fewer arrests, precisely because the criminal intelligence normally gathered after arrest is collected on the street instead. Complex systems of data storage are thereby created, allowing certain target populations to be monitored.[229] This happened on a large scale in relation to the use of anti-terrorism legislation to monitor the Irish population in Britain and Northern Ireland[230] and many Muslims (especially young men) appear now to be getting the same treatment.[231] We noted in 2.4.1 that in recent years the government has scaled back the requirement to give copies of written stop-search records to suspects, and to keep detailed records of 'stop and account' for accountability purposes.[232] But this does not mean that the police will desist from their long-standing practice of recording intelligence gleaned from stop-searches and 'stop and accounts' that *they* find useful. Indeed, intelligence gathering is becoming increasingly easy through such technological developments as digital cameras with facial recognition software, on-the-street fingerprinting devices[233] and

---

[226] Dixon et al (1989: 189); Fitzgerald (1999: ch 5); Home Office (2005e).

[227] Barton A and Evans R, *Proactive Policing on Merseyside* (Police Research Series Paper 105) (London: Home Office, 1999).   [228] Willis (1983: 15); Bridges and Bunyan (1983); Home Office (2005e).

[229] See Meehan (1993); Ericson R and Haggerty K, *Policing the Risk Society* (Oxford: Clarendon Press, 1997); Home Office (2005e).

[230] Hillyard P, *Suspect Community* (London: Pluto Press, 1993) esp ch 12, and Walker (2002: 156).

[231] Pantazis C and Pemberton S, 'From the "Old" to the "New" Suspect Community: Examining the Impacts of Recent UK Counter-Terrorist Legislation' (2009) 49(5) B J Crim 646. The notion that Muslims have become en masse a 'suspect community' is challenged by Greer S, 'Human Rights and the Struggle against Terrorism in the United Kingdom' (2008) 2 EHRLR 163.

[232] A process which cl 1 of the Crime and Security Bill (before Parliament at the time of writing) will, if enacted, take further.

[233] The BBC has reported that between 1 November 2006 and 31 October 2008, 29,000 people were stopped and fingerprinted ('optionally') using a new mobile fingerprint scanner being trialled in twenty police forces: <http://news.bbc.co.uk/1/hi/uk/7913073.stm> (accessed 5 January 2010).

the widespread use of hand-held computers which can exchange information with centralised databases.[234]

Is intelligence gathering through stop-search desirable? It could help in solving grave crimes, helping to place a suspect in a particular location at a particular time. On the other hand such intelligence can usually be obtained in less intrusive ways, such as through CCTV, or a less intrusive stop without a search (Miller et al, 2000: 37). More fundamentally, from a freedom perspective one might question whether the cost to society of using stop-search (or other forms of surveillance, including stop and account) for the systemic gathering, storage, dissemination, sharing and use of information concerning 'risky populations' justifies the crime-control benefits: 'A society fearful of being pried upon, a society in which personal data may be collected for uncontrolled speculative use, is not a free society.'[235] This argument is unlikely to persuade policy-makers given their preoccupation with crime control and the logic of risk management.[236] When the risks run as high as major terrorist incidents, such as those which occurred in the United States on September 11 2001, this is understandable.[237] But all of those who committed those outrages were subjected to the information-gathering and stop-search procedures routinely applied to air travellers as a condition of flying. Also, if particular objects or places are subjected to saturation stop-search practices terrorists will simply choose other means or places to attack; they can more easily engage in displacement than can 'normal' criminals. Broadening stop-search powers is therefore unlikely to help prevent terrorism, as the (then) Assistant Commissioner Andy Hayman (in charge of anti-terrorist operations in London) himself recognised in 2006.[238]

How are we to explain the continuing attachment to ever more extensive stop-search in the light of its limited effectiveness? Brogden argues that stop-search is actually part of a wider social control function: that historically the police have been more concerned with social control of the streets than with detecting crime.[239] From medieval times, such laws 'to keep in order the unruly' or to apprehend 'rogues, vagabonds and other disorderly persons' were common. The Head Constable of Liverpool instructed his men in 1878, for instance, to watch 'vigilantly the movements of all suspected persons... For the purposes of seeing whether his suspicions are well founded, he may

---

[234] See Home Office (2005a: 50).

[235] Sharpe S, *Search and Surveillance: The Movement from Evidence to Information* (Aldershot: Ashgate, 2000) p 223.   [236] On the self-fuelling nature of this logic see Ericson and Haggerty (1997: 449–52).

[237] On the use of risk-management in this field see Walker C and McGuinness M, 'Commercial Risk, Political Violence and Policing the City of London' in Crawford A (ed), *Crime and Insecurity: The Governance of Safety in Europe* (Cullompton: Willan, 2002).

[238] 'It's a power that's well intended: it's there to try and prevent, deter and disrupt terrorist activity. So the test is: to what extent does it achieve that aim? And I have to say, it doesn't... There's a big price to pay for probably a very small benefit': Quoted in Metropolitan Police Authority (2007: 52).

[239] Brogden (1985); and see also Brogden M and Brogden A, 'From Henry III to Liverpool 8' (1984) 12 IJ Sociology of Law 37.

stop any person...' (Brogden, 1985: 106–7). Reasonable suspicion, as found in the leg-islation of the 1970s and 1980s, was in many instances an afterthought – one which, we have seen, was increasingly dispensed with in the 1990s. Thus s 60 of the CJPO and s 44 of the Terrorism Act, far from providing a different kind of power for the police armoury, represent historical continuity. It is the attempt to impose due process on street policing which is the novelty. Stop-search, and the street policing which stop-search facilitates, is as much about monitoring, controlling and disciplining groups of 'suspicious' people, as about detecting specific crimes and specific criminals.[240] The new millennium emphasis on 'reassurance policing' (that is to say, providing highly visible policing to reassure 'the public' that order is being maintained) feeds into this long-standing phenomenon.[241]

This is where we see the importance of stop-search being limited to public places. For it is those at the bottom of the socio-economic heap who tend to gather in such places and are thus, as a group, subjected to stop-search most frequently. As Lord Scarman observed in his report on the Brixton disorders of 1981, young unemployed black people had little alternative but to make their lives on the streets:

And living much of their lives on the streets, they are brought into contact with the police who appear to them as the visible symbols of the authority of a society which has failed to bring them its benefits or do them justice.[242]

At the beginning of the twenty-first century much the same could be said of other groups of street-users including youths living in deprived areas, political protesters, the homeless, beggars, asylum seekers, drug users, and the mentally disordered. At the same time there are growing tensions evident between different groups who use the streets. Town centre managers and business leaders want protesters, drug users, the homeless and those begging to be swept out of sight to avoid harm to tourism or sales figures, fearful adults (and zero-tolerance minded policy-makers) put pressure on the police to disperse groups of youths 'hanging around', the media (with able sup-port from some senior police leaders)[243] fuels growing fears and prejudices about eth-nic minorities, youths, asylum seekers and the mentally disordered, and the potential for inter-group tensions multiplies as society becomes ever more ethnically, culturally and socially diverse. In this volatile situation, it is easy to see how stop-search could become employed by the police as much to 'reassure the public' and reassert their own authority on the streets as to detect specific crimes.

---

[240] See Choongh S, *Policing as Social Discipline* (Oxford: Clarendon Press, 1997) esp chs 2–3, and the analysis by Lister et al (2008) of the 'communicative surveillance' practised by the police on street drug users.

[241] 'In a number of forces stop and search was used as a tool for public reassurance and to prevent people who were seen as creating a public nuisance from gathering in certain places, although there was no reason-able suspicion of a crime' (Home Office 2005a: 38).   [242] Scarman (1981: para 2.23).

[243] See, for example, Waddington D, *Policing Public Disorder* (Cullompton: Willan, 2007) pp 99 and 107–8.

2.5.2 **The experience of being stopped and searched**

If being stopped and searched by the police was a one-off event in someone's life, the effect on their freedom might reasonably be assessed as relatively slight. But for those that typically attract police suspicions this scenario is increasingly implausible. We noted at the start of this chapter that several million people a year are stopped or stop-searched. The British Crime Survey indicates little change over a twenty-year period in the *proportion* of the population that are *stopped* each year,[244] but confirms a huge growth in *stop-search* activity (table 2.1) since PACE was enacted. We have also seen that some people, particularly young BME males, are likely to be stopped and searched repeatedly. Those who are stop-searched repeatedly are often well aware, and resentful, of the working assumptions and rules that underpin this pattern of police discretion. Choongh (1997: 45), for instance, found many members of ethnic minorities and people with criminal records saying the same things: 'Once you got a record or anything they're always trying to catch you on something.' Young people, in particular, report such experiences. Fitzgerald et al (2002) quote a girl saying:

They're very suspicious of teenagers...They forget they're just average normal people. If they see a group of teenagers they think 'What are they doing?' [They] just go up...because they're wearing a uniform, go up and ask them questions.[245]

Freedom is undermined not only by the frequency of stop-search, or its duration, but also by its nature. How invasive can it be? PACE Code of Practice A, which applies to all stop-search powers, states that: 'All stops and searches must be carried out with courtesy, consideration and respect for the person concerned...Every reasonable effort must be made to reduce to the minimum the embarrassment that a person being searched may experience' (para 3.1). Further, according to paras 3.5–3.7:

- a search in public should consist only of a superficial examination of outer clothing, although this can extend to feeling inside pockets, collars, socks and shoes (and within a person's hair) if this is reasonably necessary to look for the object of the search;

- when a search is in public the only clothes that can be compulsorily removed are coats/jackets and gloves (save for s 44 Terrorism Act searches where the police are allowed to remove headgear and footwear);

---

[244] Thus the BCS 1988 (Skogan (1990: table 6)) found that 15% of all adults (ie several million people) were stopped in 1987/88 – which is remarkably similar to an estimate made pre-PACE some years earlier (Southgate P and Ekblom P, *Contacts Between Police and Public* (Home Office Research Study No 77) (London: HMSO, 1984). Since that time the BCS has repeatedly found a relatively constant level of foot-stops (at around 3%) while traffic stops rose to 17% in 1991 before declining steadily since that time to a low of 10% in 2004/05: Clancy et al (2001: 61–2); Allen et al (2006: 18). It is possible that more recent BCS figures (when published) may reveal an upsurge in the proportion of the population stopped due to the rise of stop and account (see 2.2.3).   [245] See also Loader (1996: 70–1).

- a search 'out of public view' such as in a police van may be made if a more thorough search (for example requiring removal of a shirt or hat) is sought on reasonable grounds;

- if there are grounds to conduct a search which would expose intimate parts of the suspect's body such a search may take place in a police station or other nearby location, but not in a police vehicle;

- in any search going beyond the removal of headgear, footwear, coats/jackets and gloves the officer conducting the search must be of the same sex as the suspect, and no one of a different sex may be present unless requested by the suspect.

The guidance does not stop some stop-searches being humiliating, however. The very act of being forced to submit to police authority in this way is often embarrassing, as where people are searched outside their place of work or worship, or in view of their friends or family. The Metropolitan Police Commissioner himself admitted that this is 'intrusive'.[246] The feelings are still more acute when people are stopped under s 44 of the Terrorism Act, as Londoners explained to the Metropolitan Police Authority:

We heard of embarrassment and humiliation. We heard of stigmatisation, worse than that associated with being stopped under normal police powers, because the signal given out to onlookers under Section 44 Terrorism Act 2000 is not 'this person is a robber' but 'this person is a terrorist'.[247]

At the extremes stop-search is experienced as a public humiliation, particularly when the search appears arbitrary or discriminatory. In 2.2.1.2 we discussed how the Bishop of Stepney was stopped by the police. He said that he felt 'demeaned' even though it was 'only' his car, and not himself, that was the object of the officer's intended search:

When you ask and somebody doesn't give a reason and they seem to be hiding behind a uniform...that creates a feeling that they are more powerful than you and can act in any way they want over you. I just felt as if I was being treated like a little boy.[248]

In an anti-terrorism example, a woman, seven months pregnant, had travelled from England to Dublin where she had been researching for a book she was writing. She was stopped and questioned on her way back.[249] She was treated lawfully and politely. But she was questioned closely about her work, her luggage was searched twice, she was confined to a small room, her personal correspondence was read, and she was anxious about her husband and child who were waiting for her without knowing what was going on. She feared that, if they were so suspicious of her, she might be excluded from England (she was originally from Belfast) and thus permanently separated from her

---

[246] *The Guardian*, 29 January 2009.   [247] Metropolitan Police Authority (2008: 52).
[248] *The Guardian*, 24 January 2000.
[249] Under powers now contained in the Terrorism Act 2000, Sch 7.

husband and child.[250] Although well within the guidance given in the relevant Code of Practice, this examination was highly intrusive and upsetting.

As we have seen, PACE searches are commonly used to gather intelligence. Hence those using the streets can find themselves almost as closely 'examined' as those who undergo an anti-terrorism stop when seeking to enter England and Wales. As one told Choongh:

If they see me on the street they come straight over, pull my jacket off and start searching me, being rough with me. They ask me a lot of questions about my mates, who I've been with, what's happening – 'What can you tell me?', 'What can you tell us today?', that's what they say, 'Or we might have to take you down the station' (Choongh 1997: 45).

As this last example shows, not all searches conform to the Code of Practice. Hillyard recounts a number of instances where women, in particular, were humiliated by examining officers. One said that: 'It felt like rape' when her diaries and letters were read in front of her, another was both distressed and outraged when two officers read her diary (including her noting of her periods) aloud to each other. Sometimes it appears the police intend to humiliate those they search as part of a policy of intimidating those they see as 'undesirables' or 'police property'. The stop-search power becomes just one among an array of coercive devices such as the power to 'move on' those deemed to be obstructing the highway, the right to question people regardless of the level of suspicion (so long as the person questioned is not actually detained), the discretion to enforce the law harshly and the ability to make it known to someone that they are under police surveillance.[251] A homeless person quoted by Carlen (1996: 136–7) conveys this well:

They [police] pulled me up once. Had me fuckin' suitcase. He said, 'What's in there?' I said, 'Mind your own business, cos I ain't doing anything wrong.' And he said, 'We want to open it.' He checked me suitcase, got in the van and fucked off. Left me stuff all over the floor; never put it back! And they follow you. They've got a habit of when you're walking on the street – they follow you.

As does this drug user quoted by Lister et al (2008: 42):

soon as they see you, they're collaring you and they PNC'ing you[252] and they're stopping you, and they're embarrassing you in the street by making you spreadeagle on the car while they search you, or throwing you in the back of the van and strip searching you, just trying to

---

[250] All the terrorist legislation examples are from Hillyard (1993: ch 3). See ch 1, 11.2 for other examples. The specific anti-terrorist power to exclude was repealed by the Terrorism Act 2000 although Walker (2002a: 31) points out that the notion of exclusion lingers on in other legislation.

[251] See, for example, the case of the 30-year-old black social worker who appears to have been harassed in a variety of ways by officers from one police station in seven separate, but clearly related, incidents variously involving stop-search, mockery, arrest and overnight detention (case dismissed by the court the following morning), threats of arrest, handcuffing in public and a strip-search: Havis and Best (2004: 26–7).

[252] This refers to the carrying out of an identity and criminal records check using the Police National Computer.

belittle you in public. Just to embarrass you in public because people walking by are looking at you getting searched and that...it really pisses me off, it's like invading me privacy.

The invasion of liberty is felt more deeply still if it is, or is perceived to be, a product of prejudice or racism, which, in the light of the discussion in 2.3, is an understandable perception. The post-Macpherson research by Bland et al (2000: 87) confirmed that the manner in which the police exercise their powers is a crucial determinant of whether their actions were regarded as legitimate: 'It's not what they say, it's how they say it'. The result of all this is that BME people are significantly more likely than whites to report feeling upset, embarrassed or angry about being stopped (Allen et al, 2006: table 2.07). Asked what improvements they would like to see, young people who had been stop-searched asked that the police: 'Be more polite, less hostile, give reason...'; 'Stop being racist', and 'If they were less aggressive and listened to what I say...' (NACRO, 1997: 45–6). One Pakistani young adult described his interaction with the police as follows:

their exact words were, yeah (and I've got witnesses because I was with two other people, yeah) was: 'Don't fuck me about right, and I won't fuck you about, where have you got your drugs?'(Bland et al 2000: 82).

Bland et al (2000: 82) found that black people were far less likely than Asian or white people to report any positive experiences of respectful treatment by the police. Dissatisfaction is higher than average for the young and unemployed too.[253]

Vulnerable people are also likely to be badly affected by stop-search. An 11-year-old boy stop-searched at the climate camp discussed in 2.4.3 was 'crying and shaking' because he had a sticker, and heard that the police were confiscating them; he feared he would 'go to prison' for this.[254]

In other words, dissatisfaction among those who are stopped is directly related to membership of those groups which are disproportionately stopped. Either, stop for stop, the police treat members of these groups worse than they do others, or being in a group which believes itself to be targeted creates sensitivity – which is another way of saying that the stop is, or is perceived to be, a greater invasion of their freedom. In reality both of these explanatory factors are at work here. Thus, increased use of the power has an exponential effect on the resentment it causes. In many of the examples given here, the PACE and the Code of Practice were adhered to, but the encounters were nonetheless humiliating or aggravating. In evaluating the impact and value of stop-search much more needs to be examined than how far the police follow the rules. In January 2010, the European Court of Human Rights in *Gillan* adopted a similar form of analysis to that presented above, holding that:

the use of the coercive powers conferred by the legislation to require an individual to submit to a detailed search of his person, his clothing and his personal belongings amounts to a

---

[253] Bucke T, *Ethnicity and Contacts with the Police: Latest Findings from the British Crime Survey* (Home Office Research Findings No 59) (London: Home Office, 1997). Similar findings are reported by Sharp and Atherton (2007).   [254] *The Guardian*, 7 May 2009.

clear interference with the right to respect for private life. Although the search is undertaken in a public place, this does not mean that Article 8 is inapplicable. Indeed, in the Court's view, the public nature of the search may, in certain cases, compound the seriousness of the interference because of an element of humiliation and embarrassment.[255]

We welcome the realism evident in this passage (if not the unnecessarily gendered language) and wait with interest to see if the Government and the police acknowledge its force.

2.5.3 Stop-search and police-community relations

The notions of 'policing by consent' and 'community policing' are not as straightforward as they sound, and the assumptions on which they are based are questionable.[256] However, in so far as these notions are tenable and desirable, the negative impact on them of *indiscriminate* use of stop and search needs to be considered.[257] Community is itself a loaded term, of course, and the reality is that society is made up of overlapping networks of relationships based on work, age, blood, friendships, interests, geography, religion and so forth. Each 'community' will have its own set of unique relations with the police which are likely to vary over time. Space precludes fine-grained analysis of all these permutations so here we will focus on race, because, as we have seen, stop-search is experienced as particularly demeaning by large sections of ethnic minority communities.[258] While the examples in this chapter of manifestly racist stop-searches are unusual, such experiences are widely disseminated and long remembered. They form part of the collective memory of those who come frequently into contact with the police, whether as suspects, volunteers, witnesses or victims,[259] spreading out even into the ranks of 'respectable', white, middle-class society.[260] In other words a minority of racist or aggressive officers can do immense damage to police-community relations,

---

[255] *Gillan and Quinton v the United Kingdom* (App No 4158/05) Judgment 12 January 2010 [63].

[256] There is a contradiction between the aspiration to foster community solidarity and the encouragement of an informant culture, which is increasingly the direction of 'proactive policing'. See McConville M and Shepherd D, *Watching Police, Watching Communities* (London: Routledge, 1992) and Gordon P, 'Community Policing: Towards the Local Police State' in Scraton P (ed), *Law Order and the Authoritarian State* (Milton Keynes: Open UP, 1987).

[257] Even those sections of the community who experience high levels of stop-search do not generally question the need for the *existence* of this police power: Fitzgerald (1999: ch 2); Stone and Pettigrew (2000: 29); Fitzgerald et al (2002: 45). Rather the public favours more restrained, discriminating and respectful use of stop-search. Similarly, academics such as Mooney and Young (2000) argue that stop-search performance indicators should focus on 'yield' (ie the achievement of a high rate of successful detections of serious crimes) rather than 'activity' (numbers of stop-searches carried out).

[258] It is indicative that whereas the age and gender profile of those using the formal police complaints system in relation to stop-search practices is little different from the total population using that system, black complainants are responsible for 40% of all stop-search complaints compared with just 10% of all complaints (Havis and Best 2004: 47).

[259] Fitzgerald et al (2002: 49, 92–3); Bland et al (2000: 82); Britton (2000b). The fact that stop-search usually takes place in public increases its collective impact: Stone and Pettigrew (2000: 11).

[260] See Loader and Mulcahy (2003: esp 156–61).

as more enlightened officers are only too aware.[261] When the issue of racist policing becomes a matter of high public profile, as through the Stephen Lawrence Inquiry, or the broadcasting of 'The Secret Policeman', the sense of collective injustice is reinforced still further. But simply rooting out overtly racist police officers will not restore confidence in the fairness of policing, given the continuing undercurrent of more subtle forms of direct and indirect racial discrimination. What also needs to be addressed is the 'pervasive and deeply entrenched' sense amongst police officers of the 'suspicousness' of black people[262] (which leads to large-scale direct racial discrimination, albeit not accompanied by racist language), and the false assumption that the extensive use of stop-search is justified by the policing benefits it achieves (which leads to large-scale indirect racial discrimination). For the evidence is clear that these more subtle manifestations of discrimination have also provoked enormous resentment amongst ethnic minority communities.[263] This is now recognised, in relation to s 44 powers at any rate, by the Metropolitan Police anti-terrorism chief and by Lord Carlisle (the government-appointed independent reviewer of anti-terrorism legislation). The latter recently said: 'S 44 is over-used...and that is causing alienation to some communities.'[264]

Scarman blamed 'unimaginative and inflexible' tactics (culminating in stop and search sweeps such as Swamp 81) for the fact that relations in Brixton had 'been a tale of failure' (Scarman, 1981: para 4.43). At the time PACE was introduced, the Conservative MP John Wheeler understandably warned that 'the principal casualty [of the widening of stop and search powers] is likely to be a worsening of police community relations',[265] a view which was supported by Home Office research at the time.[266] Subsequent research has confirmed the tensions that now exist, particularly in economically deprived urban areas, where the police are called upon to deal with manifestations of social problems (such as high unemployment, sub-standard housing, and inadequate youth services) that are clearly not of their making. Keith quotes a police officer who says of Brixton: 'The hatred on the streets is so awful that you have to conform to the views of the rest of the [police] group to survive.'[267] A WPC working in a deprived borough of London told Fitzgerald et al (2002: 97) that '*here*, you even *dare* to say hello to anyone and you get the death stare...' And research by Hallsworth (2006: 303–7) into 'gaunt, depressing estates' in inner London found that 'the police themselves would not enter them unless in company...the sense of anger directed towards the police by local street youth was palpable...'

The police have their own collective memory in which hostile and occasionally violent interactions with black people and communities (including riots) loom much

---

[261] 'I've seen behaviour in the past that was absolutely atrocious...it only takes a couple of people to destroy all the good work': sergeant quoted by Fitzgerald (1999: ch 4).

[262] Fitzgerald M and Sibbitt R, Ethnic monitoring in police forces: A beginning (Home Office Research Study 173 (London: Home Office, 1997) p 66.   [263] See, for example, Clancy et al (2001: 73–8).

[264] The Guardian, 7 May 2009. This report also quotes the Metropolitan anti-terrorism chief, who argues for reduced use of s 44 (see 2.2.2.2).   [265] Quoted in Brogden (1985: 99–100).

[266] Clarke R and Hough M, Crime and Police Effectiveness (Home Office Research Study No 79) (London: HMSO, 1984).   [267] Keith M, Race, Riots and Policing (London: UCL Press, 1993) p 130.

larger than any positive interactions.[268] Cop culture accordingly generates anxieties which manifest themselves in the way the police deal with black people, both as suspects and victims. Fitzgerald and Sibbitt (1997: 41) quote one officer saying: 'The Japanese and the Chinese, culturally speaking, are very respectful. With black people we often prepare ourselves for the abuse in advance, or the knives (which is again a cultural thing).' Another recognised that a spiral of mutual suspicion, aggression and hostility had set in which would be difficult to break. Some officers 'conjure up an image of near warfare in terms of how they perceive the policing of the local community' (NACRO 1997: 41).

If people believe the police to be against them – whether or not this belief is justified – then they are far less likely to participate in community policing. This is important because of the huge overlap between the suspect population and the victim/witness population. For example, in London, Fitzgerald et al (2002: 49, 88) found that 55% of those stopped in the previous year by the police had also sought contact with the police in that period (typically to report a crime). They also found that black people were far less willing to help the police by reporting a crime or acting as a witness than Asian or white people. The authors of the NACRO survey found that the members of the community to whom they spoke who had been stop-searched at least once, and who were predominantly black, were in the main unwilling to help the police and would in many cases not even call the police if they needed help themselves.[269] As one said: 'If the police want co-operation they must earn it. Lack of trust is a two-way street. If they don't trust us we don't trust them either' (NACRO, 1997: 45).

Just as cop culture divides individuals into 'rough' and 'respectable', so it divides areas similarly. McConville and Shepherd (1992: 140) were discussing with an officer a 'Neighbourhood Watch' scheme in a middle class area which was surrounded by working class communities. Asked whether the new scheme would spread into the surrounding areas the officer replied, 'No, it's them that the scheme is protecting members from.' Loss of cooperation from those areas would not worry the police, who have low expectations of them in the first place. Those who become victims in these areas are less likely to be thought of as the kind of 'genuine' people the police see themselves as protecting (Reiner, 2000: 94) and this appears to be reflected in the service they receive.[270] If keeping black people in check is an implicit objective of the police, then the absence of a cooperative relationship and of information that might lead to a detection is a subsidiary matter. Exactly the same could be said in relation to Asian people about the way the Terrorism Act provisions are used. Police practices which exclude and humiliate socially marginal people and produce few of the crime

---

[268] For a discussion of how young people may be provoked by the insensitive use of police powers into defiant gestures which in turn reinforce negative police perceptions of youth see Loader (1996: 153), and Hallsworth (2006: 306–7).   [269] See, similarly, Lister et al (2008: 52) and Sharp and Atherton (2007).

[270] Fitzgerald et al (2002: 69) found that the three factors that best predicted dissatisfaction amongst victims with the police service they had received were, in order of importance, being stopped on foot, coming from a manual background, and being stopped in a car.

control benefits claimed of them are plainly unjustifiable if the objective is to protect and enhance the freedom of all.

2.6 **Conclusion**

We have seen that ss 1–3 of PACE are not of great inhibitory effect. Why? Firstly, the main legal constraint – reasonable suspicion – is too vague to act as a standard by which most police actions can be judged. Secondly, the provisions for providing information and recording of searches are difficult to enforce. Thirdly, many pedestrian stops – probably most – are in legal terms achieved without the exercise of a power, and this provides the police with the opportunity to generate grounds for a subsequent search. Fourthly, Road Traffic Act powers give the police the same opportunity in relation to vehicle stops. Fifthly, these due process provisions envisage a model of policing which does not accord with 'cop culture', the modern reality of street policing, or its history. When the police comply with PACE safeguards they do so primarily because these serve policing goals (such as securing cooperation, or building up intelligence) rather than actually protecting suspects. Sixthly, even when the police do exercise discretion in accordance with the rules, the attitudes and values which underlie their suspicions influence the *manner* in which stop-search is conducted. This exacerbates the invasion of privacy which is inherent to stop-search. Seventhly, the remedies for unlawful stop and search are uncertain in scope, inadequate in operation and insufficiently stringent in effect. Finally, there are several powers outside ss 1–3 of PACE, many of which were created in the 1990s, which allow stop-search without even the nominal requirement that there be reasonable suspicion.

The result is that the police still primarily act according to working assumptions based on 'suspiciousness', ie hunch, incongruity and stereotyping on the basis of types of people, previous records and so forth. These are all crime control norms, rooted as they are in the world of professional experience and police culture. The police sometimes discover crime when acting upon their instincts, but such suspicion as they have is seldom in relation to any particular offence, and therefore rarely is it 'reasonable' in terms of the due process norms of s 1 of PACE. Stop and search in operation corresponds far more closely to the crime control model than the due process model to which the law is purportedly oriented, which means that s 1 of PACE is primarily presentational, legitimising and enabling. One important consequence of this is the over-representation of ethnic minority people in the stop-searched population, which in turn contributes to their over-representation in the arrested, prosecuted and imprisoned populations.[271]

It might be argued that to require the police to claim that they have 'reasonable suspicion' in relation to a particular offence when in fact they are simply generally

---

[271] As documented in summary form by Phillips and Bowling (2007).

suspicious is to encourage them to treat the provisions of the law with contempt (while pretending otherwise to suspects and courts). This cannot be healthy either for the law in general or for the regard in which the police are held. Would it be better either to allow stops on grounds of general suspicion or not to allow stops at all? The former option is not attractive from a due process perspective. Laws such as these could be seen, like speed limits, as broadly inhibitory, whereby no-one expects precise compliance, but blatant transgression is rare. Relaxing the limits might only encourage the police to overstep the mark once again. Policing on the streets might then be based on random stops rather than, as now, on general suspicion. Or, more likely, 'general suspicion' could become the basis for non-random stops that are even more discriminatory than is usual now. The shift already evident in the post-PACE law away from a requirement of individualised suspicion in favour of rules enabling risk-based, actuarial policing of entire social groups (the young, ethnic minorities, the homeless etc) would then be complete.

On the other hand, attempting to 'firm up' the law and make it more inhibitory might be both undesirable and impossible. Police behaviour on the street is inherently fact-finding – ie inquisitorial – and the skilful finding of facts requires streetwise knowledge, technique, and experience. Talking to people with their consent – the starting point for many stops and often the ending point too – can and should never be prevented. Imposing an adversarial due process structure onto this craft is an attempt to deny one of the key elements of what policing is about. If policing is more about general social control than detection of specific crimes, then this is all the more true. And if the managerialist ethos identified in ch 1 continues to reward officers for their 'productivity' (including arrests arising from stops) this will be more true still.

In ch 1 we argued that the purpose of criminal justice is, or should be, to promote freedom. This chapter has shown that the freedom of actual and potential victims is protected to some extent through the arrest, deterrent and information-gathering effects of stop-search. But the freedom of suspects is hugely violated on three levels: at the community level, certain groups in society disproportionately suffer from both the actual exercise of the power and the fear that it will be exercised when in public places; at the quantitative level, the chances of being repeatedly stop-searched are very high if one is a member of one or more of those groups; and at the qualitative level, the exercise of the power, especially when it is repeated, represents suffering for the suspect which, in its different way, is as real as the suffering of many a victim. Indeed in some ways the loss of freedom of suspects and victims is similar. In many cases both groups fear that the invasion will recur. Feelings of persecution and loss of control over one's life sometimes arise. Behaviour changes, in an effort to avoid recurrence. Further, when stop-search triggers offences as a reaction to it (as in the examples given in 2.5.3 above) and leads to the alienation of the community (and hence less assistance with crime-solving) freedom which is gained by stop-search is lost in the crimes which are not solved and which are even created.

Who is to weigh up the competing demands of crime control versus liberty? Those in positions of power in this debate (Royal Commissions, Members of Parliament and the government, Home Office and Ministry of Justice officials, senior police officers, and, at the local level, councillors and residents who turn up to neighbourhood policing team meetings[272] etc) are not a representative cross-section of society. The law is reviewed, made and implemented primarily by the white, middle-aged, middle classes, while those who are stopped and searched are primarily the marginalised elements of society: the young unemployed, the homeless, the mentally disordered, the Irish, black people, Asian people, drug users and all the other 'toe rags', 'scum' and 'losers' who attract the attention of the police. One section of society shapes the law (both in books and in action) which bears down on the other. It is easy for the decision-making community to decide that it is in 'society's' interests for suspects to have their liberty compromised and their privacy invaded, when those suspects are overwhelmingly drawn from the non-decision-making community. One fundamental question raised by stop and search in a divided society is how far police powers are used to help perpetuate existing structures of inequality, subordination and social exclusion.

Further reading

Bowling B and Phillips C, 'Disproportionate and Discriminatory: Reviewing the Evidence on Police Stop and Search' (2007) 70(6) MLR 936

Goldsmith C, 'Cameras, Cops and Contracts: What Anti-social Behaviour Management Feels Like to Young People' in Squires P (ed), *ASBO Nation: The Criminalisation of Nuisance* (Bristol: The Policy Press, 2008)

Hallsworth S, 'Racial Targeting and Social Control: Looking Behind the Police' (2006) 14 Critical Criminology 293

Lister S, Seddon T, Wincup E, Barrett S and Traynor P, *Street Policing of Problem Drug Users* (York: Joseph Rowntree Foundation, 2008)

Miller J, Bland N and Quinton P, *The Impact of Stops and Searches on Crime and the Community* (Police Research Series Paper 127) (London: Home Office, 2000)

Quinton P, Bland N and Miller J, *Police Stops, Decision-making and Practice* (Police Research Series Paper 130) (London: Home Office, 2000) pp 24–5

Stenson K and Waddington P, 'Macpherson, Police Stops and Institutionalised Racism' in Rowe M (ed), *Policing Beyond Macpherson* (Cullompton: Willan, 2007)

---

[272] See Moore S, 'Street Life, Neighbourhood Policing and "The Community"' in Squires (ed) (2008).

3

Arrest

The policeman was suspended from duty after the court heard a recording
in which he allegedly told the [16-year-old] youth during an arrest that 'If
you say one more fucking word, I'll smash your fucking Arab face in... This
is one that you won't fucking get off of at court, because I'll write it up
properly.' The court dismissed the public order charge against the youth, the
judge saying, 'I cannot believe anything these officers have told me'.[1]

Key issues

- arrest and its relationship to freedom
- the lawful and unlawful purposes of arrest
- the growth of preventive forms of arrest and quasi-arrest
- the legal basis for arrest, and reasonable suspicion
- the working rules shaping the patterns of arrest
- arrest, terrorism, and the rise of young, male Muslims as the new prime suspects
- domestic violence and arrest
- race, class and arrest
- the miserable experience of being arrested
- the lack of effective remedies for wrongful arrest

3.1 **Introduction: what is an arrest?**

In *Lewis v Chief Constable of the South Wales Constabulary*[2] it was stated that:

Arrest is a matter of fact; it is not a legal concept... Arrest is a situation... Whether a person has been arrested depends not on the legality of his arrest but on whether he has been
deprived of his liberty to go where he pleases.[3]

---

[1] *The Guardian*, 20 May 2005.
[2] [1991] 1 All ER 206 at 209–10, confirming *Spicer v Holt* [1977] AC 987.
[3] This definition was endorsed in *Dawes v DPP* [1995] 1 Cr App Rep 65. In this case, the offender broke
into a car which had been set up by the police to lock automatically when the door was closed, trapping him.
This was the point at which he was held to be arrested.

There need be no explicit statement of arrest; arrest occurs if it is made clear that the arrestee would be prevented from leaving.[4] The police can use such force as is reasonable in the circumstances to effect an arrest.[5]

While every arrest involves a deprivation of liberty to go where one pleases, it is not every such deprivation that amounts to an arrest. The police can interfere with people's freedom of movement in various ways that do not amount to arrest. One example is that the courts have accepted that the police may (temporarily) detain or restrain a person or persons for their own safety or in order to prevent an imminent breach of the peace without this amounting to an arrest (or a deprivation of liberty within the meaning of Art 5 of the European Convention on Human Rights (ECHR)).[6] And police community support officers (PCSOs) can detain for up to thirty minutes those who they believe have committed one of a broad range of offences or to be acting anti-socially and who refuse to provide their name and address (or provide one reasonably believed to be false).[7] Another example is that lawful searches of the person (during which the police may use such force as is reasonable to enable the search to take place, as by forcibly detaining them) are seen by the courts as falling short of an arrest.[8] While the borderline between arrests and other forms of restraint is incapable of precise definition, the main form and (official) function of arrest is the physical apprehension of a person with a view to detaining him or her at a police station in order to facilitate the investigation of an offence and/or to secure his or her appearance in court. Arrest can also be protective (as where drunks, children or the mentally ill are detained for their own welfare) and preventive (as where someone is formally arrested to prevent a breach of the peace). As we shall see, the preventive form of arrest has grown in importance in recent years.

Arrest often renders suspects powerless, humiliated or even terrified. The Philips Commission in the 1980s recognised this:

Arrest represents a major disruption to a suspect's life ... police officers are so involved with the process of arrest and detention that they fail at times to understand the sense of alarm and dismay felt by some of those who suffer such treatment.[9]

---

[4] *Shaaban Bin Hussien v Chong Fook Kam* [1970] AC 942 at 949. For recent confirmation, see *Fiak* (2005) EWCA Crim 2381. It follows from this that a trivial restraint of an individual, by, say, tugging someone's sleeve to attract their attention, is not an arrest: *Mepstead v DPP* [1996] Crim LR 111.

[5] Criminal Law Act 1967, s 3; Police and Criminal Evidence Act 1984, s 117.

[6] *R (on the application of Jane Laporte) v (1) Chief Constable of Gloucestershire Constabulary & Others* [2006] UKHL 55; *Austin and Another v Commissioner of Police for the Metropolis* [2009] UKHL 5 (both cases are discussed in 3.3.4).

[7] Police Reform Act 2002, s 38. The purpose of the detention is to allow a police officer to attend and formally arrest the suspect. PCSOs can give a detainee the option of going to a police station with them instead of waiting to be arrested.

[8] See, for example, *DPP v Meaden* [2004] 4 All ER 75 discussed in Healy P, 'Investigative Detention in Canada' [2005] Crim LR 98.

[9] Royal Commission on Criminal Procedure (RCCP), *Report* (Cmnd 8092) (London: HMSO, 1981) para 3.75.

That arrest can be distressing without the police deliberately abusing their powers is evident from the accounts provided by arrestees, such as the following:

Two of them turned to my husband and said, 'We are arresting you under the Prevention of Terrorism Act.' I'm not kidding you, I was glad I was sitting down because I could feel my stomach going down to my feet. The Birmingham Six flashed through my mind. This is how innocent people are picked up. Up to then I had thought that the police didn't pick up people who are completely innocent....[10]

Distress can give way to humiliation or even terror when the police do abuse their arrest powers. Abuse may take many forms, including arresting for an improper purpose or conducting the arrest in a deliberately disrespectful manner. Both forms of abuse appear in the following exchange between an arrestee named Natt and a police constable:

Natt:	Why am I being arrested?
PC:	You're just a pain in the arse ain't yer?
Natt:	Oh, God.
PC:	Why don't you go and set fire to yourself or something?
Natt:	You carry on arresting me without reason. Why?
PC:	Because you are a shit.
[later] Natt:	Why beat me? Why?
PC:	Because I like it.
Natt:	You like to beat me?
PC:	I got no respect for someone like you.

We know that this is an accurate report of what happened because Natt tape-recorded it, having been verbally abused when previously stopped by police officers.[11] It is difficult, however, to quantify the extent to which arrest powers are abused and harder still to uncover the motivations of police officers and other factors (such as institutional racism, as discussed in ch 2) that might help explain their behaviour. What is unquestionable is that the arrest powers provided to the police give them the opportunity to infringe people's freedom in a variety of significant ways, and that they should therefore be subject to careful scrutiny. At the same time, sensitive and proportionate use of the arrest power is vital to the effective disruption and investigation of crime. As in other areas of criminal justice, the law can be seen as striking a balance with a view to ensuring that the freedom-enhancing aspects of arrest outweigh the threats to freedom that inhere in coercive state power. That the law may neither have got this balance right nor be respected by the police in practice are key questions for consideration here.

In this chapter we therefore look at how far the police are, and should be, allowed to infringe the freedom of the individual through arrest. In other words, we will examine

---

[10] Hillyard P, *Suspect Community* (London: Pluto Press, 1993) pp 111–13.
[11] A fuller extract is provided in Holdaway S, *The Racialisation of British Policing* (Houndmills: Macmillan, 1996) pp 72–3.

the legal rules and how effective they are in controlling the use of this power. We will also look at what reasons for arrest are lawful. We shall see that arrest is used for many purposes, some more legitimate than others. As with stop-search, this means we have to understand the informal working rules which help to structure police discretion. Section 2.1 is as applicable to arrest as it is to stop-search, and the general points made in 2.3, on race discrimination, are also relevant. We also examine some forms of detention which are not defined as arrest, since it would be artificial to ignore these closely related infringements of liberty.

3.2 **Arrest and the purposes of criminal justice**

3.2.1 **The ostensible purposes of arrest**

There are several lawful purposes of arrest, with or without subsequent detention. The *traditional* purposes include securing someone's appearance at court who has breached a court order or failed to answer a summons or requisition (a written command to attend court);[12] as part of transit between court and prison; and holding someone in custody in order to charge them. Arrests for these reasons are all to facilitate an ongoing prosecution. They pose no great problems of principle or practice, and we will not be dealing with them in this chapter.

Another traditional use of arrest is for the arrestee's own protection. For example, someone who appears to be mentally disordered and in immediate need of care or control can be taken to a place of safety for up to 72 hours in order that a medical assessment can be undertaken. This power (deriving from s 136 of the Mental Health Act 1983) is not dependent on an offence having been committed but it may be used to arrest only those found in public places where a constable believes removal is necessary in the interests of that person or for the protection of others.[13] In practice,

---

[12] Prosecutors used to secure a court summons by 'laying an information' (ie, setting out the particulars of an alleged offence) before a court. Section 29 of the Criminal Justice Act 2003 now requires *public* prosecutors to proceed instead by way of a written charge and 'requisition' to attend court to answer it. The position regarding *private* prosecutors remains unchanged. For the sake of convenience the traditional term 'summons' will be used in this chapter to cover 'requisitions', not least because at the time of writing (June 2009) s 29 had yet to be implemented across the country.

[13] Coppen estimates that 11,000 mentally ill people will be taken to police cells every year under this provision and that they spend on average 12 hours in the police station, twice as long as those arrested for criminal offences. He adds that when new mental health legislation was mooted, the Police Federation and other bodies campaigned (unsuccessfully) to have police stations removed from the definition of a place of safety, with custody officers particularly concerned at having healthcare responsibilities inappropriately placed upon them: Coppen J, 'PACE: A View from the Custody Suite' in Cape E and Young R (eds), *Regulating Policing* (Oxford: Hart, 2008) pp 87–8. Instead s 44 of the Mental Health Act 2007 merely provides an explicit power to remove the mentally disordered from one place of safety to another, still subject to the overall limit of 72 hours. Whether this will result in mentally ill arrestees spending less time in the wholly unsuitable environment of a custody suite remains to be seen.

such preventive arrest powers can be used for other purposes, such as maintaining police authority, 'reassuring' the public, or managing people seen as carriers of 'risk'. Unfortunately we have no space to explore such protective powers in depth, notwithstanding their importance.[14]

The other traditional purposes of arrest are to prevent a crime (or a further crime) taking place, and to maintain public order. Arrests for these purposes are not always to facilitate prosecution, and there may not be enough evidence to prosecute at the time of arrest (although the use of investigative powers allied to arrest may result in such evidence emerging). This type of pre-emptive arrest appears to be growing in importance and is increasingly controversial. In April 2009, for example, more than 200 police from four different forces raided a peaceful meeting of environmental protesters held in a school and arrested 114 people on suspicion of conspiracy to commit aggravated trespass and criminal damage at Ratcliffe-on-Soar power station.[15] While in custody, the arrestees had their homes searched for evidence of the conspiracy. All were released without charge, but the police nonetheless imposed bail conditions that forbade any of them from approaching any power station.[16] Thus, both the initial arrest and the subsequent bail conditions imposed were pre-emptive in nature.

Preventive quasi-arrest powers have multiplied in recent years as part of the growing emphasis on risk management described in 1.7 and 2.5.2. For example, s 16 of the Crime and Disorder Act 1998 gave the police the power to 'remove' school age children in certain circumstances from public places, and take them to their school or other appropriate place. The aim here is not to take police or court action, but to deal with truancy and the crime problems which sometimes accompany it.[17] The same Act allows local authorities and Chief Constables to introduce child curfew schemes and s 15 allows the police to remove any child (unaccompanied by a responsible adult) found in breach of such a curfew to the child's place of residence (unless the officer reasonably believes that the child would suffer significant harm if taken there).[18] Section 30 of the Anti-Social Behaviour Act 2003 provides another example of legislation seeking risk management through restricting people's freedom of movement. In brief, areas reasonably believed to suffer persistent anti-social acts by 'groups' of two or more persons may be designated as dispersal areas. Designation provides individual police

---

[14] Because protective arrests make up a small proportion of all arrests, they are under-researched. But see Bean P and Nemitz T, *Out of Depth and Out of Sight* (Loughborough: University of Loughborough, Midlands Centre for Criminology, 1994); Young H, 'Securing Fair Treatment: An Examination of the Diversion of Mentally Disordered Offenders from Police Custody'(Unpublished Phd, Birmingham University, 2002).

[15] *The Guardian*, 14 April 2009; *The Observer*, 19 April 2009.

[16] The growth in the police power to impose bail conditions is charted in Cape E, 'PACE Then and Now: 21 Years of "Re-balancing"' in Cape and Young (2008: 214–19).

[17] See Leng et al, *Blackstone's Guide to the Crime and Disorder Act 1998* (London: Blackstone, 1998) pp 37–9.

[18] As amended by ss 48 and 49 of the Criminal Justice and Police Act 2001. This power has proved unpopular in practice, and the dispersal order with its related child removal power (see below) has effectively made it redundant. The police are, however, experimenting with 'voluntary' year-round child curfews, 'encouraging' under 10s to be off the street by 8pm and under 16s by 10pm: *Daily Mail*, 20 February 2009.

officers who reasonably believe that the presence in the area of particular groups of two or more persons has resulted, *or is likely to result*, in any members of the public being intimidated, harassed, alarmed or distressed with the power to direct those persons to disperse, or to leave the relevant locality (if not a resident within it) for up to 24 hours. Failure to comply with a direction is an offence.[19] And under s 30(6) of the 2003 Act, the police may, using reasonable force, remove persons under the age of 16 found in a dispersal area between 9pm and 6am to their place of residence. As with other similar pre-emptive powers, no particular restrictions appear on the face of the statute,[20] which means that 15-year-olds popping out to late-opening shops for their parents were potentially subject to the indignity of being marched back home by the police. It has been left to the courts to remedy Parliament's slap-dash work by reading in some fairly obvious, if minimal, due process restrictions to this and other powers.[21] Research suggests that dispersal orders, and the way they are used, are often based on poor evidence, disproportionate to the harm in question, ineffective, and aimed more at some sections of society than others.[22] This appears true of all the pre-emptive measures introduced in recent years in the name of tackling anti-social behaviour,[23] including anti-social behaviour orders (ASBOs),[24] which means that the arrest powers provided to back them up are inherently problematic.

Finally, many arrests, for a variety of offences, are made, at least ostensibly, with a view to developing a case against someone suspected of having already committed a specific criminal offence. A less traditional purpose of arrest, then, which developed in the late twentieth century, is in order to obtain or secure evidence. This evidence can come from a variety of sources, including interviews with witnesses, searches of property, collection of forensic evidence and questioning of the suspects themselves.[25]

---

[19] Another broadly drawn dispersal power is contained in s 27 of the Violent Crime Reduction Act 2006. This allows the police to require people to leave a locality and not return for up to 48 hours if they deem their presence likely to cause or to contribute to the occurrence of alcohol-related crime or disorder in that locality. Failure to comply is an offence.

[20] Other than that a local authority must be notified if the power is exercised (s 32(4)). For another example of this lax attitude by Parliament, see the discussion of *Gillan* in 2.2.2.2.

[21] Thus the Court of Appeal has ruled that this power cannot be used unless the child in question is involved in, or at risk from exposure to, actual or imminently anticipated anti-social behaviour: *R (on the application of W by his parent and litigation friend PW) v Comr of Police for the Metropolis & Others* [2006] EWCA 458 at para 35. See also *Bucknell v DPP* [2006] EWCH 1888 where it was held that it was wrong for a constable to seek to disperse two groups of black and Asian schoolchildren who had congregated to chat after school on a summer's afternoon in a designated dispersal area. There was no actual behaviour by the groups indicating harassment, alarm, intimidation or distress, and no member of the public had complained about their mere presence. The court thought that 'great care' was needed where the police acted on the basis simply of 'presence', and ruled that the characteristics of these groups alone were not, in the circumstances, capable of giving rise to the necessary reasonable belief.

[22] Crawford A and Lister S, *The Use and Impact of Dispersal Orders* (London: Policy Press, 2007).

[23] See the various chapters in Squires (ed) (2008).

[24] Nixon J and Hunter C, 'Disciplining Women: Anti-social Behaviour and the Governance of Conduct' in Millie A (ed), *Securing Respect* (Bristol: Policy Press, 2009).

[25] McConville M, *Corroboration and Confessions* (Royal Commission on Criminal Justice Research Study No 13) (London: HMSO, 1993) pp 24–36. This report includes a discussion of the levels of evidence

As this is now the main form and function of arrest, let us consider how different models of criminal justice view the relationship between arrest powers and the investigation of crime.

3.2.2 Models of criminal justice and arrest

Due process

Under this model, no-one should be arrested unless it is clear that they probably committed a specific offence. Normally such a determination should be made by a magistrate who would then issue a warrant authorising the police to arrest. In situations of necessity the model would accept that the police may act without prior authority, but only on hard evidence which would be subject to subsequent judicial scrutiny.

This model accepts that these standards would impair police efficiency, and that this is the price to be paid 'for a regime that fosters personal privacy and champions the dignity and inviolability of the individual'.[26] Moreover, if the police were to be given wider powers to arrest suspects for questioning, it is unlikely that all classes of society would suffer greater interference, since the outcry would be too great. Rather, police powers would 'be applied in a discriminatory fashion to precisely those elements in the population – the poor, the ignorant, the illiterate, the unpopular – who are least able to draw attention to their plight and to whose sufferings the vast majority of the population are the least responsive'.[27]

Crime control

The adherent of this model would argue that the police need broad powers of arrest which they can deploy without prior authorisation from a judicial body. They need to be able to round up known offenders from time to time to see if they are responsible for crimes occurring in the locality. They also need the power to act on their instincts by arresting suspicious looking characters. It may be that no crime will be detected by these methods, but the very fact of arresting such persons may prevent a planned crime. Periodic infringements of the liberty of known criminals may be enough to persuade them to leave the area or desist from their illegal activities.

The innocent have nothing to fear from such broad arrest powers. In the rare case where they are arrested by mistake, release will quickly follow. The police should therefore be given powers to arrest citizens irrespective of whether they are reasonably suspected

---

possessed by the police at the time of arrest, and how 'weak' arrests are strengthened. Also see Phillips C and Brown D, *Entry into the Criminal Justice System* (Home Office Research Study No 185) (London: Home Office, 1998) pp 43–4. The police may now also seek further evidence following arrest after allowing the suspect 'street bail' under Criminal Justice Act 2003, s 4 (amending PACE, s 30). See Hucklesby A, 'Not Necessarily a Trip to the Police Station' [2004] Crim LR 803.

[26] Packer H, *The Limits of the Criminal Sanction* (Stanford: Stanford UP, 1968) p 179.
[27] Packer (1968: 180).

of committing a particular crime. The standard should be no more than that a police officer honestly thinks that an arrest will serve the goal of crime control. Alternatively, the substantive laws must be so broadly defined that the reasonable suspicion hurdle can be easily overcome. A combination of vague laws and lax standards is ideal.

Freedom

Under this model, due process and crime control considerations are both regarded as relevant, but only when applied in a 'context-sensitive' manner and only in relation to the greater goal of promoting freedom. The model cautions against wide powers, and frequent use, of arrest, because every arrest which fails to prevent or solve a crime creates a twofold loss of freedom: the arrestee loses some liberty and privacy; and the time, money and resources wasted in the arrest will have not been used to protect potential victims (eg through street patrols) or to provide non-law enforcement public services.

This model would allow wide powers if they led to a potentially greater gain in freedom – for example, in relation to particularly serious crimes or where they would be more likely to solve a crime. In some situations it will be very likely that a crime has been committed and that the offender is one of a group of people. Without arresting them all it may not be possible to find out who is responsible. A classic example is where a child is abused by one or other parent, each of whom accuses the other. Another is where a house, shared by several people, is raided and drugs found, each occupant again disclaiming responsibility.

Strict due process would not allow any arrests in any of these situations as there is nothing to suggest that any one individual probably committed the crime in question. Crime control would allow them all to be arrested as one of the suspects in each situation is undoubtedly criminal. The freedom model would weigh the certain loss of freedom to the potential arrestees against the possible gain in freedom were the crimes to be solved. Whether arrest would be allowed or not would therefore depend in part on the seriousness of the crimes and on how many people fell within the group suspected. The arrest of the two parents would be more likely to be justifiable within the freedom model than would the arrest of the multiple occupants of the house with drugs. In the latter case, context-sensitivity would also require consideration of how dangerous the drugs are and community relations considerations of the kind discussed in 2.5.4.

We might think that we could best promote complete context-sensitivity if the police are given total discretion to take all these considerations into account on a case-by-case basis. However, this approach would ignore the discussion in the previous chapter (see 2.2) of the structural and cultural biases which affect the way discretion is exercised. Further, citizens want to know, and have a right to know, whether an arrest is lawful or not. Freedom is reduced both when people experience what they believe are arbitrary interventions in their lives and when they fear such interventions.[28] We therefore need to create rules which allow context-sensitivity yet also establish clearly

---

[28] See, for example, the evidence given on behalf of W in *R (on the application of W by his parent and litigation friend PW) v Comr of Police for the Metropolis & Others* [2006] EWCA 458.

what the police can and cannot do both in general and in relation to exceptional situations. These rules would take into account offence seriousness, the probability of solving the offence through arrest, the number of people whose liberty would be infringed by arrest, and the amount of liberty that arrest would erode (that is, for how long, and how undermining of dignity it would be). The availability of other methods of crime detection would also be relevant, as the freedom model is concerned to both facilitate the detection of crime and to discourage the erosion of liberty. We will return to these issues later in this chapter.

3.2.3 The place of arrest in the criminal process

If we look back at the development of the main form and function of arrest, a shift from a due process to a crime control model can be seen. Until the early part of the nineteenth century, magistrates determined whether or not someone should be prosecuted, usually on the basis of information provided to them by other enforcement agencies or private citizens. If they were satisfied by this evidence, they could issue a warrant for arrest or a summons to the defendant to appear in court at a later time. Some people were arrested first and then immediately brought before the magistrates, who, again, decided whether or not a prosecution should follow.[29] Arrest used simply to be a mechanism for bringing offenders to court.

Arresting in order to take an offender to court was, therefore, pointless unless evidence had already been gathered sufficient to justify a prosecution. Accordingly, the police or any other law enforcer used to investigate an offence and then arrest (or not) at the end of that investigation. This means that the investigation took place (in theory) before the police exercised coercive powers. As recently as 1969, the House of Lords found itself in *Shaaban Bin Hussien v Chong Fook Kam*[30] criticising the police for making:

a premature arrest rather than one that was unjustifiable from first to last. The police made the mistake of arresting before questioning; if they had questioned first and arrested afterwards, there would have been no case against them (at 949 per Lord Devlin).

In reality, and certainly by the middle of the twentieth century, many people 'helped the police with their inquiries' in the police station: they were not formally arrested but rather were portrayed as attending the police station voluntarily. If, as a result of this 'voluntary help', the police secured enough evidence to prosecute, they would arrest and bring the suspect before the magistrates; if they did not have enough evidence, the suspect was (eventually) released. Gradually, the legal fiction of 'helping the police with their enquiries' broke down, being in detention came to be seen as being under arrest, and so arrest moved nearer to the beginning of the investigative process. Arrest's main form and function became the forcible removal of a person

---

[29] See Sanders A, 'Arrest, Charge and Prosecution' (1986) 6 LS 257.
[30] *Shaaban Bin Hussien v Chong Fook Kam* [1970] AC 942.

from conditions of freedom to conditions of detention in the police station, in order to facilitate evidence gathering through interrogation.

This was formalised by the Criminal Law Act 1967, which created a wide range of 'arrestable offences', ie offences for which the police could arrest without obtaining a warrant from the magistrates. The Police and Criminal Evidence Act (PACE) 1984 opened the door still wider to arrest by making 'non-arrestable' offences arrestable in certain circumstances (such as where the suspect's name and address – needed for the service of a summons – could not reasonably be ascertained). Section 110 of the Serious Organised Crime and Police Act 2004 subsequently made *all* offences arrestable without warrant so long as the police have reasonable grounds for believing that it is necessary to arrest the person in question 'to allow the prompt and effective investigation of the offence or of the conduct of the person in question'.

The law now makes it difficult for the police to ask detailed questions of suspects prior to arrest.[31] Questioning away from the police station has been restricted in order to protect suspects, but with the ironic result that many arrests are 'premature' in the *Shaaban* sense. Freedom is accordingly lost through a more extensive use of arrest and detention, but possibly gained through greater protection of suspects under interrogation. Whether or not these changes have led to a net gain in freedom is unclear. In the 1960s and 1970s, pre-trial detention was secured unlawfully or quasi-lawfully through the mechanism of 'helping the police with their inquiries', but now it is secured openly and lawfully through the mechanism of arrest and detention. The legal rules which we shall be discussing are therefore legitimising rules (legitimising the 'helping the police with their inquiries' fiction) and enabling rules (enabling the police to act as they wish to do without fear of legal repercussions). The extent to which they are also inhibitory, preventing abuse of power through restrictions on their use, will be a key issue in this chapter and the next two.

3.2.4 The unofficial purposes of arrest

We have seen that arrest and prosecution are now entirely separate in both theory and practice. Anything can follow arrest and detention: no action at all, an official police warning, an 'on the spot' fine,[32] a police charge (a formal allegation forming the starting point for a prosecution) or, indeed, release followed by a summons to appear at court. Studies in the 1990s found that around 50% of all arrests lead to prosecution, although the exact figures varied according to offence type, police force and even police station.[33] More recently, the Home Office has revealed that just 31% of those aged 18 or over arrested for indictable offences in England and Wales are prosecuted.[34]

Arrest is now simply an exercise of police power which does not, in itself, determine the next stage. Arrest and detention now often has 'unofficial' purposes, some of which

---

[31] See discussion of the PACE Code of Practice C in ch 5.

[32] These are also known as 'penalty notices for disorder' and are discussed in ch 6.

[33] McConville et al, *The Case for the Prosecution* (London: Routledge, 1991); Phillips and Brown (1998: 81–3).

[34] Home Office, *Statistics on Terrorism Arrests and Outcomes Great Britain, 11 September 2001 to 31 March 2008*, Statistical Bulletin 04/09 (London: Home Office, 2009a) p 2.

amount to an abuse of power. Some arrests are to secure evidence of offences unrelated to the offences for which arrests are ostensibly carried out, committed either by the arrestees or by others.[35] Another purpose is to put the 'frighteners' on arrestees – to warn them not to take certain action or to punish them for actions they are believed to have carried out. Here, there is no intention to prosecute. Arrest and detention is used as a form of 'social disciplining'[36] or summary justice. Sometimes it appears that the police arrest someone in order to distract attention away from their own malpractice.[37] Another purpose is to control individuals and groups, especially in public order situations, again with no intention of prosecuting (see 3.4.2). Yet another purpose is to facilitate the construction of useful databases, since many forms of physical evidence (such as fingerprints, photographs and DNA samples) can only be forcibly taken from those under arrest (or, increasingly, under quasi-arrest).[38] We shall see that the courts often fail to acknowledge these 'unofficial' purposes of arrest, reducing their ability to restrain the police.[39]

It follows from all this that many more people are now arrested than once happened. A careful analysis by Hillyard and Gordon found that arrests rose over the whole period from 1981 (1.27m) to 1997 (1.96m), 'with a more rapid increase since PACE became law in 1986'.[40] The Home Office indicated in the late 1990s that 'just under 2 million persons suspected of committing an offence are arrested every year'.[41] Arrests for *notifiable* offences[42] rose from 1,277,900 in 1999/2000 to almost one and a half million in 2007/08.[43] It is not known precisely how many people are arrested each year: some people are arrested more than once; arrests for 'non-notifiable' (ie minor) offences are no longer included in the official statistics; if the arrestee is released before being taken to a police station it may not be recorded;[44] and not all notifiable arrests are actually notified to those responsible for compiling the statistics.[45]

---

[35] See, for example, *Chalkley and Jeffries* [1998] 2 Cr App Rep 79, discussed in 3.4.2 below.

[36] Choongh S, *Policing as Social Discipline* (Oxford: Clarendon Press, 1997).

[37] See the distressing case of *Paul v Humberside Police* [2004] EWCA Civ 308.

[38] The growth of powers to take physical evidence from suspects since PACE was enacted is charted in Cape (2008: 210–14). The Government intends to amend the law to prohibit arrests made solely for the purpose of routinely taking fingerprints and DNA to add to national databases: Home Office, *PACE Review: Government Proposals in Response to the Review of the Police and Criminal Evidence Act 1984* (London: Home Office, 2008) paras 7.14–7.15. Once arrested, however, collection of these types of evidence will remain routine; thus the incentive to arrest solely or partly in order to enhance databases will remain.

[39] See discussion of *Plange v Chief Constable of South Humberside* in 3.4.2 below.

[40] Hillyard P and Gordon D, 'Arresting Statistics: The Drift to Informal Justice in England and Wales' (1999) 26 JLS 502 at 508.

[41] Home Office, *Statistics on Race and the Criminal Justice System 1998* (London: Home Office, 1999) p 19.

[42] Notifiable offences (notified by the police to the Home Office) include all indictable and triable eitherway offences and some closely associated summary offences.

[43] Povey and Smith, *Police Powers and Procedures England and Wales 2007/08*, Home Office Statistical Bulletin 07/09 (London: Home Office, 2009) table 1A.

[44] Under s 30(8) of PACE such releases from arrest must be recorded by the constable, but whether this always happens, and such arrests always find their way into the statistics, is not known. The legal basis for de-arresting a suspect was for some time unclear but s 4(4) of the Criminal Justice Act 2003 amends PACE by requiring the police to release without bail someone arrested outside the police station where there are no longer any grounds for keeping that person under arrest or releasing them on bail.

[45] Hillyard and Gordon (1999).

Readers may begin to be worried by now. In a population of little over 53 million people there are probably well over two million arrests per year, many of which are frightening for the arrestee. While it might be thought that these figures suggest that the police arrest whenever they can, this is far from the truth. Chapter 2 showed that the law is permissive. It allows the police to exercise all manner of powers, but does not require them to do so. In reality, the police decide not to arrest far more often than they decide to actually do so. This varies from offence to offence. Officers do not ignore bank robberies and rapes just because they are not obliged to arrest suspects. But in some situations certain types of offence are routinely ignored or dealt with informally. Waddington, for example, comments that in the early 1990s 50,000 supporters of the miners' union and 150,000 trade union demonstrators protested against pit closures without one arrest being made. 'On some occasions the police would have been lawfully entitled to make wholesale arrests, but they consciously chose not to do so.'[46] Similarly, it appears that the police rarely use the arrest powers provided under the Criminal Justice and Public Order Act 1994 in relation to 'raves' and 'trespass', although the threat to use these powers often seems effective.[47] It follows that much of what the police do is not overtly coercive. They frequently use fewer powers than they are entitled to, being influenced by the general considerations examined in 2.1. Now that arrest has become primarily a policing resource, one question for this chapter is what leads them to arrest one person, in one context, and not another person in a different context.

3.3 **The legal basis for arrest**

3.3.1 **With warrant**

The move away from arrest warrants, which is part of the general move away from judicial supervision of police powers, means that most arrests are now made by the police acting on their own knowledge and initiative rather than acting under the supervision of magistrates. It mirrors the decline in the use of summonses (issued by magistrates) and search warrants (also issued by magistrates). Nowadays, the police themselves generally decide what powers they will exercise and when. This is a crime control approach.

Warrants are nowadays mainly used when a suspect fails to appear in court to answer a summons or to answer bail. In these circumstances, the police or prosecutor

---

[46] Waddington PAJ, *Liberty and Order* (London: UCL Press, 1994) p 39.

[47] Bucke T and James Z, *Trespass and Protest: Policing under the Criminal Justice and Public Order Act 1994* (London: Home Office, 1998); Cowan D and Lomax D, 'Policing Unauthorised Camping' (2003) 30 JLS 283.

would apply to the magistrates for a warrant,[48] which would usually be granted straight away, authorising the arrest of that suspect. A relatively new device is the European Arrest Warrant, which is designed to facilitate cross-border law enforcement within the European Union. In essence, the scheme works by each EU country agreeing to enforce such a warrant issued by the judicial authorities of any other EU country.[49] This simplifies pre-existing extradition procedures, watering down domestic judicial oversight.[50]

3.3.2 Summary arrest: the withering away of the 'non-arrestable' offence

We have already noted that all offences are now arrestable without warrant. In order to appreciate the significance of this (and to enable readers to make sense of the research and statistics published prior to this change), it is crucial to understand how the law developed after the introduction of the concept of the 'arrestable offence' in the Criminal Justice Act 1967. The Royal Commission on Criminal Procedure (Philips Commission) wanted to constrain the use of the wide arrest powers introduced by the 1967 Act.[51] It believed that coercive powers like arrest were often used unnecessarily, as variations between police forces in the use of arrest, on the one hand, and summons, on the other were huge.[52] In other words, it seemed that similar offences in similar circumstances were subject to arrest, detention and charge in some areas, where in other areas they would be subject to a summons to appear in court on a specified date.

These concerns were reflected in PACE although not in the way the Royal Commission had envisaged. Under s 24 of PACE the police were entitled to arrest anyone for an 'arrestable offence' without a prior warrant. Any offence punishable by a jail term of five years or more was arrestable (PACE, s 24(1)), as were miscellaneous other offences (PACE, s 24(2) and (3) and sch 1A). This broadly re-enacted the pre-PACE law as created by the 1967 Criminal Justice Act, although many additional 'arrestable offences' were created subsequent to PACE, adding considerably to the complexity of the law.[53] The concept covered a wide range of over 100 offences, because most English legislation provides for maximum punishments much heavier than the normal punishments. Nonetheless, the use of the concept of arrestable offences meant that arrest powers were different according to which side of the 'more serious' or 'less serious' definitional divide an offence fell. For 'more serious' offences it was simply assumed by

---

[48] Under the Magistrates' Courts Act 1980, s 125, as amended by PACE, s 33.

[49] Provision for the scheme's operation in England and Wales is made by the Extradition Act 2003.

[50] See further Caolan E, 'Reciprocity and Rights under the European Arrest Warrant Regime' (2007) 123 LQR 197.

[51] Royal Commission on Criminal Procedure, Report (Cmnd 8092) (London: HMSO, 1981) paras 3.75–3.79.

[52] Gemmill R and Morgan-Giles R, *Arrest, Charge and Summons* (Royal Commission on Criminal Procedure, Research Study No 9) (London: HMSO, 1981).   [53] See Cape (2008: 196–8).

those framing the legislation that arrest should be the normal way of processing those suspected of such offences.

What of the less serious 'non-arrestable' offences? Section 25 of PACE made such offences arrestable under certain circumstances. First, the police had to have reasonable grounds for suspecting that an offence had been, or was being, committed or attempted. Unlike with arrestable offences, they could not arrest someone who was *about to* commit a non-arrestable offence unless the suspect's behaviour amounted to a criminal attempt (ie, an offence in its own right). Second, arrest for such an offence was allowed only if it appeared that service of a summons was inappropriate or impractical because any of the 'general arrest conditions' specified in s 25 were satisfied. The conditions concerned with the inappropriateness of using a summons were that the police had reasonable grounds for believing that arrest was necessary to protect a child or other vulnerable person from the suspect or to prevent the suspect hurting anyone, suffering physical injury, causing loss of or damage to property, committing an offence against public decency, or causing an unlawful obstruction of the highway. The 'impracticality conditions' were that the police did not know the name of the suspect or a suitable address for service of a summons, or had reasonable grounds for doubting whether any name or address furnished by the suspect was correct.

What the impracticality conditions were concerned with was the probability of a suspect answering a summons and being traced if he or she did not do so, for summons is the only way to proceed against someone who is not arrested. Section 25 allowed the police to arrest, even for minor offences (such as motoring or litter offences), if this was the only way of getting an offender to court. It was not enough for the police to consider that it would be more convenient or efficient to arrest rather than summons. By contrast, the inappropriateness conditions were concerned with the perceived need to arrest in order to prevent the suspect causing further harm. This opened the door to arrest for minor offences, particularly in public order contexts.

A Home Office review of PACE and its Codes and related legislation[54] gave rise to the Serious Organised Crime and Police Act 2005. In the name of modernising police powers and simplifying the 'complex and often bewildering array of [arrest] powers and procedures'[55] (which post-PACE legislation had created) the PACE distinction between arrestable and non-arrestable offences was swept away by s 110 of the 2005 Act. This section inserts a new s 24 into PACE, providing that the police may arrest without warrant anyone who is or who is reasonably suspected to be:

- about to commit an offence;
- in the act of committing an offence; or
- guilty of an offence already committed.

---

[54] On arrest, see Home Office, *Modernising Police Powers to Meet Community Needs – A Consultation Paper* (2004b).   [55] Ibid, p 4.

This power of summary arrest is exercisable only if the police have reasonable grounds for believing that it is *necessary* to arrest the person in question for any one of the reasons specified in the new s 24(5). These reasons mirror the old 'general arrest' conditions concerned with the practicality and appropriateness of proceeding by way of a summons but, crucially, add two new reasons for proceeding by way of arrest. The effect of these two additions are that the police may now arrest for any offence if they reasonably believe that arrest is necessary either to allow the prompt and effective investigation of the offence or of the conduct of the person in question, or to prevent any prosecution for the offence from being hindered by the disappearance of the person in question.

These 'enabling' rules are offensive to the 'freedom' approach. To allow arrest for *any* offence if, for instance, the offender is thought unlikely to answer a summons fails to balance the certain freedom lost by arrest with the possible loss of freedom involved when it is only feared (not known) that an offender will not answer a summons. A failure to answer a summons is not necessarily fatal to the aim of enlarging freedom through bringing offenders to justice given the availability of arrest for non-appearance. Some suspects might, of course, abscond and disappear completely, but should this possibility lead us to infringe through arrest the freedom of all suspects (the innocent as well as the guilty), no matter how trivial the offences they are suspected of? The freedom approach, in other words, would take into account such factors as seriousness of offence, the degree of probability of what is feared (non-appearance) actually occurring, and so forth. In practice the broad-brush distinction of the old PACE law between arrestable (more serious) and non-arrestable (less serious) offences might have been justifiable in order to have a workable system. The 2005 Act, however, simply prioritises considerations of police efficiency over the interests of suspects and thus eschews even such rough context sensitivity in favour of naked crime control. A further illustration of this is that the 2005 Act (unlike PACE as originally enacted) allows arrests of people who are, or who are reasonably thought to be, *about* to commit a *trivial* offence.

Finally, in principle, due process adherents might welcome the fact that the police may now only arrest where there is a genuine need to do so (even if they might consider the statutory definition of 'need' to be much too broad). The Code of Practice on arrest emphasises the importance of this necessity principle:

1.2 The right to liberty is a key principle of the Human Rights Act 1998. The exercise of the power of arrest represents an obvious and significant interference with that right.

1.3 The use of the power must be fully justified and officers exercising the power should consider if the necessary objectives can be met by other, less intrusive means. Arrest must never be used simply because it can be used. Absence of justification for exercising the powers of arrest may lead to challenges should the case proceed to court. When the power of arrest is exercised it is essential that it is exercised in an non-discriminatory and proportionate manner.[56]

---

[56] A new Code of Practice was introduced solely to cover arrests made under the amended s 24. It sets out in detail the basis on which arrest can be done, what information has to be given to arrestees etc: Home Office, PACE Code of Practice G, 2005. It took effect on 1 January 2006.

However, it is unlikely that the new statutory scheme will make any difference to actual police practice. Under PACE the police became used to arresting with a view to detaining in order to secure evidence through questioning.[57] It is implausible to suppose that they will in future often lack the belief that arrest is necessary 'to allow the prompt and effective investigation of the offence or of the conduct of the person in question'. It is equally implausible to suppose that, even if this standard procedure is challenged, the courts would pour much restrictive content into the requirement that this belief be 'reasonable'. Much more likely is an increase in the numbers of arrests for non-serious offences now that the statutory necessity principle embraces the notion of 'prompt and effective investigation'. The increase in the number of arrests since the new s 24 came into effect on 1 January 2006 supports this argument.[58] In short, the necessity principle seems to be playing a purely presentational role – giving the appearance of due process while doing nothing to promote its substance.

3.3.3 Terrorism and arrest

Terrorism-related arrests have long been subject to specific arrest powers which act as a gateway to enhanced investigatory powers such as longer than normal periods of detention for questioning. Under the 1979 Prevention of Terrorism Act (PTA) the police could arrest for various terrorist offences simply on 'suspicion' that a terrorist offence had been, or was about to be, committed. In *Fox, Campbell and Hartley v UK* (1990) 13 EHRR 157 it was held that the ECHR, Art 5(1) requirement of 'reasonable suspicion' could not be dispensed with even in the exceptional circumstances of terrorism. The PTA was replaced by the Terrorism Act 2000 and the Anti-terrorism, Crime and Security Act (ATCSA) 2001. Arrest on mere suspicion is not allowed, except that Part IV of the ATCSA originally allowed indefinite imprisonment (without trial) of foreign persons denied asylum on grounds of national security or international crimes. This required the government to derogate from the ECHR, on the grounds of the scale and nature of the threat of terrorism,[59] but the House of Lords subsequently held these grounds to be invalid.[60] The government's response to the judgment was to introduce control orders which can amount to a form of 'house arrest'.[61] Thus we saw

---

[57] This habit was reinforced by the fact that custody officers, responsible under PACE for assessing the necessity of detaining suspects presented to them at the police station, routinely authorised detention for questioning (see further ch 4).

[58] Arrests for notifiable offences fluctuated around the 1.3 million mark between 1999 and 2005 but soared to 1.48 million in 2006/07, before declining slightly to 1.47 million in 2007/08: Povey and Smith (2009: 13). The shift to making all offences arrestable is thus associated with an increase of over 100,000 arrests for notifiable offences per year, the 'necessity principle' notwithstanding.

[59] Despite the international nature of the 'war on terrorism' ushered in by '9/11', to which ATCSA was a response, the UK is the only one of 41 states ratifying the ECHR who derogated from it over this matter: Tomkins A, 'Legislating against Terror: The ATCS Act 2001' [2002] PL 205. See generally Walker C, 'Terrorism and Criminal Justice – Past, Present and Future' [2004] Crim LR 311.

[60] *A & Ors v Secretary of State for the Home Department* [2004] UKHL 56.

[61] Prevention of Terrorism Act 2005.

in 1.6.4 that 'house arrests' stretching to 14 hours per day have been upheld as lawful by the House of Lords.

There remain three other principal concerns. First, there is the main provision in the 2000 Act: s 41(1) 'A constable may arrest without a warrant a person whom he reasonably suspects to be a terrorist.' Being 'a terrorist' is not, as such, an offence. Terrorism can cover a wide range of violence – actual and threatened, to property as well as persons – and includes people who help terrorists, or (in ATCS Act 2001, s 21(2)) have 'links with an international terrorist group'. This can include those who 'support' such groups, which could be a major breach of freedom of speech,[62] or who (under s 1 of the Terrorism Act 2006) 'glorify' terrorism. One might 'support' the aims of terrorist groups whilst deploring their methods, so that Walker is concerned that, for example, animal rights protesters could be arrested under this provision, and that this would be acceptable under the ECHR.[63]

Second, what is 'reasonable suspicion' in the terrorism context? In *Fox, Campbell and Hartley v UK* (1990) 13 EHRR 157, the Court said that:

What may be regarded as 'reasonable' will however depend on all the circumstances...in view of all the difficulties inherent in the investigation and prosecution of terrorist-type offences in Northern Ireland, the 'reasonableness' of the suspicion justifying such arrests cannot always be judged according to the same standards as are applied in dealing with conventional crime. Nevertheless, the exigencies of dealing with terrorist crime cannot justify stretching the notion of 'reasonableness' to the point where the essence of the safeguard secured by Art 5 (1) is impaired...

This meant that the government had to furnish some information which could lead the court to accept the reasonableness of the suspicion. In that particular case the only basis for suspicion was the convictions of the suspects for terrorist acts seven years previously, so there was held to be a breach of Art 5 of the ECHR.

Third, for what purposes may there be an arrest? Article 5(1)(b) requires that in the absence of reasonable suspicion arrest may be made only pursuant to a 'lawful order of a court or...any obligation prescribed by law' (excepting some other technical reasons of no relevance here). In *McVeigh, O'Neill and Evans v UK* (1981) 25 DR 15 the applicants were arrested in Liverpool, when they arrived from Ireland, in order to be 'examined' (a procedure akin to extended stop, search and questioning specific to the terrorism legislation, discussed in 2.2.2). The European Commission on Human Rights (in a preliminary procedure to a Court hearing) decided that:

the existence of organised terrorism is a feature of modern life whose emergence since the Convention was drafted cannot be ignored any more than the changes in social conditions and moral opinion which have taken place in the same period...the Convention organs must always be alert to the danger in this sphere adverted to by the Court, of undermining or

---

[62] Tomkins (2002: 205).

[63] As was held in relation to similar PTA offences by the ECtHR in *Brogan* (1988) 11 EHRR 117. See Walker C, *Blackstone's Guide to the Anti-Terrorism Legislation* (Oxford: OUP, 2002), ch 5.

even destroying democracy on the ground of defending it [However] . . . some compromise between the requirements for defending democratic society and individual rights is inherent in the system of the Convention . . .

Applying that principle to the specific context of the case, the Commission decided that the requirement to be examined was a lawful obligation for the purposes of Art 5(1)(b), but only because of the limited circumstances (travel across a border), the 'threat from organised terrorism', and the fact that arrest and detention was rarely used to secure examinations.

In these cases the European Court is adopting a 'context-sensitive' approach which is consistent with the 'freedom' model.[64] However, whether its sensitivity is accurate depends on whether it is justified in its confidence that the UK government and its agencies rarely abuse these provisions. Hillyard estimates that, out of some 2,308 people arrested under the previous legislation between 1974 and 1981, 1,984 (86%) were released without any legal action being taken.[65] He argues that most of these arrests were information-gathering in purpose and that, with such a high no-action rate, it is implausible that there was reasonable suspicion in most of these cases. He points out that after major events there are often mass arrests. After the Woolwich and Guildford bombings of 1974, for example, 76 people were arrested, but only four – the 'Guildford Four' – were charged. Could there really have been 'reasonable suspicion' against the other 72, or even the majority of them?

Some have argued that, since 9/11 in 2001 and the July 2005 attacks on users of London's transport system Muslims (who make up less than 3% of the population in England and Wales) have increasingly become the new prime suspect community.[66] One high profile case occurred in April 2009 when the then Prime Minister Gordon Brown spoke of the police having foiled 'a very big terrorist plot' following a series of coordinated arrests of (mainly) Pakistanis in the north of England who had entered the country on student visas. In fact, all twelve arrestees were subsequently released without charge, even though eleven were held in police custody for a fortnight while they were interrogated and their homes and computers searched.[67] Given the breadth of the offences created under anti-terrorism laws, the objective basis for the initial suspicion against these arrestees must have been very thin indeed.

Official statistics on terrorism-related arrests and their outcomes were released for the first time in 2009, covering period of and the seven and a half years between 11 September 2001 and 31 March 2008. There were 1,471 such arrests in total and almost

---

[64] Another example of the Court's misplaced sense of context-sensitivity is its view that the Convention obligation to inform someone promptly of the reason for their arrest (discussed in 3.5) is discharged if the reason for the arrest becomes apparent in the interview. This is of little value if the reason for the provision is to reduce the initial disorientation of the suspect.   [65] Hillyard (1993: ch 4).

[66] See further Spalek et al, 'Minority Muslim Communities and Criminal Justice: Stigmatized UK Faith Identities Post 9/11 and 7/7' in Bhui H, Race & Criminal Justice (London: Sage, 2009); Pantazis C and Pemberton S, 'From the "Old" to the "New" Suspect Community: Examining the Impacts of Recent UK Counter-Terrorist Legislation' (2009) 49(5) BJ Crim 646, and 3.4.4.   [67] The Guardian, 22 April 2009.

two-thirds did not result in a charge.[68] Of the 521 charges, 222 were under terrorism legislation, 118 were for other terrorism-related criminal offences (such as conspiracy to murder or offences under the Explosive Substances Act 1883) and 162 were for non-terrorism related criminal offences (most notably, crimes of dishonesty).[69] Thus, 340 of the 1,471 arrests (23%) produced terrorism-related charges; 196 of these ended in conviction (102 of which were under terrorism legislation – the most frequent offence being possession of an article for terrorist purposes). Since 1 April 2005, 42% of terrorism-related arrestees have been of Asian ethnic appearance, although such people make up just 4.7% of the population in England and Wales; 77% of these arrestees were not subsequently charged with a terrorism-related offence.[70] Of the 117 terrorist prisoners in England and Wales on 31 March 2008, 65 self-defined their ethnicity as Asian or British Asian and 107 self-declared their religion to be Muslim.[71]

Views will naturally differ on what conclusions should be drawn from such statistics. Some of the more obvious points to make are:

- just over a dozen people a year (on average) have been convicted under terrorism legislation since 9/11;
- many of the total number of arrests and convictions are taking place under 'ordinary' (non-terrorist) legislation. It is plausible to suppose that such legislation might have served perfectly well for a large proportion of those that are now dealt with under terrorism laws. In other words, terrorism legislation may be less important than it appears to be;
- the non-charge and non-conviction rates mean that a large proportion of arrestees are being subjected to the special terrorism-related investigatory regime to no freedom-enhancing end; and
- the inherent losses of freedom this investigatory regime involves bears down on some communities more than others, thus fuelling concerns about the breadth and improper use of arrest powers.

3.3.4 Common law breach of the peace

The common law has long recognised that all citizens should have a power of arrest to prevent or end breaches of the peace. A breach of the peace is not a stand-alone offence, but a court can bind over someone arrested on this basis to be of good behaviour in future.

---

[68] 819 arrestees were released without any action being taken against them, while 131 were dealt with in some other way, most notably by being transferred to immigration authorities (n = 88): Home Office (2009a) table 2.

[69] Ibid. There were also 19 charges for failing to comply with port and border control procedures.

[70] Ibid, p 4. Earlier figures on ethnicity have not been published due to data quality concerns.

[71] Ibid, tables 10 and 13. Thus most of the 36 white and 24 black terrorist prisoners must have self-declared as Muslims.

Police may arrest if a breach of the peace is occurring, is imminent, or has recently happened and is likely to recur.[72] This means that the powers of arrest for breach of the peace are rather more restricted than most other powers of arrest. Judgement is required, not only in relation to whether the breach of the peace is occurring, but also in relation to the question of imminence and recurrence. The police have 'the right to take reasonable steps to make the person who is breaking or threatening to break the peace refrain from doing so; and those reasonable steps in appropriate cases will include detaining him against his will.'[73] Any person detained under this power should be released as soon as there are no longer reasonable grounds for fearing a further breach of the peace but otherwise be taken before a court at the earliest practicable opportunity.[74]

One problem with the concept of 'breach of the peace' is that its legal meaning is narrower than the words themselves might suggest. In *Howell*[75] the Court of Appeal confirmed the view that a breach of the peace must be related to violence: a breach of the peace occurs when harm is done or is likely to be done to any person (or, in their presence, to their property), or if someone fears being so harmed by an assault, unlawful assembly or other disturbance. Thus, despite what some law enforcement agents appear to believe, rowdy, abusive or insulting behaviour does not in itself constitute a breach of the peace, although a preventive arrest will still be lawful if a police officer reasonably regarded such behaviour as involving a threat of imminent violence.[76] Demonstrations, picketing, disputes between neighbours or intimates, disputes with police officers, street brawls and so forth are the usual context for this type of problem, although this does not mean that most demonstrations – any more than most disputes between neighbours – actually end in breach of the peace in the legal sense. The lack of precision here offends the freedom perspective, for it leaves citizens unclear about what they can and cannot do without risking a 'breach of the peace arrest'.[77] Arguably it should also cause these laws to fall foul of the ECHR's principles of legality and

---

[72] *Howell* [1981] 3 All ER 383.   [73] *Albert v Lavin* [1981] 3 All ER 878 at 880.

[74] *Chief Constable of Cleveland Police v Mark Anthony McGrogan* [2002] EWCA Civ 86.

[75] *Howell* [1981] 3 All ER 383.

[76] An example is *Hawkes v DPP* [2005] EWCA 3046 where D swore at officers and refused to get out of a police car in which her arrested son had been placed. She was arrested for having actually committed a breach of the peace. This was held to be an unlawful arrest as no violence had taken place or been threatened. The court noted that the police could, however, have used force to remove D from the police car on the basis that she was obstructing them in the course of their duty, and left open the possibility that they could have arrested in order to prevent an *imminent* breach of the peace.

[77] Note, however, that in *Bibby v Chief Constable of Essex* [2000] EWCA Civ 113 (where a bailiff seeking to enforce a debt was arrested in order to defuse a volatile situation), the circumstances in which someone *not* acting unlawfully could be arrested to avert a breach of the peace were confirmed as very narrow. The court ruled that there must be: the clearest of circumstances and a sufficiently real and present threat to the peace to justify this extreme step; the threat must be coming from the person who was to be arrested; the conduct must clearly interfere with the rights of others; the natural consequence of the conduct must be violence from a third party (that violence not to be wholly unreasonable); and the conduct of the person arrested must be unreasonable. Thus the bailiff's arrest was unlawful as his conduct did not interfere with the rights of another and any force used by the debtor to resist the bailiff would have been unreasonable.

forseeability,[78] but the ECtHR has upheld the use of this power and the 'bind-over' orders generally used to enforce it.[79]

Belief in the imminence of a breach of the peace is necessarily difficult to pin down. This was particularly evident in the miners' strike of the mid 1980s where there were several violent confrontations at pits where miners refused to strike. In *Moss v McLachlan*,[80] 60 miners were stopped by a police roadblock on the M1 motorway while on their way to picket some pits a few miles away. They carried banners and shouted abuse at a lorry driver who was passing the road block to break the strike. The men could only be arrested if it was suspected that a breach of the peace was likely to occur. Skinner J stated that, provided the police officers 'honestly and reasonably form the opinion that there is a real risk of a breach of the peace in the sense that it is in close proximity both in place and time then the conditions exist for reasonable preventive action including if necessary the measures taken in this case [that is to say arrest]'.

In this particular case, the miners were abusive and the pits to which they were travelling were nearby, so it may be that the police were justified in the arrest of the men on those grounds.[81] However, in another miners' strike incident, the police established a roadblock at the Dartford Tunnel near London, over 100 miles from the area which some miners intended to picket. The miners were turned back on the same basis as in *Moss v McLachlan*, even though it could hardly be said that a breach of the peace was imminent or proximate in these circumstances.[82]

There were many other incidents where striking miners were stopped by the police and were told when and how they could travel in the vicinity of working mines. Sometimes these miners were on their way to picket, and arguably there was a risk of a breach of the peace. However, police invocation of the breach of the peace law against striking miners spilled over into general restrictions on the liberty of striking miners and other members of mining communities. As one present put it, 'There were no justifications, just the threat of arrest if we failed to comply.'[83] It seems that a lot of police action threatened the use of these arrest powers to prevent picketing, regardless of whether there was an imminent risk of breaches of the peace. At times, such as these, of crises of law and order, legalistic models of policing may simply collapse.[84] Police powers are stretched to enable the police to fulfil wider functions than would be possible if due process principles prevailed. And the way those powers are used are

---

[78] Nicolson D and Reid K, 'Arrest for Breach of the Peace and the European Convention on Human Rights' [1996] Crim LR 764.   [79] *Steel v UK* (1988) EHRR 603.

[80] *Moss v McLachlan* [1985] IRLR 76.

[81] In *Laporte* [2006] UKHL 55 some of the speeches indicated unease about the decision in *Moss*, with Lord Brown stating that it went 'to the furthermost limits of any acceptable view of imminence, and then only on the basis that those prevented from attending the demonstration were indeed manifestly intent on violence' [118]. See also Lord Mance [150].

[82] East R and Thomas P, 'Freedom of Movement: *Moss v McLachlan*' (1985) 12 JLS 77.

[83] Green P, *The Enemy Without: Policing and Class Consciousness in the Miners' Strike* (Milton Keynes: Open UP, 1990) p 63.

[84] See Balbus I, *The Dialectics of Legal Repression* (New York: Russell Sage, 1973); and Vogler R, 'Magistrates and Civil Disorder' (November 1982) LAG Bull 12.

often aggressive, frequently to the point of violence. One result, according to a police officer, is that 'You enjoy the power it gives to inflict the collective will of the job on to a large crowd of people.... You are part of a vast crowd and if the whole thing is wrong or illegal, it's not you who's going to be picked up for it. That sort of violence becomes addictive.'[85]

By using arrest powers in respect of breach of the peace to protect the working miners, the police and judiciary elevated the freedom of strike-breakers and their employers over that of the striking miners. Nicolson and Reid argue that this could be a breach of Arts 10 and 11 of the ECHR (the protection of freedom of expression, peaceful association and assembly).[86] The excessive force in, and 'stretched' legal justification for, many of these arrests are also antithetical to the freedom model. Finally, as the last chapter showed in a less extreme form in relation to stop-search, this type of policing alienates the communities subject to this policing, as well as causing concern to other communities, groups and individuals sympathetic to those being policed in this way. That creates further losses of freedom: the police receive less cooperation from those they have already alienated, become more divided from the rest of society, and become brutalised, increasingly seeing coercion rather than cooperation as the most viable law enforcement strategy. As the officer quoted in the preceding paragraph put it, the use of direct power in these ways 'was slightly awesome but after a while it became easy'. And the chief constable also quoted there feared, as a result, 'that the whole perception of police–public relations has changed in people's minds'.[87]

The miners' strike of the 1980s may seem like a long time ago, but the same types of problem recur periodically in different contexts. Protests against the war in Iraq have provided another flashpoint, while also providing a good example of how stop-search, breach of the peace and arrest powers may interact. In the *Laporte* case[88] the police detained three coachloads of people on their way to join a protest outside a nearby airbase using the stop-search power under s 60 of the Criminal Justice and Public Order Act 1994 (see ch 2). They found a number of items on board which might have been used offensively in a protest, and one passenger was arrested for incitement to cause criminal damage relating to an earlier incident at the airbase. On the basis that they feared a breach of the peace if the coaches continued to the airbase, the police then deployed motorcycle outriders to escort the coaches on a non-stop two and a half hour journey back to London. Similarly, in the *Austin and Saxby* case,[89] the police deployed various powers in the policing of the 2001 May Day protest, when huge numbers of

---

[85] Graef R, 'A Spiral of Mutual Mistrust' *The Independent*, 12 May 1989. It is this kind of mentality that we think is likely to have lain behind the death of Ian Tomlinson, caught up in the policing of the G20 protests in April 2009. For a video of the incident see <http://news.bbc.co.uk/1/hi/england/london/7989027.stm> (accessed 5 January 2010).

[86] Nicolson and Reid (1996: 772–4). However, in the light of *Steel v UK*, op cit, it is unlikely that the ECtHR or the English courts will agree with them.

[87] See generally Townshend C, *Making the Peace: Public Order and Public Security in Modern Britain* (Oxford: OUP, 1993) ch 9.   [88] [2006] UKHL 55.

[89] *Austin and Another v Commissioner of Police for the Metropolis* [2009] UKHL 5.

protesters converged on London's Oxford Circus. First, relying on the need to prevent a breach of the peace, they cordoned off the area, preventing thousands from leaving the area for over seven hours (a practice known as 'kettling').[90] Then they sought to segregate some members of the crowd from the others by asking them questions and by using s 60 of the Criminal Justice and Public Order Act 1994 to conduct searches for offensive weapons and dangerous instruments. Finally, they entered the corralled crowd from time to time to arrest those suspected of throwing missiles at the police.

These examples show how unrealistic it is to view each police power in isolation. In practice, the police can use, or threaten to use, their powers in an overlapping, fluid manner in order to achieve broader policing objectives. In other words, police powers in a legal sense are constitutive of police power in a broader, sociological sense.[91]

In the human rights era, however, it is fair to say that there is closer scrutiny of, and more careful reflection about, police tactics. Thus in *Laporte* the courts ruled that what the police had done was unreasonable and in breach of the common law, not least because they had less restrictive alternatives open to them, such as removing known 'troublemakers' from the coaches and allowing the other passengers to continue to the demonstration (where there were sufficient officers stationed to deal with any breaches of the peace that then occurred). And in *Austin and Another* Lord Neuberger of Abbotsbury observed that if it transpired 'that the police had maintained the cordon, beyond the time necessary for crowd control, in order to punish, or "to teach a lesson" to, the demonstrators within the cordon' then 'there would have been a powerful argument for saying that the maintenance of the cordon did amount to a detention within the meaning of article 5.'[92] Moreover, police services themselves sometimes make strenuous efforts to ensure that protesters' rights to freedom of assembly and expression are not infringed disproportionately.[93] Many senior police officers are well aware of the long-term damage that may be done to police–community relations by heavy-handed tactics, and some pursue more constructive strategies. Thus in the 1990s South Yorkshire Police, under the leadership of a new Chief Constable, sought to repair its tarnished reputation following the miners' strike and the Hillsborough disaster[94] by inculcating a more restrained, professional policing style, and its new approach was reflected in its generally successful regulation of protests when the G8

---

[90] It was accepted that the two claimants (one of whom was not a demonstrator but had simply been caught up in the cordon) had done nothing to give rise to any fear that they would breach the peace, but it was held by the House of Lords that the police were justified in detaining them, along with everyone else in the demonstration, as a breach of the peace from some demonstrators was likely and no preventive alternative to the cordon was available.

[91] See further Sanders A and Young R, 'Police Powers' in Newburn T (ed), *Handbook of Policing*, 2nd edn (Cullompton: Willan, 2008) 228–9.   [92] [2009] UKHL 5 [63].

[93] See Waddington P, 'Controlling Protest in Contemporary Historical and Comparative Perspective' in della Porta D and Reiter H (eds), *Policing Protest: The Control of Mass Demonstrations in Western Democracies* (Minneapolis: University of Minnesota Press, 1998).

[94] In 1989, 96 football fans were crushed to death at the Hillsborough football stadium in Sheffield following disastrously bad decision-making by the police responsible for controlling the crowd.

summit was held in Sheffield in 2005.[95] But recent examples like *Laporte* and *Austin and Saxby* demonstrate that police services continue to seek to stretch their legal powers on occasion.[96]

Abolition of 'breach of the peace', while long overdue,[97] may not make much difference to the underlying issues and problems discussed above, given the broad powers the police now possess to summarily arrest where they reasonably suspect that an offence is *about* to be committed. Now that breach of the peace is defined in terms of threatened or actual violence it is difficult to conceive of a situation where the police could arrest for breach of the peace but not for some other offence.

3.3.5 Citizen's arrest

Before 1829, there was no organised professional police force in England and Wales, and it was many years before the police operated across the whole country. Before the establishment of the modern police, all citizens had the power to arrest suspects, and police powers were originally no greater than those of ordinary citizens. Little or no distinction was made, in theory, between the two, and arrestees had to be taken before the magistrates immediately, no matter who arrested them. Thus we find the Royal Commission on Police Powers and Procedure of 1929 saying:

The principle remains that a policeman, in the view of the common law, is only 'a person paid to perform, as a matter of duty, acts which if he was so minded he might have done voluntarily'.[98]

However true this might once have been, the police (including police community support officers)[99] are now in a completely different position from that of a citizen. In recent years in particular, police officers have been given considerably more power than ordinary citizens. The powers of arrest in the Terrorism Acts, for example, are available to police officers only. And a citizen's arrest does not act as a gateway to other powers (such as the power to search, or to take bodily samples) in the way that a police power of arrest now does.

Section 110 of the Serious Organised Crime and Police Act 2005 (inserting s 24A into PACE) now governs citizens' arrest powers. In brief, this Act preserved existing powers, extended them somewhat (broadening their application from 'arrestable offences' to all

---

[95] See Waddington D, *Policing Public Disorder: Theory and Practice* (Cullompton: Willan, 2007) ch 6.

[96] For another example, see *R (on the application of Kay) v Commissioner of Police of the Metropolis* [2008] UKHL 69.

[97] The Law Commission recommended in 1994 that the 'bind-over' associated with breach of the peace be abolished: Law Commission, *Binding Over* (Report No 222) (London: HMSO, 1994a).

[98] Cmd 3297. Quoted in Royal Commission on Criminal Procedure, *The Investigation and Prosecution of Criminal Offences in England and Wales: The Law and Procedure* (Cmnd 8092–1) (London: HMSO, 1981) p 2.

[99] Technically, police community support officers are civilians (employees of the police authority rather than sworn police officers), but they possess a distinctive set of powers deriving from s 38 of the Police Reform Act 2002, as amended by ss 7–9 of the Police and Justice Act 2006.

indictable offences) but subjected them to a necessity principle. Citizens may now arrest without warrant persons who are committing, or are reasonably suspected to be committing, an indictable offence. Where such an offence has actually been committed, citizens may arrest anyone guilty, or reasonably suspected to be guilty, of the offence. This means that citizen's arrests may lawfully take place for past and present but not future offences; and, for past offences, the offence must have been committed. It is not enough that there be reasonable suspicion that an offence occurred. There are two further conditions that must be met under s 110 for a citizen's arrest to be lawful. First, the citizen must believe that it is not reasonably practicable for a police officer to make the arrest instead. Second, the citizen must have reasonable grounds for thinking that arrest is necessary for one of the following reasons: to prevent the arrestee from causing physical injury to any person or causing loss of or damage to property; to protect the arrestee from injury to self, and to prevent the arrestee from making off before a police officer can take responsibility for him or her. While this looks like a narrower version of the 'necessity principle' discussed above in relation to police arrest powers, in practice it will usually be possible to argue that arrest was 'necessary' to stop someone 'making off'.

The citizen nonetheless faces procedural complications that do not apply to police officers. A case which illustrates this is *Self*,[100] in which the defendant was seen taking a box of chocolates out of a shop. After being followed, he was arrested for theft and for 'assault with intent to resist lawful arrest' (he hit the shop assistant who carried out the citizen's arrest). He was acquitted of theft but convicted of assault. On appeal, it was held that if he had not committed theft the arrest was unlawful, even though reasonable suspicion existed, and therefore the conviction for assault must be quashed, since it is not a crime to resist unlawful arrest.

A large number of arrests, especially for shoplifting, are made by citizens. In most of these cases, the initial arrest is carried out by a shop employee; either a security officer or store detective employed for that purpose, or a member of the management. These are ordinary citizens for the purposes of the law, so if they detain people until the police arrive, they make citizen's arrests. In practice, security staff commonly *request* suspected thieves to accompany them to a management or security office so that the police can be called, thus relying on consent rather than a legal power to achieve their aims.[101] If they then simply convey the information that led to suspicion to the police, then any subsequent arrest is that of the police, against whom any claim of unlawful arrest would then lie.[102]

The subject of a citizen's arrest must be placed in lawful custody as soon as is practicable. This is generally understood to mean either the custody of the police or (as used to be usual) that of a magistrate, but in some circumstances it might be better to take

---

[100] *Self* [1992] 3 All ER 476.

[101] Button M, *Security Officers and Policing* (Aldershot: Ashgate, 2007) pp 88–90.

[102] *Davidson v Chief Constable of North Wales* [1994] 2 All ER 597. If, however, the security staff *encourage* the police to arrest then they may be liable if the arrest turns out to be unlawful: *Shamoon Ahmed v Mohammed Shafique, Kapil Arora* [2009] EWHC 618.

the suspect briefly elsewhere. This is not covered by statute. In *John Lewis & Co Ltd v Tims*,[103] the defendant (D) was arrested by a store detective and brought before the store manager for questioning. Even though D was not brought before the police or magistrates, this was held to be valid on the grounds that the arrestor was acting for someone else. It would be far from helpful to arrestees had the law been decided otherwise; for the consequence of citizen's arrest would usually then be that the police be contacted immediately without the victim (or, more usually, a shop manager) considering whether such drastic action was desirable. Large stores often require their store detectives or employees to bring alleged thieves before the management to decide what should be done, and this can hardly be criticised.[104]

A similar situation arose in *Brewin*,[105] where a child was arrested by an ordinary person, who brought him before his father. This was held to be an unlawful arrest, since the arrest was not made on behalf of the father and there was no firm intention to take the child to the police. As a Crown Court decision, this is not authoritative, but it does illustrate the problem, and helps us understand why security staff have a strong inclination (often inculcated through training)[106] to use consent rather than arrest. Perhaps legislation should provide for citizen's arrest on the lines of the Crime and Disorder Act, s 16, which (in certain restricted circumstances) allows police officers to take truanting children from public places back to school. The danger is that something close to kidnapping could be legitimised if citizens were given this kind of power. What is needed is a more context-sensitive freedom approach. This might authorise the arrestor to bring the arrestee before whoever could most sympathetically and usefully take the next step although, as discussed in 3.2, a freedom approach also requires certainty in the law. Thus the type of person to whom the arrestee would be brought, the seriousness of the offence, and the period of time and conditions involved would all have to be specified by such a provision. This is not the most likely future trajectory for the law, however. Given the growth of 'private policing' in various forms in recent years,[107] the importance of citizen's arrest powers are likely to increase rather than diminish and pressure may grow for extending to 'citizens' the sweeping summary powers of arrest now enjoyed by police officers. While this would promote 'efficiency' and remove the procedural complications currently facing those carrying out private policing functions,[108] it would represent a further erosion of due process and jeopardise freedom.

---

[103] *John Lewis & Co Ltd v Tims* [1952] AC 676.

[104] Adu-Boyake K, 'Private Security and Retail Crime Prevention' (MSc Dissertation, University of Portsmouth, 2002) conducted a covert study as a security officer in a large inner-city supermarket and found that only 1 of the 29 people arrested for shop-theft by security staff was subsequently handed over to the police by the store managers (cited in Button M, *Security Officers and Policing* (Aldershot: Ashgate, 2007) p 88.   [105] *Brewin* [1976] Crim LR 742.

[106] Button (2007: 88).

[107] See Crawford A, Plural Policing in the UK: Policing beyond the Police' in Newburn (2008).

[108] These should not be overstated. Button (2007: 84) found that the 49 security officers he studied had a good level of knowledge about their arrest powers, and we have already noted their awareness of how to use

3.3.6 **Non-police agencies**

A considerable body of criminal law is enforced by non-police agencies. For example, health and safety laws are enforced by the Health and Safety Executive, tax laws by HM Revenue and Customs, and pollution laws by the Environment Agency. These are commonly regarded as 'regulatory offences' rather than as 'real crimes'. They are not, however, always less serious than police-enforced laws. Tax frauds involve at least as much money as dishonesty offences enforced by the police. More people die through the negligence of employers in breach of health and safety laws than die as a result of pub brawls, muggings and street fights, and pollution is more of a threat to the public's safety than is drunkenness, prostitution and criminal damage.[109]

The criminal justice system does not seem to treat these offences with the serious-ness one would expect in view of the harm they cause. More freedom is lost as a result of these offences than as a result of many offences for which the police have far more extensive freedom-taking powers. Non-police agencies do not have the arrest powers possessed by the police, so are in the position of private citizens in this respect; and many of these offences are neither indictable nor have specific arrest powers attached to them. Nor do stop and search or breach of the peace powers apply. There is therefore no equivalent of 'street policing' for these offences. Investigation is either reactive, in response to a major incident, or routine, in which case appointments are made with the potential 'criminal' to inspect the premises concerned.[110] The result is that these offences have a low profile in the criminal justice system and in society at large, creat-ing a vicious circle, whereby because they are little known, there is little concern about them, ensuring that maximum penalties remain low, ensuring that little remains known, and so on. This issue is followed up further in ch 7.

3.4 **Arrest discretion and reasonable suspicion**

3.4.1 **When the ends can justify the means**

One of the peculiarities of the law of arrest both as enacted by PACE 1994 and as subsequently amended by the Serious Organised Crime Act 2005 is that reasonable suspicion is not made a pre-condition of a lawful arrest. Thus, so far as PACE is con-cerned, the police can lawfully arrest even when they have no reasonable suspicion, so long as it turns out that the arrested person had in fact committed an offence, or

---

consent to avoid some of the potential problems the law poses. Good training is clearly important here – see also Wakefield A, *Selling Security* (Cullompton: Willan, 2003) pp 151–2.

109 See generally Slapper G and Tombs S, *Corporate Crime* (Harlow: Longman, 1999); Tombs S and Whyte S, *Safety Crimes* (Cullompton: Willan, 2007).

110 Gobert J and Punch M, *Rethinking Corporate Crime* (London: Butterworths, 2003) ch 9.

was in the course of doing so, or was about to do so (see 3.3.2 above). This is a classic crime control norm since desirable ends are regarded as justifying undesirable means. It does not matter that the arrest was speculatively made, so long as the suspect turns out to have been engaged in a crime. The police might, for instance, see a well-known burglar walking down the street and simply arrest him on a hunch that he was responsible for a burglary committed earlier that day. If, in the police station, he confessed to that crime, his guilt would be clear and his arrest would be valid as far as PACE is concerned.

However, this appears to fly in the face of Art 5 of the ECHR. This stipulates, in effect, that no-one shall be deprived of his or her liberty through arrest except 'on a reasonable suspicion of having committed an offence or when it is reasonably considered necessary to prevent his committing an offence...' The ECHR is enforceable in the English courts via the Human Rights Act 1998 (HRA), but the PACE arrest provisions have not been challenged directly. However, the ECtHR has examined cases under terrorism legislation where arrests were made using powers that did not require reasonable suspicion, and ruled that what mattered was whether *in fact* the arrest was based on reasonable suspicion.[111] Proving that a particular officer lacked reasonable suspicion might be difficult given the broad and elastic nature of that concept (see next section). What would happen if a domestic court was satisfied that an arrest was made without such suspicion and accepted that this breached Art 5? The courts can exclude evidence obtained unlawfully or unfairly – such as in this instance when an arrest is made without reasonable suspicion. However, given their past track record on similar issues, we doubt that courts will exclude evidence and refuse to convict the clearly guilty arrested in contravention of the Convention.[112]

From a freedom perspective one might say that the lack of reasonable suspicion for arrest should not matter if the person is guilty, as future victims will have their freedom enhanced by convicting such people. On the other hand, the protection of people from arbitrary interference also enhances freedom. The crucial point is that if the police are allowed to arrest people without reasonable suspicion, it is likely that many such arrestees will not be guilty and will not be charged or convicted of anything.[113]

3.4.2 Reasonable suspicion

In practice, the police will usually want to generate reasonable suspicion prior to an arrest, as this ensures that they cannot be sued for wrongful arrest should it turn out that the suspect is innocent. Whether 'reasonable suspicion' means the same across

---

[111] *Fox, Campbell and Hartley v UK* (1990) 13 EHRR 157 [31]; *O'Hara v UK* (2002) 34 EHRR 32 [41].

[112] Even though Convention rights might be regarded as 'higher rights' – on a par with constitutional rights in jurisdictions with written Constitutions – evidence is not excluded simply as a result of their breach. See *Khan* [1996] 3 All ER 289; *Khan v UK* (2000) 31 EHRR 1016. On exclusion of evidence in general, see ch 12.

[113] Similarly, we saw in ch 2 that the arrest rate produced by the use of stop-search is particularly high where no reasonable suspicion for the initial stop is required.

the contexts of stop and search and arrest is unclear in the light of the ECHR. We have noted that Art 5(1) makes reasonable suspicion an ingredient of a lawful arrest or detention. However, in *Murray v UK* (1994) 19 EHRR 193, in which Mrs Murray was held in her house for a short time under terrorism legislation, it was held by the European Court that 'The length of the deprivation of liberty at risk may also be material to the level of suspicion required' (paras 55–56). The logical conclusion of this is that the level of suspicion required for any arrest would be influenced by the length of time of (and perhaps level of distress created by) the arrest. Whilst these are relevant issues from a freedom perspective, the lack of certainty in the law thereby created is antithetical to a freedom perspective. Precisely how 'reasonable suspicion' will be interpreted in the future, and whether or not there will be one standard in all (or most) contexts is impossible to predict. It is, however, clear that reasonable suspicion is a lower standard than information sufficient to establish a prima facie case. To quote Lord Devlin in *Shaaban Bin Hussien v Chong Fook Kam*:

Suspicion arises at or near the starting point of an investigation of which the obtaining of prima facie proof is the end... Prima facie proof consists of admissible evidence. Suspicion can take into account matters that could not be put in evidence at all.[114]

This means that it is very difficult to control police discretion, although the courts have shown little inclination to exert such control. In *Castorina v Chief Constable of Surrey*,[115] for example, the police arrested a middle-aged woman for burgling the firm from which she had previously been dismissed. The grounds of suspicion were that the burglary appeared to be 'an inside job', and she was presumed by the police to have a grudge. Against this, she had no criminal record, and even the victim thought that she was an unlikely culprit. Nonetheless, the evidence was held sufficient to warrant reasonable suspicion. The court emphasised that it was not a precondition of a lawful arrest that the police believe a suspect to be guilty. The issue was whether, given the information the police had at the time of the arrest, their suspicion could be regarded as reasonable. The decision gives the police considerable freedom to follow crime control norms, in that it allows them to arrest on little hard evidence. As Clayton and Tomlinson put it:

If the police are justified in arresting a middle aged woman of good character on such flimsy grounds, without even questioning her as to her alibi or possible motives, then the law provides very scant protection for those suspected of crime.[116]

The approach used in *Castorina* was followed in *Cumming v CC Northumbria*.[117] A man was observed trying door handles, and this should have been captured on a CCTV camera. But it was not, leading the police to believe that the tape had been interfered with. They arrested (for perverting the course of justice) six CCTV operators on the

---

[114] [1970] AC 942 at 948–9. See 2.2.1 for a related discussion in the context of stop and search powers.
[115] *Castorina v Chief Constable of Surrey* [1988] NLJR 180.
[116] Clayton R and Tomlinson H, 'Arrest and Reasonable Grounds for Suspicion' (1988) 7 Sep LS Gaz 22 at p 26.   [117] *Cumming v CC Northumbria* [2003] EWCA Civ 1844.

basis that they would have had the opportunity to interfere with the tape. The Court of Appeal noted that those arrested were of good character and accepted that the arrests had caused them distress, fear and humiliation. It nonetheless upheld the legality of the arrest on the basis that where a small number of people could be clearly identified as the only ones capable of having committed the offence, that in itself could afford reasonable grounds for suspecting each of them of having committed that offence, in the absence of any information which could or should enable the police to reduce the number further.

Arrests are frequently made by officers on the basis of briefings from senior officers. In *O'Hara v Chief Constable of the RUC* an officer was told that O'Hara was suspected of a terrorist offence and that his house should therefore be raided and searched and he should be arrested. The officer did all this, and O'Hara sued for wrongful arrest, alleging the absence of 'reasonable suspicion', when it turned out that he was wrongly suspected. There was no firm evidence that the arresting officer knew any more than that the officer who briefed him claimed to have reasonable suspicion, but the House of Lords took the view that the trial judge must have inferred that some further details must have been given at the police briefing. It accordingly decided that the arresting officer did possess reasonable suspicion because, as Lord Hope stated: 'For obvious practical reasons police officers must be able to rely on each other in taking decisions as to whom to arrest.'[118] The House accepted, however, that a simple order or request to arrest could not, by itself, found the required reasonable suspicion on the part of the arresting officer.[119] This is in line with the doctrine of constabulary independence and with prior authority.[120] Where the *O'Hara* decision is open to criticism, however, is in the failure to insist that those resisting a claim of unlawful arrest should produce evidence to establish that the arresting officer did indeed have objectively reasonable grounds for suspicion. The House of Lords was surely too generous in assuming that the trial judge must have inferred that further details were given at the briefing, and any such inference on the part of that judge was similarly leaning too far towards crime control values. The presumption should be that briefing officers should give evidence in such litigation, and thus be accountable for their actions.

It is not just police powers of arrest which give the police discretion, but also many substantive laws. Vague laws give the police considerable latitude in deciding for themselves what behaviour is or is not criminal and, therefore, arrestable. Ashworth singles out the Public Order Act 1986 (POA) for particular criticism. He points out

---

[118] [1997] 1 All ER 129 at 142. This decision, which was confirmed by the ECtHR in *O'Hara v United Kingdom* (2001) 34 EHRR 32 was applied in *Hough v CC Staffordshire Constabulary* [2001] EWCA Civ 39, where a police officer's suspicion was based on information in the Police National Computer about the suspect.

[119] See also *Didier Coudrat v Commissioners of Her Majesty's Revenue and Customs* [2005] EWCA Civ 616.   [120] *Fisher v Oldham Corpn* [1930] 2 KB 364.

that the essence of a public order offence might be thought to be that it engenders fear of violence and disorder among bystanders. Yet, as he says, the 1986 Act:

goes so far as to include an express dispensation from proof that any member of the public was even at the scene, let alone put in fear – a dispensation which virtually undermines the rationale of the offence. These dispensations undoubtedly smooth the path of the prosecutor and make it correspondingly more difficult for defendants to obtain an acquittal... Does it seem right to convict a person of a serious public order offence without the need to hear the evidence from a member of the public?[121]

Ashworth's point here is that the police are enabled to prove that a public order offence occurred by virtue of what they alone saw and what they infer from what they saw. This gives the police enormous discretion in deciding what is a crime and therefore in deciding when they should or should not, and can or cannot, arrest. Thus a Home Office study found that some police officers use the most minor offence in the 1986 Act (s 5) to cover 'misbehaviour' that was not previously criminal, while other officers stated that this was unnecessary, as 'in the past, they would always have found a means to arrest if misbehaviour was sufficiently offensive'.[122] In one study of 60 disputes to which the police were called, there were six arrests. There was evidence to justify arrest on the grounds of the victims' complaints, such as criminal damage or assault, but the arrests were actually for breach of the peace, drunkenness or possession of an offensive weapon. This was because these public order charges:

only required police evidence and, therefore, did not require the production of independent evidence from witnesses or victim statements... because of the permissiveness of public order legislation, they can figure out precisely how to charge a person after they have made the arrest.[123]

The result is that police officers on the street can arrest in such a way as to make conviction much more likely. Their choice reduces the possibility that suspects will be able to challenge their actions and minimises the accountability of the police to the judiciary.

There is a parallel here with some non-police agencies. Health and safety and pollution laws require all 'practical' steps to be taken to prevent accidents, pollution and so forth. The enforcement agency decides what is, and what is not, 'practical'. This has the potential for working like public order laws, whereby evidence justifying enforcement action (failure to take practical steps to prevent the accident) also constitutes substantial evidence of guilt, just as public order laws enable arrest and conviction when an officer regards action as likely to engender fear in others. Despite the theoretical

---

[121] Ashworth A, 'Defining Criminal Offences without Harm' in Smith P (ed), *Criminal Law: Essays in Honour of J C Smith* (London: Butterworths, 1987) p 17.

[122] Brown D and Ellis T, *Policing Low Level Disorder: Police Use of section 5 of the Public Order Act 1986* (Home Office Research Study No 135) (London: Home Office, 1994) p 21.

[123] Kemp et al, 'Legal Manoeuvres in Police Handling of Disputes' in Farrington D and Walklate S (eds), *Offenders and Victims: Theory and Policy* (London: British Society of Criminology, 1992) p 73.

parallel there is a practical difference. Non-police agencies work out what is 'practical' with the firms against whom they are enforcing the law. This is like the police negotiating with Saturday night pub rowdies how many bottles they will be allowed to smash on the way home. Law enforcement is partly dictated by the law (in so far as, for instance, health and safety inspectors have no arrest powers) but also partly by policies formulated by those agencies.[124]

3.4.3 **Working rules**

The imprecision of public order laws enable them to be used as a resource for the police. Enabling rules are contained within the law itself, allowing – but not requiring – arrest in a very wide spectrum of circumstances. But if the law does not dictate when and who the police arrest, what does? We saw in relation to stop-search that, in deciding when and how to exercise their powers, the police draw on their experience and institutional objectives, as mediated by cop culture. On this basis, McConville et al identified various 'working rules' which, they argued, structure police decision-making.[125] These apply to arrest just as they do to stop and search. What are these working rules? How far are they consistent with the reasonable suspicion criterion and legality in general?

Disorder and police authority

Ever since the modern police was established in the early nineteenth century, the maintenance of public order has been its prime concern.[126] With no national riot squads and with very sparing use of armed forces in situations of disorder, the police have the lead role in these matters. Consequently, the maintenance of order is always a concern of the police, in general policy terms and at the street policing level.

The maintenance of police authority is linked to this. Since the police usually do not carry firearms, they rely on numbers and their moral and legal authority (as distinct from fear) to persuade people to do as they are told. This is particularly important when disorder is imminent (eg street fights and pub brawls) but also in 'straightforward' criminal situations such as theft and burglary, and even for minor matters such as possession of cannabis[127] or cycling on a pavement.[128] In order to maintain the authority of the police, people must believe that when police officers make requests (such as to dispose of cannabis down a street drain) or give orders they have a moral

---

[124] See eg Hutter B, *The Reasonable Arm of the Law?* (Oxford: OUP, 1988) particularly at pp 132–3; Hawkins K, *Law as Last Resort* (Oxford: OUP, 2003).

[125] McConville et al (1991: 27). Ericson uses the similar formulation of 'recipe rules' in Ericson R, *Making Crime: A Study of Detective Work* (London: Butterworths, 1981).

[126] Reiner R, *The Politics of the Police* (Oxford: OUP, 2000).

[127] Warburton et al, 'Looking the Other Way: The Impact of Reclassifying Cannabis on Police Warnings, Arrests and Informal Action in England and Wales' (2005) 45(2) BJ Crim 113.

[128] See Young R, 'Integrating a Multi-Victim Perspective through Restorative Justice Conferences' in Crawford A and Goodey J (eds), *Integrating a Victim Perspective within Criminal Justice* (Aldershot: Ashgate, 2000) at pp 240–2.

right to do so or that they can enforce compliance. Thus, as we saw in relation to 'consent' searches, the police often secure cooperation because people believe that they will have to do as requested anyway.

It follows that when there are challenges to police authority or outbreaks of disorder, the police feel the need to get on top of the situation quickly, preferably by securing voluntary submission. For this reason, threats of arrest are probably a lot more common than arrests themselves.[129] If submission is secured, and if no serious offences have been committed, the police usually take no further action. Thus Shapland and Hobbs found that only 19–25% of 'disturbances' attended by the police led to arrest.[130] Kemp, Norris and Fielding found the police taking 'immediate authoritative action' (which includes arrest, but also removing suspects, reporting the incident and so forth) in just one-third of criminal disputes.[131] However, if submission is not voluntary, the police will enforce it. Now that naked violence is unacceptable,[132] arrest (with any 'reasonably necessary' accompanying force) is all that is left to the police. In one of McConville et al's cases, the police officer explained that it 'would have been all right if he'd just gone away but he had to be Jack the Lad...I grabbed him and arrested him.' In another a police officer explained the arrest by saying 'you come to the point like a parent with a child where if you don't do something the others will all join in'.[133] When policing the night-time economy the police will often seek to neutralise potentially volatile situations by arresting and removing a suspect to a police station rather than attempt to issue an on-the-spot fine, because of what they call 'the "obvious risk" to them and others of attempting to issue a fine on the street when surrounded by the offender's mates and other interested and inebriated parties'.[134] Indeed, research indicates that 'often an arrest and placement in a cell is done only for the purpose of allowing the detainee to sober up',[135] with most drunken detainees subsequently released without charge.[136]

In the more politically charged atmosphere of major strikes, riots, confrontations with 'alternative' movements and so forth, the police – as upholders of order and the status quo – seek to arrest those who challenge their authority.[137] However,

---

[129] For an example drawn from the policing of football crowds, see Stott et al, 'Policing Football Crowds in England and Wales: A Model of Good Practice?' (2008) 18(3) Policing and Society 258 at 268.

[130] Shapland J and Hobbs R, 'Policing Priorities on the Ground' in Morgan R and Smith D (eds), *Coming to Terms with Policing* (London: Routledge, 1989).

[131] Kemp et al (1992). Also see Clarkson et al, 'Assaults: The Relationship between Seriousness, Criminalisation and Punishment' [1994] Crim LR 4.

[132] That officers would habitually mete out 'street justice' in times gone by is well documented. See eg Brogden M, *On the Mersey Beat* (Oxford: OUP, 1991) pp 96–100.   [133] McConville et al (1991: 25).

[134] Halligan-Davis G and Spicer K, *Piloting 'On the Spot' Penalties for Disorder: Final Results from a One-year Pilot, Findings 257* (London: Home Office, 2004) p 5.

[135] Hopkins M and Sparrow P, 'Sobering up: Arrest Referral and Brief Intervention for Alcohol Users in the Custody Suite' (2006) 6(4) Criminology & Criminal Justice 389 at 392.

[136] Man et al, *Dealing with Alcohol-Related Detainees in the Custody Suite, Research Findings 178* (London: Home Office, 2002) p 2.

[137] See, on the miners' strike, Green (1990: ch 3) and Fine B and Millar R (eds), *Policing the Miners' Strike* (London: Lawrence and Wishart, 1985).

the re-establishment of order frequently requires that the police take a longer view than simply arresting all and sundry: in order to retake control of the streets in the 'riots' of 1981, for example, the police sometimes allowed a remarkably large number of offences to take place without arrest.[138]

Arrests are often avoided during political demonstrations. This is in part because the police acknowledge the importance of the right to protest, in part because arrests could cause trouble to escalate, and in part because they know that the policing of the protest may be filmed, thus drawing unwelcome attention to dubious riot control tactics[139] (as the death of Ian Tomlinson at the G20 protest in April 2009 has once again illustrated).[140] The working rule of 'avoiding in-the-job trouble' means that the police seek in the main to avoid violent confrontations and arrests that would place their own legitimacy in question. Any arrests that do take place therefore tend to be strategic in nature. Thus in the policing of the G8 summit in 2005 one group of protesters was corralled in a side street for over two hours, and subjected to occasional incursions by police snatch-squads bent on arresting 'known anarchist ringleaders.' Independent observers, including a BBC reporter, were later to assert that none of those snatched from the crowd was doing anything sufficiently criminal to justify their arrest.[141] This is clearly an example of actuarial policing, with the tactics used aimed at managing and neutralising those deemed particularly 'risky'.

What does all this tell us about how far 'reasonable suspicion' is an inhibitory rule? Clearly, the 'reasonable suspicion' element is often missing from public order arrests. When asked the basis for the arrest of 'Jack the Lad', all the officer could say was 'it's Ways and Means, just to get him away, control the situation…'[142] In most situations, the flexibility of public order-type laws discussed earlier makes it difficult to say that there was insufficient evidence to arrest, for little evidence is required by them. Such laws are therefore favoured by the police precisely because they do not rely on the cooperation of witnesses, and arrests based upon them are very difficult to challenge.

Where order or authority are jeopardised, arrest is a resource for the police. It is not so much a means of getting someone to court as a means of control. Not only is prosecution not the main concern, but sometimes it is not envisaged at all, and persons arrested in this way are frequently released without charge.[143] Thus Waddington discusses a 'gay pride' demonstration which was about to disrupt a royal procession:

---

[138] Vogler R, *Reading the Riot Act* (Milton Keynes, Open UP, 1991) ch 8; Waddington P, *The Strong Arm of the Law* (Oxford: Clarendon Press, 1991) ch 6.

[139] Waddington (1994: 38–9). Overbearing, insensitive or excessively forceful arrests may trigger wider disorder within a community, as happened in Bradford in 1995: Bagguley P and Hussain Y, *Riotous Citizens* (Aldershot: Ashgate, 2008) pp 50–1.

[140] The filmed evidence of his death has prompted a major review of police public order tactics by HMIC as well as investigations by the IPCC into this and a number of other incidents during this protest. See <http://news.bbc.co.uk/1/hi/world/8000246.stm> for discussion and video footage of some of the tactics used (last accessed 5 January 2010).   [141] Waddington (2007: 157–8).

[142] McConville et al (1991: 25–6). The wryly named (and fictitious) 'Ways and Means Act' is frequently invoked in the absence of more helpful legislation.   [143] Kemp et al (1992).

'the protesters were arrested and...not charged, for the police purpose had been to maintain the dignity of the event by removing the protesters...'[144] More generally, Choongh (1997) argues on the basis of his observational study that some sections of the population are subjected to 'social discipline' by the police precisely by arresting on flimsy or no legal grounds, humiliating them while in custody, then releasing them without ever having intended to charge them. The aim is to leave them in no doubt that they are 'police property', to be treated as the police wish.

Demeanour

Even where there is reasonable suspicion, whether arrest takes place depends on a combination – all other things being equal – of offence seriousness and offender seriousness. The police judge the latter, in the absence of information about 'previous', by the attitude displayed by the suspect. Arrests for 'contempt of cop' are fairly common. Examples are given in studies by Waddington, Choongh, Brown and Ellis. One officer, referring to a police Support Unit, said '...these boys, they won't wear it [backchat from "undesirables"]...if they get any mouth, they'll drag 'em in'.[145] Another told Choongh that if someone swore at an officer he deserved to be arrested as: 'We shouldn't have to take that kind of shit, and we won't take it.' This is why, he explained to Choongh, there were often arrests for seemingly trivial matters under s 4 and s 5 of the Public Order Act 1986.[146] Brown and Ellis cite many examples throughout their report, concluding that the police view is that if those who abuse the police 'realise that they can get away with it, respect for the police will decline further, and they will be the targets of more abuse in the future...'[147] Warburton et al noted the importance of the demeanour of those found in possession of cannabis. When they asked officers whether they would arrest an individual for a first offence of possession one replied: 'It would depend on their attitude. I would have to stereotype them: their attitude toward me, society in general, and if they were apologetic.'[148] They report officers saying that if the cannabis offenders they apprehended 'had been "mouthy", then they almost certainly would have been arrested'.[149] Sometimes the police themselves directly provoke 'mouthiness', knowing that this will provide a justification for arrest. As one drug user complained:

If there's a load of them and you get pulled by them, they seem to take the piss and that, show off in front of them. But the coppers and stuff like that they try to just take the piss out of you, calling you a fucking divvy and this and that and if you call them owt back and that they'll just arrest you.[150]

---

[144] Waddington (1994: 184).   [145] Choongh (1997: 68).

[146] Choongh (1997: 75). These legislative provisions are discussed in 3.4.1 above.

[147] Brown and Ellis (1994: 42–3 and passim); also see, for one more example out of many, Waddington P, *Policing Citizens* (London: UCL Press, 1999b) p 135.

[148] Warburton et al (2005: 121); see also Lister et al, *Street Policing of Problem Drug Users* (York: Joseph Rowntree Foundation, 2008) p 23.   [149] Warburton et al (2005: 120).

[150] Quoted in Lister et al (2008: 47).

This is not to suggest that the police always arrest those that are abusive or not cooperative. The police have wider goals, as embodied in the working rules, in mind. So where one working rule (order, for example) is more powerful than another (appropriate demeanour), arrest is unlikely. Context is very important. Swearing in the context of a political or environmental protest is something the police are more likely to tolerate than when dealing with 'away' football fans, or 'rough' youths in a city centre or on a problem estate. Thus one of the senior commanders of the South Yorkshire Police responsible for the policing of the Sheffield G8 anti-poverty protests in 2005 briefed his public order units of the need for a subtler approach than they typically deployed when controlling football crowds:

So that was the tenor of the brief: only respond and react if you have to and that will be dictated to by the…commanders, the sergeants and the inspectors; no unilateral, sort of 'I'm going to arrest him because he's upset me.' In any case, they were the more professional of my public order units; they can stand around and take that sort of stuff all day.[151]

We have given qualitative examples above, but attempts have also been made to quantify the importance of demeanour in particular samples of cases. In a classic American study, Piliavin and Briar observed police decisions whether or not to arrest or warn juvenile offenders on the street: 25 juveniles were arrested or given official reprimands and 41 juveniles were released with no official action at all. These different dispositions had little to do with the juveniles' alleged offences, but had a lot to do with their demeanour. Most of the cooperative juveniles were released with no official action, while most of the uncooperative juveniles were arrested or given official reprimands. As Piliavin and Briar put it:

Assessment of character – the distinction between serious delinquents, 'good' boys, misguided youths, and so on – and the dispositions which followed…were based on youths' personal characteristics, and not their offences.[152]

In other words, the police attempted to avoid rigidity by taking action only in 'deserving' cases, but they based that judgement on rather superficial personal characteristics. In Britain, Southgate reported similar findings:

Observers noticed cases where officers enforced the law 'by the book' in response to difficult or hostile people, whereas they applied discretion to offenders of a similar kind who were more amenable.[153]

The result in Southgate's study was that official action (including arrest) was taken against 45% of 'rude, hostile' suspects, 22% of 'civil' suspects, 11% of 'friendly' suspects, and 5% of those who displayed 'particular deference'. As one officer said to

---

[151] Quoted in Waddington (2007: 150).
[152] Piliavin I and Briar S, 'Police Encounters with Juveniles' (1964) 70 AJ Sociology 206.
[153] Southgate P, *Police-Public Encounters* (Home Office Research Study No 90) (London: HMSO, 1986) p 47.

the researcher, after finding that one driver had no car tax disc: 'If he had not been so unhelpful I might not have been so determined to prosecute him'.[154] One of the authors vividly remembers being stopped one night when he might have been over the drink-drive limit. Remembering what he had written in the first edition of this book about the importance of deference to the police and being cooperative, he grovelled shamelessly and looked contrite. After allowing him to abase himself at length, the officers let him go without being breathalysed. At the other extreme are those car drivers who refuse to submit to police authority by speeding away from possible arrest. This often results in high speed car chases, road blocks and, when the duration of the chase allows, helicopter surveillance. In the six years to 2005/06 around thirty people died annually as a result of police pursuits.[155] Waddington and Wright sum up the various investigations into these incidents:

police vehicle pursuits that conclude with injuries and fatalities are prompted by often minor transgressions; are of brief duration; and those killed are usually the occupants of the pursued vehicle, which is likely to be driven by a young man under the influence of drink and/or drugs, who is disqualified from driving and/or is driving an untaxed and uninsured, and/or stolen vehicle – a profile reminiscent of many motoring offences and offenders. Reports tend to focus on the relative triviality of the initiating infraction and compliance (or lack of it) with police procedures: control rooms are often not informed that a pursuit is in progress and/or have little time to manage it; risk assessments are rarely completed; inappropriate (including defective) police vehicles take part; and long convoys of police vehicles sometimes build up.[156]

It is difficult to make sense of the disproportionate amount of police resources devoted to such offenders and offences, and of the tactics used, except by reference to macho police culture and the working rule that suspects should show the police respect by submitting to their authority.

The weak inhibitory quality of 'reasonable suspicion', combined with the overwhelming desire of the police to maintain order and authority has powerful consequences. It means that arrestees tend to be those with an 'attitude problem'. This falls disproportionately on those who dislike the police – particularly young, socially marginalised males – whose dislike is thus compounded, increasing the probability of 'attitude problems' next time round. Stop-search, which we saw in the previous chapter is disproportionately used against these people, frequently adds another twist to this spiral of mistrust. For example, Home Office research on the use of the Public Order Act shows that many stops lead to abusive responses from suspects, and consequent arrests under s 5 rather than for the suspected offences for which they were ostensibly stopped.[157]

There is another parallel here with non-police agencies. Just as suspects are arrested or not in part on the basis of their perceived moral character (as displayed by their

---

[154] Southgate (1986: 101).

[155] Docking et al, *Police Road Traffic Incidents: A Study of Cases Involving Serious and Fatal Injuries*, Paper 7 (London: Independent Police Complaints Commission, 2007) p 9.

[156] Waddington P and Wright M, 'Police Use of Force, Firearms and Riot Control' in Newburn (2008).

[157] Brown and Ellis (1994: 31–2).

attitude to the police) so this is also true of regulatory offences. Carson, for instance, found that factory inspectors only took action against those who appeared to be cavalier and disrespectful.[158] It is not just the police, then, who insist on the upholding of order and authority. However, the fact that the 'clients' of non-police agencies are generally companies or middle class individuals who are respectful of authority may partly account for the lower level of enforcement of their crimes than of the crimes with which the police are concerned. And, of course, non-police agencies, unlike the police, do not deal with people who threaten political authority or the established social order.

Suspiciousness and previous convictions

There is a line in the classic film 'Casablanca' when, following a serious crime, the police chief instructs his officers to 'round up the usual suspects'. These are, of course, people with 'form' or 'previous', meaning relevant previous convictions. It does not usually happen quite like this, although it can if the police mount a major investigation.[159] Indeed, such investigations provide a good excuse for arresting local 'villains' to see what else they will 'cough' to. Many people are arrested for serious offences because they are known to favour the modus operandi employed,[160] and many police officers spend time with arrestees in order to get to know their criminal character traits for future reference.[161]

'Previous' triggers arrest in four common ways. It is sometimes the first lead in a reported crime, the police arresting someone known to do this kind of thing or to have previously pestered the victim in question. Thus McConville et al cite examples where this was the totality of evidence; no further police action, not surprisingly, was the frequent result.[162] Secondly, the police may catch someone committing a trivial offence and then use technology to check whether they have any previous convictions. If they do, arrest is more likely.[163] Thirdly, knowledge of someone's previous convictions leads to that person being followed (either physically or by CCTV), thus allowing the suspect to be watched until he commits a crime.[164] Finally, as we saw in the previous chapter, just being a known criminal can be enough to prompt a stop and search; if this reveals, say, drugs then arrest will follow.[165] The point in these third and fourth situations is not that arrest is per se wrong (although frequently there will be no reasonable suspicion for the stop, where it occurs, which preceded it), but that if such people had no 'previous', their offences would probably not have been discovered. Again, the pattern created is one which leaves 'respectable' people out of the criminal justice net and repeatedly enmeshes those with low status. McAra and McVie looked at contacts between the police and young people over several years from the late 1990s onwards. They found that every time a youth was arrested or given a formal warning

---

[158] Carson WG, 'White Collar Crime and the Enforcement of Factory Legislation' (1970) 10 BJ Crim 383.

[159] McConville et al (1991: 24).

[160] See Smith D and Gray J, *Police and People in London* (Policy Studies Institute) (Aldershot: Gower, 1983) vol 4, p 345 and Sanders A and Bridges L, 'Access to Legal Advice and Police Malpractice' [1990] Crim LR 494.

[161] McConville et al (1991: 23).   [162] McConville et al (1991: ch 2).

[163] See Warburton et al (2005: 119–21).

[164] McConville et al (1991: 24); Wakefield (2003: 174–5); Lister et al (2008: 28).

[165] Lister et al (2008: 53).

the probability of this happening again increased, regardless of that individual's actual level of crime. Having friends who had been in trouble with the police and generally living life 'on the street' were also factors.[166] The case of the 'Arab' youth at the head of the chapter is a concrete example of this: he had previously been unsuccessfully prosecuted for rape, and it seems that at least some officers were determined to 'get him' for something.[167]

Targeting 'known criminals' is encouraged at the highest levels. In the 1990s the Audit Commission called for a greater focus on criminals rather than crimes: 'Target the Criminal', it urges, by developing an 'intelligence strategy based on target criminals . . . build an element of proactivity into all detective duties . . . encourage the use of informants.'[168] This approach continues to be endorsed by government – in its 2004 White Paper, for example, where again the call is to move (further) away from reactive to proactive policing and to target 'prolific offenders'.[169] This is part of the managerialist strategy discussed in ch 1 and the new form of proactive policing discussed in 2.1. Rather than being the neutral efficient strategy implied, the result is a skewed suspect population suffering frequent and disproportionate invasions of liberty.

Being 'known to the police' is only a special case of appearing 'suspicious', which we saw was a key working rule in relation to stop-search. Association with other criminals, such as sharing a house where drugs are dealt or being seen in public together, is particularly important. Some associates are arrested even when the police have no evidence at all of their guilt; here, arrest is used to secure witness statements and is entirely without reasonable suspicion.[170] Other 'suspicious' characteristics include appearance and attitude to the police. Attitude is related to the question of authority, discussed above. Suspects who are not cooperative when apprehended are often formally arrested without more ado, allowing further investigation to determine whether or not they are likely to be the culprits. In cases like this, it is clear that arrest has moved to the start of the investigative stage – too early in many instances for reasonable suspicion to be formed, and much earlier in any event than used to be common.

Taking account of the victim

Subject to other factors, a decision to arrest will in part depend on whether formal police action is desired by the victim (in crimes, such as assault, where there are victims). If the victim's evidence is essential to any consequent prosecution (which is by

---

[166] McAra L and McVie S 'The Usual Suspects: Street Life, Young People and the Police' (2005) 5 Criminal Justice 5. [167] *The Guardian*, 20 May 2005.

[168] Audit Commission, *Helping with Enquiries – Tackling Crime Effectively* (London: HMSO, 1993) exhibit 20.

[169] Home Office, *Building Communities, Beating Crime – A Better Police Service for the 21st Century*, CM 6360 (London: TSO, 2004a). For a general (if somewhat uncritical) review of the field, see Ratcliffe J, *Intelligence-Led Policing* (Cullompton: Willan, 2008).

[170] These specific examples are taken from several others discussed by Leng R, *The Right to Silence in Police Interrogation: A Study of Some of the Issues Underlying the Debate* (Royal Commission on Criminal Justice Research Study No 10) (London: HMSO, 1993) p 25.

no means always the case) then there may seem to be little point making an arrest without his or her agreement. Reality is not, however, so straightforward.

First, the police themselves sometimes influence the wishes of victims. When the police attend the scene of an alleged assault, for example, they are expected to use their judgement to decide which course of action (conciliation, informal warning, on-the-spot fine or arrest) would be better for the victim. They will often discuss these alternatives with the victim, who may have a preference but who will usually be open to advice. Officers who do not wish to arrest can easily make this appear to be an unattractive option, which it may indeed be.[171]

Secondly, the police always pursue grave offences. McConville et al report a serious rape case which led to mass arrests of a broad category of suspect, largely for purposes of elimination.[172] Clarkson et al (1994) examined nearly 100 assault cases. The police pursued five of the most serious cases (all meriting charges of inflicting grievous bodily harm) despite the reluctance and unreliability of the victims.

Thirdly, some victims are more influential than others. Ignoring the views of some – local businessmen and politicians, for instance – would cause more trouble for the police than ignoring others.[173] So Kemp et al[174] comment that in civil disputes, such as trespass, where no criminality is involved:

the police often take immediate action ... to end the dispute, generally by ensuring the physical removal of the 'offender' from the scene. For instance, all 11 requests made by publicans, security guards, shop/office managers, and private landlords in our 60 disputes were supported by the police.

Kemp et al point out that the police have no power to force individuals to leave, and that they could simply explain to the complainants their civil law rights. The important point for us, apart from demonstrating the willingness of the police to exercise authority even where they have no power to back it up, is that police authority is generally exercised in favour of powerful high status victims, rather than victims of low status.[175] Where the latter are concerned, Kemp et al found that:

Victims' views were basically ignored and the offence and the offender became police property to be disposed of in the manner which most suited police rather than victim priorities.[176]

---

[171] Edwards S, *Policing Domestic Violence* (London: Sage, 1989); Kemp et al (1992).

[172] McConville et al (1991: ch 2).

[173] Although the police may be reluctant to act on the wishes of high status victims if the alleged offenders are also high status, as the latter are capable of causing the police 'in-the-job trouble' by complaining about the arrest (as illustrated by the furore surrounding the arrest in November 2008 of the Opposition front bench spokesperson on immigration, Damian Green MP: <http://news.bbc.co.uk/1/hi/uk_politics/7754099.stm> – accessed 5 January 2010).   [174] Kemp et al (1992: 65).

[175] Thus the 'victims' in *Steel v UK* (op cit) were powerful arms dealers, government and grouse shoots, all of whose interests were facilitated by police arrests of the people protesting against their activities. Note, however, that it is unlawful for the police to solicit or accept financial contributions from victims to help fund an investigation, as this would jeopardise impartial and even-handed law enforcement: *R v Hounsham & Ors* [2005] EWCA Crim 1366.

[176] Kemp et al (1992: 73). See further Sanders A, 'Personal Violence and Public Order' (1988a) 16 IJ Sociology of Law 359.

The police are perhaps the most influential victims of all. This was explored earlier, in the sense that threats to their authority make them victims. But it goes further than this. Brown and Ellis found that in many of the public order arrests they looked at, the police appeared to be the only victims, even though the Public Order Act is supposed to protect the public: 'what is at issue in many of the cases...is the enforcement of respect for the police'.[177] And nothing attracts the immediate and disproportionate attention of the police quite like a serious assault on a fellow officer.

The police are acting entirely within the law in these examples, for there are no laws establishing rights for victims in relation to arrest, and the Code of Practice for Victims[178] only says that victims will be able to explain how the crime has affected them and that this will be 'taken into account' by the police and other agencies. Exactly the same findings have been made in the United States, suggesting that this is not a local or temporary phenomenon.[179] As with many aspects of the operation of police powers, it is not what was done, but who did it or who was the victim of it, that matters most.

Other factors

The other main working rules give primacy to organisational factors, 'information received' from informants or co-suspects, and workload. We examined the impact of organisational and societal factors on police discretion in general in 2.1. Arrests are as subject to such influences as any other aspect of policing. Periodic panics over vice, drugs, 'mugging' and so forth lead to surges in arrests for these offences. Sometimes individual communities or police forces adopt particular arrest policies. In an American study, the arrest rate in town A was over three times as high as in town B, giving the impression of a much lower crime rate in the latter. In reality, though, the crime rates were very similar. The true difference was that the affluent middle class residents of town B put enormous pressure on the police not to arrest their offspring.[180] Similar things happen in the UK. One study of drugs enforcement found a considerable number of arrests for possession of cannabis, while another found that the police forces it looked at had reoriented their drugs arrest policies to higher-level trafficking.[181]

The police frequently arrest suspects purely on the strength of an allegation, or 'information received'. If the allegation coincides with 'previous', so much the better, as in a case cited by McConville et al: 'you have to react on what you hear initially...when we checked his form we thought there might be a chance; the name

---

[177] Brown and Ellis (1994: 42).   [178] For discussion of the Code, see ch 13.

[179] See Buzawa E and Buzawa C, 'The Impact of Arrest on Domestic Assault' (1993) 36 American Behavioural Scientist 558.

[180] Meehan A, 'Internal Police Records and the Control of Juveniles' (1993) 33 BJ Crim 504.

[181] May T et al, *Times They are a Changing: Policing of Cannabis* (York: YPS, 2002); Newburn T and Elliott J, *Policing Anti-drug Strategies: Tackling Drugs Together 3 Years On* (London: Home Office Police Research Group, 1998).

even rang a bell to the lads...'[182] Since this arrestee did not fit the description and absolutely nothing connected him with the offence, it would have been difficult for the police to claim that they had 'reasonable suspicion'. Societal pressures often lie behind legally dubious arrests. For example, the Macpherson Inquiry's sharp criticisms of the police for failing to act quickly in arresting the prime suspects in the Stephen Lawrence case[183] resulted in a perception by senior homicide detectives in London that early arrest was now virtually mandatory ('even if knowledge and information was sparse').[184]

Workload can have all sorts of effects. Police officers avoid arresting when they have too much to do, and look for arrests when they have too little to do.[185] The weather can also be important (when it is cold and wet, almost any excuse to get back to the station will do), as can a host of other factors. Young (2002: 200) notes that the use of arrest to 'solve' problematic situations involving mentally disordered people was valued by many of the officers in her in-depth study of two police stations, not least because it was perceived to reduce future workload. This was particularly evident where the police were faced with repeated calls to attend the same address. As one officer recalled: 'On our way back to the address my colleague, of quite a few years in, was such that he said: "right, that's it, we'll just nick her, we'll have her out of there"...I didn't think it was the right thing to do, trying to put her through the system, even though, yes, it's going to save you having to go back there again during the night.' By the same token, arrests of the mentally disordered (whether for protective or prosecution purposes) were sometimes avoided because of the 'downstream workload consequences' of taking formal action. Officers felt that it was unfair (on the custody officer) to bring mentally ill people to the police station because 'they are more likely to attack police officers because they panic,...are difficult to cope with' and because the custody staff are blamed for any consequent self-harming behaviour. The standing joke of the worst custody scenario was 'a mentally disordered, juvenile, Croatian woman with children' (Young, 2002: 189–90). Thus the working norm in favour of upholding order in public has to be weighed against the working rule of avoiding disorder and disproportionate workload in the police station.

Another very important factor is the drive for 'figures' and 'quality figures' in particular. As Young says:

In this [CID] world the detection rate is of vital concern, and a succession of poor returns in the monthly or quarterly detection figures can break the ambitious detective inspector...As a result, those calls for a change of emphasis to such matters as 'crime prevention' have little or no chance of obtaining prominence...[186]

---

[182] McConville et al (1991: 30).   [183] Macpherson (1999) para 13.41.

[184] Foster J, '"It Might Have Been Incompetent, But It Wasn't Racist": Murder Detectives' Perceptions of the Lawrence Inquiry and its Impact on Homicide Investigation in London' (2008) 18(2) Policing and Society 89.   [185] Choongh (1997: 71–2).

[186] Young M, *An Inside Job* (Oxford: OUP, 1991) p 255.

Exactly the same point is made by Maguire and Norris, who observe that arrest and detection rates are still important promotion criteria; by Choongh, who observes that uniformed branches, as well as the CID, are under pressure to arrest;[187] and by officers themselves who sometimes suggest that cannabis possession arrests are easy to 'notch up' for probationers.[188] Since a charge counts as a detection regardless of the outcome (hence regardless of the evidence) the pressures to treat 'reasonable suspicion' lightly are difficult to resist. From a freedom perspective this is objectionable, because police power should be used only where it increases freedom – something that merely counting 'figures' cannot take into account. It is interesting to see that this view is voiced, in different terminology, by police officers themselves. Smith and Gray,[189] for example, report many officers saying that they end up making 'pointless...unnecessary or unjustified arrests and stops'. This is one instance where a move towards 'freedom' would not be resisted by the police[190] – perhaps because the drive for 'figures' is pure window-dressing, and therefore no more about crime control than it is about due process or freedom.

The use of working rules to guide arrest very often leads to more of a crime control than a due process approach. This is not necessarily antithetical to a 'freedom' approach. If respect for the police, for instance, allows the police to continue as a largely unarmed force, then the use of arrest to enforce respect might be acceptable if it worked. The evidence suggests, however, that the overuse of arrest is more likely to generate fear, resentment and non-cooperation than respect.[191] In other words, it generally has the same counterproductive effect as extensive stop-search practices. The same is true of 'easy' arrests for drug possession.[192] Moreover the financial cost of such arrests is huge too. It has been calculated, for example, that the cost of arrests of young recreational users for the possession of *Class A* drugs was, in 2000, nearly £3.8m. The policing costs for cannabis are far higher. It has been estimated that the average time taken by an officer to deal with a cannabis offence is five hours, yielding an overall policing commitment in 1999 of 770,000 officer hours or the equivalent of some 500 officers.[193] The adherent to the freedom perspective would ask whether resources on this scale could be put to better use in protecting vulnerable victims and/or investigating serious crimes more thoroughly. The police are aware of such

---

[187] Maguire M and Norris C, *The Conduct and Supervision of Criminal Investigations* (Royal Commission on Criminal Justice, Research Study No 5) (London: HMSO, 1992) ch 5; Choongh (1997: 69–72). See also Young H (2002: 201) who quotes a patrol officer's explanation of why 'quick fixes' were valued over the kind of complicated proactive problem-solving that might be necessary in the case of the mentally disordered.

[188] May et al (2002).   [189] Smith and Gray (1983: 60).

[190] As indicated by the views of senior police officers: Long J, 'Keeping PACE? Some Front Line Policing Perspectives' in Cape and Young (2008: 106–8); Wilding B, 'Tipping the Scales of Justice?: A Review of the Impact of PACE on the Police, Due Process and the Search for the Truth 1984–2006' in Cape and Young (2008: 146).   [191] See, for example, Brown and Ellis (1994: 43); Bagguley and Hussain (2008: 101–3).

[192] See Lister et al (2008: 48–52).   [193] May et al (2002).

opportunity costs,[194] as can be seen in this officer's comment (which provides yet another illustration of the importance of police victimhood): 'I would feel dreadful if an urgent assistance came over the radio and I was in custody dealing with a tinpot bit of cannabis whilst one of my shift were getting the shit kicked out of them.' The study from which this quote is drawn also found, however, that almost a third of the 150 officers interviewed claimed to always arrest those they found in possession of cannabis, either because they believed in strict enforcement or because they felt to 'turn a blind eye' would leave themselves open to allegations of malpractice. But for some officers, it 'depends on all the circumstances. What happens there and then, the person's demeanour, what time it is, resources, and what our reason for being there was. If our objective is something else, maybe we don't want to get tied up with cannabis'.[195] In conclusion, we can see that when the police follow working rules (which are subject to interpretation and weighting by individual officers) they do not always follow the legal rules. This is because:

(a) some working rules prescribe for the police unlawful purposes in some circumstances, and

(b) some working rules prescribe unlawful criteria for arrest in some circumstances.

Working rules and legality

What is the legality of arrests made without any intention to prosecute, or made because the police are concerned with order rather than specific offences? We have seen that the new summary power of arrest is subject to a necessity principle (see 3.3.2 above) and this may put the legality of many current arrest practices in doubt. In addition, the common law has traditionally seen arrest as a criminal justice mechanism: to either facilitate charge (or another legitimate disposition, such as a caution), or to facilitate the production of evidence relevant to the case.[196] The case law on judicial review of executive action (including that of the police) requires that powers be exercised for a proper purpose and that irrelevant considerations be excluded from the minds of those exercising powers. In *Plange v Chief Constable of South Humberside*[197] Mr Plange was accused of assault by someone who then told the police that he no longer wished to pursue the complaint. The police nonetheless arrested Plange but did not charge him. Plange sued the police for unlawful imprisonment based on the claim that the arrest was unlawful as they did not

---

[194] And this is reflected in their formal policies on cannabis enforcement, although these have shifted in recent years as the government first downgraded and then upgraded the classification of this particular drug. That these policies do not affect the doctrine of constabulary independence can be seen from *R (on the application of Mondelly) v Commissioner of Police of the Metropolis* [2006] EWHC 2370 (Admin).

[195] Warburton et al (2005: 118–19).

[196] Although many public order arrests which do not have prosecution in mind would be lawful if they were made on reasonable suspicion that a crime (or breach of the peace) was *about* to be committed.

[197] *The Times*, 23 March 1992.

anticipate, nor intend, prosecution. The judge ruled that there was no case to go before the jury, and dismissed Plange's action. On appeal, the Court of Appeal held – following the general public law principles referred to above – that, although there was no breach of any statutory provision concerning arrest, 'if it was proved that the arresting officer knew that there was no possibility of a charge, it must usually follow that he had acted upon some irrelevant consideration or improper purpose'. On this basis, the case was returned to the court of first instance for a re-trial. This decision is consistent with the view expressed by the European Commission in *McVeigh* (discussed in 3.3.3 above).[198] Arrest, it said 'must be for the purpose of securing [the] fulfilment [of an obligation prescribed by law] and not, for instance, punitive in character'.

This means that many unofficial purposes of arrest – such as to put the 'frighteners' on people, or to secure information about other people's crimes – appear to breach the common law. Commendable from both a due process and freedom viewpoint though this may be, the courts appear unaware of the large number of arrests which would be outlawed by this reasoning.

In *Chalkley and Jeffries*[199] another common police practice was questioned. The defendants were arrested for a credit card fraud for which there was reasonable suspicion. The real reason for the arrest was, however, to give other officers time to install bugging equipment in their house in order to gather evidence of a far more serious conspiracy to rob. At trial the defendants applied for this evidence to be ruled inadmissible because it was, they said, obtained unfairly. The judge refused to do this. The defendants pleaded guilty because this evidence was so incriminating, but then appealed against the conviction, saying that the judge was wrong. The Court of Appeal said that 'holding charges' (that is, arrests for one purpose while gathering evidence of a more serious charge) were entirely proper if those arrests were lawful. Whether they were lawful or not depended on whether a prosecution was possible or not – and prosecution for the fraud was a possibility (unlike the prosecution for assault in *Plange*).

From a freedom point of view the ruling in *Chalkley* might be acceptable on the ground that an arrest was made on lawful grounds, involving a small deprivation of liberty, in order to counter a more significant crime (the conspiracy to rob). This would have to be balanced against the value the 'freedom' perspective puts on honesty from the police in dealing with the public.[200]

3.4.4 Domestic violence and arrest

From a legalistic point of view, the use of arrest for domestic violence should be no different to its use for any other crime. Domestic violence is assault. Whether

---

[198] *McVeigh* (1981) 25 DR 15.   [199] *Chalkley and Jeffries* [1998] 2 Cr App Rep 79.
[200] See generally Ashworth A, 'Should the Police Be Allowed to Use Deceptive Practices?' (1998) 114 LQR 108.

it is a relatively minor common assault or a very serious GBH or attempted murder depends on the seriousness of the injuries inflicted, if any, and the intent of the violent partner. Normally, one would expect these factors (including the strength of the evidence of them), along perhaps with the wishes of the victim, to determine whether or not the suspect is arrested. However, until the early 1990s domestic violence was hardly treated as a criminal problem at all, except in the most severe cases. So the police generally arrested only when they both anticipated a successful prosecution and perceived the injuries and/or danger to the victim as grave. In a study carried out in London in the early 1980s, but which was probably representative of the general national situation, Edwards (1989) found only a 2% arrest rate. Domestic violence (along with other interpersonal violence) was unusual in that victims withdrew their complaints against perpetrators more frequently than did victims of other offences, and the police usually took this to mean that a prosecution would fail. Thus not only were the police reluctant to arrest where the victim was ambivalent, but they were reluctant to arrest also where she did ask for strong action, because they anticipated her changing her mind.[201] This created a vicious circle, insofar as many women lost confidence in the police and so were reluctant to call them, or were easily persuaded to withdraw their complaints because they expected the police to do little or nothing. This reinforced police beliefs about the victims and their lack of resolve to see their partners prosecuted.

This led the Home Office to issue a circular which urged the police to take a more interventionist approach, arresting wherever there was evidence.[202] Hoyle's evaluation of the effect of the new policy found that arrest was still infrequent, occurring in only 17% of incidents. Grace found similar results.[203] This is an interesting example of what happens when official policies (or, by extension, laws) are changed in an attempt to alter police attitudes and practices – some effect is discernible, but not as much as we would expect if only the 'normal' factors outlined in the previous paragraph were applied.[204] Hoyle found that 'cop culture' and 'working rules' still exerted a strong influence. The most important working rule, since 'suspiciousness' and 'order and authority' rarely applied, was the wishes of the victim. Whereas before the circular the police rarely arrested even when the victim wished them to, the main effect of the circular was to persuade the police to arrest usually when the victim wanted, but still very rarely otherwise. This remained so even when, later in the 1990s, several police forces adopted policies that virtually instructed the police to arrest.[205]

---

[201] Edwards (1989).

[202] *Domestic Violence* (Circular 66/90) (London: Home Office, 1990).

[203] Grace S, *Policing Domestic Violence in the 1990s* (Home Office Research Study No 139) (London: Home Office, 1995); Hoyle C, *Negotiating Domestic Violence* (Oxford: Clarendon, 1998).

[204] For a general discussion of the relationship between legal rules, policies and police action, see Dixon D, *Law in Policing* (Oxford: Clarendon, 1997).

[205] Hoyle and Sanders (2000); Wright S, 'Policing Domestic Violence: A Nottingham Case Study' (1998) 20 JSWFL 397. The US findings are similar. For a review of English and American research see Paradine K

From a due process viewpoint, this might appear laudable. Arrests were usually based on a realistic assessment of the outcome of prosecution. But why did the police adopt this legalistic approach in domestic violence cases, and not in other cases? Why not arrest in order to put the 'frighteners' on perpetrators, or as a means of controlling their violence, as in other criminal contexts?[206] Not only are the police inconsistent, but, from a 'freedom' perspective, they appear to have their priorities wrong. Hoyle (1998) found, as have all other researchers, that most domestic violence victims suffer repeat victimisation. In other words, their plight is far worse than might be suspected from any one incident to which the police are called. Arrest and, where appropriate, further action is therefore usually justifiable in terms of overall offence seriousness even if the specific offence to which the police are called is minor. Further, most women who call the police seek arrest even when they do not desire prosecution. They want the violence to stop, and time to consider their position.[207] Arrest provides this, and thus gives these victims far more freedom than is taken from perpetrators by arrest. While arrest on this basis (ie with, in many cases, reasonable suspicion but no intention or prospect of prosecution, let alone conviction) is justifiable on a freedom basis, and is common in other contexts, it would sometimes be difficult to reconcile with the law as stated in *Plange*.[208] In *Plange*, it will be recalled, the victim did not wish to testify, and – in the absence of other strong evidence – this meant that the case would not be prosecuted. This is precisely the situation in many domestic violence incidents, although if there was the danger of a breach of the peace the arrest could be justified on that ground anyway.[209]

In the 1980s and 1990s US jurisdictions increasingly adopted 'mandatory arrest' policies for domestic violence cases: the police are instructed (not merely encouraged) to arrest, if there is sufficient evidence, regardless of the wishes of the victim or of the prospects of a successful prosecution. This is partly because attempts to encourage the police to change were only partially successful, like in the UK. It is also in order to take the initiative away from victims, in recognition of the intimidation and retaliation they suffer from many perpetrators who blame them for their arrest and (where it happens) prosecution. Similarly, in 2000 the UK Government produced a revised circular for the guidance of the police that adopted a near-mandatory arrest policy (sometimes known as a 'pro-arrest' policy),[210] and the passing of the Domestic Violence, Crime

---

and Wilkinson J, *Protection and Accountability: The Reporting, Investigation and Prosecution of Domestic Violence Cases* (London: HMIC and HMCPSI, 2004).

[206] The crime control effectiveness of arrest in this context has been a matter of controversy and conflicting evidence since the mid 1980s. See Hilton et al, 'The Effect of Arrest on Wife Assault Recidivism: Controlling for Pre-Arrest Risk' (2007) 34(10) Criminal Justice and Behaviour 1334 for a review of the literature and new (Canadian) findings to the effect that 'there was a small beneficial effect of arrest, possibly in delaying recidivism' (p 1342).

[207] Hoyle C and Sanders A, 'Police Response to Domestic Violence: From Victim Choice to Victim Empowerment?' (2000) BJ Crim 40. For discussion of other research with similar findings, see Paradine and Wilkinson (2004).   [208] *The Times*, 23 March 1992, CA.

[209] *Chief Constable of Cleveland Police v McGrogan* [2002] EWCA Civ 86.

[210] Home Office: *Domestic Violence* (Circular 19/2000) paras 3 and 4.

and Victims Act in 2004 was designed to signal to the police that they should take domestic violence more seriously.

Did this new policy have the desired effect? Some indications suggest not. Research was carried out by the Inspectorates of the Police and CPS in six English police forces in 2003. In three, 'grading policy' was complied with in only around half of all incidents reported; this is the kind of situation reported in the 1970s, when domestic violence was graded so low that the police response was slow and/or inadequate. In this research the response was usually reasonable, whatever the grading, but it did sometimes take hours for the police to arrive at a potentially dangerous situation. In situations where a power of arrest was available the police arrested in between 13% and 63% of cases. It is implausible to suppose that the cases varied so much between police areas. Clearly it is the extent to which the new policy is internalised by the police that varies. The overall arrest rate where arrest was possible averaged at little more than 30%. If the circular were being fully complied with the arrest rate would have been at least twice this. It seems that the police were still allowing many factors other than strength of evidence to influence them.[211] Victims of domestic violence are among the weakest groups in our society. Even though many are middle class professionals – domestic violence knows no class or ethnic boundaries – it is their abused status and self-image which makes them, in general, weak. The working rule relating to victims – that, in general, the views and interests of powerful victims only should be influential – remained stubbornly in place.[212]

But the fundamental problem remains that the police are reluctant to arrest – legalistically speaking, correctly – when there is insufficient evidence. What constitutes 'evidence' is a matter of construction, however (see ch 7). The evidence of the victim will sometimes be vital, but this is something that requires evaluation, not an assumption, in each case. In the USA, domestic violence is increasingly prosecuted without victim participation, and there are strong arguments for, as well as concerns about, doing the same in the UK.[213] And victims may be more willing to give evidence (and support an arrest) if the criminal justice system is perceived to be more sympathetic to their needs and interests. To the Government's credit it has established and

---

[211] HMIC and HMCPSI, *Violence at Home: The Investigation and Prosecution of Cases Involving Domestic Violence* (London: HMIC and HMCPSI, 2004). Also see Hester M et al, *Domestic Violence: Making it through the Criminal Justice System* (Sunderland: University of Sunderland, 2003) and other studies discussed in Paradine and Wilkinson (2004).

[212] The same kind of analysis could probably be made of black and Asian victims. The failure to investigate properly the murder of black teenager Stephen Lawrence has been taken by many to exemplify police attitudes towards ethnic minority victims of violence. See the Macpherson Report (1999). For the argument that ethnic minority female victims of domestic violence are in a particularly weak position, and receive a poor police service in consequence, see Belur J, 'Is Policing Domestic Violence Institutionally Racist? A Case Study of South Asian Women' (2008) 18(4) Policing and Society 426.

[213] See Ellison L, 'Prosecuting Domestic Violence Without Victim Participation' [2002] 56 MLR 834; 'Responding to Victim Withdrawal in Domestic Violence Prosecutions' [2003] Crim LR 760. This is discussed further in ch 7.

maintained a high priority for domestic violence in this decade, setting up specialist domestic violence courts and creating a network of independent domestic violence advisers to help victims negotiate the criminal justice process. Together with other measures, such as specialist training for crown prosecutors, the chances of successful prosecution have probably never been higher.[214] Thus much of the traditional police reluctance to arrest may dissipate.

Even if such reluctance remains amongst patrol officers, it does not follow that the arrest rate will remain low. While street-level discretion has long been difficult to control, this is becoming increasingly less the case due to such developments as the National Crime Recording Standard (dictating how certain incidents must be classified in terms of crimes) and computerised call-handling systems, which can be used to dictate (in effect) and monitor the police response, thus rendering patrol officers vulnerable to 'in-the-job trouble' if they do not apply force policy. Thus Rowe's observational study conducted in 2004 in one English police service found that despite continued cynicism about domestic violence cases amongst many patrol officers, because all such incidents were graded as top priority by the control rooms, officers typically attended the scene rapidly. Moreover, the pro-arrest policy was always complied with, even in cases where arrest was seen as clearly counter-productive and contrary to the victim's wishes and interests – largely to avoid criticism from supervising officers who were known to monitor the outcomes of calls using the computerised logs.[215] There is obviously a danger here of the pendulum having swung too far in favour of arrest, resulting in net reductions in overall freedom, even if one only takes victims' interests into account. Rowe's research does show, however, that police service managers committed to the pro-arrest policy may now have the means to ensure that it is well-implemented in practice.

3.4.5 Race, class and arrest

It is clear from the above that police working rules do not impact equally upon all sections of society. 'Cop culture' – but not the research literature – regards some social and racial groups as more criminogenic than others. Some groups probably do commit some types of crime more than do others. For example, young socially marginalised youths are almost certainly involved in more street drug dealing and robbery than are older people in regular work; but those older people commit other drugs offences and fraudulent crimes in large numbers instead. 'Targeting' may therefore be justified, but not when considerations of equity and offence seriousness are disregarded such that

---

[214] See Inter-Ministerial Group on Domestic and Sexual Violence, *National Domestic Violence Delivery Plan: Annual Progress Report 2007/08* (available from <http://www.crimereduction.homeoffice.gov.uk/domesticviolence/domesticviolence069a.pdf> – accessed 5 January 2010).

[215] Rowe M, 'Rendering Visible the Invisible: Police Discretion, Professionalism and Decision-making' (2007) 17 (3) Policing & Society 279 (see at 290 in particular).

Table 3.1   Total arrests for notifiable offences per 1,000 population aged 10 and over, by ethnic appearance[216]

Year	Ethnic appearance of person arrested				
	White	Black	Asian	Other	Total
1998/99	26	116	44	25	28
1999/00	26	113	37	21	28
2000/01	25	121	45	24	27
2001/02	26	85	27	28	28
2002/03	26	90	29	32	28
2003/04	26	89	29	36	28
2004/05	27	91	30	36	29
2005/06	29	100	33	36	32
2006/07	29	104	34	34	31
2007/08	28	104	35	35	31

the offences which are primarily targeted are those which are, or are thought to be, committed by small, disadvantaged, sections of society.

The result of skewed targeting and the general operation of working rules based on police officers' cultural assumptions is a pattern of unjustified discrimination. For example, Stevens and Willis found that black people in deprived socio-economic conditions were no more likely to commit crimes than were white people in those conditions.[217] Yet this study (pre-PACE) and post-PACE studies such as that by Jefferson and Walker, and Fitzgerald and Sibbitt[218] found disproportionate arrest rates among black people. The official statistics are in line with this research, as can be seen from table 3.1.

These official statistics show that in 2007/08 black people were 3.8 times more likely to be arrested than white people, relative to their numbers in the population,[219] and similarly striking disproportionality ratios have been reported over the last decade. Although much of this is due to a higher proportion of black people than white people in the general population being young and socially marginal, some of it is a product of

---

[216] Source: annual publications in the 'Statistics on Race and the Criminal Justice System' available from the Home Office and Ministry of Justice websites. The statistics are usually based on estimates given problems of missing data, and are often revised when more up-to-date/complete data become available (including census data). Thus table 3.1 should be treated as providing only a reasonable approximation of disproportionality trends.

[217] Stevens P and Willis CF, *Race, Crime and Arrests* (HORS No 58) (London: HMSO, 1979).

[218] Jefferson T and Walker M, 'Ethnic Minorities in the Criminal Justice System' [1992] Crim LR 83. Fitzgerald M and Sibbitt R, *Ethnic Monitoring in Police Forces* (Home Office Research Study No 173) (London: Home Office, 1997).

[219] Ministry of Justice, *Statistics on Race and the Criminal Justice System, 2007/8* (London: MoJ, 2009b) p 72. See generally discussion by Hillyard and Gordon (1999).

proactive policing. Stevens and Willis found that black people were particularly liable to be arrested for offences such as preparatory and public order offences where 'there is considerable scope for selective perception of potential or actual offenders'.[220] Brown and Ellis, in more recent research, also found disproportionate arrests of black people for public order offences.[221] Although they do not commit themselves to an explanation for this, they say that:

it may well be that black people are more likely to perceive s 5 warnings about their behaviour as provocation, leading to an escalation of the situation. Another possibility is that the police are more ready to react adversely where they receive abuse from black people.

Public order-type offences are classic products of proactive policing. They are, in other words, usually discovered as a result of police initiative, like other 'victimless' crimes (eg drugs, prostitution).

   Around 75% of all arrests are for incidents reported to the police by the public.[222] It might be thought that this means that police bias through proactive policing would play only a small part in shaping the ethnic (and class) profile of the population of arrestees. However, just because the public report an incident, it does not follow that the public identifies the suspected offender. Phillips and Brown found that in 40% of arrests the main evidence was police evidence – evidence which is often secured through the operation of working rules.[223]

   It seems that just being black makes one suspicious and thus more liable to being arrested.[224] Fitzgerald and Sibbitt (1997) show this happening at a more general statistical level. Being young and male, as well as black, is even more risky. This is confirmed by Phillips and Brown who, as Home Office researchers, are understandably cautious in their interpretation of their figures. They show that not only are ethnic minorities over-represented among those who are arrested, but also that the evidence against ethnic minority arrestees is, on average, significantly weaker than against white arrestees. For example, in violent offences there was enough evidence to charge on arrest in 45% of white cases but only 37% and 17% respectively in cases involving black and Asian suspects, while for public order offences the corresponding figures were 84% (whites) 65% (blacks) and 64% (Asians).[225] The finding of the Official Inquiry into the failure to apprehend the murderers of black London teenager Stephen Lawrence, that the Metropolitan Police embodies 'institutional racism', fits in with our belief that simply being young and black increases the probability that one will attract police suspicion – and that ethnic minority victims are less likely than white victims to have

---

[220] Stevens and Willis (1979: 41).   [221] Brown and Ellis (1994: 33).
[222] Phillips and Brown (1998: ch 2).   [223] Phillips and Brown (1998: 41).
[224] The overall disproportionate arrest rates of blacks, as compared to whites, can only partially be explained in this way. The difference appears also to be due to the greater social deprivation of blacks and reporting and recording differences: Jefferson and Walker (1992). Note that all these studies found that Asians were arrested disproportionately infrequently, but see later discussion, post 9/11 and 7/7.
[225] Phillips and Brown (1998: 45).

their cases 'solved' by arrest.[226] The extent to which this takes place is a matter of debate.[227] But even Smith, who sets out to show that the massive over-representation of black people in prison is not due to bias, concedes that 'some bias against black people has been demonstrated at several stages of the process, and...some decision-making criteria clearly work to the disadvantage of black people...'[228] Or, as Holdaway puts it, 'It is not *either* structural factors *or* police discrimination that lead to high crime rates for black youth but both.'[229] Because as we shall see in later chapters, police and CPS prosecution decisions largely endorse the wishes of the arresting/investigating officers, one consequence is that many more cases, proportionately, involving ethnic minorities fail in court than do those involving white people.[230]

Unemployed and low-paid people are also massively over-represented in the arrest statistics, even taking into account socio-economic conditions.[231] Only one-quarter of all the arrests in Philips and Brown's random sample were of employed people.[232] Hillyard and Gordon (1999) observe that arrest rates in the poorest areas of the UK are massively higher than in wealthier areas, reinforcing the 'north-south divide'. In addition to community pressures and 'attitude' problems, these people are simply more vulnerable to being arrested, for they spend much of their time in public spaces where police powers can most easily be deployed. In 3.4.3 above we discussed research by McAra and McVie showing that youths with 'previous' were more likely to be arrested or formally warned than those with no 'previous' even after the level of their crime was taken into account. This was especially if their friends had similar experiences and if they spent much time on the streets. These youths were overwhelmingly working class. In other words, police working rules unwittingly pick out the socially marginal.[233]

How can we explain the fact that many people are arrested on little or no evidence, in defiance of 'reasonable suspicion' laws, and that poor, black and Asian people disproportionately suffer from this? We need to ask what the police want, and what they might fear, when they arrest. What they want is: to punish, by arrest and detention, those who fail to display respect; to maintain order and prevent further disorder or

---

[226] Macpherson of Cluny, Sir W, *The Stephen Lawrence Inquiry* (Cm 4262-I) (London: SO, 1999); Bowling B, *Violent Racism* (Oxford: OUP, 1998).

[227] Murder investigations post-Macpherson continue to have a racialised dimension (notwithstanding denials by the police that this is so): Foster (2008).

[228] Smith D, 'Ethnic Origins, Crime and Criminal Justice' in Maguire M, Morgan R and Reiner R (eds), *Oxford Handbook of Criminology*, 2nd edn (Oxford: Clarendon Press, 1997) p 751.

[229] Holdaway S, *The Racialisation of British Policing* (Houndmills: MacMillan, 1996) p 96. It should be borne in mind that the term 'high crime rates', in common use, relates to the recorded figures, which are a product of arrest practices as well as 'actual' crime. See pp 84–104 of Holdaway's book for a sophisticated discussion of race, crime and arrests; and also Bowling B and Phillips C, *Racism, Crime and Justice* (Harlow: Longman, 2002) ch 6.

[230] HM Crown Prosecution Inspectorate, *Thematic Review of Casework having an Ethnic Minority Dimension* (London: HMCPI, 2002).

[231] Meehan (1993); Sanders A, 'Class Bias in Prosecutions' (1985) 24 Howard JCJ 76.

[232] Phillips and Brown (1998: xii).

[233] McAra and McVie (2005). The ethnic minority dimension is not discussed, perhaps because Edinburgh, where the research was carried out, is overwhelmingly white.

crime; or to secure evidence leading to prosecution and conviction. What they fear is adverse comeback if they 'mess up'. Arresting people on 'fishing expeditions' who may provide information, arresting people for the purpose of elimination, or arresting people to enforce order is therefore viable for the police if the arrestee is unlikely to sue, make a plausible complaint, or otherwise challenge their actions.[234] This is true largely of low status people: those who are young, black/Asian or working class (and especially of those who possess all three characteristics). Hence the pattern observed in relation to stop-search is repeated and amplified at the arrest stage. Patterns of bias are created through the following of police working rules which dictate who to select for arrest out of a much larger group of arrestable suspects. The rule that the police must act only when they have 'reasonable suspicion' is sometimes ignored in this process, but the flexibility of this requirement means that breach is often not necessary. It is therefore in part an enabling rule, allowing the police to use informal norms, and in part a presentational rule with little inhibitory effect. Having said all that, it is right to highlight the efforts made by the present Government to tackle racial discrimination within the criminal justice system (even as its anti-terrorist legislation exacerbates the problem, as shown in 3.3.3) and to acknowledge that in some areas the patterns of apparent bias are not stark. For example, there is relatively little difference in the rates of arrest for Asian and white people (see table 3.1). However, it can be observed that the gap between those rates has widened somewhat since 2004/05 which may reflect increased targeting (including arrest) of Asians following the attacks on London's transport system in July 2005.

Statistics on arrest rates of 'Asians', of course, can only tell us so much about patterns of police response to such terrorist incidents. Crude racial categorisations such as 'blacks' and 'whites' can obscure as much as they reveal. For example, white people of Irish origin long suffered more at the hands of the police than the 'indigenous white' population,[235] but this was difficult to monitor when all 'white people' were lumped together in the official statistics. Similarly, many Muslims living in England and Wales would be classified by the police as white or black rather than Asian, and those classified as Asians are obviously not all followers of Islam.[236] The intensity with which the police focus their attention on Asian/Muslims may currently be very different from the policing of other Asian/faith groups such as Sikhs, Hindus or Christians. More nuanced arrest figures based on *self-defined* ethnicity were published for the first time in 2007/08 and appear to indicate exactly this: there were 20 arrests per 1,000 population aged 10 and over for people who self-defined their ethnicity as Indian

---

[234] Consider, for example, the anxiety and attempted buck-passing evident within the police when a decision had to be made regarding whether or not to arrest the former MP Neil Hamilton, and his wife Christine, in connection with (concocted) sexual assault allegations: *Miller v Associated Newspapers Ltd* [2005] EWHC 557.   [235] See Hillyard (1993).

[236] The 2001 Census was the first to collect information on religion. See Hussain S, 'An Introduction to Muslims in the 2001 Census' available at <http://www.bristol.ac.uk/sociology/ethnicitycitizenship/urcresearch.html> (last accessed 16 June 2009). See further Madood T, 'Muslims and the Politics of Difference' (2003) *Political Quarterly* 100 at 103–4 in particular.

(most of whom will not be Muslim) while the equivalent rate for those self-defining as Pakistanis or Bangladeshi (who will overwhelmingly be Muslims) was just over double this.[237] Finally, there is the point that calculating quantitative rates of arrest tells us nothing about the qualitative experience of arrest and it is to this that we now turn.

3.4.6 **The experience of arrest**

In this section of the chapter we have focused on what 'reasonable suspicion' means in the context of arrest, how far arrest discretion actually adheres to this standard, and what the impact is on socially disadvantaged groups of the pattern of arrests. We did this because 'reasonable suspicion' is the key standard set out by law, and adherence to it ought to eliminate, or at least reduce, unfair discrimination. However, it is not just the basis on which police power is exercised that is important, but also the way it is exercised. Tyler, for example, has found that most people can accept unjust results if they think the process by which those results were reached is fair.[238] If people are treated with respect and without unreasonable force when they are arrested, and detained for only as long as is necessary, their freedoms will be encroached on less than if their experience is unpleasant.[239] If we accept, as the Philips Commission did,[240] that arrest is intrinsically coercive, it follows that even a little overbearing behaviour on the part of the police encroaches significantly on the freedom of the suspect. The manner in which arrests are made is therefore of fundamental importance to a criminal justice system based on the freedom approach. And, as we saw in the previous chapter, the manner in which police powers are exerted is crucially important for police-citizen relations, which impact upon citizens' willingness to help clear up crime, which in turn impacts upon everyone's freedom.

In 3.1, and in ch 1, we gave some examples of the way in which arrest can be humiliating or even terrifying. In another example, Choongh was told by a suspect that when he told police officers who stopped him on the street to 'leave me alone', they told him he was under arrest. When he objected 'he [an officer] punched me in the balls'.[241] Some readers might doubt the credibility of such a story, but in the Internet age it is easy to observe violent arrests for oneself.[242] Examples like these often involve minority groups, such as black people and – increasingly since 9/11 – Asians. In a prevention of terrorism example, 'out of nowhere, various plain clothes detectives pounced on us from behind and threw us up against the wall . . . they spread-eagled

---

[237] Ministry of Justice (2009b) table 5.2b, p 79. Interestingly, this table shows that white Irish people (25 arrests per thousand) now have a slightly lower arrest rate than white British people (26 arrests per thousand) – which is consistent with our argument (see 3.3.3) that young, male Muslims have replaced 'the Irish' as the prime suspects so far as terrorism is concerned.

[238] Tyler T, *Why People Obey the Law* (New Haven: Yale University Press, 1990).

[239] See the discussion of the 'freedom' model in ch 1.   [240] See 3.1 above.

[241] Choongh (1997: 65).

[242] For example, at <http://news.bbc.co.uk/1/hi/england/nottinghamshire/8103707.stm> (accessed 5 January 2010).

our legs. They told us not to turn around...One of them grabbed me by the throat and dragged me into one of the Black Marias that had appeared from nowhere'.[243] CAMPACC (2003) gives examples of terrorism arrests (that proved groundless) that terrorised the arrestees.

CAMPACC also documents other serious, although probably unintended, effects of arrest for highly stigmatic 'crimes' such as terrorism. Whole Asian communities (including those studying at University)[244] have come to fear police action after a series of apparently groundless mass arrests, including that in April 2009 discussed in 3.3.3. One arrestee was ostracised by neighbours who either feared him or feared being 'tarred with the same brush' (perhaps wisely in the sense that being associated with terrorists is a ground for arrest!). Another was afraid of accepting support from an Asian charity, fearing that this would make him guilty of something by association. This was all regardless of the lack of prosecutions in these cases.

We suspect, but cannot prove, that socially marginal groups are treated disproportionately badly when arrested. We also suspect, but again cannot prove, that many arrests are unnecessarily violent, abusive or humiliating. We cannot demonstrate this because, even more than 'reasonable suspicion', the manner of arrest is almost unmeasurable. Further, it has hardly been studied and has rarely been the subject of litigation to our knowledge. This is because few of those arrested are able or willing to seek redress in the courts. Rather more use the (free of charge) option of complaining to the Independent Police Complaints Commission – some 8,600 allegations of wrongdoing relating to arrest were made by members of the public in 2007/08.[245] But most such complaints meet with little success, for reasons discussed in ch 12.

Occasionally, however, 'respectable' arrestees do challenge the manner of their arrest successfully. In *Bibby v Chief Constable of Essex* (discussed in 3.3.4), for example, a bailiff in dispute with a debtor was arrested to prevent a breach of the peace, put in handcuffs and taken to the police station where he was released an hour later. The bailiff argued that even if the arrest was lawful the use of handcuffs was unreasonable given that he had made no attempt to resist the arrest. The Court agreed, with Pill LJ observing that:

placing the bailiff in handcuffs and taking him in handcuffs through a public place and on the journey to the police station in a police car was in my view wholly unjustified. Even if the arrest had been justified, which it was not, the situation did not require that further indignity.[246]

---

[243] Hillyard (1993: 129).

[244] A particularly notorious example being the arrest in May 2008 of a University of Nottingham PhD student who had downloaded from the US justice department website an 'al-Qaida Training Manual' (a declassified document which anyone can buy from Amazon!) on to his computer in connection with his doctoral research. See Hicham Yezza, 'Britain's Terror Laws have Left Me and My Family Shattered', *The Guardian*, 18 August 2008.

[245] It can be estimated that 2,388 of these allegations related to incivility/impoliteness/intolerance, 3,645 of them to allegations of unreasonable force, and 2,573 to unlawful or unnecessary arrest/detention: Gleeson E and Grace K, *Police Complaints: Statistics for England and Wales 2007/08*, IPCC Research and Statistics Series: Paper 12 (London: IPCC, 2009) pp 7–8 and table 2.3.   [246] [2000] EWCA Civ 113.

Domestic courts must also take into account Art 2 of the ECHR, under which 'No-one shall be subjected to torture or to inhuman or degrading treatment or punishment.' The examples we have referred to in this section of the chapter seem to us to amount to 'degrading treatment', and *Bibby* indicates that the courts might agree. The best possibility of *effective* control, however, would be if police officers monitored and checked each other's behaviour (see 1.6.9). While this might seem somewhat idealistic in the light of our discussion of 'cop culture' and institutional racism in ch 2, we also noted there that there is reason to believe that attitudes within the police are slowly changing. With that in mind it is both heartening and depressing to find in a national newspaper in 2005 that: 'Recently a constable was suspended for making monkey noises at a [black] youth he was arresting. Two officers reported the incident. A third who did not was disciplined.'[247] And in the policing of protests, police officers have on occasion been observed to intervene when their colleagues use excessive force.[248] But the video of the deadly assault on Ian Tomlinson at the G20 protest in April 2009 indicates that numerous supervising officers are still prone to doing nothing when they observe a fellow officer resorting to unprovoked violence.[249]

None of this is intended to suggest that all or even most arrests are unnecessarily degrading. Sometimes the police make special efforts to arrest as clinically as possible. Waddington shows how when protests are arranged in advance, the policing strategy is also planned, usually with a view to minimising trouble for the police and disruption for the public. In an anti-poll tax riot, 'several people were arrested...the suspect was whisked away...what senior officers feared was the sight of officers struggling on the ground...'[250] In this kind of situation, behaving badly to the suspect (in public at any rate) would conflict with police working rules. But sometimes behaving badly accords with such 'rules'. We need to question the idea that 'degrading' treatment on arrest is always 'unnecessary' in the sense that it is accidental or merely an expression of prejudice. We have seen that many arrests are made largely to effect control or assert authority. Sometimes the manner of arrest is intrinsic to this.[251] Holdaway discusses how police officers often exercise powers intending 'education and punishment'. One example is where officers arrested some demonstrators who were sitting in the road. An officer told him, 'There was a bloody great puddle by the side of the road, and when

---

[247] *The Guardian*, 18 August 2005. More recently an officer who was asked in a police canteen if someone he had arrested had been black replied, 'We are sending him back to the jungle' and made a spear-throwing action. A colleague made an official complaint and the officer was required to resign by a disciplinary tribunal: reported in the *Sun*, and the *Evening Standard*, on 12 November 2008.

[248] Waddington (2007) pp 154–5.

[249] The video can be viewed at <http://news.bbc.co.uk/1/hi/england/london/7989027.stm> (accessed 5 January 2010).   [250] Waddington (1994: 56).

[251] Similarly, it may be intrinsic to a police goal of provoking resistance by the arrestee, such resistance amounting to 'revelatory knowledge' – as only the guilty would resist the police. For a sustained analysis to this effect (taken to apply equally to interrogation and other methods of evidence construction) see Green A, *Power, Resistance, Knowledge: The Epistemology of Policing* (Sheffield: Midwinter & Oliphant, 2008).

they were nicked they were swept right through this puddle.'[252] A less clear-cut example is where arrests are made at people's homes in the middle of the night. No doubt the police would argue that this method minimises the chance of violent resistance or escape but this has to be balanced against the greater infringement of liberty involved, and the risk that some officers will use this method simply in order to intimidate. As one Muslim arrested under the counter-terrorism legislation has recently put it: 'I am not saying these arrests are a bad thing, they're not, they are a good thing, but why do they have to be accompanied by middle of the night raids terrifying our children and wives?'[253]

We might therefore classify arrest-manner as follows:

(a) normal,

(b) rude/aggressive (to further working rules), and

(c) rude/aggressive (due to spite or lack of sensitivity).

We do not know the size of one group relative to another. Reducing the incidence of the third is realistic if police training and monitoring took these concerns seriously, but reducing the size of the second will be almost impossible whilst the police seek to 'discipline' large sections of society.

With that in mind, the use of 'kettling' tactics, where the police immobilise large numbers of protesters or football fans, often with a view to stop-searching or arresting 'ringleaders' or 'troublemakers', raises particular concerns about degrading treatment. This approach was deployed in the policing of the May Day protests in 2001 when several thousand people were caught within a police cordon, on a wet and chilly afternoon, for over seven hours. Conditions became increasingly squalid, as people, in the absence of toilets, were forced to relieve themselves in public. 'This and other problems bore particularly hard on some of the women.'[254]

Moreover, there is a worrying trend towards using ever more violent methods of effecting an arrest (in the name of reducing the risk of harm to police officers) which increases still further the potential for severe discipline to be inflicted on the socially marginal who challenge police authority. Thus, police officers now often resort to the use of disabling devices when arresting suspects, such as pepper spray designed to temporarily blind, and taser-guns (devices that incapacitate suspects through the delivery

---

[252] Holdaway S, *Inside the British Police* (Oxford: Blackwell, 1983) p 10. See also Choongh (1997) for the argument that many arrests are made solely for these purposes, and that humiliation is central to this process.

[253] Forum Against Islamophobia and Racism, *Counter-terrorism Powers, Reconciling Security and Liberty in an Open Society: Discussion Paper. A Muslim Response*, para 70. Available at <http://www.fairuk. org/policy.htm> (accessed 5 January 2010).

[254] Per Sir Anthony Clarke MR, *Austin and Saxby v Comr of Police for the Metropolis* [2007] EWCA Civ 989 at para 7. See also *Laporte* [2006] UKHL 55 per Lord Bingham at para 12, describing the forced (and unlawful) return of protesters' coaches from Gloucestershire to London. No toilet breaks were permitted, which caused 'acute physical discomfort and embarrassment'.

of an electric shock).[255] We suspect that the use of such levels of force is frequently objectively unreasonable, but if police officers write up the arrest 'in the right way' (see opening quote to this chapter), as by claiming that the arrestee violently resisted the arrest, challenging their actions successfully may be extremely difficult, although less so when film exists of the encounter.[256] This brings us to the question of remedies.

3.5 **Remedies for wrongful arrest**

What happens if the police arrest when they should not? Or in a way that they should not? We have seen in relation to stop-search (see ch 2) that the main problem suspects face in challenging police action is credibility. There are rarely independent witnesses to encounters on the street, and proving an absence of reasonable suspicion or reasonable belief is very difficult anyway. It may not be quite so hard to establish that unreasonable force was used, but it will often be the arrestee's word against that of several police officers and many of the latter are unlikely to report colleagues for unnecessary violence.[257] Arrest is not such a low visibility practice as it once was, however. The ubiquity of CCTV and digital recording equipment (contained in mobile phones, video cameras and so forth) in public spaces entails that many arrests are now caught on camera. The police do not welcome being filmed and sometimes respond by seizing privately owned cameras or by claiming that it is unlawful to capture their images[258] or even by arresting for obstruction.[259] But such evidence will, in any case, be more useful in detecting unlawful levels of force[260] than in exposing the fact that no grounds

---

[255] See generally Waddington and Wright (2008).

[256] Mobile phone footage of an arrest on 15 June 2009 involving repeated use of a taser (accompanied by several punches of the suspect) can be viewed at <http://news.bbc.co.uk/1/hi/england/nottinghamshire/8103707.stm> (last accessed 5 January 2010).

[257] See the self-report evidence presented by Westmarland L, 'Police Ethics and Integrity: Breaking the Blue Code of Silence' (2005) 15 Policing & Society 145 at 151–2.

[258] See the debate and video posted at <http://www.prisonplanet.com/uk-terror-law-to-make-photographing-police-illegal.html> (accessed 5 January 2010). It may now be unlawful to photograph or video the police in some circumstances (or to publish that material) as s 76 of the Counter-terrorism Act 2008 makes it an offence to 'elicit information . . . of a kind likely to be useful to a person committing or preparing an act of terrorism, or . . . publishes or communicates any such information'. It is a defence for the person concerned to prove that they had a reasonable excuse for their action. Whether the courts will agree that filming the police in an effort to hold them accountable for their actions amounts to a reasonable excuse for their action (or will simply say that such filming stretches the notion of eliciting information useful to terrorists too far) remains to be seen. But the new law does seem likely to embolden some police officers still further in their harassment of those who would seek to record their actions.

[259] See the video footage at <http://www.guardian.co.uk/environment/video/2009/jun/21/fit-watch-kingsnorth-arrests> (accessed 5 January 2010).

[260] For example, in *Wilson v Commissioner of Police for the Metropolis* [2002] EWCA Civ 434 CCTV footage was used to found a claim for damages following an unlawful and deliberate assault on an innocent bystander during an incident of disorder. In an adversarial system the significance of such footage will always be open to debate, however: Neyland D, 'Surveillance, Accountability and Organisational Failure: The Story

for an arrest existed. To these problems we can add the way the courts have interpreted the requirements of the law in such cases as *Castorina v Chief Constable of Surrey*[261] and those which we shall be examining later in this section.

Leaving such problems aside, what specific remedies are available? A complaint can be made to the Independent Police Complaints Commission. This will be examined in ch 12. Exclusion in court of evidence obtained following wrongful arrest is another possibility, although this is a discretionary matter for the court even if the arrest is proved to be unlawful. The advantage of this remedy in relation to arrest is that it might deter the police from breaking the rules. However, it only operates when the police prosecute and would otherwise win the case. In other words, exclusion of evidence on the grounds of wrongful arrest only assists defendants if they are legally guilty, ie if the offences with which they are charged can be proved. But as we have seen, arrest is lawful if a defendant is discovered to have actually committed an offence, regardless of whether the police officer had reasonable suspicion or not, and no challenge to this under Art 5 of the ECHR has yet been made.[262]

The main remedy available is to sue for wrongful arrest in the civil courts. Wrongful arrest is part of the general tort of false imprisonment, and damages can be awarded to compensate for loss. Article 5(5) of the ECHR provides a right to compensation, but – as with unlawful stop-search – it is difficult to demonstrate a significant tangible loss from unlawful arrest. Juries had been increasingly awarding large sums, especially for exemplary damages. However, in 1997 the Court of Appeal decided that basic damages of only £500 per hour of liberty removed should be awarded, up to a maximum of £3,000 for a 24-hour period. Although extra could be awarded for aggravated and exemplary damages where the arrestee suffered particularly, the Court of Appeal limited this too.[263] This is all discussed more fully in ch 12.

Wrongful arrest occurs when the statutory powers discussed in this chapter are exceeded. It also occurs when an arrest is 'unreasonable', even if no specific statutory provision is breached. This is because under administrative law principles of judicial review (known as *Wednesbury* principles) all arms of the executive are accountable to the courts for any unreasonable action. When using arrest powers, police officers must act in good faith, use the arrest powers for the purpose they were given, take into account relevant matters and disregard the irrelevant, and must not act in a way so unreasonable that no reasonable police officer could have so acted.[264] In reviewing exercises of the discretionary power to arrest, the courts must also take into account the importance of the Art 5 ECHR right to liberty which is at stake.[265] These principles,

---

of Jean Charles de Menezes' in Goold B and Neyland D (eds), *New Directions in Surveillance and Privacy* (Cullompton: Willan, 2009).

[261] [1988] NLJR 180, discussed in 3.4.2 above.   [262] See 3.4.1 above.

[263] *Thompson v Metropolitan Police Comr, Hsu v Metropolitan Police Comr* [1997] 2 All ER 762.

[264] These principles derive from *Associated Provincial Picture Houses Ltd v Wednesbury Corpn* [1948] 1 KB 223.   [265] *Cumming v CC Northumbria* [2003] EWCA Civ 1844.

by their very nature, are capable of flexible application. It is thus crucial to examine the use the courts have made of them in this context.

Should an unnecessary arrest be treated as unreasonable? In a due process system, this would certainly be regarded as a wrongful arrest, but a crime control system would allow it if it enhanced police efficiency. We have seen that the general power of summary arrest created by the Serious Organised Crime and Police Act 2005 comes complete with a meaningless 'necessity principle'. All that is necessary is that arrest should enable prompt and effective investigation of crime – a classic crime control consideration.

That this was also the pre-PACE common law position is demonstrated by the House of Lords decision in *Holgate-Mohammed v Duke*.[266] Stolen jewellery was sold to a shop by someone fitting the description of the suspect. There was therefore reasonable suspicion against the suspect. She was arrested and taken to the police station and questioned but not charged. She sued the police for wrongful arrest on the grounds that there was no need to arrest and detain her because she could have been questioned equally well at home or at work. The police conceded that she could have been questioned elsewhere and that she was not uncooperative, but they decided that she was more likely to confess if held in the police station. The arrest was not necessary, but from the police point of view it was desirable. The House of Lords declared that the question was whether the police had exercised their discretionary power to arrest in accordance with the *Wednesbury* principles. Their decision to arrest could be impugned only if they had taken into account some irrelevant factor that they should have excluded from their consideration. Since, the House of Lords decided, the greater likelihood of the suspect confessing if taken to the police station was a factor the police were entitled to take into account, it followed that they acted lawfully in exercising their power of arrest. This decision legitimised a police working rule which was then cemented into the fabric of PACE and subsequent legislation. The judges and Parliament thus seem to be agreed that the police should be encouraged to arrest whenever this would promote efficient crime control. This, again, appears to be consistent with the ECHR.

Similar considerations arise when considering whether the police have a duty to check a suspect's story on, or prior to, arrest. In Madden's case, a youth, who the police believed had been stealing, was stopped on the street.[267] They found on him a model car. Madden claimed that he had bought the car, telling the officers the name of the shop. Disbelieving him, the officers did not check the story. In the police station, he confessed to the crime but subsequently pleaded not guilty at his trial. He was acquitted, in part because he had a receipt to which the police had paid no attention. Given that his story could have been, but was not, checked, was this wrongful arrest? In other words, is there a duty on the police to seek evidence to dispel the suspicion which they may otherwise reasonably have, as one would expect if due process principles were applied? Or may the police do as they wish once a minimum threshold is reached, as

---

[266] *Holgate-Mohammed v Duke* [1984] 1 All ER 1054.   [267] See *The Guardian*, 9 March 1981.

in a crime control system? In *Castorina v Chief Constable of Surrey*,[268] the Court of Appeal faced the issue squarely, Purchas LJ stating that:

There is ample authority for the proposition that courses of inquiry which may or may not be taken by an investigating police officer before arrest are not relevant to the consideration whether, on the information available to him at the time of the arrest, he had reasonable cause for suspicion. Of course, failure to follow an obvious course in exceptional circumstances may well be grounds for attacking the executive exercise of that power under Wednesbury principles (at 181).

Under this approach, the courts may only hold that the exercise of the discretionary power to arrest is unlawful in 'exceptional circumstances' and when the course of inquiry which was not pursued was 'obvious'. Note too that when these two conditions are satisfied, the arrest is not automatically unlawful since Purchas LJ went no further than saying that in such situations there 'may well be grounds' for challenging the exercise of the arrest power. The obligation to pursue a line of inquiry which might exculpate a suspect (so avoiding an unnecessary arrest) is clearly very limited. It is therefore debatable whether either Madden or, in the 'Confait Affair',[269] Latimore (who had a very strong alibi which was not checked by the police initially) were wrongfully arrested.[270]

The judges have considerable room for manoeuvre in deciding issues arising under the *Wednesbury* principles. The cases show that they have tended to adopt a crime control approach. Judges have interpreted arrest rules in ways that enable the police to 'get on with the job', rather than seeking to inject inhibitory elements which would promote civil liberties and human rights. It is only in fairly extreme cases, as where the police arrest in order to distract attention from their own malpractice, that the courts have been prepared to countenance that discretion was exercised improperly.[271] This may be contrasted with a much more robust attitude to the actions of some other arms of the executive, where crime control considerations do not arise.[272] It is unlikely that incorporation of the ECHR will lead to a major shift in the thinking of English courts about the boundaries of lawful arrest. This is because in the cases of *Brogan* and *Murray*, discussed earlier, it was decided that it was not a breach of human rights to arrest someone on reasonable suspicion with a view to detaining them for interrogative purposes so long as the ultimate objective was to bring the person before a court to answer a criminal charge.

---

[268] *Castorina v Chief Constable of Surrey* [1988] NLJR 180.

[269] See Fisher, Sir H, *Report of an Inquiry into the Circumstances Leading to the Trial of Three Persons on Charges Arising out of the Death of Maxwell Confait and the Fire at 27 Doggett Road, London SE6* (HCP 90) (London: HMSO, 1977).

[270] Occasionally a suspect's 'alibi' is confirmed spontaneously by an independent bystander just prior to arrest, and this may lead a court to adjudge any arrest to have not been based on reasonable suspicion, as in *Conlan v Chief Constable of Northumbria* [2000] 6 CL 105.

[271] *Paul v Humberside Police* [2004] EWCA Civ 308.

[272] The patterns of judicial control of discretionary powers are charted by Griffiths J, *The Politics of the Judiciary*, 5th edn (London: Fontana, 1997). See also 1.6.4.

It used to be a clear case of wrongful arrest when an arrestee is not informed of the fact of, or the ground(s) of, his or her arrest as soon as it is reasonably practicable to do so. PACE, s 28 and the ECHR, Art 5(2) oblige the police to give the reason for arrest explicitly, however obvious it may appear to be.[273] But the police may not be subject to the degree of due process rigour that one might think from reading s 28. In *Fiak* a drunk was apprehended sitting in his car. He said that he went to his car from his house to 'cool off'. A police officer asked him to stay where he was while she asked the man's wife if this was true. She did not tell him at this point that he was under arrest but it was held that this did not matter as the arrest was 'completed' after it became obvious that he had lied.[274]

Second, what is practicable? In *Murray v Minister of Defence* (a Northern Ireland case),[275] soldiers went to the defendant (M's) house at 7am, detained everyone and searched the premises. The soldier in charge remained with M. At 7.30am, he formally informed M of her arrest and took her to an army detention centre acting under a statute giving summary arrest powers similar to those in PACE, s 24. M's de facto arrest between 7am and 7.30am would appear to breach the common law and the equivalent of s 28. Following *Shaaban Bin Hussien v Chong Fook Kam* (that, as in M's case, one is arrested if one is not allowed to leave the place in which one is kept),[276] Lord Griffiths held that M was arrested at 7am (when her detention began) rather than at 7.30am when she was told that she was arrested. However, according to Lord Griffiths, 'If words of arrest are spoken as soon as the house is entered...there is a real risk that the alarm may be raised.'[277] It was therefore not practicable in his opinion to inform M of the fact of, and reasons for, her arrest immediately, and the arrest was therefore not unlawful. This seems to assume that the alarm was not raised when the group of armed soldiers entered the house, rounded everyone up, gave it a thorough search and did not even tell the occupants what was going to happen to them. The decision in this case does not alter the principle at stake but – unless 'terrorist' cases are being treated as special cases – it does suggest that drawing the line about when something is reasonably practicable is not easy. As it happens, as we saw in 3.3.3, terrorist cases are treated differently, but where that leaves the obligation to inform 'as soon as it is reasonably practicable' is unclear.

---

[273] The reason(s) need not be a precise formulation of the law (see *Abbassy v Metropolitan Police Comr* [1990] 1 All ER 193, where the defendants were arrested for 'unlawful possession' of a car. There is no such offence, but as this encompassed all the criminal possibilities the officers had in mind, the Court of Appeal said that this was satisfactory). In *Wilson v CC Lancashire* [2000] All ER (D) 1949, the arrestee was not told enough for him to challenge the arrest, which was therefore held to be unlawful. The classic common law case is *Christie v Leachinsky* [1947] AC 573.

[274] [2005] EWCA Crim 2381. This case is interesting for two other reasons. First, it confirms the sociological point that arrest is often a process rather than an isolated event. Second, the problem for the police arose precisely because they were trying to act decently, by checking the suspect's story before they took him away (unlike in *Castorina, Madden* and the *Confait* affair).

[275] *Murray v Minister of Defence* [1988] 2 All ER 521.

[276] *Shaaban Bin Hussien v Chong Fook Kam* [1970] AC 942.   [277] [1988] 2 All ER 521 at p 527.

The European Court is no more rigorous on this human rights point than the House of Lords, with whom it agreed.[278] It was even less so a few years before in *Fox*.[279] The Court in both cases held that it became obvious in the interviews of what the suspects were suspected, and thus the actions of the police were held to comply with Art 5(2).[280] In *Fox* there was a delay of seven hours, but the Court regarded this as complying with the ECHR's requirement of 'promptness'.

What if a court does hold that an arrest was unlawful because the arrest, or reason for it, was not communicated to the suspect? In *DPP v L*[281] the suspect was arrested for an alleged public order offence, but not told this. She was taken to the police station where she assaulted an officer. She argued that she was being held unlawfully, therefore her assault was of an officer *not* executing his duty. On appeal the Divisional Court held that her initially unlawful arrest did not prevent the arrest becoming lawful when, in the police station, proper procedures were adopted. Her acquittal was therefore held to be wrong.

The less demanding the judiciary is in interpreting statutory controls on the police, the greater the play allowed to crime control principles. Even when the legislature, as in s 28 of PACE, appears to be creating strong inhibitory rules, the judiciary still manages to draw their due process sting by rendering them largely presentational, and it does not seem that the incorporation of the ECHR into English law has changed this.

3.6 **Conclusion**

The law of arrest has evolved to accommodate changes in police practice, although it has not legitimated all of these changes. The police can now use arrest to facilitate investigation, rather than just as a mechanism to bring alleged offenders before the courts. The courts and Parliament have allowed policing considerations instead of due process considerations to dictate the shape and content of the law. Crime control values underlie the law of arrest in several respects. Firstly, although the Philips Commission rightly saw arrest as intrinsically coercive and wanted to restrict it to serious offences, the police have now been given a power of summary arrest in respect of all offences, however trivial. Secondly, whereas most executive agencies are increasingly subject to searching judicial review along Wednesbury lines, this remains exceptional in respect of arrest. Thirdly, much that is a product of unlawful police action is held to be lawful, thus allowing the end to justify the means – eg where the new PACE, s 24 allows arrest without reasonable suspicion of 'anyone who is guilty', and where the courts allow an unlawful arrest to be turned into a lawful arrest. Finally, the substantive law in most

---

[278] (1994) 19 EHRR 193.   [279] *Fox, Campbell and Hartley v UK* (1990) 13 EHRR 157.

[280] An 'unacceptable dilution of a basic guarantee': Harris et al, *Law of the European Convention on Human Rights* (London: Butterworths, 1995) p 130.

[281] [1999] Crim LR 752. Discussed further in 4.3.4.

public order offences and in common law breach of the peace is so vague that the police have even more freedom to arrest according to their own priorities than they would otherwise have.

The main due process element in arrest law is the 'reasonable suspicion' requirement, but this is such a low threshold that most arrests are based on weak evidence, and many are based on virtually no evidence. More investigation would be possible prior to most arrests, but this is not required by the law except in exceptional cases. The law offers little due process protection and, instead, gives the police wide boundaries within which to operate according to their own working rules. Offence seriousness, the probability that the suspect has committed an offence and the views of the victim (although some victims more than others) all influence police decisions whether or not to arrest, but other police working rules are equally important. These are based on criteria of 'suspiciousness' and 'disorder' that – like stop and search – bear more heavily on some sections of society than others. Patterns of bias result which are a product only in part of police rule breaking. Some people are arrested as a punishment or enforcement mechanism in itself, or in order to gather information about the crimes of others, with no intention that they should ever be prosecuted. The leading cases, English as well as under the ECHR, can be read to mean that many of these arrests are unlawful, but it is so difficult to prove that the objectives of the police were unlawful that the prospects of changing police behaviour through the courts are slim. An equally great problem is that some sections of the population are constantly singled out when others are also likely to be guilty of many crimes. A skewed suspect population is constructed, which distorts the whole criminal process thereafter.

This problem can be observed on the broader socio-legal canvas when we consider non-police agencies. Though some of the criteria operated by these agencies are those used by the police (such as disrespect) the offenders are generally more 'respectable' and so application of identical criteria produces different results. In fields of employment and housing, this would be regarded as indirect and unacceptable discrimination.

As with stop-search, police-suspect interactions leading to arrest are fluid and unpredictable. As with stop-search, arrest is sometimes used in order to gather information (including DNA, fingerprint and photographic evidence) or to discipline, rather than as a prelude to court processes (thus limiting the accountability of the police to the law). Different arrest (and stop-search) patterns may not reflect different crime rates so much as different ways of securing criminal intelligence information and engaging in communicative surveillance.[282] Consequently, the police often arrest in ways that are abusive and humiliating, they do so in large numbers, and get poor results – 'poor' in the senses that detections are relatively few in number, generally for relatively minor offences, and discriminatory in the patterns they produce. The promotion of freedom is ill-served by this. For those of us who instinctively lean towards due process the response should not necessarily be to demand tighter definitions of

---

[282] See Meehan (1993) and 2.5.

'reasonable suspicion', for this strategy is unlikely to work. Instead, we might take a leaf out of the book of the non-police agencies and require the police to arrest less and use summons more, as the Philips Commission recommended. This produces less coercion and less loss of freedom. But the latest legislative developments are in the opposite direction.

If we are to accept the necessity of crime control techniques, we might none the less seek a greater say in the crimes to be controlled. We might, for example, seek more public control over the types of situation for which arrest is and is not to be regarded as appropriate.[283] To its credit, this is what the government has done in very recent years in demanding a stronger response to domestic violence, although we have seen that the police are adept at avoiding action – in this case, domestic violence arrests – that they do not favour. Adopting the 'freedom perspective' outlined in ch 1 should produce a more rational and less authoritarian approach to arrest even though traditional 'due process' standards would not always be adhered to. The use of brief periods of arrest in public order situations can protect the freedom of some citizens while impacting only marginally on the freedom of the arrestee. The same is true of near-mandatory arrest in domestic violence. Allowing arrests on the basis of 'briefings' is not contrary to 'freedom' if the briefer is called to account. Using arrest as a punishment, such as Choongh discusses, is, however, another matter entirely. And the rapid growth in the use by the police of 'on-the-spot' fines is arguably fuelling and intensifying this function of arrest.[284]

Finally, if we do accept the necessity of some methods of crime control in the interests of freedom, it does not follow that we should accept that model's assumptions about the reliability of administrative fact-finding. Instead, we should treat with scepticism police claims that, as professionals, they can be trusted not to make mistakes. No one with the amount of power the police possess should ever be trusted to that extent. The tragic killing of an innocent man, Jean Charles de Menezes, at Stockwell tube station by armed police in the aftermath of the murderous attacks on London's transport system in July 2005 underpins that conclusion.[285]

Further reading

Cape E, 'PACE Then and Now: 21 Years of "Re-balancing"' in Cape E and Young R (eds), *Regulating Policing* (Oxford: Hart, 2008)

Docking M, Bucke T, Kerry G and Dady H, *Police Road Traffic Incidents: A Study of Cases Involving Serious and Fatal Injuries*, Paper 7 (London: Independent Police Complaints Commission, 2007)

Hillyard P and Gordon D, 'Arresting Statistics: The Drift to Informal Justice in England and Wales' (1999) 26 JLS 502 at 508

---

[283] This raises broad issues concerning police accountability. See further, Reiner (2000) and Reiner and Spencer (eds), *Accountable Policing* (London: IPPR, 1993). [284] See the discussion in ch 6.
[285] See Neyland (2009). This incident is discussed in various places in the book, including chs 6 and 12.

Lister S, Seddon T, Wincup E, Barrett S and Traynor P, *Street Policing of Problem Drug Users* (York: Joseph Rowntree Foundation, 2008)

Rowe M, 'Rendering Visible the Invisible: Police Discretion, Professionalism and Decision-making' (2007) 17(3) Policing & Society 279

Waddington P and Wright M, 'Police Use of Force, Firearms and Riot Control' in Newburn T (ed), *Handbook of Policing*, 2nd edn (Cullompton: Willan, 2008) p 470

4

Detention in the police station

Vulnerable populations, particularly those with gross alcohol intoxication, are not cared for adequately in police custody...when medical crises occur in this population, police officers do not have the support, resources, skills or training to provide the emergency interventions required.[1]

Police custody staff watched 'a disturbed man throwing himself around a cell for about 20 minutes on CCTV, apparently with some amusement and making no attempt to calm him down.'[2]

IPCC investigators waited 8 months before interviewing the police officers who dealt with a mentally ill man who died in a metal cage in a police station yard because they thought 'there was nothing to suggest wrongdoing'. Yet according to the dead man's family, an officer was caught saying on CCTV 'if he dies in here we're all in the shit'. Crucial CCTV tapes that should have showed what happened to the man went mysteriously missing.[3]

Key issues

- Can the police provide an effective safeguard against abuse by the police? (And other rhetorical questions)
- The limited effectiveness of suspects' rights
- Why do so many people die in police custody?
- Defence lawyers – why aren't they more adversarial?
- Remedies (lack thereof)

[1] Best D and Kefas A, *The Role of Alcohol in Police-related Deaths: Analysis of Deaths in Custody (Category 3) between 2000 and 2001* (London: Police Complaints Authority, 2004).

[2] HMIP and HMIC, *Report on an Inspection Visit to Police Custody Suites in Cambridgeshire Constabulary* (London: HMIP and HMIC, 2009) p 9.

[3] *The Guardian*, 22 August 2009. The death of this man, Sean Rigg, is discussed in 4.4.

4.1 **Introduction**

When the police arrest suspects they usually take them to a police station, especially if they plan to subject those suspects to an intrusive investigation or to prosecute. It is only if they decide to release suspects immediately or (rarely) to report them for summons or release them on 'street bail' that they would not take this course of action.[4]

The Police and Criminal Evidence Act 1984 (PACE) regulates the rights of suspects and powers of the police in the police station.[5] In this chapter we assess the key provisions of PACE, the associated Code of Practice (Code C),[6] and subsequent developments. In the next two chapters we look at police questioning and at other forms of evidence-gathering, much of which also takes place in police stations. First we need to understand how the different models outlined in ch 1 approach the treatment of suspects in the police station.

In a crime control system, the police would have discretion to deal with arrested suspects as they thought fit in order to ascertain the truth. Suspects are most likely to cooperate with the police and reveal the truth if denied the opportunity to consult with friends, family or, in particular, a lawyer. The length of detention should be governed by considerations of efficiency alone. Suspects should be held for as long as it is thought that further questioning and custody-based evidence-gathering may provide useful information, but no longer.

In a due process system, the detention of suspects in police custody would be very tightly controlled, if it was allowed at all. Since the police should not arrest unless they first have sufficient information to prove guilt, it follows that there is no necessity to secure a confession from the suspect. Arrest should be followed by charge and judicial proceedings, not by administrative investigation.[7] There will always be some time between arresting suspects and bringing them before the courts, however. It may be in the suspect's interests to talk to the police during this period since this may dispel suspicion and lead to earlier release. But this opportunity for dialogue may be abused, so safeguards must be provided. Suspects must be told that they are under no obligation to answer questions, that it will not be held against them at court if they maintain silence, that anything said may be used in evidence, and that they are free to consult with a lawyer before answering questions.

The freedom perspective would be reluctant to allow police station detention on mere suspicion, even if it is reasonable. But the more evidence the police had, and

---

[4] Police powers consequent on arrest, including the 'street bail' power created by the Criminal Justice Act 2003, are discussed in ch 3.

[5] See Bryan I, *Interrogation and Confession* (Aldershot: Dartmouth, 1997) chs 7–9 for discussion of the pre-PACE situation.

[6] Code of Practice C: The Detention, Treatment and Questioning of Persons by Police Officers (London: SO, 2008) – available from <http://police.homeoffice.gov.uk/publications/operational-policing/2008_PACE_Code_C_(final).html> (accessed 5 January 2010).

[7] See 3.2.2 above, for discussion of the place of arrest in due process and crime control systems.

the more serious the suspected crime, the more likely it would be that, under this approach, police station detention would be allowed. Also important would be whether the police could secure the evidence they needed by means which did not encroach on the freedom of the suspect, and on how alienating the experience of custody would be for the suspect.

We will see that the law steers something of a middle course between crime control and due process, and even incorporates elements of the freedom approach, although frequently this is not how it works out in reality. PACE allows detention for the purpose of questioning, but seeks to regulate this. Police officers do not have complete discretion, but control or supervision is exercised by other (more senior) police officers. In short, PACE gave the police more powers but also provided checks and controls on the use of those powers including more safeguards and rights for suspects.

This approach is consistent with the European Convention on Human Rights (ECHR). Article 5 allows arrest and detention on various grounds. The ones that concern us in this chapter and the next are:

1.(b) ... to secure the fulfilment of any obligation prescribed by law;
1.(c) ... for the purpose of bringing him before the competent legal authority on reasonable suspicion...

One of the aims of this chapter and the next two is to see how real the checks, controls and safeguards provided in PACE are. Another is to evaluate the effect of the ECHR and the Human Rights Act (HRA) 1998.

4.2 The powers and duties of the custody officer

We saw in ch 3 that the police station has become the primary site of criminal investigation through changes in police practice. The 'Confait' scandal[8] illustrated the importance of the power of the police over detained suspects. This led to the acceptance that clear legal regulation of what goes on in the police station was necessary.

4.2.1 The custody officer

Police stations that hold suspects for significant lengths of time must have a 'custody officer' available at all times.[9] Custody officers must be at least of the rank of sergeant,[10] but need have no particular training in order to carry out their duties. Any other

---

[8] Fisher H, *Report of an Inquiry into the Circumstances Leading to the Trial of Three Persons on Charges Arising Out of the Death of Maxwell Confait and the Fire at 27 Doggett Road, London SE6* (HCP 90) (London: HMSO, 1977). See Baxter J and Koffman L, 'The Confait Inheritance – Forgotten Lessons?' [1983] Cambrian LR 14.

[9] PACE, s 36.   [10] PACE, s 36(3).

officer may carry out their functions when they are not available.[11] The post is important, however, as it is on this officer that the main responsibility rests for the maintenance of the rights of suspects.[12]

Custody officers should be independent of any investigation in which a detained
suspect is involved, so anyone acting as a custody officer must not be involved in the
process of securing evidence from or about suspects (PACE, s 36(5)). Although in
some areas custody officers do that job and no other for lengthy periods, in others it is
common to alternate this job with other duties. Brown et al found that these differing
arrangements made no difference to the way in which custody officers performed their
duties.[13] At root, custody officers are still police officers with all the typical attitudes
associated with 'cop culture' (see 2.1).

Those arrested suspects who are taken to a police station are immediately brought
before the custody officer. The principle is that nothing may happen to that suspect
prior to being 'booked in' by the custody officer. The custody officer fills in a 'custody record' form for each suspect. After some personal details (name, address and so
forth) are taken down, the custody officer has to decide whether or not to detain the
suspect and, if so, on what grounds, and whether or not to charge the suspect (and,
again, on what grounds). This is all written on the custody record.

PACE also introduced a new regime for questioning aimed at eliminating the abuses
which used sometimes to occur. The police may interrogate several times in any period
of detention, subject to the rights of the suspect discussed later. But they may normally
only do so in a room equipped for this purpose with tape recording facilities, in the
presence of an appropriate adult (if the suspect is 'vulnerable') and in the presence of a
legal adviser (if requested by the suspect). It is the responsibility of the custody officer
to ensure that all these conditions are met. For example, as we shall see in ch 5, it is up
to custody officers to ensure that police officers do not speak to suspects in their cell, in
case unfair inducements or threats are made. Details of any visits to suspects in their
cells have to be recorded on the custody record.

The custody officer also has to decide whether to seek authorisation for further
periods of detention (discussed later) and whether to allow other powers to be exercised. These include intimate and non-intimate searches of suspects, and, as we shall
see in ch 6, house searches, and the holding of identification parades. The custody
officer decides whether or not to ask the Crown Prosecution Service (CPS) to charge
and prosecute suspects (discussed in ch 7) and, if so, whether they should be held in

---

[11] PACE, s 36(4).

[12] Sections 120–121 of the Serious Organised Crime and Police Act 2005 enable, but do not require, police
services to designate civilians in their employ as 'staff custody officers'. The police resisted the civilianisa-
tion of the custody officer role and the Government has indicated that it will repeal these provisions: Home
Affairs Select Committee, *Policing in the 21st Century* HC 364-I, Seventh Report (2007–08) para 227. Many
of the detention staff working under custody officers are now civilians, however.

[13] Brown et al, *Changing the Code: Police Detention under the Revised PACE Codes of Practice* (Home
Office Research Study No 129) (London: HMSO, 1992) p 34.

custody or released on bail (discussed later in this chapter). Again this is all noted on the custody record.

Code C (which sets out the rights of suspects in the police station and the powers of the police) also requires custody officers to ensure that suspects are treated properly in terms of food, sleep, warmth, sanitary conditions, medical treatment and so on. These provisions comply with Art 3 of the ECHR whereby no-one should be subject to torture or inhuman or degrading treatment. No research has suggested that, since PACE was enacted, these provisions are frequently or systematically breached, but a recent government inspection in Cambridgeshire revealed some gross failures, such as 13 or even 24 hours elapsing between meals.[14] Later in this chapter we reveal many breaches of more serious rules (eg regarding covert surveillance – see ch 6; completion of the custody record – see Marlon Downes' case, in 4.4) and abuses leading to deaths in police custody.

Clearly the custody officer role is of central importance. But s/he is a relatively junior police officer. Moreover, according to the Police Federation spokesperson on custody issues, 'training…is a postcode lottery'.[15] He says that it varies from five days in some forces to four weeks in others; many forces do not train the (many) officers who are drafted in for hours or days at a time to cover gaps when 'real' custody officers are away; and very few forces do refresher training. And many short detentions, and all detentions lasting longer than an eight-hour shift, are supervised by more than one sergeant and gaoler. Reviews of detention are almost always conducted by different Inspectors. And when multiple medical assessments are required, detainees are often seen by different doctors. Different people interpret the same information in different ways, leading to discontinuity of protection for suspects.[16]

Throughout this and the next chapter we will see that, for these and other reasons, custody officers do not carry out their protective role as one would expect from the wording of PACE and Code C.

4.2.2 The rights of suspects[17]

Custody officers should immediately inform those suspects who are to be detained of their most important rights, both orally and by giving them a notice in writing. These include the right to consult a lawyer privately, which we will discuss in 4.5. Other rights include having someone informed of one's arrest, consulting a copy of Code C and making a telephone call to anyone of their choice. The right to have someone informed

---

[14] HMIP and HMIC (2009).

[15] Coppen J, 'PACE: A View from the Custody Suite' in Cape E and Young R (eds), *Regulating Policing* (Oxford: Hart, 2008).

[16] Young H, *Securing Fair Treatment: An Examination of the Diversion of Mentally Disordered Offenders from Police Custody* (Birmingham: Birmingham University, 2002) ch 6.

[17] The outline provided here will not attempt to discuss comprehensively these rights. A good reference text is Ozin et al, *PACE – A Practical Guide* (Oxford: OUP, 2006). Although references to Code C in this chapter are to the 2008 version, this is the same as the 2006 version (on which Ozin et al 2006 is based) in all respects other than some provisions concerning legal advice.

when arrested – otherwise known as 'intimation' – is described in Code C as the 'right not to be held incommunicado' (para 5). Under s 56(1) of PACE, a suspect may have:

One friend or relative or a person who is known to him or is likely to take an interest in his welfare told, as soon as is practicable except to the extent that delay is permitted by this section, that he has been arrested and is being detained...

The police are not allowed to stop suspects exercising this right. They may delay its exercise, but only under very strict conditions[18] and in practice rarely do so.[19] However, Note D to para 5 of Code C provides that 'In some circumstances it may not be appropriate to use the telephone' in compliance with s 56. This means that the custody officer can require that intimation be made in a written form only.

The exercise by suspects of the *separate* right to a telephone call or to contact someone by letter[20] may be delayed on a similar basis to the right of intimation. Suspects may also 'receive visits at the custody officer's discretion'.[21] Discretion is to be exercised in the light of the availability of sufficient personnel to supervise visits 'and any possible hindrance to the investigation'.[22] These last two 'rights' (to a phone call/letter and to receive visits) need not be communicated orally to suspects by custody officers on reception, or indeed at any other time. The only way in which suspects who do not already know of these rights can find them out is by consulting Code C or the written notice. Not surprisingly, very few people ask for visits, and less than 10% of suspects ask for a phone call.[23] This may well be fewer than before PACE.[24]

Although intimation is rarely formally delayed, informal delay is more common. According to Dixon et al,[25] informal delay in intimation 'may be deliberate, for example, when officers who wish to search premises wait to inform a suspect's family of arrest until they arrive to search his/her house'. Informal delay can also be an unintentional product of pressure of work. The result is that the provisions on intimation, while embodying due process values, are not fully adhered to. However, since s 56(1) merely provides that intimation should be done 'as soon as is practicable', it is difficult for suspects to demonstrate that the law has been broken. Thus there are very few cases where delay of intimation or refusal to intimate was an issue.[26] Requests for phone calls also frequently appear to be informally delayed or ignored. Brown et al[27] found that custody records noted requests in 7–8% of cases, but they observed requests being made in 10–12% of cases.[28] Further, it is no use telling suspects what rights they have

---

[18] The conditions are similar to those which apply to the delaying of a suspect's access to legal advice, discussed below in 4.5.   [19] Brown et al (1992: 54–6).

[20] Code C, para 5.6.   [21] Code C, para 5.4.   [22] Code C, Note 5B.

[23] Brown et al (1992: 55).

[24] Dixon et al, 'Safeguarding the Rights of Suspects in Police Custody' (1990a) 1 Policing and Society 118.   [25] Dixon et al (1990a: 118).

[26] See Mirfield P, *Silence, Confessions and Improperly Obtained Evidence* (Oxford: Clarendon Press, 1997) p 185 for a discussion of some of these cases.   [27] Brown et al (1992: 55).

[28] Similar findings are reported by Choongh S, *Policing as Social Discipline* (Oxford: Clarendon Press, 1997) ch 6.

if they do not understand what they are being told. The police often made little or no effort to help suspects understand their rights when PACE was first enacted, and it appears that little had changed 20 years later.[29]

Suspects detained under the anti-terrorism legislation[30] have the same rights as other suspects, but the police are allowed to delay the granting of these rights on broader grounds than usual.[31] Nearly half of all suspects held under the Prevention of Terrorism Act (PTA) 1989 (the previous legislation) requested that someone be informed, and delay was imposed (often for more than 24 hours) in around three-quarters of these cases.[32]

At first glance it might seem that whether these rights are granted or not, or whether they are delayed, is peripheral to the big issues – whether suspects are intimidated or not, whether suspects are legally detained or not, and so on. However, they can make a great difference to the *experience* of being in custody. We will see in 4.3 that, for the freedom perspective, this is crucial. And who knows how many deaths in custody (see 4.4) would be prevented if suspects were less isolated?

4.2.3 Vulnerable suspects

Some people have specific vulnerabilities, such as deafness or an inability to understand English. The custody officer must locate interpreters for such people.[33] Suspects who are 'generally' vulnerable – ie juveniles, the mentally handicapped and the mentally disordered – have special protections, in recognition of their greater welfare needs and susceptibility to coercion or suggestion.[34] The police must inform an 'appropriate adult' of their detention and ask that person – usually a parent, guardian or social worker – to attend the station;[35] and if mental disorder is suspected, or the suspect appears to need clinical attention, a police surgeon must also be called.[36] Custody officers are warned that people who are, or appear, intoxicated or dependant on alcohol or drugs may need clinical attention either because of their intoxication or dependency

---

[29] Sanders et al, *Advice and Assistance at Police Stations and the 24 Hour Duty Solicitor Scheme* (London: Lord Chancellor's Department, 1989) ch 4; Choongh (1997: ch 6); and Britton, N, 'Race and Policing: A Study of Police Custody' (2000a) 40(4) BJ Crim 639 (reporting research showing that some custody officers did not inform black detainees of a scheme established to provide extra advice and support). Unfortunately there has been little recent research.

[30] Terrorism Act 2000; Anti-terrorism, Crime and Security Act 2001; Prevention of Terrorism Act 2005. See Walker C, *Blackstone's Guide to the Anti-terrorism Legislation*, 2nd edn (Oxford: OUP, 2009), and other references in 4.3.3.   [31] Walker (2009).

[32] Brown et al (1992).   [33] Code C, para 3.12.

[34] It is no accident that in the 'Confait Affair' two of the wrongly convicted youths were juveniles, while the 18-year-old had a mental age of 13: Baxter and Koffman (1983). In more recent years, a large number of 'miscarriage' cases have concerned mentally disordered individuals. The Cardiff Newsagent Three is one notorious post-PACE case in which the coerced confession of a mentally vulnerable suspect resulted in three co-defendants serving a total of over 30 years in prison: O Brien M, *The Death of Justice* (Talybont: Y Lolfa Cyf, 2008). See also 1.4.   [35] Code C, paras 3.13–3.20.   [36] Code C, para 9.5.

or because there might be a serious underlying condition.[37] The importance of this is evident when we look at deaths in custody in 4.4.

Appropriate adults have several responsibilities: to see and advise the detainee in private, to request (if desirable) a solicitor on the detainee's behalf and to attend interviews, offering advice as needed, ensuring fairness and facilitating communication. Interviews cannot take place without an appropriate adult except in the most extreme circumstances.[38] Although there is some overlap with the role of a legal adviser (and in the early days of PACE, lawyers were frequently asked to fulfil the dual role), having an appropriate adult does not diminish the suspect's right to separate legal advice. However, in practice the police are reluctant to call a lawyer until the appropriate adult arrives,[39] even though such a delay is a clear breach of Code C.[40] An appropriate adult is unlikely to arrive for an hour or more, by which time there is a major disincentive to put up with further delay whilst waiting for a lawyer. The police know this, and sometimes exaggerate the likely delay in order to discourage requests for legal advice,[41] although this is, again, prohibited by Code C.[42]

Vulnerable suspects are by no means rare. It seems that around one-fifth of all suspects are juveniles, and in some stations the percentage is far higher.[43] Whilst suspects with other vulnerabilities may appear to be few and far between, they are not always easy to identify. People with learning disabilities or other educational or social disadvantages often try to hide these problems, and thus learn to appear confident and capable.[44] Gudjonsson et al found that, in a sample of 156 adult detainees, the police only called appropriate adults in 4% of cases.[45] Yet clinical psychologists in the research team identified 15% of the detainees as vulnerable after an interview of 10–15 minutes, and a further 5% after more extensive tests. This shows that vulnerability can sometimes be confirmed only after fairly extensive professional examination. But police

---

[37] Code C, Note 9C.

[38] However, procedures such as breathalyser tests, where time is of the essence, need not be delayed: *DPP v Evans* [2003] Crim LR 338. See related discussion in relation to legal advice in breathalyser cases in 4.5.1.

[39] Brown et al (1992: 62).

[40] Paragraph 6.5A states that the appropriate adult may seek legal advice for the juvenile, but since para 6.1 states that 'all detainees' have the right to legal advice, the power of the appropriate adult to seek advice should be interpreted as additional to that of the juvenile, not as an alternative. Delay is only allowed if Annex B applies – in the rare circumstances when this would hinder the investigation.

[41] Sanders A and Bridges L, 'Access to Legal Advice and Police Malpractice' [1990] Crim LR 494; Brown et al (1992: pp 31–4); Skinns L, '"Let's Get It Over With": Early Findings on the Factors Affecting Detainees' Access to Custodial Legal Advice' (2009a) 19 Policing and Society 58; Skinns L, '"I'm a Detainee; Get Me Out of Here" Predictors of Access to Custodial Legal Advice in Public and Privatized Police Custody Areas in England and Wales' (2009b) 49 BJ Crim 399.   [42] Code C, para 6.4.

[43] Bucke T and Brown D, *In Police Custody: Police Powers and Suspects' Rights Under the Revised Pace Codes of Practice* (Home Office Research Study No 174) (London: Home Office, 1997) p 6.

[44] Examples include the 'Tottenham Three' and 'Cardiff Three' cases: see ch 5 for discussion of these cases.

[45] Indeed, the percentage of suspects treated by the police as disordered or handicapped is generally far lower than this: only 2% in the large sample examined by Bucke and Brown (1997: p 7), and even less in the sample examined by Nemitz T and Bean P, 'The Use of the Appropriate Adult Scheme' (1994) 34 Med Sci and the Law 161.

surgeons (GPs who work part-time for the police) often have no psychiatric training at all. They therefore often fail to identify mental disorder and other vulnerabilities.[46]

Failure to identify people with a mental disability or disorder not only leads to treatment in breach of Code C and PACE, but can also lead to prosecution where diversion (see ch 7) would be more appropriate, and even to tragedy. In one case the police were concerned about a suspect, called a doctor, but then released him when the doctor pronounced him calm and 'perfectly logical'. He was in fact a paranoid schizophrenic who set himself on fire 12 hours later and died in hospital.[47] A Home Office study found that large numbers of detainees who apparently died at their own hands and who died of medical conditions (such as a fractured skull), many of whom displayed 'warning signs', had been declared 'fit' by police surgeons.[48] Moreover some 11,000 people a year are detained precisely because they are mentally ill, and many more are arrested for drink/drug-related offences for the same reasons.[49]

Custody officers often try to process cases as quickly as possible. For these and other reasons they sometimes deliberately keep appropriate adults away from suspects with relatively mild disorders or disabilities. They also frequently do not call surgeons when suspects act strangely, and some surgeons advise custody officers on the phone and then do not attend the suspect.[50] For example, Palmer reports a custody officer speaking of a suspect who the police put in a paper suit without zips (for fear he would self-harm) yet for whom they did not call a doctor or appropriate adult because they did not consider him mentally ill.[51] These are clear breaches of the Code. Not only do the police not always recognise the need for an appropriate adult or doctor, or act accordingly when they do,[52] but this help is not always secured even when it is sought. Bucke and Brown (1997) found that 91% of all juveniles had an appropriate adult with them for all or some of their time in custody, but this was true for only two-thirds of other vulnerable suspects. *Aspinall*, where the suspect was a schizophrenic, is a typical case. Two police surgeons considered him fit to be interviewed, whilst confirming his mental illness. He was interviewed without an appropriate adult, and gave answers which undermined his credibility at his trial. He was convicted of drugs offences, but won

---

[46] Laing J, 'The Mentally Disordered Suspect At the Police Station' [1995] Crim LR 371. Little more than half of all vulnerable adults had appropriate adults in their interview in a later study: Medford et al, 'The Efficacy of the Appropriate Adult Safeguard during Police Interviewing' (2003) 8 Legal and Criminological Psychology 253. Four out of 15 suspects with learning disabilities had no appropriate adult in the small study by Leggett et al, 'People with Learning Disabilities' Experiences of Being Interviewed by the Police' (2007) 135(3) British Journal of Learning Disabilities 168.

[47] *The Guardian*, 30 November 1993, cited in Laing (1995).

[48] Leigh et al, *Deaths in Police Custody: Learning the Lessons* (Home Office Police Research Series, Paper 26, 1998) pp 16, 35.

[49] Docking et al, *Police Custody as a 'Place of Safety': Examining the Use of s 136 of the MHA 1983* (London: IPCC, 2008). See, further, 4.4.

[50] Phillips C and Brown D, *Entry into the Criminal Justice System* (Home Office Research Study No 185) (London: Home Office, 1998) pp 55–6; Nemitz and Bean (1994); Jacobson J, *No One Knows: Police Responses to Suspects with Learning Disabilities and Learning Difficulties* (London: Prison Reform Trust, 2008).

[51] Palmer C, 'Still Vulnerable After All These Years' [1996] Crim LR 633.

[52] See, for example, the following critical government inspection report: HMIP and HMIC (2009).

his appeal because the absence of an appropriate adult invalidated his interview.[53] On average, the wait for an appropriate adult is a little over one hour,[54] but a study in a London police station[55] found that around one-sixth of detainees seeing appropriate adults waited more than four hours. Volunteers (as distinct from professional social workers or carers) generally have more speedy response times, and delays are usually caused by police procedures.[56] Overall, there remain serious problems in the provision of this safeguard. Thus in one Cambridgeshire police station no appropriate adults are available between 11pm and 9am (HMIP and HMIC, 2009). As we shall see (in 4.3.5), a few hours' detention can be highly stressful for even the most 'normal' people, so for vulnerable people this can be very serious indeed.

How useful to the vulnerable suspect is the presence of an appropriate adult during a police interrogation? Many 'appropriate adults' misunderstand what is happening, fail to realise how an apparently innocent series of questions and answers can be incriminating, and are just as intimidated as the suspects.[57] Bucke and Brown[58] report many family members acting as appropriate adults who clearly either did not understand or pay attention to what was happening. This is true also of many professional social workers and nominees from local victim support volunteer groups who the police select precisely because, according to one officer, they are 'on our side – on the side of the victim'.[59] Social workers have dual 'welfare' and 'control' roles, and since they have to work closely with the police it is difficult for them to act as advocates for suspects when acting as appropriate adults. There is therefore often more of an illusion of protection than the reality. Thus Dixon et al say that some parents:

are notoriously keen to help the police in obtaining confessions from their children. In one incident a mother promised to 'get my fist round his lug' (which she later did…much to the approval of the investigating officers).[60]

Bucke and Brown report similar conversations, such as the parents who asked the custody officer to give their 'lad the fright of his life'.[61] This partly reflects the contradictions in Code C about the role of the appropriate adult, which is, inter alia, 'to advise' and 'to facilitate communication'.[62] It may be proper to advise a suspect to

---

[53] [1999] Crim LR 741. On exclusion of evidence obtained in breach of PACE or the Codes, see ch 12.

[54] Phillips and Brown (1998: 56). Newburn T and Hayman S, *Policing, Surveillance and Social Control* (Cullompton: Willan, 2001) p 48 also found that a minority of obviously vulnerable suspects did not even speak on the phone to, let alone see, an appropriate adult.   [55] Newburn and Hayman (2001: 48–9).

[56] Pierpoint H 'Quickening the PACE? The Use of Volunteers as Appropriate Adults in England and Wales' [2008] Policing and Society 18: 397.   [57] Brown et al (1992: 72).

[58] Bucke and Brown (1997: 14–15).   [59] Quoted in Nemitz and Bean (1994).

[60] Dixon et al (1992: 119).

[61] Bucke and Brown (1997: 14). See also Quinn K and Jackson J, 'Of Rights and Roles: Police Interviews with Young Suspects in Northern Ireland' (2007) 47(2) B J Crim 234 at 245.

[62] Code C, para 11.17. Role conflict is exacerbated by the imposition of a crime prevention role on appropriate adults by the Crime and Disorder Act 1998 (CDA), s 37. See Williams J 'The CDA: Conflicting Roles for the Appropriate Adult' [2000] Crim LR 911.

remain silent (especially if no lawyer is present) but this cannot be said to facilitate communication. Hence not only parents, but also professional social workers, are left not understanding their proper role. Many professional social workers were horrified, after taking a training course for appropriate adults, to find that they had previously been failing to intervene in coercive interviews when they were entitled to do so.[63] The police do not help here, often failing to explain to appropriate adults the rudiments of what is *legally* expected of them,[64] despite Code C (para 11.17) saying that they should.[65] A recent survey of volunteers who act as appropriate adults (who do have some training) found that they intervene in interviews more than professionals and parents, but that they are still insufficiently interventionist.[66]

Clearly at present only a minority of vulnerable suspects secure the help they need from appropriate adults and doctors, and even with the best will in the world substantial numbers will always be missed in the absence of duty psychologists and doctors in all busy stations. Even then, to dichotomise 'vulnerable' and 'normal' people in this way is unrealistic. For when in police detention, most of us would be vulnerable to some extent, but often in unpredictable ways.

4.2.4 **Police bail**

Suspects who have no action taken against them or who are immediately cautioned (ie officially warned) or given a 'penalty notice for disorder' (see ch 7) are generally released unconditionally from detention. In most other cases, custody officers have to decide whether or not to grant bail. Bail with the stipulation that the suspect return to the station on a given date is given when the police wish to make further inquiries or to consider whether or not to charge.[67] This is used for over 20% of juvenile suspects, and 10–20% of adults. The outcome is frequently a caution in juvenile cases, but no action at all ('no further action' – NFA) for nearly half of all adults.[68] Now that the CPS have the power to charge (see ch 7), bail may be given to allow prosecutors time to consider this, and conditions may be set by the custody officer.[69]

---

[63] Hodgson J, 'Vulnerable Suspects and the Appropriate Adult' [1997] Crim LR 785 at 791.

[64] Bucke and Brown (1997: ch 2); Nemitz and Bean (1994). The police 'promote a very passive role for appropriate adults in interview': Quinn and Jackson (2007: 244).

[65] See Brown et al (1992: 72). Also see Palmer (1996); and Littlechild B, 'Reassessing the Role of the "Appropriate Adult"' [1995] Crim LR 540.

[66] Pierpoint, H 'The Performance of Volunteer Appropriate Adults' (2001) 40 Howard JCJ 255. Also see Pierpoint, H, 'Reconstructing the Role of the Appropriate Adult in England and Wales' (2006) 6 Criminology and Criminal Justice 219, Medford et al (2003) and Leggett et al (2007). The legal pitfalls, and the complex and often contradictory roles, are discussed by Parry L, 'Protecting the Juvenile Suspect: What is the Appropriate Adult Supposed to Do?' (2006) 18 Child and Family LQ 373.

[67] PACE, s 34(5). Juveniles may also be released on bail either in order to receive an official warning at a later time or in order to ascertain whether a final warning is appropriate: Crime and Disorder Act 1998, s 37. See also discussion of conditional cautions in ch 7.

[68] See Phillips and Brown (1998: 82–5); and Bucke and Brown (1997: ch 6).

[69] PACE, s 37(7) and s 47, both as amended by CJA 2003, Sch 2.

The main time when bail is considered is after suspects are charged with criminal offences.[70] The custody officer must order release, in most cases, unless:

(a) the suspect's name and address cannot be ascertained;

(b) the suspect is regarded as unlikely to appear in court to answer the charge;

(c) interference with witnesses or other obstruction of justice is likely; or

(d) it is thought that the suspect would commit an offence if released.

If one or more of these conditions is satisfied, the custody officer may keep the suspect in custody until the next magistrates' court hearing.

Most of these conditions require custody officers to predict what might happen if the suspect is released. These predictions are based on what they are told by the arresting or investigating officers and what little may be known about a suspect's previous record of appearing at court, offending on bail and so forth. It is impossible for suspects to prove that they would not do something wrong if released. Essentially, decisions are taken quickly on the basis of inadequate information. Although custody officers should protect suspects from the possible partisanship of arresting officers, most of the information they use will come from those very officers, and its quality is almost impossible to assess. Thus although custody officers are supposed to be objective, basing their decisions on reasonable grounds, subjectivism is inevitable, as is suggested by the wide disparity in bail rates from one police station to another.[71] Subjectivism and discretion allow the police to make decisions which are wholly unrelated to the nature of the individual offence or suspect. Thus at times of riot (or disorder characterised as such) 'police bail was denied *en masse* as a matter of policy'.[72]

The Criminal Justice and Public Order Act 1994 (CJPO) gives the police the power to attach conditions to bail – for instance, that suspects must not contact the victim or a particular witness.[73] The drawback is that this gives the police considerable power to control the movements of released suspects or to operate conditions as informal punishments.[74] Most suspects are more concerned about securing bail than they are about being charged.[75] Not only is a night in the cells unpleasant, but it makes it more difficult to secure court bail, which, in turn, might reduce the chances of securing acquittal or a non-custodial sentence.[76] This makes bail an important bargaining counter, particularly in relation to confessions, as we shall see in ch 5. Legal advisers can make representations about bail to the police, but lawyers rarely remain until this

[70] PACE, s 38; Magistrates' Court Act 1980, s 43, as amended by PACE, s 47.

[71] Phillips and Brown (1998: 115–18). Different offence and offender mixes will also affect bail rates.

[72] Vogler R, *Reading the Riot Act* (Milton Keynes: Open UP, 1991) p 118.

[73] CJPO 1994, s 27. This amends PACE, s 47 and the Bail Act 1976, ss 3 and 5. See ch 9 below for discussion of the principles regarding bail, which are the same for courts and the police.

[74] The dangers, as well as the benefits, of giving police this discretion are discussed by Raine J and Willson M, 'Just Bail at the Police Station?' (1995) 22(4) JLS 571. See also 3.2.1 above.

[75] Sanders et al (1989: 72–3).

[76] Morgan R and Jones S, 'Bail or Jail?' in Stockdale E and Casale S (eds), *Criminal Justice Under Stress* (London: Blackstone, 1992).

decision is made.[77] Giving the police the power to make conditions provides them with a new stack of bargaining chips.

Bucke and Brown found that 20% of suspects are refused bail, 17% are conditionally bailed, and 63% are unconditionally bailed. They found that black (though not Asian) suspects were detained disproportionately often, suspects charged with violent offences were less likely to be granted bail than other suspects, and the use of conditions varied greatly from station to station.[78] Along with other researchers, they conclude that many people who would previously have been granted unconditional bail are now only granted bail with conditions, although undoubtedly some who would previously have been detained are now given bail.[79]

Offending when on police bail does not seem to have been reduced as a result of the use of conditions, perhaps because bail conditions are so difficult to enforce. But nor has the increase in bail, as a result of conditions, led to more offending or more failure to appear in court.[80] Whether, overall, allowing the police to set bail conditions has produced a net gain or net loss of freedom is difficult to determine. However, it seems that, as usual, the freedom of the most socially marginalised – in this case, black suspects – is valued less than that of others in the criminal justice system.

4.3 **Detention without charge**

4.3.1 'Helping the police with their inquiries'

According to s 29 of PACE, anyone who is at a police station voluntarily (ie not there under arrest):

(a) shall be entitled to leave at will unless he is placed under arrest;

(b) shall be informed at once that he is under arrest if a decision is taken by a constable to prevent him leaving at will.

This is at first sight an odd provision for all it is saying is that if someone is not under arrest – that is, not deprived of their liberty – then they are not to be deprived of their liberty. This tautology can only be understood in its historical context.

Before 1964, a suspect normally could not be questioned following arrest. Arrest marked the end of the investigation, and its purpose was to enable the suspect to

---

[77] See 4.5 below.

[78] Bucke and Brown (1997: ch 7). See Raine J and Willson M, 'Police Bail with Conditions' (1997) 37(4) BJ Crim 593 and Brown D, *Offending on Bail and Police Use of Conditional Bail* (Home Office Research Findings No 72) (London: Home Office, 1998) for similar findings.

[79] Compare their post-CJPO findings with the pre-CJPO findings of Phillips and Brown (1998). Also see Raine and Willson (1997) and Hucklesby A, 'Police Bail and the Use of Conditions' (2001) 1(4) Criminal Justice 441.   [80] Brown (1998).

be brought to court (see 3.2). The solution for the police who needed extra evidence through questioning, was to put people in a situation where they could be interviewed without formally arresting them. Even then, the fiction that the police did not interrogate was still maintained, through the mechanism of the 'voluntary statement' of confession. This might mean detaining someone at their home or another place, or in the police station. The limbo in which such people were placed was known as 'helping the police with their inquiries', generally understood to mean people who were involuntarily detained but not formally arrested. A revision to the Judges Rules in 1964 made it easier for the police to interrogate following arrest but it was still common for suspects to 'help the police with their inquiries'.[81] Section 29 is designed to make it absolutely clear that this limbo is no longer allowed.

Taken on its own, s 29 appears to be an inhibitory rule providing more due process for suspects than had existed hitherto. Initially, however, it did little to affect police practices.[82] Now that PACE has bedded down it seems that the flouting of s 29 has become increasingly rare.[83] It is likely that this is because the police have come to realise that the 24-hour (and, now, 36-hour) detention time limit which applies for most offences is usually more than adequate for their purposes. It is to these time limits that we now turn.

4.3.2 Time limits for detention: non-terrorist cases

PACE originally stated that, for *serious* arrestable offences, involuntary detention could be for up to 36 hours initially, but for 'normal' offences the limit was 24 hours.[84] In an unashamedly crime control measure, the Criminal Justice Act 2003 amended PACE, s 41 to allow involuntary detention for up to 36 hours for *all* arrestable offences. The concept of an 'arrestable offence' was subsequently eliminated by the Serious Organised Crime and Police Act 2005 (see 3.3), so the 36-hour detention limit now applies to all indictable offences instead.[85] Thus any either-way offence (ie that can be tried either in the magistrates' courts or the Crown Court) is now subject to the 36-hour detention provision.

Detention has to be reviewed periodically by a senior officer independent of the investigation. This 'review officer' will be the custody officer if the suspect has been charged but an inspector or more senior officer if not.[86] Detention must be reviewed 'not later than six hours after the detention was first authorised'.[87] The second review must be 'not later than nine hours after the first' and subsequent reviews must be at intervals of not more than 12 hours.[88] To extend detention beyond 24 hours (in the

---

[81] The historical background is discussed by Dixon D, *Law in Policing* (Oxford: Clarendon Press, 1997) pp 126–47; Bryan (1997: chs 6–8).

[82] McKenzie et al, 'Helping the Police with their Enquiries' [1990] Crim LR 22.

[83] Brown D, *PACE Ten Years On* (Home Office Research Study No 155) (London: Home Office, 1997) pp 68–70.   [84] PACE, s 41(1) and 42(1).

[85] Schedule 7, s 43(7).   [86] PACE, s 40(1).   [87] PACE, s 40(3)(a).

[88] PACE, s 40(3)(b)–(c); Code C, para 15.2.

case of indictable offences) the review must be conducted by an officer of superintendent rank or above. Reviews may be postponed but only under exceptional circumstances and for as short a time as is practicable. The reviewing officer may only authorise continued detention if the original purpose of detention still holds good and if the investigation is being conducted 'diligently and expeditiously'.[89] The reviewing officer must seek and take note of any representations against continued detention which the suspect may make.[90] In reality, though:

the review procedure tends to be routinised and insubstantial, at least in its early stages; the opportunity to make representations can often consist merely of an inspector asking the suspect, 'All right mate?' through the hatch in the cell door (Dixon et al 1990: 130–1).

Indeed, reviews may even take place over the telephone.[91] Rather than this being exceptional, as was originally doubtless intended, Dixon et al (1992: 131) found this to be common. Moreover, custody record entries often failed to note this use of the telephone, giving the impression that the review was carried out in person. Frequently, Dixon et al say, 'the inspector's role is purely presentational'. Section 6 of the Criminal Justice Act 2003 legitimised impersonal review procedures by making it clear that the power to review by telephone was not subject to the condition that a review in person was impracticable. Decisions to extend detention beyond 24 hours, however, must always be made *in person* by a superintendent (Code C, Note 15F). In the previous (2007) edition of this book we said that we expected this provision to be watered down at some point too. We were right. The Home Office plans to replace reviews by a Superintendent with reviews by an Inspector, and to allow the latter to be conducted by telephone or video-conferencing. Once again the rights of suspects are to be subordinated to the convenience of senior officers.[92]

If the police wish to continue the detention beyond 36 hours (in the case of indictable offences) this is possible, up to a maximum of a further 60 hours.[93] The same criteria apply as above, but authorisation must be by an officer of the rank of superintendent or above, and the police must apply to a magistrates' court for a 'warrant of further detention'.[94] This application must generally be made before the 36-hour period has expired but, in exceptional circumstances, there is some leeway. The criteria on which magistrates decide whether or not to grant such a warrant are broadly similar to the criteria which the superintendent must apply under s 42 in deciding

[89] PACE, s 42(1)(c).

[90] PACE, s 40(12)–(14). It is not clear how wide are the purposes of reviews. See Cape E, 'Detention Without Charge: What Does "Sufficient Evidence To Charge" Mean?' [1999] Crim LR 874.

[91] PACE, s 40 (as amended by CJA 2003) and Code C, para 15.3C and 15.9–15.11. However, if video-conferencing facilities are both available and a practical option at the relevant time, they must be used instead: Code C, para 5.9B and Note 15G. We present here a simplified account of the rules on time limits and reviews, which are extremely complicated. See Ozin et al (2006: ch 4).

[92] Home Office, *PACE Review: Government Proposals in Response to the Review of the Police and Criminal Evidence Act 1984* (London: Home Office, 2008) paras 10.7–10.8 (available from <http://www.homeoffice.gov.uk/documents/cons-2008-pace-review/> (accessed 5 January 2010). [93] PACE, ss 42–43.

[94] PACE, s 43.

Table 4.1 Detention exceeding 24 hours

	Released with no charge		Warrants of further detention (over 36 hours)		
	24–36 hours	Over 36 hours	Applications	Refused	% charged
2003–4	527	94	304	0	69%
2005–6	2350	113	525	10	73%
2007–8	4079	165	630	26	73%

Source: Povey, D and Smith, K, *Police Powers and Procedures, England and Wales 2007–8* (Home Office Statistical Bulletin 07/09) (London: Home Office 2009), ch 1.

whether to authorise continued detention in the first place. If the police still wish to detain a suspect without charge after the period of further detention has expired, they may apply to a magistrate again for an extension of the warrant for further detention. Such an extension may be granted by a magistrate under s 44 as long as that extension neither exceeds 36 hours nor ends later than 96 hours after the initial 'relevant time'.[95] This means that the police may apply for, and secure, two warrants of further detention following the initial 36-hour detention. But 96 hours is the overall maximum permissible length of detention without charge.

We do not know how often the police extend detention beyond 24 hours. But as table 4.1 shows, over 4,000 detainees are now, each year, detained for 24–36 hours and then released without charge (an increase of nearly 800% since 2003). Warrants of further detention are now sought in over 600 cases each year (also a big annual increase), and are almost always granted. This is to be expected, since the magistrates apply the same criteria as the police and on the basis of information which the police provide. While the suspect will usually be legally represented, there are few grounds on which defence arguments can be made for release. For instance, if there is little evidence against a suspect, this would scarcely ever justify release since the point of the extended detention is precisely to secure more evidence. Two-thirds to three-quarters of these suspects are eventually charged.

The fact that detention beyond 24 hours is relatively infrequent does not necessarily mean that the safeguards are adequate. The police usually have no reason to detain once they consider that they have obtained full information from the suspect concerning the alleged offence. To detain any further would be inefficient. Occasionally, though, the police may wish to prolong detention, regardless of evidential or other legal considerations (as where they are seeking information on other suspects). The detention provisions, and the way in which legal duties are carried out by senior police officers, gives them the scope to do almost as they see fit in those few cases of such importance to them. Nonetheless, although Art 5(3) of the ECHR provides that

[95] PACE, s 44(3).

suspects in detention must be brought before a court 'promptly', detention for further investigation has been held not to violate the ECHR when the grounds for arrest are reasonable and when there is recourse after a reasonable period (as under PACE) to judicial oversight.[96]

Suspects must be released when either the period of detention expires or when detention is no longer necessary because the original reason for detention no longer applies. Release is either unconditional, on bail to return to the police station pending further inquiries, or (having been charged) on bail to appear in court. The only circumstances in which the suspect would not be released would be if he or she was charged and kept in custody pending the earliest available court hearing.[97] Suspects who are released because the time limit has been reached cannot be rearrested without warrant for the same offence unless new evidence is uncovered.[98]

When suspects are released on bail to return to the police station pending further inquiries the police are entitled to detain again, 'restarting the clock' where it had previously been 'stopped', but only if those inquiries produced more evidence (PACE, s 34(2)). One of the purposes of this part of PACE was to shorten the length of detention, in the interests both of suspects and police efficiency. Because there were no proper records prior to PACE it is difficult to know whether PACE has succeeded in this objective or not. Phillips and Brown (1998: 109–11) found, in the 1990s that, on average, suspects were held for around six and a half hours, but that now seems to have increased to over ten hours in one study.[99] Detention is, on average, increased when a doctor, appropriate adult or lawyer is sought, but this reflects the seriousness of the offence and other complicating factors, rather than delays caused by waiting for these people (Skinns, 2009a). Maguire concludes that PACE probably led to longer detention lengths for people who would otherwise have been kept in for very short periods (partly because of the length of time it takes to complete the paperwork and partly because of the greater numbers seeking legal advice) but quite possibly shorter periods of detention for those who would otherwise have been kept in for long periods of time.[100]

4.3.3 Time limits for detention: terrorist cases

Under the Prevention of Terrorism Act 1989 (PTA) the police used to be able to detain suspected terrorists for up to 48 hours on their own authority (with periodic reviews by senior officers); and, with the permission of the Secretary of State, for a further five days. The Terrorism Act 2000, which replaced the PTA, extended the period to 14 days, but only after judicial (not mere ministerial) approval.[101] In the wake of bombings

---

[96] *Brogan v UK* (1988) 11 EHRR 117.

[97] Or whilst advice is being sought on charging: see 4.3.4 below and 7.3.2. Police bail is discussed in 4.2.4 above.　　　　　　　　　　　　　　[98] PACE, s 41(9).　　　　　　　　　　　　　　[99] Skinns (2009a).

[100] Maguire M, 'Effects of the PACE provisions on Detention and Questioning' (1988) 28(1) BJ Crim 19.

[101] The Terrorism Act 2000, s 41 and Sch 8 originally allowed a 7-day period only. It was doubled to 14 days by the Criminal Justice Act 2003, s 306. The judicial review provision, after 48 hours of police detention, is similar to PACE provisions for further detention, complying with the ECHR – by contrast with the need

and attempted bombings in London on 7 and 21 July 2005, the government brought forward in October 2005 proposals for the law to be amended again to allow a detention period of three months. The government was defeated on these proposals but was still able to effect (through s 23 of the Terrorism Act 2006) a doubling of the detention period permissible to 28 days.

The Anti-terrorism, Crime and Security Act 2001 (ATCSA) Part IV, which allowed indefinite detention of foreign persons denied asylum who were suspected international terrorists, was even more controversial. With limited judicial oversight, and no time limit on detention, these provisions, like those of the preceding less draconian PTA, required derogation from the European Convention on Human Rights. Derogation was, however, held to be disproportionate to the threat of terrorism and discriminatory, primarily because there is no good reason to treat foreign nationals and citizens of the UK so differently.[102] The irrelevance of nationality was evident from the July bombings and attempts, at least some of which were carried out by British citizens.[103] The PTA 2005 (as amended and extended by the Counter-terrorism Act 2008) has now replaced this part of ATCSA, but is arguably even more crime control-oriented.

ATCSA established 'special advocates' to represent the interests of detainees but who were prevented from communicating to 'their clients' much of the evidence against them (evidence which, in the opinion of the Secretary of State would endanger national security). Two of these advocates resigned in 2005. They felt that effective representation was impossible, as their clients could not challenge the evidence against them as they were not able to tell them what it was. The new PTA retains special advocates, replaces indefinite detention in custody with 'control orders', and ends discrimination by making these measures applicable to UK citizens as well as foreign nationals. 'Control orders' are a form of semi-house arrest: individuals are subject to curfews; they have to report regularly (eg twice a day) to the police; and their movements away from their homes, who they see or speak to, and their other communications, are restricted and subject to electronic monitoring. The specific conditions are tailored to each individual. Breach of these orders is a criminal offence, punishable by up to five years' imprisonment. Orders cannot be made except by, or with the permission of, the courts, but the standard of proof required of the state is low. The legislation recognises that some of these orders will be so draconian that they will be incompatible with the ECHR, Art 5, and so provision is made for 'derogating' as well as 'non-derogating' control orders (though none of the former had been made at the time of writing). The former may last only six months, while the latter may be for 12 months,

---

to derogate from the ECHR (which was held to be lawful in *Brannigan and McBride v UK* (1993) 17 EHRR 539) when the PTA was in force.

[102] *A (FC) v Home Secretary* [2004] UKHL 56. See Hickman T, 'Between Human Rights and the Rule of Law: Indefinite Detention and the Derogation Model of Constitutionalism' (2005) 68(4) MLR 655 and the other articles in this special issue. See also Fenwick H, 'The Anti-terrorism, Crime and Security Act 2001: A Proportionate Response to September 11?' (2002) 65(5) MLR 724.

[103] See eg *The Guardian*, 25 August 2005.

but both types are renewable on application to the courts. Prior to the making of a control order, suspects may be detained by the police for up to 48 hours (renewable, on application to the courts, for another 48 hours).

In the 45 months since control orders were introduced, they were issued against 38 people, and at the end of 2008 15 were in force (12 against non-nationals).[104] This is many more than had been in custody under Part IV of ATCSA up to 2005.[105] Only a few of the orders no longer in force were revoked/allowed to expire; most of those subject to the rest have been deported, though some have absconded. None have been prosecuted (Bates, 2009: 123). Many, at the time of writing (September 2009), have been under this semi-house arrest for two or three years.[106] As we shall see, the experience of long periods of detention, including house arrest, can be traumatic, and the small numbers involved should not blind us to the cruelty of this legislation.

There are two human rights objections: (1) This is a deprivation of liberty (Art 5). In 2007 the House of Lords ruled that control orders do not, in general, infringe Art 5;[107] but the particular conditions in one case, where the detainee was made to live in a flat that was not his home, did do so as he suffered virtual solitary confinement for the greater part of the day.[108] (2) That withholding the evidence on which the state's case is based, despite the special advocate system, violates the Art 6 right to fair trial. In 2009 the House of Lords ruled that Art 6 was not necessarily violated if some evidence was withheld, but only if the detainee was given sufficient information to be able to challenge it.[109] Accordingly, all the cases in question were sent back to the lower courts to be dealt with on a case-by-case basis. The first result of this was the revocation of *AN*'s control order.[110] Thus while this judgement does not sweep away the special advocate system, much less control orders themselves, the continued existence of both are now in doubt.[111] As the independent reviewer of the operation of the legislation acknowledges,

---

[104] Carlisle A, *Fourth Report of the Independent Reviewer Pursuant to section 14 of the PTA 2005* (London: SO, 2009). See generally Bates E, 'Anti-terrorism Control Orders: Liberty and Security Still in the Balance' [2009] Legal Studies 29: 99.

[105] This statement, and the other material in this and the preceding paragraph concerning pre-PTA 2005 legislation, is drawn from various reports of Lord Carlisle, the Government-appointed reviewer of ATCSA and the Terrorism Acts. See especially his review of ATCSA 2001 Part IV Section 28 Review 2004 (London: SO, 2005); and Carlisle (2009).

[106] See further Campbell D 'The Threat of Terror and the Plausibility of Positivism' [2009] PL 501.

[107] *Secretary of State for the Home Department v JJ* [2007] UKHL 45.

[108] *Secretary of State for the Home Department v MB and AF* [2007] UKHL 46; E [2007] UKHL 47. Discussed by Bates (2009) and Ewing K and Tham J-C 'The Continuing Futility of the Human Rights Act' [2008] PL 668.

[109] *Secretary of State for the Home Department v N and others* [2009] UKHL 28. The House regarded itself as bound by a decision of the Grand Chamber of the ECtHR in *A v United Kingdom* [2009] ECHR 301. It was clear that several of the judges would rather have found in the government's favour. By contrast, Sedley's dissenting judgment in the Court of Appeal ([2009] 2 WLR 423 paras 107–21) makes a strong case in principle against the use of secret evidence.

[110] *Secretary of State for the Home Department v AN* [2009] EWCC 1966 (Admin).

[111] In the first control order challenge following this judgment, the government revoked the order as it was unwilling to disclose the intelligence evidence that had hitherto been withheld (*The Guardian*, 8 September 2009).

while all the control orders sought appeared justified from the written evidence, in some cases substantial doubts are raised in court hearings (Carlisle, 2009).

But the battle against control orders is far from won. The 'reasonable suspicion' threshold required to secure such an order is far lower than that needed to prosecute, and so it remains difficult to challenge: indeed, on 31 July 2009 the government issued a new control order against *AN*, making a mockery of the court revocation of his original one.[112] Counter-terrorism measures like this have been termed 'laws against law' because 'they are the antithesis of criminal justice due process'.[113] They are not proportionate responses to crime but rather devices which focus on 'pre-crime', a term that 'captures the key problematic of the counter-terrorism legal regime. Pre-crime suggests that no crime has been committed, while *simultaneously* evoking the crime that hasn't happened.'[114] A time limit that required the end of the order or a prosecution would offer some hope of resolution.[115]

The numbers detained under the anti-terrorism legislation vary from year to year, from 34 to over 200. These variations reflect frequent political changes, originally concerning Northern Ireland and, since the '9/11' attacks on the Pentagon and World Trade Center in 2001, terrorist activity carried out by al-Qaeda and similar groups. The trend is for the numbers to rise over time. In 1996, for example, there were 84 detentions (not including 'examinations' of people entering or leaving Great Britain or Northern Ireland). Only two of these people were charged under the PTA, and 15 were charged with offences under other legislation. Twenty-three of the 84 had their detention extended beyond 48 hours, of whom 10 were released without charge.[116] In 2004, by contrast, there were 162 arrests, mostly for 'international terrorism', under the Terrorism Act. One-quarter were charged, half under the Terrorism Act, and half under other legislation.[117] Since 2002/3 on average there have been 227 terrorism arrests per year, with a similar proportion charged. One-third are detained for two days or more, but several have been detained for the maximum of 28 days, not all of whom were charged.[118]

There is a striking parallel between detention under anti-terrorism legislation and stop-search: both provisions allow such a wide 'sweep' that only a minority of people subjected to these powers are ever charged (let alone convicted) with offences connected with the reason for initial suspicion. A further small minority are charged

---

[112] *Liberty*, Press Release, 31 July 2009.

[113] McCulloch J and Pickering S, 'Pre-Crime and Counter-Terrorism: Imagining Future Crime in the "War on Terror" ' (2009) 49 BJ Crim 628 at p 640. Also see Walker C (2007) 'The Treatment of Foreign Terror Suspects' 70 MLR 427.   [114] McCulloch and Pickering (2009: 641).

[115] For other examples of the government imposing 'measures that operate on the edge of human rights guarantees', see Forster S, 'Control Orders: Borders to the Freedom of Movement or Moving the Borders of Freedom?' in Wade M and Maljevic A (eds), *A War on Terror? The European Stance on a New Threat, Changing Laws and Human Rights Implications* (New York: Springer, 2009).

[116] Home Office, *Statistics on the Operation of Prevention of Terrorism Legislation* (HO Stat Bull, 4/97) (London: Home Office, 1997b).

[117] Carlisle A, *Report on the Operation in 2004 of the Terrorism Act 2000* (London: SO, 2005).

[118] Home Office, *Statistics on Terrorism Arrests and Outcomes, 2001–8* (Statistical Bulletin 04/09) (London: Home Office, 2009a). See also 3.3.3 above.

with unrelated offences. But most are released unconditionally, on classic crime control lines. In one case a man was held for a week, yet was questioned for a total of just four hours, on matters not apparently related to terrorism.[119] Is the gain in freedom achieved by these uses of police powers as great as the loss of freedom for those caught up in the net? When the risk to be averted is as great as a terrorist atrocity the answer to many might seem obvious (particularly when the 'many' cannot conceive of themselves as ever being subjected to terrorism-related powers). A question that might, however, give 'the many' pause to think is whether the draconian use of arrest and detention powers against certain prime suspects (previously the Irish, now young, male Muslims) increases the sense of alienation and bitterness amongst the communities to which they belong. While this may or may not create new terrorists, it certainly makes it less likely that these communities will identify with British security policy and actively cooperate with the police in terrorism investigations.[120]

4.3.4 The purpose of detention

Now that we have examined the *mechanisms* for authorising and reviewing detention, we need to examine the *criteria* used to decide whether or not detention should be authorised or continued. Under s 37 of PACE:

(1) The custody officer ... shall determine whether he has before him sufficient evidence to charge that person with the offence for which he was arrested and may detain him at the police station for such period as is necessary to enable him to do so.

(2) If the custody officer determines that he does not have such evidence before him the person arrested shall be released either on bail or without bail, unless the custody officer has reasonable grounds for believing that his detention without being charged is necessary to secure or preserve evidence relating to an offence for which he is under arrest or to obtain such evidence by questioning him.

(3) If the custody officer has reasonable grounds for so believing he may authorise the person arrested to be kept in police detention.

These provisions broadly follow the Philips Commission's recommendations and embody its 'necessity principle'. We saw in the chapter on arrest that the Philips Commission believed that many suspects who were arrested and charged could be reported and summonsed instead. It wished to ensure that arrests which led to detention would only be made when necessary. At least half of all formally arrested suspects are detained under s 37 for questioning.[121] In these cases, if the arrests were

---

[119] *The Guardian*, 8 February 2007.

[120] See further Mythen et al, '"I'm a Muslim, but I'm Not a Terrorist": Victimization, Risky Identities and the Performance of Safety' (2009) 49 BJ Crim 736.

[121] Brown et al (1992: 90). However, as we saw in 3.4, in public order situations in particular, many people are 'informally' arrested and then released without being taken to a police station.

on reasonable grounds and there existed sufficient evidence to prosecute, arrest will be lawful but pre-charge detention following the arrest would be unlawful. This is because s 37 requires the custody officer to charge and then either release or detain (pending a court appearance) any suspect brought into the station against whom there is already sufficient evidence to prosecute. But custody officers are rarely in a position to determine whether there is such evidence unless an arresting officer wishes them to know it, and it is not clear what duties custody officers have to seek to discover it.[122]

In practice, custody officers seem to act on the assumption that a determination of whether there is sufficient evidence to charge cannot be made until after questioning has taken place. The law envisages, however, that custody officers must make their determination as soon as the arrestee comes to the head of the queue in front of the custody desk. The obvious solution to this dilemma is to couple a determination that there is insufficient evidence to charge with a decision under s 37(2) that there are reasonable grounds for believing that detention without charge is 'necessary' in order to obtain evidence by questioning. But what does 'necessary' in this statutory context mean?

The then Home Secretary, Douglas Hurd, said in Parliament in 1984, that the question is whether 'this detention was necessary – not desirable, convenient or a good idea but necessary.'[123] A reasonable interpretation of a convenient or desirable detention would be one that was convenient in the sense that it increased the probability of confession and/or was the most cost-effective way of carrying out enquiries. A reasonable interpretation of a necessary detention would be one where there was no other practicable way of gathering, securing or preserving evidence in relation to the offence in question. If the latter interpretation was adopted by custody officers then there should be proportionately few authorisations of detention. A determination that there was insufficient evidence to charge would ordinarily be coupled with a decision that such evidence could be obtained in ways that did not require the detention of the arrestee. The presumption in s 37(2) would then apply, and the custody officer would then be obliged to release the arrestee either on bail or unconditionally.

The scenario envisaged here – of large numbers of perfectly lawful arrests being negatived by custody officers refusing to authorise detention – is not a likely scenario, nor does it correspond with reality. Research has established that virtually all arrested suspects are detained. Many of the custody officers interviewed by McConville et al[124] expressed surprise that the detention decision could be anything other than automatic.

---

[122] Cape (1999). Officers may withhold knowledge that there is sufficient evidence to charge because they may have a variety of reasons for wanting to question suspects (see 5.1). Although the CJA 2003 transfers the decision to prosecute from the police to the CPS (discussed in ch 7), this does not significantly change this process or the decision-making criteria. However, custody officers are now entitled to detain suspects after determining that they have sufficient evidence if they have good reason to seek charging advice from the CPS: PACE, s 37(7) as amended by Police and Justice Act 2006, s 11.

[123] HC Official Report, SC E, 16 February 1984, col 1229.   [124] McConville et al (1991: 44).

Thus one, when pressed on whether he would ever refuse to authorise detention, replied: 'Probably not in practice, no'. Another said:

Often the bloke's remonstrating saying 'Not me, it wasn't me. I haven't done it, you've got the wrong man', but of course I have to take the policeman's word, so I accept him on what the policeman tells me.

Most custody officers simply write out the words of s 37 – some have even asked for a rubber stamp with these words already on it[125] – and so 'reception into custody has become an essentially routinised process'.[126] In *DPP v L* the Divisional Court accepted this to the extent of saying that custody officers need not inquire into the lawfulness of an arrest.[127] Here the arrest was unlawful because the suspect had not been informed of the reason for the arrest. The Divisional Court said that this did not invalidate her detention, because, *it assumed*, in the absence of evidence to the contrary, that the custody officer gave her the reason when he 'booked her in'. Obviously the Divisional Court is unaware of the research which shows that custody officers so routinise the detention process that this is not a reasonable assumption to make. Also, in *Al-Fayed v Commissioner of the Police of the Metropolis*,[128] which endorsed the decision in *DPP v L*, suspects who attended the police station voluntarily to undergo questioning were immediately arrested and detained under s 37. The Court of Appeal held that there was no reason to think that the custody officer did not have reasonable grounds for believing that detention was necessary. Apologies for the double negative – but, faced with the obvious fact that (a) the detention of the suspects was quite obviously not necessary, and (b) the equally obvious fact that the judges do not want to stop custody officers rubber stamping arrest and detention decisions, this convoluted prose is the nearest we can get to explaining the decision. So if you know any judges, show them this passage, and ask them why they have been abdicating their responsibility to give the custody officer 'safeguard' some practical meaning.

We have seen that the function and place of arrest in relation to investigation has changed over time: whereas at one time arrests came at the end of an investigation and were the inevitable prelude to prosecution, arrest has gradually moved nearer to the beginning of the investigation. Arrest can be made on the basis of a bare reasonable suspicion, and it often is. Since that will not suffice to prosecute, the law now envisages that the police will frequently need to get more evidence in order to prosecute.[129] This development occurred gradually and along with this, of course, came the limbo of 'helping the police with their inquiries'. Section 37 of PACE formalises the process by

---

[125] McKenzie et al (1990: 24).   [126] Dixon et al (1990a: 130). See also Phillips and Brown (1998: 49).

[127] [1999] Crim LR 752, discussed in 3.5. The same position was adopted by the Court of Appeal in *Clarke v Chief Constable of North Wales Police* (Lawtel 5 April 2000; *The Independent*, 22 May 2000).

[128] *Al-Fayed v Commissioner of the Police of the Metropolis* [2004] EWCA Civ 1579.

[129] This is in fact the reality: McConville M, *Corroboration and Confessions* (Royal Commission on Criminal Justice Research Study No 13) (London: HMSO, 1993).

recognising that suspects will be detained without charge following arrest when there is insufficient evidence to prosecute and that the main purpose of this detention is to secure that evidence.

This endorses the decision in *Holgate-Mohammed v Duke*[130] (discussed in 3.5), where the House of Lords ruled that the greater likelihood of confession if a suspect was held at a police station was a legitimate reason for detention. This decision is entirely consistent with the crime control model. It is, however, entirely inconsistent with the supposed due process presumption in s 37 against detention. It is also inconsistent with the freedom model, for the freedom of those detained is traded in for the sake of police convenience. This is a bad bargain as the police could clear up crime in ways less costly to freedom. Securing evidence through custodial questioning is rarely necessary, but it is considerably more convenient for the police than securing evidence in most other ways. As investigation by questioning is envisaged in PACE and its Codes as usually taking place during detention (see ch 5), the authorisation of detention must be the norm.

Moreover, there is little to prevent pre-charge detention for questioning taking place even in cases where there is already sufficient evidence to charge (as there was in 61% of cases in one study: Phillips and Brown, 1998). Arresting officers usually want to strengthen their cases against suspects regardless of whether there already exists sufficient evidence to charge or not. In practice, they know that a taped confession from the arrestee will make the case watertight and that to get such evidence they have to question the arrestee in custody prior to charge. As we will see in ch 5, they may also have other reasons for wanting to detain suspects for questioning, such as general intelligence-gathering or the imposition of authority.[131] By not telling custody officers the full extent of the evidence already obtained against the suspect, it is easy for arresting officers to secure pre-charge detention in all cases.

The presumption against detention in s 37 is thus entirely presentational since it goes against the crime control grain of the rest of the law and practice in this area. It seems then that – rather than the police carrying out the law as made by Parliament – Parliament makes laws aimed at legitimising existing police practice. What was once part of a judicial process (arrest followed by the prosecution decision) is now part of an executive process. Not only does this mean that the police make initial decisions relating to detention (as we have seen, up to 36 hours without judicial authority) but in nearly half of all cases this detention is not followed by any judicial proceedings (see ch 7). The 2005 PTA takes matters one stage further, as this is detention without charge primarily as a means of incapacitating people against whom there is insufficient evidence to prosecute. This is the slippery slope towards an authoritarian state which prioritises risk management over all other considerations.

---

[130] *Holgate-Mohammed v Duke* [1984] AC 437.
[131] Note also that other types of evidence are often secured from suspects as a result of their detention: see ch 6.

4.3.5 **The experience of detention**

The average (non-terrorist) detention period of around nine hours appears not to be excessive. But what do those hours feel like? We all know the difference between three hours in a darkened cinema and only one in a tedious lecture. Imagine a period nine times as long as the latter, with fear thrown in, and the worry that one might be in the cells overnight. The fact that the length of detention (now up to 36 hours) is in the hands of the police leads suspects to believe that the police 'can do anything they want. They can keep you in overnight if they want.'[132]

Police control is asserted from the moment the custody officer begins the 'booking in' procedure. Suspects are immediately deprived of autonomy, and the police demand deference and obedience. Those who do not provide it are often abused or laughed at. Take this example, of a suspect who was upset and who refused to speak, observed by Choongh:

He was shouted at by both the CO [custody officer] and the arresting officers, eg 'Come on Mickey, don't be a dick'. When this failed to break his resistance, the CO shouted, 'Alright! We can play it the hard way. Put him in the cell and he can stay there until he decides to be a good boy!'[133]

Choongh observed some suspects, who responded with abuse or who refused to do what they were told, being dragged off to the cells where it sounded as if they were being beaten. As this was done while an academic researcher was observing, the police presumably felt they were behaving in a normal and unproblematic way. Choongh[134] emphasises that none of these suspects were physically threatening to the police. 'What each of them had done was to challenge the "usual procedure": challenge the right of the police to treat them as inanimate objects.' One of Choongh's interviewees under-stood what was happening in a way that only the experience of detention provides:

The bottom line is that they've got the power, yea? Like one of them said to me out there, 'You keep your mouth shut in here, because we can do whatever we want to you in here.' And that's all it boils down to.[135]

A custody officer partially acknowledged this general point when asked about the operation of a volunteer scheme for black detainees: 'We had one volunteer come, a young fella, and he was rather curt with everybody... He'd got a chip on his shoulder basically... I told him to leave the police station. I'm not having somebody shouting at me at the desk.'[136]

After being booked in, suspects are usually fingerprinted, searched and taken to a cell. Almost everything that happens next is in the hands of the police too. For drug addicts and alcoholics they control when the next 'fix' or drink becomes possible. They control food, drinks, heating and who (and what) one might share one's cell with. It

---

[132] Sanders et al (1989: 77).   [133] Choongh (1997: 89).   [134] Choongh (1997: 94).
[135] Choongh (1997: 87).   [136] Britton (2000a: 653).

may smell of the previous or co-occupant's urine or vomit. The co-occupant may look and sound violent or crazy. The police even control when and if you are allowed to use the toilet, if there is no integral sanitation – no joke if, as in one of the cases described by Hillyard,[137] you are a woman arrested after an evening in the pub and the male custody officer makes you wait four hours.[138]

Crime control adherents argue that innocent people have nothing to worry about if they are arrested. Maybe it has never happened to them. Listen to someone to whom it did happen:

There I was banged up in a jail and I hadn't done anything, and I was being taken away from my place of work, I'd been separated from my family... Here was a policeman telling me that I had nothing to fear from him and he couldn't see the stupidity of his statement.[139]

Many suspects also have to endure much of what other suspects are going through in neighbouring cells. Irving reports an almost constant din of 'rhythmic banging and hammering, shouting and cursing, groaning, screaming and crying'.[140] As one custody officer acknowledged to Britton,[141] custody areas are 'like submarines... they're pretty grim aren't they?' Detention is boring, scary, unpleasant, uncertain, isolating, disorienting and humiliating. As we saw earlier, the police control visits, phone calls and messages to the outside world. Also, personal possessions, including mobile phones, are taken away. At one and the same time one is isolated yet without privacy. Detainees are usually alone in their cells, often with no idea of the passing of time (watches are usually removed), yet able to be viewed by the police. Intimate bodily functions have to be announced to the world – the world shrinks to the police station – as one has to ask for toilet paper, for the toilet to be flushed or for sanitary towels.[142]

All suspects are fingerprinted.[143] Custody officers also have to identify all property that suspects have, and remove anything that is dangerous, illegal or evidence of crime; they can, but need not, authorise a search of the suspect for this purpose.[144] The Philips Commission recognised how invasive even a 'normal' search (involving removal of outer clothing only) is, and said that searches should not be carried out routinely,[145] but as it can be argued that only a search can demonstrate that suspects have no such articles, this recommendation has been ignored.[146] The police may, if they are still concerned, authorise strip-searches and/or intimate searches of body orifices; the latter requires authorisation by an Inspector and should be carried out by a doctor where practical.[147]

---

[137] Hillyard (1993: 151).

[138] On the importance of police control, see Leo R, 'Police Interrogation and Social Control' (1994) 3 SLS 93.   [139] Hillyard (1993: 186–7).

[140] Irving B, *Police Interrogation: A Study of Current Practice* (Royal Commission Research Paper No 2) (London: HMSO, 1980) p 122.   [141] Britton (2000a: 652).

[142] Newburn and Hayman (2001: 96–7).

[143] PACE, s 61 routinised this although the provisions were complex. The CJA 2003, s 9 amended s 61 to provide simply that everyone arrested for a recordable offence may be fingerprinted.

[144] PACE, s 54 as amended by CJA 2003. Also see Code C, para 4.1.   [145] RCCP (1981: para 3.117).

[146] Zander M, *The Police and Criminal Evidence Act 1984* (London: Sweet and Maxwell, 2005) p 194.

[147] PACE, s 55 and Code C, Annex A.

There are relatively few intimate searches each year: a little over 100 on average. Most are for drugs, and the success rate is 10–20%.[148] There are many more strip-searches: about 12% of detainees in a study in a London police station in 1999–2000. Grossed up that would amount to about 150,000 strip-searches nationally every year (no official records are collected). The factors most often associated with strip-searches were: reason for arrest, age, gender and ethnic identity (drugs offences and young black men featured most often). 'On average, being African-Caribbean rather than white European (or Irish) was associated with a virtual doubling of the probability of being strip-searched.'[149] The study found that there were fewer strip-searches after the introduction of CCTV – suggesting that officers felt less confident about doing this in unjustifiable cases when they were being watched. But the greater probability of being strip-searched if the detainee was black (regardless of age, gender and offence) *increased* rather than decreased following the introduction of filming. In other words white detainees benefited disproportionately from the greater caution being exercised – perhaps because the police fear 'comeback' more from white than black suspects.

In addition, 'intimate' and 'non-intimate' samples may be taken. Intimate samples include semen and blood. 'Non-intimate' sample taking includes having hairs plucked, fingernails scraped and your saliva examined. If someone put a gloved finger in your mouth in order to scrape out some saliva, would you see that as a 'non-intimate' act? That is how PACE sees it. At one time, the consent of suspects was needed before samples could be taken for all but the most serious offences, but as in many other instances, the Criminal Justice Act 2003 has given the police almost carte blanche in relation to non-intimate samples.[150] Hillyard comments that:

These processes are common to the initiation into many 'total institutions' and Goffman has described them as 'mortification processes' because the self is systematically, if often unintentionally, mortified through a series of debasements, degradations, and humiliations.[151]

The insistence of human rights and due process theorists on 'rights' makes little sense in these conditions:

Yea, I understood me rights, but do you get rights in here? The loo don't flush, it stinks. You get breakfast in a cardboard box and it's freezing cold…it's not the law, it's just the fucking conditions…no fags, nowhere to wash, you've no idea what time it is…'[152]

Choongh asked the suspects he interviewed how they felt when locked up.[153] He classified the 72 replies as 'intolerable', 'distressing' or 'indifferent'. One-quarter were indifferent to the experience, but one-fifth found the experience 'intolerable'. A little over half found it 'distressing', using phrases like feeling 'trapped', 'powerless' and 'angry'.

---

[148] Povey and Smith (2009: table 2e).

[149] Newburn et al, 'Race, Crime and Injustice? Strip-search and the Treatment of Suspects in Custody' (2004) 44(5) BJ Crim 677 at p 689.   [150] PACE, ss 62 and 63, as amended by CJA 2003, s 10.

[151] Hillyard (1993: 151).   [152] Choongh (1997: 178).   [153] Choongh (1997: 97–8).

Detention is not awful for everyone. Occasionally the police have to detain people who they see as allies, not as threats, such as the well-dressed and well-spoken driver in the study by Choongh[154] who had a little too much wine at lunchtime. Unlike most detainees, he did not have to 'buy' good treatment by being deferential and showing the police that they know who is in charge. Choongh also found that large numbers of suspects had such low expectations of their treatment that they were indifferent to things that most people would find outrageous. Nonetheless, it is not surprising that time in detention feels stretched, and that therefore the most important factor affecting suspects' decisions whether to ask for legal advice is the likely length of detention.[155] As one detainee in Choongh's research told him, when asked why he had not requested a solicitor, 'I'm happy I'm out, yea? That's the only thing I care about, I don't care what happens to me in court.'[156] Moreover, the significance of detention lengths is not only the actual detention length but also the threat created by the 36-hour limit. Suspects do not know that the average detention lasts 'only' nine hours or so, and rightly fear that the way they behave could lead to their being confined for longer – or could affect whether they get out at all before being hauled off to court. The subjective experience of 'only' nine hours detention, and of the threat of longer detention, is something which few legislators, judges, academics or university students are likely to have endured.

For detainees under the anti-terrorism legislation detention can be a very long time in both objective and subjective terms. Apart from anything else, police station cells provide virtually no natural light or opportunity to walk, let alone exercise. At its most extreme, indefinite detention can lead to traumatic psychological disturbance: some of the ATCSA detainees who successfully challenged their detention in 2004[157] suffered so much that by the time of the court challenge they were already in a mental hospital.

Looking at the experience of detention in the light of its purposes and time limits, we can see that crime control considerations clearly outweigh those of due process, particularly in relation to serious suspected offences. But it may be that under a 'freedom' perspective the detention of suspects in some circumstances where evidence is thin and detention not strictly necessary is justified – especially if the detention is for a short period and the offence serious. Britain used to (crudely) adopt this approach by providing great detention powers for suspected terrorism, less for 'serious arrestable offences' and less still for 'arrestable offences', but the CJA 2003 gave the police the same power for 'arrestable' as for 'serious arrestable' offences. A freedom perspective would demand more fine tuning, shorter detention periods, less isolation and degradation and more judicial supervision. Human rights perspectives, such as that of Ashworth and Redmayne (2005), are of little use here, for only the most extreme

---

[154] Choongh (1997: 206–7).   [155] Sanders et al (1989: ch 4).
[156] Choongh (1997: 149). *Aspinall* [1999] Crim LR 741 (see 4.2.3 above) concerned a particularly vulnerable suspect who was prepared to say anything to get out after being isolated for over 13 hours.
[157] *A (FC) v Home Secretary* [2004] UKHL 56.

behaviours documented in this section (beating and gross abuse) contravene the ECHR or Code C.[158] Intimate body searches, for example, have been held compatible with the Art 3 right not to be subjected to degrading treatment.[159] The same is true when detainees have all or some clothes removed, perhaps because they are seen as a suicide risk, but this is also sometimes done in a humiliating way.[160] Most of this police behaviour is not illegal or even deliberately degrading – it is simply an inevitable product of involuntary detention and of the prioritisation of crime control over freedom. Deaths in custody are another matter, however.

4.4 **Deaths in custody**

Following a death in custody the area has to be secured, the Independent Police Complaints Commission (IPCC) informed, and an investigation begun. There is then an inquest and, depending on the findings of the investigation and inquest, consideration is given to possible prosecution and/or disciplinary proceedings against the officers involved. The force in which the death occurs used to carry out that investigation – in other words, whether the police involved were held to be responsible for a death in custody was determined in large part by an investigation carried out by those officers' colleagues.

Many lawyers acting for bereaved families expressed concern about these procedures. Between 1990 and 2003, 627 people died while in police custody (an average of nearly one a week) but in only 11 were there unlawful killing verdicts and/or prosecutions, and in none of these cases was anyone convicted of a criminal offence.[161] In the five years since 2003 a further 483 have died: at over 96 per year, this is a worrying increase.[162] The definition of 'in custody' used here, as defined by PACE, s 118, is a broad one that includes death following contact with the police outside the station. Examples include Harry Stanley in 1999 (shot dead because the table leg he was carrying was mistaken for a gun),[163] Jean Charles de Menezes (shot dead in 2005 because he was wrongly thought to be one of the July 7 bombers),[164] and Ian Tomlinson (fatally assaulted by police during a demonstration in 2009 – see ch 3). They also include deadly traffic pursuits (see 3.4.2). However, in this section we are primarily concerned with

---

[158] On beating and psychologically damaging interrogation techniques, see *Ireland v UK* (1978) 2 EHRR 25.   [159] *McFeeley v UK* (App No 8317/78, (1980) 20 DR 44).

[160] See, for example, the Cambridgeshire inspection: HMIP and HMIC (2009).

[161] See Vogt G and Wadham J, *Deaths in Police Custody: Redress and Remedies* (London: Civil Liberties Trust, 2003). See ch 12 for further discussion of investigation and prosecution of police malpractice and deaths in custody.

[162] IPCC, *Annual Report and Statement of Accounts 2008/9* (London: IPCC, 2009) (adapted from p 24, table 1.1 – includes traffic deaths).

[163] For this and other cases see Inquest, *Death in Police Custody: Report on Harry Stanley* (London: Inquest, 2000, updated 2002) and the discussion in 12.2.   [164] See eg *The Guardian*, 28 July 2005.

deaths in 'custody' as understood elsewhere in this chapter. There were 128 deaths following arrest or detention in the five years to 2008/09, with the figures declining over that period from 36 (2004/05) to 15 (2008/09).[165]

Here are a few examples of some of the worst cases. In 1997 two inquest juries found that Oluwashhijibomi Lapite and Richard O'Brien had been 'unlawfully killed' while in police custody. Lapite had 45 injuries. An officer admitted kicking him in the head as hard as he could, claiming that he was the most violent prisoner he had ever encountered, but the officers involved had only superficial injuries. O'Brien had 31 injuries. The last words his wife heard him say were: 'I can't breathe, let me up, you win.'[166] Christopher Alder – another black man – was arrested and dumped half-naked and handcuffed onto a police station floor in 1998. As he lay dying, gasping for breath as blood blocked his air passages, he was accused by an officer of 'faking it'. Four other officers also watched, and only took action – too late – to save his life after he stopped breathing. For once we know the truth, because all this was caught on a 12-minute police video.[167] And in 2003 Mikey Powell – yet another black man – was deliberately hit by a moving police car, sprayed with CS gas, struck with a baton, put on the floor of a police van face down, and carried into a police cell still face down. Only then did the police realise he had stopped breathing. In December 2009 the jury at the inquest concluded that this mentally ill man (with no criminal record) had died from positional asphyxia following police restraint.[168]

We do not know how many cases there are like this. What we do know is that even some of the most suspicious circumstances do not lead to unlawful killing verdicts or prosecutions. Take the case of Marlon Downes, a young black man found hanging in his cell in 1997. The police argued that he must have committed suicide, even though the grille from which he was hanging was so high that, they said, he must have stood on two rolled-up mattresses. However:

- Police photos of the cell showed only one mattress.

- The shoelace with which he allegedly hanged himself could not have supported his weight.

- The custody record stated that he was still alive at least one hour after he actually died.

- Attempts had been made to erase an even later entry claiming he was still alive.

- His solicitor gave evidence that he had seen Marlon in a different cell, but the police denied moving him.

[165] IPCC (2009a: 24, table 1.1).

[166] *Statewatch*, July–Oct 1997, p 19; Smith G, 'The DPP and Prosecutions of Police Officers' (1997) 147 NLJ 1180.

[167] *The Guardian*, 25 August 2000. See *The Guardian*, 18 August 2005 for a discussion of these and several other cases. (Type 'Christopher Alder' into Youtube for excerpts from the police video.)

[168] <http://www.guardian.co.uk/commentisfree/libertycentral/2009/dec/27/mikey-powell-inquest-death-in-custody> (accessed 5 January 2010).

- The station cleaner cleaned the cell in which he was found before the investigation began.

The inquest recorded an open verdict, and Marlon's family will never know what really happened to their son.[169] This was not an isolated case. In a number of high profile cases in the last 30 years or so, where witnesses agreed that suspects had been subjected to more force (beaten and kicked) than was necessary to restrain them, inquest verdicts of 'justifiable homicide' and 'death by misadventure' resulted, this being one of many reasons for the inquest system coming under critical scrutiny.[170] And the suspicion of a 'cover-up' occurs in case after case (such as Rigg's, discussed below).

Two recent examples are Faisal Al-Ani, who died in hospital in 2005 of injuries sustained while being restrained by police initially in the street, then on the journey to the police station, then in the station; and Sean Rigg, who died after being arrested and dumped in a metal cage in a police station yard in 2008. The IPCC criticised the police in Al-Ani's case for using techniques 'in contravention to all guidance'. However, although officers admitted striking him several times 'in self-defence' while he was handcuffed, and the police initially claimed that their first contact with him was when he walked into the police station (a claim withdrawn later only because of CCTV evidence contradicting it), both the IPCC and inquest jury concluded that the police actions were 'reasonable'.[171]

As well as deaths in custody raising questions about police policy and practice – and, indeed, the principle established in PACE that the police should be able to use custody to facilitate their work – there is a legal dimension. The ECHR, Art 2 'right to life' not only prohibits the state from taking life except where absolutely necessary, but also imposes on it a duty to protect life and to effectively investigate deaths.[172] The procedures leading to unsatisfactory verdicts such as in Marlon Downes' case undoubtedly were in breach of Art 2[173] and so the IPCC, which is independent of the police, now takes the lead. Established only in 2004 (replacing the Police Complaints Authority – PCA), it is still too soon to be certain about the difference it is making, but its endorsement of police behaviour in the Al-Ani case, and investigative failures in Rigg's case, suggest that the police view of events continues to dominate responses to deaths in custody.[174]

---

[169] Newburn and Hayman (2001: ch 2).

[170] Scraton P and Chadwick K, *In the Arms of the Law: Coroners' Inquests and Deaths in Custody* (London: Pluto, 1987); Vogt and Wadham (2003).

[171] *The Guardian*, 2 June 2009 (Al-Ani); *The Guardian*, 22 August 2009 (Rigg). At the time of writing the IPCC report into Rigg's case had not been made public as no inquest had yet taken place.

[172] *Osman v UK* [1998] 29 [EHRR] 245; *McCann v UK* [1995] 21 ECHR 97.

[173] This is true of inquests as well as the pre-2004 investigations. See Vogt and Wadham (2003).

[174] IPCC investigators waited eight months before interviewing the officers in Rigg's case because they thought 'there was nothing to suggest wrong-doing'. Their suspicions were not alerted by the (disputed) failure of CCTV cameras covering the metal cage in which Rigg was dumped (*The Guardian*, 22 August 2009). For a good discussion of the dominance of the police view see Pemberton S, 'Demystifying Deaths in Police Custody: Challenging State Talk' (2008) 17 Social and Legal Studies 237. The IPCC and decisions about prosecution and discipline of police officers are discussed in ch 12.

In the absence of reliable investigative and judicial procedures, we have to rely on research to shed light on the causes of deaths in custody. A Home Office study of all 227 deaths between 1990 and 1996 found that *according to official sources* 63% of detainees died by their own actions (deliberate self-harm, substance abuse or accident) and 29% as a result of a medical condition. Only 6% were attributed to police actions. But, at a rate of 2–3 each year, this amounts to over 30 in the 1990–2003 period when there were just 11 adverse verdicts and/or prosecutions.[175] And, as the authors point out, 'Others might challenge the official record…working from their version of events, some of the conclusions in this study might be different.'[176] The case of Marlon Downes, where the official record was simply not credible is an obvious one, and highly typical: many of those who 'died by their own actions' in the Home Office study (around 25% of the sample of 227) actually died by hanging, just like Downes. Moreover, not only are members of ethnic minorities, especially black men, disproportionately represented in deaths in custody in general,[177] but in over one-third of black deaths in the Home Office study police actions were a possible factor (as compared to 4% of white deaths). This is consistent with the disproportionate use of police force against black people chronicled in chs 2 and 3.

The 6% of deaths attributed to police actions included a few cases where an accident occurred during a struggle (eg a police officer falling on the suspect) and rather more where the police applied faulty restraint methods, sometimes after arrest.[178] The overwhelming majority of deaths at the hands of the police are, no doubt, accidental in the sense that the killing was not intentional, or (rarely) death might be justified through, for example, self-defence. But how many detainees abuse, struggle and assault officers through fear of custody or because of what custody has done to them, especially if they are drunk, drugged or mentally unstable? Just the experience of custody leads to many of these deaths, including many who kill themselves. This is especially so as the police sometimes overlook signs of physical and mental illness that, untreated, and exacerbated by custodial conditions, cause fatalities – particularly in relation to black suspects where the police sometimes make 'racist assumptions' about why some are unpredictable or unruly in custody.[179]

A report for the PCA published in 2004[180] commented that a major warning sign was if the detainee had to be carried to the station by the police (as was true in Christopher Alder's case). The lesson has not been learned. In August 2005 Paul Coker, a young

---

[175] Legal aspects of investigations, and decisions whether to prosecute are now governed by: CPS and IPCC, Protocol between the Crown Prosecution Service Casework Directorate and the Independent Police Complaints Commission (available at <http://www.cps.gov.uk/publications/agencies/ipcc.html>).

[176] Leigh et al (1998: 6).

[177] In the year 2008/09 of the 15 people who died in police custody, three were black, two were Asian. It is not known how many of the ten white fatalities were from an ethnic minority: IPCC (2009a: 21).

[178] Leigh et al (1998: 40–50). The Al-Ani case (*The Guardian*, 2 July 2009) is an example.

[179] Bowling et al, 'Policing Ethnic Minority Communities' in Newburn T (ed), *Handbook of Policing*, 2nd edn (Cullompton: Willan, 2008). Alder's case, discussed above, is one such example, as are, again, those of Al-Ani and Rigg.   [180] Best and Kefas (2004).

black man, was arrested at his home by the police. His girlfriend, who had called the police, said that the police were upstairs struggling with Paul: '"You are killing me. You are killing me." She had never heard a man scream like that. Then it all went quiet.... when he was carried out Paul was not struggling. Police were holding his arms and legs.' He died in the police station two hours later.[181] Similarly, also in 2005, Faisal Al-Ani (see above) was carried into the police station face-down and died a few hours later. These are just two of an unknown number of cases where detainees die as a result of the police overreacting to troublesome, abusive or violent detainees, before, during or after restraining them; and where, to compound this, the police fail to seek medical attention for the detainees they injure. In the closed world of the police station in most cases the only witnesses will be police officers, and so the official records can simply not be trusted to present the full picture.

Clearly many deaths in custody are preventable. In some cases all that is needed is a speedy response to a call for help. In one study, researchers interviewing suspects in their cells were locked in on more than one occasion for half an hour or more before the police came to 'rescue' them, despite the cells having a call button (immobilised by the custody officer) and shouting and beating on the cell doors.[182] An official inspection found custody suite staff turned cell bells down rather than attending to the calls.[183] CCTV cameras that work would also be helpful, to say the least. Then we would really know what happened to people like Downes, Rigg and Al-Ani. The Home Office study found that there were warning signs or explicit warnings (such as 'suicide markers' on the PNC) in over 30% of all deaths by deliberate self-harm. Some had actually tried to commit suicide while already in police custody or shortly before. Some people who died from their medical conditions also displayed signs of major illnesses that were often mistaken for simple drunkenness.[184] On the other hand it has to be acknowledged that many attempts at self-harm and other life-threatening conditions are identified by police who prevent very large numbers of deaths and serious injuries. The number of actual deaths are dwarfed by nearly 40 times as many 'near-misses', some of which would have been fatal had it not been for police vigilance.[185]

From the freedom perspective one sets this death toll against the reasons for custodial detention. Astonishingly, most detainees in the Home Office study had been arrested for drink- or drug-related offences (49%) or minor thefts (11%).[186] There can surely be no justification for a criminal justice system that allows people to be put in a situation where *we know that some will die* when their alleged crimes are this trivial. Without denying that some police officers are culpable for deaths in custody, the main concern should be a

---

[181] *The Guardian*, 18 August 2005.   [182] Newburn and Hayman (2001: 123).
[183] HMIP and HMIC (2009).
[184] Leigh et al (1998: 8–39) and, again, Al-Ani. Code C, paras 3.6–3.10 now require custody officers to make risk assessments that include, inter alia, PNC checks.
[185] It is estimated that there are around 1,000 'near misses' per year. While many would have been fatal without police vigilance, in others only good fortune prevented a lack of vigilance leading to fatal consequences: IPCC, *Near Misses in Police Custody: A Collaborative Study with Forensic Medical Examiners in London* (London: IPCC, 2008b).   [186] Leigh et al (1998: 9).

double system-failure: that too many people are detained by the police when they should not be; and that the police are not trained or resourced to deal with circumstances that lead to deaths. As Best and Kefas (2004) concluded, 'drunken detainees should not be taken to police stations in other than the most extreme circumstances'.[187]

Part of the problem is that s 136 of the Mental Health Act 1983 (MHA) designates police stations (as well as hospitals) as 'places of safety' to which police officers can take mentally ill people in immediate need of care and control. Twice as many (over 11,000 per year) are taken to police stations as hospitals under this provision. People at risk of self-harm – as many detained under this section are – are more likely to be taken to a police station because hospitals are even less able than are the police to deal with the problem. Indeed, many drink/drug arrests are made because it is often easier for the police to arrest mentally ill people than to attempt to persuade hospitals to take them, especially where they have (as many do) drink/drug problems.[188] But as a custody officer rightly points out, 'the police are not health care providers'.[189]

4.5 **The right to legal advice**

Prior to PACE, access to legal advice was governed by the Judges' Rules. The Rules stated that a suspected person should be able to consult privately with a solicitor provided that it caused the police no unreasonable 'hindrance'. But what was or was not reasonable was never clearly established, and the Judges' Rules were not 'law' in the sense of being common law or statute. All that a suspect who was denied access to legal advice could do was to ask for the evidence obtained as a result to be excluded from trial, if there was one. Further, the Fisher inquiry into the 'Confait Affair' found that many suspects (including the wrongly convicted youths in that case) did not know they had such a right, even though the police were supposed to inform them of it. Fisher (1977) quotes a deputy assistant commissioner of the Metropolitan Police saying that 'it has never been recognised by the police...as a duty to tell a prisoner...that he has the right to consult a solicitor'.

Thus, few suspects were informed by officers of this right, fewer tried to exercise it and fewer still had their requests granted. Softley's study of four police stations found that

---

[187] A similar point, in relation to prison custody as well as police custody, is made by the Parliamentary Joint Committee on Human Rights, *Deaths in Custody* (2004). A Forum for Preventing Deaths in Custody was established by the Government in 2006 to advise the Government. It does not seem to have been effective, and was wound up in 2009. It is (at the time of writing) to be superseded by a Ministerial Council on Deaths in Custody that will be advised by an Independent Panel (<http://www.justice.gov.uk/news>). It is lamentable that all the effort seems to be in creating advisory bodies rather than in acting on the findings of the government's own research: ensuring adherence to PACE, ensuring CCTV in police stations is working and safe from tampering, and investigating deaths effectively.

[188] Docking et al, *Police Custody as a 'Place of Safety': Examining the Use of s 136 of the MHA 1983* (London: IPCC, 2008).

[189] Coppen (2008). His concern about s 136 is endorsed by a Chief Constable: Wilding B, 'Tipping the Scales of Justice?' in Cape and Young (2008) and by the IPCC research (Docking et al, 2008).

around 9% sought advice and around 7% actually secured it.[190] Even these figures are artificially high, for in one of these police stations the police were told (for the purposes of the research) that they had to inform all suspects of their right to a solicitor, whereas in the other three stations they were not so directed. In the station in which suspects were routinely informed of their rights, the numbers requesting and securing access were considerably higher than in the others. As one would expect, being told one's rights is vital. The Philips Commission recognised this, and its recommendations, which aimed to make the right to advice truly available to all, were implemented by the government in PACE.

4.5.1 The right to advice under PACE and the HRA

Section 58 of PACE states the right of access in the clearest possible terms:

(1) A person arrested…shall be entitled, if he so requests, to consult a solicitor privately at any time…

(4) If a person makes such a request, he must be permitted to consult a solicitor as soon as is practicable except to the extent that delay is permitted by this section.…

Delay in compliance with a request is only permitted…(b) if an officer of at least the rank of superintendent authorises it.

This differs from the old Judges' Rules. It is an unequivocal statutory provision although there is still no clear remedy available to suspects who are denied this right (see 4.6 below). Secondly, advice cannot be refused but merely delayed. All suspects must be permitted, if they wish, to consult a solicitor within 36 hours (the period beyond which suspects cannot be held without the authorisation of a magistrate).[191]

The 'right to consult a solicitor privately at any time' is a powerful one. As we shall see, legal advice to detainees is always available free of charge. Suspects who initially decline a solicitor can demand one later, even in the middle of an interview. And they can require that the solicitor be present in the interview and may consult with that solicitor (publicly or privately) during it.[192] As part of the ECHR 'right to a fair trial', everyone 'charged with a criminal offence' has the right to legal assistance. Suspects are 'to be given it free when the interests of justice so require'.[193] Although this only seems to apply to people being prosecuted (ie charged), the European Court held in *Murray* that it applies to suspects under arrest too if what happens when under arrest could affect the fairness of a subsequent trial: 'The concept of fairness enshrined in

---

[190] Softley P, *Police Interrogation: An Observational Study in Four Police Stations* (Royal Commission on Criminal Procedure Research Study No 4) (London: HMSO, 1980).

[191] PACE, s 58(5). Delay is only possible if the offence is indictable: PACE, s 58(6)(a) as amended by the Serious Organised Crime and Police Act 2005, Sch 7 (watering down the previous rule that delay was only permitted for serious arrestable offences).

[192] Code C, para 6.8 and notes 6B and 6D, and PACE, s 58(1).

[193] Article 6, para 3(c). See *S v Switzerland* (1991) 14 EHRR 670; *Brennan v UK* (2001) 34 EHRR 507. On the meaning of 'the interests of justice', see Ashworth A, 'Legal Aid, Human Rights and Criminal Justice' in Young R and Wall D (eds), *Access to Criminal Justice* (London: Blackstone, 1996a) pp 61–3, and 9.2.

Art 6 requires that the accused had the benefit of the assistance of a lawyer already at the initial stages of police interrogation.'[194] The Court held that a defendant could not have a fair trial if he had been interviewed while access to advice was being withheld, especially as adverse inferences could be made had he remained silent.[195]

There are obvious potential difficulties with the right of access. One is that the interview might be unduly delayed while waiting for a solicitor. If the consequences would be truly serious an officer of the rank of superintendent or above may authorise the interview in the solicitor's absence.[196] If a lawyer's advice and assistance in the interview is such that the police are 'unable properly to put questions to the suspect', the lawyer can be required to leave, but only if authorised by a superintendent (or an inspector if a superintendent is not 'readily available'), and an opportunity must be given to the suspect to be represented by a replacement lawyer.[197]

Another problem is where the police need to carry out procedures such as breath tests on suspected drunken drivers. Decisions that the 'as soon as is practicable' provision in s 58(4) means that such procedures need not wait on a legal consultation, and that this is not inconsistent with Art 6, seem sensible to us.[198] However, we do not understand why the police routinely delay even seeking a solicitor until after a sample is taken (preventing even the possibility of speedy advice), nor why the courts largely accept this.[199]

Yet another problem is the right of privacy. This is difficult to guarantee in a busy police station, though it should not be impossible if sufficient resources were allocated. As it is, the English courts make a distinction between conditions under which consultations could be overheard (which are not seen as violating the principle),[200] and deliberate attempts by police to overhear, regardless of whether or not this helps the police case (which does violate the principle).[201]

Delaying access

Section 58(8) of PACE provides that (in cases of indictable offences only):

> ...an officer may only authorise delay where he has reasonable grounds for believing that the exercise of the right...
>
> (a) will lead to interference with or harm to evidence... or interference with or physical injury to other persons; or

---

[194] *Murray v UK* (1996) 22 EHRR 29. Quoted by Cape E, 'Sidelining Defence Lawyers: Police Station Advice after *Condron*' (1997) 1 IJ E&P 386 at p 398. In this case, access to a lawyer was delayed in accordance with the PTA 1989, s 14. This allowed delay on similar, but less stringent grounds, to those of PACE, and for up to 48 hours. The current terrorist legislation is similar.

[195] See 5.3 for discussion of the right of silence.   [196] Code C, para 6.6.

[197] Code C, paras 6.9–6.10.

[198] *Campbell v DPP* [2003] Crim LR 118; *Whitley v DPP* [2004] Crim LR 585.

[199] See Commentary on *Kennedy v DPP* [2003] Crim LR 120 (which applied *Campbell*) at 121. Because breath tests provide objective evidence, courts and commentators alike see denial of advice as largely unproblematic. The value of legal advisers (and appropriate adults, where there is a similar issue – see 4.2.3) as emotional and practical supporters is routinely ignored.

[200] *La Rose* [2002] Crim LR 215, [2001] EWHC Admin 553. The ECtHR was less sympathetic to the police in *Brennan v UK* (2001) 34 EHRR 507.   [201] *Grant* [2006] QB 20.

(b) will lead to the alerting of other persons suspected of having committed such an offence...; or

(c) will hinder the recovery of any property obtained as a result of such an offence.

In *Samuel*[202] and thereafter, the courts made it clear that access could only be delayed in exceptional circumstances, such as some reason to believe that, in the particular case, access could lead to one of these consequences. The Court of Appeal went on to note that if, as in this case, the solicitor was a duty solicitor (ie not known to the suspect) this would be virtually impossible for the police to prove, since neither the police nor the suspect would know who that individual was until such time as he or she arrived at the police station.[203]

In 1987, delay was authorised in around 1% of all cases,[204] but in research covering 12,500 cases conducted in the mid 1990s, no delays were authorised at all.[205] We shall see later on that the problem now is not formal delay of access but the informal delay which results from the police bending or breaking the rules, and legal changes that reduce the value of legal advice for suspects. Delay under the terrorism legislation is still doubtless contemplated from time to time, but as we saw earlier, this is now very difficult to justify, given the way that Art 6 of the ECHR is interpreted.[206]

Notification of the right to advice and provision of advice

Not all suspects know their rights and few know them in detail. Code C is intended to deal with this:

3.1 When a person is brought to a police station under arrest or arrested at the police station having gone there voluntarily, the custody officer must make sure the person is told clearly about the following continuing rights...

(i) The right to have someone informed of his arrest...

(ii) The right to consult privately with a solicitor and the fact that free independent legal advice is available;

(iii) The right to consult these codes of practice.

This should ensure that arrested suspects are told their main rights orally, and para 3.2 provides that detainees must be given a written notice too, which sets out these and their other rights. But there are three loopholes here. Firstly, volunteers 'helping with inquiries' need not be told their rights, unless the police caution them that they are under suspicion.[207] Secondly, as noted in 4.2 above, the duty to tell suspects their rights orally does not apply to the right to a telephone call or the right to receive visits

---

[202] *Samuel* [1988] 2 All ER 135.

[203] A similar view was taken by the ECtHR in *Brennan v UK* (2001). In *Alladice* (1988) 87 Cr App Rep 380 the (differently constituted) Court of Appeal regarded itself as bound by *Samuel* but was rather more sympathetic to the police. This led them to a different view of the consequences following on from unlawful delay of access: see 12.5.

[204] Brown D, *Detention at the Police Station under the Police and Criminal Evidence Act 1984* (Home Office Research Study No 104) (London: HMSO, 1989) p 68.   [205] Bucke and Brown (1997: 23).

[206] See discussion of *Murray v UK* (1996) 22 EHRR 29 above.   [207] Code C, para 3.21.

(at the custody officer's discretion). Thirdly, the obligation begins only when the suspect is brought to the police station. Suspects who are arrested some distance from the place of the alleged crime are therefore in police custody for a long time (whilst being transported to the relevant police station) before they are informed of their rights other than the right to silence. This will not usually matter, since most questioning is prohibited before arrival at the station (discussed in ch 5). But illegal interviewing sometimes occurs anyway, and there is no prohibition on letting suspects incriminate themselves voluntarily – if that is an appropriate way of describing the actions of suspects in police custody. Thus in *Khan*[208] the defendant was arrested in Wales and driven to Birmingham by the police who alleged that he voluntarily confessed in the car.

The procedure to be adopted on arrival at the station is as follows. After authorising detention, custody officers must tell suspects of their main rights. They will be asked specifically whether they want to consult a solicitor. If so, this should be facilitated (as described below) as soon as possible. Every step in this process must be recorded on the custody record. For this set of protections to work it is essential that the police operate the system in good faith, and that a solicitor be readily available.

Solicitors are obviously not available around the clock and many suspects are arrested at night, weekends or other awkward times. Before PACE this was a major problem. Softley (1980) found that around one-quarter of all suspects who requested advice did not get any. This was sometimes because the police refused to let them see a solicitor, but often a solicitor simply could not be found. There was a clear need to provide some form of scheme which secured access within a reasonable amount of time for the sake of both the suspect and the police so that unreasonable delay was not caused. This was bound to cost a lot of money. While the government in the 1980s provided such money as was required, we shall see that this is no longer true.

Suspects requesting legal advice now have two choices. They may speak to their 'own' lawyer if they have one, if the lawyer is able to advise speedily, and if they are able to pay. Alternatively, as from 2008, they are put in contact with a national Defence Solicitor Call Centre (DSCC) which decides whether to route the request to a nationwide service, CDS Direct (this provides advice over the phone for relatively minor offences), or to an individual solicitor, if the offence is sufficiently serious, who will decide whether to attend the station. This may be a duty solicitor or a solicitor nominated by the suspect.[209] The country is divided into a number of legal aid regions, within each of which are several areas. Each area has, or should have, a duty solicitor

---

[208]   (CA: 1990, unreported). Discussed in Kaye T, *'Unsafe and Unsatisfactory?' Report of the Independent Inquiry into the Working Practices of the West Midlands Police Serious Crime Squad* (London: Civil Liberties Trust, 1991). Also see Skinns (2009a).

[209]   Pressure to reduce the amount of advice given face to face has increased over the years (discussed further below). The latest changes are made in the 2008 version of Code C, para 6.1 and Note 6B. Article 6 imposes no obligations concerning the way in which advice is provided as long as it fulfils the 'fair trial' requirement: *Salduz v Turkey* [2008] ECHR 1542.

Table 4.2 Request and consultation rates, 1988–2007

	Request rate (%)	Consultation rate (%)
1988	25	19
1991	32	25
1995–6	40	34
2007	60	48

All figures derived from Bucke and Brown (1997: ch 3) except 2007, derived from Skinns (2009b). Note this is higher than the request rate of little over 50% reported by Kemp and Balmer (2008: 23). Both studies were of relatively small samples.

scheme.[210] There is no obligation on solicitors to participate. Consequently, some schemes are overstretched, duty solicitors cannot always get to the police station quickly, and they sometimes fail to get there at all.[211]

4.5.2 The take-up of advice by suspects

Despite large increases in the request rate since 1988, less than half of all suspects receive advice (see table 4.2).

Within these general figures, there are considerable variations. For instance, advice is sought more often for serious than for minor offences (advice is sought and received in over half of all cases involving offences tried in the Crown Court)[212] and is sought more often by adults than by young offenders even though the latter are vulnerable.[213] Inexplicably great variations exist between different police stations.[214]

Despite the general increase, less than two-thirds of suspects exercise their right to advice, and fewer than half actually secure it. This seems difficult to understand at first sight. Nearly all are in the police station involuntarily. Most will be frightened or apprehensive, unsure of their rights and worried about how long they will be detained. Many perceive the police to be 'against' them – as of course they are in an adversarial system. Against this intimidating backcloth they are being offered something for nothing: a lawyer, whose sole job whilst in the station will be to help that suspect, at precisely nil cost. Yet the response of nearly half is to say 'no thanks'.

In the earliest study of PACE, Maguire (1988) observed that some suspects have a predisposition to seek advice while others do not, and some are very much easier to

---

[210] These were originally established under s 59 of PACE. See now the Access to Justice Act 1999, s 3 and Criminal Defence Service *Duty Solicitor Arrangements* 2001.   [211] Sanders et al (1989).

[212] RCCJ (1993: 35).

[213] Although trained volunteers acting as appropriate adults generally advise suspects to request advice in strong terms: Brookman F and Pierpoint H, 'Access to Legal Advice for Young Suspects and Remand Prisoners' (2003) 42(5) Howard JCJ 452.

[214] Brown et al (1992); Bucke and Brown (1997: ch 3); Skinns (2009b).

influence than are others. Suspects arrested for trivial offences like drunkenness are entitled to advice but they correctly perceive that it would usually be of little use to them. There is a low elasticity of demand among these suspects. Other suspects who reject the idea of legal advice include those who are confident that they can handle the situation and, at the opposite end of the spectrum, fatalistic suspects who believe that nothing can help them at all. Needless to say, neither the confidence nor the fatalism are always justified (Bucke and Brown, 1997: 22). Some suspects simply trust the police to deal with them so fairly that they see no need for advice or help from anyone else,[215] which will again be true only some of the time and, of course, begs the question of what is 'fair' in an adversary system.[216]

As we saw earlier, the main goal of many suspects is to get out of the station as soon as possible. These suspects refuse advice only because it might delay their departure. Most suspects who refuse advice do so because of the actual or likely wait.[217] Some suspects plan ahead by leaving messages with parents or friends that a solicitor is to be secured if they are not home by a certain time (Sanders et al, 1989). These suspects make strategic decisions based on their past experience with police and solicitors. Sometimes their bad experiences with solicitors make them reluctant to request them. Others have a low opinion of duty solicitors in particular, and so would see only their own solicitor, preferring to see no one rather than the duty solicitor: 'Duty solicitors are crap anyway, they work for the fucking police and the courts.'[218] Most suspects have no opportunity to plan ahead. The defendant in *Aspinall*[219] requested a solicitor but, because of a mix-up, he did not see one. After 13 hours in custody he signed the custody record to say that he no longer wished to see a solicitor, 'the reason being I want to get home to my missus and kid'.

Some suspects have an inflexible elasticity of demand because they always want a solicitor. Many of these are likely to be charged with serious offences, have long records or believe that a solicitor can do them no harm and may well do them some good. These suspects demand solicitors in almost any circumstances, and would do so even if the police did not have to inform them of their rights and to arrange advice for them.

Between these two groups, Maguire (1988) argued, there is a large group of suspects, accused of moderately serious crimes such as shoplifting, car theft, handling stolen

---

[215] That this attitude can contribute to major miscarriages of justice is evidenced by the post-PACE case of Sheila Bowler: Devlin A and Devlin T, *Anybody's Nightmare* (East Harling: Taverner Publications, 1998) p 87.

[216] Discussed more fully in Sanders A and Bridges L, 'The Right to Legal Advice' in Walker C and Starmer K (eds), *Miscarriages of Justice* (London: Blackstone, 1999); and in Sanders A, 'Access to Justice in the Police Station: An Elusive Dream?' in Young and Wall (1996a).

[217] Kemp V and Balmer N, *Criminal Defence Services: Users' Perspectives* (Research Paper No 21) (London: Legal Services Research Centre, 2008); Brown et al (1992: 53).

[218] Suspect quoted in Choongh (1997: 149). Sanders et al (1989) and Kemp and Balmer (2008) also found suspects who believed this. This belief is understandable in view of the way many duty solicitors used to, and sometimes still do, behave. See below.   [219] *Aspinall* [1999] Crim LR 741.

goods, burglary and deception, who have a very high elasticity of demand. Many of these suspects, when they do not seek advice, say that this is because it is 'not worth it', or that they will wait to see what happens (very few later deciding to seek advice).[220] Decisions about whether or not to seek advice are influenced by a large number of factors. These include the attitudes and practices of the police and the availability and likely quality of the advice.

4.5.3 The attitudes and practices of the police

Many suspects learn about their rights for the first time when told them by the custody officer. Others may know some of their rights but not crucial details (such as advice being free). Others may be afraid to ask for a lawyer. It follows that the way the police inform suspects of their rights – whether the choice is put as a 'question expecting the answer yes or the answer no' – could be an important influence upon them.[221] Sanders et al in the late 1980s observed the reception of suspects into custody in ten police stations and concluded that the police utilise 'ploys' to dissuade suspects from seeking advice in over 40% of all cases. Table 4.3 shows the great range of ploys used.

It is likely that ploys are (or were) even more extensively used than this study detected, since, in this context, the presence of an observer inevitably affects the process being observed. In one example given by Sanders et al,[222] two juveniles suspected of shoplifting from Mothercare were being processed by a custody officer. When the researcher walked into the custody area, he heard and saw the custody officer reading out the suspects' rights in an incomprehensible manner. The custody officer looked up, saw the researcher and said, 'Are you the chap from Mothercare?' The researcher replied, 'No, I am the chap from Birmingham University', whereupon the custody officer went bright red, stopped, and started reading out the suspects rights very slowly and clearly from the beginning.

Reading rights quickly and incomprehensibly and/or incompletely is the most frequently used ploy. In the somewhat contradictory words of a police officer:

Now, under PACE, you read them their rights as quickly as you can – hit them with it so quick they can't take it in – say 'sign here, here and here' and there you are: nothing has changed. We all know that, though you wouldn't get any policeman to admit it to you.[223]

Comments such as 'you'll have to wait in the cells until a solicitor gets here' are a dire threat to those suspects for whom length of detention is a greater concern than whether or not they are charged. Whilst the warning is true it is also incomplete: it ignores the fact that most suspects are put in the cells until they are interrogated anyway.

It is difficult to establish a causal link between the use of police ploys and actual requests for advice by suspects. Sanders et al found that there was little correlation

---

[220] See Bucke and Brown (1997: 22) and Skinns (2009a and b) who also found that the prospect of spending longer in the cells dissuaded many from seeking advice.   [221] Maguire (1988: 31).
[222] Sanders et al (1989: 63).   [223] Sanders et al (1989: 58).

Table 4.3 Police ploys

Ploy	Amount used (principal ploy only)
1. Rights told too quickly/incomprehensibly/incompletely	142 (42.9%)
2. Suspect's query answered unhelpfully/incorrectly	5 (1.5%)
3. Suspect told that inability to name own solicitor may affect right to have one contacted	2 (0.6%)
4. 'It's not a very serious charge'	1 (0.3%)
5. 'You'll have to wait in the cells until the solicitor gets here'	13 (3.9%)
6. 'You don't have to make your mind up now. You can have one later if you want to'	27 (8.2%)
7. 'You're only going to be here a short time'	25 (7.6%)
8. 'You're only here to be charged/interviewed'	14 (4.2%)
9. [To juvenile] 'You'll have to [or "do you want to"] wait until an adult gets here' [before decision can be made]	18 (5.4%)
10. [To adult] '[Juvenile] has said he doesn't want one'	8 (2.4%)
11. Combination of 9 and 10	4 (1.2%)
12. 'We won't be able to get a solicitor at this time/none of them will come out/he won't be in his office'	6 (1.8%)
13. 'You don't need one for this type of offence'	2 (0.6%)
14. 'Sign here, here and here' [no information given]	7 (2.1%)
15. 'You don't have to have one'	4 (1.2%)
16. 'You're being transferred to another station – wait until you get there'	6 (1.8%)
17. CO interprets indecision/silence as refusal	9 (2.7%)
18. 'You're not going to be interviewed/charged'	1 (0.3%)
19. 'You can go to see a solicitor when you get out/at court'	9 (2.7%)
20. 'You're (probably) going to get bail'	6 (1.8%)
21. Gives suspect *Solicitor's Directory* or list of solicitors without explanation/assistance	3 (0.9%)
22. Other	19 (5.7%)
Total	331 (100.0%)

Source: Sanders A and Bridges L, 'Access to Legal Advice and Police Malpractice' [1990] Crim LR 494.

between the two but this may have been because the police use these ploys primarily against those suspects whom they thought would ask for a solicitor anyway, or for whom they particularly did not want a solicitor involved. Brown et al considers the lack of correlation to be evidence that custody officers are not deliberately trying to obstruct suspects. They argue that:

over-speedy and unclear expositions of rights may have occurred simply because custody officers were all too familiar with what they were saying and failed to appreciate that to some suspects the information was new and unfamiliar . . . (1992: 29)

Similarly, Morgan et al found 'active discouragement, leading questions, or incomplete statement of rights' in 'only' about 14% of cases. In the rest, they say, rights were presented 'reasonably', but that 'few suspects are in a "reasonable" frame of mind at the time. There is usually no attempt to make sure the statement has been understood.'[224] Bucke and Brown (1997: ch 3) found that few suspects (almost none at all in two stations) were asked by the police why they had refused legal advice, a clear breach of Code C (para 6.5). The failure to test for understanding, or to seek reasons for decisions, is important because research carried out in the 1990s and very recently has found that many suspects think they have grasped what the police tell them, even though often unaware of important details, while many others are unsure about what is going on.[225] Clare and Gudjonsson, for example, found that only 40% of suspects could fully understand the written notice of rights provided to them.[226]

How far the police engage in 'ploys' remains a matter of debate, but the fact that they frequently break the rules is indisputable. The notification provisions of Code C were breached, in the opinion of Brown's observers, in 16% of the cases observed prior to the revision of the PACE Codes of Practice in 1991, and in 26% of the cases observed after that revision, which required the police to give more information to suspects. Brown et al (1992: 31) found that sometimes no information at all was provided. Occasionally, suspects were simply asked if they wanted a solicitor. About 7–8% of suspects were warned about the likely delay if they requested a lawyer, though Brown et al (at p 42) do not interpret this as a 'ploy'. It seems, then, that the police go through the motions of providing due process-based rights to advice, but insufficient attention is paid to ensuring that the message gets through to the vulnerable, the anxious and the less intelligent, who need them most.

Whether or not advice was originally requested, the police are supposed to remind suspects of their right to legal advice at the time of each review of detention and at the start of the interview.[227] That the police often fail to do so is evident from the following extract from the transcript of a trial:[228]

Q: [Defence Counsel]: At the end of that interview you offered the opportunity to have a lawyer?
A: [Officer]: That is correct.
Q: Why did you not do that at the beginning?
A: Because he had already been offered the opportunity to have a solicitor. If he wanted a solicitor he was welcome to have one but I am not going to encourage it.
Q: You did not offer him one for that reason?
A: No, not at the beginning of the interview.

---

[224] Morgan et al, *Police Powers and Policy: A Study of the Work of Custody Officers* (report to ESRC) (unpublished).

[225] Brown et al (1992); Choongh (1997); Kemp and Balmer (2008) (who found that 16% had 'no idea' what was going on, and as many more were not sure what was going on).

[226] Clare I and Gudjonsson G, *Devising and Piloting an Experimental Version of the Notice to Detained Persons* (Royal Commission on Criminal Justice, Research Study No 7) (London: HMSO, 1993).

[227] Code C, paras 15.4 and 11.2.   [228] Letter from the trial judge published at [1989] Crim LR 763.

Q: You suspected that if he did get a solicitor he would be advised to say nothing?
A: Yes.
Q: Which is why he was not offered one?
A: Yes.

Another complaint sometimes made is that the police try to rush people into accepting cautions without the benefit of prior legal advice, and try to avoid giving lawyers, when suspects persist with their requests, sufficient information to advise properly. In *DPP v Ara*[229] this was held to be unlawful, but this ruling seems to be ignored: in 2008 a crown prosecutor told a group of visitors to a police station that: 'We disclose the best evidence to elicit a guilty plea.'[230] (See further discussion in ch 7.)

It is clear that, whether by accident or design, many officers discourage recourse to legal advice much of the time. But it is equally clear that many suspects – those with relatively inelastic demand – increasingly persevere with their requests. The police usually accept this, and the request rate is consequently rising. However in some cases – presumably where the police are particularly keen to interrogate the suspect without a lawyer present – the police go to great lengths to block access by, for example, using multiple ploys.[231] Sometimes the police do not call the lawyer at all, which is clearly unlawful. Sometimes the call is delayed, allowing time to persuade suspects to withdraw their requests for advice, to be interrogated before the lawyer arrives, or to be informally interviewed.[232] Dixon et al (1990: 128) comment that solicitors frequently complain that on arrival at the station they are 'informed by officers that the suspect has changed his mind, agreed to talk to them, and confessed.' The suspicion is that the police play a large part in this volte face. Unfortunately, custody records give no reason for failure to secure advice in one-quarter of all such cases, thus making it difficult to account for the gap between the numbers requesting advice and those actually securing it.[233]

It would appear that giving the police the job of 'triggering' legal advice is a major obstacle to the success of the scheme. If the scheme were modified to allow solicitors to be in the police station round the clock it would almost certainly increase the advice rate, although it would be difficult and expensive to organise. Alternatively, s 58 might be amended so that advice would be provided unless actively refused. This would at least ensure that all the confused suspects who currently do not secure advice would do so. The Runciman Commission recommended none of these solutions.[234] Apart from some minor changes, it recommended that suspects who refuse advice

---

[229] [2002] 1 Cr App R 159. See Azzopardi J, 'Disclosure at the Police Station, the Right of Silence, and *DPP v Ara*' [2002] Crim LR 295.

[230] Thanks to Ed Cape – who will now probably never be invited to a police station again – for this snippet.

[231] Sanders et al (1989: 57) found that in these cases the request rate is noticeably lower than average.

[232] Sanders and Bridges (1990). All these abuses were also observed in the small-scale observational study by Choongh (1997: ch 6).

[233] Brown et al (1992: 61). The most recent research also found that a significant minority of requests were not met, and that police ploys were still widespread: Skinns (2009a and b).   [234] RCCJ (1993: 36).

'should then be given the opportunity of speaking to a duty solicitor on the telephone'. Suspects are already entitled to do this, but the Code now requires the custody officer to tell suspects who refuse advice that they can speak on the phone if they are concerned about having to wait (paras 6.4–6.5). This could have been taken further, by putting all suspects automatically into telephone contact with a duty solicitor (or, now, CDS Direct) in order to discuss the question of legal advice. The only losers, apart from crime control adherents, would be the Treasury. However, this makes assumptions about the value of telephone advice which we shall see are unwarranted.

4.5.4 The attitudes and practices of the legal profession

It would be misleading to give the impression that all, or even most, of the problems of securing legal advice in police stations are the fault of the police. Many suspects do not want legal advice because of their experiences with duty solicitors or even with lawyers in general. Delivering legal services to suspects in police custody has many difficulties.

Unavailability and contact time

We have seen that not all suspects who request advice get any. This is sometimes due to cancellation of requests because suspects do not want to wait any longer for advice to be provided. In some cases an able and willing solicitor simply cannot be located. This is bound to happen when suspects want to speak to their own solicitors, and this is what most suspects want.[235] Duty solicitor schemes are supposed to provide a safety net.

A recent study found that, on average, nearly four hours elapses between a request for advice and getting it.[236] This is a greater delay than used to be normal,[237] probably because of the new arrangements introduced in 2008 (see below). Delay is sometimes unavoidable, especially at night or if a solicitor is already dealing with a client. However, solicitors are reluctant to attend a police station simply 'to hold a suspect's hand', so they usually delay attendance until the police are ready to interview. Although understandable from the solicitors' point of view, who argue that initial phone contact should provide all the reassurance suspects need, this ignores the frightening isolation of detention discussed earlier. As one more sensitive solicitor put it: 'I think the terror of being alone in the police station is such, it [contact with a solicitor] may have no legal value whatsoever, but the psychological value of speaking to a solicitor early is not inconsiderable.'[238] It also means that many suspects, often incorrectly, think that if they refuse advice they will get out sooner.[239]

---

[235] Phillips and Brown (1998: ch 4) found that about 65% of suspects seeking advice wanted their own solicitor. Kemp and Balmer's findings (2008: 35, 48) were similar.   [236] Skinns (2009a: 63).

[237] Brown et al (1992: 62).

[238] Bridges et al, 'Quality in Criminal Defence Services' (London: Legal Services Commission, 2000) pp 67–8.

[239] Skinns (2009a) found that suspects who received advice were in custody on average for 4.6 hours longer than those who did not, but this may reflect the types of case in which advice is sought as much as delay caused by waiting for advice.

Solicitor or non-solicitor

Of those suspects who do secure advice, a large number do not see a solicitor at all, but a solicitor's clerk or trainee solicitor. This was so in around 30% of cases observed by Sanders et al in the 1980s, the proportion being rather higher for 'own' solicitors (50%) than for duty solicitors (16%). Although the numbers fluctuate, a large minority of suspects continue to see non-solicitors.[240] This proportion is likely to rise again in the future now that all 'franchised' duty solicitors are allowed to use non-solicitors who are trained or in training, although a solicitor must first speak on the phone to the suspect before a non-solicitor is allowed to advise.[241]

There is nothing wrong with the use of trained paralegals or well-supervised trainees, but in the 1980s and early 1990s many were not trained or supervised properly and there were terrible abuses.[242] Now, however, all solicitors and non-solicitors wishing to do duty solicitor work have to be trained and to pass tests, or be in training. The aim of this 'accreditation' scheme is to ensure that suspects are not disadvantaged by being advised by non-solicitors, and it appears to be successful. It seems to have led to better advice, more time spent with suspects, and a more adversarial approach in police interviews.[243] However, the level from which quality has been raised, and which was set by many quali-fied solicitors, was not very high, as we shall see. Further, some firms employ 'trainee' paralegals who are not being trained at all, then after six months replace them with other 'trainees'. Attempts are being made to prevent this evasion of training requirements.[244]

If junior staff are to be used extensively it is important that they, and the quality of their work, be supervised. Traditionally this is done in an ad hoc way, if at all, in solici-tors' firms. The Legal Services Commission (which oversees publicly-funded criminal defence work) now insists on supervision, usually in the form of reviews of completed cases, but ensuring firms do this is impossible. Research carried out in the late 1990s indicates that some firms do not take it seriously. As a senior member of a firm which had reviewed only one case in ten months wrote to his colleagues, 'We must complete the periodic reviews... We cannot afford to leave it any longer. It will not take a minute to do it'.[245] Even firms that do appear to take it seriously identify very few of the flaws in case handling that the researchers identified, and remedial action where flaws are identified appears very rare.[246]

---

[240] McConville M and Hodgson J, *Custodial Legal Advice and the Right to Silence* (Royal Commission on Criminal Justice Research Study No 16) (London: HMSO, 1993) p 17. Also see McConville et al, *Standing Accused* (Oxford: Clarendon Press, 1994); Phillips and Brown (1998: ch 4).

[241] For details see Cape E, *Defending Suspects at Police Stations*, 5th edn (London: Legal Action Group, 2006c) ch 1.

[242] See, for example, discussion in the 1st edn of this book. Also see Sanders (1996) and McConville et al (1994).

[243] Bridges L and Choongh S, *Improving Police Station Legal Advice* (London: Law Society, 1998) ch 4. But note that solicitors may advise their own clients without being accredited, so long as they hold a general criminal contract with the Legal Services Commission.

[244] Bridges and Choongh (1998); Bridges et al (2000).   [245] Bridges et al (2000: 99).

[246] Bridges et al (2000: ch 6).

Advice in person or over the telephone

About a fifth of all advice is over the phone alone.[247] Telephone advice is not necessarily inappropriate. The offence may be trivial and guilt not in doubt; the suspect may want advice on one specific thing only; the police may want to know something discrete and straightforward before, for instance, releasing on bail. Telephone advice will, however, be inappropriate where:

(a) the suspect is disputing, or unclear about, the allegations;

(b) the offence is serious;

(c) the suspect is vulnerable;

(d) detention is likely to be lengthy;

(e) the police are planning to question the suspect;

(f) the police plan to subject the suspect to an ID parade or similar; or,

(g) there may have been police malpractice.

Solicitors are professionals who ought to be able to judge these matters. Official guidance to assist them was devised, including the principle that, when in doubt, they should go to the station (and, once at the station they should stay, in all but exceptional cases, for any interview that might take place).[248] However, amendments to Code C (Note 6B), and the rules by which DSCC operate, now prevent advice being given in person in many cases (see below).

In reality, solicitors are often guided by considerations other than the needs of the suspect, and much telephone advice is unsatisfactory. Advice is sometimes given to remain silent, for instance. Although this tells suspects their rights, it does not actually help them to remain silent in the face of vigorous questioning. Sanders et al found that solicitors were wanted for many things other than the simple provision of legal advice – to witness what went on, to act as emotional supports, to secure bail, and to take action over alleged malpractice. As the legislation acknowledges, access to a solicitor is to provide not just advice but also assistance. Little assistance can be provided over the telephone.

Just as the police fail to adhere, in many cases, to their code of practice, so some solicitors fail to adhere to theirs. This was particularly evident shortly after PACE came into operation. Around 14% of all suspects in 1988 saw a legal adviser in person. Of all interrogated suspects, about 22% saw a legal adviser in person, but only about 14% had a legal adviser with them in the interrogation, because many solicitors who attended the station did not attend the interrogation.[249] The result was that many suspects might as well not have received any advice for all the use their lawyer was to them. Many suspects will not be frank with an often unknown voice on the phone: they may not

---

[247] Phillips and Brown (1998: ch 4); Pattenden R and Skinns L, 'Choice, Privacy, and Publicly-funded Legal Advice at Police Stations' (2010) 73 MLR 349. Telephone advice used to be used even more. See Brown et al (1992) and Sanders et al (1989).

[248] For details of the guidance, see Cape (2006c: paras 3.52–3.70).   [249] Sanders et al (1989: ch 6).

trust the person, and in any case the police sometimes listen to the conversation. As one suspect told Sanders et al: 'If you met him face to face you could talk.'[250] Another, asked if she would have the same solicitor again, replied 'We've not really had him have we? For all I know it might not have been a solicitor!' Cases were seen where suspects who told the solicitor that they had been assaulted were left to languish in the cells for half the weekend, and where suspects were told on the phone 'not to say anything' in the interview when it must have been known that for most suspects this advice would be impossible to follow.[251] As we have seen, many suspects are vulnerable (but not recognised as such) and many more are less than fully rational as a result of their predicament. Most of these people need the support of someone whose duty is to look after their interests.

As a result of these abuses the official guidance for solicitors on when to attend stations was tightened up in the 1990s, creating much clearer obligations for duty solicitors. In 1995–96 a large research study found that only 37% of suspects had an adviser with them in all their interviews.[252] It seems that the type of service given depends as much on the status of the client and the 'culture' of the law firm in question as the nature of the case, although solicitors deny this.[253] Many solicitors argue that, even if telephone advice is sometimes given inappropriately, this is all that can be expected of an under-remunerated profession under pressure. This will be all the more so now that solicitors are paid a fixed fee for police station visits that may be lengthy, demanding and at unsocial hours.[254] To compound the problem, in most police stations all phone conversations are held in the custody room, as are many face-to-face consultations.[255] Police officers are therefore able to listen to these conversations, sometimes on purpose but sometimes because they have to continue with their work within earshot. This has been held to breach s 58 and the ECHR, Art 6, but only if the absence of privacy is deliberate, rather than for logistical reasons.[256] In some new police stations there are in-cell intercom systems, but these work badly and the sound of suspect-solicitor telephone consultations often carries beyond the cell (Skinns, 2009b).

The quality of advice and assistance

In an adversarial system, solicitors would be expected to advise and assist suspects in the police station to the best of their abilities, regardless of how difficult this might

---

[250] Sanders et al (1989: 119–20).   [251] Sanders et al (1989: 117–26).

[252] Bucke and Brown (1997: ch 4). Most suspects are interviewed only once. Bucke and Brown found that in the minority of cases where there is more than one interview an adviser is normally, but not always, present for them all.   [253] Sanders et al (1989: ch 6); Bridges et al (2000).

[254] The 'pressure' argument is supported by Brown et al (1992: 88), but rejected by McConville et al (1994) who point out that some firms, albeit a minority, provide a very good service without noticeable financial hardship. Also see Hodgson J, 'Adding Injury to Injustice: the Suspect at the Police Station' (1994) 21 JLS 85. On the new remuneration structure, see below.

[255] Phillips and Brown (1998: ch 4); Pattenden and Skinns (2010); HMIP and HMIC (2009).

[256] The case law is contradictory. See Pattenden and Skinns (2010) and also *Roques*, discussed in 4.6 below.

make it for the police to secure evidence sufficient to prosecute. Under due process and freedom models, we would expect to find protections for suspects detained against their will, and would expect legal advisers to help suspects to use these protections. Thus in Britain there are rules which aim to prevent oppressive questioning and allow suspects to stay silent (albeit with a possible penalty – see ch 5), which solicitors should use to their clients' advantage. As Code C itself states: 'The solicitor's only role in the police station is to protect and advance the legal rights of his client' (Note 6D).

What should legal advisers do? According to Cape, a leading practitioner/academic on this topic, they should:

- advise suspects as to their best interests;
- keep an accurate record of their consultations with their clients and of the police interview;
- ensure their clients act according to their best interests (subject to not knowingly lying or actively misleading);
- ensure the police act fairly and lawfully; and
- protect clients from unnecessary pressure and distress.[257]

What all this means in concrete terms will vary from case to case. If suspects who indicated they would remain silent start to answer they can be reminded of their right to silence and, if necessary, a private consultation can be demanded. If suspects' answers are unclear, or points that could help them are not brought out, the adviser can ask clarificatory questions or suggest that the suspect may want to add something. If questioning becomes hectoring or abusive, or threatening looks or gestures are used, the adviser should intervene by, for example, objecting, asking for rephrasing, asking for a break or advising silence. Advisers have to be careful not to contravene Code C for if they do the police may require them to leave the interview.[258]

Early research into the work of legal advisers found that legal advisers did very little when they attended interrogations, frequently seeing their task as facilitating the process, rather than protecting the rights of their clients.[259] Baldwin, for example, described most legal advisers as 'essentially passive'.[260] However, Roberts pointed out that this does not mean that they fail to do their job in most cases:

if the police interviewer was behaving professionally and the suspect did not need assistance, intervention on the part of the solicitor would be quite unnecessary.[261]

---

[257] Cape (2006c: chs 3, 5, 7).

[258] Paragraphs 6.1–6.15 with accompanying notes (discussed above).

[259] See Brown et al (1992: 89), and McConville and Hodgson (1993). See also, for further examples, Sanders and Bridges (1999: 51) and Dixon D, 'Common Sense, Legal Advice, and the Right of Silence' [1991] PL 233 at p 242.

[260] Baldwin J, *The Role of Legal Representatives at the Police Station* (Royal Commission on Criminal Justice Research Study No 3) (London: HMSO, 1993b) table 1.

[261] Roberts D, 'Questioning the Suspect: The Solicitor's Role' [1993] Crim LR 369.

Without matching the behaviour of the police and of the solicitor against Code C and the official guidance, we cannot know whether non-intervention was justified or not. Bridges and Choongh did this, finding that in around one-quarter of interviews no intervention is called for. Advisers do intervene in most of those in which it is called for, but in over half of all such cases they do so less often than they should.[262] This level of performance, while not brilliant, is better than it used to be. Failure to adequately challenge police behaviour, such as objectionable police questioning can be crucial, as the 'Cardiff Three' case shows.[263] In this case, three men were convicted of killing a woman after one 'confessed'. He challenged the confession in court, but the trial judge ruled it admissible. The tapes of questioning were played to the Court of Appeal, which condemned them as contrary to Code C, quashed the convictions and criticised the defendant's lawyer for sitting through these interrogations without objecting.

The problem is that adversarialism is not a natural stance for most defence lawyers, particularly those who spend a lot of time advising suspects. To such lawyers, the police station is the workplace and maintaining good relations with work colleagues (ie the police) is important:

You've got to do the best for your client, but you've still got to live with the system many years on. So ... most solicitors do their best for their clients, but they also ... won't generally upset the police.[264]

Even Roberts, the author of the original Law Society guidance for police station advisers, is not sure what the role of the adviser should be: 'Interviews run better if the solicitor is able to establish a working relationship with the interviewer based on mutual respect.'[265] Better for whom? And at what cost are those working relationships purchased? Advisers are in a position of role conflict on potentially hostile territory. No wonder many solicitors seek to avoid this work. And, given the nature of most custodial legal advice, it is not surprising that the police are less hostile to the provision of advice than they used to be, even though advice rates have risen. The police know that advice rarely gets in the way of them carrying out their adversarial role. Yet the response of the Runciman Commission to all this evidence – which it did not challenge – was simply to call for more and better training of solicitors and paralegals, and for more monitoring.[266] As Baldwin, author of some of the research on which this recommendation was based, comments, this 'looks at best superficial'.[267]

Since PACE was passed in 1984 the numbers of suspects securing advice and assistance, and having an adviser with them in interviews, has risen dramatically. Training

---

[262] Bridges and Choongh (1998: ch 8). This research, done in the mid 1990s, shows that, despite limitations in quality, there has been a big improvement since McConville and Hodgson (1993) carried out their research in the late 1980s.   [263] *Paris, Abdullahi and Miller* (1993) 97 Cr App R 99.

[264] Solicitor, quoted in Dixon (1991: 239). Also see Baldwin (1993c: table 1).

[265] Roberts (1993: 370).

[266] RCCJ (1993: 35–9). The recommendations have been largely implemented. See Cape E, 'The Rise (and Fall?) of a Criminal Defence Profession' [2004] Crim LR 401.

[267] Baldwin J, 'Power and Police Interviews' (1993b) 143 NLJ 1194 at 1195.

for advisers has improved, and they have been made increasingly aware of their adversarial role in defending their clients. This should have led to greatly improved protection for suspects, but the improvements are limited, for various reasons.

First, it is difficult to give good advice without knowing the police case against the suspect. But the police need tell suspects and their advisers nothing.[268] Accordingly, in order to get information from the police the defence usually needs to offer something in return. That 'something' is usually information, as distinct from silence. The police are well aware of the hold they have over solicitors: 'One of the solicitors from Gutts and Co asked me why some CID officers were walking towards the cell blocks. Cheeky bastard!... He's getting no co-operation from me from now on – not until I get an apology' (Custody officer).[269]

Second, remaining silent can, as a result of the CJPO 1994, lead to great disadvantages at trial, as we shall see in ch 5. Advisers have to make very difficult judgements. Silence alone is not enough to convict a defendant. So, if the police have no admissible evidence, a client would be well advised to remain silent; but since the police need not tell suspects and their advisers what evidence they have, it is often not possible to know whether such advice is good advice.[270] Thus, paradoxically, in many cases advisers can best help their clients by encouraging cooperation with the police, even though cooperation is the antithesis of adversarialism.[271]

4.5.5 The erosion of the legal advice safeguard

The Access to Justice Act (AJA) 1999, s 12 established the Criminal Defence Service (CDS), which administers criminal legal aid for the Legal Services Commission (LSC) (established by s 1). In 2001 the CDS introduced the General Criminal Contract, which was then extended in 2004 and again in 2008 (now renamed the 'Unified Crime Contract'). Solicitors who wish to do publicly funded criminal defence work have to accept the conditions of this contract. If they wish to do duty solicitor work they additionally have to 'bid' for police station 'slots'. The major driver in these changes is to reduce the cost of legal aid, a pressure that is of increased urgency since the financial

---

[268] *Imran and Hussain* [1997] Crim LR 754; *Thirlwell* [2002] EWCA Crim 2703.

[269] Choongh (1997: 85). This is a good example of both the control that custody officers have in the station, and their lack of independence, both discussed earlier in this chapter.

[270] In a series of cases following *Condron v UK* (2001) 31 EHRR 1, the Court of Appeal has been increasingly unsympathetic, in applying s 34 of the CJPO, towards defendants who followed their lawyers' advice to remain silent. See Cooper S, 'Legal Advice and Pre-trial Silence – Unreasonable Developments' (2006) 10 IJ E&P 60. For a good practical discussion see Cape (2006c: esp chs 4–5).

[271] For further discussion of these and other ways in which advisers need to negotiate with the police, albeit from a position of inequality, in order to serve their clients' interests, see Sanders (1996). It seems that the police now disclose more to advisers than they used to: Bridges and Choongh (1998). On the problems posed by the changes to the right of silence, see Jackson J 'Silence and Proof: Extending the Boundaries of Criminal Proceedings in the UK' (2001) 5 IJ E&P 145; Leng R 'Silence Pre-trial, Reasonable Expectation and the Normative Distortion of Fact-finding' (2001) 5 IJ E&P 240.

crisis of 2008.[272] The CDS created the DSCC through which all requests for publicly funded advice must go. The DSCC now decides whether the case can be handled by telephone by the newly created CDS Direct or by a solicitor. The major changes are, in brief:[273]

(a) Publicly funded face-to-face advice is now, as previously explained, restricted. This is not, in principle, wrong, as telephone advice is sometimes adequate. But whereas in the past this was a matter of professional judgement (not always, as we have seen, professionally carried out) now decisions are for a state agency (the DSCC) that has to meet financial targets. Further, we have already seen that vulnerable people, who especially need face-to-face advice *and assistance* often miss out currently. This will be worse when DSCC has to make a judgement based on what an officer says. And as we discussed earlier, in most police stations there is no privacy when telephone advice is given.

(b) If, as happens in many cases, CDS Direct decides that the case is not suitable for telephone advice, the case is then re-referred to DSCC who then contacts a solicitor. This causes huge delays – hence the longer contact times noted earlier reported by Skinns (2009a and b and 2010).

(c) Even if CDS Direct does deal with the case it has to phone the station to give the telephone advice. An evaluation carried out for the CDS found that in nearly a quarter of all cases the phone was not answered and, equally frequently, the police said that they were 'not ready' to allow the suspect to receive the advice at that time.

(d) Much more advice than ever before is now given by duty solicitors (including CDS Direct) than before, which is generally contrary to the wishes of suspects.

(e) Police station work is now governed by fixed fees. This reduces the incentive for lawyers to spend time on cases, attend interviews, engage in lengthy consultations, argue for bail and so forth.

The CDS argues that as it sets standards for law firms who could lose their contracts if they fail to meet them, this system will not lead to reduced standards. However, as observed earlier, the (very light) supervision requirements are of limited effectiveness. Bridges et al (2000a: ch 5 and 6) set a threshold whereby essential work should be carried out in at least 70% of all cases. A total of 44% of firms in their research failed this test. In a more rigorous test of quality, 60% failed. Very few of these flaws in case handling are either identified or acted upon. Thus most firms had a long way to go in

---

[272] This was the thrust of the official government report: Carter Lord, *Legal Aid A Market-Based Approach to Reform* (London: House of Lords, 2006). Now also see Introduction to LSC, *Best Value Tendering for CDS Contracts 2010 – Consultation Paper* (London; LSC, 2009): 'The Ministry of Justice must deliver £1billion of efficiency savings up to March 2011' (p 2).

[273] This sub-section is largely based on Bridges L and Cape E, *CDS Direct: Flying in the Face of the Evidence* (London: CCJS, Kings College, London, 2008).

delivering legal advice of adequate quality even before the new financial arrangements were established. Standards are now likely to deteriorate further. Solicitors' firms are businesses. They act according to the profit motive. The less they get paid for, the less they tend to do.[274] Moreover, this scheme increases the ability of the police to discourage suspects from seeking, or waiting, for advice. They can say, with even more justification than ever, that suspects will probably have to wait a long time, and that the advice when (if) it arrives may be of little value.

It seems that suspects are at as much risk from the legal profession, legal changes (particularly to the right of silence) and the cost-cutting CDS (at the behest of government) as from the police. We have seen that the police station is police territory. When the whole purpose of due process rights is to protect suspects from the police, to make the police the main gatekeepers to these rights and to information and other needs of suspects is plainly illogical. The counter-argument would be that the purpose of the custody officer as an independent officer is precisely to stand between suspects, on the one hand, and investigating officers, on the other. Since custody officers have no specific interest in any one case, the custody officer will protect suspects by full enforcement of the rights in Code C, even if investigating officers object. This, however, relies on the rather formalistic distinction between a custody officer's duty and an investigating officer's duty. It does not take into account the shared outlook of different police officers. It also does not take into account the fact that an officer who wishes to secure the cooperation of fellow officers one day will not wish to 'get in their way' by acting out the custody officer role to perfection another day. Both custody officers and solicitors have to get on with other police officers in the latter's territory. 'Independent' operation under these conditions is hardly conceivable.

Suspects also need protecting from themselves. Voluntarism (consent) is completely misplaced when dealing with an intrinsically coercive situation.[275] Just as it is nonsense to argue that most confessions are voluntary, the same is true of decisions about advice. Some suspects are asked by lawyers on the phone whether they want them to come to the station, when the whole point about suspects in detention is that they cannot be assumed to be able to make rational or informed decisions for themselves. The rules at present are operated contrary to the interests of suspects because their interests and the interests of the gatekeepers diverge.

To make the rules work it would be necessary to install gatekeepers with the same interests as suspects, perhaps by paying solicitors or trained paralegals for effective police station work, and locating them in police stations so that they can see suspects with no delay. This might appear to be a ludicrous and expensive idea. But in 1997 a Government committee argued that police-CPS working methods could be

---

[274] For evidence from a Scottish experiment see Tata et al, 'Does Mode of Delivery Make a Difference to Criminal Case Outcomes and Clients' Satisfaction? The Public Defence Solicitor Experiment' [2004] Crim LR 120.

[275] See Young R and Wall D, 'Criminal Justice, Legal Aid and the Defence of Liberty' in Young and Wall (1996a).

improved by installing prosecutors in police stations.[276] This recommendation was speedily implemented without regard to cost or other factors (see ch 7). The Runciman Commission could have made recommendations on these lines for police station defence but did not do so. Clearly helping the police and CPS takes far higher priority than helping suspects.

Yet the future looks set to get worse, not better. First, solicitors' fees are likely in future to be determined by a process involving competitive tendering which will drive fees down and thus probably dilute the quality of their service further.[277]

Second the CDS has created a salaried 'public defence service' (PDS), again on a pilot basis in some areas of the UK, under which some defence solicitors have become part of the machinery of the criminal justice system and committed to fulfilling its objectives. These include speedy justice, which sometimes conflicts with full justice. This may lead to further role confusion for defence lawyers. At the same time one of the objectives set for the PDS is to provide examples of excellence in criminal defence work and to provide 'benchmarking' information with a view to driving up standards in private firms.[278] An interim report from a team of independent researchers found relatively few examples of excellence in the areas piloting the new service. 'Public defenders' were, however, more likely than their private practitioner counterparts to advise their clients to give a 'no comment' interview and they also compared well in an assessment of the quality of the advice given. Yet in many ways public defender offices operated similarly to private firms. For example, they were more likely to give just telephone advice if they were acting as duty solicitor rather than own solicitor, and they relied heavily on accredited representatives (in at least 45% of the cases studied) to attend police stations. And both public defenders and private practitioners did a generally poor job of recording advice they had given to suspects on their legal position and the strategy they should adopt in interview. Given the discontinuous nature of legal representation, in which a case may be dealt with by several different defence advisers during the lifetime of a case, this suggests that much criminal defence work is still poor.[279] If 'public defenders' can develop a distinctly adversarial ethos in their work we might hope that the lessons learnt will indeed be used by their paymasters to drive up standards in private practice.

As it is, most solicitors tend to discourage suspects from pleading not guilty or failing to cooperate with the police. This is not just because, as noted earlier, of the

---

[276] Home Office, *Review of Delay in the Criminal Justice System* (Narey Report) (London: Home Office, 1997a).

[277] This is so, notwithstanding the abandonment of pilots announced in December 2009: <http://www.lawgazette.co.uk/blogs/news-blog/the-bvt-pilot-decision-could-spell-trouble-lsc> (accessed 5 January 2009). For the background see Legal Services Commission, *Best Value Tendering for CDS Contracts 2010* (London: LSC, 2009).

[278] *Public Defender Service: First Year of Operation* (London: Legal Services Commission, 2002) para 6.1.

[279] The report is available on the Legal Services Commission website at <http://www.legalservices.gov.uk/criminal/pds/evaluation.asp> (accessed 5 January 2010).

pressure for reciprocal cooperation. It also stems from the non-adversarial character of the profession, the dim view some lawyers take of suspects and (especially when acting as duty solicitors)[280] the limited effort lawyers will provide for a limited reward. Compounding all of this are the institutional incentives (primarily a substantially reduced sentence) designed to encourage suspects to confess at the earliest opportunity (see further ch 8). An example of how these factors interact is the case of a lorry driver arrested for importing cannabis and ecstasy in his lorry. He declined a solicitor, and, when questioned, denied knowing anything about the drugs. He was then advised by the police to secure legal advice. The duty solicitor, without asking to hear his story, advised him that he would get six years if he pleaded guilty to knowingly importing cannabis but 12 years if he contested this and was convicted after a trial of importing both types of drug. Eventually he pleaded guilty to knowingly importing cannabis but changed his plea, citing the pressure put on him to plead guilty by the solicitor. When asked about this, the solicitor admitted not seeking the lorry driver's side of the case, saying that as a solicitor practising in Dover who had been a duty solicitor in many cases like this, he was 'only' giving his standard advice based on his experience that 99% of cases like this end in conviction.[281]

In summary, police station legal advice and assistance often provides the most bare protection because: the police are gatekeepers, allowing them to manipulate the rules and the situation to dissuade suspects from seeking advice; the law gives the police a dominant bargaining position vis-à-vis both suspect and lawyer; the financial incentives for solicitors to do a minimalist job are greater than for them to do a fully adversarial job; and the professional ideology of the majority of solicitors, similar to that of the police, holds most suspects to be guilty and unworthy of a 'Rolls Royce' service.

4.6 **Remedies**

We saw in chs 2 and 3 that rights for suspects are rarely complemented by remedies where those rights are breached. We argued there that the new right to damages for breaches of the ECHR right to liberty and security of the person (Art 5) is unlikely to have enlarged a citizen's remedies in any meaningful way. For similar reasons, most notably the apparent compatibility of English law with Convention requirements, the same is true here.[282] What of the position in home-grown domestic law?

When no specific remedies are attached to provisions creating due process safeguards, actions by aggrieved persons alleging a breach of a safeguard have to be fitted

---

[280] Choongh (1997: ch 6).

[281] Thanks to Ed Cape for details of this case. Examples of many other cases of incompetent and/or poor advice and negligent and dismissive attitudes towards clients are given in his 'Incompetent Police Station Advice and the Exclusion of Evidence' [2002] Crim LR 471.

[282] See earlier discussion of *Brennan v UK* (2001) and (below) *La Rose* (2002).

within an existing tort – in the case of wrongful arrest, for example, false imprisonment. Thus unlawful stops only have remedies available when they amount to unlawful arrests. The same is largely true where there are breaches of the rights covered in
this chapter. Thus wrongful detention is also covered by the tort of false imprisonment. Since detention is always authorised, and in a 'rubber stamp' manner, one might
have thought that many suspects would sue. In fact, there are hardly any cases challenging the initial decision to detain following a lawful arrest, and the two we know
of are distinctly discouraging.[283] The police are universally assumed to have the right
to detain in these circumstances. The main circumstance where a suspect can sue for
false imprisonment is where the time limit, overall or at the end of a review period,
expires. In one case a suspect whose review was held two hours late was awarded £500
for false imprisonment of two hours.[284] Since the purpose of periodic reviews is to
ascertain whether continued detention is justified, the failure to review was held to
create a false imprisonment until a proper review was carried out. As in other areas
of the law, however, illegality at one point in the process does not necessarily taint the
legality of what follows. In *DPP v Park*[285] the defendant was detained well beyond the
time limit, then charged with immigration offences. He argued that the charges were
invalidated by his unlawful detention. But the Divisional Court held that there was
no connection between the two, thus limiting the type of redress open to detainees in
this position.

As far as access to legal advice is concerned, denial of a solicitor is not a breach of
contract. Nor is it a tort or a crime. No specific remedy was provided for breach of
PACE, s 58, but there is a tort of breach of statutory duty. This is rarely invoked successfully[286] but in 1995 a suspect who had to speak to his solicitor on the phone while
being overheard by a police officer was successful. Section 58, it will be remembered,
provides a right to private consultation, which was denied in this case.[287] The door
may also have been opened slightly by *Cullen v Chief Constable of the RUC*,[288] but only
time will tell (see ch 12). However, most of the rights discussed in this chapter – to be
informed of one's rights, to a phone call, for vulnerable suspects and so forth – are
contained in Code C. They are not part of PACE or the ECHR. Since a Code is not

---

[283] See *Al-Fayed* [2004] EWCA Civ 1579 and *Clarke v Chief Constable of North Wales Police* (Lawtel 5
April 2000; *The Independent*, 22 May 2000) where the Court of Appeal held that a custody officer is entitled
to assume that an arrest is lawfully effected, unless there is evidence to the contrary. It went on to say that an
arrest which was lawful could not become unlawful simply because the custody officer failed to ascertain its
basis or the manner of its execution.

[284] *Roberts v Chief Constable of Cheshire Constabulary* [1999] 1 WLR 662.

[285] *DPP v Park* [2002] WL 2029132.

[286] See Sanders A, 'Rights, Remedies and the PACE Act' [1988b] Crim LR 802.

[287] *Roques v Metropolitan Police Comr* (1997) Legal Action, September, p 23. However, this was only a
first instance county court decision. In *Brennan v UK* (2001) the ECtHR held that, while denial of privacy
could breach Art 6 of the ECHR, no damages would be automatically awarded. And in *La Rose* [2001] EWHC
Admin 553 the English Divisional court found no breach of Art 6 in similar circumstances. See discussion
in 4.5 above.   [288] *Cullen v Chief Constable of the RUC* [2003] 1 WLR 1763.

a statute, breach of it is not a breach of statutory duty, and no other remedies are provided.

The situation is similar in relation to questioning. Torture is a crime.[289] It is also, along with 'inhuman or degrading treatment', contrary to Art 3 of the ECHR. But it is very rare indeed for questioning to fall into these categories. We shall see in ch 5 that PACE provides that evidence obtained through oppressive or unfair questioning may, and sometimes has to be, excluded from trial. But this provides no formal right as such to suspects in relation to questioning. And trials are an endangered species in this country. Exclusionary devices can have no purchase when the vast majority of cases are disposed of by NFA, cautions, penalty notices for disorder and guilty pleas. We shall also see that Code C provides numerous rights to contemporaneous recording, warnings and so forth, but – as with the other rights provided in Code C – these are not actionable.

The importance of the protection of suspects can be gauged by the fact that there are better remedies available for damage to reputation and trespass on one's land.[290] All suspects whose police station 'rights' are breached can do most of the time is to either make an official complaint or seek to have evidence obtained in consequence of the breach of their rights excluded from trial. These are applicable to breach of other police powers, too, and will be discussed in ch 12, along with remedies for deaths in police custody and for police violence in general. At this point we can simply note that these procedures have a limited deterrent effect on the police, making the remedial rules as much presentational as inhibitory.

4.7 **Conclusion**

The treatment of suspects in the police station is central to criminal justice. This is agreed by adherents of due process and crime control alike. For the latter, important evidence can be secured in the police station. This is precisely what worries due process adherents. Few would argue with the Runciman Commission that:

The protection of suspects from unfair or unreasonable pressure is just as important to the criminal justice system as the thoroughness with which the police carry out their investigations.[291]

Yet the police are allowed to detain for a considerable period of time in order to let them investigate even though for many people this detention is coercive in itself. We have seen that especially vulnerable people are given special protection but that vulnerability is not always recognised by the police. Further, to allocate everyone into

---

[289] Criminal Justice Act 1988, s 134.   [290] Sanders (1988b).   [291] RCCJ (1993: 25).

either a 'vulnerable' or 'normal' category is unrealistic. And the rights which apply to all suspects in detention, while an advance on what existed prior to PACE, have a limited protective effect. This is partly because of the way those rights work in practice, but also partly because of the legal rules themselves. These rules allow lawyers and police officers to behave in ways that dissuade many suspects from exercising their rights; allow police detention to be so unpleasant that many suspects are prepared to do almost anything, including waiving their rights, to get out as quickly as possible; and, especially since the changes to the right of silence in 1994, and to legal aid provisions in the last few years, make it difficult for lawyers to give useful advice and assistance to suspects.

Perhaps suspects in police custody should be *told* that they will see a lawyer, not *asked* if they want one. It is true that, in normal circumstances, people do not have things foisted on them against their will simply because someone else thinks it will be good for them. But suspects are not in normal circumstances. If they can be held in stinking conditions against their will, their mouths and hair invaded against their will, and questioned against their will why shouldn't they be given something that does them some good against their will? Vulnerable suspects are given appropriate adults whether they like it or not. This is because they are vulnerable. But in police custody, many 'normal' people are also vulnerable.

The detention regime is as offensive to the freedom perspective as it is to due process. Yet the floor of rights provided by the ECHR is so minimal that suspects are given more protection than our human rights obligations require. For example, the ECHR says nothing about vulnerable suspects, many specific rights to assistance (such as intimation and visitors) or police bail. Nor is the length of detention regulated except at the most extreme end.

The traditional way of protecting people's rights is by providing them with remedies when their rights are breached. But we have seen that the rights which we examined in this chapter are hardly protected in this way at all. The ostensible reason for this is that custody officers are supposed to safeguard the interests of suspects. Without police rule breaking, there would be no need to have custody officers. But custody officers are police officers. If suspects need protection from the police, then by what logic can custody officers be expected to provide that protection? The Runciman Commission recognised, to some extent, the failures of custody officers such as allowing cell visits by officers (see ch 5), rubber stamping detention, failing to provide clear information about rights and adopting ploys to avoid suspects receiving legal advice. Their performance, they say: 'still leaves something to be desired...it may also be unrealistic to expect a police officer to take an independent view of a case investigated by colleagues'.[292]

---

[292] RCCJ (1993: 31). Also see Choongh (1997: 172–7) for a catalogue of abuses allowed or perpetrated by custody officers.

After considering the poor performance of custody officers, the Runciman Commission then discussed (very briefly) whether another body could do the job of the custody officer. They decided that all the pressures on them would also be on a replacement body without that body even having the authority, vis-à-vis the police, of a custody officer. This was a due process/crime control crossroads. The Runciman Commission could either allow things to go on, more or less as now and accept the coercive nature of police station detention; or it could take police investigation out of the police station. It chose the former.[293] It is true that it recommended some enhancement to the custody officer role, and CCTV in custody areas and corridors leading to cells to deter malpractice.[294] Belatedly, in the late 1990s, CCTV was gradually introduced into custody areas in some police stations in most police force areas, especially where there were local police-community problems. There is some evidence that CCTV has reduced police malpractice or, at least, transferred it off-camera (such as to the back of the police van) – that, at least, is what many experienced detainees say.[295] But it did not recommend CCTV in cells because this eliminates the last vestige of privacy remaining to detainees, even though it provides added protection for them. Where CCTV has been introduced in cells this is indeed a concern among detainees, who are understandably not keen on being watched using the toilet and while being strip-searched.[296]

The privacy versus protection dilemma, which entails setting Art 2 and 3 protections against those of Art 8, only arises once it is decided, as the Runciman Commission did, that the police station should be the focus of investigation, and that the police should be free to detain suspects for 24 hours or more in order to interrogate them. This is acceptance of the crime control framework.[297] The room for due process and freedom is thereby fundamentally circumscribed. To fully appreciate the real power this puts into the hands of the police, we need to examine questioning in detail. That is the subject of ch 5.

Further reading

Cape E 'Then and Now: Twenty-one Years of Re-balancing' in Cape E and Young R (ed), *Regulating Policing: The PACE Act 1984, Past Present and Future* (Oxford: Hart, 2008)

McCulloch J and Pickering S, 'Pre-Crime and Counter-Terrorism: Imagining Future Crime in the 'War on Terror' (2009) 49 BJ Crim 628

---

[293] RCCJ (1993: 31–4).   [294] RCCJ (1993: ch 3, paras 35–38).
[295] Newburn and Hayman (2001: chs 1, 5, 6).   [296] Newburn and Hayman (2001: ch 5).
[297] For further discussion see Sanders A and Young R, 'The Rule of Law, Due Process, and Pre-Trial Criminal Justice' (1994b) 47 CLP 125.

Pemberton S, 'Demystifying Deaths in Police Custody: Challenging State Talk' (2008) 17 Social and Legal Studies 237

Shaw H and Coles D, *Unlocking the Truth: Families' Experiences of the Investigation of Deaths in Custody* (London: Inquest, 2007)

Skinns L, '"Let's Get It Over With"': Early Findings on the Factors Affecting Detainees' Access to Custodial Legal Advice' (2009a) 19 Policing and Society 58

Skinns L, *Police Custody: Governance, Legitimacy and Reform in the Criminal Justice Process* (Cullompton: Willan, 2010)

5

Police questioning of suspects

On May 14 [2008] I was arrested under section 41 of the Terrorist Act –
on suspicion of the 'instigation, preparation and commission of acts of
terrorism': an absurdly nebulous formulation that told me nothing about
the sin I had apparently committed ... the feeling that one's fate is in the
hands of the very people who are apparently trying to convict you is,
without doubt, one of the most devastating horrors a human being can
ever be subjected to. It is (to misquote Carl von Clausewitz) the continu-
ation of torture by other means ... I underwent 20 hours of vigorous
interrogation while entire days were being completely wasted by the
police micro-examining every detail of my life ... all of which became the
subject of rather bizarre questioning ...[1]

Key issues
- The expanding powers of the police to interrogate
- The multiple aims of interrogation
- The dwindling away of the right to silence
- The (inadequate) regulation of interrogation
- Traditional police interrogation tactics
- Investigative interviewing: theory and (mal)practice
- Why do the innocent confess?
- The need for a corroboration rule

5.1 Questioning: the drift from due process to crime control

In ch 4 we saw that the Police and Criminal Evidence Act 1984 (PACE) allows the police
to detain suspects in order to question them. It is not self-evident that the police should
have this power. The presumption of innocence is a basic human right: 'Everyone

---

[1] Hicham Yezza writing in *The Guardian*, 18 August 2008. See 3.4.5 for further details of his case.

charged with a criminal offence shall be presumed innocent until proved guilty by law.'[2] It is a fundamental element of both the freedom and due process perspectives that it is for the prosecution to rebut this presumption by proving guilt; it is not the suspect's duty to establish innocence. The presumption of innocence is connected with the right to remain silent and not incriminate oneself.[3] This right was recognised as an implicit element of Art 6 of the European Convention on Human Rights (ECHR) by the European Court of Human Rights (ECtHR) in *Funke v France*.[4] Building on this, in *Saunders v United Kingdom*[5] the ECtHR held that if methods of coercion or oppression are used to procure self-incriminating statements which are subsequently used in a prosecution, the suspect's right to a fair trial under Art 6 will have been breached. But neither the due process model nor the ECHR rule out all police questioning. The due process model acknowledges that suspects may wish to cooperate with the police, including by confessing. But since confession is usually not in a suspect's self-interest, police accounts of how 'voluntary' confessions were made should be viewed sceptically, and strict limits should be placed on their powers to put questions to those whom they suspect of crime.[6] The ECtHR takes a less stringent view of these matters, as we shall see. For its part, the crime control model assumes that largely unfettered police interrogation of suspects is the most efficient way of distinguishing between the guilty and the innocent.

The law used to be based on due process principles, and police questioning in custody was all but ruled out, at least in theory. This position was reflected in the original version of the Judges Rules in 1912, although this did allow the police to invite suspects to make voluntary statements. Persons making voluntary statements were not to be 'cross-examined' and only questions aimed at 'removing ambiguity' were to be asked. As the Judges Rules were transformed over the years, however, police interrogation became more acceptable. The final formulation of the Judges Rules (in force from 1964 until their replacement by PACE) no longer purported to discourage questioning but merely to regulate its methods. PACE and Code of Practice A (note 1) and Code of Practice C (para 12.5) maintained the general rule that no-one need talk to the police,[7] but made clear that the police may nonetheless persist in interrogating non-cooperative suspects in order to persuade them to talk. Changes to the right of silence in 1994 take the system even further down the crime control path. Just how far down that path we have moved, and what would be needed to incorporate a freedom perspective, is the subject of this chapter.

---

[2] ECHR, Art 6(2). The term 'charged' is interpreted to include arrested even if not charged in the English sense of prosecution being initiated.

[3] The scope of, and relationship between, these two rights has produced an enormous literature which we cannot cover here, but see Emmerson et al, *Human Rights and Criminal Justice*, 2nd edn (London: Sweet & Maxwell, 2007) paras 15.68–15.120, and Redmayne M, 'Rethinking the Privilege Against Self-Incrimination' (2007) 27(2) OJLS 209.   [4] (1993) 16 EHRR 297 [44–5].

[5] (1997) 23 EHRR 313 [68–9].

[6] Packer H, *The Limits of the Criminal Sanction* (Stanford: Stanford University Press, 1969) pp 190–2.

[7] But see 2.2.3.

5.2 **Why do the police value interrogation?**

The police are judged primarily on how successful they are in 'catching criminals' and bringing them to justice, so they naturally favour the crime control position on interviewing. It will be recalled that in *Holgate-Mohammed v Duke*[8] the police acknowledged that they arrested the suspect and took her to the police station, rather than interviewing her at home, because people are more likely to confess when interrogated while involuntarily detained. Indeed, there are confessions and incriminating statements in over half of all cases where there is an interrogation.[9] A clear and credible confession often eliminates the need to secure extra evidence, enabling more cases to be cleared up quickly than would otherwise be possible. Confessions make it difficult to plead not guilty: Phillips and Brown (1998: 158) looked at defendants prosecuted in the magistrates' courts and found that 92% of those who had self-incriminated in police interview pleaded guilty compared with 76% of those who had made no admission.

In legal terms, one key aim of interrogation is to establish evidence of the suspect's thought processes at the relevant time. The most often prosecuted (non-Road Traffic Act) criminal offences in England require evidence of mens rea (intent or recklessness) in order to convict the defendant. Assault is only a crime if a person is hurt intentionally or recklessly as distinct from someone stumbling or being careless and hurting the victim accidentally. Taking another's goods accidentally is not theft. But how are the police to prove that an item was taken, or a person injured, deliberately rather than accidentally? Sometimes there will be objective evidence of intent, such as a written plan, but this is rare. Sometimes intent can be inferred from the purposive nature of the act in question (as where somebody stabs another person repeatedly). But best of all is a statement by the person who committed the crime. Much police interrogation is geared not to establishing the objective facts – who took the articles or injured the victim, about which there is often no dispute – but what the person intended by his or her actions.[10]

There are many other functions of interrogation. Firstly, it enables the police to seek valuable information unrelated to the offence in question, such as suspects' other possible crimes. In the largest-scale study conducted to date, Phillips and Brown found

---

[8] [1984] 1 All ER 1054 discussed in 3.5.

[9] Baldwin J, 'Police Interview Techniques: Establishing Truth or Proof?' (1993) 33 BJ Crim 325, table 2; Phillips C and Brown D, *Entry into the Criminal Justice System: a Survey of Police Arrests and their Outcomes* (Home Office Research Study No 185) (London: Home Office, 1998) p 71; Bucke T and Brown D, 'In Police Custody: Police Powers and Suspects' Rights Under the Revised Pace Codes of Practice (Home Office Research Study No 174) (London: Home Office, 1997) p 33; Bucke et al, *The Right of Silence: The Impact of the CJPO 1994* (Home Office Research Study No 199) (London: Home Office, 2000) p 34.

[10] McConville et al, *The Case for the Prosecution* (London: Routledge, 1991) pp 66–75; Innes M, *Investigating Murder: Detective Work and the Police Response to Criminal Homicide* (Oxford: OUP, 2003) pp 150–1.

that 11% of suspects admitted to offences additional to those for which they were arrested.[11]

Secondly, we saw in ch 2 that policing is increasingly proactive. That is, the police target certain suspects or locations, often acting on tip-offs or surveillance-based information. Over time, the police secure sightings, film and so forth which may point to the involvement of certain suspects in particular crimes. Interrogation then is not so much to secure confessions, as to either catch offenders out in lies (such as denying being in a location where a crime was committed) or to secure silence about suspicious activities.[12] Coupled with the adverse inferences that can now be drawn against both silence and failure to account for being somewhere suspicious (see 5.3) silence or lies can be equally useful to the police. Similar tactics are also often used when the police are operating in reactive mode since routine recorded surveillance of much public and private space is now the norm thanks to the widespread use of CCTV in this country.[13] As illustrated in 5.2.6, CCTV evidence provides the police with a trap to spring on suspects in interview.

Thirdly, information about past or planned crimes in which the suspect is not involved, or general 'criminal intelligence', is also often provided.[14] This is sometimes part of a 'deal', the information being exchanged for bail, lesser charges, no prosecution at all or money. All suspects (including juveniles)[15] are treated by the police as potential informants.[16] Gathering information about possible planned crimes is particularly important in the context of terrorism; sometimes there is no intention to bring legal proceedings against the interrogatee,[17] at other times there is no 'deal' on offer other than an end to what is sometimes close to torture.[18]

Finally, interrogation by, and confession to, the police is part of a wider exercise of social and political power. Foucault identified new forms of power in modern societies which had been added to the traditional armoury of overt coercion and control. These include the allocation of space (for example, where certain categories of people are, and are not, allowed to go without permission), the regulation of time (through, for exam-

---

[11] Phillips and Brown (1998: 73); see also Bucke and Brown (1997: 34).

[12] The provisions on bad character introduced by the Criminal Justice Act 2003 (discussed in 10.4.1) entail that interrogation can now also be useful in prompting statements that amount to attacks on the character of another (such as a claim of self-defence). This can result in a suspect's previous convictions being admitted in evidence at any subsequent trial, as confirmed by *R v Lamaletie and Royce* [2008] EWCA Crim 314.

[13] The British Security Industry Association estimates that there are 4.25 million CCTV cameras in operation in the United Kingdom: <http://www.bsia.co.uk/LY8VMY74118> (accessed 5 January 2010).

[14] Maguire M and Norris C, The Conduct and Supervision of Criminal Investigations (Royal Commission on Criminal Justice, Research Study No 5) (London: HMSO, 1992) chs 5 and 7; Choongh S, *Policing as Social Discipline* (Oxford: Clarendon Press, 1997) p 175; Hillyard P, *Suspect Community* (London: Pluto, 1993) ch 8.

[15] Ballardie C and Iganski P, 'Juvenile Informers' in Billingsley et al (eds), *Informers: Policing, Policy, Practice* (Cullompton: Willan, 2001) p 120.   [16] Informants are discussed in ch 6.

[17] Gelles et al, 'Al-Qaeda-related Subjects: A Law Enforcement Perspective' in Williamson T (ed), *Investigative Interviewing: Rights, Research Regulation* (Cullompton: Willan, 2005).

[18] See *The Guardian*, 8 July 2009 and 5.5.1.3 for an example.

ple, work and school) and surveillance (through street policing and its partial replacement, CCTV cameras). He also identified specialist knowledge, in the professions and the police, as a form of power.[19] To simplify, power provides the means to gain knowledge over a subject which in turn increases the power over the now better-known subject. A central element here is confessional statements.[20] Confession, usually as a result of questioning, intrudes on the most intimate aspects of personal and social life.

The more the police are given powers to question, the more suspects are in their power. As we saw in chs 2–4, the social distribution of suspects and defendants is skewed towards the most socially marginal. Nor are these suspects merely interrogated because they are believed to have committed a specific crime. As Choongh demonstrates, the police sometimes arrest and interrogate those belonging to social groups which are regarded as 'police property' precisely because this exercise of power is a form of discipline:

Interrogation is something which the police can do to a suspect whether the suspect likes it or not...the police use the interview room as a forum to inform 'policed' communities that they can be asked any question, and in any manner, regardless of whether it relates to the original suspicion.[21]

Much the same can be said of the way the police question 'risky populations' on the street, as we saw in 2.2.3, 2.5.2 and 2.5.3.

This discussion of discipline and confessions is not entirely in line with Foucault's governmentality thesis, that power is increasingly dispersed through society. For we are arguing that the traditional criminal justice system is developing in such a way as to concentrate power in the hands of the police, power which is mostly used against the socially marginalised.[22] Foucault's insights nonetheless alert us to the value to the powerful of being able to make those with less power account to them through questioning. In the next section we consider the extent to which suspects can resist this form of 'accountability' by remaining silent.

---

[19] Foucault M, *Discipline and Punish* (London: Allen Lane, 1977). See Watson S, 'Foucault and Social Policy' in Lewis et al (eds), *Rethinking Social Policy* (Milton Keynes: Open UP, 2000) for an accessible summary of Foucault's work. See also Stenson K, 'Crime Control, Social Policy and Liberalism' in the same volume.   [20] Foucault M, *The History of Sexuality* (London: Allen Lane, 1979) vol 1.

[21] Choongh (1997: 135–6). Also see Hillyard (1993: ch 8); Waddington P, *Policing Citizens* (London: UCL Press, 1999) esp ch 5; Leo R, 'Police Interrogation and Social Control' (1994) 3 Social and Legal Studies 93.

[22] We contend this is so notwithstanding the growing importance of such forms of dispersed power as private policing and the novel forms of regulatory activity which are shaping the global economy. Braithwaite J, 'The New Regulatory State and the Transformation of Criminology' (2000) 40 BJ Crim 222 at p 299 argues that criminology, 'with its focus on the old state institutions of police-courts-prisons' is of 'limited relevance' given 'the crimes which pose the greatest risks to all of us' (on which see ch 7). This ignores that these 'old' state institutions are (a) thriving and expanding, and, (b) not just posing a 'risk' of intrusive interference with citizens' freedom, but severely (and ever more intensively) limiting that freedom for some, but certainly not 'all of us'. We think that documenting this is of more than 'limited relevance', at least to the interests of the most marginal groups in society.

5.3 **The right of silence**

The right of silence occurs at three stages in the criminal process, on the streets when grounds for suspicion arise, in the police station, and at court. On the streets, people need not speak to police officers if they are stopped and questioned, whether or not PACE s 1 stop-search powers are being exercised.[23] Further, para 10.1 of Code of Practice C provides:

A person whom there are [reasonable][24] grounds to suspect of an offence...must be cautioned before any questions about an offence, or further questions if the answers provide the [reasonable] grounds for suspicion, are put to them if either the suspect's answers or silence (i.e. failure or refusal to answer or answer satisfactorily) may be given in evidence to a court in a prosecution.

The caution begins: 'You do not have to say anything...'

On arrest, suspects must be cautioned unless this is impracticable because of the condition or behaviour of the suspect or unless the suspect had been cautioned immediately before arrest.[25] The second stage where the right of silence may be exercised is in the police station, which we shall focus on in this chapter. Thus suspects must be cautioned again at the start of any and every interrogation.[26] Finally there is the right to silence in court, looked at in ch 9. The practical value of the right of silence depends on the balance of the advantages and disadvantages which accrues to those who stand upon it. As we shall now see, the disadvantages have become acute in recent years while the advantages have been diminished.

5.3.1 **Eroding the suspect's right of silence through adverse inferences**

The ECtHR has ruled that the right of silence 'lies at the heart' of Art 6 but that it is not an absolute right: *Condron v UK*.[27] This leaves governments and courts room for manoeuvre over the extent to which this right – and the related 'privilege against self-incrimination' – should be preserved. For the due process adherent, it is up to the prosecution to find its own evidence; anything else negates the presumption of innocence. For the adherent to crime control, only the guilty have something to hide; innocent

---

[23] But note that a refusal to answer questions might have legal consequences (such as providing grounds for a stop-search or even an arrest), as discussed in 2.2.3.

[24] Paragraph 10.1 does not use the word 'reasonable', but note 10A does, and the latter (despite not being formally part of the Code – para 1.3) undoubtedly represents the law: *R v James* [1996] Crim LR 650; *Sneyd v DPP* [2006] EWHC 560.

[25] Code C, para 10.4.

[26] Code C, paras 10.1, 11.1A and 11.4 (but if there is merely a break during an interview, then the suspect need only be made aware that they remain under caution – 10.8).

[27] (2001) 31 EHRR 1.

people can only gain by assisting the prosecution. As Bentham infamously expressed this point: 'Innocence claims the right of speaking, as guilt invokes the privilege of silence.'[28]

As we have seen, there was a drift away from the due process position over the course of the twentieth century.[29] Indeed some modern statutes have adopted an extreme crime control position in order to deal with certain crimes where suspects have particular advantages. The best example is the investigation by such bodies as HM Revenue & Customs and the Department for Business, Innovation and Skills of shady financial dealings. These agencies have the power to compel answers on pain of fines for silence. As a result of *Saunders v UK*[30] the Youth Justice and Criminal Evidence Act 1999 (s 59 and Sch 3) amended the bulk of such legislation in order to prevent the admissibility in criminal proceedings of answers which are extracted in this way.[31]

It has been claimed by some that suspects retain a right of silence as long as it is no crime to remain silent.[32] Even if one accepts this approach, the right is nonetheless eroded if suspects and defendants suffer as a result of silence. Such erosion has been taking place for many years, and the process was accelerated as a result of the Criminal Justice and Public Order Act 1994 (CJPO).[33] Under the CJPO, courts may draw adverse inferences when defendants:

- rely upon facts in their defence which they did not mention to the police when questioned under caution prior to being charged (s 34);
- fail to testify at court in their own defence (s 35);
- failed (following arrest) to provide explanations for incriminating objects, substances or marks (s 36);
- failed (following arrest) to provide explanations for their presence near to the scene of crimes (s 37).

Thus the caution now says:

You do not have to say anything. But it may harm your defence if you do not mention when questioned something which you later rely on in court. Anything you do say may be given in evidence.[34]

---

[28] Quoted by Greer S, 'The Right to Silence: A Review of the Current Debate' (1990) 53 MLR 719.

[29] See 5.1. Detailed accounts are provided in Bryan I, *Interrogation and Confession* (Aldershot: Avebury, 1997) chs 1–7 and Easton S, *The Case for the Right to Silence* (Aldershot: Ashgate, 1998) ch 1.

[30] (1996) 23 EHRR 313.

[31] Not all of the potentially objectionable legislation was amended, however. For example, the Road Traffic Act 1988 requires the owner of a vehicle to declare who was driving it at a particular time; refusal is a criminal offence but there is no bar on using the information obtained in criminal proceedings. This was found to be compatible with Art 6 both by the Privy Council in *Brown v Stott* [2003] 1 AC 681, and by the European Court of Human Rights in *O'Halloran and Francis v UK* [2007] ECHR 544.

[32] This was the view of the Lord Chief Justice in *Cowan* [1996] QB 373.

[33] Mirfield P, *Silence, Confessions and Improperly Obtained Evidence* (Oxford: Clarendon, 1997) p 246. Also see Dixon D, *Law in Policing* (Oxford: Clarendon Press, 1997) ch 6.

[34] PACE Code of Practice C, para 10.5.

Typically, the adverse inference which will be drawn is that the 'fact' later relied upon in court is a post-interrogation fabrication. Previously, courts were not supposed to take into account a suspect or defendant's refusal to speak, nor the fact that the first mention of a particular defence might be in court.[35] The CJPO changes all that by eroding the right of silence in general in the police station (s 34) and in court (s 35) and in relation to certain types of circumstantial evidence (ss 36, 37).

It may seem that the CJPO allows courts to convict people merely because they are silent, or because they answer some questions but not all. While this could sometimes be the effect of the CJPO in practice, this is not what the letter of the law says. First, the CJPO itself states that no-one should have a case to answer or be convicted on the basis of adverse inferences alone (s 38(3)). This restriction has been tightened up as a result of the ECHR. In *Murray*[36] it was held by the ECtHR that a conviction must not be based 'solely or mainly' on the fact of silence. The ECtHR made clear, however, that adverse inferences could properly be drawn from silence 'in situations which clearly call for an explanation', and that those inferences may then be taken into account 'in assessing the persuasiveness of the evidence adduced by the prosecution'. The question whether failure to answer questions during interrogation is a situation which 'clearly called for an explanation' was considered in *Condron* (2001). The ECtHR ruled that adverse inferences could properly be drawn (under s 34, CJPO) from a suspect's silence in the face of police questioning, but that a jury must be told that they should not do this unless that silence could 'sensibly' be attributed *only* to the accused having no answer to the questions, or none that would stand up to cross-examination. In other words, the Court decided that silence in the face of police questions can, but does not necessarily, amount to a situation which so clearly called for an explanation that adverse inferences may be drawn.[37]

Second, inferences can only be drawn in relation to ss 36 (objects) and 37 (presence at crime-scene) if the police have first told the suspect what offence is being investigated, what facts they believe are incriminating and that adverse inferences could be drawn from failure to account for them.[38] Similarly, inferences can only be drawn under s 34 if the police through their questioning made it reasonable to expect suspects to volunteer the facts which they later rely on at trial. If, for example, the police simply read out a complainant's statement without asking the suspect to correct anything he or she disagrees with, then no adverse inference should be drawn: *Hillard*.[39]

Third, it will amount to a breach of the right to a fair trial under Art 6 ECHR if inferences are drawn from silence in the police station at a point when the suspect has not had the opportunity to take legal advice. In *Murray* the ECtHR noted that, where adverse inferences could be drawn from silence, access to legal advice was of

---

[35] There were many statutory and common law incursions into this principle: see 5.3.3 and 9.4.1.2.

[36] (1996) 22 EHRR 29 at para 47.

[37] See also 9.4.1.2. In 5.3.4 we discuss when silence can 'sensibly' be attributed only to having no good answer to police questions.   [38] Code of Practice C, para 10.11.

[39] [2004] EWCA Crim 837.

paramount importance 'at the initial stages of police interrogation' [66]. The police had denied Murray access to a solicitor for the first 48 hours of his detention and the ECtHR said that, in the circumstances, this amounted to a breach of Article 6. In response domestic legislation was changed to provide that adverse inferences cannot be drawn under ss 34, 36 or 37 in respect of a person who is at an authorised place of detention and who has not been allowed the chance to consult a solicitor prior to interview.[40]

Fourth, it is not proper under s 34 to draw an adverse inference from silence in the face of questioning if the defendant does not rely on a fact at the trial that might reasonably have been mentioned to the police. This has led to a series of cases on what counts as relying on a fact at trial and, in particular, whether a defendant who neither gives, nor calls, evidence can be said to be relying on any fact in his defence.[41] The House of Lords in *Webber* answered this question in the affirmative, ruling that a fact is relied upon 'when counsel, acting on his instructions, puts a specific and positive case to prosecution witnesses...whether or not the prosecution witness accepts the suggestion put'.[42] Thus if the defence simply probes the prosecution case (eg, 'are you sure he threw the first punch?'), without 'putting to' prosecution witnesses specific suggestions concerning 'the facts' of the case (eg, 'I put it to you that he threw the first punch') no adverse inference should be drawn.

Fifth, no adverse inference should be drawn if the fact subsequently relied upon at trial is agreed to be true.[43] There is no scope here for the inference that the explanation for silence in interview is that the fact is a post-interrogation fabrication.

Sixth, where a defendant hands a prepared statement to the police in interview of all the facts that he or she subsequently relies on at trial, no adverse inference should be drawn simply from the fact that a defendant responded 'no comment' to every police question.[44] It is not a refusal to answer questions that engages s 34 but rather a failure at this stage of the investigation to disclose facts which are subsequently relied upon.

The question of when and how adverse inferences can be drawn is evidently complex. However, one should not be blinded by the blizzard of technical detail to the fact that, sociologically speaking, fact-finders have always been able to hold silence against suspects and defendants. Prior to the introduction of the CJPO, in 80% of all Crown Court trials where defendants were silent under police questioning, this

---

[40] The Youth Justice and Criminal Evidence Act 1999, s 58 amends the CJPO to this effect. Both this legislation and *Murray* itself leave unclear whether silence in the face of an 'adverse inferences caution' administered by a police officer at the point of an arrest could damage a defendant's case at court. In practice, it may be doubted whether arresting officers will comply with all the pre-conditions necessary for an adverse inference to be drawn in relation to silence on arrest. If they did, then it would be arguable that they were in substance starting to interview the arrestee prior to their arrival at the police station, which is *generally* unlawful in any event (Code of Practice C, para 11.1).

[41] The relevant authorities were reviewed by the House of Lords in *Webber* [2004] UKHL 1.

[42] Ibid, para 34.

[43] *Wisdom and Sinclair* (Court of Appeal, 10 December 1999, Lawtel 6/1/2000, unreported elsewhere); approved by *Webber* op cit.   [44] *McGarry* [1998] 3 All ER 805; *T v DPP* [2007] EWHC 1793 (Admin).

became known to the jury.[45] Juries and magistrates probably took silence into account even when they were not supposed to. As one police officer put it,

in the past you may have actually been happy for him to give a 'no comment' interview, go to court, offer an explanation and let the jury sit and think: 'This man has already been interviewed by the police, why didn't he answer the questions then?' (Bucke et al, 2000: 35–5).

Certainly this is how many suspects think silence will be interpreted.[46] The House of Lords in *Webber* depicted the effect of s 34 as bringing the law back into line with 'common sense' (that 'common sense' being that innocent suspects would answer police questions).[47] This stance is indicative of long-standing judicial hostility to the right of silence.[48] In light of all this it is not surprising that the changes in the law brought about by the CJPO have made little difference to rates of confession or conviction (see 5.3.4).

5.3.2 Eroding the suspect's right of silence through custodial interrogation

As ch 4 showed, s 37 of PACE allows detention in a police station to be authorised in order to obtain evidence by questioning. There is nothing a suspect can gain by saying to a custody officer: 'There is no point in you holding me for questioning, because I intend to remain silent.' Suspects who refuse to speak can be held until they do so, subject to the time limits. Lengthy detention, particularly overnight, is the most feared consequence of arrest for most suspects.[49] Not only can silence lengthen detention, but in the words of Code of Practice C:

If a suspect takes steps to prevent themselves being questioned or further questioned, e.g., by refusing to leave their cell to go to a suitable interview room or by trying to leave the interview room, they shall be advised their consent or agreement to interview is not required. The suspect shall be cautioned...and informed if they fail or refuse to co-operate, the interview may take place in the cell and that their failure or refusal to co-operate may be given in evidence. The suspect shall then be invited to co-operate and go into the interview room.[50]

---

[45] Zander M and Henderson P, *Crown Court Study* (Royal Commission on Criminal Justice Research Study No 19) (London: HMSO, 1993).   [46] Choongh (1997: ch 6).

[47] *Webber*, op cit, [16–18 & 33]. See also *Hoare and Pierce* [2004] EWCA Crim 784 [53].

[48] Before 1994, trial and appellate judges often used or advised the equivalent of a 'nod and a wink' as a way of inviting juries to draw adverse inferences (eg *Gilbert* (1977) 66 Cr App R 237).

[49] Sanders A and Bridges L, 'Access to Legal Advice and Police Malpractice' [1990] Crim LR 494; Choongh (1997: ch 6); Skinns L, '"Let's Get It Over With": Early Findings On Factors Affecting Detainees' Access to Custodial Legal Advice' (2009a) 19(1) Policing & Society 58 at 63–4.

[50] Paragraph 12.5. See also Code A, note 1. Thus refusing to go into the interview room does not circumvent the adverse inferences provisions of s 34 of CJPO (as happened in *R v Johnson; R v Hind* [2005] EWCA Crim 971) so long as the police conduct a cell interview instead.

In the Cardiff Three case the suspect asserted from time to time that he had nothing further to say. Examples of police responses included:

- 'I'm never gonna leave it at that...you know that. Cause I am still gonna keep going and I'm gonna put things into you everytime because I know the truth.'
- 'Now we're going to have the truth out of you one way or...you know.'
- 'I'll keep digging and I'll keep digging because I believe you were there. I will keep digging.'[51]

In the event the interviews lasted for 12 hours and 42 minutes, spread over five days. Suspects still possess the remnants of a right to their own silence but they manifestly do not have a right to police silence.

5.3.3 Eroding the defendant's right of silence through disclosure rules

It might be thought that one advantage of standing on the right to silence is that a defendant would be able to reserve his or her defence until after the prosecution had made out a prima facie case in court. In that way the presumption of innocence would be respected, as would the dignity and privacy of the individual.[52] Suspects who remain silent in the police station may, however, be effectively compelled to provide relevant information if subsequently prosecuted. There were for many years various statutory exceptions to the principle that defendants could withhold the nature of their defence until trial.[53] The principle itself was swept away by the Criminal Procedure and Investigations Act 1996. The defence was placed under a duty by s 5 to disclose an outline of its case or risk an adverse inference being drawn at trial. In practice the sketchy information provided was found to be of little help to prosecutors.[54] Section 33 of the Criminal Justice Act 2003 accordingly imposed a much more stringent duty of disclosure. The defence *must*[55] now, in advance of trial, provide a statement which (i) sets out the nature of the accused's defence; (ii) indicates any point of law on which reliance will be placed (including any point as to the admissibility of evidence); and, (iii) provides details of any alibi witnesses. Section 34 of the same Act requires the accused to give the court and prosecutor a notice setting out the details of any other witnesses he or she plans to call to give evidence at trial; and s 39 allows for adverse inferences to be drawn

---

[51] Quoted in Gudjonsson G, *The Psychology of Interrogations and Confessions: A Handbook* (Chichester: Wiley, 2003) p 108.

[52] For the counterarguments to this position see Redmayne, M, 'Disclosure and its Discontents' [2004] Crim LR 441.

[53] For example, since 1967 defendants have been obliged to give advance warning if they wished to provide evidence of an alibi: Criminal Justice Act 1967, s 11. And under PACE, s 81 and Crown Court Rules 1987, SI 1087/716 they are obliged to disclose the contents of any expert reports on which they intend to rely.

[54] Taylor et al, *Blackstone's Guide to the Criminal Justice Act 2003* (Oxford: OUP, 2004) p 40.

[55] *R v Essa* [2009] EWCA Crim 43 [18].

where any of the duties of disclosure are breached or a defence is presented at court which is inconsistent with, or goes beyond, the initially disclosed information.

These duties of disclosure have been imposed with a view to enabling the police and prosecution to investigate the claims of the defence. There is an obvious danger here of the police 'tampering' with, or intimidating, defence witnesses or adapting the prosecution case with a view to making the defence evidence irrelevant. In the 'Confait Affair', a pathologist was persuaded to change the estimated time of the victim's death in order to neutralise the suspect's alibi.[56] In the case of the Taylor sisters, an alibi witness was arrested at dawn and told that she would face a charge of conspiracy to murder if she did not change her story.[57] Thus police power is not necessarily neutralised where suspects remain silent when interrogated. Where prosecutions take place, the police can secure much valuable information through defence disclosure instead.

5.3.4 The extent of use of the 'right' in the police station

Around one-third of all suspects deny, with some sort of explanation, the offence(s) of which they are suspected. It appears that few suspects exercise the right of silence in totality, but no proper figures are kept and estimates from research vary. Brown estimated that, between 1985 and 1994, between 5% and 9% of all interviewed suspects exercised total silence, and a similar number refused to answer some questions.[58] The rights provided to suspects in PACE as such do not appear to have led to more use of silence, although there was some increase in both the total and selective use of silence, especially in London, just before the introduction of the CJPO (Phillips and Brown 1998).

In research carried out after the introduction of the CJPO, refusal to answer all or some questions was back down to the 1985–1994 levels. This appears to be mostly because lawyers advise silence less readily than previously.[59] Table 5.1 presents figures on the use of the right of silence in eight police stations studied by Phillips and Brown (1998) just over a year before the introduction of the CJPO and in the same eight stations five months after the CJPO came into force (Bucke et al, 2000: 31). They show a fall in the proportion of suspects using the right to silence of about a third (down from 23% to 16%).

Silence has historically been higher in London than elsewhere, higher among black suspects than white and Asian suspects, and higher among those who had legal advice

---

[56] See *Report of an Inquiry into the Circumstances leading to the Trial of Three Persons on Charges arising out of the Death of Maxwell Confait and the Fire at 27 Doggett Road, London SE6* (HCP 90) (London: HMSO, 1977).

[57] *The Observer*, 13 June 1993. *Higgins* [2003] EWCA 2943 (discussed in 5.5.1.2) is another example.

[58] Brown D, *PACE Ten Years On – A Review of the Research* (Home Office Research Study No 155) (London: HMSO; 1997).

[59] Phillips and Brown (1998: 32–3) found that, following the CJPO, the use of silence fell from 39 to 22% among legally advised suspects and from 12 to 8% among those not advised. This suggests both that lawyers are now advising cooperation more frequently *and* that suspects are being cowed by the adverse inference warnings.

Table 5.1 The use of the right of silence

	Refused all questions	Refused some questions	Answered all questions
Pre-CJPO	10%	13%	77%
Post-CJPO	6%	10%	84%

than those who did not. The steepest falls in the use of silence following the CJPO occurred in these groups (Bucke et al, 2000: 31–3).

Silence seems to be more frequently exercised in serious than in trivial cases.[60] This does not necessarily mean, however, that silence helps serious criminals escape charge and conviction, as the police often claim. Leng found that in only a tiny percentage of non-prosecuted cases and acquittals was silence exercised, and that these outcomes rarely seemed to be a product of silence.[61] Few 'ambush' defences (ie defences based on 'facts' not known to the police and not disclosed in interview) were mounted in court, and none successfully. In some cases, successful defences were based on points suspects attempted to raise in interviews but to which the police refused to listen. Leng concluded that there were as many cases where the police could have acted on what suspects told them, or attempted to tell them, as where suspects refused to tell them material things. The spectre of the professional criminal avoiding justice by remaining silent in interrogation appears, therefore, to be largely a myth.

The most striking finding of the post CJPO research is that whereas the use of the right of silence has declined, the rates at which admissions are made and convictions secured have not been affected (Bucke et al, 2000: 34, 66–7). We indicated at the end of 5.3.1 why this finding should not have come as a great surprise. The notion that the right of silence prior to the CJPO 1994 was a major obstacle to convicting the guilty was seriously misconceived. The pressures and incentives to make incriminating statements in the police station were already enormous prior to the CJPO. It is therefore tempting to regard that Act as having greater symbolic-electoral value than instrumental use. But we should not forget the broader purposes of interrogation, discussed in 5.2, such as gaining general criminal intelligence, and exercising disciplinary power over suspects. The conviction rate may not have increased, but the rate at which the privacy of the citizen is invaded certainly has.

5.3.5 'Sidelining' legal advice

One of the most important pieces of advice which legal advisers can give to suspects is that they need not answer questions and, in some circumstances, that it is not in

---

60 Moston S and Williamson T, 'The Extent of Silence in Police Interviews' in Greer S and Morgan R (eds), *The Right to Silence Debate* (Bristol: University of Bristol, 1990) p 38; Phillips and Brown (1998:78).

61 Leng R, *The Right to Silence in Police Interrogation* (RCCJ Research study No 10) (London: HMSO, 1993).

their interests to do so. If, for example, the police have no objective basis for suspicion, silence should lead to release without charge, while answering questions could lead to enough evidence for charge even if the suspect is innocent. Another situation in which it may not be wise to answer police questions is when the legal adviser and suspect know too little about the police case to answer it effectively. Consistently with this, McConville and Hodgson found that when silence was advised it was most often because advisers felt that they had insufficient information about the case and when they felt that suspects might wrongly incriminate themselves.[62]

We saw in 4.5.4.4 that the police need not disclose anything about the case.[63] Legal advisers sometimes seek to secure the disclosure of the police case by advising that the client remain silent until this information is provided.[64] Bucke et al (2000: 23) found that the erosion of the right of silence brought about by the CJPO 1994 was causing legal advisers to more frequently seek disclosure of the police case on the basis that without that disclosure it was not reasonable to expect their clients to answer questions in interview. This stance flowed from s 34 which limits the drawing of adverse inferences to cases in which suspects failed to mention facts which they later relied on when it would have been *reasonable* to expect them to have mentioned them in interview. Equally, they found that the police were disclosing at least some of their case more readily now, knowing that this made the drawing of adverse inferences more probable (Ibid: 22–4). However, the police retain control. That is, they decide whether to disclose anything, what to disclose, and when to do so. Officers vary in their practices,[65] with many categorically unwilling to disclose evidence prior to a first interview, while some 'never disclose or allude to "golden nugget" or "trump card" evidence, particularly fingerprints, DNA, and CCTV'.[66]

Sometimes police disclosure of part of a case can give a misleading impression. Although no adverse inferences should be drawn if the police actively mislead the suspect, partial disclosure which has this effect is not necessarily construed as active deception.[67] Moreover, case law has made clear that neither limited disclosure of the police case, nor legal advice to remain silent, necessarily insulates the suspect from adverse inferences. In *Argent*[68] silence was advised because, it seems, the solicitor felt the police were being unusually non-cooperative and were refusing to disclose important evidence in their possession. In court it was argued that there should be no adverse inference from silence both because it was as a result of legal advice, and because the

---

[62] McConville M and Hodgson J, *Custodial Legal Advice and the Right to Silence* (Royal Commission on Criminal Justice Research Study No 16) (London: HMSO, 1993).

[63] They must disclose some relevant details, however, if they want adverse inferences to be drawn from silence (see 5.3.1). See also Toney R, 'Disclosure of Evidence and Legal Assistance at Custodial Interrogation: What does the ECHR Require?' (2001) 5 IJ E&P 39.

[64] See, for example, Quinn K and Jackson J, 'Of Rights and Roles: Police Interviews with Young Suspects in Northern Ireland' (2007) 47 BJ Crim 234 at 241.   [65] Quinn and Jackson (2007: 241).

[66] Shepherd (2007: 331).

[67] See, for example, *Imran and Hussain* [1997] Crim LR 754, discussed in 5.5(b)(vi); see also *Rosenberg* [2006] EWCA Crim 6.   [68] [1997] 2 Cr App Rep 27.

police had failed to make full disclosure of their evidence at that stage. The Court of Appeal, while accepting that the police had disclosed less evidence than normal, rejected both arguments, saying that the test in the CJPO is whether it was reasonable to have mentioned the fact subsequently relied on when initially questioned. Whether legal advice to stay silent made silence reasonable depended on what passed between lawyer and suspect. And police non-disclosure of certain evidence was relevant only if fuller disclosure was necessary in order for the suspect's silence to be regarded as unreasonable. Other appellate cases decided soon after adopted the same line.[69]

This makes it difficult for lawyers to advise silence and for suspects to know whether to follow that advice.[70] Some suspects doubtless rely on legal advice because they lack confidence in their own judgement in unfamiliar circumstances, but to convince a court of this they might have to reveal what passed between them and their lawyers.[71] This amounts to a waiver of legal professional privilege, allowing the prosecution to expose all that passed between them, which might be against the wishes or interests of the suspects[72] and which certainly undermines the potential for openness and trust on which an effective client–lawyer relationship depends (Bucke et al 2000: 51).

The ECtHR position does not remove the problems facing lawyers and their clients. In *Condron v UK*[73] suspects had been advised by their solicitor not to answer police questions because they were suffering from the symptoms of heroin withdrawal. The ECtHR said that if a defendant refuses to answer questions on the advice of a solicitor it would be wrong to allow a jury to draw an adverse inference from that silence unless they were first told that they must not do so unless they believed that silence could only sensibly be attributed to the suspect having no good answer to the questions. The ECtHR reiterated this position in *Beckles v UK*[74] when it noted that a jury should be directed to consider whether the reason for silence was a genuine one or whether, on the contrary, reliance on legal advice to remain silent was merely a convenient self-serving excuse.

It seems that the ECtHR is concerned that some (factually guilty) suspects may claim that they remained silent on legal advice in situations where they were determined to remain silent in any event in order to avoid incriminating themselves. Moreover, the court in *Condron* found nothing wrong with the fact that defendants may, because of the *Argent* decision, experience 'indirect compulsion' to reveal the content of the advice received from a lawyer. Thus, the effect of *Argent* was, at least in theory, ameliorated, rather than neutralised, by *Condron* and *Beckles*. In practice, the English courts have arguably turned something of a blind eye to these decisions, for the Court

---

[69] See *Roble* [1997] Crim LR 449; *Moshaid* [1998] Crim LR 420 and *Condron* [1997] 1 WLR 827.

[70] See Cape E, 'Sidelining Defence Lawyers: Police Station Advice After *Condron*' (1997) 1 IJ E&P 386 at p 398 and Cape E, *Defending Suspects at Police Stations*, 5th edn (London: LAG, 2006c) ch 5.

[71] See also *T v DPP* [2007] EWHC 1793 (Admin).

[72] See *Roble* [1997] Crim LR 449 and *Lisa Loizu* [2006] EWCA Crim 1719.   [73] (2001) 31 EHRR 1.

[74] (2003) 36 EHRR 13 [62]. See also *Averill v UK* (2000) 31 EHRR 36, where the ECtHR did not regard the suspect as having genuinely relied on legal advice to remain silent (so did not see the drawing of adverse inferences as unfair).

of Appeal has continued to affirm that where a defendant claims to have remained silent on legal advice adverse inferences can be drawn unless the jury believes that the defendant genuinely *and reasonably* relied on that advice.[75] At root the English courts are simply hostile to suspects remaining silent. In *Howell*,[76] for example, the Court of Appeal said that:

There must always be soundly based objective reasons for silence, sufficiently cogent and telling to weigh in the balance against the clear public interest in an account being given by the suspect to the police.

The Court went on to say that 'merely because a solicitor has so advised' it did not follow that there was a sufficiently cogent reason for remaining silent.[77]

One effect of all this is that legal advisers have to second guess what the courts would judge to be a 'good enough' reason to remain silent. Some hints have been provided that good reasons might include that the interviewing officer has disclosed little or nothing of the case against the suspect, or where the nature of the offence or of the material in the hands of the police is so complex, or relates to matters so long ago, that no sensible immediate response is feasible.[78] In *Argent* itself it was said that a jury might conclude that silence was reasonable for a 'host of reasons, such as that he was tired, ill, frightened, drunk, drugged, unable to understand what was going on, suspicious of the police, afraid that his answer would not be fairly recorded...'[79] The problem is that all these reasons involve matters of judgement on which trial judges and juries may take different views.[80] As Cape notes, given that the courts have not taken a consistent line on such matters, the defence lawyer is placed in difficulty in formulating advice whether or not to remain silent, and must now warn the client that advice to remain silent will not necessarily prevent inferences from being drawn.[81] The judiciary clearly supports the rationale of s 34 in 'flushing out innocence at an early stage or supporting other evidence of guilt at a later stage'.[82] This is the classic crime control position. The courts seem oblivious to the due process argument that there is also a 'clear public interest' in protecting (i) the privacy and dignity interests of the individual suspect (ii) the confidentiality of what passes between lawyers and their clients and (iii) the presumption of innocence. As Cooper says, 'The vulnerable suspect, in unfamiliar surroundings and emotionally weakened, accepts the professional advice he is given rather than answering the questions put, only to discover later

---

[75] See *Beckles* [2004] EWCA Crim 2766 (the case was referred back to the Court of Appeal by the Criminal Cases Review Commission). This is incompatible with the ECtHR approach – if reliance on legal advice is the genuine reason for remaining silent then there is no room for a belief that silence is attributable only to the fact that the suspect has no good answer to the questions. The question of 'reasonableness' should not arise.

[76] [2003] Crim LR 405.

[77] *Howell* was clarified and confirmed in *Knight* [2004] 1 Cr App R 9 and followed in *Hoare and Pierce* [2004] EWCA Crim 784, and *Bresa* [2005] EWCA 1414.   [78] *Roble* [1997] Crim LRW 449.

[79] *Argent* [1997] 2 Cr App Rep 27 [33E–F]. See also *Howell*, op cit, and *R v Essa* [2009] EWCA Crim 43 [15].

[80] In *Howell* itself the defence solicitor judged the police had not made sufficient disclosure but the Court of Appeal disagreed.   [81] Cape (2006c: 199–200).

[82] *Hoare and Pierce*, op cit, [54].

that by taking and acting upon that advice, the case against him has been strength-ened.... Was it ever envisaged that legal advice honestly given and genuinely received might culminate in a stronger case against a defendant?'[83]

5.3.6 Conflating silence with guilt

A major concern is that courts might convict defendants on the assumption that silence or lies are tantamount to an admission of guilt. As we saw above, under the ECHR silence should not form the main or sole basis for a conviction.[84] A model direc-tion for juries now states that jurors may take silence into account as 'some additional support' for the prosecution case.[85] But the model direction does not specifically warn juries not to view silence as direct evidence of guilt. Precisely what silence can be evidence *of* is a practical, as well as a theoretical, problem. In *Hart*,[86] for example, the main evidence of drug smuggling by the defendant, which he did not explain, was possession of an incriminating phone number. There was a bare prima facie case, and Hart was convicted. This is an example of speculation (about the defendant's motives in remaining silent) masquerading as 'common sense'.[87] As Pattenden puts it, silence becomes 'evidential poly-filler for cracks in the wall of incriminating evidence which the prosecution has built around the accused'.[88] Much depends on whether the courts interpret the CJPO in ways that assist the defence or the prosecution. Pattenden, in line with most other commentators, states that the Court of Appeal is 'so committed to crime control that at almost every turn – even when an interpretation favourable to the defence is plausible – the legislation has been construed in the prosecution's favour',[89] and the same is true of the House of Lords.[90]

5.3.7 Debating the right to silence

The right to silence has long aroused fierce debate. The Royal Commission on Criminal Procedure (Philips Commission) recommended retention.[91] Then in 1987 the matter

---

83 Cooper S, 'Legal Advice and Pre-trial Silence – Unreasonable Developments' (2006) 10 IJ E&P 60 at 68–9.   84 *Murray v UK* (1996) 22 EHRR 29.

85 Approved by the Court of Appeal in *Cowan* [1996] QB 373. See the guidance provided to trial judges on the Judicial Studies Board website at <http://www.jsboard.co.uk/criminal_law/cbb/mf_05.htm#38> (accessed 9 July 2009).

86 Unreported, 23 April 1998 (CA). Discussed by Birch D, 'Suffering in Silence' [1999] Crim LR 769.

87 Cape (1997); Easton S, 'Legal Advice, Common Sense and the Right of Silence' (1998) 2 IJ E&P 109. Hart was lucky because his conviction was quashed on appeal; as explained in ch 11 it is very difficult to win appeals.   88 Pattenden R, 'Inferences from Silence' [1995] Crim LR 602 at p 607.

89 Pattenden R, 'Silence: Lord Taylor's Legacy' (1998) 2 IJ E&P 141 at p 164.

90 In *Webber* it not only gave a very broad interpretation of a 'fact' that the defendant relies upon at trial which was not mentioned in police questioning (see 5.3.1 above), but explicitly cast doubt on two Court of Appeal decisions that had adopted a pro-defence interpretation of s 34 concerning whether adverse infer-ences should be drawn if initial silence concerned the key fact in the case.

91 Royal Commission on Criminal Procedure Report (1981: 80–91).

was raised again by the Home Secretary following complaints by the police that 'their' conviction rate was being halved. In *Alladice*[92] the Lord Chief Justice joined in on the side of the police. The Home Secretary announced in 1988 that he intended to modify the right of silence. This led to a change in the law in Northern Ireland in 1989, but proposals for England were deferred pending the report of the Royal Commission on Criminal Justice (Runciman Commission).

The Runciman Commission was split on whether to recommend that adverse inferences be drawn from silence. But the majority agreed with the Philips Commission that:

It might put strong (and additional) psychological pressure upon some suspects...This in our view might well increase the risk of innocent people...making damaging statements.[93]

They also thought that erosion of the right of silence would have little effect on experienced criminals, whose conviction rate would therefore not be substantially increased. Despite the views of Runciman, for which the government had deliberately waited before deciding what to do about the right of silence, the CJPO was nonetheless enacted.

There are good practical reasons for reverting to the pre-CJPO position. First, the changes have caused more trouble for courts than they have resolved.[94] In particular, the Court of Appeal has spoken of s 34 as a 'minefield' and cautioned trial judges not to give adverse inference directions to juries without first discussing the matter with counsel.[95] Second, they have swung the balance too far to the police by sidelining custodial legal advice. Third, they pressure vulnerable suspects into speaking against their will, but probably have little effect on professional criminals.[96] Fourth, they have not increased the rate at which suspects make incriminating statements or the rate at which conviction is achieved at court.

There is no doubt that the erosion of the right of silence by the CJPO and the other developments discussed earlier offend against the freedom principle because they have produced minimal gains to offset significant losses.

5.4 **Regulating police questioning**

5.4.1 **Questioning outside the police station**

The police question citizens in many types of situation and for many reasons. We saw in 2.2.3 that 'stop-search' often enables the police to gather intelligence through

---

[92] (1988) 87 Cr App Rep 380.
[93] Royal Commission on Criminal Justice (RCCJ), Report (Cm 2263) (London: HMSO, 1993) p 55, quoting RCCP (1981) para 4.50.   [94] Birch (1999).
[95] See, for example, *Hillard* [2004] EWCA Crim 837.
[96] Bucke et al (2000); see generally, Easton (1998*b*).

questioning. Officers also routinely gather information from those thought (at least initially) to be victims or witnesses of crime.

Thus the police only sometimes have suspicions about those they question. Once they have suspicions one might expect that the law would require the standard caution 'You do not have to say anything...' to be given, as this reminds suspects of an important due process protection (the right to silence). But the courts decided[97] that this is required only if the police have *reasonable* suspicion that they committed the offence (see 5.3). This means that the police can ask some probing questions of those against whom they have 'mere' suspicion without having to give the caution. There are a number of risks here, as can be seen from accounts of spectacular miscarriages of justice: first, that the police will avoid the cautioning requirement (and the associated risk that the suspect will seek legal advice) by acting as if they do not have reasonable suspicion when they plainly do;[98] second, that suspects will give less than considered answers or fail to grasp how their behaviour might be (mis-)interpreted when not appreciating that they are under suspicion,[99] and, third, that the police will record any answers given or behaviour observed on a selective (inculpatory) basis.[100]

Moreover, even where they do have reasonable suspicion that someone has committed an offence they are not obliged to give the caution if the questions put 'are for other necessary purposes' (Code C, para 10.1). Examples of such necessary purposes given by the Code include 'in furtherance of the proper and effective conduct of a search' or 'solely to establish their identity or ownership of any vehicle' (ibid). Thus, it appears that much of the questioning that accompanies a stop-search based on reasonable suspicion (such as 'do you have a knife in your pocket'?) does not have to be preceded by the administering of a caution. If the police search results in finding evidence of a crime (eg a knife), however, then at this point a caution must be given before further questions are put.[101]

If there is 'reasonable suspicion' in relation to a particular suspect, the police can arrest. If they decide to arrest, questioning must usually cease temporarily, as we shall see. If there is no 'reasonable suspicion', the police cannot arrest, but questioning may continue wherever it began until the suspicions are either allayed or increased. In the latter case the suspect would usually be arrested. But even if the police develop very strong suspicions, there is no obligation to arrest and so nothing to prevent further questioning.[102] Much police questioning, both of suspects and non-suspects, therefore

---

[97] Eg *Sneyd v DPP* [2006] EWHC 560.

[98] Devlin A and Devlin T, *Anybody's Nightmare: The Sheila Bowler Story* (East Harling: Taverner Publications, 1998) pp 52–64 and 158.

[99] Ibid, pp 63–4; Cannings A, with Lloyd Davies M, *Against All Odds: A Mother's Fight to Prove her Innocence* (London: Time Warner Books, 2006) pp 42–3.

[100] Devlin and Devlin (1998: 62–70); Callan K, *Kevin Callan's Story* (London: Little, Brown and Company, 1997) pp 26–7.   [101] *R v Cheb Miller* [2007] EWCA Crim 1891.

[102] See, for example, *R v Moore* [2004] EWCA Crim 1624, where the Court of Appeal accepted the evidence of customs officers that the interview of a suspect in her mother's home took place prior to a decision to arrest – and was thus lawful.

takes place outside the police station without (or prior to) arrest. This is a form of 'informal questioning' to be discussed in detail in 5.5.

Once the police decide to arrest, para 11.1 of Code of Practice C states that the suspect 'must not be interviewed about the relevant offence except at a police station…unless the consequent delay would be likely to lead to…' a number of specified possibilities such as serious damage to property or interference with evidence. In other words, where there is an urgent need to interview (sometimes referred to as a 'safety interview'), the police may do so. For example, where people are arrested on suspicion that they have just committed arson, the police can ask questions there and then about the location of the fire (see, further, 5.4.4).

PACE, s 30(1) states that the suspect 'shall be taken to a police station by a constable as soon as practicable after the arrest'. As so often with criminal justice, the phrase 'as soon as practicable' is of prime importance. Under s 30(10) the police can delay taking an arrestee to a police station 'if the presence of that person elsewhere is necessary in order to carry out such investigations as it is reasonable to carry out immediately'. So the police can take the arrested person somewhere other than a police station to conduct a safety interview. The police can also simply release an arrestee instead of taking him/her to the station if 'there are no grounds for keeping him under arrest.'[103] As we saw in 3.4.2, this is quite common in public order situations. Finally, s 4(7) of the Criminal Justice Act 2003 inserts a new s 30A into PACE which allows an arrested person to be released on bail at any time before reaching the police station. This enables the police to require the suspect to attend the police station at a time that suits the interviewing officer.

Thus, generally speaking, if people who are arrested are to be questioned, this must be only in a 'formal interview'. That is, they must be taken to a police station at once, checked in by the custody officer, offered their rights as set out in ch 4, and questioned (with recording equipment switched on) only after that. But situations are envisaged where police officers can justifiably delay taking suspects to a police station after arrest and interrogate them elsewhere. Why does this matter? There are dilemmas here which do not involve the clash of due process and crime control principles, but which create problems for due process itself and for the enhancement of freedom. Taking arrested persons to a station immediately can be seen as desirable for two main reasons. Firstly, it enables custody officers to decide whether or not arrests are justified and whether suspects are particularly vulnerable. Secondly, it allows as little time to elapse as possible after arrest before suspects have the opportunity to exercise their rights under ss 56 and 58 to consult a lawyer and to have their arrest made known to a relative or friend, thus preventing police officers from interrogating suspects incommunicado in unregulated conditions.[104] On the other hand, we saw in 3.5 that it is undesirable

---

[103] PACE, s 30(7).

[104] In *Kerawalla* [1991] Crim LR 451 the defendant was arrested in a hotel room and questioned there without being allowed to exercise his ss 56 and 58 rights. The Court of Appeal held that, while the suspect should have been taken to a police station straight away (as required by s 30 of PACE), ss 56 and 58 rights

to encourage peremptory arrest on bare reasonable suspicion if the suspect has an exonerating story. If the story can be checked by, for instance, going to a shop where the suspect says he bought allegedly stolen goods or to a place of work where an alibi could be confirmed, this must be better for the suspect than being held in custody while these investigations are made. Then there are suspects who feel, and often are, under less pressure if interrogated somewhere they feel comfortable, such as at home or in the office of their solicitor.

Section 30 is thus a messy compromise. Its imprecision provides an opportunity for the operation of crime control working rules in relation to interrogation. So, despite the fact that it might have due process potential, it is primarily a crime control enabling rule. It enables the police to insist on immediate police station interrogation except when they determine that some other course of action is preferable. The suspect has no say in the matter. This enables the police to lengthen the time between arrest and police station detention, exacerbating another problem. Incriminating statements made to the police prior to arrest, or en route to a police station or some other place envisaged in s 30(10) (such as the suspect's home or place of work), are not invalidated simply because the information was not given in the police station. This gives the police an incentive to seek a confession prior to arrival at the police station, the Code of Practice gives the police permission to do this both before and (when the safety conditions are met) after arrest, and the courts will not necessarily exclude any evidence obtained even when these already broad enabling rules are overstepped.[105]

5.4.2 **What is a police interview?**

Drawing a clear line between questioning (an interview) and a discussion or conversation is difficult. Yet it is vital to do so because Code of Practice C, para 11.1, which sets out the general (not total) prohibition against post-arrest questioning away from the police station, is only concerned with 'interviews'. According to para 11.1A of Code C:

An interview is the questioning of a person regarding their involvement or suspected involvement in a criminal offence or offences which, under paragraph 10.1, must be carried out under caution.

It is obvious that all post-arrest questioning about suspected offences should be regarded as an interview because an arrested person is, by definition, a suspect against

---

were not applicable to persons detained at premises other than a police station. This precedent was applied in *DPP v Kirkup* [2003] EWHC 2354 (where the court ruled that the right to legal advice arose in the police station only after the custody officer authorised detention). In *R v Moore* [2004] EWCA Crim 1624 [17], however, the Court of Appeal said that each case depended on its own facts, and opined that a suspect about to be questioned under caution at her mother's home should have first been advised that she could seek legal advice before giving answers (although it accepted the trial judge's view that no unfairness resulted as a result of this omission).

[105] See *Kerawalla*, op cit, and ch 12.

whom reasonable suspicion exists (and is thus covered by the para 10.1 obligation to caution).[106] This much is (usually) accepted by the courts. In *Absolam*[107] the defendant was arrested for suspected drugs offences. He was questioned in the charge room and allegedly gave incriminating answers. Only then was he read his rights and cautioned. If this was an 'interview', then the questioning was unlawful because it took place before the suspect was read his rights and before he had had the opportunity to seek legal advice. If it was not an interview, then it was not unlawful and those protections were not applicable. The Court of Appeal held that this was an interview.[108]

Interactions between the police and arrestees are often fluid, however, as are conversations between officers and mere suspects, and the less any oral exchanges 'look' like an interview, the more likely a judicial conclusion that no interview took place. Thus for some time it looked as though interviews were being defined as conversations which took place in police stations; anything which took place outside a police station was not an interview.[109] But allowing the place of the discussion to determine its legal status made little sense. If the place of the conversation was to determine whether the protection of PACE and the Code of Practice is provided, the police would simply do more interviews outside.

Another approach is to examine the intention of the officers in question. But as Field points out, it is easy for officers to claim that it was their intention merely to seek information when in fact it was not.[110] The courts have seemed gullible in this respect. In *Maguire*[111] two youths, seen pushing open the door of a flat, were told on the way to the police car, 'You've both been caught. Now tell us the truth...It's for your own good.' This was held not to be an interview. Similarly, in *Pullen*[112] the court believed that officers visited the defendant's cell 'with the object of relaxing him and...restoring some of his dignity', thus holding that only a conversation took place.[113]

Some cases, such as *Younis*[114] where the conversation took place in a police car, have been decided on the basis that an exchange is not an interview if it is initiated by the suspect. This could only be relevant if the whole discussion was on the lines initiated by the suspect, which was not so in *Younis*. In any event, whether someone needs protection depends on the nature of the discussion, rather than on where it takes place, who initiated it or on the intention of the police.[115] This seems to have been recognised in *Weekes*.[116] Here the Court of Appeal said that an 'understandable enquiry' became

---

[106] But note that para 11.1A of Code C expressly excludes procedures for testing breath, blood or urine in connection with driving whilst intoxicated offences.   [107] (1988) 88 Cr App Rep 332.

[108] Interviews were also held to have taken place in *Miller* [1998] Crim LR 209 (one question asked in the charge room) *Oransaye* [1993] Crim LR 772 (questioning at the custody officer's desk) and *Goddard* [1994] Crim LR 46 (questioning prior to being taken to the police station). Code C warns police-station based officers not to invite comments from suspects outside the context of a formal interview (paras 3.4 and 15.6).

[109] See, eg, *Maguire* (1989) 90 Cr App Rep 115 and *Younis* [1990] Crim LR 425.

[110] Field S, 'Defining Interviews under PACE' (1993) 13 LS 254.   [111] (1989) 90 Cr App Rep 115.

[112] [1991] Crim LR 457.

[113] Note, however, *Hunt* [1992] Crim LR 582, where the court was more sceptical.

[114] [1990] Crim LR 425. Similar cases are discussed by Field (1993: 261–3).

[115] See *Sparks* [1991] Crim LR 128.   [116] (1993) 97 Cr App Rep 222.

an 'interview' when the suspect started making admissions. But what good is this if the purpose of defining a conversation as an 'interview' is to prevent admissions being made without due process protections? This would be a helpful ruling only if it meant that whatever was said as a result of 'understandable enquiries' became unusable as a result of the exchange's transformation into an 'interview'.[117] This was not the line taken subsequently, however. In *James*,[118] for example, a man disappeared. His business partner was questioned without suspicion initially existing, but suspicion that he murdered the missing man grew in the course of discussions during which no caution was given. The Court of Appeal held that these were not interviews (even when they asked 'Have you killed David Martin?'), that the police were not wrong to have given no caution, and that the evidence of the discussions could be used against James.

Police–citizen encounters away from the police station are usually characterised by their low visibility. This means that what went on (who initiated the conversation, what was being sought by it, what the intentions of the officers were and so forth) is only the officers' word against the suspect's. The whole point of PACE and Code of Practice C promoting and regulating formal 'interviews' was to eradicate this problem by being able to verify what was said and done objectively. It is precisely this objective verification which the police seek to avoid by so often trying to ensure that their discussions are not classified as interviews.

Recent cases show that the problem of the pre-interview question and (incriminating) answer session has not gone away.[119] The incentive to secure, through informal questioning, confession evidence which can be used in court will still be there for as long as the rules of evidence allow it.[120]

5.4.3 Recording of interviews

Accurate recording of interviews is essential. Without knowing what was said and done, by both police officers and suspects, it is impossible to know what pressure was placed on suspects to confess or even whether they confessed at all. Prior to PACE, questions and answers were rarely tape recorded. Confessions and denials came in one of two forms. Firstly, 'verbals'; these were police officers' accounts of suspects' (supposedly) voluntary verbal statements, usually written down some time after they were made. Secondly, 'voluntary' written statements, written either by the suspect or, at the suspect's dictation, by a police officer. Both came to be challenged increasingly frequently. 'Verbals' were often said not to reflect accurately what suspects really said, and were sometimes alleged to be complete fabrications.[121] Similarly,

---

[117] See Fenwick H, 'Confessions, Recording Rules, and Miscarriages of Justice: A Mistaken Emphasis?' [1993] Crim LR 174.   [118] [1996] Crim LR 650.

[119] See, eg, *Ridehalgh v Director of Public Prosecutions* [2005] EWHC 1100; *Senior* [2004] Crim LR 749; *Sneyd v DPP* [2006] EWHC 560.

[120] See Maguire and Norris (1992: 46). Ch 12 discusses the exclusion of unlawfully obtained evidence.

[121] The Royal Commissions of 1929 and 1962, as well as the Philips Commission, were concerned about 'verbals'. See Cox B, *Civil Liberties in Britain* (Harmondsworth: Penguin, 1975) ch 4.

voluntary written statements were often said to have been the work of the officers themselves.[122]

Inaccuracy, commonly known as 'gilding the lily', took three forms. Firstly, there was alteration of the words used to create a different impression, either deliberately or inadvertently. Police officers, like everyone else, have imperfect recall, and mistakes are made when conversations are reconstructed at a later time, especially when the purpose of the reconstruction is to prove a point.[123] Secondly, there was the incomplete recording of what was said. It was common to only write down what suspects said 'when they start telling the truth', that is, when they agreed with the allegations being put to them.[124] We shall see that police tactics can lead suspects to 'confess' against their will, and this is difficult to challenge if previous denials are not recorded. Thirdly, there is fabrication. In *Blackburn*,[125] for example, a 15-year-old boy was convicted of attempted murder following his alleged voluntary confession written, so the police claimed, entirely in his own words. Blackburn spent 24 years in prison as a result. After his release expert evidence showed that the wording of the confession had been heavily prompted by the police and his conviction was quashed as unsafe.

The Philips Commission realised the dangers of all these forms of inaccuracy. It did not believe that all, or even most, alleged statements were false. But some were, as even police officers will admit.[126] The problem was in distinguishing the false from the true. The Philips Commission recommended that all exchanges be accurately written down so that the question of fabricated confessions did not arise. So, when PACE was introduced, Code of Practice C (para 11.5) required 'an accurate record' of interrogation to be made either 'during the course of the interview' (and to be a 'verbatim record') or, if this was not practicable, 'an account of the interview which adequately and accurately summarises it'.

There were several problems with this. For the police, the laborious writing down of everything said slowed the interview, gave suspects time to think, and inhibited the establishment of rapport.[127] Also, just as before, what was written down might not be accurate or complete. The only difference was that the police would have to claim that it was written contemporaneously instead of afterwards, which is only a small safeguard.[128] Finally, there was the problem of informal interviewing outside

---

[122] In a scandal of the 1960s, Sergeant Challenor and several colleagues were eventually successfully prosecuted for these practices (and many instances of corruption and brutality) when it was found that statements made by suspects he had arrested all used the same improbable phrases such as 'travelling in a northerly direction' (Cox, 1975).

[123] Stephenson G, 'Should Collaborative Testimony be Permitted in Courts of Law?' [1990] Crim LR 302.

[124] Sanders A, 'Constructing the Case for the Prosecution' (1987) 14 JLS 229.

[125] [2005] EWCA Crim 1349.   [126] See McConville et al (1991: 84–7), and 7.3.3.

[127] Maguire M, 'Effects of the PACE Provisions on Detention and Questioning' (1988) 28 BJ Crim 19.

[128] Although it was enough (eventually) in the 'Birmingham Six', 'Guildford Four', and 'Tottenham Three' cases. The convictions in all these cases were largely based on allegedly contemporaneously written confessions which later scientific evidence proved not to have been written at the time. See Rozenberg J,

the interrogation room for here it was easy for the police to claim that it had not been 'practicable' to record contemporaneously.

The glaring nature of these problems led to many eminent figures asking, well before the Philips Commission reported, for the routine tape recording of interrogations.[129] This was initially resisted by the police, but following the introduction of a new Code of Practice on Tape Recording in 1988 (Code of Practice E), the police adapted rapidly, and tape recording is now mandatory in all indictable and either-way cases except in exceptional circumstances. It is more difficult for the police to record proceedings selectively, and virtually impossible for them to fabricate recordings, but the third problem, interrogation outside the interview room, remains.[130] General conversation rarely appears on taped interviews, even though conversation between suspect and interviewer at some point is usual. This 'confirms the inadequacy of tape recording inside the police station as a wholly adequate record of all relevant verbal exchanges between suspect and interviewer'.[131]

The PACE Codes of Practice now require interview rooms to have tamper-proof tape recording facilities, and once the interview begins everything said by all parties must be tape recorded, although there is an 'if practicable' escape clause (Code of Practice E, para 3.3).[132]

Under Code C, paras 11.7–11.8, if no tape recording is made, a verbatim record or adequate summary must be written down (during the interview, if practicable, or as soon as practicable thereafter). Further, 'unless it is impracticable the person interviewed shall be given the opportunity to read the interview record and to sign it as correct or to indicate how they consider it inaccurate' (para 11.11). This is to ensure that everything that was actually said, but no more, is written down. It is also to ensure that suspects who agree that everything has been written down fairly and accurately indicate that this is their view.

There are three problems with records of interview. Firstly, even though suspects may sign what is written down, this does not mean that what was written down was

---

'Miscarriages of Justice' in Stockdale E and Casale S (eds), *Criminal Justice Under Stress* (London: Blackstone, 1992), and Walker C, 'Miscarriages of Justice in Principle and Practice' in Walker and Starmer (1999a).

[129] See especially Williams G, 'The Authentication of Statements to the Police' [1979] Crim LR 6.

[130] This is why videotaping of interrogation (used experimentally or selectively in the UK, but on a widespread basis in Australia) is of no substantial help, and may even be harmful to suspects (particularly when the camera focuses only on the suspect) both because video evidence seems so compelling, and because it can lead to amateurish assessments of demeanor by prosecutors and judges who overestimate their ability to detect deception. See McConville M, 'Videotaping Interrogations: Police Behaviour On and Off Camera' [1992] Crim LR 532; Dixon D, '"A Window into the Interviewing Process?" The Audio-visual Recording of Police Interrogation in New South Wales, Australia' (2006) 16(4) Policing & Society 323; Lassiter et al, 'Evidence of the Camera Perspective Bias in Authentic Videotaped Interrogations' (2009) 14(1) Legal and Criminological Psychology 157.

[131] Moston S and Stephenson G, *The Questioning and Interviewing of Suspects Outside the Police Station* (Royal Commission on Criminal Justice Research Study No 22) (London: HMSO, 1993) p 36.

[132] There was previously an exception to the tape-recording requirement for terrorist cases but see now the Terrorism Act 2000, Sch 8, under which has been issued a Code of Practice governing the new mandatory taping regime.

accurate, for people frequently fail to read documents which they sign. In theory, accuracy should not be a problem in the majority of formal interviews now that they are tape recorded. In practice, however, few defence or prosecution lawyers listen to these tapes and they are only very rarely played in court.[133] Instead, reliance is placed on summaries prepared by the police or, in serious cases, full transcripts. These summaries[134] and transcripts have been found to contain many inaccuracies. For example, Gudjonsson (2003) and Pearse (a senior detective) examined 20 transcripts of interviews in serious cases and concluded 'in all cases discrepancies [were identified] between the official transcripts and the audiotapes. In some of the cases the inaccuracies were seriously misleading' (p 114). An example is given of a typed transcript in which the suspect is said to have replied 'yes' to the question, 'Did you ever touch their private parts?' The audio tape showed the suspect had actually responded 'no'.[135]

The second problem with the record of interview is that although what is written down (or tape recorded) may be accurate (in the sense of reflecting what was said), it may none the less be unreliable when suspects are induced to confess, are subjected to oppressive pressure or have words put into their mouths. Not only do these things sometimes happen on tape and with a lawyer present, but they also happen before or between interviews. It is true that Code C demands that: 'A written record shall be made of any comments made by a suspect, including unsolicited comments, which are outside the context of an interview but which might be relevant to the offence' (Code of Practice C, para 11.13). But it need not be written at the time, and it need only be provided to the suspect for verification and signing 'where practicable'.[136] If these comments were made as a result of unlawful pressure, the full exchange is not likely to be fully recorded by the police and, as with pre-PACE verbals, what was said (and why) often becomes simply a matter of who is believed.

The third problem is that these provisions are not mandatory: they all have 'if practicable' escape clauses. The net result is that interviews outside the station are hardly ever contemporaneously recorded. Moston and Stephenson (1993) found that the police admitted to failing to do this in nearly two-thirds of all such interviews, and suspects were asked to check the record in little over one-quarter of such cases. The problem of lack of verification should have diminished since that research was conducted in the early 1990s as Code C (para 11.4) now requires an interviewer to

---

[133] Gudjonsson (2003: 112); Taylor C, *Criminal Investigation and Pre-Trial Disclosure in the United Kingdom: How Detectives Put Together a Case* (Lampeter: Edwin Mellen Press, 2006) p 154, n 51.

[134] Baldwin J and Bedward J, 'Summarising Tape Recordings of Police Interviews' [1991] Crim LR 671 (almost half of the summaries were adjudged unfair, misleading, distorted or of poor quality).

[135] See also Taylor (2006: 148, n 37).

[136] Moreover, para 11.13 does not apply to anything said which itself constitutes the crime in question (eg, when swearing at a police officer is labelled as a s 5 Public Order Act 1986 offence) but only to statements of a self-incriminatory nature made on or after arrest in relation to that crime: *DPP v Lawrence* [2007] EWHC 2154 (Admin).

put to the suspect at the start of an interview any significant silence or statement previously made in the presence or hearing of a police officer. The suspect is asked to confirm or deny that statement or silence and comment further if they wish. But the police are not obliged to interview at all, which means that a suspect may be denied a structured opportunity to comment on the detail of any alleged significant statement or silence until it is put forward in evidence at trial[137] (by which time a suspect's denial may be seen as less credible as human memory is known to become less reliable over time).

When alleged confessions are not contemporaneously recorded, the opportunities for dispute about what was really said are legion. In *Khan*,[138] for instance, one interview took place in the police car from Wales back to Birmingham, and one took place later in the police station. The defendant was alleged to have confessed to robbery during the journey, but he denied the offence in the police station and also denied making the earlier alleged confession. The police claimed that they took contemporaneous notes of the interview in the car (which were not shown to Khan at the time). This was accepted at his trial, and he was convicted. It later became clear that the police officers did not write the notes in the car, casting doubt on whether he really did confess, and so his conviction was quashed on appeal.

Another example is *Dunn*.[139] The defendant was interviewed with his legal adviser present and denied criminal activity. At the end, while reading through the interview notes, the police claimed that he confessed. The police said that they wrote down this alleged confession, but they did not show this record to the suspect or to his legal adviser, in clear breach of Code C. The court nonetheless allowed it to be used as evidence, as did the Court of Appeal, even though both the suspect and the legal adviser denied that the alleged confession had been made.

These examples show that even when the police are proved to have broken these provisions of Code C for no good reason, the evidence secured as a result may still be accepted, sometimes with disastrous results for the suspect. They also illustrate the wide scope the police have for breaking them, and the opportunities thus provided simply to fabricate confessions and/or impose unlawful pressure on suspects to confess. For every instance where fabrication is proved there must be a dozen where it is alleged. As *Dunn* and *Khan* show, it is often impossible to establish who is telling the truth. Sometimes, and we will never know how often, the courts get it wrong. These problems, and these mistakes, will continue for as long as confession evidence secured in the absence of an independent party remains admissible in court.

---

[137] This much is implied by the decision in *DPP v Lawrence* op cit.

[138] (1990) unreported, CA. Discussed by Kaye T, *'Unsafe and Unsatisfactory?' Report of the Independent Inquiry into the Working Practices of the West Midlands Police Serious Crime Squad* (London: Civil Liberties Trust, 1991).

[139] (1990) 91 Cr App Rep 237. Discussed in Hodgson J, 'Tipping the Scales of Justice' [1992] Crim LR 854. There are many other examples, such as *Canale* [1990] 2 All ER 187. For a case that went in the defendant's favour see *Weerdesteyn* [1995] 1 Cr App Rep 405.

5.4.4 The protection offered by legal advice and appropriate adults: safety first?

All suspects in custody are entitled to legal advice, and all vulnerable suspects must normally be accompanied in formal interviews by an appropriate adult.[140] Because the right to legal advice is a continuing one, suspects are able to request a solicitor when an interview is about to take place, or even during one, as the Code of Practice C (para 11.2) acknowledges:

Immediately prior to the commencement or re-commencement of any interview at a police station or other authorised place of detention, the interviewer should remind the suspect of their entitlement to free legal advice, and that the interview can be delayed for legal advice to be obtained...

The normal rule is that suspects may not be interviewed if they ask for solicitors who have yet to arrive, and questioning must stop if a request for legal advice is made during any interview.[141] But the police are allowed to interview even if legal advice has been requested but not yet received if a senior officer (superintendent or above) has reasonable grounds for believing that delay will involve a serious risk of harm (to evidence, persons or property) or 'unreasonable' delay.[142] Similarly, such 'safety interviews' can take place with juveniles and the mentally vulnerable without the presence of an appropriate adult.[143] In previous editions of this work we have mentioned the 'safety interview' provisions only in passing, but the recent marked shift towards preemption and public protection in criminal justice, and rising concern about terrorism, (discussed in ch 1) means that such interviews are of increasing importance, although no proper statistics are published.

In a 'safety interview' the police are meant to give the old-style pre-CJPO caution: 'You do not have to say anything, but anything you do say may be given in evidence', as no adverse inferences may be drawn from silence in a situation where the suspect has been denied the right to consult with a solicitor.[144] We saw in 3.3.4, however, that in situations that represent crises of law and order, legalistic models of policing tend to break down.

In *R v Ibrahim, Omar, Osman and Mohamed*[145] the appellants were arrested in respect of the attempted bombings in London on 21 July 2005 (two weeks after the murderous bomb attacks on London's transport system). They were interviewed under the 'emergency' provisions of the Terrorism Act 2000, Sch 8, paras 7–9[146] which, like

---

[140] These topics are discussed fully in 4.2 and 4.5.   [141] Code C, paras 6.1 and 6.6.

[142] PACE, s 58 and Code C, para 6.6 – discussed in 4.5.1. Broader exceptions apply to those detained under the Terrorism Act 2000: see Code C, Annex B.

[143] Code C, paras 11.15 and 11.18. The superintendent must be satisfied that the interview would not 'significantly' harm the suspect's physical or mental state. Amazingly, para 11.18 countenances that safety interviews may take place with those who appear 'unable to appreciate the significance of questions and their answers' or 'understand what is happening because of the effects of drink, drugs, or any illness, ailment or condition'.   [144] Code C, Annex C.

[145] [2008] EWCA Crim 880.   [146] See now Code H, para 6.7.

PACE, allows safety interviews, albeit in a wider range of circumstances. The relevant police station was holding 18 people suspected in relation to the 21 July attack. The police, who were under intense pressure to find out whether further bomb attacks were imminent, accordingly denied legal advice to Omar, Ibrahim and Mohamed for 8, 7.5 and 4 hours respectively so that safety interviews could take place without delay.[147] In a number of these interviews the police gave the wrong ('adverse consequences') caution. The suspects then told demonstrable lies whilst, at the same time, not indicating the defences later advanced at trial. The trial judge held that it was not unfair to admit as evidence what had been said in the safety interviews. While acknowledging that using the wrong caution unfairly pressured them, the trial judge ruled that the suspects were not induced to incriminate themselves but rather told deliberate, exculpatory lies.[148]

While it is difficult to feel any sympathy for these particular defendants, it is worth recalling that most of those arrested in relation to terrorism are later released without charge (see 3.3.3), and that telling lies in interview can be extremely damaging to any later *truthful* defence one might have. The suspects in this case incriminated themselves in the long run by the lies they told in interview, and the police, by giving the wrong caution, contributed to this. It goes against the grain of police culture for officers to remind suspects *accurately* of rights designed to protect the latter against those very officers – a point we wish judges would bear in mind.

Interviews may also take place following an unmet request for legal advice if suspects change their minds about wanting to see a solicitor. In these circumstances, suspects must give their agreement, in writing or on tape, to being interviewed without legal advice and an officer of the rank of inspector or above must inquire about the reasons for the change of mind and give authority for the interview to proceed.[149]

Given the rights of suspects to be accompanied by legal advisers[150] (and, where applicable, appropriate adults) why is police questioning still a problem? Firstly, questioning in the absence of a legal adviser (or an appropriate adult) is not invalid if the above provisions are complied with. And even scrupulous compliance with all due process safeguards (including telling the suspect of their right to free legal advice) does not usually result in a lawyer attending for interview. Only a relatively small

---

[147] The trial judge found that Ibrahim had been wrongfully (if unintentionally) denied access to a solicitor who was available to speak to him prior to his safety interview (ie, without causing the police any delay). He nonetheless allowed Ibrahim's statements to be used as evidence, and this was upheld by the Court of Appeal.

[148] See *Ibrahim & Ors*, op cit, [56]. The Court of Appeal agreed with the judge. It also rejected an argument that it would be good public policy to encourage suspects to speak freely in safety interviews by banning the admissibility of any self-incriminating evidence thus obtained. This case does nothing to encourage the police to take their due process responsibilities seriously. See further the case report and commentary by Andrew Roberts at [2009] Crim LR 110.   [149] Code C, para 6.6(d).

[150] Note that no such right exists under Art 6 of the ECHR. Denying a solicitor access to an interrogation is merely a factor to consider when assessing whether a defendant had a fair trial: *Brennan v UK* [2001] ECHR 596. In nearly all respects English law regulating interviews is more generous to suspects than ECHR law, which is why we say little about the latter in this chapter.

proportion of suspects who are interviewed by the police (little over one-third) have a legal adviser present to support them.[151] Even though some more suspects secure advice of some kind (eg, over the telephone, or from an 'appropriate adult') this does not wrest control of questioning from the police. In the mass of mundane criminal cases, the police can rarely delay access lawfully, and rarely try, but many suspects do not secure legal advice.[152]

Secondly, many legal advisers and appropriate adults are supine in the face of oppressive or unfair interrogation, as in the 'Cardiff Three' case and the more general research discussed in 4.5. We saw there that standards have improved in recent years, particularly amongst accredited legal representatives and volunteer appropriate adults.[153] However, it has to be recognised that, even if legal advisers or appropriate adults are minded to intervene, interrogation is controlled by the police, as in the following example:

Solicitor: ...the second clarification is the wallet.
Detective Constable: We're not on trial here; we're asking the questions, not you; we don't have to clarify anything.
Solicitor: I am entitled as any defence solicitor would be to ask for clarification – you don't need to give it, officer.
Detective Constable: We're not clarifying things here, we're not on trial. You can ask these things later when it comes to court.[154]

Legal advisers (and appropriate adults) can only intervene to prevent interrogation methods which fail to conform to the standards discussed below. But we will see that many of the key standards are unclear. Not only does this give the police considerable leeway, but it would produce uncertainty in the mind of the most assertive solicitor, let alone the average unqualified clerk, or appropriate adult.[155]

Thirdly, we should note that the police sometimes seek to maintain control over lawyer-attended interrogations by various subtle and not-so-subtle ways of undermining the legal adviser. Walkley, the police-officer author of a handbook on interrogation advises his colleagues that 'there are one or two things which the interviewer can do to mitigate the damage the presence of a solicitor can do.' These are said to include (i) introducing the lawyer to the client so that the officer is seen to be in control; (ii) selecting

---

[151] See 4.5.4. The position is likely to be even worse where other law enforcement bodies are concerned. In one study only 4% of the interviews conducted by Department of Work and Pension benefit fraud investigators were attended by a legal representative: Walsh D and Milne R, 'Keeping the Peace? A Study of Investigative Practice in the Public Sector' (2008) 13 Legal and Criminological Psychology 39 at 52.

[152] See 4.5 for discussion of how the right to legal advice operates in practice.

[153] See, for example, Pierpoint H, 'Reconstructing the Role of the Appropriate Adult in England and Wales' (2006) 6(2) Criminology & Criminal Justice 225–6. But also see Leggett et al, 'People with Learning Disabilities' Experiences of Being Interviewed by the Police' (2007) 135 BJ Learning Disabilities 168.

[154] McConville and Hodgson (1993: 127). The authors note that the solicitor made no further attempt to interrupt the interrogation. Other examples are provided by Baldwin (1993).

[155] See Medford S et al, 'The Efficacy of the Appropriate Adult Safeguard During Police Interviewing' (2003) 8 Legal and Criminological Psychology 253; Pierpoint (2006: 221 and 230).

where the lawyer sits in the interview so as to marginalise them as much as possible; (iii) dressing-up in a way designed to make the interviewer look more impressive and of higher status than the legal adviser.[156] Cape (2006c: 287) warns legal representatives that, 'it has been reported that some interview rooms have a seat in the corner, behind and out of sight of the suspect, with the label 'solicitor' on it.' And Shepherd (2007: 311) notes that some police interviewers 'put down' legal advisers who are not solicitors by pointing out their status to suspects as a way of implying that their advice is incompetent. A less subtle tactic is to dispute directly the content of legal advice given to a suspect. A legal adviser complained to Bucke et al (2000: 29) that in one interview the 'police turned round and said that "the advice you've been receiving is incorrect and an inference [from silence] can be drawn."' In these ways the police can seek both to make interventions from legal advisers less likely, and, if made, less likely to be influential.

Finally, legal advisers and appropriate adults will inevitably be absent during informal 'conversations' between the police and suspects (see 5.4.2 above and 5.5.3 below), many of which will result in admissible self-incriminating statements.

5.4.5 **When interviews must end**

When PACE was first enacted it adopted the common law position that it would be unfair to continue an interrogation once the police were satisfied that they had obtained sufficient evidence for a prosecution to succeed. The only latitude given to the police in this situation was that they were allowed to ask the suspect if they had anything further to say. But where interviewers took this opportunity to press their questions further, the courts held that this was permissible. In *McGuiness*,[157] the Court of Appeal said that, without giving the suspect a full opportunity to explain himself, including questions and answers, the police would not know whether they should prosecute.[158] A subsequent revision to Code of Practice C incorporated this greater degree of latitude. Paragraph 11.6 now provides that the interview or further interview of a person about an offence with which that person has not been charged must cease when the officer in charge of the investigation:

(a) ... is satisfied all the questions they consider relevant to obtaining accurate and reliable information about the offence have been put to the suspect, this includes allowing the suspect an opportunity to give an innocent explanation and asking questions to test if the explanation is accurate and reliable, e.g. to clear up ambiguities or clarify what the suspect said;

---

[156] Walkley J, *Police Interrogation: A Handbook for Investigators* (London: Police Review Publishing Company, 1988) pp 89–91. Gudjonsson (2003: 7) suggests that this manual 'never gained national support in Britain' (see also at p 52), but it clearly was influential amongst frontline officers, with Shepherd E, *Investigative Interviewing: The Conversation Management Approach* (Oxford: OUP, 2007) describing it as 'very popular' (p 16).

[157] Crim LR [1999] 318. *Odeyemi* [1999] Crim LR 828 was decided similarly.

[158] See also *Elliot* [2002] EWCA Crim 931 and *Howell* [2002] EWCA Crim 1.

(b) ... has taken account of any other available evidence; and

(c) the custody officer ... reasonably believes there is sufficient evidence to provide a realistic prospect of conviction ...

This wording makes clear that interrogation can continue even though the police believe they already have sufficient evidence to make conviction a realistic prospect.[159] Indeed, it is difficult to think of situations in which the police would not be able to claim that there was an outstanding need to 'clear up ambiguities' or obtain clarifications of what the suspect has already said. And if the suspect is silent in interview this provision enables the police (regardless of the strength of the case they have already assembled) to ask all relevant questions in order to lay the groundwork for adverse inferences to be drawn at trial. Even after a suspect has been charged there is provision made (Code C, para 16.5) for further interviewing but only if an interview is necessary:

(i) to prevent or minimise harm or loss to some other person, or the public;

(ii) to clear up an ambiguity in a previous answer or statement; or

(iii) in the interests of justice for the detainee to have put to them, and have an opportunity to comment on, information concerning the offence which has come to light since they were charged.

In post-charge interviews the old-style caution is given, which means that adverse inferences may not be drawn from silence.[160]

The law continues to develop in favour of greater police powers in this area. Thus, when implemented, the Counter-terrorism Act 2008, Part 2 will permit post-charge police questioning of a person about a terrorism-related offence, including after they have been sent for trial.[161] And the Government has signalled that it intends to introduce new legislation which will permit post-charge questioning in all cases, and remove the prohibition on inferences from 'silence' where a person is so questioned.[162]

Does any of this matter? For the freedom model adherent it is generally wrong to allow the police to continue to question suspects once they have sufficient evidence to prosecute. For without a cut-off point (short of the permissible maximum period of detention) they will always be able to claim that further information (or useful silences) might be forthcoming, but only under conditions of involuntary detention.

---

[159] This appears to conflict with the language of s 37 of PACE and other provisions within Code C (see Cape E, 'PACE Then and Now: 21 Years of "Re-balancing"' in Cape E and Young R (eds), *Regulating Policing* (Oxford: Hart, 2008) pp 205–8) although there seems little doubt in the light of *McGuiness*, op cit, that the courts will give full effect to the wording of para 11.6.   [160] Code C, para 16.5(a).

[161] But only if authorised by a Crown Court judge, who must be satisfied that further questioning is necessary in the interests of justice, that the investigation is being conducted diligently and expeditiously, and that questioning 'will not interfere unduly' with preparation of the defence. The judge must specify the period for which questioning is authorised (up to a maximum of 48 hours, although nothing prevents further authorisations being given) and may impose other conditions.

[162] *PACE Review: Government Proposals in Response to the Review of the Police and Criminal Evidence Act 1984*, paras 15.9–15.19 (August, 2008), available from <http://www.homeoffice.gov.uk/documents/cons-2008-pace-review/> (accessed 5 January 2010).

On the other hand, suspects who are innocent or whose mitigating circumstances point towards diversion from prosecution might benefit from the police probing further. In these circumstances adherents of the freedom perspective might be tempted to support post-charge questioning. Whether the police, as currently constituted, can be relied upon to operate in this freedom-enhancing manner is doubtful. For while the increased capacity of the police to interview suspects makes them powerful inquisitors, their objective is not a neutral 'search for the truth' but rather to obtain evidence which the prosecution can use for adversarial purposes.[163] This brings us to the subject of police interrogation tactics and strategy.

5.5 'We have ways of making you talk'

Interviewing may take place over the 24-hour period (or up to four days, for indictable offences, or 28 days for terrorist offences) of compulsory detention.[164] PACE Code of Practice C provides for this interrogation to take place under reasonable conditions, specifying adequate breaks for rest and refreshment (paras 12.2 and 12.8), adequate heating, lighting and ventilation in the interview room (12.4) and allowing the presence of a legal adviser (if requested). Code C also requires the custody officer to assess whether the detainee is fit to be interviewed. 'This means determining and considering the risks to the detainee's physical and mental state if the interview took place and determining what safeguards are needed to allow the interview to take place' (para 12.3). The purpose of all this is in part humanitarian but it is also to ensure that confessions or other information is secured by fair means, is reliable, and thus usable in court.[165] However, acceptable methods of questioning and the number of interviews are not specified. Code C (para 11.5) merely indicates in broad terms what may not be done:

No interviewer may try to obtain answers or elicit a statement by the use of oppression ... [or] ... shall indicate, except to answer a direct question, what action will be taken by the police if the person being questioned answers questions, makes a statement or refuses to do either.

Some suspects are happy to tell the police everything they know. They may be confident of their ability to establish their innocence or be anxious to clear their conscience by confessing. For many suspects, however, telling the police what they know gains them nothing and can lose them a lot. In the main, then, the interview is about

---

[163] Cape E, 'The Revised PACE Codes of Practice: A Further Step Towards Inquisitorialism' [2003] Crim LR 355 at 369. See also Walker C, 'Post-charge Questioning of Suspects' [2008] Crim LR 509, who discusses the dangers of allowing 'a process of wearing away the will of suspects until they are exhausted into a state of complicity' (p 521) and the strong due process safeguards needed to counterbalance the shift towards enabling post-charge questioning.   [164] Detention periods were discussed in 4.3.

[165] As the Code's Annex G on fitness to be interviewed puts it, a detainee should be regarded as 'at risk' if either the interview could harm their physical or mental state *or* if anything they said in the interview might be considered unreliable in subsequent court proceedings because of their physical or mental state.

negotiating release of information (in exchange for something worth gaining) and/ or attempting to persuade suspects to provide information which they do not want to provide. Whatever the situation, police strategy is first directed to establishing control. Subject to the provisions outlined above, the police control where, when and how interrogations take place, what is asked, what information is given to suspects, and what is said to suspects or solicitors outside the interrogation. This keeps suspects on the defensive, nervous, less able to exercise their normal powers of judgment, and unsure of the applicability of any rights of which they may have knowledge.

Police interrogation has to be coercive if it is to produce results in most cases, because the police have to try to induce suspects to talk about things that most do not want to talk about. At one time, before the forms of regulation discussed in the previous section were established, coercion quite frequently took the form of actual violence. Examples include the 'Sheffield Rhino whip' scandal (in the 1960s), the notorious West Midlands Police 'Serious Crime Squad'[166] (in the 1970s), and even incidents following the enactment of PACE.[167] We do not know how common this was, in part because there was even less control and monitoring of interrogations then than there is now. Probably the best evidence we have comes from an unpublished Masters dissertation by Walkley reporting 1980s' interviews with fellow police officers. Half agreed with the statement, 'It is sometimes helpful to slap a suspect round the face' but less than 10% agreed with the more extreme statement, 'If I think a suspect needs a good hiding to help him think about admitting an offence then I give him one.' The threat of violence is as important as its actual use. Thus Walkley reports that half the police officers he interviewed agreed that: 'Some suspects expect rough treatment in police stations, and, if it suits the circumstances, I don't do anything to allay their fears.'[168] The fact that arrests are often violent or accompanied by rough treatment (see 3.4.5) must create a fear of repetition in some suspects' minds. Moreover, the level of deaths in custody (see 4.4) indicates that violence in the police station has not disappeared. There is little doubt, however, that violence, and the explicit threat thereof, is now infrequent within the context of a formal police interview. The police have had to develop non-violent 'tactics' which aim at the same results through legal means.

5.5.1 Police interrogation tactics: legal standards

Nowhere does PACE or Code C specify in detail what tactics are, and are not, lawful. 'Torture' is a crime.[169] But recently revealed secret documents show that the British

---

[166] Aptly named in view of the serious crimes it committed. See further Kaye (1991).

[167] One suspect interviewed in 1987 was forced to sign a confession after having been butted and punched by a detective and threatened with injection by a syringe: *Daily Telegraph*, 20 January 1998. See also Newburn T and Hayman S, *Policing, Surveillance and Social Control* (Cullompton: Willan, 2002) pp 115 and 126.

[168] Cited in Milne R and Bull R, *Investigative Interviewing: Pyschology and Practice* (Chichester: Wiley, 1999) pp 73–4.

[169] Criminal Justice Act 1988, s 134. Evidence obtained by torture is inadmissible in English judicial proceedings: *A (FC) and Others (FC) v Secretary of State for the Home Department* [2005] UKHL 71.

government condoned its use in Pakistan, arranging for a terrorist suspect to be detained in that country for this purpose.[170] Otherwise, the standards imposed on the police arise solely through such law as there is regulating the acceptability or exclusion, at trial, of evidence. This means that breaches of these standards only affect the police adversely if they prosecute the suspect(s) in question, and seek to use evidence obtained thereby. If, for example, the police interrogate largely to discipline someone, they have nothing to fear by breaching any or all of these standards. But since the police cannot usually be certain in advance that they will not wish to use the fruits of such an interview in support of a prosecution they will generally seek to remain broadly within the legal standards. As we shall now see, however, the relevant standards are unclear and do not preclude officers from using interviews to 'put the frighteners' on suspects.

5.5.1.1 The police must not offer 'inducements'

Paragraph 11.5 of Code C (quoted above) implicitly prohibits the offering of 'inducements', such as bail or non-prosecution.[171] The ban on inducements reflects a fear that people offered inducements may say whatever they think the police want to hear, regardless of whether or not it is true. The fear is entirely justified, but it cannot be simply legislated away. The only way substantially to inhibit inducements to confess would be to reduce or eliminate the value of confessions to the police. As matters stand, 'deals' and 'bargains' in which information is exchanged for 'favours' are central to many police–suspect relationships,[172] and what is a deal other than an agreement that each side will accept the inducements offered by the other? According to one CID officer, suspects are often keen to open negotiations: 'They [suspects] always want to deal. When they're arrested they're immediately in the game of damage limitation.'[173] Suspects are in a relatively weak position in these negotiations – 'they want to deal' because of the coercive setting in which they find themselves, and the police use this to their advantage. Thus Dunninghan and Norris found that 84% of informers were either in custody or had proceedings against them when they were recruited, and in 85% of cases it was the 'handler' who initiated the discussion about becoming an informer.[174]

The rule against inducements is thus largely presentational, and rendered still more so by the courts seeking a causal connection between the inducement and the confession. In *Weeks*,[175] for example, the police implied that the suspect would be held in

---

170 *The Guardian*, 8 July 2009. See further 5.5.1.3.

171 See *Northam* (1967) 52 Cr App Rep 97 and *Howden-Simpson* [1991] Crim LR 49.

172 See, for example, McConville et al (1991: 62); Lister et al, *Street Policing of Problem Drug Users* (York: Joseph Rowntree Foundation, 2008) p 25. See also Billingsley, R 'Informers' Careers: Motivations and Change' in Billingsley et al (2001: 86). When 120 informers were asked why they had started informing, 16 said 'reduced sentence', 9 'looking for a favour', 4 'police pressure' and 2 'part of a deal'.

173 Quoted by Maguire and Norris (1992: 47).

174 Dunninghan C and Norris C, 'A Risky Business: The Recruitment and Running of Informers by English Police Officers' (1996) 19(2) Police Studies 1.   175 [1995] Crim LR 52.

custody until he told them what they wanted to hear. His partial confession was not excluded because the court did not believe that he was influenced by this. The gap between the law and reality could hardly be greater than it is here.

5.5.1.2 Interrogation must not be 'unfair'

This is not mentioned in Code C, but it arises because PACE, s 78 allows any evidence to be excluded at trial (at the discretion of the judge) if it is obtained 'unfairly'. Examples arising out of the conduct of the interrogation include lies and deception, failure to record suspects' statements contemporaneously, questioning juveniles without an appropriate adult, and failing to caution a suspect against whom there is reasonable suspicion.[176] But what a judge may regard as 'unfair' is something of a lottery, the Court of Appeal, while unpredictable,[177] rarely interferes with this discretionary power of the trial judge (see ch 12), and if a legal representative is in the interrogation this is usually regarded as sufficient protection to blunt the unfairness.[178]

A good example of the modern meaning of 'fairness' can be seen in *Higgins*.[179] The Court of Appeal noted that the police questioning in this case was 'assertive and confrontational, but not untypical of rigorous testing in cross-examination by police of suspects in interview'. The suspects had been arrested on suspicion of conspiracy to pervert the course of justice – the police alleging that the evidence for the defence that they proposed to give at the trial of X was false. The Court acknowledged that the interviews were lengthy and repetitive (focusing in minute detail on alleged inconsistencies between the suspects' initial statements and their answers to questions in interview), that they had culminated in suggestions that the suspects were lying, and that the police had warned the suspects that they would risk perjury charges if they gave evidence at the trial of X. In addition, one of the interviewing officers misled one of the suspects by claiming (untruthfully) that another of the suspects had cast doubt on his story. One of the suspects subsequently refused to give evidence at X's trial and another was so reluctant to give evidence that defence counsel decided not to put him on the witness stand. Nonetheless, the Court judged that 'viewed as a whole', the police behaviour was neither oppressive nor unfair, and that it did not believe the police had acted in 'bad faith', that is with a view to denying X a fair trial. It is evident that the fairness standard, as interpreted by the courts, covers relatively little of what might ordinarily be regarded as 'unfair'.

5.5.1.3 Interrogation must not be 'oppressive'

Section 76(8) states that oppression 'includes torture, inhuman or degrading treatment, and the use or threat of violence (whether or not amounting to torture)'. Confession

---

[176] See, respectively, *Mason* [1988] 1 WLR 139; *Canale* [1990] 2 All ER 187; *Fogah* [1989] Crim LR 141; *R v Cheb Miller* [2007] EWCA Crim 1891.

[177] Compare its reasoning in *R v Cheb Miller* [2007] EWCA Crim 1891 with that provided in *R v Rehman* [2007] Crim LR 101 and *R v Maya Devani* [2007] EWCA Crim 1926.

[178] See *R v Maya Devani* [2007] EWCA Crim 1926.   [179] [2003] EWCA Crim 2943.

evidence obtained in this way must be excluded under s 76. However, as mentioned at the start of this section, this does not mean that torture is unknown to the UK. A man, Rangzieb Ahmed, later convicted of serious terrorism offences, was effectively placed in the hands of Pakistan's secret service, who ripped out his fingernails and deprived him of sleep, and whipped, beat and sexually humiliated him over several days. British authorities effectively sub-contracted this to Pakistan, feeding agents questions to be asked about his suspected co-conspirators.[180] That this evidence could not be used in court proceedings was irrelevant, as it could be used to track down people who could then be put under surveillance.

Many practices short of torture are considered oppressive and are banned by Code C. Thus, suspects cannot be made to stand during interview (para 12.6) and individual interview sessions should not normally last more than two hours (para 12.8). On the other hand, nothing is said in the Code concerning what might constitute an oppressive style of questioning and the case of *Higgins* (see preceding sub-section) illustrates that the courts do not necessarily regard interrogation which is lengthy, repetitive, confrontational and deceitful as oppressive. In *Emmerson*[181] rude, discourteous questioning in a raised voice, peppered with swearing, was held not to be oppressive.

A relentless refusal to entertain the possibility that a suspect's answers may be truthful has, however, been regarded by the courts as amounting to oppression.[182] Gudjonsson (2003: 87–91) gives the example of an arson case in which the officer repeatedly interrupted the suspect and dismissed his replies. The 22-minute interview contained 52 such tactics, as well as the manipulation and distortion of evidence, and culminated in a confession. As Gudjonsson puts it, this 'brings into sharp focus the speed with which a person's resolve may crumble' (2003: 91). In another of his examples (2003: 91–4) a police 'question' (actually a series of abusive accusations) lasted more than five minutes, and many other forms of intimidation and persuasion were used. In both these cases the courts ruled the resultant confessions inadmissible on the grounds of oppression.

Quite when a confrontational interview becomes oppressive thus remains a matter of judgment; there are no 'bright lines' in law to guide police officers, defence lawyers or trial judges. In the Cardiff Three case the police were (eventually) adjudged to have gone too far (see 5.5.2.9 below). The Chief Constable of South Wales responded by saying that, although he did not support oppressive interviewing, two High Court judges had allowed the 'Cardiff Three' confession evidence and 'a full debate on what constituted oppressive questioning was now needed'.[183] The leading case remains *Fulling*[184] in which the defendant made incriminating statements after being told that her lover

---

[180] *The Guardian*, 8 July 2009. See also the ongoing litigation concerning the torture of Binyam Mohamed in Pakistan by the CIA (apparently with the knowledge and assistance of Britain): *Mohamed R (on the application of) v Secretary of State for Foreign & Commonwealth Affairs* [2010] EWCA Civ 65.

[181] (1990) 92 Cr App Rep 284.

[182] Gudjonsson (2003: 82), citing *Heron* (1993, unreported) and the Cardiff Three case (*Paris, Abdullahi, Miller* (1992) 97 Cr App Rep 99). [183] *The Guardian*, 17 December 1992.

[184] [1987] QB 426.

had been having an affair with the occupant of the next cell. The Court of Appeal adopted the dictionary definition of oppression, which is:

Exercise of authority or power in a burdensome, harsh, or wrongful manner, unjust or cruel treatment of subjects, inferiors etc; the imposition of unreasonable or unjust burdens.

This extremely wide definition was qualified with the view that this would normally have to include an 'impropriety' by the police. The courts do not view all 'improprie-ties' as oppressive.[185] Presumably this is why the police were held not to have acted 'oppressively' in this case, for the trick played on Fulling was undoubtedly 'cruel', although perhaps not what one would normally think of as oppressive. The recourse to the dictionary definition by Lord Lane CJ in *Fulling* was essentially rhetorical, and the courts have yet to clarify what is meant in law by oppression. This uncertainty can be useful for the police because it gives them latitude and enables them to shrug off responsibility if their tactics subsequently attract criticism. By the same token, it means that, even if the police wanted to behave ethically, they cannot know how far they can go. For example, in a murder case where the trial judge refused to accept alleged confessions secured after the police wrongly told the defendant that they had identification evidence and 'pounded him with sexual allegations', the head of CID for the force concerned said: 'It is a matter of interpretation as to what is oppressive... It is rather difficult to establish the truth by pussyfooting about.'[186]

5.5.1.4 'Unreliable' answers and statements

Under PACE, s 76(2)(b) confession evidence must be excluded if 'anything said or done' was likely to render it 'unreliable'. This overlaps substantially with 'oppression' and 'inducements' as the fruit of these would often be regarded as unreliable. The wording of s 76 makes clear that confessions which may have been obtained under circumstances conducive to unreliability (or which may have been obtained through oppression) *must* be excluded even if extrinsic evidence shows that the confession was in fact true.[187] This is an example of a strong due process rule since the crime control end of true confession evidence is not regarded as justifying the means used to secure it. However, as with all rules, much depends on how it is interpreted by the courts and it is plain that the exercise of standard police powers and procedures as provided for by Parliament will not be allowed to trigger s 76.[188] Thus, although repeated and lengthy interviewing is 'something done' to a suspect which might be thought likely to render a resultant confession unreliable within the terms of s 76, the courts can

---

[185] In *Davison* [1988] Crim LR 442, for instance, unlawful denial of access to a solicitor was held not to be oppressive. See also *Parker* [1995] Crim LR 233.

[186] *The Guardian*, 22 November 1993. This was *Heron*. See Dixon (1997: 169–77) for discussion of this and other cases illustrating the judicial approach to interrogation standards.

[187] A rule recently reaffirmed in *Blackburn* [2005] EWCA Crim 1349.

[188] For illustration, see *Kirk* [1999] 4 All ER 698, in which a 'confession' obtained after a series of interviews was not regarded as engaging s 76(2)(b), even though the police had not told the suspect the nature of the offence they suspected him of, and even though the confession contained many erroneous details.

hardly exclude such a confession without undermining the entire practice of custodial interrogation.[189]

5.5.2 Traditional police questioning tactics

Legal standards exist ostensibly to prevent questioning falling below minimal human rights standards and to attempt to ensure that confessions and other information provided is reliable. Yet we have seen that police questioning is inherently coercive. As one suspect put it:

You see, like, they tell you you don't have to talk, then they pressure you to talk. You say 'no comment, no comment', and they keep asking you questions... It's nonsense innit?[190]

It is to the nature of that pressure, steering a course between illegality and ineffectiveness, that we now turn.

5.5.2.1 Use of custodial conditions

Interrogation is nearly always on territory chosen by the police. This enables them to control suspects which is a key to productive interrogation (Leo, 1994). The manipulation of custodial conditions is particularly important. Since this, along with several other tactics, was first identified by Irving,[191] several other researchers have endorsed his findings. Just being held for interview is a 'frightener',[192] and suspects are usually placed in the cells for a while prior to interview to 'soften them up' even if there is nothing to prevent the interview going ahead immediately (Sanders et al, 1989). Similarly, the police know that drug users are more likely to cooperate if the cells are used or threatened as they will be anxious to avoid withdrawal symptoms while in custody.[193] Isolation, assertion of authority and control over details such as provision (or non-provision) of blankets or suitable alternative clothes (eg, where the suspect's own clothes have been taken for forensic examination)[194] precise times of drinks, breaks and so forth all make the experience of detention intimidating.[195]

The fact that PACE requires that suspects be provided with refreshments and breaks loosens police control to some extent but this will not necessarily be evident to

---

[189] At least so far as non-cooperative suspects in serious criminal cases are concerned (see 5.5.5). In any case, evidence discovered as a result of a confession ruled inadmissible under s 76 is not itself inadmissible (s 76(4)(a)), which rather undermines the due process pretensions of this section.

[190] Adams C, 'Balance in Pre-Trial Criminal Justice' (Unpublished PhD thesis, LSE, 1995) p 247.

[191] Irving B, *Police Interrogation: A Study of Current Practice* (Royal Commission on Criminal Procedure Research Paper No 2) (London: HMSO, 1980).

[192] Evans R, *The Conduct of Police Interviews with Juveniles* (Royal Commission on Criminal Justice Research Study No 8) (London: HMSO, 1993b) p 25.

[193] 'They don't want to be left in a cell festering away...' (Police manager quoted by Lister et al, 2008: 25).

[194] Code C, para 8.5. See Pierpoint (2006: 227) for instances where suitable clothing was not provided.

[195] See 4.3.4. For examples see Choongh (1997: 109–10).

the suspect. For example, the police can portray the provision of the required refreshments (and such bonuses as cigarettes) as doing the suspect a favour, thus capitalising on social norms 'governing gift relationships and reciprocal obligation' (Dunninghan and Norris, 1996: 8). Similarly the due process requirement that there should be breaks in the interviewing process can be presented by interrogators as allowing them to check the suspect's story, thus leaving the suspect in a state of anxiety pending the next interview. Indeed, however they are presented, breaks between interviews can serve crime control purposes in that (i) they allow interrogators (not just suspects) the chance to rest and recuperate; (ii) they give the police a chance to compare the suspect's story with other evidence with a view to exploiting any inconsistencies in the next interview and (iii) they provide time for suspects to forget precisely what they have already said to the police (particularly likely where the break takes the form of a night's sleep).[196]

In the interrogation itself police authority is crucial, for example, 'I'll decide when the interview finishes', and '...don't think we'll just let it go just because in one interview you make no replies – we're just starting'.[197] Recalcitrant suspects are often returned to the cells as a warning of how they will have to spend the rest of their 36-hour detention; a severe threat in view of the feelings of most suspects about detention. Thus Softley found that occasionally a confession was produced almost immediately on return to the cells.[198]

5.5.2.2 Police discretion

Sometimes the police allude to their discretion in relation to bail, the level and number of charges to be preferred, other suspects to be investigated and so forth. Examples include the police saying threateningly to a legal representative, in the presence of the suspect, 'We'll have to see about bail if he's not talking', and the police telling a legal representative that they would not charge his client if he confessed.[199] The interviews from one police station looked at by Baldwin contained a spate of inducements to confess on the promise that the offences would merely be 'taken into consideration' (TIC).[200] These are all examples of inducements and, as such, contrary to Code C. Estimates vary regarding how frequently unlawful inducements are used. Irving and McKenzie found none,[201] whereas McConville and Hodgson (1993) found some, but

---

[196] See also Innes (2004: 149).

[197] Both examples taken from McConville and Hodgson (1993: 126). Also see Hillyard (1993: ch 8).

[198] Softley P, *Police Interrogation: An Observational Study in Four Police Stations* (Royal Commission on Criminal Procedure Research Study No 4) (London: HMSO, 1980).

[199] McConville and Hodgson (1993: 121–2). See also Lister et al (2008: 25) and the extract from an informal interview quoted in 5.5.5 below.

[200] Baldwin (1993: 348–9). Offences taken into consideration are put before the court in abbreviated form at a normal hearing for some other offence, allowing 'the slate to be wiped clean'. See also 5.5.5 below and Gudjonsson (2003: 93).

[201] Irving B and McKenzie I, *Police Interrogation: The Effects of the Police and Criminal Evidence Act 1984* (London: Police Foundation, 1989).

not many.[202] How frequently unlawful inducements are offered outside the formal interview setting cannot be known (but see 5.5.1.1).

An entirely lawful use of discretion is the withholding, or drip-feeding, of selected items of information. As we saw in 5.3.5 (above) the police need not tell suspects what they know or suspect, and so they often use 'phased disclosure', as a bargaining chip.[203] While this is encouraged by psychologists as a way of preventing guilty suspects from fitting their false exculpatory stories to the 'known facts',[204] it also has the effect of disorienting innocent suspects and undermines the efficacy of any legal advice they may have received. Choongh (1997: 112–15) reports several suspects saying that they answered police questions in the hope that then they could discover of what they were suspected. By withholding or drip-feeding information the police can engage in active or passive deception, of which the latter is entirely lawful (see 5.5.2.6 below).

5.5.2.3 Provision of expert knowledge

This is where the police play on their specialist knowledge of the legal system to suggest what the effect will be of cooperation on the attitude of the court, likely sentence, the chance of receiving expert help and so forth.[205] In the Cardiff Three case, one of the suspects attempted to retract earlier incriminating statements he had made, and was immediately told that 'you're looking at a life sentence if this goes wrong'. He thereupon continued to confess.[206] Paragraph 11 of Code C prohibits the police from telling suspects what action they will take if they do or do not answer questions except in response to a direct question (and then only if the action is proper). This is designed to guard against the police initiating a deal (eg non-prosecution in return for a confession) with the suspect. But the police are now obliged to point out that adverse consequences may flow where suspects stand on their right to silence. Many suspects do not understand what is meant by this caution,[207] and even the police acknowledge that some suspects think that the caution requires them to answer questions. Some officers play on this by repeating the caution throughout the interview, even when asking questions that have nothing to do with the offence in question. Others find explaining the caution a useful way of building 'rapport' with the suspect or even try to present themselves as a more reliable adviser than the defence solici-

---

[202] Note, though, that they only observed cases in which there was a legal adviser present. See also Choongh (1997: 110–11).

[203] Cape (2006c: 287–8) notes that this strategy is particularly used in more serious cases and that a 'disclosure officer' may be given the job of observing interrogations and advising the interviewers on disclosure strategy.

[204] See Shepherd (2007: 334 and 338–9); Hartwig et al, 'Police Interrogation from a Social Psychology Perspective' (2005) 15(4) Policing & Society 379 at 395.

[205] See, for example, Skinns (2009a: 66–7). The sentence discount offered to those who cooperate in their own conviction is discussed in ch 8.   [206] *Paris, Abdullahi, Miller* (1992) 97 Cr App Rep 99.

[207] None of the 30 suspects in one study could provide an accurate explanation of the caution: Fenner et al, 'Understanding of the Police Caution (England and Wales) Among Suspects in Police Detention' (2002) 12 Jo Community & Applied Social Psychology 83. See also Shepherd (2007: 341).

tor.[208] Since less than one-half of suspects get legal advice (see 4.5.2) the police are the only source of advice most suspects have.

5.5.2.4 Consequences of confession

Persuasive interviewers can lead suspects to believe that confession will make them appear to be more worthy people and that non-cooperation is socially, emotionally and practically undesirable. For example, 'What's your girlfriend to think about you?', and 'sometime you'll have to stand up like a man...' (McConville and Hodgson, 1993: 123–4). The suspected 21 July 2005 terrorist Ibrahim was reminded at the start of his safety interview of his (alleged) comment on arrest that a 'good Muslim' would tell the truth.[209] Even Shepherd, who is acutely aware of the danger that suggestible people will make false confessions (2007: 16), advises interviewers to ask suspects: 'It will help all concerned if you can tell me what happened then?' (ibid: 366).

5.5.2.5 No decision to be made

While the other tactics attempt to force suspects to make a decision, this tactic suggests that there is no decision to make. The suspect is led to understand that the police have sufficient evidence anyway, so that there is no point in non-cooperation, as when an officer said: 'We've had a complaint saying you were there... There are five people to say you were there' (McConville and Hodgson, 1993: 125). This is lawful if the police are telling the truth, but not (in the sense that it is 'unfair' in terms of s 78 of PACE) if it is untrue.[210] Where, as often happens, the strength of such evidence is misrepresented, the legality of this depends on how great was the misrepresentation, whether the police were acting in a bona fide way and so forth. Since the police do not have to disclose any of their evidence to suspects or their lawyers at the interrogation (see 5.2 above) it will often not be known at that time whether such claims are true, untrue or exaggerated.

5.5.2.6 Deception

As we have seen, lying is generally regarded as 'unfair'. But there are other forms of deception, both active and passive, which the police often use, which are generally lawful.[211] For example, one of the writers once asked a detective how he got a suspect to admit to a factory break-in. The officer replied that he had asked the works manager

---

[208] Bucke et al (2000: 27–30); see also Tully B and Morgan D, 'Fair Warning?' (1997) Police Review (29 September) 24. Interviewers are not required by Code C to test whether suspects have understood the caution, and most do not do so (see 5.5.4).

[209] *R v Ibrahim, Omar, Osman and Mohamed* [2008] EWCA Crim 880 [96]. Traditional interrogation techniques are particularly likely to be deployed in safety interviews (discussed in 5.4.4), because they take place as a matter of urgency in relatively unregulated conditions and concern emotionally laden crimes: Roberts K, 'Investigative Interviewing and Islamic Extremism: The Case of Public Safety Interviews' (undated) 2(1) iIIRG Bulletin 30 (available from <http://www.tees.ac.uk/schools/SSSL/iiirg.cfm> – accessed 29 July 2009).   [210] *Mason* [1987] 3 All ER 481.

[211] Their morality is another matter of course: see Ashworth A, 'Should the Police Be Allowed to Use Deceptive Practices?' (1998) 114 LQR 108.

if anyone had a grudge against the factory. The suspect was named as being aggrieved about being sacked shortly before. When interviewed he denied the break-in. So the detective told him that he might as well confess, since his fingerprints were all over the place: a classic example of the 'no decision to be made' tactic. He did confess, the writer commented that this was not surprising given the evidence against him, and the detective fell about laughing, for the writer had fallen for the same deception as the suspect: since the suspect had worked there, of course his fingerprints were all over the place, but this was not evidence that he had broken in.

An example of 'passive' deception occurred in *Imran and Hussain*.[212] The suspects had been videotaped, without their knowledge, going into a shop where there had been an attempted robbery. The police did not tell them this, and they did not admit going into the shop. At trial this left them vulnerable under the CJPO (discussed in 5.2 above), and they contended that adverse inferences should not be drawn since the police had passively deceived them. They were convicted, and the Court of Appeal held that what the police had, and had not, said was entirely lawful.

Arrestees must be cautioned and given a valid reason for arrest,[213] but the police may give the impression that the arrest and interview are largely for one offence when in reality they have something else in mind.[214] The courts did not object to this in *Chalkley and Jeffries*[215] (see discussion in 3.4.2) where the arrest and interview were engineered simply to get the defendant out of his house while bugging equipment was installed. But the situation is different if the police use the interview to obtain incriminating evidence in relation to a matter on which they have deliberately left the suspect in the dark. In *Kirk*[216] the accused was initially arrested for burglary but re-arrested at the police station for assault and interviewed on that basis. The police deliberately chose not to disclose the crucial detail that the alleged victim had died, and that the charges they actually had in mind were robbery and manslaughter.[217] The Court of Appeal held that the trial judge had been wrong not to exclude the confession thus obtained under s 78.[218]

A tactic may be unlawful but it may still be employed if the police think they can get away with it. Waddington (1999: 136–7) gives an example of a man suspected of a series of thefts from work. The last in the series was of money that had been treated with a

---

[212] [1997] Crim LR 754. Another example is *Daly* [2001] EWCA Crim 2643.

[213] Although where an offence is vaguely defined, this reason may not be particularly illuminating, as the quote at the head of this chapter illustrates.

[214] The scope for passive deception is even greater for non-arrestees. Since those who attend at the police station 'voluntarily' (see 4.3.1) are not under arrest, the police do not need to provide accurate reasons prior to interview for wanting to speak with them. Innes (2003: 181–4) gives the example of how the police secured damaging admissions from a suspect by pretending that 'they just needed to eliminate him from enquiries'. This 'volunteer' was arrested for murder at the end of his interview.   [215] [1998] 2 Cr App Rep 79.

[216] [1999] 4 All ER 698.

[217] This phased arrest policy was evidently designed to cohere with a phased disclosure strategy as discussed in 5.2.2 above.

[218] Code C now provides (para 11.1A) that: 'Whenever a person is interviewed they must be informed of the nature of the offence, or further offence.' Whether this opaquely worded provision will lead to a change in police behaviour remains to be seen.

chemical which was supposed to show up, under UV light, on the hands of anyone who touched it. The man's hands were passed under the light, the detectives commented on the clear chemical reflection, told the suspect they had enough evidence to charge him, and then turned to the other thefts, to which the suspect confessed. In fact, unknown to the suspect, the machine was faulty and had not picked out the chemical. Since the suspect was charged only with the crimes to which he confessed (and not to the one about which he had been deceived) the police may have got away with this even if they had been challenged.[219] As a detective told an American researcher: 'Interrogation is essentially a cross between a chess game and poker: you have to carefully strategise and outsmart the suspect with each move you make, but a lot of it really comes down to how well you can bluff and deceive' (Leo, 1994: 107).[220]

5.5.2.7 Now is the time to explain

This implies to suspects who divulge only a little information that failure to explain fully will lead to unspecified harmful consequences. For example: 'It's only fair to tell you that it's in your own interests and to your benefit to give your version of events.'[221] The changes to the right of silence discussed earlier mean that sometimes this will be true,[222] but at other times the suspect (whether innocent or not) may suffer more by speaking than by keeping silent.[223] A similar tactic has been used by the police giving suspects leaflets on these lines: 'My position is one of impartiality. I am here to seek the truth.... Have you any information you can now furnish me with which would ultimately assist the CPS in making a decision not to prosecute in this matter?'[224]

5.5.2.8 Softly softly

Developing rapport with suspects is often regarded by police officers as key to a successful interview. If suspects can be misled into believing that the police 'are on their side' or have sympathy for what the suspect is alleged to have done, the suspect's defences may be lowered and useful information obtained. The following exchange between detectives and someone suspected of murdering his wife illustrates the use of this tactic:

Detective: Why is your marriage breaking up?
Suspect: She doesn't love me ... I'm just one of those wasters at the bar.
Detective: Having been through a broken marriage myself I know how difficult it can be.
             (Quoted in Innes, 2004: 151).

---

[219] Any challenge would most likely be under s 78 of PACE, whereby exclusion is a discretionary matter for the judge: ch 12.

[220] For a more recent account of the situation in the USA see Leo R, *Police Interrogation and American Justice* (Cambridge MA: Harvard University Press, 2008).

[221] McConville and Hodgson (1993: 129); Leo (1994).

[222] Similarly, those suspects who do not cooperate fully with the police deny themselves the enhanced sentencing discount on offer to those who do (see further ch 8).

[223] Shepherd (2007: 354–8) discusses 13 different reasons why the safest defence may be to exercise the right to silence, many of which apply to the innocent as well as the guilty.

[224] Extracted from a pro-forma used at one time by officers in Avon and Somerset: Cape (2006c: 289).

Empathetic stances are rarely spontaneous responses to expressions of distress by suspects, but rather are deliberately adopted in an attempt to maximise cooperation. Thus, when Innes asked a pair of detectives why they had not been more confrontational in their interview with a murder suspect, they revealed the level of planning that underlay their choice of tactic:

Detective 1:   Well we did talk about that didn't we, before we started.

Detective 2:   Yeah, we thought about it quite hard.

Detective 1:   Mmm. But after talking to the boss we came to the conclusion that if we just walked in and started banging the table and shouting and pushing him, he might just close off from us. So we decided to see if we couldn't play it a bit more 'softly, softly.'

Detective 2:   The thing is, what you're looking for is how can I get this person talking to me. You've got to think, 'what is it that I've got that I can use to my advantage over this person?' Sometimes you might decide to go in and hit 'em with it straight off and try to simply confront them with it. On other occasions, like in this case, we went in there with a 'Yeah, look we understand, we know it must be difficult for you' approach because that's what we thought would work. (Quoted in Innes, 2004: 149).

The detectives here make no reference to the legal standards governing interrogation, but rather focus on the perceived psychological vulnerabilities of the suspect.

5.5.2.9 Accusation or abuse

At the other end of the spectrum from the softly-softly approach is aggressive confrontation. In *Higgins*[225] (discussed at 5.1.2 above) the Court of Appeal acknowledged that assertive and confrontational questioning was 'not untypical' of police practice. Examples include: 'Why are they [witnesses] lying?...I asked for a reason – there isn't one – why?', 'You, young man, are a liar basically...'[226] and the infamous 'Bad cop, Good cop' routine. In the Cardiff Three[227] case, Miller – a young man with learning difficulties – was subjected to no less than 19 separate interrogations, held over a five-day period.[228] According to the Lord Chief Justice:

Miller was bullied and hectored. The officers...were not so much questioning him as shouting at him what they wanted him to say....It is impossible to convey on the printed page the pace, force, and menace of the officer's delivery.

After 300 denials Miller eventually 'confessed'. As the Court of Appeal put it: 'The officers made it clear to Mr Miller that they would go on interviewing him until he

---

[225] [2003] EWCA Crim 2943.

[226] McConville and Hodgson (1993: 128). Also see JUSTICE, *Unreliable Evidence? Confessions and the Safety of Convictions* (London: JUSTICE, 1994); Hillyard (1993: ch 8).

[227] *Paris, Abdullahi, Miller* (1992) 97 Cr App Rep 99.

[228] For an extensive analysis of the interrogation tactics used in this case (and extracts from the transcript) see Gudjonsson (2003: 106–12).

agreed with the version of events they required.' He, and two associates, were convicted of murder. They appealed. When the Court of Appeal judges began hearing the interrogation tapes, they stopped the case and allowed the appeal of all three men on the grounds of oppression before they reached the end, so shocked were they at the behaviour of the police. We have seen that in less extreme cases, however, as in *Higgins*, accusation and abuse are not regarded as either oppressive or unfair. For vulnerable people, though, even mild abuse – which is sometimes used – can be highly intimidating (Leggett et al, 2007).

Baldwin (1993: 347) also provides examples. At one point in a series of very aggressive interviews of a juvenile for murder, the officer said:

You can sit here, looking at the floor, crying and crying, but I am not going to walk out of that door; you are not going to leave here until I hear it from your own lips. Do you understand? Did you murder that boy? (Baldwin, 1993: 347).

These were not idle threats. Custodial interrogation lasted three days. For indictable offences, the police do not only have ways of making you talk. They have days to make you talk too.

5.5.3 **Informal questioning**

Some of the interviewing tactics we have just discussed, such as 'doing deals', lying about evidence, and oppressive questioning, may lead to a defence lawyer intervening or to any evidence obtained thereby being ruled inadmissible by the courts. One way for the police to avoid these possibilities is to use these tactics only in informal settings. Questioning is 'informal' if, instead of taking place in a police station interview room, it is done in the street, in the car, at the custody officer's desk or in the cells; or if proper cautions and rights are not provided and if the proceedings are not recorded.

There are many reasons why the police question suspects informally. Some of these reasons are lawful. Sometimes the police suspect an individual of a crime but cannot, or choose not to, arrest. The police therefore can continue to question, so long as they caution the individual once their suspicions cross the 'reasonable' threshold (see 5.4.1). The suspect need not answer, but usually does. Also, informal interviews are sometimes initiated by suspects who wish to 'deal' confidentially. This makes it hard to disprove police claims that informal discussions began at the behest of the suspect as said in, for instance, *Younis, Khan* (discussed in 5.4.2 and 5.4.3 above) and *Menard*.[229] And we have seen that the police are entitled to undertake informal safety interviews in situations of urgency, as where suspected terrorists are questioned by arresting officers about the possibility of explosive materials thought to still be at large.[230] Much informal questioning

---

[229] [1995] 1 Cr App Rep 306.

[230] As happened in *R v Ibrahim, Omar, Osman and Mohamed* [2008] EWCA Crim 880 [59 and 83] (informal interviews conducted of arrestees in car on the way to the police station).

is, however, clearly unlawful. This will be so where the police have reasonable suspicion in relation to an individual but do not caution him or her. And we saw in 5.4.1 that if a suspect has been arrested, the police cannot question him/her until 'booked in' at the police station, unless the provisions for safety interviews apply. Informal questioning is attractive to the police because it is uncontrolled and unsupervised, there is no time clock running, no legal adviser will be present and there are no independent witnesses or checks on the tactics used to elicit incriminating material. In short, it subverts the PACE framework of rules designed to protect the suspect.

The most obvious place to question informally is in the car on the way to or from the police station.[231] As a CID officer said to Maguire and Norris: 'You can't just sit in the car in silence' (1992: 46). Talking is not, in itself, unlawful and it need not amount to an interview but, even without the ever-present prospect of a deal, it would be unnatural for conversation not to turn to the reason for the arrest. Maguire and Norris (1992: 46) quote another officer who said that he 'would not be doing his job' if he did not talk to prisoners, thus echoing the officer who told McConville et al (1991: 58) that 'no policeman who did his job is going to say "no" if a suspect wanted to talk "off the record"'. Sometimes the police (unlawfully)[232] opt for the 'scenic route' in the knowledge that the longer the journey the more likely it is that useful information will be forthcoming.[233] Attempts to estimate the frequency with which informal interviewing takes place outside the police station are bedevilled by methodological problems, although it seems that around in one in five suspects are questioned unlawfully in this way.[234]

Informal interviewing in the police station has also been found to be prevalent. Dixon et al, for instance, found 53% of officers admitting always or often 'clarifying' suspects' accounts before beginning the 'proper' interview.[235] Many officers say that pre-interview questioning is important to establish a rapport, as might be expected given the importance of relationships and dealing. This is particularly important for the police if the suspect wants a solicitor. Some custody officers, one officer told McConville et al, 'will just bend a little bit, if you want a quick word with [suspects] to see, you know, if somebody wants a solicitor and you haven't had a chance to chat and don't want him to have a solicitor yet'.[236] The cooperation of the custody officer in allowing 'off the record' access to suspects is not essential, however, since informal interviews can take place immediately prior to the tape-recorded session. As an officer told Evans and Ferguson: 'I like to have a little chat to get things straight before I

---

231 For a recent example see Skinns L, ' "I'm a Detainee; Get me Out of Here" ' (2009b) 49(3) BJ Crim 399 at 409.

232 PACE, s 30(1), requires transfer to a police station as soon as reasonably practicable.

233 McConville M and Morrell P, 'Recording the Interrogation: Have the Police Got It Taped?' [1983] Crim LR 158; Maguire and Norris (1992: 46).

234 Moston and Stephenson (1993); Brown et al, *Changing the Code* (Home Office Research Study No 129) (London: HMSO, 1992); Choongh 1997: 169.

235 Dixon et al, 'Safeguarding the Rights of Suspects in Police Custody' (1990a) 1 Policing and Society 115.

236 McConville et al (1991: 58–9). Examples are also given by Sanders and Bridges (1990) and Choongh (1997: 175).

switch on the tape.'[237] This is unlawful, yet apparently frequent if we can judge by the number of times interviews appear to be 'little more than an attempt to validate what has already been rehearsed' (Baldwin, 1993: 347). One danger of using an informal interview to 'rehearse' the suspect's story is that the police may deliberately or inadvertently disclose facts that 'only the criminal would know' which are then incorporated by the suspect in any subsequent false confession (see further 5.6, below). This type of false confession can be very difficult to retract successfully since the initial police disclosure will usually remain hidden.

Cell visits are also prevalent.[238] Sanders and Bridges (1990), for instance, discuss a case where a CID officer admitted going to the cell of a suspect who refused to confess and secured a confession by being nice to him. According to the custody record, the suspect had asked to see the officer. The courts tend to turn a blind eye to such practices. In *Williams*[239] a suspect had been interviewed with a lawyer present and made no admissions. After the lawyer had left the police station, the interviewing officers paid an hour-long 'social visit' to the suspect in the cells. As a result, he agreed to be interviewed again in the absence of a lawyer and confessed. The Court of Appeal upheld the conviction, finding no breach of PACE had occurred. In the police area researched by Dixon et al (1990), these visits were systematically recorded as 'welfare visits', showing that custody officers allow custody records to be doctored to hide the truth. As well as cell visits, informal interviews also occur at the end of the 'official' questioning, as when a detective inspector joined other officers and proceeded to threaten the suspect in an 'unpleasant, hectoring and abusive tone'.[240] In this case, microphones installed for the purpose of a TV documentary recorded the informal interview, providing us with an insight into the behaviour of police officers when they believe themselves to be 'off the record'. The defendant had been arrested on suspicion of several burglaries but denied involvement in any of them. Once the police tape recorder was switched off, the detective inspector slipped into 'informal' mode:

DI: ...I've told you what I'm gonna do. I ain't bullshitting you, I'm gonna charge you with six [offences]. If you want six fucking charges, you can have six charges – your barrister ain't got much of a fucking argument at the end of the day. I don't really want to charge you with six fucking charges: I'd rather charge you with a couple and you can have four TICs. You can rip the fucking TICs up once you get to court – I don't really give a shit. Do you understand what I am saying?

Suspect: Mmm.
           ...

DI: Now bullshit aside now, that's the deal I can offer. Quite simply you fucking take it or leave it. You know what's going to happen if you fucking leave it. I mean you

---

[237] Evans R and Ferguson T, *Comparing Different Juvenile Cautioning Systems in One Police Force Area* (Report to the Home Office Research and Planning Unit) (1991).

[238] As are accompanied trips to a police station's exercise yard for a cigarette break, where informal conversations between officers and detainees undoubtedly take place: Skinns (2009a: 66–7).

[239] *The Times*, 6 February 1992, cited by Cape (2006c: 314).

[240] McConville (1992: 542).

	ain't going to fucking lose nothing, you don't lose anything by saying OK, I'll fucking take that.
Another detective:	Plus the fact that you've got a couple of charges, court in the morning, def the breach of curfew, 'he's got two charges of burglary, he's helped us out'. We won't oppose bail. Otherwise we get six charges, 'he didn't wanna fucking know' and remand in custody.

...

DI:	As I say, we'd lay it on heavy or we come off fucking light, it's a matter for you. The most important thing is you've got a fucking decision to make. You're either going to have six fucking charges or you're going to have two and the only fucking way you're having two is you start fucking talking to us.[241]

None of this exchange was discoverable from the official taped record of the formal questioning, and the custody officer noted in the custody record that: 'PACE codes of practice complied with' (McConville, 1992: 544–5). Informal questioning is usually officially acknowledged only when a confession is made or alleged by the police, as for example, in *Dunn*,[242] discussed at 5.4.3 above. The fact that informal interviewing is an under-recorded phenomenon does not mean, however, that its products are always unrecorded. Cape (2006c: 12) counsels legal advisers that suspects may need to be warned that their 'informal' conversations may be bugged since it has become clear that the police do sometimes (no-one knows how often) covertly place listening devices in cells and elsewhere in the police station.[243] Electronic surveillance, when installed openly, can deter some forms of informal interviewing, however. When CCTV cameras were placed in the cells (and custody suite) as an experiment in one police station, custody officers commented that this had made it harder for investigators to do deals, and have 'quick words' with detainees (Newburn and Hayman, 2002: 81).

Informal interviewing inside the station is usually a blatant breach of PACE and Code of Practice C, for it can rarely be impractical to turn an informal chat into a formal interview if one is already inside a police station. It often occurs between interviews precisely because the suspect in question does not want to talk. Since the aim of the informal chat is to change the minds of suspects, the dangers of coercion or unlawful inducements – precisely the dangers which the formal interviewing regime of PACE is ostensibly designed to combat – are obvious. Despite this, the products of these interviews are usable as evidence in court.

The wrongful conviction and jailing of *Khan* (see 5.4.3) is an example of what can happen not only when crime control practices are followed, but also when legal rules – in this case, the rule that information freely volunteered may be written down and used – contain crime control values. This is not an isolated example. Many of

---

[241] For the full exchange see McConville (1992: 542–3).   [242] (1990) 91 Cr App Rep 237.

[243] *Stephen Roberts* [1997] Crim LR 222 is an instructive example. Here the police persuaded X (in informal discussions, themselves held in breach of the Codes of Practice) to effect the 'informal interview' of X's co-suspect in a bugged cell. The resultant confession was held to be admissible. See further ch 6 for non-interrogative methods of collecting admissions, including electronic surveillance.

the infamous miscarriages of the 1990–93 period involved fabricated confessions. A more recent case is *Miller*[244] in which the defendant was alleged to have dropped a bag of Ecstasy tablets as he was being escorted to the custody room. The police officer claimed she said to him, 'I have just seen you drop this... Are these Ecstasy tablets?', to which he is alleged to have said 'Yes'. He denied dropping the tablets, having ever had them, and having the conversation. The Court of Appeal held that the judge had wrongly allowed this conversation to be used as evidence. This was an interview held in breach of the Code and, one suspects from the Law Report, the Court doubted the veracity of the police.

Despite the growing use of electronic surveillance of police–suspect interactions, informal interviewing will never be eradicated. All that can be done is to refuse to accept its products as evidence in court. The Runciman Commission, however, simply accepted that there was a considerable amount of questioning outside the station, and did not discuss informal interviewing inside the station. It commented that 'many witnesses suggested to us that spontaneous remarks uttered on arrest are often the most truthful. We agree' (RCCJ 1993: 28, 61). No evidence or reasoning was given for their agreement with this suggestion.[245] This attitude is likely to encourage police officers to provoke 'spontaneity' on the part of arrestees or, at least, to claim that remarks were spontaneously made.[246] The conclusion flowing from Runciman's approach is that courts should continue to accept evidence provided in such exchanges otherwise 'some reliable confessions might be lost' (RCCJ 1993: 60–1). The absence of concern that some unreliable confessions might also be lost betrays the crime control thinking of Runciman and its reluctance to impose inhibitory rules on the police.

5.5.4 Investigative interviewing

In the early 1990s criticism of traditional police interrogation techniques spread from the 'usual suspects' (that is, academics like us, along with a few pressure groups and defence-oriented lawyers) to the courts, Home Office officials and even the police themselves.[247] The Runciman Commission complained that there is:

an over-ready assumption on the part of some interviewing officers of the suspect's guilt and on occasion the exertion of undue pressure amounting to bullying or harassment... They entered the interview room with their minds made up and treated the suspect's explanation with unjustified scepticism.

---

[244] [1998] Crim LR 209.

[245] Vrij A, *Detecting Lies and Deceit*, 2nd edn (Chichester: Wiley, 2008a) pp 378–9 notes that many guilty suspects will prepare plausible stories in anticipation of an arrest.

[246] Again, as happened in *R v Ibrahim, Omar, Osman and Mohamed* [2008] EWCA Crim 880 [106].

[247] See, for example, Williamson T, 'Reflections on Current Police Practice', in Morgan D and Stephenson G, *Suspicion and Silence* (London: Blackstone, 1994). The availability of tape-recordings of interviews for academic and court scrutiny was undoubtedly a major factor in building the momentum necessary for reform (Shepherd, 2007: 17).

This behaviour was predominantly a product, as one would expect in a crime control system, of a belief in the suspect's guilt and of resource and legal constraints which put a premium on confession evidence. As an officer told Choongh (1997: 124), '... we certainly question on the basis that the person sitting in front of us is guilty – that's what we're paid to do, I mean we can't assume they're innocent, we'd never get the job done.' Research conducted at this time found that in over 70% of cases studied, police interviewers declared themselves sure of the suspect's guilt before the interview began, and in 80% of the cases the interviewers stated that the aim of the interview was to obtain a confession.[248]

In 1992 the Home Office issued a circular to the police setting out 'Principles of Investigative Interviewing', as follows:[249]

(1) The role of investigative interviewing is to obtain accurate and reliable information from suspects, witnesses or victims in order to discover the truth about matters under police investigation.

(2) Investigative interviewing should be approached with an open mind. Information obtained from the person who is being interviewed should always be tested against what the interviewing officer already knows or what can reasonably be established.

(3) When questioning anyone a police officer must act fairly in the circumstances of each individual case.

(4) The police interviewer is not bound to accept the first answer given. Questioning is not unfair merely because it is persistent.

(5) Even when the right of silence is exercised by a suspect, the police still have a right to put questions.

(6) When conducting an interview, police officers are free to ask questions in order to establish the truth; except for interviews with child victims of sexual or violent abuse which are to be used in criminal proceedings, they are not constrained by the rules applied to lawyers in court.

(7) Vulnerable people, whether victims, witnesses, or suspects, must be treated with particular consideration at all times.

A 'Guide to Interviewing' expanded these principles[250] and was seen by many as heralding a revolution in police interview methods. Davies, for example, argues that:

The issue in 1992 to all detectives of a new guide to investigative interviewing, based on the results of applied psychological research, marked a major turning point in police culture and attitudes.[251]

---

[248] Moston et al, 'The Effects of Case Characteristics on Suspect Behaviour During Police Questioning' (1992) 92 BJ Crim 23.   [249] Home Office Circular 22/1992.

[250] Home Office, Central Planning and Training Unit, *Guide to Interviewing* (London: HMSO, 1992a).

[251] See preface to Milne and Bull (1999: xi).

That remarkable claim requires scrutiny. The Guide set out two approaches to interviewing. The first, 'cognitive interviewing', encourages the interviewee to re-live the event in question and provide an account with minimal interference. However, although cognitive interviewing has been found to be valuable with willing participants (especially prosecution witnesses) it has not worked well with unwilling participants.[252] For this reason, no doubt, the Guide advocated the 'Management of Conversation' approach for most suspects. The interviewee is asked to provide an account of what happened. The interviewer then divides this account up, homing in on each element in turn, particularly with a view to the 'points to prove'. It is at this point that principles 4 (persistent questioning) and 5 (continued questioning notwithstanding the silence of a suspect) come into play. Effective management of the interview is seen as requiring interviewers to be aware of and manage the verbal and non-verbal behaviour of themselves, interviewees and third parties such as appropriate adults and legal advisers.[253] The guide and related training package have been revised a number of times since 1992 (eg to take account of the changes to the right of silence brought in by the CJPO 1994), but the basic approach has remained broadly the same.[254] The 'Principles of Investigative Interviewing 2007', however, seem to reflect something of an official shift back towards supporting the use of interviews to gain confessions in that investigators are told to 'recognise the positive impact of an early admission in the context of the criminal justice system'.[255]

Whichever version of investigative interviewing is studied, it is evident that the main focus is on obtaining as much information as possible from the suspect while minimising the risk of it being ruled inadmissible by a court. Thus closed or leading questions and constant interruptions are discouraged not because these practices are unfair, but rather because they can lead to the suspect 'clamming up' or to any evidence obtained being judged unreliable. Consistently with this, Bucke et al (2000: 28) found that some officers had been told during their investigative interviewing training not to probe whether a suspect had actually understood the new caution concerning adverse inferences, in part because this might reveal a lack of understanding of that caution which would put the admissibility of anything said (or not said) in doubt.[256] It is this emphasis on the admissibility of evidence rather than fairness that leads Newton to comment: 'I have difficulty in recognising this package as an ethical framework for interviewing.'[257] Moreover, investigative interviewing shares many similarities with

---

[252] Cherryman and Bull (1996).   [253] Milne and Bull (1999: 56); Shepherd (2007: 20).

[254] See now National Police Improvement Agency (NPIA), *National Investigative Interviewing Strategy 2009* (available from <http://www.npia.police.uk/en/12892.htm> – accessed 5 January 2010).

[255] Ibid, p 6, principle v.

[256] This is completely contrary to the advice of key academics in this applied field of psychology (eg Shepherd, 2007: 341–5). The problem is that most training courses will be delivered by police officers who are likely to share in, and reinforce, the predominant cop culture. In practice, testing for understanding by the suspect of the caution remains rare: Walsh and Milne (2008: 42 and 52).

[257] Newton T, 'The Place of Ethics in Investigative Interviewing by Police Officers' (1998) Howard JCJ 52 at p 66.

the traditional approach to interrogation as can be seen in its support for persistent questioning of those who remain silent,[258] 'management' of legal advisers, minute focus on inconsistencies in the suspect's story[259] and so forth.

One might still argue, however, that investigative interviewing represents a welcome shift away from the assumption that a good interviewer is one that assumes guilt and browbeats or tricks a suspect into confession. Official support for this key aspect of the 'investigative interviewing' approach is now reflected in Code of Practice C, which states that:

'In conducting an investigation, the investigator should pursue all reasonable lines of enquiry, whether these point towards or away from the suspect...' Interviewers should keep this in mind when deciding what questions to ask in an interview.[260]

This support has not merely been at the level of policy pronouncements. A massive programme to train police officers in investigative interviewing was instituted in the 1990s and, by the end of that decade, over two-thirds of police officers had received this training. The key question, however, is whether the training resulted in changes in practice.

Clarke and Milne[261] conducted a major evaluation of its effectiveness after a number of smaller-scale studies had indicated that investigative interviewing was not having the impact that some had anticipated. Their evaluation involved skilled police officers reviewing and rating the tape-recordings of interviews with suspects without knowing whether the interviewing officer had been trained in investigative interviewing or not. Compared to earlier studies, the research indicated a decline in the use of leading questions and the more frequent provision of information required by law, such as the right to legal advice. These are welcome changes but it is doubtful whether they can be attributed to the training, since trained and untrained officers were found to interview in much the same way as each other.[262] In any event, standards of interviewing indicated that the training had failed to bring about a radical change in police behaviour. For example, listening skills were rated as poor, interviews were found to be dominated by the use of closed questions,[263] and ten per cent of the interviews were considered to

---

[258] Suspects can find such tactics very distressing: Pierpoint (2006: 226).

[259] See Shepherd (2007: 349–52) who advocates doing this in a way that avoids any suggestion that the suspect is believed to be lying – a tall order for the average police officer. Vrij (2008a: 105) points out that inconsistencies are more likely to be found in truthful than untruthful accounts.

[260] Note for guidance 11B. The wording within the quote marks is taken from the Criminal Procedure and Investigations Act 1996, Code of Practice para 3.4.

[261] Clarke C and Milne R, *National Evaluation of the PEACE Investigative Interviewing Scheme*, Police Research Award Scheme Report No: PRAS/149 (London: Home Office, 2001).

[262] It is possible that the untrained had picked up better habits by watching the trained in action, but it is more plausible to suggest that the recording of formal interviews (opening them up to external scrutiny) has led to an across the board reluctance to use tactics that might render evidence obtained in that setting unreliable in judicial eyes.

[263] A closed question is one that invites a brief confirmatory answer, such as, 'Did you kick the victim in the groin?' Use of such questions enables the police to speed up the interview, reduces the possibility that the

involve possible breaches of PACE. Subsequent research into benefit fraud investigators reached broadly similar conclusions with three-quarters of those trained in investigative interviewing performing no better than those without such training.[264]

Why do interviewers not put their training more fully into practice? First, the new techniques are difficult to use. Second, many police officers argue that they simply do not have the time to interview witnesses in this way given the mass of routine crimes they deal with.[265] In response, evidence-based attempts are now underway to develop easier and more efficient interviewing techniques while still retaining core cognitive interviewing principles.[266] But there are deeper problems. Thus Clarke and Milne (2001: 110) reported that their research into interviews with victims and witnesses found 'damning' evidence of interviewers apparently looking to interviewees to confirm police suspicions rather than provide their own accounts. The research also found that there was little effective supervision of interviewing and that scant interest had been shown by police leaders in ensuring that their officers actually used the skills taught in training.[267] These research findings undermine the notion that the introduction of investigative interviewing marked a major turning point in police culture. In more realistic vein, Maguire notes that 'changing what is still a strongly ingrained element of police culture – the view that the overriding aim of an interview is to obtain a confession – is an ambitious task, and there is little doubt that poor interviewing practices still persist to a considerable extent.'[268] In short, before any ethical or cognitive approach can fully supplant the traditional approach, officers need to be adequately trained and supervised, training needs to be related to practical policing problems, this approach needs to become part of the whole ethos of policing, and officers need to be rewarded for changing the way they do things. There is little evidence of substantial progress on any of these points as yet.[269]

---

suspect will introduce exculpatory evidence into the interview, increases the risk that suggestible suspects (whether innocent or not) will compliantly incriminate themselves, and takes the pressure off skilful liars (Shepherd: 2007, 191–2).

[264] Walsh and Milne (2008: 51).

[265] Dando et al, 'The Cognitive Interview: Inexperienced Police Officers' Perceptions of their Witness Interviewing Behaviour' (2008) 13 Legal and Criminological Psychology 59 at 65.

[266] See, for example, Dando et al, 'A Modified Cognitive Interview Procedure for Frontline Police Investigators' (2009) 23 Applied Cognitive Psychology 698.

[267] See also Dando et al (2009: 65). For a (characteristically) more positive reading of the research evidence see Dixon (2005: 336–8).

[268] Maguire M, 'Regulating the Police Station: The Case of the Police and Criminal Evidence Act 1984' in McConville M and Wilson G (eds), The Handbook of the Criminal Justice Process (Oxford: Oxford University Press, 2002). See also Gudjonsson G, 'Investigative Interviewing' in Newburn et al (eds), Handbook of Criminal Investigation (Cullompton: Willan, 2007) who accepts that investigative interviews with suspects remain, in general, 'inherently guilt presumptive' (p 475). Presumptions that interviewees are guilty are just as evident amongst benefit fraud investigators and their supervisors: Walsh D and Milne R, 'Giving P.E.A.C.E. a Chance: A Study of DWP's Investigators' Perceptions of their Interviewing Practices' (2007) 85 Public Administration 525 at 535.

[269] See, for example, Choongh (1997: 128–30); Milne and Bull (1999: ch 9), Quinn and Jackson (2007: 251). A recent empirical study of CID confirms that many police remain committed to (and adept at) avoiding exculpatory lines of enquiry (Taylor: 2006, eg at pp 116, 129 and 147).

Nonetheless, the fact that there are aspirational policy statements, guides, training packages and so forth is significant. First, aspiration is the first stage in any effective reform; it is a necessary if insufficient condition of change. If nothing else, the official policy provides a yardstick by which to judge and criticise (or reward) practice and, over time, this has undoubtedly brought about some improvement. Second, the principles of investigative interviewing form a kind of 'soft law' which may have some regulatory impact. For example, Cape (2006c: 308) recommends that legal practitioners who attend interrogations should remind interviewing officers of these principles in appropriate cases, and it is possible that the courts will take account of the investigative interviewing norms when determining the admissibility of evidence. Third, the fact that Britain is seen as leading the way in ethical interviewing, with police forces from other countries such as Australia[270] and New Zealand[271] adopting many of the same techniques, means that this approach has considerable cultural prestige (at least amongst the converts) and this may help entrench better practices.[272] Fourth, the approach is evidence-based, initially drawing heavily on the work of academic psychologists,[273] many of whom now play an active part in developing, evaluating and refining best practice,[274] training packages and so forth.[275] Thus considerable momentum has now built up behind investigative interviewing. As we have seen, however, even if such interviewing were to become second nature to the police, which is far from being the case at present, the continuities with old-style interrogation would be almost as important as the discontinuities.

5.5.5 The effectiveness of interrogation tactics

When assessing the effectiveness of tactics in formal interviews, it is important to bear in mind that they are nowadays deployed primarily against non-cooperative suspects in serious cases. Many suspects readily confess in their first and only interview. Evans (1993), for example found that 92% of juveniles in the 164 interviews he studied were interviewed only once and that 77% of them confessed quickly.[276] In the remainder, persuasive tactics were more likely to be used, particularly for serious

---

[270] Dixon (2006: 328).

[271] Grantham, R, 'Investigative Interviewing in New Zealand' 1(1) iIIRG Bulletin 10.

[272] The introduction of advanced training courses for specialist interviewers (eg, of vulnerable witnesses, or murder suspects), and the positioning of these within the broader 'professionalising investigation programme' further enhances this prestige. See NPIA (2009).

[273] See, in particular, the account by Shepherd (2007: 17–33).

[274] Shepherd (2007) devotes over 500 pages to helping police officers understand the 'conversation management approach'.

[275] To gain a sense of this new academic industry, and to access relevant resources, see the website of the 'International Investigative Interviewing Research Group' at <http://www.tees.ac.uk/schools/SSSL/iiirg. cfm> (accessed 22 July 2009).

[276] When investigative interviewing techniques are used confessions are likely to come later in the interview process, although research is at an early stage in understanding why this might be: Soukara et al, 'A Study of What Really Happens in Police Interviews of Suspects' (2009) 15(6) Psychology, Crime and Law 493.

offences (see also Baldwin, 1993). Similarly, Bucke and Brown (1997: 31) report that the vast majority of suspects are interviewed only once, and that even in serious cases only just under one in five suspects were interviewed more than once. Pearse and Gudjonsson found that interviews for non-serious crimes tend to be short with little attempt made to challenge the suspect's story.[277] Following his review of the litera-ture, Gudjonsson (2003: 55) concludes that PACE brought about a marked reduction in the use of manipulative tactics in interrogations. But when the police are under pressure 'to get a result' in a high profile case they will typically deploy their full arse-nal of tactics (Gudjonsson, 2003: ch 4), notwithstanding any training in investigative interviewing.

One reason why this training has been only partially effective may relate to the con-fidence of the police in their own ability to detect lies and to reliably distinguish the innocent from the guilty.[278] If this confidence were justified police use of persuasive or deceptive tactics in interview would be less troubling. Tactics would be used only against the actually guilty, false confessions would be treated sceptically, and miscar-riages based on unreliable confession evidence would be rare. Vrij (2008a) has shown in a literature review, however, that the crime control belief in the accuracy of police judgements on these matters is contrary to the best available scientific evidence.[279] This evidence is based primarily on tests of ability to make accurate yes/no judgements as to whether someone is lying or telling the truth. In other words, a 50% accuracy rate should be achievable simply by guessing. The salient points can be summarised as follows:

   (i)   The mean average accuracy rate for professional lie-catchers (a category made up predominantly of police officers) was 55.91% compared with 54.27% found in studies with laypersons (a category predominantly comprised of undergraduates) as observers;

  (ii)   When laypersons and police officers have participated in the same experimental studies, only one study found any difference in accuracy rates between the two groups (with laypersons outperforming police investigators);

 (iii)   Police officers were more confident than students in their decision-making, suggesting that confidence is not related to accuracy. In fact confidence may impair accuracy because it tends to result in quick judgements and inadequate heuristics such as 'liars won't look you in the eye' or 'liars fidget';

---

[277] Pearse J and Gudjonsson G, 'Police Interviewing Techniques at Two South London Police Stations' (1996) 3 Psychology, Crime and Law 763. This seems to be true of interviews with juveniles in Northern Ireland too: Quinn and Jackson (2007: 239).   [278] Vrij (2008a: 164).

[279] The bulk of deception studies are rather artificial in nature (eg, based on 'laboratory experiments' involving students), and doubts can be raised about how far such findings can be generalized to real-life police interview settings. Vrij (2008a: 166–7) summarises the few studies that have examined more realistic 'high stakes' situations (as where officers are shown extracts from real-life interviews with suspects) and suggests that the results here are somewhat more positive while nonetheless concluding that 'in high-stakes situations police officers will still frequently make errors in truth/lie detection'.

(iv) Black suspects make a more suspicious impression on white police officers than do white suspects, regardless of whether they speak the truth or not. This is because black people more often exhibit behaviour (such as gaze aversion) that white police officers find suspicious;

(v) When evidence-based psychological training was provided in advance of a lie-detection exercise, accuracy rates went up in the case of students, but down in the case of police officers.[280]

Vrij speculates that a possible reason for this last finding is that police officers refused to use the information provided in the training because they did not believe it – 'the observers were told that liars typically show a decrease in hand and finger movements. This contradicts police officers' beliefs, as they typically assume that an increase in hand and finger movements indicates deception.'[281] Poor police judgement of deception increases the likelihood that tactics will be deployed against the innocent as well as the guilty. Tactics should thus be thought of as effective in terms of producing incriminating evidence (much of which will be false or unreliable) rather than 'getting at the truth'.

With any one suspect it may be difficult to guess what tactic will be effective. If one tactic does not work, the police move on to another (Hillyard, 1993: ch 8).[282] Only rarely (usually when there is an immediate confession) is no tactic used (McConville and Hodgson, 1993: 129). But tactics are thought to fail to elicit confessions as often as they succeed (Evans, 1993: 44–6), or even most of the time (Baldwin, 1993). Police interrogation in general is described in most research reports as often ineffective, clumsy, rambling, repetitious and hit and miss.[283] Effectiveness may also be affected by the presence or absence of lawyers and appropriate adults, and so forth.

The vulnerability of the suspect is crucial. The essence of interrogation tactics is to locate a particular vulnerability and exploit it.[284] In a sense all suspects are vulnerable, however. Thirty-six hours provides a lot of time to explore the vulnerabilities of the psyche. Indeed, Evans comments of juveniles that: 'The very fact that juveniles are arrested and detained for questioning by the police may render them psychologically

---

[280] Ibid, at p 162 (points i and ii), pp 164–7 and 173 (point iii) pp 179–80 (point iv) and p 400 (point v). Benefit fraud investigators working within the civil service are similarly prone to the (erroneous) belief that they can detect lies from physical behaviour: Walsh and Milne (2007: 535).

[281] Ibid, pp 400–1. But why did they get *worse* at detecting lies after the training? Perhaps the training sensitised them to hand and finger movements which they then interpreted according to ingrained police lore.

[282] For an accessible example of this strategy, see Ohrn H and Nyberg C, 'Searching for Truth or Confirmation?' (undated) 2(1) iIIRG Bulletin 11 (available from <http://www.tees.ac.uk/schools/SSSL/iiirg.cfm> – accessed 5 January 2010).

[283] See Baldwin (1993), Pearse and Gudjonsson (1996), Moston S and Engelberg T, 'Police Questioning Techniques in Tape Recorded Interviews with Criminal Suspects' (1993) 3 Policing and Society 223; Walsh and Milne (2008: 52–3). But note that academic assessments based on transcripts or tapes that interviewing is incompetent may simply reveal a misunderstanding about the interrogator's goals: Green A, *Power, Resistance, Knowledge: The Epistemology of Policing* (Sheffield: Midwinter & Oliphant, 2008) pp 14 and 172.

[284] See the comments of the homicide detectives quoted in 5.2.8 above.

vulnerable' (Evans, 1993:26). Tactics will tend to be used more when the police are convinced that a suspect is lying, a working rule which, as we have seen, will bear down most heavily on black suspects. Not surprisingly, tactics are most used where there is no ready confession and where the other evidence is weak or lacking in a crucial respect, such as intention.[285] They will also be used more when the police think the case important enough to merit the additional time and effort involved. To act on these working rules carries with it an obvious risk of grave miscarriages of justice. As Gudjonsson (2003: 624) observes:

The higher the base rate of innocent suspects interrogated, which is not uncommonly seen in terrorist cases and some notorious murder cases where the police trawl in a large number of people for interrogation, the greater the proportion of false confessions that are likely to occur. In such cases there is often a great deal of pressure on the police to solve the case and this often influences their methods of extracting confessions from suspects.

There is as yet no compelling research on the effectiveness or otherwise of interviewing tactics, although some recent exploratory studies have indicated that murderers and sex offenders may be *more* likely to confess when treated humanely (rather than subjected to insult and confrontation).[286] If the innocent are *less* likely to confess when treated humanely (as one might expect), and the police come to accept this, there might be a way of *reducing the proportion* of confessions made by innocent people. But improved questioning techniques are unlikely to *eradicate* false confessions, for reasons we will now explore.

5.6 Confessions

5.6.1 False confessions

False confessions were one of the motors driving the Philips Commission and PACE. Although the Confait Affair was the cause célèbre of the 1970s, other cases included that of Errol Madden (discussed in 3.5), who was accused of stealing a model car, and a man who 'confessed' to stealing money from his employer (Cox, 1975: 177). The claims in both cases that the confessions were false and made because of pressure from the police were verified by the fact that both the model car and the money turned out not to be stolen at all. The PACE framework of contemporaneous recording and

---

[285] Evans (1993: 31); Hakkanen et al, 'Police Officers' Views of Effective Interview Tactics with Suspects: The Effects of Weight of Case Evidence and Discomfort with Ambiguity' (2009) 23 Applied Cognitive Psychology 468.

[286] For a good summary of earlier research, as well as the presentation of new findings, see Kebbell et al, 'Sex Offenders' Perceptions of the Effectiveness and Fairness of Humanity, Dominance, and Displaying an Understanding of Cognitive Distortions in Police Interviews: A Vignette Study' (2008) 14(5) Psychology, Crime and Law 435. See further Soukara et al (2009).

interviewing in the station, together with the outlawing of oppressive treatment, was developed in order to prevent such cases.

Contrary to the expectations of some commentators, and widespread beliefs amongst police officers,[287] the overall confession rate has not been affected by the new regime for custodial interrogation ushered in by PACE. Thus, notwithstanding the decline in the actual or threatened use of violence and the most blatant forms of pressure and deception, more than half of detainees continue to confess or make self-incriminatory statements in formal interviews (see 5.2 above). What is difficult to assess is whether false confessions have also declined. Usually, it is unclear whether confessions made under pressure are false or not, but the problem of false confessions remains. In the Cardiff Three case, for example, DNA evidence resulted in a new suspect being identified and convicted in 2003, 11 years after the convictions of the original suspects had been quashed due to the oppressive nature of the police interrogation.[288] And Sean Hodgson was released in 2009 after serving 27 years in prison following his (false) confession to a crime subsequently shown by DNA evidence to have been committed by another man (David Lace). When the police reopened the investigation they found that they had records of seven men (including Hodgson and Lace) separately confessing to this crime.[289]

Occasionally it is possible both to ascertain that a convincing confession is false and to establish that it was made due to manipulative police tactics. Gudjonsson (2003: 227–30) gives another example: Mr Z made a detailed confession in 1991 to a double murder and related sexual assault of a child. This was prompted partly through lengthy custodial interrogation (five interviews over two days) and partly through a promise/threat made 'off the record' that he would get medical help if he confessed but would otherwise be sent to prison. In addition, the police blurred the line between witness interviews (which do not need to be recorded) and suspect interviews in order to accuse Mr Z (again 'off the record') of the crime at a point when he was formally being treated as a witness. The police are also alleged to have persuaded Mr Z (who had a mild learning disability) to be interviewed without an appropriate adult or solicitor present so that confession would then be less embarrassing for him. The tape-recorded confessions seemed compelling as they appeared to contain facts or 'special knowledge' that 'only the murderer could have known'. After Mr Z had spent almost ten weeks on remand in prison, DNA evidence established that he could not have sexually assaulted the murdered child. Soon afterwards the real murderer was apprehended. The apparently damning 'special knowledge' turned out to have been gleaned by Mr Z from the media and through his 'informal' interactions with the police.

In discussing false confessions we need to distinguish between innocent people who confess 'voluntarily',[290] innocent people who confess as a result of the pressure

---

[287] See Gudjonsson (2003: 138).

[288] See 5.2.9 above. For a fuller account of this case go to <http://www.innocent.org.uk/> (accessed 5 January 2010) where details of a number of other post-PACE cases can be found. For another example, in the Republic of Ireland, see O'Connell M, 'Confessions in Police Custody' Counsel Sept 2005 p 12.

[289] *The Guardian*, 18 September 2009.

[290] Occasionally people falsely confess even without police pressure.

inherent in custodial interrogation and/or police tactics; and people whose innocence is unknown, who allegedly confess but who in fact do not. The last category concerns fabricated confessions, and was discussed earlier (see 5.4.3 and 5.5.3). There are a number of reasons why people who are, or may be, innocent confess[291] but here we will concentrate on the relationship between police tactics and false confessions.

5.6.1.1 'Coerced-compliant' confessions

Here the suspect knows that the confession is false, but is prepared to confess to escape pressure. This pressure will sometimes be the result of oppressive questioning tactics, or sometimes of the 'mere' experience of custody and questioning.[292] Coerced-compliant confessions were a feature of several of the infamous miscarriage cases, including the Cardiff Three. Many of these cases involved vulnerable suspects, but people with average IQ and normal personality characteristics are also vulnerable to tactics of this type, as in a false murder confession discussed by Gudjonsson and Mackeith.[293] These confessions can also arise from strong inducements as the case of Mr Z illustrates.

5.6.1.2 'Coerced false belief' confessions

Here, suspects begin to doubt their own memory. They temporarily believe in their own guilt because of disorientation.[294] Carol Richardson, one of the 'Guildford Four' (imprisoned for terrorist offences for 14 years before having their convictions quashed), reported this experience after being told of the alleged confession of a fellow suspect.[295] Similarly, in the remarkable 'Kerry Babies' case, a whole family falsely confessed to murdering a baby as a result of the pressure to which they were subjected. One said, 'I didn't think my mind was my own...in the end I was convinced I had done it.'[296] In a post-PACE example from the early 1990s the police used an 'informal interview' to persuade Mr J that he had set fire to six caravans but had blocked out his memory of doing so. They said they had witnesses to the arson attacks (none were in fact ever identified),[297] that he must have 'done it in drink' and that they were there

---

[291] For a full discussion see Gudjonsson (2003: ch 8).

[292] See, for example, Quinn and Jackson (2007: 243).

[293] Gudjonsson G and Mackeith J, 'A Proven Case of False Confession: Psychological Aspects of the Coerced-compliant Type' (1990) 30 Med Sci Law 187.

[294] Such cases can be distinguished from 'coerced false memory' confessions, which is where suspects not only come to believe that they must have committed the crime, but actually remember (erroneously) doing so. These are probably much rarer than 'coerced false belief' confessions: Leo (2008: 220–5).

[295] Stephenson G, *The Psychology of Criminal Justice* (Oxford: Blackwell, 1992) p 127.

[296] This was an Irish case which happened in 1984 when there were no PACE-type protections. For an analysis of this fascinating case, see O'Mahony P, 'The Kerry Babies Case: Towards a Social Psychological Analysis' [1992] 13 Irish J Psychology 223.

[297] Experimental research confirms that a false confession is the likely result when suspects are misled into thinking that there is strong incriminating evidence against them: Nash R and Wade K, 'Innocent but Proven Guilty: Eliciting Internalised False Confessions Using Doctored Video Evidence' (2009) 23 Applied Cognitive Psychology 624.

to help him. Mr J, who had great faith in the police, came to believe that he must have committed the offence and accordingly tried his best to please his interviewers by constructing plausible-sounding confessions during the formal tape-recorded interviews. The case was dropped by the CPS once psychological assessments had revealed how suggestible and compliant Mr J was and how vague his 'spontaneous confession' actually was. There was no other evidence against Mr J (Gudjonsson, 2003: 239–41).

5.6.1.3 'Coerced-passive' confession

Here questioning leads suspects to 'admit' to committing an offence without necessarily adopting or even understanding the substance of this admission. In one case discussed by McConville et al, it was accepted that the suspect broke a car windscreen in the course of an argument. The question was, why? The following exchange took place:

Police: Did you intend to smash the windscreen?
Suspect: No.
Police: So you just swung your hand out in a reckless manner?
Suspect: Yes, that's it, just arguing… Just arguing, reckless, it wasn't intentional to break it. (McConville et al, 1991: 70)

Although the suspect probably did not understand this, here the interviewer was not offering a way 'out' of guilt but a way 'in' to an acceptance that the act was done with the mens rea required for criminal damage.[298] In other examples, suspects agreed that they 'stole' goods simply because they took them (not necessarily with intent permanently to deprive the owner), without understanding the legal implications of the term.

Sometimes the police will be confident that, if they can establish that a suspect committed the actus reus of the crime, no claim of lack of mens rea or justification will stand up in court. In such cases they may induce the suspect to admit to committing the act in question by suggesting that the suspect was justified in carrying it out (and thus would have a defence). A journalist who carried out an observational study of American homicide detectives saw many examples of suspects being offered such ways 'out' that were actually ways 'in'.[299] As he puts it:

The majority of those who acknowledge their complicity in a killing must be baited by detectives with something more tempting than penitence. They must be made to believe that their crime is not really murder, that their excuse is both accepted and unique, that they will, with the help of the detective, be judged less evil than they really are… the detective must let the suspect know that his guilt is certain and easily established by the existing evidence. He must then offer the Out… 'Look, bunk, I'm giving you a chance. He came at you right? You were scared. It was self-defense… He came at you right?' 'Yeah, he came at me.' The Out leads in.

---

[298] See Criminal Damage Act, s 1, which provides that criminal damage can be committed either intentionally *or* recklessly.

[299] Simon D, *Homicide: A Year on the Killing Streets* (London: Hodder & Stoughton, 1992) pp 194–207.

5.6.1.4 Interrogative suggestibility

This involves suspects receiving messages from interviewers in ways which affect their subsequent response. This can occur in all three of the confession types discussed above. 'Vulnerable' suspects are particularly susceptible,[300] as are those with 'adverse life experiences' (such as unemployment or being a victim of crime).[301] Stefan Kiszko had a mental age of 12, and was jailed for life in 1976 for murdering a schoolgirl. He had been interrogated repeatedly, and eventually 'confessed' after his sixth interrogation. In 1992, his conviction was quashed after it was found that the semen on the victim's body could not have been his. This evidence was available at the time of the trial but was not revealed.[302]

Vulnerable people now have the additional protection during questioning of an 'appropriate adult'. But as we have seen (in 4.2.3), the police often fail to identify vulnerable suspects. This was so in the 'Tottenham Three case,[303] and lower profile examples include *Brine*[304] and *Miller*.[305] In the first two of these cases, confessions were rejected by the Court of Appeal because of the vulnerability of the defendants, but this was not the result in *Miller*. There is also the problem that the police sometimes seek to undermine the protection supposedly offered by legal advisers and appropriate adults, as seen in the case of Mr Z discussed earlier in this section. Further, neither appropriate adults nor legal advice prevent the police from placing on suspects the kinds of pressures faced by the Cardiff Three.

The dangers of interrogative suggestibility are enhanced by the types of question commonly asked. If questioning was primarily fact-finding, questions would generally be of an open kind ('what did you see?', 'what did you do?') where there would be few dangers of false confessions, if only because the criminal alone would be able to provide the correct details. It may be true, as Evans (1993) argues, that most questioning is like this.[306] In Evans' study, most suspects readily confessed. The important question is what happens in questioning where suspects do not readily confess? McConville and Hodgson (1993: 137) argue that the questions then turn to admission seeking. The most important question forms of this type which they identify are, firstly, leading questions. These seek particular answers by foreclosing others (for example, 'You went down there to get the stuff and you assaulted her, didn't you?'). Secondly, there are statement questions (such as, 'You did it. You went there. There is no sign of entry, no force; whoever did it, did it by key.'); thirdly, there are legal closure questions ('So you

---

[300] Littlechild B, 'Reassessing the Role of the "Appropriate Adult"' [1995] Crim LR 540.

[301] Drake K, Bull R and Boon J, 'Interrogative Suggestibility, Self-esteem, and the Influence of Negative Life Events' (2008) 13 Legal and Criminological Psychology 299.

[302] Kiszko died, aged 41, less than two years after his release. A family friend commented: 'After being released, Stefan could not rouse himself and never recovered from what happened...He could not face the world': *The Guardian*, 24 December 1993.

[303] *Raghip, Silcott and Braithwaite* (1991) *The Times*, 9 December.   [304] [1992] Crim LR 122.

[305] [1986] 1 WLR 1191.

[306] Note, however, that his study was of juveniles only and, as he recognises, many formal interrogations were preceded by informal questioning, the content of which he was unaware.

stole the goods?'); fourthly, there are questions seeking the adoption of police opinions ('You are not innocent, you know what goes on.'). Finally, there are accusatory questions.[307] Soukara et al (2009) noted that leading questions were used in 73 out of the 80 interviews they studied.

In the process of 'asking' admission-seeking questions, the police sometimes let information slip which suspects may incorporate into their answers.[308] Whether such 'slips' are advertent or not is difficult to tell, although it seems reasonable to infer deliberate manipulation when the police disclosure takes place in an informal exchange just prior to a formal interview, as in the case of Mr Z discussed at the beginning of this section. Sometimes as the police ask for detail to confirm what they already know, and the innocent suspect gets it wrong, the suspect is contradicted until, by chance, the correct answer is produced. Gudjonsson analysed one notorious post-PACE miscarriage of justice case and observed that:

From the transcript it would appear that Heron was prompted and led in connection with almost every conceivable corroborative point. These included the point of entry to the disused building, the victim's clothing, the weapon or weapons, wounds (number and type), the position of the body and the route used inside the premises ... the weapons suggested by Heron ... included brick, hands, metal, metal pipe, sharp metal and base metal. Eventually he was asked, was it a knife?[309]

We noted at the end of 5.5 that there is now research to suggest that a strategy of treating suspects more humanely (ie, not bullying or, denigrating them) might lead to an increase in confessions amongst the guilty. We also posited that such a strategy should also reduce the confession rate amongst the innocent.[310] But whatever questioning style is adopted, custodial interrogation will remain inherently coercive, and some innocent people will continue to confess their guilt under these conditions. The radical solution to this problem is not to have custodial questioning, or at least not to rely on it so heavily. This raises the question of corroboration.

5.6.2 Corroboration

At present it is possible to convict on confession evidence alone. There is no need for independent evidence of guilt (corroboration).[311] The police frequently fail to interview

---

[307] For an illustration, see the extract from the 'Cardiff Three' interviews, quoted in 5.4 above.

[308] In the 'Cardiff Three' the police 'fed' Miller with the idea that the reason he could not 'remember' being present at the murder was that he was under the influence of drugs at the time. Also see O'Connell (2005) and Leggett et al (2007).   [309] Gudjonsson (2003: 103–5), (Heron (1993, unreported)).

[310] See also Sigurdsson J and Gudjonsson G, 'Psychological Characteristics of "False Confessors": A Study among Icelandic Prison Inmate and Juvenile Offenders' (1996) 20 Personality and Individual Differences 321 and Gudjonsson (2003: 627). This is probably because the innocent (lacking a guilty conscience or need to talk about the offence) are, on the whole, more reluctant to confess than the guilty, and are also faced with weaker police cases. See further Gudjonsson (2003: ch 6).

[311] Code C, Note for Guidance 11C, suggests that because juveniles and the mentally vulnerable are particularly prone to providing unreliable self-incriminating statements, it is important to obtain corroboration

witnesses to crimes, to secure identification evidence and to do scientific tests on fin-gerprints, blood, hair samples and so forth. In one study, reasonable steps (not includ-ing scientific tests) were taken to secure additional evidence in around 80% of the cases, but available sources were, for no apparent reason, not checked in over 10%. In most of the rest, investigation stopped after a confession was obtained because a guilty plea was anticipated.[312] It is not that further investigation was impossible in most of these cases, but that it was simply thought unnecessary to go through these costly and time-consuming processes when the law allows conviction on confession evidence alone. This attitude increases the risk of a miscarriage of justice in cases where inno-cent suspects make false confessions. Sometimes the simplest of post-interrogation steps (such as the holding of an identification parade) has not been taken and it has only been by chance that a prosecution witness has subsequently (at the trial, or even post-conviction, stage) learned of the defendant's identity and told the police that they have definitely got the wrong person.[313]

Many different types of corroboration rule are conceivable, all of which would have different effects.[314] However, McConville found that at present, in most prosecution cases, where there is a confession there is also admissible independent evidence.[315] A Home Office study carried out for the Runciman Commission found even fewer cases dependent on confession evidence alone.[316] What of the remainder, which would have fallen foul of a corroboration rule? McConville found that in many of them independent evidence existed which could have been produced at court, and in many others it may have been possible to collect such evidence. About one-third of the confession-only cases (about 3% of all prosecuted cases in which the police had interrogated) could not have satisfied a corroboration requirement. In some of these cases, this was because the confessions were so uncertain that they were incapable of being substantiated by reliable evidence. They ended in acquittal anyway. The others, which did end in conviction, would probably not have survived a corroboration rule (sometimes deservedly, given the dubious circumstances of the confessions) but were not particularly serious offences.

As McConville concludes, even the most stringent corroboration rule would affect relatively few cases and lead to few extra acquittals. However, the majority of the Runciman Commission (which was split on the issue) was concerned that the small percentage of cases which would be affected would amount to a large number in abso-lute terms, and that such a rule 'would not by itself prevent miscarriages of justice

---

of any facts admitted. This falls far short of a *general duty* to at least *seek* corroboration, not least because the Notes for Guidance are not even regarded as formally part of the Code.

[312] McConville M, *Corroboration and Confessions* (Royal Commission on Criminal Justice Research Study No 13) (London: HMSO, 1993) table 5.1.

[313] For examples, see *Brady* [2004] EWCA 2330 and Gudjonsson (2003: 230–1).

[314] See McConville (1993: 50–8); Pattenden R, 'Should Confessions be Corroborated?' (1991) 107 LQR 319. For a general discussion which includes a review of the law in Scotland and Australia, see Mirfield (1997: 345–52).   [315] This was true of 86.6% of the cases in his study: McConville (1993: 61).

[316] RCCJ (1993: 65).

resulting from fabricated confessions and the production of supporting evidence obtained by improper means'.[317] It was worried that a corroboration rule would lead to too many guilty defendants walking free, whilst offering negligible protection to the innocent; and that the benefits to be derived from such a rule would not justify the cost of more thorough investigations.

Runciman's reasoning is flawed. Firstly, it amounts to saying that a valid reason for not having a safeguard is that it might be abused by the police. In that case, we might as well do away with all safeguards for suspects, for, as we have seen, they are all abused to a lesser or greater degree. But how much abuse is likely? It is one thing for police officers to pressurise or trick suspects into confessing or to 'gild the lily' and another deliberately to frame suspects (eg, by planting incriminating evidence on them). Only rarely, in the latter case, will the risk of discipline or dismissal be seen as worthwhile.[318] It follows that a corroboration rule probably would offer significant protection.

Second, it is irrational to assert that, under a corroboration rule, the police would frame the innocent *and* let the guilty walk free. If anything, one would imagine that it would be easier to 'frame' the guilty, since there are likely to be more raw materials to work with in constructing a prosecution case if a person is actually guilty. If the police did set out to frame any suspects in such a crude fashion, the innocent would suffer no more than the guilty, and probably less so. The other side of the coin is that the innocent would stand to gain more from a corroboration rule than would the guilty, since it would be easier to corroborate a true confession than a false one. It is in this light that one must place Runciman's anxiety over the resource implications of corroboration. The main purpose of a corroboration rule would be to protect the victims of false and fabricated confessions. We know that there are such cases, we know that currently some such cases end in conviction and lengthy prison sentences, and that only a mixture of luck and hard work by those who reinvestigate cases leads to the eventual release of some of the defendants involved. There may be only a few, perhaps a few dozen, such cases each year. But if a corroboration rule led to the non-prosecution or the acquittal of at least some of these few then, to the adherent of due process or freedom, that rule would be worth its weight in gold.

5.7 **Conclusion**

The due process/crime control debate about police questioning usually revolves around the problem of false confessions and wrongful convictions. To a lesser extent it is about abuse of powers, regardless of the outcome. These are important

---

[317] RCCJ (1993: 65).

[318] Undoubtedly, however, the police do sometimes break the rules to this extent. For post-PACE examples see 7.3.3 and the *Darvell* case (1992 unreported) discussed in Gudjonsson (2003: 530–3).

matters, and civil libertarians advocating a due process approach have had some success in controlling the crime control tendencies of the police and government. This has led to the establishment of a set of standards, set out in PACE, its Codes, the ECHR and in the cases on all these provisions; and the protections analysed in ch 4, especially the right to legal advice and assistance. But this success is limited. First, we have seen that these standards are vague. Second, the value of advice and assistance (especially intervention during questioning) is blunted by lawyers not knowing what standards the police should adhere to and by the effect of the CJPO. Third, suspects who suffer from breaches of these standards usually have no remedy apart from the capricious possibility of the exclusion of evidence (discussed in ch 12).

PACE and its associated codes of practice created a legal framework which deliberately shifted suspect-focused police investigation into the police station. In this respect, and in the detailed rules provided, the change followed an established trend rather than producing a radical break with the past. As McConville and Baldwin said in 1982, before PACE was even drafted:

the really crucial exchanges in the criminal process have shifted from courts into police interrogation rooms. It is these exchanges that, in a majority of cases, colour what happens at later stages in the criminal process. Indeed they often determine the outcome of cases at trial.[319]

Restricting the police to interviewing in the police station and nowhere else could only be regarded as a due process protection if the context of detention was governed by due process standards. The reality is that, since the police station is 'police territory', it cannot be wrested from police control. Hence due process safeguards for suspects in the police station are much weaker than they appear, and manifestly fail to 'balance' the powers of the police. Crime control laws tolerate barely restricted questioning, the use in court of police evidence of what was said, and convictions based on that evidence even when it is contested and uncorroborated.

The crime control reality is hidden by the sanitised language of 'interviews' and 'questioning' but the police know very well what they are doing:

It's not an interview, let's face it. I mean most people don't want to be in there, it's not pleasant for them. We know what we want out of it. It's an interrogation, that's what it is, we just don't use the word because it doesn't sound nice (police sergeant, quoted by Choongh, 1997: 117).

What about the shift in questioning techniques over the years from violence to manipulation and the more gradual shift away from psychological tactics towards official support for 'investigative interviewing'? While welcome, its practical effect

---

[319] McConville M and Baldwin J, 'The Role of Interrogation in Crime Discovery and Conviction' (1982) 22 BJ Crim 165 at p 174.

has been much less than its advocates had claimed. This is not surprising given that it goes against the grain of police culture, and the continuing and profoundly mistaken belief of the police that they can reliably distinguish the guilty from the innocent. Then there is that great mass of cases which the police anticipate ending in NFA, a police caution, or some other pre-trial disposal (see ch 7), thus leaving any illegalities hidden, the perpetrators unaccountable, and exclusionary remedies unavailable. As Jackson argues, the police station is now the site of formal accusation and disposition as much as investigation, yet court-like safeguards, controls and remedies are badly lacking.[320]

Once it is decided that the police station should be the focus of investigation, and that confession evidence alone can form the sole basis for conviction (or other punitive disposition), the crime control framework is accepted, and the room for due process is fundamentally circumscribed. A freedom-based approach would try to counter-balance police power effectively, as would be expected in a fully adversarial system. This means not making the rights of suspects dependent on police officers, but making them either automatic or guaranteed by a genuine third party. Independent lawyers working in police stations might be a solution. Unlike most legal aid lawyers at present, however, they would need to attend all interrogations and possess an adversarial ethos. If they were based in law centres rotating with other law centre lawyers, they might not get 'captured' by the police ethos.[321]

To support this shift towards genuine adversarialism, the law could provide that no evidence obtained through questioning would be admissible in evidence unless a defence lawyer was present. If that is too much for managerialists and crime control adherents to stomach, could we not at least have a rule that rendered confessions to the police inadmissible in evidence unless tape-recorded? Where a suspect wishes to impart confidential information to the police, this could be done informally but without the evidence being directly usable in court.

Such reforms are inconceivable at present and the trend is in fact towards increasing police power in such a way that they no longer need to engage in practices that the courts find objectionable. Blatant police oppression and trickery are being replaced by latent police power and control. The attenuation of the right to silence brought about by the CJPO Act 1994 is one clear example of that, and the increase in the length of police-authorised custody for many indictable offences from 24 to 36 hours (and, with limited judicial oversight, from 7 to 28 days for terrorist offences) in the present decade (see ch 4) is another. No-one should mistake the overall trend towards increasing latent police power. Against that background, ethical custodial interrogation looks increasingly like a contradiction in terms.

---

[320] Jackson J, 'Police and Prosecutors after PACE: The Road from Case Construction to Case Disposal' in Cape and Young (2008).

[321] See the related discussion in O'Brien D and Epp J, 'Salaried Defenders and the Access to Justice Act 1999' (2000) 63 MLR 394, building on McConville et al, *Standing Accused* (Oxford: Clarendon Press, 1994) pp 296–7.

Further reading

Hartwig M, Anders Granhag P and Vrij A, 'Police Interrogation from a Social Psychology Perspective' (2005) 15(4) Policing & Society 379

Kassin S, 'Confession Evidence: Commonsense Myths and Misconceptions' (2008) 35(10) Criminal Justice and Behavior 1309

Kebbell M, Alison L and Hurren E, 'Sex Offenders' Perceptions of the Effectiveness and Fairness of Humanity, Dominance, and Displaying an Understanding of Cognitive Distortions in Police Interviews: A Vignette Study' (2008) 14(5) Psychology, Crime and Law 435

McConville M, 'Videotaping Interrogations: Police Behaviour On and Off Camera' [1992] Crim LR 532

National Police Improvement Agency (NPIA), National Investigative Interviewing Strategy 2009 (available from <http://www.npia.police.uk/en/12892.htm>)

Vrij A, 'Nonverbal Dominance Versus Verbal Accuracy in Lie Detection: A Plea To Change Police Practice' (2008b) 35(10) Criminal Justice and Behavior 1323

6

Non-interrogatory evidence

The government is backing a project to install a 'communication box' in
new cars to track the whereabouts of drivers anywhere in Europe'
(The Guardian, 31 March 2009).

Key Issues:

- Surveillance techniques; varieties of, restrictions upon, abuse and oversight
- Interviewing witnesses
- Identification evidence; procedures for obtaining and reliability
- Searches of private property
- Scientific evidence; expansion of and usefulness
- Shift in police investigative practices
- Privacy and human rights

6.1 **Introduction**

Virtually all people who are suspected of non-trivial offences, and against whom the
police are contemplating taking formal action, are arrested and detained in the police
station – the subjects of chs 3 and 4. In some cases the police will have enough evidence to prosecute or give a formal warning (the subject of ch 7) but in most cases the
police will want, or need, more evidence. Chapter 5 looked at evidence obtained from
suspects by questioning, and this chapter looks at other types of evidence and other
ways of obtaining it – usually, but not always, following arrest. So many topics fall under
this heading that what follows is merely an introduction to these topics. It is neither
detailed nor comprehensive. Nor does the chapter cover all kinds of evidence that can be
used by the prosecution, partly because some are covered elsewhere in the book.[1] Also,
the techniques covered in this chapter – informers, surveillance, phone tapping and so

---

[1] For a brief treatment of 'bad character' and hearsay evidence see ch 10. Chapter 13 discusses evidential
protections for victims and ch 12 looks at what happens to evidence obtained illegally or through police

forth – are all used by many policing agencies in addition to 'the police' as traditionally conceived. The security services are particularly important in the light of terrorism, first in the Northern Ireland context and then in the wake of the September 11 2001 (9/11) terrorist attacks on the United States and the July 2005 (7/7) bombings in London. Much of what is true of, and for, the police is true also of them, but here the focus is on the police. The aim of this chapter is to cover the main issues in sufficient depth to enable us to draw some conclusions about the nature of this aspect of criminal justice in terms of due process, crime control, freedom, human rights and the potential for miscarriages of justice.

Much of the evidence discussed here is obtained by surveillance – for example, by electronic means (such as phone taps), undercover police and informers. Some typically results from what comes after surveillance, such as entry to, and search of, private premises. This wide range of powers is controlled in various ways. The main legislation governing the use of surveillance powers is the Regulation of Investigatory Powers Act 2000 (RIPA) with its associated codes of practice.[2] There are a range of commissioners overseeing the use of surveillance powers.[3] But appeals against, or complaints about, the use of these powers go to the specially constituted Investigatory Powers Tribunal (IPT). This mainly covers the use of informers and covert policing, where authorisation to use intrusive powers (that would otherwise breach Art 8 of the European Convention on Human Rights (ECHR) – the right to privacy) is by a state official rather than by a judicial officer. The tribunal is clearly not an adequate substitute for a court.[4] There are oral hearings only if the tribunal decides this is necessary or appropriate, and the members are senior members of the legal profession.[5] It has no duty to give reasons and there is no right of appeal from its decisions. Between 2001 and 2007, 637 appeals and complaints were investigated by the tribunal. Only one (joint) complaint was upheld.[6] During 2008, 102 cases were investigated and two further complaints were upheld.[7]

A lot of the evidence discussed in this chapter is – or appears at first sight to be – 'hard' – ie by contrast with 'soft' confession evidence, which we saw in ch 5 is inherently unreliable. Scientific and electronic evidence seems to speak for itself. We shall see that appearances are, however, deceptive – as are many of the methods the police use to get evidence. The need for this chapter reflects the growth, in the last 15 years or so, of 'proactive' and 'intelligence-led' policing prompted by the Audit Commission,[8]

---

rule-breaking. The complex question of when evidence collected by the police should be disclosed to the defence is briefly discussed in ch 7.

[2] The regime is currently undergoing review: Home Office, *Regulation of Investigatory Powers Act 2000: Consolidating Orders and Codes of Practice, A Public Consultation* (London: Home Office, 2009b). For critique see *Liberty's response to the Home Office Consultation on the Regulation of Investigatory Powers Act 2000: Consolidating Orders and Codes of Practice* (London: Liberty, July 2009).

[3] These include the Chief Surveillance Commissioner and Interception of Communications Commissioner. See further *Surveillance: Citizens and the State – Constitution Committee* (House of Lords, 2008).

[4] Liberty (2009: 23–4) describes the IPT procedure as 'fundamentally flawed'.

[5] Detailed regulations are contained in RIPA 2000, Part IV.

[6] House of Commons, Written answers and statements, 23 April 2009 (Vernon Coaker MP, quoting figures from the Interception of Communications Commissioner Annual Reports 2001–7).

[7] Report of the Interception of Communications Commissioner for 2008 (HC 901, 2009) p 23.

[8] Audit Commission, *Helping with Enquiries: Tackling Crime Effectively* (London: Audit Commission, 1993). This is discussed briefly in ch 2.

and indicative, some argue, of a shift towards a 'surveillance society'. Ericson even argues that 'crime control [has been] displaced by surveillance' allowing him to define criminal justice as 'a system co-ordinated by knowledge, communication and surveillance mechanisms'.[9] The *system* is developing rights to as much knowledge as it can accrue, at the expense of everyone else's rights to privacy – described memorably as 'surveillance creep'.[10] Whilst 9/11 intensified surveillance creep the phenomenon was already well established before then.[11] Thus not only do the police have more powers than ever to acquire information – both covertly and from other organisations such as tax, social security and local government authorities[12] – but they can increasingly keep it for later, unspecified, use and share it with other national, European and global agencies.[13] We shall see that all this is not just a matter of information secured through surveillance but applies also to, for example, scientific evidence.

The threat is not just to the privacy of random people or even to everyone's privacy. By definition, proactive policing is a police initiative. It cannot target all suspected crime, so the police prioritise particular types of crime and types of suspected criminal. With the exception of a few 'Mr Bigs', this means the targeting not of individuals but of specific groups and sections of society. Together with other police working rules (see chs 2 and 3) this results in a skewed 'suspect population'. Some types of crime and some types of people become not only more heavily policed, but also more known about, than others. This reflects the priorities of the police or politically powerful lobbies. Thus drugs have been the focus of far more attention than burglary, for example.[14] The old adage that 'you can run but you can't hide' is becoming partially, but not evenly, true.

6.2 'Information received': the use of informers

Informants are, and always have been, an essential source of police knowledge…every person you deal with, and in particular offenders, should be viewed as a potential informant.[15]

---

[9] Ericson R, 'The Royal Commission on Criminal Justice System Surveillance' in McConville M and Bridges L (eds), *Criminal Justice in Crisis* (Aldershot: Edward Elgar, 1994) p 139.

[10] Marx G, *Undercover: Police Surveillance in America* (Berkeley: UCLA Press, 1988).

[11] Ball K and Webster F (eds), *The Intensification of Surveillance* (London: Pluto Press, 2003).

[12] Ericson R and Haggerty K, *Policing the Risk Society* (Oxford: Clarendon Press, 1997). The Annual Report of the Chief Surveillance Commissioner 2008–9 (HC 704) shows that drugs trafficking was the major target of surveillance authorisations (Annexes B and D).

[13] See Sharpe S, *Search and Surveillance* (Aldershot: Ashgate, 2000). For a less dated discussion of surveillance as a global phenomenon see Lyon D *Surveillance Studies: An Overview* (Cambridge: Polity Press, 2007) ch 6.

[14] Maguire M and Norris C, *The Conduct and Supervision of Criminal Investigations* (Royal Commission Research Report No 5, London: HMSO, 1992).

[15] Source: anonymised UK police force policy documents, quoted by Innes M, '"Professionalising" the Role of the Police Informant' (2000) 9 Policing and Society 357 at pp 362 and 367.

The police get information about possible crimes and suspects from a range of sources. Apart from the suspects themselves, these include informers, surveillance, and witnesses – the subjects of this and the following two sections. When the police say that they acted on 'information received' this usually means informers were involved. The Audit Commission report mentioned earlier especially encouraged the use of informers, which were already widely used anyway. It is said that about one-third of detections involve the use of informants in the widest possible sense of the term.[16] Further impetus to the practice of using informers has come with the creation of the Serious and Organised Crime Agency and the provisions in the Serious Organised Crime and Police Act (SOCPA) 2005 encouraging prosecutors to make written deals with professional criminals, offering the prospect of lighter sentences or even immunity in return for 'grassing' on associates and 'bosses'.[17]

Informers are motivated by many factors including: money;[18] promises of immunity, leniency or other 'favours' if they have themselves committed crimes; competitive advantage; revenge (common among ex-criminal associates and ex-wives/partners); dislike of a particular type of crime or person, and police pressure.[19] Gill categorises informants as follows:[20]

- *Sources:* Witnesses who give information philanthropically or as a 'one-off', with no expectations about reward. These are discussed in 6.4 below.

- *Non-participating informers:* People who are cultivated on a medium- or long-term basis for general intelligence purposes or to infiltrate specific criminal conspiracies (eg drugs rings, armed robbery gangs, fraudsters). They are 'criminal insiders',[21] usually with a history of criminal activity.

- *Participating informers:* People who actually participate in the crimes about which they are giving information to the police.

- *'Supergrasses':* People who give evidence in court about the many criminals of whom they have knowledge in exchange for immunity or massive leniency.

In this section we will only be concerned with participating and non-participating informers.[22] Sometimes the police seek to recruit specific people as informers, or informers for specific suspected criminal conspiracies. Some drugs dealers appear to

---

[16] Billingsley et al (eds), *Informers: Policing, Policy, Practice* (Cullompton: Willan, 2001) p 5.

[17] SOCPA 2005, ss 71–75. The sentence discount provisions are discussed in ch 8.

[18] 'Police Informant Payouts top £6 million', BBC News, 29 July 2009. (see <http://news.bbc.co.uk/1/hi/uk/8173638.stm> – accessed 5 January 2010).

[19] See Collison M, *Police, Drugs and Community* (London: Free Association Books, 1995) for a typology of motivations. Also see Billingsley et al (2001: ch 5).

[20] Gill P, *Rounding Up the Usual Suspects? Developments in Contemporary Law Enforcement Intelligence* (Aldershot: Ashgate, 2000) ch 8.

[21] The phrase is that of Greer S, 'Towards a Sociological Model of the Police Informant' (1995) 46 BJ Sociology 509.

[22] Supergrasses raise different issues as they are recruited as informers after arrest and are not put back into the underworld: Greer S, *Supergrasses* (Oxford: OUP, 1995).

be given a 'licence to deal' by the police in exchange for information on other dealers, giving the informers a competitive advantage.[23] An alternative strategy is for the police to make themselves disruptively visible near certain people engaged in 'shady' activities, leading those people to tell the police what they want to know in order to get them off their backs.[24] But much of the time, police officers are simply alert to the possibilities. Thus Innes gives an example of a man arrested for possession of drugs who after two hours in the cells told the arresting officer that he could not face going to prison. 'So I said to him "Well you've got to give me something and I'll see what I can do".' As it happens, for procedural reasons a prosecution would have failed, but the suspect was not told that. Instead he was told that all the charges would be dropped if he did 'some work for me. Sure enough he was good as gold and for a long time after he would pass me little bits about what was going down and where.'[25]

6.2.1 The dangers of informers

Any relationship between police officers and 'criminal insiders', other than an adversarial one aimed at ending the informer's criminality, is inevitably dangerous. First, there is the encouragement and condoning of crime. If informers are themselves criminals (as is most common), immunity can put the public at risk. Delroy Denton, for example, committed rape and murder while acting as a police informer.[26] Stephen McColl committed at least one murder while acting as an informer for Greater Manchester Police (GMP) and was so dangerous that Glasgow Police warned GMP about him.[27] Eaton Green committed armed robbery while infiltrating Jamaican gangs in London; the Metropolitan police were so keen initially to keep Green on the streets, and then to obscure their relationship with him, that they deliberately misled another police force, the CPS and a trial judge.[28] Sometimes the 'deal' is bail, a lesser charge, or a letter to the judge asking for leniency, but whenever these strategems keep informers out of jail, they are as potentially dangerous as immunity. In seeking to minimise this danger, police integrity can suffer. Thus the police sometimes 'trump up the charges' (Innes, 2000), so that what appears to be a concession is not really one, and most officers who handle informers believe that to 'run informers you have to be as devious as they are'.[29]

Even an informant who was not previously involved in crime might still be drawn into the criminal activity in question in order to gather the information sought by the police. How far the police should permit informants to become, or continue to be,

---

[23] Bean P and Billingsley R, 'Drugs, Crime and Informers' in Billingsley et al (2001). Bean P, *Drugs and Crime*, 3rd edn (Cullompton: Willan, 2008) ch 8.

[24] Hobbs D, *Doing the Business* (Oxford: OUP, 1988).

[25] Innes M, ' "Professionalising" the Role of the Police Informant' (2000) 9 Policing and Society 357 at 368.   [26] *The Guardian*, 16 July 1999.

[27] *The Guardian*, September 1 2006.

[28] *The Guardian*, 6 November 1995. The Denton and Green cases are discussed in Gill (2000: 190–1).

[29] Dunnighan C and Norris C, 'A Risky Business: The Recruitment and Running of Informers by English Police Officers' (1996) 19 Police Studies 1 at p 7.

involved in crime, and the extent of their immunity, has never been resolved. Police officers themselves express concern about 'the tail wagging the dog' in many different ways.[30] Then there are the informers who expect members of their families to benefit from the same protection that they get, and informers who cross the line to become agents provocateurs (which, as we shall see in 6.3, is legally problematic).

A second danger when police officers deal covertly with criminals without apprehending and prosecuting them is the risk of police corruption. It is easy to see how this relationship could be continued through payments from the immune criminal to the police officer. And if an officer is already corrupt, or is seeking an opportunity to make money illegally, what could be better than officially encouraged non-adversarial relationships with criminals? Historically a common factor in corruption scandals has been involvement with informers.[31] According to Clark, a high-ranking officer who led the Metropolitan police anti-corruption drive in the late 1990s, some criminals regard every arrest as an opportunity to corrupt officers, or to make contact with officers who are already corrupt. One of the many examples he gives is that of a drug dealer named Cressey who persuaded DC Donald, in exchange for a large sum of money in the early 1990s, to secure him bail (allowing him to continue criminal activity) and to try to destroy documents that were vital in securing his conviction. Cressey also agreed to pay Donald to supply him with information about planned police raids – information from which he presumably made even more money from the intended targets of the raids. This all required the two men to meet regularly, and the only way that could be facilitated was by registering Cressey as an informer. Ironically, a role reversal took place – as is common with this kind of corruption – by which the officer became the informer in exchange for the criminal's money. Both men were eventually given long prison sentences.[32] In *Davies, Rowe and Johnson* (2001) 1 Cr App R 115 the corruption consisted of some police officers conspiring with their informers to give perjured evidence in court.

Third, informers risk injury or worse if they are discovered.[33] Whether or not people who voluntarily become informers for money or immunity deserve sympathy is debatable, as they bring this danger on themselves. But not everyone is a genuine volunteer. Just as some people are deceived into believing they are guilty of a crime and thus confessing, some are similarly tricked into becoming informers. Threats are sometimes made by officers against them and/or their family and friends, who are themselves sometimes persuaded to become informers. All the techniques discussed in ch 5 to produce confessions can be used to pressure people into becoming informers, with one difference. Formal interrogations are reasonably well controlled.

---

[30] See, for example, Norris C and Dunnighan C, 'Subterranean Blues: Conflict as an Unintended Consequence of the Police Use of Informers' (2000) 9 Policing and Society 385 at p 395.

[31] Maguire M, 'Policing by Risks and Targets' (2000) 9 Policing and Society 315.

[32] Clark R, 'Informers and Corruption' in Billingsley et al (2001). This account is from the police officer's viewpoint. It is equally likely that PC Donald was the instigator and that some officers regard all encounters with well-connected criminals as opportunities to make money corruptly.

[33] Billingsley et al (2001: 8–10).

Discussions with potential informers are not controlled at all. The potential for abuse is virtually unlimited. Thus in many cases, money is less a motivator for informers (it is frequently observed that officially recorded payments are generally very small) than, as one officer put it, 'legal blackmail'.[34]

Fourth, the motivations that drive informers raise more doubts about the veracity of their evidence than that of other witnesses. In the 'murky world of informers' it may be difficult to 'know where the truth starts and ends'.[35] For example in *R v G; R v B* the Court of Appeal concluded that the evidence of an informer was not reliable because he gave information to secure a reduction in his sentence, and. commented on the 'cynical and manipulative' nature of the witness: it was difficult to know if he was truthful because he had demonstrated that he was prepared to say anything to serve his own purposes.[36] At least if information is to be used as evidence in court its veracity is normally tested openly. However, this is often impossible where informers are involved. If informers are involved in the crimes in question they can refuse to answer questions that would incriminate them.[37] Even when informers do give evidence, their identities will be protected if their lives are in danger, thus preventing the defence investigating whether motivations such as money or immunity might have distorted the evidence. An example is the 'Essex Range Rover Murders', where an informer named Nicholls could have been implicated in the murder of three drug dealers in 1995. As the trial judge told the jury, 'I need hardly stress the importance of Nicholls' evidence. So much hinges on what he said.' The two accused men, friends of Nicholls, were convicted of murder, almost wholly on his evidence. The case was returned to the Court of Appeal because it later transpired that he had sold his story, in advance, to a journalist who wrote a lurid best-seller. It is alleged that Nicholls may have been tempted to 'spice up' his evidence to enhance the appeal of the book.[38] It has also been known for 'informers' to stage crimes so that they can then provide related information to secure a benefit for themselves.[39]

Even if informers are not at risk of being incriminated, the police and prosecution may claim a public interest immunity (PII). This protects the identity of informants, preventing their questioning in court. For many years PII was granted without question as it was thought that the identity of people who give information leading to detection of crimes should be protected in the interests of their safety and, often, so they could continue to be used as informers by the police. It has now been

---

[34] Dunnighan and Norris (1996: 6); Cooper P and Murphy J, 'Ethical Approaches for Police Officers when Working with Informants in the Development of Criminal Intelligence in the UK' (1997) 26 J Social Policy 1.   [35] Bean (2008: 207).

[36] [2009] EWCA Crim 1207. See also *R v B(J)* [2009] EWCA Crim 1036. Also see Adam's case: *The Observer*, 14 January 2007.

[37] This is part of the right of silence guaranteed by the ECHR, Art 6, discussed in ch 5.

[38] *The Observer*, 1 January 2006. The book is Thompson T, *Bloggs 19* (London: Time Warner, 2000). 'Bloggs 19' was Nicholls' code-name under the police witness protection programme.

[39] See the example of Haase and Bennett, convicted prisoners who recruited others to 'fake' crimes for which they posed as informers to obtain early release. See *The Observer*, 23 November 2003.

held that ECHR, Art 6 prevents PII unless the public interest in withholding identity outweighs that of the defendant's right to a fair trial.[40] This is a very vague principle capable of a range of interpretations. The domestic courts have held that despite evidence being withheld to protect police informers, the equality of arms principle is not offended if adequate safeguards are in place to enable the defendant to argue his case effectively.[41] Defendants do not need to be given specific information; provided they know the essence of the allegations against them, information to protect an informant can be withheld.[42] Nevertheless the disclosure provisions may result in the police trying to hide their informants from superiors or the CPS,[43] avoiding using them to give evidence in court or dropping cases halfway through if required to reveal information that would identify them.[44] Many of the problems relating to the use of informers generally are heightened in the case of juvenile informers in particular. The police make considerable use of juveniles; 62 out of 75 informer handlers in one research study used them.[45] But the majority kept them hidden from their supervisory officers, some wrongly believing that the regulations for 'normal' informers (see later) did not apply to juveniles, when in fact stricter regulations apply. The potential usefulness of juvenile informers cannot be denied.[46] However, juveniles are particularly at risk of being drawn into criminal circles, and of being threatened, harmed and blackmailed by police and criminals alike. Threats and blackmail breed lies and unreliability, among other things. The police acknowledge many of these problems and some say that they keep them hidden because they fear they would, in the light of all this, not be allowed to use them. The desire to excel in detecting crime overrides both bureaucratic procedural rules and ethical considerations. In ch 7 we give an example of a juvenile criminal who was repeatedly cautioned rather than prosecuted – not because the police thought he would 'go straight', but the reverse – because he would be more use to the police on the street, passing information back every time he was arrested, than he would be locked up. One consequence of the unreliability of informer information and much of it not being tested in court is false accusations and miscarriages of justice. According to Greer, several 'supergrasses' not only reoffended, but then admitted that the evidence they had previously given at

---

[40] See, in particular, *Rowe and Davies v UK* (2000) 30 EHRR 441; *Fitt v UK* (2000) 30 EHRR 480; *Jasper v UK* (2000) 30 EHRR 1; Edwards and Lewis v UK [2003] Crim LR 891. For discussion of the disclosure aspects of the problem see ch 7. For a comparative discussion see Mares H, 'Balancing Public Interest and a Fair Trial in Police Informer Privilege: A Critical Australian Perspective' (2002) 6 IJ E&P 94. On other concerns about the abuse of PII, see *The Guardian*, 2 December 2003.

[41] *R v C; R v H* [2004] 2 AC 134. There is no blanket rule requiring the appointment of special counsel. Despite new statutory provisions for Witness Anonymity Orders following the House of Lords decision in *Davis* [2008] UKHL 36, the common law principles of PII are preserved. Anonymity orders will probably be used to protect undercover police officers rather than civilian informers, for whom the prosecuting authorities will no doubt continue to rely on PII.

[42] *R (on the application of Ajaib) v Birmingham Magistrates Court* [2009] EWHC 2127 (Admin).

[43] Norris and Dunninghan (2000).   [44] Billingsley et al (2001: 8–10).

[45] Ballardie C and Iganski P, 'Juvenile Informers' in Billingsley et al (2001).

[46] Gillespie A 'Juvenile Informers' in Billingsley R (ed) *Covert Human Intelligence Sources; The 'Unlovely Face of Police Work'* (Hampshire: Waterside Press, 2009).

trial had been false.[47] In an attempt to counter this, the Court of Appeal issued guide-lines stating that prosecutions should never be based on uncorroborated informer evidence,[48] but this does not prevent convictions being based *mainly* on informer evidence which, as in the 'Essex Range Rover Murders', might not look dodgy until years after the trial.

6.2.2 The legal regulation of informers

Traditionally, CID officers had their own 'snouts' and they resisted any attempts to control or share them with others. This exacerbated the dangers identified above, and so attempts to regulate the use of informers have concentrated on increasing the visibility of the police–informer relationship to police managers (but not to the courts or the rest of the outside world). This has, according to Innes (2000), four aims: improving the quality of information and making it more widely available within the police organisation; reducing opportunities for police corruption; pro-tecting officers from spurious accusations of corruption; and controlling the activi-ties of informants.

RIPA and its associated codes of practice (COP) represented the first systematic attempt to legally regulate surveillance.[49] Section 26 defines as 'covert human intel-ligence sources' (CHIS) people who establish or maintain a relationship with persons informed upon for the purpose of gathering information for the police. CHIS have special status and protection, and in return they have to be registered and author-ised.[50] Authorisation has to be in writing, with reasons, made by designated senior officers. Authorisation should only be granted if it is believed to be 'necessary' in the pursuit of one of a number of general objectives (including crime control and preserv-ing national security) that the CHIS be used (s 29), and that such use is proportion-ate to the particular objective pursued (COP, para 4.8). This proportionality principle applies to many of the topics discussed in this chapter.[51] Self-authorisation is allowed only exceptionally (COP, para 2). What the CHIS is authorised to do ('tasked') has to be specified in writing. Substantial changes to the 'task' must also be registered. However, the 'task' can be in general terms, so specific activities need not be identi-fied. This all has to be reviewed regularly. Separate 'handlers' and 'controllers' must be identified. There is no direct oversight by the courts over any of this.[52] So the effec-

---

[47] Greer S, 'Where the Grass is Greener? Supergrasses in Comparative Perspective' in Billingsley et al (2001).   [48] *Turner* [1975] Cr App R 67.

[49] For a critical discussion of this legislation see Akdeniz Y, 'Regulation of Investigatory Powers Act 2000: Part 1: bigbrother.gov.uk: State Surveillance in the Age of Information and Rights' [2001] Crim LR 73.

[50] For a detailed discussion see Clark D, *Bevan and Lidstone's The Investigation of Crime* (London: LexisNexis, 2004) pp 602–19. Note that CHIS include undercover officers as well as 'civilians'.

[51] The proportionality principle is essential for ECHR compliance wherever Art 8 (right to privacy) is involved, as is the case not only regarding informers but also other forms of covert policing and entry and search, both dealt with later in this chapter.

[52] Liberty's response to the recent Home Office consultation on the RIPA codes, which includes some proposals to revise the levels at which RIPA techniques including CHIS can be authorised, criticises the

tiveness of RIPA relies primarily on the honesty of the police and their willingness to comply with its regulations.

General oversight is provided by the Surveillance Commissioners. The Commissioners are judges (serving or retired) who are assisted by inspectors. Their role, which also covers covert policing (discussed in 6.3 below), includes the inspection of records. There is also the Investigatory Powers Tribunal (see 6.1) to hear complaints and provide redress. These bodies are supposed to address privacy concerns, but cannot do so. How can someone object that their Art 8 ECHR right to privacy, for example, was infringed by the placing of a CHIS in their midst when the very definition of a CHIS involves anonymity and keeping those on whom they inform in the dark about their activity? We must remember that it is not only offenders who have their Art 8 rights breached in this way: many people informed on will be innocent, for if the police knew they were guilty of anything substantial they would usually have sufficient evidence to prosecute without needing an informer. One safeguard would be to require disclosure in all cases where suspects were found to be innocent but RIPA does not do this.

One problem is that informers plausibly claiming to provide information as a result of a relationship *not* for this specific purpose are not defined as CHIS and therefore need not be registered. Even if there were a good reason for drawing this fine line, which is hard to discern, the potential for abuse is obvious. Whether or not an informer is officially authorised, their use in a particular case is often hidden by the officers involved for all manner of reasons, such as avoiding the disclosure problems mentioned earlier. Thus Norris and Dunnighan (2000), in the 1990s, found that in not one of the 114 cases involving informers that they looked at (including 31 prosecution files) was there any indication that an informer had been used. And as we saw in relation to juvenile informers earlier, the police themselves sometimes admit that they do not officially acknowledge all their informers. For all these reasons, one assumes, the Chief Surveillance Commissioner complained in 2004 that 'there is still a tendency not to recognise as CHIS, sources who should be so recognised.'[53] The basis for this judgement is not revealed. However, there were only 3,722 CHIS in place by the end of March 2009.[54] By contrast, in 1998 – before RIPA and any rigorous oversight – there were around 50,000 informers.[55] It is impossible to believe that the informer network has shrunk so dramatically in the decade since the new regime was introduced, particularly when the police are being urged to use this type of method more, not less. Clearly, most informers are simply hidden.

---

fact that authorisation is still within the organisation and does not rule out officers authorising their own activities: Liberty (2009: 12).

[53] Chief Surveillance Commissioner, *Annual Report 2004–5* (HC 444) (London: 2005) para 2.3, confirming the continued relevance of the findings of Innes (2000) and Norris and Dunnighan (2000) and others prior to the Act.   [54] Chief Surveillance Commissioner, (2009: para 4.9).

[55] This is 'a surprisingly high figure revealed for the first time by a senior police officer': *The Guardian*, 12 October 1998.

6.2.3 Conclusion

Effective use of informers requires the police to get to know suspects and their associates well so that they can assess what incentives to provide and the quality of the information they eventually produce. But encouraging police officers to form non-adversarial relationships with such people, and granting them immunity and anonymity, leads to dangers of which we know only a part. Recent law-making seeks to minimise the dangers but no one claims that they are eliminated.[56]

We have no idea how many informants are involved in criminal activity, or the extent to which the police 'authorise' this. The (hopefully) incidental criminal activity of informants as part of their information-gathering, and 'deals' made with them by the police, remains hardly regulated. Fitzpatrick argues that the use of informers who participate in crime brings the legitimacy of the criminal justice system into question. He suggests that new legislation is needed to make clearer the basis for doing this.[57] For RIPA provides no clear ethical guidelines.[58] And its emphasis on the management and recording of informers does not adhere to the principles of due process or freedom and offers only minimal compliance with human rights principles. ACPO guidance setting out standards on the use and management of informers provides little further benefit in reducing the risk associated with the police/informer relationship.[59]

Whether the benefits are worth the risks remains to be determined. One senior officer, Clark (2001), while alert to the corruption he has encountered in his career, sees the problem primarily as that of a few weak officers succumbing to temptation; while Williamson and Bagshaw, equally senior officers, find it hard to justify 'a system which coerces and deceives informers, keeps supervisors ignorant (often voluntarily) puts officers at risk of disciplinary action and dupes the courts'.[60] They conclude that it can only be justified if it is effectively controlled. This cannot be done by rules and laws alone. They argue that the police need to 'change the organisational culture which has led to so many past embarrassments.'[61] Are informers with us to stay? Academics and police officers alike agree that informers are crucial for the successful detection of

---

[56] See Harfield C 'Regulation of CHIS' ch 2 in Billingsley (2009). Harfield argues that the statutory framework gives legitimacy to CHIS and makes their use lawful in terms of human rights. However he also argues that we should not just rely on legislation but ensure other controls are in place to support the legal framework.   [57] Fitzpatrick B, 'Immunity from the Law' ch 4 in Billingsley (2009).

[58] Neyroud P and Beckley A, 'Regulating Informers: The Regulation of Investigatory Powers Act, Covert Policing and Human Rights' in Billingsley et al (2001).

[59] ACPO (2006). Guidance that was in place prior to this latest addition proved ineffective in the case of the police investigation into the death of Raymond McCord Junior: O'Loan, N, Statement by the Police Ombudsman for Northern Ireland on her investigation into the circumstances surrounding the death of Raymond McCord Junior and related matters (Belfast: 2007) – available from <http://www.policeombudsman.org> (accessed 5 January 2010).

[60] Williamson T and Bagshaw P, 'The Ethics of Informer Handling' in Billingsley et al (2001: 59).

[61] Ibid, p 64. This argument is on the same lines as that of this book – see ch 2 for discussion of police organisational culture and ch 12 on malpractice as systemic – and is far easier said than done.

relatively few cases, and of some value in only a small proportion of others.[62] There is no inevitability about such systems: 'supergrasses' were seen, for several years in the 1970s and 1980s, as the answer to both terrorism in Northern Ireland and organised crime on the UK mainland, but their unreliability and morally dubious nature led to their near-demise by the 1990s. Despite this, deals are still occasionally done. We do not know how often, because of the secrecy surrounding them. One that came to light only in 2008 concerned a deal struck by 'heroin barons' who were released one year into their 18-year sentences in the 1990s for information about crimes they had set up themselves.[63] The concern remains that supergrasses may have been replaced by a more organised, but even more secret and thus less controllable, system of informers over which RIPA merely draws a presentational veil.

6.3 **Covert policing**[64]

Covert policing falls into two main categories. First, there is undercover policing. This often takes the form of entrapment, where the police establish, for example, a bogus second-hand shop to trap dealers in stolen goods; integrity tests, such as where a van loaded with alcohol, cigarettes etc is left unlocked and the police wait for thieves; decoy operations, where officers act as 'bait' for suspected sex offenders, for example; and 'stings', where the police pose, for example, as buyers of drugs.[65] A slightly different situation arises when suspects confide in undercover officers or informants or simply speak in their presence. For example, in the 1990s, Colin Stagg was (wrongly) suspected of killing a young woman, Rachel Nickell. An undercover policewoman befriended Stagg and threatened to end their relationship unless he admitted killing Nickell.[66] Less dramatically, but more frequently, the police move an informer or undercover officer into a suspect's cell in the hope of eliciting incriminating statements. Undercover policing is perhaps most useful, and often necessary, in the uncovering of police corruption. This is ironic, as without undercover policing and the use of informants there would be less police corruption in the first place. 'In the most pessimistic scenarios, those deploying undercover tactics against officers believed to be corrupt may themselves employ measures of such dubious legality that still further miscarriages of justice may be perpetrated.'[67]

---

[62] See Innes (2000) and, for a discussion of the cost-benefit of intelligence-led policing in general, Heaton R, 'The Prospects for Intelligence-led Policing' (2000) 9 Policing and Society 337.

[63] *The Observer*, 23 November 2008.

[64] Discussion of the legal provisions in this section is highly abbreviated. For a detailed account of their complexities see Clark (2004: 578–602). For another overview see Clark D 'Covert Surveillance and Informer Handling' in Newburn et al (eds), *Handbook of Criminal Investigation* (Culllompton: Willan Publishing, 2007).

[65] All these examples are based on actual cases. They summarise a list provided by Uglow S, *Criminal Justice*, 2nd edn (London: Sweet and Maxwell, 2002) p 156. See also Ashworth A, 'Should the Police Be Allowed to Use Deceptive Practices?' (1998) 114 LQR 108.   [66] Gill (2000). See, further, below.

[67] Gill (2000: 208–9). See generally, Newburn T, *Understanding and Preventing Police Corruption* (Police Research Series Paper 110, London: Home Office, 1999).

Like much of the time when informers are used, these forms of policing involve deception. They, and the use of the resulting evidence, have therefore been challenged frequently in the courts. One ground is that of fairness (under PACE, s 78, discussed in ch 12). Another is that they sometimes trick suspects into breaching their privilege against self-incrimination and right of silence. But deception, per se, is not regarded as problematic by English courts, and the evidence that results from it has never been regarded as unacceptable;[68] and these practices are no different in principle to the many deceptive or coercive ways of securing confessions and incriminating statements discussed in ch 5. The European Court of Human Rights (ECtHR) held in *Teixeira de Castro v Portugal*[69] that if the offence was committed only because the offenders were lured into it, this is contrary to the Art 6 right to a fair trial. This was endorsed and categorised as abuse of process (see ch 12) by the House of Lords in *Looseley*.[70] Subtle and unworkable distinctions were made between what it called 'entrapment', which it condemned, and the provision of an 'unexceptional opportunity' to commit crime, which it endorsed (as long as there was reasonable suspicion and the activity was properly authorised as discussed later in this section). The main factor to be considered is therefore the degree of incitement offered to the defendant.[71] This is not a line between 'entrapment' and 'acceptable' behaviour, but between entrapment (which is allowed) and being an agent provocateur (which is not).[72]

Even when evidence is obtained by trick or deception when on the suspect's premises, the person to whom the suspect is speaking is there with the permission, implicit or explicit, of the suspect. There is therefore no need for search or other powers because no rights are being violated.[73] Stagg's case was an exception, because his 'confession' was made in conditions rendering it unreliable following inducements (from the undercover officer) during what amounted to an interview.[74] This followed from earlier cases[75] which were confirmed in *Allan*, a 'cell block' case of the type mentioned above.[76]

The second main category of covert policing is surveillance (by police officers and other law enforcement officials). This can be public or private. Public surveillance takes many forms. One is simply following people and, on occasion, photographing them in

---

[68] The leading case used to be *Smurthwaite* [1994] 1 All ER 898.

[69] *Teixeira de Castro v Portugal* (1999) 28 EHRR 101.

[70] [2001] UKHL 53. An example of a failed entrapment defence is *Shannon* [2000] Crim LR 1001.

[71] For critical comment see Ashworth A, 'Re-drawing the Boundaries of Entrapment' [2002] Crim LR 161; Ormerod D and Roberts A, 'The Trouble with *Teixeira*: Developing a Principled Approach to Entrapment' (2002) 6 IJ E & P 38.

[72] See further Squires D 'The Problem of Entrapment' (2006) OJLS 26(2) 351; Hofmeyr K 'The Problem of Private Entrapment' [2006] Crim LR 319; and *Ramanauskas v Lithuania* [2008] Crim LR 639.

[73] Sharpe (2000: ch 6); Ashworth (1998).

[74] As a result, Stagg was acquitted in 1994. In 2008 the real killer of Rachel Nickell confessed to her murder and Stagg was awarded £706,000 for the year he spent in custody awaiting trial and associated public vilification that has left him unable to secure paid work ever since. See *The Guardian*, 14 August 2008 and 18 December 2008.   [75] In particular, *Christou* [1992] 95 Cr App R 264.

[76] Crim LR [2005] 716.

public. In recent years it has become evident that the police routinely photograph and film demonstrators and retain the images even when no crimes have been committed. Though this has been ruled to be unlawful (breach of Art 8) when done indiscriminately, it can still be justified by the police on a case-by-case basis.[77] A second form is watching from a concealed place, such as a plumber's van that is actually set up to conceal officers.

An increasingly important form of public surveillance, particularly in city centres and on major roads, is CCTV. This has become a major element of the 'information' and 'security' society.[78] The UK is the 'world capital' of CCTV, with pretty much everyone being recorded repeatedly whilst going about their daily business.[79] CCTV is also used in conjunction with 'regular' policing by facilitating 'targeting' – of offenders, types of situation and event (such as football matches) and areas – by, for example, 'flagging up' particular people who are programmed into the CCTV system.[80] CCTV can give early warning to the police of gatherings that could turn violent. And when crimes take place in the vicinity of CCTV cameras one of the first things the police do is to look through the tapes for evidence. This is often with some success, but there are also dangers from the false confidence it gives some people – police officers and civilians – that they have made an accurate identification.[81] CCTV images are often very poor, yet none of this public surveillance is regulated by law, and evidence produced as a result can be used in trials.[82] This is all also true of police public surveillance by other means, such as flooding a particular area with officers or briefing patrol officers to look out for particular individuals or gang members.

A more problematic form of undercover policing is covert surveillance: the infiltrating of (potentially) criminal conspiracies. This can be done by officers or civilians (ie CHIS, discussed above). The method of operation varies. Sometimes operatives will hope to secure evidence by being 'wired' or using hidden cameras; sometimes they tip off the police about specific criminal acts and perpetrators, or about a forthcoming crime so that the police are waiting to catch them as they make the attempt; sometimes they 'cross the line' by acting as agents provocateurs such as where the police

---

[77] *The Guardian*, 22 May 2009.

[78] Lyon D, *Surveillance Society: Monitoring Everyday Life* (Buckingham: Open University Press, 2001); Coleman R, *Reclaiming the Streets: Surveillance, Social Control and the City* (Cullompton: Willan, 2004).

[79] Lyon (2007: 39). See 'Surveillance Fears for the UK', BBC News, 4 May 2009, for comment on the coupling of CCTV with face-recognition algorithms and other surveillance technology.

[80] Norris et al (eds), *Surveillance, CCTV and Social Control* (Aldershot: Ashgate, 1999); Goold B, *CCTV and Policing* (Oxford: OUP, 2004).

[81] Levesley T and Martin A, *Police Attitudes to and Use of CCTV* (Home Office On-Line Report 09/05); Costigan R, 'Identification from CCTV: The Risk of Injustice' [2007] Crim LR 591. See further 6.4.2. Note other negative findings, including the displacement effects of CCTV, that are often ignored: Lyon (2007: 39). A recent internal report for the Metropolitan police suggests a low level of detection. See '1,000 CCTV cameras to solve just one crime', *The Telegraph*, 25 August 2009.

[82] For an example of some of the consequent problems see *Chaney* [2009] Crim LR 437 and commentary at 438.

encourage crime.[83] It is difficult to know when the line is crossed, as when, for example, some of the more disorderly soccer fan groups were infiltrated in the 1990s.[84] The same is true of the infiltration of extremist groups, an example of which is discussed in 6.5. In major anti-terrorist operations the whole gamut of techniques is used.[85]

The remainder of this section concerns the other most problematic forms of covert policing: the 'bugging' of premises and cars; and the interception of telephone communications and e-mail. These activities violate Art 8 privacy rights when they are done without the permission of owners/occupiers. They can therefore only be done when authorised by a person or body in accordance with the ECHR.

6.3.1 Interception of communications

This includes not just telephone, mail, e-mail, text messages etc, but also communications data (such as itemised bills). RIPA 2000, s 1 makes it an offence to intercept communications unless this is authorised lawfully. The main circumstances are:

- Where there are reasonable grounds for believing both sender and receiver consent (s 3).
- Participant monitoring: one party consents and surveillance is authorised under s 3(2).
- No consent by either party: surveillance is authorised by a warrant from the Secretary of State under s 5.

The main concern is s 5 authorisation. Applications under s 5 have to specify the background, persons or premises to which the application relates, what is to be intercepted, and why. Consideration also has to be given to whether the intrusion is proportionate to what is hoped to be achieved and what collateral intrusion might be created. Before issuing the warrant the Secretary of State has to be satisfied:

(a) that it is necessary for one of a variety of reasons, of which the prevention or detection of serious crime is one; and

(b) that it is proportionate.

Warrants last for three months, but may be renewed. They may also be modified, either during or at the end of the three-month period. However, if the Secretary of State is satisfied that the warrant is no longer necessary at some point before it expires, he or she must cancel it. The system as a whole is supervised by an independent Interception of Communications Commissioner, who must be a serving or former judge.

---

[83] On *agents provocateurs* in general, see Norris and Dunnighan (2000); Marx (1988).

[84] Gill (2000: 197).

[85] An investigation into an IRA plot to bomb south-eastern England's main electricity sub-stations, for example, involved tens of thousands of surveillance hours and 20,000 hours of CCTV footage, among other things. Six people were jailed in 1997 for 35 years each as a result. See Wilkinson P, *Terrorism versus Democracy* (London: Frank Cass, 2001) ch 5.

Generally, intercept evidence is not admissible in court because this would reveal the product and fact of interception, thus limiting its effectiveness in future.[86] However the government set up a review of the use of intercept as evidence which concluded that it should be possible to use some material provided key conditions are met.[87] The recommended conditions include ensuring that the disclosure of material cannot be required against the wishes of the agency originating the material and not allowing the defence to conduct 'fishing expeditions' for intercept allegedly held by any agency.[88] Some trials into the use of intercept evidence apparently highlighted 'real legal and operational difficulties' which led the Interception of Communications Commissioner to urge caution in ending the ban on the use of intercept as evidence.[89] The difficulty for the prosecution is that intercept evidence is often the most compelling evidence it has. The introduction of 'control orders' for the detention of suspected terrorists adds further complications to the debate. The government argued that in some cases it would 'know' that there was evidence to justify indefinite detention even though for policy or political reasons it was not prepared to reveal that it had intercept evidence (see ch 4).[90] From a freedom perspective there are compelling reasons for bringing intercept evidence into the open to allow effective scrutiny of claims being made about terrorist suspects, provided conditions to safeguard national security are met. The courts now agree that Art 6 demands that the defence be allowed such scrutiny.[91]

There are serious concerns about whether the oversight provided by the Interception of Communications Commissioner is sufficient to address the power to issue warrants.[92] Officially, 1,503 warrants were authorised in 2008 by the Secretary of State.[93] Given the volume of authorisations can it be credibly maintained that the Secretary of State discharges effective and proper review? The Commissioner does not adjudicate on whether particular warrants are justified, but he does report on errors and breaches of the law where they are apparent. His report for 2008, for example, observed that fifty errors or breaches were reported to him during 2008, but whilst 'too high' in number, none except one were deliberate and commonly included incorrect telephone numbers.[94] The Commissioner's overall conclusion echoes that of previous years that interception is 'vital in the battle against terrorism and serious crime' and carried out

---

[86] RIPA 2000, ss 15–18. See generally, Ormerod D and McKay S, 'Telephone Intercepts and their Admissibility' [2004] Crim LR 15.

[87] Sir John Chilcot, *Privy Council Review of Intercept as Evidence* (Cm 7324, 2008).

[88] See Ryder M 'RIPA Reviewed' (2008) Archbold News 4, 6.

[89] *Report of the Interception of Communications Commissioner for 2008* (HC 901, 2009) p 4.

[90] For a robust challenge to these arguments, see Fisher J, 'Intercept Evidence' (2005) Counsel, September issue, p 9.

[91] *Secretary of State for Home Department v AF and Ors* [2009] UKHL 28. See the Home Secretary's response (*The Guardian*, 10 June 2009) and discussion in 4.3.3.

[92] Liberty argues for judicial involvement, noting that most comparable common law jurisdictions require judicial authority and judicial oversight would strengthen the case for intercept as evidence (London: Liberty, 2009: 10).

[93] *Report of the Interception of Communications Commissioner for 2008* (HC 901, 2009) p 9. A further 844 were reported as being in force.   [94] Ibid, pp 6–8.

'diligently and in accordance with the law' (para 7.1). This conclusion appears to be overly complacent.

The 'war on terror' after 9/11 prompted President Bush to authorise extensive phone tapping of citizens which he claimed was in accordance with the US constitution, although a Federal Court disagreed.[95] It seems likely that similarly dubious intelligence gathering was authorised by the UK Government to support the war in Iraq. Intercepts by British intelligence agencies are governed by regulations similar to those governing the police, but they are explicitly allowed to commit acts abroad that would be illegal in the UK.[96] So they get plenty of practice in conducting, and attempting to conceal, illegal interception.

6.3.2 Covert surveillance

Part II of RIPA and its Code of Practice regulates covert surveillance, which it defines as watching or listening in a manner designed to ensure that the objects of surveillance are unaware of the activity, with the purpose of gathering evidence or intelligence. Only surveillance aimed at securing 'private information' is regulated.[97] Authorisation may be sought to engage in covert surveillance only when it is proportionate and necessary, and collateral intrusion must be minimised. But evidence and intelligence obtained through surveillance for one purpose can be used in other investigations. Records of authorisations and the products of surveillance must be kept and be available to scrutiny by, for example, an inspector from the Office of the Surveillance Commissioner (an office established under RIPA).

A good example of common practice is the bugging of police station visiting rooms, cells and exercise yards. There is no restriction on recording conversations between suspects or between suspects and others (such as family members, friends, or informers 'planted' by the police). In *Button*, for example, covert surveillance of a police station waiting room was authorised for two murder suspects.[98] The covert surveillance of conversations between detainees and their legal advisers used to be thought to be subject to legal privilege. However in *Re C, Re M, Re McE*, detainees sought and were denied assurances that their consultations with solicitors would not be subject to covert surveillance. The House of Lords ruled that RIPA establishes exceptions to legal privilege and does not prevent the monitoring of legal consultations, but the authorisation procedure for covert surveillance of legal consultations should be the enhanced process which applies to 'intrusive' surveillance and not the internal authorisation procedure that 'directed' surveillance ordinarily requires.[99] The covert surveillance of lawyer/client communications demands a robust accountability procedure, although when such a regime is put in place (as the Secretary of State has promised) a 'chilling'

---

[95] 'Anti-terror Wiretaps Ruled Illegal': *The Guardian*, 18 August 2006.
[96] Intelligence Services Act 1994, s 7.   [97] RIPA 2000, s 26.
[98] [2005] Crim LR 572. The principle is the same as when a suspect talks to a 'plant' without a bugging device. See *Allan* [2005] Crim LR 716.   [99] [2009] UKHL 15.

effect on legal consultations will still be likely. It is also questionable whether this further erosion of defendants' rights is justifiable from a human rights or freedom perspective.

As the preceding paragraph implies RIPA distinguishes between different types of surveillance activity, of which one is the use of informers (CHIS, discussed in 6.2 above). We discuss the other categories, including directed and intrusive surveillance, below.

Property interference

This concerns actions that would otherwise amount to trespass or criminal damage, such as entering property to bug it or download information from a computer, or putting a tracking device into a car. The procedures and criteria are similar to the interception of communications. A Chief Constable or equivalent can authorise such actions for three months as long as they are proportionate and necessary to prevent or detect serious crime, and as long as the object could not reasonably be achieved by other means.[100] Details must be given of the targets, the property and the nature of the interference with it, the offences in question, and so forth. Authorisations, renewals and cancellations must be notified to the Surveillance Commissioners. In some special cases, such as when particularly sensitive material might be involved (see the three categories of material discussed in 6.5 below), only a surveillance commissioner is allowed to authorise property interference. There were 2,681 property interference authorisations in 2008/09 and 666 renewals.[101]

Intrusive surveillance

This means surveillance of private premises or a private vehicle by a person in that property or by a bugging device that gives information of the quality and detail that would be provided by a person in that property.[102] Thus while the surveillance actions might not amount to crimes or torts, they would otherwise breach Art 8 of the ECHR (right to privacy). Subject-unaware CCTV surveillance of private property or premises is included in this category. However, if, as in *Rosenburg*, someone else directs CCTV cameras at a suspect (or installs a bugging device or similar), and the police use the evidence thus obtained, no authorisation is needed. The Court of Appeal has held that this is not 'police' surveillance, hence it is not covered by RIPA.[103] It is hard to imagine a more pedantic and irrational distinction than this one, between 'police' and 'used by police'.

The procedures and criteria for 'intrusive surveillance' are similar to those for property interference but all authorisations must be sought from a surveillance commissioner except in an emergency. Most authorisations for these two categories of surveillance are for murder, drugs offences and terrorism. There were 384 intrusive surveillance authorisations granted in 2008/09 and 71 renewals.[104]

---

[100] Police Act 1997, Part III, as amended by Part 1 of the Policing and Crime Act 2009.
[101] Chief Surveillance Commissioner (2009).   [102] RIPA 2000, s 26.
[103] *Rosenburg* [2006] EWCA Crim 6.   [104] Chief Surveillance Commissioner (2009).

Directed surveillance

This is not 'intrusive' but authorisation is required when it might reveal private matters protected by Art 8. It includes surveillance over non-private premises, such as business premises. It is generally case-specific, as distinct from 'intrusive' surveillance (that need not be). There is no requirement that the crime under investigation be serious, but the procedures and criteria are otherwise similar to those for the other categories except that authorisation can be made by a middle-ranking officer (similar to those authorising the use of informers). There were 16,118 authorisations during the period April 2008 to end of March 2009 in addition to 2,708 authorisations that were still in place.[105]

6.3.3 The problems with, and potential gains from, covert policing

The problems with these provisions are legion, in part because of the danger of corruption whenever activity is low-visibility, as this type of work is, by definition. Also, there is little control over the information sought, how it is used, and with whom it is shared. With the rise of the 'information society', the police share the information they gather with a variety of agencies. Much police organisational effort is devoted to creating structures for the collation and dissemination of 'intelligence'.[106] Connections are made that will often be a complete surprise to the people under surveillance, and it can all go horribly wrong. In the wake of the July 2005 bombings in London, faulty police intelligence led armed officers to shoot dead one innocent person (Jean Charles de Menezes) and arrest, detain, interrogate and abuse numerous others such as Girma Belay (discussed in 1.9.2).

We do not know how often people are bugged and phonetapped without good reason because there is so little opportunity to know when this happens, let alone scrutinise the basis for authorisation. The Chief Surveillance Commissioner states that he is 'satisfied that the use made of the legislation for which he has oversight is proper and of a good standard'. Yet he acknowledges that he has insufficient resources to carry out more than a dip sample of authorisations, or even to investigate cases of concern that attract high profile media attention. Recent high profile alleged 'abuses' of RIPA powers have concerned local authorities that, for example, use directed surveillance to catch parents using false addresses to get their children into favoured state schools.[107] Then there is targeting of political campaigners by the police, who, as noted earlier, regularly obtain photographs and video footage of protesters which is then stored on surveillance databases.[108] Many of these surveillance activities are carried out overtly, such as the much criticised police surveillance of the climate change demonstrations in Kent in August 2008.[109] The issues with overt surveillance are of

---

[105] Ibid.   [106] See, for example, Gill (2000: esp ch 4).   [107] *The Guardian*, 21 July 2009.
[108] *The Guardian*, 6 March 2009.
[109] See <http://www.guardian.co.uk/environment/2009/jul/22/kingsnorth-police> (accessed 5 January 2010).

course different from those raised by covert surveillance, but the Court of Appeal has held that the police taking of photographs of campaigners attending peaceful meetings may constitute a violation of Art 8 of the ECHR, and that the retention of images when a person had not committed an offence for the purposes of identifying them if they committed an offence at a future event was not proportionate.[110] The House of Lords Constitution Committee recommended that the Commissioners with oversight of various surveillance activities adopt a more flexible inspection regime to investigate cases where there is widespread concern about the disproportionate use of powers. Defenders of covert policing argue that the safeguards discussed in this section guard against these dangers. But there are many obvious criticisms of these safeguards:

- Those who authorise activities (senior officers and the Secretary of State), and those who oversee them (the Commissioners and the tribunal) do not have the independence of courts or judicial officers.

- Even if these people and institutions were to be given a greater degree of independence, the only information on which they can base decisions is provided by the individuals and agencies that seek the authorisations or warrants. So, in one case an MP's conversation with a detainee was bugged. The senior officers and the office of the Surveillance Commissioner, who all authorised the bugging, did not know that an MP was being spied upon.[111]

- The agency itself will often have neither the ability nor the will to probe its officers about why the intercept or surveillance is sought or why and how the particular targets were chosen.

- The 'necessity' requirement is as meaningless as the 'necessity' requirement for police station detention discussed in ch 4.

- The proportionality requirement may deter the police from seeking surveillance hammers to crack petty crime nuts (in the unlikely event that the police were that bothered about petty crime) but whether it achieves more than this seems doubtful.

- There is no real control over the use to which information obtained by these means is put.

- Not using this information (particularly intercept information) as evidence in court, and keeping the fact of these activities from their subjects, means that when there is abuse of these powers the victims of abuse are unlikely ever to know about the interception or the abuse and will therefore not be in a position to seek redress.

- Courts are overly trusting of the police, particularly in accepting PII applications.

---

[110] *Wood v Commissioner of the Metropolitan Police* [2009] EWCA Civ 414. However the taking by police of photographs in public places does not per se engage Art 8.   [111] *The Guardian*, 22 February 2008.

- The inability of victims of abuse to seek redress and the absence of judicial oversight increases the incentives for all involved – from individual officers to the Secretary of State – to abuse these powers.[112]

A police sergeant in charge of a local drugs squad asked one of the authors to guess how often his requests for directed surveillance authorisations were rejected. A tentative 'hardly ever' was derisively swatted away: 'Never! It's just a waste of time – bureaucracy.' This sergeant said that his senior officers trusted him, and that they were right to do so. He also said that the problem was not too much surveillance but too few resources to do as much as they would like, so it was not undertaken lightly. The government's review of RIPA powers and associated codes poses the question 'What more should we do to reduce bureaucracy for the police so that they can use RIPA more easily to protect the public against criminals?'[113] The priority seems to be facilitating increased surveillance rather than ensuring that it is necessary and proportionate.[114] Whether this expansion of surveillance does result in more effective law enforcement is debatable. The shift to surveillance (proactive policing) may lead to crimes reported by the public (reactive policing) being less often detected.[115]

6.4 **Witness and identification evidence**

We saw in ch 2 that a huge number of crimes and possible crimes come to police notice through reports from members of the public. Some members of the public make a habit of looking for crimes and criminals and reporting anything vaguely suspicious to the police, something that neighbourhood watch schemes encourage. In addition, the police, along with local authorities, support 'Crimestoppers', a charitable organisation that facilitates the provision of information about crime to the police, anonymously if that is the wish of the informant.[116] This provides another way of cultivating informants – the Crimestoppers phone number is advertised on the ceiling of every police cell in London.[117] Then there are the mass of one-off reports of possible crimes

---

[112] For an example of how some of these problems come together with other forms of policing discussed in this chapter, see 6.5.

[113] *Regulation of Investigatory Powers Act 2000: Consolidating Orders and Codes of Practice – Consultation* (London: Home Office, 2009) p 4. As part of this Part 1 of the Policing and Crime Act 2009 seeks to facilitate the work of police collaborative units.

[114] Although it seems that for local authorities the levels of authorisation required for surveillance may be raised and elected counsellors given a oversight role in response to criticisms that some councils have been using their powers inappropriately. (Ibid, p 6.)

[115] Amey et al, *Development and Evaluation of a Crime Management Model* (Police Research Series Paper 18, London: Home Office, 1996).

[116] For a rosy picture written by police officers involved with Crimestoppers, see Griffiths B and Murphy A, 'Managing Anonymous Informants through Crimestoppers' in Billingsley et al (2001).

[117] Ibid, p 141.

experienced by victims or witnessed by members of the public ranging from care-less driving, drunkenness and dog fouling through to burglary, armed robbery and worse.

This brings into relief the classic problem of policing: how do, and how should, the police sift information sufficiently thoroughly so as not to miss anything important but sufficiently speedily so as not to overstretch their resources? As we saw in chs 2 and 3, the answer is to stereotype – to judge what they see, or are told, by reference to what they know of the source or think they know. Thus information from public-spirited 'police buffs' is greeted with 'weary dismay' as it is rarely thought to be of much val-ue.[118] Not only do the police have to decide who and what to take notice of, they then have to decide *how* to take notice of it. In this section we are concerned with one aspect of this only: the method and regulation of securing evidence from witnesses who are not victims. In ch 13 we examine victims (and, to some extent, non-victim witnesses) from the point of view of their involvement in the criminal justice system in general, and in giving evidence in court in particular.

6.4.1 Witnesses in general

We saw in ch 5 that police questioning of suspects is not a simple matter of eliciting objective facts from people. Some 'facts' may be matters of opinion or interpretation, such as a mental state or a response to perceived aggression. Some people will not be sure of the 'facts'. Some people may be highly suggestible and/or easily intimidated or eager to please. The police will often be objectively seeking the truth, but, unaware of these problems, will inadvertently put words or ideas into the minds and mouths of interviewees. Sometimes they are so eager to secure evidence of what they think is the truth that they do this deliberately. And sometimes they simply 'gild the lily' for a variety of thoroughly bad reasons. This is all as true of the interviewing of non-suspects as it is of suspects even though issues of coercion and ill-treatment will rarely arise with non-suspects. Such issues sometimes arise, however, where the police come to believe that a witness is hiding the truth, as some undoubtedly do. Most police officers, in common with many lay people, believe that they can 'spot a liar', but rely on techniques that are now discredited by modern research.[119] Thus both truthful and untruthful witnesses can come under pressure to change their stories.

When these problems came to light in relation to suspects the pre-PACE practice of suspects 'writing a statement' was largely abandoned, because such statements were to a greater or lesser extent written by the police themselves. Contemporaneous notes of interviews and, now, recordings and transcripts of the interviews replaced the unreli-able statements. Whilst the same problems apply to non-suspect witness interview

---

[118] Dorn et al, *Traffickers: Drug Markets and Law Enforcement* (London: Routledge, 1992).

[119] See 5.5 for discussion in relation to interviewing of suspects. And see Costigan (2007), and Heaton-Armstrong A et al (eds), *Witness Testimony* (Oxford: OUP, 2006) for reviews of the psychological evidence and its reception by the courts.

statements, the practice continues with them. Few witnesses write their own state-ments; instead the interviewer usually writes a 'good' statement. For many officers a 'warts and all' statement is a waste of time or even counterproductive. For them, a statement should satisfy, or at least not damage, the police case and the prosecu-tion evidence.[120] Research on learning-disabled witnesses has revealed that, where the police regarded the witness as credible, they would sometimes write the statement in language that the witness could not possibly have used. This creates opportunities for defence lawyers to discredit the testimony of the witness at trial as well as having the potential to distort what the witness is trying to say.[121] There are powerful arguments for recording all key witness statements in at least the most serious cases so their value can be properly evaluated in court.[122]

For these reasons, the developments in 'cognitive interviewing' discussed in ch 5 are as applicable to non-suspect interviewees as to suspects. As Milne and Bull say, '... sug-gestibility is not a property of children but is a property of their interviewing'. This is equally applicable to adults, for as they also say, 'All interviewees are vulnerable.'[123] Eliciting what the interviewee really saw/heard/knows is best done through open-ended non-leading questions, but the police also have to challenge and test what is said as any purported witness may lie or exaggerate for any number of reasons. Research indicates that, just as with the questioning of suspects, these lessons are not being internalised effectively by the police. Clarke and Milne evaluated the effectiveness of 'cognitive interviewing' training and found 'damning' evidence of police interviewers apparently looking to interviewees to confirm police suspicions, rather than to pro-vide their own accounts.[124]

All witnesses have to be treated with some caution. In 2002 four teenagers were prosecuted for the murder of a 10-year-old boy, Damilola Taylor. Much of the case rested on the evidence of one young witness, on which great doubt was cast by cross-examination. The case consequently collapsed. The fact that the guilt of the teenag-ers could not be proved did not, in itself, mean they were necessarily innocent, but the subsequent discovery of scientific evidence against people unconnected with the accused has established this beyond significant doubt (see discussion of this case in 6.6 below).

If witnesses are lying, as distinct from mistaken or confused, then cognitive inter-viewing will probably not work. This is why the police tend to adopt hostile interview-ing techniques when they believe that witnesses are lying. A good example is Dwayne Brooks, who witnessed the murder of his friend, Stephen Lawrence, but who was treated,

---

[120] Shepherd E and Milne R, 'Full and Faithful: Ensuring Quality Practice and Integrity of Outcome in Witness Interviews' in Heaton-Armstrong et al (eds), *Analysing Witness Testimony* (London: Blackstone, 1999) pp 132–3.   [121] Sanders et al, *Victims with Learning Difficulties* (Oxford: CCR, 1997).

[122] Heaton-Armstrong A and Wolchover D, 'Woeful Neglect' (2007) 157 NLJ 624.

[123] Milne R and Bull R, *Investigative Interviewing: Psychology and Practice* (Chichester: Wiley, 1999) pp 150 and 189.

[124] Clarke C and Milne R, *National Evaluation of the PEACE Investigative Interviewing Scheme* (PRAS Paper 149) (London: Home Office, 2001).

in a hostile manner, as a suspect by the police (see ch 13). In another example, a defendant charged with assault told the police that there were four witnesses who would support his claim of self-defence. They were all associates of the defendant and the police believed that they had perjured themselves for him before. They therefore interviewed them in an 'assertive and confrontational' way, and one of the interviewing officers misled, or lied to, one witness in an attempt to get him to 'tell the truth'.[125] The police clearly tried to get the witnesses to change their stories in order to support their own case theory. Unusually, this was all documented on tape because the police treated the witnesses as perjury suspects; most brow-beating of witnesses remains off-the-record.

We have focused on the way the police sometimes manipulate witnesses to make statements that fit police preconceptions to the detriment of the suspect. But sometimes the problem is the reverse. Vulnerable witnesses, such as children and the learning disabled, are often perceived by the police to be incapable of being 'good' witnesses so little attempt is made to take statements from them and those who victimise them remain unpunished.[126] This is, to some extent, because the only experience the police have is of traditional interviewing techniques, which are poor at eliciting accurate information from intimidated or suggestible people. Again, cognitive interviewing offers better opportunities to secure accurate evidence than do traditional interviewing techniques, but the police have been sluggish in taking up these opportunities and are only slowly beginning to realise that many witnesses who appear 'normal' are actually vulnerable.[127]

6.4.2 Identification evidence

Eyewitness identification is a particular aspect of witness evidence that deserves separate treatment. For it is of some importance in around 25% of all Crown Court cases,[128] yet, historically, it has been a major source of miscarriages of justice.[129] The combination of witnesses having unreasonably strong beliefs in themselves, combined with the tendency, discussed above, of the police to lead witnesses to support their cases is a recipe for error and injustice.[130] So are the classic courtroom drama scenarios where victims are asked if they can identify their attackers, whereupon the accusing finger is pointed at the dock, accompanied by a sharp intake of breath from the public gallery and a bewildered look from the suspect.[131]

---

[125] *Higgins* [2003] EWCA Crim 2943, discussed more fully in 5.5.   [126] Sanders et al (1997).

[127] Burton et al, 'Implementing Special Measures for Vulnerable and Intimidated Witnesses: The Problem of Identification' [2006] Crim LR 229.

[128] Zander M and Henderson P, *Crown Court Study* (RCCJ Research Report) (London: HMSO, 1993).

[129] Criminal Law Revision Committee, *Eleventh Report (General)*, Cmnd 4991 (London: HMSO, 1972) Valentine, T and Heaton P 'An Evaluation of the Fairness of Police Line-Ups and Video Identifications' (1999) 13 Applied Cognitive Psychology 59.

[130] See Hain P, *Mistaken Identity* (London: Quartet, 1976).

[131] This manifestly unsatisfactory form of identification evidence is frowned upon by the courts (eg *Reid* [1994] Crim LR 442) but is admissible at the discretion of the trial judge.

Where victim and defendant are not otherwise known to each other, an advance on dock identification, where there is only one candidate for the dubious honour of being fingered, was needed. And so the ID parade was born. Occasionally, in the past, police officers would 'fix' ID parades: packing them with people who looked nothing like their prime suspect, thus leading the witness to pick the suspect out, or showing the witness a photo of the suspect in advance. These abuses led to official inquiries, judicial guidelines, Home Office guidelines and then successive editions of PACE Code D that regulates ID parades in some detail – none of which stopped the police from putting a suspect in prison stripes in an ID parade as recently as 2000.[132]

All the concerns raised about witness evidence in general are equally applicable to eyewitness evidence. Memory decays over time, more than the individual witnesses often realise, and so people can be very suggestible. Moreover, witnesses are error-prone, as what is seen may have taken place in a split-second without prior warning. Psychological research shows that even when the police are trying not to influence witnesses they often inadvertently do so by, for example, their glance lingering on the suspect in an ID parade.[133] And CCTV creates nearly as many problems as it solves. For research shows that, for example, different images of the same person often resemble completely different people, yet many witnesses display high levels of confidence that do not match their accuracy. Courts have been remarkably flexible about the kind of evidence they have accepted, including from an expert on lip reading.[134]

The requirements of the Code of Practice

The 2008 version of the Code (para 3.1) requires a detailed note to be made of the first description of the suspect in every case where identification is likely to be an issue. This is so that any concrete identification made later can be compared to the witness' first statement, in an attempt to guard against 'contamination' by police manipulation. However, in the light of the earlier discussion about manipulation of witness statements this is a weak safeguard.[135] Para 3 then distinguishes between 3 situations:

- *Where the suspect is not known:* The police may, acting on a witness description, arrest someone and ask the witness if s/he is the person. Or the witness may

---

[132] *Kamara* [2000] WL 664383.

[133] Phillips et al, 'Double-Blind Photoarray Administration as a Safeguard Against Investigator Bias' (1999) 84 J Applied Psychology 940.

[134] *Luttrell and others* [2004] EWCA Crim 1344. For general discussion see Costigan (2007) and 6.3 above.

[135] One of the authors of this book once gave a (fairly vague) identification statement to a police officer having witnessed three youths breaking into a car outside his home at night. Another police officer present at the taking of the statement was given some details over his radio about the arrest of three youths nearby. On reading over the author's statement (as written down by his colleague) he asked 'didn't you say a moment ago that one of the youths had the words "Aston Villa" on the back of his coat?' The author had no recollection of saying any such thing although the question put doubt into his mind. Nonetheless, the lily remained ungilded on this point. On other points, such as the quality of street lighting, the author found much in 'his' statement that he certainly did not say.

be taken to the area where the offence occurred or be shown photographs etc. Should the suspect be identified in either of these ways, there is no point holding an ID parade for that witness, as s/he will have already picked out the suspect.[136] There is a clear danger of the police 'leading' witnesses in these procedures; this is discussed further below, but it is difficult to see what else can be done. If there are other witnesses, an identification parade for these other witnesses should be held, which does provide some safeguard.

• *Where the suspect is known to the police and is available:* A group identification (where the witness views an informal group of people, for example at a café or tube station) or identification parade can be held, but in this situation video identification is also acceptable. In fact the suspect will be initially offered video identification unless impracticable or an identification parade is more practicable and more suitable (Code D, 2008, para 3.14). Video identification has the advantage that a 'bank' of people can be built up to suit most types of suspect, enabling a speedy and appropriate set of images to be shown to witnesses.

• *Where the suspect is known but not available:* Here a video identification may be conducted.

Problems with the Code

Allowing the police to judge whether it is practical to hold an ID parade, albeit with court oversight at trial, is not ideal as is obvious from earlier discussions in this chapter and chs 1–5 about the way the police exercise discretion.[137] An example of police thinking was provided in a parade where the police could not find volunteers to match their black 6 ft 3 inch suspect, so they employed a make-up artist to change the colour of the faces of the others on the parade.[138] Lest it be thought that the police have improved in the last few years, a more recent example is *Marcus*.[139] The defendant was of unusual appearance. A video identification was arranged, but the police could not find sufficiently similar-looking people, so they 'masked' parts of their appearances, producing poor-quality footage. When the witnesses proved unable to make positive identifications on the basis of the masked footage, the police showed them 'unmasked' footage. The trial judge allowed the resulting identification evidence to be used in the trial, even though the police admitted that the defendant 'blatantly' stood out. The defendant's conviction was quashed by the Court of Appeal because this was a clear breach of Code D.[140]

---

[136] For an example see *Marsh v DPP* [2007] Crim LR 162.

[137] For discussion, see Roberts A, 'The Problems of Mistaken Identification: Some Observations on Process' (2004) 8 IJ E & P 100.   [138] *Daily Telegraph*, 25 July 1997.

[139] *Marcus* [2005] Crim LR 384.

[140] For discussion of this case and the procedural safeguards which ought to be in place to mitigate as far as possible against the deficiencies in identification evidence see Roberts A, 'Eyewitness Identification Evidence: Procedural Developments and the Ends of Adjudicative Advocacy' (2009) 6(2) International Commentary on Evidence article 3.

It would be possible to require that parades and video identifications be held 'blind' – ie organised by civilians who do not know who the suspect is. This is important, in the light of the earlier discussion about inadvertent leading of witnesses. But all the Code requires (para 3.11) is that the officer conducting the procedure not be involved in the investigation. A contemporaneous statement from witnesses about how confident they are that they have picked out the right person would also be valuable as psychological research shows that the confidence of witnesses in their choice increases once they learn that the person they identified is going on trial.[141]

Many of the examples we have given show that ID parades will always be prone to problems and bias. Volunteers on parades are inevitably more relaxed than suspects, and witnesses may get wind of this.[142] ID parades are particularly unfair for any type of suspect who is unusual in a particular area, particularly members of ethnic minorities as one is often not aware of significant differences between individuals of a different ethnic group from oneself, and ethnic minorities are overrepresented among the suspect population and under-represented in the police force. Video identification calls upon a huge bank of images that should cover most facial types, and is not 'live' and is therefore less prone to some of these problems and may produce more reliable results.[143] However, this does not make video identification entirely reliable, though some improvements are possible.[144] The identification of suspects from CCTV evidence adds an extra dimension to the problems, particularly where police officers are asked to watch CCTV film to identify suspects.[145] It is doubtful whether Code D is applicable in such circumstances, although the potential for abuse and miscarriages of justice makes a compelling case for some guidance.[146]

In the light of the above, there is the question of what weight to give identification evidence at trial. This was addressed by *Turnbull*,[147] which set out guidelines including the requirement that trial judges warn juries about the dangers of convicting on identification evidence, especially if it is weak. However the courts have shown reluctance to overturn convictions based on identification evidence even where Code D has been breached.[148] Also how 'weak' is weak? Weak in the sense of a witness not being certain,

---

[141] Wells et al, 'Distorted Retrospective Eyewitness Reports as Functions of Feedback and Delay' (2003) 9 J Experimental Psychology: Applied 42. Post-identification feedback also affects the witness's recollection of matters incidental to the witnessing of the original crime event such as how long and good a view they had of the offender, thus inflating the apparent credibility of their testimony in court.

[142] See examples given by Tinsley Y, 'Even Better than the Real Thing? The Case for Reform of Identification Procedures' (2001) 5 IJ E & P 235.   [143] Valentine and Heaton (1999).

[144] It has been argued that the use of sequential presentation of images (where the witness is required to make a decision before being shown the next image) may reduce the number of false positive identifications, but Code D requires all images to be shown at least twice before an identification is made. See Roberts (2009).   [145] *Smith and Ors* [2008] EWCA Crim 1342; [2009] Crim LR 437. And see Costigan (2007).

[146] See *The Guardian*, 18 August 2009, reporting on the wrongful conviction of a man for bank robbery based on police identification from CCTV images. DNA evidence subsequently implicated a convicted bank robber.   [147] *Turnbull* [1977] 2 QB 224.

[148] See for example *Williams* [2003] EWCA Crim 3200, discussed by Roberts (2009). He convincingly argues that where no significant adverse consequences follow the use of unreliable processes there is little

or in the sense that the witness is certain but on the basis of a fleeting glimpse? Davies, on the basis of the psychological research literature and his own experience as an expert witness, argues that consideration be given to requiring corroboration for all identification evidence. He points to the large number of convictions wholly or largely on this basis that are overturned on appeal – where the convicted person may have spent months or years in prison[149] – and the large number that are not overturned, where there are at least some grounds for thinking they should be.[150] It is true that in some of the most serious cases, such as rape, there are often no witnesses other than the victim, but advances in DNA technology make identification through scientific methods both practical and difficult for rapists to avoid if they are identified.

6.5 **Entry, search and seizure**

Police in Britain paid out more than £500,000 last year to repair doors, ceilings and even mantelpiece ornaments smashed in [3,607] raids based on wrong information. Bungles include a string of operations at properties next door to the real targets, leaving householders terrified...Northamptonshire police replaced eight doors, including one in Wellingborough belonging to Carly Payne, a 24 year old nursery nurse, who was breastfeeding her five-day-old daughter Bella when police stormed in. They arrested her partner, stepfather and a friend before realising the drug raid warrant was for next door.[151]

It has long been recognised in English law that the tort of trespass stops everyone – including the police – entering one's private property or searching one's person without good reason. It does not matter if the trespass is slight, does no tangible harm, or is done without the occupier knowing of it. The ECHR, Art 8, which we saw in 6.3 protects privacy, has a similar legal effect.[152] This is recognised in the PACE Code of Practice for entry and search (Code B) (COP), which states that these powers 'should be fully and clearly justified before use because they may significantly interfere with the occupier's privacy. Officers should consider if the necessary objectives can be met by less intrusive means' (para 1.3). It is recommended that consent be secured, if possible, before a warrant to enter and search is sought, and when executing the warrant. We shall see later that 'consent' is not straightforward.

The questions that arise for us are: for what reasons do the police seek to enter property and/or make searches, what counts in law as a 'good reason', and what does the law and practice tell us about criminal justice in general? In this section we will look

---

incentive for the police to change their ways. The process in Williams could hardly have been more suggestive (showing the suspect in handcuffs).

[149] For a recent example see *Ali* [2009] Crim LR 40.

[150] Davies G, 'Mistaken Identification: Where Law Meets Psychology Head On' (1996) 35 Howard J 232.

[151] *The Guardian*, 29 December 2009.

[152] For a discussion of the history and constitutional background of the law, see Sharpe (2000: ch 1).

at searches of property, but not at searches of people.[153] Street searches are covered in ch 2, and police station searches in ch 4. In general, powers of entry (whether with a warrant or not) allow search of premises but not of people on those premises unless *either* the premises are those to which the public has access (in which case stop-search powers can be exercised) *or* the relevant people have already been arrested. However, some legislation granting powers of entry, such as the Misuse of Drugs Act 1971, does permit search of people but only if the warrant specifies this.

The police enter property in order to: prevent breaches of the peace (not dealt with here, but see ch 3 for discussion of arrest for this), 'bug' it (see 6.3 above), question occupants, search it for evidence of crime and make arrests. For many years, entry, search and arrest were all regarded as similar as all three can amount to trespass (to the person or to property), and so a warrant was needed in all but exceptional circumstances. As with arrest warrants, search warrants have become increasingly rare as – in accord with criminal justice policy in general and crime control ideology – the police have been given more power to make decisions free of judicial oversight. Before PACE was enacted warrants were used in about 17% of searches, and now they seem to be used even less often.[154] But search warrants are still significant, not just because they are used a lot by comparison with arrest warrants, but also because many people no doubt allow search of their premises in the belief that the police have the power to obtain a search warrant anyway.

6.5.1 Entry and search without consent

To make an arrest (without a search warrant)

PACE, s 17[155] allows the police to enter any premises to 'save life and limb',[156] to prevent serious damage to property, or in order to arrest someone whom they reasonably believe to be there. This will often be to recapture someone 'unlawfully at large' (eg a prison escapee), or to arrest someone for an indictable offence. No search warrant is needed, and it would often be impractical to require one – when, for example, the police are in hot pursuit of someone they or a witness thought they saw committing an offence. Sometimes they will have an arrest warrant when seeking someone for an indictable offence or who is unlawfully at large, or for other reasons (eg because of unpaid fines, breach of injunction or failure to answer a court summons), so s 17 also allows them to enter premises to execute that warrant. In none of these circumstances

---

[153] The discussion of the legal provisions in this section is highly abbreviated. For detailed accounts of their complexities see Clark (2004: ch 4); and Stone, R, *The Law of Entry, Search and Seizure* (Oxford: OUP, 2005). Note that many governmental bodies, including gas, electricity, tax and trading standards authorities, have powers to seek search warrants. Research carried out in the 1980s found that less than 10% of all search warrants were issued to the police: Lidstone K, 'Magistrates, the Police and Search Warrants' [1984] Crim LR 449.   [154] Brown (1997: 34); Clark (2004: 122).

[155] As amended (expanded) by SOCPA 2005, Sch 7, para 43(4).

[156] Which covers saving someone from themselves as well as saving from a third party: *Baker v CPS* [2008] EWHC 299.

is a search warrant needed. The 'reasonableness' requirement in s 17, like similar requirements dealt with below, is similar to that of reasonable suspicion to stop-search and arrest (dealt with in chs 2 and 3). Thus there is no need for the evidence on which it is based to be admissible in court, nor for it to be corroborated. A tip-off from an informer, for example, will in many circumstances be adequate, and – according to a sergeant in charge of a local drugs squad in conversation with one of the authors – frequently this is the sole basis for a raid.

After arrest (without a search warrant)

People who are arrested other than at a police station may be searched at once.[157] Also the premises in which they were arrested, or left immediately before they were arrested (whoever happens to own or occupy it), may be entered and searched if the offence is an indictable one.[158] This is in order to search for evidence relating to the alleged offence in question but only if there are reasonable grounds for believing that there is such evidence there.[159] This need not be done immediately, as the police often secure evidence from questioning following arrest that would produce the suspicion required to justify a search. Stone rightly states that the time period should not be open-ended, as the police can secure a search warrant if there is time to assemble a case for doing this. Stone implicitly bases his normative argument on a due process and freedom foundation, but he then makes a logical leap to state that this *is* the law.[160] Since the only authority he cites for this is a Crown Court case from 1987[161] we have less confidence that the courts would eschew crime control thinking.

The police may, in addition, search *any* premises occupied or controlled by someone arrested for an indictable offence.[162] The power is subject to the usual 'reasonable grounds' provision and, like s 32, it can be exercised immediately after arrest or while the suspect is detained in the police station. In the latter case it must be authorised in writing by an officer of at least the rank of inspector. This seems to be the most common form of entry and search (Brown, 1997: 34).

In other circumstances (with a warrant)

The police often seek warrants when they seek evidence to assist the detection of a suspected crime, or the construction of a prosecution case, but have not yet made an arrest. They also sometimes need to seek a warrant because a substantial time has elapsed since an arrest or because they want to search premises not occupied, controlled or recently vacated by an arrestee (see above). Warrants can be obtained, in other words, to search premises occupied by people who are not suspected of any crime at all.

Applications for search warrants are normally made to a magistrate. Applications should specify the grounds for the application, the premises to be searched, and the

---

[157] PACE, s 32(1) and (2)(a).   [158] PACE, s 32(2)(b) as amended by SOCPA 2005, Sch 7, para 43(6).
[159] PACE, s 32(6).   [160] Stone (2005: 128).   [161] *Badham* [1987] Crim LR 202.
[162] PACE, s 18 (as amended by SOCPA 2005, Sch 7, para 43(5)). Again, in order to search for evidence relating to the alleged offence in question or an offence connected with, or similar to, that offence.

articles and persons sought (as far as practical).[163] The importance ascribed to this by the courts is illustrated by *Chief Constable of Thames Valley v Hepburn*,[164] where a warrant to search a pub specified 'search for drugs and associated paraphernalia' but did not mention search of anyone working or drinking there. A customer who was injured while being restrained prior to search was held to have been unlawfully assaulted by the police because holding him to search him was not authorised by the warrant.

Applications should normally be authorised by an officer of at least the rank of an inspector.[165] Under PACE as originally enacted warrants authorised entry to a specified premise or premises on one occasion only and were valid for only one month.[166] SOCPA 2005, s 114 now allows multiple entries of the same premises for a period of up to three months. It also allows the police to obtain an 'all premises' warrant allowing access to all premises occupied or controlled by a person (including premises unspecified in the application for the warrant). The potential for police harassment in these new provisions is obvious. Searches are meant, however, to take place at 'a reasonable hour'.[167] The 'reasonable hour' provision was an attempt to curb the police habit of raiding homes in the middle of the night, as this can be terrifying for the occupants, who may include young children. But as a case decided that a 6am raid was not 'unreasonable' because the early hour made it likely the householder(s) would be at home,[168] the police are not likely to be overly restrained by this provision. In any case PACE provides that the reasonable hour restriction does not apply if it appears to the police that the purposes of the search would be frustrated unless an 'unreasonable hour' was selected for the invasion to take place.[169] The spectre thus arises of repeated midnight raids on the homes of suspects, some of whom will be completely innocent of any crime. According to the drugs squad sergeant cited earlier, raids for drugs, at any rate, were always made in the early hours when the occupants were likely to be asleep and thus unable to flush drugs down the toilet.

The provisions described above are applicable to all requests for search warrants except where certain categories of material are sought (see below). Before issuing a warrant the magistrate must be satisfied as to certain conditions. PACE, s 8, which applies to 'indictable' offences only, requires reasonable grounds for believing that:

(a) the material sought will be of substantial value and admissible as evidence;

(b) the material sought is not one of various special categories of material (see below); and

(c) it is not practical to secure entry by consent without the purpose of the search being frustrated or prejudiced (eg through the concealment or destruction of the evidence).

---

[163] PACE, s 15.   [164] *Chief Constable of Thames Valley v Hepburn* [2002] EWCA Civ 1841.
[165] COP, para 3.   [166] PACE, ss 15 and 16.   [167] PACE, s 16(4).
[168] *Kent Pharmaceuticals Ltd v Director of the SFO* [2002] EWHC 3023.   [169] PACE, s 16(4).

The police need not show that other methods of obtaining the material were unsuccessfully tried, nor that such methods had been considered and rejected because they were bound to fail.[170] In other words, if the police say that they reasonably believe that they will need the power to enter without consent there is little magistrates can do to probe further – this virtual police self-certification is a classic crime control provision. In addition to these s 8 powers, many other statutes allow magistrates to issue search warrants for specific offences. Many of these are not particularly serious – they include theft, controlled drugs, obscene publications, forgery and counterfeiting, criminal damage, offensive weapons and numerous others that are fairly minor.

Research has, not surprisingly, found that virtually all applications for warrants – over 99% – are granted.[171] Thus Lidstone (1984) found that in only 4 out of 32 applications that were observed did the magistrates ask any questions of the police. Magistrates and judges are hampered in their ability to genuinely check on the police as all the information they receive is from the police. Hearings are ex parte (ie with the other party excluded). The property sought is often described vaguely (eg 'electrical goods'). Moreover, the majority of applications state, in a formulaic manner, that they are based on 'information received'. This, as we saw in 6.2, means information from one or more informers, and magistrates and judges are reluctant to risk blowing informants' cover, which the police would refuse to divulge anyway.[172] This refusal is based on 'public interest immunity', which would be upheld as ECHR, Art 6 only comes into play when guilt or innocence is at stake, not in matters of search.[173] The nature of information from informers is such that the police also frequently do not know how reliable the information is anyway. Lidstone (1984) found that there was usually little indication that the police seek to verify it. In *Keegan v Chief Constable of Merseyside Police*[174] the police were given information about a suspect for armed robbery allegedly connected with two addresses. The police obtained search warrants, broke in to one of them with a battering ram at 7 a.m., and found a completely innocent family lived there. Had the police made the most basic enquiries – eg of the electoral roll – they would have discovered this. The magistrates who granted the warrant asked if the officers were confident the information was accurate and they assured them that their grounds were reasonable. The Court of Appeal held that the negligence of the officers neither invalidated the warrant nor gave cause for any other action.[175] Lidstone also found that magistrates' working rules were similar to those of the police – for example, being happy to issue a warrant to search a house for drugs in a notorious area, but not in a 'respectable' area.[176] He also found them to be remarkably trusting of the police,

---

[170] *Billericay Justices ex p Frank Harris (Coaches) Ltd* [1991] Crim LR 559.　　[171] Clark (2004: 123).
[172] Lidstone (1984). See Brown (1997: 33) for similar findings.
[173] Clark (2004: 126); Sharpe (2000: 54–61).
[174] *Keegan v Chief Constable of Merseyside Police* [2003] 1 WLR 2187.
[175] The ECtHR subsequently found that Art 8 was violated because, although the police were not acting maliciously, their actions were not necessary in a democratic society because their misconception could have been avoided with proper precautions (*Keegan v UK* (2007) 44 EHRR 33).
[176] Lidstone (1984: 452).

quoting one magistrate as saying: 'I would issue a warrant to a member of the drugs squad because he really is a specialist. You see them dressed like they do and you think "he's under cover". He is on the scene and is more likely to have good information.'

A quarter of a century ago, the Royal Commission on Criminal Procedure (RCCP) said, 'too often they [magistrates] merely rubber stamp police requests'.[177] The Commission therefore wanted the issue of most warrants to become the responsibility of judges, but this recommendation was not implemented. The lack of due process control over the police in this area of work was clearly of little concern to the government then, and remains so now. It could be that magisterial control has improved since the RCCP and Lidstone did their work, but this is not the impression given by the later research briefly reported by Clark referred to earlier, nor by the drugs squad sergeant to whom the authors are so indebted for snippets of practical information in this chapter. The latter confirmed that most magistrates (particularly salaried magistrates, who he aims to put warrant requests in front of, in preference to lay magistrates)[178] ask no questions even when warrants only cite 'information received' as, in drugs cases, is usual. If magistrates had to keep accurate notes of hearings, this would provide a basis both for challenge and monitoring of how well they fulfil their duties. But the government cannot even be bothered to require this, even though the appellate courts in several cases have recommended this as good practice.[179] Not that judicial control is necessarily a panacea, as in at least one of the special cases where they do hear applications (see 6.5.2 below) the judge simply rubber stamped the application within a couple of minutes without knowing, or inquiring into, the applicable law.[180]

Part of the problem is that the higher courts have not adopted a consistent due process approach when hearing appeals against decisions to grant warrants by magistrates and circuit court judges. For example, in one case a warrant was challenged on the ground that there was no evidence that the magistrate had applied his mind to the relevant criteria. Since the hearing was ex parte and no notes were kept of the hearing, there was no evidence to substantiate or to challenge the assertion. The Divisional Court held that the magistrate had applied his mind appropriately simply on the basis of affidavits from the police applicant and the magistrate.[181] The courts are therefore failing to take what opportunities there are to reduce the extent to which the police self-validate their applications.

6.5.2 Seizure without consent

The police have wide powers of seizure of *almost* anything that they have reasonable grounds for believing has been obtained as a result of a crime, or is evidence of a

---

[177] RCCP, *Report* (1981) para 3.37.

[178] See ch 9 for discussion of magistrates' attitudes in England and Wales and the lay/professional distinction.   [179] Eg *CC of Warwickshire Constabulary ex p Fitzpatrick* [1998] 1 All ER 65.

[180] *Southwark CC and HM Customs and Excise ex p Sorsky Defries* [1996] Crim LR 195.

[181] *Marylebone Magistrates' Court ex p Amdrell* [1998] 148 NLJ 1230. See Sharpe (2000: 50) for further discussion.

crime.[182] We saw earlier that searches may be made only for evidence of crimes related to those for which arrest has been made, or for which warrants were issued. But if the police nonetheless find evidence of completely unrelated crimes they may seize it and use it in court proceedings. The common law went some way towards this extreme crime control position,[183] and PACE, other legislation and recent case law have continued on that path.[184] All that COP says is that, if Code B and PACE are not adhered to, evidence gained may be 'open to question' (para 1.5). Powers of seizure can only be exercised to prevent concealment, loss, alteration or destruction of the material. However, a search might reveal large quantities of material, the relevance of which requires careful consideration. To cover this situation, the police now have a 'seize and sift' power to take away everything that might be relevant, knowing that much will be returned as irrelevant.[185]

The word 'almost' was emphasised above because there are three categories of material where seizure is closely controlled and for which the police cannot obtain ordinary search warrants:[186]

Items subject to legal privilege

These are communications between a legal adviser and a client or anything relating to actual or planned legal proceedings.[187] This material cannot be seized. However, if the police doubt claims that material falls into this category they may seize it for detailed inspection.[188]

Excluded material

This includes, if held in confidence: personal records held in the course of a legitimate business or trade (eg records held by clergymen, banks or doctors); human tissue or tissue fluid taken for medical reasons; and certain categories of journalistic material.[189]

Special procedure material

This includes journalistic material not covered above and other material held in confidence. Seizure of, and applications to search for, this material and 'excluded material' must be authorised by a judge. This must normally be done 'inter partes' ie with the other party present. 'Other party' means the person or institution holding the material, not the person or institution owning the material which is suspected to be involved in a crime. While the 'other party' is not allowed to conceal or destroy the material (or otherwise obstruct the investigation, as might occur if the owner of the

---

[182] PACE, s 19.   [183] *Jeffrey v Black* [1978] QB 490.

[184] Eg *HM Customs & Excise v Michael Atkinson and others* [2003] EWHC 421. See generally, Sharpe (2000: chs 2, 3).

[185] Criminal Justice and Police Act 2001, ss 50–70 and COP paras 7.7–7.13. This is particularly important with regard to computerised information, which often takes a long time to assess.

[186] PACE, s 9 and Sch 1.   [187] PACE, s 10.   [188] Criminal Justice and Police Act 2001, s 50.

[189] PACE, ss 11–12.

material is alerted to the application),[190] judges may permit destruction when they consider this appropriate.

Generally, then, the *owners* of 'excluded' and 'special procedure' material are little or no better able to contest seizure of material they may wish to keep from public gaze than owners of 'normal' material for which search warrants are sought. Arguably such people are less well off, as at least people whose premises are searched for 'normal' material know when that has happened and can challenge it after the event. Owners of 'excluded' and 'special procedure' material may not know that their material has been seized at all. On the other hand, more stringent conditions apply than with 'normal' material: an officer of at least the rank of superintendent must authorise the request, and permission will be granted only if the judge considers it to be in the public interest. Yet more stringent conditions apply with respect to 'excluded' material. In relation to both types of material, only in exceptional circumstances (similar to those applicable to a s 8 warrant) can a warrant be sought and granted ex parte.[191]

It is worth considering why such complex procedures are in place for these relatively obscure categories of material. Most search for, and seizure of, material in these categories relates to financial crime. Access to such material was very difficult prior to PACE, making enforcement of fraud very difficult. These provisions have therefore made the enforcement of fraud law easier than before, but still difficult, when fraud is difficult enough to enforce as it is. Perpetrators of fraud are generally wealthy individuals and companies, while perpetrators of assault, theft and other crimes (where the crime control procedures described in 6.5.1 above apply) are the relatively poor and socially marginalised members of society. Bearing in mind the themes of chs 2, 3 and 7, the pattern that emerges is so obvious we will not labour the point.[192]

6.5.3 Entry, search and seizure with 'consent'

It was stated earlier that the police should seek to search property by consent if this is practical. Even when the police have a search warrant, they should seek entry from the occupier, declaring their identity and authority, unless there are reasonable grounds to believe that this would obstruct the purpose of the search or endanger anyone.[193] According again to the drugs squad sergeant cited earlier, he never seeks entry by consent, but always smashes the door in, to prevent drugs being flushed away. When asked about the presence of children who might be terrified or injured by this, he said they

---

[190] Clark (2004: 198).

[191] For a detailed discussion of this complex area of law, see Stone (2005: 139–49). For critical comment see Zuckerman A, 'The Weakness of the PACE Special Procedure for Protecting Confidential Material' [1990] Crim LR 472.

[192] As for the restrictions on seizing journalistic material, the explanation here lies in the lobbying that newspapers engaged in during the run up to PACE to maximise the degree of protection for their own interests. Once again one can see that criminal justice reflects the interests of those who are powerful enough to make their voices heard in political debates.

[193] COP, parsa 6.4–6.8. This happens frequently: Brown (1997: 36–8).

always carry out a 'risk assessment': 'looking through the letter box – and then smash-ing the door in!' As the newspaper report quoted at the head of this section indicates, on thousands of occasions the police assessment of the risks is so woeful that wholly innocent householders have their doors broken down without warning.

Around one-third of all searches are by consent. The nature of 'consent' when sought 'in the shadow of the law' is often questionable. Many people doubtless allow the police to search their homes, believing that the police have the power to do so, or to get a war-rant to do so, when this may not be so. This is particularly true of suspects in custody, who are generally not told that they need not consent, but are simply presented with a form to sign.[194]

The problem here is not simply deception of suspects (who may, in some cases, have been arrested simply to facilitate a search and may not be suspected of anything crimi-nal), but also the circumvention of the legal safeguards described earlier. Whereas the most recent versions of Code of Practice A (for stop-search) prevents searches with consent where there is no power to search (see discussion in 2.2.3), Code of Practice B (for entry and search of premises) has no equivalent provision. As we know from chs 2 and 3, police working rules, rather than such rules as 'reasonable suspicion', frequently form the basis of police decision-making.

So, to the extent that entry and search rules are inhibitory, the police will seek to cir-cumvent them. In *Sanghera*,[195] for example, a postmaster reported an alleged robbery. Acting on what seems to have been a hunch, the police conducted a thorough 'consen-sual' search of the premises and found that the allegedly stolen money had been hid-den by the 'victim'. This case also illustrates the need to obtain an explicit consent (if no warrant has been obtained or if there is no statutory power to search without war-rant) rather than an implied consent, for the police completed an authorisation for the search and ticked the 'consent' box but omitted to obtain the alleged victim's actual consent. The Court of Appeal held that even though the victim would doubtless have consented to a search, the search was illegal without it. This finding was of little use to the appellant, however, as the Court took the view that since there was no question as to the reliability of the evidence seized, the conviction should be upheld. The finding of illegality will therefore do little to deter the police from abusing their powers in future. A further problem with 'consent' searches is that, if the police decide to seize material, and can lawfully do so, this can be done without the occupier's consent.[196]

6.5.4 Case studies and conclusion

In 2002 about 20 police officers entered and searched the Stormont (NI Assembly) offices of Sinn Fein. Official sources claimed that the aim was to break an Irish Republican spy ring, and that Sinn Fein had collected confidential information that would be used to target police and prison officers. Four people were charged with

---

[194] Clark (2004: 143–6). See also Lidstone (1984: 457).   [195] *Sanghera* [2001] 1 Cr App R 299.
[196] PACE, s 19(2) and (3).

various offences, but all charges were dropped in December 2005. It then emerged that one of those charged, Denis Donaldson, a senior Sinn Fein official, was an undercover member of the security services. Rather than Sinn Fein spying on the government, it seems, the government had been spying on democratically elected members of a regional legislature. We have here entry, search and seizure based on faulty information from an undercover agent and informer. And, according to an official enquiry, no one is to blame and no official agencies did anything illegal.[197] The murky morality and dangers inherent in this area of 'policing' could scarcely be better illustrated. A more recent example is the searching of the House of Commons offices of Damian Green MP. The police did not obtain a warrant but instead put the Sergeant-at-Arms under 'considerable pressure' to consent to the search – the police having left her with the impression that otherwise she would be obstructing a serious criminal investigation. The police seem not to have made it clear, as is required by COP, that there is no obligation to consent to a search without a warrant. As the Sergeant-at-Arms put it: 'At no time was I informed that I did not have to give my consent or that I could insist on a warrant or that I could withdraw my consent at any time.'[198] The police were searching for evidence relating to leaks of confidential government information, but the CPS subsequently decided that there was insufficient evidence to prosecute Mr Green and the Home Office official allegedly involved. The police were exonerated by an internal Metropolitan Police inquiry.[199]

The experience of having one's house broken into in the early hours by people in plain clothes not immediately identifiable as police officers (as sometimes happens) is often distressing and sometimes terrifying. *Murray v Minister of Defence*[200] is just one example. This is particularly important as the people at the receiving end are often not merely thought-guilty-but-actually-innocent (as with many stopped and searched, arrested and detained), but also sometimes not even believed to be guilty: as we have seen, the police are entitled to seek warrants to search the premises of entirely innocent people if they believe that evidence of criminal offences will be found there. The same applies when they pursue people who they seek to arrest. And even if the person(s) they seek are guilty, the premises where they live that are searched often have friends and family living there who are innocent.

As with all these things, the picture is not one-sided. In London the Metropolitan Police launched the anti-burglary 'Operation Bumblebee' in the early 1990s. It used sting operations and intelligence from a variety of sources, including covert policing and informers. Over several years it mounted thousands of highly publicised 'dawn raids', leading to several thousand arrests. Burglary rates in London were claimed to have fallen dramatically, and clear-up rates to have risen. But how far these improvements were due to the covert techniques, the mass searches of premises, or other less

---

[197] *The Guardian*, 20 December 2005.
[198] House of Commons, Minutes of Evidence taken before the Committee on Issue of Privilege (Police Searches on the Parliamentary Estate), 7 December 2009, Q.701. [199] *The Telegraph*, 16 April, 2009.
[200] [1988] 2 All ER 521, discussed in ch 3.

obvious factors, is inevitably a matter of conjecture. Certainly the claims of exponents of proactive policing far outstrip the available research findings on the matter. At present there is only 'limited and relatively weak evidence on the results of proactive investigation' for volume crimes such as burglary.[201]

6.6 **Scientific evidence**

'Scientific' evidence takes many forms, including analysis and matching of bodily fluids, fibres, and other materials; analysis of voice, visual and electronic evidence; medical, psychological and psychiatric evidence and so forth. Innovations such as DNA testing and the computerised matching of fingerprint records have increased the importance of scientific evidence in recent years. Particular confidence has been placed in the National DNA Database (NDNAD) and the increased use of DNA for both investigatory and evidence purposes, sometimes portrayed as having unrivalled ability to solve crime.[202] Scientific evidence can lead the police to suspect one or more individual, or provide particular lines of investigation, that may not produce evidence as such but which may be valuable or even essential in the detection of the crime.

Since the first use of mass DNA screening in the 1980s, which eventually led to the identification of Colin Pitchfork as a double rapist and murderer, there have been some notable successes for the Forensic Science Service (FSS) in identifying potential suspects and contributing to convictions.[203] However, it is important not to overestimate the significance of the role of science in investigating crime. To take a dramatic example, in November 2000 a 10-year-old boy, Damilola Taylor was murdered. Four teenagers were prosecuted but acquitted (see discussion of the case in 6.4 above). Years later, blood and fibres that could be linked with Damilola Taylor were found on the clothes of two teenagers unconnected with the original defendants but who had been arrested and then released in the original investigation. These teenagers were subsequently tried and acquitted for murder, but convicted of manslaughter at a retrial.[204] The prosecution were not helped by the fact that the FSS was unable to explain how it had missed this scientific evidence on its initial examination (thus leaving open the possibility of innocent or corrupt contamination of the clothing prior to the re-examination) and the defence were able to put in doubt whether the defendants had been wearing the clothes at the time of Damilola's death. An independent review was set up to examine how the FSS had missed such important forensic evidence. The

---

[201] Tilley et al, 'The Investigation of High-Volume Crime' in Newburn et al (2007).

[202] This view is critiqued in McCartney C, 'The DNA Expansion Programme and Criminal Investigation' (2006a) BJ Crim 46(2) 175 and her *Forensic Identification and Criminal Justice* (Cullompton: Willan, 2006b). Also see Williams R and Johnson P, *Genetic Policing: The Use of DNA in Criminal Investigations* (Cullompton: Willan, 2008).

[203] See Case studies available at <http://www.forensic.gov.uk/>, and 'Case Closed' *The Guardian*, G2 16 January 2008.   [204] *The Times*, 9 August 2006.

review concluded that the errors were due to 'human fallibility… no scientist however experienced or skilled can ever be guaranteed to find the evidence sought'.[205]

Forensic evidence has the ability to exonerate the wrongly convicted as well as incriminate. In another case the FSS wrongly indicated that they had not retained samples which showed that Sean Hodson was not guilty of the murder for which he served 27 years in prison. The samples could have been examined 11 years sooner but for the FSS error.[206] We will look at a number of limitations of scientific evidence below, but first it is worth spelling out the role it plays more generally in crime detection:

- In large numbers of 'volume' crimes such as theft, burglary, criminal damage and assault scientific evidence is not sought.

- When it is sought, useable scientific evidence is often not found (fingerprint evidence, for example, is found in less than 5% of all burglaries).

- When it is found it is often – probably in about one-third of cases – not of use in detection.

- When it is of use in detection it is often not determinative of guilt. For example, in around 11% of cases prosecuted where there is forensic evidence there is no conviction.

- In many cases the prosecution decision and, where applicable, the verdict would have been the same without the evidence.[207]

Even apparently 'hard' scientifically determined facts about times of death, the matching of materials at the scene of a crime, fingerprints, DNA and so forth may not add much strength to a case. For example, even when there is a DNA match there is still frequently no formal action. In half such cases it is because there was no supporting evidence (frequently because the suspect claimed legitimate access).[208] McCartney (2006b) has pointed out the dilemmas of introducing DNA into criminal investigations, including the suspect interview: police guidance warns against premature disclosure which may provide an opportunity to fabricate an explanation to support legitimate access. At the same time there is a danger the lawyers may overestimate the significance of DNA matches and advise their clients to plead guilty without querying its strength or reliability.[209] Contrary to popular belief, DNA matches are not always wholly conclusive.[210]

The number of cases in which scientific evidence is obtained but discarded as useless is not known, but it seems to play a relatively small role in the prosecution process.

---

[205] Rawley A and Caddy B, *Damilola Taylor: An Independent Review of Forensic Examination of Evidence by the Forensic Science Service* (London: Home Office, 2007). Other cases where the FSS head allegedly failed to find blood and bodily fluids were examined. It was concluded that the risk of similar failings was 'low' and that there was no need to make changes to the examination procedures or the recruitment, training or management of forensic scientists by the FSS.   [206] *The Guardian*, 23 March 2009.

[207] These points and data are taken from Bradbury and Feist (2005).   [208] Ibid, p 56.

[209] See ch 8 for a fuller discussion of the role of defence lawyers in securing guilty pleas.

[210] Dror I and Charlton D, 'Why Experts make Errors' (2006) 56 J Forensic Identification 600.

Thus in 'volume crime', for example, forensic evidence is now estimated to be the primary source of evidence in around 25% of detections. Some studies have found that cases with scientific evidence are more likely to end in guilty pleas or guilty verdicts, and less likely to be discontinued, than those without it.[211] But, looking at a range of studies, the difference seems not to be huge and it varies by crime type.[212] It is clear that, despite advances in scientific knowledge and, therefore, the success of forensic scientists, the capacity of science to assist criminal justice processes will always be limited. As Bradbury and Feist (2005: 70) conclude: 'The proportion of offences in general (and volume crime in particular) that are detected by the use of forensic techniques is relatively small; most crimes are actually detected by other means.' In the rest of this section, further major limitations will become apparent.

6.6.1 Scientific evidence: value-free or constructed?

We think of scientific evidence as objective, but it, and its use, is not trouble-free. First, unlike most scientists, forensic scientists have little or no control over the material which they are testing, and the conditions in which it was collected and stored. Usually they test material collected by police officers. They have to rely on those officers not to contaminate the evidence, either deliberately or accidentally, and to report all the relevant conditions in which it was collected. Or, in the case of medical evidence, injuries may be too old to allow definite conclusions to be drawn, or medical problems may be muddied by alcohol or drugs. The material itself may be only partially adequate for testing – for example, blood may have been contaminated by other substances before the police arrived at the crime scene. And the police sometimes forward for examination evidence that might help their case but not that which might undermine it.[213] In a complex investigation there may be hundreds of actual or potential items for examination, and so there often has to be some selectivity anyway. Even in 'volume' crime investigations selectivity is needed because the time the police can give to any one routine incident is very limited. Thus most focus on fingerprint evidence, and one or more of, for example, shoe marks, organic matter, and physical matter (such as glass, plastic, fibres), markings (from tools etc).[214]

Second, unlike 'pure' science, forensic examination does not take place in a (literal or metaphorical) vacuum: scientists are asked whether particular substances can be identified, or whether a sexual assault could have occurred. This is often unavoidable,

---

[211] See especially, Burrows et al, *Understanding the Attrition Process in Volume Crime Investigations* (Home Office Research Study 295) (London: Home Office, 2005).

[212] Bradbury and Feist (2005: ch 8).

[213] Roberts P and Willmore C, *The Role of Forensic Science Evidence in Criminal Proceedings* (Royal Commission on Criminal Justice Research Study No 11) (London: HMSO, 1993). Also see, for good general discussions: Roberts P, 'Science in the Criminal Process' (1994) 14 OJLS 469; Walker C and Stockdale E, 'Forensic Science and Miscarriages of Justice' (1995) 54 CLJ 69; Jones C, *Expert Witnesses* (Oxford: OUP, 1994); Redmayne M, *Expert Evidence and Criminal Justice* (Oxford: OUP, 2001).

[214] Bradbury and Feist (2005: ch 4).

for any one substance might contain an infinite number of constituents. Without knowing what to test for, some analyses might never end. And the police always have to decide how much it is worth spending on such tests in any given case. But pointing scientists in a particular direction and restricting them from doing what scientists classically do – ie follow their own, rather than someone else's priorities – has many dangers. For example, in *Ward*, forensic scientists deliberately withheld information from the defence because they identified with the police and the desire of the police to convict Ward. As the Court of Appeal acknowledged, 'a forensic scientist conjures up the image of a man in a white coat working in a laboratory, approaching his task with cold neutrality, and dedicated only to the pursuit of the truth. It is a sombre thought that the reality is somewhat different.... Forensic scientists may become partisan.'[215] Cases like this and *Maguire* (discussed below, in which similar processes were at work) are not as unusual as one might think.[216]

Third, scientists sometimes disagree on the interpretation of their findings: scientists prefer to make clear the limits of their ability to reach black and white conclusions, but the criminal process discourages shades of grey. Scientists have to report on their findings, but cannot report on everything seen and found. They report on what appears relevant, and relevance is frequently a creation of the initial premises on which an investigation is based. In the *Maguire* case there was no doubt that the defendants had a substance on their hands that *could* have derived from nitroglycerine (an explosive). Only after the Maguires had spent several years in prison did it become clear that the forensic tests had not been sufficiently specific to justify accepting the scientists' opinion that this was a more likely source than many others, such as playing cards or plastic gloves.[217] Or take Danny McNamee, the 'Hyde Park bomber', jailed for life in 1987. His conviction was largely based on fingerprint evidence given by the police's own experts. But at his successful appeal, over 10 years later, 14 fingerprint experts gave evidence. According to the Court of Appeal: 'Remarkably, and worryingly, save for those who said the print was unreadable, there was no unanimity between them, and very substantial areas of disagreement.'[218]

Fourth, much 'science' is highly speculative. DNA evidence was wrongly used at first, leading to many erroneous convictions, because the science (including that of probability) was not properly understood.[219] Thus as Roberts points out, the newer

---

[215] Glidewell LJ in *Ward* (1992) 96 Cr App Rep 1 at 51. Judicial notice might also be taken of the fact that some forensic scientists are female.

[216] Many examples are given by Redmayne (2001: ch 2), and consider the murder convictions involving evidence given by Dr Heath, which took multiple contradictory pathologist reports to overturn (*The Guardian*, 25 November 2005, and Sekar S, 'The Failure of the Review of the Possible Wrongful Convictions Caused by Michael Heath' in Naughton (ed), *The Criminal Cases Review Commission* (London: Palgrave Macmillan, 2009). Also see the *Cannings* and *Clark* cases discussed below.

[217] See May Sir J, *Report of the Inquiry into the Circumstances Surrounding the Convictions Arising Out of the Bomb Attacks in Guildford and Woolwich in 1974, Second Report* (1992–3 HC 296).

[218] Quoted in Woffinden B, 'Thumbs Down' *The Guardian*, 12 January 1999.

[219] Roberts P, 'Science, Experts and Criminal Justice' in McConville M and Wilson G (eds), *Handbook of the Criminal Justice Process* (Oxford: OUP, 2002).

the theory or technique, the more cautious we should be. This caution clashes with the understandable desire of investigators and scientists to make especial use of new theories and techniques, for many are developed in response to problems that had not been hitherto solvable.

Two notorious miscarriages of justice in the first few years of the new millennium came about because medical scientists came to believe in such theories as 'shaken baby' syndrome so rigidly that their judgement became seriously impaired. Coupled with failures to disclose evidence to the defence, and the over-eagerness of judges and juries to defer to 'experts', this led to too little scrutiny of their evidence until some years had passed with the wrongly convicted mothers in prison.[220] These two cases led to the Attorney-General's review of infant death cases, which resulted in some cases being referred back to the Court of Appeal and a small number of convictions being quashed.[221] More important, in the long run, the courts now acknowledge that what had been thought to be medical 'fact' was now informed speculation and that evidence would usually be needed from more than one source.[222]

Another problem lies in the weight to be attributed to the evidence of the prosecution scientist. In the 'Confait Affair' the inability to fix the time of death of Confait accurately allowed the obfuscation of the facts by the prosecution which led to the wrongful conviction of the three defendants.[223] As Glidewell LJ warned in *Ward*, it is vital to recognise the lack of objectivity of much forensic science. This includes DNA evidence, which suffers from the same problems of selection and interpretation as all other scientific evidence.[224] Scientific results have to be interpreted accordingly. If scientists remain detached and relatively non-partisan they have such little control over the information they handle that their dependence upon the police becomes near-total. Alternatively, if they seek to reduce their dependence on the police by getting involved in the investigation (directing the samples to be examined for example), their partisanship will increase. In the search to blame individuals for the errors inherent in systems, scientists have frequently been blamed for taking one stance and then, only a short time later, for taking the other.[225]

---

[220] *Clark* [2003] EWCA Crim 1020; *Cannings* [2004] 1 All ER 725, Crim LR [2005] 126. See discussion by Wells C, 'The Impact of Feminist Thinking on Criminal Law and Justice' [2004] Crim LR 503; Nobles R and Schiff D, 'A Story of Miscarriage: Law in the Media' (2004) 31 JLS 221; and, more generally, Redmayne (2001: ch 7).   [221] *The Guardian*, 21 July 2005.

[222] In fact most of these cases did have corroborative evidence, which is why there were substantial doubts in so few. The CPS is rightly reluctant to prosecute unless there is corroborative evidence in 'shaken baby' cases: Cobley C, 'Prosecuting Cases of Suspected "Shaken Baby Syndrome" – A Review of Current Issues' [2003] Crim LR 93.

[223] Rozenberg J, *The Case for the Crown* (Wellingborough: Equation, 1987). The quote from Glidewell LJ above in *Ward*, some 20 years after *Confait*, indicates that the problems in the latter case were neither unique nor of only historical interest.

[224] See, for example, Redmayne M, 'Doubts and Burdens: DNA Evidence, Probability and the Courts' [1995] Crim LR 464; Redmayne M, 'The DNA Database: Civil Liberty and Evidentiary Issues' [1998] Crim LR 437; McCartney (2006b).

[225] See Jones (1994: ch 10), which includes discussion of *Confait* and several of the 'Irish' miscarriages of justice.

6.6.2 **Regulating scientific evidence**

Traditionally, the police have generally used science to corroborate existing cases against existing suspects.[226] In recent years they have increasingly used its potential to create suspects as part of the shift in emphasis towards proactive policing.[227] Either way, the need for a regulatory structure, such as governs the police in relation to the other topics in this chapter, is obvious. All that exists is a Code of Practice. Not only does this not have the force of law, but it too is open to interpretation. The Association of Chief Police Officers and FSS seem to believe that 'the forensic scientist should be treated as a member of the investigative team. His/her professionalism ensures that the independence and integrity of findings are in no way compromised by actual involvement in the process.'[228] Since, as we shall see in ch 7, a prosecution service (the CPS), independent of the police, was created precisely because it was not thought that investigators could be impartial prosecutors, this is mere piety. The idea that scientists are on a par with the police is unrealistic, too. Tilley and Ford conclude that the police treat scientists 'as technicians contracted to answer questions at the lowest possible price, rather than as partners in an integrated investigative process'.[229] The danger of partiality has become all the greater as, since the mid 1990s, governments have attempted to cut costs by subjecting the FSS to free market pressures.[230] So the police are reluctant to use the FSS if they have no prime suspect (as the money will be wasted in most cases) and when they have what they believe is a strong case. The FSS is used most when they have a weak case that they want to strengthen. Moreover, the police sometimes use independent scientists, where quality control and professional integrity may be weak, primarily because they are cheaper than the FSS. Anyone can call him or herself a forensic scientist, and there are competing 'professional' bodies. The growth of an unregulated forensic science market is an obvious cause for concern.

The other main problem of regulation is what to do with scientific evidence once a case is over – particularly when there is no prosecution or there is an acquittal. Given that fingerprints and DNA samples are routinely taken, with or without consent, from everyone detained for a recordable offence,[231] that so many arrests are based on little or no objective evidence, and the inescapable fact that some sections of the population are at more risk of arrest than others, it seems wrong that this information should be kept and perhaps used in the future in unrelated investigations. It increases the chances of the crimes of some sections of the population being detected, as compared

---

[226] Redmayne (2001: ch 2).

[227] Burrows et al (2005). This applies particularly to DNA evidence: Bradbury and Feist (2005: 50).

[228] FSS, *Using Forensic Science Effectively: A Joint Project by ACPO and the FSS* (Birmingham: FSS, 1996) p 42.

[229] Tilley N and Ford A, *Forensic Science and Crime Investigation* (Crime Prevention and Detection Series Paper 73) (London: Home Office, 1996) p 22.

[230] Roberts P, 'What Price a Free Market in Forensic Science?' (1996) 36 BJ Crim 37.

[231] Criminal Justice Act 2003, ss 9 and 10 (amending PACE, ss 61–63), allowing 'non-intimate' samples, on which DNA tests can be done, to be taken from most suspects.

with those of other sections, and is an invasion of privacy. Also, the information could be misused, to track people associated with out-of-favour political groups, for example. On the other hand, is the argument that innocent people have nothing to fear, and that DNA and fingerprint evidence, in particular, is, in itself, objective even though the use to which it is put and the weight given to it can be contested.[232] It is on this basis that PACE s 64[233] allows fingerprint evidence and samples (eg DNA) to be kept after they have fulfilled their original purpose. The national DNA database now has around 4.5 million profiles and it will continue to grow. Concerns have been raised that the 'racially skewed DNA database will exacerbate the racial bias already present in the criminal process'.[234] The extent (but not the fact) of racial disproportionality in this context is disputed by Home Office officials but one estimate has it that almost one in four black children over the age of 10 are on this database compared with 'only' one in ten of their white counterparts.[235] In addition the database contains the profiles of many people who have never been charged with a crime.

PACE, s 64 has been challenged on the grounds that it is incompatible with ECHR, Art 8 (right to privacy).[236] However, the House of Lords held (with one dissent) that Art 8(1) was not infringed, as keeping the evidence did not affect the individuals' private lives, and safeguards were in place to prevent their misuse. The majority judges went on to consider whether, if Art 8(1) had been infringed, this could have been justified on the grounds of necessity for the prevention of crime (the 'proportionality' principle in Art 8(2)). They considered that it could, as the police could not be expected to review the circumstances of each case. The ECtHR has subsequently held that the indefinite retention of fingerprint and DNA samples following acquittal or discontinuance of criminal proceedings does breach Art 8.[237] It has been argued that the decision sends a clear message to national authorities that they must tread carefully when handling personal information for the purposes of crime prevention'.[238] However, the effect of the judgement 'should not be overstated': it does not rule out the retention of samples after acquittal or discontinuance, only blanket and indiscriminate retention.[239] The UK will undoubtedly be able to craft a regime that permits retention of some samples whilst being Convention compliant.

6.6.3 **Conclusion**

There is no solution to the dilemmas discussed here, other than to recognise that since – like eyewitness evidence – science rarely provides *conclusive* proof, the *degree*

---

[232] For discussion, see Redmayne M, 'Appeals to Reason' (2002a) 65 MLR 19.

[233] As amended by the Criminal Justice and Police Act 2001: before this, samples of non-convicted suspects and defendants had to be destroyed.   [234] McCartney (2006b: 154).

[235] *The Observer*, 20 July 2009.

[236] *R (on the application of S) v CC South Yorkshire, R (on the application of Marper) v CC South Yorkshire* [2004] UKHL 39.   [237] *S v UK; Marper v UK* [2009] 48 EHHR 50.

[238] Heffernan L, 'DNA and Fingerprint Retention; *S and Marper v UK*' (2009) 34(3) European LR 491.

[239] Ibid.

of proof required should be high in order to minimise wrongful convictions. In summary, science is, like almost all other evidence:

- based, to a greater or lesser extent depending on the specific context, on speculation and theory and is therefore generally 'grey' in nature rather than 'black and white';
- subject to the biases of police and scientist;
- in need of interpretation and weighing against other evidence by juries and courts;
- in need of regulation with regard to its collection (eg how far privacy should be invaded or deception used to secure it), analysis (eg who should examine it, under what conditions), and use (eg whether it should be put to use for purposes other than it was collected).

Roberts (2002: 252) cautions us against placing, in the criminal justice context, our usual faith in the power of science; instead: 'The uses of science in the criminal process should be approached with a healthy scepticism and subjected to on-going critical scrutiny.' Should this 'healthy' scepticism go as far as regarding scientific evidence as 'negotiated constructs' like witness and confession evidence?[240] Or lead us to agree that: 'The already uneasy relationship between law and science has now reached breaking point'?[241] The Law Commission has acknowledged one aspect of the problem – use of expert evidence in court proceedings – without yet providing any answers.[242] Ultimately, it is a matter of opinion, reasoning and judgement – exactly the processes to be used when evaluating scientific evidence itself.

6.7 **Conclusion**

Misuse of many of the police powers discussed in this chapter involve the tort of trespass and breaches of ECHR, Art 8. But without any tangible damage, there is little point taking the police to court. As with most misuse of powers, the potentially most powerful remedy, if evidence is discovered as a result of the misuse and if there is a prosecution, is exclusion of that evidence. But few abuses of the powers discussed in this chapter give rise to this, and breach of Art 8 in itself does not result in exclusion.[243] As so often in this book this causes us to question the value of declaring

---

[240] Jones (1994: 273).

[241] Commentary to *Cannings* [2005] Crim LR 126 at p 127. For even greater scepticism about how far law and science can ever speak the same language, see Nobles and Schiff (2004).

[242] Law Commission, *The Admissibility of Expert Evidence in Criminal Proceedings* (Consultation Paper No 190) London: TSO, 2009. See Editorial Comment [2009] Crim LR 387. For an example see *Holdsworth* [2009] Crim LR 195. Also see Roberts A, 'Drawing on Expertise: Legal Decision Making and the Reception of Expert Evidence' [2008] Crim LR 443.   [243] See Editorial [2009] Crim LR 549.

that something – in this case, privacy – is a 'human right', at least from the standpoint of the defendant whose privacy rights were invaded.[244]

Thus while PACE, s 16(8) provides that the police may only search 'for the purpose for which the warrant was issued' any evidence discovered as a result of an illegal general search can still be used. There is therefore implicit encouragement for the police to use search warrants as licences to ransack homes and places of work. The same applies to, for example, telephone intercepts, buggings, fingerprints or DNA samples authorised for one thing but which leads to, or constitutes, evidence of something else. And *Sanghera* (discussed above)[245] illustrates the way the courts on the one hand declare the need for searches, for example, to be based on explicit consent or legal grounds, yet on the other hand allow the evidence obtained illegally to be the basis for a conviction. Again as seen in earlier chapters, many of these powers are not exercised, for 'consent' is obtained from people who doubtless believe that if they do not consent they will be given no choice anyway. Records are supposed to be kept. But with regard to the special categories of material that cannot be sought and seized except in exceptional circumstances, research has found that consent seizures were generally not recorded.[246]

There are many other common threads linking the topics in this chapter. First, what information from informers, undercover policing and surveillance, and witnesses have in common is that, by contrast with information from suspects themselves (the subject of earlier chapters), suspects usually do not know that information is being gathered about them and transmitted to the police. Thus, however inadequate the due process protections for, say, suspects in police custody, and whatever the scope for abuse, there are certain procedural standards which the police rarely now ignore. And if they do overstep the mark, suspects may become aware of this (particularly likely if – though we saw in ch 4 that it is a big 'if' – they have the assistance of a good legal adviser) and at least have the chance of redressing their grievances. But if you do not know that your cell, home or place of work is being bugged, or that there is an informer in your midst, or that a witness is being 'prepared' for an identity parade, you cannot be on your guard against abuse or know that abuse has occurred. The ability to abuse power without fear of detection increases the incentive to resort to such covert methods.

A second common thread is the importance of property rights. Whether, and under what circumstances, your property can be searched or your conversations recorded, for example, depends in large part on whether you are on your own property or not and whether the police have been invited there or not. The fact that Art 8 of the ECHR gives a right to privacy is seen as secondary to the traditional capitalistic focus of English law-makers and judges on property rights. The police can deceive but they cannot trespass. What kind of moral values are those to instil in our children?

---

[244] The main value of a successful challenge in the European Court of Human Rights is to prompt changes in the law so as to benefit (some) future suspects and defendants, as seems certain to happen in the wake of the *Marper* judgment on DNA retention.   [245] *Sanghera* [2001] 1 Cr App R 299.

[246] Clark (2004: 122–3).

Third, there is the authorisation of use of these powers. Most authorisation has to be by a senior officer although we have seen that warrants, for example, are a matter for magistrates and, in some cases, judges. Although police self-authorisation is a classic crime control and managerial approach, the level of seniority of the officer varies according to, for example, the level of intrusion. This is a partial incorporation of the 'freedom' approach, although the way the police are allowed to run their own ID parades, when impartial civilians could do it on a double-blind basis, is difficult to justify on any basis. Police self-authorisation is much criticised by academics, such as Ashworth and Redmayne,[247] who cite ECHR judgments urging judicial authorisation. It is not clear why they – and the ECtHR – think this is so important when, as we saw in 6.5, judges and magistrates exercise so little control over the police. Judicial authorisation may act as a safety net against the worst policing abuses, but its main function appears rather to be one of adding a veneer of legitimacy to the underlying crime control reality of evidence gathering. Much the same is true of human rights discourses. Certainly, the Human Rights Act 1998 has so far proved to be a rather empty vessel, full of sound and fury, signifying little. And the 'war on terror' and allied moves toward pre-empting crimes ranging from the very serious to 'anti-social behaviour', as discussed in ch 1, means that there is absolutely no prospect of reversing the continuing drift towards crime control.

Further reading

Billingsley R (ed), *Covert Human Intelligence Sources. The 'Unlovely Face of Police Work'* (Hampshire: Waterside Press, 2009)

McCartney C, *Forensic Identification and Criminal Justice: Forensic Science, Justice and Risk* (Cullompton: Willan, 2006)

Newburn T, Williamson, T and Wright A (eds), *Handbook of Criminal Investigation* (Cullompton: Willan, 2007)

Williams R and Johnson P, *Genetic Policing: The Use of DNA in Criminal Investigations* (Cullompton: Willan, 2008)

[247] Ashworth and Redmayne (2005: 114).

7

Prosecutions

[The police] don't get the offenders. And if they catch them they don't charge them. If I was to offend someone like this the police would harass me instead of turning a blind eye which is what I feel they do in case of white offenders. And the offenders feel they can do anything they like as they are always let off. [Pakistani victim of a racial incident reported to the police][1]

Key issues

- The respective roles of the police and CPS in prosecution decision-making
- How cases are constructed *for* prosecution (rarely *against*)
- The criteria for prosecution decision-making
- Diversion from prosecution
- Review of prosecution decisions and accountability
- Different treatment of 'regulatory' offences and 'real' crime

7.1 **Introduction**

Before police forces were established in 1829 and for some years thereafter, neither local nor central government accepted responsibility for day-to-day law enforcement. Prosecutions could be initiated by anyone. Suspects were generally prosecuted, if at all, by the victim. Police powers were originally no greater than those of ordinary citizens. If the police, or anyone else, wished to prosecute, they had to 'lay an information' before the local magistrates. If the latter were satisfied that there was sufficient evidence they would issue a warrant for the suspect's arrest or a summons to appear in court. Prosecution decisions were judicially controlled.

As police forces and police powers grew throughout the nineteenth and twentieth centuries, victims came to expect the police to initiate and conduct prosecutions for

---

[1] Quoted by Bowling B, *Violent Racism* (Oxford: Clarendon Press, 1998) p 237.

them. Extra arrest powers were provided to the police and they developed the practice of 'charging' suspects, whereby they took suspects before the magistrates without laying an information in advance. Magistrates lost control of prosecution decisions, but no specific prosecution powers or responsibilities were conferred on the police. Private prosecution remained the model on which police prosecutions were based, and the right of private prosecution has remained to this day.[2] In the nineteenth and twentieth centuries various agencies were created to investigate and prosecute crime in their specialist areas, such as health and safety. The statutes creating them were ad hoc and so too were the prosecution powers granted. We will look more closely at these regulatory agencies in 7.5.

In the absence of specific laws to regulate prosecutions, the police and other agencies evolved their own systems. The police prosecuted most of their own cases in the magistrates' courts, but instructed solicitors and barristers in Crown Court cases.[3] Gradually the larger police forces began to employ their own prosecuting solicitors, who had to carry out the instructions of the police.[4] If the police insisted on prosecuting a weak case to further their crime control goals, or bring more serious charges than were warranted by the evidence ('overcharging'), there was little or nothing the prosecutor could do about it.[5] These arrangements came under fire in the 'Confait Affair': three youths were wrongfully convicted of murder, partly because the prosecutor was unable, or unwilling, to act independently.[6] The Royal Commission on Criminal Procedure (Philips Commission) proposed an independent prosecution service to take over cases which the police had decided to prosecute. If the prosecutor did not agree with the police, the case could be dropped, the charges changed, or more evidence sought.[7] In the Prosecution of Offences Act 1985, the government accepted the main thrust of the Commission's proposals by establishing the Crown Prosecution Service (CPS). The Criminal Justice Act 2003 transferred the power to charge (ie to decide to prosecute) suspects from the police to the CPS in all but very minor cases.[8]

---

[2] See Sanders A, 'Arrest, Charge and Prosecution' (1986) 6 LS 257 and 7.6.4 below for further discussion of private prosecutions.

[3] See Sigler J, 'Public Prosecution in England and Wales' [1974] Crim LR 642 on the use of barristers, and for a general account of the system up to the 1970s.

[4] Sigler (1974); Weatheritt M, *The Prosecution System* (Royal Commission on Criminal Procedure, Research Study No 11) (London: HMSO, 1980); Royal Commission on Criminal Procedure (RCCP), *The Investigation of Criminal Offences in England and Wales: The Law and Procedure* (Cmnd 8092–1) (London: HMSO, 1981) pp 49–52.   [5] RCCP, *Report* (Cmnd 8092) (London: HMSO, 1981) para 6.27.

[6] See *Report of an Inquiry into the Circumstances leading to the Trial of Three Persons on Charges Arising out of the Death of Maxwell Confait and the Fire at 27 Doggett Road, London SE6* (HCP 90) (London: HMSO, 1977).   [7] RCCP, *Report* (1981: ch 7).

[8] Section 28 and Sch 2, amending PACE, s 37 (creating the new s 37B). See 'CPS, The Director's Guidance on Charging (3rd edn, 2007, available at <http://www.cps.gov.uk/publications/prosecution/dpp_guidance.html>) and Brownlee I, 'The Statutory Charging Scheme in England and Wales: Towards a Unified Prosecution System?' [2004] Crim LR 896. The impetus for this 'statutory charging scheme' was Auld LJ, *Review of the Criminal Courts of England and Wales: Report* (London: TSO, 2001). For discussion of the background covered in this section see White R, 'Investigators and Prosecutors or, Desperately Seeking Scotland: Re-formulation of the 'Philips Principle'' (2006) 69 MLR 143.

However, we shall see that the police still have the power *not* to prosecute, so when we refer to 'police prosecution decisions' we mean decisions both to not prosecute and to refer a case to the CPS to decide on charging.

The head of the CPS is the Director of Public Prosecutions (DPP).[9] Most prosecutors are based locally, in areas that match police force areas, each headed by a Chief Crown Prosecutor. The area structure has been altered several times since 1986, reflecting conflicting and changing views about what the CPS is for and to whom or what it should be accountable (see 7.6 below). This chapter will examine whether the combination of laws, policies and procedures of different prosecuting and enforcement agencies is fair, effective and freedom-enhancing.

7.2 **Discretion**

Prosecution is discretionary, like stop-search and arrest. When the police do not seek to prosecute they may: delay the decision (either releasing the suspect on bail to return at a later date or reporting the suspect with a view to a summons); release the suspect with a warning; or take no further action (NFA) at all. This is broadly true of prosecution agencies in general, which have many different reasons for deciding not to prosecute including insufficient evidence, triviality and extenuating circumstances. Sometimes immunity from prosecution is exchanged for information about other offences and other offenders.[10] In this section we examine how these discretionary decisions are regulated.

7.2.1 **'Legality' and 'opportunity'**

It is usual to describe prosecution systems as falling into one of two types. In 'legality' systems (Germany for example), the police must report all offences to the prosecutor, who must prosecute. In principle, there is no discretion, although the police screen out cases where there is no evidence. Common law countries, on the other hand, such as Britain and the United States, tend to have 'opportunity systems' in which there is complete discretion. As a former Attorney-General, Lord Shawcross put it: 'It has never been the rule in this country – I hope it never will be – that suspected criminal offences must automatically be the subject of prosecution.'[11] Legal systems do not, in reality, divide so neatly. Many, like France, combine elements of both.[12] And while police and

---

[9] The DPP was first established in 1879 to advise the police on criminal matters and to handle particularly important cases.   [10] On the importance of 'deals', see 5.1, 5.4 and 6.2.

[11] Quoted approvingly in the Attorney-General's guidelines for prosecution, which apply to the police, and in para 5.6 of the Code for Crown Prosecutors (London: CPS, 2004).

[12] Vander Becken T and Kilchling M (eds), *The Role of the Public Prosecutor in European Criminal Justice Systems* (Brussels: KVAB, 2000); Hodgson J, *French Criminal Justice* (Oxford: Hart, 2005). For comprehensive comparative surveys see Tak P (ed), *Tasks and Powers of the Prosecution Services in the EU Member States* (2 vols) (Nijmegen: Wolf, 2005).

CPS discretion in England and Wales is usually exercised in favour of prosecuting, this is not true of all law enforcement bodies within such systems. Thus discretion is usually exercised by *non*-police agencies (such as HM Inland Revenue and Customs) *against* prosecution (see 7.5 below). On the other hand, even in the most rigid legality-based systems discretion is exercised more and more frequently. This is usually a product of specific provisions, especially for juveniles, in the laws of those countries. As in Britain, juveniles, old people and motoring offences tend to be given special consideration.

So 'legality' and 'opportunity' systems sometimes produce similar practical outcomes. But because diversion in legality systems is an exception to a general rule, non-prosecution decisions are relatively strictly controlled and diversion decisions are usually made by prosecutors. The relatively small number of senior decision-makers fosters consistency and adherence to official policy.[13] In England and Wales, by contrast, discretion is not closely controlled. Neither the basis for the exercise of discretion nor the level of decision-maker is consistent throughout the system. Also, in major crimes, prosecutors (in Germany) or examining magistrates (in France) play an important part in the early stages of the investigation and prosecution process. These people are impartial, in theory at least,[14] in a way that police forces are not and never could be. In Britain, where there is no equivalent of these officials, the prosecution system is the same no matter how serious the offence.[15]

7.2.2 'Constabulary independence'

One consequence of the 'opportunity principle' in the United Kingdom is the doctrine of 'constabulary independence' which holds that, in general, no-one has the authority to tell law enforcement agencies that they must, or must not, arrest and prosecute in particular circumstances. This is exemplified by *Arrowsmith v Jenkins*.[16] The defendant (D) spoke for 30 minutes at a public meeting which obstructed a highway. She was arrested for this offence and was convicted. She appealed on the basis that many meetings had been held in that place previously and that in the past the police had not prosecuted anyone for a criminal offence. D in effect asked 'Why pick on me?' The court's answer on appeal was: 'That, of course, has nothing to do with this court. The sole question here is whether the defendant had contravened s 121(1) of the Highways Act 1959' (per Lord Parker CJ).

What of a policy not to prosecute certain offences at all? In *Metropolitan Police Comr, ex p Blackburn*[17] the policy of the Metropolitan Police at that time not to prosecute

---

[13] Jehle J and Wade M, *Coping with Overloaded Criminal Justice Systems: The Rise of Prosecutorial Power Across Europe* (Berlin: Springer, 2006); Wade M and Jehle J (eds), 'Prosecution and Diversion within Criminal Justice Systems within Europe' (2008) 14(2, 3) Euro J Crim Policy and Research (Special Issue).

[14] The reality is more complex: Hodgson J, 'The Police, the Prosecutor and the Juge d'Instruction' (2001) 41 BJ Crim 342 and Hodgson (2005).

[15] Although the DPP's consent is needed before prosecutions of particularly sensitive or serious offences (eg riot) can be launched.   [16] *Arrowsmith v Jenkins* [1963] 2 QB 561.

[17] *Metropolitan Police Comr, ex p Blackburn* [1968] 2 QB 118.

certain establishments for illegal gambling was challenged. The police altered their policy in the course of the case thus removing the need for a judicial decision. Lord Denning, however, made an obiter statement (ie not binding on future courts):

There are some policy decisions with which, I think, the court in a case can if necessary interfere. Suppose a Chief Constable were to issue a directive to his men that no person should be prosecuted for stealing any goods less than £100 in value. I should have thought that the court could countermand it. He would be failing in his duty to enforce the law (at 136).

This is powerful rhetoric, but to date, it appears that no one has successfully challenged any decisions not to prosecute or to exercise other powers that follow a coherent policy, such as community policing[18] or the need to balance offence seriousness against use of resources.[19] This autonomy in enforcement and prosecution decisions protects enforcement bodies from interference from individuals and from local and central government, but should these agencies be virtually the sole judges of when arrest and prosecution is, and is not, appropriate? We are not advocating political decisions about individual cases, but greater accountability for prosecution policies would be entirely compatible with the rule of law.[20] The Home Office does formulate policy for the police in relation to cautioning, and the CPS has a Code for Crown Prosecutors,[21] but both policies are vague, though we shall see that there are more detailed guidelines on specific topics.

The courts have developed three broad legal principles to limit the discretion of prosecution agencies. Firstly, a prosecution must not be pursued in bad faith, ie, for personal, corrupt or other similarly improper reasons. If it is, the court may hold it to be an abuse of process and dismiss the case. In *DPP v Ara* [2002] 1 WLR 815 the police offered a caution to a juvenile but refused to let his solicitor hear the tape of the interview so he could be advised. The police prosecution was stayed because this obstruction of effective legal advice was seen as an abuse of process. Though the Divisional Court did not explicitly say that the police were acting in bad faith, this was the impression given.[22] In a case of bad faith it may be possible to sue for malicious prosecution but only if the case ended in the defendant's favour (see ch 12). Here again we see the application of the crime control principle that the end justifies the means.

---

[18] *Chief Constable of Devon and Cornwall, ex p CEGB* [1981] 3 All ER 826.

[19] *Chief Constable of Sussex, ex p ITF* [1999] 1 All ER 129. Discussed in Barnard C and Hare I, 'Police Discretion and the Rule of Law: European Community Rights Versus Civil Rights' (2000) 63 MLR 581. Also see *Metropolitan Police Comr, ex p P* (1995) 160 JP 367, discussed by Evans R, 'Is a Police Caution Amenable to Judicial Review?' [1996] Crim LR 104.

[20] Jefferson T and Grimshaw R, *Controlling the Constable: Police Accountability in England and Wales* (London: Muller, 1984). See 3.4.3, for a brief discussion of these issues in relation to the policing of domestic violence. See 7.6 below for an extended discussion of accountability.

[21] The latest version of the Code for Crown Prosecutors was published in 2004 and is available on the CPS website: <http://www.cps.gov.uk/>. A consultation was launched in October 2009, with a view to producing a 6th edition of the Code in 2010.

[22] See Hilson C, 'Discretion to Prosecute and Judicial Review' [1993] Crim LR 739 for discussion of earlier cases.

No matter how malicious a prosecution might have been, a person would have no remedy if found guilty in the criminal courts.

Decisions not to prosecute which are taken in bad faith are not reviewable in these ways. There is no such thing as an action for malicious non-prosecution or abuse of no-process. A second principle, though, which applies to all prosecution decisions, positive or negative, is that they must not be *Wednesbury* unreasonable.[23] This means that courts will not interfere with the decision of the enforcement body in question unless the exercise of discretion was so offensive or incompetent that it was completely unreasonable.[24] This is the same principle that operates in relation to unlawful arrest (see ch 3). An example would be a prosecution decision (positive or negative) based on an error about the sufficiency of evidence.[25] One difficulty in challenging prosecution decisions under *Wednesbury* is that there is no general duty to give reasons for decisions or to disclose the evidence/information on which a decision was based.[26] This makes it difficult to know whether grounds for challenge exist. However, in a recent case a victim of a serious assault was able to successfully challenge the decision not to prosecute his attacker because the court decided the evidential test had not been correctly applied. The court said that the prosecutor should have left it to the jury to evaluate the victim's testimony in light of a medical report that he was suffering from a mental illness which may have affected his perception of events.[27]

Thirdly, prosecution decisions must be taken only after consideration and application of a consistent policy. Thus cautions have been successfully challenged because official guidelines on cautioning were not followed.[28] In *DPP, ex p Chaudhary* [1995] 1 Cr App R 136,[29] a decision to drop the prosecution of a man accused of non-consensual buggery of his wife was successfully challenged because the prosecutor had not considered all the possibilities laid down in the Code before the decision was taken. And in *Adaway*[30] the defendant was prosecuted by a trading standards authority and

---

[23] This concept derives from *Associated Provincial Picture Houses Ltd v Wednesbury Corpn* [1948] 1 KB 223.

[24] Thus the decision not to prosecute police officers in the *Treadaway* case was quashed as a result of a successful judicial review action. See Burton M, 'Reviewing CPS Decisions Not to Prosecute' [2001] Crim LR 374 and ch 12 for discussion. Another non-prosecution decision was quashed in *DPP, ex p Jones* [2000] IRLR 373.

[25] See, for example, *DPP, ex p Jones* [2000] Crim LR 858, discussed in 7.5 and 7.6 below; and *R (on the application of Joseph) v DPP* [2001] Crim LR 489, where the CPS were held to be wrong to discontinue a case on grounds of insufficient evidence when, on the face of it, there did appear to be substantial evidence.

[26] See *DPP, ex p Manning* [2000] 3 WLR 463: held no general duty in either English or ECHR law to give reasons for non-prosecution, although a duty could arise in exceptional circumstances. (On the facts of that case, where a coroner's jury had recorded a verdict of unlawful killing in relation to the death of a prisoner at the hands of a prison officer, the Court of Appeal ruled that there was a duty to give reasons for not prosecuting that officer.) However, we shall see that the CPS does now give reasons for non-prosecution in very serious cases.   [27] *R (on application of B) v DPP* [2009] 1 WLR 2072.

[28] *Metropolitan Police Comr, ex p P* (1996) 8 Admin LR 6; *R (on the application of Guest) v DPP* [2009] Crim LR 730. See 7.4.2.

[29] Discussed by Dingwall G, 'Judicial Review and the DPP' (1995) 54 CLJ 265.

[30] *Adaway* [2004] EWCA Crim 2831.

convicted of an offence, but the prosecution was in contravention of its stated policy. The conviction was quashed because the trial judge should have accepted the defence submission that this was an abuse of process. Generally, however, the courts exercise a light touch in controlling prosecution policy and practice.[31] The judges are right not to do the legislature's job of establishing prosecution policy, but it leaves a vacuum that agencies have to fill with their own policies and practices within the broad limits set by the courts.

It is therefore vital to examine prosecution policies, and to see how they are implemented. All agencies work within the broad framework established by the 'Attorney-General's Guidelines on Prosecution', whereby prosecution can be pursued only if there is sufficient evidence *and* it is in the 'public interest'.[32] 'If the case does not pass the evidential stage, it must not go ahead, no matter how important or serious it might be.'[33] In the next two sections we look at how the police and CPS operate these two tests, and then we look at the markedly different response of non-police agencies to the same tests.

7.3 Evidential sufficiency: police and CPS

7.3.1 Deciding that there is insufficient evidence

The police frequently decide that they have insufficient evidence to prosecute. Many arrests are of the 'wrong' suspect as one would expect when the police trawl large suspect populations in major crime enquiries, or in more minor cases, people are arrested indiscriminately or on unreliable 'information received'.[34] Sometimes the police believe that they have the right suspect, but still consider that they have insufficient evidence to take the matter further. Sometimes the evidence cannot be secured, but in other cases the police decide that it is not worth investing the time and trouble to pursue the matter further. This was their traditional attitude to 'domestics', although the situation is now changing, at least as far as domestic violence against women is concerned (see ch 3 and 7.6 below). On occasion, further action could reveal matters which the police would rather conceal, such as a case where, as a police inspector put it, prosecution 'might prove embarrassing to the police' because of racist language

---

[31] For a statement of principles from the House of Lords illustrating judicial reluctance to interfere with prosecution decisions see *DPP ex p Kebilene* [2000]. See generally, Burton (2001). For cases illustrating this, and contrary to *Metropolitan Police Comr, ex p P*, see *R v Commissioner of Police of the Metropolis* [2007] Crim LR 298; *R (Mondelly) v Commissioner of Police of the Metropolis* [2006] EWHC 2370 (and comment by Leigh L, 'The Seamless Web?' (2007) 70 MLR 654.

[32] See Sanders A, 'Prosecution Decisions and the Attorney-General's Guidelines' [1985b] Crim LR 4. For a critique of the 'public interest' test see Rogers J 'Restructuring the Exercise of Prosecutorial Discretion in England and Wales' (2006) 26 OJLS 775.

[33] Code for Crown Prosecutors (London: CPS, 2004) para 5.1.

[34] See 3.4.2 for a discussion of the working rules which shape patterns of arrest.

used during the arrest.[35] In yet other cases a 'deal' is struck in which non-prosecution is traded for information from the suspect (see 6.2). Thus, increasingly large numbers of suspects are released from detention with no further action being taken (NFA): around 8% in the 1970s,[36] 25–30% in the 1980s and 1990s[37] and well over 30% in 2008.[38] Although this might seem surprising, it must be remembered that if an arrest is made on the basis of 'reasonable suspicion' alone, more evidence will be needed before the case becomes prosecutable, and little over half of all suspects make incriminating statements.

As a result of the Philips Commission finding that large numbers of weak cases were being prosecuted, because the police used a 'prima facie case' test, the Attorney-General's guidelines for prosecution (see 7.2.2) set out a 'realistic prospect of conviction' test, under which conviction has to be more likely than acquittal. This does not require a belief in the innocence of a defendant in order for a case to be dropped, nor a belief in guilt for a case to be proceeded with. Rather it requires a prediction of what will happen in court. Thus a sophisticated fraudster may not be prosecuted because of a prediction that it would be difficult to get a jury to understand and convict on the complicated financial evidence involved.[39] To the extent that prosecutors act on such beliefs about juries, we can see that the application of the same test to people of different status leads to different results, allowing high status fraudsters to avoid prosecution. Williams argues that the test should not be whether a jury is likely to convict, but whether it ought to convict, given the admissible evidence available to the prosecutor. It is bad enough, he says, that someone believed to be guilty gets acquitted, but to spare them the anguish of the trial too is overgenerous.

The 'realistic prospect' test creates a tougher threshold for the police to surmount than did the old prima facie test. One might have hoped for fewer weak arrests, but instead there appear to be more arrests without prosecution. This has been facilitated by another development in the law: PACE. For s 37 allows suspects to be detained precisely in order to secure sufficient evidence to prosecute. Release without charge is explicitly recognised as a legitimate outcome should that evidence not be produced (see 4.3). Allowing the police to arrest, collect evidence and weed out cases which they decide do not warrant judicial proceedings is a classic crime control strategy. In practice, whether a case ends in NFA depends not just on police evaluations of evidential strength and offence seriousness but also on how much the police want to prosecute a particular individual. This in turn shapes the thoroughness and creativity

---

[35] McConville et al, *The Case for the Prosecution* (London: Routledge, 1991) p 111.

[36] Steer D, *Uncovering Crime: The Police Role* (Royal Commission on Criminal Procedure Research Study No 7) (London: HMSO, 1980) table 4.

[37] McConville et al (1991: 104) table 10; Phillips C and Brown D, *Entry into the Criminal Justice System: A Survey of Police Arrests and their Outcomes* (Home Office Research Study No 185) (London: Home Office, 1998) p 83, table 6.1.

[38] In CPS charging decisions by prosecutors, 29% are NFA, to which one has to add an unknown number of police NFA decisions. HMCPSI and HMIC, *Joint Thematic Review of the New Charging Arrangements* (London: HMCPSI/HMIC, 2008) para 3.26.

[39] Williams G, 'Letting Off the Guilty and Prosecuting the Innocent' [1985] Crim LR 115.

with which any investigation is carried out. So, for example, the prosecution collapsed in the Stephen Lawrence affair because the police had insufficient interest or competence to investigate thoroughly.[40] In other words, the degree of interest shown by the police in any particular case or category of case is crucially affected by their own working rules.

The statutory charging scheme retains the central characteristics of the 'opportunity' system – that is, constabulary independence allows the police to not prosecute as they wish, subject to the restrictions discussed in 7.2, and the police have no duty to report non-prosecuted cases to the CPS. Other agencies are in a similar position to the police, though they have fewer arrest powers. Only where the defendants are police officers or similarly placed officials do the CPS always make decisions whether or not to prosecute, but the police retain a large measure of control through the 'case construction' processes to be discussed next. For example, a British Muslim arrested in a terrorism raid in 2003 suffered 50 separate injuries while detained for six days without charge. The A&E consultant who examined him said the force used had been 'excessive' (ie unnecessary to contain him) and 'controlled' to cause pain rather than to be life-threatening: 'He was punched and kicked all over his head, torso and extremities (and)...forcefully stamped on.' Despite this, the CPS decided that there was insufficient evidence to prosecute any officers.[41] That judgement might seem surprising until one considers that it is the police themselves who control how much admissible evidence is collected and made available to the CPS.

7.3.2 Police working rules, the custody officer[42] and the statutory charging scheme

We saw in ch 3 that arrest can be used as a resource in street policing to impose police authority or control, often rendering prosecution unnecessary. But sometimes prosecution will be a natural follow-through, especially when a complaint has been made against the officer,[43] or when the latter is assaulted.[44] Waddington discusses a case where the rowdiness of the arrestee was exaggerated in order to *legally* justify an arrest which the police thought was *morally* justifiable, and essential to maintain their authority.[45] In 2009 a friend of one of the authors heard a Chief Superintendent commenting that arrest would not be normal for a particular minor offence unless the suspect 'failed the attitude test'. The working rules examined in chs 2 and 3 therefore help to shape prosecution decisions, even when the evidence is weak and the offence minor.

---

[40] Macpherson of Cluny, *The Stephen Lawrence Inquiry* (Cm 4262-I) (London: SO, 1999). See 7.6 below, and ch 3.   [41] *The Guardian*, 11 September 2004.

[42] Other officers – such as 'evidence review officers' of constable rank – are replacing the custody officer with regard to charging decisions. But arrangements vary from area to area (see HMCPSI/HMIC, 2008: ch 8 for details) so we continue to use the term 'custody officer' as shorthand.

[43] See McConville et al (1991).

[44] Clarkson et al, 'Assaults: The Relationship between Seriousness, Criminalisation and Punishment' [1994] Crim LR 4.   [45] Waddington P, *Policing Citizens* (London: UCL Press, 1999) p 135.

Conversely, where there is no public order issue in a clear-cut incident the police may regard prosecution as pointless unless they see the crime involved as serious.

The Philips Commission in the 1980s wanted to reduce the number of arrests and the number of weak cases prosecuted. Since arresting officers will often have strong personal reasons for prosecuting, it was obvious that the imposition of objective standards would be impossible without the decision to prosecute being made independently. The Commission therefore proposed the 'arrest only when necessary' principle, the 'realistic prospect of conviction' test, the custody officer and the CPS. Under its proposals, in most cases in which the police wanted to prosecute, they would have had to report the suspect. The suspect would then have been considered for summons by a senior officer (and, since 2003, a prosecutor) on the basis of a written file of evidence.

This is the system used for road traffic offences, many minor offences and non-police crimes (see 7.5). Decisions take longer than with arrest and charge but they are based on a detached consideration of the evidence, and the coercive process of arrest is avoided. However, the 'arrest only when necessary' principle was not applied in PACE to non-minor offences (ranging from theft right up to murder) (see ch 3). The result has been that a much larger proportion of cases are processed by way of arrest and charge than the Philips Commission envisaged, and more than was the case prior to PACE.[46] The safeguard offered by the Philips Commission for arrest and charge cases (enacted in PACE) was to replace the charge sergeant with the supposedly more independent custody officer. The problem with decisions taken by charge sergeants was that they were based only on the oral report(s) of the investigating officer(s). Decisions usually had to be immediate, were based on what the officer(s) said was the evidence and in the presence of those officers. This all made dispassionate decision-making virtually impossible. Thus, the Prosecuting Solicitors' Society commented that: 'As an independent check this must be almost without value.'[47]

The defect in this part of the Philips Commission's strategy is that custody officers are in exactly the same social, occupational, structural and situational position as were the old charge sergeants. Chapter 4 showed that, in relation to the rights of suspects, the custody officer is no more independent than charge sergeants used to be. The same is true in relation to decisions to charge. Research has consistently shown that it is very rare for custody officers to caution or NFA when arresting officers want to charge, or vice versa. As one custody officer told McConville et al: 'I would go along with what the arresting officers have to say.' For, as another said, 'I accept that [the officer's] got no cause to be telling lies and the [suspect] has.'[48] Giving the then-new CPS the power to drop ('discontinue') prosecutions initiated by the police in the 1980s was supposed

---

[46] Barclay G and Tavares C (eds), *Information on the Criminal Justice System in England and Wales: Digest 4* (London: Home Office, 1999) ch 4. See, for comparisons over time, McConville et al (1991: 38–40). Phillips and Brown (1998: 86). [47] Evidence to the Philips Commission (1979) para 3.3.

[48] McConville et al (1991: 119). Note that even if the custody officer does wish to hear a suspect's story, the rules on interviewing would make this difficult: see 5.4. Once again, the attempt to secure due process tends towards an opposite effect. See also Baldwin J and Hunt A, 'Prosecutors Advising in Police Stations' [1998] Crim LR 521 at p 529; Auld (2001) para 35; HMCPSI, *Thematic Review of Attrition in the Prosecution Process*

to improve police decision-making, for the CPS, like the custody officer, had to ensure that prosecution cases passed the test of evidential sufficiency. As is obvious from the research discussed above, the threat of the CPS dropping cases did not seem to have this effect. For Crown Prosecutors were in a similar position to that of the custody officer in having to rely on what they were told by police officers and this made it difficult for them to take a truly independent view of the case.

The CPS position was not, however, quite so dependent as that of the custody officer. Firstly, with no suspect in the cells awaiting a decision there was no time pressure on the CPS. Secondly, the CPS made decisions on the basis of written files in which obvious flaws would be more difficult to conceal. On the other hand, the CPS was not a decision-taker but a decision-confirmer or reverser. It is more difficult to reverse a decision of which one disapproves than it is to refuse to take it in the first place. The result was 'prosecution momentum': the continued prosecution of cases which perhaps should never have begun. We say 'perhaps' because the CPS will often, through no fault of its own, not know how weak or strong a case is when it first sees the file if, for example, identification or scientific evidence is still being processed.[49] Suppose the scientific evidence, when it arrives, is inconclusive. The problem is that it is even more difficult to reverse a decision to prosecute a case that has been ongoing for weeks or months than it is to reverse it when it is first received from the police. Consequently, as we shall see later, discontinuance rates are low even though acquittals remain high.

Auld's (2001) recommendation that charging become the responsibility of the CPS was an acknowledgment of these problems. White (2006) views this as a belated acceptance that the Scottish model was unjustly rejected by the Philips Commission. However, as we shall see in 7.4.5, the police have significant prosecution powers to issue PNDs. Further, in minor cases, especially where a guilty plea is expected, the police can charge without consulting a prosecutor – as they do in around half of all cases.[50] Under the statutory charging scheme, prosecutors are now based in police stations so that they can make prosecution decisions speedily, and with the advantage of being able to discuss cases with the investigating officers. When decisions need to be taken 'out of hours', officers can call 'CPS Direct' – a call-centre-style service headed by a Chief Crown Prosecutor. There are now the following options:[51]

   (i) *Release without charge or bail*: It is still up to the custody officer to decide whether the case should be considered for prosecution. Custody officers remain gatekeepers,

---

(*The Justice Gap*) (London: HMCPSI, 2003) (the latter two reports particularly concerning 'overcharging' by the police). Also see the anecdote about custody officers and prosecutors working together in 7.3.3 below.

   [49] Ashworth A and Fionda J, 'The New Code for Crown Prosecutors: Prosecution, Accountability and the Public Interest' [1994] Crim LR 894; and reply by Daw R, 'A Response' [1994] Crim LR 904.

   [50] CPS, *Annual Report, 2008–9* (London: SO, 2009). The exact numbers are not known, but most of these are motoring cases.

   [51] PACE, s 37A (as amended by CJA 2003) gives the DPP the power to issue guidance. See CPS, The Director's Guidance on Charging (3rd edn, 2007), available at <http://www.cps.gov.uk/publications/directors_guidance/dpp_guidance.html> (accessed 5 January 2010).

putting to duty prosecutors cases that they think should be considered for prosecution, making those decisions themselves in minor cases, and sometimes bailing suspects to return at a later date when the evidence has been collated and evaluated. The choices facing prosecutors then are to: NFA or order that one of various types of warning be given; prosecute (see (ii) below); or delay the decision (see (iii) and (iv) below).

(ii) Immediate charge: This can be done only if the usual two-stage test is satisfied – that there is sufficient evidence (a 'realistic prospect of conviction') and that prosecution is 'in the public interest'. Where suspects admit guilt and a magistrates' court hearing is anticipated, this conclusion can be reached on the basis of the key witness statements plus a summary of the interview presented by the investigating officer (since there would not normally be time to play the taped interview(s) or prepare a written version). However, this may take some hours, and PACE, s 37(7) (as amended) now provides that detention can continue until this is determined. Where a contested or Crown Court hearing is anticipated, more extensive documentation is required, often necessitating recourse to (iii) or (iv) below.

(iii) Bail pending a future decision: When presented with evidence in accord with (ii) above, prosecutors will sometimes need more evidence in order to make a definite decision. They may therefore order custody officers to bail suspects to return to the station on a specified date. Bail conditions can be applied, but this is a matter for the custody officer. Prosecutors must make 'action agreements' with investigating officers – a timetable for providing specific evidence without unnecessary delay. Custody officers may decide themselves to release suspects on bail, pending a decision by a prosecutor, if they judge there to be insufficient evidence available for a decision at that time.

(iv) Custody pending a future decision: In situations such as (iii) above, but where suspects are considered unsuitable for release on bail even with stringent conditions,[52] they may be held in custody and charged if a 'threshold test' is satisfied. In this circumstance, the suspect must be brought before the magistrates at their next sitting (as previously when a suspect was charged and held in custody). When prosecutors are not available in person or on the phone, custody officers can do this themselves when authorised by a police inspector, but the case must be brought to a prosecutor as soon as possible. The threshold test requires 'reasonable suspicion' that the suspect committed an offence and a belief that, on the face of it, it is in the public interest to prosecute. In these circumstances, as with (iii) above, there must be an action agreement with a date set on which the full two-stage test will be applied. This could be seen as no more than a reiteration of the general duty of prosecutors to review cases, and to change the original decisions in the light of new information, and applies equally to cases charged immediately or charged following a period on bail. But it can also be seen as another lurch in the direction of crime control, allowing charges to be laid on the basis of nothing more concrete than 'reasonable suspicion', and reverting to the era of the 'prima facie' case that the CPS was supposed to consign to history.

---

[52] For discussions of bail criteria and conditions, see 4.2 and 9.4.

7.3.3 **Case construction, evidential sufficiency and the CPS**

The CPS is under a duty to continuously review cases until their completion, but the 'prosecution momentum' referred to earlier is an obstacle to that. The statutory charging scheme aims to help the CPS to screen cases effectively for evidential strength by eliminating prosecution momentum in three main ways. First, some prosecutors are located in police stations to advise the police as well as to make decisions. The DPP's 'guidance' actually *requires* the police to seek advice in serious cases. Early legal advice should help the police to secure the evidence needed for successful prosecutions in more cases than hitherto. Second, it enables prosecutors to discuss possible charges with investigating officers at a point when the police, but not the CPS, may think there is sufficient evidence, again giving the police the opportunity to secure that evidence whilst, for example, the suspect is still in custody. Third, prosecutors have been made into decision-*makers*; they are no longer simply decision-*reversers*.

Very little research[53] is available at the time of writing (October 2009), so we can only guess at what difference the scheme will make, but it is unlikely to be radical, especially as the police still decide many cases themselves. Seeking and taking advice, and engaging constructively with prosecutors, requires a cultural change on the part of the police. Earlier experiments that located prosecutors in police stations found that few custody officers or investigating officers sought CPS advice on charges, despite their sometimes inadequate grasp of the relevant facts or law in particular cases.[54] And, as a senior prosecutor has warned,[55] the CPS also requires a cultural change: to assert its independence at the same time as working closer with the police is not straightforward. Thus HMCPSI/HMIC found that in a large number of face-to-face interactions between prosecutor and police, there was little or no discussion, and that 'action agreements' were frequently inadequately followed up and carried out.[56] But the problem is also structural. One reason why charge sergeants and custody officers were 'bounced' into making poor decisions by investigating officers was because all their information came – orally – from investigating officers. They could listen to suspects, but rarely did. Prosecutors in police stations are in a similar situation. Indeed, the 'threshold test' invites prosecutors to initiate prosecutions on the basis of a low level of evidence, though the bail provisions do encourage prosecutors to delay decisions where this is practical. The full evidential test should be applied when the file is complete but this is done in less than half of all such cases.[57] Prosecutors, like custody officers, now have to be speedy decision-makers – not just for 'efficiency' in the crime control sense, nor just to satisfy the custody time limits in a bureaucratic sense (see 4.3), but also because many suspects about whom decisions have to be made are

---

[53] Other than the HMCPSI/HMIC (2008) report, which is managerialist, and does not aim to be academic, though we will see that it produced some insights of value.   [54] Baldwin and Hunt (1998).
[55] Brownlee (2004).   [56] HMCPSI/HMIC (2008) paras 11.26–11.31 and 13.8–13.22).
[57] HMCPSI/HMIC (2008) paras 12.8–12.10.

waiting in the cells, often in ghastly conditions (again, see 4.3). But to be speedy, prosecutors will sometimes have little or nothing more on which to base decisions than custody officers used to have. Whilst prosecutors will, as now, later review cases on the basis of a written file, when they do this they will again be decision-reversers. Whether reversing their own colleagues' decisions will be more palatable than reversing police decisions remains to be seen.

Role-conflict is another structural problem. The government's 'Narrowing the Justice Gap' initiative requires the CPS to increase the numbers of offenders 'brought to justice'. This means more guilty pleas (on which see ch 8), more convictions in general, and fewer discontinuances (ie dropped cases).[58] The CPS Annual Reports proudly proclaim CPS progress in all these respects.[59] But the CPS is also supposed to act as a neutral truth-seeking 'Minister of Justice'.[60] This requires the discontinuance of weak (and cautionable) cases. Whilst the statutory charging scheme aims to identify and eliminate weak cases before prosecution is initiated, thus reducing the numbers of cases that should be discontinued, CPS guidance on the use of the threshold and then the full two-stage test recognises that in many cases initial decisions will be taken on inadequate information and will need to be reversed eventually. Discontinuances, then, are double-sided. The Government sees them as indicators of poor CPS decision-making because of poor case preparation, for example; but they can also be seen as indicators of CPS fairness to defendants, wishing to prosecute only those against whom the evidence is strong. For example, discontinuances in cases with ethnic minority defendants are higher than in cases with white defendants, and this is because there are more of the former cases that should not be prosecuted.[61] We need to know *why* cases are discontinued before judgment can be passed on whether discontinuance rates should rise or fall.

The proportion of cases discontinued by the CPS has declined from 12.5% for most of the 1990s to 8.7% in 2008/09 (with a spike at around 15% in 2002/03).[62] Over two-thirds of these are cases dropped for evidential insufficiency or because the prosecution is unable to proceed (eg material witnesses went missing or refused to give evidence).[63] This might suggest that the CPS is doing the job which Philips set out for it. However, between 1985 and 2009 the percentage of cases ending in conviction in

---

[58] Home Office, *Justice for All* Cm 5563 (London: TSO, 2002a) ch 1.

[59] See eg CPS, *Annual Report, 2007–8* (London: SO, 2008). Interestingly, the latest report (CPS, 2009) does not trumpet the guilty plea rate but guilty pleas remain important for the CPS. See statement on 'core quality standards' by the DPP and ensuing correspondence in *The Guardian*, 30 November and 2–4 December 2009.

[60] This ethical dimension is discussed in Young R and Sanders A, 'The Ethics of Prosecution Lawyers' (2004) 7 Legal Ethics 190.

[61] HMCPSI, *A Follow-up Review of Cases with an Ethnic Minority Dimension* (London: CPSI, 2004b) paras 11.21–3. See chs 2 and 3 for discussion of the treatment of ethnic minorities by the police.

[62] Barclay and Tavares (1999) ch 4; CPS, *Annual Report, 2008–9* (London: SO, 2009).

[63] HM CPSI, *Discontinuance (Thematic Review)* (London: HMCPSI, 2007). Similar patterns were found in HMCPSI, *Thematic Review of Attrition in the Prosecution Process (The Justice Gap)* (London: HMCPSI, 2003).

the Crown Court hovered around just 80%. The problem for the CPS is that, in any group of cases with a realistic prospect of conviction, we would expect some cases to end in acquittal, and some to end in conviction. It is impossible for the CPS to be sure which will fall into which category and so it is not surprising that there is a significant acquittal rate. To drop all cases predicted as possible acquittals would lead to convictions as well as acquittals being reduced. However, the number of judge-ordered and -directed acquittals has remained high (12.7% in 2008/09: CPS, 2009), though on a slow downward trend, and the weakness of many of these cases is obvious from the start.[64] There are therefore too few, not too many, discontinuances.[65]

So, many cases are clearly evidentially weak from the outset and only some of these are dropped, many of which the police know should be dropped. The Stephen Lawrence case was such an example: the police did charge some of the five suspects, but when the CPS discontinued the case (in consultation with the police) this came as no surprise to the senior investigating officers, and the official enquiry report regarded the CPS decision as inevitable on the basis of the evidence collected by the police (Macpherson, 1999).

Then there are the cases which appear weak, which the police do not wish to drop and which the CPS do prosecute. Sometimes this is because the police working rules which led to the initial charges embody values shared by the CPS. As one prosecutor told McConville et al, when one suspect gets 'away with it... it gets back to the others. You've got to get to know your territory – it's a bit of a policy decision' (McConville and Sanders, 1992). Despite the statutory charging scheme, some defence solicitors say the police continue 'to be influential in prosecution decision-making, by exaggerating the strength of the evidence and pushing through weak cases.'[66] Shared working rules need not always involve weakness or cynical calculation. A commitment to do whatever is reasonably possible for distressed victims has also been found to lead to prosecutions continuing despite evidential weakness.[67] At other times there is a good chance of a guilty plea (see ch 8), or the chance of a freak conviction (see chs 9 and 10). This can be made more likely by the police and prosecutors working together, manipulating their power over suspects in custody. When a colleague of

---

[64] Block et al, *Ordered and Directed Acquittals in the Crown Court* (Royal Commission on Criminal Justice Research Study No 15) (London: HMSO, 1993); HMCPSI, *Review of Adverse Cases* (London: HMCPSI, 1999b); Zander M and Henderson P, *Crown Court Study* (Royal Commission on Criminal Justice Research Study No 19) (London: HMSO, 1993) pp 184–5.

[65] McConville M and Sanders A, 'Weak Cases and the CPS' (1992) LS Gaz, 12 February, p 24. Note that in the magistrates' courts the conviction rate remains very high (only around 2% being acquitted: CPS, 2009). The disparity between conviction rates in the two levels of court is discussed in ch 9 below.

[66] Kemp V, *A Scoping Study Adopting a 'Whole-Systems' Approach to the Processing of Cases in the Youth Courts* (London: Legal Services Research Centre, 2008) p 32.

[67] On vulnerable victims, see Sanders et al, *Victims with Learning Disabilities* (Oxford: Centre for Criminological Research, 1997) summarised in Home Office Research Findings No 44 (London: HMSO, 1996) (which the CPS actually sought to publicise to deflect criticism that it was not doing enough in such cases); and see 7.6 below. On road deaths see Cunningham S, 'The Unique Nature of Prosecutions in Cases of Fatal Road Traffic Collisions' [2005] Crim LR 834 at 842.

ours visited a police station in 2008 he asked about the disclosure of evidence to suspects before interview and was told by the prosecutor: 'We disclose the best evidence to elicit a guilty plea...that is what we want.' The prosecutor also said they had a target of increasing the number of guilty pleas by 30% (although he did not say over what period) and made a point of the fact that the police and prosecutor form a 'prosecuting team'. Prosecutors do not always evaluate the evidence rigorously because they assume the defendant will plead guilty anyway. 'Continuing review' is judged inadequate by the government's own inspectorate in many cases,[68] but why look for problems in cases that are likely to end in a guilty plea? And if problems are found, why give up the possibility of a conviction for the certainty of a 'failure'? All this is not only consistent with the government's 'narrowing the justice gap' policy – it is demanded by it.

In addition, the police and CPS – like all law enforcement agencies set upon prosecution[69] – 'construct' cases to be strong. This is a natural part of the adversarial system, and would be unobjectionable if the defence had similar resources and a similar approach, but they have neither.[70] Police constructions therefore tend to dominate prosecution and court processes, giving them enormous power in the process of determining guilt and innocence. Let us examine some of the ways this is done.

7.3.3.1 Fabrication of evidence

One way of constructing cases is by creating the facts. Occasionally this may be pure fabrication. There was fabrication in many miscarriages of justice in the 1980s and 1990s, for example, the 'Guildford Four' case.[71] Another way in which the police can create prosecution evidence is by holding rigged witness identification parades. For example in *Kamara* the defendant was placed in a 'line-up' wearing prison clothes![72] Every time a scandal like this erupts the police say that they have rooted out the corruption and law-breaking and tightened up procedures, or that the law has changed to prevent it happening again. We think they do protest too much. There is no doubt that scandalous police behaviour persisted in the aftermath of PACE 1984 and the creation of the CPS the following year. Police officers have admitted planting evidence on drug offence suspects,[73] as almost certainly happened in *Somers*[74] (see 2.4.3). In July 2000

---

[68] HMCPSI (1999b). Also see Baldwin J, 'Understanding Judge Ordered and Directed Acquittals in the Crown Court' [1997] Crim LR 536 at p 547; Hoyano et al, 'A Study of the Impact of the Revised Code for Crown Prosecutors' [1997] Crim LR 556. For a contrary view, see Phillips and Brown (1998: 139).

[69] See Nelken D, *The Limits of the Legal Process* (London: Academic Press, 1983) for a study of case construction by housing officials in relation to harassment cases.

[70] McConville et al, *Standing Accused* (Oxford: Clarendon Press, 1994).

[71] Documentary analysis showed a note of interview the police claimed was contemporaneous was not. See Rozenberg J, 'Miscarriages of Justice' in Stockdale E and Casale S (eds), *Criminal Justice Under Stress* (London: Blackstone, 1992) p 94.

[72] *Kamara* [2000] WL 664383. He was picked out despite not matching the description the witness had previously given of the suspect. The murder conviction was quashed after 19 years.

[73] Keith M, *Race Riots and Policing* (London: UCL Press, 1993) p 138.

[74] *Somers* [2003] EWCA Crim 1356.

three men sentenced to 10 years each for armed robbery in 1995 were released by the Court of Appeal. The crucial evidence against them was a witness identification of one of them, and a palm print of one of the others at the scene of the crime together with the discovery in his flat of a stun gun allegedly used in the robbery; strong evidence indeed. Eventually it was discovered, because the officers involved had been subsequently convicted of a series of corruption offences, that the witness had been shown a photo of the suspect before the ID parade (another way to rig a line-up), the palm print had failed to match on the first two occasions and so the final match was, in the euphemistic words of the courts, 'unreliable', and the stun gun had probably been planted by the officers.[75] We could detail many other instances[76] of what is often termed 'noble cause corruption', the existence of which a former Metropolitan Police Commissioner himself admitted.[77]

From a freedom perspective, fabrication of evidence is an ignoble act done in an ignoble cause. It undermines the rule of law and amounts to a non-democratic arrogation of power by the police. And, of course, it leads to significant losses of freedom to those who should never have been convicted.

7.3.3.2 Interrogation and witness evidence

The process of construction is more subtle when evidence is obtained through 'interviews'. Confessions, and other self-incriminating statements, are usually the product of interrogation (ch 5). Thus even 'non-fabricated' confessions are created by the police (in conjunction with the suspect). The police construct cases both in the questions asked and in those not asked. McConville et al,[78] found an example of a store detective being advised by the police not to ask a suspected shoplifter if she had forgotten to pay, since a positive answer might provide grounds for acquittal on the grounds of no mens rea. As this example illustrates, the police do not seek all the evidence which might bear on the guilt or innocence of suspects, but only the evidence which will strengthen the case against them. As one officer put it, 'By not asking the question, you don't get the answer that you don't want sometimes.' (Taylor, 2006: 147). The same processes are at work when interviewing other witnesses and in the construction of identification evidence (ch 6). Taylor quotes an officer as follows: 'Police officers tend to look at prosecuting somebody and all they look towards is getting the evidence to secure the conviction...For example, the defendant had two mates who witnessed the assault, shall we interview them? Well, they're going to back the defendant aren't they? So the investigators don't bother going to see them...'[79]

---

[75]   *Martin, Taylor and Brown* [2000] EWCA Crim 104.

[76]   See, for example, Elks L, *Righting Miscarriages of Justice? Ten Years of the Criminal Cases Review Commission* (London: Justice, 2008) ch 10; Waddington (1999: 147-9), and the quashing in July 2000 of the convictions in 1990 of the 'M25 Three' (police found to have conspired with an informant to give perjured evidence in court): *Davis, Rowe and Johnson* [2001] 1 Cr App R 115.

[77]   *The Guardian*, 11 March 1995.   [78]   McConville et al (1991: 74).

[79]   Taylor C, *Criminal Investigation and Pre-Trial Disclosure in the UK – How Detectives Put together a Case* (Lampeter: Edwin Mellen Press, 2006), p 119.

7.3.3.3 Summaries of interviews

It is standard for the police to prepare a summary of any tape recorded interview with a suspect. In practice, both defence and prosecution lawyers tend to rely on these summaries in order to save time and money.[80] For many years these particular police constructions have been known to be inaccurate.[81] Their inaccuracy is, however, unidirectional; they nearly always overstate the extent to which a full confession or an incriminating statement was made. Prosecution files are therefore constructed to appear to be stronger than they 'really' are. In the rare event that a tape of an interview is listened to or the full transcript read, prosecution momentum will have developed. Sometimes it is only when cases are contested that different versions of the facts emerge. Thus in one case a juvenile was prosecuted instead of being cautioned because, according to the police summary, he denied the offence. Only when the defence solicitor showed the prosecutor the interview transcript was this shown not to be true (Kemp, 2008: 38). The pressures on defendants to plead guilty early in the life of a case, often before a tape can be heard or transcribed, are, however, intense (see ch 8). The provisions in the statutory charging scheme for bail in cases that are not clear-cut give prosecutors the opportunity to reduce these problems. However, prosecutors are, and will continue to be, under pressure to make concrete decisions as often as possible, particularly as charging many cases on the basis of the threshold test is allowed. In all cases, the DPP's guidance specifically allows for prosecutors to make decisions on the basis of oral summaries of evidence by investigating officers. So the new arrangements are unlikely to make much difference.

7.3.3.4 Scientific evidence

We saw in ch 6 that scientific evidence is not as solid and objective as it may seem. Forensic scientists have little or no control over the material which they are testing, and the conditions in which it was collected and stored. The material will often be incomplete or contaminated, sometimes selected to prove a point, and occasionally tampered with. Take the relatively simple matter of fingerprints: 'You might have 3 or 4 sets of fingerprints at the crime scene, one of which matches the defendant. Someone should be saying "but what about the other 3 sets? Who do they belong to?" but they never do and we never tell them.'[82] Scientists also often have to be 'led' by the police because to be asked to simply 'test' a substance will often be pointless. But the process of leading is a construction process. We also saw that much science is 'cutting edge'. This is another way of saying 'unproven'. The prosecution

---

[80] See Baldwin J and Bedward J, 'Summarising Tape Recordings of Police Interviews' [1991] Crim LR 671 at 672.

[81] See ibid; Sanders A, 'Constructing the Case for the Prosecution' (1987) 14 JLS 229; McConville et al (1991); and Baldwin J, *Preparing the Record of Taped Interview* (Royal Commission on Criminal Justice Research Study No 2) (London: HMSO, 1992).

[82] Detective, quoted by Taylor (2006: 146). Taylor observes that the existence of the other fingerprints is frequently not disclosed to CPS or defence lawyers.

will seek experts with the theories to back their cases. Overall: 'At each stage of the pre-trial process, forensic science is utilised by prosecution agencies as a tool for case construction.'[83] Or, as Taylor (2006: 12) puts it, in relation to evidence in general, including witness evidence: '... the instinctive reaction is still to seek the evidence that supports the charge.' Thus, balance is needed by providing the defence with appropriate resources, so that they can engage in counter case construction by seeking their own scientific evidence, but restrictions on legal aid funding prevent this in most cases (see ch 9).[84]

7.3.3.5 Non-disclosure of evidence

Many of the cases discussed in chs 5 and 6 illustrate another form of case construction: non-disclosure. The failure of the police to disclose relevant information can not only make cases appear strong to prosecutors, but actually to be strong in court – often leading to wrongful convictions.[85] The types of evidence in question are almost infinite. They include scientific tests and identification evidence that point to suspects other than the defendant or initial failures to match fingerprint or identification evidence with the accused; witness statements or fingerprint evidence (see the example in 7.3.3.4 above) that contradict or undermine prosecution evidence (eg that suggest the defendant was somewhere else when the crime occurred or acted in self-defence); and acknowledgement that some prosecution witnesses are informers or have other characteristics that raise doubts about their reliability (eg previous convictions). In *Ward*[86] the police hid certain evidence from the prosecution and the defence, and the prosecution hid other evidence from the defence. Government scientists had also deliberately suppressed material unhelpful to the Crown's case, and had created a distorted picture of the forensic evidence. The Court of Appeal responded by laying down strict rules for disclosure which reduced the right of the prosecution to suppress evidence. Unfortunately, this did not stop similar cases arising thereafter, such as the M25 Three[87] and the *Cannings* and *Clarke* medical scandals cases discussed in 6.6. The Criminal Cases Review Commission identified non-disclosure as the third most common reason for referring convictions to the Court of Appeal in 1999–2000, though it has dealt with relatively few non-disclosure cases in recent years.[88] The problem is not confined to the police and CPS, as prosecution non-disclosure in a '£100m fraud case' (that collapsed as a result) prosecuted by Her Majesty's Customs and Excise

[83] Roberts P and Willmore C, *The Role of Forensic Science Evidence in Criminal Proceedings* (Royal Commission on Criminal Justice Research Study No 11) (London: HMSO, 1993) p 26.

[84] This lack of funding may violate the principle of 'equality of arms' (ECHR, Art 6). See Ashworth A, 'Legal Aid, Human Rights and Criminal Justice' in Young R and Wall D (eds), *Access to Criminal Justice* (London: Blackstone, 1996).   [85] See generally Jones C, *Expert Witnesses* (Oxford: OUP, 1994) ch 10.

[86] *Ward* [1993] 1 WLR 619.

[87] Failure to disclose that a key prosecution witness was a police informant: *Davis, Rowe and Johnson* [2001].

[88] The problem was highlighted in the Commission's *Annual Reports* for 1999–2000 and 2003–4, but hardly mentioned in annual reports from 2006/07 onward, but see Elks (2008: 256–8) for non-disclosure cases involving Customs and Excise.

(HMCE) illustrates.[89] Indeed, the Court of Appeal has noted 'substantial evidence' suggesting an HMCE *policy* of non-disclosure of crucial details in drug importation cases (such as the involvement of participating informers) 'not only to the defence but also to members of HMCE's legal department, prosecuting counsel and of course trial judges'.[90]

Ward represented the high-water mark of a trend towards due process in the law of disclosure. Subsequent cases began a judicial retreat back towards crime control, supported by the Runciman Commission on the ground that *Ward* 'created burdens for the prosecution that go beyond what is reasonable'.[91] A new scheme was enacted in the Criminal Procedure and Investigations Act 1996 (hereafter CPIA) that was so crime control-oriented that the DPP himself accepted that it could lead to miscarriages of justice.[92] Although the scheme was presented in terms of 'efficiency'[93] it was actually very inefficient, so it was amended by the Criminal Justice Act (CJA) 2003.[94]

The prosecution is under a duty in most cases to disclose the case which they plan to present to the court. This is usually unproblematic given that if the prosecution do try to 'surprise' the defence through the evidence they adduce, the fact of earlier non-disclosure becomes obvious, and appropriate remedial steps can be taken by the court (such as granting an adjournment). The problem in such cases as *Ward* lies with material which the prosecution do *not* intend to present to the court but which might have been helpful to the defence. Here non-disclosure will not routinely become apparent at the trial, so some alternative mechanism designed to deal with this issue had to be devised.

The statutory scheme applies to all Crown Court cases and contested magistrates' court cases. The prosecution must now, at the earliest possible stage, disclose all material (unless it is 'sensitive' – see 392–3 below) which 'might reasonably be considered capable of undermining the case for the prosecution or of assisting the case for the accused' (CJA 2003, s 32, amending CPIA, s 3(1)(a)). In Crown Court cases the defence must respond with a statement setting out its main points, if a not guilty plea is anticipated (CPIA, s 5); as with the right of silence provisions (see 5.3) adverse inferences may be drawn in relation to major issues raised at trial that are not covered in this statement. Following this, and throughout the pre-trial and trial stages, prosecutors must keep this test under review – in other words, if they become aware subsequently of material that has not been disclosed when it should have been, they must disclose it (CJA 2003, s 37, creating CPIA, s 7A).

---

[89] *The Guardian*, 24 June 2005. This was an 'informer' case. For discussion see Taylor C 'Advance Disclosure and the Culture of the Investigator' (2005) 33 IJ Sociology of Law 118.

[90] Quoted in Elks (2008: 257). See further *R v Choudhery and others* [2005] EWCA Crim 2598.

[91] RCCJ (1993: 95). [92] *The Guardian*, 15 July 1999.

[93] Redmayne M, 'Process Gains and Process Values: the CPIA 1996' (1997) 60 MLR 79.

[94] We will only give the broadest outline of the law and its problems. For detailed discussions see Redmayne M, 'Disclosure and its Discontents' [2004] Crim LR 441; Quirk H, 'The Significance of Culture in Criminal Procedure Reform: Why the Revised Disclosure Scheme Cannot Work' (2006) 10 IJ E & P 42. Also see Attorney-General's Guidelines on Disclosure (2005 revision). Available at <http://www.attorneygeneral. gov.uk/>, and the Code of Practice issued under CPIA, s 23.

There are several problems with the law of disclosure and the way it works:

1. Prosecutors can only disclose material of which they are aware. It is up to police 'disclosure officers' to fully inform the CPS. They send the CPS 'schedules' (ie lists) of all non-used items that they think meet the test in CPIA, s 3(1)(a). These should describe the items sufficiently clearly for the CPS to decide what should be disclosed to the defence – or, at least, to decide what the CPS should examine so that informed decisions can be made. The scheme therefore depends on the competence and honesty of the police. However, most disclosure officers are inadequately trained, which they acknowledge themselves.[95] And, except in the most serious or complex cases, the disclosure officer is the main officer in the case (over 90% of the time in the HMCPSI (2008a) research), who therefore has a stake in securing a conviction.

Two problems arise. First, the way the police describe unused material much of the time makes it impossible for prosecutors to assess its likely importance (eg, 'contents of a drawer').[96] Second, relevant material is frequently missing (eg the omission of significant negative forensic findings in a child abuse case).[97] Some non-disclosure is due to laziness, antipathy to 'paperwork', error and lack of understanding. Some arises from reluctance to disclose information, because: 'If I mention something on a schedule I might get asked questions about it but if I don't mention it on the schedule...' (quoted by Taylor, 2006: 153). An example would be where informers are involved: 'I am sure that there are a lot of cases where there are informants involved and we are never ever told about it.'[98] Then there is what Taylor calls the 'ideological resistance which many officers feel towards the legislation', summed up by one detective as follows: 'The prosecution file is supposed to be "the case" and then you supply another package and that will contain ammunition for them' (2006: 89). Or, as an officer quoted by Quirk (2006: 48) commented, 'This thing where you've got to give them all your, all the weaknesses in your case. Well, if they can't find them, why should we give them?' Finally, there is the nature of police work itself. Taylor observes that the police can 'exclude material such as witness statements, not by refusing to disclose it, but by choosing not to record it at all' – for example where a witness description is, said one officer '...not what I'm trying to prove here...It should be going down that the woman in number 33 has given a contradictory description but it just won't happen' (2006: 102–3). As another put it, as in most cases officers work alone, 'If you wanted to hide something you could – easily' (p 147).

---

[95] HMCPSI, *Disclosure – Thematic Review* (London: HMCPCI, 2008a) para 4.13. This has been a consistent research finding for years: Quirk (2006); Taylor (2006: 53–6).

[96] This was a problem in around half the cases in the HMCPCI (2008a) research (paras 5.7 and 7.17).

[97] HMCPSI (2008a: para 7.17). For similar findings from pre-2003 research see Crown Prosecution Service Inspectorate, *Thematic Review of the Disclosure of Unused Material* (Crown Prosecution Service Inspectorate: London, 2000); Plotnikoff J and Woolfson R, *'A Fair Balance'? Evaluation of the Operation of Disclosure Law* (London: Home Office, 2001); Quirk (2006); Taylor (2006). On the other hand, many disclosure officers err so far on the side of caution that they disclose almost everything, having given little or no thought to its relevance: HMCPSI (2008a) para 5.9.

[98] Prosecutor, quoted by Taylor (2006: 108). On 'paperwork' see pp 108–21; 132–73.

And so there is a fundamental contradiction: the police job is to construct as strong a case as is possible without being overtly dishonest; the CPIA is designed to recognise and remedy the problem that what is left out of that construction might be more revealing of the truth than what is put in it, and so the defence should be provided with that material. However, the people given the job of identifying what the defence should be provided with are the very people who the CPIA is designed to protect the defence against! Moreover, there is little evidence that – when prosecutors are aware of omissions – the CPS do much to remedy the situation (other than to make late disclosure when they are aware of relevant material, see 2. below). Nor does the CPS seem to attempt to educate, cajole or threaten particularly poor-performing police units (HMCPSI, 2008a: para 7.18).

2. A second problem with the disclosure regime is that the CPS, like the police, have conviction-oriented goals that conflict with whatever due process philosophy underlies the CPIA. Moreover, while prosecutors are better trained than are the police, much of this preparatory work is done by paralegal CPS officers with little legal training, court experience or cultural affinity for neutral justice. One paralegal said of the way the CPIA reduced the disclosure obligation on the prosecution: 'Now we are entitled to say "on your bike, why should we do it all?" Sometimes you were ending up doing their defence work for them because you were giving them their defence' (Quirk, 2006). These views are not universally held in the CPS, and – as in all areas of criminal justice where there is discretion – practice varies between individuals and offices. The law is too imprecise to restrict discretion and judgement, as is probably inevitable when dealing with material that might assist a case (the defence) about which one knows little. Thus some officers and prosecutors disclose on the basis of interpretations of the law that are ungenerous to the defence, while others give the defence the benefit of the doubt (HMCPSI, 2000; Taylor, 2006: 98–101).

The use of barristers, particularly in the Crown Court, is a further complicating factor. Barristers tend to provide the defence with far more material than necessary, often on the day of trial (HMCPSI, 2008a: para 2.23 and ch 8). Quirk (2006) found barristers to be very opposed to the restrictive CPIA regime. This could reflect their lack of 'belonging' to any organisation or 'side', raising questions about how impartial state-salaried prosecutors can ever be. Where the police description is inadequate (as it often is) the prosecutor should inspect the material. This is actually done in less than half of all the cases where it should be (HMCPSI, 2008a: paras 7.29–7.31). The result is both failure to disclose some material that should be disclosed and over-disclosure, especially on the day of the trial.

Quirk (2006) found that relevant material is often revealed by chance during trials. Doubtless it would come to light more often if prosecutors had the time and inclination to search for it, but even those with the latter do not have the former. A change of approach would require both the cultural values of a good defence lawyer – which presumably most prosecutors do not have – different performance targets and different structural goals. The reason for such late disclosure is that in nearly half of all cases initial disclosure is inadequate (HMCPSI, 2008a: para 7.2). Continuing review is more frequently adequate (satisfactory in 71% of cases in the HMCPSI (2008a) research: para 8.2), but only because in many cases material is handed to the defence on the day of the trial, causing delays and late guilty pleas. Timely disclosure is hampered by the lack of overview by one lawyer in most cases (HMCPSI, 2008a: para 8.15). This all reflects the problems highlighted with both police and CPS.

3. A third problem is what should be done about 'sensitive' material that the prosecution believes it is not in the 'public interest' to disclose, such as from informers and from bugging and phone tapping (both discussed in ch 6)? In *Rowe and Davis v UK*[99] the prosecution withheld evidence on the grounds of 'public interest immunity' without informing either the trial judge or the defence. This was found to be in breach of the Convention duty on the prosecution to disclose 'all material evidence in their possession for or against the accused'. The solution is to ask the trial judge to rule that the information can be withheld on the grounds of public interest immunity (PII) (discussed further in 6.2).

The police are therefore now required to itemise all material that they consider to be too sensitive to be disclosed. As with disclosure generally (see problems 1. and 2. above), this is an inherently crime control-oriented provision as it ignores the key factors of competence, culture and structure within police forces and the CPS, Thus police officers told Quirk (2006) and Taylor (2006: 172) that awkward information that could undermine the case is sometimes classified as 'sensitive', in the hope the CPS would not notice or care. The test is whether disclosure would create 'a real risk of serious prejudice to an important public interest.'[100] A senior police officer should oversee this, and prosecutors should examine all material classified in this way by the police to see if the test is satisfied unless this is clear from its description. Even if this is done to the highest standard, balancing the public interest against the right of the defendant to a fair trial is sometimes impossible.[101]

But frequently it is done to a low standard. The HMCPSI research found that in only two-thirds of the cases where a disclosure officer classified some material as 'sensitive' was the material adequately described, but the prosecutor sought a copy of the item or a better description in only one-third of those with inadequate descriptions. Less than 20% of the cases said by disclosure officers to contain 'sensitive' material actually passed the test. In most cases there was no discernible input from senior officers. In over half the cases where a disclosure officer classified some material as 'sensitive' the prosecutor's reasons for agreeing/disagreeing, and that were given for whether a PII hearing was required, were inadequate. Both police and CPS were blamed by HMCPSI for these results. One consequence of this is that material which should be disclosed to the defence is not, and is often unread by the CPS too, creating: '... a significant risk that miscarriages of justice may occur' (2008a: para 9.11).[102]

---

[99] [2000] 30 EHRR 1.   [100] *H & C* [2004] Cr App R 179.

[101] For such a case see *West* [2005] EWCA (Crim) 517.

[102] And see HMCPSI (2008a: ch 9) regarding sensitive material. This is an even worse result than reported by Plotnikoff and Woolfson (2001). The HMCPSI comment that the levels of compliance regarding

The judge at a PII hearing can proceed in one of three ways:

(a) inform the defence of the application and the nature of the material and conduct an inter partes hearing;

(b) inform the defence of the application but not of the nature of the material and conduct an ex parte hearing (ie, no defence present); or

(c) conduct an ex parte hearing without even informing the defence (who, if the application is granted, will never know that material has been withheld).

The second approach can be made fairer by appointing special counsel to represent the defence, but the courts have vacillated over whether this should be usual or exceptional.[103]

4. A fourth problem with the regime is that the defence disclosure obligation, which has been expanded by the CJA 2003, could infringe the presumption of innocence enshrined in Art 6.2 because it requires the defence to assist the prosecution.[104] However, given the tendency of common law judges to interpret domestic law as already compatible with European norms, and the 'margin of appreciation' doctrine of the European Court of Human Rights, other commentators think it unlikely that a successful challenge to this aspect of the CPIA could be mounted under either the Human Rights Act 1998 or by taking a case to Strasbourg.[105]

Quirk (2006) comments: 'The statutory regime requires the culturally adversarial police to fulfil an effectively inquisitorial function; prosecutors to view material from a defence perspective; the defence to act in the interests of the administration of the justice system rather than of their clients; and defendants to cooperate with proceedings against themselves.' Hence this concern expressed by a Law Society representative in 1999 is equally valid now: 'When I go to international conferences and explain this Act to lawyers from other countries they look at me in disbelief and wonder how we can have a legal framework that is so patently unfair.'[106] In conclusion, it is clear that nondisclosure, along with the other issues discussed above, allows the police to construct cases to their advantage that increase the prospects of conviction. Prosecutors are to

---

all aspects of the disclosure rules that they discovered were lower than found by previous research because they were examining 'live' cases, and so observed non-compliance that was not evident simply from scrutiny of the files. While this is true, it is likely that research on disclosure – including that of the HMCPSI – generally understates the level of non-compliance. This is because it concentrates on contested cases. Guilty pleas are generally ignored. However, some people plead guilty because they think the prosecution case is stronger than it is, and/or they cannot find evidence to make the defence case plausible. Much of the time this may be precisely because of inadequate disclosure.

[103] See *Jasper v UK* (2000) 30 EHRR 441; *Fitt v UK* (2000) 30 EHRR 480; *H & C* [2004] 2 WLR 335; *Lewis* [2005] Crim LR 796. Discussed by Redmayne (2004) and in 6.2.

[104] See *DPP, ex p Lee* [1999] on the original CPIA. For an analysis of the new obligations, see Redmayne (2004). See 5.3.3 for further discussion in the context of the erosion of the right to silence, of which this is part.

[105] See Sharpe S, 'HRA 1998: Article 6 and the Disclosure of Evidence in Criminal Trials' [1999] Crim LR 273.

[106] Quoted by Woffinden B, 'No, You Can't See. It Might Help Your Client' *The Guardian*, 4 May 1999.

some extent unaware of these constructions, to some extent aware but supportive of them, and to some extent mediators between police and defence. But the extent to which the last point is true is insufficient to justify their characterisation as 'neutral' Ministers of Justice.[107]

The disclosure system as actually operated leads to delays, adjournments, inappropriate discontinuances and a waste of public money (HMCPSI, 2008a: chs 11 and 12). Worse, it is a continuing recipe for miscarriages of justice. The changes brought in by the CJA 2003 were made in full knowledge of this. They are ECHR-compliant, and go some way to remedying the most unjust aspects of the CPIA regime. Why not go the whole way, and simply open the police file to the defence (excepting sensitive material that could be dealt with via PII applications as now)? In France, for example, defence lawyers have access to the full prosecution dossier.[108] Or why not require certain types of information (eg previous convictions of prosecution witnesses) to always be disclosed? One answer is that in some cases there is a vast amount of material, such as CCTV footage. Who is going to pay for what, in most cases, would be lengthy and unproductive trawls? Another is that, if the police are determined to keep evidence from the defence, they might simply remove the most damaging parts anyway.

7.4 **The public interest, the police and the CPS**

If, and only if, a case passes the 'evidential' test, the police and CPS have then to consider whether prosecution is in the 'public interest'. This is a flexible concept. What is perceived as in the public interest will vary according to one's experiences and political views. In some types of case evidential and 'public interest' matters get blurred – Quick, for example, found that prosecutors were reluctant to prosecute doctors for gross negligence manslaughter, so they set their evidential requirements higher than necessary.[109]

Assisted suicide is a particularly difficult issue. It is a crime (contrary to the Suicide Act 1961, s 2) but is it in the public interest to prosecute someone who is only helping victims to do as they (lawfully) wish? Should prosecutors condone murder in the absence of a change in the law by Parliament? Should people be forced to live against their will simply because Parliament lacks the will to enter this controversy, or are there legitimate fears that some terminally ill or incapacitated victims may feel under pressure to terminate their lives? Until 2009 the CPS dealt with these cases on an

---

[107] See further Young and Sanders (2004).   [108] In theory, at any rate. See further Hodgson (2005).
[109] Quick O, 'Prosecuting "Gross" Medical Negligence: Manslaughter, Discretion and the CPS' (2006) 33 JLS 421.

ad hoc basis, though it seems it actually never prosecuted.[110] But everyone who helped loved ones to die feared they might be prosecuted. Debbie Purdy did not want to place her partner in legal jeopardy when the time came for her to want his help in dying. She persuaded the House of Lords to order the DPP to publish a policy on such cases so that people would know where they stand.[111] The result (an interim policy, with a view to a firm policy being published in 2010) does not rule out prosecutions where there is a cause for concern. But cases such as that of Purdy and James will not be prosecuted. Controversial types of crime involving the interests of the state, sometimes including grants of immunity, will be examined in 7.6.1.

The majority of cases involving the 'public interest' concern the question of warning as an alternative to prosecution. Also known as 'diversion' (that is, diversion from the courts) warnings are part of the armoury of all law enforcement agencies.[112] Police warnings (often referred to as 'cautioning') attracted little public controversy for many years until their use became so frequent that government and police spokespeople in the early 1990s began to blame them for rising crime rates. In this section we will look behind the generous facade of cautioning to see how far it increases freedom, and how far recent developments continue or reverse this trend.

7.4.1 Caution rates

The Philips Commission was concerned that, in the late 1970s, only 4% of adults (though many more juveniles) were cautioned for non-road traffic offences. At that time caution rates varied greatly from police force to police force, and still do. In 2007 the average indictable caution rate for all offenders was 40%, but police force averages varied from 49% in South Yorkshire to 25% in Greater Manchester (both urban forces) and 57% in Dyfed-Powys to 22% in North Wales (both rural).[113] Individual forces are not even consistent over time: in the previous edition, South Yorkshire force was our example of a low cautioning force. Variation between forces is less a product of the offence profiles of each force and more a product of offender mix (high cautioning forces have more offenders with no criminal record) and police forces pursuing different cautioning policies.[114] It seemed unfair to Philips that whether or not one was prosecuted depended more on where the offence was committed than on what the offence was or who did it. The government agreed, and issued caution guidelines in

---

[110] See Mullock A, 'Prosecutors Making (Bad) Law?' (2009) 17 Medical Law Review 290.

[111] *R (on the application of Purdy) v Director of Public Prosecutions* [2009] UKHL 45.

[112] For an extended discussion, see, Dingwall G and Harding C, *Diversion in the Criminal Process* (London: Sweet & Maxwell, 1998).

[113] Ministry of Justice, *Criminal Statistics England and Wales, 2007* (London: MoJ, 2008). See generally Evans R and Ellis R, *Police Cautioning in the 1990s* (Home Office Research Findings No 52) (London: HMSO, 1997).

[114] Laycock G and Tarling R, 'Police Force Cautioning: Policy and Practice' (1985) 24 Howard JCJ 81; Evans R and Wilkinson C, 'Variation in Police Cautioning Policy and Practice in England and Wales' (1990) 29 Howard JCJ 155.

1985, 1990, 1994, 2005 and yet again in 2008.[115] They exhort police forces to achieve greater consistency, and, in 1990, encouraged cautioning as:

There is widespread agreement that the courts should only be used as a last resort, particularly for juveniles and young adults; and that diversion from the courts by means of cautioning or other forms of action may reduce the likelihood of re-offending.[116]

Prosecution was therefore seen as potentially harmful, largely because of its stigmatising effects. By the early 1990s, however, the equally plausible view, that cautioning erodes the deterrent effect of the law and thus tacitly encourages crime, was being voiced by government. There is no reliable evidence on this issue one way or the other (see 7.4.2). In all probability, prosecution will harmfully stigmatise some people, while cautioning will tacitly encourage others, and many other factors, such as the manner in which prosecution or caution is administered and the developmental stage of the individual will also be important. In other words, it is almost impossible to know the best strategy for any one person, and the best aggregate strategy for society as a whole will always be contestable. The Conservative governments of the early/mid-1990s and the subsequent Labour Government of the late 1990s decided that cautioning should be restricted, more on the basis of the electoral appeal of these policies than their basis in research.[117] As we shall see later, the guidelines discourage the use of 'repeat cautions' and the Crime and Disorder Act 1998 carries that policy through into the new framework for delivering 'reprimands' and 'warnings' to 10- to 17-year-olds. Thus, as table 7.1 shows, cautioning of adults and juveniles rose sharply in the 1980s and early 1990s, and then oscillated down and up, but both remain far higher now than they were when the Philips Commission reported in the early 1980s. But only for a few years in the early 1990s was it agreed by government and its criminal justice agencies that the courts were to be used as a last resort. The 2008 Circular now states that its aims are (inter alia) to 'divert offenders where appropriate from appearing in the criminal courts' and to 'reduce the likelihood of re-offending' (para 8).

A number of issues arise from these trends. Firstly, more cautioning does not necessarily mean more consistent cautioning. Nor does it necessarily mean the right people being cautioned for the right reasons. A more fundamental problem is that of the overall level of prosecution and cautioning. Police prosecution rates remain much higher than those of other law enforcement agencies, such as the Health and Safety Executive and the Inland Revenue. Are there any good reasons for this? Underlying these issues is the most intractable problem of all: the control of prosecution and cautioning.

---

[115] Home Office, *Simple Cautioning of Adult Offenders* (Home Office Circular 016/2008) (London: TSO, 2008).

[116] Home Office, *The Cautioning of Offenders* (Home Office Circular 59/1990) (London: HMSO, 1990) para 7.

[117] Evans R, 'Cautioning: Counting the Cost of Retrenchment' [1994] Crim LR 566; Sanders A, 'What Principles Underlie Criminal Justice Policy in the 1990s?' (1998) 18 OJLS 533.

Table 7.1 Caution rates (per cent of all found guilty or cautioned for indictable offences)

	Males				Females			
	12–14	14–17	18–20	21+	12–14	14–17	18–20	21+
1982	n/k	38	3	4	n/k	65	6	12
1986	n/k	44	9	10	n/k	70	18	26
1990	n/k	58	19	16	n/k	77	34	34
1994	81	56*	34	25	94	77*	50	44
1998	72	48*	34	24	88	67*	46	39
2004	67	45*	30	21	86	68*	48	36
2007	68	46*	37	30	87	70*	57	43

* = 15–17
n/k = not known
Source: Ministry of Justice (2007) and Home Office Statistical Bulletin 21/99

7.4.2 The framework of cautioning

The process begins with the investigating officer's opinion regarding what action should be taken in a case. This is communicated to an officer of at least the rank of sergeant, who decides whether to charge, to arrange for the caution to be administered either immediately or at a later date, or to refer it to the CPS.[118] In the past, when senior officers considered the cases of juvenile suspects who were reported in either of the above ways, they often used to pass them on to a multidisciplinary juvenile liaison bureau (JLB) which would either recommend a disposition to the police or, occasionally, have the decision delegated to it by the police. Now, under the Crime and Disorder Act 1998 (CDA), juvenile caution decisions are returned to the police. JLBs – dubbed 'juvenile let-off bureaux' by some police – were seen as too 'soft'. The Act establishes, for the first time, a statutory framework for cautioning under 18s. Instead of 'cautions' it refers to 'reprimands' for first warnings (if the offence is not too serious) and 'warnings' for offenders who have been 'reprimanded' once or who commit an offence which is too serious for a reprimand. No-one who has been previously reprimanded may be reprimanded again, and no-one who has been warned may be warned again (unless two years have elapsed since the first warning).[119]

For those under the age of 18 there are two preconditions: sufficient evidence of the offender's guilt to give a realistic prospect of conviction; and admission of the offence by the offender. An 'appropriate adult' must be present if the offender is under 17.[120]

---

[118] Home Office, *The Cautioning of Offenders* (Home Office Circular 016/2008) para 27. It used to be required that this officer have appropriate training (Circular 30/2005, para 26), but no longer.

[119] CDA, s 65(1) (as amended by the Criminal Justice and Court Services Act 2000, s 56).

[120] CDA 1998, s 65(1) and (5). See 4.2.3 for discussion of 'appropriate adults'. On the CDA generally see Leng et al, *Blackstone's Guide to the Crime and Disorder Act 1998* (London: Blackstone, 1998).

For adults there are the same preconditions, plus the need for the offender's informed consent (Circular 016/2008, para 9). These preconditions are due process safeguards intended to ensure that, because a caution is a statement of guilt (which can be cited in court), the offender really is guilty and would be convicted if prosecuted.

As a mechanism for protecting innocent suspects from administrative determinations of guilt, the preconditions have been found wanting. Some cautions are administered precisely because there is insufficient evidence, and sometimes in the absence of consent or an admission.[121] Nor is consent or an admission a safeguard in reality. Young found that juveniles were prepared to admit and consent to almost anything to escape from the 'coercive jaws' of the criminal process, and Dignan (1992: 465) refers to adults having to 'bargain in the shadow of the law'.[122] In *Metropolitan Police Comr, ex p Thompson*[123] the cautioning inspector admitted that he often offered a caution and then asked the alleged offender if he understood that this amounted to an admission of the offence, with the implicit threat that if the suspect did not agree to this, he or she would be prosecuted instead of cautioned. Although the Divisional Court held that cautions offered as an inducement to confess, such as happened here, are invalid, it clearly had been a common practice and – having come to light again in 2002[124] – probably still is. Another caution was quashed by the Divisional Court after a juvenile was incorrectly told that what he did (watch his cousin shoplift) amounted to theft. It was on this basis that he admitted his 'guilt' and consented to be cautioned. But as there was insufficient evidence to prosecute, there was no informed consent.[125]

Since the Crime and Disorder Act 1998 took away the requirement that juveniles consent to reprimands and warnings, the police may be further encouraged to impose reprimands and warnings as they please. This was challenged in *R (on the application of R) v Durham Constabulary*. The defence argued that because a reprimand has a punitive element (particularly in a sex offence, such as in this case, where it results in the listing of the offender on the Sex Offenders Register) it should be defined as a 'charge' for the purposes of the ECHR, and therefore Art 6 protections, including the need to secure informed consent, should apply. The House of Lords rejected the argument that reprimands are punitive and, therefore, that Art 6 applied.[126] The preconditions to cautioning, reprimanding and warning are largely presentational rules, giving the

---

[121] Dignan J, 'Repairing the Damage: Can Reparation Be Made to Work in the Service of Diversion?' (1992) 32 (4) BJ Crim 453; Evans R, *The Conduct of Police Interviews with Juveniles* (Royal Commission on Criminal Justice Research Study No 8) (London: HMSO, 1993b) p 41; Sanders (1998); Evans R and Puech K, 'Reprimands and Warnings: Populist Punitiveness or Restorative Justice?' [2001] Crim LR 794; Holdaway S 'Final Warning: Appearance and Reality' [2003] 4 Criminal Justice 355; and other research cited in Field S 'Early Intervention and the "New" Youth Justice' [2008] Crim LR 177 at 178–9.

[122] Young R, 'The Sandwell Mediation and Reparation Scheme' (Birmingham: West Midlands Probation Service, 1987).

[123] *Metropolitan Police Comr, ex p Thompson* [1997] 1 WLR 1519.

[124] *R (U) v Metropolitan Police Commissioner* [2003], endorsing the decision in *Thompson* (above).

[125] *Metropolitan Police Comr, ex p P* (1995) 160 JP 367 discussed by Evans (1996).

[126] *R (on the application of R) v Durham Constabulary* (2005) UKHL 21; (2005) 1 WLR 1184 (HL). For critique see Gillespie A, 'Reprimanding Juveniles and the Right to Due Process' (2005) 68 MLR 1006.

appearance of due process, but having little effect on the police. It has been judicially stated that the police enjoy a wide discretion in deciding whether the conditions for cautioning are met and successful challenges to the legality of cautions will be rare.[127]

Thus deciding whether or not to caution remains nearly always a matter for the police alone. Moreover, we shall see that investigating officers who favour prosecution over caution can have the individual charged with little chance of resistance from other officers. However, the 2008 Circular (para 26) does say that offenders are entitled to legal advice (if they have been arrested) and that full disclosure of the evidence should be made.[128]

Cautioning criteria

The 2008 Circular states that, if the cautioning preconditions are met, the police should take into account the 'public interest' criteria set out in the Code for Crown Prosecutors. The Crime and Disorder Act 1998 (CDA), s 65(1) (as amended) provides similarly for the under 18s. These criteria include:

- the nature of the offence;
- the likely penalty if the offender were to be convicted;
- the offender's age, state of health, previous criminal history and attitude towards the offence (including offers to compensate victims, and so forth);
- the impact of the offence on the victim.

Factors making prosecution more likely include premeditation, the involvement of a group of offenders, a discriminatory motive, or the suspect being under a court order such as bail. In any one case many of these criteria pull in different directions. An offender may have a criminal record but commit a minor offence for which he has compensated the victim; or may commit a relatively serious offence but have no previous criminal history. The victim may favour or oppose prosecution, or simply be indifferent.

Guidelines such as these suffer many faults.[129] We mention but three here. Firstly, vagueness: how serious, for instance, is 'serious'? Seriousness is clearly a subjective matter. Police and societal judgements vary, as well as shift over time. A striking example is the reclassification of cannabis from a class 'B' to a class 'C' drug in 2003, then back again in 2008.[130] The police are now expected to warn people found with small quantities of cannabis instead of arresting and prosecuting, though only for a first offence.[131] The recent escalation in response was despite an experiment in toler-

---

[127] *Ex parte P* (1995) LEXIS 9 May 1995. In line with this approach, a challenge to a caution for simple possession of cannabis, contrary to police policy at the time, was unsuccessful: *R v Commissioner of Police of the Metropolis* [2007] Crim LR 298.

[128] But as we saw in *DPP v Ara*, discussed in 7.2.2 above, this does not always happen.

[129] See further Ashworth A, 'The "Public Interest" Element in Prosecutions' [1987] Crim LR 595.

[130] Misuse of Drugs Act 1971 (Amendment) Order 2008.

[131] Ministry of Justice Circular 2009/05, para 62.

ance in South London which saved a huge amount of police time, improved community relations and had no apparent bad effects.[132] Continuing controversy over drugs classification[133] illustrates well how offence 'seriousness' is often a fiercely contested matter.

Secondly, the criteria can be manipulated by the police. Cases can be constructed to seem more or less serious, as we shall see in relation to the views of victims of domestic violence.[134] The police are supposed to use a 'gravity factor matrix' to weigh competing factors (see the 2008 Code, para 3), but research results indicate that some, at least, use 'common sense' more (Evans and Puech, 2001; Holdaway, 2003; Field, 2008). The guidelines explicitly state that the view of the victim should be sought, but that the victim's consent is not essential to caution. No guidance is provided on how far the victim's views should outweigh other criteria. Thus research has consistently found the police justifying non-prosecution of some cases by reference to the views of the victim, but at the same time prosecuting other cases where the victim did not want prosecution.[135]

Thirdly, most of the criteria are non-prioritised, so it is impossible to say whether a given decision is right or wrong if an offender 'scores' high on one criterion and low on another. Only 'seriousness' and previous record are prioritised in the Code and 2008 guidelines.[136] In particular, the 2008 Guidelines require indictable-only offences to be referred to a prosecutor if the police wish to caution rather than prosecute (para 11). As with the preconditions discussed under the previous subheading, the application of ostensibly inhibitory criteria is left primarily to the very institution which they are supposed to inhibit. Not surprisingly, this renders the criteria largely presentational.

'Caution Plus': Juvenile warnings and conditional cautioning

There are, broadly speaking, four main responses to crime: *punitive*, where the object is to punish offenders and to deter them and others; *rehabilitative*, where the object is to encourage offenders to desist or teach them how to avoid the situations which lead to offending; *restorative*, where the object is to enable or order the offender to make good the damage caused to the victim and/or the community, and, finally, *doing*

---

[132] Warburton et al, 'Looking the Other Way: The Impact of Reclassifying Cannabis on Police Warnings, Arrests and Informal Action in England and Wales' (2005) 45 BJ Crim 113.

[133] As evidenced by the Home Secretary sacking the chief drugs adviser, Professor David Nutt, in October 2009 for critiquing drugs policy: <http://www.guardian.co.uk/politics/2009/nov/01/david-nutt-gordon-brown-drugs> (accessed 5 January 2010).   [134] Clarkson et al (1994).

[135] See, for example, Sanders A, 'Personal Violence and Public Order' (1988a) 16 IJ Soc L 359; Evans R, 'Police Cautioning and the Young Adult Offender' [1991] Crim LR 598 ; Clarkson et al (1994).

[136] In R (on the application of Guest) v DPP [2009] Crim LR 730 a caution was given for a serious assault, without consulting the victim (though the suspect had apologised and agreed to pay £200 compensation). The court, unusually, decided that the decision was wrong, and there should be a prosecution. On conviction the assailant was given a six week suspended prison sentence and ordered to pay £1,000 compensation. The case and others like it have aroused widespread concern and prompted a government review of 'out-of-court punishments' due to report in March 2010: <http://www.bbc.co.uk/blogs/panorama/2009/12/panorama_prompts_review_of_cau.html> – accessed 5 January 2010.

nothing in the belief that the offence was a 'one-off', that the offender will 'grow out of crime', that intervention of any kind will be counter-productive, or that the offence was so trivial that any official response would be an overreaction. These different ideas underlie not only sentencing but also deciding whether or not to prosecute. Most prosecutions are undertaken punitively, although not necessarily only on this basis, given the possibility of rehabilitative or restorative sentencing. Most cautioning used to be on the 'do nothing' basis, as cautioning led to little or no further action. Simple cautions and cannabis warnings, and now, for juveniles, 'reprimands' under the Crime and Disorder Act 1998 remain on this basis.

Juvenile 'warnings' under the Crime and Disorder Act 1998, however, and conditional adult cautions are intended to be primarily rehabilitative and/or restorative – and, in future, punitive elements will be attachable too.[137] Every juvenile who is 'warned' should be assessed by a 'youth offending team' for a rehabilitative or restorative programme. Participation is neither a legal obligation, nor a condition of receiving a warning, although non-participation (and any reasons given for non-participation) will be recorded and can be cited in future court proceedings.[138]

These arrangements build upon pre-existing 'restorative' or 'caution-plus' practices run in the 1980s and 1990s by many police forces, usually in relation to juveniles.[139] At one time the ethos of such schemes was primarily rehabilitative. But increasingly the cautioning process is used to encourage offenders to acknowledge the harm caused by the offence and to make restorative gestures such as apology or compensation. Some schemes build on Braithwaite's theory that deviant behaviour can best be reduced by responding to it with reintegrative shaming, and aim to make offenders ashamed of their behaviour in a way which promotes their reintegration into their community.[140] In an evaluation of one scheme offenders told their 'story' and were asked what harm they think they caused. Victims and their supporters put their 'side', and the offenders' supporters were also asked how the offence affected them.[141] It was found that, although there was little of the punitiveness that Lee observed in traditional cautioning,[142] the police emphasised the 'last chance' nature of the caution and the supposedly dire consequences of reoffending. Young and Goold argue that this element of deterrent over-

---

[137] The Police and Justice Act 2006, s 17 (amending CJA 2003, s 23) provides for punitive clauses in conditional cautions (eg fines; attendance at a day centre).

[138] CDA, s 66. However, conditional cautions which contain legal obligations are being extended to juveniles: Criminal Justice and Immigration Act 2008, s 48 and Sch 9 (amending CDA 1998, ss 65 and 66). Both this and the new punitive conditions are to be piloted in the second half of 2009.

[139] Evans and Ellis (1997). But for a discussion of a scheme catering for adults too, see Hughes et al, 'Diversion in a Culture of Severity' (1998) 37 Howard JCJ 16.

[140] Braithwaite J, *Crime, Shame and Reintegration* (Cambridge: CUP, 1989).

[141] See further Young R, 'Integrating a Multi-Victim Perspective into Criminal Justice Through Restorative Justice Conferences' in Crawford A and Goodey J (eds), *Integrating a Victim Perspective within Criminal Justice* (Aldershot: Ashgate, 2000).

[142] Lee M, *Youth, Crime, and Police Work* (Basingstoke: Macmillan, 1998). Evans and Puech (2001), on the other hand, did find extensive punitiveness. See also O'Mahoney D and Doak J, 'Restorative Justice – Is More Better? The Experience of Police-led Restorative Cautioning Pilots in Northern Ireland' (2004) 43(5) Howard JCJ 484.

kill where the offence is relatively minor could undermine the legitimacy of the process.[143] Unfortunately, warnings administered under the Crime and Disorder Act 1998 will indeed be of a 'last chance' kind, and so the police will be right to continue to emphasise this, however misguided this policy is in respect of some incidents and some offenders. And now that punitive conditions can be attached to conditional cautions, some of the most progressive changes of the last decade are being rolled back. As a result, the scheme arguably violates Art 6,[144] and is an example of the 'punitive turn' that encompasses many types of 'diversion'.[145]

The new youth justice framework and the practices taking place within it encompass an uneasy mix of penal philosophies, and many current 'restorative justice' initiatives attempt to be both rehabilitative and directly victim-oriented.[146] These objectives are laudable but not always mutually compatible. This goes to the root of the problem of multiple objectives discussed in ch 1 which gave rise to our proposed 'freedom' perspective. Restorative justice projects need to calibrate the degrees of freedom given and taken away to both offenders and victims (both current and future) by these projects, taking into account the importance of securing the human rights of all concerned, in order to assess the way in which the greatest overall amount of freedom can be secured.

Moving away from the 'do nothing' approach could be compatible with the 'freedom approach' in two ways: in reducing reoffending (increasing the freedom of future victims) and in diverting cases from prosecution where it was thought offenders need help or support or where victims would not otherwise be compensated (increasing the freedom of offenders and current victims). But doing 'something' does not seem, in aggregate, to reduce offending, at least not by much.[147] It inevitably encroaches on freedom to some extent, and as we have seen, the police cannot always be trusted to do it properly anyway. Further, so-called diversion schemes result in new populations of minor offenders being drawn into the criminal justice net or experiencing more intervention than is justified given the seriousness of their offence. Between 2005 and 2008 detections fell slightly (though, as crime rates also fell, the percentage detected rose).

---

[143] Young R and Goold B, 'Restorative Police Cautioning in Aylesbury' [1999] Crim LR 126.

[144] See Brownlee I, 'Conditional Cautions and Fair Trial Rights in England and Wales: Form versus Substance in the Diversionary Agenda?' [2007] Crim LR 129 (who reaches no firm conclusion on the point).

[145] See further Field S, 'Practice Cultures and the "New" Youth Justice in England and Wales' (2007) 47 BJ Crim 311.

[146] For good discussions of many of the problems see Gray P, 'The Politics of Risk and Young Offenders' Experiences of Social Exclusion and Restorative Justice' (2005) 45 BJ Crim 938; Fox et al, 'Restorative Final Warnings: Policy and Practice' (2006) 45 Howard J 129.

[147] Evidence of the effect of cautioning on *general* deterrence is not available and would be extremely difficult to produce. There is little evidence that restorative cautioning has any greater effect on re-sanctioning rates than traditional cautioning or other approaches: Wilcox et al, *Two-year Resanctioning Study: A Comparison of Restorative and Traditional Cautions* (Home Office Online Report 57/04) (London: Home Office, 2004); Shapland et al, *Does Restorative Justice Affect Reconviction?* (MoJ Research Series 10/08) (London: MoJ, 2008). Also see McAra L and McVie S, 'Youth Justice? The Impact of System Contact on Patterns of Desistance from Offending' (2007) 4 Euro J Criminology 315.

Prosecutions fell in line with this, but cautions have risen more. The slowly increased caution rate of the last few years looks like lowered punitiveness, when it is equally likely to be net widening.[148] This is driven in part by a deliberate attempt by government to bring more offenders into the net of formal social control through requiring the police to achieve 'measurable targets' while at the same time providing them with administratively efficient methods of 'closing cases'.[149] There are many dangers here, including that innocent people get caught up in the net and that serious offenders are not put before the courts.

One way of addressing such problems would be to take away the power of the police to determine who gets cautioned and in what way. This is not on the agenda as far as ordinary cautions, reprimands and warnings are concerned. However, the CPS controls 'conditional cautions', introduced for adults by the CJA 2003 (ss 22–27). Conditional cautions should be used when 'the public interest justifies a prosecution [but] the interests of the suspect, victim and community may be better served by the suspect complying with suitable conditions aimed at rehabilitation or reparation. These may include restorative processes.'[150] The prosecutor specifies the condition(s), but the caution, like 'simple' cautions, are administered by the police. If any condition is breached, prosecution is not automatic – it is for the CPS to decide[151] – but it would be the expected response. A Code of Practice states (para 2.2) that 'simple' cautions remain for circumstances where prosecution could not be justified (due to the offender's illness or triviality of offence, for example) or where the condition that would be imposed, such as compensating the victim, has already been voluntarily fulfilled anyway.[152] As with simple cautions, victims should be consulted, and it is envisaged that offenders will often be bailed pending consultation and possible mediation meetings between offenders and victims. Conditional cautions are not to be the 'next step' for someone who has been previously given a 'simple' caution, as someone previously cautioned for a similar offence should only exceptionally be conditionally cautioned (para 3.3). Conditions must be proportionate, achievable and appropriate (para 5.1) and may be cited in court and used in relation, for example, to the Sex Offenders' Register. Conditional cautions have been fairly slow to take off: they became a normal part of all prosecutors' weaponry only in April 2008, and in the following year only around

---

[148] Figures derived from CPS (2009) and Kershaw et al, *Crime in England and Wales, 2007/8* (Home Office Statistical Bulletin 07/08)(London: TSO, 2008) table 1.1. For earlier research showing that net widening is an endemic feature of (so-called) alternatives to prosecution see Parker et al, *Receiving Juvenile Justice* (Oxford: Basil Blackwell, 1981); Sanders A, 'The Limits to Diversion from Prosecution' (1988c) 28 BJ Crim 513; Dignan (1992); O'Mahoney and Doak (2004). The term 'net widening' derives from Cohen S, *Visions of Social Control* (Cambridge: Polity Press, 1985).

[149] See, for example, the comments of the Home Secretary on 14 December 2009 reported at <http://www.justice.gov.uk/news/newsrelease141209b.htm> (accessed 5 January 2010).

[150] Code for Crown Prosecutors, 2004, para 8.4. And see DPP's Guidance for Conditional Cautioning (2007) (available at CPS website).

[151] Criminal Justice Act 2003, s 24.

[152] Code of Practice on Conditional Cautioning, 2004. Also see DPP's Guidance (2007) (both available at <http://www.cps.gov.uk/>).

15,000 were wielded (5% of all cautions) (CPS, 2009). While we must await independent research into the working of this new scheme before reaching definite conclusions about its impact, its likely effects are not difficult to predict, as we shall now see.

7.4.3 Police working rules and cautioning

We argued above that the cautioning 'rules' do not greatly inhibit the police. Official public interest criteria are replaced in practice by unofficial police interest criteria. These working criteria may, however, lead to undesirable patterns of decision-making: cautioning of those who should be NFAd, cautioning of those who should be prosecuted, and prosecution of those who should be cautioned or NFAd.

There are two types of suspect who are cautioned when they should be NFAd: those who, as we have already observed, do not meet the preconditions, and those whose offences are so trivial that normally no action would have been taken against them. Caution is supposed to be an alternative to prosecution, not to no action. Yet we have seen that at least some of the increase in cautioning represents more offenders being drawn into the system. The reclassification of cannabis in 2003 probably led to formal 'cannabis warnings' in many cases that would have previously been subject to informal warnings, as well as many that would have previously been prosecuted (Warburton, 2005), and reclassification back to 'B' will almost certainly have displaced informal warnings still further. The same 'up-tariffing' is true for conditional cautions, some people who should have been NFAd or given a simple caution will now probably be conditionally cautioned. As some people inevitably fail to meet one of the conditions, they find themselves in court, even though the conditional caution was given in a case that should not have been prosecuted.[153] The ability to caution can make arrest worthwhile where it might otherwise be pointless (eg where there is insufficient evidence to prosecute) or too time-consuming (as cautions involve less paperwork). Moreover, if the caution is presented as a favour to the suspect, it provides, or maintains, the basis of a relationship on which future 'deals' can be built. Informers, for example, are often given informal warnings or cautions rather than prosecuted as part of maintaining a mutually beneficial relationship (see 6.2). It is no accident that control of cautioning remains largely with the investigating officer, for cautioning can be an adjunct of other aspects of policing.

Policing considerations such as order and authority, and the 'bad attitude' of the suspect, influences many officers (Field, 2008: 185). In one of many cases illustrating this examined by McConville et al (1991: 113–14), a youth with previous convictions had picked up a Mars bar and broken a piece off. Asked why they had charged rather than cautioned, the police described the defendant as a 'toe-rag' who had been suspected of

---

[153] In an early study, about one-quarter failed to comply with a condition, and most were prosecuted: Blakeborough L and Pierpoint H, *Conditional Cautions: An Examination of the Early Implementation of the Scheme* (MoJ Research Summary 7)(London: MoJ, 2007). Most of those prosecuted were given a conditional discharge – indicating that they should not, in normal circumstances, have been prosecuted.

shoplifting on several occasions but never caught. Warburton et al (2005: 120) found that officers admitted that cannabis users who they informally warned on the street would have been arrested had they been 'mouthy'. Field (2008) quotes an officer saying that suspects with criminal associates would be unlikely to be cautioned as 'they've not changed their ways have they?'[154]   And we cited (in 7.3.2) a Chief Superintendent recently endorsing the 'attitude test' to explain why some, and not others, are arrested. The same patterns of race bias which can be observed in street policing seem to operate here.[155] After reviewing several pieces of research carried out throughout the 1970s and 1980s, Fitzgerald concludes that: 'Once arrested, Afro-Caribbeans are less likely to be cautioned than whites and may be less likely than Asians to have no further action taken against them.'[156] She pins the blame on indirect factors rather than racism: Afro-Caribbeans are less likely to admit the offence (thus disqualifying themselves from a caution or warning), are more likely to be disadvantaged by the application of 'social' criteria (such as domestic circumstances) in an 'ethno-centric' way (resulting in prosecution being seen as in the public interest), and tend to have more previous convictions and cautions (possibly because of earlier biased decisions).

Some doubt on Fitzgerald's view that direct discrimination is not responsible is raised by Phillips and Brown's finding that a far higher proportion of black and Asian defendants have their cases discontinued by the CPS than do white defendants. In typically guarded Home Office-speak they say: 'The possibility must be considered that, where the defendant was from an ethnic minority group, the police were more likely to submit for prosecution cases in which the evidence was weaker than average or where the public interest was against prosecution.'[157] More recent research showing the same patterns is also 'consistent with discriminatory treatment'.[158]

The custody officer is supposed to be a protection. But as with evidential issues, the custody officer either acts as a rubber stamp or empathises with the arresting officer. Most custody officers, like police officers in general, are against extensive cautioning for adults in particular[159] and rely on the arresting officer alone for their information about the suspect: 'I'm dependent completely on what the officer says happened.'[160] What the arresting officer does and does not say determines the construction of the case as serious or trivial, and the construction of the suspect either as a public enemy or as a temporarily lapsed paragon. All this was found by Young in relation to

---

[154] Field (2008: 185).

[155] See 2.3 and 3.4, above, for related discussion in the context of street policing.

[156] Fitzgerald M, *Ethnic Minorities and the Criminal Justice System* (Royal Commission on Criminal Justice, Research Study No 20) (London: HMSO, 1993) p 33. Phillips and Brown (1998: 92) also found that both black and Asian suspects were less likely to be cautioned than were white suspects, as did Evans R, 'Comparing Young Adult and Juvenile Cautioning in the Metropolitan Police District' [1993a] Crim LR 572.

[157] Phillips and Brown (1998) p 148. See also Mhlanga (1999) summarised in: s 95 Findings no 1 (London: Home Office, 2000).

[158] Feilzer M and Hood R, *Differences or Discrimination?* (London: Youth Justice Board, 2004).

[159] Evans (1993a: 577). They are certainly against taking personal circumstances into account: Field (2008).   [160] Quoted by McConville et al (1991: 122).

the processing of mentally ill suspects. Diversion decisions were often taken when, because of mental illness, mens rea was thought to be hard to prove (that is, in cases which should not be prosecuted anyway), but less often when the mental illness was simply a mitigating factor. The wishes of influential victims and offence seriousness tended to 'trump' mental illness in determining what happened.[161]

It may well be that the relatively low cautioning rates of Afro-Caribbean (as compared to white), and poor (as compared to middle class), suspects are contrary to the Art 14 ECHR principle of equality of treatment. But the chances of any one member of a marginalised social group proving discrimination *in his or her case*, given the ability of the police to construct cases, would be vanishingly small except in particularly blatant cases. A further problem is that Art 14 is not a stand-alone provision; it only comes into play once some other Convention right is engaged. As in other areas of the criminal process, the practical value of the ECHR is not as great as might first appear.

7.4.4 Case construction, the public interest and the CPS

One of the functions of the CPS is to exercise control over the 'public interest' dimension of prosecutions. But it cannot do anything about cases which were cautioned when they should have been NFAd or prosecuted. Indeed, the police can even tie the hands of the CPS by promising that a case will be dropped. Although discontinuance is the prerogative of the CPS alone, it was held in *R v Croydon Justices, ex p Dean*[162] to be an abuse of process for prosecution to be continued after a promise, even from the police, that it would be dropped. In this case the 'deal' was discontinuance in exchange for the suspect giving evidence for the prosecution in a murder trial. This illustrates both the structurally weak position of the CPS as compared to the police, and the way the police use prosecution and non-prosecution in the 'public interest' as part of broader policing strategies.[163]

The CPS can, in principle, ensure that cautionable cases are not prosecuted by discontinuing them or, since 2003, by directing that they be cautioned.[164] As discussed in 7.4.2 above, the 'public interest' criteria in the Code for Crown Prosecutors explicitly correspond with the criteria in the Home Office cautioning guidelines. Given the research showing that many cautionable cases are still being prosecuted we would

---

[161] Young H, 'Securing Fair Treatment: An Examination of the Diversion of Mentally Disordered Offenders from Police Custody' (Unpublished Phd, Birmingham University, 2002) ch 6.

[162] *R v Croydon Justices, ex p Dean* [1993] QB 769.

[163] Although this is evidence of the power of the crime control perspective, it is not necessarily antithetical to the freedom perspective for prosecutions in relatively minor cases to be dropped in order to secure convictions in serious cases. The problem, however, is that the prosecution in the serious case may be fatally compromised once it becomes known that a key Crown witness received an inducement to give evidence. This provides the police with an incentive to suppress evidence of the 'deal'. Such deals are therefore not conducive to openness and fairness within the criminal process: a key hallmark of a free society. This illustrates the importance of not applying the freedom perspective in a crude short-term manner.

[164] CJA 2003, s 37B(3)(b).

nonetheless expect the discontinuance of at least some such cases, but this is rare. Numerous research projects carried out in the last 20 years have found that, as with evidential sufficiency, there is little incentive for the CPS to drop cases on this basis, and that the CPS and the police have similar outlooks and evaluate cases in much the same way.[165] The police still rarely consult CPS about the possibility of cautioning (Field 2008), and we have seen that the CPS relatively rarely issues conditional cautions. Take, for example, two recent drugs cases. In 1999 two charity workers running a hostel for homeless people were asked by the police for the names of people they had banned from the hostel for their drug use and/or dealing. They refused to give the names because of the charity's confidentiality policy. They were arrested and convicted of 'allowing heroin to be sold' on premises they controlled, and jailed for several years (though the sentence was reduced on appeal).[166] Then in 2007 Mark and Lezley Gibson, who had been supplying cannabis by mail order for six years, were convicted of conspiracy and sentenced to a nine-month suspended jail sentence. However, the cannabis was contained in chocolate and supplied only to MS sufferers who could prove they were indeed ill – as was Lezley.[167] What public interest was served by these prosecutions?

The most important problem for the CPS, however, is that police construction makes it often difficult and sometimes impossible to identify cautionable cases. Factors which could point towards caution or other forms of diversion are downplayed in the file, or such facts are not brought out by the police because of failure to ask appropriate questions. Thus in one of McConville et al's cases, the file did not reveal the character of the victim, giving the erroneous impression that an assault on him was unprovoked. Some prosecutors recognise this problem, although many are inappropriately – perhaps even irresponsibly – sanguine.[168] As a Scottish prosecutor told Moody and Tombs 'they [the police] usually don't do it deliberately but they can do it because they decide that the fiscal doesn't want to know that, doesn't need to know that'.[169] And, of course, there is exaggeration. Evans comments that when one digs:

beneath the legal labels of offences to assess their true seriousness...a significant number of 'trivial' offences are dealt with by the criminal justice system with legal labels attached that exaggerate their seriousness.[170]

While the CPS is undoubtedly discontinuing more cautionable cases now than it used to, the issue – as with police cautioning itself – is whether they are discontinuing as

---

[165] Crisp D and Moxon D, *Case Screening by the CPS* (Home Office Research Study No 137) (London: HMSO, 1994); Phillips and Brown (1998); McConville at al 1991; Kemp (2008).

[166] Wyner R, *From the Inside: Dispatches from a Women's Prison* (London: Aurum Press, 2003).

[167] *The Guardian G2*, 19 December 2006; *The Times*, 27 January 2007. Cannabis is well known to alleviate the symptoms, and perhaps even the advance, of MS.

[168] Crisp D, 'Standardising Prosecutions' (1993) 34 Home Office Research Bulletin 13.

[169] Moody S and Tombs J, *Prosecution in the Public Interest* (Edinburgh: Scottish Academic Press, 1982) pp 47–8. See also Gelsthorpe L and Giller H, 'More Justice for Juveniles' [1990] Crim LR 153 and Elliman S, 'Independent Information for the CPS' (1990) 140 NLJ 812 and 864.

[170] Evans (1991: 605). Also see Young (2002: ch 6) in relation to mentally disordered suspects.

often as they should and when they should. It is unlikely that they are doing either. Experimental 'public interest case assessment' (PICA) schemes (where probation officers are given the job of seeing whether there is information that would make a case cautionable) lead to more cautions, even in cases where no additional information is provided.[171] Unfortunately, the costs of running these schemes were greater than the savings achieved through diversion of these cases from the courts. However, this is partly because, despite the extra information, the CPS still did not discontinue all the cases which they could have: many of the PICA cases that continued received a conditional discharge in court, suggesting sufficient non-seriousness to warrant discontinuance.

PICA schemes show that just sensitising prosecutors to the issue leads to more (albeit insufficient) discontinuances. More important, however, is the fact that the extra information provided by PICA schemes – which the police either do not collect or which they keep from the CPS – enables the CPS to make their own independent decisions. Until schemes like this become widespread, the CPS will not be able, even if it is willing, to fulfil its statutory obligations. The Runciman Commission's recommendation that PICA schemes should be expanded 'across the country'[172] suggests that it accepted that 'prosecutors have no way of knowing what gaps there are in the information they receive'[173] and therefore cannot apply the Code satisfactorily.

7.4.5 Penalty Notices for Disorder (PNDs)

These police-administered fines were introduced by the Criminal Justice and Police Act 2001 for a small number of specified offences for adults, and subsequently extended.[174] The offences include causing harassment, alarm or distress (Public Order Act, s 5), drunk and disorderly, minor theft and criminal damage. A recent addition is a second offence of cannabis possession (a warning should normally be given for a first offence, and a third should be prosecuted).[175] The annual number of PNDs has risen sharply (over 207,000 were issued in 2007 – representing over 10% of all detected crime). Fines are fixed according to the seriousness of the offence. The payment rate is little over 50% (failure to pay then triggers court enforcement procedures), but only around 1% are challenged in court.[176]

The lack of challenge should not be taken to mean that this summary justice is necessarily fair. Fines are low (currently £80 at most) so many people pay them whether or not they feel the PND was justified, but they may not appreciate the consequences

---

[171] Crisp et al, *Public Interest Case Assessment Schemes* (Home Office Research Study No 138) (London: Home Office, 1995).   [172] RCCJ (1993: 83).

[173] Crisp (1993: 15).

[174] For details see Young R 'Street Policing after PACE: The Drift to Summary Justice' in Cape and Young (eds), *Regulating Policing: The PACE Act, Past, Present and Future* (Oxford: Hart, 2008).

[175] Ministry of Justice Circular 2009/05, under the authority of the CJPO 2001, ss 1–11.

[176] All the figures are derived from MoJ, *Criminal Statistics, England and Wales 2007* (London: MoJ, 2008), ch 7.

of this: a criminal record, likelihood of prosecution for subsequent offences and so forth. The net widening, and drawing into court of those who 'fail' these 'alternatives', that we saw happening in relation to cautioning, is almost certainly equally true of PNDs. As always, police officers driven to achieve arrest targets find the 'low-hanging fruit' all too easy to pluck.[177] Because these offences are seen as trivial, supervising officers pay even less heed than in other cases to 'quality checking' the justifiability of the arrest.

This is all particularly worrying as PNDs were extended to 16- and 17-year-olds in 2003, and were piloted for 10- to 15-year-olds in 2005/06. There are good reasons for juveniles receiving the protections we detail in ch 4, but many of these are not available at home, where most juvenile PNDs are issued (while in 90% of cases there is an appropriate adult present, few parents have legal training). Net widening was acute in the pilot studies – around half of all PNDs were issued to juveniles who would not even have been reprimanded, and many of the others replaced reprimands and warnings.[178] Thus the 'punitive turn' is made yet more acute, as reflected in 45% of the juveniles in the pilot study saying the police had been unfair.

If PNDs are only for trivial offences, why take up so much police (and court fine-enforcement) time with them? The answer is, in part, because PNDs are not so much about prosecution of individual cases as about controlling suspect populations, and should be seen as part of the wider movement to increase surveillance and control 'anti-social' behaviour. Now the police have an additional weapon to back up the order to 'move on'. And the victims who the government claims to be putting 'at the heart' of the criminal justice system? The PND scheme completely sidelines them, as it does not allow for the payment of compensation. But the victim perspective on PNDs has not been evaluated, nor the danger that ethnic minorities are likely to be over-represented (especially as ethnicity is very often not recorded),[179] nor the way poorer people are disproportionately affected by fixed penalties.

To sum up, taken together with the various forms of police and CPS caution, around one-third of crime is now prosecuted without reference to a court. The police can therefore 'get a result' with little or no scrutiny from any other agency. Yet PNDs are effectively prosecutions, and so embody all the problems of case construction, use of prosecution for policing purposes, vagueness in the case of public order offences and a cavalier attitude to evidence (Young, 2008). The growing power of the police to finalise cases leads Jackson to argue that safeguards for suspects in police stations are more important than ever – at a time when, as ch 4 shows, they are being eroded.[180]

---

[177] See Young (2008) for discussion of the research on which this is based.

[178] Amadi J, *Piloting PNDs on 10–15 Year Olds* (MoJ Research Series 19/08)(London: MoJ, 2008); Young, R, 'Ethnic Profiling and Summary Justice: An Ominous Silence?' in Runnymede Trust, *Ethnic Profiling* (London: Runnymede Trust, forthcoming 2010).   [179] Amadi (2008).

[180] Jackson J 'Police and Prosecutors after PACE: The Road from Case Construction to Case Disposal' in Cape and Young (2008). Not that this would help in the case of many PNDs and cannabis warnings, which are administered on the street. Drunk offenders are taken to the police station, however.

7.5 Non police-prosecution agencies

Substantial numbers of prosecutions are brought by non-police agencies. Health and safety offences are dealt with by the Health and Safety Executive (HSE), pollution offences by local authorities and the Environment Agency (EA), tax evasion and some drugs offences by HM Revenue and Customs (HMRC), TV licence evasion by the Television Licensing Authority (TVLA), social security benefit fraud by the Department of Social Security (DSS), and other frauds by various agencies including the Financial Services Agency, Department of Trade and Industry, and Serious Fraud Office (SFO). Many company activities are regulated by the Office of Fair Trading (OFT). Local authorities are responsible for dealing with harassment and unlawful eviction of tenants. The British 'opportunity' principle has enabled each body to develop its own prosecution policies and patterns.

Many of the 'suspects' dealt with by these agencies are companies. Their offences ought to be of major concern to policy-makers and the public. Take health and safety: in 2008/09, 180 people died at work, there were 27,594 reported major injuries, and over 350,000 other 'reportable injuries'. Over 29m working days were lost because of these illnesses and injuries.[181] The HSE estimates that in most of these incidents the employer was in breach of the Health and Safety at Work Act 1974. Thus, most of these incidents give rise to potential criminal, as well as civil, liability. In the light of under-reporting and the narrow definition of 'at work', deaths and injuries (requiring a hospital visit) at work (including to members of the public) could be around 1,400 and 50,000 per annum respectively[182] – as bad as the figures for 'normal' violence, and considerably worse than the 'official' homicide rate (648 in 2008/09).[183]

There are also a huge number of non-violent economic crimes. Criminal frauds in the UK total at least £8.75 billion per annum – £2.75 billion against individuals and £6 billion against the public sector, although its intrinsically hidden nature makes it impossible to estimate accurately. There is also an annual 'tax gap' of £30–£40 billion. If 15% of this were fraudulent the estimated fraud loss to the public sector would double.[184]

7.5.1 Patterns of enforcement

The few offences, such as those concerning benefit fraud and drugs, that are enforced by non-police agencies for which there are arrest powers are, or could be, enforced also by the police. With these offences, prosecution patterns and processes are similar to

---

[181] HSE, *Health and Safety Statistics 2008–9* (London: HSE, 2009), p 4 and 9. The HSE estimates that only 58% of all reportable accidents are actually reported (p 10).

[182] Tombs S and Whyte D, *A Crisis of Enforcement: The Decriminalisation of Death and Injury at Work* (Centre for Crime and Justice Studies Briefing No 6)(London: Kings College London, 2008). They also argue that the HSE hugely underestimates the level of under-reporting.

[183] Walker et al, *Crime in England and Wales, 2008–9* (Home Office Statistical Bulletin 11/09)(London: TSO, 2009) p 6.

[184] Levi M and Burrows J, 'Measuring the Impact of Fraud in the UK' (2008) 48 BJ Crim 293.

those of the police. But since non-police agencies cannot usually arrest, neither can they charge or detain suspects. Instead they report for summons. The decision-making structure of non-police agencies facilitates a propensity not to prosecute (Sanders, 1985a). Decisions to prosecute are always taken in the cold light of day, on the basis of a full written file, by senior officials, while decisions not to take formal action, even when there is clear evidence of crime, need not be – and frequently are not[185] – transmitted to senior officials. In principle, the approach of non-police agencies is the same as that of the police and the CPS – both the EA and HSE, for example, state that prosecution decisions should take account of the Code for Crown Prosecutors[186] – but the emphasis is usually completely different.

It is no accident that *HM Treasury* (rather than the Home Office) commissioned the Hampton Report (2005) into regulation. Its proposals aimed to make regulation more 'efficient' by reducing the 'regulatory burden' on companies and by making sanctions effective. The follow-up Macrory Report argued that regulation should be transparent, targeted, effective and proportionate, that a wider range of non-court sanctions should be created,[187] and that agencies should be prepared to take strong deterrent action when less coercive sanctions do not work (thus leaving prosecution as a last resort).[188] What could be a constructive and freedom-enhancing approach is undermined by the Regulators' Compliance Code (RCC), which states that: 'Regulators should recognise that a key element of their activity will be to allow, or even encourage, economic progress and only to intervene when there is a clear case for protection.'[189] The 'benefits' must justify the 'costs'. Prosecutions are not mentioned once.

The RCC formalises existing practice. Take the EA:

The Environment Agency regards prevention as better than cure. It offers information and advice to those it regulates and seeks to secure co-operation avoiding bureaucracy or excessive cost. . . . The purpose of enforcement is to ensure that preventative or remedial action is taken to protect the environment or to secure compliance with a regulatory system . . . the institution of a prosecution is a serious matter that should only be taken after full consideration of the implications and consequences (EA, 2008: paras 4, 6, 21).

The HSE's official policy is similarly revealing:

The ultimate purpose of the enforcing authorities is to ensure that duty holders [the people or companies under investigation] manage and control risks effectively, thus preventing

---

[185] Hawkins K, *Law as Last Resort* (Oxford: OUP, 2003).

[186] Environment Agency, *Enforcement and Prosecution Policy* (Policy EAS 8001/1/1) (2008) para 21; HSE, *Statement on Enforcement Policy* (HSE 41, 2009) para 36.

[187] Eg fines issued by regulators – similar to punitive conditions in CPS conditional cautions. See now the Regulatory Enforcement and Sanctions Act 2008.

[188] Macrory R, *Regulatory Justice: Sanctioning in a Post-Hampton World, Consultation Document* (London: Cabinet Office, 2006a). See Tombs and Whyte (2008) for a critique that identifies the bad, but not the positive, aspects of the Hampton approach.

[189] Department for Business Enterprise & Regulatory Reform, *Statutory Code of Practice for Regulators* (London: DBERR, 2007) para 3. See Whyte D, 'Gordon Brown's Charter for Corporate Criminals' (2007/08) 70 Criminal Justice Matters 31.

harm.... The enforcing authorities have a range of tools at their disposal in seeking to secure compliance with the law. (HSE, 2009: paras 1 and 3).

Paragraph 3 goes on to list the steps the agency can take, in ascending order of severity:

- give information and advice (which may include a warning that 'they are failing to comply with the law');
- serve improvement notices (requiring compliance with the law);
- serve prohibition notices (stopping work until the law is complied with);
- vary licence conditions or exemptions (relating to what the duty holder may or may not do that might be dangerous);
- issue a formal warning (on the same basis as police cautions, with the same preconditions);
- prosecute (in accordance with the evidential and public interest tests).

The 'main means' are the first four tools (para 4), and resource allocation is an explicit factor in considering not just prosecution, but any investigation at all (para 7). Other non-police agencies are similar. This approach has been characterised as comprising a 'pyramid' of sanctions, the frequency of use of each sanction decreasing as one ascends the pyramid. This strategy, some argue, will usually be as effective a deterrent as a 'first-resort' prosecution strategy, but without its disadvantages, particularly if failure to comply at one level means that the next-level sanction is the automatic result.[190]

The result is 'compliance' modes of working. Rather than treating their suspects as criminals, regulatory agencies seek to maintain continuing relationships with companies, to create 'a friendly working atmosphere',[191] to try to persuade them to comply with the law, and to avoid prosecution wherever possible. Non-police agencies and business criminals 'bargain and bluff' with each other and the threat of prosecution is perceived by regulators as often more powerful than actual prosecution.[192] But agencies are sometimes in a weaker bargaining position than the companies that they are regulating.[193] Thus Hutter comments that 'officers are to some extent dependent upon the co-operation of the regulated to comply with their demands'.[194]

Table 7.2 shows a decrease in an already low HSE prosecution rate. In 2004/05 the HSE prosecution and enforcement-notice rates were around 0.5% and 5.6%

---

[190] Ayres I and Braithwaite J, *Responsive Regulation: Transcending the Deregulation Debate* (New York: OUP, 1992), Braithwaite J, *Restorative Justice and Responsive Regulation* (Oxford: OUP, 2002). For further discussion see Baldwin R. and Black J, 'Really Responsive Regulation' (2008) 71 MLR 59. The approach was endorsed by Hampton P, *Reducing Administrative Burdens: Effective Inspection and Enforcement* (HM Treasury, London: SO, 2005) discussed later.

[191] Hutter B, *The Reasonable Arm of the Law?* (Oxford: Clarendon Press, 1988) p 189.

[192] Hawkins K, 'Bargain and Bluff' (1983) 5 L Pol Q 8; Hawkins (2003). See Dingwall and Harding (1998: ch 5) and Gobert J and Punch M, *Rethinking Corporate Crime* (London: Butterworths, 2003) ch 9 for general discussions.

[193] Richardson G, with Ogus A, and Burrows P, *Policing Pollution: A Study of Regulation and Enforcement* (Oxford: Clarendon Press, 1983).   [194] Hutter (1988: 188).

Table 7.2 HSE enforcement action

	General		Fatalities*	
	Prosecution**	Enforcement notices (prohibition and imp. notices)	Number	Prosecuted
2004–5	1,320	8,445	249	n/k
2008–9	1,231	8,054	180	n/k

* Excludes members of the public killed by work-related processes and fatalities investigated by specialised inspectorates other then the HSE.
** Number of specific offences (the number of cases is about half the numbers shown)
n/k = not known
Source: HSE (2009).

respectively.[195] Looking at all regulators, it is estimated that annually there are 400,000 warning letters, 3,400 formal cautions, 145,000 statutory notices and around 25,000 prosecutions.[196] Hawkins' study of the HSE, *Law as Last Resort*[197] was appropriately titled. One justification put forward for this approach is most corporations are 'responsible' and not 'amoral calculators' predisposed to take advantage of this 'persuasion first' policy.[198] Companies that do take advantage and hold the law in contempt are more likely to be prosecuted.[199] In addition, some aspects of financial crime, particularly major frauds enforced by the SFO, appear to be more subject to prosecution than pollution and health and safety crime.[200] And in recent years there has been some 'tough talk' on the part of government and regulator, but, as Baldwin observes, this does not necessarily mean that enforcement activity has actually become tougher.[201]

The aim of the compliance strategy is prevention rather than deterrence and punishment. This recognises, among other things, that different companies respond differently depending on a range of factors including their size and market position.[202] Whether it works or not will depend, in part, on the speed at which the pyramid is ascended, whether failure to comply automatically moves the sanction up a level and the size of its prosecution apex. But there are four questions of principle: Is the

[195] This very approximate figure was obtained by dividing the number of prosecutions and enforcement notices by the number of reported injuries reported in HSE Statistics: latest key figures for 2004/05 (HSE Web Site, Feb 2006).

[196] Macrory R, *Regulatory Justice: Making Sanctions Effective* (2006b) (available at <http://www.berr.gov.uk/files/file44593.pdf> – accessed 5 January 2009) para E3.   [197] (Oxford: OUP, 2002).

[198] Pearce F and Tombs S, 'Ideology, Hegemony and Empiricism: Compliance Theories of Regulation' (1990) 30 BJ Crim 423; Also see Cowan D and Marsh A, 'There's Regulatory Crime and then there's Landlord Crime: From Rachmanites to Partners' (2001) 64 MLR 831.

[199] Carson W, 'White-Collar Crime and the Enforcement of Factory Legislation' (1970) 10 BJ Crim 383; Hawkins (2003) ch 11.   [200] Gobert and Punch (2003: 296–303).

[201] Baldwin R, 'The New Punitive Regulation' (2004) 67 MLR 351.

[202] Lynch-Wood G and Williamson D, 'Regulatory Compliance: Organisational Capacities & Regulatory Strategies for Environmental Protection' in Quirk et al (eds), *Regulation and Criminal Justice* (Cambridge: CUP, 2010).

compliance approach an effective method of crime prevention? Are political and financial resources adequate to enable movement up the pyramid? Is it justifiable for this strategy to be adopted by non-police agencies but not by the police? Are the freedoms of all sections of society equally weighted by these different agencies?

Regarding effectiveness (and leaving the other issues to later), this is a relative matter. How effective would these agencies be if their energies were dissipated by court cases? The answer is dependent on their resources, which are minimal and declining. In the 1980s, the HSE's inspectors, for instance, were reduced in number while the traditional 'law and order' budget rose.[203] In 1999/2000 the government finally boosted spending on the HSE in real terms, but resources prevent the majority of non-fatal serious injuries from being investigated, as there are only 1,323 HSE inspectors for over 700,000 *registered* premises (HSE, 2009). So, until 1999 at any rate, only 40% of amputations at work were investigated.[204] Not even all deaths at work are investigated, and certainly not many other serious injuries.[205] Similarly, the 'SFO budget is tiny compared with (i) the size and complexity of the losses it is required to investigate … and (ii) the funds available to some of the corporations and individuals it is investigating.'[206] To take another example, it has been found that waste operators dump tons of hazardous waste in unauthorised sites (including next to shopping centres) in order to evade tax. The Environment Agency, which is supposed to inspect sites, said: 'We haven't got the resources to do it.'[207] This might be why, in 2006 there were only 744 prosecutions by the EA, of which, only 29 were against directors/senior managers: 'The majority of EA prosecutions are brought against … micro businesses'[208] who are least able to defend themselves and so are less expensive to prosecute. As Hawkins says, 'Regulatory agencies could, as a matter of policy, double or treble the number of cases prosecuted, but to do so would be at the cost of other regulatory activities deemed essential.'[209]

One measure of effectiveness is the accident rate. According to the HSE, injuries, ill-health and working days lost have gone down in the last few years. This is hardly surprising in a recession with fewer people at work, but injuries per employee have also reduced a little (HSE, 2009). Serious accidents at work predominate in factories and on building sites, not in offices and board rooms. According to a government-appointed inquiry, we tolerate a high death rate in the construction industry largely because people expect a high death rate. Many building site deaths are preventable and 'pros-

---

[203] Wells C, *Corporations and Criminal Responsibility*, 2nd edn (Oxford: OUP, 2001) p 24.

[204] Centre for Corporate Accountability, Evidence to the DoE Transport and the Regions House of Commons Select Committee (Environment Sub-Committee), September 1999.

[205] Tombs and Whyte (2008). Also see their *Safety Crimes* (Cullompton: Willan, 2007).

[206] Levi M, 'Economic Crime' in McConville and Wilson (2002).

[207] *The Guardian*, 5 April 2000.

[208] Abbot C, *Enforcing Pollution Control Regulation* (Oxford: Hart, 2009) pp 115, 150, 127. Also see Macrory (2006b: para E3).

[209] Hawkins (2002: 441). See also Middleton D, 'The Legal and Regulatory Response to Solicitors Involved in Serious Fraud' (2005) 45 BJ Crim 810.

ecutions and sentencing are ludicrously low'.[210] Moreover, EA enforcement notices are frequently not followed up.[211] Or take tax evasion: in 2008, 11,900 cases of suspected evasion by buy-to-let landlords and Internet traders were waiting to be investigated. Lack of resources also means that, according to the Chair of HMRC: 'We cannot prosecute everybody.' This is why 36 barristers repaid £605,000 to HMRC instead of being prosecuted.[212]

The enforcement of 'regulatory' offences is not, it seems, a 'law and order' matter. Questions about the methods of these agencies thus cannot be divorced from political choices about the allocation of resources. The 'pyramid' idea can only work if agencies have the resources and political backing to use all its layers effectively. In general, as Snider says:

States will do as little as possible to enforce health and safety laws. They will pass them only when forced to do so by public crisis or union agitation, strengthen them reluctantly, weaken them whenever possible, and enforce them in a manner calculated not to seriously impede profitability.[213]

Note that this is the mirror image of what takes place in 'traditional' criminal justice. Thus we have already seen in chs 2 to 5 that the state does as little as possible to enforce due process protections for suspects. It creates these only when forced to do so by public crises or international law, it strengthens them reluctantly, weakens them wherever possible, and enforces them in a manner calculated not to seriously impede the pursuit of police goals.

7.5.2 Corporate manslaughter

Since companies have legal personality, they can, in principle, commit and be convicted of criminal offences. Proving mens rea can be difficult, but few 'regulatory' offences have mens rea requirements.[214] The theoretical possibility of convicting companies for manslaughter (usually the 'gross negligence' variety) had been known for years, but until the *OLL* case in 1994,[215] there were no convictions. Between 1969 and 1993 18,151 people were killed at work.[216] Were the inadequate and unfortunate

---

[210] Donaghy R, *One Death Too Many* Cm 7657 (Norwich: Department for Work and Pensions, TSO, 2009) para 51b. Abbot (2009) also argues that a coherent deterrent strategy should be adopted using the regulatory pyramid.

[211] It is likely that other agencies have a similar follow-up problem. See Macrory (2006b: para 1.14).

[212] *The Guardian*, 9 December 2008. Tax avoidance schemes by large companies – including the newly part-government owned banks that started paying huge bonuses to senior traders again in 2010 – that may not be criminal are arguably even more of a problem. See *The Guardian*, 2 February 2009.

[213] Snider L, 'The Regulatory Dance: Understanding Reform Process in Corporate Crime' (1991) 19 IJ Soc of Law 209.

[214] *Adomako* [1995] 1 AC 171; see also *Misra and Srivastava* [2004] EWCA Crim 2375.

[215] *Kite and OLL Ltd* [1996] 2 Cr App R (S) 295.

[216] Slapper G, 'Corporate Manslaughter' (1993) 2 Social and Legal Studies 423.

Stone and Dobinson[217] really more culpable than every one of the companies which broke the Health and Safety at Work Act in these cases? It seems unlikely. Slapper estimates that in 20% of workplace deaths there is a prima facie case of manslaughter.[218] In many cases foremen, managers and/or directors are also responsible for these deaths. Hundreds of people have died in disasters like the Kings Cross fire of 1987, the Piper Alpha oil rig fire of 1988, the sinking of the 'Marchioness' in 1989 and various train crashes (Slapper, 1993). There were no prosecutions for manslaughter in any of these incidents, although there were (unsuccessful) prosecutions in the 'Herald of Free Enterprise' disaster and the Southall rail crash in 1997.[219]

If a serious crime is suspected the police investigate. If the police think prosecution is warranted the case will be passed to the CPS.[220] If the police (or CPS) decide that there is insufficient evidence for a general prosecution, the case is returned to the HSE to consider prosecution or other enforcement action under the Health and Safety at Work Act. It is true that there is usually no deliberate law-breaking in these cases (or, at least, no deliberate intention to cause injury), and these deaths occurred in the course of the perpetrators' attempts to do their legitimate jobs. But that is true also of the many surgeons and anaesthetists who have faced manslaughter charges.[221] A classic example was when Hayley Williams fell to her death from an unsafe theme park ride. The theme park operators were merely convicted of breaches of Health and Safety legislation, and fined. Hayley Williams' family condemned the fine in her case as inadequate, her aunt shouting 'I hope they will rot in hell.'[222]

The virtual immunity of companies and individual senior managers from serious criminal charges was not inevitable in practice (as Dutch experience shows),[223] or in theory. The substantive law, as developed by the judiciary, made corporate manslaughter difficult to prove. This is because fault had to be attributed to someone within the company who can be identified as its controlling mind.[224] In the mid-1990s the Law Commission therefore proposed changing the law.[225] The Government eventually pro-

---

[217] *Stone, Dobinson* [1977] 2 All ER 341. Stone and Dobinson were convicted of manslaughter after 'omitting' to adequately discharge their 'duty of care' by summoning help for someone living with them who was wasting away. That they had low IQ, had walked to the next village to try to get medical help, and had mentioned their concerns to pub staff, did not save them.   [218] *The Guardian*, 23 February 1999.

[219] *R v P&O European Ferries (Dover) Ltd* (1991) 93 Cr App Rep 72; *Attorney-General's Reference (No 2 of 1999)* [2000] 2 Cr App R 207; Wells (2001) ch 6.

[220] HSE, *Work-Related Deaths: A Protocol for Liaison* (London: HSE, 2003).

[221] Childs M, 'Medical Manslaughter and Corporate Liability' (1999) 19 Legal Studies 316; Erin C and Ost S (eds), *The Criminal Justice System and Healthcare* (Oxford: OUP, 2007).

[222] *Guardian*, 19 December 2008.

[223] Field S and Jorg N, 'Corporate Liability and Manslaughter: Should We be Going Dutch?' [1991] Crim LR 156.

[224] All of the rare successful prosecutions were of small companies. See Home Office, *Reforming the Law of Involuntary Manslaughter* (Sudbury: TSO, 2000b) para 3.16.

[225] Law Commission, *Involuntary Manslaughter* (Report No 135) (London: HMSO, 1994b); Law Commission, *Involuntary Manslaughter* (Report No 237) (London: HMSO, 1996b). For critical comment see Clarkson C, 'Kicking Corporate Bodies and Damning their Souls' (1996) 59 MLR 557; Glazebrook P, 'A Better Way of Convicting Businesses of Avoidable Deaths and Injuries?' (2002) 61 CLJ 405.

duced the Corporate Manslaughter and Corporate Homicide Act 2007. Corporations will no longer be prosecutable for the common law offence of gross negligence manslaughter (though directors and employees will). Corporations will commit the new statutory offence only 'if the way in which its activities are managed or organised by its senior management is a substantial element...' in the death (s 1(3)). The Act has been criticised as unnecessarily complex in that it requires (a) that management failure caused death, and (b) there was a gross breach of a relevant duty of care owed by the organisation to the deceased, and (c) the consent of the DPP.[226] There will be a gross breach if 'the failure in question constitutes conduct falling far below what can reasonably be expected of the organisation in the circumstances' (s 1(4)(b)). The economic, political and social factors which make agencies and governments reluctant to press prosecutions against powerful interests[227] will remain in play (see 7.6.1), making the requirement to gain DPP consent particularly worrying. The Director of Public Prosecution's reluctance to take risks in sensitive cases contrasts sharply with the Crown Prosecution Service's usual willingness to interpret the evidential test broadly. Most fundamentally, the thinking behind the Act fails to take into account the fact that deaths are the tip of an iceberg of dangerous practices leading to thousands of serious injuries each year. Legislation targeting these injuries, rather than deaths would be far more useful.[228] All these factors lead commentators to suggest that the Act will have far more symbolic than instrumental value.[229]

7.5.3 Explaining different patterns of prosecution

To summarise the above, non-police agencies usually exercise their discretion not to prosecute rather than to prosecute, preferring to use a 'compliance' strategy. Their enforcement patterns form the mirror image of those of the police, who usually use a deterrent and punitive strategy. Why do such differences arise and how are they maintained in practice?[230]

Do different crimes and criminals need different strategies?

The coercive methods characteristic of the police would be inappropriate for people and crimes dealt with by non-police agencies, if 'white collar' crime were 'self-regulating',

---

[226] Moreover, although public bodies are included in its ambit, most deaths in custody (in the broad sense discussed in ch 4) are not (see s 5 of the Act). Deaths while detained in the custody area of police stations are covered, however (s 2 (2)).

[227] Original provisions to make the Act applicable to company directors, for example, were dropped. For discussion of liability of senior managers see Wright F, 'Criminal Liability of Directors and Senior Managers for Deaths at Work' [2007] Crim LR 949.

[228] Gobert, 'The Corporate Manslaughter And Corporate Homicide Act 2007' (2008) 71 MLR 413.

[229] Gobert (2008); Ormerod D and Taylor R, 'The Corporate Manslaughter and Corporate Homicide Act 2007' (2008) Crim LR 589; Wells C, 'Corporate Manslaughter: Why Does Reform Matter?' (2006) 122 South African LJ 646.

[230] There is a sharp debate here. See Pearce and Tombs (1990) and the reply by Hawkins K, 'Compliance Strategy, Prosecution Policy, and Aunt Sally: A Comment on Pearce and Tombs' (1990) 30 BJ Crim 444.

ie these criminals keeping their crime levels as low as possible anyway. The evidence of higher levels of crime when enforcement is reduced or eliminated demonstrates that this is not so. Deterrence methods, whether straightforwardly coercive or of the 'pyramid' kind, often work better with these crimes than with street crimes. For example, the National Rivers Authority (now part of the EA) claimed that its relatively vigorous prosecution policy in the 1990s reduced pollution.[231]

The reality, as might be expected, is that some people, and some organisations, behave more morally than others. Thus Haines, for example, examining workplace deaths in Australia, found that some companies responded to deaths by trying to eliminate future risk, while others confined themselves to changes aimed at limiting their legal liability.[232] However, this is not just a matter of individual or randomly-appearing morality. Haines found that 'virtuous' organisational cultures were made less virtuous by adverse economic and financial factors. Even the most moral business people behave less morally when economic competition creates pressure to cut costs. Thus Thames Trains rejected plans to introduce an £8.2m safety system because it estimated that this would save only one life. Its valuation of a life at only £2.5m meant that the investment was thought uneconomic. In the event, 31 people died two years later when one of its trains went through a red light in an accident that the safety system would have prevented. In those two years £7.5 m was paid to shareholders.[233]

It is often said that these crimes and criminals are 'different' from those the police and CPS deal with. Braithwaite is one of the few influential figures to challenge this. He argues that the regulatory pyramid should be applied to all types of crime, defined in the broadest sense, with sanctions moving up in all cases from informal mild sanctions through restorative sanctions to 'traditional' criminal sanctions. 'Regulation' and 'law enforcement' should be available, though used sparingly, for all offences, regardless of how we classify them.[234] So far, these arguments have fallen on deaf ears. Non-police agencies are still usually referred to as 'regulatory', and their law enforcement processes as 'regulation', neutral terms from which stigma and condemnation are removed. Does a lack of social stigma lie behind the use of these terms, or do the terms contribute to the lack of stigma? Put this way, one can see that this is not a case of cause and effect, but rather of two causes operating on each other in a circular fashion. One result is that neither the public at large nor traditional text books treat 'regulatory offences' as 'real' crimes (mala in se). They are seen, instead, as mala prohibita – not things wrong in themselves, but merely things that society requires to be better regulated. It is sometimes said that the behaviour being controlled resembles acceptable business practice and hence is not mala in se. However, as Wells points out, this misses

---

[231] Dingwall and Harding (1998: 81–3). And see generally Pearce F and Tombs S, 'Hazards, Law and Class: Contextualising the Regulation of Corporate Crime' (1997) 6 Social and Legal Studies 79; Abbot (2009).

[232] Haines F, *Corporate Regulation: Beyond 'Punish or Persuade'* (Oxford: Clarendon Press, 1997).

[233] *The Times*, 12 May 2000. This was the Paddington rail crash of 1999.

[234] Braithwaite (2002). Braithwaite has successfully promoted the growth of restorative justice for 'normal' crime, and has also had some influence in relation to 'regulation'. But he has not yet persuaded governments to see the varying forms of crime as part of the *same* problem meriting the same solution.

the point that it is business people who construct the image of what practices are to be regarded as acceptable in their world. What many men regard as acceptable, by way of rape and violence, is no longer acceptable to the rest of us and nor should it be.[235] Letting criminals decide by what standards they should be judged tells us more about the sources of power in society than about the acceptability or harm of the behaviour in question.

Are different enforcement patterns the result of class bias and 'corporate capture'?

We have seen that much crime, of the conventional as well as corporate kind, imposes greater burdens on socially disadvantaged people, as does law enforcement. Class bias – like race bias – can arise indirectly through the application of criteria which bear more heavily on one section of society than another.[236] Thus Hawkins argues that, in the enforcement of 'regulatory' criminal laws, there is a 'need to preserve a fragile balance between the interests of economic activity on the one hand and the public welfare on the other'.[237] It is the unfortunate lot of the poor, the main target group for the police, that their economic activity has increasingly become non-existent through unemployment or replaceable through deskilling and globalisation.

Credence is given to this explanation by the fact that the only non-police agencies 'out of line' are those that deal with the poor and/or street criminals. First, there is the Department of Social Security fraud inspectorate which deals with social security claimants. Cook (1989) found that in 1986–87, for instance, 8,000 supplementary benefit fraudsters were prosecuted, as compared to 459 tax cheats. The Social Security Administration (Fraud) Act 1997 made prosecution of possibly fraudulent claimants even easier despite the increasing complexity of regulations that produce as many accidental errors as dishonesty; yet most of this fraud is committed by organised criminals (landlords, for example, persuading tenants to make claims) on whom few resources are expended.[238] This strategy makes sense only in ideological – rather than practical – terms. The ideologies relate to 'deserving' and 'undeserving' groups, to those who work and those who do not, and so forth. Second, there is the Customs and Excise (now part of HM Revenue and Customs), which is particularly interesting as it deals with areas as diverse as drugs (classic street crime) and corporate VAT (classic suite crime). Drug offences are enforced and prosecuted by Customs and Excise in the way that the police use the law (ie, severely), while corporate VAT fraud is enforced in the way that the Inland Revenue enforce the law (ie, lightly). Third, there is the TVLA. This agency is owned by the Post Office, which collects TV licence fees for the BBC. It is an offence not to possess a current licence if one has a TV, and officially

---

[235] Wells C, *Corporations and Criminal Responsibility*, 2nd edn (Oxford: OUP, 1993) p 25. Also see Slapper and Tombs (1999: ch 5). [236] Sanders (1985a), Slapper and Tombs (1999).

[237] Hawkins K, *Environment and Enforcement* (Oxford: OUP, 1984) p 9.

[238] McKeever G, 'Detecting, Prosecuting and Punishing Benefit Fraud: The Social Security Administration (Fraud) Act 1997' (1999) 62 MLR 261; Larkin P 'The Criminalisation of Social Security Law; Towards a Punitive Welfare State?' (2007) 34 JLS 295.

there is no way of negotiating one's way out of prosecution even though the Code for Crown Prosecutors is supposed to apply. Thousands of people – virtually all from the poorest sections of society and disproportionately women – are prosecuted every year, and literally hundreds are jailed for fine default. Yet the sums of money involved are similar to those which the Inland Revenue collects, without penalty, years after they are due.[239]

According to the related explanation of 'corporate capture', regulatory agencies become collusive as a result of their dependence on their 'suspects/ clients':

A captured agency no longer mediates between the interests of the public, which is to be protected through regulation, and the interests of the regulated industry. Instead it uses its discretion to advance the goals of regulation only so far as industry interests permit.[240]

Thus corporations act according to capitalist laws of economic behaviour rather than laws of due process or social justice. If forced to comply with laws which make processes uneconomic (or, more realistically, less profitable) firms will simply scale down or move their business. Regulatory agencies which genuinely care about their true clients (the workers within the industry they regulate) are thus forced into choosing between two unpalatable alternatives: corporate law breaking or reduced economic activity.

Do compliance strategies work better than deterrent strategies?

Slapper and Tombs argue that not only do compliance strategies work poorly, but deterrent strategies can work well, as with the pollution example mentioned earlier. Companies and business people are far more likely to 'hear' and evaluate deterrent messages than many of the low-level criminals whose thefts and robberies stem from chaotic lives. Corporate crime is usually rationally planned and continuing (rather than one-off), hence capable of being deterred if the likely costs exceed the likely gains. The Thames Trains (Paddington) rail crash, discussed above, is a tragically good example of a calculation that homicidal disaster would be cheaper to deal with than prevention. Deterrent strategies should work well with most corporate crime because detection rates are potentially high, if sufficient investigative resources are provided, due to the continuing nature of the crime and the fact that once a corporate crime is discovered the identity of the criminal is usually obvious.[241] Thus Gobert and Punch describe the SFO as '...an aggressive, well-staffed, multi-disciplinary agency, which is not reluctant to prosecute... The success of the SFO casts doubt on the claim that compliance strategies are the most effective means of controlling and deterring corporate criminality.'[242]

---

[239] Walker C and Wall D, 'Imprisoning the Poor: TV Licence Evaders and the Criminal Justice System' [1997] Crim LR 173; Panatzis C and Gordon D, 'Television Licence Evasion and the Criminalisation of Female Poverty' (1997) 36 Howard JCJ 170.

[240] Frank N and Lombness M, *Controlling Corporate Illegality* (Cincinnati: Anderson, 1988) p 97. This is not always confined to non-police agencies. Police corruption, or even honest 'undercover' work, displays these elements too. See ch 6 and Hobbs D, *Doing the Business* (Oxford: OUP, 1988).

[241] Slapper and Tombs (1999: ch 8).   [242] Gobert and Punch (2003: 303).

Ultimately, it is not possible accurately to assess the effectiveness of either strategy. First, deterrent strategies are hardly ever used in this context (and even the SFO strategy does not use the deterrent approach as fully as do the police and CPS), so no direct comparison is possible. Second, the investigative resources necessary for a deterrent strategy are never provided, although the SFO is something of an exception again. Third, since we do not know how much of this type of crime there is (partly because of inadequate investigative resources), we cannot assess the effect of enforcement (although the vast amount that we do know about is highly suggestive).

Snider, drawing on North American evidence, argues that 'if there is evidence that criminalisation does not work (which there is) there is equally compelling evidence that co-operation does not work either'.[243] Thus, when regulation fails, corporate crime is sometimes stimulated, as in the BCCI fraud case of the 1990s.[244] This is, however, too simplistic. First, whether any strategy works or not is a matter of degree, not a binary work/fail divide. Second, it ignores Haines' (1997) argument that regulatory strategies need to take account of the workplace culture to which they are applied. Third, deterrent and prosecution strategies are not necessarily synonymous. Directors and solicitors, for example, can be prevented from holding office, which appears to be highly effective; by contrast, the small fines that are levied for most health and safety offences may not deter at all. Examples given by the Hampton Report include a man who was paid £60,000 to dump toxic waste (that cost £167,000 to clean up) but was fined only £30,000 – a clear profit of £30,000; and a company that evaded waste licensing requirements for two years, saving £250,000 but was fined only £25,000 – a profit of £225,000.[245] The view of Gobert and Punch[246] that self-regulation by socially-responsible corporations would be preferable to either deterrent or compliance approaches is equally simplistic. For there is no evidence that companies are (or, as they argue, could be made to be) socially responsible unless it is profitable to be so. One of the principles of 'smart' regulation is the creation of opportunities for 'win-win' situations, 'so that, for instance, corporations can behave more responsibly and maximise profits at the same time'.[247] What might help achieve that is a context-sensitive use of the regulatory pyramid, allowing the use of whichever strategy is most appropriate in the circumstances, and encouraging compliance by applying criminal sanctions when voluntary or non-criminal methods fail.

---

[243] Snider L, *Bad Business: Corporate Crime in Canada* (Toronto: University of Toronto Press, 1993) p 142.

[244] See Clarke M, *Regulation: The Social Control of Business Between Law and Politics* (Basingstoke: Macmillan, 2000).   [245] Hampton (2005). And see Middleton (2005) and Macrory (2006b).

[246] Gobert and Punch (2003: 314, ch 10).

[247] Baldwin R, 'Is Better Regulation Smarter Regulation?' [2005] PL 485 at p 507. Baldwin discusses self-regulation, and the formidable obstacles to success that are in its path, as part of a broader 'better regulation' movement. Also see Lynch-Wood G and Williamson D, 'The Social Licence as a Form of Regulation for Small and Medium Enterprises' (2007) 34 JLS 321, who argue that small/medium firms very often fail to self-regulate and thus need a regulator to enforce environmental laws.

Are different enforcement patterns the result of the range of non-prosecution sanctions?

It might appear that traditional sanctions (fine, probation or prison) are inappropriate for many corporate crimes, but community service-style sentences could be devised for companies,[248] and prison might be a very effective deterrent for offences such as tax evasion. Equally important, diversionary measures could be used more by the police. One example is the use in Birmingham's red-light district of letters warning 'kerb crawlers' that their car registrations have been noted and that, if seen in the district again, prosecution will follow. The arrival of the post during the family breakfast was reported to have struck fear into the heart of many a well-heeled Brummie for several weeks thereafter. This sort of thing, like the conditional cautions that the CPS now control, could be extended to many offences. This has been done to some extent in the new 2008 Act. More fundamentally, thought needs to be given to what kinds of offending really are more worthy of prosecution and what kinds of offender are amenable to prosecution and alternatives to it.

7.5.4 Profit, freedom and working rules

In general, economic competitiveness is enhanced by taking a relaxed view of health and safety and environmental crime, but a harsh view of property crime. So the patterns we have explored in this section should not surprise anyone who understands that the rule of law plays second fiddle to the rule of profit. Even the relatively vigorous approach to financial crime can be explained in this way, as Britain's pre-eminence in the financial world relies on confidence in the financial markets and a 'level playing field'. It is even sometimes in the economic interests of companies to be better regulated: improved safety, and thus fewer accidents, could save money in insurance and compensation, stimulate efficiency gains and increase employee loyalty.[249] However, one effect of competition is that this will be true only if all companies in a particular sector have to comply equally. For example, if one company is allowed to undercut the others by spending less on safety the others will be tempted to stop complying. This is not an argument against the 'pyramid' approach per se, but it does mean that approach has to have a heavy deterrent 'clout' *and* be applied equally to all firms in any one sector. This is particularly difficult in a global economy. The implication of the 'smart' principle that corporate compliance should be made profitable is that where it is not profitable it will be absent unless it is imposed by law enforcement.

---

[248] Box S, *Power, Crime and Mystification* (London: Tavistock, 1983) pp 67–74; Slapper and Tombs (1999: ch 9).

[249] Tombs S, 'Law, Resistance and Reform: Regulating Safety Crimes in the UK' (1995) 4 Social and Legal Studies 343; Porter M and van der Linde C, 'Green and Competitive: Ending the Stalemate' (1995) 73 Harvard Business Review 120; Palmer et al, 'Tightening Environmental Standards: The Benefit-Cost or the No-Cost Paradigm?' (1995) 9 Journal of Economic Perspectives 119.

Non-police agencies, like the police, put their own working rules before legal rules. As Hutter puts it, 'on those occasions when the law is perceived as being discordant with popular, or individual, morality, it is morality rather than the law which takes priority'.[250] The difference is that whereas this works against the interests of suspects in the case of the police, it works in favour of suspects in the case of most non-police agencies. It seems, then, that the explanation for differential enforcement patterns lies more in the differences between different types of offender, and the different economic, political and cultural contexts of different offences, than in 'objective' differences between types of offence or agency. This is now enshrined in the Regulators' Compliance Code, 2007, para 8.1: 'Regulators should seek to reward those regulated entities that have consistently achieved good levels of compliance through positive incentives, such as lighter inspections and reporting requirements where risk assessment justifies this. Regulators should also take account of the circumstances of small regulated entities, including any difficulties they may have in achieving compliance.' Do the police 'reward' criminals that go straight, or take account of economic hardship among shoplifters?

Finally, consider the most serious crime of all: homicide. We saw earlier that only some 1% of workplace deaths are prosecuted as manslaughter. Yet the police always investigate workplace deaths and, where they wish to, they involve the CPS too. When hundreds of people die at work every year, these are surely vulnerable victims, but the relaxed approach to evidential and public interest tests taken by the police and CPS in 'normal' circumstances (that is, when the offender is poor) is not taken here. Freedom (of some), it seems, is covertly traded for profit. Thus we have the morally repugnant situation in which juvenile shoplifters receiving a caution for theft are expected to meet representatives of supermarket chains to offer their apologies and make restoration,[251] while large corporations engaged in homicidal business practices routinely evade criminal liability and moral stigma.

7.6 **Prosecution accountability**

Accountability is needed in order to ensure the appropriateness of the enforcement policy of any agency which employs discretion on the basis of the agency's own criteria and working rules.[252] This was recognised in relation to police prosecutions by the

---

[250] Hutter (1988: 202). Also see Hawkins (2002) and Slapper G, *Blood in the Bank* (Aldershot: Ashgate, 1999).

[251] Young R, 'Testing the Limits of Restorative Justice: The Case of Corporate Victims' in Hoyle C and Young R (eds), *New Visions of Crime Victims* (Oxford: Hart, 2002).

[252] For arguments drawing on the experience of other jurisdictions see Brants C and Field S, 'Discretion and Accountability in Prosecution' in Harding et al, *Criminal Justice in Europe: A Comparative Study* (Oxford: Clarendon Press, 1995); Di Federico G, 'Prosecutorial Independence and the Democratic Requirement of Accountability in Italy' (1998) 38 BJ Crim 371.

1981 (Philips) Royal Commission. Yet the even more pressing need for accountability of other regulatory/prosecution agencies, is rarely acknowledged. To whom should these agencies be accountable if the 'freedom' approach is to be pursued? The CPS, for example, is supposed to take into account the interests of the police, victims, defendants, taxpayers and the wider society as embodied in the notion of the public interest. All prosecution agencies are forced to juggle competing considerations, and the difficulty of satisfying all their 'stakeholders' might appear insuperable. However, if we set the ultimate goal of these agencies as the promotion of freedom, competing goals and interest groups can all, in theory, be catered for in a rational manner. For accountability requires an agency to explain and justify its actions in terms that appear legitimate to the various 'stakeholders'; it does not require an agency to act at the behest of any one interest group.

The second role of accountability is to consider the appropriateness of the varied enforcement policies of different agencies. Hood et al believe that these variations are due in part to the 'mutuality deficit' (the failure of regulatory agencies to communicate with each other) and the 'oversight deficit' ('no-one-in-charge-government').[253] Hence, they consider it 'not surprising that coherent principles and practices tend to be conspicuously absent in regulation within government' (1999: 212). For administrative lawyers 'regulatory legitimacy', which every agency must secure if it is 'to merit and receive public approval', is crucial.[254] Harlow and Rawlings usefully outline five possible sources of legitimacy:[255]

- *Legislative mandate:* The strong discretion of prosecution agencies means that this source cannot render their activities fully legitimate.

- *Expertise:* This is insufficient alone, as prosecution discretion involves trade-offs between competing criteria that are less a matter of expertise than of opinion and policy.

- *Efficiency and effectiveness:* The levels of all types of crime prevent this being a prime source of legitimacy.

- *Oversight:* There is far less oversight of non-police agencies than there is of the police and CPS. For example, in 7.5.1 we set out much less detailed and accurate enforcement figures for regulatory agencies than we do elsewhere for police and CPS. This is because figures, in most cases, are simply unavailable, and Macrory (2006b: para 5.8) found that only 17 of the 60 public regulators he surveyed had a publicly available enforcement policy. The CPS, by contrast, sets out policies in relation to many types of crime, such as domestic violence.[256]

---

[253] Hood et al, *Regulation Inside Government* (Oxford: OUP, 1999) p 220. Neither they nor other administrative lawyers apply their work to the police/non-police enforcement agency problem. We do not know whether they would accept the argument of 7.5 that explaining these variations requires consideration of underlying socio-economic forces in addition to the bureaucratic elements they identify.

[254] Baldwin R, *Regulation in Question* (London: LSE, 1995).

[255] Harlow C and Rawlings R, *Law and Administration*, 2nd edn (London: Butterworths, 1997) ch 10.

[256] Discussed at the start of 7.4. All these policies can be seen at <http://www.cps.gov.uk/>.

- *Due process:* Agencies can enhance legitimacy by adopting fair procedures, and by pursuing such values as consistency, equality of treatment, transparency and the participation of outside interests. We have seen these standards becoming more prevalent in the police and CPS but not in other prosecution agencies.

7.6.1 Non-accountability in 'sensitive' cases and for immunity from prosecution

Immunity from prosecution, both formal and informal, is given in some unusual circumstances. Little is known about how, and how often, these judgements are made. SOCPA 2005, s 71 provides that: 'If a specified prosecutor thinks that … it is appropriate to offer any person immunity from prosecution he may …'[257] This can still be done, as it always has been, under the common law, and the courts will not allow prosecutions that breach such promises.[258] There are several types of situation where formal or informal immunity arises. First, immunity is given to many informers with, as we saw in 6.2, often disastrous consequences.

Second, there are killings, beatings and torture by soldiers and police officers in Northern Ireland, Iraq and elsewhere, and alleged offences by police officers and other legal officials in general. Sometimes it is hard to escape the feeling that decisions to not prosecute on what are claimed to be evidential grounds are actually taken on this spurious 'public interest' ground; a shocking example is the case of the officers who arrested a Muslim in a terrorism raid in 2003 and inflicted 50 injuries on him – how could there not be a reasonable prospect of conviction in such a case?[259]

Third, there are 'political' offences against, for example, the Official Secrets Acts. These make it criminal to leak classified information that is harmful to ministers but, arguably, not to the public. Prosecutions for such offences were frequent for many years,[260] and still occur from time to time. A former civil servant, Clive Ponting, was prosecuted for revealing secret documents showing that the government and the military knew that, during the Falklands War in the 1980s, an Argentinian battle-cruiser was sunk (with the loss of hundreds of lives) as it was sailing *away* from British waters.[261] More recently, a civil servant gave to an MP's researcher a document detailing a discussion between the then US and UK leaders, Bush and Blair. This revealed that Bush wanted to bomb an Arabic TV station based in Qatar in 2004 because it had

---

[257] Discussed in Corker et al, 'Sections 71 and 72 of SOCPA: Whither the common law?' [2009] Crim LR 261.

[258] See *R v Croydon Justices, ex p Dean* [1993] QB 769 and (in the slightly different context of cautions) *Jones v Whalley* [2006] UKHL 41.

[259] The case is discussed in 7.3.1; prosecutions of police officers in general is covered in Ch 12.

[260] Edwards J, *The Attorney General, Politics and the Public Interest* (London: Sweet & Maxwell, 1984). For an up-to-date discussion see Bailin A, 'The Last Cold War Statute' [2008] Crim LR 625.

[261] Ponting C, *The Right to Know, The Inside Story of the Belgrano Affair* (London: Sphere, 1985). This account has been confirmed by Freedman L, *The Official History of the Falklands Campaign* (2 Vols) (London: Routledge, 2005).

showed pictures of an American attack on an Iraqi city which killed 1,000 citizens. The researcher passed the document on to two MPs who placed it in the hands of an American politician in the hope that if it were publicised it would undermine support for Bush in the USA. The civil servant and the researcher were prosecuted, but the MPs were not. As one said: 'It's very odd we haven't been prosecuted. My colleague Tony Clarke is guilty of discussing it with me and I have discussed it with all and sundry.'[262] The threat to prosecute can be as important as actual prosecutions. After detailed information in the document was published in one national newspaper the Attorney-General threatened other newspapers with prosecution if they did the same.[263]

Examples of double standards and selectiveness based on legally-irrational grounds abound. One man, displaying quotes from *Nineteen Eighty-Four* outside 10 Downing Street was prosecuted for illegally demonstrating (what irony!), but 100 business-men, whose demonstration breached the same laws, were not.[264] And when an intelligence officer leaked an e-mail from the US government, asking GCHQ to spy on UN Security Council delegations, she was prosecuted under the Official Secrets Acts. Her case was dropped, because if it had continued it would have revealed that on the very brink of the Iraq war the government's legal advice was ambivalent about its legality.[265] Government embarrassment should not come into it, but it frequently confers de facto immunity, as when Cabinet Ministers reveal secrets (Bailin, 2008: 629).

Finally, there are cases involving powerful economic interests. The most notorious is the 'al-Yamanah' case. The Serious Fraud Office conducted a long investigation into allegations that BAE (Britain's major weapons manufacturer) had bribed Saudi officials to sign a multi-billion pound contract for weapons. This investigation was finally dropped under pressure from the UK government because of threats by Saudi Arabia to withdraw from (a) counter-terrorism arrangements and other agreed foreign policy strategies; and (b) future arms contracts. This decision was upheld on the grounds of the danger to life in the event of (a), but commentators suspect that (b) was more powerful.[266] The Council of Europe described this as 'the most prominent example of suspected political interference in the criminal justice system in recent years.'[267]

In conclusion, it is impossible to escape the suspicion that in these cases the 'public interest' is interpreted as 'state interest', and sometimes even 'governing party interest', enabling wrongdoing to be covered up by non-prosecution, and political opposition to be silenced by prosecution or the threat of prosecution. Prosecution agencies

---

[262] *The Guardian*, 10 January 2006.   [263] Ibid.   [264] *The Observer*, 2 July 2006.
[265] *The Observer*, 29 February 2004.

[266] *R (on the application of Corner House Research) v Director of the SFO* [2008] UKHL 60. See also the former Attorney General's attempt to distinguish this case from a more recent investigation against bribery by BAE in *The Guardian*, 2 October 2009. For different views see *The Guardian*, 30 September 2009 and 1 August 2008, and <http:/www.controlbae.org/press/release2008–02-14> (accessed 14 October 2009).

[267] See Council of Europe, Parliamentary Assembly, Allegations of politically-motivated abuses of the criminal justice system in Council of Europe member states (Doc 11993, August 2009) p 10. (<http://assembly. coe.int/Documents/WorkingDocs/doc09/edoc11993.pdf> – accessed 5 January 2010).

seem to be accountable to government alone.[268] This is exactly the opposite of what we should expect of a society supposedly governed by the rule of law, and it spectacularly fails the 'due process' test identified above.

7.6.2 Organisation of the Crown Prosecution Service

The CPS was established to be independent from both the police and government because it was agreed that suspects and defendants needed an extra layer of protection. It was to be accountable, not to defendants, but to the law in a neutral fashion. The natural affinity of CPS thinking with police thinking makes this aspiration unrealistic, as we have seen. But an effort was nonetheless made to establish organisational independence. The Philips Commission recommended that for each police force area there be a Chief Crown Prosecutor, each with his/her own staff, and accountable to a local Police and Prosecutions Authority and responsive to a local democratic voice. But the government instead established the CPS as a national agency under the DPP. The CPS asserted its independence from the police by creating large areas, many of which covered several police forces; siting its offices away from police stations; and discouraging direct contact with the police. As a former DPP put it: 'Suddenly a steel curtain came down between the two services and this went a bit too far. People in both services, both the police force and ourselves, felt that we must keep our distance, we must not talk to each other, we must not communicate, the CPS is independent of the police and must be seen to be so.'[269]

The CPS therefore became increasingly bureaucratic, developing its own priorities, procedures and criteria for decision-making. Victims and the police expressed unhappiness at the remoteness of 'Fortress CPS', yet, as we have seen, there is no evidence that defendants were greatly protected by this inglorious isolation. So the CPS was reorganised into 42 areas – one for each police force, and one for London as a whole. At the same time, the government-appointed Narey (1997) and Glidewell (1998) reports recommended, among other things, that some CPS staff be stationed in police stations in order to process simple cases more speedily.[270] This 'co-location' was practised in some areas prior to the establishment of the CPS and was an example of the chumminess which the CPS was supposed to have eradicated. Thus a drop in discontinuances in one co-located area is cited by government as a positive result of prosecutors and police working together,[271] but it could equally be seen as a worrying sign of 'capture' of the CPS by the police.

---

[268] There are, of course, exceptions, such as the decision not to prosecute in the Damian Green affair (see 6.5.4). Whether the fact that Green was a front bench spokesperson for the party widely expected to form the next government in 2010 influenced the DPP's decision remains a matter of speculation.

[269] Sir Allan Green, speaking in 1989 – quoted by Glidewell (1998: 37).

[270] Home Office, *Review of Delay in the Criminal Justice System* (London: Home Office, 1997) – the Narey Report. For an evaluation, see Baldwin and Hunt (1998).

[271] Criminal Justice System, Narrowing the Justice Gap, 2002 (available at <http://www.cps.gov.uk/publications/docs/justicegap.pdf> – accessed 23 December 2009), p 12. See 7.3 above for discussion of the 'meaning' of raised or lowered discontinuance rates.

The Narey and Glidewell reforms have now been taken one step further by the 'statutory charging scheme' which, as we saw in 7.3, has as many risks in the sense of 'capture' as it does potential due process benefits in taking prosecution decisions away from the police. Not long after the establishment of the CPS in 1986, local account-ability for the police was attenuated by reducing the elected element in local police authorities.[272] Thus not only is the CPS more tied into the police than it ever has been, but the influence of locally elected bodies on the police (and therefore on the CPS) has waned. The upshot is that the police now have more influence over prosecutions than at any time since 1986.

Glidewell (1998: ch 7) set out five objectives for the CPS. Four were concerned with efficiency and quality of decision-making (including fairness to the defendant) and the fifth with 'meeting the needs of victims and witnesses...' While there is nothing wrong with these objectives the omission of the local democratic element is strik-ing. Glidewell (1998: 206–7) did recommend some 'local answerability', but explicitly rejected any involvement with local police authorities or police consultative commit-tees. The arrangements leave a gap which only the Home Office, the police and, to a limited extent, the victim, can fill. Other enforcement agencies similarly lack any local accountability. But there is an important difference. While the CPS keeps its distance from defendants (and would see this as an integral part of its 'independence'), most other agencies pride themselves on their links with offenders. In contrast to the CPS, then, where the main influence is a crime control agency (the police), the main influ-ence on these other agencies is due process or the freedom of the offender.

7.6.3 Accountability to victims

We have seen that prosecution decisions are part of a continuous process of evaluation and construction. Victims are usually involved as witnesses at the start but hardly at all as victims per se, except that the initial police/CPS decisions should 'take account' of the interests of the victim (this is not an obligation for other agencies). However, we saw in 7.4 that the police do this when it supports the action they want to take but do not necessarily do so when it does not. Just as the police construct a prime suspect out of various possible suspects they can construct 'ideal' victims when they wish to pros-ecute and 'unreliable' victims when they do not. This construction process will often not be apparent to the CPS for the reasons discussed earlier, particularly in violence cases where there is a high degree of moral and factual ambiguity.

In any one case the problems that may arise are legion. There may be evidential and/or public interest reasons not to prosecute but the victim may seek prosecution. Or the evidential and/or public interest elements may point towards prosecution but the victim may not want this. Moreover, some victims may be judged to seek solutions that are not in their interest. Even leaving aside questions of probability of conviction,

---

[272] For discussion see Jones T, 'The Accountability of Policing' in Newburn T (ed), *Handbook of Policing*, 2nd edn (Cullompton: Willan, 2008).

cost and the interests of the suspect, to whom should enforcement agencies be most accountable: future victims or the particular victim in any one case? While victims have a stake in 'their' crime, violence should be discouraged in the interests of everyone. If the victim is unlikely or unwilling to give evidence, the police and CPS are understandably unwilling to prosecute, but we should not let offenders get away with it when the reasons for victims not testifying about violence may be their fear of more violence. However, since many cases of violence will fail without the testimony of the victim we should make it easier for victims to testify.

This is easier said than done. Take vulnerable victims. Some victims are intrinsically vulnerable: the very young, very old, and mentally ill or impaired. They are unusually prey to exploitative offenders and less able to give legally compelling evidence in court.[273] Other victims are vulnerable because of their social situations: victims of sexual offences, especially 'date rapes', often find their characters attacked in court and the chances of conviction low.[274] When victims of domestic violence remain in the relationships within which violence takes place during potential court proceedings, they become particularly vulnerable to further violence.[275] And many workers in factories and building sites are vulnerable because they are in no economic position to leave their jobs or demand safer conditions.

To illustrate the problem, let us take the example of domestic violence, and revisit the discussion in 3.4.3. The traditional response of the police used to be to arrest only in the most extreme cases and to prosecute only rarely. In 1990 the Home Office encouraged the police to arrest more often. This also encouraged many forces to try to reduce the rates of NFA and 'no criming' which were far higher in domestic violence cases than average (Hoyle, 1998: ch 1). Hoyle found that this policy increased the prosecution rate but was still only about half the average rate for all arrests. This was not because the police thought the offence trivial, the victim undeserving or the idea of prosecuting 'domestics' odd. It was nearly always because the victim either refused to make a statement against the offender or withdrew a statement made earlier. In other words, the police adopted a 'let the victim decide' approach.

In recognition of the obvious downside of the 'let the victim decide' approach, pro-charge policies have developed in many police forces alongside 'pro-arrest' policies.

---

[273] Sanders et al (1997); Home Office, *Speaking Up for Justice* (London: Home Office, 1998b); Hamlyn et al, *Are Special Measures Working? Evidence from Surveys of Vulnerable and Intimidated Witnesses* (Home Office Research Study No 283) (London: Home Office, 2004). Burton et al, *Are Special Measures for Vulnerable and Intimidated Witnesses Working? Evidence from the Criminal Justice Agencies* (Home Office On-Line Report No 01/06) (London: Home Office, 2006).

[274] HMCPSI and HMIC, *Report on the Joint Inspection into the Investigation and Prosecution of Cases Involving Allegations of Rape* (London, 2002); Lea et al, 'Attrition in Rape Cases' (2003) 43 BJ Crim 583; HMCPSI/HMIC, *Without Consent: Report on the Joint Inspection into the Investigation and Prosecution of Cases involving Allegations of Rape* (London: HMCPSI, 2007); Ellison L, 'Promoting Effective Case-building in Rape Cases: A Comparative Perspective' [2007] Crim LR 691.

[275] Hoyle C, *Negotiating Domestic Violence* (Oxford: OUP, 1998); Hester M and Westmarland N, *Tackling Domestic Violence: Effective Interventions and Approaches* (Home Office Research Study 290) (London: Home Office, 2005).

In other words, all domestic violence arrests should lead to charges if they pass the evidential test. The idea is that the police would then not be able to manipulate victims into dropping their complaints and victims would not be exposed to the wrath of the violent perpetrator. To test these assumptions and to see what did influence the choice of victims, Hoyle and Sanders interviewed a sample of domestic violence victims.[276] They found that the police did not manipulate their choice, and many victims would not have welcomed the police deciding what was to happen. This was because most victims made decisions which were rational for them, given the difficult circumstances in which they found themselves. If prosecution was likely to help them, they made and pressed their complaints, but if it was not (if, for example, they wished to continue living with the perpetrator) then they did not do this. Calling the police but not prosecuting was rational for women who wanted perpetrators to be taken away until their anger or drunkenness, for example, subsided. This was no guarantee that there would not be repeated violence in future – far from it. But prosecution provided no guarantee either. Acting against the wishes of victims, but in the supposed best interests of them or of society as a whole, would therefore often be counterproductive.[277]

Hoyle and Sanders concluded that the only solution was to ensure that victims were helped into situations where they did not have to choose between the violence of their partners or other degrading situations such as the hardship of single parenthood on benefits. Domestic violence victims need to be reassured that they can be rehoused, given adequate benefits, protected from further violence, and so forth. Under this 'victim empowerment' strategy more women would choose to prosecute than now. Some police domestic violence units embody this strategy in a small way but are hampered by not having power to help victims directly with housing and other non-criminal justice problems.

There are encouraging developments, however, in the form of a number of local schemes that attempt to support victims in a variety of ways, the introduction of Special Domestic Violence Courts and the establishment of independent domestic violence advisers (IDVAs) in some areas. The attrition rate and proportion of cases in which victims seek to withdraw from the prosecution in many of these schemes is encouragingly low.[278] In general, charging and conviction numbers and rates are rising slowly, though the discontinuance rate remains higher than in 'normal' cases.[279] While Hoyle found that if victims changed their minds about prosecuting the police

---

[276] Hoyle C and Sanders A, 'Police Response to Domestic Violence: From Victim Choice to Victim Empowerment?' (2000) 40 BJ Crim 14.

[277] For discussion of research findings and the CPS Policy on domestic violence see Paradine K and Wilkinson J, *Protection and Accountability: The Reporting, Investigation and Prosecution of Domestic Violence Cases* (London: HMIC and HMCPSI, 2004) chs 2, 6. For scepticism about the deterrent value of prosecution, see Dempsey M, *Prosecuting Domestic Violence* (Oxford: OUP, 2009) p 61.

[278] Hester and Westmarland (2005: ch 5). On IDVAs see <http://www.caada.org.uk/> (accessed 5 January 2010).

[279] HMCPSI, *Violence at Home* (London: HMCPSI, 2004a) ch 6 showed slight improvement. But now see CPS, *Special Domestic Violence Courts Review 2007–8* (2008a) and CPS, *Violence against Women Report 2007–8* (2008b) (both available from CPS website).

usually dropped the case ('let the victim decide'), this has now changed to some extent. The CPS has, for many years, been supposed to satisfy itself that victims in this situation did not wish to drop cases through pressure from perpetrators. Alternatives – such as using other evidence such as photographs and other witnesses – are encouraged in the CPS's own policy, which states: 'Don't assume that a complainant giving evidence in court is the only way to prove the matter.'[280] But it is not known if there are many prosecutions without support from the victim.

Just as not all domestic violence victims want their partners prosecuted under present arrangements, so not all would even under an 'empowerment' strategy. For, to return to the discussion in 7.4 and 7.5 about diversion, many women favour rehabilitative or restorative (not necessarily punitive) strategies. These might include 'domestic violence perpetrators programmes' (DVPPs).[281] This can all be done within the framework of conditional cautioning. Whether diversion, restorative justice and/or DVPPs are appropriate in any given case needs careful evaluation (which is possible where there are IDVAs) – but just as it is wrong to simply assume that restorative justice will always be appropriate it is surely equally wrong to assert, as the CPS now does (in a remarkable change in policy over a few years) that: 'Mediation, restorative justice or diversionary measures such as conditional cautions are inappropriate in domestic violence cases' (2008: para 3). We need the type of imagination and drive that has gone into developing 'restorative justice' for juvenile offenders both as alternatives to prosecution and as part of the armoury of court dispositions in the Crime and Disorder Act 1998. The freedom of domestic violence victims (and, by extension other vulnerable victims) is surely at least as important as that of the victims of juvenile offenders – usually car, shop and home owners. Should their property losses really be regarded as worse erosions of freedom than the violence and fear suffered by millions of women, children, people with disabilities and workers in unsafe environments?[282]

The restrictive deployment of restorative justice principles in recent legislation is particularly striking in view of the real effort in the late 1990s which went into 'levelling the playing field' for vulnerable victims (that is, victims of rape, intimidated victims, and those who are vulnerable through age, illness or disability). Changes at the

---

[280] CPS – Guidance on Prosecuting Cases of Domestic Violence (2008c) Annexe D. Also see para 12. The guidance rightly stresses that the safety of the victim and any children is paramount. For discussion of 'victimless prosecutions' in the USA and how they could be developed further in the UK see Ellison L, 'Responding to Victim Withdrawal in Domestic Violence Prosecutions' [2003] Crim LR 760; Dempsey M 'Towards a Feminist State: What does 'Effective' Prosecution of Domestic Violence Mean?' (2007) 70 MLR 908; Dempsey (2009). Compelling victims to testify is sometimes suggested, but would unfairly subject victims to even more coercion and stress.

[281] Lewis R, 'Making Justice Work: Effective Legal Interventions for Domestic Violence' (2004) 44 BJ Crim 204. Lewis rightly argues that rehabilitative strategies often need deterrent strategies in the background to make offenders take them seriously: in effect, the regulatory pyramid. Also see Stubbs J 'Beyond Apology? Domestic Violence and Critical Questions for Restorative Justice' (2007) 7 Criminology and Criminal Justice 169 who warns that the applying restorative justice to domestic violence requires particular care if it is not to harm victims.

[282] For a thoughtful discussion of many aspects of these problems see Hudson B, 'Restorative Justice and Gendered Violence: Diversion or Effective Justice?' (2002) 42 BJ Crim 616.

levels of legislation, policy and practice are now being made as a result of 'Speaking up for Justice'.[283] But the apparent accountability of the police and CPS to vulnerable victims is shallow. It means that these agencies defer to their choices when those victims do not seek to prosecute, but not when they do wish to prosecute. This is particularly unacceptable when the choices of the vulnerable are so constrained by disadvantageous economic, social and personal circumstances. If the freedom of vulnerable victims is to be taken as seriously as that of the more fortunate, the criminal justice system as a whole, in conjunction with non-criminal justice agencies, needs to be made more responsive to their needs – a nettle which 'Speaking up for Justice' did not grasp. As we saw in ch 1, the criminal justice system should not be analysed in isolation from other elements of the social structure, such as housing and welfare. Freedom from crime is no more important, in principle, than freedom from poverty or illness. For many vulnerable victims freedom from the former will only be achieved when they are enabled to free themselves from the latter.

This discussion shows that the police and CPS are accountable to victims in respect of due process (in the sense set out at the start of this section) to some extent, in that those outside interests are given some limited rights to participate and to be informed. Following the recommendations of the Macpherson Report, the CPS now explains its prosecution decisions to victims in some serious cases, which is another, and welcome, step away from 'Fortress CPS'.[284] As we shall argue in ch 12, the freedom of victims can be enhanced by treating their concerns seriously, which largely requires agencies to explain their actions to them. A clear commitment to explain is better than a luke-warm commitment to consult which is neither practised consistently nor legally enforceable. It hardly needs pointing out that non-police agencies are not engaged at all in this kind of exercise even though the victims of corporate crime suffer more 'physical, economic, political, social and human suffering and damage' than those of other crimes.[285] These victims are concentrated in the poorest and least powerful sections of society. It is no coincidence that their voices and interests are drowned out by the rustle of money-making, the hustle of profit-taking, the clink of champagne glasses in corporate hospitality boxes.

7.6.4 Accountability through private prosecutions?

Accountability of the criminal justice system as a whole to victims is sometimes said to be secured by the right of private prosecution. It will be recalled that, before the police became de facto national prosecutors in the mid to late nineteenth century, most prosecutions were private. The legal form of police/CPS prosecutions remains the same,

---

[283] Home Office (1998b). This report has led to major changes to police and CPS policy and practice regarding vulnerable victims, and led to the Youth Justice and Criminal Evidence Act 1999, discussed in ch 12.

[284] Macpherson (1999). However, CPS performance is still poor, the CPS failing to communicate with victims in one-third of the cases where they should do so: HMCPSI, *File Management and Organisation: An Audit of CPS Performance* (2008b).   [285] Slapper and Tombs (1999: 84).

and so victims who are dissatisfied with police/CPS decisions not to prosecute may themselves prosecute. By this time too much time will usually have elapsed, and too many mistakes made (such as the failure by the police to prevent evidence from being destroyed) to permit successful private prosecutions.[286] This was highlighted in the Stephen Lawrence affair in which the police bungled the investigation into the murder of a young black man in 1993. As a result they had insufficient evidence to prosecute successfully the prime suspects and so the prosecution which was brought against some of them was dropped. A private prosecution of three of them in 1996 failed for the same reasons as the original prosecution.[287] The Hillsborough tragedy, in which 96 people died when the police lost control of a football crowd in 1989, was a different type of scandal. It took 10 years to mount private prosecutions against the officers who it is believed were most responsible. In July 1999 two were committed for trial when magistrates decided that there was sufficient evidence to prosecute.[288] These prosecutions were ultimately also unsuccessful (one of the officers was acquitted in July 2000, and the jury was 'hung' on the other). These cases illustrate two further functions of private prosecutions. One is symbolic, in that they can shame those responsible and highlight the suffering of the victims and their families. The second is that they can become part of the campaign against the wider social or political problems that caused the tragedies in the first place. But since private prosecutions are rarely possible (because of the money and energy required) this right does not fill the everyday 'accountability gap'.

The capacity of private prosecutions to hold enforcement agencies accountable is hampered in other ways. First, there are many offences for which only designated prosecutors may prosecute. This includes most regulatory offences, closing off yet another way of holding non-police agencies accountable. Second, there is a variety of political and obscure offences for which consent must be sought from the DPP or the law officers before they can be prosecuted. We saw in 7.6.1 that the DPP sometimes protects those that should be prosecuted (by refusing consent) and fails to protect those who should not be prosecuted (by granting consent), but this is not amenable to judicial review unless tainted by dishonesty, bad faith or some other exceptional circumstance.[289] Third, there is the power of the DPP to take over any private prosecution and then either continue or discontinue.[290] Fourth, the actions of the police and DPP 'trump' whatever a private prosecutor may wish to do. Thus a private prosecution was held to be an abuse of process when a caution was administered.[291] The DPP can use any criteria in exercising this power that he or she wishes (subject to the '*Wednesbury*' principles discussed in 7.2 above), such as to protect someone for

---

[286] But in 1995 two prostitutes scored notable successes when they successfully prosecuted a man for rape, in cases that the police and CPS were not prepared to prosecute: *The Guardian*, 18 May 1995.

[287] Macpherson (1999). Discussed further in 3.4.   [288] *The Guardian*, 21 July 1999.

[289] *DPP, ex p Kebilene* [1999] 3 WLR 972. The Law Commission proposed reducing the number of such offences: Law Commission, *Consents to Prosecution* (HC 1085) (Report No 255) (London: SO, 1998).

[290] Prosecution of Offences Act 1985, s 6(2).

[291] *Jones v Whalley* [2006] UKHL 41. See ch 12 for discussion of 'abuse of process'.

social, political or economic reasons or with whom, perhaps, the police have struck a dubious 'deal'.[292]

7.7 **Conclusion**

The police minimise the impact of external scrutiny of their prosecution decisions by choosing different dispositions (eg case construction, use of PNDs, or cautioning) according to their purposes in specific cases. The courts largely opt out of scrutiny, and neither they nor government care that different agencies adopt radically different approaches. The net result is a pattern of prosecution decisions which harmonise with economic imperatives but which, as a by-product, penalise the unfortunate and reward the powerful. The class and race differences created by stop-search and arrest practices are magnified by prosecution processes within the police and by separating police and non-police enforcement and prosecution.

This remains true despite major changes in prosecution practices since 1985. The CPS drops more weak and cautionable cases than the police used to. Some of the direct or indirect discrimination exercised by the police against ethnic minorities is blunted by CPS decision-making. Control of most charging and conditional cautioning has passed to the CPS. Government guidelines do have some effect. But these rules, guidelines and controls are all only partially inhibitory. When the police want to, they seem to secure cautions or prosecutions in breach of the rules. Little can be done about it. Inhibitory rules need to be backed up by effective sanctions, otherwise they are largely 'presentational'. There are no sanctions attached to the rules and guidelines discussed in this chapter. Alternatively, we need to achieve a change in police culture so that adherence to the rules is regarded by officers as good policing, but that will not be easy given the structural position of the police within the adversarial system, and it will be impossible for so long as the government (and others) sets their priorities in such crude terms as 'catching criminals', 'narrowing the justice gap' and 'improving public confidence'.

Despite appearances to the contrary, the CPS remains a police-dependent, rather than an independent, institution. This is partly by choice, in so far as the ethos of the two institutions are similar; partly a product of the performance indicators – conviction rates, primarily – established for it as criteria of success; and partly because the CPS is almost entirely dependent on the police for its information about cases. This structural dependency undermines the due process potential of the CPS duty to ensure that prosecution cases pass the evidential sufficiency test. Put another way, the duty of the CPS to ensure 'equality of arms' with the defence, as required by the HRA 1998, can only be carried out to the extent that the police make this possible. This is not to say that the CPS never discontinues cases that the police would have preferred to see prosecuted. Police constructions are sometimes clumsy or unconvincing and

---

[292] As happened in *Raymond v A-G* [1982] QB 839, for example.

prosecutors may in these circumstances step in to terminate an obviously flawed case. Whilst this degree of independent action is welcome it is only made possible in the first place by shoddy case construction by the police. It is thus difficult to accept that the CPS can ever be truly independent.

Is prosecution policy about fairness and keeping criminalisation as well as crime within bounds (freedom) or about balancing expediency with police working rules (crime control)? Our discussion of cautioning suggests that we may be moving back towards the latter. For although cautioning is used for humanitarian reasons, it also: increases social control through net widening; saves money where there is little to be lost by not prosecuting; punishes those against whom there is insufficient evidence of guilt to justify this; and avoids prosecuting those people who could embarrass authority. When government itself uses both prosecution and prosecution immunity to further its own narrow political causes, why should the police behave less cynically?

Cautioning and PNDs are examples of the trend noted in this book for control over criminal justice to pass from the judiciary to the police – both the dispersal of stigma and increased control over the imposition of penalties. For it used to be common for juvenile offenders, in particular, to be given absolute or conditional discharges on first and sometimes second appearances in court as a 'warning shot'. Now this is rare, for the courts see the caution as that warning shot. Indeed, it is virtually forbidden under the Crime and Disorder Act 1998 (s 66(4)). Not content with apprehending suspected offenders, the police have become triers of fact, deciders of guilt and innocence and dispensers of penalties. Giving conditional cautioning to the CPS only partially meets the problem. Just as the police cannot be expected to protect the rights of suspects, nor can we expect the CPS to do so. It is the job of defence lawyers to protect suspects' rights. But while expenditure on the CPS is rising, the legal aid budget is ever more tightly controlled (see chs 4 and 9). So, the police and CPS are no longer castigated for producing and accepting summaries of taped interrogations, but encouraged to do so under the statutory charging scheme; defence lawyers should check the accuracy of summaries, but without a remuneration structure that rewards this work, they will rarely do this, and 'fast-tracking' of cases will not give them the opportunity. Similarly, the retreat from full disclosure and restrictions on legal aid for defence forensic science also prevent defence lawyers matching the power of the prosecution.

It seems unlikely that the CPS would have prevented the infamous miscarriages of justice that gave rise to the Runciman Commission, and the fact that miscarriages of justice have continued since its inception shows it is an inadequate safeguard for suspects. Expecting it to perform a 'Ministry of Justice' role is unrealistic. What is needed is strong and committed defence advocacy to counterbalance the weighty forces lined up on the other side of the adversarial divide.

The management of 'risk' has become a major determinant of recent governmental policy in many western societies.[293] Two dimensions of 'risk' are important in this

---

[293] See Ericson R and Haggerty K, *Policing the Risk Society* (Oxford: Clarendon Press, 1997) and Braithwaite J, 'The New Regulatory State and the Transformation of Criminology' (2000) 40 BJ Crim 222.

context. First, minimising the risk of offending with an emphasis on 'community safety' and 'protecting the public' has come to be seen as outweighing the risks associated with the erosion of civil liberties and the freedom of suspects. But some 'risks' (eg posed by high status offenders) to some 'communities' (eg the vulnerable) are clearly tolerated more than others. The second dimension of 'risk', then, balances the risk of certain crime (enforced by non-police agencies) with the risk that tough enforcement will be economically disadvantageous to consumers, employees and/or wider society.[294] On this latter point, academics are listened to and their advice followed, as is evident in the government's 'better (for which, read "less") regulation' initiative and the new Regulators' Compliance Code (RCC) (2008).

In closing, let us compare the two approaches. Police and CPS are accountable to (among others) victims, as stated in both the Code for Crown Prosecutors and the Code of Practice for Victims (see ch 13). At the same time as the commitment to victims was strengthened in the Code for Crown Prosecutors, the 'case seriousness' criterion for deciding whether or not to prosecute was dropped.[295] Yet the RCC – the 'Code for Other Prosecutors' – contains no mention of victims (let alone a commitment), and the Code of Practice for Victims explicitly applies only to police and CPS. Yet while seriousness should no longer be considered by police and CPS, the RCC requires 'regulators' to ensure that enforcement action is proportionate to the crime committed and to take into account the economic impact. And while police and CPS discuss possible prosecution with victims, 'regulators' discuss this with the criminals: 'Regulators should, where appropriate, discuss the circumstances with those suspected of a breach and take these into account when deciding on the best approach' (para 8.2).

The regulation literature makes a lot of the limited instrumental value of prosecution of companies when, for example, only 50% of Health and Safety inspectors believe that prosecutions change corporate behaviour.[296] If such a high proportion of police officers thought correctly that thieves, burglars, prostitutes, street fighters and drug users responded positively to prosecution the 'crime problem' would be truly cracked. But they do not believe this. If we applied the same criterion of instrumental value to police-enforced crime, there would be very few prosecutions. But we do not do this. Similarly, underclaiming and underpayment of social security benefits exceeds the amount defrauded by claimants, partly because of the threat of prosecution for claimants who make mistakes. The risk of deterrent strategies to claimants is therefore proven to be high, but instead of this softening the strategy, it has become tougher.[297] Where prosecutions are concerned, those with economic, social or political power are regulated with a light touch, while for the rest our tolerance approaches zero.

[294] For a powerful argument on these lines see Sunstein C, 'Risk and Reason: Safety, Law and the Environment' (Cambridge: CUP, 2002), critically examined by Ericson in 31 J Law and Society (2004) 408.

[295] See the discussion by the then-DPP: Calvert-Smith D, 'The Code for Crown Prosecutors' (2000) NLJ 1494.   [296] Hawkins (2002: 282).

[297] McKeever (1999); Larkin (2007).

Further Reading

Fox D, Dhami M and Mantle G, 'Restorative Final Warnings: Policy and Practice' (2006) 45 Howard J 129

Taylor C, 'Advance Disclosure and the Culture of the Investigator' IJ Sociology of Law 33 (2005) 118

Tombs S and Whyte D, *A Crisis of Enforcement: The Decriminalisation of Death and Injury at Work* (Centre for Crime and Justice Studies Briefing No 6) (London: Kings College London, 2008)

Whyte D, 'Gordon Brown's Charter for Corporate Criminal' (2007/8) 70 Criminal Justice Matters 31

Young R, 'Street Policing after PACE: The Drift to Summary Justice' in Cape and Young (eds), *Regulating Policing: The PACE Act, Past, Present and Future* (Oxford: Hart, 2008)

8

The mass production of guilty pleas

[Defence] solicitor: Will you drop the criminal damage?
Prosecutor: But he's a pain in the arse.
Solicitor: I know, but go on, he's pleading guilty to all the other stuff.
Prosecutor: [Good humouredly] Oh, alright![1]

Key issues

- The prevalence of guilty pleas
- Types of incentives/pressures to plead guilty
- The roles of defence lawyers, prosecutors and judges in the plea bargain process
- Defendants and victims' rights in relation to bargaining
- Is plea bargaining justifiable?

8.1 **Introduction**

Prosecutions take place either in the magistrates' courts (the lower courts) or the Crown Court. The features of these courts and the allocation of cases between them are looked at in detail in chs 9 and 10. Here we discuss a phenomenon that is common to both levels of court: the mass production of guilty pleas.

One of the most remarkable features of criminal justice in England and Wales is the tiny proportion of prosecuted cases that result in contested trials. The majority of defendants give up their right to trial by pleading guilty. In 2007 the guilty plea rate in the Crown Court rose to 68%, up 3% from the year before.[2] A similarly high level of guilty pleas is evident in the magistrates' court, where 67.5% of cases in 2007/08 resulted in guilty pleas.[3] One key question for this chapter is why is it that the majority of those defendants who are presented directly with the chance to put the prosecution to proof choose not to do so?

---

[1] This quote is taken from McConville et al, *Standing Accused* (Oxford: Clarendon Press, 1994) p 195.
[2] Ministry of Justice, *Judicial and Court Statistics 2007*, Cm 7467 (London: MoJ, 2008a).
[3] *CPS Annual Report 2007–8* (London: CPS, 2008) Annex A: Casework statistics.

The phenomenon of 'cracked trials' (cases which are listed for a contested trial but on the day of the trial the case is disposed of in some other way) raises an important related question: why does the resolve of so many defendants to plead not guilty 'crack' at the last moment? In the Crown Court there were 15,380 cracked trials in 2007, representing 41.6% of all cases listed for trial. In most of these cases defendants made a last minute change of plea from not guilty to guilty.[4] In 2007 38% of cases listed for trial in the magistrates' court 'cracked', the majority due to late guilty pleas.[5]

The high rate of guilty pleas ensures that many of the most important due process protections which might apply in an adversarial system do not come into play. Crucially, the prosecution is not obliged to prove its case beyond reasonable doubt before an impartial tribunal. Its evidence is not scrutinised, witnesses are not cross-examined, and no question as to the exclusion of evidence (on the grounds that it was obtained oppressively, unfairly, or in circumstances that might render it unreliable) can arise. The defendant stands condemned merely as a result of uttering the single word 'guilty' in open court. But is this absence of due process attributable to a free and informed decision by the defendant? Or does the criminal process itself encourage defendants to waive their due process rights by pleading guilty?

Guilty pleas are likely to be motivated by a variety of factors but two important variables are the perceived likelihood of conviction, and the perceived differential between the penalty likely to be imposed on a plea of guilty and that which would follow one of not guilty. On the basis of interviewing 282 defendants convicted in the Crown Court Hedderman and Moxon concluded that: '... decisions to plead guilty were largely based on a realistic assessment of the chances of acquittal, and the potential benefits in terms of sentence severity'.[6] The researchers do not explain how they formed the view that the assessments made by defendants were 'realistic' although they do point to the crucial influence of legal advice in decisions regarding pleas. Thus, of those who changed their pleas, only one respondent said that this decision had been entirely his own; the rest said that they had been advised by their solicitor or barrister to plead guilty. It follows that in this chapter we need to look both at the systemic pressures on defendants to plead guilty, and the way that these are mediated in practice by lawyers, court officials, magistrates and judges. We need, in particular, to consider whether assessments of the chances of acquittal, and likely sentence if convicted, are 'realistic' or not.

There are four ways of securing a lighter sentence by pleading guilty: the sentence discount principle, the restrictions on the sentencing powers of magistrates, charge bargaining and 'fact bargaining'. We will examine each of these in turn.[7]

---

[4] 62.5% entered a late guilty plea, approximately 17% entered a plea to a lesser charge and a similar proportion were acquitted once the prosecution offered no evidence, with the remaining 2.1% being dealt with by way of a bind over (Judicial and Court Statistics, 2007: table 6.11).   [5] Ibid, pp 140–1.

[6] Hedderman C and Moxon D, *Magistrates' Court or Crown Court? Mode of Trial Decisions and Sentencing* (Home Office Research Study No 125) (London: HMSO, 1992).

[7] While we focus here on the most immediate pressures to plead guilty, it should not be overlooked that these are experienced differently depending on other systemic factors such as whether or not a defendant has been remanded in custody pending trial (Kellough G and Wortley S, 'Remand for Plea: Bail Decisions and

8.2 **The sentence discount principle**

The most naked attempt to persuade defendants to plead guilty lies in the sentencing principle established by the courts that defendants pleading guilty should receive a lighter sentence than those convicted after a contested trial. This principle was first put on a statutory basis by s 48 of the Criminal Justice and Public Order Act (CJPO) 1994, now replaced by the Criminal Justice Act (CJA) 2003, s 144(1). This provides as follows:

In determining what sentence to pass on an offender who has pleaded guilty to an offence before that or another court a court must take into account:

(a) the stage in the proceedings for the offence at which the offender indicated his intention to plead guilty, and

(b) the circumstances in which this indication was given.

Section 174(2)(d) of the same Act adds that 'where as a result of taking into account any matter mentioned in section 144(1), the court imposes a punishment on the offender which is less severe than the punishment it would otherwise have imposed, [it must] state that fact' in open court.

The Criminal Justice Act does not demand explicitly that any discount in fact be given. Similarly the Act does not require a sentencer to refer to the discount principle in all circumstances, but only when a discount has in fact been given as a result of a guilty plea; even then the sentencer is not obliged to say how much has been 'knocked off' the convicted person's sentence. Thus sentencers must turn to the common law for an understanding of how the discount principle is meant to work in practice. They must also 'have regard' to the definitive guideline on the subject issued by the Sentencing Guidelines Council (SGC), a body dominated by the judiciary and chaired by the Lord Chief Justice.[8] In *Last*,[9] the Lord Chief Justice noted that the SGC guideline was designed to assist judges arrive at a just sentence but that they were free to depart from it as long as valid reasons were given for doing so.[10] Although the guideline expresses reductions in percentage terms, it has been reiterated that these are 'simply guide-

---

Plea Bargaining as Commensurate Decisions' (2002) 42 BJ Crim 186 at p 199) as well as on the individual characteristics and situation of the defendant such as degree of trust in lawyers and the courts, ability to resist pressure, desire to bring proceedings to an end, willingness to take the blame so as to protect a co-defendant from conviction (Jones S, 'Partners in Crime: A Study of the Relationship between Female Offenders and their Co-defendants' (2008) 8(2) Criminology & Criminal Justice 147 at 156–7) and so forth.

[8] The guideline, first issued in December 2004 was reissued with revisions in January 2007. SGC, *Reduction in Sentence for a Guilty Plea: Definitive Guideline* (2007b) <http://www.sentencing-guidelines. gov.uk/docs/Reduction%20in%20Sentence-final.pdf> (last accessed 5 January 2010).

[9] [2005] EWCA Crim 106; applied by *McDonald* [2007] EWCA Crim 1081.

[10] See also *Peters & Ors* [2005] EWCA Crim 605.

lines' and the discounting exercise should not be undertaken in a mathematical way.[11] It is therefore important to examine judicial practice as well as the more structured approach envisaged by the SGC guideline.[12]

8.2.1 The sentence discount principle in legal theory

The rationale of the principle

The obvious rationale for encouraging an accused to plead guilty lies in the time and expense that is saved.[13] The average hearing time for a not guilty plea sent to trial is 18 hours compared with 1.5 hours for a guilty plea.[14] In the early 1990s the Home Office estimated the average cost of a contested trial was almost nine times that of a guilty plea.[15] The substantial savings involved in encouraging guilty pleas are recognised in the SGC guideline's 'statement of purpose' (para 2.2):

A reduction in sentence is appropriate because a guilty plea avoids the need for a trial (thus enabling other cases to be disposed of more expeditiously), shortens the gap between charge and sentence, saves considerable cost, and, in the case of an early plea, saves victims and witnesses from the concern about having to give evidence. The reduction principle derives from the need for effective administration of justice and not as an aspect of mitigation.

Although efficiency appears to be the primary consideration, an important subsidiary factor is a recognition that by pleading guilty early enough the defendant 'spares' any witnesses from having to attend court and from what may be the distressing experience of giving evidence. If, for example, a defendant contests a charge of rape or assault, the complainant will nearly always face lengthy cross-examination in an attempt to destroy his or her credibility as a witness.[16] The sentence discount principle thus operates as an inducement to the defendant to make life 'easier' for others.

The reference in the SGC guideline to shortening the gap between charge and sentence reflects the contemporary concern with 'bringing offenders to justice' as speedily as possible. Here, as elsewhere in the SGC guideline, the possibility that the sentence discount principle might impact on the innocent as well as the guilty is not acknowledged.

---

[11] *Ablewhite amd Ors* [2007] EWCA Crim 832.

[12] Current proposals for a Sentencing Council to replace the existing SGC may lead to an even more structured approach with less judicial discretion in the future. On the creation of the new council and its duties generally see Coroners and Justice Bill 2008–9, Part 4. On the nature of the discretion retained by the courts specifically see cl 155, which states that every court must follow the guidelines of the Council unless satisfied that it is contrary to the interests of justice to do so.

[13] Cases in which this was explicitly recognised include *Boyd* (1980) 2 Cr App Rep (S) 234, *Hollington and Emmens* (1985) 7 Cr App Rep (S) 364, and *Buffrey* (1992) 14 Cr App Rep (S) 511.

[14] Ministry of Justice (2008a: 115, table 6.21).

[15] Home Office, *Costs of the Criminal Justice System 1992* (London: Home Office, 1992b) vol 1, p 16.

[16] Brereton D, 'How Different are Rape Trials?: A Comparison of the Cross-Examination of Complaints in Rape and Assault Trials' (1997) 37 BJ Crim 242.

The argument that a plea of guilty should be rewarded because it evinces remorse is also occasionally referred to by the courts.[17] It is an unconvincing rationale. The courts have no sure way of distinguishing between guilty pleas motivated by remorse and those entered simply in order to avoid a greater degree of punishment. The SGC guideline now makes clear (para 2.4) that the issue of remorse should be addressed separately when deciding the most appropriate length of sentence '*before* calculating the reduction for the guilty plea' (emphasis in original).

The variable size of the sentence discount

The courts have long encouraged a guilty plea to be entered at the earliest opportunity on the basis that this generates the maximum savings for the system. The SGC guideline reiterates this position by declaring that (para 4.3) 'The largest recommended reduction will not normally be given unless the offender indicated willingness to admit guilt at the **first reasonable opportunity**' (emphasis in original).

Annex 1 to the SGC guideline notes that the first reasonable opportunity to indicate a willingness to plead guilty may be as early as a police interview, so long as the defendant and any legal adviser had sufficient information about the allegations. One likely consequence will be to intensify the pressure on suspects to incriminate themselves when under police interrogation, thus undermining what little is left of the right to silence (see ch 5).[18]

In addition to the 'routine' discounts available for guilty pleas there are 'further' and 'enhanced' discounts available for defendants who provide assistance to the prosecuting authorities. The common law has long recognised that defendants could expect large discounts for helping the police and prosecution to investigate and prosecute cases against their criminal associates, for example by providing information or testifying against them.[19] The 'enhanced' discount, which is in the range of one-half to two-thirds of the sentence deducted before any reduction for guilty plea, is said to operate as a pragmatic convention to incentivise defendants to provide assistance to convict serious criminals who might otherwise escape justice.[20] Sections 73 to 75 of the Serious Organised Crime and Police Act 2005 formalise 'enhanced' discounts for such assistance.[21] The SOCPA does not specify the amount of discount, but principles derived from established case law specify that the nature and extent of the assistance, and the risks and consequences for the defendant and his family in its provision, are relevant considerations; the greater the quality and quantity of assistance and the higher the risk, the larger the discount, although only in 'exceptional' cases will this

---

[17] Eg, *Turner* [1970] QB 321; *Hastings* [1995] Crim LR 661; *Karim* [2005] EWCA Crim 533 [31].

[18] See also *Peters* [2005] EWCA Crim 605. That the first reasonable opportunity can sometimes be the date of trial is illustrated by *Stringfellow* [2003] EWCA Crim 3252.   [19] *A and B* [1998] Crim LR 757.

[20] See also Kiely [2009] EWCA Crim 756.

[21] In *R v P and Blackburn* [2007] EWCA Crim 2290 it was held that the statutory regime, which applies to defendants who enter into written agreements with the prosecution to provide assistance, does not deprive defendants unwilling to enter into this formalised process of any benefit they should receive under the old common law system.

be in excess of three-quarters of the sentence which would have been imposed. While these additional forms of discount are not strictly relevant to the principle of rewarding *guilty pleas* it is evident that that principle is part of a wider strategy of encouraging various forms of cooperation from suspects. That wider strategy in turn undoubtedly helps secure the mass production of guilty pleas, since a defendant who 'fully cooperates' with the police cannot realistically plead not guilty.

How large is the sentencing discount?

The appellate courts were traditionally reluctant to specify a standard discount, arguing that sentencing is a subjective exercise to be tailored to all the circumstances of each individual case,[22] But over time it became accepted that the 'standard discount' for an early guilty plea was a third. The SGC guideline (para 4.2) provides that the deduction should be gauged on a sliding scale ranging from a maximum of one-third (where the guilty plea was indicated at the first reasonable opportunity), reducing to a maximum of one-quarter (where a trial date has been set) to a maximum of one-tenth (for a guilty plea entered just before the trial begins, or thereafter).[23] This suggests that discounts of more than a third will be rare in future.

The guideline also deals with some of the situations in which the courts had previously been reluctant to allow any discount. In *Costen*,[24] for example, the Court of Appeal said that the sentencing discount could be withheld altogether if there had been a last-minute tactical change of plea or if the offender had been caught 'redhanded' and there was no possible defence to the charge.[25] This made little sense in terms of the rationale of encouraging efficiency, and the Court of Appeal subsequently said that judges should give *some* discount for a guilty plea however strong the prosecution case may be.[26] The Court of Appeal wanted to have it both ways: it laid down a policy of requiring a discount for every guilty pleader but sometimes could not bring itself to meet its end of the bargain and introduced an exception to the policy so that a discount could be denied[27] or reduced for 'undeserving' appellants.[28] This was the rule of officials, not law.

The SGC guideline attempts to address the problem of awarding discounts to defendants against whom the prosecution case is overwhelming by stating that 'it may not be appropriate to give the full reduction that would otherwise have been given' (para 5.3). It suggests that instead of a one-third discount for a guilty plea at the first reasonable opportunity, a reduction of 20% is likely to be appropriate if the prosecution case is overwhelming (para 5.4). This shift from earlier versions of the guidance which suggested that the defendant should get 'very little, if any, discount' shows that the SGC is now keen to preserve the incentive to plead guilty despite some objections

---

[22] See, for example, *Buffrey* (1992) 14 Cr App Rep (S) 511 at 515.
[23] Cf *Attorney General's Reference No 88 of 2002* [2003] EWCA Crim 3010 in which a very late plea of guilt was seen as justifying a reduction in the minimum term from 4.5 to 3.5 years (a discount of 22.3%).
[24] (1989) 11 Cr App Rep (S) 182.   [25] Following *Morris* (1988) 10 Cr App Rep (S) 216.
[26] *Fearon* [1996] Crim LR 212.   [27] As in *Hastings* [1995] Crim LR 661.
[28] As in *Greenland* [2002] EWCA Crim 1748.

that a 20% discount is too great for defendants with a very strong case against them.[29] Despite the clear policy steer to award significant discounts to defendants caught 'red-handed', the Court of Appeal nevertheless continues to find it difficult to do for 'unde-serving' defendants.[30]

Murder, minimum sentences and public protection

Some offences have, in sentencing terms, been singled out for special treatment by Parliament and this has had a knock-on effect on the sentence discount principle. First, those convicted of murder must be given a life sentence and a minimum term to be served in prison (the 'punitive element') before release on licence can be considered. Schedule 21 of the Criminal Justice Act 2003 provides guidance on what this mini-mum term should be. Subject to the age of the offender, in the worst cases (eg, multiple murders with a sadistic element) this will be the rest of the offender's life, in the next most serious category of cases (eg, murder of a police officer) the starting point for the minimum custodial term is 30 years, while for the least serious murders the starting point is 15 years.

Considerable disquiet was expressed in the media, Parliament and elsewhere when the Sentencing Guidelines Council indicated that it intended to apply the standard sliding discount scale to the punitive element in murder cases. The SCG accordingly drew back. The guideline states that no discount at all is to be applied to 'whole life' minimum terms.[31] For all other cases of murder the discount in the minimum term to be served will be no more than a sixth and never exceed five years, with the sliding scale to apply so that there is a maximum of 5% for a late guilty plea. Finally the court should 'review the sentence to ensure that the minimum term accurately reflects the seriousness of the offence taking account of the statutory starting point, all aggravat-ing and mitigating features and any guilty plea entered' (para 6.6). The consequences of this can be seen in a case like *McDonald*,[32] where a one-sixth discount would have produced a sentence which the court regarded as too low for a domestic homicide which was 'particularly violent and ferocious'.[33] In this area, then, the rationale of pro-moting system efficiency has given ground to a concern with ensuring that the seri-ousness of the offence is reflected in the minimum term (a 'just deserts' rationale).

Secondly, there are offences where Parliament has specified a presumptive mini-mum custodial sentence. The Crime Sentences Act 1997 introduced such sentences for a third Class A drug trafficking offence (seven years) and for a third residential bur-glary (three years). These sentences were meant to achieve public protection (through deterrence or incapacitation) and that purpose could be undermined by discounting sentences for guilty pleas. As a compromise between the demands of public protection

---

[29] SGC, *Reduction on Sentence for Guilty Plea: Response to Consultation* (2007a).
[30] See, for example, *Curtis* [2007] 2 Cr App R (S) 52.
[31] In *Jones & Ors* [2005] EWCA Crim 3115 a whole life term for a murderer who had pleaded guilty was upheld.   [32] [2007] EWCA Crim 1081.
[33] See also *Mundy* [2007] EWHC 764,

and the interests of expediency, Parliament has specified that the discount in such cases should be no more than 20%.[34] A further inroad into the discount principle was created by s 287 of the CJA 2003 which introduced presumptive minimum custodial sentences (five years for adults, three years for 16- to17-year-olds) for possessing fire-arms or ammunition. Expert commentators on the Act opined that it would be highly anomalous to construe the provision as excluding the sentence discount principle.[35] The Court of Appeal duly introduced such an anomaly into the law by deciding in *Jordan* that the statutory language plainly indicated that Parliament had not wished to see its new presumptive minimums discounted in return for a guilty plea.[36]

The third category of case is where a longer than commensurate sentence is imposed on a 'dangerous' offender who has committed one of a long list of sexual or violent offences specified in Sch 15 of the CJA 2003.[37] In such cases a minimum custodial term is set by the court to reflect the seriousness of the offence committed. This 'just deserts' element, but not the additional public protection element, may be discounted in return for a guilty plea according to the normal sliding scale set out in the SGC guideline.

This discussion throws into stark relief the conflicts that lie at the heart of sentenc-ing principles and the anomalies that result. Thus we have seen that most murderers as well as repeat burglars and drug traffickers can legitimately expect to receive a dis-count for pleading guilty, but that first time firearm offenders and the worst murderers cannot.

Other benefits of pleading guilty

Prior to the SGC guideline the courts had indicated that a guilty plea could, in com-bination with other mitigating factors, make the difference between an immediate prison sentence and a non-custodial disposal.[38] The SGC guideline states that where the sentence is in doubt as to whether a custodial sentence is appropriate the discount for the guilty plea is a relevant consideration. Likewise a guilty plea is relevant when considering a fine or discharge as an alternative to a community order (para 2.3). In other words a guilty plea can make a difference to the *type* of penalty imposed. The guidance adds that where a guilty plea is a factor in the imposition of a different (lesser) penalty there is 'no need to apply a further reduction' for a guilty plea. Before we turn to look at how particular types of courts use (or abuse) the sentence discount princi-ple, it is important to stress that, notwithstanding legal constraints and guidelines, all sentencers have ample room for exercising individual judgment and discretion. An analysis by Hough et al, for example, concluded that judicial emphasis upon personal

---

[34] A provision re-enacted in the Criminal Justice Act 2003, s 144(2).

[35] See Taylor et al, *Blackstone's Guide to the Criminal Justice Act 2003* (Oxford: OUP, 2004) pp 207–8.

[36] *Jordan & Ors* [2004] EWCA Crim 3291, which also ruled that where a court decides that there are 'exceptional circumstances' which justify not applying the presumptive minimum, the discount principle may be applied.

[37] The complicated provisions are to be found in the Criminal Justice Act 2003, pt 12, ch 5 as amended by the Criminal Justice and Immigration Act 2008.

[38] *Okinikan* (1993) 14 Cr App Rep (S) 453; *Howells* [1998] Crim LR 836.

mitigation, including the elusive concept of 'remorse', rendered the sentencing exercise a 'highly subjective one'.[39]

8.2.2 The impact of the discount principle on sentencing in the magistrates' court

All sentencers, including magistrates, must now have regard to the guidance issued by the SGC on reduction of sentence for guilty plea.[40] Prior to that, the sentence discount principle in the lower courts was not formally acknowledged until a new version of the Magistrates' Association sentencing guidelines stated, in 1993, that 'a *timely* guilty plea may be regarded as a mitigating factor for which a sentencing discount of approximately one-third might be given.'[41] A study carried out by Flood-Page and Mackie in the mid 1990s could not isolate the effect of plea but found that lack of cooperative behaviour with the police did influence magisterial thinking, although 'the attempts to predict sentences on the basis of case factors were not particularly successful... [which] suggests wide differences in the way these sentences are used...'[42] In other words, sentencing was all over the place. Henham carried out a different type of study of this issue in Leicester and Nottingham Magistrates' Court in April 1998. Unfortunately the methods used in the study, and the way in which the results are reported, limits the inferences we can draw from the findings.[43] For what it is worth, Henham found that in 90% of cases sentencers indicated that the guilty plea had at least some impact on the sentence. Similarly 86.2% of sentencers claimed that they had attached at least some importance to the stage at which the guilty plea was entered.

---

[39] (Hough et al, *The Decision to Imprison: Sentencing and the Prison Population* (London: Prison Reform Trust, 2003) p 3). The multiple and sometimes conflicting aims of sentencing outlined in s 143 of the Criminal Justice Act 2003 have enlarged the judicial room for manoeuvre (Von Hirsch A and Roberts J, 'Legislating Sentencing Principles' [2004] Crim LR 639) although the SGC prioritises a just deserts approach in its guidance on the 'Overarching Principles' of sentencing (currently undergoing revision – see <http://www.sentencing-guidelines.gov.uk/>; (accessed 5 January 2010). In recent years the issue of judicial discretion has become a pressing issue as the government has looked for ways of controlling or at least predicting future levels of demand for prison places (Lord Carter, *Securing the Future: Proposals for the Efficient and Sustainable Use of Custody in England and Wales* (London: MoJ, 2007) – available at <http://www.justice.gov.uk/publications/securing-the-future.htm>–accessed 5 January 2010). This is part of the rationale behind the new Sentencing Council which, when compared with the current SGC, will have an enhanced role in monitoring the impact of sentencing decisions and policy on the prison population.

[40] Reiterated in the *Magistrates' Sentencing Guidelines* (London: Sentencing Guidelines Council, 2008) p 17.

[41] Magistrates' Association, *Sentencing Guidelines* (London: Magistrates' Association, 1993) p 3, para 2.4. Emphasis in original.

[42] Flood-Page C and Mackie A, *Sentencing Practice* (Home Office Research Study No 180) (London: Home Office, 1998) p 129. To the extent that magistrates were giving sentence discounts, white defendants benefited from the policy more often than ethnic minority defendants. This is because the latter pleaded not guilty more frequently than the former (p 117).

[43] See further Young, R 'Review of Henham R, Sentence Discounts and the Criminal Process' (2003) 7(2) Edinburgh LR 267. The magistrates knew the researcher was assessing the impact of guilty plea on sentence and were asked to indicate what effect this had in a post decision questionnaire; the replies are therefore magistrates' 'claims' about discounts.

A third of cases were said to have resulted in a sentence discount of more than one-third and around a fifth of cases less than a third; about 1 in 20 cases were claimed to have attracted no discount at all. Henham's conclusion was that the statutory encouragement of guilty pleas had 'done little to regulate the pragmatic nature of decision-making on sentence discounts';[44] in other words, magistrates remained something of a law unto themselves.

Hough et al[45] reported that the magistrates in their study said they followed the structured process required by their guidelines (which included giving a discount for a guilty plea). Whether these claims are matched by reality is debatable, however. Research by Feilzer and Hood (2004) which looked at youth offenders noted that there were considerable differences in the sentencing patterns of the youth courts they studied which could not be explained by factors that legitimately should affect outcome, such as plea, previous record and seriousness of offence. In their published findings Feilzer and Hood did not isolate the impact of plea on sentencing in the youth courts but they kindly agreed to carry out this analysis to help inform this chapter.[46] The raw data indicated:

(a) that there appeared to be no difference in sentence length according to plea in the youth court; and

(b) that amongst those who were either sentenced to custody or a community penalty involving a measure of supervision, a not guilty plea was associated with a higher risk of receiving a custodial sentence.

To investigate this second finding, a logistic regression analysis was carried out which took into account known factors that might influence the risk of custody, such as type of charge, previous convictions and so forth. The odds of not guilty cases being sentenced to custody was then (these other things being equal) found to be 1.4 that of guilty cases.[47] Plea was also found to have an effect on the pre-sentencing report prepared by the probation service in that defendants pleading not guilty were more likely (5.7%) to have been recommended for custody than those pleading guilty (3.2%). One possible explanation is that a guilty plea was taken by the probation service as a good indicator that a defendant would comply with the conditions of a community sentence. So it would seem that guilty pleas *can* result in more lenient punishments in the youth court, but not in the mechanical way presumed by the law.

Returning to Feilzer and Hood's published findings, unlike the Flood-Page and Mackie study of the sentencing of *adult* offenders, differences in guilty plea rates between male *youth* offenders of different ethnicities were relatively minor. Feilzer and Hood found, however, that ethnicity had a bearing on sentencing in a manner

---

[44] Henham R, 'Reconciling Process and Policy' [2000] Crim LR 436 at 450.
[45] Hough et al (2003b: 37).   [46] Private communication dated 29 November 2005.
[47] A statistically significant finding (p<0.040).

consistent with unfair discrimination, although this again varied from court to court.[48] This 'justice by race and geography', as the authors put it, raises further concerns about the extent to which the magistrates' courts can be relied upon to keep their end of the sentencing discount bargain.

The magistracy is an overwhelmingly white, middle-aged and middle-class institution which displays strong pro-authority attitudes and various forms of bias in all its decision-making.[49] For example, one magistrate told Flood-Page and Mackie that:

We all resent having to fine people very low amounts for no insurance. We're all sitting in court, having paid our dues, and they are taking a chance and getting away with it. If they are on income support, how can they afford to own a car?[50]

It is difficult to imagine this magistrate awarding a sentence discount to someone so obviously perceived to be 'undeserving'.

8.2.3 The impact of the discount principle on sentencing in the Crown Court

Crown Court judges are pragmatists and historically have been found to display a measure of ignorance of, or resistance to, principles established by the Court of Appeal.[51] Whether the increasing prominence of sentencing guidelines has made any difference is doubtful. The evidence from Hough et al's interviews with Crown Court judges at the start of the twenty-first century is that an 'intuitive' approach to sentencing remained in vogue.[52]

The way in which the discount principle was applied in practice prior to the CJPO was examined in three separate studies by Hood, Moxon, and Baldwin and McConville.[53] All three studies suggested that Crown Court sentencing was consistent with the overall pattern of Court of Appeal judgments in two key respects: firstly, discounts were generally being awarded for pleas of guilty, resulting in reduced sentence lengths; second, the type of sentence itself was often determined by whether or not someone pleaded guilty. This last point is crucial as the pressure exerted on defendants to plead guilty by the sentencing discount is obviously much greater if the plea can make the difference between a custodial and non-custodial sentence.

---

[48] Feilzer M and Hood R, *Differences or Discrimination?* (London: Youth Justice Board, 2004) pp 96, 100, 108, 167–8.

[49] See the discussion in 9.5.1 and, for the impact of middle-class values on sentencing, McConville et al (1994: 203–4). See further Gilchrist E and Blissett J, 'Magistrates' Attitudes to Domestic Violence and Sentencing Options' (2002) 41 Howard JCJ 348.   [50] Quoted in Flood-Page and Mackie (1998: 51–2).

[51] Dissatisfaction with and ignorance of Court of Appeal sentencing principles amongst Crown Court judges is reported by Ashworth et al (1984: 49). See also Hunter M, 'Judicial Discretion: s 78 in Practice' [1994] Crim LR 558 at 562, discussed in 12.5.3.   [52] Hough et al (2003b: 37).

[53] Hood R, *Race and Sentencing* (Oxford: OUP, 1992) p 87; Moxon D, *Sentencing Practice in the Crown Court* (Home Office Research Study No 103) (London: HMSO, 1988); and Baldwin J and McConville M, 'The Influence of the Sentencing Discount in Inducing Guilty Pleas' in Baldwin J and Bottomley A (eds), *Criminal Justice: Selected Readings* (Oxford: Martin Robertson, 1978) p 119.

One aspect of judicial practice was not consistent with the legal position, however. Late plea changers should, in legal theory, be receiving smaller discounts than those who pleaded guilty at an early stage. Yet early guilty pleas received less of a reward than late pleas in both Baldwin and McConville's study and, to a smaller extent, in that conducted by Moxon. This is consistent with a model of bargaining in which large last-minute concessions are offered by or wrung out of judges when it is clear that the defendant will otherwise stick with a plea of not guilty. This suggests that the SGC and Court of Appeal norms favouring early indications of guilty pleas will not always be honoured in practice.

The research by Hood was the most sophisticated of these studies in that it rigorously took into account all measurable factors that might affect sentence length other than plea (eg, previous record). Only three months of the 10 months aggregate difference in sentence length between guilty pleaders and those contesting their cases was found to be attributable to the plea itself.[54] Hood also discovered that Afro-Caribbeans tend to plead not guilty more frequently than whites and so are more often denied the benefit of the sentence discount principle.[55]

Henham examined 310 guilty plea cases from six Crown Court centres. He did not examine the effect of a guilty plea on sentencing except in an indirect manner. Transcripts of the judge's sentencing comments were examined to monitor the extent of 'compliance' with s 48 CJPO. Unfortunately, Henham chooses to treat an absence of sentencing comments on the effect of the guilty plea on sentence as 'non-compliance', even though he himself acknowledges that sentencers are not obliged by s 48 to make such comments if in fact they have not given any discount for a guilty plea. He made this choice on the basis that in only six of the 145 cases where no such comments were made did the sentencer explicitly say that no discount had been awarded for the guilty plea, drawing from this the 'reasonable' conclusion 'that the remainder of those 145 cases where there was a failure to state the fact that a sentence discount had been given were in reality cases where a sentence discount *was* allowed'.[56] It seems more likely to us that there were at least some cases where no discount was given for the guilty plea and the sentencer, under no obligation to explain this, confined his or her remarks to the various other matters where comment *is* obligatory. Why point out to the defendant that the system has failed to keep its side of the bargain (which it itself sought to induce) when this could threaten judicial legitimacy?

This raises the question of why no discount might be given in guilty plea cases. Perhaps Crown Court judges are like magistrates and the appellate judiciary in wanting to have it both ways. They like guilty pleas, but they do not like giving discounts to the 'undeserving'. Thus Henham found, in relation to sentencers' general approach to the discount principle in fixing sentence, that 'as many as 34.5% of sentencers considered the guilty plea as either "not particularly important" or "not important at all"'. He finds this 'surprising'. We find it predictable. In a system which plays dirty with

---

[54] Hood (1992: 125).   [55] Hood (1992: 202–3).

[56] Henham R, 'Bargain Justice or Justice Denied? Sentence Discounts and the Criminal Process' (1999) 63 MLR 515 at 527.

suspect's 'rights' at every stage in the process why should the 'right' to a sentence discount be any different?[57]

By the same token, how can we be sure, on the basis of Henham's study, that all the Crown Court judges who said they were awarding a discount for a guilty plea actually did so? In the absence of some attempt to control for all other factors that might have influenced the sentence (particularly the seriousness of the offence and previous record of the offender) we cannot be confident about this. A policy of announcing that a discount had been given but not actually making any reduction would allow Crown Court judges to have the best of what would be a particularly bad 'bargain' for defendants.

The fact that Crown Court judges are trained lawyers does not mean that their decisions will be free of bias. Indeed, Hood found evidence consistent with *direct* racial discrimination in one of the four Crown Court centres he studied, and Feilzer and Hood found that the odds of a young black male's custodial sentence at a Crown Court being 12 months or longer (once other relevant factors such as previous record, type of offence and plea were held constant) was 6.7 times the odds of a young white male receiving a sentence of a similar length.[58]

In further unpublished work they generously conducted to help inform the analysis in this book, Feilzer and Hood report:

(a) that plea appeared to have no effect on whether or not custody was imposed for those cases close to the custody threshold; and

(b) that a guilty plea was associated with shorter custodial sentences.

In investigating the second finding, logistic regression revealed that once other known factors that might influence sentence length were taken into account, defendants pleading not guilty were 1.8 times more likely to receive a sentence of two years or longer, compared with similarly situated defendants pleading guilty.[59] These findings are the mirror image of those for the youth court where Feilzer and Hood found no impact of plea on sentence length but evidence consistent with an impact on the custody/ non-custody decision.

To sum up, in the criminal courts in England and Wales the effect of a guilty plea on sentencing is variable, uncertain and often at odds with the law's requirements. To put this more bluntly, in the context of sentence discount 'bargains', large numbers of defendants are getting ripped off.

8.2.4 Communicating the discount to defendants

Sentencing remarks

One way in which defendants, particularly the courts' repeat clientele, can learn about the sentence discount is if courts regularly articulate the fact that they are giving a

---

[57] See, in particular, chs 2–5 on the extent of police compliance with suspects' rights.

[58] Hood (1992); Feilzer and Hood (2004: 112).

[59] Private communication dated 29 November 2005. Note that this finding was not statistically significant, probably due to the relatively small numbers of not guilty cases in this analysis (31).

discount and specify its size.[60] Judicial practice in relation to this is inconsistent, and it may be difficult to disentangle the impact of a guilty plea from other mitigating factors.[61] The SGC has stated that the guilty plea should be addressed separately from other mitigation and 'the court should usually state what the sentence would otherwise have been if there had been no reduction as a result of the guilty plea'.[62] However, even when the discount and amount are articulated there is no way of being certain of the veracity of a sentencer's claim.

The role of defence lawyers[63]

The defence lawyer has an ethical duty to the client 'to promote and protect fearlessly and by all proper and lawful means the lay client's best interests and do so without regard to his own interests...'[64] In a system which operates a sentence discount principle this has long meant that a defence lawyer is obliged to point out the pros and cons to the defendant of pleading guilty.[65] As Lord Parker CJ put it in *Turner*:[66]

Counsel must be completely free to do what is his duty, namely to give the accused the best advice he can and, if need be, advice in strong terms. This will often include advice that a plea of guilty, showing an element of remorse, is a mitigating factor which may well enable the court to give a lesser sentence than would otherwise be the case.

Although Lord Parker went on to say that the defendant 'having considered counsel's advice, must have a complete freedom of choice whether to plead guilty or not guilty', one may question whether such freedom can co-exist with strong advice from counsel to plead guilty.[67]

There can be little doubt that many defence solicitors in the magistrates' courts do communicate the fact of the discount 'in strong terms'. In their observational study, McConville et al (1994) found that most defence lawyers generally seek to persuade their clients to plead guilty. They argue that the main factors behind an unethical preference for trial-avoidance are a presumption that the client is guilty, and a belief that the client is unworthy and undeserving of a contested trial.[68] Where a client wishes to maintain innocence, the solicitor will emphasise (and usually exaggerate) the perils of pleading not guilty, such as increased costs, reduced scope for mitigation, and so

---

[60] Section 48(2) of CJPOA provides for the sentencer to indicate a discount has been given, but says nothing about indicating the amount.   [61] *Peters* [2005] EWCA Crim 606; *Kluk* [2005] EWCA Crim 1331.

[62] SGC (2007b: para 3.1).

[63] See generally Cape E, 'The Rise (and Fall?) of a Criminal Defence Profession' [2004] Crim LR 401.

[64] The Code of Conduct for Barristers, 8th edn (effective from 31 October 2004), para 303(a) (available from <http://www.barstandardsboard.org.uk/standardsandguidance/codeofconduct>). The code laying down equivalent professional standards for solicitors is available from <http://www.sra.org.uk/solicitors/code-of-conduct.page> (both last accessed 5 January 2010).

[65] See Blake M and Ashworth A, 'Ethics and the Criminal Defence Lawyer' (2004) 7(2) Legal Ethics 167 at pp 179–82.   [66] [1970] 2 WLR 1093 at 1097.

[67] See the critique by McConville M, 'Plea Bargaining' in McConville M and Wilson G (eds), *The Handbook of the Criminal Justice Process* (Oxford: OUP, 2002) at pp 357–60.

[68] McConville et al (1994: ch 8). This argument finds further support in Mulcahy A, 'The Justifications of Justice: Legal Practitioners' Accounts of Negotiated Case Settlements in Magistrates' Courts' (1994) 34 BJ Crim 411.

forth.[69] The sentence discount principle provides a useful additional pressure solicitors can bring to bear on defendants. It dovetails with their practice of seeking to mitigate on the basis that the defendant had cooperated with the needs of crime control, as in this example: 'I ask you to give my client credit for his plea. He was also co-operative with the police'.[70]

Many of the examples of pressure observed by McConville et al (1994) occurred on the day of the trial itself. The role of the defence solicitor in engineering changes of plea at the last moment is valuable from a crime control perspective, but more valuable still would be the communication of advice to plead guilty at an earlier stage. Amendments to the legal aid rules in recent years have been designed to ensure that it is in the financial self-interest of lawyers to drive cases forward to an early conclusion (see ch 9). Conflicts of interest may arise not only with the solicitors' own interests vis-à-vis the client but also with the duties the solicitor owes to the court, not least in terms of cooperating with policies designed to ensure efficient case management. Over the years, policy-makers have established various pre-trial initiatives designed to promote earlier case settlement. Plea before venue,[71] and the 'Narey reforms' were examples of these initiatives.[72] Under the Criminal Procedure Rules 2005 defence solicitors must assist the court in actively managing cases.[73] One of the latest initiatives *Criminal Justice: Simple, Speedy, Summary* (or CJSSS as it is known) seeks to streamline case management procedures to reduce the overall time between arrest and the case being completed, ultimately reducing the number of court hearings to just one for a guilty plea and two for a contested case.[74] It introduces a concept of 'next day justice' (defendants appearing in court within hours of the alleged offence being committed) for certain categories of crime and favours a policy of live links from the police station to allow defendants to plead guilty remotely for low level offences.[75] There is some disquiet about the impact of CJSSS on defence lawyers, particularly concerning how they can reconcile their duty to assist the court in managing the case expeditiously with their duty to act in their client's best interests.[76] The concept of a 'virtual' court, where the client may be compelled to appear without his consent via live link from the police

---

[69] See the case-studies they present at McConville et al (1994) pp 193 and 195–6 in particular.

[70] McConville et al (1994: 205).

[71] Introduced by s 49 of the Criminal Procedure and Investigations Act 1996. For more detail see ch 9.

[72] Home Office, *Review of Delay in the Criminal Justice System: A Report* (London: Home Office, 1997a). Early first hearings (EFHs) introduced a fast track procedure for 'simple' cases where defendants were expected to plead guilty; alternatively Early Administrative Hearings (EAHs) afforded an opportunity for the court and duty solicitor to advise the defendant on the consequences of maintaining a not guilty plea. See further ch 9.

[73] <http://www.justice.gov.uk/criminal/procrules_fin/rulesmenu.htm> (accessed 5 January 2010). See Rule 3.3.

[74] Department for Constitutional Affairs, *Delivering Simple, Speedy, Summary Justice* (London: DCA, 2006b).

[75] Live links from the police station have been possible since the Police and Justice Act 2006 but subject to the proviso that the defendant consents (s 57C of the Crime and Disorder Act 1988 as amended).

[76] Mountford L and Hannibal M, 'Simpler, Speedier Justice for All?' (2007) 158 Solicitors' Journal 1294.

station,[77] also raises dilemmas for defence lawyers in fulfilling their formal commitment to act in the best interest of their client.[78]

Not all defence solicitors will succumb to these pressures to expedite cases in the magistrates' court, but few need persuading that the appropriate advice for most clients is to enter a guilty plea at the earliest opportunity.

Is the position any different in the Crown Court? Baldwin and McConville's study in the 1970s of late plea changers revealed that 40% of defendants had changed their plea as a result of pressure exerted by their barristers, in over half of which 'the advice counsel gave was of such a nature that no reasonable person could say that it was fair or proper or that the final decision to plead guilty was made voluntarily'.[79] The policy of offering large sentence discounts for guilty pleas provided barristers who wished to settle cases with powerful ammunition to fire at defendants. As one explained:

The barrister then said, 'If you're found guilty you will get about 10 or 15 years but if you plead guilty you will get 4 or 5 years.' I was really shocked. I was so scared, sweating and nervous and he frightened me with this 10–15 years stuff and saying I had no chance....I agreed to plead guilty but it wasn't my decision; I had no choice about it.[80]

The study by McConville et al, conducted some 15 years later, showed that little had changed. They observed pre-trial conferences between counsel and client, held at court in order to settle the plea, and found that half the defendants involved were persuaded to enter guilty pleas immediately by their barristers 'with the remainder having to go through the same ordeal on a future occasion after their cases were adjourned without a plea'.[81] One might ask why these barristers had not advised these defendants to plead guilty at an earlier stage in the proceedings in order to earn the maximum discount on offer. The chance to press this advice is presented at pre-court conferences, but McConville et al found that any pressure applied in that setting tended to be subtle, and designed to sap the defendant's determination to go to trial rather than undermine it completely there and then. Even when the instructing solicitor told a barrister to give the client 'a talking to ... You'll have to give him a hard time' the barrister chose not to give the client an ear-wigging, justifying this afterwards by saying: 'If you get too tough at the start, they sack you!'[82]

Like solicitors, barristers are sensitive to the economic incentives represented by the fee structure made available by the state, and it can be to the financial advantage of barristers to crack cases at the last moment rather than engineer a plea of guilty at

---

[77] The Coroners and Justice Bill 2008–9 will if enacted dispense with the requirement of consent in s 57C of the CDA 1988.

[78] Guidance on 'virtual' courts is provided by the Law Society at <http://www.lawsociety.org.uk/productsandservices/practicenotes/virtualcourts.page> (accessed 5 January 2010).

[79] Baldwin J and McConville M, *Negotiated Justice* (London: Martin Robertson, 1977) p 45.

[80] Baldwin and McConville (1977a: 49–50).   [81] McConville et al (1994: 261).

[82] McConville et al (1994: 253–4).

an earlier stage or take the case to trial.[83] Like the system in the magistrates' court, there are procedures designed to ensure the routine application of pressure on defendants to plead guilty as soon as possible. The parts of the Criminal Procedure Rules applicable to Crown Court outline the process of active case management at Plea and Case Management Hearings (PCMHs) to reduce delays and late guilty pleas (cracked trials).[84] Counsel for the defence must in every case assist in the completion of a standard form, the very first question of which is: 'Has the defendant been advised about credit for pleading guilty?'[85].

Sentence indications and sentence bargaining

Should the law permit sentencers to indicate to defendants (or their lawyers) in advance what view they take of the alleged offence and what discount they would be prepared to give if a guilty plea was entered? The advantage of this would be that defendants would know exactly where they stood (although this assumes fair dealing on the part of the sentencer). The disadvantage would be that the impartiality of the court would be brought into question by such communications. It might seem as if the court had already made up its mind about the defendant's guilt and were seeking to assist the prosecution in obtaining a conviction, thus placing even more pressure on the defendant to plead guilty.

For several decades, following the key decision in *Turner*,[86] appellate judges insisted that the only acceptable advance indication of sentence was one to the effect that, regardless of how the defendant pleaded, a particular type of sentence (such as a fine) would be imposed. Anything more (such as declaring that a non-custodial penalty would follow a guilty plea but saying nothing about what would happen if the defendant was convicted following a full trial) was seen as restricting the defendant's choice as to plea. Over this same period, however, trial judges continually flouted the *Turner* rules, although the problem was very largely a Crown Court phenomenon.[87] Here, barristers and judges (who are mostly ex-barristers) formed a close-knit workgroup with shared values. Judges and counsel frequently met privately before or during the trial, and this allowed illegal forms of sentence bargaining to flourish. In the multitude of reported cases, defence counsel and Crown Court judges seemed

---

[83] For the argument that barristers' incentives in counselling clients, financial or otherwise, do not always point towards cracking trials, and that in some situations barristers may encourage or recommend guilty pleas when it is not in their own interests, see Tague P 'Barristers' Selfish Incentives in Counselling Clients' [2008] Crim LR 3. The motivations of defence barristers are further explored in 8.4.2 below.

[84] Criminal Procedure Rules 2005, Part 1V.45.

[85] The Consolidated Criminal Practice Direction, Annex E, available at <http://www.justice.gov.uk/criminal/procrules_fin/contents/practice_direction/annexE.htm> (last accessed 24 August 2009).

[86] [1970] 2 WLR 1093.

[87] There are fewer incentives and opportunities for the defence and the sentencer to conduct back-stage sentencing negotiations in the magistrates' court than in the Crown Court, particularly as there is little opportunity for informal relations to build up between part-time lay magistrates and lawyers (McConville et al, 1994: 186). That the position is probably different with professional magistrates is exemplified by the facts in *In re McFarland* [2004] UKHL 17.

to be equally implicated in sentence bargaining. Sometimes defence counsel took the initiative by going to see the judge in private, but often the judge summoned counsel to initiate discussions over sentence.[88] Trial judges, no less than barristers, are allocated more trial cases than they can handle on the assumption that some will 'go guilty' and this expectation then becomes self-fulfilling. Thus in *Nazham and Nazham*[89] in a private discussion with counsel the trial judge expressed his interest in cracking the case (scheduled for trial in Birmingham) given that he had yet to finish hearing another case and might also have to sit at Lincoln the following Friday. He said, 'this has got plea written all over it and bags of credit' and expressed his view that the defendants 'have got an eye for a deal'. The gist of this was conveyed to the defendants who pleaded guilty, thus rendering the trial judge's workload more manageable.

Research published in the early 1990s demonstrated that the Court of Appeal's attempt to inhibit sentence bargaining had met with only limited success.[90] This suggests that lawyers and judges in the Crown Court, just like the police in their milieu, habitually followed their own working rules rather than adhering to the law. The Crown Court survey conducted for the Runciman Commission provided one explanation for this flouting of the law: neither barristers nor trial judges appeared to agree with the *Turner* rules and the majority thought they should be reformed to permit full and realistic discussion between counsel and the judge about plea and sentence.[91] In the light of this evidence the Runciman Commission[92] recommended that pre-trial sentence bargaining should be legitimised by allowing judges to indicate the maximum sentence they would give if a guilty plea was entered there and then. At the time its recommendation was not acted upon. A subsequent influential review of the criminal courts by Lord Justice Auld also argued in favour of allowing pre-trial sentence indications to be made openly, noting that this was supported by the Bar Council, many of the judiciary and most criminal practitioners.[93]

Inroads into the *Turner* rules were subsequently made by Sch 3 of the CJA 2003, which applies only to the magistrates' courts. In either-way cases which the magistrates have decided would be suitable for summary trial, the defence lawyer can now request an indication from the court of whether a custodial or non-custodial sentence would be more likely if their client was to be tried summarily and plead guilty.[94] This is

---

[88] For a full list of citations to the case law from the 1970s up to the early 1990s see the 2nd edition of this book at p 424. [89] [2004] EWCA Crim 491.

[90] McConville et al (1994: 253); Morison J and Leith P, *The Barrister's World* (Milton Keynes: Open UP, 1992) p 135; Plotnikoff J and Woolfson R, *From Committal to Trial: Delay at the Crown Court* (London: Law Society, 1993a) pp 67–8. [91] Zander and Henderson (1993: 145).

[92] Runciman Commission (1993: 112–13).

[93] Auld LJ, *Review of the Criminal Courts of England and Wales: Report* (London: TSO, 2001) pp 434–44.

[94] Magistrates will presumably accede to this request whenever they want a defendant to reconsider an earlier indication of a not guilty plea *and* they regard a non-custodial penalty as an acceptable outcome. If the defendant sticks to a not guilty plea the court will not be bound by any earlier indication, 'the bargain, in other words, is off' (Taylor et al, 2004: 73).

designed to persuade more defendants in either-way cases to forego their right to elect trial by jury by pleading guilty at an early stage.

At the turn of the century it was evident that breaches of the *Turner* rules were continuing unabated,[95] and in some cases the court of Appeal seemed keen to limit the impact of their application.[96] Against this background, and taking into account the modern trend towards requiring judges to play an active role in 'case-management', in 2005 a five-strong Court of Appeal in *Goodyear*[97] decided to abandon the *Turner* rules and legitimise a form of sentence bargaining. The key points were:

(1) There was to be no watering down of the essential principle that the defendant's plea must always be made voluntarily and free from any improper pressure;

(2) For judges to respond to a request by the defendant to indicate the maximum sentence that would follow an immediate guilty plea would not constitute such improper pressure;

(3) Judges must not go further in their sentence indication by also stating what the maximum possible level of sentence would be following a contested trial. To cover all eventualities that maximum would have to be very substantial and the comparison between the two alternatives indicated would create pressure to tender a guilty plea. (Since the Court acknowledged that the sentence discount itself created pressure, we must assume here that this prohibition is designed to avoid 'improper pressure' rather than simply 'pressure'. This has now been judicially acknowledged, for example in *Clark and Ors* where it was observed 'some pressure cannot be avoided. Pressure is inherent in the giving of credit for plea'.)[98]

(4) Judges remained free, however, to indicate that the sentence, or (more likely) the type of sentence, would be the same regardless of how the defendant pleaded.

(5) While judges should not give an advance indication unless one was sought, they were entitled to remind counsel in open court, in the presence of the defendant, of the defendant's entitlement to seek an advance indication of sentence. This should be done with caution in order to avoid creating (i) pressure on the defendant to plead guilty (but see our parenthetical comment to point 3); and (ii) the perception that the judge had prejudged the issue of guilt or for some reason did not want to try the case.

(6) If, notwithstanding such a reminder from the judge, the defendant did not seek an indication of sentence, 'then, at any rate for the time being, it would not be appropriate for the judge to give or insist on giving an indication of sentence,

---

[95] For example, multiple breaches of the *Turner* rules occurred in *Bargery* [2004] EWCA Crim 816; see also *Attorney General's Reference No 44 of 2000 (Peverett)* [2001] 1 Cr App R 416 and *Attorney General's Reference No 88 of 2002* [2003] EWCA Crim 3010.

[96] *Nazham and Nazham* [2004] EWCA Crim 491.   [97] [2005] EWCA Crim 888.

[98] [2008] EWCA Crim 3221 at para 48.

unless in any event he would be prepared to give the indication permitted by *Turner*…that the sentence will or will not take a particular form' (para 51).

(7) Judges retained an unfettered discretion to decline to give a sentence indication. They might so decline in a variety of circumstances including where they believed defendants were already under pressure (but see our parenthetical comment to point 3), or were vulnerable, or had not appreciated that they should not plead guilty unless they were in fact guilty.

(8) Judges might also decline to give an indication where they considered 'that the application is no less than a "try on" by a defendant who intends or would be likely to plead guilty in any event, seeking to take a tactical advantage of the changed process envisaged in this judgment' (para 57).

(9) Any indication given by a judge binds both that judge and any other judge who becomes responsible for that case, although the indication will cease to have effect if the defendant fails to plead guilty after a reasonable opportunity to consider his or her position. In straightforward cases it would be reasonable to expect the guilty plea to be entered on the same day the indication was given.

(10) The defendant's advocate should not seek a sentence indication unless he or she had first obtained a written signed request from the defendant.

(11) Defence advocates were to be personally responsible for ensuring that defendants fully appreciate that (i) they should not plead guilty unless they are guilty; (ii) any sentence indication remains subject to the entitlement of the Attorney General to refer an unduly lenient sentence to the Court of Appeal, (iii) the indication ceases to have effect if not acted upon (by entering a guilty plea) at the first reasonable opportunity by the defendant; (iv) the indication has no bearing on ancillary matters such as confiscation proceedings.[99]

(12) Sentence indications should normally be sought at the Plea and Case Management Hearing but later requests, including during the trial itself, should not be ruled out.

(13) The request should normally take place in open court (with the public present), with a full recording of the entire proceedings, and both sides represented, in the defendant's presence.

(14) These new arrangements were only to be applied in the Crown Court. Once they had settled in, consideration might be given to extending them to summary trials in the magistrates' courts.

This guidance attempts to bring sentence bargaining into the open, regulate it, and encourage more guilty pleas. It is arguable, however, that the guidelines are too

---

[99] For examples of how confiscation proceedings can get tangled up in (and unsettle) sentence bargains, see *Mahmood and Shahin* [2005] EWCA Crim 1268 and *Karim* [2005] EWCA Crim 533.

open-ended and self-contradictory to provide a stable legal framework. For example, the use of the word 'normally' in point 13 means that private discussions about sentencing have not been banned. Some defence advocates and trial judges will no doubt in future wish to initiate such discussions in order to clarify exactly how much discount is on offer – something that the officially sanctioned indication of a maximum sentence for a guilty plea entered there and then does not reveal. The self-contradictory nature of the guidelines is evident in the slippery use of the concepts of pressure and improper pressure. Thus, while spelling out, in response to a request from the defendant, the potential difference in sentence depending on plea is regarded as improper pressure (point 3) it is regarded as proper pressure for the judge actively to prompt the defendant to request a sentence indication (point 5) and even to tell the defendant (unprompted) that the sentence would be of the same type (eg a fine) whatever the plea (point 6). Quite how such an active judge is supposed to preserve the appearance of not having prejudged the case (as required by point 5) is unclear. Finally, the operation of the guidelines remains heavily dependent on judicial judgment and discretion. Thus judges are said to have an 'unfettered discretion' to refuse to give a sentencing indication (point 7) and may refuse to give an indication where they judge a request to be a 'try-on', seeking to take tactical advantage of the new arrangements (point 8). The scope for unfair discrimination is evident.

A case decided just a few months after *Goodyear* illustrates some of these concerns. In *Attorney General's Reference (No 80 of 2005)* the defendant was charged with wounding with intent to cause grievous bodily harm, an offence that carries a maximum penalty of life imprisonment. He had attacked the new partner of his former wife with a large torch and knife after laying in wait for him. The attack was prolonged, and the victim suffered sufficiently severe lacerations to require surgery and suffered permanent injury affecting his ability to work. The defendant had four previous convictions including one for wounding. The trial judge initiated a discussion about sentencing without any request from the defence (breach of *Goodyear* point 5), out of public view in his chambers (breaching the spirit of point 13), and said that a guilty plea would result in a non-custodial outcome whereas conviction after trial would attract a long-term prison sentence (breach of point 3). The judge also said in his sentencing remarks that he was aware of the Sentencing Guideline Council's view that an appropriate reduction for a late guilty plea was one-tenth but that he was going to knock a third off. In fact he imposed a two-year suspended sentence. There could scarcely be a better illustration of the disregard of guidelines that seems to occur with some regularity in the Crown Court. In this case, however, the Court of Appeal became involved. It said that the appropriate sentence following the late guilty plea would have been four years' imprisonment and the trial judge was castigated for misapplying *Goodyear* and disregarding the SGC's views.[100] Whether the Crown will typically seek to invoke the supervision of the Court of Appeal for dodgy sentence bargains in less extreme cases

---

[100] *Attorney General's Reference (No 80 of 2005)* [2005] EWCA Crim 3367.

is uncertain but seems unlikely given that prosecuting counsel is often party to such bargains in the first place.[101] Without a proper study of Crown Court decision-making the impact of *Goodyear* will remain unknown. Unfortunately this is not the type of research that the government is likely to fund or facilitate.

One area where the *Goodyear* guidelines have created difficulty is in situations where the defendant may be sentenced for public protection under relevant 'dangerousness' provisions. The Court of Appeal has said that judges should be cautious about giving indications of sentence for plea in situations where dangerousness has yet to be decided, adding that if the judge does give an indication it should be qualified (subject to an assessment of dangerousness).[102] Such a qualified indication is unlikely to be of much use to the defendant as it provides no certainty as to the sentence he will receive if he does plead guilty. In *Seddon* the judge did give an indication but stated that he was unable to say whether a sentence for public protection would be required without a pre-sentence report. The Court of Appeal stated that an indication, which in this instance was qualified, could not bind the court in circumstances where a sentence for public protection was required.[103] In *McDonald*, where the sentencer had given an unqualified *Goodyear* indication, a later decision to impose a higher sentence imposed for public protection was quashed.[104] A reminder was given that judges retain an absolute discretion not to give an indication of sentence for plea.

One point which is clear is that a *Goodyear* indication will only bind the court if the defendant pleads guilty more or less there and then.[105] If the defendant decides to contest a case then it is no use trying to argue that the courts should not impose a sentence longer than that implied by a *Goodyear* indication, for *Goodyear* itself makes clear that it is quite proper for the judge to change his or her mind once all the evidence has been heard and the matter given more careful consideration. This is so even if the *Goodyear* indication went further than it should have (see point 3 of the *Goodyear* rules) by stipulating the likely sentence following a contested trial.[106] The fact that such cases do reach the appellate courts shows however that defendants may be being subject to 'improper pressure' by judicial indications of maximum sentences for alternative pleas.

The House of Lords seems to have a very high tolerance threshold for what constitutes acceptable levels of pressure to plead guilty. This is demonstrated by the case of *McKinnon v US* in which the defendant was fighting against extradition to the US where he faced charges relating to alleged damage caused by his hacking into US government computers.[107] He was offered a plea bargain by a US prosecutor to the effect that if he did not contest extradition and pleaded guilty he would face a 3–4 year prison

[101] See, for example, *Attorney General's Reference No 44 of 2000 (Peverett)* [2001] 1 Cr App R 416.
[102] *Kulah* [2007] EWCA Crim 1701.   [103] *Seddon* [2007] EWCA Crim 3022.
[104] As strongly emphasised in *McDonald* [2007] EWCA Crim 1117.
[105] *Patel and Ors* [2009] EWCA Crim 67.
[106] *Clark and Ors* [2008] EWCA Crim 3221; *Patel and Ors* [2009] EWCA Crim 67.
[107] [2008] UKHL 59.

sentence, most of which would be served in the UK. However if he decided to contest he was told he would face a sentence of 8–10 years without repatriation. McKinnon argued that the disparity in the outcomes subjected him to too much pressure to plead guilty and was inconsistent with *Goodyear* principles. Strictly *Goodyear* does not apply to the US plea bargaining system. However, the House of Lords was of the opinion that the differences between the US and England and Wales in respect of plea bargaining were not 'so stark' as some would contend, noting the trend towards greater formalisation of the process in England and Wales. On the issue of pressure the court said: 'In one sense all discounts for pleas of guilty could be said to subject the defendant to pressure, and the greater the discount, the greater the pressure. But the discount would have to be very substantially more than anything promised here...before it constituted unlawful pressure such as to vitiate the process'.[108] It continued that only in extreme cases, for example where the prosecutor effectively threatened homosexual rape during incarceration, would the 'encouragement' to plead guilty be unconscionable. Little, or nothing, short of threat of unlawful action would be enough. That the House of Lords is willing to countenance the level of pressure exhibited in the *McKinnon* case shows that judicial restraint of the process is weak. If the defendant does not get a strong lawyer then it seems unlikely that the *Goodyear* rules will be sufficient to safeguard him against considerable pressure to plead guilty.

8.3 **Sentencing powers and jurisdictional pressures**

There are various ways in which a plea of guilty can affect the *jurisdiction* of the criminal courts to try and sentence an offence. We will focus here on two particularly important examples which concern the threshold between non-court disposals and the magistrates' court, and the magistrates' court and the Crown Court.[109]

8.3.1 **Pleading guilty in order to escape the criminal courts**

Section 1(1) of the Youth Justice and Criminal Evidence Act 1999 (YJCEA) introduced a new procedure for youths under which a plea of guilty in court will result in the case being diverted back out of the court for 'sentencing' purposes. These 'referral orders' are available to offenders under 18 who are prosecuted for the first time, who plead

---

[108] Paragraph 38.

[109] Space constraints preclude discussion of how the prosecution can, by charging an offence which carries either a longer than commensurate sentence or a presumptive minimum sentence (see 8.2.1 above), exert enormous pressure on defendants to plead guilty to a lesser offence so as to preclude such consequences. For an example, see *Stephens* [2000] 2 Cr App Rep (S) 320, CA.

guilty, and for whom the magistrates consider that neither a custodial sentence nor an absolute discharge is warranted. The Youth Court is obliged, following conviction, to refer these 'offenders' to a 'youth offender panel' made up of trained volunteers and a youth justice professional. These panels will seek to involve offenders, their 'supporters', their victims and youth justice workers in agreeing an enforceable 'contract' designed to achieve reparation and the rehabilitation of the offender. If a contract is complied with the Youth Court conviction will be regarded as 'spent' under the provisions of the Rehabilitation of Offenders Act 1974, thus removing many of the disadvantages of a criminal record.

The introduction of these discursive panels as an adjunct to the 'current sterile structures and procedures of the youth court'[110] was welcomed in principle by commentators, although concerns were raised about many of the details.[111] But little attention was paid to the injustice likely to result from this new diversionary mechanism. The choice facing young people prosecuted for the first time is now between (a) entering a guilty plea, thereby virtually guaranteeing a referral order and (following contract compliance) avoidance of the full effects of a criminal conviction, and (b) entering a not guilty plea, thus running the risk of conviction and the consequent (non-discounted) sentence and full criminal record. Ball predicted that this dilemma would result in guilty young people pleading not guilty in order to avoid the greater intervention in their lives demanded by referral to the youth offender panel.[112] But this is to ignore the influence of lawyers who, as we have seen, are largely committed to trial avoidance, believe their clients to be guilty, and no doubt stress the advantages of the youth offender panels and downplay their disadvantages. Thus we predicted (at p 438 of the second edition of this book) an increase in the guilty plea rate for young people prosecuted for the first time, and an increase in miscarriages of justice.

Early research into Youth Offender Panels found that referral order managers were concerned that lawyers were advising clients to plead guilty to avoid more serious consequences. The researchers, however, 'found little evidence that the introduction of referral orders has had a significant impact on pleas'.[113] Since they do not explain how they investigated this issue it is difficult to know what weight to place on this statement. Subsequent research into the referral order scheme uncovered qualitative evidence that those charged with minor offences were now more likely to plead *not guilty* in order to avoid the mandatory outcome of a referral order (in line with Ball's prediction) while those charged with more serious offences were now more likely to plead *guilty* in order to ensure they received a referral order (in line with our

---

[110] Ball C, 'A Significant Move towards Restorative Justice, or a Recipe for Unintended Consequences?' [2000] Crim LR 211 at 215.

[111] See, for example, Ball (2000) and Wonnacott C, 'The Counterfeit Contract – Reform, Pretence and Muddled Principles in the New Referral Order' (1999) 11 Child and Fam LQ 209.

[112] Ball (2000: 216).

[113] Crawford A and Newburn T, *Youth Offending and Restorative Justice* (Cullompton: Willan, 2003) p 104.

prediction).[114] These offsetting trends means that it is difficult to identify the impact of the referral order process on pleas simply by examining quantitative statistics. What is undeniable is that the introduction of referral orders resulted in an increase in tactical pleading. The government responded quickly to the problem of tactical not guilty pleading by giving magistrates discretion to refrain from making a referral order in the case of non-imprisonable offences. By contrast, the problem of innocent young people pleading guilty to imprisonable offences in order to guarantee a referral order was left unaddressed. Recent changes to referral orders allow the courts to make a referral order in relation to a second offence where the defendant pleads guilty and has not previously been subject to an order.[115] The imperative to produce guilty pleas has won out again.

8.3.2 Accepting guilt in order to avoid the Crown Court

The two-tier nature of criminal courts in England and Wales puts pressure on defendants to plead guilty. The advantage to the defence of having the trial heard in the magistrates' court is that the sentencing powers of the magistrates are limited. Regardless of the statutory maxima prescribed for offences, the maximum penalty which magistrates can impose is twelve months' imprisonment.[116]

But even leaving aside the fact that magistrates' sentencing powers are limited, research shows that a de facto sentence discount can be achieved by having a case disposed of at the lower level. This is because magistrates on average sentence more leniently than do Crown Court judges, although the extent of the difference is disputed.[117] Some practitioners are sceptical of these research results,[118] but as most practitioners have experience of only a few courts this may simply reflect the variation in sentencing practice across courts noted in 8.2 above.

One way of boosting the number of summary trials was created by the 'plea before venue' procedure. For 'either way' offences, magistrates must now enquire what the defendant's plea is likely to be before deciding on whether the venue for trial should be the magistrates' court or the Crown Court. If defendants indicate an intention to plead guilty then the magistrates must proceed immediately to summary trial and record a conviction. If defendants indicate a likely not guilty plea then the magistrates

---

[114] Cap Gemini Ernst & Young, Referral Orders: Research into the Issues Raised in 'The Introduction of the Referral Order in the Youth Justice System' (March 2003) pp 36–8 (available from <http://www.yjb.gov.uk/Publications> – accessed 5 January 2010).

[115] Sections 35–37 of the Criminal Justice and Immigration Act 2008. For the current (May 2009) guidance on referral orders see <http://www.justice.gov.uk/guidance/docs/referral-order-guidance.pdf> (accessed 5 January 2010).

[116] Sentencing guidelines for magistrates can be found at <http://www.jsboard.co.uk> (last accessed 5 January 2010).

[117] Hedderman and Moxon (1992: 37); Bridges (1999); Flood-Page and Mackie (1998).

[118] Herbert A, 'Mode of Trial and Magistrates' Sentencing Powers' [2003] Crim LR 314 at 323.

move on to the mode of trial hearing and hear representations from the defence and the prosecution. If they decide that summary trial is unsuitable they must send the case to the Crown Court. If they think that summary trial is the better option it is left to the defendant to decide whether to be tried in the lower courts or the Crown Court. A substantial disincentive to a defendant who might otherwise have been willing to plead guilty in order to avoid a Crown Court sentence is the power of the magistrates to commit defendants to the Crown Court for sentencing following conviction for an either-way offence if they feel that their own sentencing powers are inadequate.[119] The risk of defendants opting for low-level trial but getting a high-level sentence was made clear following the introduction of the plea before venue system. This innovation resulted in about 15,000 fewer committals to the Crown Court for trial but about 15,000 more committals for sentence.[120] The CJA 2003 made provision for magistrates' powers of sentencing to be increased, and for their power to send defendants to the Crown Court for sentence to be radically reduced. The likely impact of these reforms was debated but now seems academic since the government has decided not to implement the provisions.[121]

Another time-honoured way of keeping a case in the magistrates' courts is for the defence to achieve a relabelling of the charge as something less serious. Summary sentencing is guaranteed if the prosecution can be persuaded to drop an either-way charge in return for a plea of guilty to a summary charge. Where the defendant is facing a charge triable only on indictment then a charge bargain which involves pleading guilty to a lesser either-way offence makes summary sentencing possible. The lower the either-way charge achieved through the bargaining process, the more likely it is that that magistrates will regard the matter as within their sentencing powers, thus negating the risk of committal to the Crown Court for sentence. The two-tier nature of the criminal courts thus fuels the practice of charge bargaining, which we discuss in the next section.

8.4 **Charge bargaining**

Charge bargaining typically involves the defendant agreeing to plead guilty in exchange for the prosecution proceeding on a less serious charge. For example, theft may be substituted for the original charge of burglary, or rape replaced by sexual assault. Alternatively, where the defendant is facing multiple charges, an agreement to plead guilty to at least one may result in the dropping of others. Unlike the sentence discount principle, where it is the law itself which exerts pressure to plead guilty, charge bargaining relies on advocates on each side of the adversarial divide reaching

---

119 The main relevant legislative provision is the Magistrates' Courts Act 1980, s 38.
120 Department for Constitutional Affairs (2005a: table 6.1).
121 Cammiss S and Stride C, 'Modelling Mode of Trial' (2008) 48(4) BJ Crim 482.

an agreement. In the magistrates' court charge bargaining takes place mainly between crown prosecutors and solicitors, whereas in the Crown Court prosecution and defence barristers take centre stage. Until recently charge bargaining has normally taken place post charge as prosecutors traditionally had very little involvement in the pre-charge process and, until the CJA 2003, charge selection. Even following the 2003 reforms which transferred charging decisions from the police to the CPS most charge bargaining occurs at a later stage in the process. However, in certain cases of serious and complex fraud a new phenomenon of pre-charge bargaining has emerged. This stems from a review of fraud in 2006 which recommended a system of more open discussions of plea bargains.[122] The alleged rationale for this was that fraud cases are particularly difficult to detect and complex and expensive to investigate and prosecute. The proposals were also presented as benefiting victims and jurors who would be spared the burden of trial.[123] A familiar cloak of victims' rights was thus cast around a crime control initiative to encourage more defendants to plead guilty at the earliest possible opportunity, in this instance before the case against them really gathers any momentum. The essence of the scheme, as embodied in the Attorney-General's Guidelines,[124] is that before charge the prosecution and suspected offender may discuss and reach an agreement as to the basis for plea. The court is not involved in these discussions. There are some safeguards built into the process for the suspect. Notably, the Criminal Justice and Immigration Act (CJIA) 2008 made provision for legal aid to be available before charge where this scheme is used.[125] The advantages of pre-charge negotiations for the defendant are said to be reduced stress as a result of early resolution. Whether this is enough to counteract the disadvantages is debatable. First, while the Guidelines note the circumstances in which admissions or information provided by suspects in the context of discussions should not be used as evidence against them should the case proceed more formally, they do not envisage an absolute bar on such material being used. Second, to a large extent it appears the defendant will be negotiating in the dark; encouraged to provide information but with limited access to the prosecution case because statutory disclosure provisions are not triggered prior to charge. Third, although the prosecutor has the ability to recommend a sentence under the new scheme the judge retains absolute discretion as to whether to accept it. Fourth, as with all forms of plea bargaining, there can be no guarantee that innocent suspects will not be subjected, and succumb, to pressure to plead guilty.

---

[122] <http://www.attorneygeneral.gov.uk/Fraud Review/Fraud Review Final Report July 2006.pdf> (last accessed 5 January 2010).

[123] See *The Introduction of a Plea Negotiation Framework for Fraud Cases in England and Wales: A Consultation* (London: Attorney General's Office, 2008); available at <http://www.attorneygeneral.gov.uk/> (last accessed 5 January 2010).

[124] *Attorney General's Guidelines on Plea Discussions in Cases of Serious or Complex Fraud* (available at <http://www.attorneygeneral.gov.uk/> – last accessed 5 January 2010).

[125] Whether defence lawyers, who may considering their own interests, will be willing to see cases fold this early is questionable. See Julian R, 'Judicial Perspectives in Serious Fraud Cases' [2008] Crim LR 764 at 778.

Pre-charge bargaining in fraud cases could be a step towards an ever expanding process for early settlement of all types of cases. Interestingly the Government is keen to deny that this form of settlement amounts to plea bargaining at all, using the term plea 'negotiation' to try to rid it of the negative connotations it perceives as attaching to the other term, particularly in its associations with the United States system: 'This is absolutely not plea bargaining, it is plea negotiation' the Attorney General has said.[126] Plea bargaining by any other name smells just as sour to us.

8.4.1 Charge bargaining in the magistrates' courts

The role of the prosecutor

The law places little constraint on the ability of prosecutors to charge bargain. Under the Prosecution of Offences Act 1985 crown prosecutors have the power to make additions, deletions or alterations to the charges, and can terminate proceedings altogether. Even on the day of the trial itself the prosecutor can secure the dismissal of the case by offering no evidence. In the past there were strong incentives for the police to 'over-charge' suspects[127] and this provided the CPS with the means and a motive to bargain with the defence. Research from the 1980s by Baldwin[128] showed that prosecutors engaged extensively in charge bargaining. The 1992 version of the Code for Crown Prosecutors which stressed 'the resource advantages both to the Service and the courts generally' of charge bargaining, made it clear that such deals were not merely tolerated but encouraged. Subsequent versions of the Code were more coy but charge bargaining remained rife in the magistrates' courts through the 1990s and beyond.[129] Overcharging by the police (and CPS failure to deal with this by reducing charges on initial review) both reflected and reinforced the normality of charge bargaining.

Charge bargains not only enable the prosecution to secure convictions in weak cases that would not have succeeded in court but may also lead to an increase in the number of such weak cases being prosecuted. Where a high guilty plea rate is achieved through such inducements there is little need for the prosecuting authorities to ensure that only properly prepared cases are brought to trial. It is interesting to note that when one United States jurisdiction 'banned' various forms of plea bargaining one effect was that prosecutors refused to proceed with weak cases and this, in turn, forced the police to investigate crimes more carefully and thoroughly from the outset.[130] Crown Prosecutors have always been directed by their Code to discontinue cases in which the evidence is weak, and this provides a theoretical safeguard against improper charge

---

[126] 'Plea Bargaining Fraudsters May Find that Truth Pays', *The Times*, 4 April 2008.

[127] See Genders E, 'Reform of the Offences Against the Person Act: Lessons from the Law in Action' [1999] Crim LR 689 at pp 692–3.   [128] Baldwin J, *Pre-Trial Justice* (Oxford: Basil Blackwell, 1985).

[129] For evidence that this remained so, see HMCPSI, *Thematic Review of Attrition in the Prosecution Process (The Justice Gap)* (London: HMCPSI, 2003) ch 5 available at <http://hmcpsi.gov.uk/> (accessed 5 January 2010).

[130] Carns T and Kruse J, 'A Re-evaluation of Alaska's Plea Bargaining Ban' (1981) 8 Alaska LR 27.

bargains. However, the due process model warns us that the prosecutor cannot be trusted to screen out weak cases any more than the police can.[131] The research by McConville et al of prosecution practices in the late 1980s provided empirical grounds for such distrust.[132] They found that crown prosecutors, for a variety of reasons, rarely took the initiative in dropping cases. As they explain:

Dropping cases on grounds of weakness will antagonize the police and may lose a successful conviction, since, as all participants in the system understand, the great majority of cases, weak or strong, are disposed of by guilty pleas. If, on the other hand, there is a weakness in the case which the defence intends to exploit, a decision to drop it, or amend the charges or drop charges in return for a bind over, may always be made once the defence have signalled their intent to contest the case...

They concluded that 'what the CPS seek is not a plea to what they can *prove*, but to what they can bluff or "arm-twist" defendants into'.[133]

McConville et al's research was conducted shortly after the CPS was created. Are their findings still valid in the light of subsequent changes? First, the CPS has taken over responsibility for determining the initial charge in non-minor cases.[134] This was meant, amongst other things, to deal with the problem of over-charging by the police. Second, the CPS has been increasingly subject to managerialist target-setting and performance monitoring, which include reducing 'unsuccessful' outcomes (discontinuances and acquittals) and increasing the guilty plea rate. This looks like a recipe for unethical over-charging and charge bargaining.[135] The call of the CPS Inspectorate for a changed ethos in which the CPS selects the right charges from the outset and then sticks to them,[136] looks pious and unrealistic. The latest edition of the Code for Crown Prosecutors states that prosecutors should not initiate or proceed with multiple charges, or more serious charges, simply in order to encourage the defendant to enter into a charge bargain (para 7).[137] Rather, prosecutors should select charges which reflect the seriousness and extent of the offending. But the Code acknowledges that defendants may be willing to plead guilty to fewer, or less serious, charges than those brought. In this situation it stipulates that:

Crown Prosecutors should only accept the defendant's plea if they think the court is able to pass a sentence that matches the seriousness of the offending, particularly where there are aggravating features. Crown Prosecutors must never accept a guilty plea just because it is convenient.[138]

It follows from this that a reduction in the number or seriousness of charges is not necessarily to be regarded as improper even though if the right charges were made in the first place, lower charges would rarely 'match the seriousness of the offending'.

---

[131] Packer H, *The Limits of the Criminal Sanction* (Stanford: Stanford UP, 1969) p 207.
[132] McConville et al, *The Case for the Prosecution* (London: Routledge, 1991).
[133] McConville et al (1991: 146, 158, 159, 166).
[134] Criminal Justice Act 2003, s 28. See 7.3 for discussion.
[135] See generally Young R and Sanders A, 'The Ethics of Prosecution Lawyers' (2004) 7 Legal Ethics 190.
[136] HMCPSI (2003: paras 5.24, 9.19–9.24).   [137] The code is available at <http://www.cps.gov.uk/>.
[138] CPS (2004: para 10).

The fluidity of prosecution cases provides another way of understanding charge reduction. While a burglary charge may have seemed appropriate at the inception of a prosecution, disclosure of defence evidence at a pre-trial review (PTR), or a change in the evidence of a crucial witness, might make a theft charge seem more appropriate. But if the original charge overstated what the defendant is alleged to have done, then it would be wrong to extract a guilty plea as the price for reducing the charge. That the Code does not make this point is indicative of its underlying assumption that charge reduction in court will take place as a result of bargaining rather than out of considerations of fairness to the defendant.

As we will see in 8.8.2 (below) the CPS has come under increasing pressure not to downgrade charges for reasons of expediency, particularly where this would be offensive to victims. However, it is questionable whether these pressures have any real effect when victims have so little direct input into the decision-making process.

Mode of trial and the regulation of pre-trial negotiation

A charge bargain involves the prosecution transforming the nature of the allegation so that a different legal label can be affixed to the case. Burglary becomes theft, rape becomes sexual assault, and so on: when cases are disposed of in this way it is the lawyers rather than the courts who effectively construct truth and determine guilt.

At one time the appellate courts discouraged the magistrates' courts from accepting jurisdiction for serious cases made to look like trivial either way cases through this kind of relabelling.[139] But the modern trend has been to entreat magistrates to accept jurisdiction in a broader band of cases than hitherto. While mode of trial guidelines issued by the Court of Appeal state that magistrates' courts should never make decisions on the grounds of convenience or expedition, they contain a presumption in favour of summary trial: 'In general, except where otherwise stated, either way offences should be tried summarily unless the court considers that the particular case has one or more ... [aggravating features] ... *and* that its sentencing powers are insufficient.'[140] The Code for Crown Prosecutors goes further still. It advises that representations to the court at mode of trial hearings should focus on those matters to which the court is obliged to have regard but then adds:

Speed must never be the only reason for asking for a case to stay in the magistrates' courts. But Crown Prosecutors should consider the effect of any likely delay if they send a case to the Crown Court, and any possible stress on victims and witnesses if the case is delayed.

This gives official endorsement to prosecutors taking into account speed when making representations to magistrates on mode of trial so long as they can combine that

---

[139] See *Bodmin Justices, ex p McEwen* [1947] KB 321 at 324; *Coe* [1968] 1 WLR 1950 at 1953; and *King's Lynn Justices, ex p Carter* [1969] 1 QB 488.

[140] *Practice Note (Mode of Trial: Guidelines)* [1990] 1 WLR 1439. The guidelines are now to be found in the Consolidated Criminal Practice Direction at para V.51 (available from <http://www.justice.gov.uk/>; accessed 5 January 2010).

with some other reason (such as avoiding stress to witnesses). So while magistrates are supposed to ignore expedition, prosecutors are expected to take it into account. Since magistrates nearly always follow the recommendations of the CPS,[141] in reality expeditiousness is a major factor in mode of trial decisions. There thus appears to be a drift towards crime control values in this part of the criminal process.

The Divisional Court in *CPS v Edgar* recognised that charge bargains were commonplace and that the integrity of criminal proceedings required that they should be adhered to. It accordingly refused to interfere with a magistrates' court decision that the reinstatement of a charge by the CPS which had been dropped as part of a charge bargain was an abuse of process.[142] But while there are elements within legal culture that remain decisively in favour of charge bargaining and other methods of cost-cutting achieved by 'defining deviance down'[143] the rise of concern for victims and witnesses has caused a rethink in some quarters. One of the attendant features of managerialism is frequent scrutiny by the various Inspectorates that now oversee the CPS, the courts and other criminal justice agencies. As noted in the preceding sub-section, the CPS Inspectorate is keen to see an end to over-charging and charge bargaining. The regulation of behaviour in the magistrates' courts is no longer just a matter of sporadic oversight by the appellate courts. How prosecutors manage the competing expectations to which they are now increasingly subject remains to be seen.

Defence lawyers and pre-trial reviews

It might be thought that, given professional codes and ethical standards, defence lawyers could be relied upon to ensure that innocent persons do not accept the offer from the prosecution of a charge bargain.[144] On the other hand, we have already seen in 8.2.4 that many defence lawyers presume their clients to be guilty and unworthy of a contested trial and accordingly put pressure on them to plead guilty, and that financial self-interest often trumps selfless promotion of the client's interests. To what extent has research uncovered evidence of unethical charge bargaining on the part of defence lawyers?

An immediate difficulty is that much pre-trial manoeuvring and negotiation is not subject to public scrutiny. Lawyers freely admit, however, that wheeling and dealing is an integral part of their trade, and last-minute negotiations can be observed taking place on a daily basis in court buildings. In the early 1980s a dozen or so magistrates' courts experimented with a more systematic approach to these negotiations. Pre-trial reviews were introduced for cases likely to be contested. Meetings between the opposing lawyers would be arranged by court clerks who would also be in attendance to make a note of any deals done. Baldwin tape-recorded the bargaining that took place

---

[141] Herbert (2003: 72–4); Cammiss S, '"I Will in a Moment Give You the Full History": Mode of Trial, Prosecutorial Control and Partial Accounts' [2006] Crim LR 38.

[142] *Crown Prosecution Service v Deborah Anne Edgar* (2000) 164 JP 471.

[143] See Garland D, 'The Limits of the Sovereign State: Strategies of Crime Control in Contemporary Society' (1996) 36 BJ Crim 445.

[144] For a discussion of the relevant ethical standards, see Blake and Ashworth (2004).

and found that defence solicitors were willing to trade information and favours with prosecutors. Prosecutors accordingly tended to see defence solicitors as their allies rather than as their opponents.[145]

The rhetorical position of the defence lawyer as the champion of the defendant makes it easy for lawyers to persuade their clients to adopt a particular course, even if this means them pleading guilty. All lawyers need do is convince defendants that they are very likely or certain to be convicted if they plead not guilty, and that there is a material advantage to be gained by pleading guilty. The legal system ensures that such advantages are there for the taking whilst prosecution disclosure provides the defence lawyer with ample material on which to base advice to defendants that their best interests lie in pleading guilty as illustrated by this example taken from Baldwin:

| Defence solicitor: | I want some ammunition...What we want is really, if you could supply it, some information about whether to lean on [the defendant]. Have you got lots of nice verbals?[146] |
| Prosecuting solicitor: | Right – I don't know about particularly nice verbals. |

[He then reads out the statements of two police officer witnesses and gives the defence solicitor a copy of the defendant's statement to the police.]

Prosecuting solicitor:	I think that should give you some of the necessary information to go back to him...Do you think you've now got sufficient to get a plea?
Defence solicitor:	Yes.
Prosecuting solicitor:	Great! Another all-day not guilty [case] bites the dust.[147]

Here the defence solicitor is not seeking disclosure of the prosecution case in order to consider how best to advise the client. Rather the client is prejudged to be guilty. The prosecution evidence is sought merely in order to help extract a guilty plea. Such encounters suggest that 'case settlement on an amicable basis is strongly favoured'[148] over adversarial battle.

The dynamics of pre-trial negotiations should have been altered by the introduction of rules in 1985 directing the prosecution to provide advance disclosure in at least summary form for cases triable either way that were to be heard in the magistrates' courts.[149] In practice, however, the extent of disclosure made by the CPS is often perceived to be inadequate by the defence, leading some solicitors to advise their clients to plead not guilty in order to obtain 'adequate information on which to base advice or conduct meaningful negotiations'.[150] Even more important, however, is the continuing preference for case settlement over a contested trial. The role of the PTR as

---

[145] Eg Baldwin (1985: 81–2).   [146] 'Verbals' is shorthand for oral confessions.

[147] Baldwin (1985: 88).

[148] Baldwin J and Feeney F, 'Defence Disclosure in the Magistrates' Courts' (1986) 49 MLR 593 at pp 604–5.

[149] Magistrates' Courts (Advance Information) Rules 1985, SI 1985/601. In summary only cases the prosecution was under no obligation to disclose its case until the issue of guidelines by the Attorney General in November 2000.   [150] Herbert (2003: 321).

a site of information-exchange and charge bargaining was thus little affected by the new disclosure regime.[151] New forms of pre-trial hearing aimed at encouraging early guilty pleas are now in place in magistrates' courts, in the shape of early first hearings and early administrative hearings.[152] But we have no reason to doubt the continued relevance of Baldwin's findings.

According to Baldwin[153] issues of real importance were resolved at nearly half of the reviews he recorded, and Mulcahy et al (1993) argue that their data show that pre-trial reviews are cost-effective. The important question for us, however, is whether a practice which appears to so undermine the adversarial system of justice is defensible in principle. Baldwin argues that bargaining is endemic in the magistrates' courts and will take place whether or not pre-trial reviews are held.[154] This leads him to the conclusion that 'the pre-trial review at least provides a forum which is open to outside scrutiny', and that the more ordered and seemly discussions they promote are to be preferred to the 'furtive business of plea negotiation in court corridors'. If plea-trial reviews are to be accepted as the lesser of two unavoidable evils, what does outside scrutiny reveal? Baldwin found that 'the participants aimed to ensure that deals and compromises about charges tallied with the gravity of the offence as revealed in the evidence...the present writer did not observe a single case in which a bargain could fairly be described as improper'.[155]

There are two main flaws in this argument. The first is that the material on which the parties base their negotiations is at best partial and at worst thoroughly misleading. For example, the opposing lawyers usually rely on summaries of tape-recordings prepared by the police.[156] As one would expect in an adversarial system, these summaries tend to exaggerate the strength of the prosecution case.[157] There may also have been failures by the police, by forensic experts and by crown prosecutors to comply with the statutory obligation of disclosure in respect of 'unused material' helpful to the defence.[158] Furthermore, as we saw in chs 5 and 6, police interviewing techniques can result in statements of evidence from suspects and witnesses omitting ambiguities and exculpatory matter. When the police themselves are the only witnesses, as in many public order situations, '...the relevant behaviour of the accused is described in the exact terms of the offence. Generally evidence of this sort is inscrutable short of cross-examination in court.'[159] There will be no cross-examination, however, if a defendant is persuaded to plead guilty on the strength of the prosecution case as it exists on paper. That case, far from allowing defendants to make a realistic assessment of their prospects of acquittal,

---

[151] See Mulcahy et al, 'An Evaluation of Pre-Trial Reviews in Leeds and Bradford Magistrates' Courts' (1993) 33 Home Office Research Bulletin 10.   [152] The reforms are discussed in 8.2.4 above.

[153] Baldwin (1985: 40).   [154] Baldwin (1985: 164–5).   [155] Baldwin (1985: 97).

[156] See 5.4.3. Defence solicitors cannot be sure that they will be reimbursed for the costs of listening to tape-recorded interviews. See, for example, Moorhead R, 'Legal Aid and the Decline of Private Practice: Blue Murder or Toxic Job?' (2004) 11(3) International Journal of the Legal Profession 160 at 182–4.

[157] Baldwin J, *Preparing the Record of Taped Interview* (Royal Commission on Criminal Justice Research Study No 2) (London: HMSO, 1992).

[158] See 7.3.3, and Redmayne M, 'Disclosure and its Discontents' [2004] Crim LR 441.

[159] McConville et al (1991: 134).

paints a systematically distorted portrait of 'the facts' which may mislead a defendant into believing that there is no option but to plead guilty. One obvious due process objection to pre-trial bargaining is thus that the lawyers are not negotiating on the basis of 'evidence' at all since the summaries and statements in the prosecution file are merely indications (or, at worst, one-sided versions) of what witnesses will say in court.

Second, Baldwin neither observed how bargains were presented to clients, nor how the clients reacted to them. McConville et al (1994) adopted a research method which allowed them to observe virtually all the key interactions between defence solicitor and client. They concluded that most bargains:

...are not struck under pressure from, or even at the suggestion of, the prosecution. It is usually the defence solicitor who decides to press the matter. Trials are overbooked and under-prepared in the expectation that clients will plead guilty on the day – an expectation that solicitors ensure is fulfilled. Clients rarely put up any resistance to suggestions to plead guilty, and accept the advice of their lawyer – the expert – even where there is no clear admission of guilt.[160]

Bargains sealed in such a manner do not strike us as proper. Moreover, pre-trial reviews do not just *legitimise* a pre-existing practice of furtive negotiation, but rather *enable* it to take place on a wider basis by *institutionalising* improper bargaining.[161]

We saw in 8.2.4 above that the Criminal Procedure Rules now require courts actively to manage cases and promote pre-trial settlement wherever possible. At every pre-trial review the court must enquire whether the prosecutor has reviewed the charges and remains satisfied that they are appropriate.[162] This will have the effect (as is no doubt intended) of continuing to encourage charge bargaining regardless of the rights of defendants.

In order to regulate pre-trial negotiation to better protect the defendant's interests we could:[163]

- require full disclosure of all prosecution cases, but we argued earlier that disclosure does not necessarily work to the advantage of the defendant;

- allow defendants to attend pre-trial reviews, but this is likely only to displace the main bargaining encounters into less visible settings;[164]

- rely on the Crown Prosecution Service to achieve higher standards of case screening, but it would make little sense in an adversarial system to rely upon prosecutorial propriety as a safeguard for defendants;

---

[160] McConville et al (1994: 198).

[161] For an illustration of the normative pressure to deal exerted by the pre-trial review see Baldwin (1985: 42–4).

[162] See <http://www.jsboard.co.uk/magistrates/adult_court/index.htm> (accessed 5 January 2010) (Adult Court Bench Book).

[163] See further Galligan D, 'Regulating Pre-Trial Decisions', in Dennis I (ed), *Criminal Law and Justice* (London: Sweet & Maxwell, 1987).

[164] As was observed to happen at the Leeds magistrates' court by Baldwin (1985: 111–12). This inhibiting effect is also noted by Mulcahy (1994: 416).

- require PTRs to be supervised by supposedly neutral officials such as magistrates or court clerks, but, as we show in ch 9, magistrates and court clerks tend to support the crime control values PTRs advance, and are not generally neutral.[165]

For pre-trial negotiation to give greater priority to due process values would seem to require, at the very least, the transformation of the ideology and culture of defence lawyers. This might be achieved, for example, by setting up 'criminal defence centres' to promote and support principled and truly adversarial criminal defence services.[166] A less ambitious strategy was pursued over the last decade or so by the Law Society and Legal Services Commission which sought to encourage an 'active defender' role for the defence solicitor.[167] Whether such a transformation in values is possible without wider cultural and structural changes in the legal system and in society itself seems doubtful. Such changes are simply not on the agenda. Indeed, the Government and the judiciary seem, if anything, to be bent on undercutting the scope for adversarial behaviour, co-opting defence lawyers still further into the pursuit of system efficiency.[168]

8.4.2 Charge bargaining in the Crown Court

In the Crown Court, just as in the magistrates' court, charge bargaining is rife, as numerous studies show. For example, 29% of the Hedderman and Moxon sample of defendants claimed to have pleaded guilty as a result of a charge bargain and the authors found plenty of evidence consistent with these claims.[169] More recently, Henham's study of six Crown Court centres found that 61.7% of defendants originally indicted for the offence of causing grievous bodily harm with intent subsequently pleaded guilty to a lesser offence.[170] Some offences seem more prone to downgrading than others; offences against the person for example.[171] And of those proportionately few alleged rapists who are convicted of something, around half are convicted of a lesser charge than rape following a charge bargain.[172]

Early studies of charge bargaining emphasised the crucial role of barristers in particular and painted a highly critical picture of rushed, last-minute negotiation which

---

[165] And see, for example, Mulcahy (1994: 411).

[166] See the proposals to this effect in McConville et al (1994: ch 11); and in Howard League, *The Dynamics of Justice* (Report of the Working Party on Criminal Justice Administration) (London: Howard League, 1993).

[167] Cape (2004); Edwards T, 'The Role of Defence Lawyers in a Re-Balanced System' in Cape E and Young R (eds), *Regulating Policing* (Oxford: Hart, 2008). [168] Cape (2004: 413–16).

[169] Hedderman and Moxon (1992: 10).

[170] Henham R, 'Further Evidence on the Significance of Plea in the Crown Court' (2002) 41 Howard JCJ 151 at 153.

[171] Genders (1999); Jeremy D, 'The Prosecutor's Rock and Hard Place' [2008] Crim LR 925.

[172] Harris J and Grace S, *A Question of Evidence? Investigating and Prosecuting Rape in the 1990s*, Research Study 196 (London: Home Office, 1999) at pp 31–2; Lea et al, 'Attrition in Rape Cases' (2003) 43 BJ Crim 583 at p 592: Kelly et al, *A Gap or a Chasm? Attrition in Reported Rape Cases*, HORS 293 (London: Home Office, 2005).

appeared to pay scant regard to defendants' rights or expressed wishes.[173] That the cracked-trial remains a barrister-centred phenomenon is well captured in Bredar's description:

This is a drama that usually unfolds in the corridors outside of court, in the barristers' robing rooms, and in the court cells. What generally happens is that prosecuting and defending counsel compare views on the strengths and weaknesses of their respective cases, and, in an indirect way, discuss what it would take from each side to get the case to 'crack.' Counsel come to a unified view about what would be an appropriate settlement of the matter, and generally that involves dismissal of one or more charges outstanding against the defendant, and guilty pleas to all the remaining charges, or to amended charges....Defending counsel discusses the option with his client and instructing solicitors, with an eye towards gaining acceptance.[174]

The role of the defence barrister

In most cases a solicitor representing a defendant hands over the conduct of the case in the Crown Court to a barrister who, on reading the brief prepared by the solicitor, may take a different view of the prospect of winning a case. The solicitor may have been over-optimistic about the prospects for the defence either due to lack of experience or a desire to keep his client happy with false expectations of success. Indeed, one of the advantages claimed for the split profession is that a barrister, with no direct relationship with the client, can be more objective about the prospects of winning a case in court. The introduction of a barrister into the case may thus lead to a change of plea being advised.[175]

It is unlikely that a defence solicitor will dissent from counsel's opinion. The barrister, after all, is the acknowledged expert in the Crown Court arena. Furthermore, as we have seen, most defence solicitors operating in the magistrates' courts seem more interested in settling than contesting cases. It is true that it is because of their advice that many defendants decide to elect trial by jury and plead not guilty. But this may not reflect any genuine commitment to adversarial due process values. Solicitors may have made tactical use of a not guilty plea to strengthen a defendant's bargaining position vis-à-vis the prosecution, to increase the chances of legal aid being granted and so on. In many instances, particularly where conferences are held on the day of the trial, the solicitor will not even be present when counsel advises a client to plead guilty, having sent one of the firm's clerks instead.[176] The high rate of guilty pleas and late plea chang-

---

[173] McCabe S and Purves R, *By-passing the Jury* (Oxford: Basil Blackwell, 1972a) pp 9–10; Bottoms A and McLean J, *Defendants in the Criminal Process* (London: Routledge and Kegan Paul, 1976) p 130; Baldwin and McConville (1977a).

[174] Bredar J, 'Moving Up the Day of Reckoning: Strategies for Attacking the "Cracked Trials" Problem' [1992] Crim LR 153 at p 155.   [175] See further, Morison and Leith (1992: 67–9).

[176] The Crown Court study conducted for the Runciman Commission noted the significant involvement of unqualified staff in Crown Court work, and that 18% of defence respondents had become involved in the case as late as the day before or on the day of the trial itself: Zander and Henderson (1993: 194–5). See generally McConville et al (1994) for a dissection of the discontinuous nature of legal representation provided for defendants and the extensive use of unqualified staff at all stages of case processing.

ing by defendants indicates that many[177] defence solicitors (and their representatives at court) are happy to allow barristers to fulfil their hired gun role of settling cases.[178]

Barristers are self-employed but group together in chambers, sharing office overheads. Barristers, like all criminal lawyers, tend to accept 'too much' work in the expectation that many cases will be settled out of court.[179] This, in itself, provides them with an incentive to try to settle cases through negotiation. But barristers may not wish to achieve a settlement until the day of trial. As noted in 8.2.4, under the legal aid scheme the graduated fees available for publicly funded Crown Court work are more generous for cracked trials than for early guilty plea cases.[180] Economic incentives such as this clearly influence the operation of labour markets and there is no evidence to suggest that lawyers are different in this regard.[181] According to Bredar, barristers deny avoiding early settlement but admit 'that their attention naturally is more focused on their cases which are at the trial (and thus more remunerative) stage, knowing that their cases which are at the earlier, plea review stage will ripen with time.'[182] The observational study by McConville et al (1994) suggests that the avoidance of early settlement is often, in fact, deliberate.[183] By the same token, given that a decent fee can be obtained by persuading a client to make a last-minute decision to plead guilty there is often little financial incentive to fight a case. As one barrister interviewed by Morison and Leith put it, 'some barristers...take the view that if they get paid the same for doing a plea as for doing a trial they will accept...the plea and go home by 11.00 o'clock in the morning.'[184] Contrary to this view, Tague (2008) argues that barristers do have a financial incentive to go to trial, asserting the monetary incentive may not be great but it nevertheless exists.[185] It seems unlikely to us that the difference would be sufficiently compelling, particularly in light of his conclusion that few of the barristers in his small scale study had actually calculated that it would be (marginally) financially advantageous for them to pursue a trial.[186]

If barristers find that they cannot conduct a case at all due to pressure of work then briefs have to be returned to solicitors and another barrister found to handle the case.

---

[177] But not all – Tague (2008) argues that some barristers may be fearful of settling cases due to sanctions that might be applied by upset solicitors who have to deal with disgruntled clients, and that the barrister's reputation with solicitors for adversarial adroitness is more important than a reputation for adept plea negotiation.   [178] Morison and Leith (1992: 67–9).

[179] Morison and Leith (1992: 64). See also 8.4.1 above for similar findings by McConville et al (1994) regarding solicitors.

[180] In theory, as we have seen, the Plea and Case Management Hearing is meant to encourage early settlement but, as the fee for such a hearing is only £100 barristers are likely to resist the pressure to resolve the case at that stage: Tague P, 'Tactical Reasons for Recommending Trials Rather than Guilty Pleas in Crown Court' [2006] Crim LR 23, n 2.

[181] See the discussion in Gray et al, 'Controlling Lawyers' Costs through Standard Fees: An Economic Analysis' in Young R and Wall D (eds), *Access to Criminal Justice* (London: Blackstone, 1996).

[182] Bredar (1992: 157). See to like effect, Plotnikoff and Woolfson (1993a: 62–5).

[183] McConville et al (1994: 253–4) and see 8.2.4 above.   [184] Morison and Leith (1992: 132).

[185] Tague (2008) provides an overview of the fee scheme.

[186] A point Tague (2008) himself concedes by noting that the non-financial incentives to trial – reputation and maintaining a relationship with the solicitor – are more effective.

This happens in nearly half of all contested cases.[187] As barristers are self-employed, a returned brief represents lost income. Barristers who are double-booked commonly wait until the last possible moment before returning a brief. As one barrister has put it: 'You say to yourself, "Well, if something happens to the other case I'll be able to do this one, whereas if I pass it now and something happens to the other case next week I'll be unemployed".'[188] Add the fact that the Crown Court issues a definitive list of the day's business it intends to transact as late as 4pm the previous day,[189] and it is not surprising that in contested cases a third of defence barristers say that they receive the brief on the day before the hearing or on the day itself.[190] In consequence, barristers commonly arrive at court ill-prepared and ill-disposed to fight on a defendant's behalf, and their conferences with defendants are often hurried last-minute affairs.[191] Defendants do not see their barrister until the day of the trial in over half of all contested and 'cracked' cases.[192]

Most Crown Court work is funded by the state at a relatively low level. As in the magistrates' courts, practitioners say that the only way to make criminal work pay is to turn over a high volume of cases in a relatively standardised fashion.[193] This is not to imply that all barristers in all cases are unethical seekers after settlement. Some have a genuine commitment to defence work, others will fight if briefed by solicitors who expect them to fight, and others are no doubt keen to contest 'good' cases in order to develop their reputations as effective advocates worthy of elevation to the ranks of Queen's Counsel or the judiciary.[194] Nonetheless, it is predictable that the most able (as well as the best connected) young barristers will tend to gravitate towards privately funded commercial work, leaving the inexperienced and the less able to eke out a living by settling cases wherever possible so as to be able to move on to the next brief.

Perhaps of equal importance to these organisational factors, however, is the role allotted to defence counsel in the legal system. Barristers are not expected to use every resource at their disposal to secure an acquittal for persons accused of crime. The professional duties of defending counsel are set out in the Code of Conduct for the Bar of England and Wales (8th edn), para 302 of which states that:

A practising barrister has an overriding duty to the Court to act with independence in the interests of justice: he must assist the court in the administration of justice and must not deceive or knowingly or recklessly mislead the court.[195]

---

[187] Zander and Henderson (1993: 32).   [188] Morison and Leith (1992: 64).

[189] Rock P, *The Social World of an English Crown Court* (Oxford: Clarendon Press, 1993) pp 271–3.

[190] Zander and Henderson (1993: 30). The barrister's clerk also plays a role here in trying to keep cases in his/her own Chambers: Rock (1993: 272). The Code of Conduct for Barristers' Clerks frowns on such tactical behaviour (see <http://www.ibc.org.uk/> – last accessed 5 January 2010) but what effect this has on practice is unknown.

[191] Defence barristers commonly claim that despite the late receipt of instructions they have sufficient time to prepare the case: Zander and Henderson (1993). This raises the question of what defence barristers regard as 'adequate' preparation, and for what purpose.   [192] Zander and Henderson (1993: 62).

[193] Morison and Leith (1992: 43–4).   [194] Tague (2008).

[195] The Code is available from <http://www.barstandardsboard.org.uk/standardsandguidance/codeofconduct> (accessed 5 January 2010).

Thus, the barrister owes a duty first and foremost to the court. In understanding what assisting the court in the administration of justice now encompasses it is necessary to turn to the Criminal Procedure Rules 2005 which require barristers, no less than solicitors (see 8.2.4 above), to assist the court in avoiding delay and 'unnecessary hearings'.[196] While the overriding objective set by these Rules is that cases should be dealt with justly, the notion of justice at work here includes dealing with the case efficiently and expeditiously (Rule 1.1). In comparison with a contested case a charge bargain represents an efficient and expeditious disposal of a case, and although this might conflict with the barrister's job to promote a client's best interests, it has been judicially acknowledged that this does not always mean contesting a case.[197] For example in *Hall* the appellant claimed that he had been pressurised into pleading guilty by his counsel. In dismissing the appeal Lord Parker stated that:

What the Court is looking to see is whether a prisoner in these circumstances has a free choice; the election must be his, the responsibility his, to plead Guilty or Not Guilty. At the same time, it is the clear duty of any counsel representing a client to assist the client to make up his mind by putting forward the pros and cons, if need be in strong language, to impress upon the client what the likely results are of certain courses of conduct.[198]

In other words, barristers are obliged by law to make plain to defendants the considerable advantages to be gained through pleading guilty as part of a charge bargain. To ensure that this obligation is discharged, the standard form used as part of the pre-trial Plea and Case Management Hearing (discussed in 8.2.4 above) asks 'might the case against a defendant be resolved by a plea of guilty to some counts on the indictment or to a lesser offence? If so, how?'[199] These pre-trial hearings, attended by the judge as well as by prosecuting and defending barristers, are clearly intended to further charge bargaining.

There are wide yet consistent variations in guilty plea rates across the circuits into which the Crown Court is organised. Thus, London has had the lowest guilty plea rate in the country for several decades, while the Midland and Oxford, and North Eastern circuits have had the highest.[200] This suggests that some local bars may have developed a culture in which the priority given to settling rather than fighting cases is particularly marked.[201] Consistently with this, one solicitor working in a firm with an adversarial ethos explained what it meant to provide a quality service to clients in the following terms: 'If there's a trial, using barristers you know will fight – we gener-

---

[196] Rules 3.2–3.3.

[197] For a general discussion of how ethical duties may conflict see Blake and Ashworth (2004). For a deeper analysis, which argues that the function of ethical codes of practice is to legitimise the repressive role of criminal courts as increasingly expressed through the encouragement of plea bargaining, see McConville M, 'Plea Bargaining: Ethics and Politics' (1998) 25 JLS 562.   [198] (1968) 52 Cr App Rep 528 at 534–5.

[199] The Consolidated Criminal Practice Direction, Annex E.

[200] See Zander M, 'What the Annual Statistics Tell Us About Pleas and Acquittals' [1991] Crim LR 252; Ministry of Justice (2008a: table 6.21).

[201] It may also explain Tague's (2008) findings that London barristers are more disposed to trials than many studies with wider geographical spread suggest.

ally use London counsel.'[202] In short, the claim of barristers that they always put the interests of their clients before their own interests simply beggars belief.

The role of prosecuting counsel

The Crown Prosecution Service gained full rights of audience in the higher criminal courts through s 36 of the Access to Justice Act 1999. In 2004 the CPS adopted a policy of increasing the proportion of cases prosecuted by its own staff and since then has, year on year, succeeded in doing this.[203] Nevertheless, barristers in private practice still handle a significant proportion of CPS Crown Court work. They have always maintained that they have an advantage over CPS advocates in not being psychologically committed to either side of the process; they may be defending one day and prosecuting the next. This suggests that in the higher courts defendants may be better protected from 'unfair' charge bargaining than in the magistrates' courts because prosecuting counsel external to the CPS are not so concerned as in-house advocates with achieving 'a result'.

The claim to objectivity needs to be seen in the light of how prosecuting and defence work is allocated and conducted in practice. Many barristers become typecast as either defenders or prosecutors. The Crown Prosecution Service, for example, maintains a panel of barristers in 'designated chambers' to whom as a matter of course briefs will be sent.[204] These barristers may well become 'prosecution-minded' and in any event would be anxious not to jeopardise an important source of business by ignoring the wishes of their institutional client. Baldwin's interviews with barristers, for example, revealed a self-interested reluctance to suggest to the CPS that weak cases should be discontinued. In explaining this reluctance one said that he would be 'too terrified of the demi-gods at the CPS, particularly in these days of preferred chambers' while another revealed that 'there are some cases – the ones that are borderline – where, for my own position (as someone who is acceptable to the CPS), I would run it because I don't want to make enemies out of these people.'[205] This desire not to upset the CPS has perhaps become more important as the amount of advocacy work the CPS keeps in-house has increased reducing the flow of work to chambers.[206]   Baldwin concluded that 'it is only on the day of the trial itself, when minds are more keenly focused than hitherto on the real issues in the case, when a decision might finally be taken to abandon a prosecution.'[207] That conclusion was reached in the context of a study of discontinued cases. But if one took a sample of all 'weak' cases one would no doubt find that prosecuting counsel prefer a last-minute charge bargain to discontinuance, as this secures 'a result' for their

---

[202] Sommerlad (2001: 347). See also Tague (2006: 24–5).

[203] HMCPSI, *Report of the Thematic Review of the Quality of Prosecution Advocacy and Case Presentation* (London: HMCPSI, 2009).

[204] Temkin J, 'Prosecuting and Defending Rape: Perspectives from the Bar' (2000) 27 J Law and Society 219 at 228.

[205] Baldwin J, 'Understanding Judge Ordered and Directed Acquittals in the Crown Court' [1997] Crim LR 536 at 552–3.   [206] See HMCPSI (2009: 92).

[207] Baldwin (1997: 554).

paymasters. Even such bargains require the blessing of the boss. According to Bredar, once counsel have agreed the appropriate settlement of the case:

Prosecuting counsel then communicates this view to a CPS law clerk or lawyer, cautiously advising in favour of the proposal.... CPS law clerks, often in consultation with CPS lawyers over the telephone, seem to be the critical decision-makers: i.e. once they 'bless' the arrangement, the trial quickly 'cracks'.[208]

This scarcely accords with the official image of the fearless independent barrister projected by the Bar.

Prosecuting counsel have much the same financial and practical interest in driving charge bargains as do their defence counterparts.[209] Zander and Henderson (1993) found that briefs were passed on by prosecuting counsel in around three-fifths of contested cases and half of prosecuting barristers received their brief either on the day before the hearing or on the day itself.[210] The fee structure may encourage barristers to take on too many cases with a view to cracking them or passing them on to less experienced members of chambers when the fees are low.[211] However, a recent report noted that since the CPS has increased in-house advocacy levels they are more frequently able to instruct and retain their barrister of choice with fewer returned briefs. Whether external counsel are less inclined to plea bargain is not really addressed by the report, although it is suggested that some in-house advocates may be more prone to crack trials due to pressure from defence counsel or fear of the judge:

The perception of several stakeholders was that some crown advocates had little appetite for contested trials which could be compounded by a listing in front of a judge who was known to be intolerant of in-house advocates.[212]

In-house CPS advocates are not necessarily less competent overall than counsel.[213] However, it does appear that they are less able when it comes to contested cases. The CPS Inspectorate found that external counsel had the edge when presenting at trial, with CPS advocates performing slightly better than external counsel at Plea and Case Management Hearings (PCMHs). Lack of confidence at trial and inexperience, particularly in cross-examination of witnesses, may add to the pressure on CPS advocates to settle cases pre trial if possible.

All advocates, whether external or internal to the CPS, are expected to consider charge bargaining as part of the PCMH.[214] As with defence barristers it would be

---

[208] Bredar (1992: 155).

[209] See O'Brien D and Epp J, 'Salaried Defenders and the Access to Justice Act 1999' (2000) 63 MLR 394 at p 397, n 30.

[210] Zander and Henderson (1993: 30–2). See also Royal Commission on Criminal Justice; Submission of Evidence by the Crown Prosecution Service, vol 1 Evidence, at p 177, footnote 66.

[211] Morison and Leith (1992: 44).   [212] HMCPSI (2009: 29).

[213] In so far as the quality of advocacy was concerned the CPS Inspectorate found it was variable across both in-house and external advocates. The majority of all advocates were judged to be competent or better but a quarter of both external and in-house advocates were said to be 'lacklustre'. Of the 7.9% judged less than competent or poor most (25/29) were in-house advocates: HMCPSI (2009: 25).

[214] See the Criminal Procedure Rules at <http://www.justice.gov.uk/criminal/procrules_fin/rulesmenu.htm> (accessed 5 January 2010).

misleading to portray a prosecuting barrister engaging in charge bargaining as having deviated from a legal duty to fight cases. The Court of Appeal has confirmed that charge bargaining is a proper part of a prosecuting barrister's duty, not a deviation from it.[215]

Keeping the customer satisfied

We have seen that counsel, whether defending or prosecuting, are expected to bargain over charges. The organisation of the courts and the Bar means that such negotiations tend to take place at a late stage between parties predisposed to compromise. The close-knit social world of a local Bar means that the negotiating parties will, in all likelihood, have concluded many similar agreements in the past and that a relationship of trust will have built up between them. Agreement is further facilitated by the fact that both sides are bound by the same code of professional ethics and owe a duty to the court to pursue the efficient (as well as the proper) administration of justice.

The interest in maintaining good relations with other barristers (and with judges seeking to manage a heavy caseload) may become more important than the interests of an individual defendant who will probably never be encountered again. As Galanter succinctly expresses it: 'Loyalty is often deflected from the one-time client to the forum or opposite party with whom the lawyer has continuing relations.'[216] In this situation, it is both tempting and easy for barristers to convince clients that their best interests lie in pleading guilty when this is not in fact so. The defence barrister's habit of lowering a defendant's expectations while creating a good impression of the legal service being offered is noted by Morison and Leith.[217] As one barrister told them:

You always give the client the worst prognosis...there is not a barrister at the criminal bar who has not learned that lesson by under estimating what the client would get and then getting the shock of his life...[218]

It is in this context that one must place the finding of the Crown Court survey that the great majority of defendants expressed satisfaction with the service provided by their legal representatives (Zander and Henderson 1993: 67). Most defence barristers are skilled advocates and it is no real surprise to find that defendants are persuaded into believing that their interests have been well served. The stark conclusion reached by Moody and Tombs[219] suggests that the defendants' perceptions are often mistaken:

there are constant factors which must be present if prosecution and defence are to agree. These centre round the notion of trust resulting in a co-alignment of interests and cooperation between traditional adversaries, while the accused, in the vast majority of cases where pleas are negotiated, stands to gain very little in material terms.

---

215 *Herbert* (1991) 94 Cr App Rep 230.
216 Galanter M, 'Mega-Law and Mega-Lawyering in the Contemporary United States' in Dingwall R and Lewis P (eds), *The Sociology of the Professions* (London: Macmillan, 1983) p 159.
217 Morison and Leith (1992: 70).   218 Morison and Leith (1992: 136–7).
219 Moody S and Tombs J, 'Plea Negotiations in Scotland' [1983] Crim LR 297 at p 307.

A decade later McConville et al observed case conferences between defence counsel and client held at court on the date fixed for settling plea.[220] They report that the 'common denominator of court conferences is the determination of counsel to secure a guilty plea to some or all of the charges... To secure this result, barristers deploy a range of techniques some of which are designed to stress the advantages of a prosecution offer and the bleakness of any alternative, and others of which are designed to encourage the client to hand the decision over to the barrister as an expert.' Thus client satisfaction was sought by describing offers of a charge bargain as 'excellent', 'the best that can be achieved' and 'better than we could have hoped for', and as something to be accepted rapidly whilst it was still on the table.[221] Most defence counsel pressed this kind of advice without having first tested whether the evidence would justify either the original charge or that now on offer. Trials may also not be anywhere as risky for defendants as their barristers may suggest given the high rate of acquittal in the Crown Court.[222] The potential for injustice is obvious.

Judicial supervision of charge bargaining in the Crown Court

If anyone could be expected to monitor the propriety of charge bargains it would surely be the judge. According to McCabe and Purves, every one of the charge bargains they identified had been expressly endorsed by the judge.[223] Zander too argues that judicial supervision provides a safeguard in this area, citing in support the 'Yorkshire Ripper' case in 1981.[224] Here, the trial judge refused to endorse the prosecution's acceptance of Peter Sutcliffe's plea of guilty to manslaughter, insisting that the original murder charge be proceeded with. However, this case was exceptional in terms of the public and media pressure to proceed with a murder charge.[225]

At one time, the appellate courts required that the charge brought should correspond to the facts alleged. In *Coe*,[226] for instance, the court deprecated charge reduction in the interests of convenience and ruled that the overriding consideration must always be the proper administration of justice. This attitude has since been replaced by a recognition of the advantages of charge bargaining. The Court of Appeal accepted in *Herbert*[227] that it was proper for prosecuting counsel to take into account the savings in public expenditure that a charge bargain could achieve. The

---

[220] McConville et al (1994: 256–7).   [221] McConville et al 1994: 257.

[222] Tague (2006). This is particularly true for rape where the conviction rate is very low (Kelly et al, 2005).   [223] McCabe and Purves (1972a: 29). See also Bredar (1992: 155).

[224] Zander M, *Cases and Materials on the English Legal System*, 9th edn (London: LexisNexis, 2003) p 310.

[225] The prosecution were left in the unfortunate position of arguing that what Sutcliffe did (brutally mutilate and kill 13 women) was rational; a response to the way he had been treated by various women, rather than a product of diminished responsibility. See Bland, L 'The Case of the Yorkshire Ripper: Mad, Bad, Beast or Male?' in Radford J and Russell D (eds), *Femicide: The Politics of Woman Killing* (New York: Twayne Publishing, 1992).

[226] (1969) 53 Cr App Rep 66. This echoed the earlier case of *Soanes* (1948) 32 Cr App Rep 136.

[227] (1991) 94 Cr App Rep 2.

Court of Appeal in *Grafton*[228] subsequently decided that the trial judge is powerless to prevent Counsel dropping or reducing any charges except where the latter seeks the seal of judicial approval for a proposed deal. Thus, if a case similar to that of Peter Sutcliffe were to go before the courts today, prosecuting counsel would be free to accept a plea of guilty to manslaughter so long as no express approval was sought from the judge.

The great majority of Crown Court judges are recruited from the ranks of the practising Bar. Many hold part-time appointments only, spending most of their time as barristers rather than judges. Prosecution and defence counsel have little to fear in seeking the approval of a judge for a charge bargain because all of the parties involved share a common outlook, all stand to gain from short-circuiting the formal trial process, and all are encouraged to enter into negotiations by the Court of Appeal. The Plea and Case Management Hearing standard form, which invites Crown Court judges to prompt pre-trial charge bargaining, should be seen as legitimising (and further enabling) a long-standing judicial practice. Sometimes judges, by indicating their desire for a speedy resolution of the case, exert direct pressure on their fellow lawyers to cut a deal. In an example given by McConville et al,[229] defence counsel had been called to see the judge privately just before a trial listed for three days was due to begin. The judge said he wanted the jury to be able to retire to consider their verdict by 11am the following morning because he was going on 'his holidays' in the afternoon of that day. This led counsel to try to persuade the client that it would be tactically astute to agree to the trial being truncated because the judge 'is a fast judge...he likes the bare bones of a case...' (The judge's desire to pack his case and rest his bones in the sun was not conveyed to the client.) The client resisted, which prompted counsel to depict the preference for a full trial as 'complete madness' and 'bloody crazy!' The client responded:

You're not the one who might go away [to prison] at the end of the day. I've lost my family and now I might lose my liberty. I want to do it properly, it *must* be done right; I don't want to rush it now' (emphasis in original).

It is a pity that more of those working in the criminal courts do not share this freedom perspective and this concern for procedural propriety.

8.5 **The prospect of conviction**

The advantages to be gained by pleading guilty explain why defendants who think they will be convicted following trial decide to plead guilty. But why do they expect to be found guilty? This expectation may be influenced by information received directly or indirectly from the court officials or from the prosecution and defence lawyers (or

---

[228] [1993] QB 101.   [229] McConville et al (1994: 265).

their staff). It may also be influenced by the realisation that prosecution witnesses are committed to giving their evidence.

8.5.1 Predictions of conviction from the bench

Nothing is more likely to cause a defendant to abandon a not guilty plea than the official(s) conducting the trial expressing a view that the defendant is guilty, will be found guilty, and is wasting the court's time by pleading not guilty. The defendant can hardly expect a fair trial in such circumstances. With the dice so heavily loaded, all the defendant then has to decide is whether to opt for a more lenient sentence by pleading guilty. In other words, there is no longer a meaningful decision to be made.[230] Thus, some of Baldwin and McConville's respondents claimed that they had been compelled to plead guilty by the judge, as in the following example:

The barrister came back from seeing the judge and said, 'Well, the judge says we can argue as long as you like but you'll be found guilty anyway.'...I think I was more forced into it [pleading guilty] than anything, personally. I was flogging a dead horse. I mean the judge had made up his mind before I even walked through the door.[231]

The Court of Appeal has made it clear that it is improper for a judge to comment on the strength of the prosecution case as a way of persuading the defendant to enter a guilty plea. This happened in Barnes[232] in which the trial judge had harangued the defendant and his barrister for their 'outrageous behaviour' in contesting a case 'without the shadow of a defence'. But reported cases continue to reveal an astonishing level of judicial interference into the conduct of a trial supposed to be conducted on adversarial principles of due process.[233]

But perhaps this is not so astonishing. So long as trial judges continue to engage in sentence bargaining the likelihood is that they will either volunteer (or become drawn into giving) their views on the likely outcome of the case. And in any case, to a defendant offered a sentence discount in return for pleading guilty, it may seem as if the judge has already decided that a conviction is not in doubt and that all that remains to be determined is the appropriate sentence. The danger of this is recognised in point 5 of the Goodyear guidelines (see 8.2.4 above) but we saw that no practical way of guarding against this was put forward by the Court of Appeal. In the world of judicial make-believe, trial judges can initiate sentence bargaining without giving the impression to defendants that their case is perceived to be a weak one.

---

[230] The problem of a bench communicating its prejudices in this way seems largely confined to the Crown Court where judges and barristers form a close-knit work group. There is less opportunity for magistrates to convey their views on the strength of the case to the parties, although the position may be different in the case of professional lawyers sitting judicially in the lower courts, as illustrated by the Northern Ireland case of In re McFarland [2004] UKHL 17.   [231] Baldwin and McConville (1977a: 33).

[232] (1970) 55 Cr App Rep 100.

[233] See, for example, Llewellyn [1978] 67 Cr App R 149; James [1990] Crim LR 815; Pitman [1991] 1 All ER 468; Pitts [2001] EWCA Crim 846; and Nazham and Nazham [2004] EWCA Crim 491.

8.5.2 Information from the prosecution

In order for the defence to assess the prospects of conviction it is obviously essential they have advance notice of the prosecution case and of any 'unused material' held by prosecution agencies which might help bolster the defence. While advance disclosure of the prosecution case is a routine feature of trials on indictment, much depends on prosecutors exercising their discretion and their duties in a fair and proper manner, and gaps remain.[234] One gap was created by the English courts deciding that, if 'unused material' relates to informants or the work of undercover police officers, the prosecution can make an ex parte application to the court for permission not to disclose such material and the defence need not be told of this application.[235] It follows that defendants may decide to plead guilty in ignorance of evidence withheld (quite lawfully) by the prosecution that would have helped to establish innocence.

A more frequent problem is that the prosecution fails to comply with the duty to disclose, sometimes through lack of care, sometimes as a result of deliberate malpractice. A failure to disclose evidence helpful to the defence has lain at the heart of most of the spectacular miscarriages of justice that have come to light in recent years. Such a failure occurred, for example, in all four of the now infamous 'terrorist' trials heard from 1974–1976.[236] There have been many other post PACE cases of a similar nature.[237]

We commented in the context of pre-trial negotiation in the magistrates' court (see 8.4.1) that what is disclosed is often as problematic as what is not, and the same is true in the Crown Court. In other words, what prosecutors disclose is a construct designed to present the best case for conviction.[238] For the defendant to rely on the contents of this dodgy dossier when assessing whether to enter the adversarial battle is fraught with danger.

8.5.3 Advice from the defence barrister

It has been argued in this chapter that defence lawyers arrive at court predisposed to settle cases for organisational and ideological reasons, and that the law provides them with the raw materials with which to fashion a negotiated settlement. A further issue is whether lawyers provide proper advice on the prospect of acquittal.[239] Research suggests that they adopt an unduly pessimistic view of the likelihood of acquittal in order to increase the pressure on defendants to plead guilty. In most cases the client is

---

[234] Our main discussion of the rules governing disclosure is in 7.3.3 and see references cited there for more detail.

[235] *Davis, Johnson and Rowe* [1993] 1 WLR 613. For subsequent developments including the views of the ECtHR see Redmayne (2004: 454–9).

[236] The 'Guildford Four', 'Birmingham Six', the 'Maguires' and Judith Ward cases.   [237] See 7.3.3.

[238] Case construction is discussed in detail in 7.3.3 and 7.4.3. Even forensic scientists are sometimes guilty of presenting their findings in a highly misleading fashion: *Ward* (1993) 96 Cr App Rep 1 provides a good example of this, and see further 7.3.3.

[239] Although we do not deal here with the part played by rules of evidence and procedure to assessments of the prospect of conviction, their importance should not be underestimated. See further 10.4.1.

simply presumed guilty and there is little attempt made to scrutinise the evidence or its relationship to legal categories of offence.[240] Some barristers in the Baldwin and McConville study were consistently described, by different defendants in different cases, as either good or bad.[241] The latter were 'seen very commonly as hurried, dismissive or in other ways unsatisfactory'. Further analysis confirmed that individual barristers did indeed vary greatly in the proportion of cases they handled that were terminated by a guilty plea.[242] We saw above how 'bad' lawyers may engage in charge bargaining or make use of the sentencing discount principle in order to pressurise defendants into pleading guilty. The defendants interviewed by Baldwin and McConville claimed that barristers commonly backed up this pressure by stating that there was little or no chance of being acquitted if the trial proceeded. Protestations of innocence were often brushed aside as irrelevant to this question, as in the following example:

My barrister pleaded guilty for me. I told him that I was innocent but he said I was a bloody nuisance and that nobody would believe me. He said, 'The judge and the others will never believe what you say in court; they will always believe the police.'[243]

More recently the observational study by McConville et al[244] has confirmed that a substantial proportion of both solicitors and barristers (and the unqualified staff they commonly use throughout the life of a case) continue to treat prosecution evidence uncritically, ignore protestations of innocence, and advise that the defendant has 'no choice' but to plead guilty. This advice was clearly contrary to the *Turner* rules under which barristers were supposed to tell clients that they must only plead guilty if they accept that they are guilty. That some barristers were prepared to tell clients that they stood no chance of acquittal notwithstanding their claims of innocence stands as a warning that defendants may not receive objective advice as regards the strength of their position. We have seen (in 8.2.4 above) that under point 11 of the *Goodyear* guidelines defence advocates are made personally responsible for ensuring that defendants fully appreciate that they should not plead guilty unless they are guilty. There is no reason to think that this will be any more effective than the *Turner* rules in ensuring that protestations of innocence are acted upon.

8.5.4 No witness, no justice

One reason why defendants might come to think conviction is likely is the sight of prosecution witnesses on the day of the trial. Monitoring of the reasons for ineffective hearings was introduced in the criminal courts following a critical report by the

---

[240]   See, in particular, McConville et al (1994: 188, 267–9). This appears to be less true of the London Bar: Tague (2006).   [241]   Baldwin and McConville study (1977a: 42).
[242]   Baldwin J and McConville M, 'Patterns of Involvement Amongst Lawyers in Contested Trials in the Crown Court' (1977b) 127 NLJ 1040.   [243]   Baldwin and McConville (1977a: 53).
[244]   McConville et al (1994: chs 7–10).

National Audit Office in 1999.[245] This monitoring revealed that an estimated 22,000 cases failed in 2002/03 due to non-attendance of the victim or other witness. As a result the government set up the *No Witness, No Justice* project which involves the police and CPS supporting witnesses more closely through the prosecution process, including arranging pre-trial familiarisation visits to the courts, and helping with travel and child-care. The project has been judged a success in reducing witness non-attendance and increasing guilty pleas.[246]

In principle greater support for prosecution witnesses is to be welcomed since it is clearly in the interests of justice for the best available evidence to be presented at court. However, the initiative is one-sided. The idea that a defence witness might need help with travel or care arrangements or that their presence at court would serve the interests of justice is overlooked by both the initiative and the report. 'No witness, no justice' can thus be deconstructed as meaning 'no prosecution witness, no conviction'. Also it is not self-evident that satisfaction with the criminal justice system will be increased by using witnesses as a means to the end of extracting guilty pleas from defendants. Cracked trials have in the past been described as causing great inconvenience and even distress to witnesses who attended court only to find their presence was not needed. This is exactly what the *No Witness, No Justice* project encourages. Witness distress may be all the greater if the cracked trial is achieved through a last minute charge bargain resulting in a relabelling of the offence in a way a victim finds objectionable.

8.6 **Fact bargains and multiple discounts**

Fact bargains are a form of deal under which the prosecution and defence agree a factual basis upon which a guilty plea is acceptable to both sides. In *Beswick*[247] the Court of Appeal attempted to regulate such agreements, stipulating that the prosecution should not agree to a fact bargain which would result in sentencing on an unreal or untrue set of facts. The extent to which fact bargains result in just such distortions is not known.[248] What *is* known is that fact bargains can combine with charge bargains and the sentence discount principle to produce an enormous discount for defendants. In *Attorney General's Reference No 44 of 2000 (Peverett)*,[249] for example, a former headmaster was faced with sixteen charges of indecent assault involving 11 of his pupils committed over a period of eight years when the victims were aged between 11 and 13. Counsel reached a charge bargain (in the presence of the trial judge) under which seven of these counts were not proceeded with, which meant that

---

[245] National Audit Office (1999).

[246] PA Consulting, *No Witness, No Justice – National Victim and Witness Care Project: Interim Evaluation Report* (December 2004) p 4.   [247] [1996] 1 Cr App Rep (S) 343.

[248] See further Ashworth A and Redmayne M, *The Criminal Process*, 3rd edn (Oxford: OUP, 2005) pp 274–5.   [249] [2001] 1 Cr App R 416.

four of the complainants dropped out of the picture altogether. In addition, a fact bargain was reached under which the nature of the conduct was transformed from spanking to fondling and 'tapping', and the motivation was agreed to be the desire to express his position of power over the children rather than sexual gratification. The final element in the bargain was that the judge promised, following a request from counsel, that a suspended sentence of imprisonment would be imposed if the defendant pleaded guilty in accordance with the terms of the charge-fact-sentence bargain. The defendant, described by the trial judge in his sentencing remarks as guilty of an 'appalling abuse of a position of immense trust', accordingly walked 'free' from court. The victims, understandably, were left feeling that they had been denied justice.[250]

Fact bargains are likely to become a routine feature of Crown Court work in future. This is because sentence indications under the *Goodyear* guidelines can only be requested from the judge once the parties have agreed the factual basis for the guilty plea. The purpose of this restriction is to safeguard against the judge becoming 'inappropriately involved in negotiations about the acceptance of pleas, and any agreed basis of plea'.[251]

8.7 Do the innocent plead guilty? (Is the Pope a Catholic?)

Many people would perhaps be prepared to tolerate sentence discounts and bargains concerning facts, charges and sentence if the net result was more convictions of the guilty and no corresponding increase in convictions of the innocent. The fact that the convictions in question may be for less serious offences than those actually committed might cause them pause for thought but the ends might nonetheless be seen to justify the means. The problem is that in practice no guarantee can be given that the innocent will not be made to suffer as a result of bargain justice despite the ostensible concern of the appellate courts to ensure that the innocent are not induced to plead guilty. Thus in *Turner* Lord Parker CJ was at pains to stress that counsel 'of course will emphasize that the accused must not plead guilty unless he has committed the acts constituting the offence charged'[252] and *Goodyear*[253] similarly makes defence barristers personally responsible for ensuring that defendants fully appreciate that they should not plead guilty unless they are guilty.

The difficulty here is that a defence lawyer will not know if a particular client is innocent or not and indeed may be anxious not to find out. Barristers to whom confessions of guilt are made are subject to strict restrictions in how they may conduct a

---

[250] 'So Why Didn't he Go to Prison?' *The Guardian*, 22 June 2000.
[251] [2005] EWCA Crim 888 [62] (see also [66]).   [252] [1970] 2 WLR 1093 at 1097.
[253] [2005] EWCA Crim 888 [65].

defence. Certain things they may still do, such as challenge the admissibility of prosecution evidence, but, according to their Code of Conduct:

...a barrister must not assert as true that which he knows to be false. He must not connive at, much less attempt to substantiate, a fraud...it would be wrong to suggest that some other person had committed the offence charged, or to call any evidence which the barrister must know to be false having regard to the confession, such, for instance, as evidence in support of an alibi. In other words a barrister must not (whether by calling the defendant or otherwise) set up an affirmative case inconsistent with the confession.[254]

Thus in one interaction observed by McConville et al,[255] counsel, on being told by a client that he had committed the offence of stealing a television as charged, feigned deafness, saying 'I don't hear so good when people make admissions.'

Many innocent persons will thus inevitably face advice from their barristers about the advantages of pleading guilty. The court in *Goodyear* implicitly recognises this in insisting that barristers must ensure that their clients appreciate that they should not plead guilty unless they are guilty. There would be no need for such an exhortation if only the guilty were to receive advice on the advantages of pleading guilty. The final choice of plea is, however, the accused's alone: 'The defendant is personally and exclusively responsible for his plea.'[256] Nothing prevents accused persons from proclaiming innocence to their lawyers yet pleading guilty in court. The defence lawyer is not deceiving the court, because the lawyer need not reveal the accused's true state of mind. Whereas barristers may not assert that defendants are innocent when they believe them to be guilty, they may conduct a case on the basis of a guilty plea while believing the defendant concerned to be innocent. As their Code of Conduct explains:

Where a defendant tells his counsel that he did not commit the offence with which he is charged but nevertheless insists on pleading guilty to it for reasons of his own, counsel should...advise the defendant that, if he is not guilty, he should plead not guilty but that the decision is one for the defendant; counsel must continue to represent him but only after he has advised what the consequences will be and that what can be submitted in mitigation can only be on the basis that the client is guilty.

The criminal justice system appears to be prepared to tolerate some frauds more than others. It discourages such frauds from coming to judicial notice (or public attention) by requiring the barrister further to explain that despite the fact that mitigation will be on the basis that the defendant is guilty, no claim of remorse can be made (as such a claim would be inconsistent with the defendant's private assertion of innocence and

---

[254] Code of Conduct, Written Standards for the Conduct of Professional Work (2004) paras 12.3–12.4 (available at <http://www.barstandardsboard.org.uk/standardsandguidance/codeofconduct/writtenstandardsfortheconductofprofessionalwork>; 5 January 2010). See the discussion by Blake and Ashworth (2004: 172–4).   [255] McConville et al (1994: 251).

[256] *Goodyear* [2005] EWCA Crim 888 [30].

thus amount to the barrister deceiving the court).[257] This creates an incentive for the client to abandon the claim of innocence so that the guilty plea can be advanced on a remorseful basis and thus attract a lower sentence than might otherwise be imposed. Whichever course a truly innocent client chooses, the court is being deceived.

Just as innocent people sometimes 'confess' to the police under interrogation, so too, it seems, (and often in consequence of having 'confessed' at an earlier stage) do innocent people plead guilty.[258] Baldwin and McConville (1977a) found that nearly half of the late plea changers in their study made substantial and credible claims of innocence. They acknowledged that they had no way of telling whether defendants were in fact innocent or not. But in a substantial number of these guilty plea cases independent assessors judged the evidence against the defendant to be weak. The more recent study by McConville et al (1994) details numerous examples of legal advisers ignoring clients' protestations of innocence[259] and failing in their legal duty to emphasise to clients that they should not plead guilty unless they were guilty. They also went on to assert in court things that they knew to be false in order to maximise the mitigating effects of the plea of guilty. McConville et al (1994: 262) write:

Thus, in a case in which the client was pressurised into a guilty plea – saying in conference that 'it makes me feel sick because I didn't do it', an observation never pursued by the barrister – counsel told the court that it was a 'spur of the moment offence' for which the client should be given credit because he had 'the courage to plead guilty today.' Similarly, in another case in which the accused asserted complete innocence but buckled after extensive pressure to accept an offer of a plea to a trivial charge... the barrister told the court that 'this is not an artificial plea at all', thereby conveying the impression that the plea was both voluntary and accurately reflected the extent of the defendant's involvement in the affair.

As to the overall scale of 'artificial pleading', the Crown Court study by Zander and Henderson[260] included a number of 'cracked trials' in which the CPS said that, had they gone to trial, the defendant would have stood a 'good' or 'fairly good' chance of acquittal. On an annual basis, this would total over 600 cracked trials where the defendant would have stood a good chance of acquittal and over 2,000 such cases with a fairly good chance of acquittal. Whilst it does not follow that defendants in these cases were all factually innocent, they may well have emerged from a contested trial legally innocent. The Crown Court study also found that 11% of defendants pleading guilty claimed to be innocent,[261] and that 6% of defence barristers were concerned that their clients had pleaded guilty despite being innocent – amounting to some

---

[257] Code of Conduct (2004: para 11.5.1) available at the Bar Standards Board website (<http://www.barstandardsboard.org.uk/>). This is not the only dilemma facing a defendant. If a claim of remorse is made then this will prejudice any future argument (on appeal) that the guilty plea was entered as a result of improper pressure and should thus be treated as a nullity: *Karim* [2005] EWCA 533 at paras 27–31. See also *Hayes* [2004] All ER 315.   [258] The phenomenon of false confession is discussed in 5.6.

[259] Eg at McConville et al (1994: 167).   [260] Zander and Henderson (1993: 157).

[261] Zander and Henderson (1993: 139). It should be borne in mind that the response rate of defendants was too low to be statistically reliable.

1,400 cases a year.[262] The annual figure for the magistrates' courts is likely to be much larger, although the only attempt to grasp the scale of 'innocent guilty pleaders' by Dell was published as long ago as 1971. In her study based on interviews with women in Holloway prison, 56 out of 527 women who had been tried in the magistrates' courts pleaded guilty to offences they claimed not to have committed.[263]

As in other areas of criminal justice, the innocent who belong to marginalised populations tend to suffer more from plea-bargaining than privileged defendants. The presumption of guilt will tend to be stronger in respect of those who are stereotyped as criminogenic or prone to lying.

8.8 **Should plea bargaining be abolished?**

The possibility of regulating or even eradicating charge bargaining has been explored by a number of domestic writers,[264] and has been attempted, with some well-documented success, in one American jurisdiction.[265] There are good reasons for trying to eradicate all plea bargaining.

8.8.1 **Plea bargaining and models of justice**

Due process objections

Encouraging defendants to convict themselves through a guilty plea undermines the principle that the burden of proof rests on the prosecution. It may seem that little harm is done to that principle by denying a discount or dropped/reduced charges, for example, to guilty defendants who stand on their right to put the prosecution to proof.[266] But there is a systemic value in requiring the prosecution to prove guilt which plea bargaining overlooks. Under a system in which guilty pleas are mass produced the prosecution of cases involving no more than vague allegations and other potential misuses of state prosecutorial power may be left unchecked. The number of weak cases prosecuted increases, as does the number of innocent persons wrongly convicted.

The risk of miscarriages of justice is exacerbated by the enhanced inducements offered to suspects to testify against their co-accused or to help the police suppress

---

[262] Zander and Henderson (1993: 138–9). The weight to be attached to this latter figure in view of the methodological weaknesses of the Crown Court survey has been much debated. Zander M, 'The "Innocent" (?) Who Plead Guilty' (1993) 143 NLJ 85 and McConville M and Bridges L, 'Pleading Guilty Whilst Maintaining Innocence' (1993) 143 NLJ 160. For further exchanges see (1993) 143 NLJ at pp 192, 228 and 276.

[263] Dell S, *Silent in Court* (London: Bell, 1971). See also the Canadian study by Kellough and Wortley (2002: 200–1).

[264] See Galligan (1987) and Bottomley A, 'Sentencing Reform and the Structuring of Pre-trial Discretion' in Wasik M and Pease K (eds), *Sentencing Reform* (Manchester: MUP, 1987).

[265] Carns and Kruse (1981).   [266] An approach taken by Auld (2001: 439, para 104).

serious crime.[267] This is because of the temptation to provide perjured testimony and to make unfounded allegations in order to further their own interests.[268] From a freedom perspective we might also want to question whether it is right for the Court of Appeal to induce defendants to cooperate with the police to such an extent that they put their own safety and that of their families in jeopardy.[269]

A related problem is the intensification of the pressure to plead guilty at a stage when the defendant may not have received adequate disclosure of the prosecution case,[270] particularly evident within the regime for pre-charge 'negotiation' in serious or complex fraud cases. The defendant may thus either feel pressurised into pleading guilty to something the prosecution could not have proved, or be penalised for refusing to indicate a guilty plea until more was known about the prosecution case. The courts are meant to take into account inadequate disclosure of the evidence when judging whether the failure to signal a willingness to plead guilty at a particular stage of the proceedings was unreasonable.[271] But the defence cannot predict with any certainty what a court will view as 'reasonable' in this regard, so the pressure to throw in the towel prematurely remains.

Another objection turns on the disjunction between plea bargaining and the rules we looked at in 5.5 that ban the police from inducing suspects to confess by offering to drop charges or grant bail. For what is the effect of enhanced discounts for cooperation with the police, and the SGC guidance that the 'first reasonable opportunity' to indicate a willingness to plead guilty may be in the police interview, other than to offer an inducement to suspects to confess to the police?[272] If inducements by the police are thought to raise too great a risk of false confessions, why is this not so with sentence, charge and fact bargaining?

Sentencing discounts, in particular, *penalise* those who stand on their right to put the prosecution to proof. This is an elementary point and yet many in the past have disputed it, claiming that discounts operate to reward those who plead guilty rather than punishing those who contest their case.[273] In his Review of the Criminal Courts, Lord Justice Auld recognised the doubletalk at work here and argued that courts should openly accept that 'once guilt has been established, there is no logical reason why a dishonest plea of not guilty should not be openly treated as an aggravating factor just as an honest plea of guilty is treated and rewarded as a mitigating factor'.[274] But, since we know that the innocent sometimes are convicted following a not guilty plea, 'logic' also tells us that the sentence discount principle results in innocent people who enter an honest plea of not guilty receiving more punishment than they would have done

---

[267] See the discussion of the formalised regime introduced by the SOCPA 2005 in 8.2.1 above.

[268] See Walker C, 'The Agenda of Miscarriages of Justice' in Walker C and Starmer K (eds), *Miscarriages of Justice* (London: Blackstone, 1999b) p 6 and references cited there.

[269] The greater the risk, the bigger the discount: *R v P and Blackburn* [2007] EWCA Crim 2290, discussed in 8.2.1 above.   [270] Discussed in 8.5.

[271] *Rafferty* [1998] Crim LR 433 at 434; SGC (2007b: annex A, para 3), provides the court must be satisfied the defendant and his adviser had 'sufficient information'.   [272] See 8.2.1 above.

[273] See, for example, *Harper* [1968] 2 QB 108 at 110.   [274] Auld (2001: 439).

had they entered a 'dishonest plea' of guilty (since 'dishonest pleas of guilty' will justify sentencing discounting no less than an 'honest plea of guilty').

This chapter has also highlighted the potential of the principle to work racial injustice. Is it acceptable that those from ethnic minorities receive longer custodial sentences than white people simply because they exercise the right to put the prosecution to proof? To the crime control adherent this pattern of sentencing would be regarded as the product of the need for efficiency, it being mere coincidence that it happens to impinge more on black people. From the due process perspective, however, it is predictable that black people would plead not guilty more often, as one would expect them more often to be at the receiving end of abuses of police and prosecutorial power.[275] Faced, as they are on average, with cases based on weaker evidence or evidence so tainted by unfairness that a reasonable argument can be made for excluding it, it is no surprise that black people have a higher rate of pleading not guilty. Plea bargaining penalises those who insist on trial, and thus works indirect racial discrimination. Auld's answer to this objection was that the root causes of any unfair discrimination (eg proportionately more black people being prosecuted on weak evidence) should be tackled and that abolishing the sentence discount principle was neither necessary nor sufficient in achieving that end.[276] To which one might reply, 'yes, but it would help'. Tackling racial discrimination is never easy and is almost bound to require that all available levers of influence are brought to bear. The real question is whether saving the system money is more important than tackling the problem of the current vast over-representation of black people in prison.[277]

The human rights perspective

Article 6(2) of the European Convention on Human Rights (ECHR) states that 'everyone charged with a criminal offence shall be presumed innocent until proved guilty according to law'. It is not contrary to that presumption for a defendant to make a free and informed decision to waive their right to a trial; a guilty plea can clearly be one way of proving guilt according to law. But it does appear contrary to that presumption for the state to seek to *induce* defendants to enter guilty pleas on the assumption that they are guilty. If the state were to offer a defendant £10,000 to induce them to plead guilty to a theft we would rightly be appalled at this attempt to negate someone's rights. But this is exactly how plea bargaining can work in practice. Further, the inducements discussed earlier could be seen as a breach of the 'right of anyone charged with a criminal offence to remain silent and not to incriminate himself'.[278] The indirect form of racial discrimination discussed earlier undermines Article 14 of the ECHR, which

---

[275] The processes resulting in the unfair treatment, and over-representation, of black people within the criminal justice system have been documented in earlier chapters.   [276] Auld (2001: 440–1).

[277] On 30 June 2008, the proportion of black prisoners relative to the general population was 6.8 per 1,000 compared to 1.3 per 1000 for white persons. See Ministry of Justice, *Statistics on Race and the Criminal Justice System 2007/8* (London: MoJ, 2009b) p 171.   [278] *Funke v France* (1993) 16 EHRR 297.

requires that the rights in the Convention 'shall be secured without discrimination on any ground such as sex, race, colour...' It is arguable that the right to be presumed innocent is currently one that is more fully enjoyed by white people than black people. And, to the extent that bargaining continues in private, it may contravene Art 6(1) (the right to a fair and public hearing).

Whether the European Court of Human Rights (ECtHR) will accept that plea bargaining is contrary to the ECHR is unclear. The most that can probably be expected would be a decision that prohibits it in private. That would represent a dilution rather than a reversal of the triumph of the crime control model in this sphere.

Crime control and managerialism

From the crime control perspective, the only problem with plea bargaining is that it does not always operate as efficiently as it should – for example, as we saw in 8.1, each year tens of thousands of people do not plead guilty until the date set for trial. This was the perspective adopted by the Runciman Commission, so it recommended that the principle that an early plea of guilty merits the largest discount be more clearly articulated so as to have greater effect.[279] This raises the question, effect on whom? The Runciman Commission accepted that it would be 'naive to suppose that innocent persons never plead guilty because of the prospect of the sentence discount'[280] but chose to place greater weight on the value to the system of encouraging the guilty to plead guilty. The Auld Report similarly argued that:

no system can guarantee that individual defendants, however innocent, will not regard the likelihood of a lesser sentence as an incentive to trade it for the risk of conviction and a more serious sentence, or that lawyers will not sometimes advise their clients badly. But these are not reasons for rejecting a sentence practice if in general it serves a proper sentencing purpose, operates justly and assists the efficient administration of justice.[281]

A sentencing practice which results in the conviction of the innocent can be described as 'in general' operating 'justly' only once one accepts that no special weight should be placed on avoiding such miscarriages of justice. Runciman and Auld went on to reject the possibility that the clearer articulation of the discount principle they advocated would increase the risk that defendants may plead guilty to offences which they did not commit.[282] Thus these review bodies adopted the self-serving assumption that one can increase the pressure on the guilty to plead guilty without increasing the pressure on the innocent to do the same.

That the Runciman Commission was wedded to crime control is also indicated by its deplorable treatment of Hood's research which had established that the discount principle works racial injustice. Its reaction was to express support for 'the recommendation made by Hood that the policy of offering sentence discounts should be

---

[279] Royal Commission on Criminal Justice (RCCJ), *Report* (Cm 2263) (London: HMSO, 1993) pp 111–12. Section 48 of the CJPO implemented this recommendation.   [280] Ibid, p 110.
[281] Auld (2001: 440, para 105).   [282] RCCJ (1993: 112); Auld (2001: 441, para 109).

kept under review'.[283] It was disingenuous of the Runciman Commission to imply that Hood had merely called for this policy to be kept under review. What he actually said was that 'it is time to consider all the implications of a policy which favours so strongly those who plead guilty, when ethnic minorities are less willing to forego their right to challenge a prosecution'.[284] What is a Royal Commission for if not to consider such implications? Although Auld's discussion of this issue is more extensive, ultimately he took much the same line by calling for the matter of unfair discrimination to be 'thoroughly researched and monitored'.[285] It is difficult to avoid the conclusion that both Reports adopted the crime control position of placing greatest weight on the need for efficiency within the criminal process.

The Runciman Commission also recommended the introduction of a 'plea canvas' so that judges could be asked by the defence to indicate the maximum sentence that would be imposed should a guilty plea be entered at that stage in the proceedings. It did so despite its acceptance that 'to face defendants with a choice between what they might get on an immediate plea of guilty and what they might get if found guilty by the jury does amount to unacceptable pressure'.[286] Yet, as Auld noted, this is exactly what the plea canvas would achieve because counsel would be ethically obliged to explain to the defendant the additional penalty that would be added to the judge's declared 'maximum sentence' should conviction follow a not guilty plea. Where Auld really differed from the Runciman Commission, however, is in declining to regard such pressure (whether emanating directly from the judge or indirectly through counsel) as unacceptable.[287] In the event, as we have discussed, *Goodyear* adopted the Runciman recommendation, effectively legitimising sentence bargaining, but preserving a modicum of judicial dignity by prohibiting judges from indicating what sentence they might give following a *not* guilty plea.[288] It may have taken 13 years, but the crime control victory sought by the Runciman Commission has now been achieved. The legal framework is now made up almost completely of legitimising and enabling rules and the due process rump is largely presentational.

The freedom model

The freedom model acknowledges the considerable resource advantages of guilty pleas, but does not accept that sentence discounts and charge bargains are the most cost-effective and freedom-enhancing way of doing justice. It seems unlikely that all, or even a majority of, defendants would plead not guilty if we left the system as it is but eliminated plea bargaining. For a start that should encourage the police and prosecutors to ensure that an appropriate charge is brought in the first place and that cases only come to court that satisfy the necessary evidential and public interest tests. Even under the current system many defendants readily accept their guilt and see no point

---

[283] RCCJ (1993: 114).   [284] Hood (1992: 182).   [285] Auld (2001: 441, para 108).
[286] RCCJ (1993: para 7.50).   [287] Auld (2001: 442, para 112).
[288] Although we have noted that Crown Court judges sometimes ignore this prohibition: *Clark and Ors* [2008] EWCA Crim 3221; *Patel and Ors* [2009] EWCA Crim 67 discussed at 8.2.4.

in putting an unarguable case before the court.[289] The proportion of defendants who felt this way should increase under a reformed system which demanded ethical charging and prosecution practices. Many more defendants would plead guilty because of the considerable incentives to do so even without plea bargaining. These incentives include less time spent inside the system (as more time is needed to prepare a contested case than a guilty plea), less time spent in court (it takes longer to fight a case than to concede it), lower court costs, the chance to mitigate on the basis of remorse, sparing any defence witnesses (such as friends or family) the ordeal of testifying, sparing oneself the ordeal of cross-examination, and so on. It might take some time for our system to adjust to a regime of non-bargain justice[290] but that fact has never stopped governments from implementing radical reforms when they favour the prosecution, as was the case with the effective abolition of the right to silence. The fact that the elimination of bargain justice is in the interests of victims, defendants and the promotion of human rights – would contribute, in other words, to a net gain in freedom – might one day convince a government that this strategy is worth pursuing. For plea bargaining is not an inevitable part of any criminal justice system but rather has its roots in particular social and political contexts.[291]

8.8.2 Sparing victims the ordeal of bargain justice?

The case of *Peverett* discussed in 8.6 provides a good example of how bargain justice can result in a conviction that bears little relation to the underlying 'facts' of a case. Another example is *Bargery*.[292] Here the CPS had indicated that they would not proceed on an affray charge if the defendant pleaded guilty to the less serious charge of using threatening behaviour. The defendant was only willing to do this if assured of a non-custodial penalty. The judge sealed the deal by giving that assurance to counsel in a private meeting, adding that if the defendant was convicted following a trial of the affray charge a prison sentence was a virtual certainty. The charge concerned the kicking and beating of two victims while on the ground. Bearing that in mind, the term 'threatening behaviour' seems to us little better than a judicially approved lie, while the punishment 'on offer' bears scant relation to the harm the offenders caused. As defence counsel put it in his record of this case: 'Given the gravity of the offence alleged and the injuries to the victims, I found this offer to be unexpected and surprising.'[293]

---

[289] See McConville et al (1994: 182–5) for supporting references and for discussion of the extent to which this point can be pressed.

[290] This is the implication of the analysis by Fisher G, 'Plea Bargaining's Triumph' (2000) 109 Yale LJ 857.

[291] On the relationship between socio-political structure and plea-bargaining see McConville M and Mirsky M, *Jury Trials and Plea Bargaining: A True History* (Oxford: Hart, 2005). See also Vogel M, *Coercion to Compromise: Plea Bargaining, the Courts and the Making of Political Authority* (Oxford: OUP, 2007).

[292] [2004] EWCA Crim 816.

[293] As this sentence indication breached the *Turner* rules and was held to have brought improper pressure to bear on the defendant resulting in a plea of guilty, the conviction was quashed by the Court of Appeal.

The clash between expediency and just deserts has been brought into sharper relief by the rise of concern for the interests of victims.[294] On the one hand devices designed to secure guilty pleas are often justified on the grounds that they spare victims the 'ordeal' of giving evidence. On the other, last minute bargains that result in offenders getting less than their just deserts may appal victims. In *Peverett*, the five victims who had attended court ready to give evidence were said to be stunned by the non-custodial outcome,[295] as was this rape victim following a cracked trial:

The judge praised [the offender for pleading guilty]. I was angry. He only did it because all my witnesses turned up. Men who leave the victim till the last minute before going into court should not be congratulated. 'Even at the last minute he saved the victim,' said the judge. No. He saved himself. They played down the violence. The violence was worse than the rape.[296]

There is also the point that many victims *want* a full-blown trial to take place, partly because this will lead to them learning more about the offence and the offender but also because they value their day in court. As one of the *Peverett* victims put it, 'The trial was going to be our chance to say "Hello. I'm back. I'm going to tell those 12 good men and women of the jury exactly what you did to me."' Instead, the victims felt that their voices had not been heard and that they had been cheated.[297]

Peverett caused such an outcry that the Attorney General immediately responded with new guidelines discouraging plea bargaining and requiring prosecutors minded to accept a plea to liaise with victims.[298] These guidelines are reflected in the most recent version of the Code for Crown Prosecutors, para 10.2 of which states that:

In considering whether the pleas offered [by the defence] are acceptable, Crown Prosecutors should ensure that the interests of the victim, and, where possible, any views expressed by the victim or victim's family, are taken into account when deciding whether it is in the public interest to accept the plea. However, the decision rests with the Crown Prosecutor.

This provision can be read as an implicit acknowledgement that charge bargains will be struck that involve the application of legal labels that victims may find offensive, as when rape is downgraded to sexual assault, or racially aggravated assault is downgraded to simple assault.[299]

---

[294] See generally Fenwick H, 'Charge Bargaining and Sentence Discount: The Victim's Perspective' (1997) 5 Int R Victimology 23.   [295] *The Guardian*, 30 October 2000.

[296] Quoted in Kelly et al (2005: 75). The public similarly regards guilty plea discounts as highly problematic: Clarke et al, *Attitudes to Date Rape and Relationship Rape: A Qualitative Study* (London: Sentencing Advisory Panel, 2002) pp 49–50, para 4.8.   [297] *The Guardian*, 22 June 2000.

[298] Attorney-General's Guidelines on the Acceptance of Pleas [2001] 1 Cr App R 28. A revised version was issued in 2005, and a further revision came into force on 1 December 2009 (available at <http://www.attorneygeneral.gov.uk/> – accessed 5 January 2010).

[299] See Burney E, 'Using the Law on Racially Aggravated Offences' [2003] Crim LR 28; Burney E, and Rose G, *Racist Offences – How is the Law Working?* (Home Office Research Study 244) (London: Home Office, 2002); Gus John Partnership (2003); HMCPSI, *Report on the Thematic Review of Casework Having a Minority Ethnic Dimension* (London: HMCPSI, 2002b) para 8.26.

Victims are not always opposed to bargains. In domestic violence cases it is not unknown for victims to be keen to downplay the impact of the offence against them, thereby supporting charge reduction, particularly where the prosecution continues without their support.[300] However, the fact that a victim approves of a charge bargain does not make it right. There are other interests in play, including those of potential future victims, and ensuring equality of treatment as between similarly situated defendants. Should those who bludgeon people into unconsciousness receive different treatment according to how understanding or forgiving their victim turns out to be?[301]

8.9 **Conclusion**

Pre-trial processes in the criminal courts, with their emphasis on case settlement, exhibit many of the hallmarks of the crime control model. But this is not just, or even primarily, a matter of lawyers seeking to make their lives easier. Rather, the system itself is geared towards the routine production of guilty pleas, as can be seen in the legal aid fee structure, the organisation of the legal profession, the sentence discount principle and so on.

At one time the legal system pretended that plea bargaining did not take place. There was a gap, in other words, between due process rhetoric and crime control reality. Developments such as the Sentencing Guideline Council's guidelines on sentence discounts, and the provisions allowing magistrates and judges to give advance indications of sentence, have been accompanied by increasingly shrill crime control rhetoric. The system is now formally, and nakedly, based on crime control norms. These developments have been sponsored by governments who have tied their political fortunes to achieving increases in the number of 'offenders brought to justice', especially through increases in guilty plea rates. The concern is with aggregate outcomes which contribute to the impression that the government has crime under control. The political context thus produces a decline in concern for miscarriages of justice and for achieving individualised justice in which sentences match offence seriousness. The adoption of crime control ideology by most solicitors, barristers and judges further oils the conveyor belt moving most defendants towards conviction. That some defendants insist on trial by jury is in some ways the most remarkable feature of the criminal justice process.

So what is to be done? The strategy of eliminating bargain justice would represent progress, but it leaves in place so many incentives to plead guilty that one might argue

---

[300] Although the charges selected in domestic violence cases may be low to start with leaving less room for reduction. This seemed to be the case in the first specialist domestic violence courts evaluated. See Cook et al, *Evaluation of Specialist Domestic Violence Courts and Fast Track Systems* (London: CPS, 2004) p 106.

[301] See the case of *Terrey* [2004] EWCA Crim 675. We discuss the appropriate role that victims should play within the criminal process as a whole in the concluding chapter.

that the presumption of innocence would still effectively be undermined. A more radical proposal would be to do away with the concept of a guilty plea altogether, or to do so for Crown Court cases at least. Inquisitorial jurisdictions have traditionally functioned without a reliance on this concept.[302] Under this proposal there would be, in every case that fell within the no-plea regime, a degree of judicial scrutiny of the prosecution case, so as to ensure that convictions were always based on relevant, sufficient, reliable and fairly obtained evidence. Defendants could be given a choice of trial by jury and judge, or trial by judge alone. Those not actively contesting guilt would be funnelled towards the latter option, whilst others could be given a more open choice.[303] Schulhofer has estimated that abolishing all systemic incentives to plead guilty in this way and replacing the guilty plea system with bench trials by judges sitting alone would increase the trial rate by some 650% but with only a 20% increase needed in judicial resources at the adjudication stage.[304] That seems a small price to pay for a more victim-centred system that better protects human rights and innocent defendants.[305]

The report of the Runciman Commission dealt with the subject of charge bargaining in a single sentence: 'We see no objection to such discussions, but the earlier they take place the better; consultation between counsel before the trial would often avoid the need for the case to be listed as a contested trial.'[306] On this subject, as on many others, the Runciman Commission failed to cite any evidence or marshal any supporting arguments to justify its preference for more crime control. The Runciman Commission thus represents a missed opportunity to reassess the fundamentals of our system of criminal justice and nothing has happened since to indicate that the reforms mooted above might find favour with policy-makers.[307] In fact the movement seems to be in the opposite direction, with increased formalisation of bargaining at ever earlier stages of the process. It is probably only a matter of time before pre-charge bargaining, now actively encouraged for serious and complex fraud cases, is rolled out to a wide range of offences.

The mass production of guilty pleas has become a systemic imperative in the criminal courts. In the new politics of criminal justice[308] defendants are constructed as 'undeserving' of due process, presumed guilty, and portrayed in public as cynical manipulators of the system who warrant swifter punishment. Yet, in reality, defendants do not commonly play the system; the system plays with them, their rights, and their freedom.

---

[302] Although more recently they have begun to succumb to the temptation to bargain away this part of their legal heritage. See Ashworth and Redmayne (2005: 265) and the sources cited there.

[303] See Doran S and Jackson J, 'The Case for Jury Waiver' [1997] Crim LR 155.

[304] Schulhofer S, 'Plea Bargaining as Disaster' (1992) 101 Yale LJ 1979.

[305] The extent to which innocent defendants are better protected under a non-bargain system is, we should acknowledge, a matter of controversy: see Scott R and Stuntz W, 'A Reply: Imperfect Bargains, Imperfect Trials and Innocent Defendants' (1992) 101 Yale LJ 2011.   [306] RCCJ (1993: 114).

[307] Auld (2001: 437–8) was dismissive of the idea that judges should not accept a guilty plea at face value.   [308] See McConville (1998).

Further Reading

R v Goodyear [2005] EWCA Crim 888; [2005] 1 WLR 2532

Attorney General's Guidelines on Plea Discussions in Cases of Serious or Complex Fraud (2009) (available at <http://www.attorneygeneral.gov.uk>)

Bredar J, 'Moving Up the Day of Reckoning: Strategies for Attacking the "Cracked Trials" Problem' [1992] Crim LR 153

McConville M, 'Plea Bargaining' in McConville M and Wilson G (eds), *The Handbook of the Criminal Justice Process* (Oxford: OUP, 2002)

McConville M, Hodgson J, Bridges L and Pavlovic A, *Standing Accused* (Oxford: Clarendon Press, 1994).

Tague P, 'Barristers' Selfish Incentives in Counselling Clients' [2008] Crim LR 3.

9

Summary justice in the magistrates' court

Just before going into court, a solicitor suddenly caught sight of
the defendant who had just arrived for trial and spoke to him in the
following terms:

Solicitor: Zip your jacket up. You should be doing better than a string
vest for court. How much gold do you have on? Take some of
that off – I don't want you looking flashy. [The client takes off
neck chain and bracelet.] And when you're in court, I don't
want you looking like you have an attitude problem; so keep
your fucking mouth shut and let me do the talking.

Client: Yeah, yeah, I know.[1]

Key issues

- The importance of the magistracy
- The involvement (and funding) of lawyers in summary justice
- Significant pre-trial decisions (including bail and mode of trial)
- How magistrates and their advisers measure up to the crime control/due process models of criminal justice
- The future of summary justice (including the impact of managerialist and 'victim rights' reforms)

9.1 **Introduction**

In England and Wales, trials are held either in the magistrates' courts or the Crown Court. There are around 360 magistrates' courts, located in most large towns and cities. All adult prosecutions begin in one of them, but the ultimate disposal of a case depends on the age of the defendant and the offence classification. There are special youth courts

---

[1] McConville et al, *Standing Accused* (Oxford: Clarendon Press, 1994) p 228.

for persons aged 10–17, although exceptionally youths can be proceeded against in the adults' magistrates' courts, or in certain cases committed to the Crown Court for trial.[2] Adult defendants charged with motoring offences or other summary offences such as common assault and drunk and disorderly have their cases heard in the magistrates' courts. Defendants charged with offences triable only on indictment, such as murder, wounding with intent to cause grievous bodily harm and rape, are tried in the Crown Court. In between there is a large band of offences which are triable either way; that is, they may be tried either summarily in the magistrates' courts or on indictment in the Crown Court. Examples of 'either way' offences are theft, burglary and assaults causing actual or grievous bodily harm. At one time, if an indictable or either-way case was to go to the Crown Court the magistrates had to decide whether there was a case to answer before 'committing' it to the Crown Court. Over the years this became a formality in most cases, and indictable-only cases are now sent to the Crown Court immediately after the defendant's first appearance without any scrutiny at all.[3]

The magistrates' court is the workhorse of the system. Table 9.1 shows the numbers of defendants prosecuted in the magistrates' courts in recent years has been steadily declining from a peak of around 2m.[4] The decline is due to an increase in the number of defendants subject to out of court disposals such as cautions and penalty notices. Around a quarter of proceedings in the magistrates' court are in respect of indictable and either-way offences, the rest concerning motoring offences and other types of summary offence. In 2007, 84,400 defendants were committed to the Crown Court for trial.[5] Over 80% of those facing either-way charges have their case heard in the magistrates' courts. The 'mode of trial' hearing held in either-way cases determines not just where but how the case should be tried. The essence of summary justice is a speedy procedure, uncluttered with elaborate judicial rituals. To try a case summarily in the magistrates' courts is to try it without many of the formalities required by the common law.[6] As we shall see, the 'formalities' absent from magistrates' courts include juries and (in most cases) professional judges, for most magistrates are unpaid, part-time amateurs.

The question of who may represent the prosecution and the defence also depends on the level of court. Barristers in private practice (lawyers who specialise in court-based negotiation and advocacy, and the drafting of legal advice) may appear in either the magistrates' courts or Crown Court to prosecute or defend, but typically appear only in the Crown Court.[7] Solicitors in private practice (traditionally regarded as the junior

---

[2] Youth courts are presided over by specially trained magistrates and are not open to the public. If cases are transferred to the Crown Court special procedures to help them cope apply. See Ball et al, *Young Offenders: Law Policy and Practice*, 2nd edn (London: Sweet & Maxwell, 2001) for analysis of the jurisdictional and procedural issues.

[3] Crime and Disorder Act 1998, s 51. See Leng et al, *Blackstone's Guide to the Crime and Disorder Act 1998* (London: Blackstone, 1998) pp 91–5.

[4] Ministry of Justice, Criminal Statistics 2007 (London: MoJ, 2008b) table 2.1.

[5] Ministry of Justice (2008b) para 2.17.

[6] See McBarnet D, *Conviction* (London: Macmillan, 1983) pp 138–43.

[7] Although members of the junior bar may act as agents for the CPS in the magistrates' court to hone their advocacy skills: HMCPSI, *Report of the Thematic Review of the Quality of Prosecution Advocacy and Case Presentation* (London: HMCPSI, 2009).

Table 9.1 Proceedings in magistrates' courts in selected years

2004	2005	2006	2007
2.02m	1.90m	1.78m	1.73m

branch of the legal profession) have historically lacked rights of audience in the Crown Court and therefore appear as advocates mainly in the magistrates' courts.[8]

The lowly status of the magistrates' courts is also reflected in the more limited rights of audience that salaried/employed lawyers traditionally possessed. Before the Access to Justice Act 1999 (AJA) Crown Prosecutors (whether qualified as barristers or solicitors) were only allowed to appear in the magistrates' courts, since it was believed that they were subject to their employer's bidding and might find it less easy to exercise independent professional judgement. Independence, it appears, was not thought so important before the lower criminal courts.[9] Since the AJA reforms paved the way for employed lawyers to appear in the Crown Court, the CPS is increasingly using its own lawyers for Crown Court advocacy work. It is also increasingly deploying staff who are not fully qualified lawyers, known as 'associate prosecutors' in the magistrates' court. The use of non-lawyers for magistrates' work reflects the belief that the skills of a lawyer are not required for the simplest cases, but the types of work that associate prosecutors are allowed to undertake are expanding. Originally non-legally qualified advocates in the magistrates' courts were allowed only for bail applications and guilty plea cases,[10] but 'associate prosecutors' can now be used for most types of non-trial hearing, and pilots are currently examining their use in a range of contested trial work. It is too early to say what the impact of this development, if more widely implemented, will be on the quality of advocacy in the magistrates' court. An inspection report in 2009 criticised some aspects of the advocacy work of CPS employees, although the worst examples were found amongst lawyers rather than associate prosecutors.[11] Nevertheless, the report notes that trials do require a broader range of skills, which, it may be speculated, associate prosecutors will lack. The use of less qualified staff is indicative of the lesser importance attached to magistrates' work and the 'ideology of triviality' that permeates the magistrates' court.

It should not be assumed that magistrates deal only with simple factual matters or guilty pleas and are never confronted with complicated matters of law, although discussion of legal issues may be resisted. A colleague of one of the authors was also a practising barrister in Yorkshire. In a rural court one day she sought to argue a point of law by reference to a leading House of Lords judgment. She was stopped before she

---

[8] Solicitors are able to obtain a 'Higher Courts Qualification' certificate (under a procedure and criteria established by the Courts and Legal Services Act 1990 amended by Access to Justice Act 1999, Part III).

[9] See Rozenberg J, *The Search for Justice* (London: Hodder & Stoughton, 1994) pp 153–62.

[10] Crime and Disorder Act 1998, s 53. See HMCPSI, *Evaluation of Lay Review and Lay Presentation* (London: CPSI, 1999a).

[11] HMCPSI (2009: ch 5).

had finished and informed that, as she was appearing before the Bogsworth magistrates, not the House of Lords, could she please get to the point?[12] This example illustrates how magistrates sometimes like to give the impression that they only deal with simple matters.

The summary nature of magistrates' courts justice is reflected, as one might expect from the above description, in lower running costs. It has been estimated that the average cost of an uncontested either-way case in the Crown Court is seven times that of an equivalent case in the magistrates' courts.[13] But is there an adequate justification for the difference in treatment meted out to defendants according to how the offence with which they are charged is classified? One argument would be that since the sentencing powers of magistrates are limited to six months' imprisonment there is less of a need for due process safeguards to apply than in the Crown Court, where (depending on the offence) a defendant may face life imprisonment on conviction.[14] Another would be that summary offences involve straightforward issues, the determination of which do not require other than a straightforward procedure. This is certainly true, for example, of many motoring offences. As nearly half of the magistrates' workload is made up of such offences, and given the very high guilty plea rate across all types of offence (see ch 8), observers in these courts might be forgiven for thinking that 'real crime' and courtroom drama were to be found elsewhere. Often, there are no observers. Journalists and curious members of the public tend to prefer the 'juicier' cases in the Crown Court. The lack of public scrutiny of these magistrates' courts is particularly helpful for white collar offenders anxious to avoid any damaging publicity.[15] To summarise, the signals given off by magistrates' courts are that they deal with trivial matters in which the issues are straightforward, defendants willingly accept their guilt and the consequences for defendants of conviction are slight. In truth, however, magistrates are responsible for decisions of far-reaching importance. They decide whether defendants should be released on bail or should lose their liberty pending trial. In 2007 magistrates remanded 52,000 defendants in prison at some stage during the court proceedings.[16] Magistrates can direct that either-way contested cases should be heard in the Crown Court, notwithstanding any objections from the defendant. They also have a role to play in supervising the work of other agencies. For example, as we have already seen (chs 4 and 6), the lower courts exercise a measure of supervision over the police in relation to such matters as periods of pre-charge

---

[12] See McConville et al (1994: 225): '…magistrates' court cases are not argued on legal issues, which are usually assumed to be inappropriate in such a forum'.

[13] The average cost of such a case in 1992 was about £210 in the magistrates' courts, and £1,400 in the Crown Court: Home Office, Costs of the Criminal Justice System 1992 (London: Home Office, 1992b) vol 1, pp 15–16.

[14] For the complex legal provisions regulating magistrates' sentencing powers see Sprack J, A Practical Approach to Criminal Procedure, 12th edn (Oxford: OUP, 2008).

[15] White collar 'regulatory' crimes are rarely prosecuted (see 7.5) ,but when they are, they are mainly kept in the magistrates and dealt with in separate sittings, reducing their visibility and helping offenders to play down the seriousness of their crimes. See the discussion by Croall H, 'Mistakes, Accidents and Someone Else's Fault: The Trading Offender in Court' (1988) 15 JLS 293.   [16] MoJ (2008a: ch 4).

detention of suspects and warrants allowing entry, search and seizure. Finally, magistrates have the ultimate power of depriving convicted defendants of their liberty. In 2007, magistrates sent 51.000 offenders to prison.[17] If they feel their sentencing powers are inadequate, they can commit defendants convicted of either-way offences to the Crown Court for sentence. This is the fate of around 17,000 people each year, over half of whom are given an immediate custodial sentence. One way or another, between a quarter and a third of the prison population is there as a result of the decisions of magistrates.

The operation of the magistrates' courts appears to be consistent with the crime control model of criminal justice. We saw in ch 8 that the high rate of guilty pleas ensures that many of the most important due process protections which might apply in an adversarial system do not come into play. This chapter will show that the antipathy towards due process values in the lower courts is deep-rooted. This is demonstrated in part at least by the approach to the provision of legal aid for criminal defence services.

9.2 Legal aid and legal representation

Legal representation is central to the functioning of the freedom, due process and human rights models, since it should guarantee that defendants are made aware of their rights and that the remedies available for any abuses of those rights are secured. The principle of equality requires that wherever the criminal process affords a theoretical right to legal representation the means should be made available to enable defendants to exercise that right. To do otherwise would place the poor and those of modest means in an unequal position with the rich. These principles appear at first sight to be enshrined in the European Convention on Human Rights (ECHR) (and, therefore, the Human Rights Act (HRA) 1998). Article 6.1 guarantees the right to a fair trial, and Art 6.3 guarantees every defendant the right '...to defend himself in person or through legal assistance of his own choosing or, if he has not sufficient means to pay for legal assistance, to be given it free when the interests of justice so require'.

For suspects detained for questioning in the police station, these due process principles are broadly accepted.[18] This may be contrasted with the position in the magistrates' courts, where legal representation is, for many, more of a privilege than a right. This is compatible with the letter (but perhaps not the spirit) of the ECHR because of the proviso in Art 6.3 concerning 'the interests of justice'.

During the last decade there have been a number of suggested and implemented reforms aimed at transforming the provision of criminal defence services. These reforms have been driven by the rising costs of legal aid and a desire to control

---

[17] Ministry of Justice, *Sentencing Statistics 2007 England and Wales* (London: MoJ, 2009e) p 13. The average prison sentence is 2.9 months. [18] See ch 4.5.

expenditure on criminal legal aid in particular.[19] In this section we provide a brief overview of the services available and examine the potential impact of reforms on the availability and quality of defence service provision in the magistrates' court. Notable developments include the introduction of a public defender service in some areas (from 2001) and controversial proposals for 'best value tendering', which many lawyers fear may put firms out of business and result in a reduction in the quality of defence services available. Currently three 'levels' of criminal defence service are available, two without means testing.[20] First, 'advice and assistance,' which largely covers police station work (see ch 4) but also covers people appearing in the magistrates' courts who may wish to apply for bail. Second, those who arrive at court unrepresented may receive 'advocacy assistance' from a duty solicitor, but must satisfy a merits test. In many of these cases the case is dealt with at that one hearing. Minor cases are not covered, and for most cases that are adjourned, the defendant will be expected to apply for full legal representation. To obtain full legal representation, the third level of service, a defendant must make an application to the Legal Services Commission (LSC) and satisfy both means and merits testing.

9.2.1 **The means test**

In 2001 the government abolished the means test for magistrates' courts work because most defendants who appear in the magistrates' courts are on low incomes and the cost of administering the test was expensive in proportion to the defendants who failed it and were required to make a contribution or pay for their defence. However, the Government failed to take into account that prior to abolition solicitors had been filtering out applications that would have failed the means test. Abolition therefore led to an unexpectedly sharp increase in the number of legally aided defendants.[21] More damagingly (in terms of critical media coverage), it also enabled some extremely rich people to defend minor criminal charges against them at public expense.[22] In October 2006 means testing was reintroduced. We would have no objection to a test which excluded the wealthiest households, but this was clearly not the intended effect. The government estimated that reintroducing means testing would save the legal aid budget £35 million a year. This can only realistically be achieved by excluding those of fairly moderate means as well as the wealthy. The government has indicated that in

---

[19] Lord Carter's Review of Legal Aid Procurement, *Legal Aid: A Market-based Approach to Reform* (2006) (<http://www.legalaidprocurementreview.gov.uk/publications.htm> – accessed 5 January 2010). Ministry of Justice, *Legal Aid: Funding Reforms* (Consultation Paper 18/09) (London: MoJ, 2009c).

[20] What follows is a very brief sketch. For details, see <http://www.legalservices.gov.uk/criminal.asp> (accessed 5 January 2010).

[21] Although quite how sharp is uncertain: Cape E and Moorhead R, *Demand Induced Supply? Identifying Cost Drivers in Criminal Defence Work* (London: Legal Services Research Centre, Legal Services Commission, 2005).

[22] Such as a footballer earning £40,000 a week, who was prosecuted in 2005 for spitting at a fan: <http://news.bbc.co.uk/2/low/uk_news/england/tees/4579265.stm> (accessed 5 January 2010).

less than three years over £80 million has been saved by the reintroduction of means testing in the magistrates' court, which is part of its rationale for wanting to extend means testing to criminal defence work in the Crown Court as well.[23] The government believes that savings can be made by fairly targeting those who can afford to contribute towards all or part of their legal costs, although others have questioned this view.[24] There is a danger that many defendants on average or middle incomes will suffer and the number of unrepresented defendants will increase.

9.2.2 The merits test

Schedule 3 of the AJA 1999 provides that representation may be granted where it appears desirable 'in the interests of justice' to do so, and specifies a number of factors which must be taken into account in determining this matter. Some of these 'Widgery' criteria[25] concern the seriousness of the consequences to the defendant of a conviction. If a defendant is facing the likelihood of loss of liberty, livelihood or reputation, more favourable consideration should be given to granting legal aid. The remaining criteria concern the inability of the defendant adequately to conduct a case in person. Thus a grant of legal aid is more likely (at least in theory) if the case requires the tracing and interviewing of witnesses, consideration of a substantial question of law or expert cross-examination, or if the defendant has inadequate knowledge of English or suffers from some mental or physical disability. One final factor to be taken into account is whether it is in the interests of another that the accused be represented. This covers situations where it might lead to difficulties if the accused had to cross-examine witnesses in person, such as in child abuse cases. This is an area in which more due process for the accused can lead to better protection for victims.

There seems little doubt that the Widgery criteria are ECHR-compliant since Art 6.3 itself uses the phrase 'interests of justice' to indicate when legal aid should be granted. And judicial interpretation of this phrase seems fully in accordance with the English position (which, if anything, is more generous). Thus, the European Court of Human Rights has repeatedly held that when assessing the interests of justice test within Art 6 regard must be had to the seriousness of the offence and the severity of the penalty at stake, and the complexity of the case.[26] The European Court has also upheld a French claim where a man who faced a very large fine was denied free legal aid,[27] showing that loss of liberty is not the only criterion.

---

[23] Ministry of Justice, *Crown Court Means Testing: Response to Consultation* (CP(R) 06/09) (London: MoJ, 2009d).   [24] Ibid.

[25] They derive from the Report of the Departmental Committee on Legal Aid in Criminal Proceedings (Cmnd 2934) (London: HMSO, 1966) para 56 (chaired by Mr Justice Widgery).

[26] See, in particular, *Quaranta v Switzerland* (1991) ECtHR Series A 205; *Benham v United Kingdom* (1996) 22 EHRR 293.

[27] *Pham Hoang v France* (1992) 16 EHRR 53, discussed by Ashworth A, 'Legal Aid, Human Rights, and Criminal Justice', in Young and Wall (eds) (1996).

The Widgery criteria are not exclusive – other factors may be taken into account.[28] For some time it seemed that it could be refused even if a case fell squarely within one or more of the statutory criteria.[29] But, especially following the Human Rights Act 1998, the Divisional Court has become increasingly willing to substitute its own view for those of decision-makers by quashing refusals to grant legal aid. It appears to take the view that Art 6 entitles it to intervene in a case where any one of the Widgery criteria are met but legal aid has been refused.[30] Much, then, relies on the correct identification of cases where the Widgery criteria apply. How much care is exercised in legal aid decision-making? Applications for state-aided representation (referred to from now, for simplicity, by the old term 'legal aid') may be made orally in open court, or, as happens much more frequently, to the justices' clerk or other designated court officer on a standard form. An application which has been refused can be renewed to the court or clerk at any time. On a renewal, a court clerk cannot refuse an application a second time, but must either grant it or refer it to the court for determination. The court retains the full power to grant or refuse. This enables the defence to have the application put before a different decision-maker, although, since the magistrates are used to relying on the advice of their clerk (who will be present in court when the application is renewed) the value of this 'second bite of the cherry' is not as great as it might be.[31]

Research by Young et al on the pre-1999 system found that grant rates were high, at 90% (although substantially less than 90% of cases were represented, as solicitors only applied in cases that had a good chance of success). Application forms were frequently completed by unqualified staff employed by the defendant's solicitor using standard wording which often exaggerated the case for granting legal aid.[32] In turn, court clerks were found to give little weight to the statutory criteria but applied a crude rule of thumb in determining an application. Defendants perceived to be charged with a 'serious' offence would almost automatically be granted legal aid, whereas those charged with a 'trivial' offence would similarly be refused. In the middle lay a grey area, which differed from court to court, wherein the chances of obtaining legal aid would depend on how

---

[28] *Liverpool City Magistrates, ex p McGhee* [1993] Crim LR 609.

[29] See, in particular, *Macclesfield Justices, ex p Greenhalgh* (1979) 144 JP 142; *Crown Court at Cambridge, ex p Hagi* (1979) 144 JP 145 and *Havering Juvenile Court, ex p Buckley* (LEXIS 554 1983).

[30] See for example *R on the Application of Luke Matara v Brent Magistrates' Court* [2005] EWHC 1829 where the defendant had applied for legal aid partly on the basis of 'inadequate English'. The magistrates' court had discounted this criterion on the basis that an interpreter would be provided, but the Divisional Court noted that the requirement that the proceedings be in a language that the defendant understood was 'merely one aspect' of the requirements of Art 6. It was satisfied that at least one of the Widgery criteria were met, the refusal of legal aid was therefore unreasonable and it was entitled to intervene.

[31] For many years, applicants had the right to appeal to an area committee of the Legal Aid Board. When the Board was abolished by the 1999 Act, so was the right of appeal. This illustrates how defendants charged with 'minor' offences are afforded few due process safeguards.

[32] Young et al, *In the Interests of Justice?* (Birmingham: Birmingham University, 1992) pp 62–86. See also Wall D, 'Keyholders to Criminal Justice' in Young R and Wall D (eds), *Access to Criminal Justice* (London: Blackstone, 1996).

well the legal aid application was argued.[33] Criteria relating to legal complexity, such as expert cross-examination, were given very little weight, and accidents of geography and adviser seemed to have a crucial bearing on whether an application was granted.

Young, with Wilcox, replicated his study in 2004, by which time grant rates had risen to nearly 95% of all applications (again, not of all cases). As before, some courts granted virtually all applications, whereas others refused one in five (previously, some refused as many as one in four). The authors judged that courts have not generally become more generous, apart perhaps from the least generous ones, but as sentencing has become tougher, and legal proceedings more complex, more cases have become deserving of assistance. Thus, whereas in 1992 only 6% of legal aid applicants had ultimately been given a custodial sentence, by 2004 the equivalent figure was 21%.[34] Some inconsistency of decision-making was found, but less than before, although it remained the case that court clerks gave little credence to claims that summary cases involved legal complexity. The authors argued that much decision-making was based on ignorance or misunderstanding of relevant appellate case law and proposed moderate reforms (such as redesigning the application form) in an attempt to address this and improve the consistency of decision-making.[35]

This research was commissioned by the LSC in anticipation of it taking over accountability for decision-making on this aspect of legal aid. Now that the Criminal Defence Service Act 2006 has effected this transfer of responsibility the LSC has entered into a 'service level agreement' with the courts. Day-to-day decision-making remains with the courts, but under the watchful eye of the LSC, which now lays down procedures to be followed and provides IT support. New guidance was issued by the Justices Clerks Society in 2007 for court decision-makers which drew on the Wilcox and Young (2006) research.[36] There is thus now the potential for more consistent decision-making although whether this is being realised in practice cannot be known until further research is undertaken.

The main problem with the discretion left to court clerks in deciding which defendants should receive legal aid is the potential it creates for subverting adversarial

---

[33] Young et al (1992: 25–39). For summaries of some of the main findings of this report see Young R, 'The Merits of Legal Aid in the Magistrates' Courts' [1993] Crim LR 336 and Young R 'Will Widgery Do?' in Young and Wall (eds) (1996).

[34] Wilcox A and Young R, *Understanding the Interests of Justice* (London: Legal Services Commission, 2006) p 126.

[35] Wilcox and Young (2006: ch 10). See also Young R and Wilcox A, 'The Merits of Legal Aid in the Magistrates' Courts Revisited' [2007] Crim LR 109. A redesigned application form along the lines advocated by Young and Wilcox was put into use for a short period but then was itself replaced due to the re-introduction of means testing and a re-design of the form to achieve this. In other words, the lessons of the research were almost immediately forgotten.

[36] Available at <http://www.legalservices.gov.uk/docs/cds_main/IofJJusticeGuidanceFinalVersion 060607.pdf> (accessed 5 January 2010). An attempt to improve upon this guidance was undertaken in 2008 by Her Majesty's Court Service and the Legal Services Commission following discussion with an 'expert panel' (on which one of the authors served – you can guess which). No new guidance had been issued by the point this chapter was finalised (25 December 2009). I really should get out more.

procedures. An adversarial system cannot work properly if there is an inequality of resources available to the prosecution and the defence. The prosecution is always represented, even if not always by a qualified lawyer,[37] however 'trivial' or 'straightforward' the case might be, so why should not the defence be treated in the same way? And, because of the way cases are constructed by the prosecution to appear strong on paper,[38] it cannot safely be predicted in advance which cases might lead to injustice if representation was not provided. Good legal representation can lead to the emergence of previously hidden aspects of the case, render problematic the prosecution version of events, and raise questions about the integrity of the procedures followed. Magistrates' cases can be complex, but the 'ideology of triviality' usually hides this successfully. It is impossible to estimate the proportion of cases in which legal aid is currently refused (or not applied for) that would benefit from legal representation. The proportion may be small, but if the system is to give priority to acquitting the innocent and other due process values, the argument for making legal aid much more widely available is strong. But, as we have seen, there is nothing in the ECHR to bolster that argument, and it is unlikely that the LSC will be allowed to foster more generous decision-making in future.

9.2.3 The cost of legal aid

For many years expenditure on criminal legal aid rose significantly, but has currently stabilised at around £1.2 billion, just over half the £2 billion total legal aid budget.[39] Nevertheless, the government believes that criminal legal aid is putting undue pressure on the budget available for civil legal aid and wishes to introduce further reforms to control criminal legal aid costs.[40] One of the most controversial 'market based' reforms in recent years is the proposal for the introduction of 'Best Value Tendering' (BVT); a process whereby every supplier who wants to take part in publicly funded criminal defence work would bid in an auction to do the work at the lowest price.[41] The Ministry of Justice announced in December 2009 that LSC pilots in two areas would not be going ahead, but made it clear that competitive tendering was still on

---

[37] We have noted an increase in non-legally qualified CPS advocates (see 9.1), and it has been stated that the fact the prosecution is legally represented does not mean that magistrates are bound to grant legal aid (*Havering Juvenile Court ex p Buckley*, Lexis CO/554/83, 12 July 1983).

[38] See McConville et al, *The Case for the Prosecution* (London: Routledge, 1991). Discussed in ch 7.

[39] For an overview of the history of legal aid and levels of expenditure see Hynes S and Robins J, *The Justice Gap—Whatever Happened to Legal Aid?* (London: LAG, 2009). See also Hynes S, 'Fixed Fees, Best Value Tendering and the CDS' *Legal Action*, March 2008, 6; Cape E, 'Legal Aid Spending: Looking the Other Way', *Legal Action*, July 2008, 8.

[40] The latest proposals, at the time of writing, included revised (lower) fixed fees for police station work. See Ministry of Justice, *Legal Aid: Funding Reforms* (CP 18/09) (London: MOJ, August 2009c). The paper also contains proposals for controlling experts' fees.

[41] *Best Value Tendering of Criminal Defence Services* (London: LSC, December 2007); *Best Value Tendering for CDS Contracts: A Consultation Paper* (London: LSC, March 2009). For further details see <http://www.legalservices.gov.uk/criminal/a_market_based_approach.asp> (accessed 22 October 2009).

its agenda.[42] In the meantime legal aid will continue to be provided by suppliers who have entered into the Criminal Defence Service (CDS) contract and are subject to a fixed fees regime. It is feared that BVT, like fixed fees before it, may price some firms out of the market with resultant gaps in services. Much of the critique about BVT is speculative at this stage and many of the criticisms have come from the Law Society which clearly has a vested interest.[43] That said, other aspects of the LSC strategy for 'transforming' criminal legal aid, including the introduction of a salaried defence service, have been independently evaluated. In conjunction with Scottish research on fixed fees, the evaluation of the salaried defender service gives us some insight into the potential impact of legal aid reforms upon the quality of criminal defence services.

9.2.4 The quality of defence work under legal aid

At around the same time as fixed fees were being introduced in England and Wales (the late 1990s) they were also introduced in Scotland (which has a separate legal system but which is similar in most respects to that of England and Wales). The rates were low and the income of specialist criminal firms initially fell sharply but then rose to the previous levels because firms increased their caseloads.[44] However, evaluative research found that the introduction of fixed fees resulted in firms reporting a decline in client contact, although they were more willing to say this had been the effect on their rivals' working practices than their own.[45]

The Scottish Legal Aid Board response to this is that client contact is not a reliable quality measure as much of it is a waste of time. But research has shown that without the unproductive parts of client interviews, one would not obtain valuable information provided in the productive parts, as a good rapport increases the probability of eliciting the maximum amount of relevant information from defendants.[46] Also, clients judge the quality of legal services in part by the nature and quality of their contact with their solicitor.[47] If it is important to take into account the way that criminal

---

[42] <http://www.solicitorsjournal.com/story.asp?sectioncode=2&storycode=15429&c=1> (accessed 5 January 2010).

[43] Links to the law society campaign against BVT can be found on their website (<http;//www.lawsociety. org.uk>). See also *The Times*, 19 June 2009. As well as forcing firms out of the market it has been predicted that some firms may make unsustainable bids with prices so low that providing a quality service becomes impossible.

[44] A similar phenomena has probably occurred in England and Wales. See Makepeace A, 'Pumping Up the Volume to Make Legal Aid Profitable' (2008) 105(03) LSG 24.

[45] Stephen et al, *Impact of the Introduction of Fixed Fee Payments into Summary Criminal Legal Aid: Report of an Independent Study* (Edinburgh: Scottish Executive, 2007) available at <http://www.scotland. gov.uk/Publications/2007/06/22104314/0> (accessed 22 October 2009).

[46] Unsurprisingly, no-one in government seems to object to the police using 'unproductive' rapport at the start of an interrogation as a way of getting suspects to lower their guards and reveal more information during the 'productive' part of the interaction: see further ch 5.

[47] For discussion of all these points see Tata C and Stephen F, 'Swings and Roundabouts: Do Changes to the Structure of Legal Aid Remuneration Make a Real Difference to Criminal Case Outcomes?' [2006] Crim

justice is experienced – as we argue throughout this book – giving time to building the solicitor–client relationship is not money down the drain.

Second, the Scottish research on fixed fees found that defence solicitors had cut other work too – such as 'precognition' of prosecution witnesses. Again, the extent to which this work is needed is a matter of dispute, and doubtless police and the CPS could also produce stronger cases if they had more resources. As well as asking whether resources suffice to enable a basic minimum of work to be done, the question is whether the level of fees and structure of remuneration puts prosecution and defence on a level playing field. The Scottish evidence is that it does not. Many firms told the researchers that they now rely wholly or largely on police reports of what witnesses say. Moreover it is not just a matter of the quality of services declining as firms cut their work to fit the fees. Fixed fees mean that firms get paid whatever they do. Some unscrupulous firms therefore make more profit per case than before, because they have allowed the quality and quantity of their preparation to fall exponentially.

Has criminal defence work, in the light of the income levels produced by such devices as low-rate standard fees, become a second-rate service? An obvious point is that low paid legal aid work may deter the best of newly qualified lawyers (and forensic scientists) from specialising in criminal defence. It also leads to experienced criminal practitioners seeking to achieve greater financial security and status by switching to more lucrative types of legal activity such as corporate and commercial work.[48] The organisation of specialist criminal practices is a key determinant of the quality of defence work.[49] The essential point here is that solicitors are business people. Either they make a profit (or at least break even) or they go out of business. Many solicitors claim that the only way to make legal aid pay is to handle large numbers of cases in a streamlined and bureaucratic fashion. Profits can be maximised by the routine allocation of legally aided work to non-solicitors. As we have already seen in 4.5, non-solicitors often attend at police stations. They are also employed in carrying out initial interviews with defendants and applying for legal aid, although the use of staff without *any* legal training seems to have declined since the early 1990s.[50] This all affects the quality of service unless training and supervision is stringent. The defendant will often meet a solicitor only on the morning of the court hearing. McConville et al observed such meetings and report that: 'Several solicitors did not even know

LR, p 722). Also see Tata et al, 'Does Mode of Delivery Make a Difference to Criminal Case Outcomes and Clients' Satisfaction? The Public Defence Solicitor Experiment' [2004] Crim LR 120.

[48] See Smith R, 'Resolving the Legal Aid Crisis' (1991) LS Gaz, 27 February, p 17. This is true also of defence experts: Roberts and Willmore (1993: 74). Moorhead R, 'Legal Aid and the Decline of Private Practice: Blue Murder or Toxic Job?' (2004) 11(3) IJ of the Legal Profession 160 at p 179 noted that a newly qualified solicitor in 2003 in London might expect to earn around £15,000 in a legal aid firm compared with £50,000 in one of the top London commercial firms.

[49] See the insightful analysis of legal aid practices by King M, *The Framework of Criminal Justice* (London: Croom Helm, 1981) pp 68–75, and the empirical study by McConville et al (1994).

[50] Compare McConville et al (1994) and Young et al (1992: 81–6), with Wilcox and Young (2006: 136–8).

their clients by sight, let alone any details of their case...'[51] Where a solicitor briefs a barrister (or a solicitor advocate)[52] to handle the case, the defendant becomes one step further removed from his or her legal representative.

Criminal legal aid representation can therefore be characterised by *routinisation, delegation* and *discontinuous representation.* Fixed fees make this more inevitable in order that criminal legal aid be efficient and cost-effective. But whether it can at the same time be 'justice-effective' is another matter. The ideal of a close client–lawyer relationship in which the lawyer conducts the case in person from the police station right through to the courts is only rarely realised in practice.

A further problem is that a legal aid (now 'legal representation') order may not cover all the work that the solicitor thinks is necessary in preparing the defence. In assessing claims for payment for legal services not covered by a fixed fee or contract price, the CDS is supposed to allow a reasonable amount in respect of all work actually and reasonably done. In practice this means that solicitors often find themselves wrangling with LSC officials over the correct level of payment to be made, or, indeed, over whether any payment at all should be forthcoming. Some solicitors have simply stopped carrying out certain preparatory steps in their cases, such as tracing and interviewing witnesses, for fear that they will not receive payment for such work.[53] Furthermore, the government is keen to cut the costs of use of experts in the same way as it aims to control criminal legal aid expenditure in general, which raises concerns about whether a suitably qualified pool of experts will remain available to the defence if rates are set too low.[54] Scientific and other forms of expert evidence are not uncontroversial and in the past have played a major part in some miscarriages of justice.[55] It is therefore important that defence firms have access to levels of funding which enable them to instruct experts to scrutinise and challenge prosecution expert evidence. The government claims that efforts to control criminal legal aid expenditure, such as fixed fees (and the new proposals for BVT), can succeed without any reduction in the quality of services available, because quality measures are in place which solicitors will have to meet if they want their relationship with the LSC to continue. This is so up to a point, but many firms struggle to provide the level of service they might otherwise have offered and some have been driven out of business. This trend, which impacts particularly on small firms, will probably continue as the squeeze on legal aid expenditure gets ever tighter. Market forces may not provide adequate scope for committed professionals, especially those providing 'niche' services.[56] We are not suggesting that solicitors are completely unprofessional and mercenary. Few would generally act unethically. But

---

[51] McConville et al (1994: 168).

[52] Solicitor-advocates (specialising, like barristers, in advocacy) are attracting an increasing market share of magistrates' courts work as they are more economic to 'brief' than barristers and operate more flexible working practices. The distinctive problems presented by the divided legal profession and the organisation of the Bar are explored in detail in ch 8. [53] See Young et al (1992: 75–6) for instance.

[54] See Ministry of Justice (2009c). [55] See the discussion in ch 6.

[56] Bridges et al (2000a: ch 8). See also Sommerlad H, '"I've Lost the Plot": An Everyday Story of the "Political" Legal Aid Lawyer', (2001) 28 JLS 335.

fee structures and other structural aspects of the system are likely to alter behaviour substantially in areas of 'ethical uncertainty'[57] – in other words, where doing a less thorough job may be an ethically defensible but less-preferred course of action – such as giving unqualified staff responsibilities that need not be done by a professional, but which would be better so done, or eliminating time spent with clients aimed at building rapport and trust. One area of 'ethical indeterminancy' – where lawyers face a choice between two courses of action but are unsure which is better for their client – might be whether to advise a guilty plea. The Scottish research referred to above found that fixed fees provided an incentive for lawyers to advise their clients to plead guilty earlier, although the lawyers were not always certain that this was in the client's interests. Overall the study concluded that while there was a range of views about whether fixed fees had impacted on the effectiveness of defence work, almost no one suggested that the impact had been positive.[58]

The creation of a salaried public defender service creates further competition for private firms offering criminal defence services. Public defender offices were opened in six sites in England and Wales between May 2001 and July 2002.[59] It might seem that such a system, by removing the profit motive from defence work, would lead to improved standards. However, this depends upon the aims and funding of the service. The development of public defender systems in the United States did not bode well in this respect,[60] although US schemes and jurisdictions vary widely and other jurisdictions such as Canada have introduced such systems with greater success.[61] A pilot scheme ran in Scotland with mixed results.[62] Prior to the setting up of the Public Defence Service (PDS) in England and Wales, concerns were raised about its independence. JUSTICE (2001) argued that this would be one of the critical factors shaping the quality of the service, arguing for an independent head of service and for the LSC to act as an independent buffer between the PDS and government. JUSTICE also argued the service should not be overloaded and competition from well resourced private firms should remain. The PDS was set up in areas where it had to compete with private sector suppliers, but most of the PDS offices had prominent shopfront locations and a higher standard of accommodation than private firms. The PDS also provided a 24-hour service, which was expensive but judged necessary to recruit and retain

---

[57] Tata and Stephen (2006); Stephen et al (2007).

[58] Stephen et al (2007). See also ch 8 for a discussion of lawyers financial incentives and guilty pleas.

[59] For details of the setting up of the service see Bridges et al, *Evaluation of the Public Defender Service in England and Wales* (2007) – available from <http://www.legalservices.gov.uk/docs/pds/Public_Defenders_Report_PDFVersion6.pdf> (accessed 5 January 2010).

[60] For a critical overview, see McConville M and Mirsky C, 'The State, the Legal Profession, and the Defence of the Poor' (1988) 15 JLS 342. For a report showing the differences within the US, see JUSTICE, *Public Defenders: Learning from the US Experience* (London: JUSTICE, 2001).

[61] See O'Brien D and Epp J, 'Salaried Defenders and the Access to Justice Act 1999' (2000) 63 MLR 394. On the dangers of making cross-jurisdictional comparisons see Tata C, 'Comparing Legal Aid Spending' in Regan et al (eds), *The Transformation of Legal Aid* (Oxford: OUP, 1999).

[62] Goriely et al, *The Public Defence Solicitors' Office in Edinburgh: An Independent Evaluation* (Edinburgh: Scottish Executive Central Research Unit, 2001); Goriely T, 'Evaluating the Scottish Public Defence Solicitors' Office' (2003) 30 J Law and Society 84; Tata et al (2004).

clients where private competition remained. The objective of the PDS was to provide a service that was as good or better than that provided by private practice, so the evaluation measured its performance by comparing the quality of service provision at three stages of the criminal process including representation at the magistrates' courts. The evaluation found that quality and practices varied across sites but in some respects the PDS seemed to be doing better than private practice. For example in relation to police station work PDS clients were more likely to make a 'no comment' interview which the researchers concluded suggests that the PDS adopts a 'more adversarial approach' than private firms.[63] In relation to magistrates' court work it was found that in general the clients of private practice firms had more hearings, but this was to be expected given that private firms had more complex caseloads and more financial incentives. There were no significant differences in bail outcomes and although the PDS had more guilty pleas they also had more discontinued cases and the levels of conviction rates for PDS and private firms were similar, as were sentencing outcomes. The researchers conclude the picture is 'broadly positive about the performance of the PDS offices relative to private practice'.[64] Outside the PDS there were generally positive perceptions about the quality of advocacy and independence of public defenders, although perhaps not surprisingly solicitors in private practice were less complimentary of the PDS in this respect. In relation to independence the majority of respondents from the police, CPS, courts and private practice thought that the PDS was as willing as private firms to challenge the police and prosecution and stand up for clients.[65] This level of service has however been provided at high costs; in the three first years of operations the PDS had substantially higher costs per case than private practice.[66] Whether it could continue to maintain a similar level of service on the more constrained funding available to private firms is clearly questionable. It is worth noting that the LSC has closed down the least cost-effective branches of the PDS (at Birmingham, Chester and Liverpool) since the pilot period, and the only branches currently operating are at Darlington, Pontypridd, Swansea and Cheltenham.[67]

The poor will always be dependent on the state to fund their defence regardless of whether legal services are based on private sector provision or salaried defenders. Either way, the state tends to draw the purse strings much tighter in relation to defence work than it does in sponsoring prosecutions. The experience on both sides of the Atlantic suggests that the state is more interested in cut-price efficient crime control than in expensive adversarial due process. There is a political dimension to this preference. Whereas cuts in spending on the police and prosecution services might be perceived as an indication that the government had gone 'soft' on crime, the due process rights of suspects present an easier target for cuts. Put crudely, there are currently more votes in crime control than in due process. The implications for the quality of defence

---

[63] Bridges et al (2007: 91).   [64] Ibid: 110.   [65] Ibid: 245–6.   [66] Ibid: 231.

[67] <http://www.legalservices.gov.uk/press/press_release23.asp> (accessed 5 January 2010). In November 2009 the Legal Services Commission was accused of not understanding the legal services market: National Audit Office, *The Procurement of Legal Aid in England and Wales by the Legal Services Commission HC 29 2009–10* (London: TSO, 2009).

services in particular, and adversarial justice in the magistrates' courts in general, seem (to us at least) obvious. Overall, the legal aid scheme provides a basic due process protection for many defendants but also nudges defence lawyers into a crime control mode of operation. This has become even more true since defence lawyers, in their criminal legal aid work, have become part of the CDS and have thus become obliged to subscribe to its goals – as a government agency – of 'bringing offenders to justice' and 'doing so efficiently'. They have become further tied into the 'efficiency agenda' by rules of criminal procedure.[68] In ch 8 we examined how this translates into pressure to deal with cases more quickly and to advise clients to plead guilty earlier. This is not what adversarialism – or, more important, justice – is supposed to be about. From a freedom perspective, the due process argument for near-universal high quality criminal aid has to be balanced against competing demands on financial resources from other sectors of society (such as education and health, as discussed in ch 1). It is relevant to ask whether the money is being spent properly. It is often said that much of the increase in the criminal legal aid bill is down to solicitors and defendants incurring unnecessary expenditure.[69] But as even the previous government's Green Paper accepted, 'demand is determined by the state' in the sense that if people were not arrested and prosecuted they would not seek criminal legal aid.[70] As Bridges points out, not only have arrests and prosecutions risen greatly over the last 30 years, but PACE in the mid 1980s authorised more police station detention than hitherto, and the Criminal Justice and Public Order Act (CJPO) in the mid 1990s further increased the need for lengthy police station attendances from legal representatives because the implications of the CJPO for each suspect are so difficult to foresee.[71] In other words, if the state is concerned about rising legal aid expenditure (as it should be) then the state should take responsibility for at least a part of the problem and alter its behaviour accordingly.

9.3 Justices' clerks and legal advisers: liberal bureaucrats?

The primary function of justices' clerks in England and Wales is to give accurate and consistent legal advice to lay magistrates.[72] Justices' clerks exercise judicial functions themselves and also delegate judicial and advisory functions to other lawyers employed

---

[68] See the Criminal Procedure Rules 2005 available at <http://www.justice.gov.uk/criminal/procrules_fin/rulesmenu.htm> (accessed 22 October 2009).

[69] See, for example, Bevan et al, *Organising Cost-Effective Access to Justice* (London: Social Market Foundation, 1994).   [70] LCD (1995: 30).

[71] Bridges L, 'The Reform of Criminal Legal Aid' in Young and Wall (eds) (1996). A more recent analysis by Cape and Moorhead (2005) is to the same effect.

[72] For a sense of the current trajectory of the justices' clerk role, see Eccles A, *A Report Following the Consultation on a Model for the Provision of Justices Clerks in England and Wales* (London: Ministry of Justice, 2007).

by the Court Service. These delegates are known as assistant justices' clerks or more commonly 'legal advisers'. Delegation is essential as the numbers of justices' clerks have been greatly reduced in recent decades; there were just 49 to cover the whole of England and Wales in 2008.[73] Justices clerks and most legal advisers are qualified lawyers[74] with specialist training. The provision of advice is essential, as most magistrates are part-time amateurs (see 9.5 below).   Justices' clerks and their staff fulfil many functions in the magistrates' courts. In addition to advising magistrates on law, procedure and sentencing they are responsible for training magistrates.[75] Through pursuing a more or less conscious policy on the determination of legal aid applications, a role which is delegated to them by the Legal Services Commission, they can influence the level of legal representation. They are meant to assist unrepresented defendants in court. Finally, they shape the conduct of proceedings in court through their role in managing the court's business.[76] Thus, they handle many pre-trial proceedings aimed at reducing delays in processing cases and they determine listing policies which might, for example, aim to dispose of as many cases in a single sitting of the court as possible. In carrying out these tasks, are clerks influenced by, and do they seek to advance, due process or crime control values?

As we have seen, court clerks have a fairly rough and ready approach to granting legal aid applications, and although some have a positive due process attitude towards legal representation, others are much less inclined to see the value of granting legal aid, particularly for guilty plea cases and for defendants charged with summary offences.[77] One common argument amongst the more restrictive court clerks in the early 1990s[78] was that, save in cases of particular difficulty or complexity, either a duty solicitor or they themselves could adequately protect a defendant's interests. This was based on a (self-fulfilling) assumption that such defendants would end up pleading guilty anyway. But Wilcox and Young (2006) found this point of view only rarely expressed, which is another sign that magistrates' courts proceedings have become more complex in recent years. Nonetheless, many unrepresented defendants still appear in the magistrates' courts and with the reintroduction of the legal aid means test their numbers will rise.

The role of the clerk in assisting unrepresented defendants has been examined by Darbyshire and Astor in separate (if now rather ancient) studies. Darbyshire found that some clerks were helpful and patient whilst others were brusque and intimidating.[79] Astor also noted varying standards of help on offer from clerks but made the important point that the 'allegiance of the clerks was ultimately not to the defendants, but to the

---

[73] Darbyshire P, *Darbyshire on the English Legal System* (London: Sweet & Maxwell, 2008) para 15–16.

[74] All legal advisers are supposed to be qualified as solicitors or barristers by 2010 but there are exemptions (eg for those in post in 1998): ibid.

[75] This latter aspect of their role is covered by Part V, para 55 of the Consolidated Criminal Practice Direction, available from <http://www.justice.gov.uk/>.

[76] The justices' clerk is responsible for case management, but the courts themselves are run by local chief executives.   [77] Young et al (1992: 34–9); Wilcox and Young (2006).

[78] Young et al (1992).   [79] See Darbyshire P, *The Magistrates' Clerk* (Chichester: Barry Rose, 1984).

rules – their insistence was that the court be run "properly", not necessarily that the defendant understood what was going on'.[80] She argues that court clerks have a genuine interest in due process, since as the magistrates' courts' legal advisers they must ensure that the legitimacy of the court is not called into question. At the same time, she acknowledges, they have a strong bureaucratic interest in efficiency and saving court time. She accordingly follows Bottoms and McClean in arguing that the model of the criminal justice process which most accurately described the values 'typically held by humane and enlightened clerks'[81] was neither crime control nor due process, but the liberal bureaucratic model.[82]

According to Bottoms and McClean, the liberal bureaucratic model differs from crime control in that the need for justice to be done and seen to be done is accepted as ultimately overriding the importance of repressing criminal conduct. Priority must be given to protecting the innocent and the importance of formal adjudicative procedures is recognised. Thus far, this sounds like a fair account of the due process model. Bottoms and McClean argue, however, that the liberal bureaucrat has a strong interest in the efficient throughput of cases. Thus, due process protections must be limited. As they put it:

If it were not so, then the whole system of criminal justice, with its ultimate value to the community in the form of liberal and humane crime control, would collapse. Moreover, it is right to build in sanctions to deter those who might otherwise use their 'Due Process' rights frivolously, or to 'try it on'; an administrative system at state expense should not exist for this kind of time-wasting.[83]

They go on to note how the pressures on defendants to elect summary trial – in particular, the fear of a heavier sentence at the Crown Court – and the pressures on defendants to plead guilty all help to smooth the administrative operation of the system. They conclude that:

despite the superficially apparent similarity of the value-systems underlying the Liberal Bureaucratic and Due Process Models, in practice the Liberal Bureaucratic Model offers much stronger support to the aims of the Crime Control Model than the Due Process Model.[84]

Bottoms and McClean contradict themselves here by claiming that 'humane and enlightened' court clerks are genuinely concerned about protecting the innocent and upholding formal adjudicative procedures, at the same time as suggesting that they support rules and sanctions designed to deter defendants from exercising their due process rights. Such rules and sanctions are, after all, quintessential to the crime control model. The essential point to grasp here is that the crime control model represents one end of a spectrum of possible criminal justice systems, at the other end of which

---

[80]   Astor (1986: 232).

[81]   Bottoms A and McClean J, *Defendants in the Criminal Process* (London: Routledge & Kegan Paul, 1976) p 228.   [82]   For a full appraisal of the due process and crime control models see 1.5–1.5.4.

[83]   Bottoms and McClean (1976: 229).   [84]   Ibid: 232.

lies the due process model. By setting up these two opposing models, Packer hoped to illuminate the competing claims and tensions within criminal justice.[85] By contrast, the so-called liberal bureaucratic model is simply a factual description of the operation of the courts. This description reveals that court procedures display elements of the due process model in that contested trials do occur (albeit rarely), legal aid is (usually) available, court clerks will (on occasion) assist unrepresented defendants and so forth. However, the predominance of guilty plea cases, and the pressures on defendants to refrain from pushing the available due process levers, means that the magistrates' courts correspond much more closely to the crime control model than its polar opposite.

To return to Astor's work, while she is undoubtedly correct in suggesting that court clerks are anxious to see the rules followed, what is overlooked is that these rules themselves often incorporate crime control values. A denial of due process can accordingly be achieved without breaking the rules and without any undermining of the court's legitimacy. Thus, the discretion given to court clerks in determining legal aid applications means that they can undermine the due process principle of equality of arms, knowing that this will make a guilty plea more likely.

An illustration of this is provided by the court clerk's role at the pre-trial stage. Clerks played a leading role in developing pre-trial reviews in the form of 'early administrative hearings' (EAHs) introduced by the Crime and Disorder Act 1998 (discussed in ch 8). The Act granted to clerks powers previously reserved to magistrates and arguably blurred the advisory and judicial line between justices' clerks and magistrates. EAHs were part of a package of measures attempting to reduce delays in the magistrates' court.[86] Providing clerks with extra powers of this kind is also an example of the managerialism discussed in ch 1. Court clerks are expected actively to encourage defence disclosure and case settlement.[87] Indeed, defence disclosure is built into the very nature of the EAH since defendants must explain why they think their case merits a grant of legal aid.[88] The enthusiasm of clerks for wheeling and dealing in informal settings, such as immediately prior to a youth court hearing,[89] is inconsistent with the liberal bureaucrat's supposed concern for justice to be done and to be seen to be done.[90] It is, however, consistent with the law and with managerial policy.

New funding methods for courts and performance-related pay for clerks, dependent on the throughput of cases, introduced in the early 1990s are another example of this managerialism. Cases handled are allocated a number of points based on such things as the seriousness of the offence, the number of defendants involved and so forth. The higher the points scored overall, the higher a court's grant (and clerks' pay) will be. Significantly, the points value of a case is not affected by whether it is disposed of by

---

[85] Packer H, *The Limits of the Criminal Sanction* (Stanford: Stanford UP, 1968). See our discussion in ch 1.
[86] Home Office (Narey Report), *Review of Delay in the Criminal Justice System: A Report* (London: Home Office, 1997a).   [87] See eg Baldwin J, *Pre-Trial Justice* (Oxford: Basil Blackwell, 1985) p 43.
[88] For discussion of the merits test see 9.2 above.
[89] See Parker et al, *Receiving Juvenile Justice* (Oxford: Basil Blackwell, 1981) pp 50–5.
[90] Bottoms and McClean (1976: 226).

a guilty plea or following a full trial lasting several hours or days.[91] The government is calling on clerks to pipe a guilty plea tune. While clerks are increasingly taking on judicial functions formerly handled by magistrates, and being pressured to do so in an increasingly managerialist way, their independence from court managers has now been legislatively enshrined.[92] We need new research on the lines of Darbyshire's or Astor's to see whether this shrine of independence is merely presentational.

9.4 **Bail or jail**

Should defendants awaiting trial (or sentencing) be imprisoned? Imprisonment without trial has three obvious attractions for adherents to the crime control model: firstly, it secures the attendance of defendants at court; secondly, it impairs the ability of defendants to interfere with prosecution witnesses; and, thirdly, it prevents defendants from committing further offences whilst awaiting trial. That imprisoned defendants might not have committed any offence in the first place hardly arises due to the factual presumption of guilt at work in this model. Contrast this with the due process model. The normative presumption of innocence is antithetical to pre-trial custody.[93] Preserving the freedom of the innocent and guarding against abuses of state power should be priorities. Pre-trial imprisonment may result in an undermining of the defendant's ability or willingness to contest the case. Punishment is unwarranted for innocent persons, regardless of whether they are ultimately acquitted or convicted on a guilty plea entered under pressure. It will be excessive for those who are guilty but who face charges which would normally attract a non-custodial or short custodial penalty.

To this the crime control adherent can retort that it is all to the good that defendants' willingness and ability to contest cases is undermined by pre-trial detention. The vast majority of defendants are factually guilty and it would put an intolerable strain on the system if they all contested that fact. Moreover, the obvious conclusion to draw from the argument that pre-trial detention may involve punishment which exceeds that likely to be imposed by a court on conviction is that sentencers are too lenient. As Packer puts it: 'For many such persons, a short period spent in jail awaiting trial is not only a useful reminder that crime does not pay but also the only reminder they are likely to get.'[94] The model nevertheless accepts that it would be counter-productive to crime control to overload police cells and the prison system with minor offenders. It maintains, however, that any limits to pre-trial detention should be governed by this consideration of crime control efficiency, rather than by any abstract notion of a right to pre-trial liberty.

---

[91] Lord Chancellor's Department, A New Framework for Local Justice (Cm 1829) (London: LCD, 1992).
[92] Courts Act 2003, s 29.
[93] Especially as custodial remands can be for months: see below. Also see Raifeartaigh U, 'Reconciling Bail Law with the Presumption of Innocence' (1997) 17 OJLS 1.   [94] Packer (1968: 212).

The freedom model shares most of the suppositions of the due process model, but would not ignore the interests of victims and witnesses in being protected from intimidation and 'further' harm by those defendants who manifest a clear and present danger of committing serious offences. It would also give weight to the fact that imprisoning people before trial does not stop them committing offences. There are plenty of opportunities for that within prison.[95] In other words, this model would seek to maximise the freedom of all involved, but in a principled way. We shall argue in this section that crime control values are more influential than those of the other models.

People charged with minor offences usually receive a summons to appear on a particular date and no further restriction on their liberty is imposed.[96] With more serious charges, the courts typically proceed by way of a series of remand hearings. The purpose of these hearings is to determine what degree of liberty defendants should be permitted to retain pending trial. Defendants may either be remanded in custody or remanded on bail. Since 1991 magistrates have been empowered to remand defendants for extended periods in custody of up to 28 days in duration.[97]

Table 9.2 shows that in 2007 about 6% of defendants appearing in the magistrates' courts (including motoring offenders and others charged with summary offences) were remanded in custody by the police pending first court appearance – about 110,000 people. The magistrates remanded 52,000 defendants (3%) in custody. Thus, although the *proportion* of defendants who are remanded in custody is relatively small, the numbers involved are large. Table 9.2 shows that the numbers peaked at the turn of the century and appear to be declining towards levels seen in the mid 1990s. Untried prisoners on remand make up around 10% of the prison population, and therefore contribute greatly to prison overcrowding. Traditionally conditions for defendants held on remand are amongst the worst that exist within the prison system. Remand prisoners have played an active role in the sporadic outbreaks of rioting that have left some establishments (most notably Strangeways in April 1990) in smouldering ruins.[98] Keeping unconvicted defendants in stinking conditions might not conflict with the letter of the law, but if the concept of human rights is to mean more than a mere sign-up to an international treaty the least we could do is to treat remand prisoners more favourably than convicted offenders.[99] Some prisoners have received

---

[95] See, for example, O'Donnell I and Edgar K, 'Routine Victimisation in Prisons' (1998) 37 Howard JCJ 266.

[96] The Criminal Justice Act 2003 (part 4) included provisions for a new procedure to replace summonsing. It gave police and prosecutors powers to issue a written charge and requisition (see Criminal Procedure Rules Part 7 at <http://www.justice.gov.uk/>).

[97] Magistrates' Courts (Remand in Custody) Order 1991, SI 1991/2667.

[98] See Morgan R and Jones S, 'Bail or Jail?' in Stockdale E and Casale S (eds), *Criminal Justice Under Stress* (London: Blackstone, 1992).

[99] See, for example, Windlesham Lord, 'Punishment and Prevention: The Inappropriate Prisoners' [1988] Crim LR 140; and Woolf, *Prison Disturbances, April 1990: Report of an Inquiry* (Cm 1456) (London: HMSO, 1991), discussed by Morgan and Jones (1992). A decade after the Woolf report, a HM Inspector of Prisons report revealed remand conditions were still a problem (*Unjust Deserts: A Thematic Review of the Chief Inspector of Prisons of the Treatment and Conditions for Unsentenced Prisoners in England and Wales* (London: Home Office, 2000).

Table 9.2 Remands in custody (%)

	1998	2002	2004	2007
Summonsed	55	54	59	56
Arrested and bailed	38	40	35	38
Arrested and remanded in custody	7 (n=143,000)	7 (n=141,000)	6 (n=135,000)	6 (n=110,000)
Remanded in custody by magistrates (subset of row 3)	5 (n=98,000)	4 (n=82,000)	3 (n=67,000)	3 (n=52,000)

Source: Ministry of Justice (2008b) tables 4.1 and 4.3.

compensation for breach of their human rights due to the lack of integral sanitation in cells of more than single occupation.[100]

9.4.1 **The principles of bail law**

As we saw in 5.3, Art 6(2) of the ECHR affirms the presumption of innocence. Although the provision that allows arrest and detention in order to bring a suspect before a court (discussed in 4.3) clearly also allows pre-trial remands in custody, this may be done only 'when it is reasonably considered necessary to prevent his committing an offence or fleeing after having done so' (Art 5(1)(c)). This is qualified by Art 5(3):

Everyone arrested or detained…shall be brought promptly before a judge…and shall be entitled to trial within a reasonable time or to release pending trial. Release may be conditioned by guarantees to appear for trial.

To comply with the ECHR (and thus the HRA 1998), then, it seems that the law:

(a) must allow remands in custody only when reasonably considered necessary;

(b) can allow conditions to be set for bail;

(c) must minimise delay for defendants remanded in custody.

English law is largely governed by the Bail Act 1976, along with some important later additions. Section 4(1) provides that a defendant 'shall be granted bail except as provided in Sch 1 to this Act'.[101] This creates a due process presumption in favour of bail (a right to bail) although the strength of that presumption depends on the nature of the exceptions set out in Sch 1. On the face of it, this complies with the ECHR,[102] but we shall see that English law does not, or may not do so (depending on how the courts apply it) in some important respects. Another important due process protection which

---

[100] <http://news.bbc.co.uk/1/hi/scotland/7060991.stm> (accessed 5 January 2010).

[101] For an account of the genesis and (limited) impact of the Bail Act 1976, see King (1981: 130–7).

[102] See, in particular, *Caballero v UK* (2000) 30 EHRR 643.

is part of the English and Welsh system is the right of appeal against adverse bail decisions. In the rest of this section we will examine each of these issues in turn, seeing how far the law corresponds with the reality, and how valuable the human rights approach is in protecting the freedom of defendants.

9.4.2 Criteria for withholding bail: the law

For defendants charged with non-imprisonable (ie relatively trivial) offences, bail need not be granted if there has been a previous failure to answer bail and the court believes that there would be a further failure to appear on this occasion. The restrictiveness of this test is welcome but its practical impact is slight because such defendants would generally be proceeded against by way of summons from the outset.

For defendants charged with imprisonable offences, the grounds for refusing bail are much wider.[103] Bail need not be granted to defendants charged with imprisonable offences which are indictable if the court is satisfied that there are 'substantial grounds' for believing that the defendant, if released on bail, would either fail to appear, commit an offence or interfere with witnesses or otherwise obstruct the course of justice. Nor need bail be granted if a court is satisfied that the defendant has previously failed to answer bail for the offence or ought to be kept in custody for his or her own 'protection' or 'welfare', or where there has been insufficient time to obtain enough information about the person for the court. In determining whether there are substantial grounds for believing that a defendant would fail to appear, commit an offence or obstruct the course of justice, Sch 1 to the Bail Act 1976 provides that the court is to have regard to, firstly, the nature and seriousness of the offence; secondly, the character, previous convictions, associations and community ties of the person; thirdly, the person's record in regard to any previous grant of bail; and finally, the strength of the evidence against the person.[104]

The due process model would object to most of the grounds for detention laid down in the 1976 Act. Whether the freedom model would object would depend on how discriminating the courts were in making use of them, and on the nature of the offences to which they were applied. We will examine here the three main grounds for refusing bail.

Obstructing the course of justice

To detain someone because they might interfere with a prosecution witness is manifestly unsatisfactory, since it penalises the defendant for a supposed disposition. Other

---

[103] Bail Act 1976, Sch 1, Pt 1, paras 2–6, although s 52 of the Criminal Justice and Immigration Act 2008 amended the Bail Act so that the grounds on which bail can be refused for imprisonable summary only offences (and criminal damage below £5,000) are more in line with non-imprisonable offences. Essentially the distinction between non-imprisonable and imprisonable summary offences was removed, but some new grounds for refusing bail in imprisonable summary cases were granted including where the court has insufficient information and where it believes the defendant may commit an offence of violence or put a person in fear of violence. [104] Bail Act 1976, Sch 1, Pt 1, para 9.

ways of reducing the risk of interference can be employed, such as offering police protection to particularly vulnerable witnesses, making bail conditional on the defendant keeping well away from such persons, or making it a crime to intimidate witnesses.[105] However, there is undoubtedly some witness intimidation,[106] and this reduces the freedom of victims and witnesses. From a freedom perspective, it would only be proper to remand in custody on this ground if there is evidence that a person has manifested a clear intent to obstruct the course of justice if left at liberty. The level of proof required for that evidence would need careful consideration.

Committing an offence

A similar objection lies against the ground that the defendant will commit an offence if released. Under this ground too, someone may be deprived of liberty because of a supposed disposition. The objection is stronger here, however, since a prediction that someone will commit an offence if released rests on the assumption that the defendant committed the offence with which he or she is currently charged. The law thus allows a factual presumption of guilt to override the normative presumption of innocence. Nor should we forget that putting someone behind bars pending trial does not stop them committing offences; 'routine victimisation' takes place in prisons.[107]

The issue of 'dangerousness' as a ground for detaining persons not yet convicted of crime, or for extending (perhaps indefinitely) the period of detention for those who have been convicted, has been much debated in the context of sentencing and parole, and a similar dilemma applies to the bail decision.[108] The due process model would argue that the defendants' interests should in every case be given special weight. But it would be an affront to common sense to say that a suspected serial killer or pathological rapist should automatically be released on bail. There is also the particular problem of people charged with offences committed while already on bail.[109] The issue of allowing bail for those accused of murder has recently become significant as a result of a number of high profile cases where murders have been committed by offenders already on bail for murder or serious violent offences.[110] The case of Gary Weddell, a police inspector who murdered his mother-in-law whilst on bail for murdering his wife, is just one of the cases which precipitated a review of the law in this area.[111]

This is where the freedom approach offers a way of reconciling conflicting interests. Under that approach it is legitimate to weigh the risk of future victimisation (as

---

[105] As it now is, under CJPO 1994, s 51.

[106] Home Office, *Speaking Up for Justice, Report of the Interdepartmental Working Group on the Treatment of Vulnerable or Intimidated Witnesses in the Criminal Justice System* (London: Home Office, 1998b) ch 4.

[107] O'Donnell and Edgar (1998).

[108] For a discussion of the 'dangerousness debate' see Padfield N, 'Bailing and Sentencing the Dangerous' in Walker N (ed), *Dangerous People* (London: Blackstone, 1996). For a study of risk based decision-making see Hood R and Shute S, *The Parole System at Work* (Home Office Research Study No 202) (London: Home Office, 2000).   [109] See ss 25 and 26 of the CJPO 1994, as amended by CJA 2003, discussed below.

[110] See provisions in the Coroners and Justice Bill 2008–09, discussed below.

[111] An inquest into his suicide revealed he possibly planned to kill more of his wife's family, *The Telegraph*, 12 April 2008.

with future intimidation as discussed above) against the freedom lost to remanded defendants. The freedom perspective also alerts us to the fact that the alternatives to a remand in custody might be more corrosive of freedom as the freedom lost by remand is certain, and that to future victims only a possibility. Thus strong safeguards are necessary. In particular, proper standards are needed to determine who may be presumed sufficiently dangerous to warrant a departure from the normative position that no-one should be imprisoned until convicted. By allowing this ground to be applied for offences which are merely imprisonable (rather than ones in which imprisonment is likely), and on the basis of little hard information, the Bail Act singularly fails this test.

Failure to answer bail

To detain defendants because of a fear that they might not attend voluntarily to answer the charges against them has greater merit, since the presumption of pre-trial liberty would quickly fall into disrepute if defendants absconded in large numbers. This fear should be properly grounded, however, and much depends on how magistrates make their predictions as to who is likely to abscond if granted bail and what level of risk they are prepared to tolerate. The factors that they are required to take into account, such as the seriousness of the offence and previous bail record, while clearly bearing on the risk of a defendant absconding, are open to wide interpretation.

For decision-making on this ground to conform to the freedom model, three things are necessary. First, the offence needs to be sufficiently serious for the loss of freedom of the detained defendant to be outweighed by the interests of the state in securing a conviction (if guilt is proved) and imposing immediate punishment. To remand in custody for, say, several weeks, someone accused of minor criminal damage for which a fine would be imposed would be disproportionate. Second, mechanisms to achieve attendance short of detention should be used wherever possible. Section 6 of the 1976 Act makes it an offence punishable by imprisonment and/or a fine to fail to answer to bail without reasonable cause. This threat should be enough to guarantee the attendance of the great majority of those facing less serious charges, while most of the rest can eventually be tracked down and punished accordingly. In addition, s 3(6) allows for persons to be released on bail subject to conditions (examined next). Finally, decision-making needs to be consistent, principled and based on high quality information (examined thereafter).

9.4.3 Conditional bail

Section 3(6) of the 1976 Act allows for persons to be released on bail subject to such conditions as appear to the court to be necessary to secure that the defendant surrenders to the court at the appropriate time, does not commit an offence on bail or obstruct the course of justice and is available for the purpose of enabling a court report to be prepared to assist in sentencing. Section 13(1) of the Criminal Justice Act (CJA) 2003 made it possible to add conditions for an adult defendant's own protection, or for a youth's welfare. Defendants released on conditional bail typically have to report to the police at periodic intervals, or must reside at a specified address (such as a bail hostel) or must keep away from certain places or people. In 2007 the government announced a Bail Accommodation and Support Service (BASS).[112] BASS is operated by a private firm providing beds for around 500 people in approximately 150 bail hostels across England and Wales. It is part of the government strategy to encourage a greater use of conditional bail for defendants thought to pose too great a risk if released unconditionally. Bail hostels are supposed to get around the problem of bailing defendants who have no suitable alternative address, although the rigour with which courts enquire into the suitability of addresses offered for conditional bail has been questioned.[113] Around half of all bail is conditional. Courts vary considerably in their use of conditions, and some use them in ways contrary to the Bail Act, such as imposing a requirement to report to the police station the day before the next court appearance so that the defendant can be reminded about that appearance.[114] This practice fits so well with the dominant managerial ethos that it can only be a matter of time before a law is passed to legitimise it. A 'precedent', should one be thought necessary, is s 54(2) of the Crime and Disorder Act 1998, which allows a condition to be attached to a grant of bail requiring a defendant to attend an interview with a legal adviser. Combined with the device of the early administrative hearing (see 9.3 above), s 54(2) is designed to ensure that defendants can be 'processed' by the court as fast as possible.

There are many difficulties with bail conditions. One is that they may impose excessive restrictions on the liberty of defendants whose alleged offences are 'political'. This is particularly so as one of the grounds for imposing a condition is to neutralise the fear that a defendant will commit an offence (any offence) if bailed. The breadth and vagueness of many criminal laws entails that highly restrictive conditions may lawfully be imposed. Thus in *Mansfield Justices, ex p Sharkey*[115] the Divisional Court upheld the legality of a condition that defendants facing charges arising out of picketing did not take part in any further demonstration connected with the trade dispute between striking miners and the National Coal Board. The court's reasoning was that those attempting to prevent miners going to work by force of numbers and threats of violence would have been guilty of at least the public order offence of threatening behaviour. Anyone attending such a demonstration must be regarded as knowingly taking part in that threatening behaviour. To guard against the risk of the defendants committing offences on bail, it was, the court argued, necessary to prevent them from picketing. However, Percy-Smith and Hillyard argue that the widespread policy of

---

[112] <http://www.justice.gov.uk/news/newsrelease180607a.htm> (accessed 5 January 2010).

[113] In the case of Anthony Peart, who killed a man who remonstrated with him for throwing chips on a bus, the defendant was bailed to live at an address which did not exist. The *Peart Review* concluded that there was 'insufficient rigour in respect of challenging the validity of proposed bail conditions' (<http://www.hmcpsi.gov.uk/index.php?id=47&docID=776> – accessed 5 January 2010).

[114] Hucklesby A, 'The Use and Abuse of Conditional Bail' (1994) 33 Howard JCJ 258; Raine J and Willson M, 'The Imposition of Conditions in Bail Decisions' (1996) 35 Howard JCJ 256.

[115] [1985] 1 All ER 193.

imposing this form of conditional bail on striking miners was motivated by a desire not to control crime, but to hamper legitimate protest.[116] Similarly, Vogler, who analysed mass custodial remands in the 'riots' of 1981, found that in Manchester, for example, curfews were used almost en masse. Many defendants charged with minor offences such as obstruction of the highway (maximum penalty: £50 fine) were being subjected to stringent restrictions for as much as four months.[117] We documented recent instances of this pre-emptive strategy, involving environmental protests against power stations, in 3.2.1. When laws are drawn in broad crime control terms there is the clear potential for them to be used in a repressive manner for political reasons.[118] The scope for variability is shown by Dhami, who also found significant reliance on extra-legal factors, as well as on factors specified in the legislation.[119] Of course, the committed political protester may simply ignore bail conditions, and hope to escape detection for breach of bail by merging with the crowd. But this is not so easy now that the Criminal Justice and Immigration Act 2008 has amended the Bail Act to make clear that electronic monitoring can be imposed as a condition of bail.[120]

The second difficulty with bail conditions is that they are sometimes unrelated to the objection to bail voiced by the CPS. For example, curfews should be used for defendants thought to pose a risk of offending, but they are sometimes used when the objection is that the defendant may abscond. This sometimes happens when solicitors offer any conditions to bolster their application for bail, or when courts simply attach conditions indiscriminately.[121] It also happens when conditions are imposed as a form of 'summary punishment' – for example, imposing a condition of residence to stop a defendant going on holiday or visiting friends.[122]

Third, conditions are imposed on some defendants who would otherwise have received unconditional bail, rather than those who were genuinely at risk of a custodial remand. The evidence on this point is somewhat unsatisfactory and equivocal in nature although it seems that some 'net widening' has taken place.[123] Raine and Willson, for example, found that many defence solicitors routinely offer bail conditions to the court in cases where they might have secured unconditional bail. And

---

116 Percy-Smith J and Hillyard P, 'Miners in the Arms of the Law: A Statistical Analysis' (1985) 12 JLS 345. See to like effect Blake N, 'Picketing, Justice and the Law' in Fine B and Millar R (eds), *Policing the Miners' Strike* (London: Lawrence and Wishart, 1985).

117 Vogler R, *Reading the Riot Act* (Milton Keynes: Open UP, 1991) p 153.

118 See our earlier discussion of this in the context of stop-search powers in ch 2.

119 Dhami M, 'Conditional Bail Decision Making in the Magistrates' Court' (2004) 43 Howard JCJ 27.

120 Bail Act 1976, s 3AB (as amended by CJIA 2008, s 51 and Sch 11). The courts may only impose such a condition if the defendant would otherwise not be granted bail.   121 Hucklesby (1994).

122 Raine and Willson (1996).

123 Consider eg the debate concerning whether bail hostels are being used to accommodate persons who would otherwise have been remanded in custody: White K and Brody S, 'The Use of Bail Hostels' [1980] Crim LR 420; Pratt J and Bray K, 'Bail Hostels – Alternatives to Custody?' (1985) 25 BJ Crim 160; and Lewis H and Mair G, *Bail and Probation Work II: The Use of London Bail Hostels for Bailees* (Home Office Research and Planning Unit Paper No 50) (London: Home Office, 1989). Also see Hucklesby (1994).

sometimes a defence solicitor and a prosecutor will strike a 'deal' that the latter will not oppose bail if the former does not oppose conditions.[124]

Although breach of a condition of bail is not an offence, it may lead to defendants being brought back before the court for reconsideration of their remand status. Indeed, defendants can be arrested if the police have 'reasonable grounds' to believe that they have broken, or *are likely to break*, any of their conditions.[125] Under any of these circumstances 'the defendant need not be granted bail'.[126] Conditions often operate in arbitrary and discriminatory ways. Financial conditions weigh far more heavily on poor people than on others, and sometimes lead to remands in custody.[127] Residence conditions similarly operate unfairly on the homeless and rootless. Most other conditions are largely unenforceable. When curfews, for example, are breached, the only defendants at any risk at all of being caught (leaving aside those who are electronically tagged) are those who the police recognise. These will usually be defendants who are 'known to the police' or who stand out – such as members of ethnic minorities in largely-white areas.[128] The opportunity for the discriminatory use of discretion is obvious.

9.4.4 Criteria for withholding bail: the decision-making process

We have seen that about 10% of all defendants who are arrested and charged (as distinct from summonsed) are remanded in custody. The custody remand rate varies considerably between different courts. Hucklesby, for example, found custody rates of 9% in two of the courts she studied, but 25% in the other court, even though the case mix was substantially the same in all three. Even in the two apparently similar courts, similar cases were treated dissimilarly. Variations between courts in the way criteria are evaluated therefore produce a 'justice by geography' effect:[129] what happens to a defendant in a borderline case depends as much on the court as on the case, just as with other aspects of magistrates' decision-making such as legal aid and sentencing. This is due largely to different 'court cultures'. One element in a court's culture is whether or not it includes a stipendiary (who, Hucklesby found, granted bail less often).[130] Nonetheless, despite the *differences* between courts, the features which are *common* to all courts are more important.

---

[124] Hucklesby A, 'Remand Decision Makers' [1997b] Crim LR 269.   [125] Bail Act 1976, s 7.

[126] Bail Act 1976, s 4. In an attempt to ensure ECHR compliance, the CJA 2003 amended provisions of the Bail Act 1976 so that courts are now required to focus on whether there are substantial grounds for fearing that a defendant charged with a non-imprisonable offence who has already failed to appear at court or breached a bail condition (etc) would *in future* fail to surrender, commit an offence or obstruct the course of justice. For details see Taylor et al, *Blackstone's Guide to the Criminal Justice Act 2003* (Oxford: OUP, 2004) p 18.

[127] Cavadino P and Gibson B, *Bail: The Law, Best Practice and the Debate* (Winchester: Waterside Press, 1993) p 170.   [128] Hucklesby (1994); Raine and Willson (1996).

[129] Similar to the effect of local police decision-making leading to cautioning variations – see 7.4.

[130] Hucklesby A, 'Court Culture: An Explanation of Variations in the Use of Bail by Magistrates Courts' (1997a) 36 Howard JCJ 129. The differences between lay and stipendiary magistrates are discussed in 9.5

The absence of adversarialism

The ECHR and the Bail Act 1976 appear to require bail to be granted, in normal circumstances, unless there is clear evidence to substantiate a belief that one of the evils envisaged by Sch 1 will occur if the defendant is released. Most remand hearings are uncontested. Hucklesby's study of 1,524 remand hearings found that in around 85% of cases the CPS did not request a remand in custody. And in only just over a half of all cases where the CPS requested a remand in custody was this opposed by the defence. It is very rare for magistrates to question these agreed proposals.[131] Hucklesby therefore argues that the real decision-makers are the police (who make recommendations to the CPS), the CPS and defence lawyers. She found that in virtually every case where unconditional bail was recommended by CPS, this was granted; in virtually every case where conditional bail was recommended by CPS, this was also granted; and in 86% of cases where custody was requested by CPS, this was granted too. And although police or prosecution objections to bail are not invariably upheld by magistrates, *unconditional* bail is hardly ever granted when bail is opposed.[132] In one respect the analysis by Hucklesby is thin. When she argues that the lack of adversarialism indicates that magistrates are less active in decision-making than are police, CPS and lawyers, she does not refer to her own findings elsewhere that these professionals know their local courts and tailor their applications accordingly. In other words, CPS will apply for remands in custody in certain types of borderline case in some courts but not others, and defence solicitors will oppose this more in some courts than others.[133]

In only a small proportion of remand hearings, then, is bail contested – less than 10%. The low percentage of cases in which the defence challenges CPS recommendations for custody has to be seen in the context of s 154 of the Criminal Justice Act 1988. This provides that, once a defendant has been refused bail, any argument may be used to support an application at the next remand hearing whether or not it has been used previously but thereafter 'the court need not hear arguments as to fact or law which it has heard previously'. Courts often interpret this as a licence to hear a maximum of two applications.[134] Thus Hucklesby found that where bail was opposed by CPS, defence lawyers usually applied for bail at the first appearance (in 85% of these cases) but did so in less than half of subsequent appearances. The lack of adversarialism also reflects the evaluation that many defence lawyers make – rightly or wrongly – of their clients' cases. Put bluntly, they do not want to lose credibility with the court, and often put that consideration above the interests of their clients.[135] Both Hucklesby and McConville et al found that when lawyers are instructed, contrary to their professional advice, to apply for bail, they let the court know that they do not have their heart in it by using

---

below. For another example showing differences between courts, see Paterson F and Whittaker C, *Operating Bail* (Edinburgh: Scottish Office, 1994).

[131] Hucklesby (1997b: 271).   [132] Hucklesby (1997b: table 1).

[133] Hucklesby (1997a). This happens in Scotland too: Paterson and Whittaker (1994).

[134] See also *Blyth Juvenile Court, ex p G* [1991] Crim LR 693 and *Dover and East Kent Justices, ex p Dean* (1991) 156 JP 357.   [135] Hucklesby (1997b); McConville et al (1994).

coded language such as 'I am instructed to say that…' Sometimes the code is not difficult to crack, as with the following lawyer's culinary comments to the bench:

He tells me – and I know you will take this with a pinch of salt, but I am instructed to say it so I shall say it – that he intended to surrender to the warrant. As I say, you may take that with a pinch of salt but I have said what I was instructed to say by my client.[136]

As Brink and Stone comment on the basis of research with similar findings:

Such an attitude is hardly unique to criminal solicitors in this country, but wherever it is found it is generally regarded as a corruption of the adversary system of justice. Lawyers, as officers of the court, have an obligation to serve the cause of justice, but in an adversary system justice is served by the strongest possible arguments being put in every case.[137]

The findings of Brink and Stone[138] are all the more striking given that their research focused on solicitors who were identified by the London Criminal Courts Solicitors' Association as 'highly qualified, experienced and respected'.

The information on which bail decisions are made

The Bail Act's presumption in favour of bail fits with the ECHR's stipulation that bail decisions be based on *evidence* (not 'speculation') and that the burden of proof be on the prosecution.[139] But Hucklesby found that bail was granted in less than 1 in 3 contested bail applications, partly because defence solicitors are seen by magistrates as less objective than the CPS. Consequently, challenging the police version of events, as put forward by the CPS, is usually unsuccessful, despite the fact that strength of evidence is supposed to be a consideration under the Bail Act.[140] Clearly defendants have an uphill struggle to overcome CPS objections to the 'right to bail'.

But how, in reality, could it be otherwise? Terms like 'prediction' and 'risk' are virtual synonyms for 'speculation', so how could it ever be *proved* that someone will abscond or commit 'further' offences? Moreover, how could it be proved *beyond reasonable doubt* as some ECHR cases seem to suggest?[141] The rhetoric is here at odds with the law, as well as the practice. As Hayes, a magistrate and academic points out:

the bail decision is a matter of guesswork, of hunches, not capable of precise explanation. Will he turn up, will he do it again? Each magistrate will apply his own criteria and his own values to his decision.[142]

---

[136] McConville et al (1994: 181).

[137] Brink B and Stone C, 'Defendants Who Do Not Ask for Bail' [1988] Crim LR 152.

[138] Brink and Stone (1998: 153).   [139] *W v Switzerland* (1993) 17 EHRR 60.

[140] Hucklesby A, 'Bail or Jail? The Practical Operation of the Bail Act 1976' (1996) 23 JLS 213.

[141] See cases cited in Burrow J, 'Bail and the Human Rights Act 1998' (2000) 150 NLJ 677. The same problem arises concerning defendants 'likely' to breach bail conditions.

[142] Hayes M, 'Where Now the Right to Bail?' [1981] Crim LR 20 at p 22. The 'values' of magistrates, and of the legal framework they operate within, may result in some women getting a raw deal: Eaton M, 'The Question of Bail' in Carlen P and Worrall A (eds), *Gender, Crime and Justice* (Milton Keynes: Open UP, 1987).

The complexity of the Bail Act's provisions and the importance of what is at stake might lead one to think that bail hearings are painstaking affairs. Go and visit your local magistrates' court and you will see for yourself the whirlwind reality. In Zander's study of London courts, the amount of time spent discussing whether defendants should retain their liberty was five minutes or less in 86% of the 261 remand cases observed.[143] Even where a remand in custody is sought, proceedings are rapid. As many as 60% of such decisions in Zander's study were reached within five minutes.[144] Magistrates' courts were castigated in the Woolf Report on prison disturbances for giving insufficient status to the bail decision; often taking decisions hurriedly on a Saturday morning.[145] Another indication that bail decision-making is cursory, if not slipshod, is that in at least some courts defendants have been convicted of the non-existent offence of breaching bail conditions.[146] Doherty and East identify the main reason for the speed with which bail decisions are taken as being the heavy workload of the magistrates' courts. The participants in the proceedings are all well known to each other and are aware that they are expected to assist in the speedy disposal of business:

In these circumstances it is probably inevitable that a camaraderie develops between the participants, and this no doubt partially explains why so few of the hearings attended were markedly adversarial in character...In a situation where there is an expectation that cases are dealt with quickly, often in a non-adversarial fashion, it is perhaps not surprising that only limited information of a low quality is made available to the courts.[147]

In addition to the limited information given to the courts, most information comes from the police. Just as the police 'construct' cases for prosecution, making cases appear stronger (or weaker) than they might otherwise appear,[148] so they can do this with remand applications and, as we have seen, the CPS generally do as the police ask, and the magistrates generally follow suit.[149] Research has also shown that a police decision to either bail a suspect from the police station or remand to next court appearance is an important factor in determining whether the CPS and the court will favour bail or remand.[150] This is something akin to prosecution momentum (see ch 7). Magistrates, with their concern for upholding authority, are naturally disinclined to 'overturn' a police decision to hold someone in custody pending trial. The police thus exert a strong influence over bail processes.

---

[143] Zander M, 'Operation of the Bail Act in London Magistrates' Courts' (1979) 129 NLJ 108.

[144] Zander (1979).

[145] See The Rt Hon Lord Justice Woolf, *Prison Disturbances April 1990, Report of an Inquiry* (Parts I and II) and His Honour Judge Stephen Tumim (Part II) (Cm 1456) (London: HMSO, 1991) para 10.80.

[146] See Cameron N, 'Bail Act 1976: Two Inconsistencies and an Imaginary Offence' (1980) 130 NLJ 382.

[147] Doherty M and East R, 'Bail Decisions in Magistrates' Courts' (1985) 25 BJ Crim 251 at p 263.

[148] McConville et al (1991); case construction is discussed in ch 7.

[149] Also see Phillips C and Brown D, *Entry into the Criminal Justice System* (Home Office Research Study No 185) (London: Home Office, 1998); Mhlanga B, *Race and the CPS* (London: SO, 1999) pp 134–5.

[150] Burrows et al, *Improving Bail Decisions: The Bail Process Project, Phase 1* (Research and Planning Unit Paper 90) (London: Home Office, 1994).

Bail information schemes might go some way towards remedying these problems. These schemes are now meant to operate in all prisons holding remand prisoners[151] as well as in magistrates' courts.[152] These schemes involve the probation service providing verified information to the CPS in cases where the police indicate an objection to bail. It is argued that such schemes are successful in persuading prosecutors and magistrates to adopt a more liberal attitude to the grant of bail without leading to more offending on bail or absconding.[153] Since some courts (albeit the smaller ones) currently operate without bail information schemes, and since many of those remanded in custody find it difficult to access prison-based schemes,[154] many magistrates have little on which to base their decisions. The effect of bail information schemes is limited. This is confirmed by Dhami, who argues that the only thing that these schemes increase is the confidence that magistrates have in their decisions.[155]

Breach of bail

The police often complain that too many defendants are released on bail. In the early 1990s they highlighted the 'growing problem' of 'bail bandits', ie persons offending while on bail.[156] The research evidence, however, tended to suggest that in fact there had been little change in the rate of known offending on bail over a 20-year period. Around 10%–17% of those bailed are known to commit an offence.[157] Many regard such levels of offending on bail as unacceptable, but it is exceptionally difficult to identify who will, and who will not, offend while on bail. The greater the number of defendants remanded in custody because of fears of offending, the more remands in custody there will be of defendants who would *not* offend while on bail. Indeed, a Scottish study found that offending on bail was hardly higher in the court with the highest bail rate than in the court with the lowest rate.[158]

---

[151] HM Prison Service, *Instruction to Governors No 67/1999 Bail Information Schemes* (London: HM Prison Service, 1999).

[152] CPS, *Annual Report, 2002–3* (London: CPS, 2004). See generally Mair G and Lloyd C, 'Policy and Progress in the Development of Bail Schemes in England and Wales' in Paterson F (ed), *Understanding Bail in Britain* (Edinburgh: Scottish Office, 1996).

[153] Mair and Lloyd (1996). The same is true of Scotland where similar schemes have been established: McIvor G, 'The Impact of Bail Services in Scotland' in Paterson (1996).

[154] HM Inspectorate of Prisons for England and Wales, *Unjust Deserts* (December 2000) pp 47–8 (available from <http://www.justice.gov.uk/inspectorates/hmi-prisons/docs/unjust-rps.pdf> – accessed 5 January 2010).

[155] Dhami M, 'Do Bail Information Schemes Really Affect Bail Decisions?' (2002) 41 Howard JCJ 245.

[156] See the articles in (1991) Police Review, 19 July and 6 September, which summarise the results of studies carried out by the Avon and Somerset and Northumbria Police, respectively. For a critique, see Hucklesby A, 'The Problem with Bail Bandits' (1992) 142 NLJ 558. And what of the politically invisible 'Remand Bandits' (remand prisoners committing crimes against other remand prisoners or prison staff)?

[157] Hucklesby A and Marshall E, 'Tackling Offending on Bail' (2000) 39 Howard JCJ 150. Also see Brown D, *Offending on Bail and Police Use of Conditional Bail* (Home Office Research Findings No 72) (London: Home Office, 1998); Morgan P and Henderson P, *Remand Decisions and Offending on Bail* (Home Office Research Study No 184) (London: Home Office, 1998).   [158] Paterson and Whittaker (1994).

Despite this, the Government in 1992 announced a number of proposals aimed at tackling 'bail banditry'.[159] One gave the prosecution for the first time the right to appeal against a grant of bail (see below). Another initiative was contained in s 26 of the Criminal Justice and Public Order Act 1994 (CJPO) aimed at reducing the likelihood of bail bandits getting further bail.[160] This was taken further by s 14 of the CJA 2003 which states that adults charged with an indictable or either-way offence committed whilst already on bail, 'may not be granted bail unless the court is satisfied that there is no significant risk of his committing an offence on bail',[161] thus introducing another exception to the ever-diminishing 'right to bail'. However, the practical impact of the provisions has probably been limited since alleged offending on bail could always have been used as a reason for refusing bail (constituting, as it does, compelling evidence of a risk of the offender committing an offence if released on bail).[162] In addition to the problem of some defendants offending on bail, about 12% of those bailed by magistrates' courts in 2007 failed to appear.[163]

All such bare statistics must be treated with caution. For example, statistics on absconding may overstate the problem in that there may be good reasons why defendants fail to appear at court (eg illness or death). Statistics of offending on bail may understate the problem, in that much offending on bail no doubt remains undetected, or may overstate it in that they take no account of the possible triviality of the offences in question or the fact that increasing delays in prosecuting cases are likely to lead to an increased offending on bail rate.[164] That people 'abscond' or offend on bail is not necessarily a sign that the remand decision was wrong.

Wrongful denial of bail

It is similarly impossible to estimate the number of defendants who are wrongly denied bail. There are three broad categories. First, in 2007, 14% of all defendants remanded in custody were acquitted or not proceeded against (table 9.3). Second, 29% of those convicted were given non-custodial sentences (table 9.4).

In total, less than half of all defendants in custody before trial are put in custody afterwards. This is, on the face of it, a gross denial of due process and freedom standards. However, the fact that many persons denied bail are not subsequently convicted may be testimony to the fairness of the courts.[165] In other words, adjudicators seem able in at least some cases to overcome the prejudicial effect created by the sight of an accused being brought up from the cells under the courtroom. Similarly, the high proportionate use of non-custodial sentences for those denied bail and subsequently

---

[159] Hucklesby and Marshall (2000).

[160] The 1994 provision made little difference to bail rates: Hucklesby and Marshall (2000).

[161] By s 15 of the CJA a similar attempt to tighten the screw is made in respect of bailed offenders who fail to surrender at the due time: Taylor et al (2004: 19–20).

[162] Hucklesby and Marshall (2000). Section 14 also changed the test for youths. For details see Taylor et al (2004: 19).

[163] Ministry of Justice (2008b: para 4.15).   [164] Hucklesby (1992: 560).

[165] Morgan and Jones (1992: 38–9).

Table 9.3 Bail and custody: acquittals and convictions (magistrates' proceedings only), 2004

	Acquit/discontinue	Fail appear	Convicted/committed for trial
Remand in custody	14%	5%	54%
Bailed	20%	12%	66%

Source: (Ministry of Justice, 2008b) table 4.6.

Table 9.4 Bail and custody: disposals (magistrates' courts and Crown Courts), 2007

	Non-custodial sentence	Custody
Remand in custody	29%	23%
Bailed	54%	5%

Source: (Ministry of Justice, 2008b) table 4.6.

convicted does not prove that the remand decision was incorrect.[166] Defendants may, for example, have been remanded for their own protection or because it was feared that they would not answer to bail.[167] Some defendants will have been judged to have suffered enough and not be given the custodial sentences that they might otherwise have got. Perhaps we should be more worried about the positive correlation between denial of bail on the one hand and conviction and custodial sentences on the other, in so far as the former may partially explain the latter. HM Chief Inspector of Prisons found that remand prisoners lacked effective access to legal reference books, had their legal correspondence opened and examined far more often than appeared justified, and experienced great difficulties in speaking to their solicitors by phone. He concluded that:

the barriers to effective communication with legal advisers constitute an obstacle to the fair and just treatment of unsentenced prisoners which may well not stand up to legal challenge under the Human Rights Act, Article 6, which guarantees rights consistent with the proper preparation and conduct of a defence, including the right to consult with a lawyer prior to and during the trial.[168]

A third category of defendants wrongly denied bail is those who would not have breached their bail. This is even more difficult to quantify. The enormous disparities in the rates at which different courts refuse bail discussed earlier shows that some, without good reason, remand more than others.[169] Moreover, bail information schemes seem to indicate that many remands in custody where such schemes do not operate

---

[166] Ibid: 39.   [167] On this, see the letters from two judges: [1993] Crim LR 324.
[168] HMIP (2000: 52).   [169] See Hucklesby (1997a); Paterson and Whittaker (1994).

are unwarranted and that the standard of decision-making can be improved.[170] As is so often the case in the criminal process, certain groups suffer more than others as a result of the law allowing a large element of discretion to those taking decisions. Hood, for example, found that black defendants had a greater likelihood of being remanded in custody than white defendants, even when all factors legally relevant to the bail decision were taken into account.[171] Ten years later, the same pattern of race discrimination was still observable, among adults and youths. Moreover, the proportions of black defendants remanded in custody who were not convicted is much higher than that of white people.[172] The framework created by the Bail Act clearly does little to prevent bad, arbitrary or even racist decision-making.[173]

Court clerks are obliged to record a court's reasons for refusing bail or imposing or varying conditions.[174] In addition, the defendant must be informed as to the reasons for any refusal of bail. These requirements are supposed to ensure that magistrates keep within the terms of the Act. But as White has observed:

it would be a poor clerk who could not formulate a reason falling within the terms of the Act and it would be a foolish magistrate who insisted on recording a personal prejudice as the reason for the decision.[175]

Further, reasons are often given by way of a pro forma which fails to explain why defence arguments were rejected. This procedure could fall foul of the ECHR.[176]

9.4.5 Appeals against bail decisions

An appeal against a refusal of bail may be made to the Crown Court under a procedure introduced in 1983, and solicitors enjoy a right of audience for this purpose.[177] Section 16 of the CJA 2003 provided the Crown Court with the power also to hear appeals against the conditions attached to a grant of bail (while s 17 abolishes the power of the High Court to hear such appeals).

The converse of defendants appealing against the refusal of bail is the prosecution appealing against its grant. The Bail (Amendment) Act 1993, gave the prosecution

---

[170] The original experiment from which these schemes developed showed that the increase in granting bail resulting from the provision of better information on defendants did not result in an increase in the failure rate, whether measured as offending on bail, breach of bail conditions or non-attendance at court. See Stone C, *Bail Information for the Crown Prosecution Service* (New York: VERA Institute of Justice, 1988). But note the concerns raised by Dhami (2002).

[171] Hood R, *Race and Sentencing* (Oxford: Clarendon Press, 1992) pp 146–9. The treatment of women is discussed in Player E, 'Remanding Women in Custody: Concerns for Human Rights' (2007) 70(3) MLR 402.

[172] Gus John Partnership, *Race for Justice* (London: CPS, 2003); Feilzer M and Hood R, *Differences or Discrimination?* (London: YJB, 2004).

[173] Compare this with the situation applying in countries which have fundamental rights enshrined in constitutional charters. See eg Padfield N, 'The Right to Bail: a Canadian Perspective' [1993] Crim LR 510.

[174] Bail Act 1976, s 5.

[175] White R, *The Administration of Justice* (Oxford: Basil Blackwell, 1985) p 84.

[176] Law Commission, *Bail and the Human Rights Act 1998* (Report 269) (London: Law Commission, 1999) para 4.21.   [177] Criminal Justice Act 1982, s 60.

for the first time the right to appeal against a grant of bail, and s 19 of the CJA 2003 considerably widened that right. Now, an appeal lies to a judge in chambers where the defendant stands charged with any imprisonable crime. A defendant must be remanded in custody pending the outcome of the appeal which must take place within 48 hours. This gives the prosecution the power, in effect, to override (albeit temporarily) a judicial decision to release on bail. The CPS has as yet no right to challenge a refusal to impose the conditions it requested in a grant of bail.

9.4.6 Time spent on remand

There are legislative time limits where defendants are in custody awaiting trial, but courts can, and usually do, grant extensions.[178] In 1990 the usual wait in custody for a Crown Court trial was 17 weeks, but only three weeks for a magistrates' court trial. By the mid 1990s the average wait for the Crown Court was down to less than ten weeks but for magistrates it was up to seven weeks, while in 2002 the average wait in custody for those committed to the Crown Court was over 12 weeks.[179] Two to four months may seem a long time to wait in prison for a trial at the conclusion of which there is an even chance of an acquittal or non-custodial sentence, but this pales into insignificance by comparison with some other countries. It seems doubtful that when delay is measured in months rather than years that any rights in the ECHR will be regarded as breached.[180] So unconvicted prisoners in the UK can expect little help from the HRA.[181]

9.4.7 A right to bail?

For most defendants the presumption in favour of bail is uncontested. But most defendants are charged with minor offences and given non-custodial sentences anyway. The situation is different when the police and CPS consider that a defendant should be remanded in custody. In these cases the crime control presumption of guilt, which operates not only on the courts but also on defence solicitors much of the time, is more powerful than legal rules and Human Rights principles. At times of stress, such as 'riots' and industrial strife, there is what Vogler describes as an 'almost complete surrender of the magistrates to policing rather than judicial priorities...'[182] When the police seek curfew conditions, the magistrates comply. Remands in custody are similarly 'rubber stamped'. Even committed defence lawyers know that there is no point

---

[178] Prosecution of Offences Act 1985 as amended. For details, see Samuels A, 'Custody Time Limits' [1997] Crim LR 260.

[179] Ashworth (1998: 219); Ashworth A and Redmayne M, *The Criminal Process*, 3rd edn (Oxford: OUP, 2005) p 220.

[180] See the cases reviewed by Emmerson et al, *Human Rights and Criminal Justice*, 2nd edn (London: Sweet & Maxwell, 2007) pp 498–501.   [181] Law Commission (1999: para 12.19).

[182] Vogler (1991: 144).

resisting these joint strategies. Vogler found that the Merseyside police 'flooded' the courts with defendants in the first week of the 1981 Liverpool 'riot':

In these circumstances, the presumption regarding bail became reversed, and the major, most severe single punishment inflicted by the court became the custodial remand rather than the post-conviction sentence.[183]

At a more obviously political level, the governments of the last 20 years have responded similarly to populist panics. Most notably, the CJPO 1994 and CJA 2003 altered bail law for high profile defendants.[184] Initially under s 26 of the CJPO defendants charged with offences allegedly committed while on bail 'need not' be presumed to be entitled to bail. And s 25 banned bail for anyone charged with rape or homicide offences (or attempts) who had a previous conviction for such an offence. The fact that courts hardly needed reminding that such defendants (especially in the s 25 category) would need a particularly persuasive argument if they were to secure bail was irrelevant: appearing 'tough' was more important than human rights or matters of principle. Sections 25 and 26 were amended by s 56 of the Crime and Disorder Act 1998 and then again by ss 14 and 15 of the CJA 2003, so that in such cases there is a rebuttable presumption against bail when an offence has been committed while on bail (and when a defendant has failed to answer bail without a reasonable excuse).[185] The provisions arguably violate the presumption of innocence because they place the burden of proof onto the defendant. The Law Commission stated s 25 was: 'liable to be . . . applied in a way which would violate the Convention'.[186] However, the House of Lords in *O v Crown Court at Harrow* held that the amended s 25 could be interpreted in such a way as to make it compatible with Art 5 of the ECHR.[187] It ruled that s 25 should not be interpreted as placing the burden of proof on the defendant to make out 'exceptional circumstances' for allowing bail. Instead, it would be enough for the defendant to point to material which might support the existence of such a circumstance.[188]

Recently the government has proposed provisions to reverse the presumption of bail in murder cases.[189] The Coroners and Justice Bill 2008–09 contains clauses creating a rebuttable presumption against bail where a defendant is charged with murder; bail

---

[183] Ibid: 143.

[184] In addition to the categories discussed in the text, s 19 of the CJA 2003 places tough restrictions on granting bail to class A drug users who decline to take part in a programme designed to curb their drug use. For details see Taylor et al (2004: 23–4), and for the particular dilemmas this creates for female remand prisoners see Player (2007: 411–12).

[185] Note that whether or not the reason for failing to attend court is reasonable is irrelevant in deciding whether a condition is breached, but 'reasonableness' is always relevant in determining whether or not this makes a further breach likely if the defendant is released on bail again: *R (on the application of Vickers) v West London Magistrates' Court* [2004] Crim LR 63.

[186] Law Commission (1999: para 9.30). Note a similar warning regarding s 26: para 6.14.

[187] [2006] UKHL 42.

[188] Arguably the defendant should not bear even this limited evidential burden: Ashworth A, 'Bail; Human Rights' [2007] Crim LR 63.

[189] *Bail and Murder: Response to Consultation*, CP (R) 11/08 (London: MoJ, 2009).

may not be granted to defendants in murder cases unless the court (in this instance a Crown Court judge) is of the opinion that there is no significant risk that the defendant would commit an offence that would cause injury. If such a provision becomes law it is unlikely to be held to violate the ECHR. By analogy with s 25 the courts would probably say that the provision should be 'read down' to ensure compatibility with Art 5. The government argues that the provision has been drafted in such a way as to make clear that it is not for the defendant to show that there is no 'significant risk', but for the prosecution to show that there is such a risk. It is therefore, in its opinion, ECHR compliant.

We may conclude by observing that the ECHR appears to have had little impact on bail decision-making either in principle or in practice[190] – speedy, slipshod decision-making has remained the order of the day. This brings us to a more general evaluation of procedural fairness in the magistrates' courts.

9.5 The quality and fairness of summary justice

When most people think of criminal prosecutions they think of jury trials. But only the Crown Court has jury trials. The most serious cases have what is assumed to be the best system, and the one that commands the most public support.[191] Leaving aside the issue of cost, the reason for magistrates' courts not having juries can therefore be only because *either* the nature of magistrates' court cases makes jury trial unsuitable; *or* the relative triviality of magistrates' court cases makes jury trial unnecessary. The former is untenable. As far as triviality is concerned we know that this is the *ideology* surrounding magistrates' work, but that it is not the reality. Consequently, we should strive to bring as many elements of judge-and-jury trial as is reasonably possible to the magistrates' courts. Doran and Glenn suggest that courts should embody three basic principles: fairness, efficiency and accountability (including commanding public confidence).[192] These principles are central to our freedom perspective, and Crown Court trials satisfy these criteria, albeit imperfectly.[193] First, the jury embodies 'social' fairness (in terms of independent fact-finding and the application of societal morality) because it is made up of ordinary people without an institutional stake in 'either side' of the criminal justice system. Juries also embody fairness because they make deci-

---

[190]   For a fuller review than is possible here, see ch 13 of Emmerson et al (2007).

[191]   Bridges et al, *Ethnic Minority Defendants and the Right to Elect Jury Trial* (London: Commission for Racial Equality, 2000b); Sanders A, *Community Justice: Modernising the Magistracy in England and Wales* (London: IPPR, 2001).

[192]   Doran S and Glenn R, *Lay Involvement in Adjudication: Review of the Criminal Justice System in Northern Ireland* (Criminal Justice Review Research Report No 11) (Belfast: SO, 2000).

[193]   See generally ch 10, where various exceptions and caveats to the points we make here are discussed.

sions after group discussions and cannot find anyone guilty unless an overwhelming majority are in favour. The judge embodies 'legal' fairness in the sense of the dispassionate application of the rule of law. Judges explain the relevant law to juries, who then adjudicate between competing factual claims. Second, the jury commands public confidence and, by its existence, makes (a small part of) the criminal justice system accountable to the community. Finally, the judge's professionalism and knowledge assist efficiency. In this section we assess the extent to which magistrates and magistrates' courts give effect to these principles by being adequate substitutes for judge-and-jury trial. This is important, as there are around four times as many magistrates' court trials as there are Crown Court trials.

9.5.1 **The magistrates**

For the last two to three hundred years, magistrates' courts have been largely presided over by lay magistrates. The exception has been Inner London, where stipendiary magistrates (full-time judges who have been practising lawyers or qualified court clerks) have traditionally heard a high proportion of cases. The AJA 1999 renamed stipendiaries 'District Judges (Magistrates Courts)' and we shall use both terms in the following analysis.

The complex separation of function and mixture of professional expertise and lay involvement in the Crown Court is in contrast with magistrates' courts proceedings. Questions of both law and fact are there decided upon by a bench of three[194] lay magistrates, or by a stipendiary magistrate sitting alone. Lay magistrates rely upon the court clerk for legal advice. A survey in the late 1990s found there were around 30,000 lay magistrates and over 100 full time stipendiary magistrates, along with about 150 part-timers, based mainly in large urban centres.[195] Seago et al found that stipendiary magistrates are increasingly being used outside of London. This means that a very substantial minority of cases in cities outside Inner London, and around half of cases in Inner London, are now handled by stipendiaries. There is no differentiation between the work done by stipendiaries and that done by lay justices, except that the occasional lengthy trial is generally given to stipendiaries. Government policy has been to resist calls to allocate lay justices one type of work and stipendiaries another because of a belief that lay justices would resent being deprived of the whole range of work.[196] The effect of this policy is that whether decisions on bail, guilt and sentencing are taken by a professional or by a group of amateurs is essentially a matter of chance. Should not some more principled basis for allocating cases be established?

Many common law-based jurisdictions have lay justices. But there are few, if any, which give lay justices sentencing powers as extensive as exist in England and

---

[194] In some circumstances two lay magistrates suffice, and for certain types of simple decision only one lay magistrate is needed.
[195] Seago et al, 'The Development of the Professional Magistracy in England and Wales' [2000] Crim LR 631.   [196] Ibid.

Wales.[197] In Scotland, for example, where lay justices in district courts handle one-third of all cases, lay justices have the power to imprison for up to 60 days, and they use this power sparingly.[198] On the other hand, professional judges sitting alone are also rarely given the power that stipendiaries have here. Stipendiaries are now even allowed to sit alone in the youth court.[199] This is surprising because, even in jurisdictions where lay magistrates are little used, it is generally thought valuable to involve lay people and/or experts in child development as well as lawyers when dealing with young people.[200] At least, under 'referral orders', youth offender panels (which have a varied membership) do much of the sentencing work of the youth court, going some way towards ameliorating this development.[201]

How well do magistrates embody the three basic principles of fairness, efficiency and accountability that we have identified? Anyone may apply to become a lay magistrate, but most people do not know that, and appointments are made on the recommendation of local advisory committees which are largely made up of local JPs. Even the Magistrates Association has described this committee system as 'a self-perpetuating oligarchy'.[202] Although the lay magistracy is now more representative of the community than it used to be, successive surveys of its membership show that it remains predominantly middle aged and middle class.[203] A typical magistrate's response to this type of point was that: 'If a person's still on the shop floor when they're of an age to be appointed then they probably haven't got what it takes to be a magistrate.'[204] Brown found that juvenile court magistrates in the late 1980s judged the families of the juveniles appearing before them by standards that were 'deeply gender and class biased'.[205] In a striking echo of what we know of the world view of the police (discussed in 2.1), she concluded that magistrates 'perceived themselves as representatives of the upright conscience....The "threat" of disorder posed by the judged to the judges, is a threat of all the other undisciplined young "out there".'[206] This may explain why some defence lawyers give clients advice or criticism about their attire; admonishing them for appearing too scruffy or 'flashy'.[207] They

---

[197] See, for a range of jurisdictions, Skyrme T, *History of the Justices of the Peace* (Chichester: Barry Rose, 1994).

[198] The lay judiciary in Scotland has been undergoing a period of reform which includes provisions for increases in sentencing powers to a maximum of 6 months' imprisonment: Criminal Proceedings (Reform) Scotland Act 2007.   [199] Crime and Disorder Act 1998, s 48; AJA 1999, Sch 11.

[200] On Northern Ireland, see Doran and Glenn (2000); in Scotland most juvenile justice is diverted to 'Children's Hearings' which are quasi-judicial and include non-lawyers.

[201] Youth Justice and Criminal Evidence Act 1999, s 1. For an evaluation see Crawford A and Newburn T, *Youth Offending and Restorative Justice* (Cullompton: Willan, 2003).

[202] Darbyshire P, 'For the New Lord Chancellor: Some Causes for Concern About Magistrates' [1997b] Crim LR 861.

[203] For example, Burney E, *Magistrate, Court and Community* (London: Hutchinson, 1979); King M and May C, *Black Magistrates* (London: Cobden Trust, 1985); Dignan J and Whynne A, 'A Microcosm of the Local Community? Reflections on the Composition of the Magistracy in a Petty Sessional Division in the North Midlands' (1997) 37 BJ Crim 184.   [204] Darbyshire (1997b).

[205] Brown (1991: 112–13).   [206] Ibid.

[207] McConville et al, *Standing Accused* (Oxford: Clarendon Press, 1994) p 228.

are attempting to create an appearance of orderliness which, although it will never equate to that of uniformed police officer witnesses, might at least offer less of a stark contrast. Magistrates have an undue respect for, and trust in, authority. The typical view, expressed to Hucklesby regarding bail, was: 'I think for the protection of the public you've got to come down on the side of the CPS or the police who say "we want this person in custody".'[208] We saw in 9.4 and in ch 6 that in politically charged situations, in particular, magistrates effectively put themselves at the disposal of police and government. They value authority, and identify with other institutions (such as the police and CPS) which wield it. There may be a lack of understanding on the bench as to why a defendant might resist arrest, or refuse to answer police questions, dissemble or make a false confession. Magistrates may have standards of behaviour which are unrepresentative of the wider community and this may be of importance in applying the law. For example, in property offences the test for whether an action is dishonest is whether ordinary people would regard the act as dishonest and whether the defendant was aware that the act would be so regarded.[209] But magistrates are not representative of ordinary people. If charged with a crime of violence you can escape liability if you acted in reasonable self-defence. Views on what would be reasonable resistance if wrongfully arrested in the presence of one's family, friends or workmates might depend on whether one has ever experienced something similar. But magistrates have seldom had adversarial contacts with the police. Juries are less susceptible to these forms of unconscious class bias.

Not only are lay magistrates less representative than juries, they are also 'insiders'. Although lay justices are unpaid part-time volunteers, they are quite different from unprepared and predominantly once-in-a-lifetime jurors. Magistrates may be only lightly trained compared to professional judges, but they serve substantial apprenticeships. Most of them sit in court once a week, some sit twice a week, and all sit at least once a fortnight. These magistrates may be lay in the sense that they are not legally qualified, but they are not untutored amateurs. By contrast, juries come fresh to the criminal courts, hear one or more cases, then leave again to return to their normal occupations. It must be difficult for magistrates to treat each case on its individual merits when they have heard the same stories countless times before. Moreover, every magistrates' court seems to have its fair share of 'regulars', defendants well known to the bench. When asked if magistrates' familiarity with the regulars was a problem, the Chief Executive of Nottingham magistrates' court replied:

If your name is Bane or Pain in Nottingham, then you're notorious. Some of them have changed their name by deed poll. The Banes and the Pains provide a lot of work for this court and everybody knows them. If it's a problem at this court, the biggest Bench in the country, with over 450 justices, then it could be a problem anywhere.[210]

---

208 Hucklesby (1997b: 276).   209 *Ghosh* [1982] 2 All ER 689.
210 Quoted by Darbyshire P, 'Previous Misconduct and Magistrates' Courts: Some Tales from the Real World' [1997c] Crim LR 105 at p 107.

So not only do magistrates (and their clerks) hear the same stories all the time, they hear them in relation to the same people. As one magistrate acknowledged to Darbyshire: 'Oh, yes. Whenever we see a certain solicitor we always know we've got Doris Day up before us and she always pleads not guilty.'[211] This level of familiarity must sometimes induce in defendants (or their solicitors) feelings of the 'que sera, sera' variety, as appears to have been the case in the following fatalistic exchange observed by McConville et al:

Solicitor: I'll suggest conditional bail, I'll see. The Chairman's not bad but the clerk's a cow – you had her last time…

Client: If I get bail, I'll be surprised![212]

Particular problems may be faced by unrepresented defendants. The work of Carlen suggests that magistrates (and their clerks) have a greater interest in maintaining social control in their courtrooms than in giving free rein to defendants to challenge authority by contesting the prosecution version of events or by, for example, raising awkward questions about behind the scenes negotiations regarding bail or plea.[213] Further, since juries are 'outsiders', lawyers have to explain things in everyday language in Crown Court trials, ensuring that justice is public in substance as well as in form, and giving defendants, victims and others a fair chance of understanding what is going on. Because magistrates are 'insiders', none of this is true. Defendants are often bewildered by magistrates' courts hearings.[214]

On the test of 'social fairness', lay magistrates are clearly a poor substitute for the jury. But stipendiaries are even less satisfactory. If we need juries to bring the world of social fairness into the Crown Court because judges are professionally and socially elite then the same applies when a district judge (magistrates' court) presides. At least a bench of lay magistrates is likely to have one person under 40 and/or one person with an average income. In areas with a large ethnic minority population, ethnic minorities are represented too, and in recent years almost in proportion to their population.[215] None of this is true of stipendiaries. Further, lay justices make most of their decisions in panels of three after group discussion, unlike lone stipendiaries.

Nor do magistrates serve to make the criminal justice system accountable to the community in the way that juries do. They are insufficiently representative of the communities they supposedly serve to be able to fulfil this function. It is true that lay magistrates stress their 'local' character, but it is not clear why 'localness' should be a virtue of justice.[216] In any case, few magistrates live in the same locales as prosecuted offenders. What is true of lay justices regarding accountability is even more true of stipendiaries, who often do not even have the dubious virtue of being 'local'.

---

[211] Ibid.   [212] McConville et al (1994: 174).

[213] Carlen P, 'Remedial Routines for the Maintenance of Control in Magistrates' Courts' (1974) 1 BJ Law & Soc 101 and Carlen P, *Magistrates' Justice* (London: Martin Robertson, 1976).

[214] Carlen (1976); McBarnet (1983).

[215] Vennard et al, *Ethnic Minority Magistrates' Experience of the Role and of the Court Environment* (DCA Research Report 3/2004) (London: DCA, 2004).   [216] Seago et al [2000] Crim LR 631.

On the test of 'legal fairness' and efficiency, stipendiaries are doubtless a good substitute for Crown Court judges, but lay magistrates are, by definition, not legally qualified. Their clerks are supposed to make up for their deficit, in the same way that judges advise juries on the relevant law. But stipendiaries are, as one would expect, much more efficient than are lay justices if we define 'efficient' as 'quick'.[217] They are also thought to adjourn cases less readily, to stand up more robustly to prosecution and defence lawyers alike, and to be better at case management.[218]

In conclusion, it seems undeniable that magistrates are a poor substitute for judge-and-jury.[219] Magistrates' court trials embody two (fairness and accountability) of the three basic principles far less well than do Crown Court trials. However, lay justices embody these principles better than do stipendiaries. Yet we are seeing more work being done by stipendiaries, rather than less. The 'efficiency' principle is implicitly being prioritised over the principles of fairness and accountability:[220] a move away from 'freedom' towards 'crime control'. Short of introducing jury trial into magistrates' court – a utopian idea in view of current moves to reduce the use of juries – what can be done?

It has been suggested that there is no need for lay magistrates' involvement in the most minor guilty pleas. Stipendiaries could handle these. For contested cases and cases of medium-seriousness, a stipendiary could sit with two lay justices.[221] This would mean much less need for lay justices than now and less need for training on their part as they would sit with a judge. Lay justices could therefore be drawn from a wider cross-section of the community than now, perhaps sitting only a handful of times per year, for a limited term of, say, five years. They would have fewer 'insider' characteristics than lay justices do currently. In this way they could be a better jury substitute than now. It is possible that lay 'wingers' could be overawed by a professional judge, but mixed panels of this kind are common in European criminal systems, and wingers are, though marginal to some extent, by no means uninfluential.[222] Any objection to the mixed panel idea on the basis that it represents some dangerous foreign device that could never take root in domestic soil can easily be countered. Mixed panels already exist within our system. As we shall detail in 11.2, convicted persons who appeal to the Crown Court are entitled to a complete rehearing before a professional judge flanked by lay magistrates. Unfortunately, they have been so neglected in the criminal justice literature that we have little idea how they work.

---

[217] Ibid: table 4.   [218] See Home Office (1997a).

[219] See Bankowski et al, *Lay Justice?* (Edinburgh: Clark, 1987) ch 9 for a discussion of the analogy between juries and lay magistrates. Note that we are talking in terms of judge-and-*jury*, and *trials*, rather than the whole range of court proceedings, because juries are not involved in Crown Court sentencing. It is not obvious that they should be left out. If the 'community' element embodied in lay justices is thought valuable for sentencing in magistrates' courts, why not similarly involve juries in the Crown Court? See Sanders (2001).

[220] Fitzpatrick et al, 'New Courts Management and the Professionalisation of Summary Justice in England and Wales' (2000) 11 Criminal Law Forum 1.

[221] Darbyshire P, 'An Essay on the Importance and Neglect of the Magistracy' (1997a) Crim LR 627; Sanders (2001).   [222] Darbyshire (1997a); Doran and Glenn (2000); Sanders (2001).

This is something that could have been looked at by Auld LJ, who was tasked by the Home Secretary with carrying out a condensed inquiry into the criminal justice system.[223] But he did not grasp this democratic nettle.[224] So defendants continue to have their fates decided by either a trio of 'half-baked professionals'[225] or a lone professional – the choice is virtually random – at the bottom of the judicial hierarchy.

9.5.2 Acquittals and convictions

Many defendants do not expect justice to be done in the magistrates' court. Typically, they regard the Crown Court as fairer and more thorough in its approach and offering a better chance of acquittal. By contrast, magistrates' courts are seen as amateurish and pro-police, but speedier and offering the prospect of a more lenient sentence.[226] There is evidence to suggest that their perceptions are accurate.[227] Vennard's study of contested cases in the magistrates' courts found that there was a tendency for magistrates to accept the accuracy of police eye witness evidence and their interpretation of events as against the defendant's denial of the alleged conduct or a claim that the act did not constitute a crime. This is consistent with what we know of contested bail applications, discussed in 9.4 above, where magistrates generally prefer to believe the police and CPS rather than the defence, turning the burden of proof on its head. Vennard found that, even where defendants' credibility was not directly impugned and there was no confession the majority of cases ended in conviction.[228] A further study by Vennard concluded that for contested either-way cases, the chances of acquittal were substantially higher in the Crown Court (57%) than in the magistrates' courts (30%).[229] More recent research, by Bridges et al (discussed below) lends support to the belief that, case-for-case, acquittal is far less likely in the magistrates' courts than in the Crown Court.

We might hope that times have changed since 1974, when the chairman of the bench said in one case: 'My principle in such cases [when the evidence of a police officer and a citizen conflicts] has always been to believe the evidence of the police officer...'.[230] But neither Darbyshire nor the research we have cited gives us reason to cling to this hope. Darbyshire (1997b) comments: 'Magistrates astonished me by supporting this

---

[223] Auld (2001).

[224] Morgan R, 'Magistrates: The Future according to Auld' (2002) 29 JLS 308; Sanders A, 'Core Values, the Magistracy and the Auld Report' (2002a) 29 JLS 324.   [225] Burney (1979: 216).

[226] See Bottoms and McClean (1976: 87–100); Gregory J, Crown Court or Magistrates' Court? (Office of Population Censuses and Surveys) (London: HMSO, 1976) and Riley D and Vennard J, Triable-Either-Way Cases: Crown Court or Magistrates' Court? (Home Office Research Study No 98) (London: HMSO, 1988) pp 16–18.   [227] On sentencing, see ch 8.

[228] Vennard J, Contested Trials in Magistrates' Courts (Home Office Research Study No 71) (London: HMSO, 1981) p 21.

[229] Vennard J, 'The Outcome of Contested Trials' in D Moxon (ed), Managing Criminal Justice (London: HMSO, 1985). Ashworth A, 'Plea, Venue and Discontinuance' [1993] Crim LR 830, who does not cite the Vennard (1981) study, argues for caution in interpreting this finding.

[230] Bingham Justices, ex p Jowitt, The Times, 3 July 1974.

statement in recent conversations.' This helps to explain the lower acquittal rate in magistrates' courts than in the Crown Court that we observed at the start of this chapter. The high success rate of appeal to the Crown Court is further evidence of poor decision-making in the magistrates' courts, as we argue in detail in 11.2.

There are a number of possible explanations for the higher acquittal rate in the Crown Court. The first is that the magistracy and juries are, as we have seen, very different. We might expect case hardened 'insiders' with little experience of the conditions to which many defendants are subjected to be sceptical of what defendants say and to be over-ready to believe the police. A defence solicitor made this telling remark:

We sometimes wonder [at the magistrates' court] who has to prove guilt or innocence. Certainly, sometimes I've felt that I'm the one who's having to do all the work – whereas really it should be the prosecution who are proving all the elements, rather than the defence having to disprove the elements of the offence.[231]

The second is simply numerical. At the Crown Court, the prosecution has to convince at least 10 out of the 12 jurors that the defendant is guilty.[232] In the magistrates' court, it is enough to convince two out of the three lay magistrates, or even just one stipendiary magistrate. As one defendant has put it:

...when you go to a magistrates' court, there is only one thing – you are guilty...at the Crown Court, you've got a better chance because you've got 12 people and at the magistrates' court, you've got either one or three people to decide.[233]

Finally, the procedures in the lower courts place defendants at a distinct disadvantage. The prosecution need not disclose its case in advance to defendants charged with summary offences[234] and legal aid is less freely available than in the Crown Court. Furthermore, magistrates, unlike jurors, are privy to much inadmissible evidence. This is because the admissibility of evidence is a question of law which can be decided by the judge in the absence of the jury in the Crown Court. Magistrates, by contrast, determine both questions of fact and law. Even if they decide, for example, that a disputed confession is inadmissible, they may still be prejudiced by the knowledge that an alleged confession exists.[235] For this reason this procedure could fall foul of Art 6 of the ECHR. A 'mixed panel' system, such as that suggested earlier, could ameliorate this problem, as the professional chair could hear the legal arguments in the absence of the lay 'wingers'. There is also some evidence that justices' clerks may occasionally,

---

[231] Bucke et al, *The Right of Silence: The Impact of the Criminal Justice and Public Order Act 1994* (Home Office Research Study No 199) (London: Home Office, 2000) p 47. See also McConville et al (1994: 226–7).

[232] Until 1967 the jury's decision had to be unanimous. Now, under the Criminal Justice Act 1967, s 13(3), the court is not supposed to consider the possibility of a majority verdict until at least two hours have elapsed since the jury retired.   [233] Quoted by Bridges L 'Taking Liberties' (2000) Legal Action, 6 July, p 8.

[234] Only once a defendant has pleaded not guilty does the Criminal Procedure and Investigations Act 1996 require the prosecutor to make 'primary disclosure'. On disclosure generally, see discussion in ch 7.

[235] See further Wasik M, 'Magistrates: Knowledge of Previous Convictions' [1996] Crim LR 851.

whether in private or in whispers, transmit opinions, prejudices and hearsay informa-tion to magistrates.[236] Magistrates' courts are also less accountable in that their pro-ceedings are not recorded in full. If the defence wish to appeal on a point of law to the Divisional Court the magistrates draw up a statement of the facts, the cases cited and their decision. This gives justices' clerks ample opportunity to cover their tracks.[237]

In its drive to increase 'efficiency', the government has implemented several reforms aimed at reducing delay. These include 'early administrative hearings' (EAHs) (see 9.3 above) and 'early first hearings' (EFH) introduced in the 1990s.[238] More recently, under the *Criminal Justice Simple Speedy Summary* (CJSS) regime[239] the aim is to dis-pose of guilty pleas in just one hearing (which might be by video link from the police station) or, in contested cases, have two hearings at most. It follows that applications to adjourn are viewed negatively, even though many defendants may appear without having had legal advice, and advance information (disclosure) from the prosecution will not have occurred. Court duty solicitors are available, but have little time to take instructions, and will not be able to see everyone due to appear in a session. 'Lay pre-senters' appear for the CPS.[240] This means that in some cases there will be not a single qualified lawyer in the court room to ensure that justice is done. To structure proceed-ings so that the police and CPS decide whether cases are, from the defendant's point of view, contestable, complex or far reaching in their consequences undermines the presumption of innocence.[241] This managerialism gone mad is completely incompat-ible with the freedom approach.

9.5.3 Mode of trial

In 'either-way' cases adult defendants have the 'right' to elect a jury trial in the Crown Court. Youths (those aged 17 or under) have no such right; they are prosecuted in the youth court, which is essentially the magistrates' court in (supposedly) more paternalistic guise.[242] Although little remarked upon in the literature, this is actually a major restriction on trial by jury. Vast numbers of citizens enter 'adulthood' with convictions for such serious offences as theft or fairly serious violence,[243] without ever

---

[236] See McLaughlin H, 'Court Clerks: Advisers or Decision-Makers' (1990) 30 BJ Crim 358 at 364.

[237] For fuller discussion see Heaton-Armstrong I, 'The Verdict of the Court...and its Clerk?' (1986) 150 JP 340, 342, 357–9.

[238] Under the EFH 'fast-track' procedure for anticipated guilty pleas in 'simple' cases, hearings are intended to be within 24 hours of charge where possible(s 46 of the Crime and Disorder Act 1998).

[239] Department for Constitutional Affairs, *Delivering Simple, Speedy, Summary Justice* (London: DCA, 2006).   [240] See 9.1 above.

[241] Bridges L, 'False Starts and Unrealistic Expectations' (1999) Legal Action, 6 October, p 6.

[242] 'Youths' can only be tried in the Crown Court if charged with a grave crime, or if they are to be co-tried with adult defendants (see Ball et al, 2001).

[243] In each year 2000–2007 over 40,000 persons aged between 10 and 17 (inclusive) were convicted in the youth court of non-summary criminal offences. This estimate is based on Ministry of Justice, *Sentencing Statistics England and Wales* (London: MoJ, 2009e) table 6.1 (available from <http://www.justice.gov.uk/publications/docs/sentencing-statistics-2007-revised.pdf> – accessed 5 January 2010).

having had the chance to contest their guilt before the 'community' as embodied by the jury. One can have sex and get married at 16, drive a car at 17, yet not be entitled to what is generally regarded as a superior form of justice until 18. Youth Court is often thought of as a liberal measure, designed to spare 'kids' the trauma of a judicial setting designed for adults. But it also results in young adults being funnelled into the conviction sausage-machine that is the magistrates' court. Once convicted, they can be committed to the Crown Court for sentence if the magistrates consider their sentencing powers to be inadequate. So young adults can get justice for kids and sentencing for adults. This puts the supposed liberality of the Youth Court mechanism in a rather different light. We will have more to say about the power of magistrates to commit for sentence below.

Not surprisingly, in view of our discussion in the preceding sub-section, many adults exercise their right to trial by jury if they intend pleading not guilty. Adults intending to plead guilty usually prefer to stay in the magistrates' court as its sentencing powers are restricted to six months' imprisonment for any one offence. This is not such a restriction as it might seem as magistrates can, as with youths, send the case to the Crown Court for sentencing following a conviction regardless of the defendant's wishes. Sometimes adult defendants want to plead not guilty in the magistrates' court but are prevented from doing so by the magistrates declining jurisdiction and committing the case for Crown Court trial. In these circumstances, the 'right' to jury trial becomes almost a duty (which can only be escaped by pleading guilty on arrival in the Crown Court). The magistrates used also to have the power to decline jurisdiction even in cases where an adult defendant was minded to plead guilty, although this has changed as we discuss below.

Hedderman and Moxon found that the perception that the Crown Court offered a fairer hearing even influenced some adult defendants who were not planning to contest their cases. Just over a quarter of defendants in their study who elected Crown Court trial did so intending to plead guilty.[244] Hedderman and Moxon also discovered that a majority of defendants who elected Crown Court trial (including some of those who intended to plead guilty), together with over a third of the solicitors interviewed, were apparently labouring under the false impression that Crown Court judges imposed lighter sentences than magistrates.[245]

The majority of either-way cases are dealt with in the magistrates' courts. Nevertheless, for several decades policy-makers have been concerned about the proportion committed to the Crown Court and sought to reduce this, primarily for reasons of economy.[246] Committal of either-way cases involves increased costs for the courts, the CPS, the probation service, the legal aid fund and the prison system. It is

---

[244] Hedderman C and Moxon D, *Magistrates' Court or Crown Court?: Mode of Trial Decisions and Sentencing* (Home Office Research Study No 125) (London: HMSO, 1992) p 23.

[245] Hedderman and Moxon (1992: 20). This finding departs from the pattern found by other studies. See further Bridges L, 'The Right to Jury Trial: How the Royal Commission Got it Wrong' (1993) 143 NLJ 1542 and Bridges (2000).

[246] Cammiss S and Stride C, 'Modelling Mode of Trial' (2008) 48(4) BJ Crim 482.

also a factor in fuelling prison overcrowding, both because defendants remanded in custody have longer to wait if committed to the Crown Court,[247] and because Crown Court judges make much more use of custodial sentences than do magistrates.[248]

On the face of it, there appear to be two types of Crown Court adult defendant in either-way cases. There are the defendants who plead guilty in the Crown Court and who could have been dealt with identically (but more quickly and cheaply) in the magistrates' courts. And there are the defendants who opt for the Crown Court because they think they are more likely to be acquitted. From a freedom perspective the option chosen by the latter group of defendants is perfectly understandable, whereas the former group's preferences are more questionable. For the crime control adherent, however, defendants who are acquitted in the Crown Court are seen to have cheated the system, whereas either-way defendants who are convicted (whether following a contested trial or not) are perceived to have wasted the time and money that would have been saved had they stayed in the lower courts. Various attempts underpinned by these crime control assumptions have been made to restrict the flow of cases committed from the magistrates' courts. Unfortunately, these attempts have not separated out the different reasons for opting for the Crown Court and so have ended up penalising those who wish to plead not guilty before a jury as well as the committed guilty pleaders.

One way to keep more cases in the magistrates' courts would be to increase their sentencing powers, but policy-makers appear to be wary of this option on the ground that it is likely to fuel prison overcrowding.[249] Another way of reducing the numbers of Crown Court cases of all kinds is simply to reclassify either-way offences as summary only. Thus, s 15 of the Criminal Law Act 1977 made a number of public order offences and drink-driving offences purely summary. Similarly, the Criminal Justice Act 1988 (ss 37 and 39) reclassified the offences of taking a motor vehicle, driving whilst disqualified and common assault as summary offences. A more subtle approach has been to encourage magistrates to accept jurisdiction in a higher proportion of cases, and to exhort CPS lawyers to suggest this to them, most notably through 'mode of trial guidelines'. This has not been a successful strategy; during the 1990s the proportion of cases committed because magistrates declined jurisdiction, rather than because defendants elected to be tried at that court, rose steadily.[250] Benches vary greatly in this respect,[251] as in all others, giving rise to further doubts about the quality of their justice. The mode of trial hearing affords both the prosecution and defence an opportunity to make representations on the appropriate venue. As with bail decision-mak-

---

[247] Morgan and Jones (1992: 38). In 2007 the average wait was around 13 weeks for those in custody (London: MoJ, 2008: table 2.2).

[248] Hedderman and Moxon (1992: 37). Although Cammiss and Stride (2008) note that this was queried by Halliday (2001).

[249] The CJA 2003, s 154 increased the maximum sentence magistrates could impose for a single offence to twelve months imprisonment, but the provision has yet to be implemented. See further <http://business.timesonline.co.uk/tol/business/law/article5941754.ece> (accessed 5 January 2010).

[250] From 63% in 1992 to 72% in 1998. Home Office (2000: 133).

[251] Herbert A, 'Mode of Trial and the Influence of Local Justice' (2004) 43 Howard J 65.

ing, there is usually a high degree of agreement between prosecutors' representations and magistrates' decisions. The reasons for this are unclear. It has been found that prosecutors tend to minimise the seriousness of allegations in domestic violence cases to try to keep them in the magistrates' court.[252] Domestic violence cases are probably affected by a double downgrading; both in the seriousness of the narrative presented to the court and the level of charge selected. If prosecutors select a summary only charge, such as common assault, they do not have to downplay the narrative to keep the offence in the magistrates.

It has been suggested that the CPS strategy has been to encourage the charging of offences which are summary only in preference to those that are triable either way. The CPS now has a range of 'Charging standards', one of which (introduced in 1994) guides decisions about which charge to bring in offences of violence.[253] While such standards have been welcomed as a step towards achieving consistency, they also have effectively broadened the band of criminal behaviour that can fall within the summary only offences. The CPS is frequently accused of charging summary offences instead of either-way offences (eg minor assaults instead of s 47 assaults), or even altering the charges to this effect once the case is under way, to keep the case in the magistrates' courts, thus depriving defendants of a Crown Court trial.[254] Since 1997, adult defendants have had to indicate their plea before the trial court is decided. If they indicate a guilty plea in an 'either way' case, the magistrates have to deal with it themselves.[255] While these measures have led to a drop in the numbers of cases sent to the Crown Court for trial by magistrates, this is more than compensated for by a sharp rise in the numbers sent to the Crown Court for sentence.[256] Nonetheless, there are likely to have been some cost savings as Crown Court contested trials are far more expensive than Crown Court sentencing proceedings. On the other hand, the plea before venue procedure, by advancing the moment at which defendants are asked to indicate their plea, has increased the pressure to plead guilty. This is because the sentence discount principle (discussed in ch 8) works by offering the greatest discounts to those that plead guilty at the earliest opportunity.

We should note that these crime control approaches are frequently at odds with the wishes, and sometimes the interests, of victims. Many victims, especially of sexual offences, seek charges, procedures and sentences that fit what they believe to be the seriousness of the crime.[257]

The Runciman Commission also advocated the keeping of more cases in the magistrates' court, but by an even more radical step of removing the defendant's right to

---

[252] Cammiss and Stride (2008).

[253] Crown Prosecution Service Charging Standards are now incorporated in the CPS 'legal guidance' available at <http://www.cps.gov.uk/legal>.

[254] Genders (1999); Jeremy D, 'The Prosecutor's Rock and Hard Place' [2008] Crim LR 925.

[255] See Criminal Procedure and Investigations Act 1996, s 49 for this 'plea before venue' procedure.

[256] Bridges (1999).

[257] See Fenwick H, 'Charge Bargaining and Sentence Discount: the Victim's Perspective' (1997) 5 Int R Victimology 23. The issue is discussed more fully in chs 8 and 13.

elect jury trial. The government tried to enact this proposal in two unsuccessful mode of trial bills.[258] Although there are no current proposals to proceed with removing the defendant's right to elect, it would be naive to think it might not be revived at some point. It is unclear why the Runciman Commission felt that defendants should not be able to choose the court that they feel is fairer, when the Commission was well aware of the higher acquittal rate in the Crown Court and simply asserted that magistrates could be trusted to try cases fairly[259] rather than commissioning any research as to whether this is the case.

The Runciman Commission, whilst relying on Hedderman and Moxon's research that the majority of defendants electing Crown Court trial pleaded guilty, overlooked the fact that the study was of convicted defendants only and that, since just under half of those pleading not guilty in the Crown Court are eventually acquitted, their figures significantly understate the number of defendants who maintain not guilty pleas following election.[260] None the less, it is clearly the case that substantial numbers of defendants do change their plea to guilty following committal. Instead of regarding extensive plea changing as a puzzling phenomenon to be explored, the Runciman Commission took the view that 'the facts speak for themselves'[261] and that there was self-evidently a waste of resources that ought to be eliminated. But unless we understand why plea changing occurs, we cannot rationally decide what the appropriate response should be.[262] It seems that no official body wanted to countenance the possibility that it is not defendants who are abusing the system, but the system that is abusing defendants.[263]

Targeting defendants' decisions to elect is in any event misguided given that the majority of triable either-way cases in the Crown Court are there as a result of magistrates' decisions to decline jurisdiction.[264] There is no need to erode further the due process right of defendants charged with either-way offences to elect trial by jury in order to relieve pressure on the Crown Court. For if magistrates lost their power to commit cases to the Crown Court for sentence, many more defendants might voluntarily elect for trial in the lower courts,[265] especially if the fairness of those trials was enhanced. Removing the right of magistrates to decline jurisdiction in either-way cases would also relieve much pressure on the Crown Court. The suspicion must be that the government's attempt to abolish the right to elect jury trial was motivated by other concerns, such as increasing the rates of guilty pleas and convictions, almost regardless of whether this is justified by the strength of the prosecution evidence.

---

[258] Criminal Justice (Mode of Trial) Bill 2000.

[259] Royal Commission on Criminal Justice, *Report* (Cm 2263) (London: HMSO, 1993) p 88.

[260] Hedderman and Moxon (1992: 11). A point made also by Bridges (1993).

[261] Here, we are quoting Michael Zander, a member of the Royal Commission, giving a presentation at the British Society of Criminology Conference held in Cardiff on 29 July 1993.

[262] For our analysis of the main reasons for changes of plea see ch 8.

[263] See ch 8 and Bridges (2000).   [264] See, for example, the figures reproduced by Bridges (1999).

[265] See Legal Action Group, *Preventing Miscarriages of Justice* (London: LAG Education and Service Trust Ltd, 1993) p 5.

Research by Bridges et al in the mid/late 1990s fills some of the gaps left by the 'Royal Omission on Criminal Justice'.[266] They looked at the reasons for electing jury trial in a sample of defendants. They found that the defendants fell into two main groups. First, there were those that denied the charges, pleaded not guilty and were either tried by a jury or had the case dropped. Second, were defendants who contested one or more of the (often several) charges against them or the seriousness of the charge(s). Most of this group pleaded guilty to lesser charges when these were offered by the prosecution, or contested the charges they disagreed with. In most cases in the second group the 'deals' could have been done without going to the Crown Court, but it was the unwillingness of the CPS, not the defence, to alter its position that led to the unnecessary Crown Court appearances. Often, it was only moving 'up' to a court with a 'proper' judge (and, perhaps, having to instruct an independent barrister to prosecute) that prompted the CPS to scrutinise its case sufficiently to let itself 'deal'. In many of these cases, it must be remembered, pressure to drop or reduce charges comes from the judge who has read the committal papers, so this is not simply a matter of the CPS having no stomach for a fight. If the defendant's right to a Crown Court trial were removed, it is not just the chances of acquittal that will be reduced for many defendants, but the pressure to negotiate. Who knows what would have happened if the cases in which the CPS dropped or reduced charges had gone to trial before less independently minded magistrates? When Bridges et al looked at the cases in their sample which were tried in the magistrates' court they found that only one (out of 14) ended in acquittal.[267]

The loss of the right to choose Crown Court trial would not impact evenly across all types of adult defendant. Cases with ethnic minority defendants are disproportionately discontinued, dismissed and acquitted. This makes up, to some extent, for their disproportionate presence in the stop-search, arrest and charge statistics. It seems that when the CPS, juries and (to a lesser extent) magistrates are put to the test, they see the flaws in many weak cases and act accordingly. This benefits ethnic minority defendants, the prosecution cases against whom are disproportionately weak.[268] Perhaps surprisingly, in a recent study ethnic minority Crown Court defendants were less happy, and perceived more racism, than did ethnic minority defendants in the magistrates' courts. However, though their perceptions of justice were more favourable than the researchers expected, a significant minority perceived some decision-making in both types of court to be unfair, and particularly so due to perceived racism.[269] Whilst perceptions and reality are not the same, the appearance of justice is important. Bridges et al show that, much of the time, it is election for Crown Court trial that puts the rest of the criminal justice system to the test. The more that cases are kept in the magistrates' courts, the less will be the ability of the defence to put pressure on the CPS, and this will have a disproportionately adverse impact on ethnic minority defendants.

---

[266] The joke is by Darbyshire (1997a).   [267] Bridges et al (2000b). Summarised in Bridges (2000).
[268] Phillips and Brown (1998).
[269] Shute et al, *A Fair Hearing? Ethnic Minorities in the Criminal Courts* (Cullompton: Willan, 2005).

9.6 **Specialist magistrates**

In recent years a new phenomenon has emerged of specialist courts in the summary jurisdiction. This is based on policy-makers looking over the Atlantic at a range of 'problem solving' courts that exist in the United States, particularly to deal with issues such as drugs-related offending and domestic violence.[270] As a result there has been a programme for introducing drugs courts,[271] community justice courts[272] and domestic violence courts into England and Wales. By far the most significant of these specialist courts, in numerical terms at least, are domestic violence courts. These now exist in over 100 magistrates' courts in England and Wales. A feature of these courts, which vary slightly in their modes of operation and characteristics, is that all the magistrates are specially trained on domestic violence and are thus supposed to be alert to the power dynamics that exist in violent relationships and to appropriate attitudes and responses to display in court.[273] In specialist domestic violence courts (SDVCs) the magistrates work in partnership with other agencies, both from within and outside the criminal justice system, with the dual aims of improving victim satisfaction and safety and increasing offender accountability. Thus, unlike in traditional non-specialist courts, the victim has an 'advocate' who may speak to the prosecution on her behalf and thereby communicate information to the magistrates.[274] It is debatable whether having SDVCs has any significant effect on the outcomes of domestic violence cases in the magistrates' courts. Research has shown that victim retraction rates are still high, and ways of continuing prosecutions without the victim's support (for example through use of other evidence collected via enhanced evidence gathering policies) are yet to make a big impact in many of the SDVCs. However, some SDVCs have increased their conviction rate through increased guilty pleas and convictions following trial.[275] Increasing the conviction rate dovetails with a crime control agenda and so it is possible to view specialist courts as part of a phenomenon, observed in the Canadian context by Roach (1999),[276] of harnessing victims' rights in pursuit of crime control. There is variation in the experiences of victims using the SDVCs; not all received a good response from the magistrates or other criminal

---

[270] Plotnikoff J and Woolfson R, *Review of the Effectiveness of Specialist Courts in Other Jurisdictions* (London: Department for Constitutional Affairs, 2005).

[271] Matrix Knowledge Group, *Dedicated Drug Court Pilots; A Process Report* (London: Ministry of Justice, 2008).

[272] Brown R and Payne S, *Process Evaluation of Salford Community Justice Initiative* (London: Ministry of Justice, 2007).

[273] For research on the first domestic violence courts in England and Wales, which provided the basis for the programme for national roll out, see Cook et al, *Evaluation of Specialist Domestic Violence Courts/Fast Track Systems* (London: Crown Prosecution Service and Department for Constitutional Affairs, 2004).

[274] These 'advocates' are from a range of voluntary sector support agencies such as women's aid (see Cook et al, 2004).

[275] See Burton M, *Legal Responses to Domestic Violence* (Abingdon: Routledge-Cavendish, 2008) ch 7.

[276] See discussion in Ch 1.

justice agencies.[277] Of those who had experience of the magistrates' courts before specialisation, some did not feel that outcome or process had improved that much for them. Victims of domestic violence are as much interested in the process of the case as in the outcome. From a freedom perspective one of the recurring issues for victims of crime, particularly domestic violence, is the frequency with which defendants breach their conditional bail and are regranted bail. This erodes victim confidence in the ability of the criminal justice system to protect them and perhaps contributes to the high level of victim withdrawal. But conditional bail is, as we have seen, a convenient way to deal with the resource implications of remanding defendants into custody. It might then be fair to conclude that SDVCs are not primarily about enhancing victims' rights but about pursuing traditional criminal justice goals which may pay scant attention to either the victim's interests or the defendant's due process rights.

9.7 **Conclusion**

It is no exaggeration to say that magistrates' courts are crime control courts overlaid with a thin layer of due process icing, or in the case of specialist courts, victim orientated icing. At every twist and turn in the process, defendants are saddled with handicaps which undermine their willingness or ability to stand on their rights in court. Some are denied legal aid, some are denied bail and a majority do not receive proper assistance and advice from their legal advisers. Some will not receive advance disclosure of the prosecution case and many more will receive inadequate or misleading disclosure. Some defendants will be offered tempting oven-ready deals prepared by prosecutors and served up by legal advisers.[278] Many adult defendants will be told that longer delays and a higher sentence can be expected if they elect trial by jury but that the prospects of acquittal before the magistrates are bleak. Many will already know this from previous experience. Youths who would like to contest their guilt before a jury have no choice but to lump magistrates' court trial.

For defendants, the process must seem like an obstacle course with formidable impediments to them continuing to maintain their innocence. Meanwhile managerialist reforms hurry and harry the defendant on to the ever-more smooth path of least resistance, the guilty plea. Some will end up pleading guilty to, or being found guilty of, crimes they did not commit.

These miscarriages of justice are not the stuff of headline news. The possibility that innocent people will plead guilty is even now little recognised and excites little concern. Appreciation of the role that more due process could play in protecting us against the abuse of police and prosecutorial power is very limited, but this is to be expected. For it tends to be marginalised groups (black people, the unemployed and the poor) who suffer most from whatever abuse of power takes place. It is easy for the rest of us to

---

[277] Burton (2008) Ch 7.   [278] See ch 8.

turn a blind eye to this as we gratefully focus instead on the high conviction rate that our courts achieve in seeking to repress crime on our behalf.

This is all done in the name of 'efficiency' or sometimes in the guise of victims' rights. Efficiency is consistent with the freedom perspective, but not at any cost. The cost appears small because these low-profile courts appear to deal with trivia. But in reality they deal with a vast amount of serious issues. The processes and sentencing outcomes in many cases are enormously intrusive, yet most adjudication is done by either a bench of case-hardened lay magistrates or a similarly case-hardened lone professional judge – chosen, in any one case, at random. Doris Day, and other 'regular' defendants, will continue to be caught between an all too familiar rock and a hard place, with diminishing prospects of being allowed to take their case before a jury. Despite the HRA, the ECHR has failed to bolster the fairness of trial by magistrates. A programme of managerial reforms have reduced the jury-like qualities of the magistracy. The government seems to be less interested in the rights of victims and defendants to a fair trial than it is in the responsibility of defendants to plead guilty and the responsibility of magistrates' courts to convict. From a freedom perspective we would hope for a more genuine attempt to address the needs of victims, such as those experiencing domestic violence, without further eroding defendants' rights.

Further Reading

Cammiss S and Stride C, 'Modelling Mode of Trial' (2008) 48(4) BJ Crim 482

Darbyshire P, 'An Essay on the Importance and Neglect of the Magistracy' (1997) Crim LR 627

McConville M et al, *Standing Accused* (Oxford: Clarendon Press, 1994)

Young R and Wilcox A, 'The Merits of Legal Aid in the Magistrates' Courts Revisited' [2007] Crim LR 109

10

Trial by judge and jury

[In our observational study of Crown Court trials we] collected a rich set
of hard-to-follow exchanges between lawyers and witnesses [including]:
PROSECUTION: 'Was there no sexual intercourse?'
DEFENCE: 'Yes.'
PROSECUTION: 'Are you admitting it or denying it?'
One problematic construction is the double negative . . . A defendant with
acknowledged learning difficulties was asked 'you can't be certain that
you think it was not possible that you filled in the first side of the form?'[1]

Key issues

- The influence of the judge on the trial process and outcome
- How jury composition affects perceptions of the fairness and legitimacy of jury trial
- The impact of jury composition and juror attitudes on verdicts
- Whether key evidential rules unduly favour the defence or prosecution
- Attempts to further erode the practical significance of jury trial

Jury trial is the public face of the criminal justice system, the image with which we are all familiar from countless news reports and fictionalised accounts. The jury is a key battleground for the due process and crime control models, because jury trial is used in the most serious cases such as murder, rape and terrorism. A high rate of guilty verdicts is thus essential to the strategy of effective crime control. The deterrent aim of the system would be undermined if in 'too high' a proportion of these widely publicised cases the defendants were allowed to walk free from the court. Similarly, the very authority of the state might be called into question if juries acquitted too readily, especially in obviously political cases concerning official secrets, terrorist activities and so forth.

---

[1] Fielding N, *Courting Violence: Offences against the Person Cases in Court* (Oxford: OUP, 2006) pp 177–8.

Trials by jury can be sharply contested affairs in which the case construction techniques used at earlier stages of the criminal process (see chs 1–7) are exposed to 12 members of the public. These dozen jurors have to choose who to believe, and their choice may depend to a large extent on their backgrounds and prior experiences, as well as the mores, prejudices and panics of the wider society in which they live. Sometimes it may come down to little more than whether people have faith in the police or not; people who have experienced negative encounters with the police may perhaps be willing to believe that the police might, for example, fabricate evidence.

Although jury trial offers a measure of external scrutiny to the case constructions of criminal justice professionals it is statistically speaking largely an irrelevance. Some have argued that the jury's symbolic or legitimising function far outweighs its practical significance.[2] Of all defendants proceeded against in the criminal courts, less than 1% have their fate determined by a jury. The vast majority of criminal proceedings (over 95%) are concluded in the magistrates' courts.[3] Of those cases committed to the Crown Court the majority end up not as jury acquittals but as guilty pleas or judge ordered or directed acquittals.[4] This pattern of acquittals gives us one indication of the importance of the trial judge.   Even where it is left to the jury to decide whether the prosecution has proved guilt beyond reasonable doubt, judges often exert a strong influence on the outcome and are far from being the passive impartial referee as depicted in adversarial theory.[5] Their influence has been increasing in recent years as they have been called upon to play an even more active part in managing cases.[6] Trial by jury may be thought of as 'a cornerstone of our system of criminal justice',[7] and may command considerable support from the public[8] and members of the senior judiciary,[9] but it is important to remember the significant role of the judge in 'trial by judge and jury'.

---

[2] See in particular Darbyshire P, 'The Lamp That Shows That Freedom Lives – Is it Worth the Candle?' [1991] Crim LR 740 and, by the same author, 'An Essay on the Importance and Neglect of the Magistracy' [1997] Crim LR 627.

[3] Around two million defendants are proceeded against each year in the magistrates' courts, compared to just 96,992 committed to the Crown Court in 2007–08: CPS, *Annual Report 2007–8* (London: CPS, 2008).

[4] In 2007–08, 71.4% of defendants pleaded guilty in the Crown Court and a further 13.9% were acquitted by the judge (London: CPS, 2008).

[5] See further Jackson J and Doran S, *Judge Without Jury* (Oxford: Clarendon Press, 1995) pp 99–110.

[6] See Rule 3.2 of the Criminal Procedure Rules (<http://www.justice.gov.uk/criminal/procrules_fin/rulesmenu.htm>– accessed 5 January 2010); see further *K & Ors* [2006] EWCA Crim 724.

[7] Home Office, *Juries in Serious Fraud Trials* (London: Home Office Communication Directorate, 1998a) para 2.2.

[8] Roberts J and Hough M, *Public Opinion and the Jury: An International Literature Review* (Ministry of Justice Research Series 1/09) (London: Ministry of Justice, 2009).

[9] Lord Phillips 'Trusting the Jury', Kalisher Lecture 23 October 2007 (<http://www.judiciary.gov.uk/docs/speeches/lcj_trusting_juries_231007.pdf>– accessed 5 January 2010).

10.1 **Directed and ordered acquittals – weak cases?**

The formal distinction between directed and ordered acquittals is not difficult to grasp. If the prosecution indicates that it will not be offering evidence at trial, the judge orders the jury to acquit. A directed acquittal, by contrast, occurs on the instigation of the prosecutor, the defence or the judge, after the trial has begun 'Where the judge comes to the conclusion that the prosecution evidence, taken at the highest, is such that a jury properly directed could not properly convict upon it, it is his duty, upon a submission being made, to stop the case.'[10]

In 2007–08 there were 12,356 judge ordered and 1,189 judge directed acquittals. There has been a small reduction in the percentage of judge ordered and directed acquittals in recent years, but there are still more than twice as many judge ordered acquittals than acquittals following trial.[11] In the years immediately following the creation of the CPS in the mid 1980s the proportion of Crown Court proceedings which resulted in non-jury acquittals rose steadily, although the reasons for this were a matter of dispute.[12] As we discussed in ch 7, the level of directed and ordered acquittals raises the question of whether the prosecution is adequately discharging its duty in the Code for Crown Prosecutors to continue only with those cases where a court is more likely than not to convict. That it is not so doing is suggested by research showing many acquittals are foreseeable.[13] Bureaucratic pressures or professional misjudgement may explain the failure to discontinue some foreseeably weak cases, or the prosecution may simply be hoping the defendant will plead guilty.[14] If a defendant calls the prosecution's bluff by insisting on trial by jury, one natural response is to drop the case by offering no evidence.

Block et al (1993) noted that around half of the directed acquittals occurred before the end of the prosecution case at the intervention of the judge. There were also cases in which the judge pressured the prosecution into offering no evidence by revealing that the result of the case would be a bind over whether or not the prosecution went

---

[10] *Galbraith* [1981] 1 WLR 1039 at 1042.

[11] Judge ordered acquittals fell from 13.8% of Crown Court case outcomes in 2005–06 to 12.7% in 2007–08 and judge directed acquittals fell from 1.6% to 1.2%. Jury acquittals comprised 5.4% of all Crown Court outcomes in 2007–08 (CPS, 2008). See also *Judicial and Court Statistics 2007* (London: MoJ, 2008): table 6.8 shows that in 2007, 60% of acquittals were judge ordered, 10% judge directed and 29% by the jury.

[12] See Baldwin J, 'Understanding Judge Ordered and Directed Acquittals in the Crown Court' [1997] Crim LR 536 at p 537 and Lewis P, 'The CPS and Acquittals by Judge: Finding the Balance' [1997] Crim LR 653.

[13] Block et al, *Ordered and Directed Acquittals in the Crown Court* (Royal Commission on Criminal Justice, Research Study No 15) (London: HMSO, 1993a). The results are summarised by the authors in 'Ordered and Directed Acquittals in the Crown Court: A Time of Change?' [1993b] Crim LR 95. Baldwin (1997: 541). But note that Baldwin's sample over-represents cases likely to cause prosecutor difficulty: Lewis (1997).

[14] See McConville et al, *The Case for the Prosecution* (London: Routledge, 1991) ch 8; Baldwin (1997: 548).

ahead.[15] In the researchers' view, the seriousness of the offence and the strength of the evidence in many such instances was such that the case should have been left to the jury to decide. From a due process perspective it could be said that by directing or ordering acquittals judges are giving priority to ensuring innocent defendants are not convicted. But it can also be argued that crime control concerns may explain why at a relatively late stage in the process judges and prosecutors might abandon weak cases; they may take the view that less serious cases, such as assault, theft or burglary do not merit the resources of jury trial in circumstances where the defendant maintains a not guilty plea. It is perhaps more difficult to explain why judges would acquit in strong cases of serious crime but seriousness and strength of evidence are both factors that are open to interpretation. Some trial judges may simply be taking a different view from prosecutors, police or researchers as to what counts as an important enough case to justify the resources involved in a Crown Court contest, perhaps because they feel less susceptible to the pressure that the police and CPS have come under in recent years to pursue cases involving vulnerable victims (eg rape, domestic violence and child abuse).[16]

The study by Block et al (1993) raises further questions about the propriety of defence solicitors or counsel advising defendants that, given the 'strength' of the prosecution case, they should plead guilty (see ch 8). The strength of the case on paper will often not be reflected in court should the defence decide to fight. It should be noted, however, that the Block et al study was not one of weak cases per se, but of cases that ended in an ordered or directed acquittal (some of which were in fact strong). It would be wrong to assume that all weak cases end in acquittal. Some end in conviction. In the Crown Court study conducted by Zander and Henderson, judges, defence barristers, and prosecution barristers agreed that around one-fifth of all contested cases were based on a weak prosecution case. Although the great majority of these cases ended in acquittal, the respondents reported that between 4–8% ended in conviction.[17] Conversely, strong cases do not always end in conviction – the acquittal rate in such cases was between 21 and 27% according to barristers and judges.[18]

Clearly, the outcome of contested cases is often uncertain. This helps explain why the CPS prosecutes so many weak cases. Where the CPS drop a case, a conviction is lost, whereas one which is continued may result in conviction, notwithstanding its apparent weakness. The police know this, and also know that most cases will, in any event, terminate with a guilty plea. To attempt to secure more evidence in order to 'firm up' a prosecution case, or to clarify ambiguous statements made by witnesses,

---

[15] The bind over is best described as a 'suspended fine' and may be imposed on anyone involved in court proceedings, whether found guilty of an offence or not.

[16] The influence on the police of changing public attitudes to offences involving vulnerable victims is discussed in Gregory J and Lees S, 'Attrition in Rape and Sexual Assault Cases' (1996) 36 BJ Crim 1 at pp 2–8. For the attitude of prosecutors see Baldwin (1997: 543).

[17] Zander M and Henderson P, *Crown Court Study* (Royal Commission on Criminal Justice, Research Study No 19) (London: HMSO, 1993) pp 184–5.   [18] Ibid: 185.

'would often be, from the police point of view, wasted effort'.[19] Baldwin[20] found the same attitude among some of the CPS lawyers he interviewed. McConville et al conclude that:

Many [not guilty] verdicts, even when judge-directed, were impossible to predict. Indeed, most contests, and many non-contested cases, represent intrinsically ambiguous situations or situations in which the 'facts' were simply incomplete in vital ways. These were cases which the police may have been able to clarify but did not, cases in which clarification was not possible or potentially strong cases which – because of their relative or absolute triviality – the police and/or CPS could not be bothered to fight over… The idea that the pattern of acquittals and convictions reflects either real situations 'out there' or the product of the obstacle course of Due Process just does not stand up to scrutiny.[21]

The outcome of cases is also dependant on the level of preparatory work carried out by the prosecution and the defence. In reality the defence rarely does more than respond to the prosecution case, and it is the level of care and effort that the police commit to a case that is the crucial factor in determining outcome. As earlier chapters have shown, police commitment is more a product of their own informal working rules and assumptions than officially sanctioned criteria such as the seriousness of the case.[22] As a corollary, the minority of Crown Court cases that go before a jury for determination range from the fairly trivial to the very serious, from the evidentially weak to those in which the prosecution appears to hold all the aces. It is important to keep this point in mind when we consider (in 10.4 and 10.5 below) the various attempts that have been made to evaluate the performance of the jury and whether the acquittal rate by the jury is 'too high'.

We have suggested that practice in this area has been influenced by both due process and crime control values. These models do not help us determine how these tensions should be resolved and they leave out of consideration the interests of victims. From a freedom perspective, however, we can accept the importance of ensuring that evidentially weak cases are either discontinued or strengthened, regardless of whether or not the victim is vulnerable.[23] It is not acceptable to have defendants run the risk of conviction, particularly in a serious case, where the evidence is weak. But because resources are limited, this perspective contends that strengthening would be the better option in cases of seriousness, and discontinuing the better option in relatively trivial matters. In the 1990s, Crown Prosecutors considered that, even if they were inclined to do so, they did not have the time or resources (legal, financial and organisational) to review cases thoroughly or to arrange for their strengthening.[24] It was simply unrealistic to expect the CPS to be able to reorient itself towards the

---

[19] McConville et al (1991: 171).   [20] Baldwin (1997: 548).   [21] McConville et al (1991: 171).

[22] See ch 7 in particular.

[23] A further alternative is to remove the relatively non-serious cases from the expensive setting of the Crown Court and handle them in the magistrates' court instead. As we saw in ch 8, this approach seems to prioritise economic considerations over those of justice.

[24] See Baldwin (1997: 547). Managerialism is discussed in 1.7.

freedom model in the absence of support for that model amongst the political and legal elites which determine the goals and resources of such public agencies. But following changes made under the Criminal Justice Act 2003, the CPS has taken over from the police the power to choose which charges to bring against suspects. The government has also placed growing emphasis on the CPS advising the police on what is needed to strengthen a case at the investigation stage. Unfortunately, the government's interest here is not so much to enhance freedom as to ensure that more offenders are brought (efficiently, effectively and economically) to justice, so the temptations to prosecute weak cases (given the realistic expectation that many of these will be disposed through guilty pleas) remain.[25]

The freedom model would also demand that vulnerable victims are empowered so that, for example, they felt able to attend court and give evidence if that is what they wished to do.[26] It is too easy to assume that the retraction of a witness statement or the failure of a prosecution witness to appear at court is 'unforeseeable' and thus nobody's fault. Decisions by witnesses are not taken in a vacuum but are crucially affected by socio-economic factors and the shadow of the law and legal processes (see Gregory and Lees, 1996). For example, one of us worked on the Baldwin study of non-jury acquittals (cited above) and saw from a reading of CPS files how vulnerable witnesses sometimes braved a court appearance only to find that the case was adjourned by the trial judge at the last minute. One can imagine the anxiety, inconvenience and frustration this may have caused. Not surprisingly some of these witnesses failed to appear subsequently. The time and convenience of civilian witnesses has historically ranked low in the priorities of those operating the Crown Court.[27] If the rules of criminal procedure and evidence, and the practices of trial judges and court administrators, were more sensitive to the problems of witnesses, without prejudicing the right of the defendant to a fair trial, the level of ordered and directed acquittals could be reduced in a freedom-enhancing way. The government has belatedly recognised that inadequate 'witness care' has led to adjourned hearings, discontinuances and acquittals, and responded by setting up a *No Witness, No Justice* initiative. This requires the police and the CPS to support witnesses more closely through the prosecution process, including arranging pre-trial familiarisation visits to the courts, and helping with travel and childcare.[28] While this is clearly a good idea in itself, the effect it is having on directed and ordered acquittals has yet to be documented. There has been a reduction in the discontinuance rate since the mid 2000s[29] but, as we noted in 7.3, we need to know *why* cases are, or are not, being discontinued (and what kind of cases they are)

[25] This is more fully discussed in 7.3 and 8.4.

[26] See ch 13 for discussion of the provisions of the Youth Justice and Criminal Evidence Act 1999 designed to support vulnerable witnesses.

[27] See Rock P, *The Social World of an English Crown Court* (Oxford: Clarendon Press, 1993) ch 7.

[28] See PA Consulting, *No Witness, No Justice – National Victim and Witness Care Project: Interim Evaluation Report* (December 2004).

[29] In Crown Prosecution Service, *Annual Report 2007/08* (London: CPS, 2008) notes the discontinuance rate has dropped to just 9.9%.

before we can reach a judgement as to whether this is to be welcomed or not. There is an urgent need for independent research into the new prosecution arrangements and their effect on the pattern of case disposal in the Crown Court.

10.2 **The composition of the jury**

In legal theory, jurors are selected at random so that juries will be reasonably socially representative. In practice, however, this principle has always been subject to important exceptions and modifications. For centuries eligibility to serve on a jury was tied to a property qualification. Following the Juries Act 1974 (as amended), a person is eligible for jury service if aged between 18 and 70, included on the electoral register and resident in the UK for at least five years since the age of 13. Whether the electoral register should be used as the only juror source list has been debated in recent years as certain groups, such as ethnic minorities, the 20–24 age group, and renters, are likely to be under-represented on the register. The register could be supplemented by references to other lists such as those of the vehicle licensing authority.[30] However, Thomas has argued that there is no need to alter the juror source list to increase the proportion of ethnic minorities summoned as they are currently summoned in proportion to their representation in the juror catchment area in almost every Crown Court.[31] Thomas claims to have busted a long-standing myth that ethnic minorities are under-represented on juries but, as we discuss below, her findings still provide grounds for unease about the racial composition of juries.

Prior to the Criminal Justice Act 2003, many of those falling within the basic eligibility criteria were nonetheless ineligible, disqualified or excusable from jury service. The ineligible included those who might have an undue influence on a jury's deliberations, such as lawyers, judges and the police, and those who are seen as unsuited for a judgmental role, such as nuns, monks and the clergy. The disqualified included anyone who had received a serious criminal penalty following conviction. Members of Parliament, the armed services and the medical profession had the right to be excused if summoned, while any person could be excused service if they could show good cause. Airs and Shaw (1999) found that of 50,000 people summoned for jury service in June–July 1999, only one-third were available, about half of whom were allowed to defer their service until a later date. Of the remaining two-thirds, 13% were ineligible, disqualified or excused as of right, 15% failed to attend court or their summons was returned 'undelivered' and 38% were excused. The many excusals and exemptions were not randomly distributed across different populations, distorting the

---

30 Airs J and Shaw A, *Jury Excusal and Deferral* (Home Office Research Findings No 102) (London: Home Office, 1999).

31 Thomas C, *Diversity and Fairness in the Jury System* (Ministry of Justice Research Series 2/07) (London: Ministry of Justice, 2007). See also Thomas C, 'Exposing the Myths of Jury Service' [2008] Crim LR 415.

representativeness of juries.[32] In particular, observed Lord Justice Auld in his Review of the Criminal Courts, juries were being deprived 'of the experience and skills of a wide range of professional and otherwise successful and busy people'.[33] To counter the impression that 'jury service is only for those not important or clever enough to get out of it'[34] he recommended that everyone should be eligible for jury service, save for those who are disqualified by reason of mental disorder or a serious criminal record (as before).[35] This was accepted and s 321 and Sch 33 of the Criminal Justice Act 2003 eliminated excusals as of right (except for serving military personnel) and the categories of ineligibility. Thomas found that the changes to the eligibility rules made by the Criminal Justice Act increased the proportion of jurors serving from 54% to 64% and that the number of those disqualified fell by one-third and excusals by one-quarter. The research found income and employment status were the most important factors predicting whether a summoned juror would serve, with low income, retired and unemployed people least likely to serve. According to Thomas (2007, p 197): 'The reality is that the highest rate of jury service for summoned jurors are among middle to high-income earners, and that those of higher status profession are fully represented among serving jurors.' Juror service may no longer only be for those not important or clever enough to avoid it,[36] but jury composition is still distorted in certain complex cases, where the anticipated length of the trial means that those with professional commitments may be unable or unwilling to take time off to serve.[37] And Thomas' findings suggest that poorer people are now under-represented on juries.

Since the disqualification for various criminal justice professionals sitting on juries was removed there have been a steady stream of appeals against convictions alleging the appearance of jury bias.[38] In *Abdroikov*[39] the House of Lords stated that the test to be applied was whether a fair minded and informed observer would conclude there was a real possibility of unfairness beyond the reach of standard judicial warnings. Lord Bingham observed 'most adult human beings, as a result of their background,

---

[32] Darbyshire P, with research by Maughan A and Stewart A, 'What Can We Learn from Published Jury Research? Findings for the Criminal Courts Review' [2001] Crim LR 970 at p 971. This is a summary of the research literature which omits citations, but a citation rich version can be found at <http://www.kingston.ac.uk/~ku00596/elsres01.pdf> (accessed 5 January 2010).

[33] Auld LJ, *Review of the Criminal Courts of England and Wales: Report* (London: TSO, 2001) para 5.13.

[34] Ibid. For discussion of Auld's proposals on jury reform see McEwan et al, 'Evidence, Jury Trials and Witness Protection – The Auld Review of the English Criminal Courts' (2002) 6 E & P 163.

[35] Anyone sentenced in the past ten years to a community order, drug order, or prison cannot serve as a juror and those who have at any time been sentenced to prison for five years or more are disqualified for life. For full details see Sch 33 of the 2003 Act.

[36] Issue has been taken with the way some of the findings are presented. See Darbyshire P and Thomas C, 'Exposing Jury Myths – Letters to the Editor' [2008] Crim LR 888.

[37] Julian R, 'Judicial Perspectives on the Conduct of Serious Fraud Trials' [2007] Crim LR 751. Senior judges interviewed supported the principle of random selection but acknowledged that professionals may get excused from long trials. See also 10.6 below.

[38] In the first of these, *Pintori* [2007] EWCA Crim 1700, the Court of Appeal quashed the conviction because a juror in the case knew three police witnesses and had worked closely with one of them.

[39] [2007] UKHL 37.

education, experience, harbour certain prejudices and predilections of which they may be conscious or unconscious… the safeguards established to protect the impartiality of the jury, when properly operated, do all that can reasonably be done to neutralise the ordinary prejudices and predilections to which we are all prone'.[40] Nevertheless he acknowledged that the allegations against police and prosecutors were not that they were subject to 'ordinary prejudices' but those which might stem from being professionally committed to one side of the adversarial conflict. This led the court to conclude that a CPS prosecutor should never sit as a juror in a CPS prosecution but could sit in a case where the prosecution was being brought by another prosecuting authority. Baroness Hale observed that junior CPS employees might also be allowed to sit as jurors for CPS prosecutions brought by areas other than where they were employed. The court concluded that since Parliament had made police officers eligible to serve there was no basis for disqualifying them simply because of their occupation; they should only be excluded if a challenge to police evidence comprised an important part of the case or if there was some connection between the police juror and a police witness beyond the fact they were from the same police area. Baroness Hale argued there was more distance between the police and the 'prosecution process' than is the case with a CPS lawyer, as police officers are only identified with the 'fight against crime generally rather than the prosecution process in particular'.[41] Those defendants who are unlucky enough to have random selection throw up a police officer on their jury, may not be much comforted by Baroness Hale's questionable distinction.

The Court of Appeal seems to have taken a wide approach to interpreting *Abdroikov* which leans towards allowing criminal justice professionals to serve. In *Khan*,[42] the Court of Appeal considered the convictions of several defendants whose juries variously comprised serving police officers, prison officers and a CPS employee. The police officer juror in one trial knew a police witness in the case but the conviction was upheld as the court concluded an objective observer would not suspect bias. Another conviction was upheld in the case of a police officer juror called upon to assess a conflict between the evidence of the defendant and police witness, as the court said that the issue in conflict was of 'little significance'.[43] The CPS employee was a former caseworker employed as a press officer for the CPS at the time of the trial. The court said this did not create an appearance of bias because the prosecution was being brought by a non-CPS authority. In relation to prison officers it was stated that there was unlikely to be any bias or appearance of bias against the defendant because this could only stem from suspicion that the prison officer juror might recognise the defendant as a former prisoner. The jurors in this case had not encountered the prisoners whilst they had been in prison on remand and in any event it was said knowledge of bad character would not automatically result in the juror ceasing to be independent

---

[40] At [23].   [41] At [52].   [42] [2008] 2 Cr App R 13.

[43] To similar effect see *Burdett* [2009] EWCA Crim 543 in which there were an issue between the defendant and a police witness (the sole prosecution witness) but the court upheld the conviction despite a police officer sitting as a juror (and becoming the jury foreman) in the case.

and impartial. The court concluded by stating that trial judges be made aware of any connection, past or present, potential jurors have with the administration of justice so that they can address the question of bias. However the decision creates an impression that judges should work with the statutory expectation of eligibility and that the discretion to disqualify jurors who are criminal justice insiders should be sparingly exercised.

Judges are clearly reluctant to interfere with the principle of random selection to remove jurors who may be biased, or appear to be biased, against the defendant because of their professional occupation. However, the principle of random selection has never been sacrosanct. There is a long history of attempts to rig the composition of the jury.[44] In certain cases the prosecution can carry out preliminary investigations into potential jurors, known as jury vetting, and use the information to 'stand by' (ie exclude) jurors before the trial begins.[45] The practice came to light in modern times in the 1978 'ABC trial' of a soldier and two journalists for offences under the Official Secrets Act. As a result of a secret prosecution application to the judge, an 82-member panel from which a jury was to be chosen was vetted for 'loyalty'. Defence objections to this process were strengthened when it was discovered that the prosecution had failed to act on information that two members of the jury so selected had signed the Official Secrets Act and that the foreman was an ex-member of the SAS (Special Air Services regiment). As a result of the public outcry which followed, the Attorney-General published the guidelines for the vetting of jury panels which had existed as a 'restricted document' for three years previously.[46] It was admitted in Parliament that jury vetting had been going on 'at least since 1948, and probably since a great deal earlier than that'.[47] Soon after the Court of Appeal upheld the practice of routine Criminal Records Office checks. There would be no objection to this if the purpose of the check was merely to establish whether any juror fell foul of the disqualification provisions in the Juries Act 1974. But the Court went on to say that the prosecution could justifiably exclude a juror with a criminal conviction not serious enough to trigger a statutory disqualification.

The Court of Appeal refrained from commenting on jury vetting which went beyond checking criminal records, but the most recent redraft of the Attorney-General guidelines states that additional checks may be made with the security services and the police special branch in security and terrorist cases. This is to counter the perceived 'danger that a juror's political beliefs are so biased as to go beyond normally reflecting the broad spectrum of views and interests in the community to reflect the extreme views of sectarian interest or pressure groups to a degree which might interfere with his fair assessment of the facts of the case or lead him to exert improper pressure on his

---

[44] See Freeman M, 'The Jury on Trial' (1981) CLP 65 at pp 75–6 for examples drawn from the eighteenth and nineteenth centuries. For further examples from an even earlier period see Masschaele J, *Jury, State, and Society in Medieval England* (New York: Palgrave Macmillan, 2008) ch 3.

[45] On the right to stand by see McEldowney J, 'Stand by for the Crown – An Historical Analysis' [1979] Crim LR 272.   [46] The guidelines were published in *The Times* on 11 October 1978.

[47] HC Deb 5th Series, vol 958, col 28, 13 November 1978.

fellow jurors'.[48] Since 'extreme views' is a term capable of wide interpretation there is clearly scope for abuse here.[49] A safeguard is that the Attorney-General must author- ise each request for such additional checks, but this clearly does not constitute an independent check on state malpractice. It was said of the 2002 trial of David Shayler (a former MI5 officer charged with disclosing secret information) that the request to the Attorney General to authorise security checks into the jury panel was the first since Labour came to power in 1997.[50] There may have been more checks since then, particularly given the number of recent trials for terrorist offences. But the focus of any critical scrutiny should not merely be on the frequency with which authorisation is given, but also on the nature of the cases which trigger the procedure, the reliability of the information held or gathered by the security services, and the impact on jury selection.

The extent, nature and consequences of jury vetting are not known. The secrecy surrounding the practice is itself a denial of due process values. A further problem is that the prosecution is placed under no duty to 'stand by' jurors when checks suggest that they might be biased against the defendant. Instead the guidelines provide that in such a situation:

the defence should be given, at least, an indication of why that potential juror may be inimi- cal to their interests; but because of its nature and source it may not be possible to give the defence more than a general indication.[51]

This falls a long way short of mandating full disclosure to the defence. Moreover, the Association of Chief Police Officers has recommended that the police should only make checks on behalf of the defence if requested to do so by the Director of Public Prosecutions.[52] There is no law which stops the defence from vetting a jury panel itself, although it might have difficulty in securing the names sufficiently in advance. The problem is most defendants do not have abundant resources and the Criminal Defence Service[53] would be unlikely to pay for a vetting exercise. The evidence suggests that the state authorities are more concerned with ensuring a 'fair' hearing for the prosecution than for the defendant.

Other restrictions on the ability of the defence to influence the composition of the jury support this conclusion. The defence were traditionally allowed to exclude pro- spective jurors without the need to give any reason. The number of such 'peremptory challenges' allowed was reduced from 20 to seven in 1948 and to three (per defendant)

---

[48] Attorney-General's Guidelines on the Exercise of the Crown of its Right of Stand-by (1988) 88 Cr App Rep 123 [5].

[49] See, for example, East R, 'Jury Packing: A Thing of the Past?' (1985) 48 MLR 518 at 527–8.

[50] *The Guardian*, 29 July 2002.   [51] Attorney-General's guidelines (1988) 88 Cr App Rep 123 [11].

[52] The recommendations are published as an annex to the Attorney-General's guidelines: (1988) 88 Cr App Rep 123. For the CPS guidance on jury vetting, see <http://www.cps.gov.uk/legal/h_to_k/jury_vetting/ index.html> (accessed 5 January 2010).

[53] The Criminal Defence Service administers criminal legal aid under the auspices of the Legal Services Commission, both bodies created by the Access to Justice Act 1999.

in 1977 before being abolished by s 118 of the Criminal Justice Act 1987. In the White Paper which preceded the 1987 Act the government accepted that peremptory challenge might be used for proper reasons such as to adjust the age, sex or race balance on the jury, but contended that the defence sometimes abused the right so as to remove jurors thought to have too much respect for the law.[54] If the system was serious about prioritising the acquittal of the innocent, one might think that the occasional 'abuse' of the right of peremptory challenge would be regarded as a price worth paying for more representative juries. At the very least one would expect that the right of peremptory challenge in proper circumstances (as described in the White Paper) would be preserved in any reform of the law. Yet despite the timely publication of research showing that peremptory challenges had no discernible impact on the likelihood of acquittal,[55] the government successfully pressed through its plan to abolish this defence right in its entirety.[56] By contrast, the government resisted the powerful argument that fairness demanded that the prosecution should simultaneously lose its equivalent right to 'stand by' (ie exclude) jurors without cause. Instead the Attorney-General issued guidelines exhorting, but not requiring, prosecutors to exercise this right more sparingly in future.[57]

The defence continues to share with the prosecution the right to challenge any juror 'for cause', but this is of little practical use since jurors may not be questioned about their beliefs or background unless counsel knows of facts to justify such questioning.[58] Where the fruits of a prosecution vetting are passed on to the defence, the generality of the information supplied (see above) may not be enough to support a challenge for cause. Usually defence counsel know no more than a juror's name and address.

The defence can form a visual impression as to the racial, class and age balance on the jury, and this raises the question of whether challenges can be made for cause to achieve a more mixed jury. A Practice Note issued in 1973 stressed that it would be wrong to allow the exclusion of jurors on such 'general' grounds as race, religion, political beliefs or occupation.[59] The Court of Appeal subsequently followed this up by

---

[54] *Criminal Justice, Plans for Legislation* (Cmnd 9658) (London: Home Office, 1986) para 33.

[55] See Vennard J and Riley D, 'The Use of Peremptory Challenge and Stand By of Jurors and their Relationship to Final Outcome' [1988] Crim LR 731.

[56] Critiqued by Gobert J, 'The Peremptory Challenge – An Obituary' [1989] Crim LR 528.

[57] The guidelines are to be found at (1988) 88 Cr App Rep 123.

[58] See *Chandler (No 2)* [1964] 1 All ER 761. See further Buxton R, 'Challenging and Discharging Jurors' [1990] Crim LR 225. If there is prejudicial publicity in advance of the trial, the judge may direct that the jury should answer a questionnaire to test for bias, but this will only be done in fairly extreme cases: see *Andrews (Tracey)* [1999] Crim LR 156 and accompanying commentary. Compare this with the position in the United States where questioning of prospective jurors is standard practice: May R, 'Jury Selection in the United States: Are There Lessons to be Learned?' [1998] Crim LR 270. See also the consultation paper issued by the Home Office (1998a), para 4.4 of which states that prosecution and defence counsel have in 'some recent fraud trials' devised a questionnaire for potential jurors to test for personal hardship grounds for excusal and knowledge of, or bias against, the defendants. The Government has indicated that it is against any widespread use of jury vetting: Department for Constitutional Affairs, *Jury Research and Impropriety, Response to Consultation* (CP 04/05) (London: DCA, 2005b) p 17.   [59] [1973] 1 All ER 240.

declaring in *Ford*[60] that a judge had no discretion to discharge a juror in order to secure a racially-mixed jury nor otherwise to influence the overall composition of the jury. For the Court, '"fairness" is achieved by the principle of random selection'.[61] Whereas the government had suggested in its 1987 White Paper that it would be proper to peremptorily challenge so as to achieve a socially mixed jury, the courts subsequently denied the defence the ability to challenge for cause on just this basis. Again, the fear seems to be that the defence will seek to 'rig' the jury in its favour. Yet little concern is evident that *random* selection from the available pool of jurors can never guarantee a *representative* jury.

The research by Thomas (2007), which we discussed earlier, looked at the racial composition of juries and the influence of race on jury decision-making. It found that there was no under-representation of BME (black and minority ethnic) groups sitting on juries in most of the Crown Court centres studied. However, this headline finding is less reassuring when one considers that the same research revealed that racially mixed juries are only likely to exist where BME people make up at least 10% of the juror catchment area. Only just over one-fifth of Crown Court centres fit this description, so in most centres there is little likelihood of BME representation on the jury. Thomas concluded that this was a problem for courts where there were significant pockets of BME populations in the catchment area, as in such places a high proportion of BME defendants and victims faced all white juries.[62]

The importance of the racial composition of juries needs to be considered in the context of the influence that race may have on jury deliberations and verdicts. It has been argued that where the defendant is from an ethnic minority group and there is no BME representation on the jury there is 'the distinct possibility that the different life style, mentality and experience arising from membership of an ethnic minority will not be taken sufficiently into account'.[63] But more worrying still is the likelihood that all juries will be influenced by (at worst) conscious and (at best) unconscious racial biases when interpreting evidence and assessing witness credibility, and that these will remain unexamined and unchallenged if juries are drawn from too homogenous an ethnic background.[64] As Daly and Pattenden put it:

To dismiss self-defence because those with dark skins are believed to incline to aggression is unacceptable. Other dangerous – but unfortunately all too common – stereotypes include: black people look much the same, do not respect the law and are sexually promiscu-

---

[60] [1989] 3 All ER 445; followed in *Tarrant* [1998] Crim LR 342 where a conviction was quashed on the basis that the judge was wrong to discharge a jury on the basis that 11 out of 12 of them came from the same postal district, and wrong to direct that the new jury should be drawn from a panel brought in from outside the court's normal catchment area. [61] [1989] 3 All ER 445 at 449.

[62] Thomas (2007: 193–6). See also Thomas (2008).

[63] Bohlander M, '"…By a Jury of his Peers" – The Issue of Multi-racial Juries in a Poly-ethnic Society' [1992] XIV(1) Liverpool LR 67.

[64] We invite readers in doubt about this point to take the Race IAT test at <https://implicit.harvard.edu/implicit/uk/selectatest.jsp> (accessed 5 January 2010).

ous; Muslims are terrorists or terrorist sympathizers; Jews are greedy; Asians are devious liars.[65]

Thomas attempted to explore the impact of ethnic composition of juries on outcome by using case simulations with 29 juries made up of real discharged jurors. The jurors saw a version of a filmed trial for assault in which a number of variables such as the ethnicity of the defendant and the nature of the charge (racially aggravated/non aggravated) were altered. All the juries were racially mixed. The study found that there was some evidence of same race leniency influencing the votes of individual jurors; BME jurors were more likely to show this leniency, which Thomas suggests was possibly because they felt the criminal justice system is racially biased. However, she concludes: 'The main finding of the decision-making study is that, while ethnicity can have a significant effect on the votes of some jurors in some cases, the verdicts of racially mixed juries on which these jurors sat did not discriminate against defendants based on the defendant's race.'[66] This finding of lack of racial bias in the verdicts of mixed juries is however likely to be of little comfort to BME defendants who face all white juries. Thomas concedes that the crucial question is whether all white juries, which make up the vast majority of juries in the Crown Court, discriminate against BME defendants.[67]

Juries themselves believe that diversity is important in reaching a sound verdict free of bias,[68] and despite Thomas' research there is evidence from around the world that the racial composition of a jury does make a difference to verdicts.[69] There is also the point that justice should be seen to be done. In a recent study of perceptions of fairness, 10 out of 30 black interviewees who had been tried in the Crown Court thought that the jury was racially biased or prejudiced against them.[70] In high-profile cases heard by all white juries it is not just ethnic minority defendants (or victims) who may feel a sense of injustice, but also the community from which they are drawn. While noting that there is little English research on public attitudes to the racial composition of juries, Roberts and Hough (2009) cite one survey in which one-quarter of white respondents, but almost twice as many BME respondents, said that they would be concerned about the racial composition of the jury if they were on trial.[71] An extreme example of the

---

[65] Daly G and Pattenden R, 'Racial Bias and the English Criminal Trial Jury' (2005) 64(3) CLJ 678 at p 681 (internal citations omitted).   [66] Thomas (2007: 201).

[67] Thomas is doing further research on this question for the Ministry of Justice (which commissioned her original study). See Thomas (2008). Thomas (2010) suggests that all white juries do not discriminate against BME defendants.

[68] Matthew et al, *Jurors' Perceptions, Understanding, Confidence and Satisfaction in the Jury System: A Study in Six Courts*, Online Report 05/04 (London: Home Office, 2004) available at <http://www.homeoffice.gov.uk/rds/>.

[69] Darbyshire et al (2001: 16–20). For a contrary view see McEwan et al (2002). See also Sommers S and Ellsworth P, 'How Much Do We Really Know about Race and Juries? A Review of the Social Science Theory and Research' (2003) Chicago-Kent LR 997.

[70] Hood et al, *Ethnic Minorities in the Criminal Courts: Perceptions of Fairness and Equality of Treatment* (Research Series No 2/03) (London: DCA, 2003) pp 39–40.

[71] BBC race survey cited in Roberts and Hough (2009: 27).

dangers involved is the Rodney King case in which a jury with no African-American jurors failed to convict white Los Angeles police officers of misconduct even though they had been videotaped kicking and beating an African-American suspect as he lay on the ground. This 'triggered the worst race riot in American history, two days of violence that cost 58 lives and nearly one billion pounds in property damage'.[72] Whilst the fraught history of unjust race relations in the United States provided the tinder box for this conflagration, it would be naive to think that England and Wales could never experience such problems.[73] As we have seen in earlier chapters, ethnic minorities often suffer disproportionately from the exercise of police powers and pre-trial discretion, and damage has been done to police–community relations as a result. There is a sense of racial injustice amongst some communities in this country that could be dangerously exacerbated by convictions (or acquittals, where the defendant is white but the victim is not) delivered by all white juries.

The incorporation through the Human Rights Act of the European Convention on Human Rights (ECHR) has not resulted in any great change in English law and practice concerning jury selection or jury composition. Whilst Art 6 gives defendants the right to a fair trial by an independent and impartial tribunal, the European Court of Human Rights (ECtHR) presumes that members of a tribunal are impartial unless there is evidence of subjective bias.[74] The argument that it is nigh impossible to produce such evidence in the British context, where juries do not give reasons for their decision, and that therefore the subjective presumption should not apply, was rejected by the ECtHR in *Pullar v UK*.[75] The Court accepts, however, that if an objective observer would have any ground for a legitimate doubt about a tribunal's impartiality that this is sufficient for a violation (objective bias). Would an all white jury trying a black defendant give rise to such a doubt? It seems not. In *Gregory v UK*,[76] the black defendant was convicted of robbery on a majority verdict and sentenced to six years' imprisonment. One hour after the jury had retired to consider its verdict, one juror sent a note to the judge reading 'jury showing racial overtones, one member to be excused'. The judge recalled the jury and told them that 'any thoughts of prejudice of one form or another, for or against anybody, must be put out of your minds' and that they must decide the case on the evidence alone. The ECtHR held that this redirection was sufficiently forceful to dispel any objectively held misgivings about the impartiality of the jury. Do you think Mr Gregory will have seen it that way? If you were one of his friends would you not have wanted the judge to identify the jurors showing 'racial overtones' and to have discharged them?[77] In answering these questions it is

---

[72] Alschuler A, 'The All-white American Jury' (1995) 145 NLJ 1005.

[73] See further Herbert P, 'Racism, Impartiality and Juries' (1995) 145 NLJ 1138. For some evidence of racial prejudice affecting juries see 10.5.2 below.

[74] See, for example, *Sigurdsson v Iceland* (2003) 40 EHRR 15 [37].

[75] *Pullar v UK* (1996) 22 EHRR 391.   [76] *Gregory v UK* (1997) 25 EHRR 577.

[77] The Juries Act, s 16 allows a jury to continue to hear a case with as few as nine members. Under s 17, a nine-member jury must be unanimous, whereas juries with 10 or 11 members can bring in verdicts so long as there is not more than one dissentient.

important to bear in mind the body of psychological research which shows that warnings are often ineffective in preventing or remedying prejudicial reasoning.[78] Given the judgment that a violation of the Convention did not occur in this case, it is simply inconceivable that a violation would be found on the sole ground that an all white jury had determined the fate of an ethnic minority defendant.

In the later case of *Sander v UK*[79] the ECtHR (by four votes to three) found a breach of Art 6 in fairly similar circumstances. Here a juror in the trial of two Asian defendants sent a note to the judge alleging that at least two other jurors were making racist remarks and jokes and that there was a danger that a racist conviction would follow. The judge informed the jury of the complaint and asked them to consider whether they felt able to try the case free of prejudice, solely on the evidence. The next day the judge received two inconsistent letters, one from the whole jury which denied the allegation and affirming their commitment to reach an unprejudiced decision, and one from an individual juror admitting to making racist jokes but denying he was racially biased. The judge decided not to discharge the jury, or any juror, and one of the defendants was convicted. Here the ECtHR decided that there was legitimate grounds for fearing that the tribunal was not impartial (objective bias) even if it could not be sure that the jury was actually prejudiced (subjective bias). Its reasoning is interesting in that it justified its decision in part on the basis that 'generally speaking, an admonition or direction by a judge, however clear, detailed and forceful, would not change racist views overnight' (para 30). That is consistent with the psychological research referred to above, but seemingly inconsistent with the ECtHR's stance in *Gregory*. That case was distinguished, however, on the basis that the complaint of racism was vague and not admitted by any juror. So, following *Sander*, it seems that if a precise and substantiated allegation of racism is made, the only course available to a trial judge may be to discharge the jury, or at least those jurors believed to be biased. This is a fairly minor inroad into the problem of jury bias, and more radical proposals, such as tape-recording jury deliberations,[80] have not found favour with government.[81] It is worth adding that the courts are generally unwilling to investigate allegations of racism, or indeed other kinds of alleged juror bias, once a verdict has been given.[82]

Jury vetting presents a dilemma for the state. It cannot be seen to interfere with the composition of the jury too readily as this will undermine the useful legitimising effect

---

[78] See Daly and Pattenden (2005: 690–1) and the many studies cited there.

[79] *Sander v UK* (2001) 31 EHRR 44.   [80] Daly and Pattenden (2005).

[81] Its preference is to allow the common law to develop its own regulatory strategies for dealing with 'jury impropriety': DCA (2005b).

[82] See also *Mirza* [2004] 1 AC 1118 where a four-to-one majority of the House of Lords decided that the common law position that appellate courts could not investigate allegations of racism once a verdict had been delivered was compatible with Art 6 (discussed by Quinn K, 'Jury Bias and the European Convention on Human Rights: A Well-kept Secret?' [2004] Crim LR 998). This makes it all the more important that trial judges deal with racial bias prior to verdict. A practice direction issued in the wake of *Mirza* now requires trial judges to warn jurors that they should bring any concerns about the behaviour of other jurors to their attention.

of jury trial on the criminal process as a whole.[83] Interference on security grounds also makes its refusal to countenance non-random selection to address the problem of racial bias look somewhat perverse. On the other hand, the desire to influence the outcome of a particular trial is sometimes overwhelming. The law both reflects this tension and provides for its resolution by enabling interference to take place on a covert basis. The prosecution may simply stand by a juror without giving any reason and the defence need not be told that jury vetting has taken place.[84] The prosecution's duties and powers are governed by broadly-drawn administrative directions and guidelines which provide no sanctions for breach. In stark contrast, the defence has to state reasons for challenging jurors and its more limited powers are governed by restrictive case law. The different treatment of prosecution and defence by the state authorities (including Parliament, the government and the courts) is revealing as to the dominant values in our political and legal culture.

10.3 **The verdict of the jury**

10.3.1 **Majority verdicts**

For centuries jury verdicts had to be unanimous but the Criminal Justice Act 1967 permitted a majority of not less than 10 out of 12, so long as the jury has been deliberating for at least two hours. This change has been seen by some critics as undermining the requirement that the prosecution proves guilt beyond reasonable doubt. As Freeman puts it, 'If one or two jurymen conscientiously feel strong enough to dissent from the majority view that demonstrates to my satisfaction that there is reasonable doubt as to the guilt of the accused.'[85] Others have seen majority verdicts as merely a means to prevent rogue jurors blocking convictions or acquittals.[86] The rationale for the 1967 reform was ostensibly to prevent professional criminals escaping conviction by the expedient of bribing or intimidating individual jurors. That this occasionally happens is undeniable. But the question remains of whether the majority verdict is the correct response to that problem.

In answering, one must consider the effect of the change. The introduction of majority verdicts led to a trebling of the rate at which juries fail to reach unanimity and nearly one in five (18%) of guilty verdicts are now by majority.[87] As Freeman explains:

juries when told by judges that they may consider a non-unanimous verdict simply stop deliberating when they reach the requisite majority. This may save time and money and it

---

[83] Duff P and Findlay M, 'Jury Vetting – The Jury under Attack' (1983) 3 LS 159 at pp 171–3.

[84] If the CPS vetting guidelines (<http://www.cps.gov.uk/>) are followed, however, the defence can work this out, as prosecutors are only supposed to stand-by jurors if *either* the juror is manifestly unsuitable 'but only if the defence agree', *or* in a terrorist or security case where the Attorney General has authorised this course following a security check.   [85] Freeman (1981: 69).

[86] Auld (2001: para 5.75).

[87] See Freeman (1981: 70) and MoJ (2008: 109). In 1992 the figure was nearer one in eight: Judicial Statistics 1992 (Cm 2268) (London: HMSO, 1993) p 62, table 6.10.

may be 'convenient' but how relevant should these considerations be? When managerial efficiency becomes the dominant consideration, justice can soon take a back seat.[88]

Researchers who have investigated the dynamics of jury decision-making have concluded that allowing juries to reach verdicts by a majority has resulted in them undertaking a less thorough investigation of the evidence and law.[89] This is probably because those inclined to one view have less of a need to demonstrate convincing reasons why their opponents are wrong. Instead of allowing their deliberations to be 'evidence-driven' the majority reaches for the verdict it thinks right and then constructs a narrative story of the case that fits that verdict.[90] Unsurprisingly, heterogeneous juries (where differing interpretations of the facts are to be expected) are more likely to engage in lengthy evidence-led deliberations than homogeneous ones.[91] This increases the case against all white juries that we set out above.

Majority verdicts have thus prodded jury trial in the direction of crime control. The argument that this was necessary in order to guard against 'jury nobbling' is similar to that used to deny bail to defendants on the ground that they might otherwise interfere with prosecution witnesses.[92] In both cases the argument appears to give greater weight to the conviction of the guilty at the expense of the acquittal of the innocent. In both cases there is a more appropriate response, which is to safeguard the administration of justice by other means, such as more effective protection for witnesses and jurors. The judge can, for example, make a jury protection order, under which the police will provide protection for members of the jury during the course of the trial.[93] The vast majority of trials do not involve professional criminals and so the risk of 'jury nobbling' is low. The solution adopted, allowing (in all cases) the views of one-sixth of the jury to be dismissed as 'unreasonable', appears grossly disproportionate to the supposed problem. Moreover, the determined big-time 'nobbler' can evade the supposed safeguard by the simple expedient of intimidating three or more jurors. In August 2002, for example, the trial of six defendants in Liverpool for serious drug offences collapsed after two jurors were threatened and a third offered £10,000 to return a verdict of not guilty.[94]

It is interesting to note recent legislative innovations designed to deter and perhaps remedy intimidation of jurors. While there has long been a common law offence of perverting the course of justice, Parliament created a new offence of intimidating witnesses and jurors by s 51(1) of the Criminal Justice and Public Order Act 1994. Two

---

[88] Freeman (1981: 70). See also Darbyshire P, 'Notes of a Lawyer Juror' (1990) 140 NLJ 1264 at p 1266.

[89] See, in particular, Hastie et al, *Inside the Jury* (Cambridge, MA: Harvard UP, 1983). An accessible summary to the research in this area is provided by Darbyshire et al (2001: 29–32).

[90] Note that this is rather like the problem with inquisitorialism, where facts that do not fit with one's pre-existing case theory tend to be ignored: see ch 1.

[91] Arce R, 'Evidence Evaluation in Jury Decision-Making' in Bull R and Carson D (eds), *Handbook of Psychology in Legal Contexts* (Chichester: Wiley, 1995).   [92] On bail, see ch 9.

[93] The potential prejudice or fear this might cause in the minds of the jury should be addressed by some explanatory remarks by the trial judge: *Comerford* [1998] 1 Cr App Rep 235. The same case decides that a trial judge may take the precautionary step of having the members of the jury referred to by numbers instead of the more usual procedure of stating their names in open court as they are sworn in.

[94] For this and other examples see Hansard HL col 1963 (19 November 2003).

years later it went further by enacting a new procedure for re-opening acquittals allegedly tainted by interference with the administration of justice.[95] Seven years on came
s 44 of the Criminal Justice Act 2003. This allows the prosecution to apply to a Crown
Court judge to make an order for non-jury trial. The judge must make this order if there
is evidence of a 'real and present danger that jury tampering would take place' and
that notwithstanding any steps (including the provision of police protection) which
might reasonably be taken to prevent tampering, the likelihood that it would take place
would be so substantial as to make it necessary in the interests of justice for the trial to
be heard without a jury. Strikingly, the creation of these new 'safeguards' against jury
nobbling did not lead to any reassessment by the Government of the 'need' for majority verdicts. As in other areas of the criminal process, once a due process safeguard is
dismantled or weakened, the chances of it being resurrected are slim.

The argument that majority verdicts allow the views of extremists to be neutralised
is defective. By definition, people of extreme views are in a minority in the populace
at large. Most juries will have no such jurors and so the problem will rarely arise.
Moreover, the views of an extremist will seldom have a bearing on the decision-making process: if a white defendant is alleged to have burgled a shop run by white owners,
would not the racist be as open-minded as the next person on the question of guilt?
The danger of an extremist very occasionally blocking a justifiable conviction (or
acquittal) has to be weighed against the overall due process cost of allowing a majority
verdict to be returned in any and every criminal case.

In so far as the 'extremist' argument is used to justify majority verdicts, there is a
double standard at work. Like the argument for jury vetting, it claims that the random selection principle cannot be trusted in cases where fierce ethnic or political
conflicts are involved. There is some truth in this and that is precisely why ethnic
minorities demand some black people on juries when the defendant is black. Yet this
has been rejected by the government and the courts. In short, the argument that random selection is defective is accepted when this serves prosecution interests, but not
otherwise.[96]

Majority verdicts also apply to acquittals in the sense that a defendant is acquitted if at least 10 out of 12 jurors vote for a verdict of not guilty. Otherwise, the jury is
said to be 'hung' and the prosecution may opt for a retrial. This symmetry with the
requirement for a guilty verdict is impossible to reconcile with the presumption of
innocence. For whenever between three and nine jurors vote for acquittal, the prosecution has failed to prove guilt and the presumption of innocence would demand that

---

[95] Criminal Procedure and Investigations Act 1996, ss 54 to 57. Whilst these complex provisions are
unlikely to be used with any frequency, 'from a constitutional perspective they represent a major inroad
into the fundamental rule against double jeopardy': Leng R and Taylor R, *Blackstone's Guide to the Criminal
Procedure and Investigations Act 1996* (London: Blackstone, 1996) p 91. That major inroad was subsequently
extended by Part 10 of the Criminal Justice Act 2003: Taylor et al (2004: ch 7).

[96] But note that it might well serve prosecution interests to have black jurors when the defendant is white
and the victim black. If the Government is serious about putting victims 'at the heart of criminal justice' (see
ch 13) it may need to rethink its position on this issue.

the defendant be acquitted. Instead, the English system allows guilt or innocence to remain an open question pending a retrial.[97]

10.3.2 The conduct of the trial by the judge

Judges can influence jury verdicts. Historically juries were commonly told by judges what verdicts to return and, although juries had the right in legal theory to rebel, they seldom did so. The advent of defence lawyers in the eighteenth century broke up this cosy relationship between judge and jury and caused the criminal trial to move much closer to the adversarial ideal of a passive and impartial judge.[98] The judgment by Lord Denning in *Jones v National Coal Board*[99] is generally regarded as the classic statement of the modern position:

The judge's part in [an adversarial trial] is to hearken to the evidence, only himself asking questions of witnesses when it is necessary to clear up any point that has been overlooked or left obscure; to see that the advocates behave themselves seemly and keep to the rules laid down by law; to exclude irrelevancies and discourage repetition; to make sure by wise intervention that he follows the points the advocates are making and can assess their worth;... If he goes beyond this, he drops the mantle of a judge and assumes the robe of an advocate...

Moreover, it is now (at last!) clear law that a judge may not direct a jury to convict in any circumstances.[100] Since judges may direct an acquittal but not a conviction the law on this point reflects the due process stance that wrongful convictions are a greater evil than wrongful acquittals. The same position underlies the duty of the judge to put before the jury any defence which arises from the evidence even if not explicitly raised by defence counsel.[101] But other aspects of the legal framework governing trials reveals that conviction-minded judges are given ample scope to influence the jury.

The judgment in *Jones v National Coal Board* accepts that judges may properly ask some questions and make some interventions, but its tone suggests that these should be limited in number and scope. The reality is that the Court of Appeal has allowed judges a large degree of freedom in conducting trials.[102] In *Webb; Simpson*,[103] for example, the Court noted that:

The judge asked 175 questions, and it is clear that at times he was assuming the role of a prosecutor and was not displaying appropriate judicial impartiality. Even when he was factually in error defence counsel was not permitted to intervene to correct him.

---

[97] Statistics on this issue are not published as a matter of course although it is known that some 370 retrials of hung cases were heard in 1981. Butler S, *Acquittal Rates* (Home Office Research and Planning Unit Paper 16) (London: HMSO, 1983) p 7.

[98] Langbein J, 'The Criminal Trial Before Lawyers' (1978) 45 U Ch LR 263 at p 314.

[99] *Jones v National Coal Board* [1957] 2 QB 55 at 64.   [100] *Wang* [2005] UKHL 9.

[101] See Doran S, 'Alternative Defences: The "Invisible" Burden on the Trial Judge' [1991] Crim LR 878.

[102] For reviews of the case law, see Doran S, 'Descent to Avernus' (1989) 139 NLJ 1147, and Jackson and Doran (1995: 104–10).   [103] *Webb; Simpson* [2000] EWCA Crim 56.

The conviction was nonetheless upheld as safe. Part of the problem here is the Court of Appeal's tendency to focus on whether the conviction is reliable (factually accurate) rather than on whether it was fairly obtained (see further ch 11). What should matter is whether the degree of intervention from the bench compromised the appearance or substance of judicial impartiality.[104] The appellate courts seem unable or unwilling to grasp this point. In *Hircock*,[105] the trial judge had muttered 'Oh God', and groaned and sighed throughout defending counsel's closing speech. Surely such gross discourtesy undermined the fairness of the trial. The Court of Appeal decided, however, that the judge's behaviour did not reflect any view of the defendant's case, but was simply implicit criticism of the conduct of the case by defence counsel. One cannot help wondering whether the jury appreciated this subtle distinction. In more extreme cases, interventions may be so frequent and hostile as to amount to a denial of the defendant's right to have his evidence considered by the jury. Where this is so, the appellate courts have little choice but to declare the trial unfair. An example is *Perren*[106] in which the trial judge frequently interfered in the examination in chief in a manner which was hostile and suggested incredulity. The Court of Appeal held that the defendant's story might have been highly improbable but he was entitled to have it heard without being subjected to 'sniper fire'. It appeared to be of particular significance that the judge had effectively subjected the defendant to cross-examination before the prosecution got the opportunity to perform what is, in the adversarial system, their designated role.

Much judicial behaviour is relatively immune from subsequent challenge as it will not appear on the transcript of court proceedings. In *Bryant*,[107] however, a defence barrister and a solicitor's representative both made witness statements to the effect that a trial judge had shown bias during the development of the defence case by sighing, rolling his eyes, and throwing down his pen or papers in exasperation. And Counsel for the Crown conceded that this judge was well known for making such gestures when impatient with the conduct of those appearing before him. The Court of Appeal said it was wholly impermissible for a judge to indicate to a jury in this way that he or she favoured one side or the other, so the conviction was quashed (and a retrial ordered). We can only guess how often this trial judge, and others like him, gets away with such behaviour. It is further worth noting that the appellate judiciary are unable to criticise or remedy excessive interventions by the trial judge which result in an acquittal. This is because there is generally no appeal from an acquittal.[108] Thus it is open to a trial judge to harangue or undermine prosecution lawyers and witnesses with little fear that the case will result in an appeal.

The appellate cases just discussed give an indication of the scope for judicial intervention and provide some extreme examples of behaviour by trial judges. By their nature they cannot, however, tell us the frequency with which trial judges *typically*

---

[104] ECtHR case law on the ECHR, Art 6 requirement for an *impartial* tribunal (see 10.2 above) would seem to support this position.   [105] [1969] 1 All ER 47.

[106] [2009] EWCA Crim 348.   [107] [2005] EWCA Crim 2079.

[108] The exceptions are briefly noted in 10.3.1 above.

question witnesses or interrupt counsel, the nature of those interventions, or whether such interventions are welcomed by other participants. What little research evidence there is makes it clear that there is considerable variation between judges.[109] Jackson and Doran[110] studied 17 jury trials in Northern Ireland presided over by nine different judges. They found that of the 77 judicial objections to counsel's questioning, two-thirds (54) were made by just two judges in three of the trials. By contrast, four of the judges made no more than one objection per trial they heard. This study also found that one judicial question was asked every 5.5 minutes during the taking of oral evidence from witnesses.[111] Much of this questioning was legitimate in that it was designed to clarify evidence, but 14% of defence witnesses (compared with 6% of prosecution witnesses) were subjected to inquisitorial questioning designed to elicit new information.[112] In other words, the judges often did take on the robe of an advocate. The authors were unable to settle upon an explanation for this greater tendency to probe defence witnesses but note that it may have been that the judges observed were simply more disposed to believe the prosecution evidence. Not surprisingly, they found that 'prosecution counsel were generally happier about judicial questioning than defence counsel'.[113] In England and Wales, the Crown Court survey carried out for the Runciman Commission found no support from either prosecuting or defence counsel for more 'robust interventions' from the judge. Where judges had intervened in trials, the interruptions favoured the prosecution much more frequently than they did the defence.[114]

The Runciman Commission[115] advocated that judges should be more interventionist in conducting trials in order to save time and money and because shorter trials would make it easier for jurors to recall the essential facts. It also wanted judges to prevent witnesses being 'subjected to bullying and intimidatory tactics by counsel or to deliberately and unnecessarily prolonged cross-examination'. It brushed aside the suggestion that such interventions might give the 'impression of bias' and failed to acknowledge the impact its proposals would have on the adversarial theory of justice which asserts that the production and presentation of evidence must be left to the parties in dispute.[116] Moreover, its proposals evince a degree of trust in judicial impartiality which scarcely seems justified on the track record of the courts.

A number of developments since Runciman have required trial judges to take a more interventionist stance.[117] In particular, we saw in ch 8 how judges are now expected actively to manage cases (eg by ensuring that evidence, whether disputed or not, is presented in the clearest and shortest way)[118] and also to encourage plea bargaining. We saw above that in *Bryant*,[119] the trial judge went too far in demonstrating his impatience

---

[109] See Fielding (2006: 145–58). [110] Jackson and Doran (1995: 122, table 5.4).
[111] Ibid: 132. [112] Ibid: 154, table 6.10. [113] Ibid: 160–2.
[114] Zander and Henderson (1993: 137–8). [115] RCCJ (1993: 122). [116] See 1.3 for discussion.
[117] See Doran S, 'The Necessarily Expanding Role of the Criminal Trial Judge' in Doran S and Jackson J (eds), *The Judicial Role in Criminal Proceedings* (Oxford: Hart, 2000).
[118] Rule 3.2(e), Criminal Procedure Rules (<http://www.justice.gov.uk>).
[119] [2005] EWCA Crim 2079.

with those conducting the defence. But the Court of Appeal said that it would support trial judges who helped cases to proceed at a reasonable speed, and who, with that end in mind, robustly rebuked counsel who developed their cases too sluggishly. This illustrates the tightrope that trial judges must now walk. There is an inevitable clash here between such values as efficiency, procedural fairness and crime control. This is not just a simple clash between due process and crime control principles, however. Neither model adequately caters for victims and other witnesses.[120] When the conduct of the case is left to defence and prosecution lawyers, victims often suffer.[121] Concern at the treatment of rape victims in court, in particular, leads naturally to the position that judges ought to be more interventionist.[122] There is a difficulty that the judge may not know in advance what direction questioning is going to take.[123] Once a question is asked the damage may be done whether or not the judge intervenes.

From a freedom perspective we would want arguments and policy decisions about judicial intervention to be grounded in clear principles which take into account the various interests at stake. The ECtHR has provided an important lead here in suggesting that victims' interests, not just defendants' rights, are part of the Art 6 right to a fair trial.[124] In similar vein the Court of Appeal ruled in *Brown (Milton Anthony)*[125] that: 'It is the clear duty of the trial judge to do everything he can, consistently with giving the defendant a fair trial, to minimise the trauma suffered by other participants....' Parliament, through the Youth Justice and Criminal Evidence Act 1999, has provided trial judges with various new 'special measures' and devices, such as video-recorded examination in chief and giving evidence by live link, to encourage them to safeguard the interests of fearful or vulnerable witnesses in court.[126] Whilst this legislative concern for victims and witnesses is welcome, there remain some troubling aspects to these developments. First, the new Act overlooks the fact that trial judges are sometimes directly responsible through their own questioning for the 'trauma' suffered by witnesses in court. Second, there has been no recognition by criminal justice policy-makers that some trial judges can and do exhibit bias, more often than not against the defence, through their interventions during a trial. As we have seen such behaviour is inadequately regulated by the senior judiciary. Third, the accused is specifically excluded from the new 'special measures' introduced by the Youth Justice and Criminal Evidence Act. Yet this overlooks that defendants can be vulnerable or fearful in the same way as victims. They may find the experience of cross-examination by the prosecution just as humiliating or offensive as complainants find cross-examination

---

[120] See 1.8.

[121] See Brereton D, 'How Different are Rape Trials? A Comparison of the Cross-Examination of Complainants in Rape and Assault Trials' (1997) 37 BJ Crim 242, and Rock (1993: ch 2).

[122] See the discussion by Ellison L, 'Cross-Examination in Rape Trials' [1998] Crim LR 605.

[123] For example, questions suggesting a rape complainant's mental illness affects her credibility. See Ellison L 'The Use and Abuse of Psychiatric Evidence in Rape Trials' (2009d) 13 IJEP 28. Ellison suggests evidential rules might be required to prevent a complainant's being questioned about mental illness except where the judge is satisfied that the probative value of psychiatric evidence outweighs its prejudicial effect.

[124] See *Doorson v Netherlands* (1996) 23 EHRR 330 and the discussion in ch 1.

[125] [1998] 2 Cr App Rep 364 at 391.   [126] These special measures are discussed in ch 13.

by the defence.[127] The legislation also seems to be based on the faulty assumption that defendants and victims are distinct groups of people.[128] In showing concern for victims it is important not to lose sight of the need to address the conduct (and powers) of the trial judge in relation to the defence case in general, and the defendant in particular. The new legislation advances the freedom of victims and most other witnesses but it has turned a blind eye to the plight of defendants in court. This is discussed further in the concluding chapter.

10.3.3 Summing up by the judge

The last word in a contested trial before the jury retires to consider its verdict is always that of the judge. The judge explains the law to the jury and provides them with a summary of the evidence.[129] This gives judges another opportunity to influence the outcome of the trial, and some famous miscarriages of justice have resulted. Thus in the case of Derek Bentley (hanged in 1953) the eminent trial judge (Lord Goddard CJ) suggested in his summary of the evidence that, as witnesses, the police were likely to be accurate and reliable, and defendants inaccurate and unreliable. When the case was referred back to it in 1998, the Court of Appeal concluded that: 'The language used was not that of a judge but of an advocate…Such a direction by such a judge must in our view have driven the jury to conclude that they had little choice but to convict….'[130] The most notorious modern example of a biased summing up was in the trial of the 'Birmingham Six', where Bridge J over a three-day summing up skilfully led the jury by the nose to a verdict of guilty.[131] He began by telling the jury that 'however hard a judge tries to be impartial, inevitably his presentation of the evidence is bound to be coloured by his own view'. He then left them in no doubt as to what that view might be.[132] For example, he sought to depict the defence contention that the police had fabricated evidence and lied in court as far-fetched:

If the defendants are giving you honest and substantially accurate evidence, there is no escape from the fact that the police are involved in a conspiracy to commit a variety of crimes which must be unprecedented in the annals of British criminal history.

Other defence witnesses were similarly discredited, such as the prison doctor who gave evidence of injuries to the accused and their probable infliction by the police:

Can you believe one single word of what Dr Harwood says? There are inescapably many perjurers who have given evidence. If Dr Harwood is one of them, is he not the worst?

---

[127] As where racial stereotypes are invoked against black defendants: Kalunta-Krumpton A, 'The Prosecution and Defence of Black Defendants in Drug Trials' (1998) 38 BJ Crim 561.

[128] For a critique of this assumption see 1.9.

[129] On the extent of this judicial obligation see *Amado-Taylor* [2000] Crim LR 618 and accompanying commentary.   [130] *Bentley (Deceased)* [1998] EWCA Crim 2516; [1999] Crim LR 330.

[131] Excerpts from the transcript of the trial are reproduced (with critical commentary) by Wood J in Walker C and Starmer K (eds), *Miscarriages of Justice* (London: Blackstone, 1999) p 226. See also in the same book the discussion by Jackson J, 'Trial Procedures' (at p 199) on the summing up in the Carl Bridgewater case.

[132] After the jury convicted, the judge commented that the evidence in the case was the clearest and most overwhelming he had ever heard.

Mr Justice Bridge made this performance virtually appeal-proof, however, by continually reminding the jurors that it was for them, not him, to decide where the truth lay.[133] Where this formalistic incantation is omitted, the Court of Appeal has sometimes intervened. Thus in *Berrada* (1989) 91 Cr App Rep 131, the judge observed that the defendant's allegations of police misconduct were 'really monstrous and wicked'. The Court of Appeal rebuked the judge, declaring that her duty was to sum up impartially without seeking to inflate evidence by 'sarcastic and extravagant comment'.[134] And in *Wood* [1996] 1 Cr App R 207, the Court of Appeal accepted that the degree of permissible adverse comment was substantially less than 50 years earlier. More temperate language from the judge is all that the law requires, however. In *DPP v Stonehouse*, for example, Lord Salmon opined that it would be in order for a judge in an appropriate case to sum up to the jury 'in such a way as to make it plain that he considers the accused is guilty and should be convicted'.[135] And in *Kelleher* the Court of Appeal said trial judges, when they think a not guilty verdict would be perverse, may say to the jury 'you may think that there can only be one verdict in this case and that is one of guilty...'[136]

One danger in giving judges such freedom of manoeuvre is that they are privy to much inadmissible evidence, including the defendant's previous convictions (if any), and may therefore be biased against the defendant. Zander and Henderson (1993: 135) found that in cases where judges summed up for conviction and where the defendant had a previous record the summation was in line with the evidence as often as it was against the weight of the evidence. On this basis, they argue that judges do not appear to be influenced by knowledge of prior convictions. This is a crude analysis, however. One would need to control for all factors that might lead to a judge summing up for conviction (such as race, class or sex of the defendant, political/media pressures to clamp down on particular crimes, and so on) in order to establish whether knowledge of a defendant's previous record played a part. Also, if judges sum up for conviction against the evidence they are plainly prejudiced – whether by knowledge of previous record or not is hardly important! On the other hand, judges sometimes make clear in their summary of the evidence that they think an acquittal the right result, as in the Stephen Waldorf case in which the two police officers on trial had

---

[133] In the third (and successful) appeal by the Birmingham Six the Court of Appeal acknowledged the forceful nature of the summing up by Bridge J, but did not accept that this had vitiated the proceedings. As Lloyd LJ put it, 'the judge also made it clear throughout the summing-up that it was for the jury, and not for him, to determine where the truth lay': *McIlkenny* (1991) 93 Cr App Rep 287 at 293. But see *Mears* [1993] 1 WLR 818 at 822 where the Privy Council approved the position that a fundamentally unbalanced summing up cannot be saved by the constant repetition of the phrase 'these are matters for you, the jury, to decide'.

[134] See also *Osborne-Odelli* [1998] Crim LR 902 and *Gibbons and Winterburn* (22 June 1993) in which convictions were quashed because of an unfair summing up by the trial judge. Amongst many other prejudicial comments the trial judge in the latter case had referred to the defendant as an 'an old lag trying to go straight'. See the discussion by Robertshaw P, *Summary Justice* (London: Cassell, 1998) pp 26–8.

[135] [1978] AC 55 at 80. See also the speech by Lord Edmund-Davies.

[136] [2003] EWCA Crim 3525, per Mantell LJ, whose judgment was described by the House of Lords in *Wang* [2005] UKHL 9 to be 'a very lucid and accurate exposition of the law.' See also *Bryant* [2005] EWCA Crim 2079.

shot and pistol-whipped an innocent man by mistake.[137] In general, judges simply get case-hardened and sceptical about defendants, particularly when they are not seen as respectable characters. As we saw in ch 9, in relation to magistrates, this is one of the central arguments for employing a jury to decide questions of fact. Extensive judicial intervention introduces into trials the very problem that the use of juries is meant to avoid – prejudice.

How frequent is the problem of a biased summing up? Zander and Henderson (1993) report that, according to prosecutors, in over 1,000 cases in 1992 the judge summed up against the weight of the evidence, while the figure was more than 2,000 (nearly 10% of all cases tried by jury) according to defence barristers. Prosecuting barristers tended to think that where the summing up was against the weight of the evidence, it favoured an acquittal. According to defence barristers, however, in 92% of the cases where the summing up was identified as biased in this sense, the bias was towards conviction.[138] In half of these cases the jury convicted.[139]

The Court of Appeal sometimes defends trial judges making comments 'one way or the other' on the basis that juries 'are more robust than people often give them credit for'.[140] How can we know that juries ignore biased comments in the absence of any research evidence? Theoretically, one would expect there to be at least some influence. First, the summaries are clearly intended to influence the jury else there would be no point in making them. Second, as Robertshaw[141] points out, members of the jury are symbolically and physically constructed as passive and silent observers from the sidelines during the trial. By contrast, the judge is raised up on high, centre stage, and given the 'superior status indicators of wig and robes...All procedural moves and sequences pass through the judge, to whom deferential behaviour and speech forms are routine.... The role-expectation for the jury throughout the trial is one of dependence on the judge.'

In the United States, a historical distrust of officialdom is reflected in the rule in most state jurisdictions that the judge in a criminal trial must express no opinion on the weight or credibility of the testimony of a witness, or on the merits of either side of the case.[142] In some continental jurisdictions, such as France, the other extreme of the argument may be seen, in that judges are allowed to retire with juries in order to determine the verdict. The evidence suggests that this co-decision model produces a much lower acquittal rate than when matters are left in the hands of the jury alone.[143] A model nearer to hand is that of Scotland which limits trial judges to directing on the

---

[137] See *The Times*, 19 October 1983.

[138] Note that this does not mean that prosecution and defence counsel were disagreeing about where the bias lay in particular cases, since they may well have been talking about different cases. Prosecutors will tend to be alive to bias against their interests but not notice when the bias runs in their favour, and the same is true of defence lawyers.   [139] Zander and Henderson (1993: 135–6).

[140] Eg *Spencer (John)*, *The Times*, 13 July 1994, discussed in Robertshaw (1998: 32–3).

[141] Robertshaw (1998: 15, 192–3).

[142] See Wolchover D, 'Should Judges Sum up on the Facts?' [1989] Crim LR 781.

[143] See Munday R, 'Jury Trial, Continental Style' (1993) 13 LS 204 at p 216 in particular.

law and explaining how the evidence is relevant to the legal ingredients of each charge. This seems to ensure greater respect for the jury's role as fact-finder and ultimate determiner of guilt.[144] If we think it important that our long-term freedom should not be taken away by a process effectively dominated by state-paid professionals then there is much to be said for the Scottish approach. Even judicial commentators have noted that judges have been too ready in the past to make overtly biased comments about the evidence and questioned whether any judicial comment on the evidence is 'necessary, appropriate or fair'.[145] Rather than ignoring judicial activism, it would be better to 'forge out a theory of judicial truth finding which does not lead to unfairness'.[146] One solution might be to try to build more checks and balances into the trial process itself; for example allowing counsel to comment on judicial summaries of evidence before they are presented to the jury.[147]

10.4 Trial: procedure, evidence and law

10.4.1 Procedure and evidence

In an adversarial system the decision-makers are meant to be passive. It is not part of the jury's role to investigate matters for itself away from the courtroom.[148] There have been examples recently of jurors using the Internet to carry out their own research, but where this has come to light trials have been abandoned and convictions overturned.[149] Jurors can ask questions of witnesses in court but rarely do so.[150] Any question is meant to be passed in writing to the judge who will then relay it to a witness if appropriate. The artificiality of this procedure undoubtedly deters jurors from a more proactive role in the trial and they receive little encouragement to assert themselves.[151] It follows that juries should reach their verdicts on the material that is placed before them by counsel for the prosecution and defence. This material is itself shaped by the rules of criminal procedure and evidence. This body of law accordingly forms yet another battleground for Packer's two models of the criminal process.

---

[144] Robertshaw (1998: 23–5, 179–93).

[145] Madge N 'Summing Up – A Judge's Perspective' [2006] Crim LR 817.

[146] Jackson J, 'Judicial Responsibility in Criminal Proceedings' (1996) 49 Current Legal Problems 59 at p 92.   [147] Doran (2000: 15–17).

[148] To do so may amount to a serious irregularity vitiating any subsequent conviction. See *Davis, Rowe and Johnson* [2001] 1 Cr App R 115.

[149] *KaraKaya* [2005] EWCA 346. Berlins, M 'Jury's Out on the Net Generation', *The Guardian*, 10 November 2008. See also *Hambleton* [2009] EWCA Crim 13 where a conviction had to be quashed after it was discovered that a discharged juror had made a prejudicial comment about a defendant to one of the jurors hearing the case which was then repeated within the jury retiring room.

[150] In the Crown Court study, under half of jurors had wanted to ask a question and less than a fifth of this number had actually done so: Zander and Henderson (1993: 213).

[151] Nearly a third of jurors in the Crown Court study had not been informed at any stage that they could ask questions: ibid, p 213.

The clarion call for the crime control model was sounded by the then Commissioner of the Metropolitan Police, Sir Robert Mark, in his Dimbleby Lecture of 1973.[152] Arguing that the jury acquits an unacceptably high proportion of those whom the police believe to be guilty, Mark pinned the blame on procedural rules and crooked lawyers, asserting 'technical rules' such as those relating to disclosure, the right to silence and evidence of bad character gave 'every advantage to the defence'.[153] Mark's claims were contested by academics, who argued that there was little evidence that the jury acquittal rate was too high,[154] bent lawyers were helping criminals escape justice,[155] or that professional criminals were exploiting the rules.[156]

In the decades since Mark's comments many of the 'technical' rules of procedure and evidence have been significantly altered. If we examine the rules on disclosure, right to silence and bad character, as we do briefly below, they seem to have lurched significantly in a crime control direction, in a way that erodes defendants' freedom whilst doing little or nothing to enlarge freedom overall.

Advance disclosure of prosecution and defence evidence

The requirement that the prosecution should give advance disclosure of its evidence to the defence is intended to redress an imbalance between the parties to the case. As was noted by Lloyd LJ in the successful Birmingham Six appeal, a 'disadvantage of the adversarial system may be that the parties are not evenly matched in resources... But the inequality of resources is ameliorated by the obligation on the part of the prosecution to make available all material which may prove helpful to the defence.'[157] The resources of the police and prosecution far outweigh those available to the defence.[158] Moreover, the police are involved in the case from the outset, whereas the defence will not begin to operate until a suspect is arrested. In these circumstances, it is not possible for the defence to carry out an adequate independent investigation of an offence. Advance prosecution disclosure should not be seen as advantaging the defence, but as a means of

---

[152] Mark was the first high-profile police officer to seek openly to influence criminal justice policy-making, although many have subsequently followed his lead. Loader I and Mulcahy A, 'The Power of Legitimate Naming: Part I – Chief Constables as Social Commentators in Post-war England' (2001a) 41(1) BJ Crim 41; Loader I and Mulcahy A, 'The Power of Legitimate Naming: Part II – Making Sense of the Elite Police Voice' (2001b) 41(3) BJ Crim 252; Wilcox A and Young R, 'How Green was Thames Valley?: Policing the Image of Restorative Justice Cautions' (2007) 17(2) Policing and Society 141.

[153] Mark R, Minority Verdict (The 1973 Dimbleby Lecture) (London: BBC, 1973).

[154] Commentators typically pointed out that most Crown Court defendants plead guilty and that of those found not guilty by the jury most are acquitted on the order or direction of the judge, a pattern that holds true today (see 10.1).

[155] See Baldwin and McConville (1979: 118), and, by the same authors, 'Allegations Against Lawyers' [1978] Crim LR 744.

[156] Contrast Mack J, 'Full-time Major Criminals and the Courts' (1976) 39 MLR 241 with Sanders A, 'Does Professional Crime Pay? – A Critical Comment on Mack' (1977) 40 MLR 553. See also Baldwin J and McConville M, Jury Trials (Oxford: OUP, 1979) pp 110–12.

[157] McIlkenny (1991) 93 Cr App Rep 287 at 312.

[158] See Barclay G and Tavares C, Information on the Criminal Justice System in England and Wales: Digest 4 (London: Home Office, 1999) (<http://www.homeoffice.gov.uk/rds/digest41.html>) ch 9.

attempting to redress a structural disadvantage. Indeed, unless accused persons are told what the details of allegations against them are, they cannot prepare a defence.

The duty to disclose was by no means as absolute in 1973 as Mark implied. The common law imposed increasingly strict duties on the prosecution over the next two decades. But the police, the CPS and other prosecution agencies often failed to comply,[159] claiming that these duties were too onerous.[160] So the common law was replaced by the Criminal Procedure and Investigation Act 1996. The prosecution duty to disclose was cut back at the same time as a new defence duty to disclose its 'case' was introduced. As discussed in 7.3.3.5, research into the operation of the 1996 Act uncovered evidence of significant levels of wrongful non-disclosure. Partly in consequence, Part 5 of the Criminal Justice Act 2003 somewhat widened the prosecution duty to disclose, but at the same time widened very substantially the defence duties of disclosure. As explained in 5.3.3, the defence must now, in advance of trial, provide a statement which sets out the nature of the accused's defence, indicates any point of law on which reliance will be placed (including any point as to the admissibility of evidence), and provides details of any alibi witnesses. The accused must also give the court and prosecutor a notice setting out the details of any other witnesses he or she plans to call to give evidence at trial. Adverse inferences may be drawn where any of the duties of disclosure are breached or a defence is presented at court which is inconsistent with, or goes beyond, the initially disclosed information.

The police have got their way. Disclosure rules are no longer binding only on the prosecution, so no longer do they fulfil their old function of helping to redress the structural imbalance within the adversarial system. Indeed, one could reasonably argue that they now unduly favour the prosecution. And where disclosure is perhaps most needed, by the police in advance of their interrogation of the suspect, no duty to disclose exists.[161] This was true at the time Mark made his claims and it remains true today. What has changed since Mark's time is that, if suspects remain silent when questioned by the police, the odds of adverse inferences being drawn against them at trial have shot up. The 'rules' on disclosure are now indeed somewhat one-sided – in favour of the police.

The right of silence

Mark acknowledged the inroad made into the right of silence by s 11 of the Criminal Justice Act 1967 which requires alibi defences to be notified to the police in advance of the trial, so that they may be 'checked'. What he failed to mention was the limited extent to which the right of silence was respected by the courts.[162] The Court

---

[159] See O'Connor P, 'Prosecution Disclosure: Principle, Practice and Justice' in Walker C and Starmer K (eds), *Justice in Error* (London: Blackstone, 1993) and our discussion of disclosure at 7.3.3 in particular.

[160] See, for example, the views expressed by the then Chief Constable of Thames Valley Police, Pollard C, 'A Case for Disclosure' [1994] Crim LR 42.   [161] See 5.3.5.

[162] For a full review of the relevant case law, see the four-part article by Wolchover D (1989) 139 NLJ at 396, 428, 484 and 501, and also Starmer K and Woolf M, 'The Right to Silence' in Walker C and Starmer K (eds), *Miscarriages of Justice* (London: Blackstone, 1999) pp 100–2.

of Appeal in *Gerard*[163] declined to intervene when a trial judge commented that an accused's silence before charge might appear 'perhaps a little curious' and 'a little odd'. In *Chandler*[164] the Court of Appeal ruled that where an accused and an accuser were on equal terms it would be in order to invite the jury to consider whether silence in the face of an accusation or question amounted to an acceptance of what had been said. This equal terms doctrine was in accordance with earlier cases such as *Parkes*[165] but the new departure was to assert that suspects might be adjudged as on level or even superior terms vis-à-vis police officers. Thus in *Chandler*, a police officer was held to be on equal terms with a suspect because the latter had his solicitor present during questioning.[166] None of this seems consistent with the view of Mark that procedural rules developed so as to give every advantage to the defence.

Since Mark wrote there have been several major statutory developments.[167] As we have just seen, the Criminal Procedure and Investigations Act 1996 placed a positive duty on the defence to disclose its 'case' prior to trial, and that duty has been greatly increased by Part 5 of the Criminal Justice Act 2003 (see further 5.3.3). This is a clear departure from the right to silence. That right had already been emasculated by the Criminal Justice and Public Order Act 1994. The most significant aspects of the 1994 Act were analysed in depth in 5.3. That is where the reader should turn for discussion of the principles involved, and the evidence that bears on the costs and benefits of the right to silence. Our focus there was on those sections of the 1994 Act which allow the jury to draw adverse inferences against suspects if they remain silent *during the investigation* of the alleged crime. Here we look briefly at the sections which allow the jury to draw adverse inferences against accused persons who decline to give evidence *in court*, and which allow the prosecutor to make adverse comment if a defendant remains silent.[168]

Section 35(2) imposes a duty on the court, at the end of the prosecution case, to make accused persons aware of the possibility of the drawing of adverse inferences if they choose not to give evidence or refuse to answer any question on giving evidence. Section 38 sets out some restrictions on this new crime control power by stipulating that a person shall not have a case to answer or be convicted of an offence 'solely' through an adverse inference. This section must now be read in the light of subsequent judicial interpretation. In the leading case of *Cowan*[169] the Court of Appeal set out five points which a trial judge must convey to the jury before an adverse inference can be drawn under s 35:

(a) the burden of proof remains on the prosecution at all times;

(b) the defendant is entitled to remain silent;

---

[163] *Gerard* (1948) 32 Cr App Rep 132.

[164] [1976] 1 WLR 585. See also *Osborne* [2005] EWCA Crim 3082.   [165] (1976) 64 Cr App Rep 25.

[166] See also the case of *Horne* [1990] Crim LR 188 where the equal terms doctrine was applied to silence in response to a victim's accusation made in the presence of police officers.

[167] There were many other statutory inroads into the right to silence, particularly from the 1980s onwards: see 5.3 for discussion.

[168] See the analysis by Wasik M and Taylor R, *Blackstone's Guide to the Criminal Justice and Public Order Act 1994* (London: Blackstone, 1995) pp 62–8.

[169] [1996] QB 373. Approved by the House of Lords in *Becouarn* [2005] UKHL 55.

(c) an inference from failure to give evidence cannot on its own prove guilt;

(d) the jury must be satisfied that the prosecution established a case to answer before drawing any adverse inferences from the defendant's silence;

(e) the jury may draw an adverse inference if it concludes that the silence can only sensibly be attributed to the accused having no good answer to the prosecution case.[170]

In *Murray v UK*[171] the ECtHR accepted that there was no absolute right to not have adverse inferences drawn from silence. But it also held that it was incompatible with the immunity from self-incrimination to base a conviction 'solely or mainly' on a refusal to give evidence at trial. This is a more stringent requirement than s 35 which only expressly prevents a conviction which is based 'solely' on such a refusal.[172] But the fourth *Cowan* requirement requires a jury to believe that there is a case for the defendant to answer before they consider whether to *add* to that prosecution case by drawing an adverse inference from the defendant's silence in court. It is arguable that this requirement of an independent prima facie case means that a conviction will not be based either solely *or mainly* on silence. Not surprisingly, in *Birchall*[173] the Court of Appeal ruled that it was essential that the fourth condition in *Cowan* formed part of the direction to juries in s 35 cases, and that a failure to include it rendered a conviction unsafe. It thus seems that the Convention has softened the crime control impact of the 1994 Act. Nonetheless, whereas at one time, as Mark put it, the police had to keep reminding suspects that they need not say anything, nowadays police, prosecutors and trial judges may or must remind suspects that they need to say something if they want to avoid seriously damaging the chances of acquittal.

The jury's ignorance of the defendant's criminal record

The historical rationale for the principle that juries should not ordinarily be told of a defendant's previous convictions (or otherwise be informed that the defendant is of bad character) is that the prejudicial impact of this information outweighs its probative value.[174] Some empirical support for such a prejudicial effect was provided by research done for the Law Commission by Lloyd-Bostock.[175] Using mock juries she found that knowledge of previous convictions similar to the offence charged increased the perceived probability of guilt. To the extent that previous behaviour is a good predictor of future behaviour (which it sometimes is) this is arguably an example of probative value outweighing prejudicial effect.[176] But Lloyd-Bostock's research also found

---

[170] The Court of Appeal indicated that there might be other circumstances in which a trial judge might think it right to direct or advise against drawing an adverse inference.   [171] (1996) 22 EHRR 29.

[172] As confirmed by *Cowan*: see point (c) in the above paragraph.   [173] [1999] Crim LR 311.

[174] See *Selvey v DPP* [1968] 2 All ER 497.

[175] Law Commission, *Evidence in Criminal Proceedings: Previous Misconduct of a Defendant* (Consultation Paper No 141) (London: HMSO, 1996a) Appendix D. Also reported in Lloyd-Bostock S, 'The Effects of Hearing About the Defendant's Previous Criminal Record: A Simulation Study' [2000] Crim LR 734.

[176] Redmayne M, 'The Relevance of Bad Character' (2002b) 61 CLJ 684.

that convictions for offences which provoke an all-round negative evaluation of the perpetrator, such as indecent assault on a child, are likely to be particularly prejudicial to a defendant whatever the current offence charged. Given the level of hysteria[177] and vigilante violence against sex offenders 'named and shamed' by the 'red top' press we might indeed doubt whether anyone known to have previously been convicted of a sexual offence involving a child could receive a fair trial for any offence. This is a good example of the need to situate analyses of criminal justice within a wider social context (see ch 1). We can hardly expect juries to be unprejudiced if drawn from a society consumed with such hatred and fear.

Whether one sees the principle of not admitting previous convictions into evidence as unduly favouring the defendant depends, in part, on a judgement as to how reliable the police are at identifying the probably guilty in the first place. As we have shown in earlier chapters (see 2, 3 and 6 in particular), the police tend to focus their attention upon 'known criminals'. Statistically, this strategy may be effective in increasing the number of guilty persons detected, but, by giving insufficient attention to independent evidence of guilt, it also increases the risk that innocent people will be drawn into the criminal process. From a due process perspective, this insight would strengthen the argument for keeping the defendant's past record from the jury. Denied this knowledge, the jury is forced to focus on the essential issue – is there sufficient evidence that the defendant committed the offence as charged?

As Mark recognised, the bad character rule has never been applied rigidly, and there were long-standing exceptions to it; for example, evidence of the defendant's bad character could be admitted under the 'similar facts' rule,[178] or where the defendant gave evidence suggesting he was of good character, or where he gave evidence against a co-accused. A fourth exception allowed bad character evidence to be admitted if the defence attacked the character of a prosecution witness, sometimes known as the 'tit for tat' rule. Research showed that defendants were often deterred from attacking the character of police witnesses, for example by alleging they had fabricated evidence, because their lawyers advised them it would be counterproductive.[179] Interestingly this advice was sometimes given even when the defendant was of good character so at no risk of convictions being disclosed under the bad character rules.

McConville et al's post-PACE study found many examples of defence lawyers advising their clients not to challenge 'the veracity of statements made in custody which the defendant alleged were, in some measure, the product of police malpractice'.[180] From

---

[177] On 30 August 2000, BBC News 24 reported that vigilantes had vandalised the home of a paediatrician under the mistaken belief that this is the label applied to sex offenders.

[178] If the facts alleged were similar to the facts of previous incidents involving the defendant then the jury could be told of the latter, even if those incidents were the subject of acquittals.

[179] In one study of late plea changers (discussed in ch 8), two-fifths of sampled defendants alleged in interview that the police had falsely attributed to them verbal admissions, and a third of those claiming to be innocent made such allegations. However their counsel almost invariably advised no challenge to the police evidence since the police would be believed and the judge might be sufficiently annoyed to impose a heavier sentence (Baldwin J and McConville M, *Negotiated Justice* (London, Martin Robertson 1977) pp 68–9.

[180] McConville et al, *Standing Accused* (Oxford: Clarendon Press, 1994) p 217.

a due process perspective the tit for tat exception is objectionable. It increases the risk that the innocent will plead or be found guilty and encourages the police to fabricate evidence. In Zander and Henderson's Crown Court study 77% of defendants had previous convictions and the jury were told of these in one-fifth of cases,[181] but we have no way of knowing how many more defendants decided to plead guilty because of the chilling effect of the bad character rules.

The Criminal Justice Act 2003 made it even easier to introduce evidence of the defendant's bad character.[182] Its provisions are complex and we refer readers to specialist works for more detailed analysis,[183] confining ourselves here to providing some examples of the crime control thrust of the legislation. The Act introduces a series of 'gateways' through which bad character evidence can be admitted. The gateways make it easier to admit evidence of the defendant's bad character than other witnesses. Under s 100, evidence of the bad character of witnesses other than the defendant is only admissible with the leave of the court if it has 'substantial probative value' and is of 'substantial importance in the context of the case as a whole'. By contrast, evidence of the defendant's bad character does not need to be of 'substantial' value – it may be admitted through the gateway in s 101(1)(d) if it is merely 'relevant to an important matter in issue between the prosecution and defence'. It is evidently regarded as more important to protect prosecution witnesses from the upset that might be caused by attacks on their character than to protect defendants from similar upset *and* the risk of wrongful conviction.

Although the gateway under s 100(1)(d) overlaps with the similar facts rule that previously existed at common law it has much broader scope.[184] Section 103 spells out that matters in issue between the prosecution and defence include 'propensity to be untruthful' and the 'propensity to commit offences of the kind' with which the defendant is charged. This may be established, 'without prejudice to any other way of doing so', by evidence that the defendant has committed an offence of the 'same description' or 'same category' as the one charged. The government subsequently used its power under s 103(4) to prescribe categories of offences in wide terms.

Given the breadth of the legislation the role of the judiciary in interpreting its application is clearly crucial. In *Hanson*[185] the Court of Appeal upheld the conviction of a defendant who entered a guilty plea to stealing money from a bag in a bedroom to which he had access when the judge ruled he would allow the admission of evidence of his previous convictions for dishonesty. However, Rose LJ asserted that where

---

[181] Zander and Henderson (1993: paras 4.6.1–4.6.8). For the position in the lower courts see Wasik M, 'Magistrates: Knowledge of Previous Convictions' [1996] Crim LR 851, and Darbyshire P, 'Previous Misconduct and Magistrates' Courts – Some Tales from the Real World' [1997] Crim LR 105.

[182] The government mischaracterised the pre-legislation framework as one where previous convictions were generally inadmissible, when the truth was that 'any evidence of bad character which was more probative than prejudicial was admissible'. See Tapper C, 'Evidence of Bad Character' [2004] Crim LR 533 at 538.

[183] Spencer J, *Evidence of Bad Character* (Oxford: Hart Publishing, 2006a); Mirfield P, 'Character and Credibility' [2009] Crim LR 135.   [184] Spencer (2006a: 61).

[185] [2005] EWCA Crim 824.

evidence of bad character is admitted to show propensity, either to commit offences or be untruthful, the judge should warn the jury against placing undue reliance on previous convictions: 'Evidence of bad character cannot be used simply to bolster a weak case, or to prejudice the minds of the jury against the defendant' (at para 18).

It has recently been found that the propensity gateway the most commonly used provision for admitting bad character evidence, and that the prosecution sought to rely on it even where the defendant's previous convictions were not similar to the alleged offence.[186] The success rate for applications was high and defence lawyers were not particularly robust in contesting applications.[187] Although prosecutors claimed that the decision in *Hanson* had made them more selective in their approach, one also admitted that the defence might be put on notice of an application to admit evidence of bad character to try to force the defendant to plead guilty. This is an important reminder of the impact of evidential rules on not just the trial itself but the pre-trial processes. It is tempting to conclude that the Criminal Justice Act 2003 gave the prosecution greater freedom to use bad character rules to their advantage, although the decision in *Hanson* may have had some limited inhibitory effect.

It should be noted that the meaning of 'bad character' is broader than simply previous convictions and includes 'reprehensible behaviour'. What amounts to 'reprehensible behaviour' is unclear,[188] and very few applications appear to be made to admit evidence of this type of behaviour.[189] However, such applications might be useful in cases of domestic violence where there may be a history of violence which is not reflected in previous convictions. One study found a 'widespread view' amongst practitioners that the new rules were a 'backward step' in domestic violence cases, where it was said to be previously possible to introduce background evidence, such as an incident log, without giving advance notice.[190] In ch 1 we noted our view that the rights of victims and defendants are not in automatic opposition. In principle from a freedom perspective the admission of evidence of a history of violence towards the complainant or other partners might be justifiable. If the prosecution wish to assert that the defendant has a history of domestic violence not resulting in convictions then admitting that evidence might be problematic, but if he has previous convictions for domestic abuse then these should be readily admissible under the propensity gateway to argue that the defendant has propensity to commit offences of a similar type. How relevant are they to the issue of credibility? In *Campbell*[191] the defendant was charged with falsely imprisoning and assaulting a woman with whom he had a sexual relationship. The prosecution applied for the defendant's convictions for assaulting two other female partners to be admitted

---

[186] Morgan Harris Burrows LLP, *Research into the Impact of Bad Character Provisions on the Courts* (Ministry of Justice Research Series 5/09)(London: MoJ, 2009). In this study of six courts, which included three Crown Courts, most applications related to similar offences but 13% were applications for previous convictions for dissimilar crimes to be admitted.

[187] 78% of applications were successful in full or part.

[188] Munday R, 'What Constitutes "Other Reprehensible Behaviour" under the Bad Character Provisions of the Criminal Justice Act 2003?' [2005] Crim LR 24.   [189] Morgan Harris Burrows LLP (2009: 18).

[190] Ibid: p 19.   [191] [2007] EWCA Crim 1472.

in evidence under s 100(1)(d). The judge allowed the evidence and directed the jury that it was relevant to both propensity to commit offences of the same type (violence against women) and credibility (whether the defendant was being truthful when he denied assaulting and falsely imprisoning the complainant). The defendant was convicted and appealed on the basis that the convictions were not relevant to his credibility. The Court of Appeal held that the gateway through which the convictions were admitted did not limit the purposes for which they could be used. Thus, in this case it did not matter that the convictions were admitted as evidence of propensity to commit offences; 'the jury could attach significance to them in any respect in which they were relevant'. However, the court also stated it would be rare for the propensity for 'truthfulness' to be an important matter in issue between the prosecution and defence. Lord Phillips argued that the jury were as a matter of 'common sense' likely to reach the conclusion that a defendant who has committed an offence is more likely to lie about it: 'whether or not the defendant is telling the truth to the jury is likely to depend simply on whether or not he committed the offence charged. The jury should focus on the latter question rather than on whether or not he has a propensity for telling lies'. He has reiterated his view extra-judicially, arguing juries can be trusted to give bad character evidence no more weight than it deserves.[192] The old common law rules in his view demonstrated 'a lack of trust of the jury' and 'were part of a criminal system that seemed to weight the scales in favour of the defence'. The new rules 'place greater trust in the ability of the jury to apply common sense to relevant evidence'. It has been suggested, however, that it may be 'premature' to abandon juries to their common sense understanding of bad character: 'It might be argued that the greater the volume of (prejudicial) evidence which legislation makes potentially admissible, the greater the obligation on the trial judge to guide the jury on how to approach it.'[193]

Whilst many opposed the bad character provisions of the Criminal Justice Act 2003 and argued that they would erode the safeguards against wrongful conviction of the innocent, they have their supporters. Spencer acknowledges that evidence of bad character is now admissible in many situations where it would previously have been excluded, but argues admission is not inherently unfair provided that there is other solid evidence that links the defendant to the offence.[194] However, as Redmayne observes, this appears to be precisely what the jury at the retrial of Barry George for the murder of Jill Dando were invited by the prosecution to do; convict on the basis of his 'bad character' with weak supporting evidence from eyewitnesses.[195] The prosecution presented the jury with extensive information about George's behaviour, suggesting that he was, to quote the media coverage, a 'celebrity and gun obsessed stalker with a grudge against the BBC'.[196] Although he was acquitted, if the coverage is accurate it

---

[192] Phillips (2007).   [193] Ormerod D, 'Editorial' [2008] Crim LR 337.

[194] Spencer (2006a).

[195] Redmayne, M, Book review of *Evidence of Bad Character* and *Hearsay Evidence in Criminal Proceedings* by J Spencer (2009) Howard JCJ 108–10.

[196] 'George Not Guilty of Dando Murder', BBC News, 1 August 2008.

does not present a picture of prosecutorial restraint in the face of rules which seem now to be stacked in their favour. Redmayne comments that it is difficult 'to see what sort of rule can be used to prevent weak cases being propped up by unimpressive character evidence, without going back to the unnecessarily strict standards of the old law'.[197] Were they really so strict and unnecessarily so? In our view reasoned and careful law reform that represents a principled balancing of the interests at stake has been abandoned in the Government's illiberal pursuit of 'bringing more offenders to justice'. The tragic and predictable result will be that more innocent defendants will be brought to injustice.

Other rules of evidence

We have shown above that Mark's three examples of rules that favour the defence were neither so absolute nor so one-sided as he contended, and that they have subsequently been remoulded so as to make it still easier to secure convictions. There are many other important procedural and evidential rules that favour the prosecution rather than the defence. For instance, there is no requirement that the prosecution produce evidence to corroborate the confession of an accused yet, as 5.6 demonstrated, extreme caution in this area is vital.

Where the evidence against the accused rests substantially on identification evidence the case of *Turnbull*[198] requires that the judge should direct an acquittal if the quality of the evidence is poor (unless there is other evidence which goes to support the correctness of the identification),[199] but otherwise should warn the jury of the need for caution before convicting on such evidence.[200] Arguably these guidelines do not go far enough in protecting accused persons from wrongful conviction given the inherently unreliable nature of identification evidence, and the role such evidence is known to have played in miscarriages of justice.[201] Furthermore, the senior judiciary are not consistent in their stipulations concerning when this due process safeguard is needed. Jackson noted in 1999 that earlier cases like *Curry*[202] confined the impact of *Turnbull* to 'fleeting glimpse' sightings, but that 'it is now clear that the cases in which the warning can be dispensed with are "wholly exceptional"'.[203] Since then the Court of Appeal has reheated *Curry* by observing[204] that *Turnbull* was intended primarily to deal with

---

[197] Redmayne (2009: 109).   [198] *Turnbull* [1977] QB 224.

[199] A point confirmed by *Davies* [2004] EWCA Crim 2521.

[200] Voice identification is also subject to the *Turnbull* principles but requires even greater caution according to *Davies* [2004] EWCA Crim 2521. See also the two articles by Ormerod D: 'Sounds Familiar: Voice Identification Evidence' [2001] Crim LR 595; 'Sounding Out Expert Voice Identification' [2002] Crim LR 771.

[201] See 6.4.2, and Roberts and Zuckerman (2004: 490–6) for fuller discussion. For a recent review of the conditions under which eyewitnesses tend to make mistakes see Memon et al, *Psychology and Law: Truthfulness, Accuracy and Credibility of Victims, Witnesses and Suspects*, 2nd edn (Chichester: John Wiley, 2003).   [202] [1983] Crim LR 737.

[203] Jackson (1999: 195), citing *Shand v R* [1996] 1 All ER 511.

[204] *Beckles and Montague* [1998] EWCA Crim 1494; [1999] Crim LR 148, relying on the view expressed by Lord Widgery CJ (who gave the judgment in *Turnbull*) in *Oakwell* [1978] 66 Cr App R 174.

cases of fleeting encounters. Trying to derive clarity from this case law is liable to give you indigestion.[205]

A key rule of evidence is that a statement made out of court is inadmissible as evidence of any fact stated. The rules prohibiting the admission of such hearsay evidence (already subject to many exceptions) are weakened considerably by s 114 of the Criminal Justice Act 2003, which introduces a general inclusionary discretion where 'the court is satisfied that it is in the interests of justice for it to be admissible'. The hearsay provisions in the 2003 Act run from ss 114–136 and there is little to be gained by attempting to summarise them here. We instead refer readers to specialist literature on the subject.[206] But three general observations are worth making. First, the old hearsay rules sometimes worked as much against defendants as in their favour (as when a confession made by some other person could not be admitted in evidence to show that the defendant was unlikely to have committed the offence).[207] Second, the new hearsay rules are not as tilted against the defence[208] as the bad character provisions of the CJA 2003 (see preceding sub-section). Third, the new rules 'enhance the value of material acquired during what might (loosely) be termed the investigative phase of a criminal prosecution' thus reducing one of the distinctions between inquisitorial and adversarial systems 'though without putting in place the former's regulatory safeguards'.[209] To put this more bluntly, it is now easier for the prosecution to adduce evidence that was fabricated or constructed by the police at the pre-trial stage. For example, under s 120(6) of the CJA 2003, statements made by witnesses can be adduced if they were made when matters were fresh in their memory and they cannot reasonably be expected to remember them well enough to give oral evidence of them in court. There has thus been created a new incentive for the police to 'gild the lily' to the detriment of suspects when taking witness statements (see further 6.4).

To illustrate the human rights implications of admitting hearsay, it is helpful to examine the issue of 'absent witnesses'. Section 23 of the Criminal Justice Act 1988 allowed first-hand documentary evidence to be admitted if the maker was dead, ill, could not be located and brought to court, or if the statement was made to a police officer and the maker did not give oral evidence through fear or because the authorities deemed it important to keep the witness out of the public arena. Leave was required to introduce such evidence, and the courts had to consider whether it was in the interests of justice to admit the statement, bearing in mind the difficulty of challenging the statement if the maker did not give oral evidence. As the Court of Appeal pointed out

---

[205] This is another sphere in which judicial bias may become evident. In *Shervington* [2008] EWCA Crim 648 the judge prefaced his comments on identification evidence by saying that the jury should not allow an over-sophisticated approach to become 'a muggers' charter'; the conviction was nonetheless upheld.

[206] Spencer J, *Hearsay Evidence in Criminal Proceedings* (Oxford: Hart Publishing, 2008a); Worthern T, 'The Hearsay Provisions of the Criminal Justice Act 2003: So far, Not So Good?' [2008] Crim LR 431.

[207] See *Beckford and Daley* [1991] Crim LR 833; *Lawless* [2003] EWCA Crim 271.

[208] See the analysis by Birch D, 'Hearsay: Same Old Story, Same Old Song' [2004] Crim LR 556.

[209] Durston G, 'Previous (In)Consistent Statements after the Criminal Justice Act 2003' [2005] Crim LR 206 at 214.

'you cannot conduct an argument with, nor ask questions of, a piece of paper'.[210] That Court policed the boundaries of s 23, for example by discouraging judges from allowing juries to speculate that the reason a person did not give oral evidence was fear of the defendant.[211] Nonetheless, as Jackson notes, s 23 'increased the ability of the prosecution to submit dubious documentary evidence against the accused'.[212] Section 116 of the Criminal Justice Act 2003 replaces s 23 of the 1988 Act and extends the admissibility of evidence by absent witnesses to all first-hand hearsay evidence. The leave requirement was abolished for absent witnesses other than the fearful. This will result in the automatic admission of a greater amount of hearsay evidence than previously, unless judges accede to applications to exclude the evidence on the grounds of fairness under s 78 of PACE.[213] By contrast, in the case of 'fearful witnesses' the leave requirement was tightened, by directing the court to consider whether a 'special measures' direction under the Youth Justice and Criminal Evidence Act 1999 (see 10.3.2 above) might be a fairer way of proceeding. These 'special measures' include the use of live-link video or screens to avoid confrontation, thus avoiding the need for the witness to come face-to-face with the defendant yet allowing cross-examination to take place. This is a welcome development although much will now depend on how trial judges exercise their discretion (see ch 13).

This is one area in which the ECHR safety net has had some effect, albeit not as much as one might have expected given its wording. Article 6(3)(d) of the European Convention sets out the minimum right of everyone charged with a criminal offence 'to examine or have examined witnesses against him'. At first sight, admitting the evidence of absent witnesses would seem to breach this right, but the Court of Appeal has held that statutory provisions which allow this are not in themselves contrary to Art 6 so long as the more general right to a fair trial is not breached.[214] From the ECtHR's perspective, the question of whether the admission of evidence from absent witnesses produces breaches of the Convention is likely to turn on the strength of the rest of the prosecution case, and the provision of compensating safeguards for defendants, such as the warning provided to juries about the danger of relying on statements not subjected to cross-examination.[215] In *PS v Germany*[216] a conviction of sexual abuse of a child was based on hearsay evidence reported to the court by the child's mother and a police officer. The defence here were prevented from challenging the key evidence of the child so a violation was found. By contrast in *SN v Sweden*[217] no violation was found in similar circumstances because pre-trial questioning of the child on behalf of the defence had taken place. The danger of hearsay evidence should not be viewed in

---

[210] *Radak, Adjei, Butler-Rees and Meghjee* [1999] Crim LR 223.

[211] See *Wood and Fitzsimmons* [1998] Crim LR 213. Trial judges are also meant to warn the jury of the dangers of accepting witness evidence not subject to cross-examination, but the warning need not take any specific form: *Batt and Batt* [1995] Crim LR 240.   [212] Jackson (1993: 139).

[213] Section 78 is discussed in ch 12.

[214] *Thomas, Flannagan, Thomas and Smith* [1998] Crim LR 887; *D* [2002] 2 Cr App R 361.

[215] See Ashworth A, 'Article 6 and the Fairness of Trials' [1999] Crim LR 261 at 268–9.

[216] (2000) 30 EHRR CD301, [2002] Crim LR 312.   [217] [2002] Crim LR 831.

isolation but in combination with other rules of evidence, such as bad character, which have moved in a pro-prosecution direction.

We conclude by recalling that Sir Robert Mark argued that jury trials were lop-sided affairs in which the prosecution was bound by rules whilst the defence could play dirty. In the interests of even-handed analysis let us record that the prosecution authorities are not above foul play themselves. We saw in earlier chapters how these authorities seek to construct cases so as to ensure the outcome they seek, and that this can involve such unethical practices as fabricating and tampering with evidence.[218] Two cases which came to light in the 1990s show that it would be wrong to assume that they would not dare 'tamper' with the jury itself. In *Kaul*[219] the police improperly took away from the court a rucksack already admitted into evidence and even more improperly placed items in it which were prejudicial to the defendant, returning it to court the following day. This only came to light because the jury, having taken the rucksack with them when retiring to consider their verdict, sent a note to the judge querying why the contents of the rucksack had not been mentioned during the trial. The Court of Appeal in quashing the conviction referred to its earlier unreported decision in *Ellis* (10 June 1991) in which 'documents which should not have been shown to the jury were "accidentally" given to them, allegedly by a police witness'.[220] In one sense it is understandable that the police stoop to such tactics. As we saw in 10.1, despite all the supposed safeguards, weak cases do end up in front of the jury. The police are naturally sometimes tempted to strengthen them through a last minute piece of case construction.

10.4.2 Substantive law and the definition of offences

In understanding how juries come to be convinced of guilt beyond reasonable doubt it is also necessary to look at the structure of substantive criminal law. We can do no more than scratch the surface of this issue here, but the links between criminal law and criminal justice are too important to ignore.[221] We commented in earlier chapters on how the breadth of the criminal law has implications for police powers of arrest and stop and search, and the implications are no less important at the trial stage. The essential point is that the fewer the elements that have to be proved by the prosecution, and the easier the law makes it to prove those elements, the more likely it is that juries will convict. All-encompassing offence definitions are antithetical to due process since they cover a variety of acts and states of mind ranging from the venal to the virtuous. To be presumed innocent is of little significance if the prosecution need do little to prove guilt (see 1.2). This is precisely what makes such definitions attractive to crime control adherents, since they assist in curtailing inefficient and pointless adversarial

---

[218] See especially 6.4 and 7.3.3.   [219] [1998] Crim LR 135.
[220] Commentary to *Kaul* [1998] Crim LR 135 at p 137.
[221] See further Lacey N, 'Legal Constructions of Crime' in Maguire et al (eds), *Oxford Handbook of Criminology*, 4th edn (Oxford: OUP, 2007).

trials. Moreover, they may deter defendants from opting for trial in the first place and thus contribute to maintaining a high guilty plea rate.

Many examples of broadly drawn offences could be given. McBarnet[222] pointed out in the early 1980s that crimes such as theft and assault cover a much wider range of behaviour than the lay person generally realises, and the reach of the criminal law has grown still further since then. Under the Theft Act 1968, the actus reus of theft is the appropriation of property belonging to another, and any assumption of any one right of the owner amounts to an appropriation: *Morris*.[223] Moreover, the House of Lords held in *Gomez*[224] that it is an appropriation notwithstanding that the owner authorises the taking or moving of property. Thus simply taking down a bottle of whisky from a supermarket shelf amounts to an appropriation and if there is, in addition, evidence of dishonesty and an intention to permanently deprive the supermarket of the whisky, then a conviction for theft could follow. As the only evidence of a defendant's state of mind in this situation is likely to be a confession, it is dangerous to reduce the conduct element of the crime of theft to this minimum. As we saw in ch 5, the risk of false confessions is great and it would be more in accordance with due process principles to require that the defendant did some act which was strongly corroborative of a criminal purpose (such as concealing the whisky under a coat).

General principles of liability further extend the prodigious reach of the criminal law. For example, s 1(1) of the Criminal Attempts Act 1981 makes it an ('inchoate') offence to do an act which is more than merely preparatory to the commission of an indictable offence if done with intent to commit such offence. To take our earlier example, merely reaching to pick up the bottle of whisky from the shelf may be classified as a criminal attempt. Principles of secondary liability (covering those who assist the principal offender), and of mens rea, are similarly broad in scope, rendering a vast range of behaviour subject to criminalisation. Thus it has been noted that:

The cumulation of secondary liability with the group offences of riot affray and violent disorder under the [Public Order Act] 1986 increases the flexibility of an already broad and inclusive area of criminal regulation...The further cumulation with inchoate offences makes possible applications of criminal law which are of staggering breadth.[225]

We may also note that the criminal law generally ignores the defendant's motive in defining what counts as a guilty state of mind.[226] Defendants charged with theft of food will not be heard to say in their defence that they were hungry, nor will those who enter a boarded-up building as trespassers, intending to chop up floorboards for firewood, be allowed to defend a charge of burglary by arguing that they were cold and homeless. Juries are enjoined to do justice according to law, but the law incorporates a particular kind of justice which skates over awkward problems arising from gross

---

[222] McBarnet (1983: 13–14).   [223] [1984] AC 320.   [224] [1993] 1 All ER 1.

[225] Lacey et al, *Reconstructing Criminal Law*, 3rd edn (London: LexisNexis, 2003) p 215.

[226] See the discussion by Norrie A, *Crime, Reason and History* (London: Weidenfeld and Nicolson, 1993) pp 36–47.

inequalities in society.[227] In this way too, the issues to be debated at trial are narrowed and the potential for adversarial challenge is reduced.

Finally, we should not forget the discussion in 1.2, regarding the burden of proof. As noted there, in 1996 it was calculated that 219 out of the 540 indictable (ie triable in the Crown Court) offences then in common use involved a reversal of the burden of proof. In other words, in relation to some elements of offence definitions the defendant was effectively placed under a duty to prove his or her innocence.[228] Quite when it is acceptable under the ECHR to place a burden of proof on the defendant is still being established, but, as we noted in our ch 1 discussion of this point, many reverse onuses are undoubtedly here to stay. This further undermines Sir Robert Mark's implicit claim, set out at the start of this section, that the burden of proof lay only on the prosecution and that the rules 'were designed to give every advantage to the defence'.

10.5 Evaluating the jury's performance

It was argued in ch 9 that magistrates are more likely than jurors to embrace crime control ideology. This is largely because jurors are outsiders, free of the administrative concerns of dealing speedily with a large caseload. Moreover, unlike magistrates, jurors bear no direct responsibility for sentencing,[229] and are accordingly less likely to see themselves as instruments for upholding law and order. As jury service is statistically a less than once in a lifetime opportunity, it seems unlikely that in such circumstances jurors will in general subscribe to the crime control view that their task is to trust the prosecution evidence and convict without more ado. On the other hand, one must not simply assume that the jury operates according to due process principles. This is all the more so when we recall the concerns we raised in 10.2 about the pro-prosecution bias in the law and practice of jury selection. Rather, we must question whether juries in practice set aside their prejudices, seek hard evidence of guilt, and apply the appropriate standard of proof.

An immediate problem is that juries are not required to articulate reasons for the conclusions they reach at the end of a case. They deliberate in private and, on their return to the court, merely give a general verdict of 'guilty' or 'not guilty'.[230] Moreover, a stifling and all-embracing concern to protect the secrecy of the jury has prevented

---

[227] There is a striking contrast here with non-police agencies. Immunity from prosecution (and hence conviction) for crimes which are a product of the economic facts of life is almost universally accepted. See 7.5 for further discussion.

[228] Ashworth A and Blake M, 'The Presumption of Innocence in English Criminal Law' [1996] Crim LR 306.

[229] In some jurisdictions jurors do bear some responsibility for sentencing: see Munday (1995).

[230] In the case of a 'guilty' verdict the jury foreman will be asked to state the number of jurors voting for and against conviction. To avoid 'second-rate acquittals', this question is not put if a 'not guilty' verdict is returned.

any systematic study based on direct observation or recording of its deliberations. For many years the exact legal position was unclear on this point, although a convention of jury secrecy was maintained. But s 8 of the Contempt of Court Act 1981 made it a contempt to 'obtain, disclose or solicit any particulars of statements made, opinions expressed, arguments advanced or votes cast by members of a jury in the course of their deliberation.' It is sometimes said that such a rule is necessary to protect individual jurors from reprisals or to preserve the finality of jury verdicts, although closer analysis suggests that the purpose of s 8 was to 'preserve public confidence in regard to the adjudication of issues of fact'.[231]

Do juries deserve public confidence? The answer to this can only be equivocal since the existing studies in England and Wales are either based on individual jurors' accounts, or general surveys, or based on the impressions of judges, lawyers and police officers, or on simulations with 'shadow' or 'mock' juries.[232] To this motley collection can be added surveys of views on the jury. We will look at each type of evidence in turn.

10.5.1 General impressions

Individual jurors have published their recollections of their period of service both before and after the Contempt of Court Act 1981. Some have been disillusioned or even dismayed by their experiences while others have reported broad satisfaction with the jury process.[233] A full review of the 33 (then) available accounts is given in Darbyshire et al.[234] The people who choose to write about their experiences give fascinating insights into jury dynamics but are self-selecting and probably unrepresentative of jurors in general. Moreover, they may have felt moved to write because their experiences were in some sense extraordinary. Some defence lawyers are reportedly concerned about the effects of the publication of the views and experiences of jurors in individual cases.[235]

One way in which such accounts can undoubtedly be valuable is to alert researchers to questions requiring more systematic study. For example, individual jurors have revealed that the standard of proof applied in practice ranges from the balance of probabilities to 100% certainty (neither of which accords with the legal standard of

---

[231] Jaconelli J, *Open Justice: A Critique of the Public Trial* (Oxford: OUP, 2002) p 244. Thus if a foreman wrongly declares the verdict of guilty to be 'unanimous' the Court of Appeal will refuse to inquire into the matter: *Hart* [1998] Crim LR 417; *Millward* [1999] Crim LR 164. See also Quinn (2004).

[232] Another approach, which is ruled out by s 8 in England and Wales, is to interview jurors immediately after verdict. This produced illuminating results in New Zealand: Tinsley Y, 'Juror Decision-Making: A Look Inside the Jury Room' Selected Papers from the British Criminology Conference, vol 4 (2001), available on <http://www.britsoccrim.org/volume4/004.pdf> (accessed 5 January 2010).

[233] See, for example, the five accounts published in (1990) 140 NLJ 1264–76.

[234] Darbyshire et al (2001). Since then several more accounts have emerged, such as by the jurors in the case of a childminder convicted of murdering a child in her care. See 'Juror Speaks Out; "The Court Saw Us as Idiots"', *The Times*, 29 January 2008.

[235] 'Why Juries Just Can't Keep Quiet', *The Times*, 18 March 2008.

beyond reasonable doubt).[236] The problem seems to stem, at least in part, from the standard direction to the jury which tells them that they must feel sure of guilt before convicting.[237] Zander tested this direction on 1,763 members of the public and found that 51% equated 'sure' with 100% proof (as did almost a third of magistrates and other legal professionals).[238] It is not possible here, however, to explore all the qualitative points that arise from individual jurors' accounts and we remain somewhat sceptical as to the value of doing so given their unrepresentative nature. For the same reason we do not dwell upon the oddities revealed by case law.[239]

The large-scale Crown Court survey carried out for the Runciman Commission[240] found that 80% of jurors rated trial by jury as a good or very good system and only 5% rated it as poor or worse. Jurors typically claimed that they had little difficulty in understanding or remembering the evidence, in coping with legalistic language or in following directions on the law from the judge.[241] The judges surveyed thought the jury system was good or very good in terms of 'generally getting a sensible result' in 79% of cases, the prosecution barristers in 82% and defence barristers in 91%. The survey found that 8% of judges rated the system as poor or very poor, compared with 4% of prosecuting barristers and 2% of defence barristers.[242] While such ratings of trial by jury as 'good' or 'bad' are somewhat crude and subjective, the findings of this survey nonetheless reveal a high level of support for this institution. Even more positive support was found by Matthews et al (2004). They interviewed 361 jurors who had recently completed jury service at six Crown Court centres in 2001/02. Out of those interviewed, 95% regarded juries as either quite (33%) or very (62%) important to the justice system and just under two-thirds had a more positive view of the jury system after completing their service than they did before. What made jurors so positive about their experience? The most important factor was the perceived benefits of having a diverse jury drawn from different social and economic backgrounds with different viewpoints and experiences. Jurors were also impressed by the fairness of the trial process, praising the performance, commitment and competence of judges, and the way in which the rights of defendants were respected.

Large-scale surveys evidently produce a more rosy picture than individual jurors' accounts. This discrepancy might be accounted for by the greater representativeness

---

[236] Darbyshire et al (2001: 55).

[237] Available on the Judicial Studies Board website: <http://www.jsboard.co.uk/downloads/specimen directions_oct08.doc> (accessed 5 January 2010).

[238] Zander M, 'The Criminal Standard of Proof – How Sure is Sure? (2000) 150 NLJ 1517, building on the earlier findings of Montgomery J, 'The Criminal Standard of Proof' (1998) 148 NLJ 582. But as McEwan et al (2002) point out, given the high conviction rate which obtains in the criminal courts, these results are most likely artefacts of the research.

[239] Such as: the foreman who, after the jury retired, produced his own list of the defendant's previous convictions (*Thompson* (1961) 46 Cr App Rep 72); the profoundly deaf jury member who missed half of the evidence and all of the summing up (*Chapman and Lauday* (1976) 63 Cr App Rep 75); and the members of a jury who consulted a 'ouija board' for help in reaching their verdict (*Young* [1995] 2 Cr App Rep 379).

[240] Zander and Henderson (1993).   [241] Zander and Henderson (1993: 232, 206, 208, 212, 216).

[242] Ibid: 172–3.

of survey data, but it is equally plausible to argue that survey-type questioning conducted within the constraints of s 8 of the Contempt of Court Act is liable to produce general and superficial claims that tell us little about the actual functioning of trial by judge and jury. Jurors may believe that they are doing a great job, but what do other people think?

10.5.2 Professional disagreement with juries

A number of studies have examined the extent of disagreement with jury verdicts in particular cases. In the USA, Kalven and Zeisel examined 3,576 trials and found that judges agreed with the decision reached by the jury in 75% of cases.[243] This is not a particularly high level of agreement. Stephenson observes that the most striking finding of this study is that judges, as well as agreeing with nearly all jury decisions to convict, would also have convicted 57% of the 1,083 persons whom the jury acquitted.[244] Judges attributed the disagreement between themselves and the juries they instructed to a range of factors. In nearly a third of cases they thought juries had been swayed by their dislike for the law and had exercised jury equity. In 15% of cases they acquitted, in the judge's view, because either the defendant or defence counsel had made a favourable impression upon them. In 54% of cases the judge thought that the jury had taken a different approach to the evidence.[245]

The early English studies that measured the extent of agreement amongst lawyers and police officers with jury verdicts concluded that these groups for the most part had no quarrel with the jury's decision.[246] The most substantial study of this type, conducted by Baldwin and McConville in the mid 1970s, painted a more critical picture. Of 370 randomly selected cases heard in one Crown Court centre, 114 ended in acquittal. Of the latter, serious doubts were expressed about the jury's verdict by the judge in 32% of cases, by the police in 44%, by prosecuting solicitors in 26% and by defence solicitors in 10% of cases.[247] Baldwin and McConville defined a 'questionable acquittal' as one where the judge and at least one other respondent thought the acquittal was not justified. They considered whether jury equity explained the high incidence of questionable acquittals (36% of all acquittals), but concluded that it did not. The proportion of convictions that were questioned was much smaller, but in 15 cases (6% of all convictions) two or more of the parties to the case had serious doubts about the jury's verdict. Whereas the judge had reservations in eight of these cases, it

---

[243] Kalven H and Zeisel H, *The American Jury* (Boston: Little, Brown, 1966).

[244] Stephenson G, *The Psychology of Criminal Justice* (Oxford: Basil Blackwell, 1992) pp 180–1.

[245] Kalven and Zeisel (1966: 115).

[246] See McCabe S and Purves R, *The Jury at Work*, (Oxford: Basil Blackwell, 1972b) and Zander M, 'Are Too Many Professional Criminals Avoiding Conviction?' (1974) 37 MLR 28. For a critique of such research, see Freeman (1981) pp 85–97.

[247] Baldwin and McConville (1979: 45–7). See also Zander and Henderson (1993: 162–72), for the reactions of lawyers, police officers and judges to particular jury verdicts. As with Baldwin and McConville, 'problematic' acquittals were found to be more prevalent than problematic convictions.

is striking that the police doubted the verdict in all but two instances. The researchers considered that the most likely explanation for these doubtful convictions was that the jury had failed to appreciate the high standard of proof required in criminal cases and that it had lacked comprehension of the issues involved.[248] There was also evidence to suggest that in some of these cases the jury might have been swayed by racial prejudice.[249] This, from a due process point of view, is the flip side of 'jury equity' and it must be taken into account by those who find attractive the idea of a jury following 'its conscience' rather than the law.[250] Cases like that of Clive Ponting, acquitted by the jury when he was prosecuted under the Official Secrets Act for revealing details of government duplicity during the Falklands War,[251] perhaps show merit in allowing the jury to take a broader view of the justice of the case.[252] However, the power to return verdicts in the face of the law and evidence may result in greater susceptibility to emotional biases.[253]

Two points need to be made concerning Baldwin and McConville's work. The first is that their method for assessing questionable jury acquittals is itself highly questionable. Of the four parties to the case whose views they sought, two (prosecuting solicitor and police) are clearly conviction minded, one (the judge) is, as this chapter has argued, very often pro-conviction, and only one is likely to be pro-acquittal (defence solicitor). Whereas defence solicitors had serious doubts about acquittals in 10% of all acquittal cases, the other three groups had such doubts in much larger proportions ranging from 26% to 44%. By defining a questionable acquittal as one in which the judge and one other party to the case thought the jury's verdict to be wrong, Baldwin and McConville built into their measurements an inherent prosecution bias. That juries were found to be acquittal-prone by the standards of state officials and representatives is not surprising given the state's commitment to crime control values. This methodological flaw was avoided in a recent New Zealand study, where the researchers scrutinised the evidence given at trial for themselves, and interviewed jurors about their decision-making once the verdict had been given. They counted a verdict as questionable only if:

(a) the judge disagreed with the jury;

(b) the researchers agreed that the verdict was questionable on the basis of the data they had collected; and

---

[248] Baldwin and McConville (1979: 76).

[249] Ibid: 80–1.This could be addressed by ensuring a more representative racial mix on the jury: see 10.2 above.

[250] See also Gordon J, 'Juries as Judges of the Law' (1992) 108 LQR 272 at 278; Matravers M, '"More Than Just Illogical": Truth and Jury Nullification' in Duff et al (eds), *The Trial on Trial: Truth and Due Process* (Oxford: Hart, 2004).

[251] Ponting C, *The Right to Know, The Inside Story of the Belgrano Affair* (London: Sphere, 1985).

[252] As has occurred in a number of celebrated cases throughout legal history: Cornish W, *The Jury* (London: Penguin, 1968) ch 5 and Freeman (1991: 90–3).

[253] Horowitz et al, 'Chaos in the Courtroom Reconsidered: Emotional Bias and Juror Nullification' (2006) 30 Law and Human Behaviour 163.

(c) an independent barrister experienced in both defence and prosecution work
     agreed with the researchers.

Whereas the judge disagreed with the jury in 24 out of 48 trials, only three of these
were categorised as questionable by the researchers and independent counsel, and
there was little evidence of jury equity or of verdicts being influenced by sympathy
for the defendant.[254] As Tinsley (2001) puts it, 'overall juries were conscientious in
approaching their task and were not usually swayed, as a unit, from making a decision
based on the evidence and the law'.

The second point to ask in relation to Baldwin and McConville's work is what meaning to attribute to evidence of disagreement between professionals and lay jurors. If
juries always reached verdicts of which judges approved what would be the point of
having a jury? One of the strongest arguments for retaining trial by jury is to avoid
leaving the fate of defendants to be determined by professionals, applying professional
standards. Thus, Mungham and Bankowski contend that since there is no consensus
about what constitutes a 'good' jury decision, and because the lawyer's view of a case
is not the only sensible or rational interpretation, professional disagreement with jury
verdicts tells us nothing meaningful about jury competence.[255]

If one accepts that law is not an absolute but must always be interpreted and applied
in specific contexts and circumstances it follows that jurors may take a different view of
what the law requires in a particular case from that adopted by lawyers. The institution
of the jury represents a policy preference for the process by which this judgment is to be
reached to be left ultimately in the hands of lay people rather than professionals. This
injection of a lay element into the administering of justice does not have to be justified
on the ground that the jury is more reliable or efficient as a finder of fact than a professional judge. Rather, one can argue that lay involvement is necessary in order to allow
jury equity to be exercised (if we think this to be desirable) and also to ensure that law
and justice do not become monopolised by professionals.[256] From a freedom perspective, there are good reasons why professional expertise should be challenged and laid
bare before the community as represented by the 12 individuals on the jury. This seems
consistent with the current government's encouragement of 'active citizenship' and its
oft-repeated view that 'with rights come responsibilities'. There is evidence that serving
on a jury can lead to a sense of pride in the accomplishment of an important civic duty
and a more general interest in, and understanding of, the administration of justice.[257]

[254] Young et al, *Juries in Criminal Trials: A Summary of the Research Findings* (Preliminary Paper 37,
Vol 2) (Wellington, New Zealand: Law Commission, 1999), available from <http://www.lawcom.govt.nz>
(accessed 5 January 2010).

[255] Mungham G and Bankowski Z, 'The Jury in the Legal System' in Carlen P (ed), *The Sociology of Law*
(Keele: University of Keele, 1976) p 209. See also Freeman (1981: 85–8, 95–7).

[256] See Mungham and Bankowski (1976) and Freeman (1981) for extended treatment of this theme. See
also 9.5, where we illustrate how juries, when compared with social elites, such as magistrates or lawyers,
may reach a different (and, arguably, better) view of what the law requires.

[257] Munday R, 'What do the French Think of their Jury?' (1995) 15 LS 65 at pp 68–71; Matthews et al
(2004).

Lay participation in criminal justice, whether in the form of lay magistrates or the jury, is an element of democracy.[258] Jury service, by furthering transparency and accountability within criminal justice, is a safeguard of a free society.

10.5.3 Shadow and 'mock' juries

An obvious difficulty with all studies that simply measure professional disagreement with verdicts is that they are based on indirect measurements of the jury's work. It is possible that observation of the jury's deliberations would have indicated to Baldwin and McConville a satisfactory explanation (whether of an evidential or equitable nature) for many of the verdicts they classified as questionable. The New Zealand study discussed above suggests exactly that, although it in turn suffered from the drawback that it relied for its understanding of what took place in the deliberation room on interview material rather than direct observation.

Direct observation of 'shadow' juries – where a panel of people observe or listen to trials in tandem with the real jury, and then retire to consider their 'verdict' – have provided some insight into the dynamics of the jury room. All such studies show a fairly high level of correspondence between the verdicts of the real and the shadow juries, suggesting that the latter approach their simulated task in a reasonably realistic manner. In a study of 30 cases, McCabe and Purves concluded that:

The 'shadow' juries showed considerable determination in looking for evidence upon which convictions could be based; when it seemed inadequate, they were not prepared to allow their own 'hunch' that the defendant was involved in some way in the offence that was charged to stand in the way of an acquittal... There was little evidence of perversity in the final decisions of these thirty groups. One acquittal only showed that sympathy and impatience with the triviality of the case so influenced the 'shadow' jurors' view of the evidence that they refused to convict.[259]

More recently, McConville reported on a televised study of five real cases heard by a shadow jury:

Although not dealing with the fate of actual defendants, the shadow jury's deliberations have an authentic ring, marked by fierce debate, acute analysis, common sense, personal experience, stubbornness and occasional whiffs of prejudice... Overall, the quality and power of the argument within the shadow jury room, and the high level of correspondence between the verdicts of the real and shadow juries, suggests that confidence in the jury is well-placed.[260]

Another kind of research, even more artificial than shadow jury studies, involves 'mock juries' in which panels of people observe and then deliberate on mock trials.[261]

---

[258] Gobert J, *Justice, Democracy and the Jury* (Aldershot: Dartmouth, 1997); Bankowski et al, *Lay Justice?* (Edinburgh: T & T Clark, 1987) chs 1, 9.

[259] McCabe S and Purves R, *The Shadow Jury at Work* (Oxford: Basil Blackwell, 1974).

[260] McConville M, 'Shadowing the Jury' (1991) 141 NLJ 1588 at pp 1588 and 1595.

[261] The Lloyd-Bostock research (2000) was of this type: see 10.4.2 above. See also the study by Honess et al 'Juror Competence in Processing Complex Information: Implications from a Simulation of the Maxwell

For example, a study of decision-making in sexual assault cases shows that jurors are influenced by a previous consensual sexual relationship between the victim and defendant and are less likely to find the defendant credible when such a relationship exists. This may perhaps explain the low prosecution and conviction rate in cases of 'domestic' or marital rape. A variety of extra legal factors, including stereotypes about behaviour, may enter into jury decision-making: 'the conceptualisation of jurors as rational decision-makers embarking on a fact-finding mission based on the rules of logic and the principles of law is not a valid representation of what happens in jury trials'.[262]

Finch and Munro's study of the impact of complainant intoxication in rape trials used mock juries to investigate how knowledge of intoxication influenced jurors' attribution of blame.[263] They recognise the problems of this method[264] such as ensuring adequate sampling[265] and that mock jurors are given realistic stimuli.[266] Their mock jury sample relied on self selecting members of the public who responded to advertisements for the research. They were exposed to 75 minute 'mini' trials using actors performing in a university classroom rather than courtroom. Despite these limitations, the researchers argue that their study involved more adequate sampling and realistic stimuli than many. In line with the shadow jury research described above they found that mock jurors undertook their task seriously even though no-one's fate really hung in the balance. The ability to observe the group deliberation process was an important advantage of the method.[267] The substantive findings of their research show the importance of stereotypes in jury decision-making in rape trials.

This has been explored further by Ellison and Munro in a separate study of rape trials again using the mock jury approach.[268] Their research suggests that jurors cannot leave their personal prejudices and stereotypes behind at the door of the courtroom. Jurors make assumptions about the presence or absence of resistance and injury, delay in reporting and the calm demeanour of complainants. For example,

---

Trial' [1998] Crim LR 763 discussed in 10.6 below. Thomas' research, discussed in 10.2 above, involved real discharged jurors observing mock trials.

[262] Temkin J and Krahe B, *Sexual Assault and the Justice Gap* (Oxford: Hart Publishing, 2008) p 71.

[263] Finch E and Munro V, 'Breaking Boundaries?: Sexual Consent in the Jury Room' (2006) Legal Studies 303; Finch E and Munro V, 'The Demon Drink and the Demonised Woman: Socio-Sexual Stereotypes and Responsibility Attribution in Rape Trials Involving Intoxicants' (2007) Social and Legal Studies 591.

[264] Finch E and Munro V, 'Lifting the Veil: The Use of Focus Groups and Trial Simulations in Legal Research'(2008) JLS 30.

[265] One problem with mock juries has been the tendency to rely on students because these are the easiest group for academic researchers to recruit but are obviously not representative of the wider community from which real jurors are drawn.

[266] Often mock jurors are given written vignettes as stimuli, depriving them of the opportunity to assess non-verbal behaviour in the courtroom. Also the vignettes might be deliberately limited in order to enable the researchers to try to isolate the impact of particular variables more clearly, inviting the criticism that they produce the effect they are intended to observe.

[267] Whilst this is also possible with shadow juries, mock jury simulations allow the researcher to try to isolate particular variables more effectively (as by varying the 'story' for some juries).

[268] Ellison L and Munro V, 'Reacting to Rape' (2009a) 49(2) BJ Crim 202. See also Ellison L and Munro V 'Of "Normal Sex" and "Real Rape": Exploring the Use of Socio-Sexual Scripts in (Mock) Jury Deliberation' (2009b) 18 (3) Social and Legal Studies 291.

many believed that injury was required to corroborate a complaint of real rape, to the extent that jurors expected unrealistically high levels of injury, some even doubting whether non-consensual penetration was possible without vaginal injury. Treatment of delayed reporting was not uniform across mock juries but some saw a three-day delay in reporting as a serious obstacle to conviction whereas victims who called the police immediately were often evaluated positively. Jurors were perplexed when complainants presented as emotionally flat and held calmness against them, although (in a classic double-bind) a 'distressed' complainant was not always seen positively with some jurors suspecting a managed performance.

These findings provide useful insights into the influence of stereotypes on jury decision-making in rape cases and should inform the policy debate as to what type of instructions or evidence, if any, jurors should be given to counter prejudices they might have which are not supported by psychological and sociological evidence.[269]

The research is also valuable for the insights it offers into the nature of jury deliberations. Past research has shown two broad approaches to deliberation; 'verdict driven' (where the jurors take an early vote and deliberations are driven by their voting positions) and 'evidence driven' (where voting is postponed and the deliberations are guided by a discussion of the evidence). Ellison and Munro found that some of the mock juries in their study tended to be more verdict driven than others, but the approaches are not polar opposites and most juries fell on a continuum between the two.[270] Those juries who were verdict driven tended to be more competitive and confrontational in their deliberations whilst the evidence driven juries tended to be more collaborative. Their research also suggests that the foreperson may influence deliberations, which could be significant in the context of their finding that there was a tendency where such a person was elected, for the person to be an older male. It might be expected from previous research that this would compound a male gender bias against rape victims in jury decision-making but in fact Ellison and Munro found that victim blaming was not limited to male jurors and in some cases male jurors were the most vocal in challenging stereotypes. Their research also confirmed that jurors are confused about the standard of evidence required for conviction, with some jurors expressing the view that this required 100% certainty. However, they suggest that this may simply have been a strategy to persuade other jurors away from conviction.

10.5.4 Jury research in context

Criminal justice has undergone a series of fundamental changes over the last quarter of a century. Notable amongst these are PACE, the inception of the Crown Prosecution

---

[269] In *R v D* [2008] EWCA Crim 2557 the judge gave a warning to the jury regarding the effect of the delay on the credibility of a complainant in a rape case. The government has been considering whether juries should be given expert evidence to counteract so called 'rape myths'. See Ellison L, 'Promoting Effective Case-building in Rape Cases' [2007] Crim LR 691; Ellison L and Munro V, 'Turning Mirrors into Windows? Assessing the Impact of (Mock) Juror Education in Rape Trials' (2009c) 49(3) BJ Crim 363.

[270] See Ellison L and Munro V (forthcoming in *Legal Studies* 2010).

Service, and amongst the many other recent 'reforms' to the law of evidence, the major attenuation of the right to silence. The impact of all this on the workings of jury trials has yet to be charted properly. The weight of the evidence to date suggests, however, that juries do conform much more closely to due process values than to crime control ideology. But since, as demonstrated earlier, it is not the jury, but the judge, who is the central directing figure in a trial, and since judges lean towards crime control positions, juries are in reality unlikely to base decisions on anything like a pure due process approach.

Juries do not act in a vacuum, nor do they act as finders of the truth.[271] They simply decide 'a case'. The case that is presented to the jury is shaped by rules of evidence, procedure and substantive law, the presentation skills of opposing counsel, the preparatory work by the police, the influence of the judge and a host of other factors. We have argued throughout this book that all pre-trial and trial processes are imbued, to a greater or lesser degree, with crime control values. No matter how due process oriented juries might be, they cannot be relied upon to spot the crime control workmanship that went into building the case put before them. To expect the jury to deconstruct the case and re-examine it under a due process microscope is simply unrealistic. The fact that every major miscarriage of justice case was preceded by a guilty verdict from a jury is evidence of this. But judges are no different from juries in this respect. They too can only deal with the case as presented. And that will have been shaped by the processes covered in chs 2–7 of this book. This is a point worth bearing in mind when we consider, in the next section, the value of 'Diplock courts'.

10.6 **Narrowing the jury's domain**

The prevailing attitude of the state seems to be that juries are costly and too prone to acquit, so it has repeatedly attempted to restrict juries from hearing certain categories of case altogether. There are now so few contested Crown Court trials that the chances of doing jury service 'have been whittled down to one in six'.[272] Here we review briefly the trend *away* from trial by jury and consider some of the broader implications of the move *towards* other modes of trial.

In 1973 'Diplock courts' were introduced in Northern Ireland for defendants charged with offences deemed to be terrorist-related to be tried by a single judge sitting without a jury.[273] The introduction of these courts was justified on the grounds that firstly, the

---

[271] See Mungham and Bankowski (1976: 206, 212–13).

[272] Darbyshire P, 'Strengthening the Argument in Favour of the Defendant's Right to Elect' [1997] Crim LR 911.

[273] See the Northern Ireland (Emergency Provisions) Act 1973. The criteria and methods for directing cases to single judge courts are rough-and-ready and resulted in the diversion of many cases lacking a terrorist connection away from juries: see Jackson J and Doran S, 'Diplock and the Presumption Against Jury Trial: A Critique' [1992] Crim LR 755.

circumstances of that province left jurors exposed to intimidation and, second, that jurors were likely to return perverse verdicts borne of partisanship.[274] However, the thrust of the report which proposed these courts was to dismantle a series of procedural rights and safeguards for suspects so as to ease the path towards a conviction.[275] As no empirical evidence existed to justify the supposed concerns about jury trials, the suspicion must be that the change was in reality part of the strategy to secure more guilty verdicts. The annual number of cases heard in Diplock courts was always small, falling from over 1,000 in the mid 1970s to around 400 in the 1990s[276] but they represented an area of criminal activity in which, for obvious reasons, the state is particularly keen to secure a high conviction rate. The IRA 'ceasefire' left Diplock courts dealing with a dwindling number of cases, and the Justice and Security (Northern Ireland) Act 2007 began the process of replacing Diplock courts with jury trial, but the Act still allows the DPP to certify judge-only trial if he believes that there is a risk of jury intimidation or interference with the Administration of Justice.[277]

Research examining Diplock courts gives us some insights into the impact of judge-only trial. It was suggested that Diplock judges became increasingly prone to accepting police and prosecution evidence in preference to that of the defence and that this 'case-hardening' led to a decline in the acquittal rate,[278] although the evidence was not clear cut. Jackson and Doran[279] highlighted a more important point; that trial by jury produces a higher average acquittal rate than Diplock trial. Their own comparison of Diplock trials with jury trials suggests one reason for this is that Diplock judges confine their consideration of the case to the strict legal issue of guilt or innocence. In other words, these judges eschew the broader jury role of considering the merits (or morality) of prosecuting and punishing a particular defendant.[280] That role tends to work in the defendant's favour, but does not invariably do so as juries may wish to punish certain individuals even though the legal elements of the offence may not be made out. Counsel interviewed by Jackson and Doran claimed that sexual cases were particularly difficult to defend before juries. As one put it: 'It would suit me nearly as well not to have a jury at all because I would rather the case was dealt with in a colder, unemotional fashion because there's enough emotion to start with.'[281] This chimes with our earlier comments in 10.4.2 about the dangers of jury trial for individuals who

---

[274] *Report of the Commission to Consider Legal Procedures to Deal with Terrorist Activities in Northern Ireland* (Cmnd 5185) (London: HMSO, 1972). The Commission was chaired by Lord Diplock.

[275] See Hillyard P, 'The Normalization of Special Powers: from Northern Ireland to Britain' in Scraton P (ed), *Law, Order and the Authoritarian State* (Milton Keynes: Open UP, 1987) pp 285–6.

[276] Jackson and Doran (1995: 33–6).

[277] The Act also contained provisions increasing juror anonymity and abolishing the defence right of peremptory challenge. Since the 2007 Act consultations have taken place on widening the jury pool in line with changes made England and Wales by the Criminal Justice Act 2003 to allow previously ineligible people, such as police officers and prosecutors, to serve as jurors (Northern Ireland Court Service, *Widening the Jury Pool* (Belfast: NICS, 2008).   [278] See Jackson and Doran (1995: 294).

[279] Jackson and Doran (1995: 33–6).   [280] Jackson and Doran (1995: 291–4).

[281] See Jackson J and Doran S, 'Judge and Jury: Towards a New Division of Labour in Criminal Trials' (1997) 60 MLR 759 at pp 764–5.

are liable to be stereotyped or stigmatised during the proceedings. Doran and Jackson suggest that one solution would be to allow defendants to waive trial by jury. Instead trial would be by a professional judge.[282] In a climate deeply hostile to the creation of new rights for defendants it is highly unlikely that the government would favour giving defendants who are tried in the Crown Court any right to opt for the mode of trial they thought gave them the best chance of an acquittal, and it is not self-evident that we should give guilty defendants that right in any event.[283]

In England and Wales jury trial has come under attack in a number of ways, which in recent years includes persistent attempts to introduce judge-only trial in serious and complex fraud cases. The government cajoled parliament into passing s 43 of the Criminal Justice Act 2003, which, subject to conditions, would allow a judge to order non-jury trial in complex or lengthy fraud cases. The controversial nature of the provision was such that further parliamentary action was required to bring it into force and the government has been unsuccessful in successive attempts to do this.[284] There is a long history of debate about the wisdom of asking lay juries to act as fact-finders in complex fraud trials. In 1986 the Roskill Committee recommended that such trials might better be heard by a special tribunal.[285] But the Runciman Commission[286] concluded that, in the absence of research evidence on the workings of jury trials, there was no basis on which to recommend dispensing with juries for complex frauds or other lengthy cases. The difficulty of achieving or sustaining convictions in these cases has kept this issue alive. From a freedom perspective we welcome this as we would not wish to see powerful fraudsters granted effective immunity from conviction. There is some basis for questioning whether ordinary juries can, as matters stand, return fair and accurate verdicts on matters as complex as insider trading, bond-washing and so forth. In 1998 the government published a consultation document which canvassed various options for change, such as screening potential jurors for competence, judge-only trials, or a mixed judge and lay member tribunal.[287] It also noted the continuing lack of empirical information on whether and to what degree juries failed to grasp the evidence and issues in complex fraud trials. Research published by Honess, Levi and Charman, based on a simulation of the trial of Kevin Maxwell, found that 'with some screening and more focused help for the jury, non-specialist jurors are sufficiently competent to understand and deal with the information relevant to their verdicts'.[288] This view is also supported by research examining the experience of jurors in the Jubilee Line case.[289] The trial notoriously collapsed 21 months after it was begun at a cost of several million pounds to the taxpayer. Interviews with the discharged jurors

---

[282] Doran S and Jackson J, 'The Case for Jury Waiver' [1997] Crim LR 155.

[283] See the discussion by Redmayne M, 'Theorising Jury Reform' in Duff et al (eds), *The Trial on Trial: Judgment and Calling to Account* (Oxford: Hart, 2006) at pp 109–11.

[284] The latest attempt was defeated by the House of Lords in March 2007.

[285] *Report of the Departmental Committee on Fraud Trials* (London: HMSO, 1986).

[286] RCCJ (1993: 136).   [287] Home Office (1998a).

[288] Honess et al (1998) Crim LR 763 at p 773.

[289] Lloyd-Bostock, S, 'The Jubilee Line Jurors: Does their Experience Strengthen the Argument for Judge-only Trial in Long and Complex Fraud Cases?' [2007] Crim LR 255.

found that they had a good understanding of the evidence and, although they had different levels of specialist knowledge and immediate understanding, they worked cooperatively and took their task seriously. Given the importance of lay involvement in criminal justice we hope that heed is taken of this research. What it suggests is needed is a reappraisal of the way jurors are selected and then treated during the trial. The treatment of the Jubilee Line trial jurors varied greatly over the course of the trial, deteriorating enormously towards the end. With long trials jurors may need special help during and after the trial to alleviate some of the burdens of jury service.[290]

Jackson and Doran,[291] on the basis of their comparative study of jury and non-jury trial, have similarly argued that if juries are to maximise their fact-finding potential they should be encouraged to engage in more active inquiry during the trial. In this way any areas of potential confusion, prejudice or misunderstanding on their part could be exposed and addressed, thus allowing the jury to make better sense of the case as it develops and to reach more justifiable verdicts.[292] There is undoubtedly a problem here. According to Matthews et al[293] jurors currently feel frustrated that evidence is 'not always presented in the clearest ways', visual aids are underutilised and jurors are unsure whether they can take notes and ask questions. The Jubilee Line jurors echoed some of these concerns; some felt the pace of evidence was too slow resulting in boredom, and some expressed frustration that they were not allowed to use notes outside the courtroom. Darbyshire et al (2001) identify many ways in which jurors could be helped in their work including judges giving written copies of their directions to juries.[294] Lord Judge has also recently commented that the Internet generation may be better suited to information presented in a written or visual format.[295]

The problem of jury comprehension needs to be seen within the context of an adversarial system in which each side may be more concerned with 'winning' than 'truth-finding'. This can result in barristers invoking social stereotypes of 'good' and 'bad' behaviour,[296] and in their use of questions designed merely to trap, confuse or mislead witnesses (such as those which include double-negatives, or multiple clauses, or statements dressed up as questions).[297] Tighter judicial regulation of the

---

[290] Jurors may feel that they are being kept 'on tap' when they are inadequately informed of reasons for delays and when they will be required. Long trials can have detrimental impact on employment. As Redmayne (2006: 110) notes, case-length poses a greater problem for jurors than complexity.

[291] Jackson and Doran (1997: 775–8).

[292] This argument is amply supported by research from the United States where, since the mid 1990s, the practice has developed in most states of encouraging jurors to ask questions. For a good review of the issues and evidence see Shafer B and Wiegand O, 'It's Good to Talk – Speaking Rights and the Jury' in Duff et al (eds), The Trial on Trial: Judgment and Calling to Account (Oxford: Hart, 2006).

[293] Matthews et al (2004: 3).   [294] See also Madge (2006).

[295] Lord Judge 'The Criminal Justice System in England and Wales: Time for Change?', Speech to the University of Hertfordshire, 4 November 2008.

[296] See, for example, Temkin J, 'Prosecuting and Defending Rape: Perspectives from the Bar' (2000) 27(2) JLS 219.

[297] A good summary of the research evidence of the effects of such questioning techniques is provided by Kebbell M and Gilchrist E, 'Eliciting Evidence from Eyewitnesses in Court' in Adler J (ed), Forensic Psychology: Concepts, Debates and Practice (Cullompton: Willan, 2004). They also show how such techniques might be regulated without putting the impartiality of the judge in question.

kind of cross-examination quoted at the head of this chapter would promote fairness to witnesses, save time, and make the jury's job of assessing credibility more straightforward.

The strategy we have sketched above is at least worth a try, especially as public opinion tends to be opposed to restricting jury trial.[298]   To jump immediately to the option of dispensing with the jury in complex fraud cases is likely to set a precedent which will make it harder to resist further whittling away in future.

Over the years the jury has also come under indirect attack as Parliament has reclassified many previously 'either way' offences as summary only in order to remove them from the province of the jury. At the turn of the century the 'New Labour' government made strenuous (but ultimately unsuccessful) efforts to go further by ending the right of defendants in 'either way' offences to choose jury trial. Such moves seem primarily to be driven by cost-cutting but a useful side-effect of channelling cases away from juries, from the crime control point of view, is that magistrates are more likely to convict in these cases.[299] This may be particularly important in public order situations where legitimate protest (picketing, anti-racist marches, demonstrations against capitalism or visits by heads of totalitarian states, and so forth) spills over (allegedly) into criminal acts. Such threats to public order, like terrorist offences, amount to threats to the authority of the state itself. Usually the prosecution evidence in such cases consists entirely of police accounts. A not guilty verdict by a jury would, therefore, both call into question the integrity of the police and undermine the moral authority of the state. Small wonder then that the state seeks to ensure that the vast majority of public order offences are heard in the magistrates' courts.

To sum up, the Criminal Justice Act 2003 can be seen as presaging a new strategy of gradually hiving off particular categories of serious cases to judge-only trial on the basis that the jury cannot cope with too much complexity or stress. We should also expect to see some further reclassification of either-way offences so that they become triable only in the magistrates' courts. By nibbling away at both ends of the spectrum of cases currently heard in the Crown Court, the government will be able to narrow the jury's domain still further.

10.7 Conclusion

The one recommendation of the Runciman Commission[300] that received unequivocal support from the academic community is that s 8 of the Contempt of Court Act 1981 should be amended so as to permit proper (direct) research into real jury decision-making. The government did not support this proposal and so currently we must rely on other, less satisfactory, approaches to evaluating trial by jury. The available research tends to suggest that juries conform more to due process principles than

---

[298] Roberts and Hough (2009).   [299] See 9.5.   [300] RCCJ (1993: 2).

other components of the criminal justice system, but that evidence is neither so satis-factory, nor so unequivocal, as to be conclusive. Jury trial could probably be improved, with the cases of ethnic minority defendants facing all white juries and juries in sex-ual assault cases relying on outmoded stereotypes being two examples in point. We support the need for further research into jury decision-making but would urge that such research should not be confined to an examination of the workings of the jury. Rather, a comparison should be attempted between different possible modes of trial, including: trial by lay magistrates; by a district judge sitting with or without lay col-leagues (see 9.5); by a Crown Court judge sitting with lay magistrates (see 11.2.1) and by a Crown Court judge alone. For while jury trial undoubtedly has its faults, the real question is whether other modes of trial are, or could be made to be, any better. Where comparisons have been attempted they have tended to flatter jury trial.[301] We noted in 9.5 that research by Vennard suggests that juries approach prosecution evidence with more circumspection than do magistrates.[302] The empirical evidence concerning the gathering and presentation of evidence by the police and the CPS (reviewed in chs 2–7) shows that a degree of wariness is justified. This may convince some of the force of due process arguments in favour of the jury, but the committed crime control adherent may still prefer to see priority given to maintaining a high conviction rate at low cost. Arguments about the future development of the criminal justice system should be informed by facts, but can rarely be resolved by them.

Finally, one should bear in mind that for the vast majority of defendants, arguments about modes of trial are essentially meaningless given the high rate of guilty pleas. Whilst the public think that the right for a defendant charged with a serious offence to be tried by a jury is a very important right,[303] many defendants waive their right to a trial by judge and jury. Thus, perhaps the single most important reform of the system would be to require that judges should not accept a plea of guilty without first exam-ining closely the adequacy of the prosecution case.[304] Such a reform could scarcely be effective, however, without a strong cultural commitment to due process amongst trial judges and appeal courts. The research and case law examined in this chapter, for example relating to judicial interventions and summing up, suggest that commitment is sometimes sadly lacking. Evidential rules, once lamented as being overgenerous to the defence, are now openly commended for favouring the prosecution. Relying on the judiciary to restrain the use of potentially prejudicial evidence seems like an overly optimistic strategy. From this perspective, the jury's injection of due process into a predominantly crime control system might appear to be little more than a placebo. Nevertheless, from a freedom perspective that 'little more' is well worth preserving both for symbolic and practical reasons.

---

[301] This is certainly our reading of Jackson and Doran (1995), the best such comparative study within a domestic setting.

[302] See Vennard J, *Contested Trials in Magistrates' Courts* (Home Office Research Study No 71) (London: HMSO, 1981) p 21.   [303] Julian and Hough (2009).

[304] Jackson and Doran (1995: 301).

Further Reading

Darbyshire P, with research by Maughan A and Stewart A, 'What Can We Learn from Published Jury Research? Findings for the Criminal Courts Review' [2001] Crim LR 970

Ellison L and Munro V, 'Of 'Normal Sex' and 'Real Rape': Exploring the Use of Socio-sexual Scripts in (Mock) Jury Deliberation' (2009) 18(3) Social and Legal Studies 291

Finch E and Munro, V 'The Demon Drink and the Demonised Woman: Socio-Sexual Stereotypes and Responsibility Attribution in Rape Trials Involving Intoxicants' (2007)16(4) Social and Legal Studies 591

Sommers S and Ellsworth P, 'How Much Do We Really Know about Race and Juries? A Review of the Social Science Theory and Research' (2003) 78 Chicago-Kent LR 997

Thomas C, *Are Juries Fair?* (Ministry of Justice Research Series 1/10) (London: MoJ, 2010)

Thomas C with Bulmer N, *Diversity and Fairness in the Jury System* (Ministry of Justice Research Series 2/07) (London: MoJ, 2007)

11

Appeals against conviction

Was he free? Was he happy? The question is absurd; Had anything been
wrong, we should certainly have heard.[1]

Key issues
- The values that should underpin an appeals system
- The relatively generous right(s) of appeal for those convicted of a relatively trivial offence in the magistrates' courts
- The restrictive nature of the right of appeal for those convicted of serious offences in the Crown Court
- The role of the Criminal Cases Review Commission in referring cases back to the appeal courts once normal appeal rights are exhausted

11.1 What values should underpin appellate procedures?

Appeals can fulfil a number of functions, and express a variety of values. In this intro-duction we use Packer's models to begin exploring the various possibilities, and adopt the freedom perspective to help us choose amongst them. Part of the common ground that exists between the crime control and due process models is that the criminal sys-tem's potential for error necessitates some form of appellate review. The two models differ sharply as to the desirable scope of such review.

11.1.1 Crime control

The crime control model rests on the assumption that the administrative procedures operated by police and prosecutors reliably screen out the probably innocent at an early stage, as is evident from the fact that most defendants plead guilty. Where defendants

---

[1] From 'The Unknown Citizen' by W. H. Auden.

plead not guilty, any remaining doubts about guilt should be resolved by the court of first instance. The aim of ensuring certainty and finality within the criminal process would be undermined if appeals were the norm. They should therefore be so discouraged that only those with the clearest grounds for complaint should be financially assisted to pursue the matter. Moreover, the grounds for appeal should be narrow, focused primarily on whether a blatant error has been made about the issue of actual guilt.[2]

If on a review of the evidence, the appellate court concludes that the accused's factual guilt was adequately established at trial, the conviction must be upheld regardless of the fairness of the proceedings. Any procedural error, such as the admission at trial of evidence produced by oppressive police questioning, should be the subject of remedies that operate independently of the criminal trial (for example, disciplinary action or re-training).

11.1.2 Due process

The demand for finality is low in this model. It should remain possible to reopen a case whenever there is an allegation of factual error that has not received an adjudicative hearing in a fact-finding context. Appellate review is also seen as a crucial means of upholding the moral integrity of the criminal process. Reversal of criminal convictions is seen as a 'small price' for upholding the values of the process and deterring abuses of power by the police, prosecutors and trial judges.[3] Any infringement of the basic rights of an accused person, such as unlawful arrest, oppressive interrogation or the wrongful admission of evidence at trial, should suffice for the quashing of a conviction, regardless of the strength of the evidence against the appellant. Even minor infringements of procedural rules may justify this course if their cumulative effect is significant.

Finally, legal aid must be available to underwrite the cost of appealing. If convicted persons are unable to afford legal advice and representation the chances are that they will neither appreciate whether grounds for appeal exist nor be able to present their case effectively.

11.1.3 Freedom

The main way in which crime control claims to promote freedom is by general deterrence: apprehending and punishing a reasonably high percentage of the guilty ensures extensive compliance with the norms of the criminal law. But it seems doubtful that this deterrent effect would be significantly undermined by allowing convicted persons to appeal. Because the presumption of innocence is displaced by a finding of guilt,[4] the

---

[2] Packer H, *The Limits of the Criminal Sanction* (Stanford: Stanford UP, 1968) p 228.

[3] Packer (1968: 232).

[4] In England and Wales sentences are executed immediately – an outstanding appeal does not prevent the imposition of punishment. To continental European eyes, this is 'both shocking and astonishing': Spencer J, 'Does our Present Appeal System Make Sense?' [2006b] Crim LR 677.

trial court will be able to publicly censure the offending behaviour through its sentence and any remarks that sentencers choose to make. The reporting of the sentence and accompanying remarks is what produces most of any general deterrent effect.[5] While post-conviction denunciation will lose its immediate power if the frequent or expected response is that it will be successfully challenged, if large numbers of convicted people successfully appeal there would be something badly wrong with the earlier stages of the criminal process. If those stages are working properly there should usually be clear evidence of guilt established in a fair manner by the time defendants reach court. We can expect most defendants to plead guilty when faced with such evidence – if only to get the case over with as quickly as possible. Similarly, we can expect that only a minority of those who are convicted following a not guilty plea will appeal. It follows that a fair system should not lose its deterrent power.

The freedom perspective, like crime control, is concerned about resources. All things being equal, both perspectives would seek to discourage large numbers of appeals when the resources they consume could be better spent elsewhere. Thus it makes little sense to provide convicted persons with unfettered rights to re-litigate a criminal matter; the right of appeal is there to correct error, not simply to give convicted persons another throw of the dice. Some deference to the decision-making capacity of the trial courts must therefore be shown by appellate bodies.[6] This deference can be reflected in the way that the scope of grounds for appeal is defined, and by a requirement that an appellant specifies adequate grounds for appeal in advance. Any further filtering devices (such as a procedural requirement to obtain leave to appeal) should be focused squarely on whether appellants have arguable cases, rather than take the form of deterrent devices (such as potential costs orders) since the latter will tend to discriminate on the basis of factors other than merits (the rich will not be deterred by costs orders). If courts are unable to cope with the number of potentially meritorious appeals heading in their direction, they should lobby the government for more resources (or identify and, where possible introduce, reforms that would reduce the number of errors at first instance) rather than introduce rationing 'by the back door'.[7]

Overall it seems that the social freedom to be achieved by affording only minimal rights of appeal is largely speculative and relatively slight. By contrast the freedom lost to people who are factually innocent but convicted is tangible and significant.[8] There may be losses of reputation, housing, relationships, self-esteem, job prospects, actual employment, money (where one is fined), or freedom to determine one's own actions (as where one is imprisoned or ordered to perform community service). The families of these people often suffer too. To deny a right of appeal would be to ensure that such

---

[5] For a more sophisticated analysis of mechanisms of deterrence than is possible here, see von Hirsch et al, *Criminal Deterrence and Sentence Severity* (Oxford: Hart, 1999).

[6] See the discussion by Nobles R and Schiff D, 'The Right to Appeal and Workable Systems of Justice' (2002) 65(5) MLR 676.   [7] See also Spencer (2006b: 694).

[8] See further Naughton M, *Rethinking Miscarriages of Justice* (Houndmills: Palgrave Macmillan, 2007) ch 8.

wrongful losses of freedom could not be redressed or at least minimised. Moreover, it would virtually guarantee that the criminal 'case' remained closed, thus insulating any person who in fact committed the crime (assuming a crime was committed at all) from investigation and apprehension.

What of 'the victim'? It is true that an appeal may cause difficulties for victims, such as delaying their sense of 'closure' and perhaps requiring them to submit to further stressful courtroom experiences. But a victim has no legitimate interest in denying convicted persons the chance to have a wrongful conviction overturned. Moreover, a wrongful conviction which cannot be corrected virtually ensures that victims will never see 'their' offender brought to justice. In any case, as we pointed out in ch 1, defendants and victims are not separate groups of people. Thus, even if we were to concede that providing appeal rights favoured 'defendants' more than 'victims' we would not be privileging one group of people over another – rather we would be determining that, in the long run, the promotion of freedom is best achieved for everyone by allowing liberally framed (but not absolute) rights of appeal.

So far we have only dealt with the issue of convictions which are wrong in the sense that a factually innocent person has been convicted (which we might term 'miscarriages of justice at first instance').[9] But what about quashing convictions where factual guilt has been established beyond reasonable doubt but the conviction is tainted by procedural error or malpractice? To quash a conviction in these circumstances leaves someone who has offended at large (assuming no retrial is ordered), causing important losses of freedom, not least to victims. On the other hand, the occasional quashing of convictions on the ground of procedural unfairness should have no more impact on the general deterrence achieved through the practices of conviction, denunciation and punishment than the quashing of convictions on any other ground. This is so even leaving aside the point that the moral message communicated by a verdict of guilty may be weakened or destroyed where it was produced in an unfair way.[10]

By contrast, quashing a reliable but unfair conviction may make a significant difference to the respect shown by the police, prosecutors, magistrates, judges and others to the rules and principles of criminal procedure. For while criminal justice actors know that most defendants will not seek to put their guilt in dispute or overturn their convictions, they cannot know for sure which few defendants will contest these matters. The safe option is therefore to keep to the rules, just in case. For the quashing of a conviction in these circumstances will not only lead to a guilty person walking free, but might lead to scrutiny and criticism of the practices that led to this happening. From the freedom perspective the quashing of unfairly obtained convictions helps ensure that invasions of liberty which take place within criminal justice processes do so within the rule of law. The freedom of everyone (including victims) is enhanced if we know that officials will not ignore our rights when it suits them or

---

[9] See further Naughton (2007: ch 2).
[10] See Dennis I, 'Convicting the Guilty: Outcomes, Process and the Court of Appeal' [2006] Crim LR 955 and Spencer J, 'Quashing Convictions for Procedural Irregularities' [2007] Crim LR 835 at 836.

otherwise invade our liberty in an arbitrary fashion. That is surely a truer mark of a free society than one which has a lower than average crime rate. And, by definition, other remedies for unfairness within the criminal process (eg civil actions, disciplinary procedures, prosecution of corrupt police officers) are not sufficient deterrents to malpractice. If they were, we would not be discussing the need to quash a conviction on the ground of procedural unfairness. If the police and other criminal justice actors want to avoid the quashing of reliable convictions all they have to do is abide by the rules. Our broad brush preliminary conclusion is that freedom is best served by affording broadly drawn appeal rights in which the grounds for quashing a conviction include procedural unfairness. But it seems unlikely that freedom is best served by allowing obviously guilty defendants to overturn convictions merely because of a relatively minor procedural error.[11] The question of where the boundary line is, and should be, drawn between 'minor' and 'non-minor' error is examined below, as is the question of whether a retrial should be ordered in cases where convictions are quashed on grounds of procedural error.

11.2 Appeals from the magistrates' courts

11.2.1 Rehearings in the Crown Court

The rights of appeal in the English system differ markedly according to whether the defendant was convicted in the magistrates' court or the Crown Court.[12] Partly as a result of historical accident, and partly due to the unsatisfactory nature of summary justice, magistrates' courts convictions are subject to more extensive forms of appellate review. No leave is required for an appeal from this court to the Crown Court, and the appeal takes the form of a complete rehearing of the case before a professional judge and two or more magistrates who took no part in the original trial.[13] The grounds for appeal are unrestricted and fresh evidence will be admitted. This form of appellate review is not as generous or effective as might at first appear, however.

To begin with, an appeal against conviction does not lie to the Crown Court if the defendant pleaded guilty.[14] This automatically excludes around three-quarters of all defendants tried in the lower courts. Many may be aggrieved by the circumstances of

---

[11] Not least because, if the courts are prepared to overturn convictions in these circumstances, 'crude populist' attempts to remove the power to appeal for procedural error (however gross) are more likely to succeed: Spencer J, 'Quashing Convictions for Procedural Irregularities' [2008b] CLJ 227.

[12] For a comprehensive account see Pattenden R, *English Criminal Appeals 1844–1994* (Oxford: Clarendon Press, 1996).

[13] Supreme Court Act 1981, s 74; rule 63.10 of the Criminal Procedure Rules (available at: <http://www.justice.gov.uk/criminal/procrules_fin/rulesmenu.htm> (accessed 5 January 2010). In exceptional circumstances a judge may sit with just one magistrate: CPR rule 63.10(c).

[14] Magistrates' Courts Act 1980, s 108; *Crown Court at Birmingham, ex p Sharma* [1988] Crim L R 741.

the police investigation, the conduct of the prosecution or the behaviour of the magistrates' court itself, yet have felt themselves to have had little option but to plead guilty (see ch 8). Only if the plea of guilty can be said to have been entered equivocally or under duress can a complaint be made to the Crown Court. If the complaint is found to have substance the Court must remit the case back to the magistrates' court so that a full trial can take place there.[15] Of course, the degree of pressure on a defendant to plead guilty which would qualify as 'duress' is much more narrowly defined in a system which operates on crime control lines than one in which due process principles prevail. The Court of Appeal insists, for example, that while defendants who plead guilty as a result of a charge bargain may face difficult choices between unpalatable alternatives, that is no ground for arguing that the plea of guilty was not freely made.[16] Not surprisingly, few defendants convicted on a guilty plea in the magistrates' courts mount successful challenges.[17]

An appeal to the Crown Court must be commenced within 21 days of the conclusion of the proceedings in the magistrates' courts.[18] Defendants who were legally aided[19] in the magistrates' courts may receive preliminary advice, at public expense, on whether they have grounds for appeal, and this will cover preparing the notice of appeal. Those who were not legally aided may receive advice from a duty solicitor at court or may receive £500 worth of legal advice under the advice and assistance scheme.[20] In all cases, however, a grant of full legal aid for appellate proceedings is subject to the application of a merits test[21] and, until its abolition in April 2001, a means test. Virtually all applications for legal aid for appellate purposes are granted but a large proportion of those appealing against conviction in the Crown Court have historically not made an application. The reasons for this are unclear. Some of those not legally aided are wealthy enough to fund their own representation while others may choose to appear unrepresented. Presumably, others have not made an application following advice that they would be unable to meet either the means or the merits test. When the means test was abolished in 2001 an increase in the proportion of appellants who were legally aided resulted. But even now many appellants do not apply for legal aid. For example, in 2007, of the 5,849 appellants against conviction appearing in the Crown Court, 2,869 were legally aided, and 2,980 were privately represented

---

[15] *Crown Court at Huntingdon, ex p Jordan* [1981] QB 857.   [16] *Herbert* (1991) 94 Cr App Rep 230.

[17] Only 35 appeals to the Crown Court were remitted to the magistrates' courts in 1996: Mattinson J, *Criminal Appeals England and Wales, 1995 and 1996* (Research and Statistical Bulletin 3/98) (London: Home Office, 1998) table 4. More recent figures are not available.

[18] Rule 63.2(2) of the Criminal Procedure Rules. Rule 63.2(3) allows an applicant to seek an extension of this time limit, but there is no right to an oral hearing or to reasons for a refusal to grant an extension: *Crown Court at Croydon, ex p Smith* (1983) 77 Cr App Rep 277.

[19] The terminology 'legal aid' was dropped in the wake of the Access to Justice Act 1999, which saw the replacement of the Legal Aid Board with the Legal Services Commission, but it is retained here for the sake of convenience.   [20] The scheme is discussed in 11.4.2.2.

[21] Access to Justice Act 1999, s 12(2). The merits test is discussed in ch 9.

or not represented.[22] A financial deterrent remains in place following abolition of the means test, in that a recovery of costs order can be made at the termination of the case.[23] Costs orders are unlikely to be made against the poor, but pose a realistic threat to those of moderate means. Since the wealthy can fund their appeals regardless of the merits of the case (there being no direct filter to prevent unmeritorious appeals to the Crown Court), and are unlikely to be deterred by the prospect of a costs order, the procedural rules breach the due process equality principle. The rules provide a screening device in all but name for all but the rich. That device is shortly to become more stringent as the government has committed itself to reintroduce means testing for Crown Court proceedings across the country from April to June 2010. In future, unsuccessful appellants against conviction with a disposable annual income above £3,398 will be required to pay £500.[24] The deterrent effect of this on those of modest means remains to be seen.

The rehearing itself is a relatively perfunctory affair. The average hearing time for an appeal is about an hour, compared with just over eight hours for a normal Crown Court trial.[25] The absence of a jury is one obvious factor lying behind this speed. Another is likely to be the lack of enthusiasm of legally aided lawyers to argue the case as fully as they perhaps should. Given that they are paid a fixed fee for this work, economics dictate that the faster they can dispose of the matter the better.[26] Moreover, this type of work is routinely allocated to inexperienced barristers, preparation on both sides tends to be minimal and prosecution disclosure of fresh evidence is almost unknown.[27] Where the appellant is unrepresented, there is no legally qualified court clerk to offer any help (unlike in the magistrates' court) and no duty solicitor (or barrister) scheme either. Imagine a layperson trying to counter the arguments of a prosecution barrister in an oak panelled courtroom presided over by a bewigged judge.

A further off-putting feature of these appeals is the wide power of the Crown Court to vary the decision appealed or make any order it wishes.[28] In one case the Crown Court ordered the appellant to pay £28,000 in costs, which included £14,000 for the costs incurred by the prosecutor in the magistrates' court. This was despite the fact that the magistrates' court had already made its own costs order (of £260). This power to reopen the initial costs decision was upheld by the Divisional Court in *Hamilton-Johnson v RSPCA*.[29] The Court stated prosecutors should give written notice to appellants if they intended to seek a higher cost order so that the appellant's mind could be focused on the possible consequences of appeal. Thus prosecutors have a mechanism

---

[22] Ministry of Justice, *Judicial and Court Statistics 2007*, Cm 7467 (London: MoJ, 2008) table 10.6. The following year's statistics were not broken down by type of appeal.   [23] Access to Justice 1999, s 17(2).

[24] See Ministry of Justice, *Crown Court Means Testing, Response to Consultation* (CP(R) 06/09) (London: MoJ, 2009a) para 162.

[25] *Judicial and Court Statistics 2008*, Cm 7697 (London: Ministry of Justice, 2009a). The average hearing for offences that must be tried on indictment is close to twenty hours: ibid (this table, unfortunately, aggregates appeals against sentence with those against conviction).

[26] Nation D, 'He Can Always Appeal' (1992) 156 JP 521.   [27] Pattenden (1996: 242).

[28] Supreme Court Act 1981, s 48.   [29] [2000] EWHC Admin 300.

to deter appeals. Another possible consequence is a higher sentence. Unlike the Court of Appeal, which has no power to change a sentence on hearing an appeal against conviction, it is open to the Crown Court to impose a severer sentence than that imposed by the magistrates.[30] This is done only infrequently,[31] but how can convicted people be sure that the Crown Court will not impose a stiffer punishment to mark its disapproval of what it sees as a 'frivolous' appeal?[32] In a system which is organised around the principle of penalising defendants for resisting conviction (as expressed through sentence discounts for those pleading guilty) it is easy to understand a prospective appellant's fears. The uncertainty of outcome and the possibility of being punished (in effect) for appealing, plus delay, expense, a reluctance to face the ordeal of a rehearing, and a wish for finality, surely dissuades many from taking matters further, and causes about 30% of those who do decide to challenge their convictions to later abandon their appeals.[33] In 2007 1,351,000 defendants were found guilty at the magistrates' courts,[34] yet there were only 5,531 appeals against conviction in that year,[35] giving an appeal rate of 0.4%. But around three-quarters of completed CPS cases in the magistrates' courts are terminated by a guilty plea,[36] thus disqualifying the defendants in those cases from appealing. Thus the 'true' appeal rate is probably around 3%.

From 2004–2008, the success rate for appeals has been about 40%, with around 2,000 appellants a year overturning their convictions. If, however, one calculates the success rate by reference only to those appeals that were heard (omitting all those abandoned) then the success rate climbs to around 55%. These figures raise doubts about the quality of justice in the magistrates' courts. However, there is virtually no research into the adequacy of Crown Court appellate review, or the kinds of cases that it rehears. Nearly all of the literature in this area concerns itself with the more glamorous matter of appeals to the Court of Appeal following trials on indictment. Yet the Crown Court hears over ten times as many appeals as the Court of Appeal.[37] Most of these are motoring cases.[38] We suspect that relatively wealthy 'white collar defendants' are responsible for a substantial proportion of appeals to the Crown Court, which is why so few appeals are legally aided.

Section 11 of the Criminal Appeal Act 1995 permits the Criminal Cases Review Commission (CCRC) to refer suspect convictions produced by the magistrates'

---

[30] Supreme Court Act 1981, s 48(4). Any new sentence must be within the sentencing limits which apply to the magistrates' court.

[31] In 1996, 112 of those appealing against conviction to the Crown Court were given an increased sentence of the same type: Mattinson (1998) table 4. More recent statistics are not available.

[32] Pattenden (1996: 219), states that the power to increase a sentence is 'intended as a deterrent to frivolous appeals'.

[33] See Mattinson (1998: table 4); MoJ (2009a: table 6.10). This is not always allowed if the appeal has begun, or is about to begin: *Munden v Southampton Crown Court* [2005] EWHC 2512 (Admin).

[34] Ministry of Justice, *Criminal Statistics: England and Wales 2007, Statistics Bulletin* (London: MoJ, 2008b) table 1.1.   [35] MoJ (2009a) table 6.10.

[36] MoJ (2008b: table 2.6). The equivalent figures for non-CPS prosecutions are not available.

[37] MoJ (2009a) table 1.7 (Court of Appeal figures) and table 6.10 (Crown Court figures). See further Naughton (2007) ch 2.   [38] Mattinson (1998) table 6.

courts – regardless of whether the defendant pleaded guilty or not. This is a due process safety net and recognises that miscarriages of justice should be seen to be undone not only in high profile cases (such as the Birmingham Six, which originated in the Crown Court) but also in situations of low visibility. Whether the CCRC provides effective redress for low-level miscarriages of justice will be examined later in this chapter.

A proposal to abolish the right to a rehearing was made in the Auld Report. While this has not (yet!) been taken forward by the government, it is worth assessing Auld's reasoning. He suggested the right was a throwback to times when magistrates' courts were seen as 'police courts' and there was a lack of confidence in their competence and impartiality. The modern standing of the courts did not, in his view, justify a right to rehearing.[39] Whilst we saw in ch 9 that there are still some concerns about the quality of summary justice, the unfettered right to a rehearing makes little sense and in practice tends to favour the wealthy, so Auld's proposal to require leave to appeal might be justifiable. The real difficulty with his proposal, however, is that the current system produces, as we have seen, a low rate of appeals with a high rate of success. Filtering out more appeals might, therefore, easily result in an increase in the number of unsafe convictions that are not subject to appellate review.[40]

11.2.2 Appeals by way of case stated to the High Court

An appeal lies to the Divisional Court where it is claimed that a 'conviction, order, determination or other proceeding' by the magistrates' court was in excess of jurisdiction or wrong in law.[41] For example, it would be wrong in law for the magistrates to convict when they had heard no evidence to support such a decision. Since a full record of proceedings is not kept in the magistrates' court, the clerk to the justices is required to state the details of the case including the question(s) for determination by the Divisional Court. The latter Court hears only legal argument and no evidence.

In principle this procedure gives defendants convicted of relatively trivial crimes access to the senior judiciary, thus allowing high quality supervision of some aspects of summary justice, not only determining the case in question but also creating binding precedents for the future. But the applicant must ask the magistrates' court to state a case within 21 days of the final determination of the case;[42] the justices may refuse to state a case if they consider the application 'frivolous'[43] (which Auld LJ defined as meaning 'futile, misconceived, hopeless or academic');[44] and the court may require the prospective appellant to enter into a means-related recognisance to pay any costs

---

[39] Auld LJ, *Review of the Criminal Courts of England and Wales: Report* (London: TSO, 2001) p 617, para 17.

[40] See the discussion by Malleson K and Roberts S, 'Streamlining and Clarifying the Appellate Process' [2002] Crim LR 272 at 273–5.

[41] Magistrates' Courts Act 1980, s 111; Supreme Court Act 1981, s 28; Criminal Procedure Rules, part 64.   [42] Magistrates' Courts Act 1980, s 111(2).

[43] Magistrates' Courts Act 1980, s 111(5).

[44] Auld (2001) p 618, para 19 (thus proving that judges do have a sense of humour).

ultimately awarded against him.[45] Moreover, the right to appeal by way of rehearing in the Crown Court is extinguished once an application has been made under the case stated procedure.[46] Legal aid is available for this type of appeal but is subject to the usual merits test[47] and the court may make a defence costs order at the end of the case depending on an appellant's means.[48] A backlog of cases creates delays of several months;[49] in 2008 the High Court received 72 appeals from the magistrates' courts by way of case stated and determined 57 (a further two were withdrawn). The court itself is usually made up of a Lord Justice of Appeal and another High Court judge and 16 of the appeals in 2008 were determined by a single judge.[50] The appeal fails in a two-judge court if the bench is divided.[51] If the appellant does persuade both judges that an error of law has occurred it is open to the Divisional Court to order a retrial in the magistrates' court,[52] although this should not be done if a rehearing would be oppressive (eg where a fair trial was no longer possible) or inappropriate (eg the offence in question is trivial).[53]

The prosecution has the same right to appeal as does the defence, thus providing an exception to the usual rule that the prosecution cannot appeal against an acquittal.[54] The Divisional Court may dispose of the case in various ways, including remitting the case to the magistrates' court with a direction to convict. It appears that the appellate courts do not regard the concept of 'jury equity' (see ch 10) as having any application in the magistrates' courts.

Appeal by way of case stated is of little practical significance to the average person convicted in the magistrates' courts. Of the 57 appeals determined in 2008, 30 were successful.[55] Some of these will have concerned the civil jurisdiction of the magistrates' court, others will have been prosecution appeals, and a proportion of the defence appeals will have been in relation to a decision other than one to convict. The typical defendant-initiated appeal against conviction probably concerns allegations of white collar crime.[56] Business people and corporations convicted of the latter type of crime can afford to pursue the matter and will be more concerned than the average defendant to establish a precedent that their routine activities are not against the criminal law.

11.2.3 **Judicial review**

Applications for judicial review provide an alternative way of mounting a challenge (by either the prosecution or the defence) to a magistrates' court decision (including

---

[45] Magistrates' Courts Act 1980, s 114; *Newcastle-upon-Tyne Justices, ex p Skinner* [1987] 1 All ER 349.
[46] Magistrates' Courts Act 1980, s 111(4).   [47] Access to Justice Act 1999, s 12(2)(b).
[48] AJA 1999, s 17(2).   [49] Pattenden (1996: 223).   [50] MoJ (2009a: table 1.13).
[51] *Flannagan v Shaw* [1920] 3 KB 96.   [52] See, eg, *Jeffrey v Black* [1978] 1 All ER 555.
[53] *Griffith v Jenkins* [1992] 1 All ER 65. Where the Divisional Court decision entails the innocence of the appellant the conviction will usually be quashed forthwith: Pattenden (1996: 224).
[54] For an example, see *DPP v P* [2007] EWHC (Admin).   [55] MoJ (2009a: table 1.13).
[56] Pattenden (1996: 223).

acquittal[57] or conviction) in the Divisional Court.[58] The purpose of such an action is to obtain a ruling that the proceedings in the lower court were tainted by illegality and to secure an appropriate remedy. For example, where the rules of natural justice have been breached, the Divisional Court may quash the magistrates' decision. An unreasonable refusal to 'state a case' can also be the subject of a judicial review action.[59] A number of procedural hurdles face the potential judicial review applicant. The application must be initiated 'promptly' – and in any event within three months of the time at which the grounds for judicial review arose.[60] Civil legal aid is available to help with the costs of mounting a judicial review application but this is subject to both a means and merits test. Permission to apply must always be obtained from the Divisional Court and in practice about three-quarters of applicants are denied this and are thus weeded out of the system. 81 out of 298 applications for permission to apply for judicial review of criminal proceedings were granted in 2008, a success rate of only 27%.[61] It is not known how many of the successful applications resulted in the overturning of a conviction. A single judge of the Court initially determines whether permission should be granted and this is usually done on the papers. In the event of a negative decision, the application may be renewed orally before the full Court. The Divisional Court is supposed to grant permission if on a quick perusal of the material presented it thinks that it discloses what might on further consideration turn out to be an arguable case in favour of granting the relief sought.[62] However, it seems that the Court in practice often applies a more stringent test in order to ensure that judicial workloads remain 'manageable'.[63] There is no appeal against a decision by the full Court to refuse permission.

Obtaining permission places the applicant halfway down the obstacle course but not yet in sight of the finishing line. A delay of between four and eight months in having the case heard can be expected,[64] and in some cases the delays are much worse.[65] Furthermore, the remedies available through this procedure are discretionary. This means that a convicted person may 'win' the argument but be denied a remedy because of some perceived broader interest of fairness or due administration of justice. An example is *Peterborough Justices, ex p Dowler*[66] in which the Divisional Court decided that, because a procedurally unfair conviction might be remedied through an appeal by way of a rehearing in the Crown Court, certiorari would not

---

[57] It is easier for the prosecution to challenge an acquittal by way of case stated rather than judicial review, however, as case law suggests that the latter will not result in the quashing of an acquittal unless the trial itself was a nullity: *R v Hendon Justices ex parte DPP* [1994] QB 167.

[58] Supreme Courts Act 1981, ss 29–31 and Civil Procedure Rules, Part 54.

[59] *Sunworld Ltd v Hammersmith and Fulham LBC* [2000] 2 All ER 837.

[60] Civil Procedure Rules 54.5.   [61] MoJ (2009: table 1.12).

[62] *IRC, ex p National Federation of Self-Employed and Small Businesses Ltd* [1982] AC 617.

[63] See Le Sueur A and Sunkin M, 'Applications for Judicial Review: The Requirement of Leave' [1992] PL 102, and the discussion by Harlow C and Rawlings R, *Law and Administration*, 2nd edn (London: Butterworths, 1997) pp 530–6.   [64] Pattenden (1996: 227).

[65] In *R v Liverpool City Magistrates* [2006] EWHC 887 (Admin), for example, leave was granted in October 2004 but the case was not determined until March 2006.   [66] [1996] 2 Cr App Rep 561.

issue. If it does quash a conviction, the Divisional Court can remit the case to the magistrates' court with directions on how to reconsider it, which might be by way of retrial.[67]

There is clearly an overlap between the case stated and judicial review procedures as both are concerned with errors of law. Generally speaking the Divisional Court encourages the use of the appeal by way of case stated as this procedure enables the facts as found by the magistrates, as well as the legal determinations based on those facts, to be set out clearly.[68] On the other hand, if the rules of natural justice are breached (eg, the defence was not allowed a fair opportunity to present its case) this would not emerge from a case stated so judicial review should be pursued instead. Similarly, a refusal by a magistrates' court to state a case could by definition only be challenged by way of judicial review.[69]

At one time, the view seemed to be that judicial review might only be employed to correct defects or irregularities in the trial itself.[70] A broader approach was established in *Leyland Justices, ex p Hawthorn*[71] where, following conviction, it emerged that the police had not told the defence of two witnesses whose statements were helpful to the defendant. This omission had prevented the court from giving the defendant a fair trial, so the conviction was quashed. Given the importance of pre-trial procedure in set-tling the fate of the defendant, this decision represented a significant shift towards due process values. Subsequent cases suggest, however, that the Divisional Court will not quash a conviction simply because the prosecution failed in its duty to bring all mate-rial evidence before the court. Rather that failure must have resulted in an 'unjust or potentially unjust decision'.[72] This is in line with the general stance of the senior judi-ciary to unlawful police or prosecutor behaviour, since the focus is primarily on the factual accuracy of the conviction rather than the fairness of the procedures followed (see further 11.3.2.1).

11.2.4 Evaluating appeals against magistrates' court convictions

We have seen that the right to a rehearing in the Crown Court is not so generous as it might appear, and appeal by way of case stated and judicial review are even less use to the vast majority of defendants. Too few summary cases enter these channels to enable proper judicial oversight of the quality of magistrates' courts justice, and the overlap

---

[67] *R v Hereford Magistrates' Court, ex p Rowlands* [1998] QB 110.

[68] See *Morpeth Justices, ex p Ward* (1992) 95 Cr App R 215 at 222.

[69] For further discussion of the complex question of which 'appellate' procedure should be pursued in a given circumstance see Pattenden (1996: 229–39) and Auld (2001: 617–20).

[70] See *West Sussex Quarter Sessions, ex p Albert and Maud Johnson Trust Ltd* [1974] QB 24, per Orr LJ.

[71] [1979] 1 All ER 209.

[72] See *Crown Court at Liverpool, ex p Roberts* [1986] Crim LR 622. For discussion of the case law, see Spencer J, 'Judicial Review of Criminal Proceedings' [1991] Crim LR 259.

between the different procedures is complex and confusing, creating procedural traps for appellants.[73]

Replacing three avenues of appeal with one would improve this. A low threshold filter of 'an arguable case' could be introduced alongside a period within which to launch an appeal of three months (extendable if special circumstances arose). Legal aid should be granted in order to enable counsel to make an application to the relevant court for leave to appeal. If permission is granted, legal aid should automatically be made available for the conduct of the appeal and financial deterrents that discriminate in favour of the wealthy should be removed. Decisions concerning the appropriate appellate procedure should be governed by legislation rather than being left to judicial whim. Discretion regarding remedies should similarly be better structured through statutory criteria. The costs of any increase in the number of appeals could be more than offset by the benefits of a reduction in the number of unfair trials. Indeed, it is possible that the pool of unfair trials will shrink sufficiently to lead to an overall decline over time in the number of appeals. Are such reforms at all likely? If one takes an historical perspective the deficiencies in the appeals process evident at the beginning of the last century are less obvious these days,[74] but there is still a compelling case for reform.[75]

Better information about the social consequences of the present arrangements would further strengthen the case for reform. Research is needed to uncover the factors influencing decisions concerning whether or not to appeal, how people experience the appeal procedures in practice, and whether some social groups (eg ethnic minorities, women, the young, the poor) encounter greater difficulties than others in pursuing an appeal. Above all, light needs to be shed on the impact of appeal processes and decisions on the quality of magistrates' justice.

11.3 **Appeals from the Crown Court to the Court of Appeal**

An appeal lies to the Court of Appeal from the Crown Court only on the ground that the conviction was 'unsafe'. Those convicted on indictment do not have the right to a rehearing. Instead, the Court of Appeal's role is essentially that of *reviewing* the

---

[73] See, for example, the observations made by Collins J in *R v Liverpool City Magistrates* [2006] EWHC 887 (Admin).   [74] For the historical perspective see Pattenden (1996: 215–16).

[75] They are certainly likelier now than at any time over the last few decades, as the anomalies within the appeals process have attracted much recent critique, notably by Auld (2001) and Spencer (2006b). A simplification of the appeal mechanisms in relation to Crown Court proceedings is proposed in Law Commission, *The High Court's Jurisdiction in Relation to Criminal Proceedings* (Consultation Paper No 184) (London: Law Commission, 2007). The implications for appeals from the magistrates' courts are considered at pp 124–133. A further report containing revised proposals is to be published in 2010 according to the Law Commission website (accessed 5 January 2010).

fairness of the Crown Court proceedings or, exceptionally, the accuracy of the result produced by the trial.

11.3.1 Applications for leave to appeal

Leave to appeal must be sought (normally within 28 days of conviction).[76] Most applications for leave are determined by a single High Court judge.[77] If an application for leave is refused, it may be renewed to the full Court of Appeal which will consider the matter afresh. The test to be applied when determining leave is whether the appeal seems 'reasonably arguable'.[78] These various preliminary filters are supposed to weed out 'weak' appeals. As we shall now see, however, 'weakness' may be the product of the legal and social processes through which an appeal is funnelled rather than an objective quality.

11.3.1.1 Financial considerations: legal aid and costs

It is standard for a representation order (legal aid) to be granted for trials on indictment. This also covers the cost of counsel advising on the prospect of a successful appeal against conviction.[79] If counsel advises that there are, or may be, grounds for appeal, then legal aid also funds the professional drafting of these grounds. Alternatively, if counsel's initial advice is that there are no grounds for appeal, then the initial representation order is effectively terminated and the appellant must either pay for legal assistance privately, find a lawyer willing to act either under the more limited 'advice and assistance scheme'[80] or for free (pro bono), or try to pursue an appeal unassisted. Initial advice from counsel that grounds for appeal do not exist can thus operate as a filter, since many convicted persons may be deterred from pursuing an appeal if denied access to legal assistance.[81]

Once the application for leave is lodged, the Registrar of the Court of Appeal will usually refer the matter to a single judge but may bypass that stage and refer the matter to the full court. Where the matter is referred by the Registrar to the single judge, it is normal for the leave application to be determined on the papers. Counsel can request an oral hearing but the Registrar will grant legal aid for this purpose 'only in very rare circumstances'.[82] If Counsel are allowed to argue the application before the single

---

[76] See Criminal Appeal Act 1968, s 18, sub-section 3 of which empowers the Court of Appeal to extend the time allowed for seeking leave to appeal.

[77] Section 31 of the Criminal Appeal Act 1968 enables a single judge to exercise various Court of Appeal powers. Leave is not required in the rare cases which are certified as suitable for appeal by the trial judge under the power given by s 1(2)(b). The Court of Appeal has actively discouraged trial judges from using this power: Pattenden (1996: 95–6).   [78] Auld (2001: 637), para 73.

[79] Access to Justice Act 1999, s 26.   [80] This scheme is discussed in 11.4.2.2 below.

[81] In one study, approximately half of the prisoners who did not appeal gave as one of their reasons the fact that a lawyer had advised them not to do so: Plotnikoff J and Woolfson R, *Information and Advice for Prisoners about Grounds for Appeal and the Appeals Process* (Royal Commission on Criminal Justice, Research Study No 18) (London: HMSO, 1993b) p 78.

[82] Her Majesty's Court Service (HMCS), *A Guide to Commencing Proceedings in the Court of Appeal Criminal Division* (London: HMCS, 2008) para A9–1 (<http://www.hmcourts-service.gov.uk/docs/proc_guide.pdf> – accessed 5 January 2010).

judge, the expectation is that they will do so privately funded or pro bono.[83] This again privileges the rich and the lucky. The single judge can grant or refuse leave, or refer the matter to the full Court of Appeal. Whenever a case is referred to the full Court of Appeal (whether by the Registrar or by the single judge) a representation order is almost invariably granted to cover the preparation and presentation of the appeal, although the order is normally restricted to counsel only.[84]

If, on the other hand, the single judge refuses leave to appeal, the applicant is given just 14 days in which to renew their application to the full court. If an extension of time is sought this must be supported by 'cogent reasons'.[85] Challenging a single judge's refusal to grant leave is not straightforward as full reasons for the negative decision need not be provided although the appellant will be notified by the Registrar of 'any observations which the Judge *may* have made…'[86]

A representation order is never granted by the Registrar to cover the legal costs of renewing an application to the full court. Counsel must therefore be prepared to undertake the work privately or on a pro bono basis. If the application for leave is successful then the Court of Appeal will at that point normally grant a representation order to cover that appearance.[87] It follows that an appellant may fail in a renewed application to the Court of Appeal purely because they lacked professional help in preparing the legal paperwork and presenting their case.[88] Since the rich can afford the legal costs involved regardless of the strength or weakness of the particular case, the legal aid rules once again breach the due process principle of equality of access to justice.

An unsuccessful appellant may be ordered to pay whatever costs the Court of Appeal considers 'just and reasonable'[89] and a recovery of defence costs order 'shall' also be made except in specified circumstances.[90] An explicit warning that unsuccessful appellants may have costs awarded against them is included in the standard form used to initiate an application for leave to appeal.[91] All this might be defensible if the filters in operation succeeded in weeding out only unarguable cases but, as we shall see, this is not so.

Another aspect of the appeals process which is shaped by the legal aid rules is the type and amount of work which lawyers will undertake in preparing appeals. As with legal aid generally, claims made for work done or costs incurred may be reduced or even refused if considered unreasonable.[92] In one study, between a quarter and a third

---

[83] Ibid.   [84] Ibid, A11–1–A11–3.   [85] Ibid, A12–2.   [86] Ibid, A12–1. Our emphasis.

[87] Ibid A12–3.

[88] See the discussion by Malleson K, *Review of the Appeal Process* (Royal Commission on Criminal Justice, Research Study No 17) (London: HMSO, 1993) pp 29–30.

[89] Prosecution of Offences Act 1985, s 18(2).

[90] Criminal Defence Service (Recovery of Defence Costs Orders) (Amendment) Regulations 2008 (SI 2008/2430), reg 4, amending Criminal Defence Service (Recovery of Defence Costs Orders) Regulations 2001. Youths, those on benefits, and those with few assets are the main exceptions.

[91] Form NG, available from <http://www.hmcourts-service.gov.uk/> (accessed 5 January 2010).

[92] Criminal Defence Service (Funding) Order 2007, Sch 4, para 1.

of solicitors and barristers complained that they had lost money because of these rules. It was claimed by 20% of solicitors that they no longer bothered to charge for work done in the 28 days following conviction. Some were clearly offering what they themselves regarded as a sub-standard service in order to stay within the legal aid rules:

> Many lawyers talked of a policy on the part of determining officers of reducing claims without reason or explanation and a total lack of understanding of the amount of work involved in properly serving the interests of one's client…Despite the obligation to communicate with their client, many solicitors said that the costs of visiting a prison to discuss an appeal were never allowed and some now refused to make such visits for this reason.[93]

It generally takes much longer than 28 days to find the fresh evidence or argument usually needed to win leave to appeal, and legal aid (if available at all) covers relatively little of this work. Angela Cannings spent almost two years in prison while her legal team put together her appeal with the help of medical experts, all 'working for nothing because the majority of legal aid funding isn't granted until a case is won'.[94] This meant that a certain line of exculpatory inquiry was not pursued due to lack of funds, and it was only when a BBC documentary team became interested in the case and looked into the matter for themselves that the exculpatory evidence was found.[95] Not all convicted persons are this 'lucky'.

11.3.1.2 The quality of legal advice

Plotnikoff and Woolfson's research for the Runciman Commission established that large numbers of convicted defendants were not given advice on appeals at all, were advised by unqualified staff, or were advised wrongly on important points – such as that their sentences might be increased if their appeal was unsuccessful. Whilst the Crown Court can increase a sentence following an appeal from the magistrates' court, the Court of Appeal has no such power.[96] Yet the fear of an increased sentence was a major factor in decisions taken by prisoners convicted in the Crown Court not to appeal.[97]

The guidelines prepared by the Court of Appeal now require solicitors to address the issue of appeal without waiting for a request for advice from their clients. 'Immediately following the conclusion of the case, the legal representatives should see the defendant and counsel should express orally his [sic] final view as to the prospects of a successful appeal…'[98] Where the advice is positive, counsel must draft and send signed grounds of appeal to the defence solicitor 'as soon as possible'.[99] The defence solicitor must then notify the client, and lodge the appeal papers at the Crown Court. Counsel are warned

---

[93] Plotnikoff and Woolfson (1993b: 83).

[94] Cannings A, with Lloyd Davies M, *Against All Odds: A Mother's Fight to Prove her Innocence* (London: Time Warner Books, 2006) p 223. The case is discussed at 11.3.2.3.   [95] Ibid.

[96] Whilst the loss of time rules (discussed later in the text) might reasonably (if somewhat misleadingly) be portrayed by legal advisers as a de facto power to increase sentence they are rarely applied in practice and could not in any case result in a substantially 'increased sentence'.

[97] Plotnikoff and Woolfson (1993b: 82).   [98] HMCS (2008: A1–1).   [99] Ibid.

that they must not sign grounds of appeal 'unless they are reasonable, have some real prospect of success' and they are prepared to argue them before the court – grounds must not be included merely because the appellant so instructs.[100] It is impossible to assess, in the absence of recent research, whether these guidelines are proving any more effective then earlier versions. Anecdotally, we may note that counsel still sometimes provide the misleading advice to clients that the Court of Appeal has the power to increase a sentence following an unsuccessful appeal.[101]

Bottoms and McClean reported that many of the convicted persons they interviewed saw the appeals process 'as a somewhat remote affair, a lawyer's procedure where they essentially had to rely on the professionals'.[102] This heavy reliance on counsel has drawbacks. Counsel are particularly unlikely to advise that errors by lawyers might provide grounds for appeal, which probably accounts for the low number of appeals drafted by counsel which assert this compared with those drafted by convicted persons themselves.[103] Legal advice, when offered at all, is predominantly against appealing, or overestimates the risks involved, deterring all but the most committed of convicted persons from taking any further action.

A safeguard for convicted persons given a custodial sentence is provided by each prison designating one of its staff as a 'legal services officer', with responsibility to assist prisoners on how to obtain legal advice on appeals.[104] They are directed to meet with prisoners within a day of their initial reception into prison. In practice, however, these prison officers are diverted by other demands on their time:

These problems are reflected in the fact that only 32% of inmates claimed to have received advice on appeals from the prison and in the widespread ignorance of the appeals process demonstrated by prisoners in their responses.[105]

11.3.1.3 Temporal factors: time limits, delays and the loss of time 'rules'

The four-week time limit for lodging an appeal causes difficulties for some appellants, especially those that do not receive legal advice (as they are supposed to) after their trial ends in conviction. Those wrongfully convicted are often in shock at the conclusion of the trial, are not told or do not understand the time limit, and understandably lack confidence in their legal representatives. Obtaining fresh legal representation and

---

100 Ibid: A2.6. 101 As counsel did in *R v Hart and Others* [2006] EWCA Crim 3239 [42].

102 Bottoms A and McClean J, *Defendants in the Criminal Process* (London: Routledge & Kegan Paul, 1976) p 178. 103 Pattenden (1996: 105–6).

104 For details, see Prison Service Order 2605 (available at <http://pso.hmprisonservice.gov.uk/PSO_2605_legal_services_officer.doc> (accessed 5 January 2010).

105 Plotnikoff and Woolfson (1993b: 118). No independent research is available to test the claim (Interim Government Response, Royal Commission on Criminal Justice, February 1994, pp 36–7) that arrangements for providing appeals assistance to prisoners were improved in the aftermath of the Runciman Report. An inspection of the experiences of remand prisoners in accessing legal advice indicates that problems are likely to remain: HMIC, *Unjust Deserts: A Thematic Review of the Chief Inspector of Prisons of the Treatment and Conditions for Unsentenced Prisoners in England and Wales* (London: Home Office, 2000) pp 45–53.

acting swiftly in mounting an appeal is far from straightforward, especially for those sent to prison.[106]

The limit can be waived by either the single judge or the full Court of Appeal if a reasoned application is lodged at the same time as the application for leave to appeal,[107] but in practice this is unlikely unless the proposed appeal has obvious merit. Historically, the Court of Appeal has been unsympathetic to applicants who have tried to excuse their failure to meet the 28-day deadline by reference to financial difficulties[108] or to a barrister's (perhaps bad) advice against appealing.[109] Sometimes the common law is 'clarified' in such a way that convictions based on the old understanding of the law were wrongful. The Court has refused to allow such convictions to be reopened by an out-of-time appeal, even in the case of an applicant whose 28-day period had only just expired.[110] The 14-day limit for seeking to overturn a single judge's refusal to grant leave to appeal is even less likely to be extended. Generally, it is clear that the Court of Appeal places great weight on the value of finality when considering requests for out-of-time appeals, particularly when those requests originate from those seen as morally undeserving.[111] There is something of a lottery here, however.[112]

The incentive to appeal is much reduced for those imprisoned citizens who are due to be released before the appeal can be heard.[113] Delays in hearing cases will therefore be one determinant of the overall level of appeals. The defendant who is wrongly convicted of a serious crime can expect to spend an average of 11 months in prison awaiting the chance to have his legal innocence established.[114] The expedition required by the appellant in initiating appeals is not similarly required of judges. This is not the fault of the judges, with their 'crushing' case load[115] but of government in not providing adequate

---

[106] See, for example, the account by Callan K, *Kevin Callan's Story* (London: Little Brown and Company, 1997) pp 79–83.   [107] HMCS (2008: A3–3–A3–4).

[108] *Moore* (1923) 17 Cr App Rep 155; *Cullum* (1942) 28 Cr App Rep 150.

[109] *Burnett* [1964] Crim LR 404.

[110] See *Ramsden* [1972] Crim LR 547. For discussion of the post Criminal Appeal Act 1995 case law on this point see Kerrigan K, 'Unlocking the Human Rights Floodgates' [2000] Crim LR 71 at 76–7 and, for the CCRC implications, Cooper S, 'Appeals, Referrals and Substantial Injustice' [2009] Crim LR 152.

[111] For example, *Richardson* [1999] Crim LR 563 where the Court refused an application for leave to appeal out of time even though it conceded that the delay was not the applicant's fault and that his conviction was undoubtedly 'unsafe'.

[112] *Mullen* [1999] Crim LR 561 illustrates that not every 'morally undeserving' applicant for a late appeal is rebuffed.

[113] 11% of those deciding not to appeal gave this as one of their reasons in the study by Plotnikoff and Woolfson (1993b: 104).

[114] Court of Appeal Criminal Division, Review of the Legal Year 2007/2008 para 1.3 (<http://www.hmcourts-service.gov.uk/cms/1497.htm> – accessed 5 January 2010). Appellants can be granted bail but this is done only in exceptional circumstances: See generally Pattenden (1996: 55, 111–12).

[115] Pattenden (1996: 56). The case-load has been added to in recent years because of the Government's determination to increase prosecution appeal rights. Most notably, the Criminal Justice Act 2003 granted the prosecution (but not the defence) the right of interlocutory appeal to the Court of Appeal against rulings by a trial judge (eg regarding the admissibility of evidence), but at the price (s 58(8)) that if the appeal fails an acquittal will necessarily follow: *R v Y* [2008] EWCA Crim 10 (where the introduction of this provision was described [19] as a 'significant shift of rights towards the Crown as against an individual' – see commentary

resources. In an effort to minimise delay, the judges sometimes appear to cut corners. Lord Justice Auld observed that provisional notes made by judges allotted to give judgment, whilst speeding up the processing of cases, 'often suggests to those in the court that they have made their mind up before hearing argument in the matter'.[116]

Malleson argues that it is difficult to 'overturn' the preliminary view constructed by the Court before it even hears the appeal. The Court 'decides cases in hours which have occupied the trial courts for days, weeks or even months.'[117]

A further off-putting feature of the appeals process is the loss of time 'rule', under which the Court of Appeal may order that some or all of the time spent appealing will not count towards a sentence of imprisonment.[118] This is likely to have the greatest deterrent effect on those serving short custodial sentences. Those given non-custodial sentences are not affected and the threat of an additional month or year in custody is unlikely to register in the same way upon someone serving a life imprisonment as it would on someone serving a short prison sentence. The loss of time rule is a classic crime control device aimed at deterring prisoners from exercising their 'right' of appeal. Changes in the 1960s which removed some of the disincentives to appealing and made it easier for convictions to be quashed , resulted in a quadrupling of applications to the Court of Appeal. The Lord Chief Justice responded by announcing that in future single judges hearing applications for leave deemed 'frivolous' could, and should, order loss of time.[119] The number of applications was instantly halved and remained at the lower figure of around 6,000 a year for several years. A subsequent affirmation of this judicial policy sternly warned those contemplating an appeal without professional assistance that a loss of time direction 'will normally be made unless the grounds are not only settled and signed by counsel, but also supported by the written opinion of counsel'.[120]

The Practice Direction (Criminal Proceedings Consolidation) [2002] 1 WLR 2870 contained the additional warning that a loss of time direction given by a single judge on refusing leave might be supplemented by a further loss of time direction should the applicant have the temerity to renew the application to the full court.

In *R v Hart and Others* [2006] EWCA Crim 3239 [43] the Court noted that even those acting on the advice of counsel were at risk of a loss of time direction. It stated:

We hope that both applicants and counsel will heed the fact that this court is prepared to exercise its power and will do so more frequently in the future than it has done so in the past.

by Ormerod to the case report at [2008] Crim LR 466. See also *R v O, J and S* [2008] EWCA Crim 463; [2008] Crim LR 892 (where it is noted that by that time there had already been 60 reported cases concerning this type of prosecution appeal).

[116] Auld (2001: 644, para 85).

[117] Malleson K, 'Decision-making in the Court of Appeal: The Burden of Proof in an Inquisitorial Process' (1997) I JE&P 175 at 186.   [118] Criminal Appeal Act 1968, s 29.

[119] *Practice Note* [1970] 1 WLR 663. Recently reaffirmed in *Kuimba* [2005] All ER (D) 110.

[120] *Practice Note* [1980] 1 All ER 555.

To emphasise the deterrent message still further, the single judge who refuses leave to appeal 'will also now be asked to identify where the Court should consider using this power should the application be renewed to the Court' and such applicants will themselves be asked for their representations as to why such a loss of time direction should not be made.[121] The form on which appeals must be lodged spells out the loss of time provisions and requires appellants in custody to confirm by signature that they appreciate their significance.[122] And Legal Services Officers in prison are also required to bring the loss of time rules to prisoners' attention.[123] These deterrent messages make it still more unlikely that convicted persons whose lawyers advise against an appeal (or fail to give any advice at all) will pursue the matter. Denied legal aid, and faced with the potent threat of loss of time, the prospect of launching an appeal is scarcely an enticing one. One might seek to justify this from a freedom perspective by arguing that deterring 'frivolous' appeals enables the court to devote more resources to expediting the appeals of other appellants with stronger cases. But we cannot assume that appeals which are not supported by counsel are inherently weak. As we have seen, legal advice can be difficult to obtain and, when provided, may simply be wrong. Moreover, the difficulty of separating out the frivolous cases from the 'reasonably arguable' is shown by the disagreement rate on questions of leave, calculated as the percentage of applications for leave granted by the full court following refusal by a single judge. This varied between 26% and 36% in the years 2000–2008.[124] As Pattenden notes: 'If the single judge can get it wrong that often, so presumably can counsel.'[125]

Most lawyers fail to point out to their clients that loss of time orders are actually quite rare and, when made, do not exceed 28 days.[126] This information is also omitted from both the standard appeal form and the Prison Service official advice to its staff acting as Legal Services Officers. Malleson's examination of the Court's decisions on 65 renewed applications for leave to appeal found that the loss of time rules were never mentioned, still less applied. This was so even though some of these applications were obviously regarded by the Court of Appeal as groundless, being described in such terms as 'disgraceful', 'a tissue of lies' or a 'cock and bull story'.[127] The gap between the formal time loss rules, the stern deterrent messages associated with them, and the actual practice of the court is not hard to explain. The court is able to have it both ways: its rules are so effective in keeping down its workload that, by almost never applying the rules in individual cases, it can give the appearance of adhering to due process values. There seems little prospect of getting rid of the loss of time rules. They chime with the managerial

---

[121] The Court of Appeal Criminal Division, Review of the Legal Year 2006/2007, para 7.2.

[122] 'Form NG' can be viewed on: <http://www.hmcourts-service.gov.uk> (accessed 5 January 2010).

[123] Prison Service Order 2605, para 6.6 (available at <http://pso.hmprisonservice.gov.uk/PSO_2605_legal_services_officer.doc> (accessed 5 January 2010).

[124] MoJ (2009a: table 11.5) and DCA (2005: table 1.7). See also table 11.1 below.

[125] Pattenden (1996: 115). See also at p 99 where she highlights considerable variation in the frequency with which leave is granted between single judges.

[126] See Plotnikoff and Woolfson (1993b: 79). In *R v Hart and Others* [2006] EWCA Crim 3239 the two loss of time directions made were both for 28 days.   [127] Malleson (1993: 15).

Table 11.1 Applications for leave to appeal against conviction originally determined by single judge

	2004	2005	2006	2007	2008
Applications granted by single judge	348	360	291	288	212
Applications refused by single judge	1,187	1,111	843	881	774
Percentage of applications determined by single judge that were **refused**	77%	76%	74%	75%	78%
Refused applications renewed to the full Court	545	557	481	520	400
Percentage of applications refused by single judge that were **not** renewed to full Court	54%	50%	43%	41%	48%
Renewed applications **refused** by the full Court	401	416	344	395	254
Percentage of renewed applications **refused** by the full Court	74%	75%	72%	76%	64%
Percentage of all applications originally determined by single judge which were **granted** leave to appeal by either that judge or by the full Court	32%	34%	38%	35%	36%

ethos that has become so prominent within the courts and a challenge to them on the basis that they infringe the European Convention on Human Rights has failed.[128]

11.3.1.4 Appeal rates in context

Table 11.1 shows the figures for those applications for permission to appeal that were originally determined by the single judge (as opposed to being referred directly to the full Court).[129] It may be observed that the typical pattern is for three-quarters of applications to be refused leave by the single judge, with around half of applicants giving up at this point. Of those that renew their applications to the full Court, around three-quarters are refused leave. Thus around two-thirds of those subjected to this double-filter are weeded out of the process and do not succeed in having their appeal heard.

The success rate in terms of grant of leave of those who have their applications referred directly to the full Court is, as one would expect, higher. But such applicants have only won the right to have their appeal heard. Most of those whose appeals are actually heard by the Court fail to overturn their convictions. Between 2002 and 2007 inclusive, of all applicants who finally managed to get their appeal heard, only just over a third were successful.[130] Between 2004 and 2007 inclusive, the chances of final success for those who set out on this obstacle process can be calculated as about one in eight.[131]

---

[128] *Monnell and Morris v United Kingdom* (1987) 10 EHRR 205. For a critique of the reasoning in this decision see Ashworth A and Redmayne M, *The Criminal Process*, 3rd edn (Oxford: OUP, 2005) pp 341–2.

[129] Adapted from MoJ (2009a: table 1.6).   [130] MoJ (2009a: table 1.7).

[131] Based on MoJ (2009a: tables 1.6 and 1.7).

The number of successful appeals against Crown Court convictions is proportionately very low, averaging out at 361 per year from 1997 to 2007.[132] The Court of Appeal proudly observed that in the year to September 2008 'less than 1% of [Crown Court] convictions result in successful appeals. This clearly demonstrates good reason for confidence in the criminal justice system...'[133] But the statistics demonstrate no such thing. They need to be understood rather as the product of the dominant value of finality as woven into appellate law and procedure. Walker, relying on Home Office figures, suggests that there was a relatively short-lived rise in applications to the Court of Appeal and 'quashings around the time of the major Irish miscarriage of justice cases' in the early 1990s.[134] Thus it seems that the Court of Appeal became more sensitive to due process values when public concern about miscarriages of justice was at its height.

Those who reach the court are not necessarily the appellants with the strongest cases. As Malleson notes, serious offences attracting long custodial sentences, relatively rare in the Crown Court, are the staple diet of the Court of Appeal.[135] Since more run of the mill cases are allocated to less experienced Crown Court judges (under whom miscarriages of justice might be expected to occur more frequently) it appears that the system operates so as to exclude the majority of potential appeals: 'The appeal process can be likened to an obstacle race: only the determined, strong and well prepared will reach the end – and they are likely to be found in the higher reaches of the offence and sentence scale' (Malleson 1991: 328). The true function of the various filters within the appeal system is not so much to weed out weak appeals as to deter all but the most committed from challenging their conviction.[136] The strength of this commitment will depend as much on such factors as the availability of legal advice and legal aid, the quality of legal advice, sentence length, and the fear of loss of time, as on the merits of the case or the intensity of grievance nursed.

11.3.2 The grounds for appeal

It is self-evident that the narrower the grounds for appeal, the harder it is to obtain leave to challenge a conviction. In understanding why relatively few of those convicted

---

[132] MoJ (2009a: table 1.7).

[133] Court of Appeal Criminal Division, Review of the Legal Year 2007/2008, para 1.7 (available from <http://www.hmcourts-service.gov.uk/cms/1497.htm> – accessed 5 January 2010).

[134] Walker C, 'The Judiciary' in Walker C and Starmer K (eds), *Miscarriages of Justice* (London: Blackstone, 1999c) p 221.

[135] Malleson K, 'Miscarriages of Justice and the Accessibility of the Court of Appeal' [1991] Crim LR 323 at 325. This is confirmed by more recent statistics: Mattinson (1998: table 14).

[136] For the sake of completeness we should here mention that a further appeal may lie (with leave) to the House of Lords but only if the Court of Appeal is prepared to certify that a point of law of general public importance is involved. In recent times leave to appeal from the Court of Appeal Criminal Division has been sought in about 20–25 cases a year, with only around half succeeding in gaining a hearing, and only about half of these winning their appeal (8 won their appeals in 2008): MoJ (2009a: tables 1.3–1.4); Dickson B, 'The Processing of Appeals in the House of Lords' (2007) 123 LQR 571 at 583–6.

in the Crown Court challenge their convictions it is therefore crucial to examine the grounds on which people may appeal.

11.3.2.1 Fairness and reliability: the meaning of an unsafe conviction

Section 2(1) of the Criminal Appeal Act 1968 used to provide as follows:

...the Court of Appeal shall allow an appeal against conviction if they think:

(a) that the [conviction] of the jury should be set aside on the ground that under all the circumstances of the case it is unsafe and unsatisfactory; or

(b) that the judgment of the court of trial should be set aside on the ground of a wrong decision of any question of law; or

(c) that there was a material irregularity in the course of the trial, and in any other case shall dismiss the appeal:

Provided that the court may, notwithstanding that they are of opinion that the point raised in the appeal might be decided in favour of the appellant, dismiss the appeal if they consider that no miscarriage of justice has actually occurred.

This formulation gave the Court ample discretion in determining the outcome of appeals, as it was clearly open to it to say that a procedural error was not such as to render the conviction 'unsafe and satisfactory', or did not amount to a 'material' irregularity (but only a minor one) or that the defendant would have been properly convicted of the offence charged even if the 'wrong decision in law' had not been made. This 'harmless error' doctrine was reinforced by the last sentence in s 2(1) which set out what was known as 'the proviso' – a device dating back to the creation of the Court of Criminal Appeal by the Criminal Appeal Act 1907 – which allowed the upholding of a conviction even in the face of a *material* irregularity or a *crucially* wrong decision on a question of law.[137] This discouraged the Court of Appeal from adopting a pure due process posture in which the integrity of procedural justice must be upheld at virtually any cost. Rather it was prodded into the crime control approach of focusing ultimately on the appellant's factual guilt. But since the proviso merely gave the court the freedom to overlook procedural errors rather than mandating that it should do so,[138] the Court of Appeal was left to chart its own course between the poles of due process and crime control. Let us briefly review its navigational tendencies.

An extensive analysis of criminal appeals by Knight published in 1970 demonstrated that the proviso was frequently applied even in cases where there were serious errors at trial.[139] Knight's analysis did, however, uncover the occasional case in which a serious fault resulted in the quashing of a 'factually accurate' conviction (Knight 1970: 30–7),

---

[137] See, for example, *McHugh* (1977) 64 Cr App R 92 discussed by Spencer (2007: 839).

[138] A point either missed or underplayed by Nobles R and Schiff D, 'Miscarriages of Justice: A Systems Approach' (1995) 58 MLR 299, and by the same authors in 'Criminal Appeal Act 1995: The Semantics of Jurisdiction' (1996) 59 MLR 573 at 576–7.

[139] Knight M, *Criminal Appeals* (London: Stevens, 1970) pp 15–21.

and commentators have identified other such cases in more recent times.[140] In line with Knight's findings, Malleson's (1993) survey for the Runciman Commission found no consistent pattern in the use of the proviso. Generally, it seems that a serious error or instance of malpractice at or before the trial was a necessary but not a sufficient condition for quashing a conviction.[141] We think that there is a plausible explanation for this apparently arbitrary pattern of discretion. The default position of the senior judiciary throughout the bulk of the twentieth century was to use the device of the proviso to prevent the factually guilty from escaping justice 'on a technicality'.[142] But where the conduct of a trial was *blatantly* unfair, especially where this might or did become public knowledge, the court declined to apply the proviso to avoid bringing the criminal justice system into disrepute. The need for a 'proviso' was somewhat reduced once the Court gained the limited power in the mid-1960s to order a retrial when it quashed a conviction because new evidence emerged, and substantially reduced when it was given a general power to order a retrial when quashing a conviction (for whatever reason) in the late 1980s.[143] From that point onwards the Court was not forced to choose between upholding the tainted conviction of someone believed guilty or quashing that conviction and letting that person walk free. Now it could be seen to uphold due process values (by quashing tainted convictions) while still pursuing crime control goals (by ordering a retrial).[144]

Then the Criminal Appeal Act 1995 came along. Section 2 abolished the proviso and substituted for the three pre-existing grounds of appeal the single ground that the Court of Appeal thinks the conviction 'is unsafe'. But unsafe in what sense? The Act does not say. One possible interpretation was that the 1995 Act required the Court to dismiss an appeal if in no doubt that an appellant was guilty of the offence committed, regardless of any procedural errors or malpractice associated with the prosecution and trial. This apparent shift towards crime control was not acknowledged in Parliament during the passing of the legislation, however. Ministers asserted that the new law merely restated the existing practice of the Court of Appeal and that the senior judiciary were of the same view.[145] But in *Chalkley and Jeffries*[146] the Court of Appeal interpreted s 2 as meaning that the Court could not overturn a reliable guilty verdict however unfair the trial might have been. Moreover, in the case of *MacDonald*[147] Auld LJ expressed his doubts that the jurisdiction to quash a conviction where the trial was

---

[140] See, for example, Clarke A, 'Safety or Supervision? The Unified Ground of Appeal and its Consequences in the Law of Abuse of Process and Exclusion of Evidence' [1999] Crim LR 108.

[141] Although Spencer (2007: 839–40) shows that, prior to obtaining the power to order a retrial, the Court sometimes quashed a conviction even though the procedural irregularities were *minor* in nature.

[142] Whereas the senior judiciary resisted the introduction of an appeal against conviction on the facts in 1907, the device of the proviso was welcomed: Pattenden (1996: 182).

[143] See Spencer (2007: 841) for the details.

[144] Retrials have grown rapidly in number since the late 1980s, reaching a high of 83 in 2007: DCA (2009: table 1.7).

[145] See Smith J, 'The Criminal Appeal Act 1995: (1) Appeals against Conviction' [1995] Crim LR 920.

[146] [1998] 2 All ER 155. This case is also examined in ch 3 (arrest) and in ch 11 (in discussing exclusion of evidence).   [147] For a discussion of this unreported case and the issues it raises see Clarke (1999).

adjudged to be not merely unfair but an abuse of process[148] had survived the change in the law brought about by the Criminal Appeal Act 1995. One commentator suggested that Auld LJ's judgment showed that he was 'troubled' by the restriction in the Court of Appeal's powers brought about by the 1995 Act, and that it suggested 'a court belatedly coming to terms with a radical diminution of its power'.[149] But can this be right given that the senior judiciary commented during the Act's passing that it represented no change to their existing practice? In doing so the appellate judges were acknowledging that their existing practice was predominantly based on crime control values. In particular, the Court of Appeal has throughout its history consistently championed the value of finality (not least through its harmless error doctrine) over that of procedural fairness.[150] Nonetheless, an interpretation of the Criminal Appeal Act which ruled out *any* possibility of quashing a factually reliable conviction, even when the trial had been tainted by blatant unfairness, would mark a break with the past. It would also pose a threat to the legitimacy of the courts.

In the subsequent case of *Mullen*[151] the Court of Appeal changed tack by revisiting the question of whether abuse of process rendered a conviction 'unsafe'. It opted for an examination of the parliamentary history of the new legislation and determined that the intention of Parliament had been to restate the existing practice of the Court. On that basis it concluded that 'unsafe' did (or at least, could) include a conviction achieved through an abuse of process.

This is one area in which the growing influence of the human rights perspective can be detected.[152] Article 6 of the European Convention secures to an accused the right to a 'fair' trial. If unfairness at a trial could not lead in itself to the quashing of a conviction, the Court of Appeal would arguably be failing to protect a fundamental human right. The denial of a fair trial and the failure of the appellate courts to cure this defect could then lead to an adverse finding against the UK by the European Court of Human Rights.

This is exactly what occurred in *Condron v UK*[153] in which the European Court opined that 'the question whether or not the rights of the defence guaranteed to an accused under Art 6 of the Convention were secured in any given case cannot be assimilated to a finding that his conviction was safe in the absence of any enquiry into the issue of fairness'. Acknowledging that ruling, and preferring the approach of *Mullen* to that of *Chalkley and Jeffries*, the Court of Appeal in *Davis, Johnson and Rowe*[154] subsequently accepted that a conviction 'may be unsafe even where there is no doubt about guilt but the trial process has been "vitiated by serious unfairness

---

[148] See Choo A, *Abuse of Process and Judicial Stays of Criminal Proceedings*, 2nd edn (Oxford: OUP, 2008) for a scholarly account of the abuse of process doctrine.   [149] Clarke (1999: 114–15).

[150] See generally Malleson K, 'Appeals against Conviction and the Principle of Finality' (1994) 21 JLS 151; Nobles and Schiff (1995). For a critique of Nobles and Schiff's position see Walker C, 'Miscarriages of Justice in Principle and Practice' in Walker and Starmer (1999a: 42–3).   [151] [1999] 2 Cr App Rep 143.

[152] For a review of the relevant case law, see Emmerson et al, *Human Rights and Criminal Justice*, 2nd edn (London: Sweet & Maxwell, 2007) paras 17-25–17-41.   [153] (2001) 31 EHRR 1.

[154] [2001] 1 Cr App R 8 [56].

or significant legal misdirection."' The use of the word 'may' in this formulation is crucial. The Court went on to note that 'the effect of any unfairness upon the safety of the conviction will vary according to its nature and degree' and rejected the argument that a breach of Art 6 would inexorably lead to a conviction being quashed. In short, the Court's view is that only when *it* takes the view that serious procedural unfairness has occurred may otherwise reliable convictions become 'unsafe'.[155] Even then, the Court will take into account the countervailing 'principle' that those reliably but unfairly convicted of grave crimes should have their convictions upheld on appeal.[156] That judicial wiggle room is valued by the Court is also evident from the case of *Togher*[157] in which two remarkable statements were made: (i) 'if it would be right to stop a prosecution on the basis that it was an abuse of process, this Court would be *most unlikely* to conclude that if there was a conviction despite this fact, the conviction should not be set aside'; (ii) 'we consider that if a defendant has been denied a fair trial it will *almost be inevitable* that the conviction will be regarded as unsafe' [our emphasis]. The House of Lords has also expressed conflicting views across different cases on the question of whether unfairness at trial (not in itself impinging on the reliability of the verdict) required or merely allowed a conviction to be adjudged unsafe.[158]

It is deplorable that there should have been such judicial vacillation for several years over a matter as important as this. Parliament should also bear some of the blame for its failure to spell out what an 'unsafe' conviction might be. Nobles and Schiff rightly argue that the Court of Appeal has always resisted being tied to statutory formulae, responding as much to their own perceptions and experience of 'justice', and to pressures on them, as to any 'literal' interpretation of statutory language.[159] Nonetheless, it would have been difficult for the Court to ignore a clear direction from Parliament to quash all reliable convictions obtained unfairly, especially if it had defined unfairness as amounting to a breach of the Art 6 right to a fair trial (and/ or where the unfairness amounted to an abuse of process such that the trial should never have taken place in the first place). No such clarity was achieved in the 1995 Act.[160] Perhaps the government feared associating itself with an explicit statement

---

[155] See also *R v Caley-Knowles; R v Jones (Iorwerth)* [2007] 1 Cr App R 13 (holding that a wrongful direction to a jury to convict does not necessarily render the conviction unsafe).

[156] *Alfrey* [2005] EWCA Crim 3232.   [157] [2001] 3 All ER 463.

[158] Compare *A* [2001] UKHL 25 with *Lambert* [2001] 3 WLR 206, and note also its surprising willingness in *R v Clarke and McDaid* [2008] UKHL 8 to set aside convictions for what many would regard as a minor procedural error. See further the discussion by Taylor N and Ormerod D, 'Mind the Gaps: Safety, Fairness and Moral Legitimacy' [2004] Crim LR 266 at pp 274–5.

[159] Nobles R and Schiff D, *Understanding Miscarriages of Justice* (Oxford: OUP, 2000) ch 3 and their 'Due Process and Dirty Harry Dilemmas: Criminal Appeals and the Human Rights Act' (2001) 64 MLR 911, at p 922.

[160] Auld (2001) called for clarification of the statutory ground for quashing convictions so as to 'make clear whether and to what extent [the test] is to apply to convictions that would be regarded as safe in the ordinary sense of the word but follow want of due process before or during the trial.' He refrained from advocating any particular resolution in his Report, perhaps because his own crime control preferences were made abundantly clear in *Chalkley and Jeffries*.

that the 'obviously guilty' must go free when this is necessary to uphold the value of procedural fairness.[161] The irony is that in many such cases it would be possible to quash a conviction on the ground of unfairness yet order a retrial – hence the guilty would not walk free at all. That would be a preferable approach to the current, although not invariable, practice of upholding tainted but reliable convictions except in cases of blatant and gross procedural injustice. Even when it comes to the latter kind of case, the Court is disinclined to quash convictions except where the defendant was brave enough to maintain innocence at trial (thus foregoing the sentence discount available to those pleading guilty as discussed in ch 8).[162] This stance can again be linked to the Court's concern with maintaining public confidence in the criminal process. For in cases where the defendant fails to contest guilt, there is little risk of the criminal courts falling into disrepute – the media and public are likely to view the guilty plea as sufficient moral justification for conviction and punishment, notwithstanding any taint of procedural unfairness.

While it is impossible to be certain, it seems unlikely that the European Court of Human Rights will insist in future that substantially greater weight be placed on breach of Convention rights when assessing the 'safety' of jury verdicts.[163] One difficulty in it so insisting is that the Convention itself merely requires an effective remedy (Art 13) for a breach of one of its rights, while s 8 of the Human Rights Act 1998 confers discretion on the Court of Appeal to grant such relief or remedy as it considers just and appropriate.[164] Thus, one technique for upholding a conviction obtained through proceedings tainted by unfairness is for the Court to claim that it has removed the taint through its own examination of the evidence. *Togher* celebrates this power while subsequent cases appear to be broadening the circumstances in which it may be used.[165] The difficulty here, of course, is that the Court of Appeal is likely to be influenced by its awareness that the jury arrived at a guilty verdict, and by its knowledge of matters that may have been kept from the jury precisely because they were thought more prejudicial than probative (such as previous convictions). More importantly, while the relatively open-ended nature of the powers available to the criminal courts in determining whether to uphold reliable but unfairly obtained convictions may enable them to do substantive justice (as they see it), the result is an unstable and unpredictable

---

[161] As part of its infamous 'rebalancing' of the system in favour of victims and the 'law-abiding majority' the government in 2006 announced that it was committed to removing the power to quash convictions on 'purely procedural grounds' – for critique see Dennis (2006) and Spencer (2007). In the face of biting criticism the government eventually backed down.

[162] See Nobles and Schiff (2001a: 915–17); *Brown* [2006] EWCA Crim 141. And even in this small minority of cases the Court of Appeal 'will usually order a retrial': Spencer (2007: 837).

[163] See: *Khan (Sultan) v UK* [2000] Crim LR 684 and accompanying commentary; Taylor and Ormerod (2004: 283) (who conclude that the ECHR's concept of fairness 'appears too flexible to provide the desired principled context'), and Nobles and Schiff (2001a: 917–22).

[164] See further Dennis I, 'Fair Trials and Safe Convictions' (2003) 56 Current Legal Problems 211.

[165] Taylor and Ormerod (2004) at p 276 et seq. For a recent example see *Steele & Ors* [2006] EWCA Crim 195 [37].

body of appellate case law.[166] This offends rule of law ideals, making it difficult for defence lawyers and others to judge when an appeal is worthwhile.

11.3.2.2 Reviewing 'mistakes' by juries: lurking doubts

Another basis on which a conviction might be regarded as 'unsafe' is where, despite the lack of any procedural error or unfairness, the jury is thought to have reached the wrong conclusion. It was not until the Criminal Appeal Act 1907 that convicted persons were given the opportunity to appeal on the basis that a factual mistake about their guilt had been made by a jury. The grounds for an appeal were stated in s 4(1) in broad terms. The Court of Appeal was directed to allow an appeal if it thought the verdict of the jury was 'unreasonable' or could not be supported 'having regard to the evidence' or that 'on any ground there was a miscarriage of justice'. The Court chose to interpret these powers in the narrowest possible way. Prior to the mid 1960s, it refused to overturn the verdict of the jury unless it was one which no reasonable jury could have arrived at. The fact that members of the court thought that they themselves would have returned a different verdict was, according to the judgment in *Hopkins-Husson*, 'no ground for refusing to accept the verdict of the jury, which is the constitutional method of trial in this country.'[167] The value of finality was clearly paramount.

This stance had a certain logic to it given that the Court of Appeal was not set up to rehear cases. Whereas the jury sees the witnesses and exhibits, and hears oral evidence, the Court of Appeal usually does no more than review the conduct of the trial as recorded in writing at the time. The jury might thus appear to be in a better position to assess the issue of guilt.[168] And to overturn jury verdicts on a frequent basis would call into question the assumption that trial procedures routinely produce correct verdicts, and that the job of deciding guilt properly lies with the jury, thus draining confidence in criminal justice.[169] On the other hand a concern with protecting the innocent might justify giving the benefit of any appellate doubt about guilt to a convicted person. It seems that it was the latter approach that Parliament sought to encourage in passing the 1907 Act.[170] The Court of Appeal preferred to act as if it had been given narrower powers. Parliament eventually tried again by passing the Criminal Appeal Act 1966

---

[166] This level of unpredictability is, in our view, far greater than that conceptualised as 'the law's capacity to evolve' by Nobles R and Schiff D, 'Theorising the Criminal Trial and Criminal Appeal: Finality, Truth and Rights' in Duff et al (eds), *The Trial on Trial Vol 2: Judgment and Calling to Account* (Oxford: Hart, 2006) 255. That it is possible to introduce greater certainty and legal principle here is demonstrated by Spencer (2007).

[167] (1949) 34 Cr App Rep 47, per Lord Goddard CJ. Note that jury trial is in fact used in relatively few criminal cases: ch 10.

[168] Appearances can be deceptive though. Just as in the interrogation context (see 5.5) assessments of reliability based on mode of speech, appearance or behaviour are likely to be flawed, reflecting misconceptions about how liars present themselves. See McEwan J, *The Verdict of the Court* (Oxford: Hart, 2003) pp 104–14.

[169] See further Nobles and Schiff (2006: 252). Similar arguments no doubt influence the Court of Appeal in its discouragement of appeals on the basis that a judge has made a mistake of fact (eg in determining whether a confession was obtained by oppression and thus should not be heard by the jury): Pattenden R, 'The Standards of Review for Mistake of Fact in the Court of Appeal, Criminal Division' [2009] Crim LR 15.   [170] Pattenden (1996: 141).

which directed the Court to quash a conviction which was 'unsafe or unsatisfactory'. At first it seemed that the Court under Lord Chief Justice Widgery had taken heed, introducing the 'lurking doubt' test in *Cooper*:[171]

the court must in the end ask itself a subjective question, whether we are content to let the matter stand as it is, or whether there is not some lurking doubt in our minds which makes us wonder whether an injustice has been done.

In *Cooper*, there was no complaint about the way in which the case had been put in court – it was simply asserted that the jury had come to the wrong verdict. At first blush it would seem that the lurking doubt test hoisted the value of avoiding wrongful convictions above that of finality. However, relatively few convictions (less than one a year on average) have ever been quashed on this basis.[172] Whatever the rhetorical significance of *Cooper*, it was crime control business as usual for the Court of Appeal in the decades that followed. The Criminal Appeal Act 1995 does nothing to encourage more frequent quashings under the lurking doubt test.[173] And the Court of Appeal stated in *B* that 'It is a discretion which must be exercised in limited circumstances and with caution'.[174] Roberts (2004) examined 300 appeals considered in 2002 and found only one in which a conviction was quashed on the basis of a 'lurking doubt'.

The Court of Appeal's practice in this area has always exhibited a restrictive interpretation of its legislatively granted powers. Indeed, in an eerie echo of the reception of the Criminal Appeal Act 1995, Lord Chief Justice Widgery had claimed during a debate on the 1966 legislation that the new power to quash 'unsafe or unsatisfactory' convictions merely codified and legitimised the existing practice of the Court.[175]

11.3.2.3 The admission of fresh evidence at appeal

When the Court of Appeal was set up in 1907 it was given the power to go beyond merely reviewing the papers relating to the original trial. Under s 9 it could order the production of any document, exhibit or other thing connected with the proceedings and order that witnesses attend for examination either before the Court or a commissioner appointed by the court. It could also refer questions to a special commissioner for reports, and appoint expert assessors. Parliament's intention was to allow the Court ample power to reopen a case and get at the truth. The Court of Appeal

---

[171] [1969] 1 QB 267 at 271.

[172] Malleson (1993: 24); Pattenden (1996: 146–7); Roberts S, 'The Royal Commission on Criminal Justice and Factual Innocence: Remedying Wrongful Convictions in the Court of Appeal' (2004) 1(2) Justice Journal 86.

[173] Malleson K, 'The Criminal Cases Review Commission: How Will It Work?' [1995] Crim LR 929 at 934–6.

[174] *B* [2003] EWCA Crim 319 per Woolf CJ (in line with the views of Lord Bingham CJ as expressed in *Criminal Cases Review Commission ex p Pearson* [1999] 3 All ER 247). Careful analysis of the circumstances in which this discretion has been exercised indicates that the Court proceeds by way of reasoned analysis rather than 'mere visceral or inchoate reaction' but also that it '...is not always easy to predict when a court will take an expansive approach towards the review of verdicts and when it will not': Leigh L, 'Lurking Doubt and the Safety of Convictions' [2006] Crim LR 809.   [175] See Pattenden (1996: 146).

interpreted these powers restrictively and refused to admit new evidence on appeal except in very narrow circumstances. Most notably, the Court imposed a requirement that the evidence which an appellant wished to call must not have been available (in the sense that it could have been produced with reasonable diligence) at the trial.[176] It wanted to:

- review, not to rehear, cases;
- to guard against appellants 'playing the system' by trying one line of defence at trial, reserving another for their appeal;
- to protect the notion that the constitutional responsibility for convicting persons of serious crime rested with juries, not appellate judges.

These are legitimate considerations but they have to be weighed against the interest in avoiding miscarriages of justice. Parliament responded in 1964 by introducing a new power which would allow the Court to order a retrial after the admission on appeal of fresh evidence.[177] But the Court's restrictive approach to the reception of fresh evidence was maintained.[178] So Parliament tried again. It imposed a duty on the Court to admit credible evidence which would have been admissible at trial whenever there was a reasonable explanation for the failure to adduce it earlier.[179] In practice, however, the Court remained reluctant to step outside what it conceived to be its review function by admitting fresh evidence. Where the failure to adduce evidence at the original trial was attributable to a mistake on the part of the defendant's lawyers, the court rarely permitted that evidence to be heard on appeal.[180]

In the infamous 1972 case of Luke Dougherty, a veritable busload of witnesses could have provided the defendant with a cast-iron alibi on a shoplifting charge, but only two were called at trial:[181] one was Dougherty's girlfriend and the other had previous convictions. The jury believed neither, and convicted. Dougherty faced a 15-month prison sentence for a crime he plainly did not commit. Leave to appeal was refused by the single judge, who ruled that the fresh evidence from others who went on the same bus trip as Dougherty could not be heard. The Court of Appeal subsequently confirmed that the single judge's stance was correct. It was only when the case was referred back to the Court of Appeal by the Home Secretary that the alibi witnesses were heard and the conviction quashed. But by this time Dougherty had already spent nine months in prison.

The Court has occasionally received new evidence of matters arising subsequent to the trial. As such evidence, by definition, could not have been adduced at trial, its

---

[176] Pattenden (1996: 130–2).   [177] Criminal Appeal Act 1964, s 1.   [178] Pattenden (1996: 137).

[179] Criminal Appeal Act 1966, s 5. The fresh evidence provisions were subsequently re-enacted in the Criminal Appeal Act 1968, s 23.

[180] The current position on 'incompetence cases' is that there must be conduct or failure by counsel which can be criticised and which resulted in the subsequent conviction being unsafe: *Grey* [2005] EWCA Crim 1413 [62].

[181] The case is discussed at length in ch 2 of the Report of the Departmental Committee on Evidence of Identification in Criminal Cases, HCP 338 (1976).

reception amounts to an implicit acknowledgement that the Court's function goes beyond reviewing the propriety of what happened in the lower courts. But the grudging nature of the Court's stance in this regard belies any commitment to protecting the innocent from wrongful conviction. Witnesses who wish to retract their trial testimony should not expect to be welcomed by the Court as converts to the pursuit of truth and justice. As a judgment in 1990 put it: 'the mere fact that a prosecution witness chooses to come forward after the trial to assert that his evidence at trial was perjured will rarely provide a basis for permitting him to give evidence or for interfering with the conviction.'[182]

Malleson's study for the Runciman Commission demonstrated a continuing judicial distaste for fresh evidence: 'Only in very limited circumstances will such evidence be admitted and if admitted form the basis for a successful appeal.'[183] This broader approach is most likely where the case is grave and the fresh evidence of innocence overwhelming. One such unusual case was *Cannings*.[184] The death of a baby was attributed to 'shaken baby' syndrome, but there were no visible injuries to back up the medical theory that the baby must have suffered non-accidental injury because it was statistically highly improbable that the causes of death could have been medical. The fresh evidence that led to the child's mother's conviction being quashed was new medical thinking rejecting this statistical approach. It is difficult to avoid the conclusion that what chiefly influences the Court in these matters is whether it is likely to attract criticism for failing to reopen a case that has aroused public concern.[185] Otherwise, the value of finality dominates its thinking and the inaccuracy of the original verdict is of subsidiary concern.

The Criminal Appeal Act 1995 entrenched this ordering of values. Section 4 abolishes the rarely used power to rehear evidence presented at the trial, as well as the duty to admit fresh evidence in the circumstances laid down in the mid-1960s legislation. The Court of Appeal is left with a discretion to admit fresh evidence having regard to factors which are worded similarly to those which it has long applied.[186] In 2002, 6% of the grounds raised by appellants concerned fresh evidence, compared with 7% of the grounds raised by appellants in an equivalent study of 1990 cases. The success rate for 'fresh evidence' appeals was, at 27%, actually lower in 2002 than it had been in 1990 (35%).[187] The history of the Court of Appeal demonstrates that the limited impact of fresh evidence does not stem from the definition of its powers but rather reflects judicial working rules. In *ex parte Pearson* the Court of Appeal reviewed its own practices as revealed in decided cases. It concluded that all applications to adduce fresh evidence turned on their own

---

[182] *Turner* cited in Malleson (1993: 10).

[183] Malleson (1993: 11). See also O'Connor P, 'The Court of Appeal: Re-Trials and Tribulations' [1990] Crim LR 615 at 619.   [184] [2004] 1 All ER 725. Discussed in 6.6.

[185] See the discussion of the case law in Pattenden (1996: 135).

[186] The factors are the credibility, admissibility and relevance of the evidence and whether there is a reasonable explanation for the failure to adduce the evidence at trial: Criminal Appeal Act 1968, s 23(2).

[187] Roberts (2004).

peculiar facts, adding that 'judicial reactions, being human, are not uniform.'[188] In other words, appellants should not regard cases where fresh evidence was admitted as establishing binding precedents. Recent cases have adopted the same approach[189] reflecting the judges' distaste for, and discouragement of, fresh evidence cases. The typical appeal continues to consist of no more than legal argument between opposing counsel. The Court of Appeal remains, by stubborn inclination, a reviewing court.

Once fresh evidence has been admitted, how should the Court of Appeal determine its effect on the safety of the conviction? The leading case following the Criminal Appeal Act 1995 is the House of Lords decision in *Pendleton*.[190] This holds that the Court of Appeal should assess the impact of the new evidence for itself, but *may* test its provisional view by posing the hypothetical question of whether that evidence, if presented at the original trial, might reasonably have affected the jury's decision to convict.[191]

We saw above that the Court of Appeal is reluctant to admit fresh evidence of innocence on the basis that jury trial is the proper place for hearing and weighing evidence. This works against appellants' interests. But if fresh evidence is admitted, how a jury might have reacted to that evidence becomes, at best, a matter to which the court may have regard. This also works against appellants' interests. Whereas a jury at a retrial would not know of the quashed conviction, of the defendant's previous convictions and so forth, the Court of Appeal is privy to such prejudicial material. Given the Court's historical stance of rarely ordering retrials in fresh evidence cases, the next best option from an appellant's point of view is for the judges to put themselves in an imaginary jury's shoes. Instead the judges have decided that they will decide the matter from their own point of view. It seems that the jury's role of determining guilt or innocence is regarded as constitutionally sacrosanct only when that works against the interests of appellants. But does it matter all that much whether the Court of Appeal evaluates fresh evidence from its own, or from a jury's, point of view? In legal theory, it should, but in reality it probably does not. Given that the Court of Appeal is privy to much prejudicial information, if it is set upon upholding a conviction it can easily justify this whichever test it applies. One only has to read appellate judgements to discover how easy it is to manipulate the relevant tests in order to arrive at a desired result.[192]

11.3.4 Evaluating appeals against Crown Court convictions

From a freedom perspective it is evident that a number of obstacles to appealing against a Crown Court conviction need to be removed. First, legal services need to be made more readily available to those convicted, and especially to those imprisoned. The defendant's

---

[188] See *Criminal Cases Review Commission, ex p Pearson* [1999] Crim LR 732 and accompanying commentary.   [189] See, especially, *R v Erskine; R v Williams* [2009] EWCA Crim 1425.

[190] [2002] 1 WLR 72.

[191] The 'jury impact test' was held to be equally applicable to 'fresh argument' cases: *Poole and Mills* [2003] EWCA Crim 1753 [64].

[192] See further Nobles R and Schiff D, 'The Criminal Cases Review Commission: Establishing a Workable Relationship with the Court of Appeal' [2005] Crim LR 173 at pp 186–8.

own legal representatives should have their legal aid bills cut by a large percentage in any case in which they failed to comply with their duty to advise in writing, immediately following conviction, on the prospects of an appeal. To ensure compliance, no legal aid bill should be paid unless a copy of counsel's written advice on this matter was attached to the claim for payment. But because legal advice is sometimes wrong, and because the defendant's own legal representatives may be unable or unwilling to identify their own mistakes, convicted persons should be provided with the means to get a second opinion. One possibility is for each prison to be visited by a duty barrister once a month in order to give general advice about appeal rights and offer specific advice to those interested in taking the matter further. This should encourage some barristers to become expert in appellate law and practice and thus lead to high-quality provision of advice. Their work could be supported in each prison by the prison officer designated as 'legal services officer'. That support could encompass such matters as publicising the duty barrister scheme, ensuring that reference books are kept up to date, and helping with the administration of the scheme. Second, the legal aid rules should be changed so that they place less weight on the advice of the defendant's original legal representatives and the views of the single judge. If a barrister giving a 'second opinion' thinks there is an arguable case, legal aid should be granted to make the application to the single judge. If the single judge refuses it, that should not result in the termination of legal aid if counsel, having considered the single judge's reasons, thinks the case is still an arguable one. Third, as with appeals from the magistrates' courts, a more generous time limit is needed, especially if our proposed duty barrister scheme is to work. Fourth, there should be a more relaxed leave test which would filter out only 'unarguable' cases. The loss of time rules should be abolished. As they stand, they deter not only the 'frivolous' time-wasting appeal but also many worthwhile ones. They are also arbitrary in their application in that they only apply to those serving prison sentences. It should be regarded as a sufficient filter that leave to appeal can be refused in any case that is plainly unarguable, and a sufficient deterrent to 'frivolous appeals' that unsuccessful appellants run the risk of an order for costs being made against them. Beyond that the disadvantages of applying more stringent filtering and deterrent mechanisms outweigh the possible benefits.

These reforms would increase the number of appeals. These should not be choked off by new procedural hurdles. Instead, more resources are needed, though government is unlikely to grant them. But there is little point in stimulating more appeals if the judges remain reluctant to quash convictions. Malleson argues that their reasons are based on due process concerns such as respect for jury verdicts, the need for speedy justice, and the fear that juries would, if they knew that an appellant had a generous right of appeal, deliberate less carefully and convict on weaker evidence.[193] But this misunderstands the due process model, at least as developed by Packer, which prefers to protect an individual's right against wrongful conviction to upholding 'respect for the jury', and prefers extensive appeal rights to the 'need' for a speedy post-conviction resolution. As for the 'fear' that

---

[193] Malleson (1994: 156).

juries would become too conviction-prone, Malleson accepts too readily that this factor actually motivates judges rather than being a rhetorical smokescreen designed to disguise crime control reasons for restricting appeal rights. Perhaps the only way to persuade the judiciary of the need for more due process is to demonstrate that miscarriages of justice remain a frequent occurrence. This brings us to the subject of post-appeal review.

11.4 **Post-appeal review: The Criminal Cases Review Commission**

A convicted person may only appeal once through the normal judicial channel: *Pinfold*.[194] A second appeal is not allowed even if the matter to be raised at the second appeal would have been different from that dealt with at the first. But once the standard appeal channels have been exhausted the case may be referred back to the Court of Appeal via the Criminal Cases Review Commission. Prior to the establishment of the Commission, by the Criminal Appeal Act 1995, the Home Secretary had a statutory power to refer cases back to the Court of Appeal. In order to appreciate the significance of this change, it is necessary to say something about the pre-Act position.

11.4.1 **References by the Home Secretary to the Court of Appeal (prior to 1997)**

On average, the Home Office received 700–800 requests each year to reopen cases in this way, but agreed to only seven cases per annum.[195] Legal aid was not available for the preparation of petitions and, in consequence, many were ill-conceived or poorly presented. Yet petitions needed to be detailed and convincingly argued to stand a chance of success. They were considered by a small number of legally unqualified civil servants within the Home Office who lacked the resources to carry out further investigation and research into particular grievances. Occasionally the police were asked to re-examine evidence but critics argued that the police were more likely to cover up their own wrongdoing than root it out.[196] More fundamentally, the Home Office was reluctant to refer many cases to the Court of Appeal for fear of being seen as interfering with the judicial function. Moreover, the Home Office had potentially conflicting roles, since it was responsible for the police and the maintenance of law and order. In practice the few cases it referred were those in which there was fresh evidence or some other new consideration of substance that had yet to be put before the court.[197]

---

[194] [1988] QB 462.
[195] Royal Commission on Criminal Justice (RCCJ), *Report* (Cm 2263) (London: HMSO, 1993) p 181.
[196] Mansfield M and Taylor N, 'Post-Conviction Procedures' in Walker C and Starmer K (eds), *Justice in Error* (London: Blackstone Press, 1993) p 164.   [197] RCCJ (1993: 181–2).

From the appellants' point of view, the unavailability of legal aid made it almost essential to enlist the aid of lawyers prepared to act on a voluntary basis and, better still, public figures, bodies or campaigning journalists prepared to fight their corner. How else was fresh evidence to be found when the convicted person remained incarcerated in prison, and how else could the Home Office be persuaded to act in this sensitive area? Luke Dougherty (discussed in 11.3 above) would not have achieved even the limited degree of success that he did were it not for the campaigning group 'Justice' taking up the case on his behalf. A House of Commons select committee noted in 1982 that in practice the 'chances of a petition being ultimately successful might sometimes depend less on its intrinsic merits than on the amount of external support and publicity it was able to attract.'[198] The Guildford Four secured the endorsement of a number of high profile 'worthies,'[199] the Birmingham Six did not.

Lord Denning MR, in terminating the civil action brought by the 'Birmingham Six' for assault against the police, refused to countenance that the police were guilty of perjury and using violence and threats to extract involuntary confessions, entailing as it would a pardon or the Home Secretary remitting the case to the Court of Appeal. He described this as an 'appalling vista'.[200] Evidently it was more important to him that the criminal justice system preserve its good name (even if undeserved) than that possibly innocent persons are given the chance to regain theirs.

The Home Office did, years later, remit the case to the Court of Appeal, but Lord Lane indicated his distaste for the reference procedure in his closing remarks:

> As has happened before in references by the Home Secretary to this court under s 17 of the Criminal Appeal Act 1968, the longer this hearing has gone on the more convinced this court has become that the verdict of the jury was correct. We have no doubt that these convictions were both safe and satisfactory.[201]

This was a criticism of the referral not only in the particular case but other 'hopeless' references.[202] The 'Birmingham Six' remained in prison another three years. Only after a further reference from the Home Secretary were their convictions finally quashed, by which time they had collectively lost 96 years of freedom.

11.4.2 The Criminal Cases Review Commission in action

The restrictive approach of the Court of Appeal, combined with the caution shown by the Home Office, led to repeated calls for reform over a period of some 25 years. But in the late 1980s and early 1990s there had been an unprecedented number of high-profile miscarriages of justice, many of which – like the Birmingham Six – had

---

[198] Home Affairs Committee, *Report on Miscarriages of Justice* (HC 421) (1981–82) para 10.

[199] Mansfield and Taylor (1993: 166).

[200] *McIlkenny v Chief Constable of the West Midlands* [1980] 2 WLR 689 at 706.

[201] Quoted by Rozenberg J, 'Miscarriages of Justice' in Stockdale E and Casale S (eds), *Criminal Justice Under Stress* (London: Blackstone, 1992) p 104.   [202] Rozenberg (1992: 104).

initially not been recognised as such by the Home Secretary and Court of Appeal. So the Runciman Commission recommended that a 'Criminal Cases Review Authority' should be set up to consider alleged miscarriages of justice and to refer appropriate cases back to the Court of Appeal.

Critics of the recommendation noted a number of problems, including that the new body would rely heavily on the police to carry out any necessary investigations, would not be subject to appeal and, when referring cases to the Court of Appeal, would have no power to make any recommendation as to outcome. Furthermore, legal aid would not normally be made available during the period in which the Authority was investigating a case. The proposed body looked very similar to the process it was to replace.[203] Not surprisingly, the Conservative Government was content to accept the Runciman Commission's conservative blueprint more or less as it stood and made provision for the new Criminal Cases Review Commission (CCRC) in the Criminal Appeal Act 1995. It is not even particularly independent, as the selection procedure for appointments to the Commission is run by the Home Office. Half of the first body of Commissioners to be appointed came from business, prosecution or police backgrounds whilst none came from a background of campaigning to root out miscarriages of justice.[204]

The CCRC assumed responsibility for referring cases back to the appellate courts on 31 March 1997. It refers cases based on challenges to sentences as well as to convictions and its statistical reports rarely distinguish the two. In its first three years of operation it received 3,193 applications, consisting of 279 transferred from the Home Office, 1,105 new cases in 1997/98, 1,035 in 1998/99, and 774 in 1999/2000.[205] Thus, following an initial surge in applications, the average annual intake settled down to roughly the same level as that the Home Office dealt with. The following decade saw a gradual increase in the annual number of new applications, levelling off at 919 in 2008/09.[206] This increase may be in part attributable to the implementation of the Human Rights Act 1998 in October 2000,[207] in part due to the CCRC's advertising/marketing strategies, and in part due to a rising prison population. Even now, however, the CCRC is receiving only about one-fifth more cases than the Home Office used to.

In the 12 years since the Commission commenced operations, it has referred more than 420 cases to the Court of Appeal, an average of 35 a year. It has thus shown itself substantially more ready to refer cases than the Home Office used to be, but the vast majority of applications still do not result in a referral. By 30 September 2009, the CCRC had referred 440 (3.85%) of 11,423 cases completed.[208] In other words an

---

[203] Thornton P, 'Miscarriages of Justice: A Lost Opportunity' [1993] Crim LR 926 at p 929.

[204] Taylor with Mansfield, 'Post-conviction Procedures' in C Walker and K Starmer (eds), *Miscarriages of Justice* (London: Blackstone Press, 1999) pp 235–6.

[205] Criminal Cases Review Commission (CCRC), *Annual Report 1999–2000* (London: TSO, 2009), p 17.

[206] *CCRC Annual Report and Accounts 2008/09* (HC 857) (London: TSO, 2009).

[207] See on this point Kerrigan (2000).

[208] See <http://www.ccrc.gov.uk/cases/case_44.htm> (accessed 5 January 2010).

Table 11.2 Referral statistics of CCRC from 1 April 1997 to 25 February 2005

	Crown Court	magistrates' courts	Both courts
Applications	7,008	475	7,483
Proportion of all applications	94%	6%	100%
Referrals	257	9	266
Proportion of all referrals	97%	3%	100%
Referral rate (proportion of applications that are referred)	3.7%	1.9%	3.55%

applicant to the Commission has about a 1 in 26 chance of success of getting their case back before the Court of Appeal.

11.4.2.1 The CCRC and summary convictions

The high failure rate amongst applicants to the CCRC is particularly pronounced for those seeking to overturn summary convictions. Table 11.2[209] shows application and referral data broken down by the court in which the original trial took place.

As can be seen, just 6% of applications to the CCRC have concerned summary convictions, amounting to an average of 60 a year.[210] Given that some three thousand appeals to the Crown Court are dismissed each year (see 11.2.1 above), the application rate is clearly very low. This is perhaps because, first, potential applicants will have already had two full hearings (including at least one before a professional judge) and may see little point in taking the matter further. Second, they will have usually received either short custodial, or non-custodial sentences which will have been served by the time the CCRC completed its work on their case. The applicants own desire for finality (ie to put the matter behind them) may outweigh the desire to address any lingering sense of injustice.[211]

As Kerrigan (2006: 133–5) has pointed out, however, it is harder to explain the fact that the CCRC appears more willing to refer cases back to the Court of Appeal (referral rate of 3.7%) than to the Crown Court (1.9%). The Commission may only refer cases in the restricted circumstances set out in s 13 of the Criminal Appeal Act 1995. It must consider that there is a 'real possibility' that the appellate court will not uphold the conviction or sentence. The framework within which appeals will be heard following a

---

[209] This table was constructed by Kevin Kerrigan on the basis of statistics supplied to him by the CCRC. See his 'Miscarriage of Justice in the Magistrates' Court: The Forgotten Power of the Criminal Cases Review Commission' [2006] Crim LR 124 at 126.

[210] Kerrigan (2006: note 10) observes that the CCRC sometimes asks a magistrates' court to reopen matters under s 142 of the Magistrates' Courts Act 1980 but that no formal statistics are kept of this 'extra statutory request'.

[211] Successful applicants to the CCRC do not risk the imposition of a higher sentence if their case is referred back to the Crown Court: Criminal Appeal Act 1995, s 11(6).

CCRC referral is no different from the legal framework governing the initial appeal.[212] It follows that the CCRC is obliged to take into account the narrow way in which the Court of Appeal interprets its own powers[213] and equally obliged to take into account the fact that a Crown Court must conduct a full rehearing once a case has been referred back to it. All other things being equal, it follows that there should be a high referral rate of cases back to the Crown Court since it would be hard for the CCRC to conclude on the basis of its necessarily limited investigation that there is no real possibility of the defence raising a reasonable doubt about guilt if given a fresh and complete rehearing. The statutory test in this context seems to place too low a value on finality, creating something very close to an open-ended, absolute right to appeal.

So how are we to explain the fact that the CCRC has referred an average of just one summary case per year so far? It is likely that in practice the CCRC exercises discretion by declining to refer cases back to the Crown Court unless it considers that the applicant is actually innocent or the original conviction is tainted by a substantial breach of due process.[214] It further seems likely that the CCRC would not think it reasonable to refer a case that it regarded as 'trivial'. At present, the law seems too expansive, and the practice of the CCRC too restrictive. In the interests of transparent and accountable decision-making it is arguable that the statutory test for referring cases should be amended for summary convictions so as to strike a more reasonable balance between the values of finality and the quashing of wrongful convictions.[215] The 'one test fits all' approach of the Criminal Appeal Act 1995 is indicative of the scant attention paid by Parliament to the possibility of summary miscarriages of justice and how best to guard against or remedy them. So far the evidence suggests that the CCRC is making only a tiny contribution to this objective.

11.4.2.2 The CCRC and convictions on indictment

We have seen that the 'real possibility' test entails that the CCRC is forced to apply the same criteria to the merits of appeals as does the Court of Appeal. So it is not surprising that the CCRC mirrors the Court of Appeal's practice of weeding out most putative appellants. Moreover, applicants must already have exhausted their appeal rights, and the Commission must consider that the case involves some argument or evidence not previously put forward at the trial or the appeal stage.[216] These last two conditions do not apply only if the Commission considers there are 'exceptional circumstances' justifying the making of a referral.[217] Once referred, the appeal may be argued on any ground identified by the CCRC, and any other ground with leave of the Court of

---

[212] Criminal Appeal Act 1995, s 9(1).

[213] As confirmed by *Criminal Cases Review Commission, ex p Pearson* [1999] 3 All ER 498.

[214] Kerrigan (2006: 137–8). The existence of such discretion has been recognised in the context of referrals back to the Court of Appeal: *Smith (Wallace Duncan)* [2004] EWCA Crim 631 [29].

[215] Kerrigan (2006: 139).   [216] Criminal Appeal Act 1995, s 13(1)(b) and (c).

[217] Criminal Appeal Act 1995, s 13(2). An example would be where an applicant has not exhausted appeal rights but the CCRC has already decided to refer a related case involving a co-defendant: CCRC, Annual Report 1999–2000, p 8.

Appeal.[218] In cases where the CCRC refers on narrow grounds only, the Court can, by refusing leave to expand those grounds, greatly restrict the ambit of an appeal. Where this happens it becomes impossible for appellants to put their cases holistically, thus reducing the likelihood that the conviction will be found unsafe.[219] Moreover, the Court will not depart from its own previous reasoning absent exceptional circumstances.[220] This is a difficult test to satisfy:

the exceptional circumstances, whatever they are, would have to be such as would convince the Court that if the matter had been arguable and argued in that way before the previous Court, it would – not might – have quashed the conviction. The Court should in any such cases be very slow to differ from its previous judgment.[221]

Generally, then, it is clear that the CCRC provides a means by which the applicant may be allowed to bring further appeals but only when there is something new and legally relevant to say. This is no different from the position that previously obtained under the old Home Office referral route. Without fresh evidence or new legal arguments the applicant to the CCRC is almost doomed to fail. Applicants who simply assert that the jury 'got it wrong' or that the CCRC should refer the case on the basis of a 'lurking doubt' make little headway.[222] As Auld LJ put it in *Poole and Mills*, the Court must keep in mind 'alongside the safety of convictions, the public and private interests in an orderly, as well as just, system that secures finality of decisions'.[223]

No provision for legal aid was made in the legislation setting up the CCRC. Thus another point of continuity with the old Home Office procedure was that the only help available initially was through what used to be known as the 'Green Form' scheme, which essentially was limited to two hours of initial advice. This was wholly inadequate given the complexities involved in maximising the chances of a successful application to the CCRC.[224] The results were predictable. After opening for new business, the CCRC was deluged with hopeless applications (for example, where normal appeals processes had yet to be exhausted) submitted by non-legally represented applicants – in the first year only 10% of applicants were helped by lawyers, commonly acting on

---

[218] See s 14 of the Criminal Appeal Act 1995. The leave requirement was added by s 315 of the Criminal Justice Act 2003.

[219] Eady D, 'The Failure of the CCRC to Live Up to its Stated Values?: The case of Michael Attwooll and John Roden' in Naughton M (ed), *The Criminal Cases Review Commission* (London: Palgrave Macmillan, 2009).

[220] The courts have recognised that this might be the case where a cogent argument advanced at a previous appellate hearing was not as fully developed as it might have been, or where there has been a development of the law which might require a different approach by the Court of Appeal to an issue before it, or where there has arisen a tension between overlapping principles: *Thomas* [2002] EWCA Crim 941; *Poole and Mills* [2003] EWCA Crim 1753.

[221] *Thomas* [2002] EWCA Crim 941 at para 74. This restrictive approach was reiterated in *Stack* [2008] EWCA Crim 1862 (and see the commentary by Nick Taylor at [2009] Crim LR 188).

[222] See further Malleson (1995); Eady (2009: 74); Nobles R and Schiff D, 'After Ten Years: An Investment in Justice?' in Naughton (2009). [223] *Poole and Mills* [2003] EWCA Crim 1753 [61].

[224] See Taylor with Mansfield (1999) and the second edition of this book at pp 652–3.

a pro bono basis.[225] After only two years in full operation the CCRC had a backlog of cases which it estimated would take it between three and four years to clear.[226]

This situation prompted the CCRC to proclaim through its literature the virtues of legal representation. It evidently wanted lawyers to help it carry out its work in three key ways: first, by taking on some of the investigative work that the CCRC would otherwise have to do; second, by filtering out hopeless applications before they reached the Commission; and, third, by making it easier for the Commission to grasp quickly the essential issues in those applications it receives. In its third Annual Report the CCRC reported that the percentage of legally represented applicants had risen to 30%. Nonetheless, about a third of applications were screened out as ineligible shortly after receipt, and in the vast majority of cases proceeding past that stage the ultimate decision was not to refer.[227]

A distinct improvement was brought about by the creation of the Legal Services Commission in 2000, and the replacement of the 'Green Form' scheme with 'Advice and Assistance'. The new scheme, which is means tested, funds those legal advisers who have a general criminal contract with the Legal Services Commission to conduct an 'initial screening' of a case, not normally exceeding two hours. This period is supposed to cover taking instructions from the client, considering any relevant papers or records, and the provision of initial advice on law and procedure. Bird argues that it is 'patent nonsense' to suggest that this can be done within two hours but notes that in practice the limit does not stop the solicitor getting paid if more time is spent on this stage.[228] The lawyer should reject the case after this screening process 'if it is clear that there is no reasonable prospect of a referral by the CCRC'.[229] Indeed, the solicitor must cease work immediately it becomes apparent that there will be no 'sufficient benefit' to the client to justify even this limited amount of public funding.[230] It will be easier to satisfy this test when the solicitor confines the investigation and advice to whether there was some procedural error at trial rather than looking into the much broader question of whether evidence can be found of actual innocence.[231]

If the case survives initial screening then further work can be undertaken at public expense, including further forensic testing, and the obtaining of witness statements and counsel's opinion. If an application is made to the CCRC the Legal Services Commission envisages that 'the solicitor will be involved in gathering and rationalising the material, preparing a chronology of events, and preparing the submission of any legal arguments required'.[232] The solicitor can also continue to assist the client by liaising with the CCRC once the application has been made. Advice and assistance is limited, however, to £300 (about six hours work at current rates) or £500 (ten hours) for

---

[225] CCRC, *Annual Report 1997–98*, p 18.   [226] CCRC, *Annual Report 1998–99*, p 12.

[227] CCRC, *Annual Report 1999–2000*, pp 17–20.

[228] Bird S, 'The Inadequacy of Legal Aid' in Naughton (2009) p 140.

[229] Legal Services Commission, Notes for Legal Representatives (available at <http://www.ccrc.gov.uk/108.htm> – accessed 5 January 2010).   [230] Bird (2009: 136).

[231] Ibid: 146–7.   [232] LSC, Notes for Legal Representatives, op cit.

initial appeal and CCRC matters respectively. After that, the solicitor needs to apply to the Legal Services Commission for authority to incur further costs, at which point, if authority is granted, a new upper limit is set. This process can be repeated but the LSC keeps a close eye on whether the work actually done is reasonable and corresponds with that which the solicitor originally indicated was necessary, and fees claimed are sometimes reduced on 'audit'.[233] Hodgson and Horne found that a high proportion of claims against this scheme (for cases where an application to the CCRC had been made) were in the £500 to £999 bracket.[234] Nonetheless, that the advice and assistance scheme is more generous than the green form scheme it replaced is suggested by the CCRC assertion that in the two years to March 31 2005 almost two-thirds of applicants were legally represented,[235] although independent research indicates that the actual representation rate is considerably lower than this at around a third.[236]

Thus, even under these new legal aid arrangements most applicants to the CCRC lack legal representation, probably because there are insufficient solicitors willing to take on legally aided appeals work, which continues to pay very poorly indeed compared to the income that can be generated from privately paying clients. Even those firms who undertake appeals work turn many potential clients away, not least because they receive no payment for appeals work until the CCRC either closes the case or refers it to the Court of Appeal.[237] Moreover, such firms find it difficult to justify allocating accepted cases to staff of the seniority required to assess whether the police, CPS, defence lawyers and courts have erred in their handling of the pre-trial and trial stages.[238] As one put it:

It is so badly paid and with the very low rates generally for crime, senior practitioners cannot spend time doing this work, not least travelling to see the clients [in prison]. The need to keep one's head above water drives senior solicitors to do work that pays, as opposed to work that does not, and unfortunately miscarriage work is regarded by many as at the bottom of the pile, purely because of finances.[239]

Despite the higher rates of legal representation now found amongst those cases that are lodged with the CCRC, over a third of applications are screened out by the CCRC as ineligible shortly after receipt, with a further 14% identified as having 'no reviewable grounds' and thus concluded with little or no investigation.[240] Moreover, as we have seen (table 11.2), the referral rate remains very low.

[233] Bird (2009: 139 and 143–4).

[234] Hodgson J and Horne J, *The Extent and Impact of Legal Representation on Applications to the Criminal Cases Review Commission* (CCRC) (Warwick: Warwick University, 2008) p 37.

[235] CCRC (2005: 38).

[236] See Hodgson and Horne (2008: 10–11). Nonetheless, the trend towards a greater level of legal representation is clear. [237] Bird (2009: 138). [238] Ibid.

[239] Ewen Smith, a partner with 30 years' experience, quoted in Arkinstall J, 'Unappealing Work: The Practical Difficulties Facing Solicitors Engaged in Criminal Appeal Cases' (2004) 1(2) Justice Journal 95.

[240] Hodgson and Horne (2008: para 1.7).

The fact that the screening out rate has changed little since the CCRC was set up raises further doubts about the quality of legal representation that applicants are receiving. The CCRC position is that good legal representation helps expedite its work, but does not increase the chances of a referral being made. Independent research suggests a more nuanced picture. Hodgson and Horne estimate that in the 2001–2007 period unrepresented applicants had a 2.1% chance of having their case referred to the Court of Appeal compared with a 7.6% chance for represented applicants, although to an unknown extent this will reflect the fact that lawyers tend to attach themselves to strong cases (where public funding is more assured) rather than indicating that the application was strengthened by legal representation.[241] That legal representation *often* improves the chances of success seems incontrovertible in the light of this research[242] but this is not so in every case.[243] The Miscarriages of Justice Organisation (MOJO), co-founded by one of the Birmingham 6, Paddy Hill, has asserted that 'many lawyers assist in the preparation of applications to the CCRC without sending for and fully reviewing the defendants trial files, leading to submissions that are bound to fail' and notes that such cases divert CCRC resources from well-founded ones, thus increasing delays for wrongly convicted persons.[244] Some solicitors do little more than add their name to the 'client's' application form, proving reluctant thereafter to engage with the process of case review, with some lacking even a basic understanding of the CCRC's role.[245] We have discussed, in this and earlier chapters, the poor standard of much criminal defence work, and it appears that post-appeals work is no better in this regard. That said, the impact of the 'economically impractical rate of £49.70' per hour currently available under the advice and assistance scheme needs to be taken into account.[246] Glyn Maddox worked on what was effectively a pro bono basis for 12 years in helping Paul Blackburn overturn his conviction (in May 2005) for which the latter had spent almost a quarter of century in prison.[247] How many solicitors could realistically 'fully engage' with the CCRC for years on end without going bust?

Initial impressions of the CCRC in its infancy were generally positive, suggesting that its low referral rate was not attributable to faulty investigative practices.[248] There are a number of welcome features of CCRC case-handling when compared with what went before. Cases considered prima facie eligible, and which raise significant new

---

[241] Ibid: 12–13.

[242] Ibid: 14–17. Firms that handle relatively large numbers of CCRC cases have noticeably better success rates: ibid: 17–18.   [243] Ibid: para 17.5.

[244] Memorandum submitted by MOJO to Select Committee on Home Affairs, December 2003 (available from <http://www.publications.parliament.uk/>) p 2. The CCRC agrees about poor standards (Evidence given to Select Committee on Home Affairs on 27 January 2004, Q50–Q56), as does the Criminal Appeals Lawyers Association (Arkinstall (2004: 101–2).

[245] Maddox G and Tan G, 'Applicant Solicitors: Friends or Foes?' in Naughton (2009) at pp 126–8; Hodgson and Horne (2008: 15).   [246] Maddox and Tan (2009: 127)

[247] Ibid: 119.

[248] See James et al, 'The Criminal Cases Review Commission: Economy, Effectiveness and Justice' [2000] Crim LR 140.

evidence or argument, are reviewed with care,[249] although some case review managers are no doubt more thorough and proactive than others.[250] The CCRC assembles the primary materials (exhibits, court transcripts and so forth), obtains fresh evidence and expert advice, and interviews witnesses (usually itself, rather than relying on the police to do this).

Criticisms and problems remain, however, and have grown in recent years. For example, all of the external investigating officers appointed by the Commission so far have been police officers.[251] Commentators have recorded their disappointment at this replication of Home Office practices and at the fact that the CCRC tends to draw external investigating officers from the same police force which initiated the original prosecution (James et al, 2000: 145). On the other hand, the CCRC reports that where it has turned to the police for help it 'has been well satisfied by the depth and thoroughness of the investigations that it has commissioned'.[252] Whether that satisfaction is warranted is unclear in the absence of independent research on the matter. Those who have had close dealings with the CCRC argue that its investigations are sometimes far too superficial.[253] Research is also needed to determine the fairness of the initial screening out of cases on the basis that they are ineligible or raise no new matters. Those lacking legal representation may be relying on the CCRC launching an investigation so as to discover the new matters which the CCRC looks for before accepting a case for investigation. As Malleson (1995: 933) observes, this is a Catch-22 situation.

Another problem is that the CCRC suffers from various handicaps in investigating a case: its power to obtain materials from any public body is of decreasing value as more bodies become privatised (eg telecommunication companies and the Forensic Science Service). In addition, the CCRC is not included among the agencies which can make use of existing mechanisms for international cooperation and mutual assistance in criminal justice: 'In one recent case we estimate that the absence of such powers delayed completion of the review by almost two years'.[254] The Home Office has been sluggish in responding to such concerns.[255]

The Criminal Appeals Lawyers Association has raised further concerns that the CCRC case review managers rarely visit prisoners or meet with their representatives, and are insufficiently open about the investigative steps they are taking, leaving applicants unsure whether they should be seeking themselves to make certain inquiries

---

[249] One indication of this is that in some 15% of the referred cases examined in depth by Hodgson and Horne (2008: para 6.5), none of the issues on which referral was based had been identified by either the applicant or the applicant's solicitor.   [250] Maddox and Tan (2009: 123–4).

[251] CCRC, *Annual Report 2006–2007*, p 14 (more recent annual reports are silent on this issue).

[252] CCRC, *Annual Report 1999–2000*, p 15.

[253] Eady (2009); Green A, 'Challenging the Refusal to Investigate Evidence Neglected by Trial Lawyers', and Sekar S, 'The Failure of the Review of the Possible Wrongful Convictions Caused by Michael Heath' all in Naughton (2009).   [254] CCRC (2005: 34).

[255] CCRC (2005: 8); CCRC, Memorandum Submitted [to the Justice Committee] by the Criminal Cases Review Commission (2009b), para 8 (available at <http://www.publications.parliament.uk/pa/cm200809/cmselect/cmjust/343/9031004.htm> – accessed 5 January 2010).

before evidence is lost or the trail goes cold.[256] MOJO has expressed similar sentiments and described the statement of reasons given to unsuccessful applicants to the CCRC as bland and mechanical.[257] What both bodies are most concerned about, however, is the low referral rate to the Court of Appeal, which they attribute to the excessive caution of the CCRC in applying the 'real possibility' test. Are they right to be so critical?

About 70% of the total of 411 cases heard by the Court of Appeal (by 31 December 2009) following a referral from the CCRC have resulted in the quashing of a conviction or sentence.[258] Rather than this being 'a strong vindication of the Commission's judgment',[259] it seems that the CCRC may be applying a test which is substantially more demanding than the civil standard of proof, also known as the 51% test.[260] In *ex parte Pearson* the Lord Chief Justice described the 'real possibility' test as 'plainly' denoting a contingency which 'is more than an outside chance or a bare possibility, but which may be less than a probability or a likelihood or a racing certainty.'[261] Since a probability or likelihood can be thought of as anything more than an evens chance, this judicial formulation suggests that the CCRC should take a less restrictive approach and allow its success rate to fall from 70% to, say, 30%. At this lower level the cases concerned would on average have a 'more than an outside chance', and 'less than a probability' of success. While this new policy would result in a higher proportion of failed cases, it should also mean that many more miscarriages of justice could be brought to light. It does seem, then, that the CCRC is excessively cautious in its referral decision-making[262] and the possible reasons for this will be explored in the next section. There is little prospect that the CCRC will change its ways, however. The second Chair of the CCRC commented that while a 98% success rate would be cause for concern, a 70% success rate confirms 'that we are applying the test in a way that is reasonable...'[263] There has as yet been no independent scrutiny of the correctness of decisions not to refer cases to the Court of Appeal, however, (beyond the occasional

---

[256] Memorandum submitted by the Criminal Appeal Lawyers Association to the Select Committee on Home Affairs, January 2004 (available from <http://www.publications.parliament.uk/>). See also Maddox and Tan (2009: 121–3).

[257] Memorandum submitted by MOJO to Select Committee on Home Affairs, December 2003, p 4.

[258] Source: CCRC website – <http://www.ccrc.gov.uk/cases/case_44.htm> (accessed 5 January 2010). About 90% of referrals are of convictions rather than sentences: Justice Committee, Minutes of Evidence: The Work of the Criminal Cases Review Commission (2009) q 18 (available at <http://www.publications. parliament.uk/pa/cm200809/cmselect/cmjust/343/9031001.htm> – accessed 5 January 2010).

[259] Dennis I, Editorial [2003] Crim LR 663.

[260] It is difficult to be certain about this absent independent scrutiny of the strength of cases both referred and not referred. As the CCRC has (correctly) pointed out, the fact that it has a 70% 'success rate' does not mean that it only refers cases that are 70% likely to succeed: Justice Committee (2009) q 25. Some cases referred with a lower chance of success will be 'balanced out' by others with a higher chance.

[261] *Criminal Cases Review Commission, ex p Pearson* [2000] 1 Cr App R 149.

[262] As Green (2009: 51–2) notes, the Court of Appeal is inconsistent and is sometimes more flexible in its reception of fresh arguments and evidence (even if they could have been presented at the initial trial) than the CCRC seems to believe. See also Newby M, 'Historical Abuse Cases: Why They Expose the Inadequacy of the Real Possibility Test', and Malone C, 'Only the Freshest Will Do' both in Naughton (2009).

[263] Examination of Witnesses before the Select Committee on Home Affairs on 27 January 2004, Q27.

judicial review case), and the CCRC is not subject to external inspection in the way that most criminal justice agencies are. Any self-satisfaction on the part of the CCRC seems as yet unjustified, as the third Chair of the CCRC (appointed in November 2008) appears to recognise.[264]

The effect of inadequate resources

The capacity of the CCRC to investigate cases is limited by lack of adequate resources. From the outset the CCRC did not have enough case workers in post to process the case load in a thorough and timely manner. A considerable backlog of cases built up and the Home Office, after initially rejecting calls to increase the number of case-workers, eventually agreed to fund 50,[265] which still fell short of what the CCRC felt it needed.[266]

By 31 March 2009, following successive budgetary squeezes, freezing of recruitment and stingy pay settlements which left staff 'angry and dispirited',[267] the figure had fallen to 44.[268] The number of Commissioners has also fallen over time from 16 to 11 (the minimum allowed by statute.) As a result, and despite recent changes to working methods which have boosted efficiency, applicants to the CCRC continue to encounter significant delays. For 90% of cases the applicant can expect to wait an average of 18 months for the CCRC to reach a decision,[269] but the delay experienced by any particular applicant may range from a few months to several years. In cases where the applicant is in custody it typically takes three months for the case to be screened for eligibility and then closed or allocated to a case reviewer; for those at liberty the corresponding delay is between 9 and 12 months. Case review itself can take a long time. In 2008/09 there were 35 Category C (more complex) cases allocated for review more than 18 months previously and which had still not reached even a provisional decision stage. The average age of these 35 cases was 32.5 months (substantially reduced from the corresponding figure of 42 months for the year before). The target for such cases is that a provisional decision should be reached within 18 months for 50% of them, and this was (narrowly) missed in 2008/09.[270] The CCRC has said that it continues 'to make strenuous efforts to improve our caseworking efficiency and find ways of working more quickly and cheaply, but we cannot compromise on the quality of the work we do.'[271] Laudable as these sentiments are, one may be a little sceptical at the notion that any such 'efficiency gains' are having no impact on the quality of case review.[272] This is another area where independent research would be of value.

We need to consider the implications of the CCRC backlog for the patterns of application and referrals. In its first Annual Report 1997/98 the CCRC revealed (p 18)

---

[264] Justice Committee (2009) q13.   [265] CCRC, *Annual Report 1999–2000*, p 5.
[266] CCRC, *Annual Report 1998–99*, p 12.   [267] CCRC, *Annual Report and Accounts 2007/08*, p 4.
[268] CCRC (2009a: 16).   [269] Justice Committee (2009) q7.   [270] CCRC (2009: 69).
[271] CCRC (2005: 7).
[272] For a detailed discussion of the investigation stage, and the potential clash between efficiency/economy and quality, see Nobles R and Schiff D, 'The Criminal Cases Review Commission: Reporting Success?' (2001) 64 MLR 280 at pp 286–91.

that two-thirds of applicants were in custody at the date of application, of whom over three-quarters were serving sentences of six years or more. Those serving shorter prison sentences (or the lawyers they approach)[273] may think the game not worth the candle. From their point of view what matters most is how quickly the conviction can be quashed. Thus, to the delays within the CCRC must be added judicial delays on receipt of referrals. In 2007/08 average waiting times in respect of all appeals against conviction disposed of by the full court was 11.1 months. The average delay for appeals referred by the CCRC will presumably have been somewhat longer given that the Court of Appeal considers these cases 'to be notoriously complex'.[274] The CCRC affords priority to 'in-custody' cases over 'at-liberty' cases.[275] Even so, those sentenced to terms of imprisonment of less than five years with cases of any complexity are unlikely to see the CCRC as of much relevance. By the time they have exhausted their normal appeal rights, secured a referral from the CCRC, and had their referred case heard, they are likely to be at liberty again anyway. If a prisoner is due to be released before a fresh appeal is likely to be heard the incentive to pursue the matter is much reduced. While some will still want to 'clear their names', those with previous convictions of a similar type will presumably not see much point in doing this. As table 11.2 above suggests, the priority given by the CCRC to in-custody cases means that those wrongfully convicted in the magistrates' courts receive from the CCRC least attention of all.

Two other aspects of the order in which the CCRC deals with cases are worthy of mention. First, the CCRC chose to prioritise the cases it inherited from the Home Office, many of which were very old but high-profile in nature. Thus eight of the first 54 cases to be referred involved deceased convicted persons, including Derek Bentley, who was hanged in 1952.[276] Second, the CCRC (2009: 73) has said that it may assign priority to cases 'of particular significance to the criminal justice system where, for example, public confidence is an issue'. This might mean prioritising cases which bring systemic defects in the system to the attention of the Court of Appeal,[277] or perhaps less commendably, prioritising high profile cases which have attracted media attention. The CCRC has accepted that its capacity for systemic review is limited, thus the second interpretation seems more likely. The CCRC has stated it believes that old cases should continue to be reviewed because they may be 'a matter of public debate and controversy.'[278] Notorious cases have continued to loom large in the CCRC's work. The rethinking of 'shaken baby' syndrome led to several cases that had originally been

---

[273] Arkinstall (2004: 96).

[274] Court of Appeal Criminal Division, Review of the Legal Year 2007/2008, para 1.3 (statistic) and para 7.2 (quote). Giving evidence before the Select Committee on Home Affairs on 27 January 2004 the Chair of the CCRC estimated the average length of time between referral and hearing to be 'around 18 months, a year to 18 months' (Q30).

[275] CCRC (2009: 73). Other influential factors are the age or health of applicants or witnesses, and the possibility of deterioration of evidence (ibid).

[276] For critical discussion see James et al (2000: 149–50); Nobles and Schiff (2005a: 179–81).

[277] See Zellick G, 'The Criminal Cases Review Commission and the Court of Appeal: The Commission's Perspective' [2005] Crim LR 937 at 949.   [278] Paragraph 18. See also para 22.

rejected by the Court of Appeal being referred back again by the CCRC, several of them being quashed.[279] It was the Court of Appeal itself, in *Cannings* (above) and the Attorney-General's review of all the 'shaken baby' cases that initiated this, the CCRC then responding to these events (see 6.6).

Our overall assessment is that, on the pattern to date, the CCRC, just like the Home Office before it, is dealing mainly in high-profile cases involving those sentenced to long periods of imprisonment. And it is proving to be unreasonably cautious in its decision-making concerning referrals to the Court of Appeal. As a result, the criticisms previously directed at the Home Office are increasingly being directed at the CCRC. For example, according to MOJO: 'The view expressed by experienced professionals who deal with [miscarriage of justice] cases is that you have to fight and battle with the Commission to get a referral and it is becoming as difficult to work with as its predecessor.'[280] Naughton has gone even further in suggesting that in many ways C3 (in the Home Office) was preferable to the CCRC, not least because the focus of the former was firmly on the wrongful conviction of the innocent. Moreover, its operation within the political realm ensured that MPs, the media and campaigning organisations took a keen interest in such convictions. By contrast the CCRC has neutered criticism of the criminal justice system while doing little to investigate and overturn convictions of those claiming actual innocence as opposed to claiming that their trial was vitiated by unfairness or procedural error.[281]

11.4.3 The response of the Court of Appeal to the new referral process

In the late 1980s miscarriages of justice were rarely out of the headlines. Of the 38 appellants involved in cases referred back to the Court of Appeal by the Home Office in 1989–91, 37 had their convictions quashed.[282] The uncovering of a string of sensational miscarriages of justice in the late 1980s and early 1990s amounted to both a cause and an effect of the Court of Appeal's greater willingness in more recent times to contemplate 'appalling vistas' of police and prosecution malpractice. The strongly worded judgment in *Judith Ward*[283] in which the Court of Appeal laid down clear rules governing the prosecution duty to disclose, is one example of this. Another example

---

[279] Eg *Clark* (Sally) [2003] EWCA Crim 1020; *Anthony* [2005] EWCA Crim 952.

[280] Memorandum submitted by MOJO to the Select Committee on Home Affairs, 15 December 2003, p 2. Concern at the inadequacies of the CCRC has led to the creation of the 'Innocence Network', made up of projects (usually housed in universities) devoted to publicising, investigating and remedying the wrongful conviction of the innocent. See further Naughton M and McCartney C, 'The Innocence Network UK' (2005) 7(2) Legal Ethics 150. The value of such projects is debated by Quirk H, 'Identifying Miscarriages of Justice: Why Innocence in the UK is Not the Answer' (2007) 70(5) MLR 759 and Roberts S and Weathered L, 'Assisting the Factually Innocent: the Contradictions and Compatibility of Innocence Projects and the Criminal Cases Review Commission' (2009) 29(1) OJLS 43.

[281] Naughton M, 'The Importance of Innocence for the Criminal Justice System' in Naughton (2009).

[282] Two of these were ordered to be retried and were subsequently acquitted: see RCCJ (1993: 181).

[283] [1993] 1 WLR 619.

is the decision in *Edwards*[284] in the aftermath of the disbanding of the West Midlands Serious Crimes Squad in 1989 because of mounting allegations that its officers were fabricating evidence. The Court of Appeal here ruled that the prosecution had a duty to disclose a police officer's disciplinary record to the defence. It also said that the defence could put before the jury the fact that police witnesses in the case had previously been disbelieved by juries in earlier trials.[285] The development of due process principles in cases such as these showed that the judiciary was no longer blind to the possibility of systematic malpractice by the police and prosecution agencies. Has this greater readiness to act on referrals carried on under the new system?

The initial signs were, on the whole, encouraging. In the very first case referred, the Court of Appeal acknowledged that 'the Criminal Cases Review Commission is a necessary and welcome body, without whose work the injustice in this case might never have been identified'[286] – even though this injustice could not be adequately remedied as Mr Mattan was hanged in 1952. The presiding judge in the Court of Appeal added his stamp of approval in *Criminal Cases Review Commission, ex p Pearson*.[287] Lord Bingham CJ declared that: 'It is essential to the health and proper functioning of a modern democracy that the citizen accused of crime should be fairly tried and adequately protected against the risk and consequences of wrongful conviction.'[288] Although the CCRC does not have the power to make any recommendation to the appellate courts, its Statement of Reasons for making the reference have been cited in judgments 'and have clearly been of material assistance in many of the appeals'.[289] Similarly, the Court of Appeal had made plain its appreciation for the rigorous and prompt way the CCRC has carried out any investigation requested by the judiciary.[290]

In some cases, however, the Court of Appeal has implicitly or expressly criticised the CCRC decision to refer. A striking example is *Knighton* in which the relevant conviction was of a man who had been dead for 75 years. The Court expressed itself 'troubled that this conviction was referred at all' noting that there 'are here no issues of exceptional notoriety, and therefore public interest...'.[291] As Nobles and Schiff (2005: 176) put it, 'the continuing work of the CCRC represents a significant ongoing threat to the Court of Appeal's ability to manage its role within the criminal justice system.' Tensions are bound to arise as the two bodies seek to develop a workable relationship.[292]

---

[284] [1991] 2 All ER 266.

[285] This decision has nonetheless been seen as placing undue limits on the defence's ability to cast doubt on a police officer's credibility. See Pattenden R, 'Evidence of Previous Malpractice by Police Witnesses and *Edwards*' [1992] Crim LR 549 and the critical commentary accompanying *Twitchell* [2000] Crim LR 468.

[286] *Mattan, The Times*, 5 March 1998.   [287] [1999] 3 All ER 498.

[288] This position has also been forcefully articulated by Lord Steyn in *Secretary of State for the Home Department, ex p Simms* [1999] 3 All ER 400.   [289] CCRC, *Annual Report 1999–2000*, p 18.

[290] Eg *Azam & Ors* [2006] EWCA Crim 161 [60]; Court of Appeal Criminal Division, Review of the Legal Year 2006/2007, para 4.7.

[291] *Knighton* [2002] EWCA Crim 2227 at para 73. The case is discussed more fully by Nobles and Schiff (2005a: 179–81) and by Zellick (2005: 942–4). See also *R v Gore (deceased)* [2007] EWCA Crim 2789 [42].

[292] See also Zellick (2005) (replying to Nobles and Schiff (2005a) and Nobles R and Schiff D, 'A Reply to Graham Zellick' [2005] Crim LR 951.

It is implausible to think that the CCRC has been unaffected by judicial criticism; one of the CCRC's ex-Commissioners has written of the 'bruising outcome' of referrals that irked the judiciary.[293] In practice, as we have seen above, the CCRC tends to excessive caution in referring cases. That said, it has on occasion tested the boundaries of the Court's willingness to reopen cases through the referral process. Thus, for example, it has referred cases where the law has developed since the time of the original trial, presumably with a view to testing whether convictions can become vulnerable in the light of more modern standards of due process.[294] The Court of Appeal has sent out contradictory signals on this[295] and a number of other points.[296]

The CCRC is bound to take notice of such signals given that it may only refer convictions where it considers there is a real possibility that the Court will quash them. Thus one might expect the referral rate to increase as the Court of Appeal lays down clearer norms in this area. But perhaps this is to expect too much. We argued earlier that it is relatively easy for appellate judges to manipulate legal resources (such as the *Pendleton* test) to arrive at the decision they instinctively favour. Just like the rest of us, judges are torn between due process and crime control values, with some more towards the crime control end of the spectrum than others, and all prone to being swayed one way or another by the particular facts of cases. Further incoherence is generated by what the second Chairman of the CCRC described as the 'occasionally uneven' quality of the court's work.[297] For example the, judges may not be specialists in criminal law, or the court's case law may be 'conflicting, unclear, or underdeveloped'.[298]

The more one examines appellate judgments the less one expects to find clear norms which are consistently applied. Consider again the case law vacillation over such crucial jurisdictional points as whether a reliable conviction can nevertheless be so tainted by unfairness as to be unsafe. The difficulty of the CCRC's position then becomes evident. If the Court of Appeal continues to tack between the poles of due process and crime control, the CCRC will have no choice but to follow queasily in its wake.

---

[293] Elks L, *Righting Miscarriages of Justice? Ten Years of the Criminal Cases Review Commission* (London: Justice, 2008) p 110.   [294] See James et al (2000: 143–4) for discussion of this line of referrals.

[295] See (in chronological order) *Bentley* [1999] Crim LR 330; *Gerald* [1999] Crim LR 315; *O'Brien* [2000] Crim LR 676 and *Kansal (No 2)* [2001] 2 Cr App R 30. More recent decisions have emphasised that the Court must focus on the safety of the conviction, albeit with a view to what modern standards of fairness require and imply: *Hussain* [2005] EWCA Crim 31 and *Steele & Ors* [2006] EWCA Crim 195. The Human Rights Act 1998 was also thought likely to have a bearing on this issue (Kerrigan, 2000) but the House of Lords has ruled that this Act does not have retrospective application: *Lambert* [2001] 3 WLR 206, *Kansal* [2001] 3 WLR 107 and *Benjafield* [2003] 1 AC 1099.

[296] See, generally, Zellick (2005). The CCRC's ability to refer cases where a development in the law subsequent to conviction put that conviction in doubt was disliked by the Court of Appeal (*R v Cottrell and Fletcher* [2008] 1 Cr App R 7), which regained control over its ability to decide whether to entertain such appeals by the insertion of s 16C into the Criminal Appeal Act 1995 by s 42 of the Criminal Justice and Immigration Act 2008. See Nobles R and Schiff D, 'Absurd Asymmetry' (2008) 71(3) MLR 464, and Cooper (2009) for critique, and *R v Rowe* [2008] EWCA Crim 2712 [21] for discussion of the difference between a 'change of law' and a 'declaration of previously undefined law'.   [297] See also Elks (2008) eg at p 185.

[298] Zellick (2005: 938–9). For an example of such a referral see *Kennedy* [2005] EWCA Crim 685.

11.5 **Conclusion**

The major miscarriage of justice cases show why the crime control demand for finality within the criminal process needs to be resisted. The Maguires, for example, had been convicted at trial in 1976 and had failed to have their convictions overturned through the normal appeal channel in 1977. An attempt to have the case referred back to the Court of Appeal foundered in 1987. The Home Office took the view that there was insufficient evidence to cast doubt on the validity of the prosecution's forensic evidence which suggested that the Maguires had handled explosives. The Home Office refused to set up a committee of scientists to reconsider that evidence. But when the 'Guildford Four' were released in 1989, Sir John May was asked by the Home Office to inquire into the circumstances of the convictions of the related Maguires' case. At last, adequate resources were committed to testing theories which might undermine the prosecution case. Sir John May's inquiry duly found that the Maguires might not have handled explosives at all; they could simply have picked up traces of nitro-glycerine from drying their hands on a towel. This finding led directly to the quashing of the Maguires' convictions. It also led to the forensic evidence in the 'Birmingham Six' case being scientifically reviewed. The findings this time were even more remarkable. It now appeared that tests which the prosecution had relied upon as demonstrating that the men had handled nitro-glycerine were thoroughly unreliable. The 'positive results' could equally well have been attributed to the soap used to wash the laboratory dishes prior to samples being tested or to the fact that the men smoked cigarettes.[299] In other cases, it has been a matter of sheer good luck that evidence of fabricated confessions, in the form of supposedly contemporaneous notes of interview, have not been destroyed or misplaced.

It follows that prosecution cases which appear to the trial court and the Court of Appeal as unshakeable at first, second and even third sight may be merely artful constructions built on foundations of sand.[300] In the 1988 appeal of the 'Birmingham Six', Lord Lane CJ said that fresh evidence had made the court sure that one of the men had had nitro-glycerine on his hand, 'for which there is and can be no innocent explanation.'[301] Three years later, the Court was forced to admit that a number of innocent and plausible explanations could be advanced to account for this fresh evidence. In 1988, the court had concluded that they were 'certain' that the superintendent in charge of the inquiry into the pub bombings in Birmingham, who the 'Birmingham Six' accused of fabricating evidence and perjury, had not sought to deceive them. In 1991 the Court said, 'On the evidence now before us, Superintendent Reade deceived the court.'[302] There could be few better illustrations of the point that the courts are not dealing in moral certainties and absolute truth, despite their frequent claims to do

---

[299]   For a fuller account of this sequence of events see Rozenberg (1992).

[300]   See ch 6 on scientific evidence, and ch 7 for a general discussion of how prosecutions are 'constructed' to appear strong, as distinct from simply being an assemblage of 'facts'.

[301]   Quoted in Rozenberg (1992: 104).   [302]   Rozenberg (1992: 106).

just that, but in degrees of proof. An awareness of the realities of case construction by police and prosecution agencies strengthens the argument for always leaving open the possibility of a further challenge to the factual basis for a conviction.

From our freedom perspective we argued above that challenges should also be permissible to the moral basis for a conviction. Where convictions are tainted by unfairness there are strong arguments for quashing them regardless of how reliable they might be. The crime control arguments against this position are not without all force, however. It is important in particular to look for ways to reduce the frequency with which convictions of factually guilty persons have to be quashed on the ground of procedural unfairness. One way would be to say that only procedural errors made in 'bad faith' or which were 'significant' or which 'prejudiced the defendant' should lead to the loss of a conviction.[303] But as we will see in our discussion of s 78 of PACE (in ch 12), such a strategy allows the courts too much latitude to overlook breaches of the rule of law.

A more productive strategy would be to improve the system of alternative 'remedies' for such unfairness (eg civil actions) so that they exert as much deterrent influence as possible. Better still, we might persuade the police and other criminal justice actors that the end of conviction can never justify breaking the law (even if minor procedural errors might be excusable). Breaking adherence to crime control values will not be easy, but couching our exhortations in the language of freedom rather than in the non-goal-oriented language of due process or 'human rights' may help. We can go further in buttressing our arguments. The law gives suspects and defendants rights to certain forms of 'fair' treatment. These rights are sometimes bound to impair the efficient pursuit of the truth and the conviction of the guilty. There is a trade-off in values here which is a deliberate choice of public policy.[304] It follows that it would be fundamentally undemocratic for criminal justice officials 'to take the law into their own hands' by imposing their own views of a 'just' allocation of power and 'rights' as between the state and individual citizens. Upholding convictions where the police have, for example, bamboozled suspects into 'signing away their rights' undermines democracy as well as freedom.

Achieving a freedom-oriented appellate system will not be easy. In one of the earliest studies of the appeals process, Bottoms and McClean (1976) highlighted the conflict that exists between fairness and justice, on the one hand, and the demands of efficient administration, on the other. The central issue for them was the status of the appeals process. Was an appeal to be a general right for all defendants, or a special procedure designed to correct the occasional wrong? The history of the Court of Appeal suggests that it is the latter that was intended from the outset.

---

[303] A strategy favoured by Dennis I, 'Fair Trials and Safe Convictions' (2003b) 56 Current Legal Problems 211 for example.

[304] See also Nobles and Schiff (1995) and, by the same authors, 'The Never Ending Story: Disguising Tragic Choices in Criminal Justice' (1997) 60 MLR 293.

In the nineteenth century the law provided no means for correcting the errors of juries in criminal trials. This was in marked contrast to the position in civil trials, which were tried by the same judges and juries. As Pattenden observes it is 'difficult to explain this discrepancy except...as reflecting a greater concern for property than life or liberty.'[305]

Only a wealthy minority had much property to speak of, and the life or liberty of those typically subjected to criminal proceedings did not concern those with the power to change the law. In consequence, 30 Bills designed to create a right of criminal appeal failed in Parliament between 1844 and 1906. The judiciary and Parliament refused to accept, or care, that innocent persons could be wrongly convicted. In addition there were problems of costs, no accurate record of trials, and insufficient judges to cope with the anticipated level of appeals. But as Pattenden notes the legislature and their friends were not the ones most frequently prosecuted, it was: 'the "criminal class", who were seen as a threat to the stability of the social order and the sanctity of private property' and so the law makers had it their own way.[306]

The Court of Appeal was eventually created in 1907 in response to an outcry over a particularly gross miscarriage of justice; the case of Adolf Beck who was wrongfully convicted on two occasions for crimes committed by another man. As Malleson (1991: 331) convincingly argues, the Court of Appeal was set up:

to sift out and put right such serious and rare cases which generated public concern and brought the Criminal Justice System into disrepute...The present design of the system, the limited and narrow powers of the Court and the hazardous path to that institution are not accidental or a mistake but persist because there has never been the will or intention to have a system the size and scope of which is determined by the numbers of miscarriages of justice occurring.

Nobles and Schiff (2000) also argue that appeal reforms throughout the twentieth century were designed to mollify public (especially media) opinion, rather than to solve the underlying problems. However, they argue that these problems are insoluble anyway, dooming the efforts of 'reformists' to failure. This is because the only thorough appeal process is one that puts the investigation and court processes themselves on trial. The scope for uncovering error is infinite. Whilst this is true, it is a valid criticism only of a purist due process position. The freedom perspective would not seek infinite appeals or infinite thoroughness because it holds that the scarcity of resources is a legitimate concern. This does not prevent us from critiquing the current appeal system.

The English system of appellate review is moulded by what can be seen as its crime control heritage. The crime control model is reluctant to concede that its procedures are likely to produce miscarriages of justice. From this perspective every acquittal and every successful appeal serves to sap public confidence in the reliability of the system in distinguishing the innocent from the guilty. This undermines the deterrent efficacy

---

[305] Pattenden (1996: 6).   [306] Ibid: 19.

of the criminal law and threatens the entire crime control project. But public confidence might drain away altogether if the system failed to right its mistakes in a timely fashion. However, the processes of case construction and evidential constraints (such as the reluctance on appeal to admit fresh evidence) ensures that, although errors are legion, few become obvious. Even then, it is only when major public campaigns are mounted that the public takes an interest in the fate of convicted persons. The Court of Appeal exists to ensure that convictions in such high-profile cases are either quashed or given the seal of approval by the senior judiciary. Because miscarriages of justice occurring in more run-of-the-mill cases attract minimal public interest, there is no need to ensure that they are subject to appellate review and much to be said for suppressing appeals.

Where does the CCRC fit within this analysis? On the one hand its work has resulted in more miscarriages of justice coming to light, which might in the long run prompt systemic reforms aimed at eradicating the conditions which generated them. On the other hand the CCRC itself takes the view that its work has allayed pubic concern about the system. As the second Chairman put it:

It should not be forgotten that our work is critical to confidence in the criminal justice system, which is a prominent aim of the Government's criminal justice policy: the public want to be assured that, when things have gone wrong, there is a mechanism which can ensure they are put right and they also want assurance, which we can give, that the majority of criminal prosecutions appear to result in a satisfactory outcome.[307]

This is an extraordinary claim to make, not only because the CCRC does not review anything like 'the majority of criminal prosecutions' but also because of the problematic issues that surround its own functioning. Why then was it made? It is contained in the Foreword to the 2005 Annual Report addressed to the Home Secretary. One is driven to the conclusion that the CCRC is trying to justify itself in terms that it knows are likely to be palatable to the hand that feeds it. In consequence, just like the Court of Appeal, it has got into the habit of focusing almost exclusively on 'exceptional', high-profile, heavy-end miscarriages and is developing an ever blinder eye to the possibility (in our view, probability) that wrongful convictions of innocent persons remain mundane and routine features of the system. Maintaining public confidence in the appearance of justice is the order of the day.

Naughton has argued that the status quo might most fruitfully be challenged by the production and deployment of 'counter discourse'. This would be achieved through the unearthing and publicizing of new miscarriages of justice, especially those that highlight previously unaddressed issues, with a view to generating a public crisis of confidence in the implicated parts of the criminal process. The 'reform window' thus created (as where a Royal Commission or other inquiry is set up) might then be used to

---

[307] CCRC (2005: 8). See also Zellick (2005: 949): 'I very much doubt whether the 6,000–7,000 completed non-referred cases would disclose much of value if disinterred and interrogated. Most, I suspect, would reveal nothing of interest – hence the decision to reject…'

achieve progressive reforms. He accepts, however, that during such reform moments, conflicting discourses will also come into play.[308] At present the political mood-music suggests that further reform will be fiercely resisted. Tony Blair asserted in a major speech on 18 June 2002 that: 'it's perhaps the biggest miscarriage of justice in today's system when the guilty walk away unpunished'.[309] His successor has shown no sign of adopting the counter-discourse of due process and it is difficult to imagine this changing once Brown has left the stage.

Further reading

Elks, L, *Righting Miscarriages of Justice? Ten Years of the Criminal Cases Review Commission* (London: Justice, 2008)

Naughton M, *Rethinking Miscarriages of Justice: Beyond the Tip of the Iceberg* (Houndmills: Palgrave Macmillan, 2007)

Naughton M (ed), *The Criminal Cases Review Commission* (Houndmills: Palgrave Macmillan, 2009)

Spencer J, 'Does our Present Appeal System Make Sense?' [2006] Crim LR 677

Spencer J, 'Quashing Convictions for Procedural Irregularities' [2007] Crim LR 835

---

[308] Naughton M, 'Miscarriages of Justice and the Government of the Criminal Justice System: An Alternative Perspective on the Production and Deployment of Counter-Discourse' (2005) 13 Critical Criminology 211. But see also Nobles and Schiff (2001b: 294–8) who suggest that there are inherent limits to what can be achieved through garnering media attention.

[309] <http://www.number-10.gov.uk/output/Page1717.asp> (accessed 5 January 2010).

12

Remedying police malpractice

Scotland Yard faced calls for an 'ethical audit' of all officers in its controversial riot squad last night after figures revealed that they had received
more than 5000 complaint allegations [in 4 years], mostly for 'oppressive
behaviour'... only nine were 'substantiated' after an investigation by the
force's complaints department.... The figures either mean thousands of
members of the public are taking the trouble to make fabricated complaints... [or] it is virtually impossible for officers in the unit to be held to
account for their actions.[1]

Key issues

- The (non-) prosecution of police officers
- Of civil rights and remedies: a threadbare patchwork?
- The police complaints system: give up hope most of ye who enter here
- Trial remedies: the exclusion of evidence and the abuse of process doctrine
- Understanding police malpractice: rotten apples, rotten barrel, or business as usual?

12.1 **Introduction**

In criminal justice, as in other systems, a balance has to be struck between guarding against error and injustice on the one hand, and facilitating efficiency on the other. The way that balance is and should be struck has been an important theme of this book. The imposition of controls on the police and the provision of rights to suspects and defendants are, at least in part, attempts to guard against error and injustice. Since these attempts will never be entirely successful, it follows also that error and injustice have to be anticipated and procedures have to be established for their identification, correction and compensation. This is recognised by the European Convention on

---

[1] *The Observer*, 7 November 2009.

Human Rights (ECHR), most of which has now been incorporated into English law by the Human Rights Act 1998 (HRA). For example, Art 5(5) provides an enforceable right to compensation to anyone 'who has been the victim of arrest or detention in contravention of the provisions of this Article'. But the more general catch-all provision in Art 13, which requires that states provide an 'effective' remedy for a breach of any Convention right, has not been incorporated into English law. People who wish to make use of Art 13 must embark on the long slow march to the European Court of Human Rights (ECtHR).

Chapter 11 looked at appeal procedures. These are concerned with wrongful convictions, some of which are a result of police malpractice. Exposing miscarriages of justice can expose malpractice, helping to prevent future abuses, but they do nothing directly to deal with the police at fault or to compensate the defendant. Then there are the cases in which conviction was not wrong – the defendant may even have pleaded guilty – but in which the defendants' rights were in some way abused (eg being assaulted or denied a solicitor). Finally, there are many cases of malpractice where the defendant was not even prosecuted – or died in custody like Sean Rigg or Faisal Al-Ani, discussed in ch 4 – and so appealing to expose an abuse does not arise. For all these cases, remedies are needed.

The role of remedial procedures is very different in different models of criminal justice. Due process is sceptical about the reliability of administrative fact-finding processes. It therefore expects errors and injustices to be legion. The model argues that to maintain public confidence the system should own up to, and correct, error and injustice. The exclusionary remedy, which operates at the trial stage, can serve this purpose. Errors that affect the reliability of evidence must be corrected by the trial judge ruling that evidence inadmissible. But even where the evidence obtained unlawfully is shown to be reliable, exclusion must still follow, so the system can uphold its own integrity and remove the incentive for the police to break the rules. If the collapse of prosecution cases following exclusion adversely affects the morale of the police, the answer lies in their hands, since if they kept to the rules they would not lose convictions in this way. Other remedies must also be provided, however, since exclusionary rules can only affect that tiny percentage of criminal cases which are both prosecuted and contested, and may, in any case, be ineffective in punishing and deterring the particular police officers responsible for malpractice. Thus civil remedies, criminal prosecution and disciplinary mechanisms are also needed. A strong system of remedies is bound to impair police efficiency and reduce the conviction rate, but these are prices worth paying for enhancing fairness, individual liberty, and the protection of the factually innocent.

The crime control model concedes that error and injustice will occur but not on the scale envisaged by the due process adherent. Only errors which undermine confidence in the reliability of the evidence put before the court and the accuracy of the finding of guilt require an exclusionary remedy. It would be intolerable to allow a guilty person to go free because of some technical procedural error. To do so would undermine both police morale and public confidence in the system, whilst having little effect on police practices. The availability of other remedies should be limited so that only those with serious and genuine grievances will complain. The best way to tackle police rule-breaking is through disciplinary mechanisms which focus on how to make individual officers more efficient in future, emphasising that the primary aim of these rules is not to protect suspects, but to ensure the reliability of evidence. Officers who are unable to judge accurately when it is rational to break the rules in the search for the truth should be regarded as terminally inefficient and dismissed.

The approach of the freedom model is close to that of due process, but less extreme in its effects. The test is whether the freedom lost to the suspect by the malpractice (and which will be lost to future suspects if the malpractice is allowed to continue) is greater or less than the loss of freedom created by punishing and preventing the malpractice. Since most malpractice is simply a short cut for the police, and is uncertain in its crime control effects anyway, in most cases the balance will come down in favour of using whatever remedies best eradicate the malpractice. The freedom model also takes account of what it feels like to be on the receiving end of malpractice. Loss of freedom is a qualitative as well as quantitative matter. This has the further implication that if malpractice consists of a suspect being treated with contempt, for example, remedies which provide monetary compensation, or exclusion of evidence, may not provide what the suspect is looking for. An admission of poor behaviour and sincere apology can sometimes count for a lot more.

All three models accept that errors may be dealt with in many different ways but differ on what the purpose of a remedy should be. In reality, any one remedy may serve a variety of purposes, including apology, punishment, deterrence and righting the wrong. These are all remedies for individual victims of malpractice. In theory, individual remedies should reduce malpractice in general, to which all the models aspire. However, it would be wrong to assume that any of them are much use in this respect. We therefore need to think also about why malpractice occurs and what can be done at an organisational level to reduce it.

12.2 **Prosecutions**

Where there is any reason to investigate a possibly criminal incident, such as the shooting of Jean Charles de Menezes in July 2005, the investigation is carried out by the Independent Police Complaints Commission (IPCC) or, in less serious cases, by the police (perhaps under IPCC supervision: see 12.4 below). If the investigation concludes that there 'may be evidence' of crime, the case is passed to the Crown Prosecution Service (CPS) for a decision according to the evidential and public interest tests as in any other case (see ch 7).[2] Again as in any other case, the police and/or IPCC may seek

---

[2] There is no agreed threshold defining 'may be evidence' and practice differs from area to area: HMIC/HMCPSI, *Justice in Policing: A Joint Thematic Review of the Handling of Cases Involving an Allegation of a Criminal Offence by a Person Serving with the Police* (London: HMIC/HMCPSI, 2007) paras 4.10–4.19.

the advice of the CPS, and are strongly encouraged to do so.[3] A HQ Division of the CPS (the Special Crime Division) handles the most serious cases, while the majority are passed onto CPS Areas that do not correspond with the police force area in question (this is to facilitate independent decision-making). A decision against prosecution is not necessarily the end of the matter, however, because the CPS now gives reasons for such decisions, enabling victims and their families to pursue lines of enquiry that the police may have neglected.[4]

12.2.1 The evidential test

The difficulty of proving a case where it is usually one citizen's word against that of one or more police officers weighs heavily against prosecution. From a due process perspective, police officers are rightly protected from prosecution when the case is weak. However, according to the then Metropolitan Police Commissioner Paul Condon in 1997, corrupt police officers know the law so well that they can usually cover their tracks to ensure that the case against them is weak.[5] In other words, the same type of construction technique that the police use against 'normal' suspects to make a weak case strong (discussed in ch 7) is used by the 'suspect' police officer at risk of prosecution to make what could be a strong case weak. The *Harry Stanley* case is a classic – and tragic – example. He was shot in 1999 while walking home with a table leg in a plastic bag. A member of the public thought the table leg looked like a gun, and called the police. Two armed officers confronted him and shot and killed him. Initially it was decided to discipline, but not to prosecute, the officers. Following further investigations and reviews, particularly in the light of an inquest verdict of unlawful killing, the IPCC finally concluded that there was insufficient evidence to discipline or prosecute the officers. This was partly because there was insufficient reason to disbelieve the officers whose accounts were identical. The IPCC clearly suspected that the police constructed their defence by 'cooking' their accounts, together with their solicitor, as it recommended that in future police officers in situations like this be treated like other witnesses – not be allowed to confer, nor to secure legal advice, before making a formal statement; and that if they do want legal advice they should be treated like suspects: 'The police cannot have it both ways.'[6] For the time being, however, as we shall see in

---

[3] CPS and IPCC, Protocol between the Crown Prosecution Service Casework Directorate and the Independent Police Complaints Commission, 2005 (available at <http://www.cps.gov.uk/publications/agencies/index.html> – accessed 5 January 2010).

[4] Following *DPP, ex p Manning* [2000]. For further discussion, see Burton M, 'Reviewing CPS Decisions Not to Prosecute' [2001] Crim LR 374.   [5] *The Guardian*, 5 December 1997.

[6] IPCC, *The Death of Harry Stanley* (2006). Available at <http://www.ipcc.gov.uk/stanley_ipcc_decision_feb_06.pdf>. This was based on an investigation by Surrey Police: <http://www.ipcc.gov.uk/stanley_report_to_ipcc_03.02.06_for_publication.pdf> (both accessed 5 January 2010). Also see Inquest, *Death in Police Custody: Report on Harry Stanley* (London: Inquest, 2000, updated 2002) and *The Guardian*, 10 February 2006. The IPCC again criticised the police for colluding with each other when writing statements in its report on the shooting of Jean Charles de Menezes (*The Guardian*, 9 November 2007).

12.4, the police do get away with this type of behaviour, and so hardly any complaints, whether of criminal conduct or other kinds of rule-breaking, are 'substantiated' (ie proved on the balance of probabilities).

Even where there does seem to be sufficient evidence the decision is often taken not to prosecute. Take the notorious West Midlands Police Serious Crime Squad. The inquiry in the early 1990s into its alleged fraud, perjury, corruption, fabrication of evidence and assault cost £4m. At least 15 people convicted on evidence produced by the squad were released by the Court of Appeal. Not one police officer was prosecuted, despite the West Yorkshire police investigation into the squad recommending some prosecutions.[7] In *DPP, ex p Treadaway*[8] the Divisional Court ordered the Director of Public Prosecutions (DPP) to reconsider the decision not to prosecute four of these officers, said by the High Court judge in a civil action five years earlier, to have 'tortured' Treadaway.[9]

The ubiquity of CCTV and mobile phone cameras makes it easier to find evidence of assault. In the G20 protests in April 2009 where Ian Tomlinson was killed after being struck by an officer (the videos were viewed by millions on YouTube), CCTV caught an officer repeatedly striking a 35-year-old woman. He is now being prosecuted for assault.[10] But in 2003, CCTV footage clearly showed two officers holding a black man down while another kicked him, yet there were no prosecutions in that case.[11] Similarly, Faisal Al-Ani's fatal mistreatment by police was captured on CCTV but, again, no officers were prosecuted.[12]

Even when officers are prosecuted, convictions are rare. In 1998 armed police raided James Ashley's house. Naked and unarmed, he was shot by PC Sherwood, who was prosecuted. CPS then discontinued the prosecution, saying that 'the depth of corporate failure in Sussex Police was too great to make any individual responsible'.[13] In another case, PC Jones and five other officers were accused of assaulting and racially abusing two teenagers of Asian origin. They all gave evidence backing each other up, and were acquitted in July 2009 despite evidence corroborating the victims' account by an officer who witnessed the arrest. The jury had not been told of the 31 complaints made against Jones, mostly of assault against BME people, nor of the £60,000 paid in damages by Metropolitan police because of a racist assault he committed in 2003.[14] These cases show why the CPS often justifies its reluctance to prosecute

---

[7] *The Guardian*, 28 July 1994; House of Commons, Home Affairs Select Committee, Police Disciplinary and Complaints Procedure, 1st Report (HC 258–1, 1998) paras 24, 91.

[8] Legal Action, October 1997, p 15.

[9] Treadaway was awarded £50,000 compensation. See Smith G, 'The DPP and Prosecutions of Police Officers' (1997) 147 NLJ 1180, 8 August.

[10] *The Guardian*, 29 September 2009. At the time of writing the case had not been decided. Nor has any decision yet been taken regarding Tomlinson's death.   [11] *The Guardian*, 9 August 2005.

[12] See <http://www.cps.gov.uk/news/press_releases/156_07/> (accessed 5 January 2010).

[13] Hansard 11 Feb 2002 Col 47. This and the subsequent civil case is discussed in Palmer P and Steele J, 'Police Shootings and the Role of Tort' (2008) 71 MLR 801.

[14] *The Guardian*, 4 November 2009. The assault was against Babar Ahmad: see 12.3.3.

by the need for a 'reasonable prospect of conviction'. And many less serious assault allegations are not prosecuted because the police counter-punch by prosecuting the complainant. By the time that case is concluded the six month time limit (applicable in common assault cases) has usually passed[15] – especially if the complainant pleads not guilty as would be usual if the police were prosecuting merely to undermine a valid complaint.

Another serious concern over the years has been deaths in police custody. Like deaths at work, it is a reasonable prima facie assumption that these deaths occur because of a breach of duty on the part of the police (or, in the case of deaths at work, the employer). Manslaughter by omission (ie gross negligence manslaughter) should be prosecuted if death or GBH is foreseeable. If the death is caused by an unlawful act, say an assault, then constructive manslaughter, whereby only some harm need be foreseeable, should be prosecuted. As with deaths at work, manslaughter prosecutions are very rare. Occasionally, though, a particularly disturbing case comes to light. In 1997 two inquest juries found that Oluwashhijibomi Lapite and Richard O'Brien had been 'unlawfully killed' while in police custody. Lapite had 45 injuries. O'Brien had 31 injuries. The DPP nonetheless decided not to prosecute in either case. Only when these decisions were judicially reviewed, were officers prosecuted (but acquitted) for the death of O'Brien.[16]

These deaths in custody were the subject of an official report by a former judge who decided that there was no pro-police bias and that there was no police-CPS conspiracy.[17] As Smith observes, this misses the point that the CPS is dependent on the police (and now, where applicable, IPCC) investigation.[18] Only occasionally does enough independent evidence emerge to convince a civil court or inquest that the weak police construction is faulty. There has never, in recent years, been enough evidence to secure a conviction for a death in custody. Having said that, when inquest juries give verdicts of unlawful death, and civil courts award damages for torts that also constitute crimes, as happened in several of these cases, it is hard to see how there cannot be a reasonable prospect of conviction. Civil cases generally require proof only on a balance of probabilities, and that is precisely what is meant by 'a reasonable prospect of conviction' (Burton 2001). When Christopher Alder died in custody the violence and gross negligence of the police was caught on a 12-minute video. But the DPP only decided to review the decision not to prosecute for manslaughter after an inquest decided that he had been unlawfully killed.[19]

---

[15] HMIC/HMCPSI (2007: paras 7.26–7.27).

[16] Smith (1997); Coles D and Murphy F, 'O'Brien: Another Death in Police Custody' (1999) Legal Action, Nov, p 6. The DPP reaffirmed the decision not to prosecute the officers in the Lapite case: Burton (2001).

[17] Butler G, Inquiry into Crown Prosecution Service Decision-Making in Relation to Deaths in Custody and Related Matters (London: SO, 1999).

[18] Smith G, 'The Butler Report: An Opportunity Missed?' (1999b) 149 NLJ 20 August. Also see Smith G, 'Police Complaints and Criminal Prosecutions' (2001) 64 MLR 372.

[19] The Guardian, 25 August 2000. The judge at the manslaughter trial ordered the acquittal of the officers involved, who were eventually pensioned off without further action: The Guardian, 24 December 2004.

12.2.2 **The public interest test**

Althea Burnett, a blind mother of three, was playing with her children one Sunday afternoon in July 1996 when there was a knock at the front door of her South London home. She was surprised to be confronted by a man and a woman who identified themselves as police officers. 'The woman said that somebody had taken a taxi from my address the previous day and left without paying,' she says. The police were reluctant to believe her when she said she was unable to identify the woman whom she had met only once… 'I was getting frightened. The children were also getting frightened,' says Burnett. 'I told the police I was blind and couldn't see what the woman looked like, but they kept asking me to identify her.' Burnett began to shut the door. As she did so, it flew open and 'my arm was grabbed for what felt like a long time'…

Burnett says that by now she could hear many more police and she was dragged into the street without her shoes, while her children were screaming. Both Burnett and her mother repeatedly told the police she was blind but she claims she was given no guide as she was manhandled to a police van. 'I was pleading with them to let go and for someone to guide me.'

She was detained for more than an hour before being released without charge. She was given a warning for what the police claim was an assault on one of their officers but she denies any offence, saying that the supposed assault occurred when she put her arm out as the police grabbed her.

Since the incident, she has been diagnosed as suffering from chronic post-traumatic stress disorder. She has had bars put on the windows and is nervous of opening the door. 'My children are still upset and my son doesn't want to go to school.'

The Crown Prosecution Service wrote to her solicitor admitting that 'the arrest was unlawful and therefore constituted an assault and false imprisonment.' But after two years no police officer had been charged with an offence or disciplined. A CPS letter in April [1998]…says: 'We concluded that these offences were somewhat of a technical nature…A criminal court was unlikely to impose more than a very small penalty…the loss of liberty lasting in total one hour and a quarter.'[20]

In the above example, there was no doubt that there was sufficient evidence to justify prosecution, but the CPS (displaying an appalling lack of empathy) concluded that it was not in the public interest to bring proceedings. That this is a general problem is indicated by table 12.1. This shows that there were just 23 prosecutions of police officers for non-traffic offences in 2003/04 arising from substantiated complaints – that is, there were prosecutions in about 18% of the (very few) cases where on balance it was believed that one or more officers had indeed committed crime. Even young juveniles are prosecuted in higher proportions than this. Another way of counting probable crimes that are not prosecuted was given in 4.4, where research showed that only about one-third of deaths attributable to police actions are prosecuted.[21]

---

[20] *The Guardian*, June 1998.
[21] See further Leigh et al, *Deaths in Police Custody: Learning the Lessons* (Home Office Police Research Series, Paper 26) (London: TSO, 1998).

Table 12.1 Prosecutions of police officers following a substantiated complaint of a criminal character (2003/04)

	Number of substantiated complaints	Number of substantiated complaints which led to prosecution
Assault	99	
Perjury/irregular evidence	26	
Corrupt practices	5	
Total	130	23

Source: Cotton J, *Police Complaints and Discipline* 2003–4, Statistical Bulletin, 17/04 (London: Home Office, 2004) tables 7 and 8. Note these are the most up-to-date statistics available as they are no longer published. Though IPCC statistics indicate that there were 15 convictions of officers for assault following complaints in 2004/05, these tables have also been discontinued.

It follows that the overwhelming majority of cases are not prosecuted on 'public interest' grounds, which means the DPP behaves towards police officers rather as the Health and Safety Executive behaves towards companies (see 7.5). Something akin to the 'compliance' approach appears to operate, as in 2003/04 there were more resignations (31) than there were prosecutions – an either/or approach that is rarely offered to 'normal' people who commit crimes of violence or dishonesty in the course of their work. It was commended by a Chief Constable thus: 'We have rectified the wrong ... do we now still need to prosecute?'[22] In thinking about this, consider the following cases. Five men were tried for murder. The trial was stopped by the judge and declared an 'abuse of process'[23] when it emerged that he had been lied to by the Detective Chief Inspector in charge of the investigation. For this crime of perjury the DCI was neither prosecuted nor disciplined. Instead, he was allowed to retire and collect his pension.[24] And in 2003 four officers were condemned as 'vicious cowardly racists' by a judge who awarded one of their victims £250,000 in damages for, among other injuries, a partially paralysed arm. The CPS decided not to prosecute because of 'the passage of time'.[25]

These non-prosecution decisions are inconsistent with the Code for Crown Prosecutors, which states that: 'A prosecution is likely to be needed if ... the defendant was in a position of authority or trust' (para 5.9) and with the police discipline regulations that require the 'public interest' to be considered in deciding whether to allow officers to retire and thus avoid disciplinary charges.[26] Nor should discipline be

---

[22] Quoted in Smith (2001: 383).   [23] 'Abuse of process' is discussed in 12.5 below.

[24] *Manchester Metro News*, November 26 2004. See further: Quinton P, *An Evaluation of the New Police Misconduct Procedures* (Home Office Online Report 10/03) (London: Home Office, 2003).

[25] *The Guardian*, 27 September 2006.

[26] See *R (on the application of Coghlan) v Chief Constable of Greater Manchester; R v Chief Constable of Devon and Cornwall ex p Hay*, both discussed in 12.4 below.

a substitute for prosecution, but a study by HMCPSI 'revealed some examples where this factor had received some consideration'.[27] HMCPSI disagreed with three of the 80 police complaint cases it examined, all of which were non-prosecution decisions. In two the 'public interest' had worked to the advantage of the officers concerned.[28]

There are also more fundamental questions: first, how malpractice in general is investigated (see 12.4 below).[29] Second, why these suspect/alleged criminal offences are treated differently from 'normal' crimes in some respects (not recorded as crimes, and treated initially as mere discipline matters) but inappropriately similar in another (the police, in most cases, investigating allegations against fellow officers).[30] Third, a third of the fifteen people who died following their arrest or detention by the police in 2008/09 were from ethnic minorities.[31] Butler stated that he could discern no bias against 'any section of the community' in the way the cases were dealt with, but did not express concern that police stations are disproportionately dangerous for ethnic minorities as compared to white people.

However, the most important reason why most malpractice and law-breaking is not prosecuted is because it is not contrary to the criminal law. This might seem a non sequitur. After all, there are all sorts of things that we might like to be criminal but which are not, like the humiliation of students by egotistical academics in tutorials. But what the police do is different because of their power. 'Normal' people cannot make you stop and explain yourself time after time. The police can (see ch 2). Doing it wrongly breaks the law, but it does not break the criminal law. The same applies to detaining you when it is not 'necessary', exiling you to a cell between interrogations, exerting improper pressure on you for information when your solicitor is not there to protect you, not telling your family why you have disappeared and that you are (relatively) safe, denying you bail so you spend another night in a cell stinking of vomit and urine, 'fixing' ID parades, tapping your phone or turning your house over without authorisation, and putting you through the prosecution mill only to drop the case weeks or months later (see chs 4–7). Girma Belay (see 1.9.2) was shattered by what the police did to him as much as if he had been the victim of a street gang. In an age when it is a crime to drop a crisp packet, to swear at a football match, or to forget to buy a TV licence, but not a crime to abuse people in these ways, it looks like the freedom perspective is yet to be recognised by modern governments.

---

[27] HMCPSI, *Review of HQ Casework* (London: HMCPSI, 2002a) para 2.25.

[28] Ibid, paras 2.19–2.20 and annexe 2. The later HMIC/HMCPSI (2007) report disagreed with very few of the decisions it examined.

[29] For a critical discussion, see Amnesty International, *Deaths in Police Custody: Lack of Police Accountability* (London: AI, 2000).

[30] Smith G, 'Police Complaints and Criminal Prosecutions' (2001) 64 MLR 372. And see his 'Rethinking Police Complaints' (2004) 44 BJ Crim 15. Also see Vogt G and Wadham J, *Deaths in Police Custody: Redress and Remedies* (London: Civil Liberties Trust, 2003) whose analysis is similar to ours, particularly in relation to the CPS, and who make several recommendations for reform.

[31] IPCC, *Annual Report and Statement of Accounts 2008/9* (London: IPCC, 2009a) p 21.

12.3 **Civil actions**

12.3.1 **Causes of action**

Earlier chapters showed that numerous statutes have defined a large number of police powers and rights for suspects. But, typically, no specific enforcement mechanisms or civil remedies accompany these provisions. Section 67(10) of PACE, for example, provides that a failure on the part of a police officer to comply with any of their provisions 'shall not of itself render him liable to any criminal or civil proceedings'.[32] People whose ECHR rights are infringed (eg Art 6 rights to a fair trial as a result of improper interrogation, or Art 8 rights to privacy as a result of an illegal bugging or house search) may sue and be compensated.[33] But unless a breach of legislation or a code of practice breaches the ECHR, claimants must make such use as they can of existing tortious remedies, developed many years before police forces and modern investigative techniques were created. We look here at the torts which might be used by people suspected or accused of crime (remedies for victims and witnesses are discussed in ch 13).[34]

(a) *False imprisonment:* This applies to unlawful police detention. It should include detention in breach of the 'necessity' rule in s 37 of PACE but the only case on s 37 that has been appealed makes that 'rule' entirely presentational.[35] A two-hour delay in a review of detention has also been held to be false imprisonment even though detention was confirmed, and so the complainant would have been in custody for the two hours concerned anyway.[36] In the light of this, the courts' decisions that unlawful detention conditions (eg denying suspects refreshment or sleep) do not make the detention itself unlawful,[37] are bizarre: compensating someone who has not suffered but not compensating someone who has, even though both types of loss are at the hands of the police in police stations, reflects the absence of appropriate remedies.

False imprisonment also applies to wrongful arrest[38] as it involves the unlawful infliction of bodily restraint. Bodily restraint is the essence of arrest, police station detention and stop-search. It should therefore follow that unlawful stop-search be subject to the tort of false imprisonment, but, once again, we know of no such successful actions. There is, otherwise, no specific civil action available in relation to stop-search.

---

[32] PACE, s 67(8) made a breach of its Codes of Practice a disciplinary offence, but this was repealed in 1996.

[33] HRA 1998, ss 7 and 8. See further, Naughton M, 'Redefining Miscarriages of Justice' (2005) BJ Crim 165 at 175.

[34] For details of all the torts discussed here see: Harrison et al, *Police Misconduct: Legal Remedies*, 4th edn (London: LAG, 2005).

[35] *Al-Fayed v Commissioner of the Police of the Metropolis* [2004], discussed in 4.3.

[36] *Roberts v Chief Constable of Cheshire Police* [1999] 1 WLR 662.

[37] See eg *Williams v Home Office (No 2)* [1981] 1 All ER 1211.

[38] See eg *Wershof v Metropolitan Police Comr* [1978] 3 All ER 540, discussed in 12.3.3 below.

(b) *Trespass:* If the police enter property without lawful authority, an action for trespass may follow. This can occur when an arrest warrant is invalid, or in the purported exercising of other police powers, such as search and/or seizure of property (see ch 6).

(c) *Assault and intimidation:* Anything in excess of 'reasonable force' to effect an arrest is an assault, as in *Adorian v MPC*, where a man subsequently conditionally discharged for obstructing the police suffered, in the course of arrest, multiple head, leg and hip fractures: 'a class of injury associated with head-on car crashes or falls from a significant height'.[39] But it is 'reasonable', for example, to allow a dog to inflict 'very nasty' injuries on a fleeing drink-drive suspect.[40] The threat of an unlawful act (for example, unreasonable use of force) is intimidation.[41] This may also occur if the police try to secure a confession through threats.[42]

(d) *Malicious prosecution and malicious process:* If a prosecution is initiated both without prima facie evidence and maliciously, the defendant may sue for malicious prosecution.[43] Few cases are successful, for courts give prosecutors considerable latitude in determining that there was prima facie evidence,[44] and proving the subjective state of mind of 'malice' is intrinsically difficult. In *Paul v CC Humberside*[45] two men had a fight. One later died in police custody – the infamous *Alder* case (see 12.2 above). Paul tried to break up the initial fight and later came forward as a voluntary witness. The police arrested and prosecuted him for murder. When it was established that the blow he allegedly struck was unconnected with Alder's death the charge was changed to GBH, and subsequently the case was discontinued. Paul claimed that the police prosecuted him simply to divert attention from their own contribution to Alder's death – ie maliciously. The claim failed initially as the trial judge removed the issue from the jury. Paul successfully appealed against this ruling and a retrial was ordered. At the retrial an eight-strong jury decided unanimously that that it was 'more likely than not that the police charged [Mr Paul] with causing GBH with intent to deflect potential criticism of the circumstances of Christopher Alder's death' and seven of them concluded that the initial arrest was similarly motivated. Paul was awarded £30,500.[46] The first trial illustrates how hard it is to convince a judge that the police acted wrongly, even though the use of prosecution to cover up their own misdeeds is a well-known police tactic.[47] 'Malicious process' – such as securing a search warrant maliciously – is

---

[39] [2009] EWCA Civ 18 per Sedley LJ. [40] *Roberts v CC Kent* [2008] EWCA Civ 1588.

[41] See eg *Allen v Metropolitan Police Comr* [1980] Crim LR 441.

[42] See, for example, the case of George Lewis, discussed in (e) below.

[43] The police would still be liable, despite statutory charging, if (as is usual) the CPS based its actions solely on the file submitted to it by the police: *Clifford v CC Hertfordshire* [2008] EWHC 3154 QB.

[44] See for example *Coudrat v Commissioners of HM Revenue and Customs* [2005] EWCA Civ 616.

[45] *Paul v CC Humberside* [2004] EWCA Civ 308.

[46] See <http://news.bbc.co.uk/1/hi/england/humber/4656112.stm> (accessed 5 January 2010).

[47] Smith G, 'Actions for Damages against the Police and the Attitudes of Claimants' (2003) 13 Policing and Society 413. Also see ch 7 and several of the cases in 12.3.3 below. For a rare example of a successful claim in such a case, see *Thompson v Metropolitan Police Commissioner* [1997] 2 All ER 762.

similar, and negligence is not enough.[48] In both actions the prosecution has to have been resolved in the defendant's favour either through discontinuance or acquittal.[49] This is an application of the crime control principle that the end justifies the means. No matter how malicious a prosecution might have been, a person has no remedy if convicted.

(e) *Wrongful conviction:* Statutory compensation for wrongful conviction is normally only available where the conviction is overturned 'on the ground that a new or newly discovered fact shows beyond reasonable doubt that there has been a miscarriage of justice', and only if this follows a referral by the Criminal Cases Review Commission rather than 'within time' standard appeal procedures.[50] It can take many years for compensation to be settled, leaving victims of miscarriages of justice virtually penniless in the meantime. An example of a successful claimant is George Lewis who was arrested by the infamous West Midlands Police Serious Crime Squad in 1987. He was head-butted, punched, racially abused and threatened with a syringe unless he signed blank sheets of interview notes. Police officers said he confessed in the car. He was convicted of armed robbery and spent over five years in jail until the Court of Appeal ordered a retrial (which the CPS abandoned). Eventually, in 1998, he received £200,000 compensation.[51] An exceptional case was that of Colin Stagg who spent a year in custody awaiting trial for the murder of Rachel Nickell (discussed in 6.3). He received £706,000 from a discretionary government scheme even though he was not convicted (the actual killer, Robert Napper, was eventually convicted),[52] partly because, in the words of the judge at his trial, the police engaged in 'a blatant attempt to incriminate [him] by positive and deceptive conduct of the grossest kind'.[53] The discretionary scheme has now been scrapped, leaving those outside the statutory scheme with no remedy other than to sue for compensation in the civil courts.[54]

(f) *Breach of statutory duty:* This arises where no other remedy is available. However, it is unclear whether this action is possible in respect of all or even any breaches of PACE, and it certainly does not apply to rights found in the codes of practice only (such as the right to be informed of one's rights and the right not to be held incommunicado) as the latter are not statutes. In *Cullen v Chief Constable of the RUC*[55] the

---

[48] See the search warrant case of *Keegan v Chief Constable of Merseyside Police* [2003] 1 WLR 2187, discussed in 6.5.1.   [49] See, for example, *Martin v Watson* [1996] AC 74.
[50] CJA 1988, s 133, as amended (restrictively) by s 61 of the Criminal Justice and Immigration Act 2008. The interpretation of these provisions is not straightforward: Roberts S, 'Unsafe Convictions: Defining and Compensating Miscarriages of Justice' (2003) MLR 441. See also *R (Mullen) v Home Secretary* [2004] UKHL 18; *R (Allen) v Justice Secretary* [2008] EWCA Civ 808; *R (Adams) v Justice Secretary* [2009] EWHC 156 Admin. For other possibilities see <http://www.cjsonline.gov.uk/the_cjs/how_it_works/wrongful_conviction/> (accessed 5 January 2010).   [51] *The Guardian*, 20 January 1998.
[52] *The Guardian*, 19 December 2008.
[53] *The Guardian*, 14 August 2008. The scheme is discussed in *R(Niazi and Ors) v Home Secretary* [2008] EWCA Civ 755.
[54] See <http://business.timesonline.co.uk/tol/business/law/article4619822.ece> (accessed 5 January 2010).   [55] *Cullen v Chief Constable of the RUC* [2003] 1 WLR 1763.

police in Northern Ireland breached the equivalent of s 58 PACE by not giving reasons for denying a suspect in custody access to legal advice. The House of Lords held that as the denial was justified, no real harm was done, so the action failed, but left the door open for similar claims.

12.3.2 Rights but what remedies?

Just as the biggest obstacle in the way of prosecuting the police is that much malpractice which would be criminal if done by 'normal' people is not criminal when done by the police, the same is true of suing the police. No civil actions are possible in respect of much of the subject matter of this book, such as the right to legal advice, not to be kept incommunicado, and to be informed of one's rights; and the duties of the police to interrogate in accordance with Code of Practice C. These provisions are at the centre of the 'balance' struck by the Royal Commission on Criminal Procedure (Philips Commission): a quid pro quo for increasing police powers (regarding stop-search and pre-charge detention, for example). It was supposedly because these safeguards were so powerful that the right of silence had to go (see 5.3). Loss of reputation can be compensated by suing for libel. Homeless travellers can be ejected from one's holiday cottage, development land or empty office block and sued for the owner's loss of amenity. But there is no such remedy if one is isolated from a lawyer and/or induced into a false confession through lies or deception.[56] The human rights perspective has little to say about the inadequate protection of the rights of suspects and the ECHR has barely increased the remedies available.[57]

How well do civil remedies work at the general level of deterring or controlling malpractice? Since torts are not crimes, punishment and deterrence are not the main objectives, so 'damages' are awarded simply to compensate for loss. But since torts are wrongs, it is sometimes possible to award 'punitive' or 'exemplary' damages. In the classic American Ford Pinto case huge punitive damages were awarded against Ford because it knew that the Pinto car had a dangerous design fault, but calculated that it would be cheaper to pay the occasional fatal damages claim than to change the design.[58] Punitive damages can be awarded against public bodies in relation to 'oppressive, arbitrary or unconstitutional action by the servants of government'[59] where 'the official acted intentionally or maliciously… with a reckless disregard for its legality'.[60] This is to punish and deter, but when the police lose an action it is not the individual officers who pay the damages but the police organisation, blunting the potential

---

[56] Sanders A, 'Rights, Remedies and the Police and Criminal Evidence Act' [1988b] Crim LR 802.

[57] Ashworth A and Redmayne M, *The Criminal Process*, 3rd edn (Oxford: OUP, 2005), the first edition of which blazed the trail for the human rights perspective on criminal justice in this country, does not even discuss the issue.   [58] See <http://www.calbaptist.edu/dskubik/pinto.htm> (accessed 5 January 2010).

[59] *Rookes v Barnard* [1964]. Now also see *Holden v Chief Constable of Lancashire* [1987].

[60] Cane P, *Tort Law and Economic Interests* (Oxford: OUP, 1996) p 301.

impact of punitive damages. Exemplary damages are not awarded if the police were provoked by the plaintiff[61] or if the police made a genuine mistake.[62]

Actions for damages against the Metropolitan Police in particular increased in the early 1990s (see 12.3.3 below) with large amounts of exemplary damages frequently awarded. Matters came to a head in *Thompson v Metropolitan Police Comr, Hsu v Metropolitan Police Comr* [1997] 2 All ER 762. In these two separate cases Miss Thompson was lawfully arrested for drink-driving. She objected to being put in a cell, and was assaulted by four or five officers. She was charged with assault, kept in custody and prosecuted. She brought a civil action and was awarded damages for assault, false imprisonment and malicious prosecution. In Mr Hsu's case, two officers demanded entry to his home because of a complaint by a former lodger of Hsu's that he had some of her belongings and would not let her collect them. Hsu refused to let them in as they had no search warrant. They attempted to force their way in. When Hsu tried to stop them they assaulted him several times (including a kick that caused internal injuries), racially abused him, arrested and detained him in the police station for over an hour and refused to take him home even though he had no shoes on. The jury awarded Hsu £220,000, £200,000 of which was punitive damages, and awarded lesser amounts to Thompson. The Court of Appeal reduced Hsu's punitive damages to £15,000; said that Thompson should only have received £25,000; and set an absolute limit for sums of punitive damages in cases against the police of £50,000.[63] The civil juries in these cases decided that the police officers committed crimes and so naturally people feel a need for elements of deterrence and punishment. That need would be better served through prosecutions, but we have already seen how rare this is, and the officers in these cases were not prosecuted. A more vigorous prosecution policy would enable civil actions to focus on the issue of compensation. As it is, we have a lackadaisical prosecution policy and an increasingly strait-jacketed civil regime.

12.3.3 Pursuing civil actions

Having the right to sue does not mean that one is always able to sue. The first problem is establishing a case on the balance of probabilities (the civil standard of proof), when it is usually just one person's word against another's. Evidence of previous malpractice by the officers concerned can assist. But it is hard to obtain because the main way in which malpractice can be demonstrated is the deeply flawed complaints system (see 12.4). In *Scott v Chief Constable of South Yorkshire* [2006] 3 All ER (D) 412 (Mar). an officer who appears to have made an unlawful arrest was given 'advice' instead of being brought before a disciplinary hearing. This meant that the complaint was

---

[61] *O'Connor v Hewitson* [1979] Crim LR 46: police unnecessarily punched person who resisted arrest.

[62] *Wershof v Metropolitan Police Comr* [1978] 3 All ER 540: solicitor arrested in public and marched down a street in a half-nelson.

[63] For detailed discussion see Dixon B and Smith G, 'Laying Down the Law: The Police, the Courts and Legal Accountability' (1998) 26 IJ Soc of Law 419.

'unsubstantiated' and therefore did not need to be disclosed in a later action against the same officer for similar malpractice. The second problem is that many people cannot afford the cost of their own lawyers, let alone those hired by the police, and suspects are disproportionately drawn from the poorest sections of society. Legal aid is, in principle, available for those who cannot afford to sue. However, the means test has been steadily tightened up over the last 25 years, making an ever smaller proportion of the population eligible for legal aid. Although 'no win, no fee' agreements are now possible, the case has to be strong and financially attractive before a solicitor will take it on.[64] The third problem is the 'merits' test. Legal aid is generally only granted if the action would be worth bringing were it to be privately funded. The considerations are: likelihood of success; whether there is an alternative remedy; and cost in relation to the likely level of damages.[65] Legal aid may be provided if: 'The likely benefits of the proceedings justify the likely costs, having regard to the prospects of success and all other circumstances.'[66]

How does this work in practice? The Court of Appeal in *Hsu and Thompson*[67] set out 'starting points' for non-punitive damages. These were (in the late 1990s): £500 for each hour of unlawful detention on a reducing scale. Presumably, then, a wrongful stop-search or arrest which did not lead to police station detention would attract far less than £500. Such a brief detention, even if accompanied by an assault not causing injury, would not attract significant damages even if a claim of assault was upheld, so legal aid would generally not be provided.[68] Malicious prosecution would be a different matter. In *Hsu* it was decided that damages for malicious prosecution should begin at £2,000 because the suffering is drawn-out while fighting one's case.

Serious malpractice can attract significant damages. In *Hsu* the Court of Appeal decided that each plaintiff should receive £20,000 in non-punitive damages. Opinions on whether that was sufficient compensation for the degrading and unlawful actions of the police might legitimately differ. But it is hard for us to understand the psychological impact of such treatment if we have not experienced it ourselves.

Most cases are settled out of court. The plaintiff generally accepts a lower level of damages but avoids the delay involved in pursuing court proceedings and the risk of losing. However, the opportunity that a public court hearing would have provided for bringing police officers to account is lost. When police forces settle they avoid the

---

[64] See, for discussion of Conditional Fees Agreements, Legal Action, March 2000, p 17 and Harrison et al (2005: 417–18).

[65] These matters are all governed by the Funding Code of the Legal Services Commission (LSC) and the 2005 Legal Services Commission guidelines, made under the Access to Justice Act 1999. See generally Harrison et al (2005: ch 11).   [66] LSC Funding Code, section 8 and para 5.7.3.

[67] *Hsu and Thompson* [1997] 2 All ER 762.

[68] However, legal aid can be granted where the applicant's status, reputation or dignity was particularly harmed even if the monetary amount is small. See Blake C, 'Legal Aid: Past, Present and Future' (2000) Legal Action, Jan, p 6. See generally Harrison et al (2005: ch 11). Also, punitive damages can be awarded for 'misfeasance in a public office', where the misfeasance interferes with the claimant's constitutional rights: *Watkins v Home Secretary* [2006] UKHL 17. The extent to which abuses of police power are regarded as breaches of constitutional rights remains to be seen.

shame of a public hearing and adjudication and do not admit liability. Thus most civil actions do little to punish, deter or genuinely compensate for the suffering. Take Leslie Burnett, who in 1988 was stopped by two officers who said they saw him tampering with a car. He was kicked, stamped and racially abused. At the police station: 'They all came to look at me like I was an exhibit in a zoo…and laughing.' Charged with assaulting the police, he was acquitted. In 1991 the Metropolitan Police settled out-of-court, awarding him £40,000 plus costs. But the police did not admit liability nor apologise to him. Mr Burnett said: 'I feel very bitter.…I see the officers in the street and they laugh at me. Why are they still in the police?'[69]

Since 1988 history has repeated itself several times. Babar Ahmad was arrested in 2003 for suspected terrorism. A civil jury awarded £60,000 to compensate him for being punched, stamped on, kicked and strangled. Yet the officer who did this remained in the police and continued to attract complaints of racist assault and was (unsuccessfully) prosecuted in 2009.[70] In the infamous Stephen Lawrence case, Duwayne Brooks was one of the victims but was treated by the police as a suspect. He was arrested for the murder of his friend simply because a) he was there; and b) he was black. He was then repeatedly charged with offences, all of which failed in court. The police finally agreed to settle the case for £100,000 in 2006 – 13 years after the initial assault.[71] Not by coincidence, Francisco Borg is another black man who, with a friend, was attacked by a gang in 1997, and asked the police for help. Instead, he was sprayed with CS gas, arrested and prosecuted. After the police dropped the charges Mr Borg began civil proceedings. The police gave him £40,000 in an out-of-court settlement in 2003, after the arresting officer admitted giving 'incorrect information'. Like Burnett, he remained aggrieved at the police attitude.[72]

Overall, tens or even hundreds of millions of pounds have been paid to victims of malpractice over the last 30 years. For example, in the 17 years from 1991 to 2008, the Metropolitan Police alone paid out some £30m.[73] Table 12.2 shows that, although the amount of compensation and number of successful actions has declined from its peak in the late 1990s, each year still sees well over 100 successful actions, costing over £1m/year in compensation alone. No figures are available for the English and Welsh police as a whole, which is in itself scandalous. But there must be hundreds of successful cases, at a cost of several million pounds against the police as a whole each year, despite all of the obstacles strewn in the path of those wanting to sue the police.

From the due process viewpoint a growth in successful civil actions represents justice, and no more need be said. But both crime control and freedom perspectives suggest the money could be better spent on more positive aspects of policing. The crime

[69] *The Guardian*, 2 July 1991.

[70] *The Guardian*, 4 November 2009. This officer, PC Jones, is a member of the squad referred to in the quote at the start of this chapter and in 12.2.1.   [71] *The Guardian*, 10 March 2006.

[72] *The Guardian*, 24 April 2003. Claimants are generally more concerned that their grievances get an airing, and that the police recognise their mistakes and put measures in place to reduce the risk of recurrence, than to secure large amounts of money in compensation: Smith (2003).

[73] See Metropolitan Police Commissioner, Annual Reports.

Table 12.2 Successful civil actions against the Metropolitan Police

	1991/92	1997/98	2000/01	2003/04	2005/06	2007/08
Actions resulting in compensation paid	127	389	235	166	126	144
Amount paid	Nk	Nk	£2.7m	£1.7m	£1.9m	£1.1m

Source: Metropolitan Police Commissioner, Annual Reports and Metropolitan Police Service, *Metropolitan Police Service and Police Authority Annual Report* 2004/05 and 2007/08 (London: MPS/MPA, 2005 and 2009). It is not known why the number of successful actions and sums awarded have fallen in the last few years, though the 'counting rules' changed in 2005/06.

control adherent would first act, as the Court of Appeal did in *Hsu*, to reduce the amount of money paid out. And, second, do as the Legal Services Commission has done, and insist that the police complaints system is normally used first on the questionable assumption that under the IPCC it is a less biased system than previously.[74]

For us, the answer is to tackle the problem at source by reducing the amount of malpractice so that there are fewer victims and less money paid out. This means creating organisational structures and cultures which discourage malpractice. For cases like Leslie Burnett's seem to have done little either to change police behaviour or to protect the freedom of people like him. Clearly civil actions do not succeed well in deterring malpractice, otherwise the number and value of civil claims would be fewer now than 15 years earlier, not greater.

12.4 **Complaints against the police**

Nicola Dennis was grabbed from her doorway and held face-down at gunpoint on a pavement with her hands bound behind her back for over 15 minutes by the police. 'I thought I was going to die.' The police officer who later visited her at her home explained that she was 'in the wrong place at the wrong time'. A court later condemned the view of the IPCC (which oversees complaints against the police) that the complaint be resolved by offering only 'words of advice' to the officer concerned, but at the time of writing nothing else has happened.[75]

Most bureaucracies and public agencies maintain some form of grievance procedure for handling complaints by citizens of shoddy treatment. The 1964 Police Act required

[74] Discretion is retained to by-pass the complaints system: Legal Services Commission, Funding Code Amendments 2005. This followed a proposal on these lines in a Consultation Paper: Legal Services Commission, *A New Focus for Civil Legal Aid* (London: LSC, 2004) paras 4.7–4.10. See <http://www.legalservices.gov.uk/civil/guidance/funding_code.asp> (accessed 15 December 2009).

[75] *Legal Action* June 2008, p 4. See *R (Dennis) v IPCC* [2008] EWHC 1158 (Admin).

that all complaints against the police be recorded and investigated by either a senior officer from the force or, where complaints were particularly serious, from a different force. Reports of the investigation generally went to the deputy chief constable, who decided whether or not there was evidence of:

(a) a criminal offence, in which case the file was sent to the DPP, who decided whether or not to prosecute;

(b) a disciplinary offence (including abuse of police power or the rights of suspects), in which case a disciplinary hearing might (but need not be) arranged; or

(c) no offence at all, in which case no action was taken.

For the police to investigate themselves, decide whether or not the investigations revealed grounds for complaint, and then (in non-criminal allegations) decide whether or not the complaint was proven, was crazy. The Police Act 1976 established a civilian Police Complaints Board (PCB). All procedures remained as before except that, where the police decided that there was no evidence for any proceedings, the file was passed onto the Board. In the nine years of its existence (1976–1985), the Board recommended charges in just 210 cases. This failed to enhance public confidence. PACE replaced the PCB with the Police Complaints Authority (PCA). But this, in itself, made little difference as the system was almost unchanged, except regarding the most serious complaints (where police investigations were supervised by the PCA). By the late 1980s, there were a huge number of investigations into, for example, incompetence (eg in the Hillsborough tragedy),[76] bribery and corruption, the planting of evidence, assault and the fabrication of confessions.[77]

Public confidence was low, and falling. In 1996, for the first time, more people did not trust the police to investigate themselves (40%) than did trust them (37%). Moreover, the percentage believing the PCA to be independent and impartial was 39% and 37% respectively.[78] Even the Police Federation's survey, conducted in 1997, produced similar results.[79] The lack of confidence was particularly marked in black communities, especially in the wake of the Stephen Lawrence scandal.[80] A drop in cases of complaints was mirrored by a rise in civil actions: the civil courts were filling a gap that

---

[76] See <http://www.contrast.org/hillsborough/> (accessed 5 January 2010).

[77] See Kaye T, 'Unsafe and Unsatisfactory?' Report of the Independent Inquiry into the Working Practices of the West Midlands Police Serious Crime Squad (London: Civil Liberties Trust, 1991) app A.

[78] Police Complaints Authority, Annual Report, 1995/6 (London: SO, 1996). See also Maguire M and Corbett C, A Study of the Police Complaints System (London: HMSO, 1991) pp 147–8, and Waters I and Brown K, 'Police Complaints and the Complainants' Experience' (2000) 40 BJ Crim 617. Both studies found that the majority of complainants were dissatisfied.

[79] House of Commons, Home Affairs Select Committee, Police Disciplinary and Complaints Procedure, 1st Report (HC 258-1, 1998), p 194. All these surveys are discussed in Harrison J and Cuneen M, An Independent Police Complaints Commission (London: Liberty, 2000).

[80] Sir William Macpherson of Cluny, The Stephen Lawrence Inquiry (Cm 4262-I) (London: SO, 1999). This was also found by the PCA's surveys.

the complaints system should fill.[81] The European Committee for the Prevention of Torture and Inhuman or Degrading Treatment or Punishment criticised the fact that 'the police themselves maintain a firm grip upon the handling of complaints against them.'[82] The Committee's view was based, in part, on its examination of Metropolitan Police files in which the police had settled cases where suspects were injured in police custody but there had been no prosecutions or disciplinary proceedings. We cannot make an independent assessment of whether the Committee's conclusions were justified, for the government censored these sections.[83] In *Khan*[84] an unlawful bugging was held to breach the ECHR Art 8. Under Art 13 everyone has a right to seek an effective remedy against allegedly unlawful actions. The English police complaints system did not provide this, according to the ECtHR, because of its lack of independence.

The momentum was unstoppable.[85] Under the Police Reform Act 2002 (PRA), Part 2, the PCA was replaced in 2004 by the IPCC. This is a civilian body with a staff of around 80 investigators, plus administrators, case workers and lawyers. The police still investigate the majority of (relatively minor) complaints themselves, but relatively serious cases are supervised by the IPCC, more serious ones are 'managed' by the IPCC, and the most serious are investigated by the IPCC itself. Conduct leading to death or serious injury is investigated by the IPCC whether or not there is a complaint.[86]

12.4.1 Investigation of complaints

The way in which the police investigate complaints is still the key to the process since only a very small number of cases are investigated by the IPCC: 106, in 2008/09, out of around 10,000 investigated cases (in addition, 117 were 'managed' and 167 were 'supervised'). Overall, then, around 95% are handled exactly as they were under the old system – the police investigate themselves. But whereas in the past the PCA scrutinised all police reports of their formal investigations (only a small proportion of all complaints, but several thousand a year), now the IPCC only looks at appeals by complainants (of which it upholds a relatively large proportion, though numbering only around 500 per year).[87]

Investigation used always to be by a senior officer who presented the report of the investigation to the appropriate assistant or deputy chief constable. Regardless of the seriousness of the complaint, or the wishes of the complainant, the procedure was the same. This was, for the majority of less serious complaints, disproportionate, over-bureaucratic and ineffective both in terms of helping officers improve their behaviour and reassuring complainants about this. Most cases are now handled differently, either

---

[81] Dixon and Smith (1998).   [82] Quoted in Harrison and Cuneen (2000: 1).

[83] *The Guardian*, 13 January 2000.   [84] *Khan (Sultan) v United Kingdom* [2000] Crim LR 684.

[85] For a discussion of this history of 'scandal and reform' see Smith G, 'A Most Enduring Problem: Police Complaints Reform in England and Wales' (2006) 35 J Social Policy 121.

[86] The more general role of the IPCC is discussed at the end of this section. For a detailed account of the powers, structure and work of the IPCC see Harrison et al (2005: ch 4).

[87] IPCC, *Annual Report and Accounts, 2008/9* (London: IPCC, 2009a).

through conciliation procedures (informal resolution: see 12.4.3) or new procedures as a result of the Taylor Review (see 12.4.5).

As far as 'supervised' investigations are concerned, Maguire and Corbett's (1991) study is still relevant. Initially the PCA (now IPCC) receives basic documentation (for example, the custody record, if the complainant was arrested) and can decide which officer from which force should investigate. It will also be given regular progress reports by investigating officers. Where this is all that supervision involves (and 60% of Maguire and Corbett's sample involved little or no discussion between the PCA and the investigating officer) it can be termed 'passive'. 'Active' supervision entails substantive discussion of the progress of investigations and occasional observation of interviews with witnesses, and comprised around 30% of their sample. In 10% or less was supervision 'directive', in the sense that investigating officers were formally requested to pursue particular lines of inquiry. Under the PRA, 'managed' cases are similar to 'directive' supervision, the idea being that IPCC control will be exercised on a day-to-day basis.

The report of a supervised investigation is sent to the IPCC and the police, in the first instance. The IPCC can request more information or further interviews. When the supervising member of the IPCC thinks that little more is to be gained from further investigation it accepts the report, which is then transmitted to the police. What action, if any, should follow from the investigation is considered by other IPCC members separately. Maguire and Corbett[88] found that at this stage PCA members frequently 'noted a lack of thoroughness' in investigation by which time nothing could be done about it. Even if all the investigation of all cases were supervised, and even if that supervision were not so inadequate, the notion of investigation by the police would still be fundamentally flawed. This is because the IPCC (like the PCB and PCA before it and, indeed, like the deputy chief constable) is in a similar position to that of the CPS. None of these bodies assesses the facts of the incidents complained of, except in those few cases where supervision is directive or the case is 'managed'. What they assess are reports of the facts, compiled by investigators whose job is to present a case. Since those investigators are police officers, the case they are generally predisposed to present will be that there is insufficient evidence to proceed. For although investigating officers are investigating alleged wrongdoing by other officers, much of this wrongdoing is part of everyday policing, is consistent with police working rules and will have been engaged in by themselves and/or their close colleagues. Writing in 1975, Box and Russell argued that the police psychologically neutralise the apparently deviant nature of their rule-breaking by using 'techniques of neutralisation' common to all occupational and cultural groups.[89] These techniques include 'condemning the condemners' and 'denying the victim', ie either blaming the complainant or disputing a crucial alleged fact about the complainant's injuries or loss. Such techniques enable the police to shrug off most complaints with a clear conscience.

---

[88] Maguire and Corbett (1991: 143).

[89] Box S and Russell K, 'The Politics of Discreditability: Disarming Complaints Against the Police' (1975) 23 Soc Rev 315.

Just as cases against ordinary suspects can be constructed to justify prosecution, cases against police suspects can be constructed to justify no further action, not least by methods intended to discredit the complainant. Arrest and/or prosecution of the complainant is one such method for it transforms the identity of the complainant from 'good citizen' to 'criminal suspect'. This makes denial by the police of the allegations more plausible and provides an explanation for what is claimed to be a false complaint (ie a complainant is said to be trying to use the complaints system to justify their own (alleged) violent resistance to arrest). Previous criminal record, a past record of mental illness and alleged drunkenness are other 'facts' used to discredit complainants.

The result is not just a generally low rate of substantiation, but a particularly low rate for those people whose complaints can be easily discredited. In Box and Russell's sample, 32% had two or more 'discredits' against them. None of their complaints was substantiated. One in ten of those with one discredit, but four in ten of those with no discredits, had their complaints substantiated. One result of this was that working class people had little success (8% of their complaints were substantiated, as against 28% of the complaints of middle class people). It is, of course, possible that drunks, criminals and the mentally ill really do make more false complaints than do other people. But the failure of the complaints mechanism in notorious cases such as *Police Complaints Board, ex p Madden* (1983) and the 'Confait Affair'[90] leads one to suspect that, however true this may be in part, the investigative process is intrinsically faulty.

Since the research by Maguire and Corbett suggests that the advent of the PCA made little difference to the substance of the investigative process as described by Box and Russell, the new IPCC is unlikely to make much difference either. Box and Russell[91] detected 'a certain amount of "stereotyping" by police (including investigating) officers – for instance, a belief that almost all complaints by certain kinds of people are made purely in order to cause trouble for the police, or a tendency to treat complainants as either "deserving" or "non-deserving" of serious attention, depending on their background and character.' Investigating officers, in other words, are steeped in 'cop culture' (see 2.1) and are unable to avoid viewing policing and rule-breaking through the eyes of that culture:

What a police officer may honestly (and perhaps justifiably) regard as totally 'reasonable force' to manoeuvre an intoxicated person quickly and effectively into a police van, may appear to the person – or to bystanders – as totally unreasonable force.[92]

Sometimes these attitudes were noticed by the PCA, and commented upon adversely, but it could do nothing about this, short of demanding a new investigation. How the IPCC performs in this respect will be a crucial determinant of the success of the new system. The signs are not encouraging. In 2004, shortly after the birth of the IPCC, its Chairman stated that 'there will be no such thing as a completely independent

---

90 See Baxter J and Koffman L, 'The Confait Inheritance – Forgotten Lessons?' [1983] Cambrian LR 14.
91 Box and Russell (1975: 130).
92 Maguire M, 'Complaints against the Police: Where Now?' (unpublished manuscript).

investigation'.[93] A few years on, the National Audit Office suggested abolishing 'supervised' investigations since, as indicated above, 'supervision' does little other than create an extra bureaucratic layer.[94]

12.4.2 Adjudication and discipline

Table 12.3 shows the number of complaints made in various years between 1986 and 2008/09 and the results of the investigations into them. The 2006/07 and 2008/09 figures relate to the 'IPCC era'. Except where the IPCC investigates itself or manages the investigation, decisions about disciplinary action are taken by the Chief Constable (or a very senior officer to whom this is delegated), but this is now changing (see 12.4.5).

The table shows that around a quarter of all complaints are withdrawn or 'dispensed with', the latter being when, for a variety of reasons, cases cannot or should not be investigated. Over 40% are dealt with by conciliation procedures. Both are discussed later. Very few complaints are substantiated, and in even fewer are there disciplinary or criminal charges. Look at the figures for 2008/09 (and, for comparison, 2003/04, the last year of the PCA, in brackets): there were 158 (112) prosecutions and discipline charges taken together. These were:

- 0.3% (0.4%) of all complaints made;
- 0.5% (0.7%) of all complaints minus those informally resolved;
- 0.9% (1.4%) of all complaints investigated;
- 8.7% (12%) of all complaints substantiated.

Or we could look at the substantiation rate. In 2008/9 (and 2003/4), this was:

- 3.6% (3.8%) of all complaints made;
- 6.1% (5.8%) of all complaints minus those informally resolved;
- 10% (12.4%) of all complaints investigated.

The substantiation rate is very low, but the gap between substantiated complaints and those where action was taken (ie those not dealt with 'by other means') is equally dramatic. Under the superintendence of the IPCC it is getting worse (and indeed, the figures were worse in 2003/4 than in the 1990s). Some of those who are not disciplined despite the complaint being upheld retire early or are given 'advice', and so forth. But even of the 121 disciplined in 2008/9, 85 were merely warned or had no action at all taken against them.

The impact of the IPCC is clearly as minimal as was the PCA, except that the number of people making complaints (and therefore the number of substantiations, though

[93] Quoted in Smith, 2006.

[94] National Audit Office, The IPCC (House of Commons, 14 November 2008, accessible at <http://www.nao.org.uk/>). The investigation into Nicola Dennis' complaint (at the head of the chapter) was 'supervised': see judicial condemnation of it in 12.4.5.

Table 12.3 Complaints against the police and outcomes in selected years

	1986	1991	1995/96	1998/99	2003/04	2006/07	2008/09
Total complaints	29,178	35,346	35,840	31,653	25,376	41,584	50,369
Complaints investigated	13,805	12,142	8,653	9,202	7,761	12,683	18,137
	(47%)	(34%)	(24%)	(29%)	(31%)	(30%)	(36%)
Complaints withdrawn	11,335	14,224	15,535	11,423	8,701	9,334	11,798
(including cases 'dispensed with')	(39%)	(40%)	(43%)	(36%)	(34%)	(22%)	(23%)
Informally resolved	4,038	8,980	11,652	11,028	8,914	19,567	20,434
	(14%)	(25%)	(33%)	(35%)	(35%)	(47%)	(41%)
Substantiated	1,129	813	749	745	961	1,389	1,810
Prosecuted (non-RTA)	(NK)	(NK)	10	38	23	(NK)	37*
Disciplined	(NK)	(NK)	162	122	89	(NK)	121
Dealt with 'by other means'	(NK)	(NK)	577	585	867	(NK)	(NK)

* recommended for prosecution, but outcome NK.
(NK = not known)

Sources: Cotton (2004); IPCC (2009a); IPCC, Police complaints and discipline, 2008/09 (London: IPCC, 2009b)

not charges) is rising. This probably reflects more malpractice and/or greater public confidence.[95] The overwhelming majority of disciplinary charges are the decisions of the police themselves (IPCC, 2009b). The situation under the IPCC is little different from the pre-PACE situation before the PCA replaced the PCB. For the fundamental problem – the police investigating themselves – remains.

Lest it be thought that complaints are generally trivial, let us look at the case of Leroy McDowell and Wayne Taylor, black men in their early 30s. They were stopped and searched late one night because they were in a 'drugs-related area'. No drugs were found. They complained about being stopped, and were arrested and accused of threatening behaviour. They asked for medical help, because they suffer from sickle cell anaemia, but were instead locked in a cell. They were offered a caution which they refused. They were prosecuted and acquitted in 1995. They brought civil actions for wrongful arrest, malicious prosecution, trespass and (in relation to the medical issue) negligence. They each settled for £19,000 and the police did not accept liability. And the police officers? The arresting officers were 'admonished' and the custody officer 'given advice'.[96] Little has changed, as shown by the case of Nicola Dennis, cited at the head of the chapter.

Research shows that the overwhelming majority of complainants – successful as well as unsuccessful – are dissatisfied because of inadequate penalties, the time taken to complete the investigation, the lack of apology and the lack of information provided (for example, about what the investigation found and about disciplinary proceedings). Poor communication is almost as much of a problem as the nature and quality of the investigation and subsequent decisions about disciplinary or criminal proceedings.[97] The 'Taylor reforms' (referred to earlier and discussed in 12.4.5) are aimed, in part, to meet these concerns.

There are many reasons for the low rate of substantiation of complaints. Firstly, there is the process of case construction and discrediting, discussed earlier. Secondly, there is the closing of ranks by police officers who might have witnessed the events complained of and the inherent difficulty that people mistreated in police custody have in finding independent witnesses. 'Cop culture', in other words, creates evidential problems.[98] We saw earlier that the IPCC has repeatedly complained about officers colluding when preparing witness statements, but if the IPCC responded to, for example, criminal complaints and deaths in custody as if they were potential crimes (as the police do when 'civilians' are the suspects) the police would have fewer of these opportunities.[99] Only

---

[95] The IPCC's surveys chart increasing confidence. See IPCC 2009a.

[96] *The Guardian*, 22 November 1997. Police officers tend to regard the outcome of 'words of advice' as confirmation that they have not done anything 'that wrong': Hill et al, *Meeting Expectations* (Occasional Paper No 21) (Oxford: Centre for Criminological Research, 2003b) pp 62–3.

[97] Maguire and Corbett (1991); Waters and Brown (2000); Hill et al (2003: ch 7); IPCC (2009a).

[98] Lustgarten (1986). See also the 'Manchester case' discussed in Loveday B, 'Recent Developments in Police Complaints Procedure' (1989) Local Gov Studies May/June 25.

[99] See, for example, earlier discussions of the deaths of Faisal Al-Ani, Sean Rigg and Jean Charles de Menezes. Also see Inquest, Briefing on the death of Ian Tomlinson (Inquest, June 2009: <http://inquest.org. uk/publications> – accessed 5 January 2010).

when a court made its disapproval of collusion clear did the IPCC concede that it could have ordered the police not to collude in serious cases.[100] As a result new police guidance now 'advises' officers not to collude. But this is not statutory, is not from the IPCC and only applies to shootings.[101] Of the officers Maguire and Corbett interviewed, 60% 'admitted the existence of something like a "Code of Silence" among junior officers'. Loveday (1989: 29) said that, 'Breaking through the "blue curtain" has in practice proved as difficult for the PCA as for its predecessor body, the PCB' and the same is true of the IPCC. There is now a new 'standard of professional behaviour' requiring officers to report the misconduct of other officers, and we wait to see what difference, if any, this will make.[102] Another problem is the 'double jeopardy' rule, which was abolished years ago, but the effects of which linger on (see 12.4.5).

Finally, we saw in 12.2 that officers under investigation often take early retirement or resign for 'medical' reasons and thus avoid discipline or criminal charges. This is a form of plea bargain. Like all plea bargaining, the interests of the victim are set aside: from the police force's point of view the problem is dealt with easily, speedily and without publicity that would question why the malpractice occurred and what was being done to prevent recurrence; while the officers concerned lose their jobs but protect their record and pension rights. Occasionally complainants, backed by the IPCC (and, in the past, the PCA) successfully challenge this on the grounds that the discipline regulations require that disciplinary charges be pursued if that is in the public interest.[103] The practice is still very common, though, so presumably most Chief Constables consider that, in most cases, the public interest lies in a quick low-key exit rather than a proper investigation. The obvious reform required is to move the decision to allow 'medical' or early retirement in such cases from Chief Constables to the IPCC.

If the police reject disciplinary proceedings but the IPCC insist on them – which, under the PCA, was rare – the IPCC can present the case. This should remedy the problem noted in successive years by the Police Complaints Authority, which criticised police forces for presenting cases with such a lack of 'clarity and vigour' that they often failed.[104] But fitting the punishment of police officers to the offence remains a matter for the police alone in most cases.

Examination of the effects on the complaints and discipline process of proceedings in the ordinary courts is revealing. Over the five years 1988–1992 inclusive, 80% of the Metropolitan Police officers involved in civil actions where over £10,000 was paid in damages or settlements had no disciplinary action taken against them.[105] The

---

[100] *R (Sanders and Tucker) v IPCC* [2008] EWHC 2372 (Admin).

[101] <http://www.wm-ireland.com/polfed/issues/acpo1008.pdf> (accessed 5 January 2010).

[102] Schedule to the Police (Conduct) Regulations 2008 (SI 2864/2008). For these and the other discipline regulations see Home Office Circular 025/2008 ('The Taylor Reforms – police conduct, performance and associated regulations').

[103] *R (on the application of Coghlan) v Chief Constable of Greater Manchester* [2005] 2 All ER 890; *R v Chief Constable of Devon and Cornwall Ex p Hay* [1996] 2 All ER 711.

[104] Hall A, 'Police Complaints; Time for a Change' (1990) Legal Action, August p 7.

[105] *The Guardian*, 15 April 1993.

Runciman Commission was concerned that action was frequently not taken in this situation, nor where 'police malpractice has contributed to a miscarriage of justice', nor 'where a prosecution has been dismissed because of a more than technical breach of PACE or its codes and the actions of the police have been publicly criticised by the judge.'[106] Runciman found that the police had no mechanism for noting and acting upon judicial criticism of officers. This remains true and the IPCC has not changed it. Take Babar Ahmad's case. The police settled this case when it came to court, paying Ahmad £60,000 to compensate for their 'serious, gratuitous and prolonged attack' when his home was raided in 2003; yet none of the officers who saw this happen, but refused to give evidence, were disciplined.[107]

A key element of the rule of law is that the police (along with all other arms of government) should be accountable to 'the law'. The reality, in this context, clearly falls well short of the rhetoric. Not only is the failure to discipline most officers found to have done wrong (let alone those against whom this could not be proved) unacceptable in itself, but as we saw earlier, the courts have held that apparently valid complaints that do not lead to disciplinary charges need not be disclosed in civil actions.[108] Thus the failures of the remedies 'system' compound themselves over time, and the condoning of malpractice allows yet more malpractice to flourish unpunished.

12.4.3 Informal (or local) resolution

One source of dissatisfaction among complainants discovered by Brown[109] was that making a complaint was 'all or nothing' regardless of the seriousness of the incident. Many of them wanted nothing more than an apology and a recognition of how they felt about their treatment by the police. PACE therefore allowed the 'informal resolution' of complaints if this was the wish of both chief officer and complainant, and if the matter was insufficiently serious for it to be dealt with through disciplinary proceedings even if proven.[110] There is no requirement that the officer complained of give consent for the use of this procedure. This is now renamed 'local resolution', but is largely unchanged, in the PRA (Sch 3), except that complainants no longer have the right to insist on formal proceedings. In practice[111] it consists of a meeting between the 'appointed officer' (handling the case on behalf of the police service) and the complainant, followed by a meeting between the appointed officer and the officer complained against (at which the complainant's views are conveyed, and the police officer given a chance to respond).

Informal resolution is now used for over 40% of all complaints. Does this mean that a large proportion of complaints are relatively trivial? Not necessarily; in one study 46%

---

[106] RCCJ (1993: 48). Also see House of Commons, Home Affairs Select Committee, *Police Disciplinary and Complaints Procedure*, 1st Report (HC 258-1, 1998) paras 25–6.

[107] *The Guardian*, 19 and 26 March 2009.

[108] *Scott v Chief Constable of Yorkshire* [2006] 3 All ER (D) 412 (Mar).

[109] Brown D, *Police Complaints Procedure* (Home Office Research Study No 93) (London: HMSO, 1987).

[110] PACE, s 85 has now been replaced by s 69 of the Police Act 1996, but there has been no material change.   [111] Hill et al (2003b: 22–4).

of complainants subject to this procedure said that the incident had upset or shocked them, with 17% suffering physical injury, 9% inconvenience and 7% property damage or loss.[112]

In reality, informal resolution is more popular with police services than it is with either complainants or the officers complained against. Many complainants are 'nudged' into it, or even presented with a fait accompli.[113] Hill et al (2003b), who were allowed to observe what went on, found that in 42% of cases complainants were dissuaded from opting for a formal investigation by the police stressing how long this would take and how little would be achieved, while in another 29% of cases informal resolution was presented as the only option. Moreover, the potential of informal resolution to achieve disciplinary or educative ends was exaggerated. The following explanation given by an appointed officer to a complainant is fairly typical of the salesmanship the researchers observed:

You know, realistically, going down a formal route, you're looking at eight or nine months before you get a result. The result in all likelihood is going to be exactly the same, he'd [the officer] probably get advice. What I'm suggesting to you is that the informal resolution, it is informal because it's not a formal interview, [but] it is a formal discipline.[114]

This is misleading because local resolution involves no formal admission of guilt and is not noted on the officers' records. Indeed, Hill et al[115] found that appointed officers spent much of the time in their meetings with officers complained against reassuring them that the matter would not be recorded on their personal files, that they did not necessarily agree with the complaint, and so forth. Nonetheless, it is unpopular among the officers concerned (Maguire and Corbett, 1991; May et al, 2007a). Warburton et al (2003) identified an important reason for this: some police services keep a centralised file on officers against whom complaints are made. If multiple complaints are received then a superior officer interviews the officer concerned, regardless of whether the complaints were disposed of by way of informal resolution.[116] Some forces even dock officers' pay in this situation which is probably a harsher sanction than they would have received had the complaint been substantiated following formal investigation.[117]

---

[112] Hill et al, *Introducing Restorative Justice to the Police Complaints System: Close Encounters of the Rare Kind* (Occasional Paper No 20) (Oxford: Centre for Criminological Research, 2003a) p 11.

[113] Corbett C, 'Complaints Against the Police: The New Procedure of Informal Resolution' (1991) 2 Policing and Society 47; Maguire and Corbett (1991) Waters I and Brown K, 'Police Complaints and the Complainants' Experience' (2000) 40 BJ Crim 617; May T et al, Local Resolution: The Views of Police Officers and Complainants (London: IPCC, 2007a).

[114] Hill et al (2003b: 19). These findings are also set out in Young et al, 'Informal Resolution of Complaints Against the Police: A Quasi-Experimental Test of Restorative Justice' (2005) 5 Criminal Justice 279 at pp 287–8.   [115] Hill et al (2003b: 22–4).

[116] Warburton et al, *Opposite Sides of the Same Coin: Police Perspectives on Informally Resolved Complaints* (London: The Police Foundation, 2003).

[117] IPCC (2005), Making the new police complaints system work better: statutory guidance (available from <http://www.ipcc.gov.uk/stat_guidelines.pdf> – accessed 5 January 2010) para 5.3.6.

Against that background, it is not surprising that Hill et al[118] found officers criticising informal resolution on the basis that it assumed their guilt and ignored their views of whether the use of this procedure was appropriate.

Many complainants are disappointed when they receive a letter from the police service announcing blandly that the matter is now regarded as closed, with no information provided about the officer's reaction to the complaint, and no apology from either that officer or the police service itself. In other words, the process raises citizens' expectations of a conciliatory spirit, only to dash them (Hill et al, 2003b; May et al, 2007a). Over half of the complainants expressed an interest to Hill et al (2003b: 28–9) in meeting the officer complained against so that each could hear the other's point of view, but this was arranged only rarely. Young et al (2005: 290) conclude that informal resolution at best 'results in an indirect transmission of views from the complainant to the officer complained against (which is all that some complainants want); at worst it is a means of suppressing a dispute and of bringing premature, bureaucratic closure to an incident.' The potential that informal resolution appears to offer for officers and complainants to come to understand each other's behaviour and views is rarely realised in practice, in part because of inadequate resourcing, training and support (May et al 2007a). The IPCC has the power to prod recalcitrant forces into becoming more 'complainant focused' but chooses not to exercise it.[119]

12.4.4 Withdrawn complaints

The low level of substantiation of complaints against the police could reflect a high level of bogus complaints as much as unfair investigation processes. Were this so, one would expect most people with a grudge against the police – whether justified or not – to complain wherever possible. If anything, however, the reverse is true. All research studies agree that the vast majority of complainants have not previously made a complaint against the police, even though they may have felt like doing so, and that people who are 'anti-police' are less likely to complain about them than are others (because they lack confidence in the system).[120] Like the 'hidden figure' of unreported crime, there is a 'hidden figure' of unreported complaints: in 2004/05 17% of adults reported having been 'really annoyed' by the police in the previous five years. But only 11% of those who felt this way said they had made or tried to make a complaint. Of those who did not complain despite being 'really annoyed', two-thirds explained that they could see no point in doing so. Of those who did try to complain only around a quarter were very or fairly satisfied with the way the matter was handled by the police; the numbers who were dissuaded from lodging a formal complaint or who were persuaded to withdraw such a complaint are not

---

[118] Hill et al (2003b: 25–6).

[119] May T et al, *From Informal to Local Resolution: Assessing Changes to the Handling of Low-level Police Complaints* (London: Police Foundation/IPCC, 2007b).

[120] Maguire and Corbett (1991: 43); Waters and Brown (2000: 626); Hill et al (2003a: 12); Wake et al, *Public Perceptions of the Police Complaints System* (London: IPCC, 2007).

known.[121] Some groups are particularly sceptical about the police complaints process or disinclined to use it, including ethnic minorities, those with previous negative experiences of the police and those from lower-class backgrounds.[122] Whatever the merits of a particular complaint, pursuing it is clearly not something done lightly.[123]

Most putative complainants try to start the process by contacting (in person or by phone) their local police station – which is often the location of the incident being complained about. At this stage, many are dissuaded from formally lodging their complaints by the police. Waters and Brown[124] found that 58% of all their survey respondents, and 41% of those whose cases were eventually informally resolved, felt that the police were trying to discourage them from making their complaint.[125] These figures take no account of those who actually were dissuaded and therefore never entered the formal complaints process. Those who continue are interviewed by an appointed officer, after which around one-third of complainants withdraw their complaints.

Pressure to withdraw can take the form of inducements (for example, an offer to drop charges), charm (as when apologies are offered), threat (as where the possibility of charges against the complainant or associates is raised), dissuasion (explaining that success is very unlikely) or moral pressure (asking the complainant to consider the likely impact on the officer's career). Sometimes what is said satisfies complainants, who then withdraw, but most feel pressured into giving up and are left feeling resentful. Officers do not dispute the fact that they often advise withdrawal but they generally claim that they do this only where appropriate. Like most police work, interviews between appointed officers and complainants are hidden from view, making what the police do largely unaccountable. The only researchers to have directly observed such meetings have confirmed, however, that complainants are encouraged to 'define police deviance down' by accepting appointing officers' promptings to opt for informal resolution or even complete withdrawal rather than seek formal investigation.[126] Table 12.3 is encouraging insofar as the number of complaints is rising, and the number and percentage that are withdrawn is dropping. This is doubtless because people can now complain directly to the IPCC itself, via 'access points' such as CABx, and on-line.

12.4.5 An interim assessment of the new system

Despite major changes in the system over the past 30 years or so, the complaints system still largely allows the police to follow their own informal norms. This is partly because

---

[121] Allen et al, *Policing and the Criminal Justice System – Public Confidence and Perceptions: Findings from the 2004/05 British Crime Survey* (Home Office Online Report 07/06) (London: Home Office, 2006) pp 21–2.

[122] Docking M and Bucke T, *Confidence in the Police Complaints System: A Survey of the General Population* (London: IPCC, 2006) available from <http://www.ipcc.gov.uk/confidence_survey.pdf> (accessed 5 January 2010).

[123] Contrast this with the belief of most police officers that most complainants are malicious and/or time wasting: Maguire and Corbett (1991: ch 5).   [124] Waters and Brown (2000: 626).

[125] See also Hill et al (2003a: 16–17).   [126] Hill et al (2003b: ch 4).

investigating deviance by anyone (including criminals) is intrinsically difficult and likely to fail in the majority of cases.[127] It is also because processes requiring articulate argument, polite persistence and so forth favour highly educated middle class adults. Since most complainants are from more marginal sections of society, they are less likely to succeed in their complaints.[128] Little can be done about these problems, but more can be done about the way the system deals with complainants and the investigation of the police by the police in addition to the positive changes already noted.

Investigative powers

For the first time in the UK, an independent body has powers of its own to investigate police complaints. Indeed, the IPCC has many of the same powers, when investigating the police, as do the police when investigating crime. These include surveillance powers of the type discussed in ch 6.[129] The shooting of Menezes in 2005, and the alleged attempted cover-up of it by the Commissioner of the Metropolitan Police, was therefore investigated by the IPCC itself – not, as would have happened before, by another force under the supervision of an independent body. There are two main problems. First, the IPCC will only ever be able to investigate a tiny minority of all alleged wrongdoing (the resource problem is addressed below). Second, independent investigation by 'civilian' investigators or civilian review boards is not a panacea. Many jurisdictions, such as Toronto and several American cities, have similar systems. The difficulties include obstruction of investigators by the police, civilian investigators over-identifying with the problems of the police, the creation of cumbersome procedures to protect officers from the new outside body, and a lack of understanding of policing on the part of civilians.[130] This last problem both impedes investigators in finding out what really happened, as officers can erect smokescreens more easily and pull the wool over the eyes of novices, and could lead to lack of understanding of why certain malpractice takes place, reducing the possibility of effective punishment and prevention measures.[131] This is certainly the impression given by the way the IPCC handled the de Menezes affair and many others since, such as the death of Ian Tomlinson.[132] It is also

---

[127] See Goldsmith A, 'External Review and Self-Regulation' in Goldsmith A (ed), *Complaints Against the Police: the Trend to External Review* (Oxford: OUP, 1991); Walsh D, '20 years of Handling Police Complaints in Ireland: A Critical Assessment of the Supervisory Board Model' (2009) 29 Legal Studies 305.

[128] Box and Russell (1975).

[129] PRA, s 19 and IPCC (Investigatory Powers) Order 2004, SI 815/2004.

[130] For good surveys, see Loveday (1989) and McMahon M, 'Police Accountability: The Situation of Complaints in Toronto' (1988) 12 Contemporary Crises 301. Also see Goldsmith A and Farson S, 'Complaints against the Police in Canada: A New Approach' [1987] Crim LR 615; Goldsmith (ed) (1991); Harrison and Cuneen (2000); and Prenzler T, 'Civilian Oversight of Police: A Test of Capture Theory' (2000) 40 BJ Crim 659.

[131] Bayley D, 'Getting Serious about Police Brutality' in P Stenning (ed), *Accountability for Criminal Justice* (Toronto: University of Toronto Press, 1995).

[132] For a good general discussion, focusing especially on the de Menezes affair, see Smith G, 'Citizen Oversight of Independent Police Services: Bifurcated Accountability, Regulation Creep and Lesson Learning' (2009b) 3 Regulation & Governance 422. See also <http://latestnews.virginmedia.com/news/uk/2009/05/26/ipcc_probe_clears_menezes_officer> (accessed 5 January 2010).

said that civilians who have not experienced 'the street' could 'not easily tell the difference between an officer "trying honestly to do his job, but perhaps making mistakes", and a truly deviant officer "who should not be in uniform".'[133] Many of the problems can be summed up as those of breaking into police culture, which, as we saw in ch 2, is very powerful. Nonetheless, where 'external' involvement in investigation is more than merely supervisory its impact can be considerable.[134]

Independence

Nicola Dennis (see story at the head of the chapter) was so disgusted by the IPCC's decision that the officer who caused her to fear for her life merely deserved 'words of advice' (this was a supervised investigation) that she took the IPCC to court. The judge agreed with her.[135] This was no isolated case. A review of dozens of cases found the IPCC:

failing to order proper inquiries; accepting police evidence without challenge; failing to disclose documents to complainants; misunderstanding the law; and rejecting complaints on weak grounds...failure to interview witnesses, failure even to interview the police officers involved, failure to collect CCTV footage (eventually retrieved in one case by the complainant's mother) and failure to gather medical evidence of alleged assault.[136]

One complaint, for example, was that an officer committed perjury. The magistrates believed this, saying the officer's evidence was 'not credible' but the IPCC did not. As in the past, complainants who had been paid compensation by the police had still not had their complaints upheld by the IPCC. For example, a man who was shot in the shoulder and held for a week on suspicion of terrorism because of faulty police information was simply told the police should have apologised. In that raid all the 11 occupants of the house were taken to a police station even though only two were formally arrested. The IPCC accepted that three were assaulted by the police but made no disciplinary recommendations.[137] Sean Rigg died after being put in a police station cage, with CCTV cameras mysteriously not working, yet the IPCC put out a press statement that incorrectly accepted the police story, and justified waiting eight months before interviewing the police because 'there was nothing to suggest wrongdoing'.[138] In 2008 100 members of the Police Action Lawyers Group withdrew their backing for the IPCC, and two of the group's representatives resigned from the IPCC's advisory board in protest at its deference to the police.[139] The charity INQUEST concludes with some justification that, like the PCA, the IPCC has been 'captured' by the police.[140] A similar verdict was made by a former Commissioner who 'could no longer support an organisation

---

[133] Maguire (undated) (quoting police officers).

[134] Goldsmith (ed) (1991). Disputed by Bayley (1995).

[135] *R (Dennis) v IPCC* [2008] EWHC 1158 (Admin).   [136] *The Guardian*, 25 February 2008.

[137] *The Guardian*, 14 February 2007.   [138] *The Guardian*, 22 August 2009.

[139] *Legal Action*, June 2008, p 4.

[140] Inquest response to IPCC stock take consultation 2008 (Inquest, October 2008) (<http://inquest.org.uk/publications> – accessed 5 January 2010). See also Shaw H and Coles D, *Unlocking the Truth: Families' Experiences of the Investigation of Deaths in Custody* (London: Inquest, 2007).

producing the worst of all outcomes – timidity towards police accountability and redress for complainants, combined with a drawn-out bureaucratic approach…'[141]

Resources

Limited resources held back the PCA, which had to decline to supervise 70–80% of the cases referred to it by the police.[142] Even when the infamous West Midlands Police Serious Crime Squad affair erupted, the Authority initially avoided involvement.[143] While the IPCC is far better funded than was the PCA, it remains grossly under-resourced.[144] This is partly because of its success in encouraging more complaints and appeals (particularly against the outcomes of police investigation: 1,838 in 2006/07), and the need to investigate more deaths and near-deaths as a result of European Court rulings.[145] Lack of resources is the most charitable explanation for the delay in investigating numerous cases, even deaths in custody in suspicious circumstances, such as noted earlier, and the investigative failures noted above.[146]

'Self-regulation'

There will never be sufficient resources for the IPCC to investigate all serious complaints or even to supervise them. The police will inevitably continue to investigate most themselves. It is common for complaints about professions to be investigated by those professions. However, the police are not like doctors and lawyers. First, while self-regulation is by no means ever perfect, the record of police complaints investigation is particularly lamentable (although not just in the UK). Second, the police have uniquely coercive powers, giving them greater opportunity for malpractice of a kind that carries very serious consequences for the individual citizen. Third, there is usually some element of choice on the part of people using doctors, lawyers, accountants and so forth, which is not true of suspects. Citizens cannot choose their police officers or control when they come into contact with them.

Finally, the police have a greater ability to hide malpractice than other professions because of their greater power and their capacity to choose the time, place and manner of their interaction with citizens. The IPCC, like the PCA and PCB before it, receives reports of police investigations. Police 'case constructions' continue. A solicitor specialising in this area commented, 'Most internal police complaints departments that I have come across are behaving as though the Police Reform Act never happened.'[147] A test of the IPCC is how far it is prepared to challenge these constructions in public. In all these respects the IPCC has the power and right to do this, as part of its 'guardianship

---

[141] Crawley J, 'The Worst of All Outcomes' *Society Guardian*, 8 April 2009.

[142] Maguire and Corbett (1991: 12).   [143] Kaye (1991).

[144] Public Accounts Committee, *Independent Police Complaints Commission* (HC335)(London: TSO, 2009) (also available as the Fifteenth Report of Session 2008–09 from the Committee's website).

[145] Especially *Ramsahai* (ECtHR Chamber Judgment 2005). See generally IPCC, *Building on Experience* ('Stocktake Consultation') (London: IPCC, 2008).

[146] *The Guardian*, 25 February 2008. In some cases discussed in this report, inadequate resources were cited by Commissioners to justify failings.   [147] *Law Society Gazette*, 9 March 2006, p 22.

role'.[148] Its waspish comments about police behaviour in the Harry Stanley and other cases is a good sign, though its failure to insist on an end to police collusion, its failure to recommend disciplinary charges in the Stanley case, (see discussion in 12.2 above) and the overall failure to increase the substantiation and discipline rates are not.

The conflation of crime investigation with discipline investigation

The police complaints system continues to force the investigation of complaints of a criminal nature (eg assault, perjury) into the same system for investigating complaints of a disciplinary nature (eg neglect of duty, incivility, abuse of power) (Smith, 2004). However, since so many complaints are both about discipline (eg abuse of powers) and crime (that abuse including assault or perjury) it is hard to see how investigation of the two types of complaint could be separated. Under the new, as under the old, system the investigating body decides whether or not there is any evidence of criminal activity; if there is, the file is sent to the DPP. Complainants can now see the report and object to a decision not to refer the case to the DPP.

Deciding whether or not to prosecute

Liberty suggests that thought be given to transferring the power to decide whether or not to prosecute from the CPS to the IPCC (Harrison and Cuneen, 2000). This would be unlikely to make any substantive difference. Whatever body makes decisions on the basis of reports and investigations by another body will be dependent on that other body in the sense that it is led by that body's often hidden working rules and cultural norms. On the other hand, retaining the power within the CPS has an advantage. At present the DPP's decisions regarding police officers can be contrasted unfavourably with those regarding civilians, when the criteria regarding both should be the same. If prosecutions of officers were hived off to the IPCC, there is the danger that, like prosecution decisions by non-police agencies in 'regulatory crimes' (discussed in ch 7), they would come to be seen as 'different'. The best way of ensuring that prosecution decisions are taken in the way that other decisions are taken is by the development and application of the case law discussed in 12.2 (above) and ch 7, by establishing robust accountability mechanisms, and by treating complainants like other alleged victims of crime (ie assumed to be victims unless proved otherwise – see ch 13). If any of this is to be effective, far more openness in relation to prosecution and adjudication decisions will be needed. One of the tasks of the IPCC will be to press the DPP for more transparency in these matters and to publicise cases where the DPP does not prosecute but where it judged there to be sufficient evidence.

The Taylor reforms

In 2005 the Government-commissioned Taylor Review recommended several changes aimed at improving the cost-effectiveness of the complaints and discipline system and

---

[148] See <http://www.ipcc.gov.uk/guardianship0402.pdf> (accessed 5 January 2010).

securing 'a significant shift of emphasis towards development and improvement more than blame and sanction'.[149] The main changes (which apply to all possible misconduct and performance failures whether or not the subject of complaint), which were implemented by Home Office Circular 025/2008, are:

- early assessment of allegations as either 'misconduct' or 'gross misconduct' (though this is subject to reassessment in the light of investigation or further information);

- the investigation (if there is one) of 'misconduct' by a line manager;

- 'gross misconduct' has to be investigated, and is done so by the force's 'professional standards department';

- 'misconduct' will be resolved through management action or 'misconduct meetings', while 'gross misconduct' will be resolved through 'misconduct hearings'; the former is conducted at a local level by an officer at least one rank above the officer concerned, while the latter is conducted by three senior officers;

- the only formal outcomes from misconduct meetings is management action or a warning, while misconduct hearings can lead to these outcomes and to more serious measures, including dismissal; and

- despite the double jeopardy rule, which prevented officers from being charged with disciplinary offences which are similar to criminal offences with which they had been charged and acquitted, being abolished in 1999[150] the police were still, until recently, encouraged by the Home Office to take no action following failed prosecutions. Moreover, disciplinary proceedings always waited until possible criminal proceedings were resolved, even though prosecutions are vanishingly rare. This is no longer to happen. Unless there is a compelling reason to wait, investigation and proceedings are now to proceed (if appropriate) regardless of possible criminal matters.

At the time of writing these changes had been in force for too short a time for their impact to be assessed. On the face of it, these measures direct investigative resources at the most serious matters, and the structure of 'meetings' and 'hearings' could, in less serious cases, facilitate officers accepting responsibility and learning from their actions. On the other hand, the scope for the police sweeping matters under the carpet is greater now than ever, as they themselves make a preliminary judgement about the seriousness of the possible misconduct, and then still handle subsequent processes themselves in most cases. As to what is 'mere' misconduct and what is 'gross', Taylor's

[149] Taylor W, *Review of Police Disciplinary Arrangements* (London: Home Office, 2005) para 0.10 (<http://press.homeoffice.gov.uk/documents/police-disciplinary-arrangements/report.pdf> – accessed 5 January 2010).

[150] This was done by activating a provision of the Police and Magistrates' Courts Act 1994. See Smith G, 'Double Trouble' (1999a) 149 NLJ 1233.

assessment does not inspire confidence. His examples of misconduct (2005, para 5.3) include 'incivility', and those of gross misconduct include serious assault and racial or sexual harassment. But abuse of power – unlawful stop-search, wrongful arrest, breach of the PACE Codes, for example – is not mentioned.

The rights of complainants

These have improved, but there is still some way to go. Despite non-police 'access points' for complainants, the first interview is still conducted by a police officer. Many complainants find this disconcerting or even intimidating. Perhaps someone else – an IPCC member or CAB worker, for example – should do this. Another change is that complainants in 'supervised' and 'managed' cases now have the right to speak to the IPCC member in charge of the case to discuss progress. Even in other cases, if a complainant feels, for example, that a witness should be interviewed, s/he can ask the IPCC to intervene.

A major criticism of the old system was a presumption against disclosure to the complainant of documents found or produced in the course of the investigation. The presumption is now in favour of disclosure.[151] Disclosure of witness statements is not a straightforward matter, particularly where a prosecution is possible. In *R (Green) v PCA* [2004] UKHL 6 the complainant sought witness statements in a case that could lead to the prosecution of the officers complained about. The risk that the complainant might tailor his evidence to fit that of other witnesses was found to be too great to allow disclosure. However, these problems do not apply to disclosure of provisional findings and the final report. Complainants are informed of the progress of the case, which should tackle another major fault of the old system.

Complainants also now have various appeal rights – after 'local resolution', at the end of police-investigated cases, and when cases are judged not to need investigation, for example. Appeals may be made against findings, discipline decisions, and (non-)disclosure, but not against decisions not to uphold (substantiate) a complaint or send the file to the DPP. We have seen that though the appeal rate is low, many appeals are successful.

Complainants used to be excluded from disciplinary hearings. They, along with IPCC members, may now attend until the point at which it is decided whether the officer acted wrongly. This, along with the IPCC being able to present cases against officers in some circumstances, should increase justice and the appearance of justice. But hearings are rare, and conciliation is common, and complainants no longer have the right to insist on formal proceedings (ie misconduct hearings).

The injection of restorative values

Young et al (2005) evaluated an initiative by Thames Valley Police in which complainants were offered the chance to meet the officer complained about in the presence of a

---

[151] PRA, s 20 and Sch 3.

facilitator trained in such restorative justice principles as promoting active listening, ensuring full exchange of views and achieving a focus on harm and its repair. Of the 49 cases handled by a special Conflict Resolution Team, in 47 the complainants were offered a face-to-face meeting of this kind, and in 22 cases both police officer and complainant agreed. Where the offer was rejected indirect mediation was offered instead and this was taken up in 19 cases, with the facilitator transmitting information between the parties. The extent to which this was productive depended on the ability of those parties to think and behave in a restorative (rather than argumentative or aggressive) manner. The researchers drew careful comparisons with a sample of cases dealt with in Hampshire using the standard informal resolution procedure. Of the significant differences between the Hampshire and Thames Valley respondents, the most important were the greater degree of satisfaction amongst complainants who experienced restorative justice and the improvement in their attitudes towards the officer complained against. There was also a tendency for officers who had experienced a restorative meeting to learn or benefit directly from hearing the complainant's perspective, with one officer saying that he would no longer think about things with a 'blinkered policeman's attitude [but] think about how it affects other people' (2005: 307). Local resolution and many of the Taylor reforms are ostensibly aimed at helping police forces and officers to learn from unhappy encounters and be more open about problems and failings. But so far neither complainants nor officers generally feel this is the usual result (May et al, 2007b). Complainants clearly welcome and benefit from the chance to enter into dialogue with the officer complained about – and this could be the start of a more general dialogue between the police and the public. So why does it rarely happen?

Towards a freedom approach to complaints

The main value of reforms such as appeal rights for complainants and the use of restorative justice principles lies less in establishing the 'truth' or in securing more 'wins' for complainants than in opening up investigation and police processes to public scrutiny and debate. Such a reform programme may not succeed in making the complaints system conform to due process values, but at least the limitations of the system might become more widely recognised. Less would be claimed for the system and less expected of it.

The police complaints procedure used not to exist for those who set it in motion – complainants – but was essentially an internal matter for the police and the PCA. For example, the detective superintendent in charge of the inquiry into the murder of PC Blakelock (which led to the wrongful conviction of the 'Tottenham Three') was put before a disciplinary tribunal by the Police Complaints Authority (PCA). The assistant commissioner of the Metropolitan Police is reported to have urged the PCA to drop proceedings 'on grounds including the damage which substantiation of the allegations would do to force morale'.[152] The success of civil actions relative to that of complaints is

---

[152] *The Guardian*, 12 May 1990.

striking. Smith (2003) found that most claimants whose cases got as far as a court were satisfied with the civil process, even if they lost, because they thought the process was fair (despite the many years most cases take). By contrast, most complainants, even those whose complaints are upheld, remain dissatisfied with the process. Significantly, claimants have substantial control over their civil actions, but still have little input into 'their' complaints and prosecutions.

The complaints procedure has been grafted onto the police disciplinary procedure and the IPCC has been grafted onto that. This was implicitly acknowledged by the Taylor Review, but the reforms it produced were, in turn, grafted onto the existing system. The system still allows considerable latitude for crime control-oriented police working rules by prioritising morale, efficiency and cost considerations. Taylor made it clear that his reforms are not intended to punish and deter most breaches of the legal rules, and only aim to protect suspects and defendants indirectly and in the long term. But the freedom approach would not adopt the due process demand for punishment for all malpractice. Complainants generally seek a restoration of respect, an apology and an assurance that the police will alter their practices and attitudes. For people who complain about the police are generally those who come into repeated, and repeatedly adversarial, contact with the police. They do not generally seek punishment except in very serious cases.[153] The Taylor reforms and the IPCC's 'lesson learning' approach rightly aims to see malpractice as a process and to make dealing with complaints individually a lower priority. But this requires civilian oversight of police management, with particular emphasis on those aspects of management related to malpractice, as well as IPCC-style investigation of serious complaints (Smith 2009). Civilians, in other words, can help to pressure police management to tackle malpractice at all levels, including that of system incentives and system obstacles, and public confidence will remain low, whatever the reality, unless this is done.[154] This, along with the other principles underlying the IPCC and Taylor reforms, is now internationally recognised as a human rights requirement where death is involved, and so by implication, in relation to police misconduct in general.[155]

Consequently, perhaps the most important role of the IPCC is to identify and publicise general problems and suggest reforms. The legislation gives it this role, but in steering a course between exposing, and working with, the police it usually favours the latter. The IPCC also has the job of building confidence in the system among the public. The danger is that this will be seen as an objective in itself, rather than a natural by-product of a better system. Perhaps this is why the IPCC called in the police to investigate a leak in the de Menezes inquiry, leading to the arrest of a journalist

---

[153] The international literature bearing on these points is reviewed in Young et al (2005).

[154] Bayley (1995).

[155] See Council of Europe Commissioner for Human Rights, Opinion concerning independent and effective determination of complaints against the police (<http://www.coe.int/t/commissioner/> dated 12 March 2009 – accessed 5 January 2010), commented on by Smith G, 'European Complaints' *Legal Action* April (2009a) p 38.

and an IPCC employee and months of investigation: it seemed to be more concerned about bad publicity than discovering what the police knew about the fatal shooting of an innocent man.[156] We conclude that the IPCC has currently got its priorities badly wrong.

12.5 **Trial remedies**[157]

One of the great dilemmas of any system of criminal justice is what to do about evidence obtained in the course of rule-breaking by police and other officials. The crime control position is that the only sensible test of evidence is its probative value – ie its reliability. If evidence is obtained wrongly, the officials responsible should be dealt with and the wronged defendant should be compensated, in proceedings designed for those purposes. Excluding reliable evidence at trial (that is, the use of an 'exclusionary rule') – or, worse, halting the trial altogether – so that a guilty person walks free, punishes the innocent public along with the guilty police. The purpose of the criminal trial is to establish whether guilt has been proved beyond reasonable doubt, not to provide a system of 'trial remedies', so legal niceties should not obstruct the search for the truth.

The due process position is that the best way of deterring future breaches of the rules is by preventing the police from benefiting from them. Moreover, in so far as due process protections have value in themselves as ethical standards, a system which accepts evidence secured in breach of those standards is tainted. If citizens are to respect the law, the criminal justice system has to set an example. The crime control adherent argues that the ends justify the means. The due process adherent argues that the means themselves must have moral integrity, regardless of what ends are being pursued, and that trial remedies are one way of securing that.

There are a number of problems with both positions. For instance, both make assumptions about the value of all these remedies and controls without a firm factual basis for those assumptions. What discredits the criminal justice system more: ignoring apparently reliable evidence and allowing the apparently guilty to go free, or using illegally obtained evidence and, by doing so, condoning illegal police behaviour which may not be subject to any other sanction? What is the best way of controlling police illegality? Is it the threat of civil or disciplinary sanctions, given what we have said about them earlier in this chapter? Is halting the whole trial using a sledgehammer to

---

[156] *The Guardian, Media Suppt*, 15 May 2006.

[157] The literature on this topic is enormous and only a brief outline is given here. For detailed discussions see, for instance: Mirfield P, *Silence, Confessions and Improperly Obtained Evidence* (Oxford: OUP, 1997); Grevling K, 'Fairness and the Exclusion of Evidence' (1997) 113 LQR 667; Sharpe S, *Judicial Discretion and Criminal Investigation* (London: Sweet & Maxwell, 1998); Corker D and Young D, *Abuse of Process and Fairness in Criminal Proceedings* (London: Butterworths, 2003); Ashworth and Redmayne (2005: chs 9, 11).

crack a nut? Does the exclusion of illegally obtained evidence operate equally quixotically, 'punishing' police officers only when illegal behaviour occurs in cases with not enough lawfully obtained evidence to support a conviction? And how valuable are trial remedies as protections? They provide no comfort for suspects who are not tried; that is, who are not charged or who plead guilty or who may have suffered greatly through having had their home unlawfully searched, being interrogated roughly or being denied access to legal advice.

Advocates of crime control and due process do share some common ground. If a minor rule were breached (for example, refreshments to a suspect held in cells being provided 10 minutes late) even the most ardent due process adherent would not advocate that all evidence secured thereafter should be excluded. And in the second edition of this book we confidently stated that no civilised systems would countenance the use of evidence secured through torture, no matter how reliable it might be. However, until the House of Lords overruled it, that is precisely what the Court of Appeal did endorse.[158] It seems that the limits to civilisation are unpredictable, even for sceptics like us, but there are no systems in democratic societies which use absolute all-embracing inclusionary or exclusionary rules. Can the freedom model assist us in reaching a principled compromise?

Since minor breaches reduce freedom insignificantly, reliable evidence obtained following them would not be excluded. The point at which a minor breach became, for this purpose, a major breach, would depend on the loss of freedom created by such breaches in comparison with the loss of freedom that occurred as a result of exclusion. In weighing up the former, the value or otherwise of the other remedies discussed in this chapter would be assessed, as would the loss of confidence people would have in the system in the event either of condoning police rule-breaking or of acquittals stemming from the rejection of reliable evidence. Weight would also have to be given to the nature of the suspects' rights that the police had infringed, since some rights (such as the right of access to a lawyer) are so fundamental that even relatively minor infringements of them pose a fundamental threat to freedom. This would be so even if the general populace would prefer evidence obtained through such an infringement to be admitted at trial, since one of the purposes of a system of democratically established rights is to defend the interests of unpopular minorities against the preferences of the majority.

Historically, the common law position on exclusion was at the crime control end of the spectrum. In Sang[159] (where evidence was obtained by an agent provocateur) it was held that judges had no general discretion to exclude non-confession evidence (eg fingerprints) simply because of the duplicitous or oppressive way in which it was obtained. However, confession evidence was treated differently, because of the peculiar

---

[158] A v Secretary of State for the Home Department (No 2) [2005] UKHL 71, briefly discussed below.

[159] [1980] AC 402. For a concise modern history of the pre- and post-PACE situation, see Ormerod D and Birch D, 'The Evolution of the Discretionary Exclusion of Evidence' [2004] Crim LR 767. Also Sharpe (1998): ch 2 on the common law, and ch 3 on the background to the 1984 legislation.

difficulty of reconciling confession-inducing questioning with the right of silence. The Judges' Rules, which codified the common law, stated that 'it is a fundamental condition of the admissibility in evidence' of a confession that 'it shall have been voluntary' and not secured 'by oppression' (or by inducements: see ch 5 above).

When PACE was drafted, the government intended largely to re-enact these common law rules. What is now s 76 provides for the exclusion of confession evidence obtained oppressively or in conditions making it likely to be unreliable. And what is now s 82(3) provides that nothing '... in this Part of this Act shall prejudice any power of a court to exclude evidence... at its discretion'. In addition, s 78 allows judges to exclude, at their discretion, any evidence obtained 'unfairly'. This criterion need not relate to reliability at all. Thus it covers most situations covered by s 82(3), some situations covered by s 76, and many other situations not previously covered by the common law.[160] In addition to these statutory provisions, we have to consider the common law abuse of process doctrine under which prosecutions can be halted entirely.

12.5.1 Principles underlying trial remedies

PACE, s 78 was a movement towards due process. The extent of that movement depends on the way 'unfairness' (plus s 76 and the abuse of process doctrine) is interpreted by the judges and how they use their discretion. Interpretation now has to comply with the ECHR (Art 6, the right to a fair trial). The meaning given to 'fairness' depends largely on the principles which judges implicitly – and occasionally explicitly – apply. Predicting which will be prominent in any one case is impossible. These principles are:[161]

Reliability: Evidence which is unreliable will be excluded. This hardly needs stating as a matter of principle, and is enshrined (in relation to confessions) in s 76. What is, or is not, regarded as reliable is, however, not at all straightforward, and some court evaluations here are based implicitly on the other principles set out below.[162] A pure crime control approach would adopt this principle alone.

Disciplinary: Sometimes evidence is excluded to discipline the police if the court considered that the police behaved especially badly or oppressively. Use of this principle in relation to all rule-breaking would be a hallmark of a pure due process approach.

Voluntarism: In keeping with the due process origins of English law (in theory, although not in practice), evidence obtained through compulsion used to be excluded, but is no longer. For example, bodily samples may in some circumstances be taken forcibly, and interrogation is imposed, not requested (see ch 4 and 5). The courts and legislature have attempted to put broad limits on the compulsion that can be adopted (banning violence, oppression and so forth), but otherwise this

---

[160] See Birch D, 'The PACE Hots Up: Confessions and Confusions Under the 1984 Act' [1989] Crim LR 95.   [161] These principles are set out in Sharpe (1998: ch 2) and in Mirfield (1997: ch 2).
[162] See Sharpe (1998: 132).

principle is rarely referred to, and it appears to be even more rarely relied upon, even implicitly.[163]

Judicial integrity: Evidence should be excluded if this best preserves the moral integrity of the legal system and/or public confidence in it, and included if this best fulfils that aim. This effects some kind of compromise between due process and crime control positions, but such compromises, as we suggested earlier, tend to be based on unarticulated and untested assumptions (about, for example, what may or may not erode public confidence), lack of principle and inconsistency from case to case. Thus is integrity eroded more by a minor deviation from the rules which was motivated by dishonesty on the part of the police, or by a major deviation from the rules which was the result of honest error by the police? What relevance, if any, is the effect on the defendant of the breach? We shall see that this principle is articulated usually in relation to abuse of process. The use of evidence obtained by torture has been held to undermine the principle.[164]

Protective: The essence of this principle is that where a defendant has been disadvantaged by a breach of the rules, the evidence obtained should be excluded. This could be seen as a variant on the 'judicial integrity' principle, in that it preserves moral integrity by preventing the system from profiting from a breach. Where a breach does not lead to a profit for the system (for example, if a detention review is late but would have led to continued detention had it been at the right time), the evidence obtained thereafter is useable. This principle has the merit of effecting a principled compromise between due process and crime control positions, although as we shall see, in practice it has been misused by the courts.

12.5.2 PACE, s 76: oppression and reliability

Confession evidence cannot be presented in court unless the prosecution proves that it was not obtained:

(a) by oppression of the person who made it; or

(b) in consequence of anything said or done which was likely, in the circumstances existing at the time, to render [it] unreliable...' (s 76(2)).

We saw in ch 5 that 'oppression' is not defined in PACE or elsewhere. It includes the ECHR, Art 3 prohibition on 'torture, inhuman or degrading treatment, and the use or threat of violence...' (s 76(8)) but is not confined to such extreme circumstances.[165] In *Fulling*, it was stated, obiter, that oppression must almost necessarily 'entail some impropriety'.[166] However, not all law-breaking, such as denial of access to legal advice,

---

[163] However, for a positive endorsement of the principle by the House of Lords, see *Mushtaq* [2005] 1 WLR 1513.   [164] *A and others v Secretary of State for the Home Department (No 2)* [2005] UKHL 71.
[165] See generally Sharpe (1998: 114–19).
[166] [1987] QB 426. The case is more fully discussed in 5.4. See, similarly, *Heaton* [1993] Crim LR 593.

is oppressive.[167] Not knowing just what behaviour will, and will not, be excluded under this heading limits its value as a deterrent to malpractice.[168] Circumstances 'likely' to render confession evidence 'unreliable' is similarly vague, and of similarly limited value as a deterrent. In *W*, for example, a confession made by a 13-year-old was held to be 'reliable'. Yet her 'appropriate adult' was her mother, who was psychotic at the time and therefore not capable of protecting or supporting her daughter.[169] Since anything which is excludable under s 76 is also, as we shall see, excludable under s 78, most defence lawyers argue under the latter. There is therefore little case law to clarify the scope of s 76.

Judicial interpretation of s 76 focuses on police intentions rather than the effects of their behaviour on suspects even though s 76 was intended to protect suspects. In *Miller*[170] a paranoid schizophrenic was questioned at length. This produced hallucinations and delusions, along with a confession. The Court of Appeal held that the fact that the defendant experienced the interrogation as oppressive did not make it so in law, for this was not the intention of the police and would not have been the result in normal circumstances. This was small comfort to Miller. The decision ignored the fact that few suspects experience custodial interrogation as normal, that the application of pressure is a natural police interrogation tactic, and that many more suspects are 'vulnerable' than are ever officially recognised as such, as we saw in ch 5. However, the 'reliability' rule should cater for such cases, and the Court of Appeal has frequently held that confessions by vulnerable suspects with very low IQs should be excluded on this basis.[171]

Since the courts only apply s 76 when the police are at fault, suspects who behave unreliably or feel oppressed because of their custodial circumstances do not benefit from this exclusionary provision, even though (as we saw in ch 5) it is the police who determine what those custodial circumstances are, and whether the suspect should be in custody. Thus in *Wahab*[172] the defendant and members of his family were arrested for drugs offences. Wahab asked his solicitor to negotiate with the police the release of his family in exchange for a confession. The responses of the police and solicitor were non-committal, but Wahab confessed anyway. He asked for the confession to be excluded on the ground that it was unreliable as it was made to secure his family's release. The Court of Appeal held not simply that the judge was right to regard it as reliable, as many factors could have led him to confess, but also that since the inducement to confess (release of his family) was self-induced, reliability was irrelevant – although,

---

[167] *Parker* [1995] Crim LR 233.

[168] However, the due process rationale of the rule was underlined in *Mushtaq* [2005] 1 WLR 1513, where the House of Lords held that, regardless of the ruling of the trial judge, if a jury considers a confession to have been obtained through oppression they should disregard it – even if they believe it to be true.

[169] [1994] Crim LR 130. See 4.2 for discussion of vulnerable suspects and the 'appropriate adult'.

[170] [1986] 1 WLR 1191.

[171] See eg *Everett* [1988] Crim LR 826; *Delaney* (1988) 88 Cr App Rep 338; and the 'Tottenham Three' case: *Re Raghip, Silcott and Braithwaite* (1991) *Times*, 9 December. Also see *Mackenzie* (1992) 96 Cr App Rep 98; *Sylvester* [2002] EWCA Crim 1327.   [172] [2003] 1 Cr App R 15.

had his relatives been wrongly arrested, this would have been taken into account. Another major limitation on the potential power of s 76 to increase freedom or due process is the refusal of UK courts to adopt the 'fruit of the poisoned tree' doctrine under which evidence obtained as a result of oppressively obtained confessions is no more admissible than the confessions themselves.[173]

12.5.3 **PACE, s 78: fairness**

Section 78(1) provides that:

...the court may refuse to allow evidence...if it appears to the court that, having regard to all the circumstances in which the evidence was obtained, the admission of the evidence would have such an adverse effect on the fairness of the proceedings that the court ought not to admit it.

Whereas s 76 applies to confession evidence alone, s 78 applies to all evidence. Unlike in s 76, the burden of proof in s 78 is on the defence.[174] The test is one of 'fairness' and if the court is satisfied on this it must then exercise a discretion (unlike s 76 where exclusion is mandatory if the 'oppression' or 'reliability' tests are satisfied). The decision not to adopt a hard and fast rule, combined with the sheer volume and diversity of unfair police practices, has resulted in a flood of reported appellate cases on exclusion (s 78 is said by Grevling (1997) to be the most cited provision of PACE). There is no consistent pattern in the deluge of appellate decisions. As Zuckerman puts it, 'The notion of fairness...can refer to a multitude of aspects and merely furnishes an excuse for achieving whatever result is wanted without rigorous justification.'[175]

The changes to the right of silence and the development of covert policing techniques stimulated this flow yet further in the late 1990s and early part of this century respectively.[176] These appellate decisions must form only a small fraction of the cases on which judges rule in the Crown Court. We have little idea of how Crown Court judges exercise their discretion, although in a small interview study most said that they decided on the basis of 'fairness' – which, in the light of Zuckerman's comment, tells us nothing. Few, if any, of the judges interviewed articulated the principles discussed earlier. One said that if his colleagues 'were asked about these principles they would not know what you were talking about'.[177] Asked by one of the authors how he decided s 78 cases, one Court of Appeal judge who, not unusually, had a commercial law background, replied, 'by the seat of my pants'. All that is clear is that a pure 'disciplinary' rule is disallowed, for a court which automatically excluded evidence obtained

---

[173] Indeed, s 76(4)(a) provides that exclusion does not affect the admissibility 'of any facts discovered as a result of the confession.' See Mirfield (1997: 221–5) and Mirfield P, 'Successive Confessions and the Poisonous Tree' [1996] Crim LR 554. Note that exclusion of collateral evidence can always be considered under s 78.   [174] See the commentary on *Keenan* [1989] Crim LR 720.

[175] Zuckerman A, 'Illegally Obtained Evidence: Discretion as a Guardian of Legitimacy' [1987] CLP 55.

[176] Ormerod and Birch (2004).

[177] Hunter M, 'Judicial Discretion: s 78 in Practice' [1994] Crim LR 558 at 562.

in breach of legal rules would not be exercising discretion properly.[178] What principles, including those outlined in 5.1 above and some others too, seem to predominate?

Bad faith

Two contrasting cases illustrate the view often taken by the courts, as in s 76 cases, that it is the motivation of the police, rather than the effect of the unfair behaviour on the defendant, that is the issue. In *Alladice*,[179] the police delayed access to legal advice under s 58. They thought that they were entitled to do this but the Court of Appeal decision in *Samuel*[180] intervened, making what they thought was lawful into an unlawful act. The confession evidence secured in the absence of a solicitor was held admissible due, in part, to what the Court of Appeal regarded as their good faith. In *Mason*,[181] by contrast, the police deliberately deceived the defendant (D) and his solicitor, saying that they had found D's fingerprints on an item when in fact they had not. D confessed. It was held that the confession should have been excluded, even though the police lies were not characterised as unlawful. However, only rarely is it held that behaviour which does not breach PACE or other legislation such as RIPA (see ch 6) should be excluded, trickery which does not involve lying is not regarded as per se unfair, and where it is only defendants (not their lawyers) who are deceived the courts are far less sympathetic.[182]

How valuable in protecting suspects is this approach? Alladice suffered no less through the police making an honest mistake than he would have done if they had acted out of malice. Good or bad faith is, in any case, difficult to ascertain. With no solicitor present, and no other independent witness, it was the officers' word against that of Alladice. It is also questionable whether good and bad faith are meaningful concepts in the context of police interrogation. After all, if suspects do not wish to speak, it is the job of the police to persuade them to do so. Like inducements, 'bad faith' is part of the game. Finally, Alladice, like many other defendants,[183] not only disputed the offence, but also disputed making the alleged confession to it. One of the purposes of having a right to a solicitor is to have a witness to the interrogation precisely to avoid such disputes.[184] Unlawful denial of the right to a solicitor deprives suspects of the chance of calling independent evidence to corroborate their claims that they did not make the confessions attributed to them. The most powerful argument for excluding

---

[178] Consider this rejection of the due process position by the then Lord Chief Justice: 'the object of a judge in considering the application of s 78 is not to discipline or punish police officers or custom officers...' (*Hughes* [1994] 1 WLR 876 at 879). Similarly strong statements were made in *Chalkley and Jeffries* [1998] 2 All ER 155.   [179] (1988) 87 Cr App Rep 380. Similarly see *Marsh* (below).

[180] [1988] QB 615.   [181] [1987] 3 All ER 481.

[182] See eg *Maclean and Kosten* [1993] Crim LR 687, *Bailey and Smith* (1993) 97 Cr App Rep 365, and *Looseley* [2001] UKHL 53. See ch 6 for discussion of a variety of deceptive covert policing tactics that have been held to be fair. For further cases following the reasoning of *Alladice*, see *Mason* [2002] 2 Cr App R 38 and *Gill* [2003] EWCA Crim 2256.

[183] For example, *Samuel*. See ch 5 for discussion of interrogation and confession problems.

[184] *Dunn* (1990) 91 Cr App Rep 237.

evidence in such circumstances, whatever the motives of the police, is that this is the only way of ensuring that suspects do not suffer from the wrongs done to them by the police.

Protective

This principle would be consistent with the freedom approach if courts were able or willing to ascertain when defendants would be prejudiced, were the disputed evidence to be admitted.[185] In *Alladice* (1988) the Court of Appeal considered that, leaving aside the issue of good faith, the confession was rightly admitted because, had Alladice seen a solicitor, the solicitor would only have told him of the rights of which he was already aware. No consideration was given to whether Alladice would have been better able to exercise his rights (particularly to silence) had his lawyer been present or, of course, to Alladice's 'right' to have a witness to what he did say to the police. Yet in *Dunn* (1990), when an informal interview was not recorded (a breach of Code of Practice C) the Court of Appeal held that the evidence was rightly admitted because Dunn's solicitor was present to witness the discussion, and so the defendant was not put at risk.[186] The Court of Appeal is clearly selective about how it applies this principle, in order to reduce its protectiveness. And it ignores the realities of police interrogation – that knowing one's rights and having the resilience to exercise them when under pressure to speak are entirely different things (see ch 5) – preferring to pretend that knowledge of one's rights puts one on a level footing with the police.

Significant breach

Several s 78 cases have held that some breaches of PACE or the codes of practice are so serious that exclusion of evidence is justified regardless of the intentions of the police or what the consequences of that breach might have been. They include *Keenan*,[187] where contemporaneous notes were not taken; *Canale*,[188] *Scott*[189] and *Oransaye*,[190] in each of which the police blatantly breached the rules on, among other things, contemporaneous recording;[191] and *Weekes*,[192] where a 'conversation' was said by the Court of Appeal to be an 'interview'. However, the principle has been diluted: first, in *Walsh*[193] where the Court of Appeal held that it was not enough that there be a substantial breach; there must also be 'such an adverse effect that justice requires the evidence to

---

[185] As they failed to do in *Dunford* (1990) 91 Cr App Rep 150. See Sanders A, 'Access to a Solicitor and s 78 PACE' (1990) LS Gaz 31, October, p 17 and Hodgson J, 'Tipping the Scales of Justice: The Suspect's Right to Legal Advice' [1992] Crim LR 854. More recent cases where this principle was implicitly invoked to justify not excluding evidence were *Senior and Senior* [2004] 2 Cr App R 12 and *Rehman* [2006] EWCA Crim 1900.

[186] The presence of a solicitor in the interrogation was similarly used to justify using unfairly obtained evidence in *Maya Devani* [2007] EWCA Crim 1926.   [187] [1989] 3 All ER 598.

[188] [1990] 2 All ER 187.   [189] [1991] Crim LR 56.   [190] [1993] Crim LR 772.

[191] Doubtless the 'good faith' principle also operated in these cases.   [192] [1993] Crim LR 211.

[193] [1989] Crim LR 822. It is hard to discern consistency. In the later case of *Raphaie* [1996] Crim LR 812 a straightforward 'substantial breach' test was adopted, but in *Forbes* [2001] AC 473 the House of Lords held that identification evidence obtained in breach of the Code of Practice should be allowed as it was reliable.

be excluded'. The result was the decision in *Dunn*, discussed above, where the breach was, by any standards, substantial. Secondly, in *Marsh*,[194] the 'good faith' test was another obstacle placed in the path of defendants. Thirdly, in *Attorney-General's Reference No 3 of 1999*,[195] Lord Steyn said, by way of justifying the use of evidence that would not have been obtained were it not for prior illegal action by the police, 'There must be fairness to all sides.... the position of the accused, the victim and his or her family, and the public.'[196]

The merit of the undiluted 'significant breach' test is that it enables judges to exercise discretion on the basis of the objective significance of the law in question. This is more certain and fairer than the other two tests which require subjective judgments and, in the case of the protective principle, a guess as to what defendants would have done had they been allowed by the police to exercise their rights. However, what is a substantial breach is itself a matter of subjective interpretation. One might have thought that any breach of the ECHR would be 'significant' – that is what makes something a 'human right'. However, this is not the view of the courts, as regards the 'right to privacy' (Art 8) at any rate. Thus confessions recorded illegally and covertly, for example, have not been excluded.[197] Given the disadvantages of a complete exclusion rule, and in the light of the unwillingness or inability of the Court of Appeal to use the protective principle to protect defendants, the significant breach principle would be the most effective way of reducing miscarriages of justice. Otherwise, implicit encouragement will be given to the current culture of police malpractice.

12.5.4 Halting criminal prosecutions: the abuse of process doctrine

It has long been a principle of common law that trials could be halted by the judge if malpractice by police officers or prosecutors made the trial an 'abuse of process'.[198] Traditionally, it has been reserved for the most deplorable behaviour. Thus, in two major cases in the 1990s, where the defendants were effectively kidnapped unlawfully by the police and security services and brought to the UK against their will, the doctrine was invoked and charges were dismissed on appeal. This was despite the

---

[194] [1991] Crim LR 455.   [195] [2001] 2 AC 91.

[196] At p 118. See Grevling (1997) on the consideration of interests other than those of the defendant in s 78 cases. The idea that victims, or some notion of their rights, should influence trial outcomes is bizarre, yet increasingly used to promote crime control measures. See Jackson J, 'Justice for All: Putting Victims at the Heart of Criminal Justice?' (2003) 30 JLS 309 and ch 13.

[197] *Mason* [2002], followed in *Button* [2005] Crim LR 571. Endorsed in *Khan v UK* [2001] 31 EHRR 45 and in *PG v UK* [2002] Crim LR 308 by the ECtHR. See ch 6 for discussion of covert policing. See generally, Ormerod D, 'ECHR and the Exclusion of Evidence: Trial Remedies for Art 8 Breaches?' [2003] Crim LR 61. Failure to caution before questioning – undoubtedly a 'significant breach' – was regarded as irrelevant in *Senior and Senior* (2004), Shillibier [2006] EWCA Crim 793 and *Rehman* (2006). See criticism in Crim LR [2007] 102.

[198] For the background, see Choo A, 'Halting Criminal Prosecutions: The Abuse of Process Doctrine Re-visited' [1995] Crim LR 864.

reliability of the evidence against them not being in doubt. In *Mullen* [1999] the Court of Appeal said that the unlawful deportation of the defendant was:

a blatant and extremely serious failure to adhere to the rule of law ... the need to discourage such conduct on the part of those who are responsible for criminal prosecutions is a matter of public policy to which ... very considerable weight must be attached.[199]

The application of the 'disciplinary' principle in this judgment is more apparent than real, as the Court held that judges must exercise a 'discretionary balance' (as with PACE, s 78). This applies the 'judicial integrity' principle, as in the notorious case concerning the suspected 'September 11' terrorists against whom there was evidence allegedly obtained in another country by torture;[200] and in a case where solicitor-client confidentiality was breached by unlawful police bugging of a police station exercise yard.[201] In these three cases it was eventually decided that the 'balance' should be exercised in the defendants' favour. But the vagueness and unpredictability of this principle has led the 'balance' to come down against defendants in other cases where – in our opinion – officials behaved almost as reprehensibly.[202] These other cases include other types of situation where, for example, agents provocateurs are involved[203] and unused evidence that should have been disclosed to the defence is lost or destroyed by the police or prosecution witnesses.[204] The inconsistency of the case law in all these situations shows that the judiciary does not always accept the need to discourage blatant and extremely serious failures to adhere to the rule of law. Is it right to convict citizens following trials tainted by such gross failures? Has not the verdict been deprived of all moral and condemnatory force by the illegal behaviour of the very officials charged with upholding the law?

12.5.5 The need for reform

We have seen that decisions on s 78 are generally crime control-based, the reliability principle usually outweighing the other principles except in cases of gross misconduct. However, what is 'gross' depends on a multitude of factors, not least the attitudes of the particular judges in the case. The crime control approach was endorsed by the ECtHR

---

[199] The invocation of the 'rule of law' here follows the House of Lords' judgment in *Horseferry Road Magistrates Court, ex p Bennett* [1994] 1 AC 42. For discussion of the rule of law in this context see Sanders A and Young R, 'The Rule of Law, Due Process and Pre-Trial Criminal Justice' (1994) 47 CLP 125.

[200] *A and others v Secretary of State for the Home Department (No 2)* [2005] UKHL 71.

[201] *Grant* [2005] 2 Cr App R 28.

[202] For a defence of the judicial integrity principle see Ashworth A, 'Testing Fidelity to Legal Values: Official Involvement and Criminal Justice' (2000) 63 MLR 633.

[203] Ormerod D and Roberts A, 'The trouble with *Teixeira*: developing a principled approach to entrapment' (2002) 6 IJ Evidence and Proof 38. See *Latif and Shazad* [1996] 1 All ER 353 and *Looseley* (2001). But in *Moon* [2004] the clear entrapment was held to be an abuse of process and the Court of Appeal said that proceedings should have been halted.

[204] Martin S, 'Lost and Destroyed Evidence: The Search for a Principled Approach to Abuse of Process' (2005) 9 IJE&P 158.

in *Khan* [2000], which agreed that it did not automatically follow from the defendant's privacy being violated (Art 8 ECHR) that the evidence should have been excluded. In every other House of Lords case in recent years it has been held that evidence obtained in 'non-s 76 circumstances' (for example, illegal bugging or entrapment) should not be excluded under s 78 except in exceptional circumstances; and that, if there is to be a trial remedy, it should normally be a halt to the prosecution on the ground of abuse of process. As we have seen, this is also only done in exceptional circumstances.[205] As Choo and Nash point out, this leads to the ludicrous position that in some circumstances judges can halt proceedings entirely even though they cannot take the less drastic action of excluding the offending evidence: 'What is at stake is surely the same fundamental question: should the prosecution be deprived of the fruits of the pre-trial police impropriety?'[206] Ironically, the development of the 'abuse of process' doctrine provided the excuse to narrow down the ambit of the s 78 discretion. This would not matter were it not for the reluctance of the courts in practice to use 'abuse of process' to halt prosecutions.

The crime control desire to facilitate policing often distorts the courts' normal reasoning processes. For example, in *Latif and Shazad* a customs officer acted as a go-between who encouraged one of the defendants to come to England and take part in the conspiracy. The argument that evidence should be excluded because of the unfairness of this was rejected by the House of Lords largely on the grounds of Shazad's general criminality.[207] Second, in some of these cases, such as *Christou*[208] and *Maclean and Kosten*[209] there were arguably breaches of PACE Code C, as the suspects were 'interviewed' without being cautioned. The view of the Court of Appeal was that, since cautioning would blow the officers' cover, it was not required.

Although this discussion of trial remedies has only scratched the surface of the problem, it should be clear that there are a multitude of potentially relevant considerations involved. The courts take all of them into account at one time or another but not in a rational or principled manner. Unfortunately, the Runciman Commission's evaluation of trial remedies was less than profound. Its complacent contribution amounted to a single sentence: 'We are satisfied generally with the way in which section 78 has worked in practice and propose no changes to it.'[210] How could anyone be satisfied with such confusion and contradiction? The only rationality in this pattern of decisions is that if an appropriate adult and/or legal adviser is present during interrogation, exclusion rarely follows. This is on the ground that suspects have been protected. Thus even when advisers or appropriate adults do their jobs badly,[211] or when breaches of Code C

---

[205] See especially *Latif and Shazad* [1996]; *Chalkley and Jeffries* [1998] 2 All ER 155 (see ch 3); *Looseley* [2001] (see ch 6). For discussion see Ashworth and Redmayne (2005: 322).

[206] Choo A and Nash S, 'What's the Matter with s 78?' [1999] Crim LR 929. See, similarly, Robertson G, 'Entrapment Evidence: Manna from Heaven, or Fruit of the Poisoned Tree?' [1994] Crim LR 805.

[207] This approach is similar to that taken in many US states but not in other common law jurisdictions: Sharpe S, 'Covert Policing: A Comparative View' (1996) 25 Anglo-Am LR 163.

[208] [1992] 4 All ER 559.   [209] [1993] Crim LR 687.   [210] RCCJ (1993: 58).

[211] *W* [1994] Crim LR 130.

take place in front of them,[212] the evidence is allowed. Paradoxically, the protections which PACE and its Code provide to give some effect to due process values are used to justify the application of crime control values at the trial and appeal stages. Opinions may legitimately differ as to the proper scope of exclusionary rules, but the attempt to hide the reality behind a facade of incoherent legal reasoning is unacceptable.

Since Runciman reported, the situation has become more complicated. The changes to the right of silence introduced in the Criminal Justice and Public Order Act 1994 have caused immense problems for the courts as well as for defendants, defence lawyers and prosecutors. And the shift in policing tactics from reactive to proactive policing means that s 78 cases increasingly concern covert operations, surveillance, bugging, the use of informers and so forth. It seems that, insofar as any clear pattern can be discerned, the courts do not impose the same level of protections for suspects in these cases as with police interrogation. Yet many of the people involved in these cases, such as informers, are even less trustworthy than the police, and when the police are undercover the scope for malpractice is at its height (see ch 6 and the investigation into the murder of the Belfast solicitor discussed in 12.6 below). When protection and control are most needed the courts fail to provide it.[213] At worst, major corruption and malpractice have been encouraged and now flourish; at best, it is a crisis waiting to happen.

A major inquiry now needs to decide: what principles should govern trial remedies; the extent to which those principles should apply equally in different situations (eg interrogation, covert policing, identification, retention of scientific evidence); whether particular weight should be given to breaches of the ECHR; whether s 78-type remedies and abuse of process, which are currently hopelessly blurred, should be merged. These evaluations should be made in furtherance of the 'freedom' approach – in other words, they should be neither blindly crime control oriented (for the real crime control gains would be outweighed by the inadequate protection given to the rights and freedoms of defendants), but nor should they be blindly due process or human rights-based, for it is wrong to jeopardise cases in which there are no significant losses caused by rule-breaking. In making these evaluations we need to take into account not just formal legal principles and matters of 'internal' legal logic, but also the reality of the criminal justice process – for example, whether or not a legal adviser or appropriate adult actually protected a defendant who was denied a particular right is more important than their presence when the malpractice occurred; that knowing one's rights and having the confidence to exercise them in coercive situations are not the same thing. Finally, this should be done alongside an appraisal of the degree of protection

---

[212] *Dunn* (1990).

[213] See Sharpe S, 'Covert Police Operations and the Discretionary Exclusion of Evidence' [1994] Crim LR 793. For a different view, see Birch D, 'Excluding Evidence from Entrapment: What is a Fair Cop?' [1994] CLP 73; Ormerod and Roberts (2002). For a general critique, using comparisons with Commonwealth countries, see Choo A and Nash S, 'Improperly Obtained Evidence in the Commonwealth: Lessons for England and Wales?' (2007) 11 IJ E&P 75.

and remedial possibilities provided by other remedies discussed in this chapter – for although, arguably, an effective complaints system would provide a better remedy against malpractice than the exclusion of evidence, if there is no such alternative, exclusion of evidence is better than nothing.

12.6 **Malpractice: individual fault or the system at work?**

Like most sets of facts amounting to possible crimes, most statistics can be presented in two or more ways. This chapter has made a lot out of the hundreds of substantiated complaints, millions of pounds in damages and hundreds of excluded confessions that every year point to widespread police malpractice and error. And that is not including the malpractice and error that is not proven, not challenged, and not even known about by the victims (such as illegal covert surveillance). But another way of looking at this dismal picture is to observe that, in a country with over 100,000 police officers, who arrest one million suspects each year, a few hundred (or even a few thousand) mistakes per year are only to be expected, especially as many are fairly trivial. Both views are plausible until one looks at the source and nature of malpractice and error. In reality, there is so much that the police can do in furtherance of their goals within the rules that there is rarely much need to breach them. In low visibility situations, police officers may nonetheless break the rules on a systematic basis. In other words, just because malpractice and rule-breaking is (relatively) rare, it does not follow that it is aberrant. Instead of malpractice being different in nature from normal policing, it may just be one end of the spectrum of normal policing; and instead of rule-breaking officers being unusually incompetent, unethical or corrupt, it may be that most officers break rules for normal policing purposes some of the time.

If it is true that rule-breaking is systemic, then it should be tackled at the level of the criminal justice system through structural reform. However, with the partial exception of recent changes to the police complaints and discipline system, all the remedies discussed in this chapter are individualistic, that is, they all treat alleged wrongs and errors as individual problems arising from individual mistakes. Although legal processes usually individualise conflict, the structural nature of some problems are glaringly obvious. Even then, when the Police Complaints Authority belatedly launched an inquiry into the West Midlands Police Serious Crime Squad, this took the form of pursuing individual malpractices, rather than investigating the squad and its working practices as a whole.

But the response need not be individualistic. In *Edwards*[214] the Court of Appeal accepted that some police officers break the law on a systematic basis and that defence

---

[214]   [1991] 2 All ER 266.

lawyers should be able to discredit them by referring to their past deeds. Similarly, in *Judith Ward*[215] the Court of Appeal responded to evidence of the systematic non-disclosure of evidence by the police, government forensic scientists, the Director of Public Prosecutions and prosecuting counsel by laying down, for the first time, a systematic statement of the common law requirements on disclosure (see 7.3.3). And wide-ranging inquiries into policing, its context and its consequences are possible, as Lord Scarman's (1981) inquiry into the Brixton disorders of 1981 demonstrates. But the government did not repeat the Scarman experiment until it established the Macpherson inquiry into the Stephen Lawrence affair in the late 1990s (Macpherson, 1999). And, as a result of his enquiry into the murder of a Belfast solicitor, the then Metropolitan Police Commissioner found that: 'Widespread collusion between the security forces and loyalist paramilitaries in Northern Ireland continued unchecked for years because a culture of "gross unprofessionalism and irresponsibility" allowed officers to create a climate in which Catholics could be murdered with near impunity.'[216]

It is one thing to point to systemic malpractice by one squad, or to finally accept that there is institutionalised racism in the police (as the Macpherson inquiry did), and another to claim that the great bulk of police malpractice is systemic (ie a natural product of the criminal justice system). There are several possible explanations for police malpractice; they are not mutually exclusive.

Firstly, there is the 'rotten apple' theory, beloved of senior police officers and politicians, whereby a few unscrupulous or incompetent officers commit all the wrongs. Such rotten officers will be detected and removed from the barrel before the great mass of law-abiding police officers become infected through contact. This ignores the evidence of widespread rule-breaking uncovered by research; the 'code of silence' operated by senior as well as junior officers to cover it up; and the failure to discipline adequately most of those few officers who are found to have broken the rules. This is not to deny that there are some particularly violent, racist, sexist, homophobic or corrupt cops who disgust their fellow officers as much as the rest of us. But if malpractice is a result of rotten apples, they must have infected the barrel as well as its contents.

Secondly, there is the 'technical failure' theory. We all make mistakes, rules are misunderstood, training needs improvement, technology needs development. There is some truth in this. But for it to be generally true we would expect many more even-handed 'errors': as many summaries of interrogation which wrongly suggest that no incriminating statements were made as suggest the opposite; non-authorisation of detention when it is necessary, as well as authorisation when it is not; police contact with solicitors, friends or family when it was not clear that this was the wish of the suspect, as well as non-contact in these circumstances; and contact with a psychologist or social worker when a suspect might be, but probably is not, vulnerable, as well as non-contact when suspects might not be, but probably are, vulnerable. The 'errors' we

215 [1993] 1 WLR 619.   216 *The Guardian*, 14 June 2002.

detected as we have examined each stage of the criminal process in turn can scarcely be described as even-handed.

These two theories are primarily individualistic. The individualistic remedies we have discussed are directed at 'the problems' as conceived (individualistically) by these theories, and are inadequate in the light of the evidence discussed in this book. The final two theories are systemic. Irving and Dunnighan apply a systems approach to police work similar to that applied by social psychologists in other fields of work.[217] This approach assumes that humans naturally err and that the best systems are those that accept this as inevitable but which also work on the basis that this is undesirable. Prevention and correction of error should therefore be designed into the system through quality control procedures as with factories and other production systems. Irving and Dunnighan found that the CID has no systems for identifying the sources of error, that training does not direct itself to sources of error, and that there is little, if any, supervision which aims to identify error.[218]

The implications of Irving and Dunnighan's theory are that individualistic remedies will be far less effective as preventive measures than will training and supervision which focuses on error combined with a complete redesign of police structures. But they seem to assume that systemic error in legal terms is also systemic error in terms of the organisation and production of criminal justice. The evidence discussed in this book suggests that this is rarely so. Arrest without reasonable suspicion is often functional for the system; so is fiddled scientific evidence and ID procedures, illegal surveillance, unnecessary detention and informal interviews. And the issue goes beyond the police. Prosecutors prosecute in breach of prosecution guidelines, judges engage in plea bargaining and defence lawyers do little by way of defence, even if these things are not always and everywhere the same. Much of this behaviour involves rule-breaking but it is all grist to the crime control mill. A slightly different example is that of London Underground, which was fined £225,000 for health and safety offences. In 'sacrificing safety in favour of profits' it allowed a manager to force employees to work alongside live rails that led to many getting electrical shocks, causing one to be hospitalised. The manager's rule-breaking was functional for the system: 'He tried to intimidate the inspector by saying it would be his fault if the Central Line was closed down and ordered his men to continue working.' The manager was also convicted, and appealed on the basis that: 'I feel that I always abided by the rules. I received commendations for my work on the London Underground and received nothing but praise from my bosses.'[219]

Systemic rule-breaking, on this theory, then, is a product of the lack of fit between due process rules (to the extent that they are due process in content) and crime control

---

[217] Irving B and Dunnighan C, *Human Factors in the Quality Control of CID Investigations* (Royal Commission on Criminal Justice, Research Study No 21) (London: HMSO, 1993).

[218] On the inadequacy of supervision, see also Baldwin J and Moloney T, *Supervision of Police Investigation in Serious Criminal Cases* (Royal Commission on Criminal Justice Research Study No 4) (London: HMSO, 1992) and Maguire M and Norris C, *The Conduct and Supervision of Criminal Investigations* (Royal Commission on Criminal Justice, Research Study No 5) (London: HMSO, 1992).

[219] *The Guardian*, 11 January 2002.

roles, objectives and working rules. On this theory, unlike in Irving and Dunnighan's, it is not in the interest of the organisation to discover and correct most rule-breaking because rule-breaking is, from its perspective, almost always functional. This could explain why there are no quality control systems, why complaints procedures 'fail' to uncover malpractice, and why court-based remedies are so inadequate. The Taylor review (2005) implicitly adopted this approach, recognising that it would be counter-productive to identify most malpractice, or even to treat it as such. The Taylor reforms allow the police to condone useful malpractice and correct or condemn that which is dysfunctional. There are only two ways to eradicate malpractice: either eradicate the whole crime control environment so that roles, objectives and working rules are transformed and infused with due process values (unrealistic in the current political climate) or eradicate the due process rules so that practices are no longer malpractices. Taylor was not willing to lose crime control efficiency by adopting the first solution, or the veneer of due process respectability by adopting the second solution.

However, to the extent that some malpractice is attributable to the first three theories we examined, malpractice can be reduced without such drastic change. To correct and prevent error, the fullest information is needed. To secure this, especially in a low visibility occupation like the police, the cooperation is needed of those who know what is happening. If either of the two individualistic theories are valid, cooperation would be expected: information would be provided by the 'good' officers against the 'bad'. This rarely seems to happen, indicating that only a small amount of malpractice can be explained using those two theories; and when it does, whistleblowing officers are not always believed.[220]

Where malpractice is systemic, it will be perceived as unfair to punish one person for something that is routine and condoned by senior officers. The protection of colleagues, oneself and one's organisation is a natural response if discovery of malpractice is likely to lead to adverse consequences for those 'found out' or for organisational morale. On the other hand, if information and cooperation are required only to correct and prevent error, with no disciplinary or punitive consequences, cooperation and information are much more likely to be forthcoming. In other words, systems of discipline are incompatible with systems of diagnosis and prevention.[221] Even the brutality of the Holloway Road scandal – which could well have had a 'bad apple' element to it – was opened up only after limited immunity was offered.[222]

This suggests that the only way malpractice can be tackled systematically, if at all, whilst retaining a genuine system of remedies (ie which punish and/or compensate), is by having two systems working in parallel: a management information system and a complaints and remedies investigation system, whereby no 'leakage' would be allowed from the former to the latter. Prior to the PRA 2002 no 'leakage' was allowed from complaints

---

[220] As in the case against PC Jones, discussed in 12.2.1. But see the new 'standard' discussed in 12.4.2.

[221] Bayley (1995).

[222] See East R, 'Police Brutality: Lessons of the Holloway Road Assault' (1987) 137 NLJ 1010 and by Hilliard B, 'Holloway Road – Unfinished Business' (1987) 137 NLJ 1035.

investigations to civil actions, although the discipline and criminal prosecution processes continue to share the same information. It seems that if we want to alter police practices systematically we not only have to accept Irving and Dunnighan's optimistic theory of malpractice, we would also have to reverse the decision to make complaints files available to civil litigants, and agree to keep investigations into error separate from investigations into possible criminal acts by officers. This might be too high a price to pay for the hope of improving police practices in general, but only if those individualistic remedies are of true value. This is questionable, as the prosecution process rarely 'bites' on police officers; complaint investigation remain largely in the hands of the police; civil actions, like the complaints system, was largely designed (insofar as it was designed at all) for other purposes; and there is no coherent and predictable basis on which to decide the admissibility of wrongly obtained evidence. Our system of remedies is primarily enabling, legitimising and presentational in relation to police working rules.[223]

This might seem an unduly negative and cynical conclusion. We seem to be stuck with accepting a crime control culture, where a fairly high level of wrongful convictions are inevitable and many more suspects suffer indignity and deprivation. But scepticism about the way systems work need not be cynical. Irving and Dunnighan's work in effect applies to the police the sceptical model of analysis which sociologists have long applied to all occupations. Their aim, like ours, is to improve the police system, not to undermine it. The first step to successful reform is accurate identification of the problem to be addressed. Reforms are unlikely to succeed if the system they are applied to is not understood in the first place. The second step is to encourage a frank debate in which the police are open about what they do, lawfully and unlawfully, and what they can deliver without rule-breaking. If what can be delivered legally is not enough, then we have to consider such options as legitimising some illegal practices, reducing or changing our expectations of the police, or tackling crime in some other way, as by alleviating the conditions which are associated with violence, theft and so forth.

12.7 Conclusion

Remedial procedures exist in order that abuse of power by officials (the police, prosecutors and trial judges) acting for, or in tandem with, the executive may be checked and redressed. Yet it is the executive which determines how well resourced these

---

[223] Nonetheless there is reason for a little cautious optimism. The IPCC (2009a: 8), for all its faults, realises that it is vital that the causes of malpractice be tackled, even at some cost to the resolution of specific complaints. Whether it is able or willing to deal sufficiently robustly with the police to do this is doubtful, but at least the IPCC is at last asking the right questions. See further Inquest response to IPCC stock take consultation 2008 (Inquest, October 2008) (<http://inquest.org.uk/publications> – accessed 18/11/09) and Shaw H and Coles D, *Unlocking the Truth: Families' Experiences of the Investigation of Deaths in Custody* (London: Inquest, 2007).

procedures shall be. There is a conflict of interest here. In practice, remedial procedures are starved of the necessary resources. Legal aid is being cut for civil actions, is
not available for police complaints and does not get through to convicted people who
might have grounds for appeal. Like the Criminal Cases Review Commission (see
ch 11), the IPCC does not have the resources needed to assert true independence from
the executive, and the same is increasingly true of defence lawyers. The former two
bodies are forced into deterring, sifting out and not acting upon the majority of cases
which potentially fall within their jurisdictions, whilst the most important decision
most of the latter have to make is the precise level of poor practice at which they will
operate. But the problems run much deeper than a lack of resources.

First, the IPCC and CPS are not fully independent of the police. This is partly a
matter of case construction (as discussed in ch 7), in that most IPCC and CPS decisions are taken on the basis of investigation by some police officers into other police
officers. It is also a cultural matter: both bodies often regard investigation of potentially criminal police actions as of little importance. Time after time the IPCC initially accepts the police version of events (eg the de Menezes, Rigg and Faisal Al-Ani
cases) until proven wrong. How often, when complainants and their families cannot
prove the police version wrong, do the IPCC simply accept the police version? And
is it not the IPCC's job to question the police version? Nor, all too often, does either
body act with any sense of urgency – as in, for example, Rigg's case where officers
were not interviewed for months. In some 50% of cases it takes 'a disproportionate
length of time' for the police or IPCC to send a file to the CPS (HMIC/HMCPSI,
2007: para 7.4). There are then unaccountable delays of several months before the
CPS makes a decision in many cases. The importance with which the CPS regards
police wrongdoing is indicated by it not even having a system for tracking how many
such cases it deals with, how long it takes to deal with cases, and what proportions
are prosecuted and end in conviction (HMIC/HMCPSI, 2007: paras 4.7, 5.1–5.16,
7.10–7.24). 'These cases should be dealt with . . . in the same way as any other', pro-
claims the HMIC/HMCPSI report (para 7.2), but the fact is that they are not. The
same report goes on to say that some delays are because it is 'difficult to facilitate
interviews under caution or to contact police officers who may be suspended from
duty' (para 7.11). If we really want to deal with all cases 'the same way' and reduce
delay, the answer is simply and not even costly. Why not arrest the suspect police
officers?

Second, none of the remedies we have discussed provides adequate protection for
some of the most central 'rights' in the criminal justice system. Rules restricting stop-
search, roadblocks and unsuitable identification procedures, and rights, for instance,
to a lawyer, to silence, and to be treated with respect when in police custody, are not
catered for at all by civil and criminal remedies; equivocally by exclusionary rules; and
only half-heartedly by appeal procedures. These rights have no effective remedies. It
seems that many police actions take place in a legal wilderness, such that officers can
roam at will without the restraint of the rule of law.

Further reading

Choo A and Nash S, 'Improperly Obtained Evidence in the Commonwealth: Lessons for England and Wales?' (2007) 11 IJ E&P 75

Crawley J, 'The Worst of All Outcomes' *Society Guardian*, 8 April 2009 (<http://www.guardian.co.uk/society/2009/apr/08/police-complaints-commission> – accessed 5 January 2010)

Palmer P and Steele J, 'Police Shootings and the Role of Tort' (2008) 71 MLR 801

Shaw H and Coles D, *Unlocking the Truth: Families' Experiences of the Investigation of Deaths in Custody* (London: Inquest, 2007) (executive summary available from <http://inquest.gn.apc.org/pdf/unlocking_the_truth_executive_summary.pdf> – accessed 5 January 2010)

13

Victims, the accused and the future of criminal justice

A shop assistant who was hurt apprehending a shoplifter wrote the following in her victim personal statement (for use by the prosecution and the courts): '...continuously feeling sick whenever I have to go to work...cannot walk through shops to take children to their grand-ma's...if I walk outside at night I break out in a hot sweat.'[1]
A victim at the end of his case, having made a statement at the start: 'the police were great at first, then they left us to it. No phone calls, nothing.'[2]

Key issues

- How developments in criminal justice have affected suspects' rights (especially 'proactive' policing)
- Different types of victims' 'rights'
- Do and should victims have (legally) enforceable rights? If so, in relation to what matters?
- Enhancing victims' rights (especially those of vulnerable victims) without eroding defendants' rights
- Concluding thoughts on our 'freedom' perspective

13.1 **Introduction**

In this book we have tried to show that in criminal justice trade-offs cannot be avoided. One of the main trade-offs is that in the course of catching and convicting more criminals, one will catch and convict more innocent people too. Another is that the system cannot always do what victims want, especially if different victims ask

---

[1] Morgan R and Sanders A, *The Uses of Victim Statements* (London: Home Office, 1999) p 10.
[2] Hoyle et al, *Evaluation of the 'One Stop Shop' and Victim Statement Pilot Projects* (London: Home Office, 1998) p 32.

for different things, without prejudicing other important values, such as equality of treatment. Criminal justice rules and policies reflect the natural ambivalence most of us feel when faced with uncomfortable reality, but unwillingness to accept this lesson fully has led to many rules and policies being unworkable.

This is not to say that due process-based rules, for example, are necessarily unworkable, nor that they are continually broken. The police probably stick to most of the rules most of the time. However, most of the time, the rules enable the police to do their job without difficulty. The problem arises when they get in the way. Due process rules are unworkable in the sense that, in those circumstances, the police have the incentive and the opportunity to break them with little fear of negative consequences. The same is true of procedures for taking account of victims.

The working rules of the law enforcement bureaucracies are not in harmony either with those legal rules which are due process-based or with those which seek to give effect to the interests of victims. And so we have a significant (but unquantifiable) level of rule-breaking by law enforcement agencies, some of which leads to (legally speaking) wrongful conviction, and much of which leads to unnecessary and unpleasant pre-charge detention. But many legal rules are inspired by crime control ideology, so we also have a significant (and also unquantifiable) level of wrongful conviction which is a product of the police following the legal rules, just as much unpleasant pre-charge detention is perfectly lawful. The same is true of victims – sometimes what they want is ignored, in defiance of applicable policies, and sometimes what they want is ignored in accordance with applicable policies. The criminal justice system encompasses largely crime control-oriented rules and even more profoundly crime control-oriented policies and practices. It follows that the criminal justice system is not due process or freedom oriented. Several important consequences flow from this, which we shall briefly survey in this final chapter.

13.2 **Taking suspects' rights seriously**

We saw in chs 3 to 6 that, over the course of the twentieth century, the police station became the central site of police investigation. Not only have interrogation-based confessions become steadily more central to the prosecution case, but other investigative procedures take place in, begin from, or are authorised in the police station by the police. PACE and subsequent developments legitimised and facilitated these evolving processes. Take the initiation of prosecutions: arrest and charge (which entail initial detention) have now almost entirely supplanted the use of report and summons (which does not) for all but the most minor offences; and the police themselves are increasingly disposing of cases by warnings, cautions, and Penalty Notices for Disorder (PNDs). Furthermore, much police power is used to further policies and strategies such as pre-empting protests, gathering information, disciplining 'suspect populations' and so forth, whereby there is no intention of prosecuting. There is nothing new in this, nor in police station detention being used as part of these tactics, but the legitimisation of all this has probably increased its scale, such that around half of all arrests do not result in any further action. A core crime control value is trust in the police, and trends in criminal justice show that policy-makers do indeed have blind faith in them.

Against our argument, one might contend that the police are closely regulated and that the system is 'in balance'. After all, everything that takes place in the station is regulated by custody officers, records, time limits, recordings (in the case of interrogations), special safeguards where suspects are vulnerable (such as appropriate adults, doctors and so forth) and access to free legal advice for all. There are guarantees of proper treatment and freedom from coercion and violence. And the CPS protects defendants by dropping weak cases. None of this works perfectly, but one might still argue that these protections operate satisfactorily most of the time. Most suspects who do not secure legal advice, for example, choose not to seek it and come to no harm as a result of not securing it.

There is some truth in these counterarguments. But there are two main problems with them.

First, they ignore wider developments which have effectively circumvented the PACE regime. For while PACE made some policing controllable in the station, much policing has moved back outside, bringing in its wake several of the old problems and many new ones. Thus the ever-increasing practices of stop and account, stop-search and other forms of 'informal interviewing' (both inside and outside the station) enable the police to sidestep the controls now associated with formal interrogation. Moreover, many people who might otherwise have been forced to 'confess' are now simply tricked into committing crime while informers and undercover officers or surveillance devices look on. And many PNDs and warnings are administered outside the station by front-line officers free of any effective supervision.

Second, the police mainly regulate themselves: the officer carrying out the stop-search fills in the stop-search form, the police investigate complaints against themselves, and so forth. Self-regulation only works when it is in the interest of the organisation to secure compliance. This is not, in the main, the case with the police. Effective regulation requires that power be dispersed – which, in the case of the police station, would mean giving defence solicitors, say, many more rights over the police than they have at present.[3] As it is, there is less accountability with each new development, creating more scope for malpractice and corruption.

The move to proactive and pre-emptive policing and on-street dispositions shows the resourcefulness of the government and its agencies to achieve the same goals as before but to find new ways of doing so when legal rules get in the way. However, proactive policing can only supplement, not supplant, reactive policing.[4] To organise a police force solely around 'targeted' crime and not to react to serious 'non-targeted'

---

[3] Sanders A 'Can Coercive Powers be Effectively Controlled or Regulated?' in Cape E and Young R (eds), *Regulating Policing* (Oxford: Hart, 2008); Shearing C and Froestad J, 'Nodal Governance and the Zwelethemba Model' in Quirk et al (eds), *Regulation and Criminal Justice* (Cambridge: CUP, 2010).

[4] See, for example, Heaton R, 'Intelligence-Led Policing and Volume Crime Reduction' (2009) 3 Policing 292.

offending is unthinkable. Moreover, the police are neither structured nor sufficiently culturally attuned to make effective use of crime intelligence and scientific data to the extent required by the 'intelligence-led' model .[5]

Serious crimes will always be committed without the police's prior knowledge, thus calling for an investigative reaction. The police have to have some powers if there is to be a reasonable conviction rate without unreasonable expenditure of resources. Thus, at the same time as proactive policing was developing in order to counteract the effect of PACE on police 'success' rates, the government virtually abolished the right to silence, sidelining legal advice and reducing the need to intimidate to secure confessions, because silence is equally incriminating. A main plank of the so-called 'balanced' system was removed.   There are no remedies available to suspects who suffer from many of these rules being broken, and the remedies that are available are deeply flawed. Unfairly and illegally obtained evidence is frequently used at trial (ch 12). And we know from chs 8 to 10 that trials are rare anyway, for a host of reasons that have only a tenuous link with factual guilt and innocence. Further, the main reason why so many people do as the police tell them on the street, or refuse legal advice and make incriminating statements, is that they experience policing – especially in the station – as coercive, frightening and humiliating. Suspects make coerced choices without the police having to be overtly threatening or hostile. This crime control-based system subjects the police to the rule of law only in a minimalist and largely rhetorical manner.[6] The Human Rights Act, and the ECHR generally, has made little difference, acting only as the lowest of safety nets. As for the CPS acting as a safeguard, if the objective is to protect suspects and defendants would it not be better to put more resources into funding defence lawyers, into strengthening the defence side of the adversarial system?

A different challenge to our view of the system as primarily crime control oriented comes from Ericson and Haggerty. As we saw in ch 6, they argue that criminal justice has been completely transformed.[7] This rests on a wider argument that developed societies are becoming ever more obsessed with 'risk'. Institutions and individuals increasingly expect 'security', and the more breaches of that security there are, the more that (unfulfillable) demand swells. Risk assessment and risk management, based on progressively expanding information, have therefore become key tools in the attempt to increase security. The police are one of the key providers of information, particularly as their information-gathering powers increase. Hence the growth of powers to secure

---

[5] Maguire M and John T, *Intelligence, Surveillance and Informants: Integrated Approaches* (Police Research Series Paper 64) (London: Home Office, 1995); Barton A and Evans R, *Proactive Policing on Merseyside* (Police Research Series Paper No 105) (London: Home Office, 1999); on 'crime analysis' see Cope N, 'Intelligence Led Policing or Policing Led Intelligence?' (2004) 44 BJ Crim 188; on police failings in collating simple information, particularly in relation to the murders of Jessica Chapman and Holly Wells, see Gill P, 'Policing in Ignorance?' (2004) 58 Criminal Justice Matters 14.

[6] See further Sanders A and Young R, 'The Rule of Law, Due Process and Pre-Trial Criminal Justice' (1994b) 47 Current Legal Problems 125.

[7] Ericson R and Haggerty K, *Policing the Risk Society* (Oxford: Clarendon Press, 1997).

surveillance and other types of information, such as keeping DNA records of around a million arrested people who have not even been prosecuted.[8] Then there is a ratcheting effect: according to the government's own human genetics commission many people are arrested simply in order to justify taking a DNA sample.[9] So powers are created to take samples, then other powers are stretched in order to facilitate taking as many samples as possible. Other examples include 'public protection' (MAPPA) monitoring of people who have been acquitted,[10] registration requirements and other forms of surveillance of sex offenders and 'foreign students', the accumulation of information on people subject to anti-social behaviour orders (ASBOs), briefly discussed in ch 1, and new powers to freeze the funds of suspected terrorists (who have never been even charged with offences remotely connected with terrorism).[11] It is sometimes claimed that developments like this represent a shift in focus from 'post-crime' (that is, dealing with crimes that have been committed) to 'pre-crime' (that is, crime prevention and apprehension of crime at the planning stage).[12]

These developments are common to many western societies.[13] We can infer from this that the structural roots of these changes go deeper than the particular political or legislative fads of any one moment. It is not only the police but many other agencies (such as local authorities) who are increasing their information-gathering and surveillance powers and sharing information with each other resulting in government-by-information (or 'governmentality', as it is characterised by Foucault and his followers) – dispersing state power more widely than had been the case in earlier times.

Whilst these analyses accurately describe current developments up to a point, their 'either/or-ism' (crime control or surveillance control, state power or dispersed power, pre-crime or post-crime) is unnecessary. These processes are consistent with our argument that the system is an increasingly crime control one. The two go hand-in-hand. As some crime control techniques, such as coercive interrogation methods, become more difficult to use – because there are some due process developments, and some of them are effective to some extent – surveillance techniques and scientific methods develop to fill the gap. Risk analysis does not displace crime control, but rather shores it up. Further, as criminal methods become more sophisticated, so the methods of detecting it have to develop accordingly. Old methods are not replaced; they are supplemented by new ones so that a 'menu' of detection methods is available to cover

---

[8] Keeping these records indefinitely is contrary to Art 8 of the ECHR: *Marper v UK* [2008] ECHR 1581. See 6.6.2.

[9] Human Genetics Commission, *Nothing to Hide, Nothing to Fear?* (London: HGC, 2009) See *The Guardian*, 24 November 2009.

[10] Such as Barry George who was acquitted of the murder of Jill Dando. His MAPPA order requires him to keep the police informed of his address and movements. He is challenging this in court: *The Guardian*, 30 November 2009.   [11] *The Guardian*, 3 November 2008.

[12] Zedner L, 'Pre-Crime and Post-Criminology?' (2007) 11 Theoretical Criminology 261; McCulloch and Pickering (2009). For example, the HGC (2009) argues that the DNA database creates 'pre-suspects'.

[13] See, for example, Fijnaut C and Marx G (eds) *Undercover: Police Surveillance in Comparative Perspective* (The Hague: Kluwer, 1996).

increasingly varied needs. Take terrorism legislation. The first edition of this book (1994) hardly mentioned it, as we actually believed that it could be, as the government claimed, 'temporary'. It became evident in the late 1990s that this was not true, so we did discuss it in the second edition. By the time that edition was published, in 2000, the conflict in Northern Ireland looked like it was going to be concluded peacefully, and we wondered whether we had been right the first time. How naive we were. Not only have new targets of this legislation been found, but the provisions have got much tougher and many of them have found their way into 'normal' criminal justice processes (such as extended detention periods). We have seen that terrorists, many more innocent people suspected of terrorism, and people like journalists and tourists innocently photographing public buildings who are no more likely to be terrorists than anyone else[14] are the subject of the most heavy-handed crime control methods *and* the most sophisticated covert policing methods. It would not be so bad if this Orwellian surveillance-control combination provided a safeguard against innocent people being detained for days. It doesn't. It doesn't even stop some of them being abused, and occasionally even being shot dead.

Moreover, risk analysis is not a neutral process. By targeting high-crime social groups as well as high-risk individuals it draws on the 'knowledge' the criminal justice system has generated about marginalised sections of society that is a product of skewed thinking in the first place. In other words, risk analysis reproduces, instead of reconceptualising, existing patterns in order better to control or punish them.[15] Proactive policing would have to increase hugely before reactive policing was so diminished that crime control truly gave way to surveillance control. And the powers acquired by local authorities and regulatory agencies do not challenge or weaken police power but add to it. The information-gathering process is greater than the sum of its parts.

It is possible to envisage a different kind of system altogether, based on our freedom perspective. Without compulsory detention for all suspected offences except the most serious, the police would have to investigate more thoroughly before arrest. This would be less intrusive and therefore less eroding of freedom. Interviews could be conducted at home, work or anywhere suspects felt most comfortable. Most suspects would be happy to wait for a legal adviser or supporter to arrive in those circumstances. Covert methods and searches would be allowed, but would be better controlled – by, for example, the judiciary or a multidisciplinary body of part-time lay people on Parole Board lines. The police could be obliged to disclose their case to suspects and their advisers so that they knew what allegations they were answering and so that advisers did not have to barter their clients' rights. This system would lead to fewer confessions, fewer convictions and, on the face of it, greater expenditure of police resources (although the improvement in police-community relations it could lead to would increase public cooperation which should counterbalance, to an unknown extent, what the police

---

[14] See eg *The Independent*, 4 December 2009.
[15] See, in relation to 'crime analysis' for example, Innes et al, 'The Appliance of Science?: The Theory and Practice of Crime Intelligence Analysis' (2005) 45 BJ Crim 39.

lose in effectiveness). It is true that there would be fewer convictions of the guilty. But there would also be fewer convictions of the innocent, as well as less coercion of all suspects, whether guilty or not. Also, the latitude currently given to the police allows discretion to be exercised in unfairly discriminatory ways in terms of ethnic group, socio-economic group, age and gender. Our ideal system would prioritise due process and freedom. The current system does not and cannot. To pretend otherwise is to delude ourselves.

13.3 **Taking victims' rights seriously**

This chapter has been concerned so far with the erosion of the freedom of suspects and defendants. We should be equally concerned with the freedom of victims. It is justifiable to reduce freedom for suspects if this leads to more freedom for victims, to the extent of a net gain in freedom.[16] It is not possible to be sure about whether this has happened over the last 20 years or so, but it seems unlikely. As we saw in ch 1, victims and offenders are not distinct groups. There is considerable overlap between them. Further, what victims want most is not increased punishment or even detection, but some confidence that it will not happen again.[17] The kind of detection, prosecution and conviction methods detailed in this book create resentment and marginalisation on the part of suspects, offenders, their families and their communities. One result is stigmatisation and the enhancement of anti-authority attitudes which deintegrate rather than reintegrate, and which leads to more crime, not less. Time after time, newspaper stories report victims of wrongful arrest, for example, who say that they had not been in trouble before and had always respected the police, but do so no longer.[18] The reconviction rate is very high. In other words, taking freedom away from suspects and offenders in order to increase conviction rates does little to increase the freedom of victims. Restorative processes, which are less coercive and aim to reintegrate, are used increasingly, but they still only nibble away at the edges of conventional justice processes, and their effect on re-conviction rates is typically small.[19]

It could be argued that crime control methods do at least lead to relatively high arrest and prosecution rates, without which people would commit even more offences. Indeed one of the (unlawful) reasons for mass stop-search is precisely to intimidate suspect populations and deter them from offending. But this argument also ignores the point that members of the public (especially victims) are the main sources of

---

[16] Whilst this sounds like a form of utilitarianism we show in ch 1 that this perspective can accommodate giving special weight to human rights, fundamental democratic values, and legal principles such as the rule of law.

[17] On victims of domestic violence, for example, see Hoyle C and Sanders A, 'Police Response to Domestic Violence: From Victim Choice to Victim Empowerment' (2000) 40 BJ Crim 14.

[18] Type the phrase 'used to respect the police' plus the word 'arrest' into Google and you'll see what we mean.   [19] See further 7.4.2 and 8.3.

information about the identity of offenders. In other words, crime control methods lead to relatively few arrests and prosecutions in relation to crimes of any seriousness. What are the most upsetting offences that occur frequently? There are sex offences, which have particular detection and conviction difficulties which no amount of police powers will ever be able to do much about; street robberies, where victims can often give descriptions and where the detection rate is reasonably high; and burglaries, where offenders are rarely seen in the act, and which usually remain undetected. Changes to police powers make very little difference to the detection and conviction rates of any of these offences. It could be argued that even if crime control methods do not reduce crime, at least they ease the fears and assuage the anger of victims. Again, however, this wrongly assumes that victims and offenders are different people. Do crime control systems have the interests of victims at heart? We cast doubt on this in ch 1, because in an adversarial system the two parties are the state and the suspect/defendant and as such victims have no rights in 'their' cases.[20] The interests of the state and those of victims do not always coincide, for example in relation to plea bargaining, which is driven by the desire to conserve resources and to secure convictions in what might be weak cases. Some victims may benefit: they are saved from giving evidence and are guaranteed at least some kind of 'result', but not all will see it this way. In some of the most distressing and dangerous offences of all, that is, domestic violence and sexual offences, plea bargaining is both most rife and potentially most upsetting to victims. We should also remember that some weak (and indeed some strong) cases are mounted against innocent people. Just as due process-oriented systems do not help victims when guilty people are acquitted, equally, crime control-oriented systems do not help victims when innocent people are convicted. Pressure to plea bargain reduces the capacity of innocent (as well as guilty) people to contest guilt. Crime control systems ill-serve one group of victims in particular. These are victims of crime about which the state cares little: mostly those dealt with by non-police agencies (see 7.5). The Code of Practice for Victims of Crime, discussed below, applies to the police, CPS and courts, but explicitly excludes the HSE and victims of crime dealt with by the HSE (paras 2.1, 3.1, 3.7 and 3.9).

In recent years the 'victim movement' has become politically influential. The political parties now compete with each other for the mythical 'victims' vote', and heed must also be paid to various international obligations.[21] The idea of 'victims' rights' has become increasingly important, both in substance[22] and in rhetoric: a crime control approach may not be synonymous with increased rights for victims, but crime

---

[20] See Doak J, 'Victims' Rights in Criminal Trials: Prospects for Participation' (2005) 32 J Law and Society 294.

[21] For reviews see Doak J 'The Victim and the Criminal Process: An Analysis of Recent Trends in Regional and International Tribunals' (2003) 23 Legal Studies 1 and Van Dijk J and Goenhuijsen M, 'Benchmarking Victim Policies in the Framework of European Union Law' in Walklate S (ed), *Handbook of Victims and Victimology* (Cullompton: Willan, 2007).

[22] For a detailed account of government policy-making 1997–2001, see Rock P, *Constructing Victims' Rights* (Oxford: OUP, 2004).

control policies are often (spuriously) justified in this way.[23] Four types of right can be identified.

13.3.1 'Substantive rights'

A person or organisation can be sued for negligence by someone who suffers reasonably foreseeable loss or harm because of failure to carry out a duty to that person. Whether the police have duties to particular victims of crime depends on whether it is 'fair, just and reasonable' to impose such a duty. The tort of negligence in general is a huge topic, and the circumstances under which it applies to the police–victim relationship demands far more discussion than we have space for. What follows is therefore an extremely simplified account.[24]

In *Hill v Chief Constable of West Yorkshire*[25] the mother of the 'Yorkshire Ripper's' last victim sued the police for negligence. While it is true that, had the police been more competent, they might have caught the 'Ripper' earlier, thus preventing the death of the claimant's daughter, the House of Lords decided that no duty of care is owed to potential victims. If the victim's family had succeeded, police resources and time would from then onwards have been diverted from suppressing crime into ensuring that no offence or harm was caused to a potential victim or witness, which would not be in the interests of society in general. Although not framed in these terms, this is a good application of the 'freedom approach'. The decision in *Hill* was reaffirmed in *Brooks v Commissioner of the Police of the Metropolis*.[26] Brooks witnessed the murder of his friend, Stephen Lawrence,[27] but the police treated him as a suspect, causing or exacerbating his post-traumatic stress disorder. As in *Hill* it was stated that to establish a duty in such a case would distort police activity and remove from the police the autonomy they need to apply their resources effectively.[28] However, this assumes that treating specific witnesses with respect is costly, when in many cases it costs more to treat them as suspects. There seems little recognition that the groups of marginalised people identified in this book as particularly at risk from police actions need special protection. To say, as Lord Steyn did in this case, that people in Brooks' situation would be better off pursuing a complaint than suing the police ignores the evidence set out in ch 12 about how that system works and the fact that many victims of malpractice consequently prefer civil actions to the complaints system.

The virtual immunity that the police enjoy from negligence claims where they have failed to protect victims from the criminal acts of third parties has been challenged in

---

[23] Discussed briefly in ch 1. Also see *Attorney-General's Reference No 3 of 1999*, discussed in 12.5.3. For good general discussions see Garland D, *The Culture of Control* (Oxford: OUP, 2001); Jackson J, 'Justice for All: Putting Victims at the Heart of Criminal Justice?' (2003) 30 JLS 309; and, Roach, K (1999b) *Due Process and Victims' Rights: The New Law and Politics of Criminal Justice* (Toronto: University of Toronto Press).

[24] See further Harrison et al, *Police Misconduct: Legal Remedies*, 4th edn (London: LAG, 2005) ch 8.

[25] [1989] AC 53.   [26] [2005] UKHL 24.   [27] The Lawrence case is discussed in ch 3 and 12.

[28] [2005] UKHL 24. Discussed by Smith G, 'Comment on *Brooks v Commissioner of the Police of the Metropolis*' (2005) 69 J Crim L 4.

the European Court of Human Rights. In *Osman* a victim was known to be at risk. A teacher was obsessed by a former pupil. Numerous complaints of a serious nature had been made to the police, who did not arrest the teacher. He then injured the former pupil and killed his father. The English courts held that it would not be 'fair, just and reasonable' to impose a duty of care in these circumstances.[29] The ECtHR said this was wrong, but its decision was based on a misunderstanding of the English law, as it acknowledged in a later case.[30] Had the former pupil died, it would have been another matter, as his Art 2 'right to life' rights would have been breached. As it was, in *Osman* the police had no reason to fear for the life of the person who actually lost his life, so no duty was owed to him.

The scope of the obligations imposed by *Osman* are not particularly onerous; there is a high threshold of knowledge required before the police are expected to take 'reasonable' steps to prevent a risk to life materialising. Art 2 is only engaged where the police 'knew or ought to have known' of a 'real and immediate risk to the life of an identifiable individual'. In *Van Colle* the House of Lords emphasised that the degree of risk is to be assessed on the basis of what the police knew at the time and not with the benefit of hindsight.[31] The victim in this case was killed by a man whom he was due to testify against in a theft trial. Both he and other witnesses had received threats and experienced damage to their property, and many of these incidents had been reported to the police. However, the court held that there was no violation of Art 2 because the police could not have appreciated at the time he was killed that there was a 'real and immediate' risk to the deceased's life.

This restrictive interpretation of the knowledge test limits the potential liability of police considerably.[32] This may be especially pertinent in domestic violence cases where the onus will be on the victim to draw to the police attention information to contextualise isolated incidents of abuse which may not, on their own, result in the police having sufficient knowledge of the life-threatening risk faced by the victim. The Strasbourg court has held that the police and prosecuting authorities in Turkey violated Art 2 in a case where victims of domestic abuse repeatedly complained to the police that their lives were in danger and received an inadequate response.[33] However, they reiterated the *Osman* threshold so in most cases it is likely to continue to be difficult for victims' families to successfully claim a breach of Art 2 when their relatives have been killed despite the police being previously alerted to the criminal acts of the killer.

The appeal in *Van Colle* was heard jointly with the case of *Smith* in which the victim wished to sue the police in negligence for failing to protect him from the violent acts of his former same-sex partner. The police had been alerted to messages received by the

---

29 *Osman v Ferguson* [1993] 4 All ER 344.

30 *Osman v UK* (1998) 29 EHRR 245; *Z v UK* (2002) 34 EHRR 3.

31 *Chief Constable of the Hertfordshire Police v Van Colle; Smith v Chief Constable of Sussex Police* [2008] UKHL 50.   32 Burton M 'Failing to Protect: Victims' Rights and Police Liability' (2009) 72 MLR 283.

33 *Opuz v Turkey* (2009) Application No 33401/02.

victim, including death threats, but had done little to investigate despite assuring the victim that the case was 'progressing well'. The majority of the House of Lords upheld the *Hill* public policy principle against imposing liability on the police. They were particularly concerned that the police should retain discretion not to act in domestic violence cases free from the spectre of negligence claims. The reasoning behind this was the alleged ambiguity about who is a 'genuine' victim and the 'hysteria and exaggeration' which often surrounds claims of domestic abuse.[34] This illustrates the continuing difficulty that victims of domestic violence have in getting their cases taken seriously at all levels of the criminal justice process. The opportunity to use the ECHR to provide victims of crime with substantive rights to redress for police inaction was ducked. However, where the police simply fail to investigate a serious crime they probably do have a duty: a rape report lay unrecorded and uninvestigated for two months. By the time it was investigated, crucial potential CCTV evidence had been destroyed. The complainant sued the police and received an out-of-court settlement for £3,500.[35]

So far we have been talking about the failure of the police to protect individuals from third parties but what happens when suspects die at the hands of the police and their loved ones wish to sue? In chs 4 and 12 we discussed the scandal of deaths in custody. Those discussions concerned criminal acts by officers causing death. But most deaths are a result of self-harm or 'accident' (arising from alcohol or drugs in particular). It is now well-established that the police owe a duty of care to suspects in custody who die in such circumstances.[36] As a result, the police now assess the risk to suspects. While this should lead to fewer deaths, the risk cannot be eliminated. In *Orange v Chief Constable of the West Yorkshire Police*[37] a suspect hanged himself, but as the police were not aware that he was a suicide risk, and the risk assessment that they carried out was negative, their failure to take further precautions was held not to breach their duty of care. The fact that, as we saw in ch 4, custodial conditions are so coercive that *everyone* should be seen as vulnerable, has escaped the courts' attention. Earlier chapters also commented on fatal shootings, such as Menezes, in the wake of the July 2005 bombings, and Harry Stanley. These tragedies are covered by the tort of negligence and ECHR, Art 2 as well. There is no doubt about whether a duty is owed, the issue always being whether it was discharged negligently or without lawful justification. In *Bubbins v UK*[38] a man was shot who, like Stanley and Menezes, appeared to present a threat by pointing a firearm at the police but he had only an imitation gun. There were a number of unsatisfactory features of the police operation. For example, none of the local force's trained negotiators went to the scene because all bar one were at a negotiators' conference; the other was playing five-a-side football and claimed that his pager had been left switched on but had not bleeped. The ECtHR said that deprivations of life must be subject to the most careful scrutiny and any use of force must be absolutely necessary. But the use of force by agents of the state based on an honest and

---

[34] [2008] UKHL 50 at paras 76 and 107.   [35] *The Guardian*, 1 December 2009.
[36] See, for example, *Reeves v Commissioner of Police of the Metropolis* [2000] 1 AC 360.
[37] [2002] QB 347.   [38] [2005] ECHR 159.

reasonable belief in its necessity to protect their own lives did not amount to a breach of Art 2. And the court did not believe that the planning and control of the operation had been sufficiently botched to amount to such a breach. It thus seems that only the most gross errors would violate Art 2.

Although this discussion has concerned how far the tort of negligence and the ECHR can be used to create or enforce the rights of victims in relation to the police or prosecution, some victims suffer from the deliberate, as well as negligent, actions of those agencies. Two types of example have been discussed in this book. First, there is non- or selective enforcement. In the *ITF* case[39] (discussed in 7.2) a company was the victim of breaches of the peace. The police devoted only limited resources to the problem, leading to financial losses for the company. No rights were conceded to the victims, in recognition of the almost infinite resources that would be required to satisfy all victims of crime. The second example is where a prosecution agency decides not to prosecute (discussed in ch 7). Judicial reviews of these decisions have had some success, though only in tightly prescribed circumstances. We cannot yet say that victims have the 'right' to see 'their' offenders prosecuted when there is sufficient evidence. Although victims appear to have the right to demand that agencies apply their policies rationally they do not have the right to influence those policies or to demand that different agencies are consistent with each other.

13.3.2 'Service rights': the Code of Practice for Victims of Crime

The Victims' Charter, first introduced in 1990, and revised in 1996, told victims that they are entitled to 'proper' services. This was replaced by a more robust Code of Practice in 2006,[40] supposedly with oversight from a Commissioner for Victims and Witnesses (an unsuccessful attempt to recruit one in 2006 cost £96,625).[41] In 2009 Sara Payne, mother of a 9-year-old murder victim, accepted a one-year appointment as 'victims champion', a role meant to pave the way for the appointment of the first Commissioner in 2010.[42] One of the most important service rights is the offer of appropriate support, both in general and (where applicable) prior to court proceedings. The police are crucially important here, in putting victims in touch with Victim Support, an independent, but government-funded, charity (Code, paras 5.3–5.6). Other important rights are to be provided with appropriate facilities in court[43] and to be given information about their cases by agencies such as the police and the CPS. Because victims have no standing, they have traditionally had no right to know what was happening in 'their' cases and

---

[39] *Chief Constable of Sussex, ex p ITF Ltd* [1999] 1 All ER 129.

[40] Office of Criminal Justice Reform, *Code of Practice for Victims of Crime* (London: SO, 2005). See Domestic Violence, Crime and Victims Act 2004, ss 32, 48–53 and Sch 8, as amended by s 142 of the Coroners and Justice Act 2009.   [41] Hansard, HC Deb 1 April 2009 c 1204W.

[42] <http://news.bbc.co.uk/1/hi/uk/7850785.stm> (accessed 5 January 2010).

[43] Improvements have been made in recent years but more are needed: Sanders A and Jones I, 'The Victim in Court' in Walklate (ed) (2007). Now see the Code, para 8.

may, for example, find themselves bumping into the alleged offender because the latter is let out on bail, has had the case dropped or been given a non-custodial sentence.

In the mid 1990s the government established some experiments whereby, in selected police areas, victims in cases where someone had been charged would be asked whether they wanted information about 'their' cases. About two-thirds of victims who were asked did want this information, but many victims did not get all that they wanted, and many wanted to know not just *what* happened, but *why*. If a decision is unpalatable, the more that one is told, the more one wants to discuss and challenge it so that it can at least be *understood*. In other words, giving victims a 'right to know' raises expectations which, in many cases, are dashed.[44] Moreover, in most cases no-one is charged. Failure to identify or charge a suspect can be upsetting – an understatement in a murder case like that of Stephen Lawrence, whose family were denied information, given misinformation, and then given unhelpful information about the investigation into the murder of their son.[45] This cannot be justified from a freedom perspective, as this is a form of 'secondary victimisation' which erodes freedom.[46]

The Code attempts to meet some of these problems by requiring the police to provide information such as whether a suspect has been arrested (and, if so, what happened subsequently) and, where applicable, whether a defendant has been given bail (this being information that victims want but were not previously given) (paras 5.9–26); by requiring police/CPS witness care units to provide information and support to victims in contested cases (para 6); and requiring the CPS to provide information about decisions for which it is primarily responsible (including offering to meet victims in particularly serious cases) (para 7). The Code also provides 'enhanced' service rights for vulnerable and intimidated victims (see 13.3.3). Although the 'right' of victims of crime to *understand* is still limited, the CPS claims that it increasingly provides better information.[47] However, a different picture emerges from the Crown Prosecution Service Inspectorate. Two surveys found that Direct Communication with Victim (DCV) letters were not sent to between 23% and 31% of victims seeking them; and the computer system that enables special categories of victim to be identified and treated with particular sensitivity was not used in nearly half such cases.[48]

---

[44] Sanders et al, 'Victim Impact Statements: Don't Work, Can't Work' [2001] Crim LR 447. Later research similarly found frustration that requests to be kept informed were not fulfilled: Graham et al, *Testaments of Harm: a Qualitative Evaluation of the Victim Personal Statements Scheme* (London: National Centre for Social Research, 2004).

[45] See Macpherson of Cluny, Sir W, *The Stephen Lawrence Inquiry* (Cm 4262-I) (London: SO, 1999).

[46] On 'secondary victimisation' see Wolhuter L et al, *Victimology: Victimisation and Victim's Rights* (Abingdon: Routledge, 2009). Also see Sebba L, *Third Parties: Victims and the Criminal Justice System* (Columbus: Ohio State UP, 1996).

[47] CPS *Annual Report for 2008/9* (London: CPS, 2009). Under the 'Direct Communication with Victims' (DCV) initiative detailed letters are now provided in serious cases, and less detailed letters in all other cases where victims request them.

[48] HMCPSI, *File Management and Organisation: An Audit of CPS Performance* (London: HMCPSI, 2008b) paras 6.12–6.15, 8.1–8.5; HMCPSI/HMICA/HMIC, *Report of a Joint Thematic Review of Victim and Witness Experiences in the Criminal Justice System* (London: HMCPSI, 2009) paras 3.32–3.44.

No rights in any real sense are provided, because these provisions, like those of the Charter before it, are not enforceable in the courts. Like many rights of suspects, there is no proper remedy for people who are deprived of this type of entitlement:[49] 'Where a person fails to comply with this Code, that does not, of itself, make him or her liable to any legal proceedings.... Breaches of this Code should be referred initially to the service provider(s) concerned' (Code, para 1.3 and 1.4). If that does not lead to a satisfactory result, the case can then be referred to the Parliamentary Ombudsman who can award a 'consolatory' (not compensatory) payment. This seems to herald the creation of a new class of 'semi-right' – for a semi-party to proceedings? Victim-oriented pressure groups have been competing for rights for some time and are unlikely to be satisfied with a consolation prize, particularly as 'the service to victims is neither consistent across the country, nor at the level envisaged by the DCV scheme or the Victims' Code' (HMCPSI 2009 para 3.44).

13.3.3 Vulnerable victims and witnesses

It was recognised 25 years ago that child victims of crime were less likely to have 'their' cases prosecuted, and more likely to suffer secondary victimisation, than adult victims. Children were often afraid to report crimes, were frequently not believed, had difficulty explaining or remembering exactly what happened, and could be made to appear untruthful or confused in court. Police officers and prosecutors were therefore reluctant to prosecute, and these children suffered greatly under cross-examination if there was a prosecution.[50] Once this was documented by research, and became a matter of public scandal because of revelations of widespread sexual abuse, court procedures were amended to facilitate prosecutions. The government established the Pigot Committee in 1988 and, as an interim measure, child witnesses were permitted to give evidence via CCTV.[51] Pigot recommended that child witnesses should be allowed to give all their evidence via pre-recorded video tape,[52] but this recommendation was only half implemented.[53]

People who are learning disabled or mentally ill suffer from similar problems, so it made no sense to prevent them from being helped in the way children were helped.[54] Sadly, what makes these groups of people vulnerable in the criminal justice system also makes them especially vulnerable to crime.[55] Some of the most exploited groups in society were receiving less protection than 'normal' victims. At the same time,

---

[49] The lack of remedies for many 'rights' is discussed in ch 12. See also Fenwick H, 'Rights of Victims in the Criminal Justice System' [1995] Crim LR 843.

[50] Morgan J and Zedner L, *Child Victims* (Oxford: Clarendon Press, 1992).

[51] Criminal Justice Act (CJA) 1988, s 32.

[52] Pigot Judge T, *Report of the Advisory Group on Video-Recorded Evidence* (London: HMSO, 1989).

[53] CJA 1991, s 54 inserting s 32A into the CJA 1988.

[54] This was noted by Pigot (1989). See also Sanders et al, *Victims with Learning Disabilities* (Oxford: Centre for Criminological Research, 1997) summarised in Home Office Research Findings No 44 (London: Home Office, 1997).

[55] Again noted by Pigot (1989). Also see Williams C, *Invisible Victims: Crime and Abuse Against People with Learning Disabilities* (Bristol: Norah Fry Research Centre, 1995).

concern was developing about witnesses being intimidated by defendants and their friends or family in some cases.[56] A Home Office working party therefore made wide-ranging proposals to support all these vulnerable and intimidated witnesses.[57] Many of these were enacted in the Youth Justice and Criminal Evidence Act (YJCE) 1999 (Part II), but numerous police, prosecution and court procedures (and the attitudes and culture which lie behind them) which are not laid down in the law also needed to be changed. We do not attempt here to discuss all these changes in detail, but it is important to provide a brief overview.[58]

The first problem which vulnerable victims face is whether or not to report the offence. Sometimes reluctance to report stems from the fact that their 'authority figures' (parents, teachers, carers) are the abusers or are close to the abusers. This is a structural feature of vulnerability about which little, regrettably, can be done. But traditionally some reluctance has been because of fear at how the police and courts would treat their complaint. This fear is justified in many cases. Sanders et al (1997) found that the police were often dismissive of crimes against the learning disabled which may have been objectively minor but which, to the victims, were traumatic. These fears often remain, with some justification. Similarly, efforts by the police over the last decade or so to improve their service to rape and domestic violence complainants have not been an unqualified success.[59] The position is even less satisfactory in the courts.[60] And if victims fear being humiliated in court they will frequently not report the matter at all. Even when they do, they often seek to withdraw their complaint or choose not to give evidence in court, usually causing the case to collapse.

The police need to show vulnerable witnesses care and respect, but first they need to identify witnesses as vulnerable. Then they need to interview them in ways which elicit the best evidence without distorting their recollections or intimidating them. Further, compared with 'normal witnesses', vulnerable witnesses tend to have greater difficulties in telling a traumatic story of victimisation several times. The police should adopt 'cognitive interviewing' techniques, but skill is needed both to identify mild cases of vulnerability and to use these techniques. The police are poor in both respects, and training and resources are inadequate.[61]

---

[56] Maynard W, *Witness Intimidation: Strategies for Prevention* (PRG Crime Detection and Prevention Series Paper 55) (London: Home Office, 1994); Tarling et al, *Victim and Witness Intimidation: Findings from the British Crime Survey* (Home Office Research Findings No 124) (London: Home Office, 2000).

[57] Home Office, *Speaking Up for Justice* (London: Home Office, 1998b).

[58] Much of this legislation is exceptionally and unnecessarily complex. The April 2000 issue of the Criminal Law Review contains several articles which dissect the Act in detail. Also see Ellison L, *The Adversarial Process and the Vulnerable Witness* (Oxford: OUP, 2001).

[59] See, for example, Belur J, 'Is Policing Domestic Violence Institutionally Racist? A Case Study of South Asian Women' (2008) 18(4) Policing and Society 426; HMCPSI/HMIC, *Without Consent, a Report on the Joint Inspection into the Investigation and Prosecution of Cases Involving Allegations of Rape* (London: HMCPSI/HMIC, 2007), available from <http://www.hmcpsi.gov.uk/> (accessed 15 December 2009).

[60] See, for example, Ellison L, 'The Use and Abuse of Psychiatric Evidence in Rape Trials' (2009) 13(1) International Journal of Evidence & Proof 28.

[61] See 6.4.1 and Keenan et al, 'Interviewing Allegedly Abused Children with a View to Criminal Prosecution' [1999] Crim LR 863. Interviewing is guided by Home Office, Achieving best evidence in

The next stage is the prosecution decision. The two tests discussed in ch 7 are applied here as in all cases. Because of the difficulties of these cases, many fall at the 'evidential' hurdle. It is not suggested by government (or us) that the tests should change. Instead, full and prompt investigation by the police is needed so that fewer cases are evidentially weak,[62] and the police need to inform the CPS of the problems which the vulnerability in question could cause. For there are ways of mitigating vulnerabilities so that evidence can be better presented in court, reducing the prospects of acquittal and thus feeding back to the prosecution decision, making a negative decision both less justifiable and less likely. A particularly important example is pre-court familiarisation (in the form of visits, videos and so forth), which reduces the fear many witnesses, particularly vulnerable witnesses, have of giving evidence. But even when witnesses are identified as vulnerable, the police often do not tell the CPS, and neither agency is good at seeking the views of witnesses on whether they want this type of help.[63] Police and CPS are supposed to meet in difficult cases to discuss strategy (in 'early special measures meetings') but they actually take place rarely.[64]

Support for witnesses is seen by police and prosecutors primarily in terms of the 'special measures' in court provided in the YJCE. These include judges and barristers removing wigs and gowns, screening off the defendant from the sight of the witness, providing interpreters and communication aids (important not only for people who have difficulty with English but also for some learning disabled people who have difficulty speaking at all), and giving evidence via CCTV from a room outside the courtroom. Assessments are made in each case of which, if any, of these special measures would help the particular witness (because each vulnerability and every way of alleviating it is different) so that preparation and, where necessary, application to the court can be made in good time. Where appropriate, interviews should have been videotaped in advance and played in court, but this depends on proper identification at the start. Something approaching the full Pigot proposals are contained in the legislation but have not been, and are unlikely to be, implemented, despite much criticism of the

criminal proceedings: *Guidance for Vulnerable and Intimidated Witnesses, Including Children* (London: Home Office, 2001a). See also Burton et al, 'Implementing Special Measures for Vulnerable and Intimidated Witnesses: The Problem of Identification' (2006b) Crim LR 229 and HMCPSI/HMICA/HMIC (2009) 2.5–2.9 for similar findings (nearly 40% of vulnerable and intimidated witnesses not identified as such).

[62] See, for example, Ellison L, 'Promoting Effective Case-building in Rape Cases: A Comparative Perspective' [2007] Crim LR 691.

[63] Burton et al, *Are Special Measures for Vulnerable and Intimidated Witnesses Working? Evidence from the Criminal Justice Agencies* (Home Office Online Report No 01/06) (London: Home Office, 2006a). See also HMCPSI/HMICA/HMIC (2009) paras 2.10–2.19.

[64] Never, in the sample taken by Burton et al (2006a) soon after implementation of the legislation. A larger sample taken a little later, in 2003/04, found meetings took place in 2% of cases (but there were phone discussions in a further 7% of cases): Cooper D and Roberts P, *Special Measures for Vulnerable and Intimidated Witnesses: An Analysis of CPS Monitoring Data* (London: CPS, 2005). And see their 'Monitoring Success: Special Measures under the YJCE 1999' (2005) 9 E&P 269. It is not credible that less than 10% of these cases are difficult. Similar results were found in HMCPSI/HMICA/HMIC (2009) paras 3.1–3.21.

halfway house enacted in the CJA and which still applies.[65] All these measures have been available for children for some time, the YJCE extends them to other vulnerable witnesses, and the CJA 2003 extends many of them to any witness who the judge or magistrate believes would benefit from them.[66] This latter provision is a welcome recognition that *anyone* can be vulnerable in an artificial and intimidating situation like a court, no matter how 'normal' they may otherwise be. Special measures are not automatically available for those who request them, except for most child witnesses for whom CCTV and the admission of prior recorded evidence in chief is automatic. But it is rare for applications to be rejected (Cooper and Roberts, 2005), and there is no doubt that this whole raft of measures has gone a substantial way to meeting the less-intractable problems of vulnerable witnesses.[67]

Finally, there are the actual procedures in court. There is the potential in all types of case for witnesses to find cross-examination, and sometimes questioning from the judge, upsetting and challenging. This can ruin an otherwise strong case as well as weak cases. It is sometimes hard to know whether testimony lacks credibility because it really is untrue or mistaken, or because questioning unfairly tripped up or confused the witness. In an adversarial system it is essential that the defence be allowed to test prosecution evidence, and if there is reasonable doubt about its strength, there should be an acquittal. Drawing the line between what is robustly fair and what is viciously destructive of the character of the witness is often difficult. Judges have the power to stop oppressive cross-examination,[68] but they dare do this only in the most extreme circumstances. For victims will not be helped if convictions are quashed on the ground that judges did not give defence counsel full opportunities to cross-examine. One possibility is for judges or intermediaries to 'translate' intimidating or convoluted questioning for witnesses, but the problem can only really be alleviated through changing the culture of the Bar, which is a long-term and indeterminate prospect.[69]

The nature of the adversarial system puts limits on how far secondary victimisation of victims in the witness box can be reduced, as trashing, trapping and tripping is all part of proving and disproving cases.[70] Further, there remains too little understanding of the variety of types of vulnerability and the ways in which vulnerabilities – particularly learning disabilities – are manifested. This means that often witnesses are

[65] Cooper D, 'Pigot Unfulfilled: Video-recorded Cross-Examination under s 28 of the YJCE 1999' [2005] Crim LR 456.   [66] YJCE, ss 23–30; CJA 2003, ss 51–56 and ss 137–138.

[67] Burton et al (2006b); Hamlyn et al, *Are Special Measures Working? Evidence from Surveys of Vulnerable and Intimidated Witnesses* (Home Office Research Study 283) (London: Home Office, 2004); HMCPSI/ HMICA/HMIC (2009). However, for a note of caution regarding giving evidence through a live link see Mulcahy L, 'The Unbearable Lightness of Being? Shifts Towards the Virtual Trial' (2008) 35 JLS 464.

[68] *Milton Brown* [1998] 2 Cr App Rep 364. They rarely do this. See for example, Davis et al (1999).

[69] Blake M and Ashworth A, 'Some Ethical Issues in Prosecuting and Defending Criminal Cases' [1998] Crim LR 16 at pp 25–26; Ellison L, 'The Mosaic Art? Cross-examination and the Vulnerable Witness' (2001) 21 Legal Studies 353. Intermediaries are briefly discussed later.

[70] McBarnet D, 'Victim in the Witness Box – Confronting Victimology's Stereotype' (1983) 7 Contemporary Crises 293; Ellison (2001a).

thought, wrongly, to lack credibility[71] but there is little in this programme of action to deal with this problem. Police officers and prosecutors are supposed to seek the views of vulnerable victims and witnesses about the help they want or need, but they still do this inadequately or not at all in most cases, perhaps because they wrongly believe that they cannot evaluate their own needs or express their wishes coherently.[72] Thus while the use of special measures has gone up significantly,[73] leading to a much better deal for these witnesses, many are still not getting what they want and need.[74]

For victims of sexual offences, in particular, aggressive and humiliating questioning in court has been a major cause of attrition – that is, acquittals and, further back down the line, withdrawals and decisions not to report.[75] For these victims, and those of certain other crimes, there are provisions to prevent defendants cross-examining in person[76] and to prevent certain types of evidence (on the witnesses' sexual history in particular) being elicited.[77] But while lack of consent, which is often impossible to prove,[78] remained an element in most sexual offences, the rate of acquittals and secondary victimisation of witnesses in court was inevitably higher than in most other offences. Changes to the definition of sexual offences in 2003 offered some hope of improvement[79] but substantial difficulties remain.[80]

We should not fool ourselves into thinking that that legal solutions can ever completely solve the problems faced by vulnerable victims. That is not because of a lack of will on the part of government or criminal justice agencies, or (primarily) a lack of resources. The fact is that vulnerable victims are in structurally weak positions in society. That is what makes them vulnerable. Social and cultural change might alleviate this for the victims of sexual offences and domestic violence, but not for the aged and mentally vulnerable. People with very low actual or mental ages, for example, simply have less comprehension than other people. There comes a point when a witness has to be regarded as not competent to give evidence or, in some cases, not competent to give evidence on matters of detail or in relation to forgotten events. The YJCE tries to deal with this problem more intelligently than the law used to do, by providing for 'intermediaries' to 'translate' questioning for witnesses who cannot cope (s 29), and by a new 'competence' test of 'understanding' (s 53). It was feared that both

---

[71] Sanders et al (1997).   [72] Hamlyn et al (2004); Burton et al (2006a).

[73] Cooper and Roberts (2005).   [74] Burton et al (2006a); HMCPSI/HMICA/HMIC (2009) ch 5.

[75] Kelly et al, *A Gap or a Chasm? Attrition in Reported Rape Cases* (Home Office Research Study 293) (London: Home Office, 2005).

[76] YJCE, s 35. There are also provisions giving judges discretion to prohibit cross-examination in person in any other case: ss 36 and 37.   [77] YJCE, s 41.

[78] Harris J and Grace S, *A Question of Evidence? Investigating and Prosecuting Rape in the 1990s* (Home Office Research Study 196) (London: Home Office, 1999); HMCPSI and HMIC, *A Report on the Joint Inspection into the Investigation and Prosecution of Cases Involving Allegations of Rape* (London: HMCPSI, 2002).

[79] Sexual Offences Act 2003. See McEwan J, 'Proving Consent in Sexual Cases: Legislative Change and Cultural Evolution' (2005) 9 E&P 1.

[80] McGlynn C and Munro V (eds), *Rethinking Rape Law: International and Comparative Perspectives* (Abingdon: Routledge-Cavendish, 2010).

would be problematic.[81] However, early experience with well-trained intermediaries is very positive, particularly with learning disabled people who can understand what is being asked if it is put in simple terms.[82] It may be tempting in future to allow witnesses who understand very little of what is happening to give evidence, but this would be a further attenuation of the already-eroded rights of suspects and defendants. Along with further restrictions on cross-examination and the method of cross-examination to help vulnerable witnesses, this would harm the prospects of acquittal of innocent defendants. It hardly needs to be said that not all alleged victims and witnesses, whether vulnerable or not, tell the truth;[83] not all are correct in their beliefs and recollections; and some defendants are innocent even when victims tell the truth if, for example, a defence is proved or there is a lack of mens rea. But in an era of crime control-mindedness this could all be forgotten or brushed aside.

There would be no need for trials at all if we automatically accepted what victims and other witnesses said. We may soon reach the point when vindication of more victims' cases will only be achievable by failing to vindicate defence cases. This is the classic dilemma running through this book. The government deserves to be congratulated, in this respect at least, for not falling into this trap in the main. Most of these measures for vulnerable witnesses, legislative and otherwise, attempt to put vulnerable witnesses on a level playing field with other witnesses without eroding significant rights of defendants. However, the non-entitlement of vulnerable child *defendants* to special measures on an equal footing with other witnesses has been criticised.[84] This may in practice lead to prosecution witnesses being denied measures that they might otherwise have benefited from, leading to *two* people having to suffer unnecessarily.[85]

13.3.4 **Procedural rights**

These are rights to be *involved* in one's case. As with service rights, the freedom perspective is concerned to reduce secondary victimisation. So if being involved achieves this, without any loss of freedom to suspects or defendants, it is to be encouraged. This

---

[81] Ellison L, 'Cross-examination and the Intermediary: Bridging the Language Divide?' [2002] Crim LR 114. On s 53 see Birch D, 'A Better Deal for Vulnerable Witnesses?' Crim LR [2000] 223 (but note that it was applied satisfactorily in *D* [2003] Crim LR 274).

[82] Plotnikoff J and Woolfson R, 'Making the Best Use of the Intermediary Special Measure at Trial' (2008) Crim LR 91.

[83] An unusual example was that of a teenager who claimed that she had been raped in a park by a tramp. A young man was later arrested on a minor charge and his DNA sample matched the one taken from the young woman. When the police questioned her again, because the man's description did not match that of the 'tramp', she admitted that she had had consensual sex with him. She was later jailed for six months: *The Guardian*, 27 September 2000.

[84] In *Camberwell Youth Court ex parte D, ex p DPP* [2005] 1 WLR 353 the accused and the main witness were of similar age and capability yet special measures were provided for the latter (as was mandated by the YJCE) but not the former (specifically excluded by the YJCE). The House of Lords expressed misgivings about this disparity, but stated that just because it was unfair that the accused was denied special measures it did not follow that a prosecution witness should be.   [85] Burton et al (2006a: ch 6).

is difficult in relation to plea bargaining, which in some cases will be distressing for victims and coercive to defendants yet in others might be beneficial for one or other. Victims should now be consulted. But this will rarely go as far as a genuine discussion, and prosecutors need take no notice of what the victim says, for victims have no rights over 'their' cases, which are technically not theirs at all (discussed in 8.8).

In relation to other aspects of proceedings, different legal systems provide a variety of ways of being involved, such as by providing information to the prosecutor or court through a 'victim personal statement' (VPS) as in some common law systems; by being a secondary party of some kind to the case as in many civil law systems;[86] or by being fully involved as in restorative processes.[87] This chapter will be concerned only with 'mainstream' Anglo-American criminal justice where, traditionally, victims have not been involved at all.

Involvement can, in principle, take various forms – an opportunity to discuss, to be consulted, or to actually participate in decision-making. Whatever type of involvement is provided, it can take place at one or more of various stages of the criminal process: in particular, the decision to prosecute, bail/remand decisions, decisions to reduce or drop charges, sentencing and early release from prison.

In the USA, where the victims' movement took off earlier than in the UK, involvement began to take the form of making a VPS to police or probation officers, who relayed the information provided by the victim to the court and/or the prosecutor. In England and Wales the 1996 Victims' Charter included a requirement that the police and CPS take the interests of victims 'into account', and announced experimental VPS schemes in the same areas as the 'right to know' schemes. The VPS supplements the original witness statement with another written statement detailing the medical, psychological, financial and emotional harm caused by the crime. Unlike in some American states,[88] only facts are sought, not opinions about what victims think should happen to the offender.[89] This is, in other words, not a consultative process. Victims' interests are to be taken into account but not, it seems, their views about what is in their interests. Sanders et al (2001) found that a large minority of victims who opted to make a VPS were disappointed. Many who said, at the start of their case, that they were pleased that they participated, said at the end that they no longer felt this way. Thus one victim observed: 'I think it's all a gimmick. It achieves nothing. I took the victim impact statement very seriously and I'd suffered a very serious attack but I doubt that anyone even looked at it. It clearly didn't influence anything... a totally

---

[86] Doak (2005). Defence witnesses in general are not treated with the same care in court as are prosecution witnesses (HMCPSI/HMICA/HMIC, 2009: ch 5).

[87] For good discussions see Strang H, *Repair or Revenge: Victims and Restorative Justice* (Oxford: OUP, 2002); Dignan J, *Understanding Victims and Restorative Justice* (Maidenhead: Open UP, 2005).

[88] For an example of the way this works even in capital punishment cases where juries, who in some states decide whether to order the death penalty, can be influenced by emotive appeals from victims' families, see Sebba L, 'Sentencing and the Victim: The Aftermath of *Payne*' (1994) 3 Int Rev Victimology 141. For a general survey of the use of victim impact statements in the USA, see Erez E, 'Victim Participation in Sentencing: And the Debate Goes On' (1994) 3 Int Rev Victimology 17.

[89] Practice Direction (Victim Personal Statements) [2001] 4 All ER 640.

useless outcome.'[90] But Erez claims on the basis of her research that VPS is good for victims, because it 'empowers' them by making them visible to criminal justice officials who can thus no longer ignore their interests.[91] She argues that this has two beneficial consequences. First, she claims that participation is cathartic. Her findings and those of Sanders et al are reconcilable in that for some victims they are cathartic; but Sanders et al found this was so more at first than at the end of the case. Whether, on balance, they produce a net cathartic benefit is hard to say. The second beneficial consequence claimed by Erez is that VPS can influence decisions.[92] She is here referring to sentencing only. Sanders et al (2001) found that VPS, in the Victims' Charter schemes at any rate, had virtually no effect on sentencing or on any of the pre-trial stages: a prosecutor observed 'You don't see impact statements having much of an impact',[93] and a judge referred to their 'PR value'[94] thus implying that they had no other utility. Again, there is little contradiction here, as Erez concedes that most research, including her own, found the effect to be slight. This partly explains why VPS is so unsatisfactory for so many victims. They expect VPS to make a difference, and when it does not they are disappointed. Victims remain ignored even if not forgotten. Sanders et al found that few prosecutors, judges or magistrates were willing to take any notice of a VPS even though they almost universally subscribed to the rhetoric of victims' rights. And in some areas of both the UK and the USA a large number of impact statements are neither read nor put in the prosecution file.[95] Being treated like this hardly restores the self-respect of victims or reduces their secondary victimisation. The victims' movement complaint was that victims were used by the system: their witness statements were taken and then they were ignored. And now under the VPS scheme? Two statements are taken (witness and personal), and then they are both ignored. Hardly a revolutionary change. As Erez herself complains, the limited use of VPS represents a compromise between supporters and opponents of victims' rights, 'maintaining the time-honoured tradition of excluding victims from criminal justice with a thin veneer of being part of it'.[96] We do not regard this as empowerment.

Despite these findings, VPS schemes have been introduced nationwide. The statement is taken, by the police, at the same time as the witness statement with the opportunity to add to it at a later point.[97] Although this remedies one defect of the pilot

---

[90] Hoyle et al (1998: 32).

[91] Erez E, 'Who's Afraid of the Big Bad Victim? Victim Impact Statements as Victim Empowerment *and* Enhancement of Justice' [1999] Crim LR 545. Also see Erez E and Rogers L, 'The Effects of Victim Impact Statements on Criminal Justice Outcomes' (1999) 39 BJ Crim 216.

[92] Many writers object to VPS precisely for this reason. See, for example, Ashworth A, 'Victim's Rights, Defendant's Rights, and Criminal Procedure' in Crawford A and Goodey J (eds), *Integrating a Victim Perspective within Criminal Justice* (Aldershot: Ashgate, 2000); Sarat A, 'Vengeance, Victims and the Identities of Law' (1997) 6 Social and Legal Studies 163.   [93] Morgan and Sanders (1999: 22).

[94] Ibid: p 7.

[95] Henley et al, 'The Reactions of Prosecutors and Judges to Victim Impact Statements' (1994) 3 Int Rev Victimology 83; HMCPSI/HMICA/HMIC (2009: para 2.33).   [96] Erez and Rogers (1999: 234–5).

[97] Home Office information booklet, *Making a Victim Personal Statement* (London: Home Office, 2003a); VPS were introduced experimentally in Scotland a little later: Scottish Executive, *Making a Victim Statement: Guidance for Victims* (Edinburgh: Scottish Executive, 2003).

scheme, the take-up is now so low that a planned statistical survey had to be abandoned in favour of a study of just 28 participants (only 22 of whom actually completed a VPS).[98] Generalisation is difficult from such a small study. For what it is worth, as in the earlier research, some victims were unhappy because they did not know what use, if any, had been made of the VPS, and felt that they had been sidelined; and some would not have made a VPS had they understood the scheme at the time (eg some had thought it would help secure a conviction).[99] The scheme was thought to be working so badly by the government inspectorates that they recommended that it needs to be relaunched (HMCPSI, 2009: 33). Less dissatisfaction is reported from a much larger evaluation of the equivalent Scottish scheme, although only 15% of these eligible victims made a VPS and, of those, 38% said that making the VPS made them feel worse; and, again, a substantial number wrongly thought that the VPS would assist conviction.[100] The authors of the Scottish evaluation nonetheless critique Sanders et al (2001) for being unduly pessimistic. There is not room here to debate the evidence and the issues in more detail, but readers are urged to read both articles and make up their own minds.

In one sense there is no stopping the trend towards the provision of victim information to criminal justice officials and the courts. This is partly because, in the political sphere, no-one dares argue against 'victims' rights'. It is also because sentencing legitimately takes account of harm done (including emotional and psychological harm). Many courts (especially the Crown Court) have been receiving, and sometimes even seeking,[101] such information in cases concerning serious sexual offences, robbery and violence for some years.[102] However, statement schemes are not the best way of involving victims and of ensuring that relevant information is transmitted.[103] Nor are court actions, such as those brought against the DPP following deaths in custody and at work. We saw in chs 7 and 12 that in these actions the DPP is sometimes forced to reconsider not prosecuting, but these are expensive, lengthy and distressing strategies, best reserved for the worst cases only.[104] More effective ways of taking account of victims' interests and reducing secondary victimisation, modelled on civil law or restorative procedures, are more expensive than statement schemes. They would also

---

[98] Effort is being put into increasing the take-up rate; on a small sample taken in 2004, it rose from 2% to 19%: *No Witness, No Justice Pilot Evaluation* (London: CPS and ACPO, 2004) Executive Summary, p 9.

[99] Graham et al (2004).

[100] Note this evaluation also found take-up to be very low even though the Scottish scheme is post-charge. See Chalmers et al, 'Victim Impact Statements: Can Work, Do Work (For Those who Bother to Make Them)' [2007] Crim LR 360.

[101] Morgan and Sanders (1999).

[102] See, for example, *Perks* [2000] Crim LR 606, in which, following a review of several cases in which victim impact statements were considered, the relevant principles of sentencing are set out. Also: Edwards I, 'The Place of Victims' Preferences in the Sentencing of "Their" Offenders' [2002] Crim LR 689.

[103] There are far more effective ways of enhancing their freedom: Sanders et al (2001).

[104] See, for example, *DPP, ex p Manning* [2000] 3 WLR 463. But note the failure of the victim in *C* (*The Guardian*, 9 March 2000) to secure a ruling that the police and DPP should consult with her before dropping 'her' case.

require us to rethink the role of victims in adversary processes.[105] For a crime control system which only pays lip service to the interests of victims, this is not even on the agenda. The penalty which will be paid is that, as victims continue to be dissatisfied, their concerns will be hijacked by populist politicians to justify ever greater incursions on the liberties and rights of suspects, defendants and prisoners.[106]

It is evident that there is no clear policy about how influential, if at all, victims should be.[107] Decisions about prosecution, bail, plea bargaining, discontinuance, sentence and release from prison are all now to be made with varying degrees of input from, and discussion with, those relatively few victims who wish to be involved. The new Code does not shed any light on how much notice agencies should take of victims because it is concerned solely with service rights. The opportunity to provide for procedural rights on a consistent basis was not taken. This is because of a formalistic distinction between 'service' and 'procedural' rights that fails to recognise the interconnection between the two.[108]

13.4 **Rhetoric and reality: managing the gap**

It is sometimes rhetorically said that it is better that ten guilty people should escape justice rather than one innocent person be wrongly convicted. In addition to proclaiming the greater importance of acquitting the innocent than convicting the guilty, and recognising the trade-off between the two, the fact that the number stated is ten, rather than ten thousand, also recognises that we do not insist upon absolute certainty in the courtroom and nor could we. Statistically, it follows that some convicted defendants will in fact be innocent. The system is not, and never will be, perfect.

The real problem with this rhetoric is that it does not adequately characterise the reality, or even the rules, of the criminal justice system. There is a gap between the rhetoric of the system as a whole (largely due process), the rules (displaying a mixture of values) and the reality (largely crime control). We say that the rhetoric is *largely* due process-oriented, for governments increasingly favour crime control rhetoric, rules and reality. This is usually dressed up in the language of caring for victims and 'the law-abiding majority': for example, by Lord Williams, for the government,

---

[105] Strang (2002); Dignan (2005); Doak J, *Victims' Rights, Human Rights and Criminal Justice* (Oxford: Hart 2008).

[106] See Elias R, *Victims Still: The Political Manipulation of Crime Victims* (London: Sage, 1993) and Sarat (1997). See also Roach (1999b) for an insightful analysis of punitive and non-punitive (ie restorative) victims' rights models.

[107] In relation to sentencing see Edwards I, 'Victim Participation in Sentencing: The Problems of Incoherence' (2001) 40 Howard JCJ 39.

[108] This distinction is attributable to Ashworth A, 'Victim Impact Statements and Sentencing' [1993] Crim LR 498. However, in addition to having to add to these two categories, as we do here, the apparently clear distinction is not, on further investigation, so clear-cut: Sanders et al (2001).

trying to justify the sexual history provisions of the YJCE 1999 in this way;[109] by the Home Office, seeking to 'rebalance the criminal justice system';[110] and the then Prime Minister stating ominously in 2005 that the 'rules of the game are changing' (see ch 1). Occasionally there is a little more honesty, as in the CPS *Annual Report 2008/9* which states: 'Victims and witnesses have a central role to play in the prosecution process. The CPS recognises that it relies on the evidence of victims and witnesses, without whose co-operation prosecutions may not be able to take place, and justice may not be served.' Victims need to be treated well so that they will be more likely to cooperate.

The idea that victims should have the same rights as the accused (for example, to be protected and heard) is seductive. But the reason why accused people have these rights is because they stand to lose their liberty wrongly if they are deprived of them. The victim is not in the same position.[111] This is why the freedom perspective gives some, but less, weight, to the interests of victims than those of the accused. The new victim-centred rhetoric is therefore flawed, but it is also deceitful because it disguises the crime control drift.[112]

This process could continue until we have a totalitarian 'police state', at least so far as the poor, youths, protesters, and other 'problem populations' are concerned, but this is unlikely as it would be too politically dangerous. Within all the major political parties, there is sufficient attachment to the rhetoric and substance of due process to rule out the possibility of introducing an undiluted and naked system of crime control. There is also an ideological reason. By arguing that the criminal justice system has become too heavily tipped towards the interests of suspects, the Government has chosen to lock itself into the discourse of 'balance' in which more crime control can be justified by reference to bits and pieces of due process. In this sense, rather than in the crude sense implied by McBarnet,[113] due process is for crime control. But it also means that some genuine due process safeguards are sure to be retained, since one cannot create the appearance of due process if there is no substance to such safeguards.[114] Finally, the Human Rights Act 1998 and ECHR will ensure that there is an irreducible minimum of due process safeguards.

We have seen that the gap between rhetoric and reality is no smaller when we consider the plight of victims. For vulnerable victims, there are real improvements. But most victims have 'rights' which are totally unenforceable, and are therefore even less

---

[109] Discussed by Kibble (2000: 290).   [110] *Justice for All* (2002) Cm 5563, para 0.3.

[111] Edwards I, 'An Ambiguous Participant: The Crime Victim and Criminal Justice Decision Making' (2004) 44 BJ Crim 967.   [112] Garland (2001); Jackson (2003).

[113] McBarnet (1981: 156): 'the law on criminal procedure in its current form does not so much set a standard of legality from which the police deviate as provide a licence to ignore it. If we bring due process down from the dizzy heights of abstraction and subject it to empirical scrutiny, the conclusion must be that due process is for crime control'. This argument assumes that we must characterise rules of procedure as due process even when they served the goals of crime control. This is mistaken, in our view. Rules of procedure can be either due process or crime control in orientation as Packer H L, *The Limits of the Criminal Sanction* (Stanford: Stanford UP, 1968) himself pointed out.

[114] In this, we follow Thompson E P, *Whigs and Hunters* (London: Allen Lane, 1975) pp 259–65. See further Cole D, ' "An Unqualified Human Good": E.P. Thompson and the Rule of Law' (2001) 28(2) JLS 177.

substantial than many of the rights of suspects and defendants. Indeed, government decided to expand the VPS scheme despite research evidence showing that it is useless or even unhelpful to as many victims as it is helpful. Even the recent Scottish evaluation, which produced more positive results than the English one, found that victims overwhelmingly sought improvements to the information they get about their cases in preference to involvement in decisions.[115] In other words, service rights are more highly valued by victims than are procedural rights, but the latter are more headline grabbing so this is where the money and publicity are centred. Crime control systems make use of the rhetoric of the rights of the victim, but not the reality, for the rights of victims get in the way almost as much as the rights of defendants. For victims, just as much as innocent suspects and defendants, want the *right people* to be convicted. This is not the same as wanting the *criminal population* to be controlled (the crime control objective).

The powers of police and prosecution are therefore available to be used both for and against both suspects/defendants and victims – or without a care for either group. It may appear surprising that the crime control system serves victims as badly as it serves defendants until we remember that prosecution (in the minority of cases that get that far) requires the presentation of a case. All cases are constructions, and become the property of the side which built it. Cases often become far removed from the facts which provided their initial impetus and therefore, not infrequently, as far removed from anything the victim recognises as from anything the defendant recognises.

Thus while official rhetoric argues that the system is unbalanced in favour of 'offenders' and against victims, in reality, suspects/defendants/offenders and complainants/witnesses/victims are in a similar position, because the search for truth (whoever's version that might be) is subordinated to other priorities. Members of the public, whatever role they happen currently to be occupying, have no significant leverage on the agencies and officials about what should happen, when, and to whom. Contrary to government rhetoric, most victims are more concerned that the system should help prevent future reoffending – in our terms, to increase the sum total of freedom – than to be punitive per se. By restricting genuine victim participation in most cases the criminal justice system is exclusionary to both the accused and the victim, missing opportunities to enhance freedom.[116] It is therefore not surprising to find that surveys have consistently found that victim and witness satisfaction is highest with Victim Support and court witness services[117] – for, unlike the police, CPS and courts, these are the only agencies whose sole aim is to serve victims. The other agencies, rightly, have other objectives too.

[115] Chalmers et al (2007).

[116] Sanders A, 'Victim Participation in an Exclusionary Criminal Justice System' in Hoyle C and Young R (eds), *New Visions of Crime Victims* (Oxford: Hart, 2002). Doak (2008: 248) wrongly characterises our approach as anti-participation, when it is the current form of participation with which we take issue. His solution is to entrench victims' rights in a human rights framework, and to replace the adversary system with inquisitorial and restorative approaches. Ironically, he says the freedom approach is 'not...straightforward'!

[117] Eg, HMCPSI/HMICA/HMIC (2009: ch 5).

The criminal justice system will continue to represent a site of struggle and conflict. Many skirmishes will result in victories for due process (as where evidence is excluded on the grounds of unfairness), even some battles may be temporarily won (as with the creation of court and police station duty solicitor schemes), only for ground to be taken back again (as with the restricted right of silence sidelining legal advice in many cases, and the formalisation of plea bargaining). The Court of Appeal sometimes quashes convictions to express its disapproval of police malpractice even though there is reliable evidence of guilt, some police officers behave ethically and advocate progressive reforms, and some defence lawyers provide an outstanding service to their clients, often at great emotional and financial cost to themselves. But these events and people are exceptional, tending to occur in high-profile contexts (as with the dramatic freeing of the 'Birmingham Six', Angela Cannings and Colin Stagg), creating an appearance of far more due process than is really the case. So the war will continue. Crime control cannot be imposed by an open show of naked force, since its ideological justification is that it increases real freedom and liberty, but nor are we asked to give our *informed* consent to it. Instead we are presented with a picture of a system – neatly balancing due process rights, crime control powers and the rights of victims – which is a gross distortion of reality.

Part of this distortion is achieved by judges and legislators proclaiming the virtues of due process at the same time as they are acting on crime control instincts. For example, the case law on exclusion provides the judges with a wide scope as to which precedents to follow, which tests to apply and which decisions to reach. The open texture of the law means that, and on this point we follow McBarnet (1981: 166), 'judges can both uphold, even eulogise, the rhetoric yet simultaneously deny its applicability...' Thus in *Fulling*[118] (discussed in ch 5), we saw the Court of Appeal adopt a broad definition of oppression, which clearly covered the case in question, yet the appellant still lost. The protections introduced by PACE and the Codes of Practice are used against suspects, so that when a solicitor is present, this is usually judged to be sufficient protection to condone rule-breaking such as failure to caution, record questioning properly, and so forth. Similarly, in examining the Court of Appeal's powers, we saw how malpractice by police or prosecution agencies might be condemned but the conviction upheld. And, at other times, such as when informers or undercover officers are involved, the courts are happy to admit to discarding due process protections in favour of crime control.

The use of rhetoric bearing little relation to reality is not confined to English governments and courts. The ECtHR is equally guilty. For example, we saw in ch 9 that according to the ECtHR the bail decision has to be based on evidence (not speculation) and it has to be proven beyond reasonable doubt that someone is likely to breach bail. This is plainly ridiculous. Bail decisions in reality have to be based on risk and prediction (that is, *intelligent* speculation). This is a probabilistic, and not evidence-based, process and we doubt that anyone in the ECtHR believes otherwise.

---

[118] [1987] QB 426.

The uneven distribution of due process protections across society is as worrying as their general erosion. At various points in this book, we have seen that disadvantaged sections of society are disproportionately at the receiving end of state power. 'We' are taken in by the ideological self-portrait of criminal justice because we have so little experience of the system and have no incentive to question its operation. It does not threaten 'our' interests, but appears to serve them. Ask people who regularly come into contact with the system, whether as victims or offenders, and they will have a different story to tell. We saw that this led to so much dissatisfaction with the police complaints system that it was radically reformed, but this disaffection – bordering on disbelief in the rule of law – can be seen in many other criminal justice contexts (such as stop-search) where no change is on the cards.

Widespread disbelief in the rule of law is hardly surprising, for when we look at the rule of law another gap between rhetoric and reality is revealed. As we argue elsewhere,[119] two vital elements of the rule of law are equality before the law (as between citizens in different communities and as between citizens and officials) and the accountability of state officials to the courts. We have seen that, despite the rhetoric, neither of these conditions apply in many situations. The gap is managed, however, because they *appear* to apply. For example, anyone can ask anyone else a question without requiring an answer. Whether on the street or in the station, this is held to apply equally to police officers as to citizens. But treating people *the same* in this way is not treating them *equally*. By ignoring the power which police officers exert over citizens, whether unstated (as often happens on the street) or overt (as in the station), the citizen is not treated equally and the police are not made subject to legal control – 'consent' searches of people's homes, for example, are not subject to the restrictions, such as they are, of PACE.[120] Moreover, because some communities are disadvantaged by comparison with others in the way this type of power is exercised, people are treated unequally in an *institutionalised* manner, thus further violating the rule of law. And the relative lack of accountability of enforcement agencies – police, CPS and non-police agencies – means that they almost never have to account for this or its effects, violating the rule of law yet further.

We cannot expect, and nor would we advocate, the adoption of either a consistent crime control philosophy and all that goes with it, nor the adoption of the due process model and all that that would imply. Unfortunately, the freedom approach which we advocate is also unlikely to materialise unless politicians take a lead in raising the debate as distinct from raising their opinion poll ratings. Looked at in this way, the prospects for an open, rational and fair system of justice are bleak.

---

[119] See Sanders and Young (1994b) in relation to police practices.

[120] The fact that 'consensual stop-searches' have now been effectively outlawed in the light of evidence that the police were abusing this device to evade the controls of PACE (see ch 2) suggests that it is not inevitable that the government will turn a blind eye to this problem; although it requires a lot of evidence and persistent argument before this kind of power is taken away from the police. Contrast this with the scant evidence and argument required to justify increasing police powers (as in the case of stop-search powers that do not require reasonable suspicion – see ch 2).

Our negative tone might be criticised on the grounds that the English system is, for all its faults, the best in the world. It is probably true that it is better than most, and undoubtedly true that it is better than some. This is as it should be, as we are still one of the wealthiest societies in the world. We ought to be able to afford the best justice. And if we are as civilised as we would like to think, we should aspire to have the best system. The argument of this book is that the system neither achieves, nor aspires to achieve, such a high standard. The due process and crime control models help us understand the tensions within the system as it stands. But they cannot help us make out a persuasive argument for a transformation of that system. We need a new language in which to express our aspirations, and the language of freedom seems to us to provide a vocabulary most likely to persuade the various entrenched interest groups of the need for change. It is time to set the primary goal of the criminal justice system as the promotion of freedom of all citizens and social groups alike.

Further reading

Doak J, *Victims' Rights, Human Rights and Criminal Justice* (Oxford: Hart, 2008)

Gill P, 'Policing in Ignorance?' (2004) 58 Criminal Justice Matters 14

Sanders A and Jones I, 'The Victim in Court' in Walklate S (ed), *Handbook of Victims and Victimology* (Cullompton: Willan, 2007)

Van Dijk J and Goenhuijsen M, 'Benchmarking Victim Policies in the Framework of European Union Law' in Walklate S (ed), *Handbook of Victims and Victimology* (Cullompton: Willan, 2007)

Zedner L, 'Pre-Crime and Post-Criminology?' (2007) 11 Theoretical Criminology 261

Bibliography

ABBOT C (2009) *Enforcing Pollution Control Regulation* (Oxford: Hart).

ADAMS C (1995) *Balance in Pre-Trial Criminal Justice* (Unpublished PhD, LSE).

AINSWORTH P (2002) *Psychology and Policing* (Cullompton: Willan).

AIRS J and SHAW A (1999) *Jury Excusal and Deferral* (Research Findings No 102) (London: Home Office).

AKDENIZ Y (2001) 'Regulation of Investigatory Powers Act 2000: Part 1: bigbrother.gov.uk: State Surveillance in the Age of Information and Rights' Crim LR 73.

ALLEN J, EDMONDS S, PATTERSON A and SMITH D (2006) *Policing and the Criminal Justice System – Public Confidence and Perceptions: Findings from the 2004/05 British Crime Survey* (Home Office Online Report 07/06)(London: Home Office).

ALSCHULER A (1995) 'The All-white American Jury' 145 NLJ 1005.

AMADI J (2008) *Piloting PNDs on 10–15 Year Olds* (Ministry of Justice Research Series 19/08)(London: MOJ).

AMEY P, HALE C and UGLOW S (1996) *Development and Evaluation of a Crime Management Model* (Police Research Series Paper 18)(London: Home Office).

AMNESTY INTERNATIONAL (2000) *Deaths in Police Custody: Lack of Police Accountability* (London: AI).

AMOS M (2007) 'The Impact of the Human Rights Act on the United Kingdom's Performance before the European Court of Human Rights' Public Law 655.

ARANELLA P (1996) 'Rethinking the Functions of Criminal Procedure' reprinted in WASSERSTROM S and SNYDER C, *A Criminal Procedure Anthology* (Cincinnati: Anderson).

ARCE R (1995) 'Evidence Evaluation in Jury Decision-Making' in BULL R and CARSON D (eds), *Handbook of Psychology in Legal Contexts* (Chichester: Wiley).

ARKINSTALL J (2004) 'Unappealing Work: The Practical Difficulties Facing Solicitors Engaged in Criminal Appeal Cases' 1(2) Justice Journal 95.

ASHWORTH A (1978) 'A Threadbare Principle' Crim LR 385.

ASHWORTH A (1979) 'Prosecution and Procedure in Criminal Justice' Crim LR 490.

ASHWORTH A (1987a) 'Defining Offences Without Harm' in SMITH P (ed), *Criminal Law: Essays in Honour of J C Smith* (London: Butterworths).

ASHWORTH A (1987b) 'Public Order and the Principles of English Criminal Law' Crim LR 153.

ASHWORTH A (1987c) 'The "Public Interest" Element in Prosecutions' Crim LR 595.

ASHWORTH A (1993a) 'Plea, Venue and Discontinuance' Crim LR 830.

ASHWORTH A (1993b) 'Victim Impact Statements and Sentencing' Crim LR 498.

ASHWORTH A (1996a) 'Crime, Community and Creeping Consequentialism' Crim LR 220.

ASHWORTH A (1996b) 'Legal Aid, Human Rights and Criminal Justice' in YOUNG R and WALL D (eds), *Access to Criminal Justice* (London: Blackstone).

ASHWORTH A (1998a) *The Criminal Process*, 2nd edn (Oxford: OUP).

ASHWORTH A (1998b) 'Should the Police Be Allowed to Use Deceptive Practices?' 114 LQR 108.

ASHWORTH A (1999) 'Article 6 and the Fairness of Trials' Crim LR 261.

ASHWORTH A (2000a) 'Testing Fidelity to Legal Values: Official Involvement and Criminal Justice' 63 MLR 633.

ASHWORTH A (2000b) 'Victim's Rights, Defendant's Rights, and Criminal Procedure' in CRAWFORD A and GOODEY J (eds), *Integrating a Victim Perspective within Criminal Justice* (Aldershot: Ashgate).

ASHWORTH A (2001) 'Criminal Proceedings after the Human Rights Act: The First Year' Crim LR 855.

ASHWORTH A (2002a) 'Re-drawing the Boundaries of Entrapment' Crim LR 161.

ASHWORTH A (2002b) 'Responsibilities, Rights and Restorative Justice' 42(3) BJ Crim 578.

ASHWORTH A (2004) 'Criminal Justice Reform: Principles, Human Rights and Public Protection' Crim LR 516.

ASHWORTH A and BLAKE M (1996) 'The Presumption of Innocence in English Criminal Law' Crim LR 306.

ASHWORTH A and FIONDA J (1994) 'The New Code for Crown Prosecutors: Prosecution, Accountability and the Public Interest' Crim LR 894.

ASHWORTH A and REDMAYNE M (2005) *The Criminal Process*, 3rd edn (Oxford: OUP).

ASHWORTH A, GENDERS E, MANSFIELD G, PEAY J and PLAYER E (1984) Sentencing in the Crown Court (Occasional Paper No 10) (Oxford: Oxford Centre for Criminological Research).

ATTORNEY GENERAL (2003) Review of the Role and Practices of the CPS in Cases Arising from a Death in Police Custody: available at <http://www.lslo.gov.uk/pdf/deathincustody.pdf>.

ATTORNEY GENERAL (2005a) Guidelines on Disclosure; available at <http://lslo.gov.uk/guidelines.htm>.

ATTORNEY GENERAL (2005b) The Review of Infant Death Cases: Addendum to Report on Shaken Baby Syndrome: <http://www.lslo.gov.uk/>.

AUDIT COMMISSION (1993) *Helping with Enquiries: Tackling Crime Effectively* (London: Audit Commission).

AULD LJ (2001) *Review of the Criminal Courts of England and Wales: Report* (London: The Stationery Office).

AUSTIN R (2007) 'The New Powers of Arrest' Crim LR 459.

AYRES I and BRAITHWAITE J (1992) *Responsive Regulation: Transcending the Deregulation Debate* (New York: OUP).

AYRES M and MURRAY L (2005) *Arrests for Recorded Crime (Notifiable Offences) and the Operation of Certain Police Powers under PACE: England and Wales, 2004/05, Home Office Statistical Bulletin 21/05* (London: Home Office).

AZZOPARDI J (2002) 'Disclosure at the Police Station, the Right of Silence, and *DPP v Ara*' Crim LR 295.

BAGGULEY P and HUSSAIN Y (2008) *Riotous Citizens* (Aldershot: Ashgate).

BAKER E (1998) 'Taking European Criminal Law Seriously' Crim LR 361.

BAILIN A (2008) 'The Last Cold War Statute' Crim LR 625.

BALBUS I (1973) *The Dialectics of Legal Repression* (New York: Russell Sage).

BALDWIN J (1985) *Pre-Trial Justice* (Oxford: Basil Blackwell).

BALDWIN J (1992) *Preparing the Record of Taped Interview* (Royal Commission on Criminal Justice Research Study No 2) (London: HMSO).

BALDWIN J (1993a) 'Police Interview Techniques: Establishing Truth or Proof?' 33 BJ Crim 325.

BALDWIN J (1993b) 'Power and Police Interviews' 143 NLJ 1194.

BALDWIN J (1993c) *The Role of Legal Representatives at the Police Station* (Royal Commission on Criminal Justice Research Study No 3) (London: HMSO).

BALDWIN J (1997) 'Understanding Judge Ordered and Directed Acquittals in the Crown Court' Crim LR 536.

BALDWIN J and BEDWARD J (1991) 'Summarising Tape Recordings of Police Interviews' Crim LR 671.

BALDWIN J and FEENEY F (1986) 'Defence Disclosure in the Magistrates' Courts' 49 MLR 593.

BALDWIN J and HUNT A (1998) 'Prosecutors Advising in Police Stations' Crim LR 521.

BALDWIN J and McCONVILLE M (1977a) *Negotiated Justice* (London: Martin Robertson).

BALDWIN J and McCONVILLE M (1977b) 'Patterns of Involvement Amongst Lawyers in Contested Trials in the Crown Court' 127 New Law Journal 1040.

BALDWIN J and McCONVILLE M (1978a) 'Allegations Against Lawyers' Crim LR 744.

BALDWIN J and McCONVILLE M (1978b) 'The Influence of the Sentencing Discount in Inducing Guilty Pleas' in BALDWIN J and BOTTOMLEY A (eds), *Criminal Justice: Selected Readings* (Oxford: Martin Robertson).

BALDWIN J and McCONVILLE M (1979) *Jury Trials* (Oxford: OUP).

BALDWIN J and MOLONEY T (1992) *Supervision of Police Investigation in Serious Criminal Cases* (Royal Commission on Criminal Justice Research Study No 4) (London: HMSO).

BALDWIN J and MULVANEY A (1987) 'Advance Disclosure in the Magistrates' Courts: How Useful are the Prosecution Summaries?' Crim LR 805.

BALDWIN R (2004) 'The New Punitive Regulation' 67 Modern Law Review 351.

BALDWIN R (2005a) 'Is Better Regulation Smarter Regulation?' Public Law 485.

BALDWIN R (2005b) *Regulation in Question* (London: LSE).

BALDWIN R and BLACK J (2008) 'Really Responsive Regulation' 71 MLR 59.

BALL C (2000) 'A Significant Move Towards Restorative Justice, or a Recipe for Unintended Consequences?' Crim LR 211.

BALL C, McCORMAC K and STONE N (2001) *Young Offenders: Law, Policy and Practice*, 2nd edn (London: Sweet & Maxwell).

BALL K and WEBSTER F (eds) (2003) *The Intensification of Surveillance* (London: Pluto Press).

BALLARDIE C and IGANSKI P (2001) 'Juvenile Informers' in BILLINGSLEY R, NEMITZ T and BEAN P (eds), *Informers: Policing, Policy, Practice* (Cullompton: Willan).

BANKOWSKI Z, HUTTON N and McMANUS J (1987) *Lay Justice?* (Edinburgh: T & T Clark).

BANTON M (1964) *The Policeman in the Community* (London: Tavistock).

BAR COUNCIL (2004) Code of Conduct, Written Standards for the Conduct of Professional Work: available at <http://www.barcouncil.org.uk/>.

BARCLAY G and TAVARES C (1999) *Information on the Criminal Justice System in England and Wales: Digest 4* (London: Home Office).

BARNARD C and HARE I (2000) 'Police Discretion and the Rule of Law: European Community Rights Versus Civil Rights' 63 MLR 581.

BARTON A and EVANS R (1999) *Proactive Policing on Merseyside* (Police Research Series Paper 105) (London: Home Office).

BATES E (2009) 'Anti-terrorism Control Orders: Liberty and Security Still in the Balance' 29 Legal Studies 99.

BAXTER J and KOFFMAN L (1983) 'The Confait Inheritance – Forgotten Lessons?' Cambrian LR 14.

BAYLEY D (1994) *Police for the Future* (Oxford: OUP).

BAYLEY D (1995) 'Getting Serious about Police Brutality' in STENNING P (ed), *Accountability for Criminal Justice* (Toronto: University of Toronto Press).

BEAN P (2008) *Drugs and Crime*, 3rd edn (Cullompton: Willan).

BEAN P and BILLINGSLEY R (2001) 'Drugs, Crime and Informers' in BILLINGSLEY R, NEMITZ T and BEAN P (eds), *Informers: Policing, Policy, Practice* (Cullompton: Willan).

BEAN P and NEMITZ T (1994) *Out of Depth and Out of Sight* (Loughborough: University of Loughborough, Midlands Centre for Criminology).

BELUR J (2008) 'Is Policing Domestic Violence Institutionally Racist? A Case Study of South Asian Women' 18(4) Policing and Society 426.

BENNETTO J (2009) *Police and Racism: What has Been Achieved 10 Years After the Stephen Lawrence Inquiry Report?* (London: Equality and Human Rights Commission).

BERLIN I, *Liberty* (edited by Hardy H) (Oxford: OUP, 2002).

BERRY J (2009), Reducing Bureaucracy in Policing: Interim Report (available from <http://police.homeoffice.gov.uk/publications/police-reform/reducing-bureaucracy-report.html>).

BEST D and KEFAS A (2004) *The Role of Alcohol in Police-related Deaths: Analysis of Deaths in Custody (Category 3) Between 2000 and 2001* (London: Police Complaints Authority).

BEVAN G, HOLLAND T and PARTINGTON M (1994) *Organising Cost-Effective Access to Justice* (London: Social Market Foundation).

BHATT MURPHY (Solicitors), Inquest and Liberty (2002) Response to consultation paper on Attorney General's review of the role and practices of the CPS in cases of deaths in custody.

BILLINGSLEY R (2001) 'Informers' Careers: Motivations and Change' in BILLINGSLEY R, NEMITZ T and BEAN P (eds), *Informers: Policing, Policy, Practice* (Cullompton: Willan).

BILLINGSLEY R (2009) *Covert Human Intelligence Sources; The 'Unlovely Face of Police Work'* (Hampshire: Waterside Press).

BILLINGSLEY R, NEMITZ T and BEAN P (eds) (2001) *Informers: Policing, Policy, Practice* (Cullompton: Willan).

BIRCH D (1989) 'The PACE Hots Up: Confessions and Confusions Under the 1984 Act' Crim LR 95.

BIRCH D (1994) 'Excluding Evidence from Entrapment: What is a Fair Cop?' CLP 73.

BIRCH D (1999) 'Suffering in Silence' Crim LR 769.

BIRCH D (2000) 'A Better Deal for Vulnerable Witnesses?' Crim LR 223.

BIRCH D (2004) 'Hearsay: Same Old Story, Same Old Song' Crim LR 556.

BIRD S (2009) 'The Inadequacy of Legal Aid' in Naughton M (ed), *The Criminal Cases Review Commission* (London: Palgrave Macmillan).

BLAKE C (2000) 'Legal Aid: Past, Present and Future' Legal Action, Jan, p 6.

BLAKE M and ASHWORTH A (1998) 'Some Ethical Issues in Prosecuting and Defending Criminal Cases' Crim LR 16.

BLAKE M and ASHWORTH A (2004) 'Ethics and the Criminal Defence Lawyer' 7(2) Legal Ethics 167.

BLAKE N (1985) 'Picketing, Justice and the Law' in FINE B and MILLAR R (eds), *Policing the Miners' Strike* (London: Lawrence and Wishart).

BLAKEBOROUGH L and PIERPOINT H (2007) *Conditional Cautions: An Examination of the Early Implementation of the Scheme, MoJ Research Summary* (London: MOJ).

BLAND L (1992) 'The Case of the Yorkshire Ripper: Mad, Bad, Beast or Male?' in RADFORD J and RUSSELL D (eds), *Femicide: The Politics of Woman Killing* (New York: Twayne Publishing).

BLAND N, MILLER J and QUINTON P (2000) *Upping the PACE? An Evaluation of the Recommendations of the Stephen Lawrence Inquiry on Stops and Searches* (Police Research Series Paper 128) (London: Home Office).

BLOCK B, CORBETT C and PEAY J (1993a) *Ordered and Directed Acquittals in the Crown Court* (Royal Commission on Criminal Justice, Research Study No 15) (London: HMSO).

BLOCK B, CORBETT C and PEAY J (1993b) 'Ordered and Directed Acquittals in the Crown Court: A Time of Change?' Crim LR 95.

BOHLANDER M (1992) '"...By a Jury of His Peers" – The Issue of Multi-racial Juries in a Poly-ethnic Society' XIV(1) Liverpool LR 67.

BONNER D (2007) *Executive Measures, Terrorism and National Security: Have the Rules of the Game Changed?* (Aldershot: Ashgate).

BOTTOMLEY A (1987) 'Sentencing Reform and the Structuring of Pre-trial Discretion' in WASIK M and PEASE K (eds), *Sentencing Reform* (Manchester: MUP).

BOTTOMS A and McCLEAN J (1976) *Defendants in the Criminal Process* (London: Routledge).

BOWLING B (1998) *Violent Racism* (Oxford: Clarendon).

BOWLING B and PHILLIPS C (2002) *Racism, Crime and Justice* (Harlow: Longman).

BOWLING B and PHILLIPS C (2003) 'Policing Ethnic Minority Communities' in NEWBURN T (ed), *Handbook of Policing* (Cullompton: Willan).

BOWLING B and PHILLIPS C (2007) 'Disproportionate and Discriminatory: Reviewing the Evidence on Police Stop and Search' 70(6) MLR 936.

BOWLING B, PARMAR A and PHILLIPS P (2008) 'Policing Ethnic Minority Communities' in NEWBURN T (ed), *Handbook of Policing*, 2nd edn (Cullompton: Willan).

BOX S (1983) *Power, Crime and Mystification* (London: Tavistock).

BOX S and RUSSELL K (1975) 'The Politics of Discreditability: Disarming Complaints Against the Police' 23 Soc Rev 315.

BRADBURY S and FEIST A (2005) *The Use of Forensic Science in Volume Crime Investigation: A Review of the Research Literature* (Home Office Online Report 43/05) (London: Home Office).

BRAITHWAITE J (1989) *Crime, Shame and Reintegration* (Cambridge: CUP).

BRAITHWAITE J (2000) 'The New Regulatory State and the Transformation of Criminology' 40 BJ Crim 222.

BRAITHWAITE J (2002) *Restorative Justice and Responsive Regulation* (Oxford: OUP).

BRAND S and PRICE R (2000) *The Economic and Social Costs of Crime* (Home Office Research Study 217) (London: Home Office).

BRANTS C and FIELD S (1995) 'Discretion and Accountability in Prosecution' in HARDING C, FENNELL P, JORG N and SWART B (eds), *Criminal Justice in Europe: A Comparative Study* (Oxford: Clarendon).

BREDAR J (1992) 'Moving Up the Day of Reckoning: Strategies for Attacking the "Cracked Trials" Problem' Crim LR 153.

BRERETON D (1997) 'How Different are Rape Trials? A Comparison of the Cross-Examination of Complainants in Rape and Assault Trials' 37 BJ Crim 242.

BRIDGES L (1992a) 'The Fixed Fees Battle' Legal Action, November, p 7.

BRIDGES L (1992b) 'The Professionalisation of Criminal Justice' Legal Action, August, p 7.

BRIDGES L (1993) 'The Right to Jury Trial: How the Royal Commission Got it Wrong' 143 NLJ 1542.

BRIDGES L (1996) 'The Reform of Criminal Legal Aid' in YOUNG R and WALL D (eds) (1996) *Access to Criminal Justice* (London: Blackstone).

BRIDGES L (1999) 'False Starts and Unrealistic Expectations' Legal Action, October, 6.

BRIDGES L (2000) 'Taking Liberties' Legal Action, July, p 6.

BRIDGES L and BUNYAN T (1983) 'Britain's New Urban Policing Strategy – The Police and Criminal Evidence Bill in Context' 10 JLS 85.

BRIDGES L and CHOONGH S (1998) *Improving Police Station Legal Advice* (London: Law Society).

BRIDGES L, CAPE E, ABUBAKER A and BENNETT C (2000a) *Quality in Criminal Defence Services* (London: Legal Services Commission).

BRIDGES L, CHOONGH S and McCONVILLE M (2000b) *Ethnic Minority Defendants and the Right to Elect Jury Trial* (London: Commission for Racial Equality).

BRIDGES L, CAPE E, FENN P, MITCHELL A, MOORHEAD R and SHERR A (2007) Evaluation of the Public Defender Service in England and Wales (<http://www.legalservices.gov.uk/docs/pds/Public_Defenders_Report_PDFVersion6.pdf>).

BRITTON, N (2000a) 'Race and Policing: A Study of Police Custody' 40(4) BJ Crim 639.

BRITTON N (2000b) 'Examining Police/Black Relations: What's in a Story' 23(4) Ethnic and Racial Studies 696.

BROGDEN M (1985) 'Stopping the People' in BAXTER J and KOFFMAN L (eds), *Police: The Constitution and the Community* (Abingdon: Professional Books).

BROGDEN M (1991) *On the Mersey Beat* (Oxford: OUP).

BROGDEN M and BROGDEN A (1984) 'From Henry III to Liverpool 8' 12 IJ Sociology of Law 37.

BROOKMAN F and PIERPOINT H (2003) 'Access to Legal Advice for Young Suspects and Remand Prisoners' 42(5) Howard JCJ 452.

BROWN A (2004) 'Anti-Social Behaviour, Crime Control and Social Control' 43 Howard JCJ 203.

BROWN D (1987) *Police Complaints Procedure* (Home Office Research Study No 93) (London: HMSO).

BROWN D (1989) *Detention at the Police Station under the Police and Criminal Evidence Act 1984* (Home Office Research Study No 104) (London: HMSO).

BROWN D (1997) *PACE Ten Years On: A Review of the Research* (Home Office Research Study No 155) (London: HMSO).

BROWN D (1998) *Offending on Bail and Police Use of Conditional Bail* (Research Findings No 72) (London: Home Office).

BROWN D and ELLIS T (1994) *Policing Low Level Disorder: Police Use of Section 5 of the Public Order Act 1986* (Home Office Research Study No 135) (London: Home Office).

BROWN D, ELLIS T and LARCOMBE K (1992) *Changing the Code: Police Detention under the Revised PACE Codes of Practice* (Home Office Research Study No 129) (London: HMSO).

BROWN K, 'Charting the Expansion in the Number of Civil Orders to Tackle Criminal and Sub-Criminal Behaviour' (unpublished).

BROWN R and PAYNE S (2007) *Process Evaluation of Salford Community Justice Initiative* (London: Ministry of Justice)

BROWNLEE I (2004) 'The Statutory Charging Scheme in England and Wales: Towards a Unified Prosecution System?' Crim LR 896.

BROWNLEE I (2007) 'Conditional Cautions and Fair Trial Rights in England and Wales: Form Versus Substance in the Diversionary Agenda?' Crim LR 129.

BRYAN I (1997) *Interrogation and Confession* (Aldershot: Dartmouth).

BUCKE T (1997) *Ethnicity and Contacts with the Police: Latest Findings from the British Crime Survey* (Home Office Research Findings No 59) (London: Home Office).

BUCKE T and BROWN D (1997) *In Police Custody: Police Powers and Suspects' Rights Under the Revised Pace Codes of Practice* (Home Office Research Study No 174) (London: Home Office).

BUCKE T and JAMES Z (1998) *Trespass and Protest: Policing under the Criminal Justice and Public Order Act 1994* (London: Home Office).

BUCKE T, STREET R and BROWN D (2000) *The Right of Silence: The Impact of the Criminal Justice and Public Order Act 1994* (Home Office Research Study No 199) (London: Home Office).

BULLOCK S (2008) *Police Service Strength* (Home Office Statistical Bulletin 08/08) (London: Home Office).

BURNEY E (1979) *Magistrate, Court and Community* (London: Hutchinson).

BURNEY E (2003) 'Using the Law on Racially Aggravated Offences' Crim LR 28.

BURNEY E and ROSE G (2002) *Racist Offences – How is the Law Working?* (Home Office Research Study No 244) (London: Home Office).

BURNS R (2004) 'The Distinctiveness of Trial Narrative' in DUFF A, FARMER L, MARSHALL S and TADROS V (eds), *The Trial on Trial: Truth and Due Process* (Oxford: Hart).

BURROW J (2000) 'Bail and the Human Rights Act 1998' 150 NLJ 677.

BURROWS J, HENDERSON P and MORGAN P (1994) *Improving Bail Decisions: The Bail Process Project, Phase 1* (Research and Planning Unit Paper 90) (London: Home Office).

BURROWS J, HOPKINS M, HUBBARD R, ROBINSON A, SPEED M and TILLEY N (2005) *Understanding the Attrition Process in Volume Crime Investigations* (Home Office Research Study No 295) (London: Home Office).

BURTON M (2001) 'Reviewing CPS Decisions Not to Prosecute' Crim LR 374.

BURTON M (2008) *Legal Responses to Domestic Violence* (Abingdon: Routledge-Cavendish).

Burton M (2009) 'Failing to Protect: Victims' Rights and Police Liability' 72(2) MLR 283.

Burton M, Evans R, Sanders A (2006a) *Are Special Measures for Vulnerable and Intimidated Witnesses Working? Evidence From the Criminal Justice Agencies* (Home Office Online Report No 01/06) (London: Home Office).

Burton M, Evans R and Sanders A (2006b) 'Implementing Special Measures for Vulnerable and Intimidated Witnesses: the Problem of Identification' Crim LR 229.

Butler G (1999) *Inquiry into CPS Decision-Making in Relation to Deaths in Custody and Related Matters* (London: SO).

Butler S (1983) *Acquittal Rates* (Home Office Research and Planning Unit Paper 16) (London: HMSO).

Button M (2007) *Security Officers and Policing* (Aldershot: Ashgate).

Buxton R (1990) 'Challenging and Discharging Jurors' Crim LR 225.

Buzawa E and Buzawa C (1993) 'The Impact of Arrest on Domestic Assault' 36 American Behavioural Scientist 558.

Callan K (1997) *Kevin Callan's Story* (London: Little Brown and Company).

Cameron N (1980) 'Bail Act 1976: Two Inconsistencies and an Imaginary Offence' 130 NLJ 382.

Cammiss S (2006) ' "I Will in a Moment Give You the Full History": Mode of Trial, Prosecutorial Control and Partial Accounts' Crim LR 38.

Cammiss S and Stride C (2008) 'Modelling Mode of Trial' 48(4) BJ Crim 482.

Campbell D (2009) 'The Threat of Terror and the Plausibility of Positivism' Public Law 501.

Campbell S (2002) *A Review of Anti-social Behaviour Orders* (Home Office Research Study 236) (London: Home Office).

Campbell T (2006) *Rights: A Critical Introduction* (London: Routledge).

Cane P (1996) *Tort Law and Economic Interests* (Oxford: OUP).

Cannings A, with Lloyd Davies M (2006) *Against All Odds: A Mother's Fight to Prove her Innocence* (London: Time Warner Books).

Caolan E (2007) 'Reciprocity and Rights under the European Arrest Warrant Regime' LQR 197.

Cap Gemini Ernst & Young (1993) Referral Orders: Research into the Issues Raised in 'The Introduction of the Referral Order in the Youth Justice System' (March): available at <http://www.youth-justice-board.gov. uk/Publications>.

Cape E (1997) 'Sidelining Defence Lawyers: Police Station Advice After *Condron*' 1 IJ E & P 386.

Cape E (1999) 'Detention Without Charge: What Does "Sufficient Evidence To Charge" Mean?' Crim LR 874.

Cape E (2002) 'Incompetent Police Station Advice and the Exclusion of Evidence' Crim LR 471.

Cape E (2003) 'The Revised PACE Codes of Practice: A Further Step Towards Inquisitorialism' Crim LR 355.

Cape E (2004) 'The Rise (and Fall?) of a Criminal Defence Profession' Crim LR 401.

Cape E (2006a) *Police Station Advice: Advising on Silence* (Criminal Practitioners' Newsletter No 63, special edition) (London: Law Society).

Cape E (2006b) 'Police Station Law and Practice Update' Legal Action, April, p 10.

Cape E (2006c) *Defending Suspects at Police Stations*, 5th edn (London: LAG).

Cape E (2007) 'Modernising Police Powers – Again?' Crim LR 934

CAPE E (2008) 'Then and Now: Twenty-one Years of Re-balancing' in Cape E and Young R (eds), *Regulating Policing: The PACE Act 1984, Past Present and Future* (Oxford: Hart).

CAPE E (2008) 'Legal Aid Spending: Looking the Other Way' July *Legal Action* 8.

CAPE E and MOORHEAD R (2005) *Demand Induced Supply? Identifying Cost Drivers in Criminal Defence Work* (London: Legal Services Research Centre, Legal Services Commission).

CAPE E and YOUNG R (eds) (1998) *Regulating Policing* (Oxford: Hart).

CARLEN P (1974) 'Remedial Routines for the Maintenance of Control in Magistrates' Courts' BJ Law & Soc 101.

CARLEN P (1976) *Magistrates' Justice* (London: Martin Robertson, 1976).

CARLEN P (1996) *Jigsaw: A Political Criminology of Youth Homelessness* (Buckingham: Open University Press).

CARLISLE, LORD (2005) *Report on the Operation in 2004 of the Terrorism Act 2000* (London: SO).

CARLISLE A (2009) *Fourth Report of the Independent Reviewer Pursuant to Section 14 of the PTA 2005* (London: SO).

CARNS T and KRUSE J (1981) 'A Re-Evaluation of Alaska's Plea Bargaining Ban' 8 Alaska LR 27.

CARSON W (1970) 'White-Collar Crime and the Enforcement of Factory Legislation' 10 BJ Crim 383.

CARTER I (1999) *A Measure of Freedom* (Oxford: OUP).

CARTER, Lord (2006) *Legal Aid: A Market-Based Approach to Reform* (London: Ministry of Justice).

CARTER, Lord (2007) *Securing the Future: Proposals for the Efficient and Sustainable Use of Custody in England and Wales* (London: Ministry of Justice).

CASHMORE E (2001) 'The Experiences of Ethnic Minority Police Officers in Britain: Under-recruitment and Racial Profiling in a Performance Culture' 24(4) Ethnic and Racial Studies 642 .

CASHMORE E and McLAUGHLIN E (eds) (1991) *Out of Order?* (London: Routledge).

CAVADINO M (1997) 'A Vindication of the Rights of Psychiatric Patients' 24 JLS 235.

CAVADINO P and GIBSON B (1993) *Bail: The Law, Best Practice and the Debate* (Winchester: Waterside Press).

CCRC (2005) *Annual Report and Accounts 2004–2005* (HC 115) (London: TSO).

CCRC (2009a) *Annual Report and Accounts 2008/09* (HC 857) (London: TSO).

CCRC (2009b) Memorandum Submitted [to the Justice Committee] by the Criminal Cases Review Commission, <http://www.publications.parliament. uk/pa/cm200809/cmselect/cmjust/343/ 9031004.htm>

CENTREX (2004) *Practical Guide to Investigative Interviewing* (Centrex).

CHAKRABORTI N (2007) 'Policing Muslim Communities' in ROWE M (ed), *Policing beyond Macpherson* (Cullompton: Willan).

CHALMERS J, DUFF P and LEVERICK F (2007) 'Victim Impact Statements: Can Work, Do Work (For Those Who Bother to Make Them)' Crim LR 360.

CHAN J (1996) 'Changing Police Culture' 36 BJ Crim 109.

CHAN J (1997) *Changing Police Culture: Policing in a Multicultural Society* (Cambridge: Cambridge University Press).

CHERRYMAN J and BULL R (1996) 'Investigative Interviewing' in LEISHMAN F, LOVEDAY B and SAVAGE S (eds), *Core Issues in Policing* (Harlow: Longman).

CHIEF SURVEILLANCE COMMISSIONER (2005) *Annual Report 2004-5* (HC 444) (London).

CHIEF SURVEILLANCE COMMISSIONER (2009) *Annual Report 2008-9* (HC 704) (London).

CHILDS M (1999) 'Medical Manslaughter and Corporate Liability' 19 Legal Studies 316.

CHILCOT, Sir John (2008) *Privy Council Review of Intercept as Evidence* (Cm 7324).

CHOO A (1995) 'Halting Criminal Prosecutions: The Abuse of Process Doctrine Re-visited' Crim LR 864.

CHOO A (2008) *Abuse of Process and Judicial Stays of Criminal Proceedings*, 2nd edn (Oxford: OUP).

CHOO A and NASH S (1999) 'What's the Matter with s 78?' Crim LR 929.

CHOO A and NASH S (2007) 'Improperly Obtained Evidence in the Commonwealth: Lessons for England and Wales?' 11 IJ E&P 75.

CHOONGH S (1997) *Policing as Social Discipline* (Oxford: Clarendon).

CHOONGH S (1998) 'Policing the Dross: A Social Disciplinary Model of Policing' 38 BJ Crim 623.

CHOUDRY S and HERRING J (2006a) 'Righting Domestic Violence' International Journal of Law, Policy and Family 95.

CHOUDRY S and HERRING J (2006b) 'Domestic Violence and the Human Rights Act 1998: A New Means of Legal Intervention?' PL 752.

CLANCY A, HOUGH M, AUST, R and KERSHAW C (2001) *Crime, Policing and Justice: The Experience of Ethnic Minorities, Findings from the 2000 British Crime Survey* (Home Office Research Study 223) (London: Home Office).

CLARE I and GUDJONSSON G (1993) *Devising and Piloting an Experimental Version of the Notice to Detained Persons* (Royal Commission on Criminal Justice, Research Study No 7) (London: HMSO).

CLARK D (2004) *Bevan and Lidstone's The Investigation of Crime* (London: LexisNexis).

CLARK D (2007) 'Covert Surveillance and Informer Handling' in NEWBURN T, WILLIAMSON T and WRIGHT A (eds), *Handbook of Criminal Investigation* (Culllompton: Willan).

CLARK R (2001) 'Informers and Corruption' in BILLINGSLEY R, NEMITZ T and BEAN P (eds), *Informers: Policing, Policy, Practice* (Cullompton: Willan).

CLARKE A (1999) 'Safety or Supervision? The Unified Ground of Appeal and its Consequences in the Law of Abuse of Process and Exclusion of Evidence' Crim LR 108.

CLARKE A, MORAN-ELLIS J and SLENEY J (2002) *Attitudes to Date Rape and Relationship Rape: A Qualitative Study* (London: Sentencing Advisory Panel).

CLARKE C and MILNE R (2001) *National Evaluation of the PEACE Investigative Interviewing Scheme* (Police Research Award Scheme Report No: PRAS/149) (London: Home Office).

CLARKE M (2000) *Regulation: The Social Control of Business Between Law and Politics* (Basingstoke: Macmillan).

CLARKE R and HOUGH M (1984) *Crime and Police Effectiveness* (Home Office Research Study No 79) (London: HMSO).

CLARKSON C (1996) 'Kicking Corporate Bodies and Damning their Souls' 59 MLR 557.

CLARKSON C (2005) 'Corporate Manslaughter: Yet More Government Proposals' Crim LR 677.

CLARKSON C, CRETNEY A, DAVIS G and SHEPHERD J (1994) 'Assaults: The

Relationship between Seriousness, Criminalisation and Punishment' Crim LR 4.

CLAYTON R and TOMLINSON H (1988) 'Arrest and Reasonable Grounds for Suspicion' 7 Sep LS Gaz 22.

CLEMENTS L, 'Winners and Losers' (2005) 32(1) JLS 34.

COBLEY C (2003) 'Prosecuting Cases of Suspected "Shaken Baby Syndrome" – A Review of Current Issues' Crim LR 93.

COHEN S (1985) Visions of Social Control (Cambridge: Polity Press).

COLE D (2001) '"An Unqualified Human Good": E.P. Thompson and the Rule of Law' 28(2) JLS 177.

COLEMAN R (2004) Reclaiming the Streets: Surveillance, Social Control and the City (Cullompton: Willan).

COLES D and MURPHY F (1999) 'O'Brien: Another Death in Police Custody' Legal Action, Nov, p 6.

COLLISON M (1995) Police, Drugs and Community (London: Free Association Books, 1995).

COOK D, BURTON M, ROBINSON A and VALLELY C (2004) Evaluation of Specialist Domestic Violence Courts and Fast Track Systems (London: CPS).

COOPER D (2005) 'Pigot Unfulfilled: Video-recorded Cross-examination under Section 28 of the Youth Justice and Criminal Evidence Act 1999' Crim LR 456.

COOPER D and ROBERTS P (2005) Special Measures for Vulnerable and Intimidated Witnesses: An Analysis of CPS Monitoring Data (London: CPS).

COOPER D and ROBERTS P (2005) 'Monitoring Success: Special Measures under the YJCE 1999' 9 E&P 269

COOPER P and MURPHY J (1997) 'Ethical Approaches for Police Officers when Working with Informants in the Development of Criminal Intelligence in the UK' 26 J Social Policy 1.

COOPER S (2006) 'Legal Advice and Pre-trial Silence – Unreasonable Developments' 10 IJ E&P 60.

COOPER S (2009) 'Appeals, Referrals and Substantial Injustice' Crim LR 152.

COPE N (2004) 'Intelligence Led Policing or Policing Led Intelligence?' 44 BJ Crim 188.

COPPEN J (2008) 'PACE: A View from the Custody Suite', in CAPE E and YOUNG R (eds) Regulating Policing (Oxford: Hart).

CORBETT C (1991) 'Complaints Against the Police: The New Procedure of Informal Resolution' 2 Policing and Society 47.

CORKER D and YOUNG D (2002) Abuse of Process and Fairness in Criminal Proceedings (London: Butterworths).

CORKER D, TOMBS G and CHISHOLM T (2009) 'Ss 71 and 72 of SOCPA: Whither the Common Law?' Crim LR 261.

CORNISH W (1968) The Jury (London: Penguin).

COSTIGAN R (2007) 'Identification from CCTV: The Risk of Injustice' Crim LR 591.

COUNCIL OF EUROPE (1985) The Position of the Victim in the Framework of Criminal Law and Procedure (COUNCIL OF EUROPE).

COUNCIL OF EUROPE, PARLIAMENTARY ASSEMBLY (2009) Allegations of Politically-Motivated Abuses of the Criminal Justice System in Council of Europe Member States (Council of Europe).

COWAN D and LOMAX D (2003) 'Policing Unauthorised Camping' 30 JLS 283.

COWAN D and MARSH A (2001) 'There's Regulatory Crime and then there's Landlord Crime: From Rachmanites to Partners' 64 MLR 831.

COX B (1975) Civil Liberties in Britain (Harmondsworth: Penguin).

CRAIG P (1997) 'Formal and Substantive Conceptions of the Rule of Law: An Analytical Framework' Public Law 467.

CRAWFORD A (1997) *The Local Governance of Crime* (Oxford: Clarendon).

CRAWFORD A (2007) '"Reassurance Policing: Feeling is Believing"' in HENRY A and SMITH D (eds), *Transformations of Policing* (Aldershot: Ashgate).

CRAWFORD A (2008a) 'Dispersal Powers and the Symbolic Role of Anti-Social Behaviour Legislation' 71(5) MLR 753.

CRAWFORD A (2008b) 'Plural Policing in the UK: Policing Beyond the Police' in NEWBURN T (ed), *Handbook of Policing*, 2nd edn (Cullompton: Willan).

CRAWFORD A and LISTER S, *The Use and Impact of Dispersal Orders* (London: Policy Press, 2007).

CRAWFORD A and NEWBURN T (2003) *Youth Offending and Restorative Justice* (Cullompton: Willan).

CRAWLEY J (2009) 'The Worst of All Outcomes' *Society Guardian*, 8 April.

CRETNEY A and DAVIS G (1995) *Punishing Violence* (London: Routledge).

CRETNEY A, DAVIS G, CLARKSON C and SHEPHERD J (1994) 'Criminalising Assault: The Failure of the "Offence Against Society" Model' 34 BJ Crim 15.

CRIMINAL LAW REVISION COMMITTEE (1972) *Eleventh Report (General)*, Cmnd 4991 (London: HMSO).

CRISP D (1993) 'Standardising Prosecutions' 34 Home Office Research Bulletin 13.

CRISP D and MOXON D (1994) *Case Screening by the CPS* (Home Office Research Study No 137) (London: Home Office).

CRISP D, WHITTAKER C and HARRIS J (1995) *Public Interest Case Assessment Schemes* (Home Office Research Study No 138) (London: Home Office).

CROALL H (1988) 'Mistakes, Accidents and Someone Else's Fault: The Trading Offender in Court' 15 JLS 293.

CROWN PROSECUTION SERVICE (1998) Discontinuance Survey (November) (unpublished: cited in Criminal Justice System, Narrowing the Justice Gap, 2002 available at <http://www.cps.gov.uk/publications/docs/justicegap.pdf>.

CROWN PROSECUTION SERVICE (CPS) (2003) *Guidance on Prosecuting Cases of Racial and Religious Crime* (London: CPS).

CROWN PROSECUTION SERVICE (CPS) (2004a) *Annual Report, 2002–3* (London: CPS).

CROWN PROSECUTION SERVICE (CPS) (2004b) *Code for Crown Prosecutors* (London: CPS) available at <http://www.cps.gov.uk/>.

CROWN PROSECUTION SERVICE (CPS) (2005) *Annual Report, 2004–5* (London: SO).

CROWN PROSECUTION SERVICE (CPS) (2007) *The Director's Guidance on Charging*, 3rd edn (London: CPS).

CROWN PROSECUTION SERVICE (CPS) (2008a) *Special Domestic Violence Courts Review 2007–8* (London: CPS).

CROWN PROSECUTION SERVICE (CPS) (2008b) *Violence Against Women Report 2007–8* (London: CPS).

CROWN PROSECUTION SERVICE (CPS) (2008c) *Guidance on Prosecuting Cases of Domestic Violence* (London: CPS).

CROWN PROSECUTION SERVICE (CPS) (2008d) *Annual Report 2007–8* (London: SO).

CROWN PROSECUTION SERVICE (CPS) (2009) *Annual Report, 2008–9* (London: SO).

CROWN PROSECUTION SERVICE (CPS) and ASSOCIATION OF CHIEF POLICE OFFICERS (ACPO) (2004) *No Witness, No Justice Pilot Evaluation* (London: CPS and ACPO).

CROWN PROSECUTION SERVICE (CPS) and INDEPENDENT POLICE COMPLAINTS COMMISSION (IPCC) (2005) Protocol between the Crown Prosecution Service CaseworkDirectorateandtheIndependent Police Complaints Commission: available at <http://www.cps.gov.uk/publications/agencies/index.html>.

CUNNINGHAM S (2005) 'The Unique Nature of Prosecutions in Cases of Fatal Road Traffic Collisions' Crim LR 834.

DALY G and PATTENDEN R (2005) 'Racial Bias and the English Criminal Trial Jury' 64(3) CLJ 678.

DAMASKA M (1973) 'Evidentiary Barriers to Conviction and Two Models of Criminal Procedure: A Comparative Study' 121 U Penn LR 506.

DAMASKA M (1986) The Faces of Justice and State Authority (New Haven: Yale).

DANDO C, WILCOX R and MILNE R (2008) 'The Cognitive Interview: Inexperienced Police Officers' Perceptions of their Witness Interviewing Behaviour' 13 Legal and Criminological Psychology 59.

DANDO C, WILCOX R, MILNE R and HENRY L (2009) 'A Modified Cognitive Interview Procedure for Frontline Police Investigators' 23 Applied Cognitive Psychology 698.

DARBYSHIRE P (1984) The Magistrates' Clerk (Chichester: Barry Rose, 1984).

DARBYSHIRE P (1990) 'Notes of a Lawyer Juror' 140 NLJ 1264.

DARBYSHIRE P (1991) 'The Lamp That Shows That Freedom Lives – Is it Worth the Candle?' Crim LR 740.

DARBYSHIRE P (1997a) 'An Essay on the Importance and Neglect of the Magistracy' Crim LR 627.

DARBYSHIRE P (1997b) 'For the New Lord Chancellor: Some Causes for Concern About Magistrates' Crim LR 861.

DARBYSHIRE P (1997c) 'Previous Misconduct and Magistrates' Courts – Some Tales from the Real World' Crim LR 105.

DARBYSHIRE P (1997d) 'Strengthening the Argument in Favour of the Defendant's Right to Elect' Crim LR 911.

DARBYSHIRE P (2008) Darbyshire on the English Legal System (London: Sweet & Maxwell).

DARBYSHIRE P and THOMAS C (2008) 'Exposing Jury Myths-Letters to the Editor' Crim LR 888.

DARBYSHIRE P, with research by MAUGHAN A and STEWART A (2001) 'What Can We Learn from Published Jury Research? Findings for the Criminal Courts Review' Crim LR 970.

DARBYSHIRE P, MAUGHAN A and STEWART A (2001) 'What can the English Legal System Learn from Jury Research Published up to 2001?', available at <http://www.kingston.ac.uk~ku00596>.

DAVIES G (1996) 'Mistaken Identification: Where Law Meets Psychology Head On' 35 Howard J 232.

DAVIS G, HOYANO L, KEENAN C, MAITLAND L and MORGAN R (1999) Assessment of the Admissibility and Sufficiency of Evidence in Child Abuse Prosecutions (London: Home Office).

DAW R (1994) 'A Response' Crim LR 904.

DE MAS S (2003) 'Protecting the Legal Rights of the Travelling Citizen: Easier Said than Done' Crim LR 865.

DE SCHUTTER O and RINGELHEIM J (2008) 'Ethnic Profiling: A Rising Challenge for European Human Rights Law' (2008) 71(3) MLR 358.

DELL S (1971) Silent in Court (London: Bell).

DEMBOUR M-B (2006) Who Believes in Human Rights? (Cambridge: Cambridge University Press).

DEMPSEY M (2007) 'Towards a Feminist State: What does 'Effective' Prosecution of Domestic Violence Mean?' 70 MLR 908.

DEMPSEY M (2009) *Prosecuting Domestic Violence* (Oxford: OUP).

DENNIS I (1993) 'Miscarriages of Justice and the Law of Confessions' Public Law 291.

DENNIS I (2002) *The Law of Evidence*, 2nd edn (London: Sweet & Maxwell).

DENNIS I (2003a) 'Editorial' Crim LR 663.

DENNIS I (2003b) 'Fair Trials and Safe Convictions' 56 Current Legal Problems 211.

DENNIS I (2005) 'Reverse Onuses and the Presumption of Innocence: In Search of Principle' Crim LR 901.

DENNIS I (2006) 'Convicting the Guilty: Outcomes, Process and the Court of Appeal' [2006] Crim LR 955.

DEPARTMENT FOR BUSINESS ENTERPRISE & REGULATORY REFORM, *Statutory Code of Practice for Regulators* (London: DBERR, 2007).

DEPARTMENT FOR CONSTITUTIONAL AFFAIRS (DCA) (2005a) *Judicial Statistics: England and Wales for the Year 2004* (Cm 6565) (London: TSO).

DEPARTMENT FOR CONSTITUTIONAL AFFAIRS (DCA) (2005b) *Jury Research and Impropriety, Response to Consultation* (CP 04/05) (London: DCA).

DEPARTMENT FOR CONSTITUTIONAL AFFAIRS (2006a) *Review of the Implementation of the Human Rights Act* (London: DCA).

DEPARTMENT FOR CONSTITUTIONAL AFFAIRS (2006b) *Delivering Simple, Speedy, Summary Justice* (London: DCA).

DEPARTMENTAL COMMITTEE ON FRAUD TRIALS (1986) *Report* (London: HMSO).

DEPARTMENTAL COMMITTEE ON LEGAL AID IN CRIMINAL PROCEEDINGS (1966) *Report* (Cmnd 2934) (London: HMSO) (chaired by Mr Justice Widgery).

DEVLIN A and DEVLIN T (1998) *Anybody's Nightmare* (East Harling: Taverner Publications).

DHAMI M (2002) 'Do Bail Information Schemes Really Affect Bail Decisions?' 41 Howard JCJ 245.

DHAMI M (2004) 'Conditional Bail Decision Making in the Magistrates' Court' 43 Howard JCJ 27.

DI FEDERICO G (1998) 'Prosecutorial Independence and the Democratic Requirement of Accountability in Italy' 38 BJ Crim 371.

DICKSON B (2007) 'The Processing of Appeals in the House of Lords' LQR 571.

DIGNAN J (1992) 'Repairing the Damage: Can Reparation Be Made to Work in the Service of Diversion?' 32(4) BJ Crim 453.

DIGNAN J (2005) *Understanding Victims and Restorative Justice* (Maidenhead: Open UP).

DIGNAN J and CAVADINO M (1996) 'Towards a Framework for Conceptualising and Evaluating Models of Criminal Justice from a Victim's Perspective' 4 Int R Victimology 153.

DIGNAN J and WHYNNE A (1997) 'A Microcosm of the Local Community? Reflections on the Composition of the Magistracy in a Petty Sessional Division in the North Midlands' 37 BJ Crim 184.

DINE J (1993) 'European Community Criminal Law?' Crim LR 246.

DINGWALL G and HARDING C (1998) *Diversion in the Criminal Process* (London: Sweet & Maxwell).

DIXON B and SMITH G (1998) 'Laying Down the Law: The Police, the Courts and Legal Accountability' 26 IJ Soc of Law 419.

DIXON D (1991) 'Common Sense, Legal Advice, and the Right of Silence' Public Law 233.

DIXON D (1997) *Law in Policing* (Oxford: Clarendon).

DIXON D (2005) 'Regulating Police Interrogation' in WILLIAMSON T (ed), *Investigative Interviewing: Rights, Research Regulation* (Cullompton: Willan).

DIXON D (2006) '"A Window into the Interviewing Process?" The Audio-visual Recording of Police Interrogation in New South Wales, Australia' 16(4) Policing and Society 323.

DIXON D, BOTTOMLEY A, COLEMAN C, GILL M and WALL D (1989) 'Reality and Rules in the Construction and Regulation of Police Suspicion' 17 IJ Sociology of Law 185.

DIXON D, BOTTOMLEY K, COLEMAN C, GILL M and WALL D (1990a) 'Safeguarding the Rights of Suspects in Police Custody' 1 Policing and Society 115.

DIXON D, COLEMAN C and BOTTOMLEY K (1990b) 'Consent and the Legal Regulation of Policing' 17 JLS 345.

DOAK J (2003) 'The Victim and the Criminal Process: An Analysis of Recent Trends in Regional and International Tribunals' 23 Legal Studies 1.

DOAK J (2005) 'Victims' Rights in Criminal Trials: Prospects for Participation' 32 JLS 294.

DOAK, J (2008) *Victims' Rights, Human Rights and Criminal Justice: Reconceiving the Role of Third Parties* (Oxford: Hart).

DOCKING M and BUCKE T (2006) *Confidence in the Police Complaints System: A Survey of the General Population* (London: IPCC) available from <http://www.ipcc.gov.uk/confidence_survey.pdf>.

DOCKING M, GRACE K and BUCKE T (2008) *Police Custody as a "Place of Safety": Examining the Use of s 136 of the MHA 1983* (London: IPCC).

DOHERTY M and EAST R (1985) 'Bail Decisions in Magistrates' Courts' 25 BJ Crim 251.

DONAGHY R (2009) *One Death Too Many* (Cm 7657) (Department for Work and Pensions) (Norwich: TSO).

DORAN S (1989) 'Descent to Avernus' 139 NLJ 1147.

DORAN S (1991) 'Alternative Defences: The "Invisible" Burden on the Trial Judge' Crim LR 878.

DORAN S (2000) 'The Necessarily Expanding Role of the Criminal Trial Judge' in DORAN S and JACKSON J (eds), *The Judicial Role in Criminal Proceedings* (Oxford: Hart).

DORAN S and GLENN R (2000) *Lay Involvement in Adjudication: Review of the Criminal Justice System in Northern Ireland* (Criminal Justice Review Research Report No 11) (Belfast: SO).

DORAN S and JACKSON J (1997) 'The Case for Jury Waiver' Crim LR 155.

DORN N, MIRJI K and SOUTH N (1992) *Traffickers: Drug Markets and Law Enforcement* (London: Routledge).

DOUZINAS C (2007) 'Left or Rights?' 34 JLS 617.

DRAKE K, BULL R, BOON J (2008), 'Interrogative Suggestibility, Self-esteem, and the Influence of Negative Life Events' 13 Legal and Criminological Psychology 299.

DROR I and CHARLTON D (2006) 'Why Experts make Errors' 56 J Forensic Identification 600.

DUFF P (1998) 'Crime Control, Due Process and "The Case for the Prosecution"' 38 BJ Crim 611.

DUFF P and FINDLAY M (1983) 'Jury Vetting – The Jury under Attack' 3 LS 159.

DUFF P and HUTTON N (eds) (1999) *Criminal Justice in Scotland* (Aldershot: Dartmouth).

DUNNIGHAN C and NORRIS C (1996) 'A Risky Business: The Recruitment and Running of Informers by English Police Officers' 19 Police Studies 1.

DURSTON G (2005) 'Previous (In)Consistent Statements after the Criminal Justice Act 2003' Crim LR 206.

DWORKIN R (1981) 'Principle, Policy, Procedure' in TAPPER C (ed), *Crime, Proof and Punishment* (London: Butterworths).

EADY D (2009) 'The Failure of the CCRC to Live Up to its Stated Values?: The Case of Michael Attwooll and John Roden' in NAUGHTON M (ed), *The Criminal Cases Review Commission* (London: Palgrave Macmillan).

EAST R (1985) 'Jury Packing: A Thing of the Past?' 48 MLR 518.

EAST R (1987) 'Police Brutality: Lessons of the Holloway Road Assault' 137 NLJ 1010.

EAST R and THOMAS P (1985) 'Freedom of Movement: *Moss v McLachlan*' 12 JLS 77.

EASTON S (1998a) 'Legal Advice, Common Sense and the Right of Silence' 2 IJ Evidence & Proof 109.

EASTON S (1998b) *The Case for the Right to Silence* (Aldershot: Ashgate, 1998).

EATON M (1987) 'The Question of Bail' in CARLEN P and WORRALL A (eds), *Gender, Crime and Justice* (Milton Keynes: Open UP).

EDWARDS I (2001) 'Victim Participation in Sentencing: The Problems of Incoherence' 40 Howard JCJ 39.

EDWARDS I (2002), 'The Place of Victims' Preferences in the Sentencing of "Their" Offenders' Crim LR 689.

EDWARDS I (2004) 'An Ambiguous Participant: The Crime Victim and Criminal Justice Decision Making' 44 BJ Crim 967.

EDWARDS J (1984) *The Attorney General, Politics and the Public Interest* (London: Sweet & Maxwell).

EDWARDS S (1989) *Policing Domestic Violence* (London: Sage).

EDWARDS T (2008) 'The Role of Defence Lawyers in a Re-Balanced System' in CAPE E and YOUNG R (eds), *Regulating Policing* (Oxford: Hart).

EKBLOM P and HEAL K (1982) *The Police Response to Calls from the Public* (Research and Planning Unit Paper No 9) (London: Home Office).

ELIAS R (1993) *Victims Still: The Political Manipulation of Crime Victims* (London: Sage).

ELKS L (2008) *Righting Miscarriages of Justice? Ten Years of the Criminal Cases Review Commission* (London: Justice).

ELLIMAN S (1990) 'Independent Information for the CPS' 140 NLJ 812.

ELLISON L (1998) 'Cross-Examination in Rape Trials' Crim LR 605.

ELLISON L (2001a) *The Adversarial Process and the Vulnerable Witness* (Oxford: OUP).

ELLISON L (2001b) 'The Mosaic Art? Cross-examination and the Vulnerable Witness' 21 Legal Studies 353.

ELLISON L (2002) 'Prosecuting Domestic Violence Without Victim Participation' 56 MLR 834.

ELLISON L (2002) 'Cross-examination and the Intermediary: Bridging the Language Divide?' Crim LR 114.

ELLISON L (2003) 'Responding to Victim Withdrawal in Domestic Violence Prosecutions' Crim LR 760.

ELLISON L (2007) 'Promoting Effective Case-building in Rape Cases: A Comparative Perspective' Crim LR 691.

ELLISON L and MUNRO V (2009a) 'Reacting to Rape' 49(2) BJ Crim 202.

ELLISON L and MUNRO V (2009b) 'Of 'Normal Sex' and 'Real Rape': Exploring the Use of Socio-sexual Scripts in (Mock) Jury Deliberation' 18(3) Social and Legal Studies 291.

ELLISON L and MUNRO V (2009c) 'Turning Mirrors in Windows? Assessing the Impact of (Mock) Juror Education in Rape Trials' 49(3) BJ Crim 363.

ELLISON L (2009d) 'The Use and Abuse of Psychiatric Evidence in Rape Trials' 13 IJEP 28.

EMMERSON B, ASHWORTH A and MACDONALD A (2007) *Human Rights and Criminal Justice*, 2nd edn (London: Sweet & Maxwell).

EREZ E (1994) 'Victim Participation in Sentencing: And the Debate Goes On' 3 Int Rev Victimology 17.

EREZ E (1999) 'Who's Afraid of the Big Bad Victim? Victim Impact Statements as Victim Empowerment *and* Enhancement of Justice' Crim LR 545.

EREZ E and ROGERS L (1999) 'The Effects of Victim Impact Statements on Criminal Justice Outcomes' 39 BJ Crim 216.

ERICSON R (1981) *Making Crime: A Study of Detective Work* (London: Butterworths).

ERICSON R (1982) *Reproducing Order: A Study of Police Patrol Work* (Toronto: University of Toronto Press).

ERICSON R (1994) 'The Royal Commission on Criminal Justice System Surveillance' in MCCONVILLE M and BRIDGES L (eds), *Criminal Justice in Crisis* (Aldershot: Edward Elgar).

ERICSON R and HAGGERTY K (1997) *Policing the Risk Society* (Oxford: Clarendon).

ERICSON R and HAGGERTY K (1999) 'Governing the Young' in SMANDYCH R (ed), *Governable Places: Readings on Governmentality and Crime Control* (Aldershot: Ashgate).

ERIN C and OST S (eds) (2007) *The Criminal Justice System and Healthcare* (Oxford: OUP).

EVANS M and MORGAN R (1992) 'The European Convention for the Prevention of Torture: Operational Practice' 41 ICLQ 590.

EVANS R (1991) 'Police Cautioning and the Young Adult Offender' Crim LR 598.

EVANS R (1993a) 'Comparing Young Adult and Juvenile Cautioning in the Metropolitan Police District' Crim LR 572.

EVANS R (1993b) *The Conduct of Police Interviews with Juveniles* (Royal Commission on Criminal Justice Research Study No 8) (London: HMSO).

EVANS R (1994) 'Cautioning: Counting the Cost of Retrenchment' Crim LR 566.

EVANS R (1996) 'Is a Police Caution Amenable to Judicial Review?' Crim LR 104.

EVANS R and ELLIS R (1997) *Police Cautioning in the 1990s* (Home Office Research Findings No 52) (London: HMSO).

EVANS R and PUECH K (2001) 'Reprimands and Warnings: Populist Punitiveness or Restorative Justice?' Crim LR 794.

EVANS R and WILKINSON C (1990) 'Variation in Police Cautioning Policy and Practice in England and Wales' 29 Howard JCJ 155.

EWING K and THAM J-C (2008) 'The Continuing Futility of the Human Rights Act' Public Law 668.

FAULKNER D (1996) *Darkness and Light: Justice, Crime and Management for Today* (London: Howard League).

FEELEY M and SIMON J (1994) 'Actuarial Justice: The Emerging New Criminal Law' in NELKEN D (ed), *The Futures of Criminology* (London: Sage).

FEILZER M and HOOD R (2004) *Differences or Discrimination?* (London: Youth Justice Board).

FELDMAN D (2002) *Civil Liberties and Human Rights in England and Wales*, 2nd edn (Oxford: OUP).

FELDMAN D (2006) 'Human Rights, Terrorism and Risk: The Roles of Politicians and Judges' Public Law 364.

FENNER S, GUDJONSSON G and CLARE I (2002) 'Understanding of the Police Caution (England and Wales) Among Suspects in Police Detention' 12 J Community & Applied Social Psychology 83.

FENWICK H (1993) 'Confessions, Recording Rules, and Miscarriages of Justice: A Mistaken Emphasis?' Crim LR 174.

FENWICK H (1995) 'Rights of Victims in the Criminal Justice System' Crim LR 843.

FENWICK H (1997) 'Charge Bargaining and Sentence Discount: The Victim's Perspective' 5 Int R Victimology 23.

FENWICK H (2002) 'The Anti-Terrorism, Crime and Security Act 2001: A Proportionate Response to September 11?' 65(5) MLR 724.

FIELD S (1993) 'Defining Interviews under PACE' 13 LS 254.

FIELD S (2007) 'Practice Cultures and the "New" Youth Justice in England and Wales' 47 CJ Criminology 311.

FIELD S (2008) 'Early Intervention and the "New" Youth Justice' Crim LR 177.

FIELD S and JORG N (1991) 'Corporate Liability and Manslaughter: Should we be going Dutch?' Crim LR 156.

FIELD S and THOMAS P (eds), (1994) Justice and Efficiency? The Royal Commission on Criminal Justice (London: Blackwell) (also published as (1994) 21 JLS no 1).

FIELDING N (1985) Community Policing (Oxford: Clarendon).

FIELDING N (1988) Joining Forces (London: Routledge).

FIELDING N (2006) Courting Violence: Offences against the Person Cases in Court (Oxford: OUP).

FIJNAUT C and MARX G (eds) (1996) Undercover: Police Surveillance in Comparative Perspective (The Hague: Kluwer).

FINCH E and MUNRO V (2006) 'Breaking Boundaries?: Sexual Consent in the Jury Room' Legal Studies 303.

FINCH E and MUNRO V (2007) 'The Demon Drink and the Demonised Woman: Socio-Sexual Stereotypes and Responsibility Attribution in Rape Trials Involving Intoxicants' Social and Legal Studies 591.

FINCH E and MUNRO V (2008) 'Lifting the Veil: The Use of Focus Groups and Trial Simulations in Legal Research' JLS 30.

FINE B and MILLAR R (eds) (1985) Policing the Miners' Strike (London: Lawrence and Wishart).

FISHER G (2000) 'Plea Bargaining's Triumph' 109 Yale LJ 857.

FISHER H (1977) Report of an Inquiry into the Circumstances leading to the Trial of Three Persons on Charges arising out of the Death of Maxwell Confait and the Fire at 27 Doggett Road, London SE6 (HCP 90) (London: HMSO).

FISHER J (2005) 'Intercept Evidence' Counsel, September issue, p 9.

FITI R, PERRY D, GIRAUD W and AYRES M (2008) Statistical Bulletin: Motoring Offences and Breath Test Statistics England and Wales 2006 (London: Ministry of Justice).

FITZGERALD M (1993) Ethnic Minorities and the Criminal Justice System (Royal Commission on Criminal Justice, Research Study No 20) (London: HMSO).

FITZGERALD M (1999) Stop and Search: Final Report (London: Metropolitan Police).

FITZGERALD M and SIBBITT R (1997) Ethnic Monitoring in Police Forces: A Beginning (Home Office Research Study 173) (London: Home Office).

FITZGERALD M, HOUGH M, JOSEPH I and QUERESHI T (2002) Policing for London (Cullompton, Willan).

FITZPATRICK B (2009) 'Immunity from the law' in BILLINGSLEY R (ed), *Covert Human Intelligence Sources; The 'Unlovely Face of Police Work'* (Hampshire: Waterside Press).

FITZPATRICK B, SEAGO P, WALKER C and WALL D (2000) 'New Courts Management and the Professionalisation of Summary Justice in England and Wales' 11 Criminal Law Forum 1.

FLANAGAN R (2008) *The Review of Policing: Final Report* (London: HMIC).

FLOOD-PAGE C and MACKIE A (1998) *Sentencing Practice: An Examination of Decisions in Magistrates' Courts and the Crown Court in the Mid-1990s* (Home Office Research Study No 180) (London: Home Office).

FLOOD-PAGE C, CAMPBELL S, HARRINGTON V and MILLER J (2000) *Youth Crime: Findings from the 1998/99 Youth Lifestyles Survey* (Home Office Research Study 209) (London: Home Office).

FORENSIC SCIENCE SERVICE (2005) *Annual Report, 2004–5* (London: SO).

FORSTER S (2009) 'Control Orders: Borders to the Freedom of Movement or Moving the Borders of Freedom?' in: WADE M and MALJEVIC A (eds), *A War on Terror? The European Stance on a New Threat, Changing Laws and Human Rights Implications* (New York: Springer).

FORUM AGAINST ISLAMOPHOBIA and RACISM (2004) Counter-terrorism Powers, Reconciling Security and Liberty in an Open Society: Discussion Paper. A Muslim Response, available at <http://www.fairuk.org/policy12.htm>.

FOSTER J (2003) 'Police Cultures' in NEWBURN T (ed), *The Handbook of Policing* (Cullompton: Willan).

FOSTER J (2008) ' "It Might Have Been Incompetent, But It Wasn't Racist": Murder Detectives' Perceptions of the Lawrence Inquiry and its Impact on Homicide Investigation in London' 18(2) Policing and Society 89.

FOSTER J, NEWBURN T and SOUHAMI A (2005) *Assessing the Impact of the Stephen Lawrence Inquiry* (Home Office Research Study 294) (London : Home Office).

FOUCAULT M (1977) *Discipline and Punish* (London: Allen Lane).

FOUCAULT M (1979) *The History of Sexuality* vol 1 (London: Allen Lane).

FOX D, DHAMI M and MANTLE G (2006) 'Restorative Final Warnings: Policy and Practice' 45 Howard J 129.

FRANK N and LOMBNESS M (1988) *Controlling Corporate Illegality* (Cincinnati: Anderson).

FRANKEL M (1975) 'The Search for the Truth: An Umpireal View' 123 U Penn LR 1031.

FREEDMAN L (2005) *The Official History of the Falklands Campaign* (2 Vols) (London: Routledge).

FREEMAN M (1981) 'The Jury on Trial' CLP 65.

FULLER L (1978) 'The Forms and Limits of Adjudication' 92 Harv LR 353.

GALANTER M (1983) 'Mega-Law and Mega-Lawyering in the Contemporary United States' in DINGWALL R and LEWIS P (eds), *The Sociology of the Professions* (London: Macmillan).

GALLIGAN D (1987) 'Regulating Pre-Trial Decisions' in DENNIS I (ed), *Criminal Law and Justice* (London: Sweet & Maxwell).

GALLIGAN D and SANDLER D (2004) 'Implementing Human Rights' in HALLIDAY S and SCHMIDT P (eds), *Human Rights Brought Home* (Oxford: Hart).

GARLAND D (1990) *Punishment and Modern Society* (Oxford: Clarendon).

GARLAND D (1996) 'The Limits of the Sovereign State: Strategies of Crime

Control in Contemporary Society' 36 BJ Crim 445.

GARLAND D (1999) '"Governmentality" and the Problem of Crime' in SMANDYCH R (ed), *Governable Places: Readings on Governmentality and Crime Control* (Aldershot: Ashgate).

GARLAND D (2001) *The Culture of Control* (Oxford: OUP).

GEARTY C (2005) '11 September 2001, Counter-terrorism, and the Human Rights Act' 32 JLS 18.

GEARTY C (2006) *Can Human Rights Survive?* (Cambridge: Cambridge University Press).

GELLES M, McFADDEN R, BORUM R and VOSSEKUIL B (2005) 'Al-Qaeda-related Subjects: A Law Enforcement Perspective' in WILLIAMSON T (ed), *Investigative Interviewing: Rights, Research, Regulation* (Cullompton: Willan).

GELSTHORPE L and GILLER H (1990) 'More Justice for Juveniles' Crim LR 153.

GEMMILL R and MORGAN-GILES R (1981) *Arrest, Charge and Summons: Arrest Practice and Resource Implications* (Royal Commission on Criminal Procedure, Research Study No 9) (London: HMSO).

GENDERS E (1999) 'Reform of the Offences Against the Person Act: Lessons from the Law in Action' Crim LR 689.

GENERAL COUNCIL of the BAR (2004) Code of Conduct for Barristers, 8th edn (effective from 31 October 2004) available at <http://www.barcouncil.org.uk/>.

GILCHRIST E and BLISSETT J (2002) 'Magistrates' Attitudes to Domestic Violence and Sentencing Options' 41 Howard J 348.

GILL O (1976) 'Urban Stereotypes and Delinquent Incidents' 16 BJ Crim 312.

GILL P (2000) *Rounding up the Usual Suspects? Developments in Contemporary Law Enforcement Intelligence* (Aldershot: Ashgate).

GILL P (2004) 'Policing in Ignorance?' 58 Criminal Justice Matters 14.

GILLESPIE A (2005) 'Reprimanding Juveniles and the Right to Due Process' 68 MLR 1006.

GILLESPIE A (2009) 'Juvenile Informers' in BILLINGSLEY R (ed), *Covert Human Intelligence Sources; The 'Unlovely Face of Police Work'* (Hampshire: Waterside Press).

GLAZEBROOK P (2002) 'A Better Way of Convicting Businesses of Avoidable Deaths and Injuries?' 61 CLJ 405.

GLEESON E and GRACE K (2009) *Police Complaints: Statistics for England and Wales 2007/08* (IPCC Research and Statistics Series: Paper 12) (London: IPCC).

GLIDEWELL I (1998) *Review of the Crown Prosecution Service: A Report* (Cm 3960) (London: HMSO).

GOBERT J (1989) 'The Peremptory Challenge – An Obituary' Crim LR 528.

GOBERT J (1997) *Justice, Democracy and the Jury* (Aldershot: Dartmouth).

GOBERT J and PUNCH M (2003) *Rethinking Corporate Crime* (London: Butterworths).

GOBERT J (2008) 'The Corporate Manslaughter And Corporate Homicide Act 2007' 71 MLR 413.

GOLDING B and SAVAGE S (2008) 'Leadership and Performance Management' NEWBURN T (ed), *The Handbook of Policing*, 2nd edn (Cullompton: Willan).

GOLDSMITH A (1990) 'Taking Police Culture Seriously: Police Discretion and the Limits of the Law' 1 Policing and Society 91.

GOLDSMITH A and FARSON S (1987) 'Complaints against the Police in Canada: A New Approach' Crim LR 615.

GOLDSMITH A (1991) 'External Review and Self-Regulation' in GOLDSMITH A (ed), *Complaints Against the Police: The Trend to External Review* (Oxford: OUP).

GOLDSMITH C (2008) 'Cameras, Cops and Contracts: What Anti-social Behaviour Management Feels like to Young People' in SQUIRES P (ed), *ASBO Nation: The Criminalisation of Nuisance* (Bristol: The Policy Press).

GOOLD B (2004) *CCTV and Policing: Public Area Surveillance and Police Practices in Britain* (Oxford: OUP).

GORDON J (1992) 'Juries as Judges of the Law' 108 LQR 272.

GORDON P (1987) 'Community Policing: Towards the Local Police State' in SCRATON P (ed), *Law Order and the Authoritarian State* (Milton Keynes: Open UP).

GORIELY T (2003) 'Evaluating the Scottish Public Defence Solicitors' Office' 30 JLS 84.

GORIELY T, McCRONE P, DUFF P, KNAPP M, HENRY A, TATA C, LANCASTER B and SHERR A (2001) *The Public Defence Solicitors' Office in Edinburgh: An Independent Evaluation* (Edinburgh: Scottish Executive Central Research Unit).

GRACE S (1995) *Policing Domestic Violence in the 1990s* (Home Office Research Study No 139) (London: Home Office).

GRAHAM J, WOODFIELD K, TIBBLE M and KITCHEN S (2004) *Testaments of Harm: A Qualitative Evaluation of the Victim Personal Statements Scheme* (London: National Centre for Social Research).

GRANTHAM, R, 'Investigative Interviewing in New Zealand' iIIRG Bulletin, Vol 1(1) p 10.

GRAY A, FENN P and RICKMAN N (1996) 'Controlling Lawyers' Costs through Standard Fees: An Economic Analysis' in YOUNG R and WALL D (eds), *Access to Criminal Justice* (London: Blackstone).

GRAY P (2005) 'The Politics of Risk and Young Offenders' Experiences of Social Exclusion and Restorative Justice' 45(6) BJ Crim 938.

GREEN A (2008) *Power, Resistance, Knowledge: The Epistemology of Policing* (Sheffield: Midwinter & Oliphant).

GREEN A (2009) 'Challenging the Refusal to Investigate Evidence Neglected by Trial Lawyers' in NAUGHTON M (ed), *The Criminal Cases Review Commission* (London: Palgrave Macmillan).

GREEN P (1990) *The Enemy Without: Policing and Class Consciousness in the Miners' Strike* (Milton Keynes: Open UP).

GREER S (1990) 'The Right to Silence: A Review of the Current Debate' 53 MLR 719.

GREER S (1994) 'Miscarriages of Criminal Justice Reconsidered' 57 MLR 58.

GREER S (1995) 'Towards a Sociological Model of the Police Informant' 46 BJ Sociology 509.

GREER S (1995) *Supergrasses* (Oxford: OUP).

GREER S (2001) 'Where the Grass is Greener? Supergrasses in Comparative Perspective' in BILLINGSLEY R, NEMITZ T and BEAN P (eds), *Informers: Policing, Policy, Practice* (Cullompton: Willan).

GREER S (2005) 'Protocol 14 and the Future of the European Court of Human Rights' Public Law 83.

GREER S (2006) *The European Convention on Human Rights: Achievements, Problems and Prospects* (Cambridge: Cambridge University Press).

GREER S (2008) 'Human Rights and the Struggle against Terrorism in the United Kingdom' 2 EHRLR 163.

GREGORY J (1976) *Crown Court or Magistrates' Court?* (Office of Population Censuses and Surveys) (London: HMSO).

GREGORY J and LEES S (1996) 'Attrition in Rape and Sexual Assault Cases' 36 BJ Crim 1.

GREVLING K (1997) 'Fairness and the Exclusion of Evidence' 113 LQR 667.

GRIFFITH J (1997) *The Politics of the Judiciary*, 5th edn (London: Fontana).

GRIFFITHS B and MURPHY A (2001) 'Managing Anonymous Informants through Crimestoppers' in BILLINGSLEY R, NEMITZ T and BEAN P (eds), *Informers: Policing, Policy, Practice* (Cullompton: Willan).

GROSSKURTH A (1992) 'With Science on their Side' Legal Action, May, p 7.

GUDJONSSON G (2003) *The Psychology of Interrogations and Confessions: A Handbook* (Chichester: Wiley).

GUDJONSSON G (2007) 'Investigative Interviewing' in NEWBURN T, WILLIAMSON T and WRIGHT A (eds), *Handbook of Criminal Investigation* (Cullompton: Willan).

GUDJONSSON G and MACKEITH J (1990) 'A Proven Case of False Confession: Psychological Aspects of the Coerced-compliant Type' 30 Med Sci Law 187.

GUS JOHN PARTNERSHIP (2003) *Race for Justice: A Review of CPS Decision Making for Possible Racial Bias at Each Stage of the Prosecution Process* (London: CPS) available at <http://www.cps.gov.uk/>.

HAIN P (1976) *Mistaken Identity* (London: Quartet).

HAINES F (1997) *Corporate Regulation: Beyond 'Punish or Persuade'* (Oxford: Clarendon).

HAKKANEN H, ASK K, KEBBELL M, ALISON L and ANDERS GRANHAG P (2009) 'Police Officers' Views of Effective Interview Tactics with Suspects: The Effects of Weight of Case Evidence and Discomfort with Ambiguity' 23 Applied Cognitive Psychology 468.

HALL A (1990) 'Police Complaints: Time for a Change' Legal Action, August, p 7.

HALL S, CRITCHER C, JEFFERSON T, CLARKE J and ROBERTS B (1978) *Policing the Crisis* (London: Macmillan).

HALLIDAY J (2001) *Making Punishments Work: Report of a Review of the Sentencing Framework for England and Wales* (London: Home Office).

HALLIGAN-DAVIS G, and SPICER K (2004) *Piloting 'On the Spot' Penalties for Disorder: Final Results from a One-year Pilot* (Findings 257) (London: Home Office).

HALLSWORTH S (2005) *Street Crime* (Cullompton: Willan).

HALLSWORTH S (2006) 'Racial Targeting and Social Control: Looking Behind the Police' 14 Critical Criminology 293.

HAMLYN B, PHELPS A, TURTLE J and SATTAR G (2004) *Are Special Measures Working? Evidence from Surveys of Vulnerable and Intimidated Witnesses* (Home Office Research Study 283) (London: Home Office).

HAMPTON P (2005) *Reducing Administrative Burdens: Effective Inspection and Enforcement* (HM Treasury, London: SO).

HARDING C, FENNELL P, JORG N and SWART B (1995) *Criminal Justice in Europe: A Comparative Study* (Oxford: Clarendon).

HARFIELD C (2009) 'Regulation of CHIS' in BILLINGSLEY R (ed), *Covert Human Intelligence Sources; The 'Unlovely Face of Police Work'* (Hampshire: Waterside Press).

HARLOW C and RAWLINGS R, *Law and Administration*, 2nd edn (London: Butterworths, 1997).

HARRIS D, O'BOYLE M and WARBRICK C, *Law of the European Convention on Human Rights* (London: Butterworths, 1995).

HARRIS J and GRACE S (1999) *A Question of Evidence? Investigating and Prosecuting Rape in the 1990s* (Home Office Research Study 196) (London: Home Office).

HARRISON J and CUNEEN M (2000) *An Independent Police Complaints Commission* (London: Liberty).

HARRISON J, CRAGG S and WILLIAMS H (2005) *Police Misconduct: Legal Remedies*, 4th edn (London: LAG).

HART H (1961) *The Concept of Law* (Oxford: Clarendon).

HARTLESS J, DITTON J, NAIR G and PHILLIPS S (1995) 'More Sinned Against than Sinning: A Study of Young Teenagers' Experience of Crime' 35 BJ Crim 114.

HARTWIG M, ANDERS GRANHAG P and VRIJ A (2005) 'Police Interrogation from a Social Psychology Perspective' 15(4) Policing and Society 379.

HASTIE R, PENROD SD and PENNINGTON N (1983) *Inside the Jury* (Cambridge, Mass: Harvard UP).

HAVIS S and BEST D (2004) *Stop and Search Complaints: A Police Complaints Authority Study* (London: Police Complaints Authority).

HAWKINS K (1983) 'Bargain and Bluff' 5 L Pol Q 8.

HAWKINS K (1984) *Environment and Enforcement* (Oxford: OUP).

HAWKINS K (1990) 'Compliance Strategy, Prosecution Policy, and Aunt Sally: A Comment on Pearce and Tombs' 30 BJ Crim 444.

HAWKINS K (2003) *Law as Last Resort* (Oxford: OUP).

HAYES M (1981) 'Where Now the Right to Bail?' Crim LR 20.

HEATON R (2000) 'The Prospects for Intelligence-Led Policing' 9 Policing and Society 337.

HEATON R (2009) 'Intelligence-Led Policing and Volume Crime Reduction' 3 Policing 292.

HEATON-ARMSTRONG I (1986) 'The Verdict of the Court…and its Clerk?' 150 JP 340.

HEATON-ARMSTRONG A, SHEPHERD E, GUDJONSSON G, and WOLCHOVER D (eds) (2006) *Witness Testimony* (Oxford: OUP).

HEATON-ARMSTRONG A and WOLCHOVER D (2007) 'Woeful Neglect' 157 NLJ 624.

HEDDERMAN C and MOXON D (1992) *Magistrates' Court or Crown Court? Mode of Trial Decisions and Sentencing* (Home Office Research Study No 125) (London: HMSO).

HEFFERNAN L (2009) 'DNA and Fingerprint Retention; *S and Marper v UK*' 34(3) Euro LR 491.

HENHAM R (1999) 'Bargain Justice or Justice Denied? Sentence Discounts and the Criminal Process' 63 MLR 515.

HENHAM R (2000) 'Reconciling Process and Policy: Sentence Discounts in the Magistrates' Courts' Crim LR 436.

HENHAM R (2002) 'Further Evidence on the Significance of Plea in the Crown Court' 41 Howard J 151.

HENLEY M, DAVIS R and SMITH B (1994) 'The Reactions of Prosecutors and Judges to Victim Impact Statements' 3 Int Rev Victimology 83.

HER MAJESTY'S COURT SERVICE (HMCS) (2008) *A Guide to Commencing Proceedings in the Court of Appeal Criminal Division* (London: HMCS).

HER MAJESTY'S CROWN PROSECUTION SERVICE INSPECTORATE (HMCPSI) (1999) *Evaluation of Lay Review and Lay Presentation* (London: HMCPSI).

HER MAJESTY'S CROWN PROSECUTION SERVICE INSPECTORATE (HMCPSI) (1999) *Review of Adverse Cases* (London: HMCPSI).

HER MAJESTY'S CROWN PROSECUTION SERVICE INSPECTORATE (HMCPSI) (2000) *Thematic Review of the Disclosure of Unused Material* (London: HMCPSI).

HER MAJESTY'S CROWN PROSECUTION SERVICE INSPECTORATE (HMCPSI) (2002) *Review of HQ Casework* (London: HMCPSI).

HER MAJESTY'S CROWN PROSECUTION SERVICE INSPECTORATE (HMCPSI) (2002) *Report on the Thematic Review of Casework Having a Minority Ethnic Dimension* (April) (London: HMCPSI).

HER MAJESTY'S CROWN PROSECUTION SERVICE INSPECTORATE (HMCPSI) (2003) *Thematic Review of Attrition in the Prosecution Process (The Justice Gap)* (London: HMCPSI).

HER MAJESTY'S CROWN PROSECUTION SERVICE INSPECTORATE (HMCPSI) (2004a) *Violence at Home* (London: HMCPSI).

HER MAJESTY'S CROWN PROSECUTION SERVICE INSPECTORATE (HMCPSI) (2004b) *A Follow-up Review of Cases with an Ethnic Minority Dimension* (London: HMCPSI).

HER MAJESTY'S CROWN PROSECUTION SERVICE INSPECTORATE (HMCPSI) (2007) *Discontinuance – Thematic Review* (London: HMCPSI).

HER MAJESTY'S CROWN PROSECUTION SERVICE INSPECTORATE (HMCPSI) (2008) *Disclosure – Thematic Review* (London: HMCPSI).

HER MAJESTY'S CROWN PROSECUTION SERVICE INSPECTORATE (HMCPSI) (2008) *File Management and Organisation: An Audit of CPS Performance* (London: HMCPSI).

HER MAJESTY'S CROWN PROSECUTION SERVICE INSPECTORATE (HMCPSI) (2009) *Report of the Thematic Review of the Quality of Prosecution Advocacy and Case Presentation* (London: HMCPSI).

HER MAJESTY'S CROWN PROSECUTION SERVICE INSPECTORATE (HMCPSI) and HER MAJESTY'S INSPECTORATE OF CONSTABULARY (HMIC) (2002) *Report on the Joint Inspection into the Investigation and Prosecution of Cases Involving Allegations of Rape* (London: HMCPSI).

HER MAJESTY'S CROWN PROSECUTION SERVICE INSPECTORATE (HMCPSI) and HER MAJESTY'S INSPECTORATE OF CONSTABULARY (HMIC) (2004) *Violence at Home: The Investigation and Prosecution of Cases Involving Domestic Violence* (London: HMCPSI).

HER MAJESTY'S CROWN PROSECUTION SERVICE INSPECTORATE (HMCPSI) and HER MAJESTY'S INSPECTORATE of CONSTABULARY (HMIC) (2007) *Without Consent: Report on the Joint Inspection into the Investigation and Prosecution of Cases Involving Allegations of Rape* (London: HMCPSI).

HER MAJESTY'S CROWN PROSECUTION SERVICE INSPECTORATE (HMCPSI) and HER MAJESTY'S INSPECTORATE of CONSTABULARY (HMIC) (2008) *Joint Thematic Review of the New Charging Arrangements* (London: HMCPSI).

HER MAJESTY'S CROWN PROSECUTION SERVICE INSPECTORATE (HMCPSI), Her MAJESTY'S INSPECTORATE OF COURT ADMINISTRATION (HMICA) and HER MAJESTY'S INSPECTORATE of CONSTABULARY (HMIC) (2009) *Report of a Joint Thematic Review of Victim and Witness Experiences in the Criminal Justice System* (London: HMCPSI).

HER MAJESTY'S INSPECTORATE of CONSTABULARY (HMIC) and HER MAJESTY'S CROWN PROSECUTION SERVICE INSPECTORATE (HMCPSI) (2007) *Justice in Policing: A Joint Thematic Review of the Handling of Cases Involving an Allegation of a Criminal Offence by a Person Serving with the Police* (London: HMIC).

HER MAJESTY'S INSPECTORATE of PRISONS and HER MAJESTY'S INSPECTORATE of CONSTABULARY HMIC (2009) *Report on an Inspection Visit to Police Custody Suites in Cambridgeshire Constabulary* (London: HMIP and HMIC).

HERBERT A (2003) 'Mode of Trial and Magistrates' Sentencing Powers: Will Increased Powers Inevitably Lead to a Reduction in the Committal Rate?' Crim LR 314.

HERBERT A (2004) 'Mode of Trial and the Influence of Local Justice' 43 Howard J 65.

HERBERT P (1995) 'Racism, Impartiality and Juries' 145 NLJ 1138.

HESTER M and WESTMARLAND N (2005) *Tackling Domestic Violence: Effective Interventions and Approaches* (Home Office Research Study 290) (London: Home Office).

HESTER M, HANMER J, COULSON S, MORAHAN A and RAZAK A (2003) *Domestic Violence: Making it Through the Criminal Justice System* (University of Sunderland).

HICKMAN T (2005) 'Between Human Rights and the Rule of Law: Indefinite Detention and the Derogation Model of Constitutionalism' 68(4) MLR 655.

HICKMAN T (2008) 'The Courts and Politics after the Human Rights Act: A Comment' Public Law 84.

HILL R, COOPER K, HOYLE C and YOUNG R (2003a) *Introducing Restorative Justice to the Police Complaints System: Close Encounters of the Rare Kind* (Occasional Paper No 20) (Oxford: Centre for Criminological Research).

HILL R, COOPER K, YOUNG R and HOYLE C (2003b) *Meeting Expectations: The Application of Restorative Justice to the*

Police Complaints Process (Occasional Paper No 21) (Oxford: Centre for Criminological Research).

HILLIARD B (1987) 'Holloway Road – Unfinished Business' 137 NLJ 1035.

HILLYARD P (1987) 'The Normalization of Special Powers: from Northern Ireland to Britain' in SCRATON P (ed), *Law, Order and the Authoritarian State* (Milton Keynes: Open UP).

HILLYARD P (1993) *Suspect Community* (London: Pluto Press).

HILLYARD P and GORDON D (1999) 'Arresting Statistics: The Drift to Informal Justice in England and Wales' 26 JLS 502.

HILLYARD P, PANTAZIS C, TOMBS S and GORDON D (eds) (2004) *Beyond Criminology: Taking Harm Seriously* (London: Pluto Press).

HILTON N, HARRIS G and RICE M (2007) 'The Effect of Arrest on Wife Assault Recidivism: Controlling for Pre-Arrest Risk' 34(10) Criminal Justice and Behaviour 1334.

HILSON C (1993) 'Discretion to Prosecute and Judicial Review' Crim LR 739.

HOARE J AND FLATLEY J (2008) *Drug Misuse Declared: Findings from the 2007/08 British Crime Survey* (London: Home Office).

HOBBS D (1988) *Doing the Business* (Oxford: OUP).

HOBBS D, HADFIELD P, LISTER S and WINLOW S (2003) *Bouncers: Violence and Governance in the Night-time Economy* (Oxford: OUP).

HODGSON J (1992) 'Tipping the Scales of Justice: The Suspect's Right to Legal Advice' Crim LR 854.

HODGSON J (1994) 'Adding Injury to Injustice: the Suspect at the Police Station' 21 JLS 85.

HODGSON J (1997) 'Vulnerable Suspects and the Appropriate Adult' Crim LR 785.

HODGSON J (2001) 'The Police, the Prosecutor and the Juge D'Instruction' 41 BJ Crim 342.

HODGSON J (2003) 'Codified Criminal Procedure and Human Rights: Some Observations on the French Experience' Crim LR 165.

HODGSON J (2005) *French Criminal Justice* (Oxford: Hart).

HODGSON J and HORNE J (2008) *The Extent and Impact of Legal Representation on Applications to the Criminal Cases Review Commission (CCRC)* (Warwick: Warwick University).

HOFMEYR K (2006) 'The Problem of Private Entrapment' Crim LR 319.

HOLDAWAY S (1983) *Inside the British Police* (Oxford: Blackwell).

HOLDAWAY S (1996) *The Racialisation of British Policing* (Houndmills: Macmillan).

HOLDAWAY S (2003) 'Final Warning: Appearance and Reality' 4 Criminal Justice 355.

HOLDAWAY S and O'NEILL M (2007) 'Where has All the Racism Gone? Views of Racism within Constabularies after Macpherson' 30(3) Ethnic and Racial Studies 397.

HOME AFFAIRS COMMITTEE (1981–82) *Report on Miscarriages of Justice* (HC 421).

HOME AFFAIRS COMMITTEE (1998–99) *The Work of the Criminal Cases Review Commission* (HC 569).

HOME AFFAIRS SELECT COMMITTEE (2007–08) *Policing in the 21st Century*, Seventh Report (HC 364-I).

HOME OFFICE (1992a) Central Planning and Training Unit, *Guide to Interviewing* (London: HMSO).

HOME OFFICE (1992b) *Costs of the Criminal Justice System 1992*, vol 1 (London: Home Office).

HOME OFFICE (1997a) *Review of Delay in the Criminal Justice System: A Report* (Narey Report) (London: Home Office).

HOME OFFICE (1997b) *Statistics on the Operation of Prevention of Terrorism Legislation* (Statistical Bulletin, 4/97) (London: Home Office).

HOME OFFICE (1998a) *Juries in Serious Fraud Trials* (London: Home Office Communication Directorate).

HOME OFFICE (1998b) *Speaking Up for Justice, Report of the Interdepartmental Working Group on the Treatment of Vulnerable or Intimidated Witnesses in the Criminal Justice System* (London: Home Office).

Home Office (1999) *Statistics on Race and the Criminal Justice System 1998* (London, Home Office).

HOME OFFICE (2000) *Reforming the Law on Involuntary Manslaughter* (London: Home Office).

HOME OFFICE (2001a) *Achieving Best Evidence in Criminal Proceedings: Guidance for Vulnerable and Intimidated Witnesses, Including Children* (London: Home Office).

HOME OFFICE (2001b) *Statistics on the Operation of Prevention of Terrorism Legislation* (Statistical Bulletin 16/01) (London: Home Office).

HOME OFFICE (2002a) *Justice for All* (Cm 5563) (London: TSO).

HOME OFFICE (2003a) *Making a Victim Personal Statement* (London: Home Office).

HOME OFFICE (2003b) *Safety and Justice: The Government's Proposals on Domestic Violence* (Cm 5847) (London: TSO).

HOME OFFICE (2004a) *Building Communities, Beating Crime – A Better Police Service for the 21st Century* (CM 6360) (London: TSO).

HOME OFFICE (2004b) *Modernising Police Powers to Meet Community Needs – A Consultation Paper* (London: Home Office).

HOME OFFICE (2004c) *National Policing Plan 2005–2008: Safer, Stronger Communities* (London: Home Office).

HOME OFFICE (2004d) *An Evaluation of the Phased Implementation of the Recording of Police Stops* (London: Home Office).

HOME OFFICE (2005a) *Stop & Search Manual* (London: Home Office, 2005).

HOME OFFICE (2005b) *Criminal Statistics England and Wales 2004* (Home Office Statistical Bulletin 19/05) (London: Home Office).

HOME OFFICE (2008) *PACE Review: Government Proposals in Response to the Review of the Police and Criminal Evidence Act 1984* (Policing Powers and Protection Unit) (London: Home Office).

HOME OFFICE (2009a) *Statistics on Terrorism Arrests and Outcomes Great Britain, 11 September 2001 to 31 March 2008* (Statistical Bulletin 04/09) (London: Home Office).

HOME OFFICE (2009b) *Regulation of Investigatory Powers Act 2000: Consolidating Orders and Codes of Practice, A Public Consultation* (London: Home Office).

Home Office (2009c) *Crime in England and Wales: Quarterly Update to December 2008* (Statistical Bulletin 06/09) (London: Home Office).

HOME OFFICE, DEPARTMENT FOR CONSTITUTIONAL AFFAIRS AND YOUTH JUSTICE BOARD (2003) Important Changes to Referral Orders from 18 August 2003: available at <http://www.youth-justice-board.gov.uk>.

HONESS T, LEVI M and CHARMAN E (1998) 'Juror Competence in Processing Complex Information: Implications from a Simulation of the Maxwell Trial' Crim LR 763.

HOPKINS M and SPARROW P (2006) 'Sobering Up: Arrest Referral and Brief Intervention for Alcohol Users in the Custody Suite' 6(4) Criminology & Criminal Justice 389.

HOOD C, JAMES O, JONES G, SCOTT C and TRAVERS T (1999) *Regulation Inside Government* (Oxford: OUP).

HOOD R (1992) *Race and Sentencing* (Oxford: OUP).

HOOD R and SHUTE S (2000) *The Parole System at Work* (Home Office Research Study No 202) (London: Home Office).

HOOD R, SHUTE S and SEEMUNGAL F (2003) *Ethnic Minorities in the Criminal Courts: Perceptions of Fairness and Equality of Treatment* (Research Series No 2/03) (London: DCA).

HOOKER B (2000) 'Rule-Consequentialists' in LA FOLLETTE H (ed), *The Blackwell Guide to Ethical Theory* (Oxford: Blackwell).

HOROWITZ I, KEER N, PARK E and GOCKEL, C (2006) 'Chaos in The Courtroom Reconsidered: Emotional Bias and Juror Nullification' 30 Law and Human Behaviour 163.

HOUGH M and MAYHEW P (1985) *Taking Account of Crime* (Home Office Research Study No 111) (London: HMSO).

HOUGH M, JACOBSON J and MILLIE A (2003) *The Decision to Imprison: Sentencing and the Prison Population* (London: Prison Reform Trust).

HOUSE OF COMMONS HOME AFFAIRS SELECT COMMITTEE (1998) Police Disciplinary and Complaints Procedure, 1st Report (HC 258–1).

HOWARD LEAGUE (1993) *The Dynamics of Justice* (Report of the Working Party on Criminal Justice Administration) (London: Howard League).

HOYANO A, HOYANO L, DAVIS G and GOLDIE S (1997) 'A Study of the Impact of the Revised Code for Crown Prosecutors' Crim LR 556.

HOYLE C (1998) *Negotiating Domestic Violence* (Oxford: Clarendon).

HOYLE C and SANDERS A (2000) 'Police Response to Domestic Violence: From Victim Choice to Victim Empowerment' 40 BJ Crim 14.

HOYLE C, CAPE E, MORGAN R and SANDERS A (1998) *Evaluation of the 'One Stop Shop' and Victim Statement Pilot Projects* (London: Home Office).

HUCKLESBY A (1992) 'The Problem with Bail Bandits' 142 NLJ 558.

HUCKLESBY A (1994) 'The Use and Abuse of Conditional Bail' 33 Howard JCJ 258.

HUCKLESBY A (1996) 'Bail or Jail? The Practical Operation of the Bail Act 1976' 23 JLS 213.

HUCKLESBY A (1997a) 'Court Culture: An Explanation of Variations in the Use of Bail by Magistrates Courts' 36 Howard JCJ 129.

HUCKLESBY A (1997b) 'Remand Decision Makers' Crim LR 269.

HUCKLESBY A (2001) 'Police Bail and the Use of Conditions' 1(4) Criminal Justice 441.

HUCKLESBY A (2004) 'Not Necessarily a Trip to the Police Station' Crim LR 803.

HUCKLESBY A and MARSHALL E (2000) 'Tackling Offending on Bail' 39(2) Howard JCJ 150.

HUDSON B (2002) 'Restorative Justice and Gendered Violence: Diversion or Effective Justice?' 42 BJ Crim 616.

HUGHES G, PILKINGTON A and LEISTAN R (1998) 'Diversion in a Culture of Severity' 37 Howard JCJ 16.

HUMAN GENETICS COMMISSION (2009) *Nothing to Hide, Nothing to Fear?* (London: HGC).

HUNTER M (1994) 'Judicial Discretion: s 78 in Practice' Crim LR 558.

HUSSAIN S (2002) 'An Introduction to Muslims in the 2001 Census': available at <http:www.bristol.ac.uk/sociology/ethnicitycitizenship/urcresearch.html>.

HUTTER B (1988) *The Reasonable Arm of the Law?* (Oxford: OUP).

HYNES S (2008) 'Fixed Fees, Best Value Tendering and the CDS' March, Legal Action, 6.

HYNES S and ROBINS J (2009) *The Justice Gap – Whatever Happened to Legal Aid?* (London: LAG,).

INDEPENDENT POLICE COMPLAINTS COMMISSION (IPCC) (2005) *Making the New Police Complaints System Work Better: Statutory Guidance* (London: IPCC) available at <http:www.ipcc.gov.uk/stat_guidelines.pdf>.

INDEPENDENT POLICE COMPLAINTS COMMISSION (IPCC) (2006) The Death of Harry Stanley (London: IPCC) available at <http://www.ipcc.gov.uk/stanley_ipcc_decision_feb_06.pdf>.

INDEPENDENT POLICE COMPLAINTS COMMISSION (IPCC) (2008a) *Building on Experience* ('Stocktake Consultation') (London: IPCC).

INDEPENDENT POLICE COMPLAINTS COMMISSION (IPCC) (2008b) *Near Misses in Police Custody: A Collaborative Study with Forensic Medical Examiners in London* (London: IPCC).

INDEPENDENT POLICE COMPLAINTS COMMISSION (IPCC) (2009a) *Annual Report and Statement of Accounts 2008/9: Incorporating our Report on Deaths During or Following Police Contact* (London: IPCC).

INDEPENDENT POLICE COMPLAINTS COMMISSION (IPCC) (2009b) *Police Complaints and Discipline, 2008/9* (London: IPCC).

INNES M (2000) '"Professionalising" the Role of the Police Informant' 9 Policing and Society 357.

INNES M (2003) Investigating Murder: Detective Work and the Police Response to Criminal Homicide (Oxford: OUP).

INNES M, FIELDING N and COPE N (2005) 'The Appliance of Science?: The Theory and Practice of Crime Intelligence Analysis' 45 BJ Crim 39.

INQUEST (2000) Death in Police Custody: Report on Harry Stanley (London: Inquest).

IRVING B (1980) Police Interrogation: A Study of Current Practice (Royal Commission on Criminal Procedure Research Paper No 2) (London: HMSO).

IRVING B and DUNNIGHAN C (1993) Human Factors in the Quality Control of CID Investigations (Royal Commission on Criminal Justice, Research Study No 21) (London: HMSO).

IRVING B and McKENZIE I (1989) Police Interrogation: The Effects of the Police and Criminal Evidence Act 1984 (London: Police Foundation).

JACKSON J (1993) 'Trial Procedures' in WALKER C and STARMER K (eds), Justice in Error (London: Blackstone).

JACKSON J (1995) 'Evidence: Legal Perspective' in BULL R and CARSON D (eds), Handbook of Psychology in Legal Contexts (Chichester: Wiley).

JACKSON J (1996) 'Judicial Responsibility in Criminal Proceedings' 49 Current Legal Problems 59.

JACKSON J (2001) 'Silence and Proof: Extending the Boundaries of Criminal Proceedings in the UK' 5 IJ E&P 145.

JACKSON J (2003) 'Justice for All: Putting Victims at the Heart of Criminal Justice?' 30 JLS 309.

JACKSON J (2008) 'Police and Prosecutors after PACE: The Road from Case Construction to Case Disposal' in CAPE E AND YOUNG R (eds), Regulating Policing (Oxford: Hart).

JACKSON J and DORAN S (1992) 'Diplock and the Presumption against Jury Trial: A Critique' Crim LR 755.

JACKSON J and DORAN S (1995) Judge without Jury (Oxford: OUP).

JACKSON J and DORAN S (1997) 'Judge and Jury: Towards a New Division of Labour in Criminal Trials' 60 MLR 759.

JACOBSON J (2008) No One Knows: Police Responses to Suspects with Learning Disabilities and Learning Difficulties (London: Prison Reform Trust).

JACONELLI J (2002) Open Justice: A Critique of the Public Trial (Oxford: OUP).

JAMES A, TAYLOR N and WALKER C (2000) 'The Criminal Cases Review Commission: Economy, Effectiveness and Justice' Crim LR 140.

JEFFERSON T and WALKER M (1992) 'Ethnic Minorities in the Criminal Justice System' Crim LR 83.

JEHLE J and WADE M (eds) (2006) Coping with Overloaded Criminal Justice Systems: The Rise of Prosecutorial Power Across Europe (Berlin: Springer).

JEREMY D (2008) 'The Prosecutor's Rock and Hard Place' Crim LR 925.

JOINT Inspectorates (2003) Streets Ahead: A Joint Inspection of the Street Crime Initiative (London: Home Office Communication Directorate).

JONES C (1994) Expert Witnesses (Oxford: OUP).

JONES S (2008) 'Partners in Crime: A Study of the Relationship between Female Offenders and their Co-defendants' 8(2) Criminology & Criminal Justice 147.

JONES T (2003) 'The Governance and Accountability of Policing' in NEWBURN

T (ed), *The Handbook of Policing* (Cullompton: Willan).

JONES T (2008) 'The Accountability of Policing' in Newburn T (ed), *The Handbook of Policing*, 2nd edn (Cullompton: Willan).

JONES T and NEWBURN T (2002) 'The Transformation of Policing? Understanding Current Trends in Policing Systems' 42(1) BJ Crim 129.

JONES T, NEWBURN T and SMITH D (1996) 'Policing and the Idea of Democracy' 36 BJ Crim 182.

JORG N, FIELD S and BRANTS C (1995) 'Are Inquisitorial and Adversarial Systems Converging?' in HARDING C, FENNELL P, JORG N and SWART B (eds), *Criminal Justice in Europe* (Oxford: Clarendon).

JUDICIAL STUDIES BOARD (2005) Adult Court Bench Book, <http://www.jsboard. co.uk/magistrates/adult_court/index. htm>

JULIAN R (2007) 'Judicial Perspectives on the Conduct of Serious Fraud Trials' Crim LR 751.

JULIAN R (2008) 'Judicial Perspectives in Serious Fraud Cases' Crim LR 764.

JUSTICE (1994) *Unreliable Evidence? Confessions and the Safety of Convictions* (London: JUSTICE).

JUSTICE (2001) *Public Defenders: Learning from the US Experience* (London: JUSTICE).

JUSTICE COMMITTEE (2009) Minutes of Evidence: The Work of the Criminal Cases Review Commission <http:// www.publications.parliament.uk/pa/ cm200809/cmselect/cmjust/343/9031001. htm>

KALUNTA-KRUMPTON A (1998) 'The Prosecution and Defence of Black Defendants in Drug Trials' 38 BJ Crim 561.

KALVEN H and ZEISEL H (1966) *The American Jury* (Boston: Little Brown).

KASSIN S (2008) 'Confession Evidence: Commonsense Myths and Misconceptions' 35(10) Criminal Justice and Behavior 1309.

KAYE T (1991) *'Unsafe and Unsatisfactory?' Report of the Independent Inquiry into the Working Practices of the West Midlands Police Serious Crime Squad* (London: Civil Liberties Trust).

KEBBELL M and GILCHRIST E (2004) 'Eliciting Evidence from Eyewitnesses in Court' in Adler J (ed), *Forensic Psychology: Concepts, Debates and Practice* (Cullompton: Willan).

KEBBELL M, ALISON L and HURREN E (2008) 'Sex Offenders' Perceptions of the Effectiveness and Fairness of Humanity, Dominance, and Displaying an Understanding of Cognitive Distortions in Police Interviews: A Vignette Study' 14(5) Psychology, Crime and Law 435.

KEENAN C, DAVIS G, HOYANO L and MAITLAND L (1999) 'Interviewing Allegedly Abused Children with a View to Criminal Prosecution' Crim LR 863.

KEITH M (1993) *Race, Riots and Policing* (London: UCL Press).

KELLOUGH G and WORTLEY S (2002) 'Remand for Plea: Bail Decisions and Plea Bargaining as Commensurate Decisions' 42 BJ Crim 186.

KELLY L, LOVETT J and REGAN L (2005) *A Gap or a Chasm?: Attrition in Reported Rape Cases* (Home Office Research Study 293) (London: Home Office).

KEMP C, NORRIS C and FIELDING N (1992) 'Legal Manoeuvres in Police Handling of Disputes' in FARRINGTON D and WALKLATE S (eds), *Offenders and Victims, Theory and Policy* (London: British Society of Criminology).

KEMP V (2008) *A Scoping Study Adopting a 'Whole-Systems' Approach to the Processing of Cases in the Youth Courts* (London: Legal Services Research Centre).

KEMP V and BALMER N (2008) *Criminal Defence Services: Users' Perspectives* (Research Paper No 21) (London: Legal Services Research Centre).

KERRIGAN K (2000) 'Unlocking the Human Rights Floodgates' Crim LR 71.

KERRIGAN K (2006) 'Miscarriage of Justice in the Magistrates' Court: The Forgotten Power of the Criminal Cases Review Commission' Crim LR 124.

KERSHAW C, NICHOLAS S and WALKER A (2008) *Crime in England and Wales, 2007/8* (Home Office Statistical Bulletin 07/08) (London: Home Office).

KIBBLE N (2000) 'The Sexual History Provisions' [2000] Crim LR 274.

KIBBLE N (2005) 'Judicial Perspectives on the Operation of s.41 and the Relevance and Admissibility of Prior Sexual History: Four Scenarios' Crim LR 190.

KING M (1981) *The Framework of Criminal Justice* (London: Croom Helm).

KING M and MAY C (1985) *Black Magistrates* (London: Cobden Trust).

KNIGHT M (1970) *Criminal Appeals* (London: Stevens).

KOFFMANN L, 'Holding Parents to Account: Tough on Children, Tough on the Causes of Children' (2008) 35(1) JLS 113.

LACEY N (2007) 'Legal Constructions of Crime' in MAGUIRE M, MORGAN R and REINER R (eds), *Oxford Handbook of Criminology*, 4th edn (Oxford: OUP).

LACEY N, WELLS C and QUICK O (2003) *Reconstructing Criminal Law*, 3rd edn (London: LexisNexis).

LAING J (1995) 'The Mentally Disordered Suspect at the Police Station' Crim LR 371.

LANGBEIN J (1978) 'The Criminal Trial Before Lawyers' 45 U Ch LR 263.

LARKIN P (2007) 'The Criminalisation of Social Security Law; Towards a Punitive Welfare State?' 34 JLS 295.

LASSITER G, WARE L, RATCLIFF J and IRVIN C (2009) 'Evidence of the Camera Perspective Bias in Authentic Videotaped Interrogations' 14(1) Legal and Criminological Psychology 157.

LAW COMMISSION (1994a) *Binding Over* (Report No 222) (London: HMSO).

LAW COMMISSION (1994b) *Involuntary Manslaughter* (Report No 135) (London: HMSO).

LAW COMMISSION (1996a) *Evidence in Criminal Proceedings: Previous Misconduct of a Defendant* (Consultation Paper No 141) (London: HMSO).

LAW COMMISSION (1996b) *Involuntary Manslaughter* (Report No 237) (London: HMSO).

LAW COMMISSION (1998) *Consents to Prosecution* (HC 1085) (Report No 255) (London: SO).

LAW COMMISSION (1999) *Bail and the Human Rights Act 1998* (Report No 269) (London: Law Commission).

LAW COMMISSION (2009) *The Admissibility of Expert Evidence in Criminal Proceedings* (Consultation Paper No 190) (London: TSO).

LAYCOCK G and TARLING R (1985) 'Police Force Cautioning: Policy and Practice' 24 Howard JCJ 81.

LE SUEUR A and SUNKIN M (1992) 'Applications for Judicial Review: The Requirement of Leave' Public Law 102.

LEA S, LANVERS U and SHAW S (2003) 'Attrition in Rape Cases' 43 BJ Crim 583.

LEE M (1998) *Youth, Crime, and Police Work* (Basingstoke: Macmillan).

LEE R (2005) 'Resources, Rights and Environmental Regulation' 32 JLS 111.

LEGAL ACTION GROUP (1993) *Preventing Miscarriages of Justice* (London: LAG Education and Service Trust Ltd).

LEGAL AID BOARD (1999) *Annual Reports 1998–99* (HC 537) (London: SO).

LEGAL SERVICES COMMISSION (2002) *Public Defender Service: First Year of Operation* (London: Legal Services Commission) available at <http://www.legalservices.gov.uk/criminal/pds/evaluation.asp>.

LEGAL SERVICES COMMISSION (2004) *A New Focus for Civil Legal Aid* (London: LSC) available at <http://www.legalservices.gov.uk/civil/guidance/funding_code.asp>.

LEGAL SERVICES COMMISSION (2007) *Best Value Tendering of Criminal Defence Services* (London: LSC).

LEGAL SERVICES COMMISSION (2009) *Best Value Tendering for CDS Contracts 2010 – Consultation Paper* (London: LSC).

LEIGH A, JOHNSON G and INGRAM A (1998) *Deaths in Police Custody: Learning the Lessons* (Home Office Police Research Series, Paper 26) (London: Home Office).

LEIGH L (2006) 'Lurking Doubt and the Safety of Convictions' Crim LR 809.

LEIGH L (2007) '"The Seamless Web?" Diversion from the Criminal Process and Judicial Review' 70 MLR 654.

LEIGH L and ZEDNER L (1992) *A Report on the Administration of Criminal Justice in the Pre-Trial Phase in England and Germany* (Royal Commission on Criminal Justice, Research Study No 1) (London: HMSO).

LEGGETT J, GOODMAN W and DINANI S (2007) 'People with Learning Disabilities' Experiences of Being Interviewed by the Police' 135 British Journal of Learning Disabilities 168.

LENG R (1993) *The Right to Silence in Police Interrogation: A Study of Some of the Issues Underlying the Debate* (Royal Commission on Criminal Justice Research Study No 10) (London: HMSO).

LENG R (2001) 'Silence Pre-trial, Reasonable Expectation and the Normative Distortion of Fact-finding' 5 IJ E&P 240.

LENG R and TAYLOR R (1996) *Blackstone's Guide to the Criminal Procedure and Investigations Act 1996* (London: Blackstone).

LENG R, TAYLOR R and WASIK M (1998) *Blackstone's Guide to the Crime and Disorder Act 1998* (London: Blackstone).

LEO R (1994) 'Police Interrogation and Social Control' 3 Social and Legal Studies 93.

LEO R (2008) *Police Interrogation and American Justice* (Cambridge MA: Harvard University Press).

LEVESLEY T and MARTIN A (2005) *Police Attitudes to and Use of CCTV* (Home Office Online Report 09/05) (London: Home Office).

LEVI M (2002) 'Economic Crime' in MCCONVILLE M and WILSON G (eds), *The Handbook of the Criminal Justice Process* (Oxford: Oxford University Press).

LEVI M and BURROWS J (2008) 'Measuring the Impact of Fraud in the UK' 48 BJ Crim 293.

LEWIS H and MAIR G (1989) *Bail and Probation Work II: The Use of London Bail Hostels for Bailees* (Home Office Research and Planning Unit Paper No 50) (London: Home Office).

LEWIS J (2007) 'The European Ceiling on Human Rights' Public Law 720.

LEWIS P (1997) 'The CPS and Acquittals by Judge: Finding the Balance' Crim LR 653.

LEWIS R (2004) 'Making Justice Work: Effective Legal Interventions for Domestic Violence' 44 BJ Crim 204.

LIBERTY (2009) *Home Office Consultation on the Regulation of Investigatory Powers Act 2000: Consolidating Orders and Codes of Practice* (London: Liberty).

LIDSTONE K (1984) 'Magistrates, the Police and Search Warrants' Crim LR 449.

LISTER S, SEDDON T, WINCUP E, BARRETT S and TRAYNOR P (2008) *Street Policing of Problem Drug Users* (York: Joseph Rowntree Foundation).

LITTLECHILD B (1995) 'Reassessing the Role of the "Appropriate Adult"' Crim LR 540.

LIVINGSTONE S and MURRAY R (2004) 'The Effectiveness of National Human Rights Institutions' in HALLIDAY S and SCHMIDT P (eds), *Human Rights Brought Home* (Oxford: Hart).

LLOYD-BOSTOCK S (2000) 'The Effects of Hearing About the Defendant's Previous Criminal Record: A Simulation Study' Crim LR 734.

LLOYD-BOSTOCK S (2007) 'The Jubilee Line Jurors: Does their Experience Strengthen the Argument for Judge-only Trial in Long and Complex Fraud Cases?' Crim LR 255.

LOADER I (1996) *Youth Policing and Democracy* (Basingstoke: Macmillan Press).

LOADER I and MULCAHY A (2001a) 'The Power of Legitimate Naming: Part I – Chief Constables as Social Commentators in Post-war England' 41(1) BJ Crim 41.

LOADER I and MULCAHY A (2001b) 'The Power of Legitimate Naming: Part II – Making Sense of the Elite Police Voice' 41(3) BJ Crim 252.

LOADER I and MULCAHY A (2003) *Policing and the Condition of England: Memory, Politics and Culture* (Oxford: Oxford University Press).

LONG J (2008) 'Keeping PACE? Some Front Line Policing Perspectives' in CAPE E and YOUNG R(eds), *Regulating Policing* (Oxford: Hart).

LORD CHANCELLOR'S DEPARTMENT (LCD) (1992) *A New Framework for Local Justice* (Cm 1829) (London: LCD).

LOVEDAY B (1989) 'Recent Developments in Police Complaints Procedure' Local Gov Studies, May/June 25.

LUSTGARTEN L (2003) 'The Future of Stop and Search' Crim LR 603.

LUSTGARTEN L (2006) 'Human Rights: Where Do We Go From Here? 69(5) MLR 843.

LYNCH-WOOD G and WILLIAMSON D (2007) 'The Social Licence as a Form of Regulation for Small and Medium Enterprises' 34 JLS 321.

LYNCH-WOOD G and WILLIAMSON D (2010) 'Regulatory Compliance: Organisational Capacities & Regulatory Strategies for Environmental Protection' in SEDDON T and SMITH G (eds), *Regulation and Criminal Justice* (Cambridge: CUP).

LYON D (2001) *Surveillance Society: Monitoring Everyday Life* (Buckingham: Open UP).

LYON D (2007) *Surveillance Studies: An Overview* (Cambridge: Polity Press).

MACDONALD S (2006) 'A Suicidal Woman, Roaming Pigs and a Noisy Trampolinist: Refining the ASBOs Definition of Anti-Social Behaviour' 69 MLR 183.

MACDONALD S and TELFORD M (2007) 'The Use of ASBOS against Young People in England and Wales: Lessons from Scotland' 27(4) Legal Studies 604.

MACK J (1976) 'Full-time Major Criminals and the Courts' 39 MLR 241.

MAKEPEACE A (2008) 'Pumping Up the Volume to Make Legal Aid Profitable' 105(03) LSG 24.

MCKINNON C (2006) *Are Women Human?* (Harvard: Harvard University Press).

MACPHERSON of CLUNY, SIR W (1999) *The Stephen Lawrence Inquiry* (Cm 4262-I) (London: SO).

MACRORY R, (2006a) *Regulatory Justice: Sanctioning in a Post-Hampton World, Consultation Document* (London: Cabinet Office).

MACRORY R (2006b) *Regulatory Justice: Making Sanctions Effective* (London: Cabinet Office).

MADDOX G AND TAN G (2009) 'Applicant Solicitors: Friends or Foes?' in NAUGHTON M (ed), *The Criminal Cases Review Commission* (London: Palgrave Macmillan).

MADGE N (2006) 'Summing Up – A Judge's Perspective' Crim LR 817.

MADOOD T (2003) 'Muslims and the Politics of Difference' Political Quarterly 100.

MAGISTRATES' ASSOCIATION (1993) *Sentencing Guidelines* (London: Magistrates' Association).

MAGUIRE M (1988) 'Effects of the PACE Provisions on Detention and Questioning' 28(1) BJ Crim 19.

MAGUIRE M (2000) 'Policing by Risks and Targets' 9 Policing and Society 315.

MAGUIRE M (2002) 'Regulating the Police Station: The Case of the Police and Criminal Evidence Act 1984' in MCCONVILLE M and WILSON G (eds), *The Handbook of the Criminal Justice Process* (Oxford: Oxford University Press).

MAGUIRE M (undated) 'Complaints against the Police: Where Now?' (unpublished manuscript).

MAGUIRE M and CORBETT C (1991) *A Study of the Police Complaints System* (London: HMSO).

MAGUIRE M and JOHN T (1995) *Intelligence, Surveillance and Informants: Integrated Approaches* (Police Research Series Paper 64) (London: Home Office).

MAGUIRE M and NORRIS C (1992) *The Conduct and Supervision of Criminal Investigations* (Royal Commission on Criminal Justice, Research Study No 5) (London: HMSO).

MAGUIRE M, MORGAN R AND REINER R (eds) (2007) *Oxford Handbook of Criminology*, 4th edn (Oxford: OUP).

MAIMAN R (2004) ' "We've Had to Raise our Game": Liberty's Litigation Strategy under the Human Rights Act 1998' in HALLIDAY S and SCHMIDT P (eds), *Human Rights Brought Home* (Oxford: Hart).

MAIR G and LLOYD C (1996) 'Policy and Progress in the Development of Bail Schemes in England and Wales' in PATERSON F (ed), *Understanding Bail in Britain* (Edinburgh: Scottish Office).

MALLESON K (1991) 'Miscarriages of Justice and the Accessibility of the Court of Appeal' Crim LR 323.

MALLESON K (1993) *Review of the Appeal Process* (Royal Commission on Criminal Justice, Research Study No 17) (London: HMSO).

MALLESON K (1994) 'Appeals against Conviction and the Principle of Finality' 21 JLS 151.

MALLESON K (1995) 'The Criminal Cases Review Commission: How Will It Work?' Crim LR 929.

MALLESON K (1997) 'Decision-making in the Court of Appeal: The Burden of Proof in an Inquisitorial Process' Int J of Evidence and Proof 175.

MALLESON K and ROBERTS S (2002) 'Streamlining and Clarifying the Appellate Process' Crim LR 272.

MALONE C, 'Only the Freshest Will Do' in Naughton M (ed), *The Criminal Cases Review Commission* (London: Palgrave Macmillan).

MANSFIELD M and TAYLOR N (1993) 'Post-Conviction Procedures' in WALKER C and STARMER K (eds), *Justice in Error* (London: Blackstone).

MARES H (2002) 'Balancing Public Interest and a Fair Trial in Police Informer Privilege: A Critical Australian Perspective' 6 IJ E&P 94.

MARK R (1973) *Minority Verdict* The 1973 Dimbleby Lecture (London: BBC).

MARKS S (1995) 'Civil Liberties at the Margin: the UK Derogation and the European Court of Human Rights' 15 OJLS 68.

MARTIN S (2005) 'Lost and Destroyed Evidence: The Search for a Principled Approach to Abuse of Process' 9 IJ E&P 158.

MARX G (1988) *Undercover: Police Surveillance in America* (Berkeley: UCLA Press).

MASSCHAELE J (2008) *Jury, State, and Society in Medieval England* (New York: Palgrave Macmillan).

MATRAVERS M (2004) '"More Than Just Illogical": Truth and Jury Nullification' in DUFF A, FARMER L, MARSHALL S and TADROS V (eds), *The Trial on Trial: Truth and Due Process* (Oxford: Hart).

MATRIX KNOWLEDGE GROUP (2008) *Dedicated Drug Court Pilots; A Process Report* (London: Ministry of Justice).

MATTHEWS R, HANCOCK L and BRIGGS D (2004) *Jurors' Perceptions, Understanding, Confidence and Satisfaction in the Jury System: A Study in Six Courts* (Online Report 05/04) (London: Home Office).

MATTINSON J (1998) *Criminal Appeals England and Wales, 1995 and 1996* (Research and Statistical Bulletin 3/98) (London: Home Office).

MAY R (1998) 'Jury Selection in the United States: Are there Lessons to be Learned?' Crim LR 270.

MAY T, WARBURTON H, TURNBULL P and HOUGH M (2002) *Times they are a Changing: Policing of Cannabis* (York: YPS).

MAY T, HOUGH M, HERRINGTON V and WARBURTON H (2007a), *Local Resolution: The Views of Police Officers and Complainants* (London: IPCC).

MAY T, HOUGH M, HERRINGTON V and WARBURTON H (2007b) *From Informal to Local Resolution: Assessing Changes to the Handling of Low-level Police Complaints* (London: Police Foundation/IPCC).

MAY, SIR J (1992–3) Report of the inquiry into the circumstances surrounding the convictions arising out of the bomb attacks in Guildford and Woolwich in 1974, Second Report (1992–3 HC 296).

MAYNARD W (1994) *Witness Intimidation: Strategies for Prevention* (PRG Crime Detection and Prevention Series Paper 55) (London: Home Office).

MCARA L and MCVIE S (2005) 'The Usual Suspects: Street Life, Young People and the Police' 5 Criminal Justice 5.

MCARA L and MCVIE S (2007) 'Youth Justice? The Impact of System Contact on Patterns of Desistance from Offending' 4 European J Criminology 315.

MCBARNET D (1983a) *Conviction* (London: Macmillan).

MCBARNET D (1983b) 'Victim in the Witness Box – Confronting Victimology's Stereotype' 7 Contemporary Crises 293.

MCCABE S and PURVES R (1972a) *By-passing the Jury* (Oxford: Basil Blackwell).

MCCABE S and PURVES R (1972b) *The Jury at Work* (Oxford: Basil Blackwell).

MCCABE S and PURVES R (1974) *The Shadow Jury at Work* (Oxford: Basil Blackwell).

MCCAHILL M (2002) *The Surveillance Web: The Rise of Visual Surveillance in an English City* (Cullompton: Willan).

McCartney C (2006a) 'The DNA Expansion Programme and Criminal Investigation' 46(2) BJ Crim 175.

McCartney C (2006b) *Forensic Identification and Criminal Justice* (Cullompton: Willan).

McColgan A (2000) *Women Under the Law: The False Promise of Human Rights* (London: Longman).

McConville M (1991) 'Shadowing the Jury' 141 NLJ 1588.

McConville M (1992) 'Videotaping Interrogations: Police Behaviour On and Off Camera' Crim LR 532.

McConville M (1993) *Corroboration and Confessions: The Impact of a Rule Requiring that No Conviction Can Be Sustained on the Basis of Confession Evidence Alone* (Royal Commission on Criminal Justice Research Study No 13) (London: HMSO).

McConville M (1998) 'Plea Bargaining: Ethics and Politics' 25 JLS 562.

McConville M (2002) 'Plea Bargaining' in McConville M and Wilson G (eds), *The Handbook of the Criminal Justice Process* (Oxford: OUP).

McConville M and Baldwin J (1981) *Courts, Prosecution and Conviction* (Oxford: OUP).

McConville M and Baldwin J (1982) 'The Role of Interrogation in Crime Discovery and Conviction' 22 BJ Crim 165.

McConville M and Bridges L (1993) 'Pleading Guilty whilst Maintaining Innocence' 143 NLJ 160.

McConville M and Bridges L (eds) (1994) *Criminal Justice in Crisis* (Aldershot: Edward Elgar).

McConville M and Hodgson J (1993) *Custodial Legal Advice and the Right to Silence* (Royal Commission on Criminal Justice Research Study No 16) (London: HMSO).

McConville M and Mirsky C (1998) 'The State, the Legal Profession, and the Defence of the Poor' 15 JLS 342.

McConville M and Mirsky M (2005) *Jury Trials and Plea Bargaining: A True History* (Oxford: Hart).

McConville M and Morrell P (1983) 'Recording the Interrogation: Have the Police Got it Taped?' Crim LR 158.

McConville M and Sanders A (1992) 'Weak Cases and the CPS' LS Gaz, 12.

McConville M and Shepherd D (1992) *Watching Police, Watching Communities* (London: Routledge).

McConville M and Wilson G (eds) (2002) *The Handbook of the Criminal Justice Process* (Oxford: Oxford University Press).

McConville M, Hodgson J, Bridges L and Pavlovic A (1994) *Standing Accused* (Oxford: Clarendon).

McConville M, Sanders A and Leng R (1991) *The Case for the Prosecution* (London: Routledge).

McCulloch J and Pickering S (2009) 'Pre-Crime and Counter-Terrorism: *Imagining Future Crime in the "War on Terror"*' 49 BJ Crim 628.

McEldowney J (1979) 'Stand by for the Crown – An Historical Analysis' Crim LR 272.

McEwan J (1989) 'Documentary Hearsay Evidence – Refuge for the Vulnerable Witness?' Crim LR 629.

McEwan J (2004) 'The Adversarial and Inquisitorial Models of Criminal Trial' in Duff A, Farmer L, Marshall S and Tadros V (eds), *The Trial on Trial* (Oxford: Hart).

McEwan J (2005) 'Proving Consent in Sexual Cases: Legislative Change and Cultural Evolution' 9 E&P 1.

McEwan J, Redmayne M and Tinsley Y (2002) 'Evidence, Jury Trials and Witness Protection—The Auld Review of the English Criminal Courts' (2002) 6 E&P 163.

McGlynn C and Munro V (eds) (2010) Rethinking Rape Law: International and Comparative Perspectives (Abingdon: Routledge-Cavendish).

McIvor G (1996), 'The Impact of Bail Services in Scotland' in Paterson F (ed), Understanding Bail in Britain (Edinburgh: Scottish Office).

McKeever G (1999) 'Detecting, Prosecuting and Punishing Benefit Fraud: The Social Security Administration (Fraud) Act 1997' 62 MLR 261.

McKenzie I, Morgan R and Reiner R (1990) 'Helping the Police with their Enquiries' Crim LR 22.

McLaughlin E (2007) The New Policing (London: Sage).

McLaughlin E and Murji K (1995) 'The End of Public Policing? Police Reform and "The New Managerialism"' in Noaks L, Levi M and Maguire M (eds), Contemporary Issues in Criminology (Cardiff: University of Wales Press).

McLaughlin H (1990) 'Court Clerks: Advisers or Decision-Makers?' 30 BJ Crim 358.

McMahon M (1988) 'Police Accountability: The Situation of Complaints in Toronto' 12 Contemporary Crises 301.

Medford S, Gudjonsson G, and Pearse J (2003) 'The Efficacy of the Appropriate Adult Safeguard during Police Interviewing' 8 Legal and Criminological Psychology 253.

Meehan A (1993) 'Internal Police Records and the Control of Juveniles' 33 BJ Crim 504.

Memon A, Vrij A and Bull R (2003) Psychology and Law: Truthfulness, Accuracy and Credibility of Victims, Witnesses and Suspects, 2nd edn (Chichester: John Wiley).

Metropolitan Police Authority (2007) Counter-Terrorism: The London Debate (London: MPA).

Mhlanga B (1999) Race and the CPS (London: SO).

Middleton D (2005) 'The Legal and Regulatory Response to Solicitors Involved in Serious Fraud' 45 BJ Crim 810.

Miller J, Bland N and Quinton P (2000) The Impact of Stops and Searches on Crime and the Community (Police Research Series Paper 127) (London: Home Office).

Miller S (1999) Gender and Community Policing: Walking the Talk (Boston MA: North Eastern University Press).

Millington T and Williams S, The Proceeds of Crime (Oxford: OUP, 2007).

Milne R and Bull R (1999) Investigative Interviewing: Pyschology and Practice (Chichester: Wiley).

Ministry of Justice (2008a) Judicial and Court Statistics 2007 (Cm 7467) (London: MoJ).

Ministry of Justice (2008b) Criminal Statistics England and Wales, 2007 (London: MoJ).

Ministry of Justice (2008c) Arrests for Recorded Crime (Notifiable Offences) and the Operation of Certain Police Powers under PACE England and Wales 2006/07 (London: MoJ).

Ministry of Justice (2008d) Statistics on Race and the Criminal Justice System 2006/7 (London: MoJ).

Ministry of Justice (2009a) Judicial and Court Statistics 2008 (Cm 7697) (London: MoJ).

MINISTRY OF JUSTICE (2009b) *Statistics on Race and the Criminal Justice System, 2007/8* (London: MoJ).

MINISTRY OF JUSTICE (2009c) *Legal Aid: Funding Reforms, Consultation Paper 18/09* (London: MoJ).

MINISTRY OF JUSTICE (2009d) *Crown Court Means Testing: Response to Consultation* (CP(R) 06/09) (London: MoJ).

MINISTRY OF JUSTICE (2009e) *Sentencing Statistics 2007 England and Wales* (London: MoJ).

MIRFIELD P (1996) 'Successive Confessions and the Poisonous Tree' Crim LR 554.

MIRFIELD P (1997) *Silence, Confessions and Improperly Obtained Evidence* (Oxford: OUP).

MIRFIELD P (2009) 'Character and Credibility' Crim LR 135.

MOECKLI D (2007) 'Stop and Search Under the Terrorism Act 2000: A Comment on *R (Gillan)* v *Commissioner of Police for the Metropolis*' 70 MLR 654.

MONTGOMERY J (1998) 'The Criminal Standard of Proof' 148 NLJ 582.

MOODY S and TOMBS J (1982) *Prosecution in the Public Interest* (Edinburgh: Scottish Academic Press).

MOODY S and TOMBS J (1983) 'Plea Negotiations in Scotland' Crim LR 297.

MOONEY J and YOUNG J (2000) 'Policing Ethnic Minorities: Stop and Search in North London' in MARLOW A and LOVEDAY B (eds), *After Macpherson: Policing after the Stephen Lawrence Inquiry* (Lyme Regis: Russell House).

MOORE S (2008) 'Street Life, Neighbourhood Policing and "The Community"' in SQUIRES P (ed), *ASBO Nation: The Criminalisation of Nuisance* (Bristol: Policy Press).

MOORHEAD R (2004) 'Legal Aid and the Decline of Private Practice: Blue Murder or Toxic Job?' 11(3) IJ of the Legal Profession 160.

MORGAN J and ZEDNER L (1992) *Child Victims* (Oxford: Clarendon).

MORGAN P and HENDERSON P (1998) *Remand Decisions and Offending on Bail* (Home Office Research Study No 184) (London: Home Office).

MORGAN R (2002) 'Magistrates: The Future according to Auld' 29 JLS 308.

MORGAN R and JONES S (1992) 'Bail or Jail?' in STOCKDALE E and CASALE S (eds), *Criminal Justice Under Stress* (London: Blackstone).

MORGAN R and NEWBURN T (1997) *The Future of Policing* (Oxford: OUP).

MORGAN R and SANDERS A (1999) *The Uses of Victim Statements* (London: Home Office).

MORGAN R, REINER R and McKENZIE I, *Police Powers and Policy: A Study of the Work of Custody Officers* (report to ESRC) (unpublished).

MORGAN HARRIS BURROWS LLP (2009) *Research into the Impact of Bad Character Provisions on the Courts* (Ministry of Justice Research Series 5/09) (London: MoJ).

MORISON J and LEITH P (1992) *The Barrister's World* (Milton Keynes: Open UP).

MOSTON S and ENGELBERG T (1993) 'Police Questioning Techniques in Tape Recorded Interviews with Criminal Suspects' 3 Policing and Society 223.

MOSTON S and STEPHENSON G (1993) *The Questioning and Interviewing of Suspects Outside the Police Station* (Royal Commission on Criminal Justice Research Study No 22) (London: HMSO).

MOSTON S and WILLIAMSON T (1990) 'The Extent of Silence in Police Interviews' in GREER S and MORGAN R (eds), *The Right to Silence Debate* (Bristol: University of Bristol, 1990).

Moston S, Stephenson G and Williamson T (1992) 'The Effects of Case Characteristics on Suspect Behaviour During Police Questioning' 92 BJ Crim 23.

Mountford L and Hannibal M (2007) 'Simplier, Speedier Justice for All?' 158 Solicitors' Journal 1294.

Moxon D (1988) *Sentencing Practice in the Crown Court* (Home Office Research Study No 103) (London: HMSO).

Mulcahy A (1994) 'The Justifications of Justice: Legal Practitioners' Accounts of Negotiated Case Settlements in Magistrates' Courts' 34 BJ Crim 411.

Mulcahy A, Brownlee I and Walker C (1993) 'An Evaluation of Pre-Trial Reviews in Leeds and Bradford Magistrates' Courts' 33 Home Office Research Bulletin 10.

Mulcahy L (2008) 'The Unbearable Lightness of Being? Shifts Towards the Virtual Trial' 35 JLS 464.

Mullock A (2009) 'Prosecutors Making (Bad) Law?' 17 Medical LR 290.

Munday R (1993) 'Jury Trial, Continental Style' 13 LS 204.

Munday R (1995) 'What do the French Think of their Jury?' 15 LS 65.

Munday R (1996) 'Inferences from Silence and European Human Rights Law' Crim LR 370.

Munday R (2005) 'What Constitutes "Other Reprehensible Behaviour" under the Bad Character Provisions of the Criminal Justice Act 2003?' Crim LR 24.

Mungham G and Bankowski Z (1976) 'The Jury in the Legal System' in Carlen P (ed), *The Sociology of Law* (Keele: University of Keele).

Munro V (2008) 'Of Rights and Rhetoric: Discourses of Degradation and Exploitation in the Context of Sex Trafficking' 35 JLS 240.

MVA and Miller J (2000) *Profiling Populations Available for Stops and Searches* (Police Research Series Paper 131) (London: Home Office).

Mythen G, Walklate S and Khan T, (2009) '"I'm a Muslim, But I'm Not a Terrorist": Victimization, Risky Identities and the Performance of Safety' 49(6) BJ Crim 736.

NACRO (1997) *Policing Local Communities: The Tottenham Experiment* (London: NACRO).

Nation D (1992) 'He Can Always Appeal' 156 JP 521.

National Audit Office (2000) Criminal Justice: Working Together HC 29 Session 1999–00 executive summary available from <http://www.nao.org.uk/publications/nao_ reports/990029es.pdf>.

National Audit Office, *The Procurement of Legal Aid in England and Wales by the Legal Services Commission HC 29 2009–10* (London: TSO, 2009).

National Police Improvement Agency (NPIA), National Investigative Interviewing Strategy 2009 (available from <http://www.npia.police.uk/en/12892.htm>).

Naughton M (2005a) 'Miscarriages of Justice and the Government of the Criminal Justice System: An Alternative Perspective on the Production and Deployment of Counter-Discourse' 13 Critical Criminology 211.

Naughton M (2005b) 'Redefining Miscarriages of Justice' 45 BJ Crim 165.

Naughton M (2007) *Rethinking Miscarriages of Justice* (Houndmills: Palgrave Macmillan).

Naughton M (2009) 'The Importance of Innocence for the Criminal Justice System' in Naughton M (ed), *The Criminal Cases Review Commission* (Houndmills: Palgrave Macmillan).

NAUGHTON M (ed) (2009) *The Criminal Cases Review Commission* (Houndmills: Palgrave Macmillan).

NAUGHTON, M and McCARTNEY C (2005) 'The Innocence Network UK' 7(2) Legal Ethics 150.

NELKEN D (1983) *The Limits of the Legal Process* (London: Academic Press).

NEMITZ T and BEAN P (1994) 'The Use of the Appropriate Adult Scheme' 34 Med Sci and the Law 161.

NEWBURN T (1999) *Understanding and Preventing Police Corruption* (Police Research Series Paper 110) (London: Home Office).

NEWBURN T (ed) (2008) *Handbook of Policing*, 2nd edn (Cullompton: Willan).

NEWBURN T and ELLIOTT J (1998) *Policing Anti-drug Strategies: Tackling Drugs Together 3 Years On* (London: Home Office Police Research Group).

NEWBURN T and HAYMAN S (2001) *Policing, Surveillance and Social Control* (Cullompton: Willan).

NEWBURN T, SHINER M and HAYMAN S (2004) 'Race, Crime and Injustice? Strip-Search and the Treatment of Suspects in Custody' 44(5) BJ Crim 677.

NEWBURN T, WILLIAMSON T and WRIGHT (eds) (2007) A *Handbook of Criminal Investigation* (Cullompton: Willan).

NEWTON T (1998) 'The Place of Ethics in Investigative Interviewing by Police Officers' 37 Howard JCJ 52.

NEWBY M (2009) 'Historical Abuse Cases: Why They Expose the Inadequacy of the Real Possibility Test' in NAUGHTON M (ed), *The Criminal Cases Review Commission* (London: Palgrave Macmillan).

NEYLAND D (2009) 'Surveillance, Accountability and Organisational Failure: The Story of Jean Charles de Menezes' in GOOLD B and NEYLAND D (eds), *New Directions in Surveillance and Privacy* (Cullompton: Willan).

NEYROUD P and BECKLEY A (2001) 'Regulating Informers: The Regulation of Investigatory Powers Act, Covert Policing and Human Rights' in BILLINGSLEY R, NEMITZ T and BEAN P (eds), *Informers: Policing, Policy, Practice* (Cullompton: Willan).

NICOL D (2006) 'Law and Politics after the Human Rights Act' Public Law 722.

NICOLSON D and REID K (1996) 'Arrest for Breach of the Peace and the European Convention on Human Rights' Crim LR 764.

NIXON J and PARR S (2006) 'Anti-social Behaviour: Voices from the Front Line' in FLINT J (ed), *Housing, Urban Governance and Anti-Social Behaviour* (Bristol: Policy Press).

NIXON J and HUNTER C (2009) 'Disciplining Women: Anti-social Behaviour and the Governance of Conduct' in MILLIE A (ed), *Securing Respect* (Bristol: Policy Press).

NOBLES R and SCHIFF D (1995) 'Miscarriages of Justice: A Systems Approach' 58 MLR 299.

NOBLES R and SCHIFF D (1996) 'Criminal Appeal Act 1995: The Semantics of Jurisdiction' 59 MLR 573.

NOBLES R and SCHIFF D (1997) 'The Never Ending Story: Disguising Tragic Choices in Criminal Justice' 60 MLR 293.

NOBLES R and SCHIFF D (2000) *Understanding Miscarriages of Justice* (Oxford: OUP).

NOBLES R and SCHIFF D (2001a) 'Due Process and Dirty Harry Dilemmas: Criminal Appeals and the Human Rights Act' 64 MLR 911.

NOBLES R and SCHIFF D (2001b) 'The Criminal Cases Review Commission: Reporting Success?' 64 MLR 280.

NOBLES R and SCHIFF D (2002) 'The Right to Appeal and Workable Systems of Justice' 65 (5) MLR 676.

NOBLES R and SCHIFF D (2004) 'A Story of Miscarriage: Law in the Media' 31 JLS 221.

NOBLES R and SCHIFF D (2005a) 'The Criminal Cases Review Commission: Establishing a Workable Relationship with the Court of Appeal' Crim LR 173.

NOBLES R and SCHIFF D (2005b) 'A Reply to Graham Zellick' Crim LR 951.

NOBLES R and SCHIFF D (2006) 'Theorising the Criminal Trial and Criminal Appeal: Finality, Truth and Rights' in DUFF A, FARMER L, MARSHALL S and TADROS V (eds), The Trial on Trial Vol 2: Judgment and Calling to Account (Oxford: Hart).

NOBLES R and SCHIFF D (2008) 'Absurd Asymmetry' 71(3) MLR 464.

NOBLES R and SCHIFF D (2009) 'After Ten Years: An Investment in Justice?' in NAUGHTON M (ed), The Criminal Cases Review Commission (London: Palgrave Macmillan).

NORRIE A (1993) Crime, Reason and History (London: Weidenfeld and Nicolson).

NORRIE A (1998) ' "Simulacra of Morality?" Beyond the Ideal/Actual Antinomies of Criminal Justice' in DUFF A (ed), Criminal Law: Principle and Critique (New York: CUP).

NORRIS C (2003) 'From Personal to Digital: CCTV, the Panopticon, and the Technological Mediation of Suspicion and Social Control' in LYON D (ed), Surveillance as Social Sorting: Privacy, Risk and Digital Discrimination (London: Routledge).

NORRIS C and DUNNIGHAN C (2000) 'Subterranean Blues: Conflict as an Unintended Consequence of the Police Use of Informers' 9 Policing and Society 385.

NORRIS C, FIELDING N, KEMP C and FIELDING J (1992) 'Black and Blue: An Analysis of the Influence of Race on Being Stopped by the Police' 43 BJ Sociology 207.

NORRIS C, MORAN J and ARMSTRONG G (eds) (1999) Surveillance, CCTV and Social Control (Aldershot: Ashgate).

O'BRIEN D and EPP J (2000) 'Salaried Defenders and the Access to Justice Act 1999' 63 MLR 394.

O BRIEN M (2008) The Death of Justice (Talybont: Y Lolfa Cyf).

O'CONNOR P (1990) 'The Court of Appeal: Re-Trials and Tribulations' Crim LR 615.

O'DONNELL I and EDGAR K (1998) 'Routine Victimisation in Prisons' 37 Howard J 266.

O'LOAN N (2007) Statement by the Police Ombudsman for Northern Ireland on her Investigation into the Circumstances Surrounding the Death of Raymond McCord Junior and Related Matters (Belfast).

O'MAHONY P (1992) 'The Kerry Babies Case: Towards a Social Psychological Analysis' 13 Irish J Psychology 223.

O'MAHONEY D and DOAK J (2004) 'Restorative Justice – Is More Better? The Experience of Police-led Restorative Cautioning Pilots in Northern Ireland' 43(5) Howard JCJ 484.

OHRN H and NYBERG C (undated) 'Searching for Truth or Confirmation?' 2(1) iIIRG Bulletin 11

ORMEROD D (2001) 'Sounds Familiar: Voice Identification Evidence' Crim LR 595.

ORMEROD D (2002) 'Sounding Out Expert Voice Identification' Crim LR 771.

ORMEROD D (2003) 'ECHR and the Exclusion of Evidence: Trial Remedies for Article 8 Breaches' Crim LR 61.

ORMEROD D and BIRCH D (2004) 'The Evolution of the Discretionary Exclusion of Evidence' Crim LR 767.

ORMEROD D and McKAY S (2004) 'Telephone Intercepts and their Admissibility' Crim LR 15.

ORMEROD D and ROBERTS A (2002) 'The Trouble with *Teixeira*: Developing a Principled Approach to Entrapment' 6 IJ E&P 38.

ORMEROD D and ROBERTS A (2003) 'The Police Reform Act 2002 – Increasing Centralisation, Maintaining Confidence and Contracting Out Crime Control' Crim LR 141.

ORMEROD D and TAYLOR R (2008) 'The Corporate Manslaughter and Corporate Homicide Act 2007' Crim LR 589.

OVEY C (1998) 'The European Convention on Human Rights and the Criminal Lawyer: An Introduction' Crim LR 4.

OXFORD T (1991) 'Spotting a Liar' Police Review 328.

OZIN P, NORTON H and SPIVEY P (2006) *PACE – A Practical Guide* (Oxford: OUP).

PA CONSULTING (2004) *No Witness, No Justice – National Victim and Witness Care Project: Interim Evaluation Report* (London: PA Consulting).

PACKER H (1968) *The Limits of the Criminal Sanction* (Stanford: Stanford UP).

PADFIELD N (1993) 'The Right to Bail: a Canadian Perspective' Crim LR 510.

PADFIELD N (1996) 'Bailing and Sentencing the Dangerous' in WALKER N (ed), *Dangerous People* (London: Blackstone).

PADFIELD N (2003) *Text and Materials on the Criminal Justice Process*, 3rd edn (London: LexisNexis).

PALMER C (1996) 'Still Vulnerable After All These Years' Crim LR 633.

PALMER K, OATES W and PORTNEY P (1995) 'Tightening Environmental Standards: The Benefit-Cost or the No-Cost Paradigm?' 9 J of Economic Perspectives 119.

PALMER P and STEELE J (2008) 'Police Shootings and the Role of Tort' 71 MLR 801.

PANATZIS C and GORDON D (1997) 'Television Licence Evasion and the Criminalisation of Female Poverty' 36 Howard JCJ 170.

PANTAZIS C and PEMBERTON S (2009) 'From the "Old" to the "New" Suspect Community: Examining the Impacts of Recent UK Counter-Terrorist Legislation' 49(5) BJ Crim 646.

PARADINE K and WILKINSON J (2004) *Protection and Accountability: The Reporting, Investigation and Prosecution of Domestic Violence Cases* (London: HMIC and HMCPSI).

PARKER H, CASBURN M and TURNBULL D (1981) *Receiving Juvenile Justice* (Oxford: Basil Blackwell).

PARLIAMENTARY JOINT COMMITTEE ON HUMAN RIGHTS (2004) Deaths in Custody. HL 15 session 2003–4, HC 137 session 2003–4.

PARRY L (2006) 'Protecting the Juvenile Suspect: What is the Appropriate Adult Supposed to Do?' 18 Child and Family Law Quarterly 373.

PATERSON F and WHITTAKER C (1994) *Operating Bail* (Edinburgh: Scottish Office).

PATTENDEN R (1991) 'Should Confessions be Corroborated?' 107 LQR 319.

PATTENDEN R (1992) 'Evidence of Previous Malpractice by Police Witnesses and *R v Edwards*' Crim LR 549.

PATTENDEN R (1995) 'Inferences from Silence' Crim LR 602.

PATTENDEN R (1996) *English Criminal Appeals 1844–1994* (Oxford: Clarendon).

PATTENDEN R (1998) 'Silence: Lord Taylor's Legacy' 2 IJ Evidence and Proof 141.

PATTENDEN R (2009) 'The Standards of Review for Mistake of Fact in the Court of Appeal, Criminal Division' Crim LR 15.

PATTENDEN R and SKINNS L (2010) 'Choice, Privacy and Publicly-funded Legal Advice at Police Stations' 73 MLR 349.

PEARCE F and TOMBS S (1990) 'Ideology, Hegemony and Empiricism: Compliance Theories of Regulation' 30 BJ Crim 423.

PEARCE F and TOMBS S (1997) 'Hazards, Law and Class: Contextualising the Regulation of Corporate Crime' 6 Social and Legal Studies 79.

PEARSE J and GUDJONSSON G (1996) 'Police Interviewing Techniques at Two South London Police Stations' 3 Psychology, Crime & Law 763.

PEMBERTON S (2008) 'Demystifying Deaths in Police Custody: Challenging State Talk' 17 Social and Legal Studies 237.

PERCY-SMITH J and HILLYARD P (1985) 'Miners in the Arms of the Law: A Statistical Analysis' 12 JLS 345.

PHILLIPS C and BOWLING B (2007) 'Ethnicities, Racism, Crime, and Criminal Justice' in MAGUIRE M, MORGAN R and REINER R (eds), *Oxford Handbook of Criminology*, 4th edn (Oxford: OUP).

PHILLIPS C and BROWN C (1998) *Entry into the Criminal Justice System: A Survey of Arrests and their Outcomes* (Home Office Research Study 185) (London: Home Office).

PHILLIPS M, MCAULIFF B, KOVERA M and CUTLER B (1999) 'Double-Blind Photoarray Administration as a Safeguard Against Investigator Bias' 84 J Applied Psychology 940.

PHILLIPSON G (2007) 'Bills of Rights as a Threat to Human Rights: The Alleged "Crisis of Legalism"' Public Law 217.

PIERPOINT H (2001) 'The Performance of Volunteer Appropriate Adults' 40 Howard JCJ 255.

PIERPOINT H (2006) 'Reconstructing the Role of the Appropriate Adult in England and Wales' 6(2) Criminology & Criminal Justice 225.

PIERPOINT H (2008) 'Quickening the PACE? The Use of Volunteers as Appropriate Adults in England and Wales' 18 Policing and Society 397.

PIGOT JUDGE T (1989) *Report of the Advisory Group on Video-Recorded Evidence* (London: HMSO).

PLAYER E (1989) 'Women and Crime in the City' in DOWNES D (ed), *Crime and the City* (Basingstoke: Macmillan).

PLOTNIKOFF J and WOOLFSON R (1993a) *From Committal to Trial: Delay at the Crown Court* (London: Law Society).

PLOTNIKOFF J and WOOLFSON R (1993b) *Information and Advice for Prisoners about Grounds for Appeal and the Appeals Process* (Royal Commission on Criminal Justice, Research Study No 18) (London: HMSO).

PLOTNIKOFF J and WOOLFSON R (1998) *Witness Care in Magistrates' Courts and the Youth Court* (Home Office Research Findings No 68) (London: Home Office).

PLOTNIKOFF J and WOOLFSON R (2001) '*A Fair Balance*'? *Evaluation of the Operation of Disclosure Law* (Home Office: London).

PLOTNIKOFF J and WOOLFSON R (2005) *Review of the Effectiveness of Specialist Courts in Other Jurisdictions* (London: Department for Constitutional Affairs).

PLOTNIKOFF J and WOOLFSON R (2008) 'Making the Best Use of the Intermediary Special Measure at Trial' Crim LR 91.

POLICE COMPLAINTS AUTHORITY (PCA) (1996) *Annual Report, 1995/6* (London: SO).

POLLARD C (1996) 'Public Safety, Accountability and the Courts' Crim LR 152.

PONTING C (1985) *The Right to Know, The Inside Story of the Belgrano Affair* (London: Sphere).

PORTER M and VAN DER LINDE C (1995) 'Green and Competitive: Ending the Stalemate' 73 Harvard Business Review 120.

POVEY D and SMITH K (eds), (2009) *Police Powers and Procedures, England and Wales 2007/08* (Home Office Statistical Bulletin 7/09) (London: Home Office).

PRATT J and BRAY K (1985) 'Bail Hostels – Alternatives to Custody?' 25 BJ Crim 160.

PRENZLER T (2000) 'Civilian Oversight of Police: A Test of Capture Theory' 40 BJ Crim 659.

PRIME J, WHITE S, LIRIANO S and PATEL K (2001) *Criminal Careers of Those Born Between 1953 and 1978* (Home Office Statistical Bulletin 4/01) (London: Home Office).

QUICK O (2006) 'Prosecuting "Gross" Medical Negligence: Manslaughter, Discretion and the CPS' 33 JLS 421.

QUINN K (2004) 'Jury Bias and the European Convention on Human Rights: A Well-kept Secret?' Crim LR 998.

QUINN K and JACKSON J (2007) 'Of Rights and Roles: Police Interviews with Young Suspects in Northern Ireland' 47 BJ Crim 234.

QUINTON P (2003) *An Evaluation of the New Police Misconduct Procedures* (Home Office Online Report 10/03) (London: Home Office).

QUINTON P, BLAND N and MILLER J (2000) *Police Stops, Decision-making and Practice* (Police Research Series Paper 130) (London: Home Office).

QUIRK H (2006) 'The Significance of Culture in Criminal Procedure Reform: Why the Revised Disclosure Scheme Cannot Work' 10 E&P 42.

QUIRK H (2007) 'Identifying Miscarriages of Justice: Why Innocence in the UK is Not the Answer' 70(5) MLR 759

RAIFEARTAIGH U (1997) 'Reconciling Bail Law with the Presumption of Innocence' 17 OJLS 1.

RAINE J and WILLSON M (1995) 'Just Bail at the Police Station?' 22(4) JLS 571.

RAINE J and WILLSON M (1996) 'The Imposition of Conditions in Bail Decisions' 35 Howard JCJ 256.

RAINE J and WILLSON M (1997) 'Police Bail with Conditions' 37(4) BJ Crim 593.

RATCLIFFE J (2008) *Intelligence-Led Policing* (Cullompton: Willan).

RAWLEY A and CADDY B (2007) *Damilola Taylor: An Independent Review of Forensic Examination of Evidence by the Forensic Science Service* (London: Home Office).

REDMAYNE M (1995) 'Doubts and Burdens: DNA Evidence, Probability and the Courts' Crim LR 464.

REDMAYNE M (1997) 'Process Gains and Process Values: the CPIA 1996' 60 MLR 79.

REDMAYNE M (1998) 'The DNA Database: Civil Liberty and Evidentiary Issues' Crim LR 437.

REDMAYNE M (2001) *Expert Evidence and Criminal Justice* (Oxford: OUP).

REDMAYNE M (2002a) 'Appeals to Reason' 65 MLR 19.

REDMAYNE M (2002b) 'The Relevance of Bad Character' 61 CLJ 684.

REDMAYNE M (2004) 'Disclosure and its Discontents' Crim LR 441.

REDMAYNE M (2006) 'Theorising Jury Reform' in Duff A, Farmer L, Marshall S and Tadros V (eds), *The Trial on Trial: Judgment and Calling to Account* (Oxford: Hart).

REDMAYNE M (2007) 'Rethinking the Privilege Against Self-Incrimination' 27(2) OJLS 209.

REDMAYNE, M (2009) Book review of *Evidence of Bad Character* and *Hearsay Evidence in Criminal Proceedings* by J Spencer, 48 HJCJ 108.

REDMOND D (2005) 'License to Live?' 155 (7182) NLJ 962.

REINER R (2000) *The Politics of the Police*, 3rd edn (Oxford: OUP).

REINER R (2007) 'Success or Statistics? New Labour and Crime Control' 67 Criminal Justice Matters 4.

REINER R and SPENCER J (eds) (1993) *Accountable Policing* (London: IPPR).

RICHARDSON G with OGUS A and BURROWS P (1983) *Policing Pollution: A Study of Regulation and Enforcement* (Oxford: Clarendon).

RILEY D and VENNARD J (1988) *Triable-Either-Way Cases: Crown Court or Magistrates' Court?* (Home Office Research Study No 98) (London: HMSO).

ROACH K (1999a) 'Four Models of the Criminal Process' 89 J Crim Law and Criminology 671.

ROACH K (1999b) *Due Process and Victims' Rights: The New Law and Politics of Criminal Justice* (Toronto: University of Toronto Press)

ROBERTS A (2004) 'The Problems of Mistaken Identification: Some Observations on Process' 8 IJ E&P 100.

ROBERTS A (2008) 'Drawing on Expertise: Legal Decision Making and the Reception of Expert Evidence' Crim LR 443.

ROBERTS A (2009) 'Eyewitness Identification Evidence: Procedural Developments and the Ends of Adjudicative Advocacy' 6(2) International Commentary on Evidence 3.

ROBERTS D (1993) 'Questioning the Suspect: the Solicitor's Role' Crim LR 369.

ROBERTS J and HOUGH M (2009) *Public Opinion and the Jury: An International Literature Review* (Ministry of Justice Research Series 1/09) (London: MoJ).

ROBERTS P (1994) 'Science in the Criminal Process' 14 OJLS 469.

ROBERTS P (1996) 'What Price a Free Market in Forensic Science?' 36 BJ Crim 37.

ROBERTS P (2002) 'Science, Experts and Criminal Justice' in MCCONVILLE M and WILSON G (eds), *Handbook of the Criminal Justice Process* (Oxford: OUP).

ROBERTS P (2008) 'Comparative Criminal Justice Goes Global' 28 OJLS 369.

ROBERTS P and WILLMORE C (1993) *The Role of Forensic Science Evidence in Criminal Proceedings* (Royal Commission on Criminal Justice Research Study No 11) (London: HMSO).

ROBERTS P and ZUCKERMAN A (2004) *Criminal Evidence* (Oxford: OUP).

ROBERTS S (2004) 'The Royal Commission on Criminal Justice and Factual Innocence: Remedying Wrongful Convictions in the Court of Appeal' 1(2) Justice Journal 86.

ROBERTS S and WEATHERED L (2009) 'Assisting the Factually Innocent: The Contradictions and Compatibility of Innocence Projects and the Criminal Cases Review Commission' 29(1) OJLS 43.

ROBERTSHAW P (1998) *Summary Justice* (London: Cassell).

ROBERTSON G (1994) 'Entrapment Evidence: Manna from Heaven, or Fruit of the Poisoned Tree?' Crim LR 805.

ROCK P (1993) *The Social World of an English Crown Court* (Oxford: Clarendon).

ROCK P (2004) *Constructing Victims' Rights* (Oxford: OUP).

ROGERS J (2006) 'Restructuring the Exercise of Prosecutorial Discretion in England and Wales' 26 OJLS 775.

ROSE D (1996) *In the Name of the Law: The Collapse of Criminal Justice* (London: Jonathan Cape).

ROWE M (2007) 'Rendering Visible the Invisible: Police Discretion, Professionalism and Decision-making' 17(3) Policing and Society 279.

ROYAL COMMISSION ON CRIMINAL JUSTICE (RCCJ) (1993) *Report* (Cm 2263) (London: HMSO).

ROYAL COMMISSION ON CRIMINAL PROCEDURE (RCCP) (1981a) *Report* (Cmnd 8092) (London: HMSO).

ROYAL COMMISSION ON CRIMINAL PROCEDURE (RCCP) (1981b) *The Investigation and Prosecution of Criminal Offences in England and Wales: The Law and Procedure* (Cmnd 8092–1) (London: HMSO).

ROZENBERG J (1987) *The Case for the Crown* (Wellingborough: Equation).

ROZENBERG J (1992) 'Miscarriages of Justice' in STOCKDALE E and CASALE S (eds), *Criminal Justice Under Stress* (London: Blackstone).

ROZENBERG J (1994) *The Search for Justice* (London: Hodder & Stoughton).

RUMNEY P (2006) 'False Allegations of Rape' 65(1) CLJ 128.

RYDER M (2008) 'RIPA Reviewed' Archbold News 4.

SAMUELS A (1997) 'Custody Time Limits' Crim LR 260.

SANDERS A (1977) 'Does Professional Crime Pay? – A Critical Comment on Mack' 40 MLR 553.

SANDERS A (1985) 'Class Bias in Prosecutions' 24 Howard JCJ 76.

SANDERS A (1986) 'Arrest, Charge and Prosecution' 6 LS 257.

SANDERS A (1987) 'Constructing the Case for the Prosecution' 14 JLS 229.

SANDERS A (1988a) 'Personal Violence and Public Order' 16 IJ Sociology of Law 359.

SANDERS A (1988b) 'Rights, Remedies and the Police and Criminal Evidence Act' Crim LR 802.

SANDERS A (1988c) 'The Limits to Diversion from Prosecution' 28 BJ Crim 513.

SANDERS A (1990) 'Access to a Solicitor and s 78 PACE' LS Gaz, 31 October, p 17.

SANDERS A (1996) 'Access to Justice in the Police Station: An Elusive Dream?' in YOUNG R and WALL D (eds), *Access to Criminal Justice* (London: Blackstone).

SANDERS A (1998) 'What Principles Underlie Criminal Justice Policy in the 1990s?' 18 OJLS 533.

SANDERS A (1999) *Taking Account of Victims in the Criminal Justice System* (Edinburgh: Scottish Office).

SANDERS A (2001) *Community Justice: Modernising the Magistracy in England and Wales* (London: IPPR).

SANDERS A (2002a) 'Core Values, the Magistracy and the Auld Report' 29 JLS 324.

SANDERS A (2002b) 'Victim Participation in an Exclusionary Criminal Justice System' in HOYLE C and YOUNG R, *New Visions of Crime Victims* (Oxford: Hart).

SANDERS A (2008) 'Can Coercive Powers be Effectively Controlled or Regulated?' in Cape E and Young R (eds), *Regulating Policing* (Oxford: Hart).

SANDERS A and BRIDGES L (1990) 'Access to Legal Advice and Police Malpractice' Crim LR 494.

SANDERS A and BRIDGES L (1999) 'The Right to Legal Advice' in WALKER C and STARMER K (eds), *Miscarriages of Justice* (London: Blackstone).

SANDERS A, BRIDGES L, MULVANEY A and CROZIER G (1989) *Advice and Assistance at Police Stations and the 24 Hour*

Duty Solicitor Scheme (London: Lord Chancellor's Department).

SANDERS A, CREATON J, BIRD S and WEBER L (1997) *Victims with Learning Disabilities* (Oxford: Centre for Criminological Research).

SANDERS A, HOYLE C, MORGAN R and CAPE E (2001) 'Victim Impact Statements: Don't Work, Can't Work' Crim LR 447.

SANDERS A and JONES I (2007) 'The Victim in Court' in WALKLATE S (ed), *Handbook of Victims and Victimology* (Cullompton: Willan).

SANDERS A and YOUNG R (1994) 'The Rule of Law, Due Process and Pre-Trial Criminal Justice' 47 Current Legal Problems 125.

SANDERS A and YOUNG R (2008) 'Police Powers' in NEWBURN T (ed), *Handbook of Policing*, 2nd edn (Cullompton: Willan).

SARAT A (1997) 'Vengeance, Victims and the Identities of Law' 6 Social and Legal Studies 163.

SAVAGE S and CHARMAN S (1996) 'Managing Change' in LEISHMAN F, LOVEDAY B and SAVAGE S (eds), *Core Issues in Policing* (Harlow: Longman).

SCARMAN SIR L (1981) *The Brixton Disorders: 10–12 April 1981* (Cmnd 8427) (London: HMSO).

SCHULHOFER S (1992) 'Plea Bargaining as Disaster' 101 Yale LJ 1979.

SCHWARTZ J (1997) 'Relativism, Reflective Equilibrium, and Justice' 17 LS 128.

SCOTT R and STUNTZ W (1992) 'A Reply: Imperfect Bargains, Imperfect Trials and Innocent Defendants' 101 YLJ 2011.

SCOTTISH EXECUTIVE (2003) *Making a Victim Statement: Guidance for Victims* (Edinburgh: Scottish Executive).

SCRATON P and CHADWICK K (1987) *In the Arms of the Law: Coroners' Inquests and Deaths in Custody* (London: Pluto).

SEAGO P, WALKER C and WALL D (2000) 'The Development of the Professional Magistracy in England and Wales' Crim LR 631.

SEBBA L (1994) 'Sentencing and the Victim: The Aftermath of *Payne*' 3 Int Rev Victimology 141.

SEBBA L (1996) *Third Parties: Victims and the Criminal Justice System* (Columbus: Ohio State UP).

SEKAR S (2009) 'The Failure of the Review of the Possible Wrongful Convictions Caused by Michael Heath' in NAUGHTON M (ed), *The Criminal Cases Review Commission* (London: Palgrave Macmillan).

SENTENCING GUIDELINES COUNCIL (SGC) (2007a) *Reduction in Sentence for Guilty Plea: Response to Consultation* (London: SGC).

SENTENCING GUIDELINES COUNCIL (SGC) (2007b) *Reduction in Sentence of Guilty Plea: Definitive Guideline* (London: SGC).

SHAFER B and WIEGAND O (2006) 'It's Good to Talk – Speaking Rights and the Jury' in Duff A, Farmer L, Marshall S and Tadros V (eds), *The Trial on Trial: Judgment and Calling to Account* (Oxford: Hart).

SHAPLAND J, ATKINSON A, ATKINSON H, DIGNAN J, EDWARDS L, HIBBERT J, HOWES M, JOHNSON J, ROBINSON G and SORSBY A (2008) *Does Restorative Justice Affect Reconviction?* (MoJ Research Series 10/08) (London: MoJ).

SHAPLAND J, WILLMORE J and DUFF P (1985) *Victims in the Criminal Justice System* (Aldershot: Gower).

SHARP D and ATHERTON S (2007) 'To Serve and Protect? The Experiences of Policing in the Community of Young People from Black and Other Ethnic Minority Groups' 47(5) BJ Crim 746.

SHARPE S (1994) 'Covert Police Operations and the Discretionary Exclusion of Evidence' Crim LR 793.

SHARPE S (1996) 'Covert Policing: A Comparative View' 25 Anglo-Am LR 163.

SHARPE S (1998) *Judicial Discretion and Criminal Investigation* (London: Sweet & Maxwell).

SHARPE S (1999) 'HRA 1998: Article 6 and the Disclosure of Evidence in Criminal Trials' Crim LR 273.

SHARPE S (2000) *Search and Surveillance: The Movement from Evidence to Information* (Aldershot: Ashgate).

SHAW H and COLES D (2007) *Unlocking the Truth: Families' Experiences of the Investigation of Deaths in Custody* (London: Inquest).

SHEARING C and FROESTAD J (2010) 'Nodal Governance and the Zwelethemba Model' in QUIRK H, SEDDON T and SMITH G (eds), *Regulation and Criminal Justice* (Cambridge: CUP).

SHEPHERD E (2007) *Investigative Interviewing: The Conversation Management Approach* (Oxford: OUP).

SHEPHERD E and MILNE R (1999) 'Full and Faithful: Ensuring Quality Practice and Integrity of Outcome in Witness Interviews' in HEATON-ARMSTRONG A, SHEPHERD E and WOLCHOVER D (eds), *Analysing Witness Testimony* (London: Blackstone).

SHINER M (2006) 'National Implementation of the Recording of Police Stops' (London: Home Office).

SHUTE S, HOOD R and SEEMUNGAL F (2005) *A Fair Hearing? Ethnic Minorities in the Criminal Courts* (Cullompton: Willan).

SIGLER J (1974) 'Public Prosecution in England and Wales' Crim LR 642.

SIGURDSSON J and GUDJONSSON G (1996) 'Psychological Characteristics of "False Confessors": A Study among Icelandic Prison Inmate and Juvenile Offenders' 20 Personality and Individual Differences 321.

SIMESTER A and VON HIRSCH A (eds) *Incivilities: Regulating Offensive Behaviour* (Oxford: Hart, 2006).

SIMON D (1992) *Homicide: A Year on the Killing Streets* (London: Hodder & Stoughton).

SISSON S (1999) *Cautions, Court Proceedings, and Sentencing: England and Wales, 1998* (London: Home Office).

SKINNS L (2009a) ' " Let's Get It Over With": Early Findings on Factors Affecting Detainees' Access to Custodial Legal Advice' 19(1) Policing and Society 58.

SKINNS L (2009b) ' "I'm a Detainee; Get Me Out of Here" ' 49(3) BJ Crim 399.

SKOGAN W (1990) *The Police and Public in England and Wales: A British Crime Survey Report* (Home Office Research Study 117) (London: HMSO).

SKOGAN W (1994) *Contacts between Police and Public – Findings from the 1992 British Crime Survey* (Home Office Research Study 134) (London: Home Office).

SKYRME T (1994) *History of the Justices of the Peace* (Chichester: Barry Rose).

SLAPPER G (1993) 'Corporate Manslaughter' 2 Social and Legal Studies 423.

SLAPPER G (1999) *Blood in the Bank: Social and Legal Aspects of Death at Work* (Aldershot: Ashgate).

SLAPPER G and TOMBS S (1999) *Corporate Crime* (Harlow: Longman).

SMITH D (1991) 'Origins of Black Hostility to the Police' 2 Policing and Society 6.

SMITH D (1997a) 'Case Construction and the Goals of Criminal Process' 37 BJ Crim 319.

SMITH D (1997b) 'Ethnic Origins, Crime and Criminal Justice' in MAGUIRE M, MORGAN R and REINER R (eds), *Oxford*

Handbook of Criminology, 2nd edn (Oxford: Clarendon).

SMITH D and GRAY J (1983) *Police and People in London* vol 4 (Policy Studies Institute) (Aldershot: Gower).

SMITH G (1997) 'The DPP and Prosecutions of Police Officers' 147 NLJ 6804.

SMITH G (1999a) 'Double Trouble' 149 NLJ 1223.

SMITH G (1999b) 'The Butler Report: An Opportunity Missed?' 149 NLJ 20 August.

SMITH G (2001) 'Police Complaints and Criminal Prosecutions' 64 MLR 372.

SMITH G (2003) 'Actions for Damages against the Police and the Attitudes of Claimants' 13 Policing and Society 413.

SMITH G (2004) 'Rethinking Police Complaints' 44 BJ Crim 15.

SMITH G (2005) 'Comment on *Brooks v Commissioner of the Police of the Metropolis* 69 J Crim L 4.

SMITH G (2006) 'A Most Enduring Problem: Police Complaints Reform in England and Wales' 35 J Social Policy 121.

SMITH G (2009a) 'European Complaints' April, Legal Action 38.

SMITH G, (2009b) 'Citizen Oversight of Independent Police Services: Bifurcated Accountability, Regulation Creep and Lesson Learning' 3 Regulation & Governance 422.

SMITH J (1995) 'The Criminal Appeal Act 1995: (1) Appeals against Conviction' Crim LR 920.

SMITH R (1991) 'Resolving the Legal Aid Crisis' (1991) LS Gaz, 27 February, p 17.

SNIDER L (1991) 'The Regulatory Dance: Understanding Reform Process in Corporate Crime' 19 IJ Soc of Law 209.

SNIDER L (1993) *Bad Business: Corporate Crime in Canada* (Toronto: University of Toronto Press).

SOFTLEY P (1980) *Police Interrogation: An Observational Study in Four Police Stations* (Royal Commission on Criminal Procedure Research Study No 4) (London: HMSO).

SOMMERLAD H (2001) ' "I've Lost the Plot": An Everyday Story of the "Political" Legal Aid Lawyer' 28 JLS 335.

SOMMERS S and ELLSWORTH P (2003) 'How Much Do We Really Know about Race and Juries? A Review of the Social Science Theory and Research' Chicago-Kent LR 997.

SOUKARA S, BULL R, VRIJ A and TURNER M (2009) 'A Study of What Really Happens in Police Interviews of Suspects' 15(6) Psychology, Crime and Law 493.

SOUTHGATE P (1986) *Police–Public Encounters* (Home Office Research Study 90) (London: Home Office).

SOUTHGATE P and EKBLOM P (1984) *Contacts Between Police and Public* (Home Office Research Study 77) (London: HMSO).

SPALEK B, LAMBERT R and HAQQ BAKER A (2009) 'Minority Muslim Communities and Criminal Justice: Stigmatized UK Faith Identities Post 9/11 and 7/7' in BHUI H (ed), *Race & Criminal Justice* (London: Sage).

SPENCER J (1991) 'Judicial Review of Criminal Proceedings' Crim LR 259.

SPENCER J (2006a) *Evidence of Bad Character* (Oxford: Hart).

SPENCER J (2006b) 'Does our Present Appeal System Make Sense?' Crim LR 677

SPENCER J (2007) 'Quashing Convictions for Procedural Irregularities' Crim LR 835.

SPENCER J (2008a) *Hearsay Evidence in Criminal Proceedings* (Oxford: Hart).

SPENCER J (2008b) 'Quashing Convictions for Procedural Irregularities' CLJ 227.

SPRACK J (2008) *A Practical Approach to Criminal Procedure*, 12th edn (Oxford: OUP).

SQUIRES D (2006) 'The Problem of Entrapment' 26(2) OJLS 351

SQUIRES P (ed) (2008) *ASBO Nation: The Criminalisation of Nuisance* (Bristol: Policy Press).

STENSON K (2000) 'Crime Control, Social Policy and Liberalism' in LEWIS G ET AL (eds), *Rethinking Social Policy* (Milton Keynes, Open UP).

STENSON K and WADDINGTON P (2007) 'Macpherson, Police Stops and Institutionalised Racism' in Rowe M (ed), *Policing Beyond Macpherson* (Cullompton: Willan).

STEPHEN F and TATA C with the assistance of SWEENEY L, FAZIO G and CHRISTIE A (2007) *Impact of the Introduction of Fixed Fee Payments into Summary Criminal Legal Aid: Report of an independent study* (Edinburgh: Scottish Executive).

STEPHENSON G (1992) *The Psychology of Criminal Justice* (Oxford: Blackwell).

STEVENS P and WILLIS CF (1979) *Race, Crime and Arrests* (HORS No 58) (London: HMSO).

STOCKDALE R and WALKER C (1999) 'Forensic Evidence' in WALKER C and STARMER K (eds), *Miscarriages of Justice* (London: Blackstone).

STONE C (1988) *Bail Information for the Crown Prosecution Service* (New York: VERA Institute of Justice).

STONE V and PETTIGREW N (2000) *The Views of the Public on Stops and Searches* (Police Research Series Paper 129) (London: Home Office).

STONE R (2005) *The Law of Entry, Search and Seizure* (Oxford: OUP).

STOTT C, LIVINGSTONE A and HOGGETT J (2008) 'Policing Football Crowds in England and Wales: A Model of Good Practice?' 18(3) Policing and Society 258.

STRANG H (2002) *Repair or Revenge: Victims and Restorative Justice* (Oxford: OUP).

STUBBS J (2007) 'Beyond Apology? Domestic Violence and Critical Questions for RJ' 7 Criminology and Criminal Justice 169.

SUNSTEIN C (2002) 'Risk and Reason: Safety, Law and the Environment' (Cambridge: CUP).

TAGUE P (2000) 'Economic Incentives in Representing Publicly-Funded Criminal Defendants in England's Crown Court' 23 Fordham International LR 1128.

TAGUE P (2006) 'Tactical Reasons for Recommending Trials Rather than Guilty Pleas in Crown Court' Crim LR 23.

TAGUE P (2008) 'Barristers' Selfish Incentives in Counselling Clients' Crim LR 3.

TAK P (ed) (2005) *Tasks and Powers of the Prosecution Services in the EU Member States* (2 vols) (Nijmegen: Wolf).

TAPPER C (2004) 'Evidence of Bad Character' Crim LR 533.

TARLING R, DOWDS L and BUDD T (2000) *Victim and Witness Intimidation: Findings from the British Crime Survey* (HO Research Findings No 124) (London: Home Office).

TATA C (1999) 'Comparing Legal Aid Spending' in REGAN F, PATERSON A, GORIELY T and FLEMING D (eds), *The Transformation of Legal Aid* (Oxford: OUP).

TATA C and STEPHEN F (2006) 'Do Changes to the Structure of Legal Aid Remuneration Make a Real Difference to Criminal Case Outcomes?' Crim LR 722.

TATA C, GORIELY T, McCRONE P, DUFF P, KNAPP M, HENRY A, LANCASTER B and SHERR A (2004) 'Does Mode of Delivery Make a Difference to Criminal Case Outcomes and Clients' Satisfaction? The

Public Defence Solicitor Experiment' Crim LR 120.

TAYLOR C (2005) 'Advance Disclosure and the Culture of the Investigator' 33 IJ Sociology of Law 118.

TAYLOR C (2006) *Criminal Investigation and Pre-Trial Disclosure in the United Kingdom: How Detectives Put Together a Case* (Lampeter: Edwin Mellen Press).

TAYLOR N and ORMEROD D (2004) 'Mind the Gaps: Safety, Fairness and Moral Legitimacy' Crim LR 266.

TAYLOR R with MANSFIELD M (1999) 'Post-conviction Procedures' in WALKER C and STARMER K (eds), *Miscarriages of Justice* (London: Blackstone).

TAYLOR R, WASIK M and LENG R (2004) *Blackstone's Guide to the Criminal Justice Act 2003* (Oxford: OUP).

TAYLOR W (2005) *Review of Police Disciplinary Arrangements* (London: Home Office).

TEMKIN J (2000) 'Prosecuting and Defending Rape: Perspectives from the Bar' (2000) 27 JLS 219.

TEMKIN J and KRAHE B (2008) *Sexual Assault and the Justice Gap* (Oxford: Hart).

THOMAS C with BULMER N (2007) *Diversity and Fairness in the Jury System* (Ministry of Justice Research Series 2/07) (London: Ministry of Justice).

THOMAS C (2008) 'Exposing the Myths of Jury Service' Crim LR 415.

THOMAS C (2010) *Are Juries Fair?* (Ministry of Justice Research Series 1/10) (London: MoJ).

THOMPSON E P (1975) *Whigs and Hunters* (London: Allen Lane).

THOMPSON T (2000) *Bloggs 19* (London: Time Warner).

THORNTON P (1993) 'Miscarriages of Justice: A Lost Opportunity' Crim LR 926.

TILLEY N, ROBINSON A and BURROWS J (2007) 'The Investigation of High-volume Crime' in NEWBURN T, WILLIAMSON T and WRIGHT A (eds), *Handbook of Criminal Investigation* (Cullompton: Willan).

TILLEY N and FORD A (1996) *Forensic Science and Crime Investigation* (Crime Prevention and Detection Series Paper 73) (London: Home Office).

TINSLEY Y (2001a) 'Even Better Than the Real Thing? The Case for Reform of Identification Procedures' 5 IJ E&P 235.

TINSLEY Y (2001b) 'Juror Decision-Making: A Look Inside the Jury Room' Selected Papers from the British Criminology Conference, vol 4, available on <http://www.britsoccrim.org/volume4/004.pdf>.

TOMBS S (1995) 'Law, Resistance and Reform: Regulating Safety Crimes in the UK' 4 Social and Legal Studies 343.

TOMBS S and WHYTE D (2007) *Safety Crimes* (Cullompton: Willan).

TOMBS S and WHYTE D (2008) *A Crisis of Enforcement: The Decriminalisation of Death and Injury at Work* (Centre for Crime and Justice Studies Briefing No 6) (London: Kings College London).

TOMKINS A (2002) 'Legislating Against Terror: The ACTS Act 2001' Public Law 205.

TONEY R (2001) 'Disclosure of Evidence and Legal Assistance at Custodial Interrogation: What Does the ECHR Require?' 5 IJ E&P 39.

TOWNSHEND C (1993) *Making the Peace: Public Order and Public Security in Modern Britain* (Oxford: OUP).

TYLER T (1990) *Why People Obey the Law* (New Haven: Yale University Press).

UGLOW S (2002) *Criminal Justice*, 2nd edn (London: Sweet and Maxwell).

VALENTINE T and HEATON P (1999) 'An Evaluation of the Fairness of Police Line-

Ups and Video Identifications' 13 Applied Cognitive Psychology 59.

VAN DIJK J (2000) 'Implications of the International Crime Victims Survey for a Victim Perspective' in CRAWFORD A and GOODEY J (eds), *Integrating a Victim Perspective within Criminal Justice* (Aldershot: Ashgate).

VAN DIJK J and GOENHUIJSEN M (2007) 'Benchmarking Victim Policies in the Framework of European Union Law' in WALKLATE S (ed), *Handbook of Victims and Victimology* (Cullompton: Willan).

VANDER BECKEN T and KILCHLING M (eds) (2000) *The Role of the Public Prosecutor in European Criminal Justice Systems* (Brussels: KVAB).

VENNARD J (1981) *Contested Trials in Magistrates' Courts* (Home Office Research Study 71) (London: HMSO).

VENNARD J (1985) 'The Outcome of Contested Trials' in MOXON D (ed), *Managing Criminal Justice* (London: HMSO).

VENNARD J and RILEY D (1988) 'The Use of Peremptory Challenge and Stand By of Jurors and Their Relationship to Final Outcome' Crim LR 731.

VENNARD J, DAVIS G, BALDWIN J and PEARCE J (2004) *Ethnic Minority Magistrates' Experience of the Role and of the Court Environment* (DCA Research Report 3/2004) (London: DCA).

VOGEL M (2007) *Coercion to Compromise: Plea Bargaining, the Courts and the Making of Political Authority* (Oxford: OUP).

VOGLER R (1982) 'Magistrates and Civil Disorder' (November) LAG Bull 12.

VOGLER R (1991) *Reading the Riot Act* (Milton Keynes: Open UP).

VOGLER R, *A World View of Criminal Justice* (Aldershot: Ashgate, 2005).

VOGT G and WADHAM J (2003) *Deaths in Police Custody: Redress and Remedies* (London: Civil Liberties Trust).

VON HIRSCH A, BOTTOMS A, BURNEY E and WILKSTROM P-O (1999) *Criminal Deterrence and Sentence Severity* (Oxford: Hart).

VRIJ A (2008a) *Detecting Lies and Deceit*, 2nd edn (Chichester: Wiley)

VRIJ A (2008b) 'Nonverbal Dominance Versus Verbal Accuracy in Lie Detection: A Plea To Change Police Practice' 35(10) Criminal Justice and Behavior 1323.

WADDINGTON D (2007) *Policing Public Disorder* (Cullompton: Willan).

WADDINGTON P (1991) *The Strong Arm of the Law* (Oxford: Clarendon).

WADDINGTON P (1994) *Liberty and Order* (London: UCL Press).

WADDINGTON P (1998) 'Controlling Protest in Contemporary Historical and Comparative Perspective' in DELLA PORTA D and REITER H (eds), *Policing Protest: The Control of Mass Demonstrations in Western Democracies* (Minneapolis: University of Minnesota Press).

WADDINGTON P (1999a) 'Police (Canteen) Sub-Culture: An Appreciation' 39 BJ Crim 286.

WADDINGTON P (1999b) *Policing Citizens* (London: UCL Press).

WADDINGTON P, STENSON K and DON D (2004) 'In Proportion: Race, and Police Stop and Search' 44(6) BJ Crim 889.

WADDINGTON P and WRIGHT M (2008) 'Police Use of Force, Firearms and Riot Control' in Newburn T (ed), *Handbook of Policing*, 2nd edn (Cullompton: Willan).

WADE K (2009) 'Innocent but Proven Guilty: Eliciting Internalised False Confessions Using Doctored Video Evidence' 23 Applied Cognitive Psychology 624.

WADE M AND JEHLE J (eds) (2008) *Prosecution and Diversion within Criminal Justice Systems within Europe* Vol 14 (2, 3): Special Issue, European J Crim Policy and Research.

WADHAM J, MOUNTFIELD H and EDMUNDSON A (2007) *Blackstone's Guide to the Human Rights Act 1998*, 4th edn (Oxford: OUP).

WAKE R, SIMPSON C, HOMES A and BALLANTYNE J (2007) *Public Perceptions of the Police Complaints System* (London: IPCC)..

WAKEFIELD A (2003) *Selling Security* (Cullompton: Willan).

WALKER C (1999a) 'Miscarriages of Justice in Principle and Practice' in WALKER C and STARMER K (eds), *Miscarriages of Justice* (London: Blackstone).

WALKER C (1999b) 'The Agenda of Miscarriages of Justice' in WALKER C and STARMER K (eds), *Miscarriages of Justice* (London: Blackstone).

WALKER C (1999c) 'The Judiciary' in WALKER C and STARMER K (eds), *Miscarriages of Justice* (London: Blackstone).

WALKER C (2002a) *Blackstone's Guide to the Anti-terrorism Legislation* (Oxford: OUP).

WALKER C (2002b) 'Miscarriages of Justice' in MCCONVILLE M and WILSON G (eds), *The Handbook of the Criminal Justice Process* (Oxford: OUP).

WALKER C (2004) 'Terrorism and Criminal Justice – Past, Present and Future' Crim LR 311.

WALKER C (2007) 'The Treatment of Foreign Terror Suspects' 70 MLR 427.

WALKER C (2008) 'Post-charge Questioning of Suspects' Crim LR 509.

WALKER C (2009) *Blackstone's Guide to the Anti-terrorism Legislation*, 2nd edn (Oxford: OUP).

WALKER C and MCGUINNESS M (2002) 'Commercial Risk, Political Violence and Policing the City of London' in CRAWFORD A (ed), *Crime and Insecurity: The Governance of Safety in Europe* (Cullompton: Willan).

WALKER C and STOCKDALE E (1995) 'Forensic Science and Miscarriages of Justice' 54 CLJ 69.

WALKER C and WALL D (1997) 'Imprisoning the Poor: TV Licence Evaders and the Criminal Justice System' Crim LR 173.

WALKLEY J (1988) *Police Interrogation: A Handbook for Investigators* (London: Police Review Publishing Company).

WALL D (1996) 'Keyholders to Criminal Justice' in YOUNG R and WALL D (eds), *Access to Criminal Justice* (London: Blackstone).

WALSH D (2009) '20 Years of Handling Police Complaints in Ireland: A Critical Assessment of the Supervisory Board Model' 29 Legal Studies 305.

WALSH D and MILNE R (2007) 'Giving P.E.A.C.E. a Chance: A Study of DWP's Investigators' Perceptions of their Interviewing Practices' 85 Public Administration 525.

WALSH D and MILNE R (2008) 'Keeping the Peace? A Study of Investigative Practice in the Public Sector' 13 Legal and Criminological Psychology 39.

WARBURTON H, MAY T and HOUGH M (2003) *Opposite Sides of the Same Coin: Police Perspectives on Informally Resolved Complaints* (London: The Police Foundation).

WARBURTON H, MAY T, and HOUGH M (2005) 'Looking the Other Way: The Impact of Reclassifying Cannabis on Police Warnings, Arrests and Informal Action in England and Wales' 45 BJ Crim 113.

WASIK M (1996) 'Magistrates: Knowledge of Previous Convictions' Crim LR 851.

WASIK M and TAYLOR R (1995) *Blackstone's Guide to the Criminal Justice and Public Order Act 1994* (London: Blackstone).

WATERS I and BROWN K (2000) 'Police Complaints and the Complainants' Experience' 40 BJ Crim 617.

WATSON S (2000) 'Foucault and Social Policy' in LEWIS G et al (eds), *Rethinking Social Policy* (Milton Keynes: Open UP).

WEATHERITT M (1980) *The Prosecution System: Survey of Prosecuting Solicitors' Departments* (Royal Commission on Criminal Procedure, Research Study No 11) (London: HMSO).

WELLS C (2001) *Corporations and Criminal Responsibility*, 2nd edn (Oxford: OUP).

WELLS C (2004) 'The Impact of Feminist Thinking on Criminal Law and Justice: Contradiction, Complexity, Conviction and Connection' Crim LR 503.

WELLS C (2006) 'Corporate Manslaughter: Why Does Reform Matter?' 122 South African LJ 646.

WELLS G, OLSON E and CHARMAN S (2003) 'Distorted Retrospective Eyewitness Reports as Functions of Feedback and Delay' 9 J Experimental Psychology: Applied 42.

WESTMARLAND L (2005) 'Police Ethics and Integrity: Breaking the Blue Code of Silence' 15 Policing and Society 145.

WESTMARLAND L (2008) 'Police Cultures' in NEWBURN T (ed), *The Handbook of Policing*, 2nd edn (Cullompton: Willan).

WHITE K and BRODY S (1980) 'The Use of Bail Hostels' Crim LR 420.

WHITE R (1985) *The Administration of Justice* (Oxford: Basil Blackwell).

WHITE R (2006) 'Investigators and Prosecutors or, Desperately Seeking Scotland: Re-formulation of the "Philips Principle"' 69 MLR 143.

WHYTE D (2007/8) 'Gordon Brown's Charter for Corporate Criminals' 70 Criminal Justice Matters 31.

WILCOX A and YOUNG R (2006) *Understanding the Interests of Justice* (London: Legal Services Commission).

WILCOX A and YOUNG R (2007) 'How Green was Thames Valley?: Policing the Image of Restorative Justice Cautions' 17(2) Policing and Society 141.

WILCOX A, YOUNG R and HOYLE C (2004) *Two-year Resanctioning Study: A Comparison of Restorative and Traditional Cautions* (Home Office Online Report 57/04) (London: Home Office).

WILDING B (2008) 'Tipping the Scales of Justice?: A Review of the Impact of PACE on the Police, Due Process and the Search for the Truth 1984–2006' in CAPE E and YOUNG R (eds), *Regulating Policing* (Oxford: Hart).

WILKINS G and ADDICOT C (2000) *Operation of Certain Police Powers Under PACE* (Statistical Bulletin 9/00) (London: Home Office).

WILKINSON P (2001) *Terrorism versus Democracy* (London: Frank Cass).

WILLIAMS C (1995) *Invisible Victims: Crime and Abuse Against People with Learning Disabilities* (Bristol: Norah Fry Research Centre).

WILLIAMS G (1979) 'The Authentication of Statements to the Police' Crim LR 6.

WILLIAMS G (1985) 'Letting off the Guilty and Prosecuting the Innocent' Crim LR 115.

WILLIAMS J (2000) 'The CDA: Conflicting Roles for the Appropriate Adult' Crim LR 911.

WILLIAMS R and JOHNSON P (2008) *Genetic Policing: The Use of DNA in Criminal Investigations* (Cullompton: Willan).

WILLIAMSON T (1994) 'Reflections on Current Police Practice' in MORGAN D and STEPHENSON G (eds), *Suspicion and Silence* (London: Blackstone).

WILLIAMSON T and BAGSHAW P (2001) 'The Ethics of Informer Handling' in BILLINGSLEY R, NEMITZ T and BEAN P (eds), *Informers: Policing, Policy, Practice* (Cullompton: Willan).

WILLIS C (1983) *The Use, Effectiveness and Impact of Police Stop and Search Powers* (Home Office Research and Planning Unit Paper No 15) (London: Home Office).

WINDLESHAM Lord (1988) 'Punishment and Prevention: The Inappropriate Prisoners' Crim LR 140.

WOFFINDEN B (1999a) 'No, You Can't See. It Might Help Your Client' *The Guardian*, 4 May.

WOFFINDEN B (1999b) 'Thumbs Down' *The Guardian*, 12 January.

WOLCHOVER D (1989) 'Should Judges Sum Up on the Facts?' Crim LR 781.

WOLHUTER L, OLLEY N and DENHAM D (2009) *Victimology: Victimisation and Victim's Rights* (Abingdon: Routledge).

WONNACOTT C (1999) 'The Counterfeit Contract – Reform, Pretence and Muddled Principles in the New Referral Order' 11 Child and Fam LQ 209.

WOOD J (1999) 'Appendix – Extracts from the Transcript of the Trial of the Birmingham Six, Lancaster, June 1975' in WALKER C and STARMER K (eds), *Miscarriages of Justice* (London: Blackstone).

WOOLF (1991) *Prison Disturbances April 1990, Report of an Inquiry by The Rt Hon Lord Justice Woolf (Parts I and II) and His Honour Judge Stephen Tumim (Part II)* (Cm 1456) (London: HMSO).

WOOLF (2000) *Unjust Deserts: A Thematic Review of the Chief Inspector of Prisons of the Treatment and Conditions for Unsentenced Prisoners in England and Wales* (London: Home Office).

WORTHERN T (2008) 'The Hearsay Provisions of the Criminal Justice Act 2003: So Far, Not So Good?' Crim LR 431

WRIGHT F (2007) 'Criminal Liability of Directors and Senior Managers for Deaths at Work' Crim LR 949.

WRIGHT S (1998) 'Policing Domestic Violence: A Nottingham Case Study' 20 JSWFL 397.

WYNER R (2003) *From the Inside: Dispatches from a Women's Prison* (London: Aurum Press).

YOUNG H (2002) 'Securing Fair Treatment: An Examination of the Diversion of Mentally Disordered Offenders from Police Custody' (Unpublished PhD, Birmingham University).

YOUNG J (1994) *Policing the Streets – Stops and Search in North London* (London: Islington Council).

YOUNG J (1999) 'The Politics of the Human Rights Act' 26(1) JLS 27.

YOUNG M (1991) *An Inside Job* (Oxford: OUP).

YOUNG R (1987) *The Sandwell Mediation and Reparation Scheme* (Birmingham: West Midlands Probation Service).

YOUNG R (1993) 'The Merits of Legal Aid in the Magistrates' Courts' Crim LR 336.

YOUNG R (1996) 'Will Widgery Do?' in YOUNG R and WALL D (eds) (1996) *Access to Criminal Justice* (London: Blackstone).

YOUNG R (2000) 'Integrating a Multi-Victim Perspective into Criminal Justice Through Restorative Justice Conferences' in CRAWFORD A and GOODEY J (eds), *Integrating a Victim Perspective within Criminal Justice* (Aldershot: Ashgate).

YOUNG R (2002) 'Testing the Limits of Restorative Justice: The Case of Corporate Victims' in HOYLE C and YOUNG R (eds),

New Visions of Crime Victims (Oxford: Hart).

YOUNG R (2003) Review of Henham R, *Sentence Discounts and the Criminal Process* 7(2) Edinburgh LR 267.

YOUNG R (2008) 'Street Policing after PACE: The Drift to Summary Justice' in CAPE E and YOUNG R (eds), *Regulating Policing* (Oxford: Hart).

YOUNG R (forthcoming 2010) 'Ethnic Profiling and Summary Justice: An Ominous Silence?' in RUNNYMEDE TRUST, *Ethnic Profiling* (London: Runnymede Trust).

YOUNG R and GOOLD B (1999) 'Restorative Police Cautioning in Aylesbury' Crim LR 126.

YOUNG R, HOYLE C, COOPER K and HILL R (2005) 'Informal Resolution of Complaints Against the Police: A Quasi-Experimental Test of Restorative Justice' 5 Criminal Justice 279.

YOUNG R, MOLONEY T and SANDERS A (1992) *In the Interests of Justice?* (Birmingham: Birmingham University).

YOUNG R and SANDERS A (1994) 'The Royal Commission on Criminal Justice: A Confidence Trick?' 15 OJLS 435.

YOUNG R and SANDERS A (2005) 'The Ethics of Prosecution Lawyers' 7(2) Legal Ethics 190.

YOUNG R and WALL D (eds) (1996a) *Access to Criminal Justice* (London: Blackstone).

YOUNG R and WALL D (1996b) 'Criminal Justice, Legal Aid and the Defence of Liberty' in YOUNG R and WALL D (eds), *Access to Criminal Justice* (London: Blackstone).

YOUNG R and WALL D (eds) (1996) *Access to Criminal Justice* (London: Blackstone).

YOUNG R and WILCOX A (2007) 'The Merits of Legal Aid in the Magistrates' Courts Revisited' Crim LR 109.

YOUNG W, CAMERON N and TINSLEY Y (1999) *Juries in Criminal Trials: A Summary of the Research Findings* (Preliminary Paper 37, Vol 2) (Wellington, New Zealand: Law Commission) available from <http://www.lawcom.govt.nz>.

ZANDER M (1974) 'Are Too Many Professional Criminals Avoiding Conviction?' 37 MLR 28.

ZANDER M (1979) 'Operation of the Bail Act in London Magistrates' Courts' 129 NLJ 108.

ZANDER M (1991) 'What the Annual Statistics Tell Us About Pleas and Acquittals' Crim LR 252.

ZANDER M (1993) 'The "Innocent" (?) Who Plead Guilty' 143 NLJ 85.

ZANDER M (2000) 'The Criminal Standard of Proof – How Sure is Sure?' 150 NLJ 1517.

ZANDER M (2003) *Cases and Materials on the English Legal System*, 9th edn (London: Butterworths).

ZANDER M (2005) *The Police and Criminal Evidence Act 1984*, 5th edn (London: Sweet & Maxwell).

ZANDER M and HENDERSON P (1993) *The Crown Court Study* (Royal Commission on Criminal Justice Research Study No 19) (London: HMSO).

ZEDNER L, 'Pre-Crime and Post-Criminology?' (2007) 11 Theoretical Criminology 261.

ZELLICK G (2005) 'The Criminal Cases Review Commission and the Court of Appeal: The Commission's Perspective' Crim LR 937.

ZUCKERMAN A (1987) 'Illegally Obtained Evidence: Discretion as a Guardian of Legitimacy' CLP 55.

ZUCKERMAN A (1990) 'The weakness of the PACE Special Procedure for Protecting Confidential Material' [1990] Crim LR 472.

INDEX